More Than Just a Textbook

Log on to **ca.gr3math.com** *to…*

Access your book from home

- **Online Student Edition**
- **Student Workbooks**

See mathematical concepts come to life

- **Personal Tutor**
- **Concepts in Motion**

Practice what you've learned

- **Chapter Readiness**
- **Extra Examples**
- **Self-Check Quizzes**
- **Vocabulary Review**
- **Chapter Tests**
- **Standards Practice**

Try these other activities

- **Cross-Curricular Features**
- **Game Time**

Macmillan McGraw-Hill

California Mathematics

Concepts, Skills, and Problem Solving

3

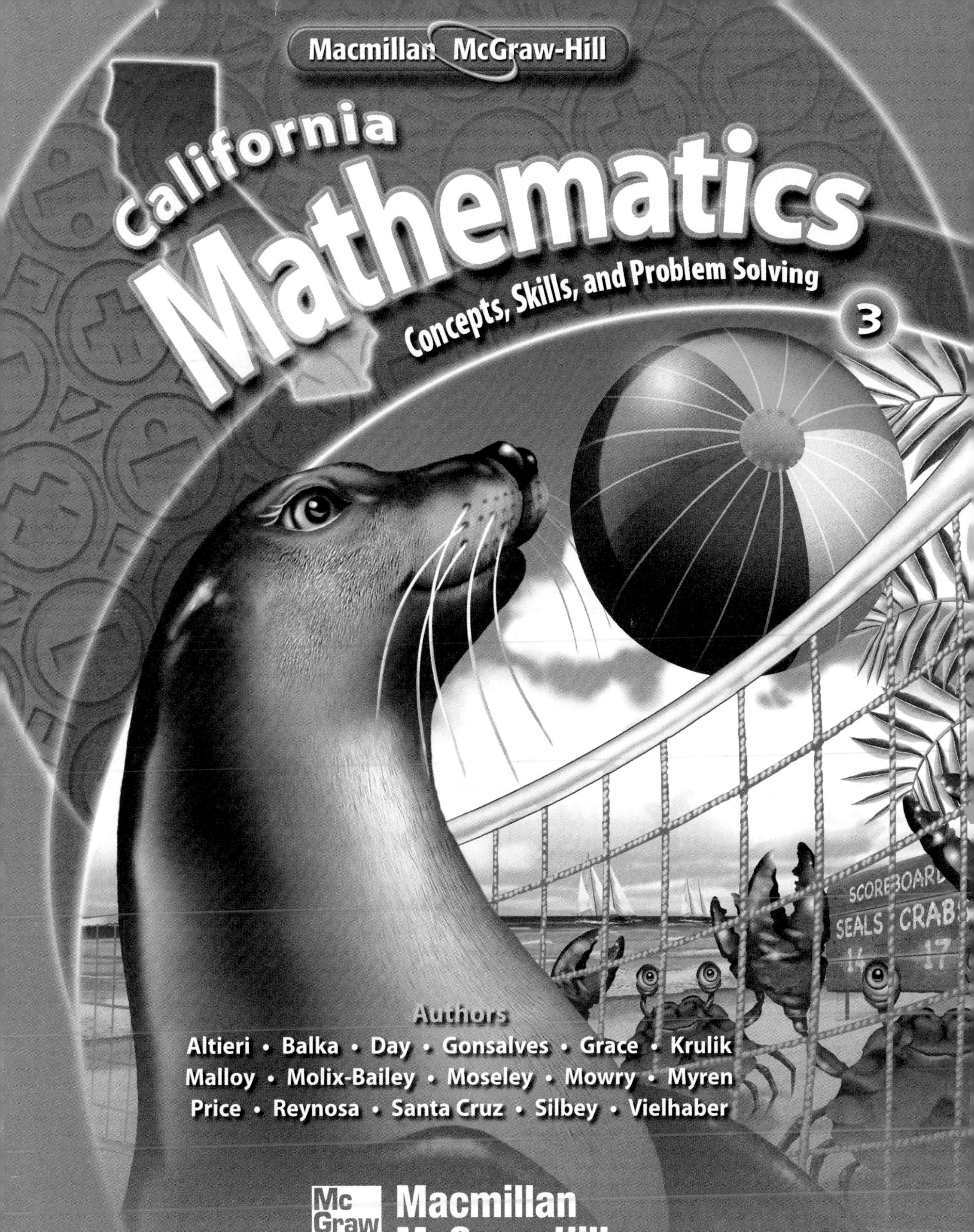

Authors

Altieri • Balka • Day • Gonsalves • Grace • Krulik
Malloy • Molix-Bailey • Moseley • Mowry • Myren
Price • Reynosa • Santa Cruz • Silbey • Vielhaber

Macmillan McGraw-Hill

About the Cover

California Focus Beach volleyball is a popular sport in California. And there are over 1,264 miles of beaches to enjoy. Even the crabs seem to be having fun.

About the Graphics

Mathematics Focus This year you will learn about multiplication. There are two sailboats on the cover. Each one has 3 sails. There are 6 sails in all. You can write the multiplication fact $2 \times 3 = 6$. Use the pictures on the cover to write another multiplication fact.

Macmillan McGraw-Hill

The McGraw-Hill Companies

Send all inquiries to:
Glencoe/McGraw-Hill
8787 Orion Place
Columbus, OH 43240-4027

ISBN-13: 978-0-02-105709-2
ISBN-10: 0-02-105709-5

Printed in the United States of America.

3 4 5 6 7 8 9 10 079/055 15 14 13 12 11 10 09 08

Contents in Brief

Start Smart

Chapter 1 Place Value and Number Sense

Chapter 2 Addition

Chapter 3 Subtraction

Chapter 4 Multiplication Concepts and Facts

Chapter 5 More Multiplication Facts

Chapter 6 Division Concepts and Facts

Chapter 7 More Division Facts

Chapter 8 Measurement: Customary System

Chapter 9 Measurement: Metric System

Chapter 10 Measurement and Geometry

Chapter 11 Statistics: Data, Graphs, and Probability

Chapter 12 Fractions

Chapter 13 Fractions and Decimals

Chapter 14 Multiply by One-Digit Numbers

Chapter 15 Divide by One-Digit Numbers

Standards Review

Looking Ahead to the Grade 4 Standards

Authors

Mary Behr Altieri
Putnam/Northern Westchester BOCES
Yorktown Heights, New York

Don S. Balka
Professor Emeritus
Saint Mary's College
Notre Dame, Indiana

Roger Day, Ph.D.
Mathematics Department Chair
Pontiac Township High School
Pontiac, Illinois

Philip D. Gonsalves
Mathematics Coordinator
Alameda County Office of Education and California State University East Bay
Hayward, California

Ellen C. Grace
Consultant
Albuquerque, New Mexico

Stephen Krulik
Professor Emeritus
Mathematics Education
Temple University
Cherry Hill, New Jersey

Carol E. Malloy
Assistant Professor of Mathematics Education
University of North Carolina at Chapel Hill
Chapel Hill, North Carolina

Rhonda J. Molix-Bailey
Mathematics Consultant
Mathematics by Design
Desoto, Texas

Lois Gordon Moseley
Staff Developer
NUMBERS: Mathematics Professional Development
Houston, Texas

Brian Mowry
Independent Math Educational Consultant/Part-Time Pre-K Instructional Specialist
Austin Independent School District
Austin, Texas

Math Online Meet the Authors at ca.gr3math.com

Christina L. Myren
Consultant Teacher
Conejo Valley Unified School District
Thousand Oaks, California

Jack Price
Professor Emeritus
California State Polytechnic University
Pomona, California

Mary Esther Reynosa
Instructional Specialist for Elementary Mathematics
Northside Independent School District
San Antonio, Texas

Rafaela M. Santa Cruz
SDSU/CGU Doctoral Program in Education
San Diego State University
San Diego, California

Robyn Silbey
Math Content Coach
Montgomery County Public Schools
Gaithersburg, Maryland

Kathleen Vielhaber
Mathematics Consultant
St. Louis, Missouri

Contributing Authors

Viken Hovsepian
Professor of Mathematics
Rio Hondo College
Whittier, California

Donna J. Long
Mathematics Consultant
Indianapolis, Indiana

FOLDABLES™ **Dinah Zike**
Educational Consultant
Dinah-Might Activities, Inc.
San Antonio, Texas

California Mathematics Advisory Board

Macmillian/McGraw-Hill wishes to thank the following professionals for their invaluable feedback during the development of the program. They reviewed a variety of instructional materials at different stages of development.

Cheryl L. Avalos
Mathematics Consultant
Hacienda Heights, California

William M. Bokesch
Rancho Bernardo High School
San Diego, California

Patty Brown
Teacher
John Muir Elementary
Fresno, California

David J. Chamberlain
Secondary Mathematics Resource Teacher
Capistrano Unified School District
San Juan Capistrano, California

Eppie Chung
K-6 Teacher
Modesto City Schools
Modesto, California

Lisa Marie Cirrincione
Middle School Teacher
Lincoln Middle School
Oceanside, California

Carol Cronk
Mathematics Program Specialist
San Bernardino City Unified School District
San Bernardino, California

Ilene Foster
Teacher Specialist–Mathematics
Pomona Unified School District
Pomona, California

Grant A. Fraser, Ph. D.
Professor of Mathematics
California State University, Los Angeles
Los Angeles, California

Suzanne Bocskai Freire
Teacher
Kingswood Elementary
Citrus Heights, California

Beth Holguin
Teacher
Graystone Elementary
San Jose, California

Donna M. Kopenski, Ed. D.
Mathematics Coordinator K-5
City Heights Educational Collaborative
San Diego, California

Kelly Mack
6th Grade Teacher
Captain Jason Dahl Elementary
San Jose, California

Juvenal Martinez
Dual Immersion/ESL Instructor
Aeolian Elementary
Whittier, California

John McGuire
Associate Principal
Pacific Union School
Arcata, California

Dr. Donald R. Price
Teacher, Adjunct Professor
Rowland Unified School District
Rowland Heights, California

Kasey St. James
Mathematics Teacher
Sunny Hills High School
Fullerton, California

Arthur K. Wayman, Ph. D.
Professor of Mathematics Emeritus
California State University, Long Beach
Long Beach, California

Beverly Wells
First Grade Teacher
Mineral King Elementary School
Visalia, California

Frances Basich Whitney
Project Director, Mathematics K-12
Santa Cruz County Office of Education
Capitola, California

Consultants

Macmillan/McGraw-Hill wishes to thank the following professionals for their feedback. They were instrumental in providing valuable input toward the development of this program in these specific areas.

Mathematical Content

Viken Hovsepian
Professor of Mathematics
Rio Hondo College
Whittier, California

Grant A. Fraser, Ph.D.
Professor of Mathematics
California State University, Los Angeles
Los Angeles, California

Arthur K. Wayman, Ph.D.
Professor of Mathematics Emeritus
California State University, Long Beach
Long Beach, California

Assessment

Jane D. Gawronski
Director of Assessment and Outreach
San Diego State University
San Diego, California

Cognitive Guided Instruction

Susan B. Empson
Associate Professor of Mathematics and Science Education
University of Texas at Austin
Austin, Texas

English Learners

Cheryl Avalos
Mathematics Consultant
Los Angeles County Office of Education, Retired
Hacienda Heights, California

Kathryn Heinze
Graduate School of Education
Hamline University
St. Paul, Minnesota

Family Involvement

Paul Giganti, Jr.
Mathematics Education Consultant
Albany, California

Literature

David M. Schwartz
Children's Author, Speaker, Storyteller
Oakland, California

Vertical Alignment

Berchie Holliday
National Educational Consultant
Silver Spring, Maryland

Deborah A. Hutchens, Ed.D.
Principal
Norfolk Highlands Elementary
Chesapeake, Virginia

California Reviewers

Each California Reviewer reviewed at least two chapters of the Student Edition, giving feedback and suggestions for improving the effectiveness of the mathematics instruction.

Sherry G. Anderson
Teacher/G.A.T.E. Coordinator
Will Rogers Elementary
Lynwood, California

Ysaaca Axelrod
Kindergarten Teacher
El Monte Elementary
Concord, California

Cathy Bullock
Teacher
Capri Elementary
Encinitas, California

Michelle Callender
Teacher
Morgan/Kincaid Preparatory School of Integrated Studies
Victorville, California

M. Olivia Campos
4th Grade Teacher
Morrison Elementary
Norwalk, California

Malaura Page Easton, M.S.
Kindergarten Teacher
La Pluma School
La Mirada, California

Priscilla S. Edwards
5th Grade Classroom Teacher
David Reese Elementary
Sacramento, California

Lisa B. Friedberg
4th Grade Teacher
Alderwood Basics Plus School
Irvine, California

Wendy Smith Hernandez
Kindergarten Teacher
Herndon-Barstow Elementary
Fresno, California

Beth Holguin
Teacher
Graystone School
San Jose, California

Kristi Iverson
First Grade Teacher
Village Oaks Elementary
Stockton, California

Sheri Leiken
Teacher
Weathersfield Elementary
Thousand Oaks, California

Sarab H. Lopes
Teacher
Anza Elementary
El Cajon, California

Karen E. Lund
5th Grade Teacher
Meadow Park Elementary
Irvine, California

Efrain Melendez
Teacher
Livermore Valley USD
Livermore, California

Jean A. Nelson
Teacher
Fremont Elementary School
Alhambra, California

Tara Pahia
Elementary Teacher
Bear Gulch Elementary
Rancho Cucamonga, California

Dr. Donald R. Price
Teacher, Adjunct Professor
Rowland Unified School District
Rowland Heights, California

Kitty Ritz, M.A.
Teacher
Monte Vista Elementary
Rohnert Park, California

Corinne E. Schwartz
First Grade Teacher
Lincrest Elementary School
Yuba City, California

Deborah Shapiro
5th Grade Teacher
Nancy Cory
Lancaster, California

Maureen Smith
Curriculum Specialist
Fremont Unified School Dist. (retired 6/2006)
Fremont, California

Joseph M. Snodgrass
3rd Grade Teacher
Park Elementary School
Alhambra, California

Marie W. Stevens
Elementary Mathematics Coordinator
LAUSD
Los Angeles, California

Jane Traut
Classroom Teacher
Lang Ranch Elementary School
Thousand Oaks, California

Rachel C. Trowbridge
Teacher
Evergreen Elementary
San Jose, California

Cynthia H. Vandemoortel
Educator
Alderwood Basics Plus School
Irvine, California

Norine Yale
Teacher
Justin Elementary
Simi Valley, California

Dr. Darlene York
Education Consultant
Associate Professor
Antioch University
Seattle, Washington

Contents

Start Smart

1. Problem Solving: The Great Giants 2
2. Number Sense: Now That's Hot! 4
3. Algebra and Functions: At the Aquarium 6
4. Measurement: Measure Away 8
5. Geometry: Food and Geometry 10
6. Statistics, Data Analysis, and Probability: How Fast Can You Go? 12

WRITING IN ▸MATH 3, 5, 7, 9, 11, 13

Chapter 1 Place Value and Number Sense

Are You Ready for Chapter 1? 16

1-1 **Algebra:** Number Patterns 17

1-2 **Problem-Solving Skill:** Use the Four-Step Plan 20

Explore **Math Activity for 1-3:** Place Value 22

1-3 Place Value through 1,000 24

1-4 Place Value through 10,000 28

Mid-Chapter Check 31

1-5 **Problem-Solving Investigation:** The Four-Step Plan 32

1-6 Compare Numbers 34

1-7 Order Numbers 38

Problem Solving in Geography: The Mighty Mississippi 42

1-8 Round to the Nearest Ten and Hundred 44

Game Time: Round Numbers 47

1-9 Round to the Nearest Thousand 48

ASSESSMENT

Study Guide and Review 52

Chapter Test 59

California Standards Practice 60

California Standards Practice

- 27, 31, 37, 41, 51, 59, 60, 61

H.O.T. Problems
Higher Order Thinking
19, 27, 30, 37, 41, 46, 51

WRITING IN MATH 19, 21, 23, 27, 30, 31, 33, 37, 41, 46, 51, 59

CHAPTER 2 Addition

Are You Ready for Chapter 2? 64

2-1 **Algebra:** Addition Properties 65

2-2 **Problem-Solving Skill:** Estimate or Exact Answer 68

2-3 Estimate Sums 70

2-4 Two-Digit Addition 74

Mid-Chapter Check 77

2-5 Add Money 78

Problem Solving in Geography: A Walk in the Park 82

2-6 **Problem-Solving Investigation:** The Four-Step Plan 84

Explore **Math Activity for 2-7:** Add Three-Digit Numbers 86

2-7 Three-Digit Addition 88

Game Time: How Low Can You Go? 91

2-8 Add Greater Numbers 92

ASSESSMENT

Study Guide and Review 96

Chapter Test 101

California Standards Practice 102

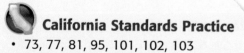

California Standards Practice

- 73, 77, 81, 95, 101, 102, 103

H.O.T. Problems
Higher Order Thinking
67, 73, 76, 81, 90, 95

WRITING IN ►MATH 67, 69, 73, 76, 77, 81, 85, 87, 95, 101

Chapter 3 Subtraction

Are You Ready for Chapter 3? 106

3-1 Two-Digit Subtraction 107

3-2 Estimate Differences 110

3-3 Subtract Money 114

Mid-Chapter Check 117

Problem Solving in Music: The Sounds of the Symphony 118

3-4 **Problem-Solving Skill:** Reasonable Answers 120

Explore **Math Activity for 3-5:** Subtract Three-Digit Numbers with Regrouping 122

3-5 Three-Digit Subtraction with Regrouping 124

3-6 **Problem-Solving Investigation:** Choose a Strategy 128

3-7 Subtract Greater Numbers 130

Game Time: Do Not Zero Out 133

3-8 Subtract Across Zeros 134

3-9 **Algebra:** Expressions and Number Sentences 138

ASSESSMENT

Study Guide and Review 142

Chapter Test 149

California Standards Practice 150

California Standards Practice

• 113, 117, 127, 137, 141, 149, 150, 151

H.O.T. Problems
Higher Order Thinking
109, 113, 116, 127, 132, 137, 141

WRITING IN MATH 109, 113, 116, 117, 121, 123, 127, 129, 132, 137, 141, 149

CHAPTER 4

Multiplication Concepts and Facts

Are You Ready for Chapter 4? **154**

Explore **Math Activity for 4-1:** Meaning of Multiplication **155**

4-1 Multiplication as Repeated Addition **157**

4-2 Arrays and Multiplication **160**

4-3 Multiply by 2 .... **164**

Mid-Chapter Check **167**

4-4 Multiply by 4 .... **168**

Game Time: Factor Power **171**

4-5 **Problem-Solving Skill:** Extra or Missing Information **172**

4-6 Multiply by 5 .... **174**

Facts Practice **177**

4-7 Multiply by 10 .... **178**

Problem Solving in Science: Lots of Arms and Legs **182**

4-8 **Problem-Solving Investigation:** Choose a Strategy **184**

4-9 Multiply by 0 and 1 .... **186**

Facts Practice **189**

ASSESSMENT

Study Guide and Review **190**

Chapter Test **195**

California Standards Practice **196**

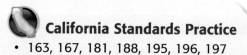

California Standards Practice
- 163, 167, 181, 188, 195, 196, 197

H.O.T. Problems
Higher Order Thinking
159, 163, 166, 170, 176, 181, 188

WRITING IN MATH 156, 159, 163, 166, 167, 170, 173, 176, 181, 185, 188, 195

CHAPTER 5 More Multiplication Facts

Are You Ready for Chapter 5? 200

Explore Math Activity for 5-1: Multiplication Table 201

5-1 Multiply by 3 203

5-2 Multiply by 6 206

Facts Practice 210

Game Time: Three in a Row 211

5-3 Problem-Solving Strategy: Look for a Pattern 212

5-4 Multiply by 7 214

Mid-Chapter Check 217

5-5 Multiply by 8 218

5-6 Multiply by 9 222

Facts Practice 225

5-7 Problem-Solving Investigation: Choose a Strategy 226

5-8 Algebra: Associative Property 228

Problem Solving in Art: Not Just a Blanket 232

5-9 Algebra: Find a Rule 234

ASSESSMENT

Study Guide and Review 238

Chapter Test 245

California Standards Practice 246

California Standards Practice

- 209, 217, 221, 231, 237, 245, 246, 247

H.O.T. Problems
Higher Order Thinking
205, 208, 216, 221, 224, 231, 237

WRITING IN MATH 202, 205, 208, 213, 216, 217, 221, 224, 227, 231, 237, 245

Chapter 6 Division Concepts and Facts

Are You Ready for Chapter 6? ... **250**

Explore **Math Activity for 6-1:** Understand Division ... **251**

6-1 Relate Division and Subtraction ... **253**

Explore **Math Activity for 6-2:** Relate Multiplication to Division ... **256**

6-2 Relate Multiplication to Division ... **258**

6-3 **Problem-Solving Skill:** Choose an Operation ... **262**

6-4 Divide by 2 ... **264**

Mid-Chapter Check ... **267**

6-5 Divide by 5 ... **268**

Problem Solving in Community: Communities within Communities ... **272**

6-6 **Problem-Solving Investigation:** Choose a Strategy ... **274**

6-7 Divide by 10 ... **276**

Game Time: Number Cubes ... **279**

6-8 Division Properties ... **280**

ASSESSMENT

Study Guide and Review ... **282**

Chapter Test ... **287**

California Standards Practice ... **288**

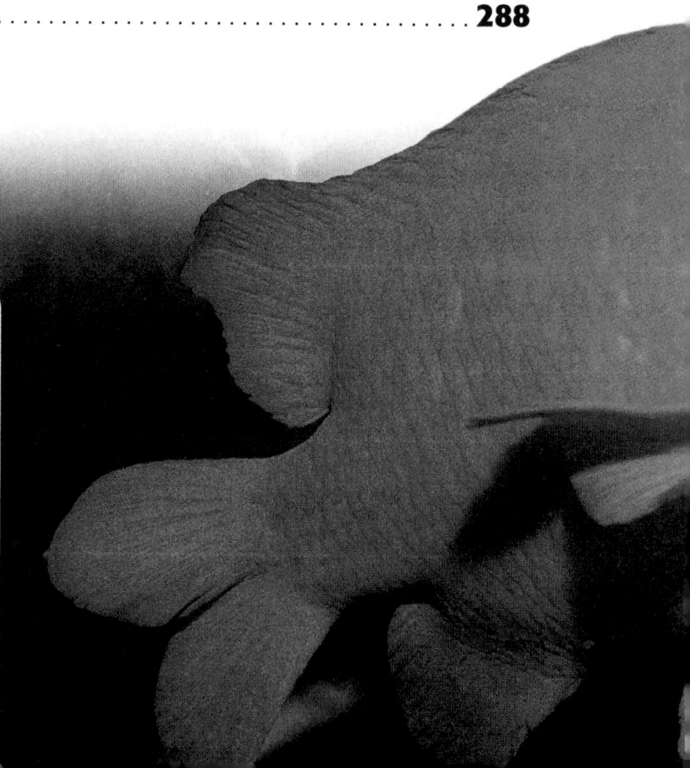

California Standards Practice

- 261, 267, 271, 278, 287, 288, 289

H.O.T. Problems
Higher Order Thinking
255, 261, 266, 271, 277, 281

WRITING IN MATH 252, 255, 257, 261, 263, 266, 267, 271, 275, 277, 281, 287

CHAPTER 7 More Division Facts

Are You Ready for Chapter 7? 292

Explore Math Activity for 7-1: Divide Using a Multiplication Table 293

7-1 Divide by 3 295

7-2 Divide by 4 298

7-3 **Problem-Solving Strategy:** Make a Table 302

7-4 Divide by 6 and 7 304

Mid-Chapter Check 307

Problem Solving in Civics: Stars and Stripes 308

7-5 Divide by 8 and 9 310

Game Time: Facts Roll 313

7-6 Determine Unit Cost 314

7-7 **Problem-Solving Investigation:** Choose a Strategy 318

7-8 **Algebra:** Expressions and Equations 320

7-9 **Algebra:** Translate Words to Expressions 324

ASSESSMENT

Study Guide and Review 328

Chapter Test 335

California Standards Practice 336

California Standards Practice

• 301, 307, 317, 323, 327, 335, 336, 337

H.O.T. Problems

Higher Order Thinking

297, 301, 306, 312, 317, 323, 327

WRITING IN MATH 294, 297, 301, 303, 306, 307, 312, 317, 319, 323, 327, 335

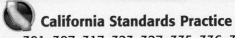

Chapter 8 Measurement: Customary System

Are You Ready for Chapter 8? 340

Explore Measurement Activity for 8-1: Length to the Nearest Inch 341

8-1 Length to the Nearest Half Inch 343

8-2 Customary Units of Length 346

8-3 Problem-Solving Strategy: Work Backward 350

Explore Measurement Activity for 8-4: Capacity 352

8-4 Customary Units of Capacity 354

Game Time: Capacity Guess 358

Mid-Chapter Check 359

8-5 Problem-Solving Investigation: Choose a Strategy 360

8-6 Customary Units of Weight 362

Problem Solving in Science: Lengths, Heights, and Weights, Oh My! 366

8-7 Convert Units of Time 368

ASSESSMENT

Study Guide and Review 372

Chapter Test 377

California Standards Practice 378

California Standards Practice
- 349, 357, 359, 365, 371, 377, 378, 379

H.O.T. Problems
Higher Order Thinking
345, 349, 357, 365, 371

WRITING IN MATH 342, 345, 349, 351, 353, 357, 359, 361, 365, 371, 377

CHAPTER 9 Measurement: Metric System

Are You Ready for Chapter 9? **382**

Explore **Measurement Activity for 9-1:** Millimeter and Centimeter **383**

9-1 Metric Units of Length **385**

Game Time: Hit the Target **389**

9-2 **Problem-Solving Strategy:** Guess and Check **390**

9-3 Metric Units of Capacity **392**

Mid-Chapter Check **395**

9-4 **Problem-Solving Ivestigation:** Choose a Strategy **396**

9-5 Metric Units of Mass **398**

Problem Solving in Science: A Visit to the Supermarket **402**

9-6 Metric Unit Conversions **404**

ASSESSMENT

Study Guide and Review **408**

Chapter Test **413**

California Standards Practice **414**

California Standards Practice

- 388, 395, 401, 407, 413, 414, 415

H.O.T. Problems
Higher Order Thinking
388, 394, 401, 407

WRITING IN ▸MATH 384, 388, 391, 394, 395, 397, 401, 407, 413

CHAPTER 10 Measurement and Geometry

Are You Ready for Chapter 10? **418**
10-1 Geometry: Polygons **419**
10-2 Measurement: Perimeter **422**
Explore **Measurement Activity for 10-3:** Area **426**
10-3 Measurement: Area **428**
10-4 Problem-Solving Strategy: Solve a Simpler Problem **432**
10-5 Triangles and Angles **434**
Mid-Chapter Check **437**
10-6 Geometry: Quadrilaterals **438**
10-7 Problem-Solving Investigation: Choose a Strategy **442**
10-8 Geometry: Solid Figures **444**
Game Time: Guess the Shape **447**
10-9 Complex Solid Figures **448**
Problem Solving in Art: Gardens Under Glass **450**
Explore **Measurement Activity for 10-10:** Volume **452**
10-10 Measurement: Find Volume **454**

ASSESSMENT
Study Guide and Review **458**
Chapter Test **465**
California Standards Practice **466**

California Standards Practice
• 425, 431, 437, 441, 446, 457, 465, 466, 467

H.O.T. Problems
Higher Order Thinking
421, 425, 430, 436, 441, 446, 449, 457

WRITING IN ▸MATH 421, 425, 427, 430, 433, 436, 437, 441, 443, 446, 449, 453, 457, 465

CHAPTER 11 Statistics: Data, Graphs, and Probability

Are You Ready for Chapter 11? **470**

Explore **Graphing Activity for 11-1:** Make a Bar Graph **471**

11-1 Bar Graphs **473**

11-2 Line Plots **476**

11-3 **Problem-Solving Strategy:** Make an Organized List **480**

Mid-Chapter Check **482**

Game Time: Catch Me if You Can! **483**

11-4 Identify Probability **484**

Problem Solving in Science: Eggs! **488**

11-5 **Problem-Solving Investigation:** Choose a Strategy **490**

Explore **Probability Activity for 11-6:** Outcomes **492**

11-6 Make Predictions **494**

ASSESSMENT

Study Guide and Review **498**

Chapter Test **503**

California Standards Practice **504**

California Standards Practice

- 479, 482, 487, 497, 503, 504, 505

H.O.T. Problems
Higher Order Thinking
475, 478, 487, 497

WRITING IN MATH 472, 475, 478, 481, 482, 487, 491, 493, 497, 503

CHAPTER 12 Fractions

Are You Ready for Chapter 12? 508

12-1 Parts of a Whole 509

12-2 **Problem-Solving Investigation:** Choose a Strategy 512

Explore **Math Activity for 12-3:** Equivalent Fractions 514

12-3 Find Equivalent Fractions 516

Game Time: Fraction Concentration 519

12-4 **Problem-Solving Strategy:** Draw a Picture 520

12-5 Compare Fractions 522

Mid-Chapter Check 525

Explore **Math Activity for 12-6:** Add Like Fractions 526

12-6 Add Like Fractions 528

Problem Solving in Science: The Buzz on Insects 532

Explore **Math Activity for 12-7:** Subtract Like Fractions 534

12-7 Subtract Like Fractions 536

ASSESSMENT

Study Guide and Review 540

Chapter Test 545

California Standards Practice 546

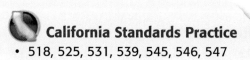

California Standards Practice

- 518, 525, 531, 539, 545, 546, 547

H.O.T. Problems
Higher Order Thinking
511, 518, 524, 531, 538

WRITING IN MATH 511, 513, 515, 518, 521, 524, 525, 527, 531, 535, 538, 545

CHAPTER 13 Fractions and Decimals

Are You Ready for Chapter 13? **550**

Explore **Math Activity for 13-1:** Fractions and Decimals **551**

13-1 Tenths **553**

Game Time: Fractoes and Decimoes **557**

13-2 Hundredths **558**

Mid-Chapter Check **561**

Problem Solving in Science: Continents **562**

13-3 **Problem-Solving Strategy:** Act It Out **564**

Explore **Math Activity for 13-4:** Fractions, Decimals, and Money **566**

13-4 Decimals and Money **568**

13-5 **Problem-Solving Investigation:** Choose a Strategy **572**

ASSESSMENT

Study Guide and Review **574**

Chapter Test **579**

California Standards Practice **580**

California Standards Practice

- 556, 561, 571, 579, 580, 581

H.O.T. Problems
Higher Order Thinking
556, 560, 571

WRITING IN ▸MATH 552, 556, 560, 561, 565, 567, 571, 573, 579

CHAPTER 14 Multiply by One-Digit Numbers

Are You Ready for Chapter 14? **584**

14-1 Multiply Multiples of 10, 100, and 1,000 .... **585**

14-2 **Problem-Solving Strategy:** Use Logical Reasoning **588**

14-3 Estimate Products **590**

Mid-Chapter Check **593**

14-4 Multiply by a One-Digit Number **594**

14-5 **Problem-Solving Investigation:** Choose a Strategy **598**

Explore **Math Activity for 14-6:** Multiplication with Rerouping **600**

14-6 Multiply Two-Digit Numbers **602**

14-7 Multiply Greater Numbers **606**

Game Time: High and Low **609**

14-8 Multiply Money **610**

Problem Solving in Art: Stamp Collecting **614**

ASSESSMENT

Study Guide and Review **616**

Chapter Test **621**

California Standards Practice **622**

California Standards Practice
- 593, 597, 605, 613, 621, 622, 623

H.O.T. Problems
Higher Order Thinking
587, 592, 597, 605, 608, 613

WRITING IN MATH 587, 589, 592, 593, 597, 599, 601, 605, 608, 613, 621

CHAPTER 15 Divide by One-Digit Numbers

Are You Ready for Chapter 15? 626

15-1 Divide Multiples of 10, 100, and 1,000 627

15-2 Estimate Quotients 630

Explore **Math Activity for 15-3:** Division 634

15-3 Two-Digit Quotients 636

Mid-Chapter Check 639

15-4 **Problem-Solving Strategy:** Work Backward 640

15-5 Three-Digit Quotients 642

Game Time: That's Close! 645

Problem Solving in Science: Roller Coaster Physics 646

15-6 **Problem-Solving Investigation:** Choose a Strategy 648

15-7 Divide Money 650

ASSESSMENT

Study Guide and Review 654

Chapter Test 659

California Standards Practice 660

California Standards Practice

- 633, 639, 653, 659, 660, 661

H.O.T. Problems
Higher Order Thinking
629, 633, 638, 644, 653

WRITING IN MATH 629, 633, 635, 638, 639, 641, 644, 649, 653, 659

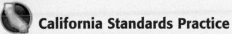

California Standards Review

Tips for Success CA1
Multiple-Choice Questions CA2
Practice by Standard CA4

Looking Ahead
to the Grade 4 Standards

1 Algebra: Function Tables (+/−) 664

2 Algebra: Function Tables (×/÷) 668

3 Ordered Pairs 672

4 Geometry: Congruent Figures 676

5 Geometry: Symmetry 678

Student Handbook

Built-In Workbooks

Extra Practice R2

Facts Practice R41

Reference

English-Spanish Glossary R49

Photo Credits R69

Index R70

H.O.T. Problems
Higher Order Thinking
667, 671, 675, 677, 679

WRITING IN ▸MATH 667, 671, 675, 677, 679

California Standards for Mathematics Grade 3

🔑 denotes Key standards

Standard	Text of Standard	Primary Citations	Supporting Citations
Number Sense			
1.0	**Students understand the place value of whole numbers:**	17–19, 22–30, 34–51, 70–73, 110–113	17–19, 24–25, 28–29, 34–41, 44–51, 68–81, 88–90, 93–95, 115, 120–121, 590–597, 602–606, 611–613, 646–647, 650–653
1.1	Count, read, and write whole numbers to 10,000	17–19	24–25, 28–29, 34–35, 38–35, CA4, CA5, CA6
1.2	Compare and order whole numbers to 10,000.	34–41	17–19, 44–51, CA4, CA6
🔑 **1.3**	Identify the place value for each digit in numbers to 10,000.	22–30, 42–43	34–41, 44–51, CA4, CA5, CA6
1.4	Round off numbers to 10,000 to the nearest ten, hundred, and thousand.	44–51, 70–73, 110–113	68–81, 88–90, 93–95, 115, 120–121, 590–597, 603–606, 611–613, 646–647, 650–653, CA5, CA6
🔑 **1.5**	Use expanded notation to represent numbers (e.g., 3,206 = 3,000 + 200 + 6).	24–30	594–597, 602–603, CA5, CA6
2.0	**Students calculate and solve problems involving addition, subtraction, multiplication, and division:**	20–21, 32–33, 65–69, 74–76, 82–87, 107–137, 155–159, 164–181, 184–189, 201–210, 214–227, 232–233, 251–281, 293–301, 304–319, 360–361, 396–397, 490–491, 512–513, 585–608, 614–615, 627–638, 640–653	70–73, 78–81, 88–90, 182, 211, 350–351, 432–433, 442–443,585–587, 590–608, 614–615, 627–629, 640–641, 648–653
🔑 **2.1**	Find the sum or difference of two whole numbers between 0 and 10,000.	20–21, 32–33, 65–69, 74–76, 82–87, 107–137, 490–491, 512–513, 588–589, 640–641	70–73, 78–81, 88–90, CA7, CA8, CA9
🔑 **2.2**	Memorize to automaticity the multiplication table for numbers between 1 and 10.	155–159, 164–181, 184–185, 189, 201–210, 214–227, 232–233	211, 182, 585–587, 590–608, CA9
🔑 **2.3**	Use the inverse relationship of multiplication and division to compute and check results.	251–281, 293–301, 304–312, 318–319, 636–638, 642–644	640, 650–663, 614–615, CA7, CA9
🔑 **2.4**	Solve simple problems involving multiplication of multidigit numbers by one-digit numbers (3,671 × 3 = _).	585–587, 590–608, 614–615	442–443, , CA7, CA9
2.5	Solve division problems in which a multidigit number is evenly divided by a one-digit number (135 ÷ 5 = _).	627–638, 642–649	640–641, CA8
2.6	Understand the special properties of 0 and 1 in multiplication and division.	186–188, 280–281	585–587, 627–629, CA8, CA9
2.7	Determine the unit cost when given the total cost and number of units.	314–317, 360–361, 650–653	350–351, CA2, CA3, CA8
2.8	Solve problems that require two or more of the skills mentioned above.	360–361, 396–397	350–351, 432–433, 648–649, CA9
3.0	**Students understand the relationship between whole numbers, simple fractions, and decimals:**	78–81, 88–95, 114–116, 509–511, 514–524, 526–539, 551–557, 572–573, 610–613, 650–653	512–519, 526–539, 551–565
3.1	Compare fractions represented by drawings or concrete materials to show equivalency and to add and subtract simple fractions in context (e.g., 1/2 of a pizza is the same amount as 2/4 of another pizza that is the same size; show that 3/8 is larger than 1/4).	509–511, 514–524	526–539, CA10

Standard	Text of Standard	Primary Citations	Supporting Citations
3.2	Add and subtract simple fractions (e.g., determine that $1/8 + 3/8$ is the same as $1/2$).	526–539	514–519, 555, CA11, CA12
3.3	Solve problems involving addition, subtraction, multiplication, and division of money amounts in decimal notation and multiply and divide money amounts in decimal notation by using whole-number multipliers and divisors.	78–81, 88–95, 114–116, 572–573, 610–613, 650–653	512–513, CA11, CA12
3.4	Know and understand that fractions are two different representations of the same concept (e.g., 50 cents is 1/2 of a dollar, 75 cents is 3/4 of a dollar).	566–571	551–565, CA11, CA12
Algebra and Functions			
1.0	**Students select appropriate symbols, operations, and properties to represent, describe, simplify, and solve number relationships:**	65–67, 138–141, 160–163, 182–183, 228–231, 320–327, 368–371, 404–407	65–66, 206–209, 214–227, 347, 355, 362–365, 522–524, 600–601
1.1	Represent relationships of quantities in the form of mathematical expressions, equations, or inequalities.	65–67, 138–141, 182–183, 320–327	600–601, CA13, CA15
1.2	Solve problems involving numeric equations or inequalities.	320–323	65–66, 522–524, CA13, CA14
1.3	Select appropriate operational and relational symbols to make an expression true (e.g., if 4 _ 3 = 12, what operation symbol goes in the blank?).	138–141, 320–323	324–327, CA13, CA15
1.4	Express simple unit coversions in symbolic form (e.g., _ inches = _ feet $\times$ 12).	368–371, 404–407	347, 355, 362–365, CA14, CA15
1.5	Recognize and use the commutative and associative properties of multiplication (e.g., if $5 \times 7 = 35$, then what is 7×5? And if $5 \times 7 \times 3 = 105$, then what is $7 \times 3 \times 5$?).	160–163, 228–231	206–209, 214–224, 320–323, CA14, CA15
2.0	**Students represent simple functional relationships:**	212–213, 234–237, 302–303	157–159, 165, 168, 175, 178, 203–209, 212–213, 302–303, 314–317, 610–613
2.1	Solve simple problems involving a functional relationship between two quantities (e.g., find the total cost of multiple items given the cost per unit).	234–237	212–213, 302–303, 314–317, 610–613, CA16, CA17, CA18
2.2	Extend and recognize a linear pattern by its rules (e.g., the number of legs on a given number of horses may be calculated by counting by 4s or by multiplying the number of horses by 4).	212–213, 234–237, 302–303	157–159, 165, 168, 175, 178, 203–209, 360–363, CA16, CA17, CA18
Measurement and Geometry			
1.0	**Students choose and use appropriate units and measurement tools to quantify the properties of objects:**	341–349, 352–357, 362–371, 383–394, 398–407, 422–433, 442–443, 452–457	366–367, 385–388, 392–394, 398–401, 404–407, 419–421, 432, 450–453, 480–481
1.1	Choose the appropriate tools and units (metric and U.S.) and estimate and measure length, liquid volume, and weight/mass.	341–349, 352–357, 362–365, 383–394, 398–403	366–367, 404–407, CA19
1.2	Estimate or determine the area and volume of solid figures by covering them with squares or by counting the number of cubes that would fill them.	426–431, 442–443, 452–457,	480–481, 432, CA20, CA21
1.3	Find the perimeter of a polygon with integer sides.	422–425, 432–433	450–451, 419–421, CA16, CA17, CA18

Standard	Text of Standard	Primary Citations	Supporting Citations
1.4	Carry out simple unit conversions within a system of measurement (e.g., centimeters and meters, hours and minutes).	346–349, 354–357, 362–371, 404–407	352–353, 385–388, 392–394, 398–401, CA21
2.0	**Students describe and compare the attributes of plane and solid geometric figures and use their understanding to show relationships and solve problems:**	419–421, 434–441, 444–446, 448–449, 450–451, 605	419–421, 425–431, 441, 446, 444–447, 450–451, 539
2.1	Identify, describe, and classify polygons (including pentagons, hexagons, and octagons).	419–421, 450–451	425, 431, CA22, CA24
2.2	Identify attributes of triangles (e.g. two equal sides for the isosceles triangle, three equal sides for the equilateral triangle, right angle for the right triangle).	434–436	441, 450–451, 539, CA22, CA23, CA24
2.3	Identify attributes of quadrilaterals (e.g. parallel sides for the parallelogram, right angles for the rectangle, equal sides and right angles for the square).	438–441	419–421, 446, CA23, CA24
2.4	Identify right angles in geometric figures or in appropriate objects and determine whether other angles are greater or less than a right angle.	434–441	426–431, CA24
2.5	Identify, describe, and classify common three-dimensional geometric objects (e.g., cube, rectangular solid, sphere, prism, pyramid, cone, and cylinder).	444–446	447, CA23
2.6	Identify common solid objects that are the components needed to make a more complex solid object.	448–449	444–446, CA24
Statistics, Data Analysis, and Probability			
1.0	**Students conduct simple probability experiments by determining the number of possible outcomes and make simple predictions:**	471–479, 484–489, 492–497	471–483, 492–497
1.1	Identify whether common events are certain, likely, unlikely, or improbable.	484–489	492–497, CA26, CA27
1.2	Record the possible outcomes for a simple event (e.g., tossing a coin) and systematically keep track of the outcomes when the event is repeated many times.	492–493	480–481, 495, CA25
1.3	Summarize and display the results of probability experiments in a clear and organized way (e.g., use a bar graph or a line plot).	471–479	483, 492–493, CA26, CA27
1.4	Use the results of probability experiments to predict future events (e.g., use a line plot to predict the temperature forecast for the next day).	494–497	471–479, CA27
Mathematical Reasoning			
1.0	**Students make decisions about how to approach problems:**	*Used throughout the text.* For example, 20–21, 184–185, 480–481.	
1.1	Analyze problems by identifying relationships, distinguishing relevant from irrelevant information, sequencing, prioritizing information, and observing patterns	20–21, 32–33, 128–129, 184–185, 212–213, 262–263, 274–275, 350–351, 390–391, 480–481, 490–491, 648–649	360–361, 366–367, 396–397, 426–427, 432–433, 512–513, 640–641, CA28, CA29

Standard	Text of Standard	Primary Citations	Supporting Citations
1.2	Determine when and how to break a problem into simpler parts.	360–361, 432–433, 448–453, 572–573, 640–641	350–351, 585–587, 627–629, 634–635, CA28
2.0	**Students use strategies, skills, and concepts in finding solutions:**	*Used throughout the text.* For example, 74–81, 222–224, 556–567.	
2.1	Use estimation to verify the reasonableness of calculated results.	74–81, 88–95, 426–431, 590–592, 602–608, 630–633, 640–641	110–121, 343–349, 354–357, 362–365, 442–443, 452–457, 594–597, 650–653, CA30
2.2	Apply strategies and results from simpler problems to more complex problems.	86–87, 492–493, 585–587, 600–601	155–159, 177, 186–189, 210, 225, 253–255, 264–271, 324-327, 343–345, 432–441, 444–453, 528–531, 536–539, 627–629, CA31
2.3	Use a variety of methods, such as words, numbers, symbols, charts, graphs, tables, diagrams, and models, to explain mathematical reasoning.	155–159, 203–209, 222–224, 251–261, 264–271, 341–342, 352–353, 396–397, 512–515, 526–527, 534–535, 564–565, 588–589, 634–635	22–23, 32–33, 68–69, 84–85, 107, 160–181, 184–185, 274–281, 302–303, 320–323, 426–431, 434–443, 490–497, 509–511, 551–552, 558–560, 566–567, 636–641, CA30
2.4	Express the solution clearly and logically by using the appropriate mathematical notation and terms and clear language; support solutions with evidence in both verbal and symbolic work.	566–567	65–67, 228–231, 234–237, 324–237, 568–571, 642–644, CA31
2.5	Indicate the relative advantages of exact and approximate solutions to problems and give answers to a specified degree of accuracy.	68–73	383–388, 590–592, 630–633, CA31
2.6	Make precise calculations and check the validity of the results from the context of the problem.	130–137	78–81, 128–132, 134–137, 512–513, 642–644, CA31
3.0	**Students move beyond a particular problem by generalizing to other situations:**	*Used throughout the text.* For example, 120–121, 293–294, 494–497.	
3.1	Evaluate the reasonableness of the solution in the context of the original situation.	120–121, 124–127	78–81, 324–327, 588, 589, 602–605, CA32, CA33
3.2	Note the method of deriving the solution and demonstrate a conceptual understanding of the derivation by solving similar problems.	293–294, 551-552	86–95, 134–137, 295–306, 310–312, 341–342, 404–407, 448–449, 452–453, 512–513, 551–556, CA32, CA33
3.3	Develop generalizations of the results obtained and apply them in other circumstances.	22–23, 201–202, 471–472, 494–497	293–294, 426–427, 484–487, 610–613, CA33

Scavenger Hunt

Chapter 1

Let's Get Started

Use the Scavenger Hunt below to learn where things are located in each chapter.

1. What is the title of Chapter 1?
2. What is the Main Idea of Lesson 1-1?
3. How do you know which words are vocabulary words?
4. What are the vocabulary words for Lesson 1-3?
5. What is the key concept shown in Lesson 1-9?
6. How many Examples are presented in Lesson 1-4?
7. What is the web address where you could find extra examples?
8. On page 29, there is a Remember tip box. How does the Remember tip help you?
9. How many exercises are there in Lesson 1-5?
10. Suppose you need more practice on a concept. Where can you go for Extra Practice?
11. Suppose you're doing your homework on page 36 and you get stuck on Exercise 18. Where could you find help?
12. What is the web address that would allow you to take a self-check quiz to be sure you understand the lesson?
13. On what pages will you find the Chapter 1 Study Guide and Review?
14. Suppose you can't figure out how to do Exercise 7 in the Study Guide and Review on page 53. Where could you find help?

Math? Symbols?

Start Smart

Let's Review!

1 Problem Solving 2
2 Number Sense 4
3 Algebra and Functions 6
4 Measurement 8
5 Geometry 10
6 Statistics, Data Analysis, and Probability 12

The California Sea Otter

Reinforcement of Standard 2NS2.2 Find the sum or difference of two whole numbers up to three digits long.

START 1 SMART

Problem Solving

The Great Giants

California is home to some of the tallest trees in the world. A Coast Redwood tree is the tallest at 321 feet tall. A Coast Douglas Fir is the second tallest at 301 feet tall.

How much taller is the Coast Redwood than the Coast Douglas Fir?

You can use the four-step plan to solve math problems. The four steps are Understand, Plan, Solve, and Check.

Understand

- **Read the problem carefully.**
- **What facts do you know?**
- **What do you need to find?**

You know the height of the Coast Redwood and the Coast Douglas Fir. You need to find how much taller the Coast Redwood is than the Coast Douglas Fir.

Plan

- **Think about how the facts relate to each other.**
- **Make a plan to solve the problem.**

To find how much taller the Coast Redwood is than the Coast Douglas Fir, you can use subtraction.

Solve

- **Use your plan to solve the problem.**

321 feet	Coast Redwood
− 301 feet	Coast Douglas Fir
20 feet	

The Coast Redwood is 20 feet taller than the Coast Douglas Fir.

Check

- **Look back at the problem.**
- **Does your answer make sense?**
- **If not, solve the problem another way.**

You can check the subtraction by using addition. $20 + 301 = 321$. So, the answer is correct.

Did you Know?

The third tallest tree is the General Sherman Tree in Sequoia National Park. It is 275 feet tall and is still growing!

CHECK What You Know **Multiplication and Division**

1. List the four steps of the Four-Step Problem-Solving Plan.

2. WRITING IN ▸MATH Describe each step of the four-step problem-solving plan.

Reinforcement of Standard 2NS1.3 Order and compare whole numbers to 1,000 by using the symbols <, >, =.

START SMART 2

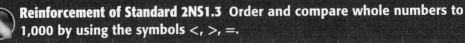

Number Sense

Now That's HOT!

Death Valley National Monument contains many mountain peaks. It also contains the lowest point in North America, 282 feet below sea level.

CHECK What You Know — Place Value

The model shows the value of each digit in 282.

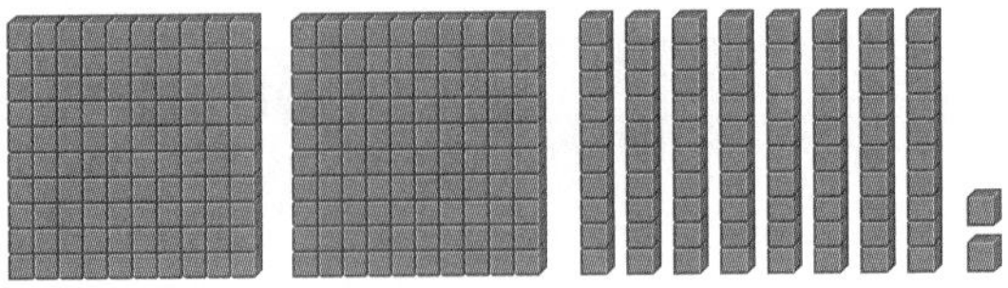

1. Copy and complete the place value chart below.

Number	Hundreds	Tens	Ones
282	2	8	2
134	■	■	■
120	■	■	■
903	■	■	■

2. Write each number in Exercise 1 in expanded form.

✓ CHECK What You Know Compare and Order Numbers

There are 307 species of birds and 36 species of reptiles found in Death Valley, California. Since 307 is greater than 36, you can write 307 > 36.

Compare. Write <, >, or =.

3. 87 ● 108 **4.** 425 ● 45 **5.** 307 ● 310

6. 313 ● 313 **7.** 580 ● 508 **8.** 919 ● 929

Did you Know?

Death Valley is one of the hottest places on earth. The temperature once reached 134 degrees Fahrenheit (°F).

Death Valley is known as the warmest location in North America. The table shows the average temperature in Death Valley for four months of the year.

Month	June	July	August	September
Average Temperature	109° F	115° F	113° F	106° F

9. Which month is the warmest?

10. Which month is the least warm?

11. Order the temperature from greatest to least.

12. **WRITING IN ▸MATH** Explain how to order numbers from greatest to least.

Reinforcement of Standard 2AF1.2 Relate problem situations to number sentences involving addition and subtraction.

START SMART 3

Algebra and Functions

At the Aquarium

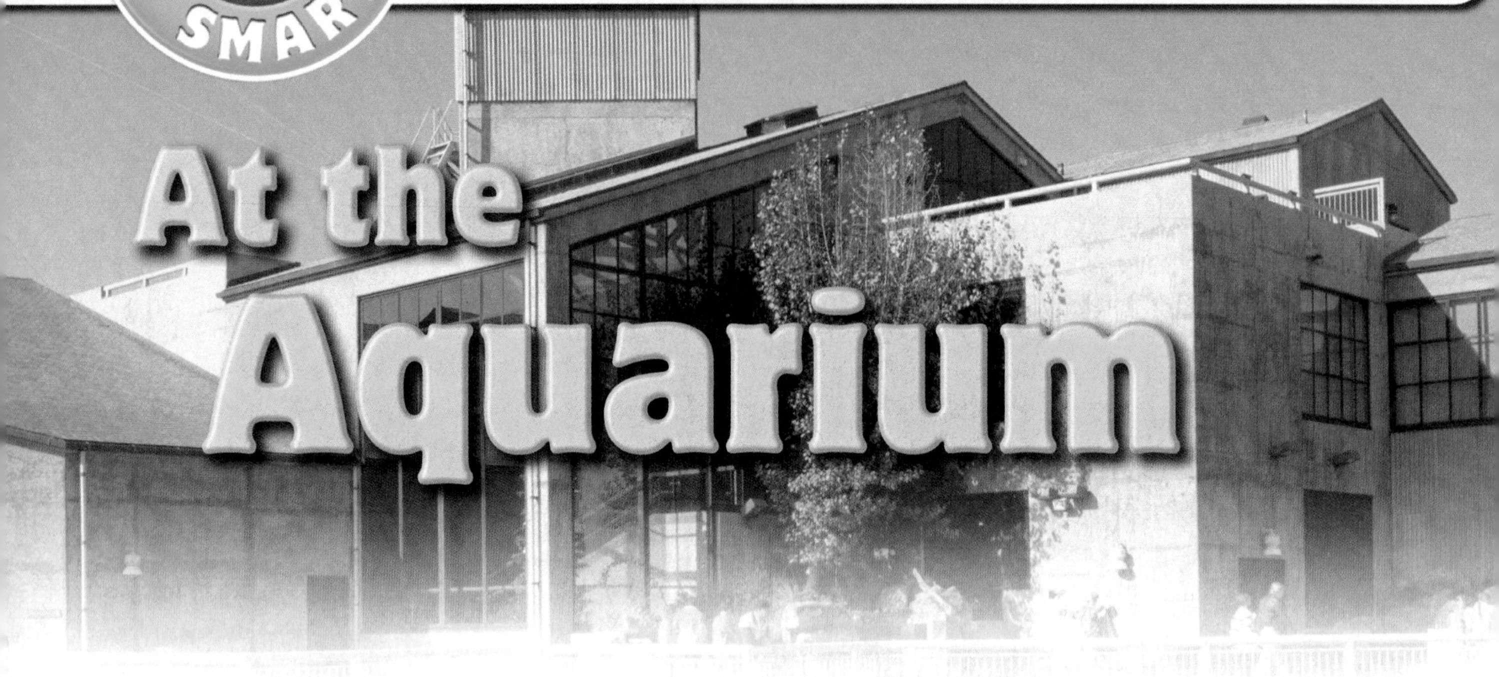

The Monterey Bay Aquarium is home to sea life such as sea stars, sharks, stingrays, penguins, jellyfish, and giant octopuses.

CHECK What You Know — Addition Rules

Ming sees 3 sharks and 4 penguins. Tomás sees 4 penguins and 3 sharks. The sum in $3 + 4 = 4 + 3$ is the same since the order in which numbers are added does not change the answer.

1. Hernando sees 5 sea otters and 8 sharks. Draw a picture using circles to show that $5 + 8 = 8 + 5$.

2. Draw a picture to show that $3 + 2 + 4 = 2 + 4 + 3$.

Tell what number is missing in each number sentence.

3. $3 + \blacksquare = 2 + 3$

4. $\blacksquare + 6 = 6 + 5$

5. $10 + 7 + 1 = 1 + 7 + \blacksquare$

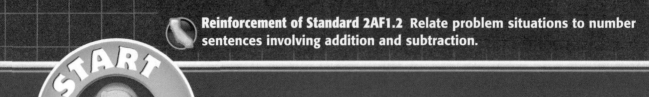

6. $9 + 12 + 3 = 3 + \blacksquare + 9$

CHECK What You Know   Number Sentences

Suppose 25 students went on a field trip to the Monterey Bay Aquarium. There were 12 boys. How many girls went? The number sentence shows this problem situation.

Number of boys		Number of girls		Total students
12	+	■	=	25

25 − 12 = 13. So, 13 girls went on the field trip.

Did you Know

A variety of sea stars can be found at the Monterey Bay Aquarium. The Sunflower Star can have up to 24 arms.

Choose the number sentence that can be used to solve the problem. Then solve the problem.

7. Carlos had $12. He bought a toy shark. He now has $5. How much did the shark cost?

8. Twelve penguins are standing on a rock. Seven jump into the water. How many are now on the rock?

A. 12 − ■ = 5

B. 7 + 12 = ■

C. 5 + ■ = 12

D. 12 − 7 = ■

9. There were 5 fish in a tank. Now there are 12 fish. How many fish were added?

10. A toy star fish costs $7. A stuffed octopus costs $12. What is the total cost?

11. **WRITING IN ▶MATH** Lydia adds 7 + 5 and then adds the result to 10. Will she get the same number if she adds 7 to the result of 5 + 10? Explain.

Reinforcement of Standard 2MG1.3 Measure the length of an object to the nearest inch and/or centimeter.

START SMART 4

Measurement

Measure Away

California's state quarter was released in January 2005. The U.S. Mint made more than 520 million California quarters.

CHECK What You Know **Customary Units**

One customary unit of measurement is the inch. One California state quarter has a length of about 1 inch.

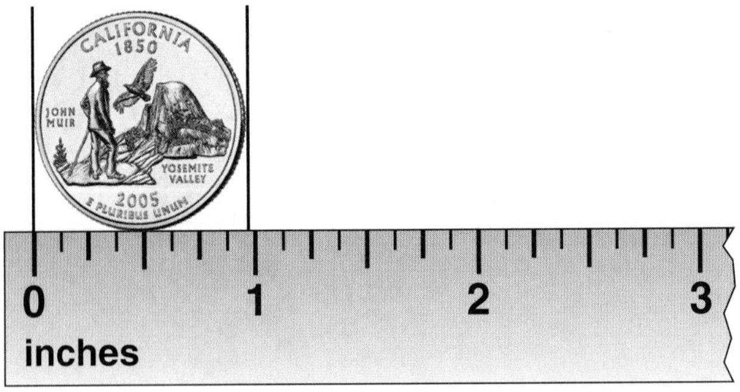

Estimate the length of each set of coins to the nearest inch. Then use a ruler to measure the length to the nearest inch.

1. 

2. 

3. How many pennies in a row would measure about 5 inches?

CHECK What You Know — Metric Units

One metric unit of measurement is the centimeter. Two California state quarters are about 5 centimeters in length.

Did you Know

The California quarter was the thirty-first state quarter to be released since California was the thirty-first state to be admitted into the Union.

Estimate the length of each set of coins to the nearest centimeter. Then use a ruler to measure the length to the nearest centimeter.

4. 

5. 

6. 

7. How many nickels in a row would measure about 10 centimeters?

8. WRITING IN ▸MATH Explain how to use a ruler to measure in inches and in centimeters.

Reinforcement of Standard 2MG2.1 Describe and classify plane and solid geometric shapes (e.g. circle, triangle, square, rectangle, sphere, pyramid, cube, rectangular prism) according to the number of faces, edges, and vertices.

START 5 SMART

Geometry

Food and Geometry

California grows more crops than any other state. Crops grown in California include strawberries, grapes, and oranges.

CHECK What You Know — Three-Dimensional Figures

Many food items are examples of three-dimensional figures. A three-dimensional figure has length, width, and height.

1. What shape does an orange resemble?

A cylinder **C** cube

B sphere **D** pyramid

2. What shape does a strawberry resemble?

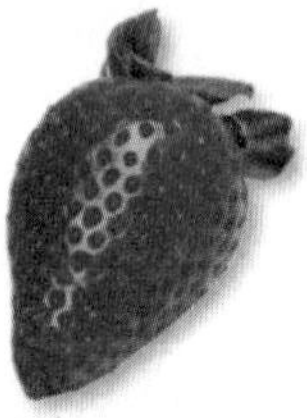

A cone **C** sphere

B cylinder **D** cube

CHECK What You Know — Two-Dimensional Figures

A two-dimensional figure is a shape with length and width. A circle and a square are two-dimensional figures.

Copy and complete the table.

	Figure	Name	Sides
3.			
4.	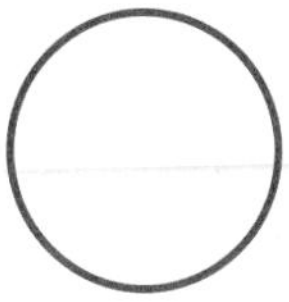		
5.			
6.	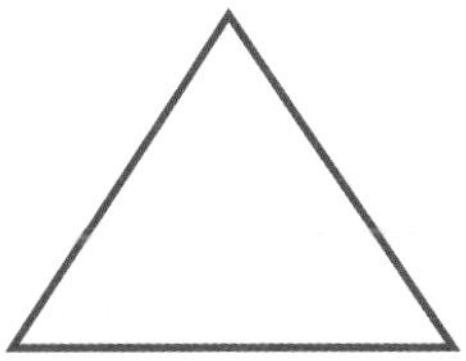		

Did you Know

Each year, California grows more than 1,400,000,000 pounds of strawberries!

7. **WRITING IN ▸MATH** How is a square different than a cube? How they are they alike?

Reinforcement of Standard 2SDAP1.4 Ask and answer simple questions related to data representations.

START SMART 6

Statistics, Data Analysis, and Probability

How Fast Can You Go?

There are about 30 amusement parks in California. These parks have a total of 72 roller coasters.

CHECK What You Know Pictograph

Justin asked his friends which kind of amusement park ride they like best. He put their answers in a pictograph.

Favorite Amusement Park Rides	
Roller coaster	☺ ☺ ☺ ☺
Ferris wheel	☺ ☺
Water ride	☺ ☺ ☺ ☺ ☺
Merry-go-round	☺ ☺ ☺

Key ☺ = 2 student

1. How many friends did Justin survey?

2. Which kind of ride is most liked?

3. How many more friends like roller coasters than Ferris wheels?

CHECK What You Know — Tally Chart and Bar Graph

Alicia asked her friends how many times they rode a roller coaster last summer. She recorded the results in a tally chart.

Ride a Roller Coaster?

Name	Tally	Total
Marcos		7
Samuel		3
Bonny		2
Star		10

Did you Know?

The Silver Bullet, a roller coaster at Knott's Berry Farm in Buena Park, California, thrills 1,300 riders each hour.

4. Copy and complete the tally chart.

5. How many friends did Alicia survey?

6. How many times did they ride a roller coaster in all?

7. How many more times did Star ride a roller coaster than Bonny?

8. Copy the table below. Use the data above and X's to make a bar graph. The data for Marcos is shown.

Ride a Roller Coaster?

Marcos	X	X	X	X	X	X	X			
Samuel										
Bonny										
Star										

9. WRITING IN MATH Explain the difference between a pictograph and a tally chart.

CHAPTER 1

Place Value and Number Sense

BIG Idea What is the place value of a digit in a number?

Place value is the value given to a digit by its place in a number.

Example Every 5 seconds, a cat purrs about 125 times. The number 125 is read *one hundred twenty-five.*

Hundreds	Tens	Ones
1	2	5
↑ 100	↑ 20	↑ 5

What will I learn in this chapter?

- Count, read, and write whole numbers.
- Identify place value of whole numbers.
- Compare and order whole numbers.
- Round numbers to the nearest ten, hundred, and thousand.
- Use the four-step problem-solving plan.

Key Vocabulary

pattern

place value

equal to

round

Math Online **Student Study Tools at** ca.gr3math.com

FOLDABLES™ Study Organizer

Make this foldable to help you organize information about place value and number sense. Begin with one sheet of 11″ × 17″ paper.

1. **Fold** the paper in half as shown.

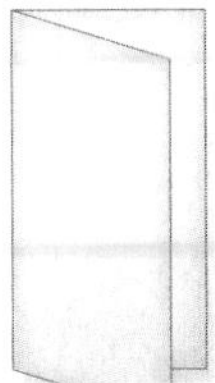

2. **Unfold** and fold one side up 5 inches.

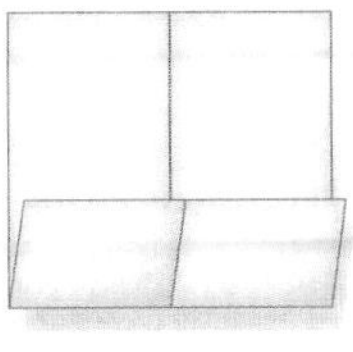

3. **Fold** again so the pockets are inside. Glue the edges.

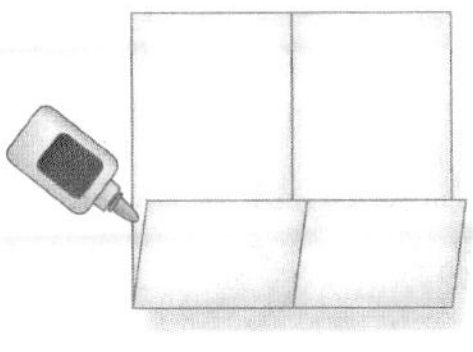

4. **Label** as shown. Record what you learn.

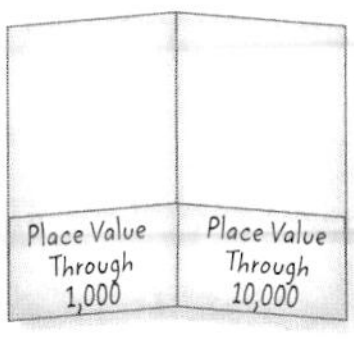

ARE YOU READY for Chapter 1?

You have two ways to check prerequisite skills for this chapter.

Option 2

Math Online Take the Chapter Readiness Quiz at ca.gr3math.com.

Option 1

Complete the Quick Check below.

QUICK Check

Write each number. (Prior grade)

1.

Hundreds	Tens	Ones
	1	4

2.

Hundreds	Tens	Ones
	3	3

3.

Hundreds	Tens	Ones
1	1	0

4. 1 ten 5 ones

5. 1 hundred 2 ones

6. twenty-four

7. one hundred thirty eight

Write the number of tens and ones in the following numbers. (Prior grade)

8. 12 **9.** 26 **10.** 31 **11.** 85

12. Manuel and his family went to the circus. They paid $45 for the tickets. They also bought food for $20. They spent a total of $65. Name how many tens and ones are in 65.

Find a pattern and write the next two numbers. (Prior grade)

13. 2, 4, 6, 8, ■, ■

14. 1, 3, 5, 7, ■, ■

15. 5, 10, 15, 20, ■, ■

16. 10, 20, 30, 40, ■, ■

17. Sonja read 4 pages the first day, she read 8 pages the second day, and 12 pages the third day. If the pattern continued, how many pages did she read on the fourth day?

1-1 Number Patterns

GET READY to Learn

Number patterns are everywhere. Look at the speed limit signs shown. What number pattern do you see?

MAIN IDEA

I will find patterns in numbers.

Standard 3NS1.1 Count, read, and write whole numbers to 10,000.

New Vocabulary

pattern

A **pattern** is a series of numbers or figures that follow a rule. A hundreds chart shows many number patterns.

1	2	3	4	5	6	7	8	9	10
11	12	13	14	15	16	17	18	19	20
21	22	23	24	25	26	27	28	29	30
31	32	33	34	35	36	37	38	39	40
41	42	43	44	45	46	47	48	49	50
51	52	53	54	55	56	57	58	59	60
61	62	63	64	65	66	67	68	69	70
71	72	73	74	75	76	77	78	79	80
81	82	83	84	85	86	87	88	89	90
91	92	93	94	95	96	97	98	99	100

EXAMPLE Find and Extend a Number Pattern

1 Identify a pattern in 15, 25, 35, 45, ■. Then find the missing number.

The pattern shows that 10 is added to each number.

15, 25, 35, 45, ■

+10 +10 +10 +10

The missing number is 55.

Real-World EXAMPLE

Remember

When looking for a pattern, see how the next number changes from the one before it.

2 READING **Lakeisha is reading a book. If the pattern continues, how many pages will she read on Saturday?**

Pages Lakeisha Read

Day	Pages
Monday	3
Tuesday	6
Wednesday	9
Thursday	12
Friday	15
Saturday	■

Each day, Lakeisha reads 3 more pages than the day before.

3, 6, 9, 12, 15, 18

+3 +3 +3 +3 +3

So, Lakeisha will read 18 pages on Saturday.

Online Personal Tutor at ca.gr3math.com

Real-World EXAMPLE

3 SPORTS **Mia's bowling scores are 150, 145, 140, ■, 130, ■. Find the missing numbers in the pattern.**

Notice that 5 is subtracted from each number.

150, 145, 140, 135, 130, 125

−5 −5 −5 −5 −5

The missing numbers are 135 and 125.

CHECK What You Know

Identify a pattern. Then find the missing numbers. See Examples 1–3 (pp. 17–18)

1. 10, 12, 14, 16, ■, 20

2. 5, 10, 15, 20, ■, 30

3. 20, ■, 40, 50, ■, 70

4. 110, 107, ■, 101, 98, ■

5. A track team runs 4 laps on Day 1, 6 laps on Day 2, and 8 laps on Day 3. The pattern continues. How many will they run on Day 5?
See Example 3 (p. 18)

6. Talk About It Suppose you start at 20 and skip count to 36. Is the pattern skip counting by 3s? Explain.

Practice and Problem Solving

EXTRA PRACTICE See page R2.

Identify a pattern. Then find the missing numbers. See Examples 1–3 (pp. 17–18)

7. 10, 14, 18, ■, 26, 30

8. 13, 18, 23, ■, 33, 38

9. 28, 24, 20, ■, 12, 8

10. 63, 60, ■, 54, 51, 48

11. 34, 36, ■, 40, ■, 44

12. 71, 76, 81, ■, 91, ■

13. 105, 100, ■, 90, ■, 80

14. 100, 110, 120, ■, ■

15. Each soccer player has a number. If the pattern continues, what is Takisha's number?

Soccer Players' Numbers	
Name	**Number**
Kisho	3
Kayla	5
Michael	7
Lenora	9
Takisha	■

16. Dillon is saving his allowance. How much money will he have saved at week 5? at week 10?

Dillon's Savings	
Week	**Total Saved**
1	$4
2	$8
3	$12
4	$16
5	■

17. Elki draws 6 stars, 10 stars, 14 stars, and then 18 stars. If he continues the pattern, how many stars will he draw in the next row?

18. Measurement A school bell rings at 8:15, 8:45, 9:15, and 9:45. If the pattern continues, when will the bell ring next?

H.O.T. Problems

19. OPEN ENDED Create a number pattern. Explain your pattern.

NUMBER SENSE Copy and complete. Use a hundreds chart if needed.

20.

	57		
	67		
76			

21.

51			
		63	

22.

44		
		66

23. WRITING IN ▸MATH Describe the pattern that can produce the numbers 104, 99, 94, 89, ... What number is next?

1-2 Problem-Solving Skill

MAIN IDEA I will use the four-step plan to solve problems.

Standard 3MR1.1 Analyze problems by identifying relationships, distinguishing relevant and irrelevant information, sequencing and prioritizing information, and observing patterns. Standard 3NS2.1 Find the sum or difference of two whole numbers between 0 and 10,000.

Daniela's family went to a zoo. They learned that a roadrunner is 1 foot tall. An African elephant is 12 feet tall. How much taller is an African elephant than a roadrunner?

Roadrunner

Understand

What facts do you know?

- The roadrunner is 1 foot tall.
- The African elephant is 12 feet tall.

What do you need to find?

- You need to find how much taller an African elephant is than a roadrunner.

Plan

To find out how much taller an African elephant is than a roadrunner, subtract.

Solve

$$\begin{array}{r} 12 \\ -\ 1 \\ \hline 11 \end{array}$$

12 ← height of elephant
1 ← height of roadrunner

So, the elephant is 11 feet taller than the roadrunner.

Check

Since addition and subtraction are inverse operations, you can use addition to check the subtraction.

$$\begin{array}{r} 11 \\ +\ 1 \\ \hline 12 \end{array} \qquad \begin{array}{r} 12 \\ -\ 1 \\ \hline 11 \end{array}$$

So, the answer is correct.

ANALYZE the Skill

Refer to the problem on the previous page.

1. Explain why you subtract 1 from 12 to find how much taller an elephant is than a roadrunner.

2. Suppose an elephant is 8 feet tall. How much shorter would a roadrunner be?

3. Suppose a roadrunner is 3 feet tall. How much taller would an elephant be than the roadrunner?

4. Look back at Exercise 3. Check your answer. How do you know that it is correct? Explain.

PRACTICE the Skill

EXTRA PRACTICE
See page R2.

Solve. Use the *four-step plan*.

5. Cameron and Mara walk 2 blocks and then they turned a corner and walk 4 blocks. How many blocks do they need to walk to return to their starting place?

6. **Algebra** Find the missing numbers.

Input	16	■	24	28	32
Output	18	22	■	■	34

7. Rachel sold 4 glasses of lemonade. How much money did she make?

8. Lola read a book that has 24 more pages than the book Fran read. Fran's book has 12 pages. How many pages does Lola's book have?

9. If the pattern continues, what number will be the 6th and 7th number in the pattern?

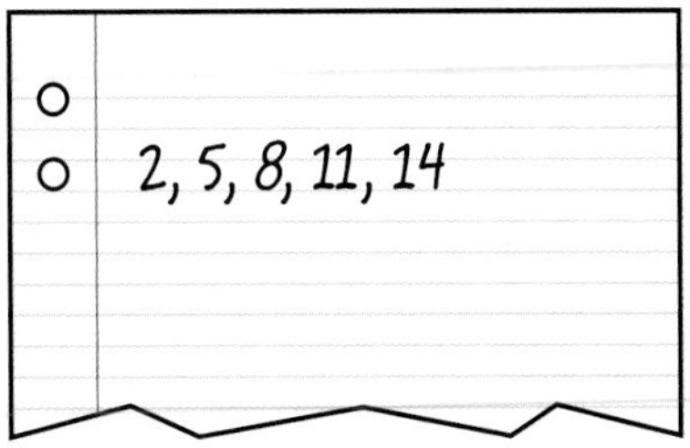

10. Cortez and Gloria went to the store to buy some bread. Each bought 3 different loaves of bread. How many different loaves of bread did they buy?

11. Darnell drew 4 pictures Monday. He drew 8 pictures Tuesday and 12 on Wednesday. If the pattern continues, how many pictures will he draw on Thursday?

12. WRITING IN MATH Explain how the four-step plan helps you solve a problem.

Explore

Math Activity for 1-3
Place Value

A **digit** is any symbol used to write whole numbers. The numbers (0, 1, 2, 3, 4, 5, 6, 7, 8, 9) are all digits. The **place value** of a digit tells what value it has in a number. Base-ten blocks can be used to explore place value.

MAIN IDEA

I will use models to explore place value through thousands.

Standard 3NS1.3 Identify place value for each digit in numbers to 10,000.

Standard 3MR3.3 Develop generalizations of the results obtained and apply them in other circumstances.

You Will Need
base-ten blocks

ACTIVITY

1 Use base-ten blocks to show 142 in two ways.

One Way **Use hundreds, tens, and ones.**

Another Way **Use tens and ones.**

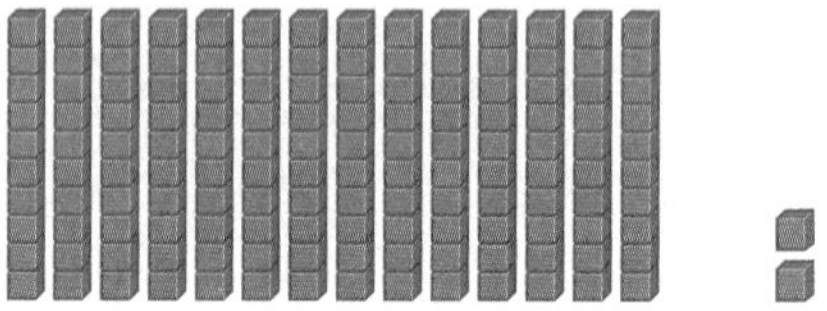

Concepts in Motion

Animation
ca.gr3math.com

Hands-On Activity

ACTIVITY

2 Use base-ten blocks to show 1,025 in two ways.

One Way **Use thousands, hundreds, tens, and ones.**

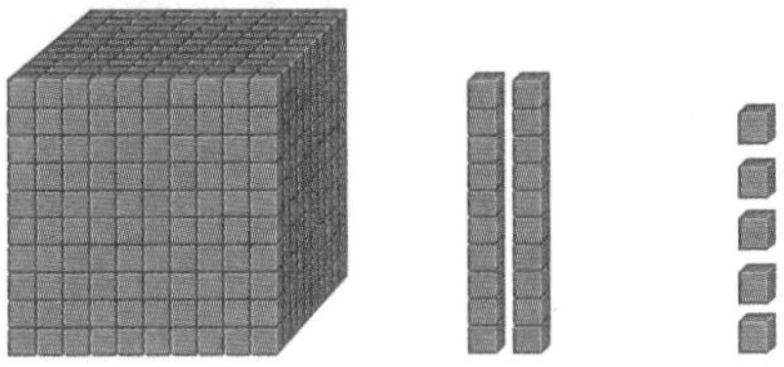

1 thousand 2 tens 5 ones

Another Way **Use hundreds, tens, and ones.**

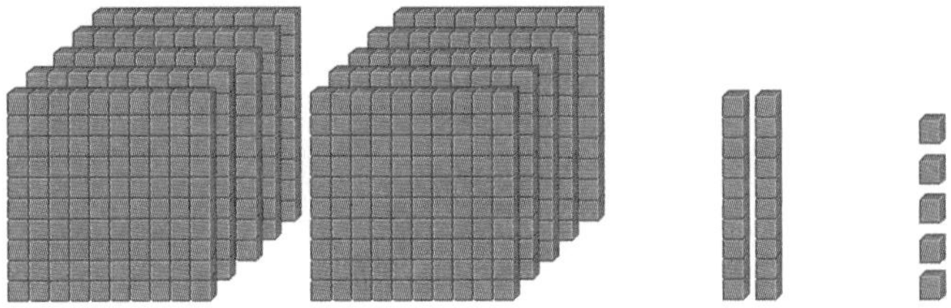

10 hundreds 2 tens 5 ones

Think About It

1. Why can you use different combinations of thousands, hundreds, tens, and ones to show the same number.

CHECK What You Know

Use base-ten blocks to show each number in two ways.

2. 135 **3.** 304 **4.** 1,283 **5.** 1,890

Write each number.

6.

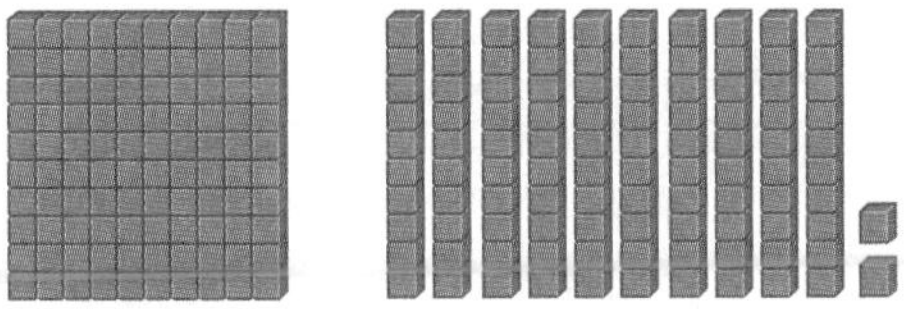

7.

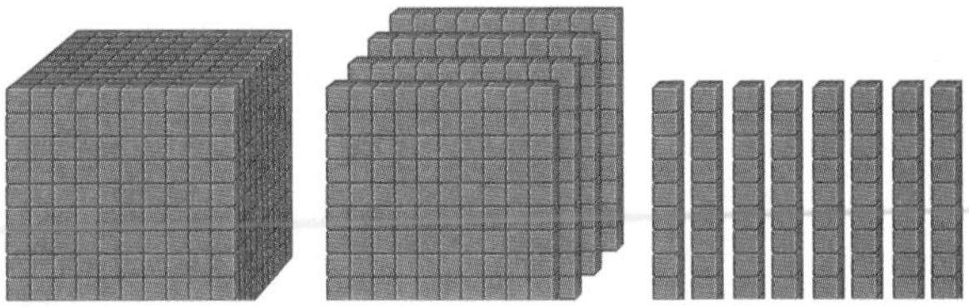

8. WRITING IN ▸MATH Explain how base-ten blocks are helpful in understanding numbers.

1-3 Place Value through 1,000

GET READY to Learn

The Statue of Liberty recently celebrated her 120th birthday. The height from the top of the base to the torch is 1,813 inches.

MAIN IDEA

I will read, write, and identify place value of whole numbers through thousands.

Standard 3NS1.3 Identify place value for each digit in numbers to 10,000.

Standard 3NS1.5 Use expanded notation to represent numbers (e.g., 3,206 = 3,000 + 200 + 6).

New Vocabulary

digit
place value
standard form
expanded form
word form

The number 1,813 has four **digits**. A digit is any symbol used to write whole numbers. The **place value** of a digit tells what value it has in a number.

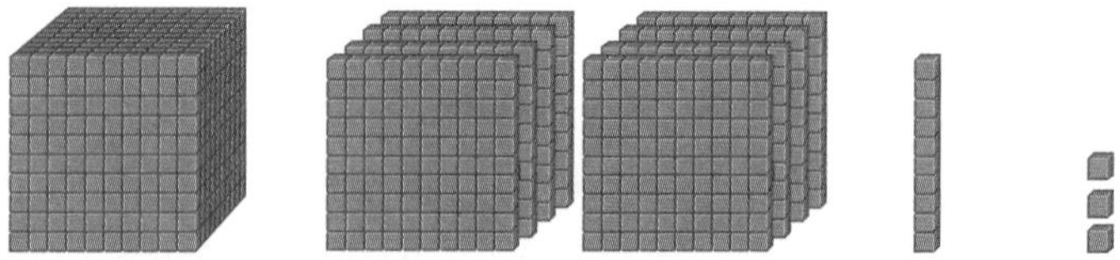

A place value chart can help you understand place value.

EXAMPLE Identify Place Value

1 Identify the place value of the underlined digit in <u>1</u>,813. Then write the value of the digit.

Thousands	Hundreds	Tens	Ones
1	8	1	3

- The value of the 1 is 1,000. 1 × 1,000
- The value of the 8 is 800. 8 × 100
- The value of the 1 is 10. 1 × 10
- The value of the 3 is 3. 3 × 1

The value of the underlined digit is 1,000.

Real-World EXAMPLE

2 STATUES If ten people climb the stairs to the top and back down the Statue of Liberty, they will have walked 7,080 steps. Identify the place of the underlined digit in 7,0̲80. Then write its value.

The place value chart shows 7,080.

Thousands	Hundreds	Tens	Ones
7	0	8	0

A comma is placed between periods.

Remember

In 7,080, there are two place holders. The zero in the hundreds place and the zero in the ones place.

The underlined digit, 0, is in the hundreds place. Its value is zero. There are no hundreds. When 0 is used in a number, it is sometimes called a place holder.

Numbers can be written in different ways. **Standard form** shows only the digits. **Expanded form** shows the sum of the value of the digits. **Word form** uses words.

Real-World EXAMPLE Write Numbers

3 TRAVEL It is 2,781 miles from Los Angeles to the Statue of Liberty in New York City. Write 2,781 in three ways.

The place value chart shows 2,781.

Thousands	Hundreds	Tens	Ones
2	7	8	1

Standard Form 2,781

Expanded Form 2,000 + 700 + 80 + 1

Word Form two thousand, seven hundred eighty-one

Online **Personal Tutor at** ca.gr3math.com

CHECK What You Know

Write the place of the underlined digit. Then write the value of the digit. See Examples 1 and 2 (pp. 24–25)

1. $\underline{8}$70 **2.** $\underline{2}$,312 **3.** 7,5$\underline{0}$9

Write each number in standard form. See Example 3 (p. 25)

4. 800 + 50 + 6 **5.** one thousand, six hundred four

Write each number in expanded form and word form.
See Example 3 (p. 25)

6. 375 **7.** 5,230 **8.** 9,909

9. Lindsey uses each digit 3, 8, 0, and 1 once. Find the greatest whole number she can make.

10. Talk About It How do you tell the place value of each digit when given a number?

Practice and Problem Solving

EXTRA PRACTICE See page R2.

Write the place of the underlined digit. Then write the value of the digit. See Examples 1 and 2 (pp. 24–25)

11. $\underline{5}$01 **12.** 5,77$\underline{2}$ **13.** 1,0$\underline{2}$0

14. 4,81$\underline{0}$ **15.** $\underline{3}$,176 **16.** 8$\underline{0}$4

Write each number in standard form. See Example 3 (p. 25)

17. 4,000 + 600 + 70 + 8 **18.** 3,000 + 20 + 1

19. seven thousand, six hundred forty-one

20. eight thousand, seven hundred sixty

Write each number in expanded form and word form. See Example 3 (p. 25)

21. 4,332 **22.** 1,324 **23.** 6,219

24. 6,503 **25.** 8,150 **26.** 1,001

27. A motorcycle costs $3,124. What is the value of each digit?

28. Write all of the three-digit numbers that have 3 in the tens place and a 5 in the ones place.

H.O.T. Problems

29. CHALLENGE Carlos is thinking of a four-digit number. The thousands digit is double the ones digit. The sum of these two digits is 9. What is the number? Explain your work.

30. FIND THE ERROR Julio and Caitlyn are writing 2,013 in word form. Who is correct? Explain your reasoning.

Julio
Two hundred thirteen

Caitlyn
Two thousand, thirteen

31. WRITING IN MATH Explain why a zero needs to be used when writing the number four thousand, sixty-eight in standard form.

Standards Practice

32 Marcus has 1,270 baseball cards. Which of these equals 1,270? **(Lesson 1-3)**

A 1 + 2 + 7 +0

B 100 + 20 + 7

C 100 + 200 + 70

D 1,000 + 200 + 70

33 Which number is 7 more than 1,097? **(Lesson 1-2)**

F 1,004

G 1,104

H 2,004

J 2,007

Spiral Review

34. Josefina had 15 math problems for homework on Monday night. On Tuesday night, she had 18. How many math problems did she have in all? **(Lesson 1-2)**

ALGEBRA Identify a pattern. Then find the missing numbers. **(Lesson 1-1)**

35. 19, ■, 23, ■, 27

36. 145, ■,165, ■, ■,195

1-4 Place Value through 10,000

GET READY to Learn

Scientists found that a gooney bird once traveled 24,983 miles in just 90 days. That is almost the distance around the Earth.

gooney bird

MAIN IDEA

I will read, write, and identify place value of whole numbers through ten thousands.

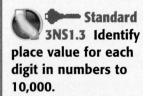

Standard 3NS1.3 Identify place value for each digit in numbers to 10,000.

Standard 3NS1.5 Use expanded notation to represent numbers (e.g., 3,206 = 3,000 + 200 + 6).

New Vocabulary

period

A place value chart can be used to help read large numbers. A group of 3 digits is called a **period**. Commas separate the periods. At each comma, say the name of the period.

EXAMPLES Place Value

1 Identify the place of the underlined digit in <u>2</u>4,983. Then write its value.

The place value chart shows 24,983.

Thousands Period			Ones Period		
hundreds	tens	ones	hundreds	tens	ones
	2	4,	9	8	3

The underlined digit, 2, is in the ten thousands place. So, its value is 20,000.

2 Write 24,983 three ways.

Standard Form 24,983

Expanded Form 20,000 + 4,000 + 900 + 80 + 3

Word Form twenty-four thousand, nine hundred eighty-three

Real-World EXAMPLES Write and Read Numbers

PLANETS **While studying planets, Mario found a chart comparing the width of the three largest planets in our solar system.**

> **Remember**
> Place a comma between the thousands and hundreds place.

3 **Write the width of Uranus in expanded form.**

31,518 = 30,000 + 1,000 + 500 + 10 + 8

4 **Write the width of Jupiter in word form.**

eighty-six thousand, eight hundred twenty-two

Online Personal Tutor at ca.gr3math.com

CHECK What You Know

Write the place of each underlined digit. Then write its value. See Example 1 (p. 28)

1. 62,57$\underline{4}$ **2.** 38,$\underline{0}$35 **3.** $\underline{5}$3,456 **4.** 1$\underline{2}$,345

Write each number in standard form. See Example 2 (p. 28)

5. 50,000 + 1,000 + 300 + 3 **6.** twelve thousand, four

Write each number in expanded form and word form.
See Examples 2–4 (pp. 28–29)

7. 23,472 **8.** 49,602 **9.** 52,220 **10.** 71,002

11. A car's mileage is thirty-six thousand, five hundred twenty-three miles. Write this number in standard and expanded form.

12. Talk About It Dominic said that the number 61,903 is the same as 60,000 + 1,000 + 90 + 3. Is he correct? Explain.

Practice and Problem Solving

EXTRA PRACTICE
See page R3.

Write the place of each underlined digit. Then write its value. See Example 1 (p. 28)

13. 15,388 **14.** 19,756 **15.** 30,654 **16.** 43,543

17. 57,081 **18.** 69,003 **19.** 70,000 **20.** 86,060

Write each number in standard form. See Example 2 (p. 28)

21. 20,000 + 4,000 + 200 + 20 + 2 **22.** 10,000 + 1,000 + 100 + 10 + 1

23. forty thousand, three hundred eighty **24.** thirty-two thousand, twenty-five

Write each number in expanded form and word form.
See Examples 2–4 (pp. 28–29)

25. 12,194 **26.** 28,451 **27.** 39,234 **28.** 51,160

29. 60,371 **30.** 73,100 **31.** 81,001 **32.** 99,027

Real-World PROBLEM SOLVING

Science

Data File The table lists the location and altitude of the world's largest telescopes.

33. Which altitudes have a digit in the ten thousands place?

34. Write the altitude of the Palomar Mountain observatory in word form.

35. Which observatory's altitude has a digit with a value of 700?

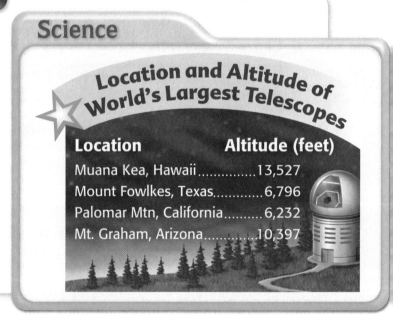

Location and Altitude of World's Largest Telescopes

Location	Altitude (feet)
Muana Kea, Hawaii	13,527
Mount Fowlkes, Texas	6,796
Palomar Mtn, California	6,232
Mt. Graham, Arizona	10,397

H.O.T. Problems

36. OPEN ENDED Write three different numbers that have 5 in the thousands place.

37. WRITING IN MATH Explain the difference between standard form and expanded form.

Math Online Self-Check Quiz at ca.gr3math.com

CHAPTER 1 Mid-Chapter Check

Lessons 1-1 through 1-4

Identify a pattern. Then find the missing numbers. **(Lesson 1-1)**

1. 20, ■, 60, 80, ■

2. 5, 15, ■, 35, ■

3. Hong has saved $37. He spends $19 on school clothes. He earns $15 for mowing the neighbor's yard. How much money does Hong have now? Use the *four-step plan.* **(Lesson 1-2)**

Write the place of each underlined digit. Then write its value. **(Lesson 1-3)**

4. $5\underline{4}9$

5. $3,\underline{5}20$

6. **STANDARDS PRACTICE** How is five thousand, three hundred nineteen written in standard form? **(Lesson 1-3)**

A 5,193

B 5,309

C 5,319

D 5,391

7. A hippopotamus at a zoo weighs 3,525 pounds. Write this number in expanded and word form. **(Lesson 1-3)**

Write the place of each underlined digit. Then write its value. **(Lesson 1-4)**

8. $\underline{1}6,846$

9. $\underline{2}8,950$

Write each number in standard form. **(Lesson 1-4)**

10. twenty-three thousand, seven hundred forty-two

11. 60,000 + 4,000 + 8

Write each number in expanded form. **(Lesson 1-4)**

12. Jennifer hopes to read 10,240 pages this summer.

13. Forty-five thousand, sixty-seven people.

14. **STANDARDS PRACTICE** Which digit is in the ten thousands place in the number 92,108? **(Lesson 1-4)**

F 0

G 1

H 2

J 9

15. **WRITING IN ▸MATH** Describe the pattern that can produce the numbers shown below. What number is next? **(Lesson 1-1)**

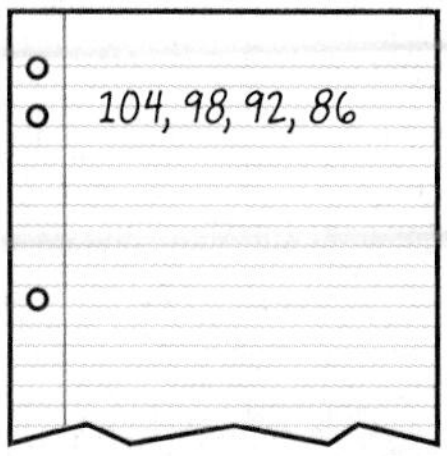

1-5 Problem-Solving Investigation

MAIN IDEA Use the four-step plan to solve a problem.

Standard 3MR1.1 Analyze problems by identifying relationships, distinguishing relevant and irrelevant information, sequencing and prioritizing information, and observing patterns. **Standard 3NS2.1 Find the sum or difference of two whole numbers between 0 and 10,000.**

P.S.I. TEAM +

DERRICK: My sister gave me drawing paper for my birthday. There were 32 sheets. I want to make it last 8 days.

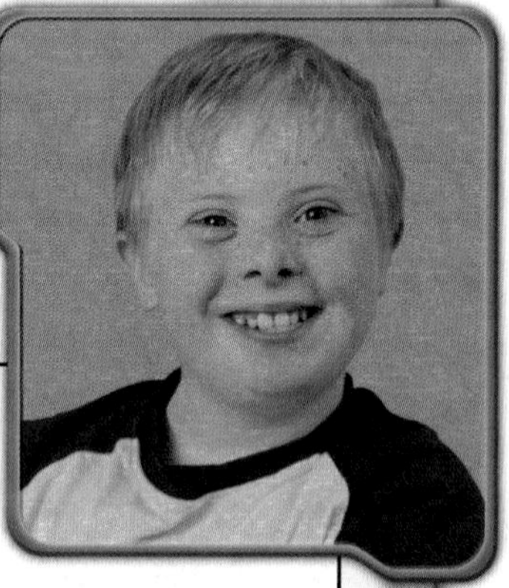

YOUR MISSION: Find how many sheets Derrick can use each day if he uses the same number of sheets each day.

Understand

There are 32 sheets of paper to last for 8 days. Find how many sheets he can use each day.

Plan

You know the total number of sheets of paper and how many days they need to last. You can show this using counters.

Solve

Use 32 counters to represent the 32 sheets of paper. Make 8 equal groups, placing the counters one at a time into each group until gone.

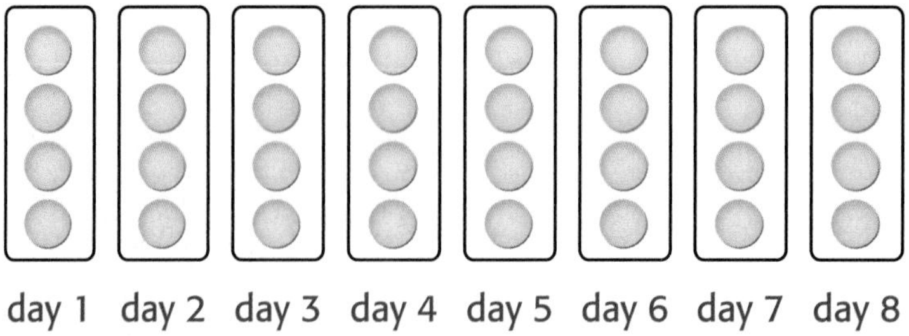

So, he can use 4 sheets of paper each day.

Check

Look back at the problem.

$4 + 4 + 4 + 4 + 4 + 4 + 4 + 4 = 32$

So, the answer is correct.

Mixed Problem Solving

EXTRA PRACTICE
See page R3.

Use the four-step plan to solve each problem.

1. Juan exercised 20 minutes yesterday. Today he is going to exercise twice as much. How long does Juan plan to exercise today? Explain how you found the answer.

2. What is the next figure in the pattern shown?

3. Mr. Hernandez brought pretzels to share with his 36 students. Only 18 of his students ate the pretzels. How many students did not eat the pretzels?

4. Marjorie baked 48 pancakes for the school breakfast. Elian ate some of the pancakes, and now Marjorie only has 43 pancakes. How many pancakes did Elian eat?

5. Gabriela buys the following items. She gives the cashier $20. How much change will she receive?

6. Joshua gets up at 8:30 A.M. He needs to be ready for school by 9:00 A.M. How many minutes does he have to get ready?

7. Uncle Ramos is putting up a fence in the shape of a triangle. How much fencing is needed?

Side A	Side B	Side C
36 feet	half of side A	same as side A

8. Austin's garden has 5 rows of 6 plants. How many plants does Austin have in his garden?

9. Look at the table. How many pens do Cesar and Pamela have in all? How many more pens does Carmen have than Pamela?

Name	Pens
Pamela	7
Cesar	9
Carmen	20

10. Mrs. Reinhart read her students one book each day for 2 weeks. If there are 5 days in each school week, how many books did she read in all? Explain your reasoning.

11. **WRITING IN ►MATH** Explain how the plan step is different than the solve step in the four-step plan.

1-6 Compare Numbers

MAIN IDEA

I will compare numbers through ten thousands.

Standard 3NS1.2 Compare and order **whole numbers to 10,000.**

New Vocabulary

is less than (<)

is greater than (>)

is equal to (=)

GET READY to Learn

The table lists the maximum speeds of two kinds of go-carts. Which go-cart is faster?

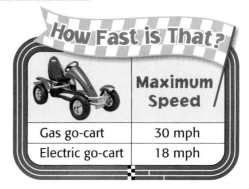

How Fast is That?

	Maximum Speed
Gas go-cart	30 mph
Electric go-cart	18 mph

When comparing two numbers, the first number is either **less than**, **greater than**, or **equal to** the second number.

Symbol	Meaning
<	is less than
>	is greater than
=	is equal to

Real-World EXAMPLE **Use a Number Line**

1 MEASUREMENT **Which go-cart is faster, the gas go-cart or the electric go-cart?**

You can use a number line to compare 30 and 18.

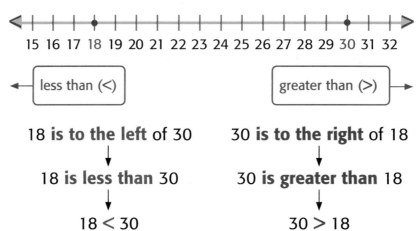

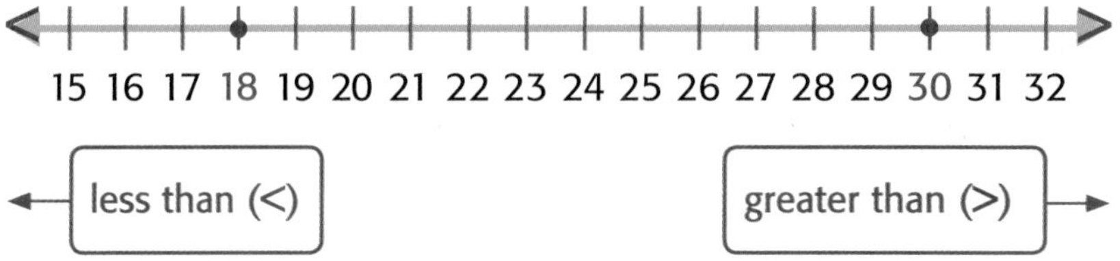

18 **is to the left** of 30 → 18 **is less than** 30 → 18 < 30

30 **is to the right** of 18 → 30 **is greater than** 18 → 30 > 18

So, the gas go-cart is faster than the electric go-cart.

Real-World EXAMPLES Use a Place Value Chart

2 **TRAVEL The Tyee family is planning a road trip to the Grand Canyon. One route from Sacramento is 835 miles. Another route through Las Vegas is 840 miles. Which route is shorter?**

Compare 835 and 840 to see which route is shorter.

Step 1 Line up the numbers by place value

Hundreds	Tens	Ones
8	3	5
8	4	0

Step 2 Compare. Start with the greatest place value position.

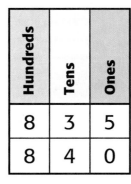

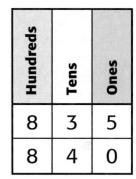

Hundreds	Tens	Ones
8	3	5
8	4	0

same (Hundreds)

different 3 tens < 4 tens (Tens)

> **Remember**
>
> Always line up the numbers by their place value and start to compare from the left.

Since 3 is less than 4, the number 835 is less than 840. So, 835 < 840. The route from Sacramento is shorter.

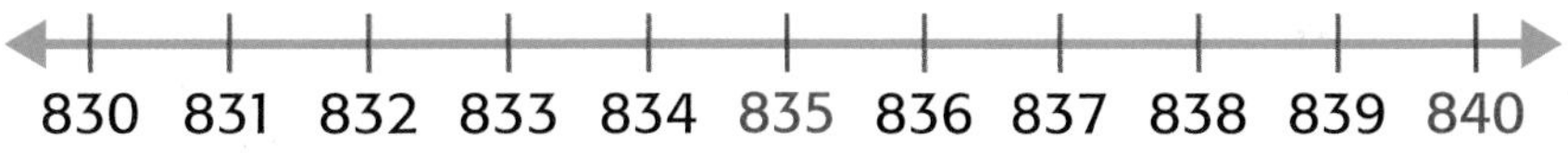

3 **Which is greater, 987 or 1,400?**

You need to compare 1,400 and 987. Line up the numbers. Then compare.

Thousands	Hundreds	Tens	Ones
1	4	0	0
	9	8	7

1,400 has 1 thousand but 987 has 0 thousands

1 thousand is greater than 0 thousands.
So, 1,400 > 987.

Online Personal Tutor at ca.gr3math.com

CHECK What You Know

Compare. Write >, <, or =. See Examples 1–3 (pp. 34–35)

1. 60 ● 59 **2.** 88 ● 98 **3.** 100 ● 85

4. 64 ● 46 **5.** 1,000 ● 1,000 **6.** 2,345 ● 2,357

7. The Flips Gymnastics Club has 131 members. The Tumblers have 113 members. Which club has more members? Explain.

8. Talk About It Why is it not necessary to compare the ones digits in the numbers 4,365 and 4,378?

Practice and Problem Solving

EXTRA PRACTICE See page R3.

Compare. Write >, <, or =. See Examples 1–3 (pp. 34–35)

9. 55 ● 72 **10.** 99 ● 99 **11.** 70 ● 80

12. 93 ● 83 **13.** 121 ● 112 **14.** 657 ● 765

15. 303 ● 330 **16.** 998 ● 989 **17.** 8,008 ● 8,080

18. 2,753 ● 2,735 **19.** 7,654 ● 7,654 **20.** 9,999 ● 1,000

Algebra Compare. Write >, <, or =.

21. 65 ● 62 + 3 **22.** 35 + 4 ● 39 **23.** 209 ● 200 + 90

24. The table shows the number of tickets sold for a movie. Which showing sold more tickets?

Revenge of Dinosaurs	
Showing	**Tickets sold**
5:00 P.M.	235
7:00 P.M.	253

25. **Measurement** Which day was warmer in the desert, Tuesday or Wednesday?

Desert Temperature	
Day	**Temperature**
Tuesday	119°F
Wednesday	109°F

26. There are 165 students in the third grade. There are 35 students in each of the 5 classes in the second grade. Which has more students? Explain.

27. Keith's family bought a computer for $1,200. Margareta's family bought a computer for $1,002. Which computer costs less? Explain.

H.O.T. Problems

28. OPEN-ENDED Write the largest and smallest number you can make using the numerals 3, 6, 7, and 9.

29. WHICH ONE DOESN'T BELONG? Identify the number that is not more than 4,259.

4,295   4,260   4,300   4,209

30. WRITING IN MATH Explain the first step to comparing 2,032 and 203. Which number is greater? Explain.

Standards Practice

31 Which number will make the number sentence true? **(Lesson 1-6)**

1426 > ■

A 1425   **C** 1452

B 1426   **D** 1524

32 Mrs. Phillips' class is having a party. There are 30 students. Each pizza is cut into 10 pieces. If each student gets one piece, how many pizzas are there? **(Lesson 1-5)**

F 3   **H** 7

G 5   **J** 10

Spiral Review

Write each number in expanded form and word form. **(Lesson 1-3)**

33. 982   **34.** 2,045   **35.** 1,900

Identify the place of each underlined digit. Then write the value of the digit. **(Lesson 1-3)**

36. 2$\underline{4}$,981   **37.** 6,$\underline{0}$79   **38.** 2,76$\underline{1}$

39. Ricardo said the word form of 60,287 is six thousand, two hundred eighty-seven. Is this correct? If not, write the correct word form. **(Lesson 1-2)**

40. Identify the pattern of Byron's stamp collection. **(Lesson 1-1)**

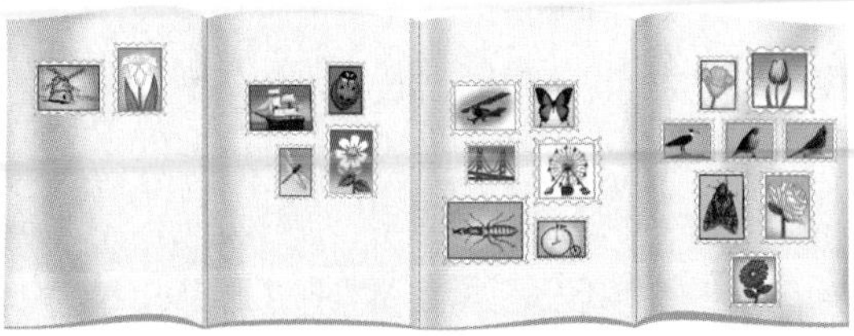

1-7 Order Numbers

MAIN IDEA

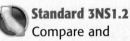

I will use a number line and place value to order numbers through ten thousands.

Standard 3NS1.2 Compare and **order whole numbers to 10,000.**

GET READY to Learn

The table shows the length of three whales. Which whale is the longest? Which is the shortest?

Average Length of Whales

Whale	Length (inches)
Orca Whale	264
Blue Whale	1,128
Humpback Whale	744

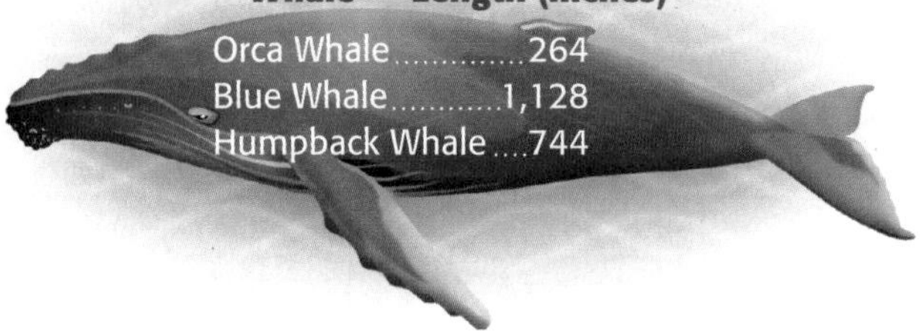

Comparing numbers can help you to order numbers.

Real-World EXAMPLE **Order Least to Greatest**

1 **MEASUREMENT** **Order the lengths from least to greatest.**

One Way: Use a Number Line

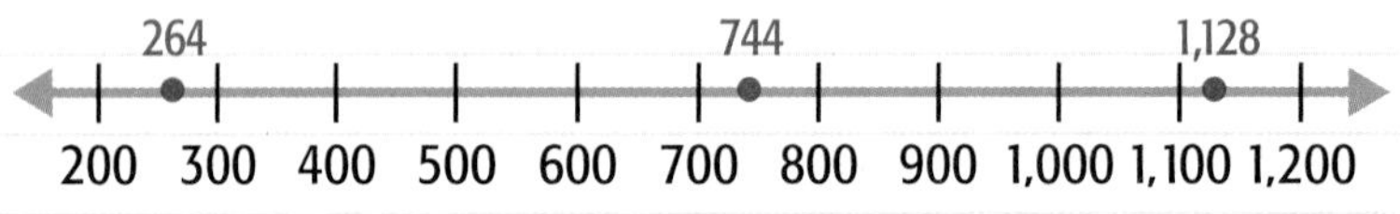

264 < 744 < 1,128

Another Way: Use a Place Value Chart

Line up the numbers by their place value. Compare from the left.

Thousands	Hundreds	Tens	Ones
	2	6	4
1,	1	2	8
	7	4	4

1 thousand is the greatest number. → (1,128)

7 hundreds > 2 hundreds → (744)

The order is 264 inches, 744 inches, and 1,128 inches.

Real-World EXAMPLE Order Greatest to Least

> **Remember**
> When you move to the left on the number line, the numbers get smaller.

2 **MEASUREMENT The table shows the distances whales travel to feed in the summertime. This is called migration. Order these distances from greatest to least.**

Whale Migration

Whale	Distance (miles)
Humpback Whale	3,500
Gray Whale	12,000
Orca Whale	900

Use the place value chart to line up the numbers by their place value. Compare from the left.

Ten Thousands	Thousands	Hundreds	Tens	Ones
	3,	5	0	0
1	2,	0	0	0
		9	0	0

12,000 is the greatest number.

3 thousands > no thousands so 3,500 is the next greatest number.

The order from greatest to least is 12,000 miles, 3,500 miles, and 900 miles.

Online Personal Tutor at ca.gr3math.com

CHECK What You Know

Order the numbers from least to the greatest. See Example 1 (p. 38)

1. 39; 32; 68

2. 224; 124; 441

3. 202; 2,202; 220

Order the numbers from greatest to the least. See Example 2 (p. 39)

4. 231; 136; 178

5. 1,500; 150; 15

6. 9,009; 909; 6,999

7. Team A won 19 games, Team B won 40 games, and Team C won 22 games during the season. What place did each team earn for the season?

8. Talk About It Order these numbers from the greatest to the least: 435; 345; 3,453. Explain how you can tell which number is the greatest.

Practice and Problem Solving

EXTRA PRACTICE
See page R4.

Order the numbers from the least to the greatest. See Example 1 (p. 38)

9. 303; 30; 3,003
10. 4,404; 4,044; 4,040
11. 39; 78; 123
12. 1,234; 998; 2,134
13. 598; 521; 3,789
14. 2,673; 2,787; 2,900

Order the numbers from greatest to the least. See Example 2 (p. 39)

15. 60; 600; 6,006
16. 288; 209; 2,899
17. 49; 43; 60
18. 3,587; 875; 2,435
19. 451; 409; 415
20. 999; 1,342; 2,000

21. Carra's dad bought the 3 items below. Which item costs the most?

22. Kurt wants to buy a parrot, lizard, or hamster. Order the animals from the least to the most expensive.

23. Three elementary schools have 2,500 students, 3,002 students, and 2,536 students. Which is the least number of students?

24. In a set of numbers, 59 is the least number and 10,000 is the greatest. Write 4 ordered numbers that could come between these numbers.

Real-World PROBLEM SOLVING

Animals The lengths of three different whales are shown.

25. Order the lengths from greatest to least.

26. Which whale is the longest?

27. How much longer is the humpback whale compared to the orca whale?

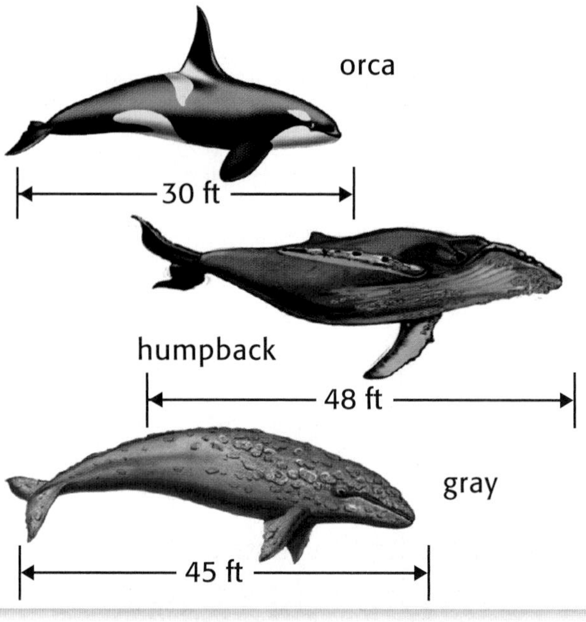

Math Online Self-Check Quiz at ca.gr3math.com

H.O.T. Problems

28. FIND THE ERROR Juliana and Alex are ordering a set of numbers from least to greatest. Who is correct? Explain.

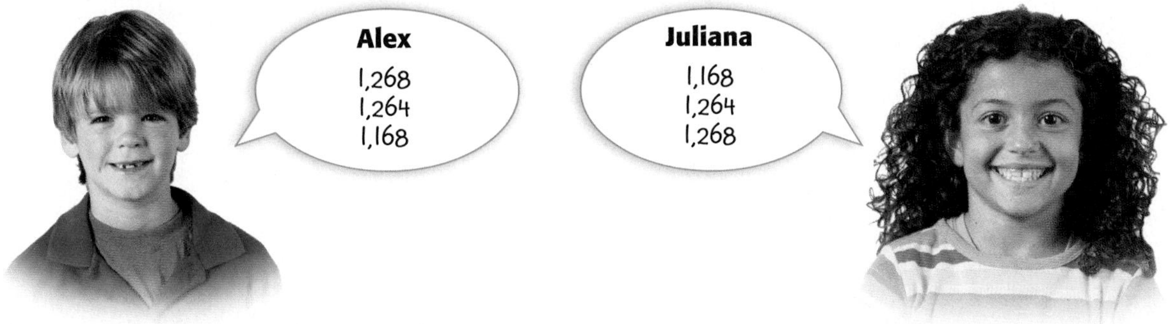

29. NUMBER SENSE Between which two numbers will 567 be placed if we are placing the numbers 467; 980; 745 in order from greatest to least?

30. WRITING IN ▶MATH Write a real-world problem that asks to order numbers from least to greatest.

Standards Practice

31 Which number sentence is false? **(Lesson 1-6)**

A 227 > 232

B 368 < 386

C 958 > 887

D 1587 > 1547

32 Which set of numbers is in order from greatest to least? **(Lesson 1-7)**

F 2587, 3610, 5846, 8745

G 1587, 567, 987, 1453

H 362, 542, 464, 558

J 268, 251, 158, 119

Spiral Review

Compare. Write >, <, or =. **(Lesson 1-6)**

33. 29 ● 38

34. 69 ● 58

35. 98 ● 85

36. Measurement Mrs. Garrison needs the longest string. Whose string does she need? **(Lesson 1-5)**

Student	Tracy	Nichelle	Collin
String	24 inches	36 inches	28 inches

Problem Solving in Geography

THE MIGHTY MISSISSIPPI

The Mississippi River is part of the largest river system in North America. The river begins in Minnesota and empties into the Gulf of Mexico. The Mississippi River system extends from the Rocky Mountains in the western United States to the Appalachian Mountains in the east.

The Mississippi River is about 2,340 miles long. The shallowest point is 3 feet. The deepest point is 198 feet. It's no wonder that the Mississippi River is called the "Mighty Mississippi."

MAJOR RIVERS OF THE MISSISSIPPI RIVER SYSTEM

River	Length (miles)
Arkansas	1,469
Mississippi	2,340
Missouri	2,540
Ohio	1,310
Red	1,290

Source: United States Geological Survey

Standard 3NS1.3 **Identify the place value for each digit in numbers to 10,000.**

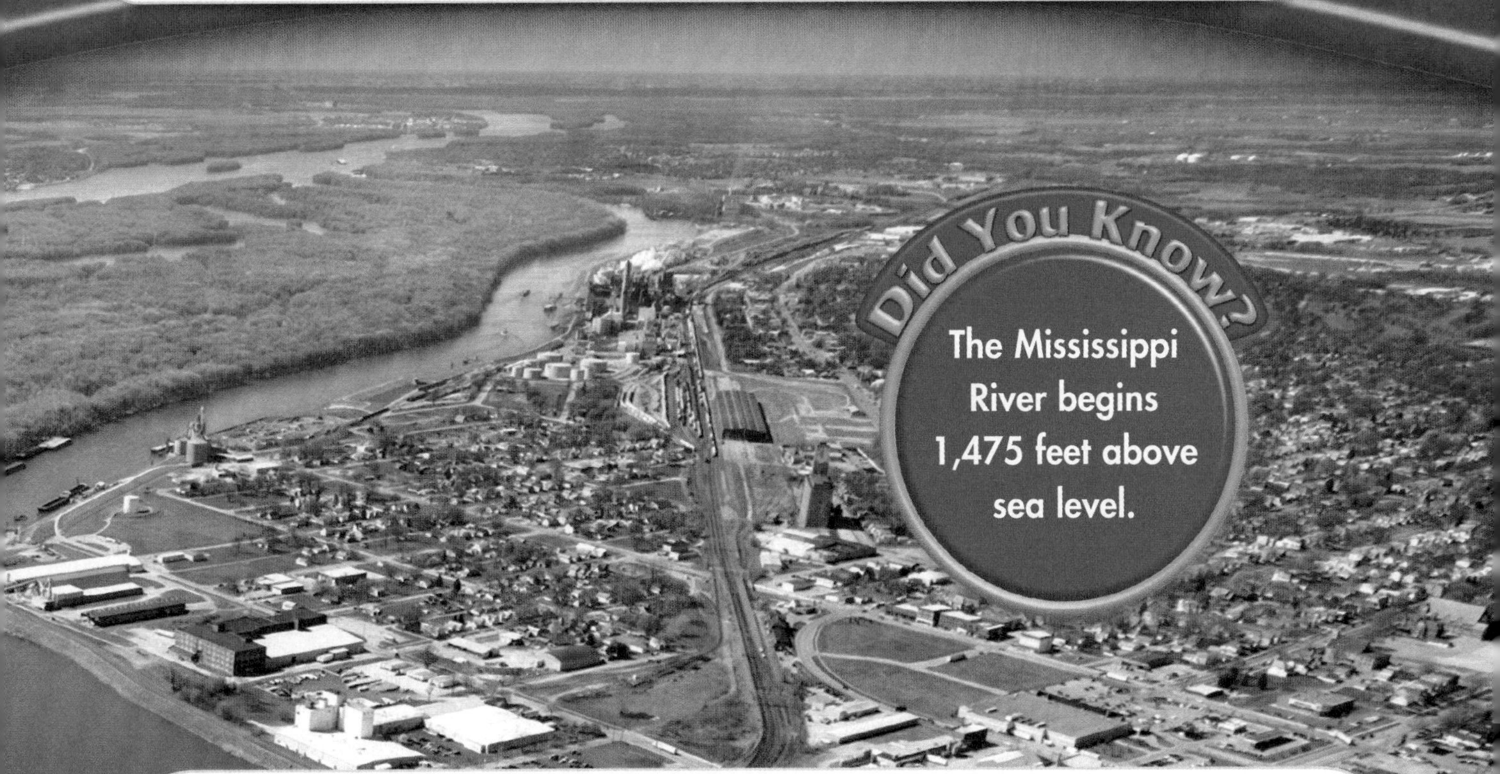

Did You Know?

The Mississippi River begins 1,475 feet above sea level.

Real-World Math

Use the information on page 42 to answer each question.

1. Which river is the longest?
2. Which river lengths have the same value for the hundreds place? What is that value?
3. Write the length of the Arkansas River in expanded form.
4. The total of the lengths of the Missouri River and Mississippi River is 4,880 miles. How is this number written in words?
5. How does the length of the Red River compare to the lengths of the other 4 rivers? Use $>$, $<$, or $=$ for each comparison.
6. Which is the third longest river?
7. Which rivers, when rounded to the nearest hundred, are 1,300 miles long?
8. Write the length of the Ohio River in words.
9. What is the difference in the depths of the Mississippi from its shallowest point to its deepest point?
10. The Amazon River in South America is 3,920 miles long. Which river is longer, the Amazon or the Missouri?

1-8 Round to the Nearest Ten and Hundred

MAIN IDEA

I will round numbers to the nearest ten and hundred.

Standard 3NS1.4 Round off numbers to 10,000 to the nearest ten, hundred, and thousand.

New Vocabulary

round

GET READY to Learn

Cassandra used 62 minutes of time on her family's cell phone plan. Her brother Matao used 186 minutes of time. About how many minutes did each person use?

To **round** is to change the value of a number to one that is easier to work with. You can use a number line to round.

Vocabulary Link

round means *about how many*

Real-World EXAMPLES Round to the Nearest Ten

1 TECHNOLOGY About how many minutes did Cassandra use? Round to the nearest ten.

The closest ten *less than* 62 is 60. The closest ten *greater than* 62 is 70. Use a number line from 60 to 70.

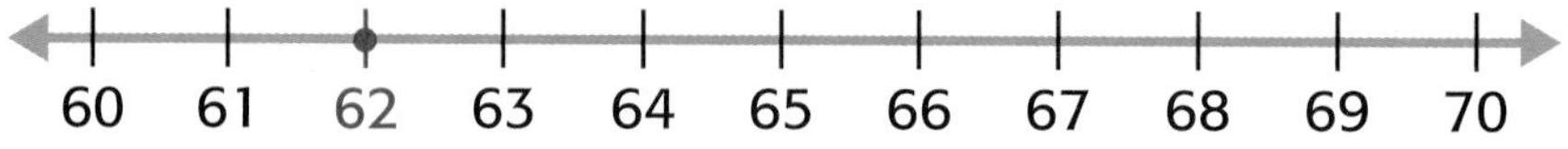

Since 62 is closer to 60 than to 70, round 62 to 60.

2 TECHNOLOGY About how many minutes did Matao use? Round to the nearest ten.

The closest ten *less than* 186 is 180. The closest ten *greater than* 186 is 190. Use a number line from 180 to 190.

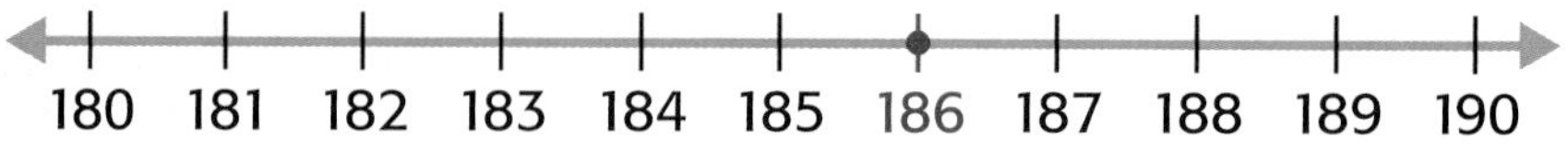

Since 186 is closer to 190 than to 180, round 186 to 190.

You can also round numbers to the nearest hundred.

Real-World EXAMPLES

> **Remember**
> When rounding 5, round up to the next higher number.

3 **BOOKS** **Bruno read a book that was 267 pages long. To the nearest hundred, how many pages did he read?**

The closest hundred *less than* 267 is 200. The closest hundred *greater than* 267 is 300.

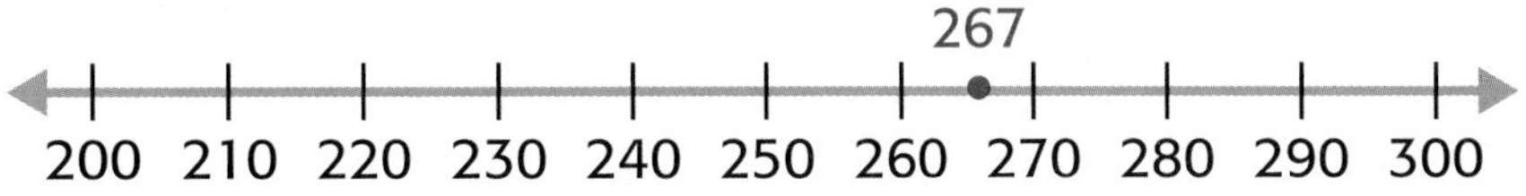

267 is closer to 300 than to 200. Round 267 to 300.

4 **SHELLS** **Olivia collected shells. To the nearest hundred, how many seashells did she collect?**

The closest hundred *less than* 1,423 is 1,400. The closest hundred *greater than* 1,423 is 1,500.

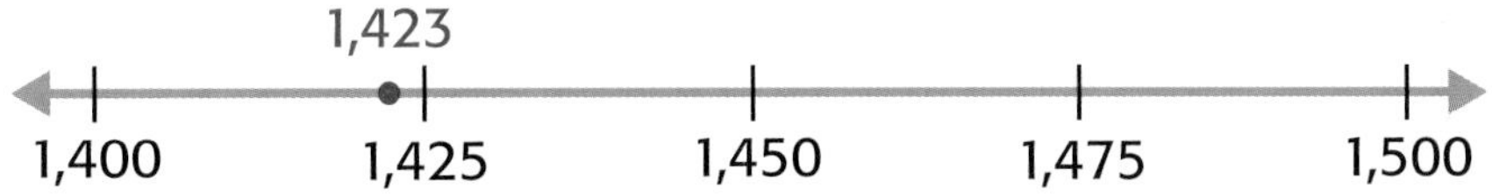

Since 1,423 is closer to 1,400 than to 1,500, round 1,423 to 1,400.

Online **Personal Tutor at** ca.gr3math.com

CHECK What You Know

Round to the nearest ten. See Examples 1 and 2 (p. 44)

1. 58 **2.** 62 **3.** 685 **4.** 552

Round to the nearest hundred. See Examples 3 and 4 (p. 45)

5. 449 **6.** 473 **7.** 415 **8.** 1,450

9. Kayla has to read 67 pages for homework tonight. To the nearest ten, how many pages does she need to read?

10. Talk About It What should you do to round a number that is exactly halfway between two numbers?

Practice and Problem Solving

EXTRA PRACTICE
See page R4.

Round to the nearest ten. See Examples 1 and 2 (p. 44)

11. 77 **12.** 67 **13.** 13 **14.** 21

15. 285 **16.** 195 **17.** 157 **18.** 679

Round to the nearest hundred. See Examples 3 and 4 (p. 45)

19. 123 **20.** 244 **21.** 749 **22.** 750

23. 353 **24.** 850 **25.** 1,568 **26.** 4,829

27. Myron has 179 baseball cards. He says he has about 200 cards. Did he round the number of cards to the nearest ten or hundred? Explain.

28. Measurement A passenger train traveled 1,687 miles. To the nearest hundred, how many miles did the train travel?

29. Coco collected 528 cans of food for the school food drive. If she collects 25 more cans, what will the number of cans be, rounded to the nearest hundred?

30. Mrs. Boggs ran for mayor. She received 1,486 votes. Mrs. Swain received 1,252 votes. What is the difference in the number of votes to the nearest ten?

Real-World PROBLEM SOLVING

Sports Danilo is practicing bowling. The table shows his scores for one week.

31. Round all scores to the nearest hundred. Which days were the scores about 300?

32. To the nearest ten, what was the score on Tuesday?

33. Which day's score rounds to 250?

BOWLING SCORES

Monday	252
Tuesday	83
Wednesday	164
Thursday	256
Friday	290
Saturday	283
Sunday	173

H.O.T. Problems

34. OPEN ENDED I am thinking of a number that when it is rounded to the nearest hundred is 400. What is the number? Explain.

35. WRITING IN MATH Explain why 238 can be rounded to 240 or 200.

 Math Online Self Check Quiz at ca.gr3math.com

Round Numbers

Round to the Nearest Hundred

You will need: pencil and paper

Get Ready!

Players: 2 players

Get Set!

Each player draws the game board.

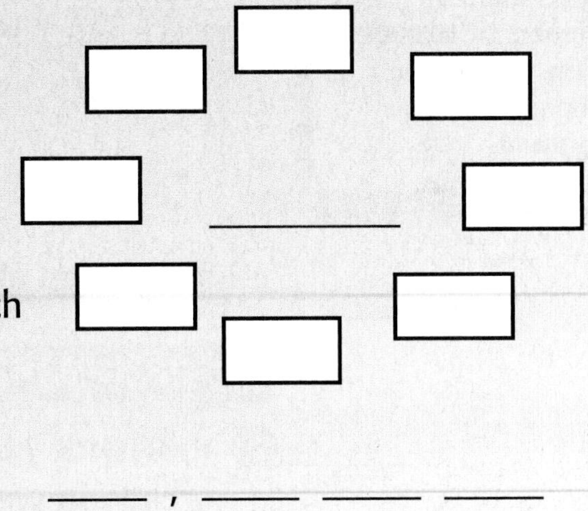

Go!

- Each player secretly writes a 4-digit number.
- In the center of the game board, each player writes their 4-digit number rounded to the nearest hundred.
- Player 1 guesses 1 digit that he or she thinks is in the other player's secret number.
- If the digit is correct, Player 2 writes it on the correct line. If it is incorrect, Player 2 fills in one space.
- Player 2 takes his or her turn guessing Player 1's secret number.
- Play continues until a number is guessed or all spaces are filled in.

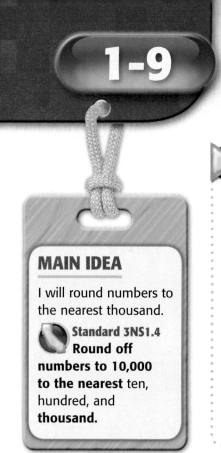

1-9 Round to the Nearest Thousand

GET READY to Learn

Mr. Chou's Arcade keeps a record of how many visitors it has each week. About how many people visited the arcade during week 3?

MAIN IDEA

I will round numbers to the nearest thousand.

Standard 3NS1.4 Round off numbers to 10,000 to the nearest ten, hundred, and **thousand.**

Numbers can also be rounded to the nearest thousand.

Real-World EXAMPLES Use a Number Line

1 VISITORS **About how many visitors came to the arcade in week 3? Round to the nearest thousand.**

The closest thousand *less than* 4,684 is 4,000. The closest thousand *greater than* 4,684 is 5,000.

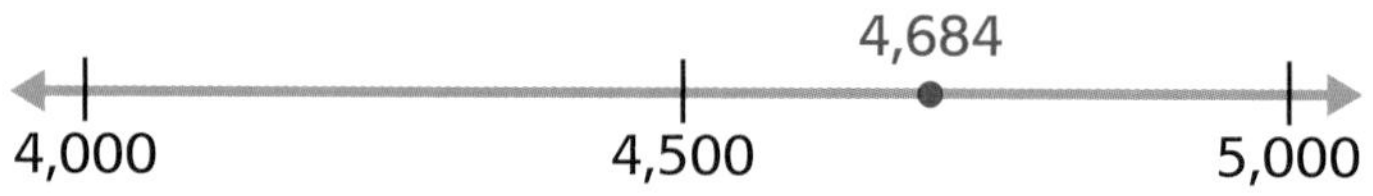

Since 4,684 is closer to 5,000 than to 4,000, round 4,684 to 5,000.

2 **About how many visitors were there in week 2? Round to the nearest thousand.**

The closest thousand *less than* 2,341 is 2,000. The closest thousand *greater than* 2,341 is 3,000.

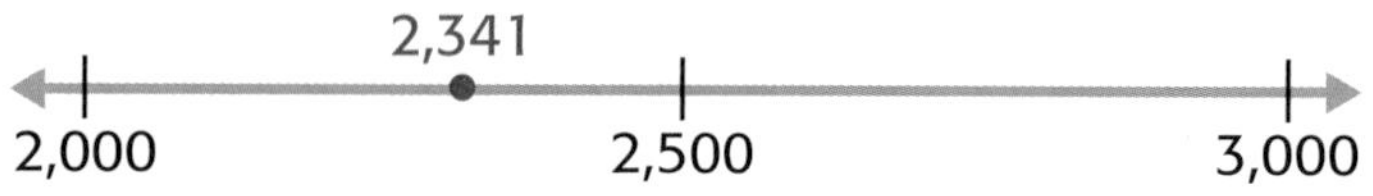

Round 2,341 to 2,000.

You can use rounding rules to round a number.

KEY **CONCEPT** — Rounding Whole Numbers

Step 1 Underline the digit to be rounded.

Step 2 Look at the digit to the right of the place being rounded.

Step 3 If the digit is 4 or less; do not change the underlined digit. If the digit is 5 or greater, add 1 to the underlined digit.

Step 4 Replace all digits after the underlined digit with zeros.

Real-World **EXAMPLE** Use Rounding Rules

Remember

Use rounding rules for rounding in *all* place values.

3 ZOO **A zoo had 5,499 visitors last week. To the nearest thousand, about how many people visited the zoo?**

You need to round 5,499 to the nearest thousand.

Step 1	Underline the digit in the place to be rounded. In this case, the 5 is in the thousands place.	5,499
Step 2	Look at the 4, the digit to the right of the underlined digit.	5,499
Step 3	This digit is less than 5, so do not change the underlined digit.	5,499
Step 4	Replace all digits after the underlined digit with zeros.	5,000

To the nearest thousand, 5,499 rounds to 5,000.

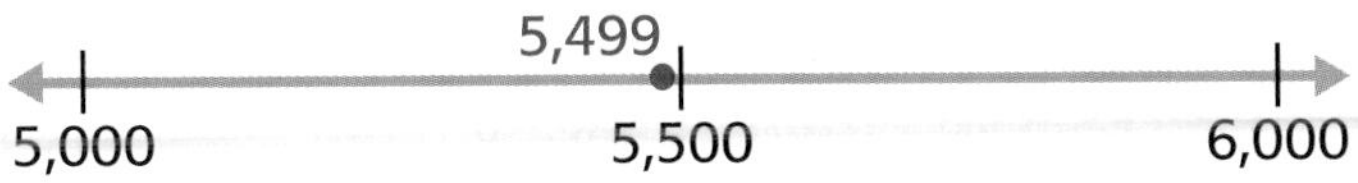

Online **Personal Tutor at** ca.gr3math.com

CHECK What You Know

Round to the nearest thousand. See Examples 1–3 (pp. 48–49)

1. 3,922
2. 2,798
3. 7,099
4. 1,499
5. 2,500
6. 3,601

7. There are 1,250 houses in our city. Round the number of houses to the nearest thousand.

8. Talk About It Explain how you would use the rounding rules to round 5,299 to the nearest thousand.

Practice and Problem Solving

EXTRA PRACTICE See page R4.

Round to the nearest thousand. See Examples 1–3 (pp. 48–49)

9. 8,611
10. 3,651
11. 1,099
12. 4,243
13. 2,698
14. 1,503
15. 1,257
16. 5,598
17. 5,299
18. 1,500
19. 2,400
20. 3,789

21. The fourth-grade class read a total of 2,389 pages this week. Round the number of pages read to the nearest thousand.

22. The attendance at a recent high school football game was 1,989. What is the attendance rounded to the nearest thousand?

23. To the nearest thousand, what will the cost be for the third grade to take a trip to the zoo?

24. Irene's scores on her favorite video game got better each day. What is her score on Wednesday rounded to the nearest thousand?

Video Game Scores	
Day	**Score**
Monday	1,735
Tuesday	2,200
Wednesday	2,585

25. Alton and his friends collected 1,683 rocks. How many rocks is that rounded to the nearest thousand?

26. **Measurement** Chong rode a train 2,156 miles one way. To the nearest thousand how many miles did he ride the train both ways?

H.O.T. Problems

27. NUMBER SENSE Describe all the four digit numbers that when rounded to the nearest thousand the result is 8,000.

28. WHICH ONE DOESN'T BELONG? Identify the number that is not rounded correctly to the nearest thousand. Explain.

2,184 → 2,000	5,500 → 5,000	3,344 → 3,000	8,456 → 8,000

29. WRITING IN ▸MATH Round 499 to the nearest hundred. Then round 499 to the nearest ten. Are the two answers the same? Explain.

Standards Practice

30 Which number is 549 rounded to the nearest ten? **(Lesson 1-8)**

A 500 **C** 540

B 600 **D** 550

31 Margo rounded the number of beads in her craft set to 4,000. What number could be the exact number of beads? **(Lesson 1-9)**

F 2,989 **H** 4,576

G 3,576 **J** 5,004

Spiral Review

Round to the nearest ten. (Lesson 1-8)

32. 89 **33.** 319 **34.** 5,568 **35.** 8,728

Order the numbers from greatest to the least. (Lesson 1-7)

36. 1,234; 998; 2,134 **37.** 598; 521; 3,789 **38.** 2,673; 2,787; 2,900

39. Elias purchased the following items. He also bought a book about sports for $8. How much did he spend in all? **(Lesson 1-5)**

CHAPTER 1

Study Guide and Review

FOLDABLES™ Study Organizer GET READY to Study

Be sure the following Key Vocabulary words and Key Concepts are written in your Foldable.

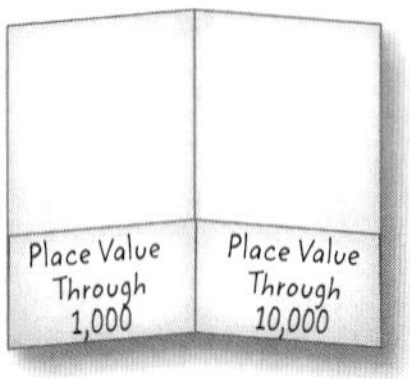

BIG Ideas

- A **pattern** is a sequence of numbers, or figures that follows a rule. (p. 17)

5, 15, 25, 35, 45, 55

+ 10 + 10 + 10 + 10 + 10

- **Place value** is the value given to a digit by its place in a number. (p. 24)

Hundreds	Tens	Ones
9	8	3

- To compare numbers use **is less than** <, **is greater than** >, or **is equal to** =. (p. 34)

$46 < 50$ 46 is less than 50.

$125 > 89$ 125 is greater than 89.

$60 = 60$ 60 is equal to 60.

Key Vocabulary

equal to (p. 34)
pattern (p. 17)
place value (p. 24)
round (p. 44)

Vocabulary Check

Choose the vocabulary word that completes each sentence.

1. In the number 12,354 the digit 5 is in the tens place. This shows its ___?___.

2. A series of numbers or figures that follow a rule is called a ___?___.

3. The number 887 ___?___ eight hundred eighty-seven.

4. When you ___?___ 87 to the nearest 10, you get 90.

5. The order of the numbers 50, 60, 70, and 80 is an example of a ___?___.

6. The value of a digit in a number is its ___?___.

Math Online Vocabulary Review at ca.gr3math.com

Lesson-by-Lesson Review

1-1 Number Patterns (pp. 17–19)

Example 1

Identify a pattern in 140, 135, 130, ■, 120, ■. Then find the missing numbers.

The pattern shows that 5 is subtracted from each number.

140, 135, 130, ■, 120, ■

−5 −5 −5 −5 −5

The missing numbers are 125 and 115.

Identify a pattern. Then find the missing numbers.

7. 85, ■, 105, 115, ■, 135

8. 200, 400, ■, ■, 1,000, 1,200

9. 120, 110, ■, 90, 80, ■

10. The first four numbers in a pattern are 27, 30, 33, and 36. If the pattern continues, what are the next four numbers?

1-2 Problem-Solving Skill: Use the Four-Step Plan (pp. 20–21)

Example 2

Estella runs 1 mile the first week, then doubles her miles each week after that. How many weeks will it take for her to run 8 miles?

The first week Estella ran 1 mile. She doubles that each week. Find how many weeks it will take to run 8 miles.

You can start with 1 and keep doubling it until you reach 8.

1 mile	Week 1
$1 + 1 = 2$ miles	Week 2
$2 + 2 = 4$ miles	Week 3
$4 + 4 = 8$ miles	Week 4

She reached 8 miles by week 4.

Solve each problem.

11. Raini wants a bike that costs $65. Raini's father will match any amount of money Raini saved. Raini has $30. With his father's help, can he buy the bike? Explain.

12. Vincent played soccer for 3 seasons. Mitchell has played for 3 years. If there are 2 seasons each year, who has played more seasons? Explain.

13. Bo brought 25 pencils to school the first week. He used 5 the first week and 7 the second week. How many are still unused?

CHAPTER 1

Study Guide and Review

1-3 Place Value Through 1,000 (pp. 24–27)

Example 3
Write 3,456 in expanded form and word form.

The number 3,456 is written in standard form.

Standard Form 3,456

Expanded Form 3,000 + 400 + 50 + 6

Word Form three thousand, four hundred fifty-six

Write each number in expanded form and word form.

14. 4,013 **15.** 6,047

Write each number in standard form.

16. 7,000 + 600 + 20 + 2

17. 4,000 + 50 + 6

18. one thousand, two hundred three

19. two thousand eight hundred seventy-five

1-4 Place Value Through 10,000 (pp. 28–30)

Example 4
Write the place of the underlined digit in 23,456. Then write its value.

The place value chart shows 23,456

Thousands Period			Ones Period		
hundreds	tens	ones	hundreds	tens	ones
	2	3,	4	5	6

The underlined digit, 2, is in the ten thousands place. So, its value is 20,000.

Write the place of each underlined digit. Then write its value.

20. 46,887 **21.** 63,004

Write each number in expanded form and word form.

22. 60,457 **23.** 54,010

Write each number in standard form.

24. 80,000 + 7,000 + 400 + 3

25. forty-seven thousand, nine hundred seventy-one

1-5 Problem-Solving Investigation: Use the Four-Step Plan (pp. 32–33)

Example 5
Bart lives 30 miles from a water park. Clancy lives 25 miles more than Bart from the same water park. How many miles does Clancy live from the water park.

Understand You know that Bart lives 30 miles from the park. Clancy lives 25 miles further than Bart. You want to find out how many miles Clancy lives from the water park.

Plan You can use addition to find the total.

Solve Add the distance Bart lives from the water park and how much further Clancy lives from the park.

30	distance Bart lives
+ 25	distance further Clancy lives
55	total distance Clancy lives

So, Clancy lives 55 miles away from the water park.

Check Look back at the problem. Check by subtracting.

$$\begin{array}{r} 55 \\ -\ 25 \\ \hline 30 \end{array}$$

The answer is correct.

Use the four-step plan to solve each problem.

26. **Algebra** Garth has twice as many model cars as Luke. Luke has 12. How many cars do they own?

27. For each coupon book Julie sells, she earns 100 points. If she sold 4 books last week and 5 this week, does she have enough points for an 800-point prize? Explain.

28. **Measurement** Mr. Jonas needs to put a fence around part of his yard for his dog. How many feet of fence will he need?

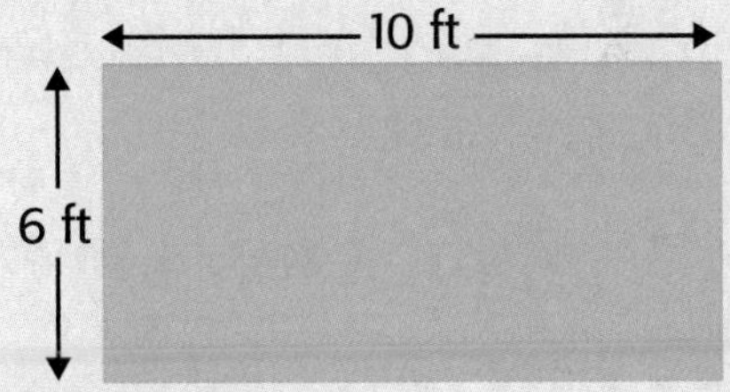

29. Mrs. Cassady made tea for her grandchildren. She used 3 tea bags for one pitcher. If she makes 4 pitchers, how many tea bags will she use?

30. Star gave each of her 6 friends 5 pieces of paper. She kept the rest of the paper. The pack now has 70 pieces of paper left. How much did she have to begin with?

1-6 Compare Numbers (pp. 34–37)

Example 6
Compare 679 ● 686.

You can use a number line.

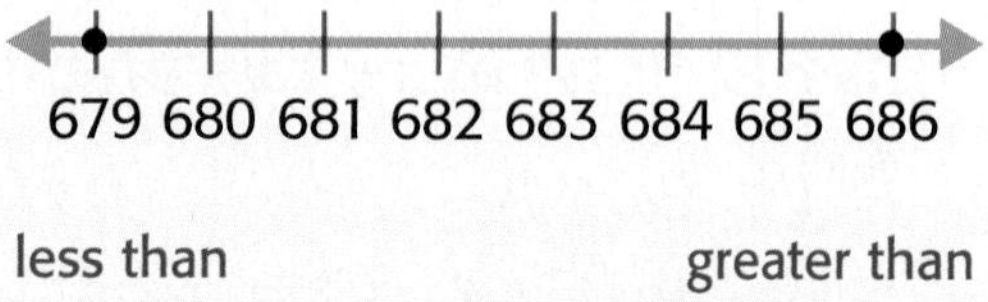

679 is to the left of 686

679 is less than 686

679 < 686

Compare. Write >, <, or =.

31. 2,045 ● 2,405

32. 201 ● 1020

33. 10,567 ● 10,657

34. 5,801 ● 8,051

35. A school sold 235 tickets for the 3rd grade play. There were 253 tickets sold for the 4th grade play. Which play had more people? Explain.

1-7 Order Numbers (pp. 38–41)

Example 7
Order the numbers from the least to the greatest.

7,541; 5,300; 6,108

Use a place value chart to compare.

Thousands	Hundreds	Tens	Ones
7,	5	4	1
5,	3	0	0
6,	1	0	8

5,300 < 6,108 < 7,541

Order the numbers from the least to the greatest.

36. 36,201; 35,201; 36,102

37. 450; 540; 405

Order the numbers from greatest to the least.

38. 89,554; 98,554; 87,554

39. 603; 630; 306

40. Explain how you know which number is the greatest without comparing the value of the digits.
535; 354; 4,435

1-8 Round to the Nearest Ten and Hundred (pp. 44–46)

Example 8

MEASUREMENT The students played on the playground for 78 minutes. To the nearest ten, about how many minutes is this?

The closest ten *less than* 78 is 70. The closest ten *greater than* 78 is 80.

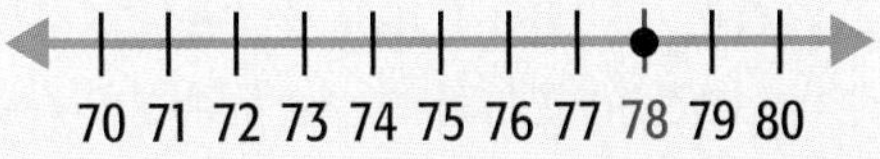

78 is closer to 80, so round 78 to 80.

Example 9

Jordan has 236 toy cars. To the nearest hundred, about how many toy cars does he have?

The closest hundred *less than* 236 is 200. The closest hundred *greater than* 236 is 300.

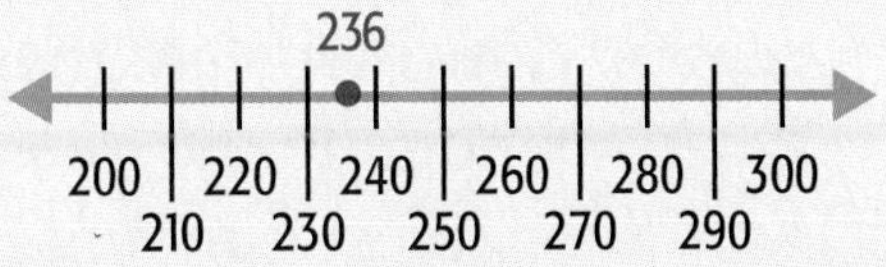

236 is closer to 200, so round 236 to 200.

Round to the nearest ten.

41. 56 **42.** 32

43. 801 **44.** 652

Round to the nearest hundred.

45. 569 **46.** 858

47. 1,593 **48.** 1,263

49. Coty has 465 marbles. Rounded to the nearest hundred, how many does he have?

50. Anita read 39 pages. Lisa read 33 pages. Rounded to the nearest ten, how many did they each read?

51. Raul says he has 200 army men when he rounds the total to the nearest hundred. How many men could Raul have? Explain how you know.

52. This is May's rock collection. What is the total number of rocks in her collection to the nearest ten?

1-9 Round to the Nearest Thousand (pp. 48–51)

Example 10

Round 5,256 to the nearest thousand.

You can use a number line.

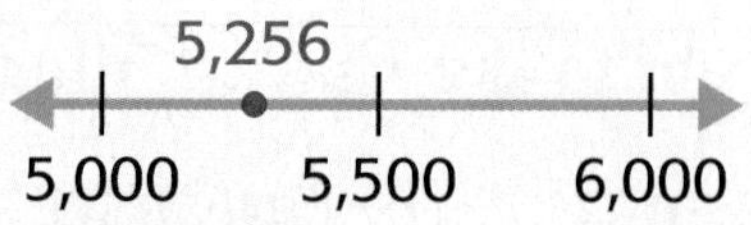

So, 5,256 is closer to 5,000 than to 6,000.

Example 11

Round 5,789 to the nearest thousand.

You can also use the rules of rounding.

Step 1 Underline the digit to be rounded.

5,789

Step 2 Look at the digit to the right of the place being rounded.

5,789

Step 3 This digit is more than 5, so, add 1 to the underlined digit.

6,789

Step 4 Replace all digits after the underlined digit with zeros.

6,000

So, 5,789 rounded to the nearest thousand is 6,000.

Round to the nearest thousand.

53. 4,509 **54.** 4,905

55. 3,980 **56.** 3,089

57. 8,097 **58.** 8,709

59. Gayla found the receipt below. What is the total amount spent rounded to the nearest thousand?

The Sports Store

Treadmill	$ 2,500
Weight set	$ 2,000
Volley Ball set	$ 150
Total	$ 4,650

CUSTOMER COPY

60. There are 4,210 students in the school. How many are there when rounded to the nearest ten? the nearest hundred? the nearest thousand?

61. Paula visited a city that has a popluation of 14,671. What is the population rounded to the nearest thousand?

CHAPTER 1

Chapter Test

For Exercises 1 and 2, tell whether each statement is *true* or *false*.

1. The number 3,578 is written in standard form.

2. Expanded form is a way to write a number in words.

Identify a pattern. Then find the missing number.

3. 30, ■, 50, 60, ■

4. 5, 10, ■, 20, ■

Identify the place of the underlined digit. Then write its value.

5. <u>3</u>,720

6. 5<u>2</u>9

7. Darlene noticed that the meter on her family's new car showed they have driven two thousand, eight hundred eighteen miles so far. How is that number written in standard form?

Write each number in expanded form and word form.

8. 6,191

9. 19,804

10. **STANDARDS PRACTICE** How is four thousand, three hundred twenty-one written in standard form?

A 3,421

B 4,021

C 4,231

D 4,321

11. There are 62 students in line to buy lunch. If 14 more students are in line to buy milk, how many students are there in all?

Compare. Write >, <, or =.

12. 8,415 ● 8,541

13. 500 + 80 + 9 ● 589

14. Order the numbers from least to greatest.

4,804; 4,408; 8,440

15. Order the number of baskets from least to greatest.

Career Baskets

Player	Baskets
Roz	2,308
Marquez	2,803
Amada	2,083

Round each number to the nearest ten, hundred, and thousand.

16. 2,942

17. 9,267

18. **STANDARDS PRACTICE** Which digit is in the thousands place in the number 92,108?

F 1

G 2

H 8

J 9

19. **WRITING IN MATH** Give an example of when it would be appropriate to round numbers rather than be exact. Explain.

CHAPTER 1

California Standards Practice

Cumulative, Chapter 1

Standards Example

The pet shop sold 1372 turtles. Which of these equals 1372?

A 1 + 3 + 7 + 2

B 1 + 30 + 70 + 2000

C 100 + 300 + 70 + 2

D 1000 + 300 + 70 + 2

Read the Question

You need to find which equals 1372.

Solve the Question

You can use a place value chart to find the value of each digit in 1372.

Thousands	Hundreds	Tens	Ones
1	3	7	2

1372 = 1000 + 300 + 70 + 2. So, the answer is D.

Online Personal Tutor at ca.gr3math.com

Choose the best answer.

1 **Which point on the number line names 415?**

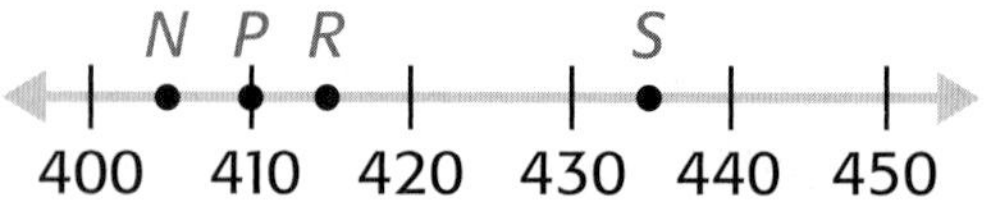

A *N*

B *P*

C *R*

D *S*

2 **Which is the standard form for three hundred forty-two?**

F 234

G three hundred twenty-four

H 342

J 300 + 40 + 2

3 **Leonardo has 158 baseball cards in his collection. Which of these equals 158?**

A 1 + 5 + 8

B 1 + 50 + 800

C 100 + 80 + 5

D 100 + 50 + 8

4 **How is five thousand, thirty-two written in standard form?**

F 5023 **H** 5230

G 5032 **J** 5320

5 **Which set of numbers is in order from greatest to least?**

A 583, 834, 994, 998

B 834, 583, 998, 994

C 994, 998, 583, 834

D 998, 994, 834, 583

6 **Mark put 8 stickers and 2 balls in each party favor bag. How many favors are in each bag?**

F 10 **H** 14

G 12 **J** 16

7 **What is 6639 rounded to the nearest thousand?**

A 7500 **C** 6700

B 7000 **D** 6600

8 **What is this number in standard form?**

Thousands Period			Ones Period		
hundreds	tens	ones	hundreds	tens	ones
		1,	3	4	2

F 1432 **H** 1234

G 1342 **J** 132

9 **Bertram played with 5 toy sailboats in the pool. He gave 2 to his friend to use. How many sailboats does Bertram have now?**

A 1 **C** 3

B 2 **D** 7

10 **What number is 3737 rounded to the nearest ten?**

F 3740 **H** 3800

G 3780 **J** 4000

CHAPTER 2

Addition

BIG Idea When will I use addition?

Addition is helpful when you want to buy something.

Example Renato wants to buy the skateboard items shown. What is the total cost of the items?

What will I learn in this chapter?

- Use the properties of addition.
- Add money.
- Estimate sums.
- Add two-digit, three-digit, and four-digit numbers.
- Decide if an *estimate or exact answer* is needed.

Key Vocabulary

Commutative Property of Addition
Identity Property of Addition
Associative Property of Addition
regroup
estimate

Math Online **Student Study Tools at ca.gr3math.com**

FOLDABLES™ Study Organizer

Make this Foldable to help you organize information about addition. Begin with one sheet of $8\frac{1}{2}'' \times 11''$ paper.

1. **Fold** the sheet of paper as shown.

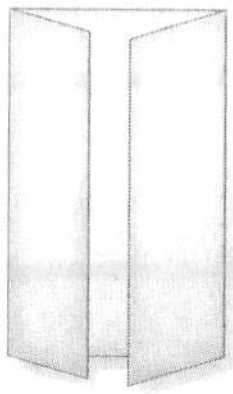

2. **Fold** again in half as shown.

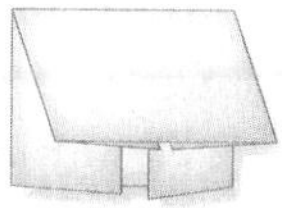

3. **Unfold** and cut along the two inside valley folds.

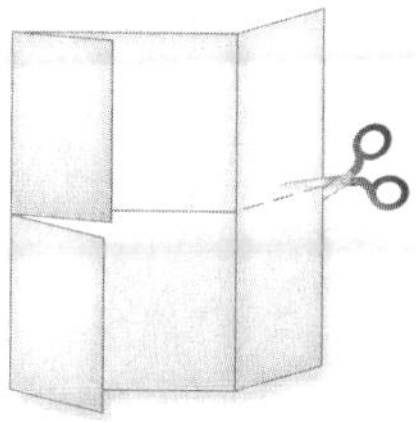

4. **Label** as shown. Record what you learn.

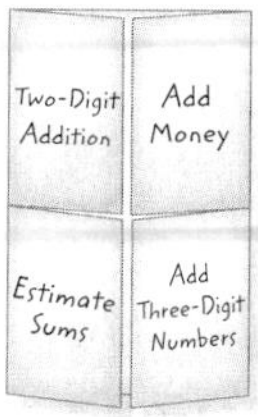

ARE YOU READY for Chapter 2?

You have two ways to check prerequisite skills for this chapter.

Option 2

Math Online Take the Chapter Readiness Quiz at ca.gr3math.com.

Option 1

Complete the Quick Check below.

QUICK Check

Add. **(Previous grade)**

1. $\begin{array}{r} 5 \\ +\ 4 \\ \hline \end{array}$ **2.** $\begin{array}{r} 6 \\ +\ 7 \\ \hline \end{array}$ **3.** $\begin{array}{r} 3 \\ +\ 9 \\ \hline \end{array}$ **4.** $\begin{array}{r} 7 \\ +\ 7 \\ \hline \end{array}$

5. 9 + 2 **6.** 4 + 6 **7.** 8 + 3 **8.** 9 + 8

9. Percy swam 8 laps today and 4 laps yesterday. How many laps did he swim the 2 days?

Find each sum. **(Previous grade)**

10.

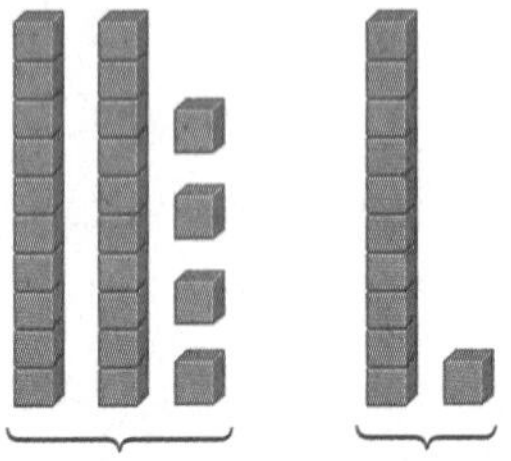

24 + 11

11.

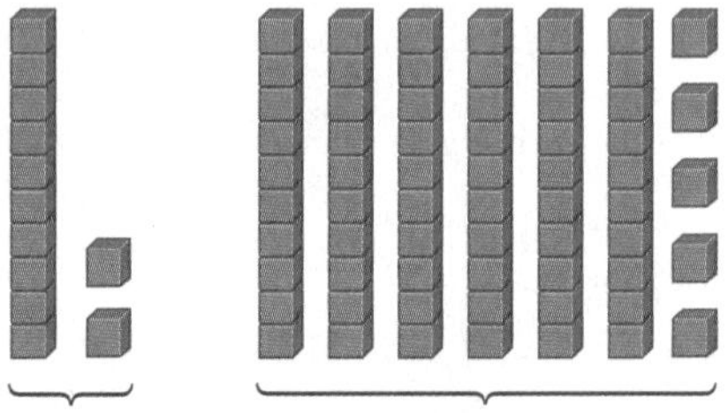

12 + 65

Round to the nearest ten. **(Lesson 1-8)**

12. 72 **13.** 19 **14.** 55 **15.** 89

Round to the nearest hundred. **(Lesson 1-8)**

16. 450 **17.** 771 **18.** 301 **19.** 149

20. 99 **21.** 505 **22.** 75 **23.** 651

2-1 Addition Properties

MAIN IDEA

I will use addition properties to add whole numbers.

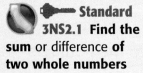

Standard 3NS2.1 Find the sum or difference **of two whole numbers between 0 and 10,000.**

Standard 3AF1.1 Represent relationships of quantities in the form of mathematical expressions, equations, or inequalities.

New Vocabulary

Commutative Property of Addition

Identity Property of Addition

Associative Property of Addition

GET READY to Learn

Sal has 2 pieces of quartz and 3 pieces of granite in his rock collection. Ruby has 3 pieces of quartz and 2 pieces of granite in her collection. They both have the same number of rocks.

$$2 + 3 = 3 + 2$$

In math, properties are rules you can use with numbers.

KEY CONCEPT — Properties

Models

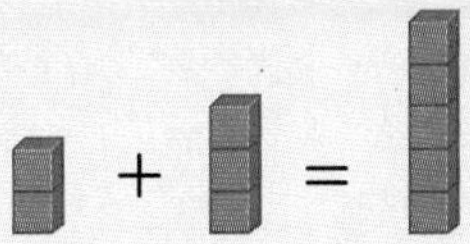

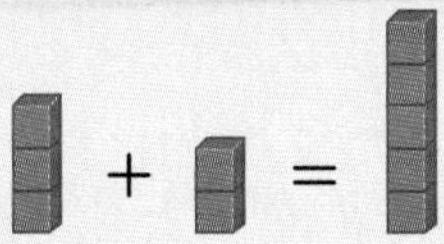

Examples $2 + 3 = 5$ $\quad$ $3 + 2 = 5$

Words **Commutative Property of Addition** The order in which the numbers are added does not change the sum.

Examples $3 + 0 = 3$ $\quad$ $0 + 3 = 3$

Words **Identity Property of Addition** The sum of any number and zero is the number.

Examples $(3 + 2) + 4 =$ $\quad$ $3 + (2 + 4) =$

$5 + 4 =$ $\quad$ $3 + 6 =$

9 $\quad$ 9

Words **Associative Property of Addition** The way the addends are grouped does not change the sum.

EXAMPLE Use Properties to Add

1 **Find the sum. Identify the property.**

$4 + 5 = \blacksquare$ and $5 + 4 = \blacksquare$

The sum is 9. The order in which the numbers are added does not change the sum.

This is the Commutative Property of Addition.

Online Personal Tutor at ca.gr3math.com

Real-World EXAMPLE Associative Property

2 ANIMALS **A zoo has 4 owl chicks, 2 cheetah cubs, and 6 lion cubs. How many baby animals are at the zoo?**

You need to find 4 + 2 + 6. Rearrange the numbers so they are easier to add.

$(4 + 2) + 6$

$= (2 + 4) + 6$ ← Commutative Property of Addition.

$= 2 + (4 + 6)$ ← Associative Property of Addition. The grouping of the addends does not change the sum.

$= 2 + 10$

$= 12$

So, there are 12 baby animals.

CHECK What You Know

Find each sum. Identify the property. See Examples 1 and 2 (p. 66)

1. $6 + 5 = \blacksquare$
$5 + 6 = \blacksquare$

2. $(5 + 7) + 3 = \blacksquare$
$5 + (7 + 3) = \blacksquare$

3. $0 + 12 = \blacksquare$

4. **Algebra** Write a number sentence to show how many shells were collected. What property did you use?

Seashell Collection			
Day	Friday	Saturday	Sunday
Shells	6	7	4

5. Talk About It Describe how you can use the Commutative and Associative Properties of Addition to add 7, 8, and 3.

Practice and Problem Solving

EXTRA PRACTICE See page R5.

Find each sum. Identify the property. See Examples 1 and 2 (p. 66)

6. $0 + 9 = ■$

7. $9 + 2 = ■$
$2 + 9 = ■$

8. $(2 + 5) + 8 = ■$
$2 + (5 + 8) = ■$

9. $2 + 8 = ■$
$8 + 2 = ■$

10. $100 + 0 = ■$

11. $4 + (6 + 3) = ■$
$(4 + 6) + 3 = ■$

Algebra Find each missing number. Identify the property.

12. $6 + ■ = 6$

13. $(7 + 9) + 3 = (9 + ■) + 3$

14. $9 + ■ = 2 + 9$

15. $(8 + 3) + ■ = 8 + (3 + 2)$

Find each sum mentally.

16. $\begin{array}{r} 1 \\ 7 \\ +\ 9 \\ \hline \end{array}$

17. $\begin{array}{r} 5 \\ 7 \\ +\ 5 \\ \hline \end{array}$

18. $\begin{array}{r} 4 \\ 2 \\ 6 \\ +\ 2 \\ \hline \end{array}$

19. $\begin{array}{r} 2 \\ 1 \\ 9 \\ +\ 3 \\ \hline \end{array}$

Solve.

20. Necie has 3 dogs. Simona has 5 fish and 6 birds. Peyton has 1 snake. How many pets do the children have?

21. Luis drew the picture below. Write two number sentences that would be examples of the Associative Property of Addition.

22. Mrs. Jackson bought 6 blue, 2 red, and 2 yellow notebooks. There are 7 notebooks left on the store's shelf. How many were there to begin with?

H.O.T. Problems

23. OPEN ENDED Describe three different ways to find the sum of 7 + 9 + 3. Which properties of addition did you use? Explain the way that you find easiest.

24. WRITING IN ▸MATH Is there a Commutative Property of Subtraction? Explain.

2-2 Problem-Solving Skill

MAIN IDEA I will decide whether an estimate or an exact answer is needed to solve a problem.

Standard 3MR2.5 Indicate the relative advantages of exact and approximate solutions to problems and give answers to a specified degree of accuracy. **Standard 3NS2.1 Find the sum** or difference **of two whole numbers between 0 and 10,000.**

To celebrate Arbor Day, a town planted trees one weekend. On Saturday, 53 trees were planted. Another 38 trees were planted on Sunday. About how many trees were planted in all?

Understand

What facts do you know?

- On Saturday, 53 trees were planted.
- On Sunday, 38 trees were planted.

What do you need to find?

- Find *about* how many trees were planted in all.

Plan

You need to decide whether to estimate or find an exact answer. Since the question asks *about* how many trees were planted, you need to estimate.

Solve

- First, find about how many trees were planted each day. Estimate by rounding to the closest ten.

$53 \rightarrow 50$ ← Round 53 to 50.
$38 \rightarrow 40$ ← Round 38 to 40.

- Then, add.

$$\begin{array}{r} 50 \\ +40 \\ \hline 90 \end{array}$$

So, about 90 trees were planted in all.

Check

Look back at the problem. If the question asked for an exact answer you would find $53 + 38 = 91$. The estimate is close to the exact answer. So, the estimate makes sense.

ANALYZE the Skill

Refer to the problem on the previous page.

1. How do you know when to find an estimate or an exact answer?
2. Describe a situation when an exact answer is needed.
3. Would under-estimating ever cause difficulty? Explain.
4. Explain one reason why only an estimate is needed for the number of trees planted.

PRACTICE the Skill

EXTRA PRACTICE
See page R5.

Tell whether an estimate or an exact answer is needed. Then solve.

5. During a career day, the students gave an author stories they wrote. How many stories were written?

Student Stories	
2nd grade	26
3rd grade	35

6. **Measurement** Kishi cut 2 lengths of rope. One was 32 inches long. The other was 49 inches long. Will he have enough rope for a project that needs 47 inches and 29 inches of rope? Explain.

7. There are enough seats for 60 students on the bus. Can all 32 boys and 26 girls ride the bus? Explain.

8. The number 7 septillion has 24 zeros after it. The number 7 octillion has 27 zeros after it. How many zeros is that altogether?

9. **Measurement** If each tablespoon of mix makes 1 glass of lemonade, will 96 ounces be enough for 15 glasses of lemonade? Explain.

Lemonade Directions	
Water	**Mix**
32 ounces	4 tablespoons
64 ounces	8 tablespoons
96 ounces	12 tablespoons

10. The directions on a treasure map told Rosaline to walk 33 paces forward. She was then to walk 15 paces right. How many paces does she need to walk?

11. WRITING IN MATH Write two real-world problems. One should involve estimation and the other should involve an exact answer.

2-3 Estimate Sums

GET READY to Learn

The students at Glenwood Elementary School had an art show. The number of visitors is shown. About how many people visited the art show over the two days?

MAIN IDEA

I will estimate sums using rounding and front-end estimation.

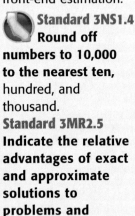

Standard 3NS1.4 Round off numbers to 10,000 to the nearest ten, hundred, and thousand.

Standard 3MR2.5 Indicate the relative advantages of exact and approximate solutions to problems and give answers to a specified degree of accuracy.

New Vocabulary

estimate
front-end estimation

The word *about* means that you do not need an exact answer. You can estimate. When you **estimate**, you find an answer that is close to the exact answer. You can use rounding to estimate.

Real-World EXAMPLE **Estimate by Rounding**

1 SCHOOL **About how many people in all visited the art show on Friday and Saturday?**

To find the total, find 47 + 34. Since, the question says *about* how many people, estimate 47 + 34.

Step 1 Round each number to the nearest ten.

47 ⟶ 50 ⟵ Round 47 to 50.
34 ⟶ 30 ⟵ Round 34 to 30.

Step 2 Add.

$$\begin{array}{r} 47 \\ +\ 34 \\ \hline \end{array} \longrightarrow \begin{array}{r} 50 \\ +\ 30 \\ \hline 80 \end{array}$$

So, *about* 80 people visited the art show.

Remember

See Lesson 1-8 to review rounding of whole numbers.

Online **Personal Tutor at** ca.gr3math.com

Real-World EXAMPLE Estimate by Rounding

2 **BAGELS Mrs. Cruz bought 36 honey bagels and 32 blueberry bagels for an awards breakfast. About how many bagels did Mrs. Cruz buy?**

You need to estimate 36 + 32.

$$\begin{array}{rcr} 36 & \longrightarrow & 40 \\ 32 & \longrightarrow & +\ 30 \\ \hline & & 70 \end{array}$$

Round 36 to 40.
Round 32 to 30.

So, Mrs. Cruz bought *about* 70 bagels.

In **front-end estimation**, you add the front digits of the numbers.

Remember

When using front-end estimation, the sum is always less than the real sum.

Real-World EXAMPLE Front-End Estimation

3 **SNACKS During the circus, 85 boxes of popcorn and 79 beverages were sold. About how many popcorn and beverages were sold?**

Use front-end estimation to find 85 + 79.

$$\begin{array}{rcr} 85 & \longrightarrow & 80 \\ +\ 79 & \longrightarrow & +\ 70 \\ \hline & & 150 \end{array}$$

Use the front digits. Change the remaining digits to 0.

So, *about* 150 popcorn and beverages were sold.

CHECK What You Know

Estimate each sum using rounding. See Examples 1 and 2 (pp. 70–71)

1. $\begin{array}{r} 31 \\ +\ 57 \\ \hline \end{array}$

2. $\begin{array}{r} 38 \\ +\ 59 \\ \hline \end{array}$

3. $\begin{array}{r} 35 \\ +\ 28 \\ \hline \end{array}$

Estimate each sum using front-end estimation. See Example 3 (p. 71)

4. 33 + 56

5. 91 + 94

6. 52 + 17

7. This week, a movie theater will show 53 movies. Next week, 45 movies will be shown. About how movies will they show in the two weeks?

8. Talk About It Look back at Exercise 7. How could it be rewritten so an exact answer is needed?

Practice and Problem Solving

EXTRA PRACTICE See page R5.

Estimate each sum using rounding. See Examples 1 and 2 (pp. 70–71)

9. $64 + 34$

10. $75 + 11$

11. $56 + 22$

12. $13 + 39$

13. $81 + 10$

14. $23 + 25$

15. 11 + 72

16. 49 + 20

17. 18 + 41

Estimate each sum using front-end estimation.
See Example 3 (p. 71)

18. $23 + 28$

19. $84 + 14$

20. $83 + 15$

21. 33 + 37

22. 80 + 89

23. 11 + 72

24. 48 + 39

25. 91 + 14

26. 13 + 31

27. About how many racers were in the Summer Fun Race?

Summer Fun Race		
Start time	**Group**	**Entrants**
9:00 A.M.	runners	79
10:00 A.M.	race walkers	51

FINISH

28. What would be a reasonable estimate for attendance at the school fair?

School Fair Attendance	
Saturday	**Sunday**
62	92

29. Noshie made 2 bunches of balloons. One bunch had 9 blue and 12 yellow balloons. The other bunch had 14 red and 16 yellow balloons. About how many yellow balloons were there in all?

30. Team A has 112 soccer players and Team B has 74. Match the correct number of boys and girls to each team.

Team A and Team B's Players	
Boys	**Girls**
55	33
41	57

31. Measurement Two walls of a room measure 21 feet each, and the other two measure 26 feet each. Estimate the total length of all four walls.

H.O.T. Problems

32. OPEN ENDED Using the digits 1, 2, 3, and 4 once, write two 2-digit numbers whose estimated sum is less than 50.

33. FIND THE ERROR Ed and Jayden are estimating 26 + 47. Who is correct? Explain your reasoning.

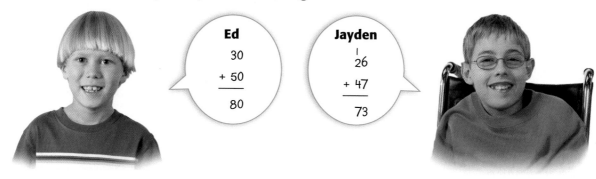

Ed

$$\begin{array}{r} 30 \\ +\ 50 \\ \hline 80 \end{array}$$

Jayden

$$\begin{array}{r} {}^{1} \\ 26 \\ +\ 47 \\ \hline 73 \end{array}$$

34. WRITING IN ▸MATH Write about a real-world situation where using front-end estimation would not be the best way to estimate a sum.

Standards Practice

35 For the party, Evelina made 39 celery sticks and 58 egg rolls. About how many snacks does she have for the party? **(Lesson 2-2)**

A 60   **C** 90

B 70   **D** 100

36 Mr. Moseley will plant 12 flowers in each of his 4 window boxes. About how many flowers does he need to buy? **(Lesson 2-3)**

F 12   **H** 35

G 20   **J** 50

Spiral Review

Algebra Find each missing number. Identify the property. **(Lesson 2-1)**

37. (8 + 4) + 7 = ■
■ + (4 + 7) = 19

38. 25 + ■ = 25

39. 9 + ■ = 16
7 + ■ = 16

40. It rained 12 days in March and 26 days in April. About how many days did it rain these two months? **(Lessons 2-2 and 2-3)**

41. Measurement Miss Sylvia drove 7 miles to the store. Then, she drove another 16 miles to work. At the end of the day, she drove home. How many miles did she drive that day? **(Lesson 1-2)**

2-4 Two-Digit Addition

MAIN IDEA

I will regroup ones to add two-digit numbers.

Standard 3NS2.1 Find the sum or difference **of two whole numbers between 0 and 10,000. Standard 3MR2.1 Use estimation to verify the reasonableness of calculated results.**

New Vocabulary

regroup

GET READY to Learn

Hands-On Mini Activity

Step 1
Use models to show 28 + 7.

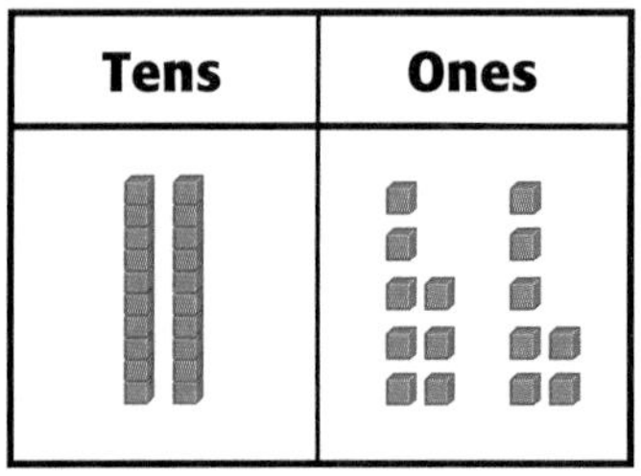

Step 2
Add the ones. Regroup 10 ones as 1 ten.

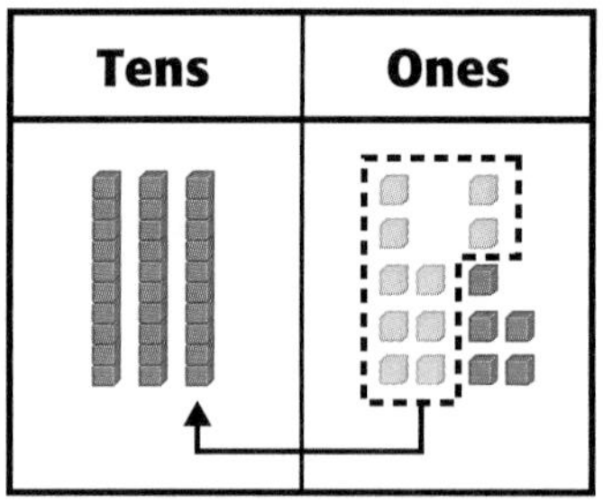

1. What is 28 + 7?
2. Explain when you need to regroup.
3. How would you use regrouping to find 13 + 9?

When you add, you sometimes need to regroup. **Regroup** means to rename a number using place value.

Real-World EXAMPLE Add With Regrouping

1 GAMES **Gaspar has 8 game tokens. His brother has 24 tokens. How many tokens do they have in all?**

You need to find the sum of 24 and 8.

Estimate 24 + 8 ⟶ 20 + 10 = 30

Step 1 Add the ones.

$$\begin{array}{r} {\scriptstyle 1} \\ 24 \\ +\ 8 \\ \hline 2 \end{array}$$

4 ones + 8 ones = 12 ones
12 ones = 1 ten and 2 ones

Step 2 Add the tens.

$$\begin{array}{r} {\scriptstyle 1} \\ 24 \\ +\ 8 \\ \hline 32 \end{array}$$

1 ten + 2 tens = 3 tens

Check for Reasonableness

Compare 32 to the estimate. The answer is reasonable. ✓

Real-World EXAMPLE — Partial Sums

2 DOGS There are 26 golden retrievers and 17 beagles. What is the total number of dogs?

You need to add 26 and 17. You can use partial sums.

Estimate 26 + 17 ⟶ 30 + 20 = 50

$$\begin{array}{rl} 26 & \\ +\ 17 & \\ \hline 30 & \text{Add the tens.} \\ +\ 13 & \text{Add the ones.} \\ \hline 43 & \text{Add the partial sums.} \end{array}$$

Check for Reasonableness

Compare 43 to the estimate. The answer is reasonable. ✓

Sometimes you do not need to regroup.

Remember

Line up the ones column and line up the tens column to add.

EXAMPLE — Add Without Regrouping

3 Find 51 + 23.

Estimate 51 + 23 ⟶ 50 + 20 = 70

$$\begin{array}{rl} 51 & 1 \text{ one} + 3 \text{ ones} = 4 \text{ ones} \\ +\ 23 & 5 \text{ tens} + 2 \text{ tens} = 7 \text{ tens} \\ \hline 74 & \end{array}$$

Check for Reasonableness

Compare 74 to the estimate. The answer is reasonable. ✓

Online Personal Tutor at ca.gr3math.com

CHECK What You Know

Add. Check for reasonableness. See Examples 1–3 (pp. 74–75)

1. $\begin{array}{r} 27 \\ +\ 2 \\ \hline \end{array}$ **2.** $\begin{array}{r} 42 \\ +\ 9 \\ \hline \end{array}$ **3.** $\begin{array}{r} 17 \\ +\ 26 \\ \hline \end{array}$ **4.** 20 + 79

5. In the park, 13 children are riding bikes, and 18 children are on skateboards. How many children are on bikes and skateboards?

6. Talk About It When adding, why do you need to line up the columns for the ones and tens digits?

Practice and Problem Solving

EXTRA PRACTICE
See page R6.

Add. Check for reasonableness. See Examples 1–3 (pp. 74–75)

7. $44 + 5$

8. $62 + 3$

9. $43 + 7$

10. $57 + 7$

11. $75 + 12$

12. $72 + 13$

13. $26 + 34$

14. $61 + 19$

15. 22 + 7

16. 32 + 8

17. 78 + 12

18. 53 + 25

19. There were 25 words on last week's spelling list. This week's list has 19 words. How many words is this in all?

20. In two hours, 47 trucks and 49 cars passed through a tunnel. How many vehicles is this altogether?

21. Pasha and her father picked 38 red apples and 18 yellow apples at an orchard. They used 11 of them in pies. How many apples are there now?

22. One tray makes 24 ice cubes. Another tray makes 36. Are there enough ice cubes for 25 cups if each cup gets 2 ice cubes? Explain.

Real-World PROBLEM SOLVING

Data File Rodeos have a great tradition in California. A rodeo has several events where the person with the fastest time wins.

Rodeo

RED BLUFF ROUNDUP

Event	Winning Time (seconds)
Steer wrestling	23
Team roping	27
Tie down	38
Barrel racing	53

23. What is the combined time for steer wrestling and barrel racing?

24. What is the combined time for all four events?

H.O.T. Problems

25. **OPEN ENDED** Explain how to find 33 + 59 mentally.

26. **WRITING IN ▶MATH** Miki had 60 minutes before her swim lesson. It took 45 minutes to do her homework and 18 minutes to eat a snack. Did she get to her lesson on time? Explain.

Math Online Extra Examples at ca.gr3math.com

Chapter 2 Mid-Chapter Check

Lessons 2-1 through 2-4

Find each sum. Identify the property. (Lesson 2-1)

1. $9 + 0 = ■$

2. $(3 + 4) + 2 = ■$
$3 + (4 + 2) = ■$

Algebra Find each missing number. Identify the property shown. (Lesson 2-1)

3. $2 + (7 + ■) = (2 + 7) + 3)$

4. $■ + 4 = 4 + 7$

5. $6 + ■ = 6$

6. **STANDARDS PRACTICE** Look at the number sentence below.

$$(7 + 2) + 9 = ■$$

Which number will make the number sentence true? (Lesson 2-1)

A 18 **C** 81

B 23 **D** 126

7. The window washer washed 41 windows today and 54 yesterday. How many windows were washed in the two days? (Lesson 2-2)

8. Fina bought 8 daffodils and 13 daisies for her mother. About how many flowers did she buy? (Lesson 2-2)

Estimate each sum using front-end estimation. (Lesson 2-3)

9. $\begin{array}{r} 41 \\ +\ 35 \\ \hline \end{array}$

10. $\begin{array}{r} 19 \\ +\ 36 \\ \hline \end{array}$

11. Mrs. Barnes bought supplies for the classroom. Estimate the total number of items by rounding. (Lesson 2-3)

Add. Check for reasonableness. (Lesson 2-4)

12. $\begin{array}{r} 58 \\ +\ 3 \\ \hline \end{array}$

13. $\begin{array}{r} 73 \\ +12 \\ \hline \end{array}$

14. **STANDARDS PRACTICE** (Lesson 2-4) There are a total of 38 second graders and 59 third graders at a school. How many students are in the second and third grades?

F 87 **H** 107

G 97 **J** 151

Algebra Find each missing digit. (Lesson 2-4)

15. $\begin{array}{r} 38 \\ +■2 \\ \hline 60 \end{array}$

16. $\begin{array}{r} ■9 \\ +32 \\ \hline 61 \end{array}$

17. **WRITING IN MATH** Explain what it means to regroup. Give an example. (Lesson 2-4)

2-5 Add Money

GET READY to Learn

Claudio paid Rey 35¢ for one goldfish and 50¢ for one angelfish. How much money did Claudio pay for the two fish?

MAIN IDEA

I will learn to add money.

Standard 3NS3.3 Solve problems involving addition, subtraction, multiplication, and division **of money amounts in decimal notation** and multiply and divide money amounts in decimal notation by using whole-number multipliers and divisors.
Standard 3MR2.1 Use estimation to verify the reasonableness of calculated results.

New Vocabulary

- **dollar sign ($)**
- **cents sign (¢)**
- **decimal point**

Adding cents is like adding whole numbers. You place a **cent sign (¢)** *after* the sum. You can also add dollars. In this case, you place a **dollar sign ($)** *before* the sum of dollars and a **decimal point** *before* the cents.

35¢ = $0.35 50¢ = $0.50

Real-World EXAMPLES Add Money

1 MONEY **How much money did Claudio pay for the two fish?**

You need to find the sum of 35¢ + 50¢.

Estimate 35¢ + 50¢ ⟶ 40¢ + 50¢ = 90¢

One Way: **Add Cents**		Another Way: **Add Dollars**	
35¢	Add the ones.	$0.35	Line up the decimal points.
+ 50¢	Add the tens.	+ $0.50	
85¢	Place cents sign *after* the sum.	$0.85	

So, Claudio paid 85¢ or $0.85 for the two fish.

Check for Reasonableness

85¢ is close to the estimate of 90¢. So, the answer is reasonable. ✓

Real-World EXAMPLE Add Money

2 TICKETS Ted spent $27 for a ticket to a San Francisco Giants baseball game, and $18 a ticket to an Anaheim Angels game. How much did Ted spend for the two tickets?

You need to add $27 and $18.

Estimate $27 + $18 ⟶ $30 + $20 = $50

1 $27	Add the ones and regroup.
+$18	Add the tens.
$45	Place the dollar sign before the sum.

So, Ted spent $45 for the tickets.

Check for Reasonableness

$45 is close to the estimate of $50. So, the answer is reasonable. ✓

Online **Personal Tutor at** ca.gr3math.com

CHECK What You Know

Add. Use estimation to check for reasonableness.

See Examples 1 and 2 (p. 78–79)

1. 86¢ + 11¢

2. $12 + $78

3. $39 + $18

4. 19¢ + 30¢

5. 59¢ + 20¢

6. 42¢ + 37¢

7. $17 + $9

8. $0.66 + $0.14

9. Rory earns $6 allowance each week. Aida earns $4 each week. If Rory and Aida put 2 weeks of their allowance together, what three different things could they buy to spend as much of their combined allowance as possible?

10. Talk About It Tell where to place the dollar sign and decimal point when adding dollars.

Practice and Problem Solving

EXTRA PRACTICE
See page R6.

Add. Use estimation to check for reasonableness. See Examples 1 and 2 (pp. 78–79)

11. 12¢ + 23¢

12. 30¢ + 38¢

13. 49¢ + 19¢

14. 36¢ + 19¢

15. \$0.21 + \$0.38

16. \$53 + \$45

17. \$17 + \$26

18. \$69 + \$13

19. 25¢ + 4¢

20. 21¢ + 2¢

21. 68¢ + 6¢

22. 8¢ + 74¢

23. \$27 + \$71

24. \$55 + \$41

25. \$0.34 + \$0.08

26. \$7 + \$66

27. A market sells oranges for 37¢ each. How much would 2 oranges cost?

28. A computer program is \$19. The guidebook is \$15. You have \$25. Do you have enough money to buy both? Explain.

For Exercises 29–31, use the poster.

29. Beverly spent \$0.85 at the store today. What 2 items did she buy?

30. Which list would cost Beverly more to buy? Explain.

List
Sunglasses
checkers game
flower seeds

List
Shampoo
Sunglasses

31. What is the greatest number of items Beverly can buy without spending more than \$1? Explain.

Real-World PROBLEM SOLVING

History The cost for many items has increased over the years. Find each sum.

32. a stamp and a gallon of milk in 1900

33. a loaf of bread, a gallon of milk, and a stamp in 1940

Prices Then and Now

Year	Bread	Milk	Stamp
1900	3¢	30¢	2¢
1940	8¢	51¢	3¢
1980	48¢	\$2	15¢
2000	\$2	\$3	34¢

Source: Somethingtoremembermeby.org

H.O.T. Problems

34. CHALLENGE Benny has $36. He wants to buy screw drivers and a hammer. Kali has $42 and wants to buy wrenches and a tool box. Who has enough money to buy the items they need? Explain.

35. WRITING IN ▶MATH Write about a time when you needed to know how to add sums of money.

Standards Practice

36 Look at the number sentence below. **(Lesson 2-4)**

79 + 13 = ■

Which sum would make it true?

A 96

B 93

C 92

D 90

37 Alexandra buys the two items.

What was the total cost? **(Lesson 2-5)**

F $32 **H** $42

G $35 **J** $51

Spiral Review

Find each sum. (Lesson 2-4)

38. 22 + 68 **39.** 75 + 13 **40.** 79 + 87

41. Booker took the first tray of cookies out of the oven at 1:08. If he continues this pattern, what time will he take the fourth and fifth trays out? **(Lesson 1-1)**

Time to Take Cookies Out

Tray	Time
1	1:08
2	1:16
3	1:24

Problem Solving in Geography

A Walk in the PARK

Yellowstone National Park is located in Montana, Wyoming, and Idaho. It is home to hot springs, bubbling mud holes, and fountains of steaming water. These fountains shoot water more than 100 feet into the air.

Yellowstone is also home to 290 species of birds, 50 species of mammals, 6 species of reptiles, and 18 species of fish. What a place to visit! A seven-day visitor's pass to the park costs $10 for one person to hike, or $20 for a carload of people.

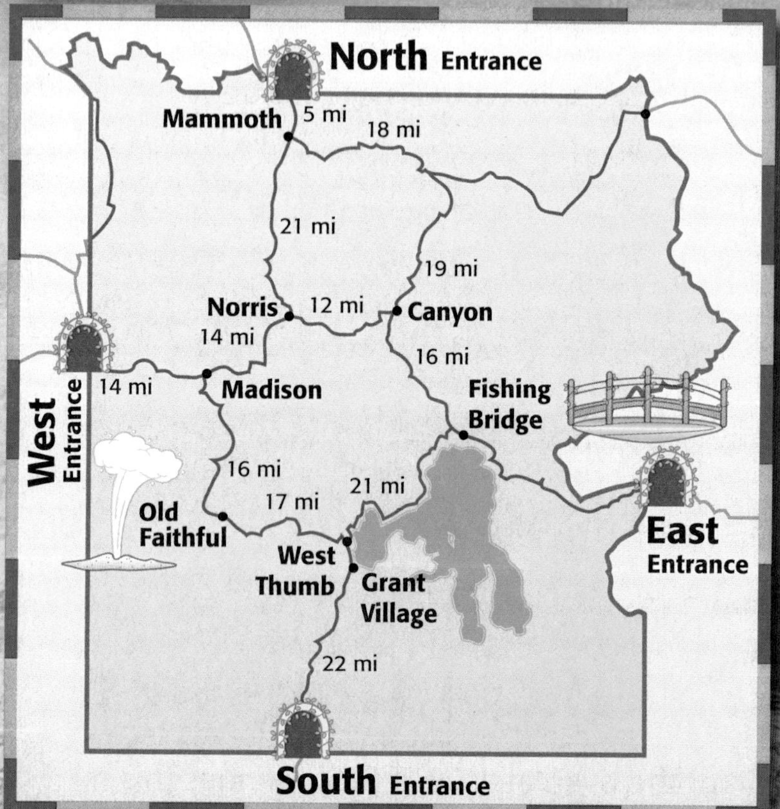

Standard NS2.1 Find the sum or difference of two whole numbers between 0 and 10,000.

Did You Know?

The tallest waterfall in Yellowstone is 308 feet high.

Real-World Math

Use the information and map on page 82 to answer each question.

1. What is the total number of species of birds, mammals, fish, and reptiles in Yellowstone?

2. Five people will visit the park. If they travel by car, they need two cars. Does it cost less for them to drive or hike? Explain.

3. Suppose you walk from the Fishing Bridge to West Thumb and then to Old Faithful. How many miles will you walk?

4. The Diaz family drives from Mammoth to the Fishing Bridge. If their trip was 49 miles long, what route did they take?

5. What is the shortest distance you can walk from the North Entrance to Canyon?

6. A group of visitors travels from the West Entrance to Norris and then to Canyon. Another group travels from the West Entrance to Madison and then to Canyon. Did they travel the same distance? Explain.

7. A group of visitors wants to travel to Norris from the South Entrance. They want to pass the lake. About how long is this route?

2-6 Problem-Solving Investigation

MAIN IDEA I will choose the best strategy to solve a problem.

Standard 3MR1.1 **Analyze problems by identifying relationships, distinguishing relevant and irrelevant information, sequencing and prioritizing information, and observing patterns.** Standard 3NS2.1 **Find the sum or difference of two whole numbers between 0 and 10,000.**

P.S.I. TEAM +

KIRI: My father and I needed to catch at least 10 fish. During the first hour, we caught 9 fish but threw 4 back. The second hour we caught 16 fish and threw 9 back.

YOUR MISSION: Find if they caught and kept at least 10 fish.

Understand	You know how many fish they caught and how many they threw back. Find if they caught and kept at least 10 fish.
Plan	You need to find an exact answer. Use addition and subtraction and write number sentences.
Solve	First, subtract to find out how many fish they kept. Hour One: 9 − 4 = 5 (fish caught − threw back = total each hour) Hour Two: 16 − 9 = 7 Next, add the total for each hour. first hour 5 + second hour 7 = total 12 Kiri and her father caught and kept 12 fish.
Check	Look back at the problem. Yes, Kiri and her father caught and kept at least 10 fish. They caught 12.

Mixed Problem Solving

EXTRA PRACTICE
See page R6.

Use the four-step plan to solve each problem.

1. Neva has a hamster and Sherita has a turtle. If they each have a $5 bill, how much change will each receive when they buy food for their pets?

Pet Food	
Hamster	**Turtle**
$3.95	$4.25

2. It takes one hour to make 4 pizzas. How many pizzas can be made in 4 hours and 30 minutes?

3. Rudy left for his vacation at 5 A.M. If the trip takes 10 hours, will he be at his destination by 3 P.M.? Explain.

4. Blaine built a cube staircase. How many cubes in all are needed to build 6 steps?

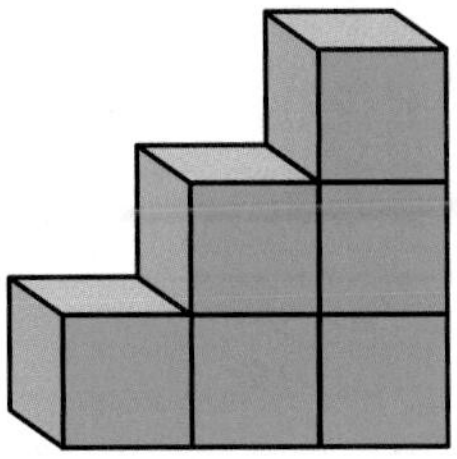

5. There are 4 snack-packs of yogurt. Each snack-pack has 6 yogurts. How many more snack-packs are needed for a total of 30 yogurts?

6. There are 3 children in line. Cami is right after Brock. Bo is third. What place is each child in line?

7. There are 37 stores on the first floor of a 2-floor mall. The second floor has 29 stores. About how many stores are at this mall?

8. The space museum gift shop opened at 10:30 A.M. In the morning, 15 model spaceships were sold. During the afternoon, 23 models were sold. How many spaceship models were sold that day?

9. At one campsite there are 3 tents with 5 people in each tent. Another campsite has 3 tents with 4 people in each. How many campers in all?

10. Mom's watering can holds 2 gallons. Each day she needs to water 12 large flower pots and 10 small pots. How many times will she need to fill her watering can?

Pots that can be watered with 2 gallons	
Large pots	4
Small pots	5

11. WRITING IN MATH The children in Mr. Robinson's class are designing a flag. The flag's background can be red or green with a blue or a purple stripe. How many flags can they design? Explain how you solved the problem.

Explore

Math Activity for 2-7
Add Three-Digit Numbers

MAIN IDEA

I will use models to explore regrouping with addition.

Standard 3NS2.1 Find the sum or difference **of two whole numbers between 0 and 10,000.**

Standard 3MR2.2 Apply strategies and results from samples to more complex problems.

You Will Need
base-ten blocks

Concepts in Motion
Animation
ca.gr3math.com

Base-ten blocks can also be used to model three-digit addition.

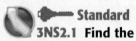

ACTIVITY **Add 148 + 153.**

Step 1 **Model 148 and 153.**

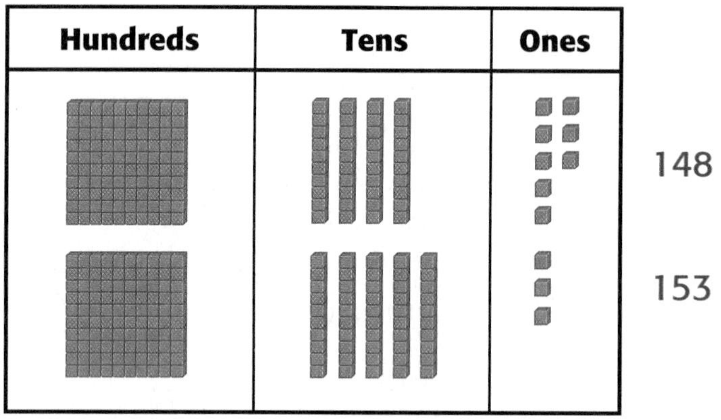

Step 2 **Add the ones.**

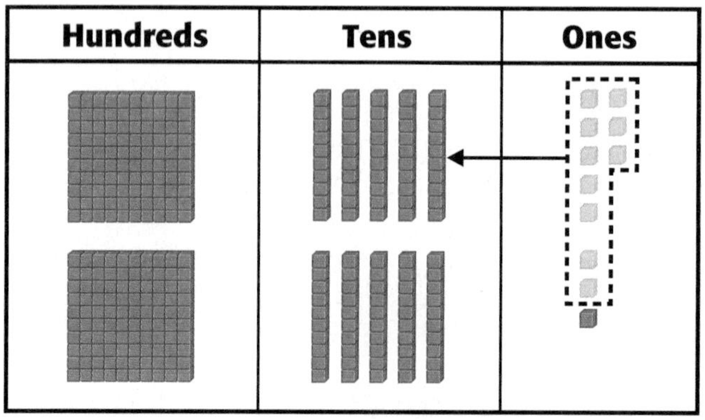

8 ones + 3 ones = 11 ones

Regroup 11 ones as
1 ten and 1 one.

Step 3 **Add the tens.**

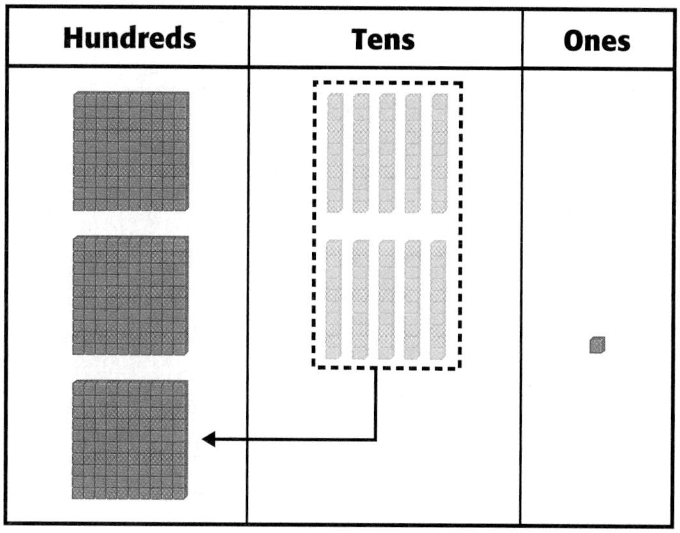

5 tens + 5 tens = 10 tens

Regroup 10 tens as 1 hundred and 0 tens.

Step 4 **Add the hundreds.**

1 hundred + 1 hundred + 1 hundred = 3 hundreds
So, 148 + 153 = 301.

Think About It

1. Describe the sum of the digits that needed to be regrouped.

2. Why were the ones and the tens regrouped?

3. Does changing the order of the addends make a difference in whether you need to regroup? Explain.

CHECK What You Know

Add. Use base-ten blocks if needed.

4. 259 + 162 **5.** 138 + 371 **6.** 362 + 172

7. 541 + 169 **8.** 261 + 139 **9.** 285 + 75

10. WRITING IN ▸MATH Write a rule that would explain when to regroup.

2-7 Three-Digit Addition

MAIN IDEA

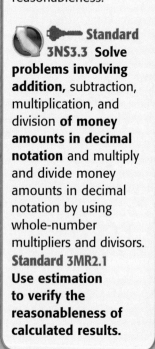

I will add three-digit numbers and use estimation to check for reasonableness.

Standard 3NS3.3 Solve problems involving addition, subtraction, multiplication, and division **of money amounts in decimal notation** and multiply and divide money amounts in decimal notation by using whole-number multipliers and divisors.

Standard 3MR2.1 Use estimation to verify the reasonableness of calculated results.

GET READY to Learn

During the annual backyard bird count, birdwatchers in the state of California reported sighting 127 marsh wrens and 68 bald eagles. How many birds is that total?

In the Explore lesson, you used base-ten blocks to add three-digit numbers. You can also use paper and pencil.

Real-World EXAMPLE — Add with Regrouping

1 BIRDS **How many wrens and eagles did the bird watchers in California report?**

You need to add 127 + 68.

Estimate

$$\begin{array}{lcr} 127 & \rightarrow & 130 \\ 68 & \rightarrow & +\ 70 \\ \hline & & 200 \end{array}$$

Step 1 Add the ones.

$$\begin{array}{r} {}^{1} \\ 127 \\ +\ 68 \\ \hline 5 \end{array}$$

7 ones + 8 ones = 15 ones
Regroup 15 ones as 1 ten and 5 ones.

Step 2 Add the tens and hundreds.

$$\begin{array}{r} {}^{1} \\ 127 \\ +\ 68 \\ \hline 195 \end{array}$$

1 ten + 2 tens + 6 tens = 9 tens
Bring the 1 hundred down.

So, the bird watchers reported 195 wrens and eagles.

Check for Reasonableness

195 is close to the estimate of 200. The answer is reasonable. ✓

Online **Personal Tutor at** ca.gr3math.com

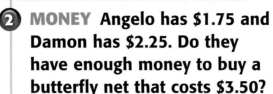

Real-World EXAMPLE — Add with Regrouping

2 MONEY Angelo has \$1.75 and Damon has \$2.25. Do they have enough money to buy a butterfly net that costs \$3.50?

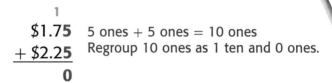

Find \$1.75 + \$2.25 to determine if they can buy the net for \$3.50.

Step 1 Add the ones.

$$\begin{array}{r} \scriptstyle 1 \\ \$1.75 \\ +\ \$2.25 \\ \hline 0 \end{array}$$

5 ones + 5 ones = 10 ones
Regroup 10 ones as 1 ten and 0 ones.

Step 2 Add the tens.

$$\begin{array}{r} \scriptstyle 1\,1 \\ \$1.75 \\ +\ \$2.25 \\ \hline .00 \end{array}$$

1 ten + 7 tens + 2 tens = 10 tens
Regroup 10 tens as 1 hundred + 0 tens.

Step 3 Add the hundreds.

$$\begin{array}{r} \scriptstyle 1\,1 \\ \$1.75 \\ +\ \$2.25 \\ \hline \$4.00 \end{array}$$

1 + 1 + 2 hundreds = 4 hundreds

Together, Angelo and Damon have enough money to buy the butterfly net.

Remember

When adding money, line up the decimal points. Bring the decimal point straight down in the sum.

CHECK What You Know

Find each sum. Use estimation to check for reasonableness.

See Examples 1 and 2 (pp. 88–89)

1. 164 + 17

2. 156 + 255

3. $\begin{array}{r} 468 \\ +\ 35 \\ \hline \end{array}$

4. $\begin{array}{r} 227 \\ +\ 26 \\ \hline \end{array}$

5. $\begin{array}{r} \$3.55 \\ +\ \$1.56 \\ \hline \end{array}$

6. $\begin{array}{r} \$2.72 \\ +\ \$1.48 \\ \hline \end{array}$

7. Chase has 176 video games. Estaban has 238 games. What is the total number of games they have?

8. Talk About It Why is it important to check for reasonableness?

Practice and Problem Solving

EXTRA PRACTICE
See page R7.

Find each sum. Use estimation to check for reasonableness. See Examples 1 and 2 (pp. 88–89)

9. $759 + 19$

10. $445 + 26$

11. $3.45 + $0.93

12. $4.27 + $2.17

13. $597 + 51$

14. $599 + 59$

15. $2.98 + $4.08

16. $2.87 + $4.53

17. 43 + 217

18. 607 + 27

19. $1.73 + $5.91

20. $1.08 + $5.89

21. 635 + 285

22. 398 + 355

23. $7.97 + $1.85

24. $4.90 + $2.88

25. A 10-speed bike is on sale for $199, and a 12-speed racing bike is on sale for $458. How much are the two bikes altogether?

26. Measurement Russell's bean stalk grew 24 inches the first month and 27 inches the second month. How tall was Russell's bean stalk after two months?

27. Measurement Use the map at the right. What is the total distance from the entrance of the park to Leonora's house and back to the park again?

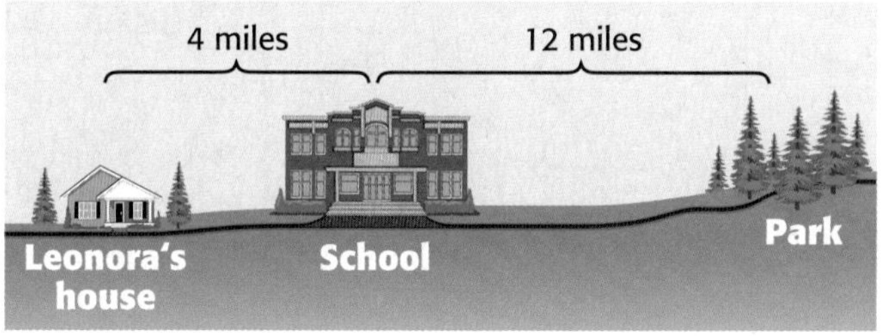

Algebra Find each missing number. Identify the property.

28. 240 + 679 = ■ + 240

29. (13 + 24) + 6 = ■ + (24 + 6)

30. 989 + ■ = 989

31. (565 + 6) + 39 = 565 + (■ + 39)

H.O.T. Problems

32. OPEN ENDED Write an addition problem whose sum is between 450 and 500.

33. CHALLENGE Use the digits 3, 5, and 7 to make 2 three-digit numbers. Use each digit one time in each number. Write an addition problem that would make the greatest sum possible.

Game Time

How Low Can You Go?

Add Three-Digit Numbers

You will need: spinner

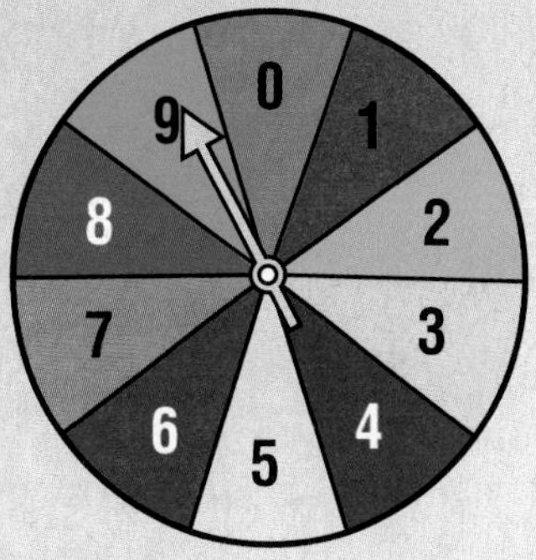

Get Ready!

Players: 2 players

Get Set!

- Divide and label a spinner as shown.
- Make two game sheets.

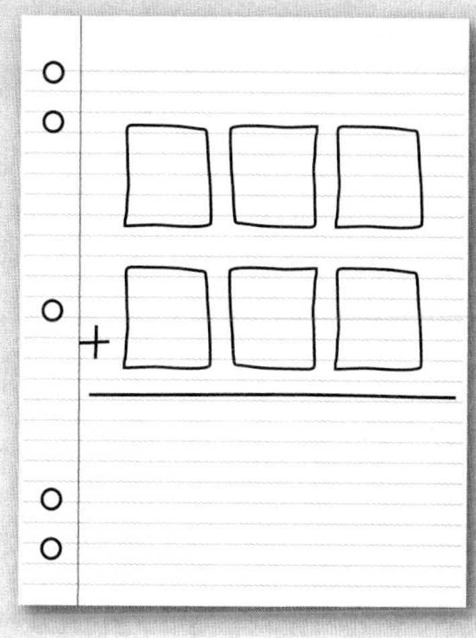

Go!

- Player 1 spins the spinner and records the digit in any box on his or her game sheet.
- Player 2 spins the spinner and records the digit in any box on his or her game sheet.
- Players repeat taking turns and recording numbers until all boxes are filled in.
- Players find the sums of their numbers. The least sum wins.

2-8 Add Greater Numbers

GET READY to Learn

In the United States, 869 radio stations play rock music. There are 2,179 news/talk radio stations. How many radio stations play these two formats?

MAIN IDEA

I will add three- and four-digit numbers with regrouping.

Standard 3NS3.3 Solve problems involving addition, subtraction, multiplication, and division **of money amounts in decimal notation** and multiply and divide money amounts in decimal notation by using whole-number multipliers and divisors.
Standard 3MR2.1 Use estimation to verify the reasonableness of calculated results.

Add 2,179 and 869 just like you add two-digit numbers.

Real-World EXAMPLE

1 RADIO Add 2,179 + 869 to find how many radio stations play these two formats.

Step 1 Add the ones.

$$\begin{array}{r} {}^{1} \\ 2{,}179 \\ +\ 869 \\ \hline 8 \end{array}$$

9 ones + 9 ones = 18 ones
Regroup as 1 ten and 8 ones.

Step 2 Add the tens.

$$\begin{array}{r} {}^{11} \\ 2{,}179 \\ +\ 869 \\ \hline 48 \end{array}$$

1 ten + 7 tens + 6 tens = 14 tens
Regroup as 1 hundred and 4 tens.

Step 3 Add the hundreds.

$$\begin{array}{r} {}^{111} \\ 2{,}179 \\ +\ 869 \\ \hline 3{,}048 \end{array}$$

1 hundred + 1 hundred + 8 hundreds = 10 hundreds
Regroup as 1 thousand and 0 hundreds.

Step 4 Add the thousands.

$$\begin{array}{r} {}^{111} \\ 2{,}179 \\ +\ 869 \\ \hline 3{,}048 \end{array}$$

1 thousand + 2 thousands = 3 thousands

So, 3,048 radio stations play the two formats.

Real-World EXAMPLE **Addition Methods**

2 **PLANES The world's fastest plane can fly 2,139 miles in 32 minutes. What is the total distance if it flew another 2,314 miles?**

You need to find 2,139 + 2,314.

Estimate

$$\begin{array}{r} 2{,}139 \\ +2{,}314 \\ \hline \end{array} \longrightarrow \begin{array}{r} 2{,}100 \\ +2{,}300 \\ \hline 4{,}400 \end{array}$$

Remember

To check if your answer makes sense, estimate first. Than compare the answer to the estimate.

One Way: **Partial Sums**		Another Way: **Expanded Form**
2,139		2,139 = 2,000 + 100 + 30 + 9
+ 2,314		+ 2,314 = 2,000 + 300 + 10 + 4
13	Add ones.	4,000 + 400 + 40 + 13
40	Add tens.	400
400	Add hundreds.	40
+ 4,000	Add thousands.	+ 13
4,453		4,453

Check for Reasonableness

4,453 is close to 4,400. So, the answer is reasonable. ✓

To add money, add as you would with whole numbers.

Real-World EXAMPLE **Addition of Money**

3 **SPORTS Dekland bought a new helmet for $32.95 and skate shoes for $39.99. How much did he spend?**

Estimate $32.95 + $39.99 ⟶ $30 + $40 = $70

Find $32.95 + $39.99.

1 1 1	
$32.95	Line up the decimal points.
+39.99	Add.
$72.94	Place the dollar sign in front of the dollars.
	Place the decimal point in the answer.

Check for Reasonableness

$72.94 is close to $70, the answer is reasonable. ✓

Online Personal Tutor at ca.gr3math.com

CHECK What You Know

Find each sum. Use estimation to check for reasonableness.

See Examples 1–3 (pp. 92–93)

1. 3,345 + 654

2. 4,234 + 500

3. \$32.05 + \$17.09

4. 678 + 4,789

5. \$34.45 + \$65.47

6. \$92.99 + \$7.01

7. Lou's dad's car uses 1,688 gallons of gas a year. His mom's car uses 1,297 gallons. Find the total gallons used.

8. Talk About It How is finding the sum of 3-digit numbers like finding the sum of 4-digit numbers?

Practice and Problem Solving

EXTRA PRACTICE
See page R7.

Find each sum. Use estimation to check for reasonableness.

See Examples 1–3 (pp. 92–93)

9. 6,999 + 543

10. \$19.98 + \$3.00

11. \$25.07 + \$28.99

12. \$82.85 + \$14.56

13. \$23.90 + \$34.90

14. 5,555 + 3,555

15. 2,865 + 5,522

16. 3,075 + 5,640

17. \$16.03 + \$35.09

18. \$57.88 + \$25.50

19. \$39.99 + \$48.00

20. 1,250 + 1,520

21. Write a number sentence to represent the total number of minutes each group read this month. Use > or <.

Time Spent Reading	
Group	**Minutes**
A	2,600
B	2,574

22. How many people were surveyed?

23. The Appalachian Trail is 2,174 miles long. How many miles is it if you hike it one way and then back?

24. Keisha has \$76.81. Randall has \$14.06 more than Keisha. How much do they have altogether?

H.O.T. Problems

25. CHALLENGE Use the digits 2, 3, 4, 5, 6, 7, 8, and 9 to create two four-digit numbers whose sum is greater than 10,000. Use each digit once.

26. FIND THE ERROR Selina and Elliott have found the sum for 4,573 + 2,986. Who is correct? Explain.

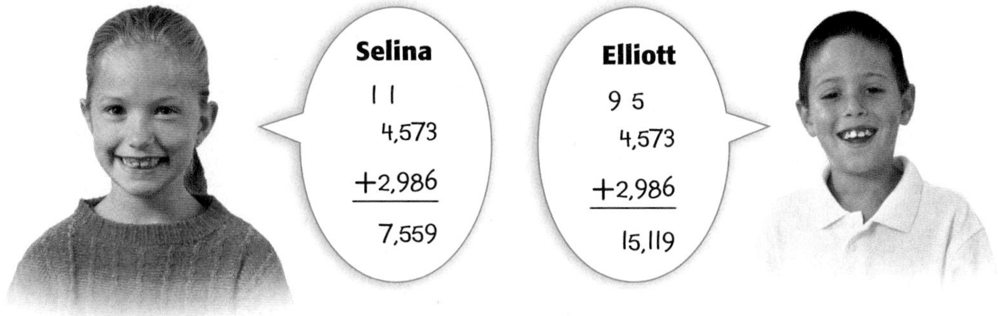

27. WRITING IN ▸MATH Explain what it means to check for reasonableness.

Standards Practice

28 Yesterday's attendance at a baseball game was 4237. Today's attendance was 3176. What is the attendance for the two days? **(Lesson 2-7)**

A 7313

B 7403

C 7413

D 7611

29 What is the total cost? **(Lesson 2-8)**

F $12.27 **H** $14.73

G $12.53 **J** $14.79

Spiral Review

Find each sum. **(Lesson 2-7)**

30. 78 + 19 **31.** $0.24 + $0.53 **32.** $46 + $46

33. Rita's mom bought eggs, milk, and bread. She paid with a $5 bill. Does she have enough money left to buy a smoothie for $1? Explain. **(Lesson 2-6)**

Shopping List	
Eggs	$0.89
Milk	$2.59
Bread	$0.99

CHAPTER 2 Study Guide and Review

FOLDABLES™ Study Organizer GET READY to Study

Be sure the following Key Vocabulary words and Key Concepts are written in your Foldable.

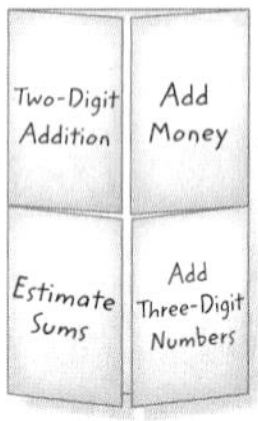

BIG Ideas

Addition Properties (p. 65)

- **Commutative Property of Addition**

  $4 + 3 = 7 \qquad 3 + 4 = 7$

- **Identity Property of Addition**

  $6 + 0 = 6$

- **Associative Property of Addition**

  $(2 + 5) + 1 = 2 + (5 + 1)$

Estimate Sums (p. 70)

56	→	60	← Round 56 to 60
+ 21	→	+ 20	← Round 21 to 20
		80	

Addition with Regrouping (p. 74)

1 1	4 ones + 7 ones = 11 ones
474	Regroup 11 ones as 1 ten and 1 one.
+ 237	1 ten + 7 tens + 3 tens = 11 tens
711	Regroup 11 tens as 1 hundred and 1 ten.

Key Vocabulary

Associative Property of Addition (p. 65)
Commutative Property of Addition (p. 65)
estimate (p. 70)
Identity Property of Addition (p. 65)
regroup (p. 74)

Vocabulary Check

Choose the vocabulary word that completes each sentence.

1. When you ___?___, you find an answer that is close to the exact answer.

2. The ___?___ states that the sum of any number and zero is the number.

3. To rename a number using place value is to ___?___.

4. The ___?___ states that grouping the addends does not change the sum.

5. 2 + 4 = 6 and 4 + 2 = 6 is an example of the ___?___.

Math Online Vocabulary Review at ca.gr3math.com

Lesson-by-Lesson Review

2-1 Addition Properties (pp. 65–67)

Example 1
Find the sum in 2 + 7 = ■ and 7 + 2 = ■. Identify the property.

Both sums are 9. The order does not change the sum. This is the Commutative Property of Addition.

Example 2
Find 8 + 0 = ■. Identify the property.

The sum is 8. The sum of any number and 0 is that number. This is the Identity Property of Addition.

Find each sum. Identify the property.

6. 0 + 10 = ■

7. 11 + 2 = ■
2 + 11 = ■

8. Algebra Find the missing number. Identify the property.

$$(6 + 9) + 5 = 6 + (■ + 5)$$

Find each sum mentally.

9. $\begin{array}{r} 4 \\ 6 \\ +\ 0 \\ \hline \end{array}$

10. $\begin{array}{r} 8 \\ 6 \\ +\ 2 \\ \hline \end{array}$

2-2 Problem-Solving Skill: Estimate or Exact Answer (pp. 68–69)

Example 3
LaVonne saved $35. Her sister saved $29. About how much money do the two girls have in all?

You need to estimate $35 + $29. Round each amount to the nearest ten. Then add.

$$\begin{array}{rcr} \$35 & \rightarrow & \$40 \\ +\ \$29 & \rightarrow & +\ \$30 \\ \hline & & \$70 \end{array}$$

The girls have about $70.

Tell whether an estimate or exact answer is needed. Then solve.

11. To enter a dance competition, Viviana needs $35 for an entrance fee and $75 for her costume. How much money does Viviana need?

12. Cole practices violin 45 minutes three nights a week. Two other nights he has soccer practice for 25 minutes. About how many minutes does Cole spend practicing each week?

Study Guide and Review

2-3 Estimate Sums (pp. 70–73)

Example 4
An artist created a piece of art with 66 round glass beads. There are 17 more beads in the shape of a heart. About how many beads are there altogether?

You need to estimate 66 + 17. Round each number to the nearest ten. Then add.

$$\begin{array}{r} 66 \\ +\ 17 \\ \hline \end{array} \quad \begin{array}{c} \longrightarrow \\ \longrightarrow \end{array} \quad \begin{array}{r} 70 \\ +\ 20 \\ \hline 90 \end{array}$$

So, there are about 90 beads

Estimate each sum using rounding.

13. $\begin{array}{r} 76 \\ +\ 12 \\ \hline \end{array}$ **14.** $\begin{array}{r} 52 \\ +\ 21 \\ \hline \end{array}$

Estimate using front-end estimation.

15. $\begin{array}{r} 33 \\ +\ 58 \\ \hline \end{array}$ **16.** $\begin{array}{r} 18 \\ +\ 47 \\ \hline \end{array}$

17. 31 + 68 **18.** 97 + 28

19. There are about 2,000 earthquakes each year in Yellowstone National Park. Is this an estimate or an exact number? Explain.

2-4 Two-Digit Addition (pp. 74–76)

Example 5

Find 25 + 3.

$\begin{array}{r} \mathbf{25} \\ +\ \mathbf{3} \\ \hline \mathbf{28} \end{array}$ 5 ones + 3 ones = 8 ones; 2 tens + 0 tens = 2 tens.

So, 25 + 3 = 28.

Example 6

Find 32 + 9.

$\begin{array}{r} ^{1} \\ \mathbf{32} \\ +\ \mathbf{9} \\ \hline \mathbf{41} \end{array}$ 2 ones + 9 ones = 11 ones; 11 ones = 1 ten and 1 one; 1 ten + 3 tens = 4 tens

So, 32 + 9 = 41.

Add. Check for reasonableness.

20. $\begin{array}{r} 32 \\ +\ 4 \\ \hline \end{array}$ **21.** $\begin{array}{r} 19 \\ +\ 3 \\ \hline \end{array}$

22. Karly's math class has 21 students. Landon's math class has 29 students. How many math students are there in the two classes?

23. There are 18 juice boxes in the refrigerator and 12 on the shelf. How many juice boxes are there altogether?

2-5 Add Money (pp. 78–81)

Example 7
At school, Vito bought yogurt for 65¢ and milk for 25¢. How much money did he spend?

Find 65¢ + 25¢. To add money, add as you would with whole numbers.

```
   1
  65¢
+ 25¢
  90¢
```

Place the cents sign *after* the sum.

Example 8

Find $0.39 + $0.45.

```
   1
  $0.39
+ $0.45
  $0.84
```

Place the dollar sign and the decimal point.

Add. Check for reasonableness.

24. 13¢ + 43¢

25. $54 + $35

26. 74¢ + 6¢

27. $90 + $19

28. Rondell's piggy bank has $23. For his birthday, his grandmother gave him $15. How much money does he have now?

29. Edgardo found 36¢ on the sidewalk. If he combines this with the 27¢ he has left from his lunch money, how much will he have altogether?

2-6 Problem-Solving Investigation: Choose a Strategy (pp. 84–85)

Example 9
A music group bought two new guitars. Each guitar cost $488. How much did the guitars cost?

Since each guitar cost the same, add $488 two times.

```
   11
  $488
+ $488
  $976
```

So, the guitars cost $976.

Solve.

30. While fishing, Augusto and his uncle caught 17 catfish, 21 trout, and 6 bass. About how many fish did they catch?

31. Carolyn walked 2 blocks south to meet Tiffany. They walked 3 blocks east and 1 block north to Fabio's house. Does Fabio live on Carolyn's street? Explain.

2-7 Three-Digit Addition (pp. 88–90)

Example 10
Joel read one book with 175 pages and another with 409 pages. How many pages did Joel read total?

Find 175 + 409. Add the ones.

```
   1
  175   5 ones + 9 ones = 14 ones
+ 409   14 ones = 1 ten + 4 ones
    4
```

Add the tens. Then hundreds.

```
   1
  175   1 ten + 7 tens = 8 tens
+ 409   1 hundred + 4 hundreds =
  584   5 hundreds
```

So, 175 + 409 = 584.

Add. Check for reasonableness.

32. 377 + 26 **33.** 657 + 245

34. $67 + 25 **35.** $3.25 + 2.56

36. Flavio and Felix each bought airline tickets for $213. Their rental car and hotel are $378. How much will they spend on these vacation expenses?

37. Last year Ithaca had a record snowfall of 124 inches. This year it snowed 117 inches. What was the total snowfall for the two years?

2-8 Add Greater Numbers (pp. 92–95)

Example 11
Find the total number of students surveyed.

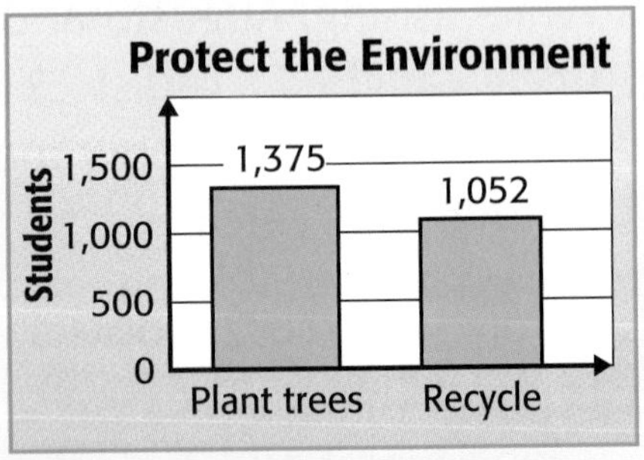


```
  1,375
+ 1,052
  2,427
```

Add. Check for reasonableness.

38. 1,003 + 7,927

39. 3,042 + 4,517

40. $8,385 + $1,476 **41.** $21.90 + $37.90

42. A chess set costs $24.95. The collector's edition, costs $12.95 more. How much will the collector's edition cost?

CHAPTER 2

Chapter Test

Identify each property shown.

1. $5 + 3 = 3 + 5$
2. $0 + 2 = 2$
3. $(1 + 2) + 3 = 1 + (2 + 3)$

Estimate each sum using rounding.

4. $54 + 29$

5. $18 + 23$

6. **STANDARDS PRACTICE** At a movie theater, 64 bags of popcorn were sold before the movie. During the movie, 29 bags of popcorn were sold. How many bags of popcorn were sold?

   A 90 **C** 103
   B 93 **D** 113

7. How many tickets were purchased the last two weeks?

Add. Use estimation to check for reasonableness.

8. $281 + 674$

9. $\$3.13 + \$7.31$

10. $403 + 879$

11. $5,545 + 3,545$

For Exercises 12 and 13, tell whether you need an estimate or an exact answer. Then solve.

12. Toshi wants to buy new school supplies. She has \$5. Does she have enough money? Explain.

School Supplies		
paper	crayons	pencils
\$1.75	\$0.70	\$1.25

13. There are 3 office buildings on a block. About how many offices are in the three buildings? Explain.

Number of Offices by Building		
A	B	C
2,114	3,112	2,295

14. **STANDARDS PRACTICE** Gen spent \$378 at the mall. Her sister spent \$291. About how much did the sisters spend together?

   F \$700 **H** \$600
   G \$670 **J** \$400

15. Abby's bird club counted 328 birds. Nita's bird club spotted 576 birds. Did the two bird clubs spot more than 915 birds? Explain.

16. **WRITING IN MATH** How do you know when you need to regroup when adding? Include an example.

CHAPTER 2

California Standards Practice

Cumulative, Chapters 1–2

Standards Example

Becky bought a tennis racket for $69.95 and tennis balls for $4.99. How much did she spend in all?

A $64.94

B $64.96

C $73.84

D $74.94

Read the Question

You need to find how much Becky spent in all.

Solve the Question

Add to find the amount.

$$\begin{array}{r} {}^{1\,1\,1} \\ \$69.95 \\ +\ \$\ \ 4.99 \\ \hline \$74.94 \end{array}$$

So, Becky spent $74.94 in all.
The correct choice is D.

Online Personal Tutor at ca.gr3math.com

Choose the best answer.

1 **Ryder bought a notebook for $4.59, a pen for $3.25, and a marker for $2.99. What is the total cost of these items?**

A $7.58

B $7.84

C $10.75

D $10.83

2 **What number makes this number sentence true?**

$$2 + 5 + 8 = 2 + 8 + ■$$

F 2

G 5

H 8

J 15

3 **What is the total number of people in the park on Friday?**

People in the Park	
Activity	**Number of People**
Biking	12
Walking	22
Running	45
Reading	18

A 86 **C** 93

B 87 **D** 97

---

4 **What is 64 + 128 rounded to the nearest ten?**

F 200 **H** 180

G 190 **J** 150

---

5 **The River School sold 3428 banners. The Gibson School sold 4636 banners. How many banners were sold in all?**

A 7252 **C** 7954

B 7952 **D** 8064

---

6 **Kurt and his brother have 783 marbles. Which of these equals 783?**

F 700 + 80 + 3 **H** 7 + 80 + 3

G 700 + 8 + 3 **J** 7 + 8 + 3

---

7 **Which point on the number line names 174?**

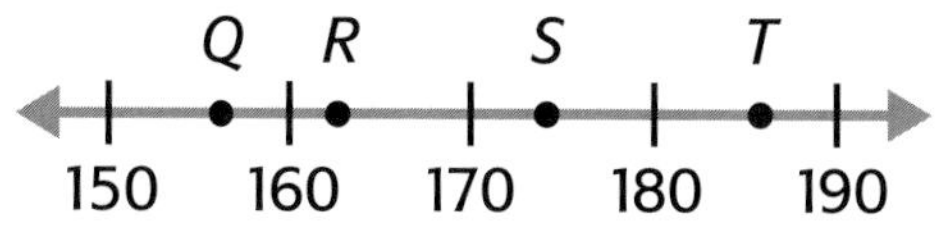

A *Q* **C** *S*

B *R* **D** *T*

---

8 **Tia received 94, 81, 90, and 89 points on the last four math tests. How many total points did Tia have?**

F 354 **H** 344

G 351 **J** 244

---

9 **How is two thousand, one hundred forty-six written in standard form?**

A 2416 **C** 1246

B 2146 **D** 214

---

10 **Mrs. Vallez bought 2 packages of 127 stickers each. She added these to the 219 stickers she already has. How many stickers does she have total?**

F 346 **H** 446

G 348 **J** 473

CHAPTER 3 Subtraction

BIG Idea What is subtraction?

Subtraction is an operation that tells the difference, when some or all are taken away.

Example Tanisha has red and green apples. There are 30 apples in all. If 17 of the apples are green, 30 – 17 or 13 apples are red.

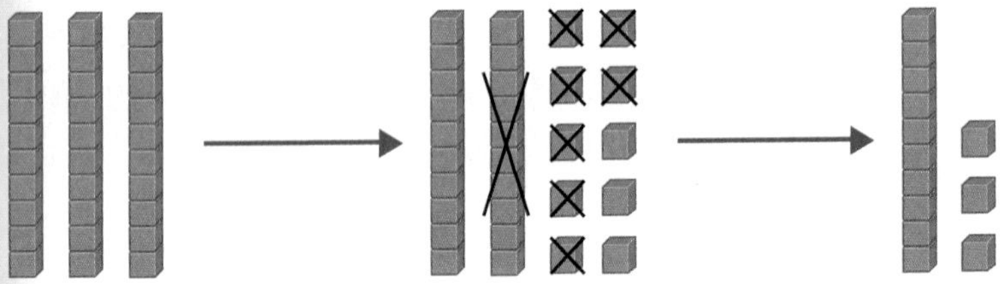

30 – 17 = 13

What will I learn in this chapter?

- Subtract multiples of 10, 100, and 1,000.
- Subtract two-, three-, and four-digit numbers.
- Estimate differences.
- Write expressions and number sentences.
- Decide whether an answer is reasonable.

Key Vocabulary

difference

expression

Math Online **Student Study Tools at** ca.gr3math.com

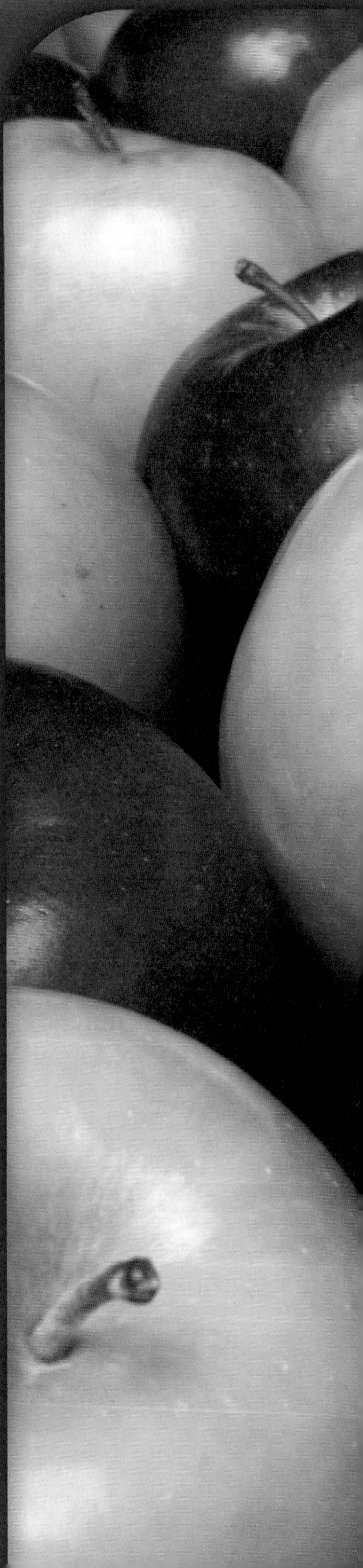

FOLDABLES™
Study Organizer

Make this Foldable to organize information about subtraction. Begin with four sheets of $8\frac{1}{2}'' \times 11''$ paper

1. **Stack** 4 sheets of paper as shown.

2. **Fold** upward so all layers are the same distance apart.

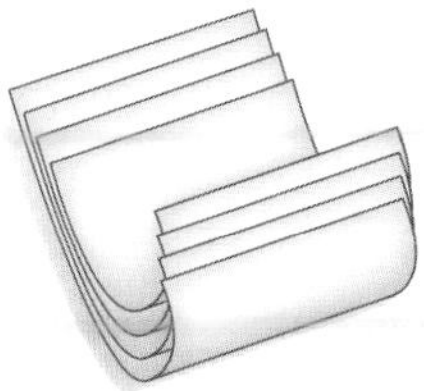

3. **Crease** well. Open and glue together as shown.

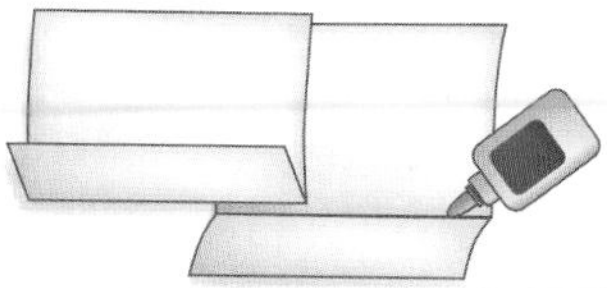

4. **Label** with the lesson titles. Record what you learn.

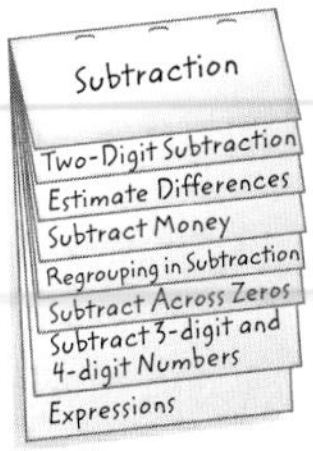

ARE YOU READY for Chapter 3?

You have two ways to check prerequisite skills for this chapter.

Option 2

Math Online Take the Chapter Readiness Quiz at ca.gr3math.com.

Option 1

Complete the Quick Check below.

QUICK Check

Subtract. **(Prior grade)**

1. $\begin{array}{r} 15 \\ -\ 9 \\ \hline \end{array}$ **2.** $\begin{array}{r} 12 \\ -\ 4 \\ \hline \end{array}$ **3.** $\begin{array}{r} 13 \\ -\ 6 \\ \hline \end{array}$ **4.** $\begin{array}{r} 17 \\ -\ 9 \\ \hline \end{array}$

5. $\begin{array}{r} 50 \\ -\ 20 \\ \hline \end{array}$ **6.** $\begin{array}{r} 70 \\ -\ 10 \\ \hline \end{array}$ **7.** $\begin{array}{r} 25 \\ -\ 15 \\ \hline \end{array}$ **8.** $\begin{array}{r} 61 \\ -\ 31 \\ \hline \end{array}$

9. Dalila had a package of 36 pens. She gave 14 to her friends. How many pens does she have left?

10. Abram took 27 magazine orders. He needs 50 orders in all. How many more does he need to get?

Round to the nearest ten. **(Prior grade)**

11. 76 **12.** 55 **13.** 32 **14.** 99

Round each number to the nearest hundred. **(Prior grade)**

15. 273 **16.** 923 **17.** 156 **18.** 501

Estimate. **(Prior grade)**

19. 52 − 42 **20.** 49 − 18 **21.** 67 − 25 **22.** 88 − 61

3-1 Two-Digit Subtraction

MAIN IDEA

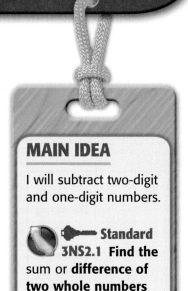

I will subtract two-digit and one-digit numbers.

Standard 3NS2.1 Find the sum or **difference of two whole numbers between 0 and 10,000.**

GET READY to Learn

The table shows that a tiger sleeps 16 hours a day. A cat sleeps 12 hours each day. How much longer does a tiger sleep than a cat?

Hours of Sleep Each Day

Animal	Time (hr)
python	18
tiger	16
cat	12
horse	3

You can use subtraction to solve the problem.

Real-World EXAMPLE **No Regrouping**

1 ANIMALS **How much longer does a tiger sleep than a cat?**

You need to find 16 − 12.

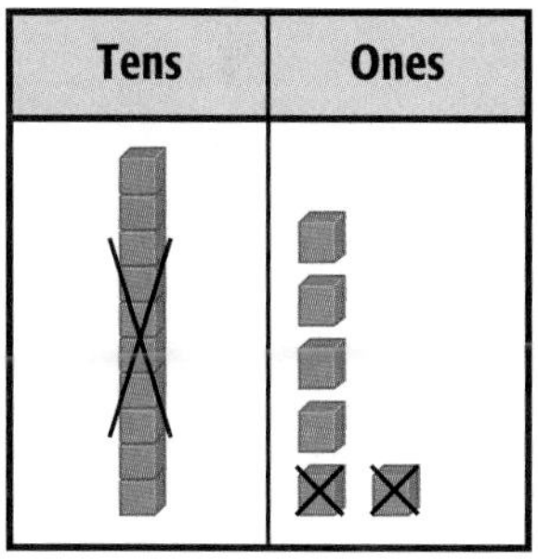

Step 1 Subtract ones

$$\begin{array}{r} 16 \\ -\ 12 \\ \hline 4 \end{array}$$ 6 ones − 2 ones = 4 ones

Step 2 Subtract tens

$$\begin{array}{r} 16 \\ -\ 12 \\ \hline 4 \end{array}$$ 1 ten − 1 ten = 0 ten

So, a tiger sleeps 4 hours more than a cat.

Check You can use addition to check your answer.

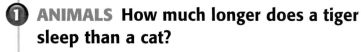

same

$$\begin{array}{r} 16 \\ -\ 12 \\ \hline 4 \end{array} \qquad \begin{array}{r} 4 \\ +\ 12 \\ \hline 16 \end{array}$$

So the answer is correct. ✓

Remember

1 ten = 10 ones

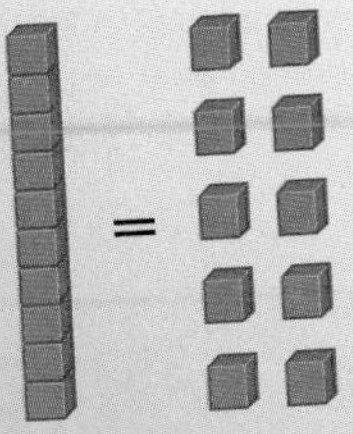

Sometimes when you subtract, there are not enough ones to subtract from. In this case, you need to regroup.

Real-World EXAMPLE Regrouping

2 CARS At one time, Preston had 54 toy cars. He lost 18. How many does he have now?

You need to find 54 − 18.

Step 1 Subtract ones.

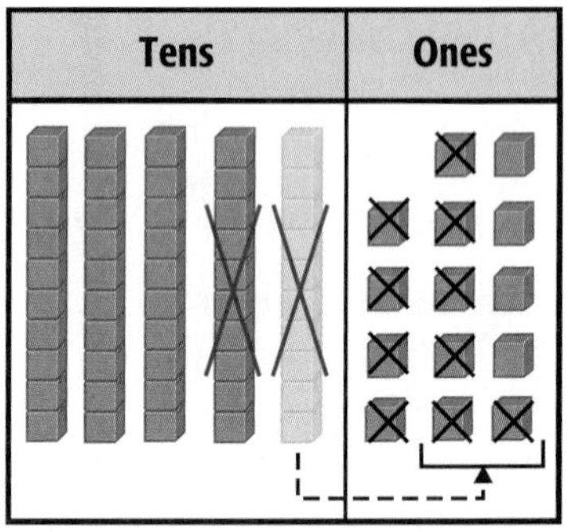

You cannot take 8 ones from 4 ones.

Regroup 1 ten as 10 ones.

4 ones + 10 ones = 14 ones

14 ones − 8 ones = 6 ones.

$$\begin{array}{r} {}^{4}\,{}^{14} \\ \not{5}\not{4} \\ -\ 18 \\ \hline 6 \end{array}$$

Step 2 Subtract tens.

$$\begin{array}{r} {}^{4}\,{}^{14} \\ \not{5}\not{4} \\ -\ 18 \\ \hline 36 \end{array}$$

4 tens − 1 ten = 3 tens.

Check You can use addition to check your answer.

$$\begin{array}{r} 54 \\ -\ 18 \\ \hline 36 \end{array} \qquad \begin{array}{r} 36 \\ +\ 18 \\ \hline 54 \end{array}$$

same

So the answer is correct. ✓

Online Personal Tutor at ca.gr3math.com

CHECK What You Know

Subtract. Check your answer. See Examples 1 and 2 (pp. 107–108)

1. $\begin{array}{r} 39 \\ -\ 4 \\ \hline \end{array}$

2. $\begin{array}{r} 79 \\ -\ 8 \\ \hline \end{array}$

3. $\begin{array}{r} 94 \\ -\ 5 \\ \hline \end{array}$

4. $\begin{array}{r} 63 \\ -\ 46 \\ \hline \end{array}$

5. Nell brought lemonade and juice to the picnic. Of the 26 drinks, 8 were lemonade. How many are juice?

6. Talk About It Why do you start subtracting with the ones?

Practice and Problem Solving

EXTRA PRACTICE
See page R7.

Subtract. Check your answer. See Examples 1 and 2 (pp. 107–108)

7. $\begin{array}{r} 28 \\ -\ 16 \\ \hline \end{array}$

8. $\begin{array}{r} 74 \\ -\ 13 \\ \hline \end{array}$

9. $\begin{array}{r} 45 \\ -\ 8 \\ \hline \end{array}$

10. $\begin{array}{r} 54 \\ -\ 5 \\ \hline \end{array}$

11. $\begin{array}{r} 99 \\ -\ 35 \\ \hline \end{array}$

12. $\begin{array}{r} 34 \\ -\ 21 \\ \hline \end{array}$

13. $\begin{array}{r} 32 \\ -\ 27 \\ \hline \end{array}$

14. $\begin{array}{r} 41 \\ -\ 15 \\ \hline \end{array}$

15. 70 − 48

16. 30 − 14

17. 96 − 68

18. 57 − 39

19. **Measurement** Howie is 43 inches tall. His brother is 51 inches tall. Find the difference in their heights.

20. There are 28 days left of summer vacation. If there were 90 days total, how many days have passed?

21. Elijah had 42 pieces of chalk. He gave 13 to Amado and 15 to Wapi. How many were left?

22. Ramona made 28 bracelets. Some are red and some are blue. If 17 are blue, how many are red?

Real-World PROBLEM SOLVING

Animals For Exercises 23–26, use the table shown.

23. How much faster does a lion run than the fastest human?

24. What is the difference between the fastest animal and the slowest?

25. Which animal is 38 miles per hour slower than the lion?

26. Name two animals whose speeds have a difference of 7 miles per hour.

FAST MOVERS

Animal	Speed (mph)
Cheetah	70
Lion	50
Greyhound	39
Dragonfly	36
Rabbit	35
Giraffe	32
Fastest human	28
Elephant	25
Squirrel	12

H.O.T. Problems

27. **NUMBER SENSE** Without subtracting, how do you know if 31 − 19 is greater than 20?

28. **WRITING IN MATH** Refer to the table in Exercises 23–26. Write a real-world subtraction problem about the animal data in which the answer is 34.

3-2 Estimate Differences

GET READY to Learn

Toya had a choice to buy a 64-ounce bag of cat food or a 48-ounce bag of cat food. About how much more food is in the larger bag of cat food?

MAIN IDEA

I will estimate differences using rounding.

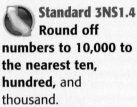

Standard 3NS1.4 Round off numbers to 10,000 to the nearest ten, hundred, and thousand.

Standard 3NS2.1 Find the sum or **difference of two whole numbers between 0 and 10,000.**

Remember

You can review rounding whole numbers in Lessons 1-8 and 1-9.

An exact answer is not needed. You can use rounding to make an estimate that is close to the exact answer.

Real-World EXAMPLE Estimate Differences

1 PET FOOD **About how much more food is in the larger bag of cat food?**

You need to estimate 64 − 48.

Step 1 Round each number to the nearest ten.

64 → 60
48 → 50

Round 64 to 60.
Round 48 to 50.

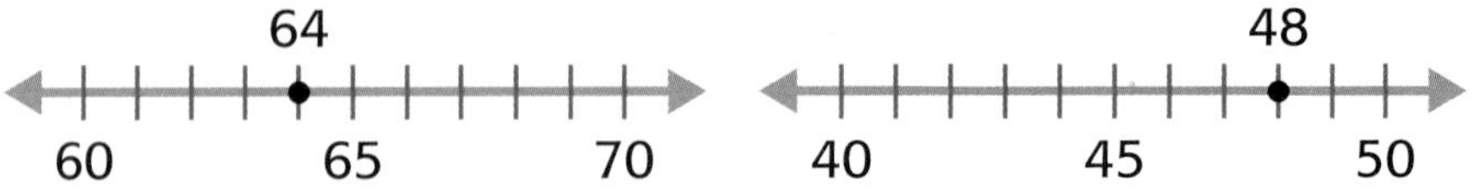

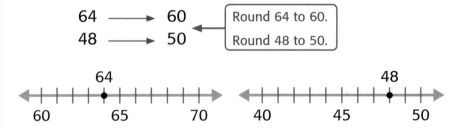

Step 2 Subtract.

$$\begin{array}{r} 64 \\ -\ 48 \\ \hline \end{array} \longrightarrow \begin{array}{r} 60 \\ -\ 50 \\ \hline 10 \end{array}$$

So, there are *about* 10 ounces more in the larger bag.

Online Personal Tutor at ca.gr3math.com

You can also round to the nearest hundred when estimating.

Remember

There can be several reasonable estimates when solving a problem.

Real-World EXAMPLE — Estimate Differences

2 **TRAVEL Yosemite National Park is 92 miles from Fresno, but Los Angeles is 219 miles from Fresno. About how many miles farther is Los Angeles from Fresno than Yosemite?**

You need to estimate 219 − 92.

Step 1 Round each number to the nearest hundred.

219 ⟶ 200
92 ⟶ 100

Round 219 to 200.
Round 92 to 100.

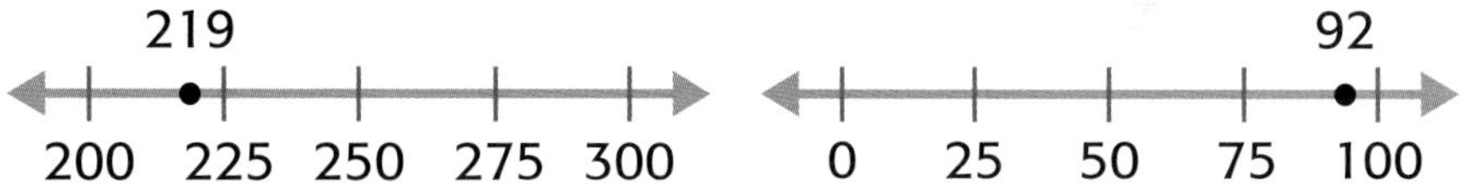

Step 2 Subtract.

$$\begin{array}{r} 219 \\ -92 \\ \hline \end{array} \longrightarrow \begin{array}{r} 200 \\ -100 \\ \hline 100 \end{array}$$

So, Los Angeles is *about* 100 miles farther from Fresno.

CHECK What You Know

Estimate. Round to the nearest ten. See Example 1 (p. 110)

1. 84 − 61

2. 91 − 37

3. 46 − 23

Estimate. Round to the nearest hundred. See Example 2 (p. 111)

4. 176 − 64

5. 341 − 183

6. 365 − 119

7. Pedita invited 112 friends to a party. Of those, 37 could not come. About how many people will come?

8. Talk About It Explain the steps you would take to round 789 to the nearest hundred.

Practice and Problem Solving

EXTRA PRACTICE See page R8.

Estimate. Round to the nearest ten. See Example 1 (p. 110)

9. 55 − 37

10. 91 − 73

11. 72 − 49

12. 88 − 32

13. 86 − 68

14. 57 − 41

Estimate. Round to the nearest hundred. See Example 2 (p. 111)

15. 901 − 260

16. 775 − 191

17. 381 − 265

18. 880 − 114

19. 322 − 199

20. 671 − 156

Real-World PROBLEM SOLVING

Data File The Pomo Indian culture of California is famous for beautiful baskets.

21. When rounded to the nearest ten, which basket is the same size as the cooking basket?

22. About how many centimeters wider is the cooking basket than the serving basket?

23. Estimate the difference in width of the storage basket and the water bottle.

Art

Baskets

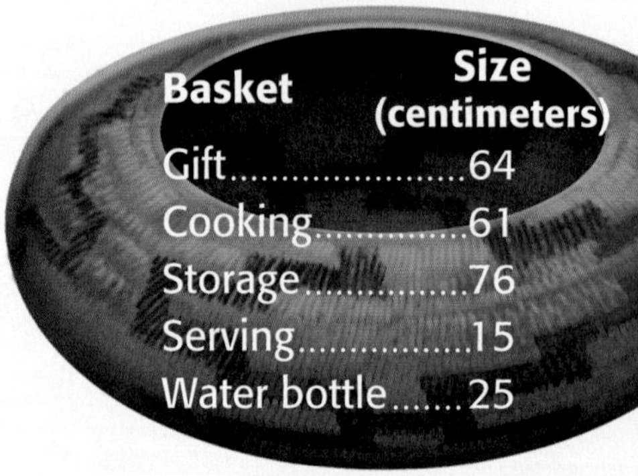

Basket	Size (centimeters)
Gift	64
Cooking	61
Storage	76
Serving	15
Water bottle	25

24. A gale has a wind speed up to 54 miles per hour. A breeze has a wind speed of 18 miles per hour. Estimate the difference between the two speeds.

25. The students are working to earn enough money to buy 78 books for the school library. So far, they have bought 49 books. Estimate how many more books they need to buy to reach their goal.

26. Bernard is on a trip that is 105 miles one way. Estimate the number of miles left in his trip if he has traveled 56 miles so far.

27. Margaret ordered 275 school T-shirts for the first day of school. Estimate the number of T-shirts left if she sold 183.

H.O.T. Problems

28. FIND THE ERROR Flor and Kenny estimated the difference of 78 and 45. Who is correct? Explain.

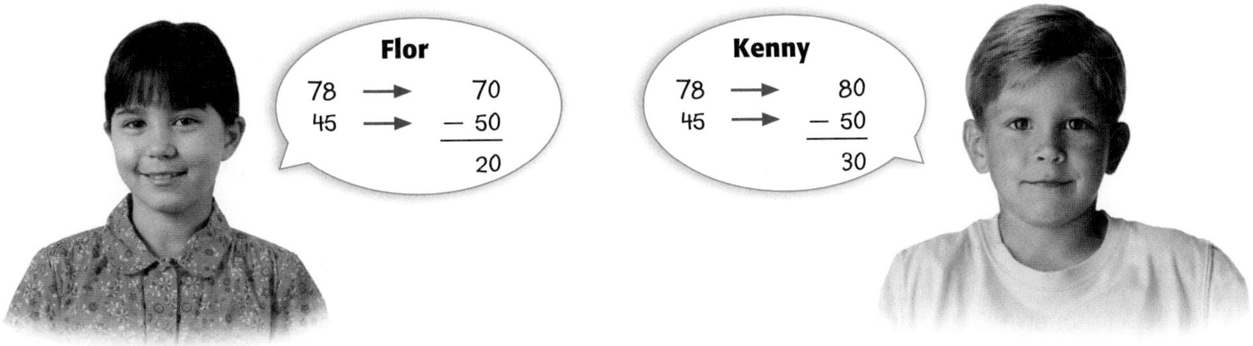

29. WRITING IN MATH Write a real-world problem about a situation when you would use estimation.

Standards Practice

30 The temperature this morning was 59 degrees. This afternoon it warmed up to 87 degrees. What is the difference in temperature? **(Lesson 3-1)**

A 28 **C** 38

B 32 **D** 146

31 There are 92 pumpkins and 38 cornstalks in a field. About how many more pumpkins are there than cornstalks? **(Lesson 3-2)**

F 40 **H** 50

G 44 **J** 60

Spiral Review

Subtract. Use addition to check. (Lesson 3-1)

32. 45 − 28 **33.** 51 − 16 **34.** 37 − 9

35. Leandro has $4. Does he have enough money to buy all of the items in the table? Explain. **(Lesson 2-5)**

Box of pencils	$1.00
Pad of paper	$1.25
Pack of gum	$1.00

36. About how much money would Kele need to buy the items in the shop window? **(Lesson 2-3)**

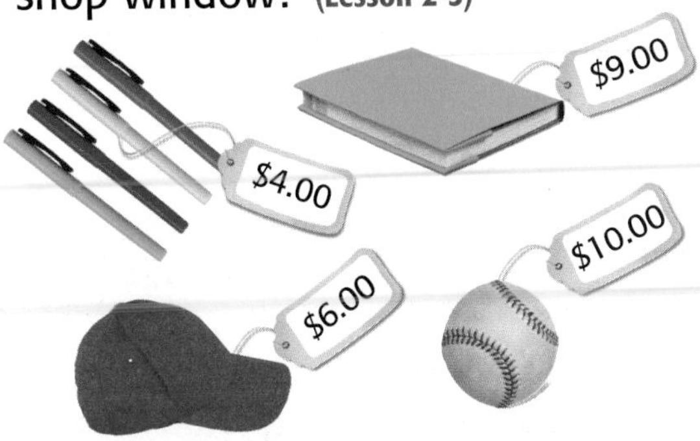

3-3 Subtract Money

MAIN IDEA

I will subtract money.

Standard 3NS2.1 Find the sum or difference of two whole numbers between 0 and 10,000.

Standard 3NS3.3 Solve problems involving addition, subtraction, multiplication, and division **of money amounts in decimal notation** and multiply and divide money amounts in decimal notation by using whole-number multipliers and divisors.

GET READY to Learn

Large posters sell for 94¢ and small posters sell for 42¢. What is the difference in price?

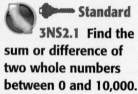

Subtracting money is just like subtracting whole numbers.

Real-World EXAMPLE — Subtract Cents

1 POSTERS What is the difference in the price of the large and small posters?

You need to find the difference between 94¢ and 42¢.

One Way: Subtract Cents		Another Way: Subtract Dollars	
94¢	Subtract the ones.	$0.94	Bring down the dollar sign and decimal point.
− 42¢	Subtract the tens.	− $0.42	
52¢	Place the cents sign *after* the difference.	$0.52	

So, the difference in price is 52¢.

Check Use addition to check your subtraction.

same

```
  94¢      52¢
 −42¢     +42¢
  52¢      94¢
```

So, the answer is correct. ✔

Online Personal Tutor at ca.gr3math.com

When you subtract money, you often need to regroup.

Real-World EXAMPLE Subtract Dollars

2 SKATING **Carson paid $59 for in-line skates. Luandra paid $75. How much more did Luandra pay for her skates?**

You need to find the difference between $75 and $59.

Estimate $75 − $59 ⟶ $80 − $60 = $20

615	Regroup 1 ten as 10 ones.
$~~75~~	Subtract the ones.
−$59	Subtract the tens.
$17	Place the dollar sign *before* the difference.

So, the difference is $16.

Check for Reasonableness

Since $16 is close to the estimate, the answer is reasonable. ✓

Check Use addition to check your subtraction.

$75	$16
−$59	+$59
$16	$75

same

So, the answer is correct. ✓

Remember

When you write money amounts and there are no cents, you can drop the zeros to the right of the decimal point.

Example:
$31.00 = $31

CHECK What You Know

Subtract. Check your answer. See Examples 1 and 2 (pp. 114–115)

1. 29¢ − 23¢

2. $77 − $45

3. $0.45 − $0.16

4. 75¢ − 6¢

5. $32 − $27

6. $0.56 − $0.48

7. The Westville Garden Club wants to make $65 on their flower sale. So far they have made $29. How much more money do they need?

8. Talk About It Explain how you know when you need to regroup a ten for 10 ones in a subtraction problem.

Practice and Problem Solving

EXTRA PRACTICE
See page R8.

Subtract. Check your answer. See Examples 1 and 2 (pp. 114–115)

9. $52 − $41

10. $78 − $37

11. $0.66 − $0.25

12. 67¢ − 9¢

13. 74¢ − 7¢

14. $0.52 − $0.13

15. 93¢ − 42¢

16. $0.63 − $0.42

17. $0.73 − $0.31

18. 81¢ − 56¢

19. $28 − $19

20. $0.32 − $0.16

21. Cooper wants to buy 2 rubber snakes. Each snake is 39¢ and he has 95¢ to spend. Does he have enough money to buy a rubber spider also, for 15¢? Explain.

22. Enzo and his grandfather each paid $17 to go deep sea fishing. How much change did they receive from $40?

For Exercises 23–26, use the picture at the right. See Example 2 (p. 115)

23. Angel has $20. How much change will she get when she buys the baseball cap?

24. How much more does the tennis racket cost than the baseball bat?

25. Isabel has $60. She buys the tennis racket. Bryce has $40. He buys the baseball bat. Who gets more change back? Explain.

26. Coach paid for three things with four $20 bills. He got $10 in change back. What were the three things he bought?

H.O.T. Problems

27. OPEN ENDED A subtraction problem has an answer of 23. What could be the subtraction problem?

28. WRITING IN ► MATH Write about a real-world situation when knowing how to make change will be helpful.

CHAPTER 3

Mid-Chapter Check

Lessons 3-1 through 3-3

Subtract. Check your answer. (Lesson 3-1)

1. $\begin{array}{r} 28 \\ -\ 3 \\ \hline \end{array}$

2. $\begin{array}{r} 37 \\ -\ 5 \\ \hline \end{array}$

3. 70 − 19

4. 99 − 69

5. Akira had 38 ribbons for the art project. He gave 14 to Katsu and 12 to Brendan. How many did he have left for himself? (Lesson 3-1)

6. Fritz has 23 baseball cards. He gave 6 of them to his best friend. How many baseball cards does Fritz have now? (Lesson 3-1)

7. **STANDARDS PRACTICE** (Lesson 3-1)

97 − 65 =

A 23

B 32

C 33

D 172

Estimate. Round to the nearest ten. (Lesson 3-2)

8. $\begin{array}{r} 83 \\ -62 \\ \hline \end{array}$

9. $\begin{array}{r} 38 \\ -18 \\ \hline \end{array}$

10. 63 − 28

11. 46 − 12

Estimate. Round to the nearest hundred. (Lesson 3-2)

12. $\begin{array}{r} 742 \\ -614 \\ \hline \end{array}$

13. $\begin{array}{r} 567 \\ -113 \\ \hline \end{array}$

14. 889 − 279

15. 335 − 142

16. Kaitlyn purchased a new blouse and skirt. The blouse was \$19 and the skirt was \$7. She paid with two \$20 bills. How much change did she receive? (Lesson 3-3)

Subtract. Check your answer. (Lesson 3-3)

17. $\begin{array}{r} 34¢ \\ -14¢ \\ \hline \end{array}$

18. $\begin{array}{r} \$69 \\ -\$35 \\ \hline \end{array}$

19. **STANDARDS PRACTICE** Vanesa compared the prices of two cartons of milk. The table shows the prices. (Lesson 3-3)

Brand	Cost
A	\$0.99
B	\$0.81

How much more does Brand A cost than Brand B?

F \$0.17

G \$0.18

H \$0.53

J \$0.70

Subtract. Check your answer. (Lesson 3-3)

20. \$64 − \$6

21. \$0.73 − \$0.52

22. **WRITING IN MATH** Explain how subtracting money is like subtracting whole numbers and how it is different.

Problem Solving in Music

The Sounds of the Symphony

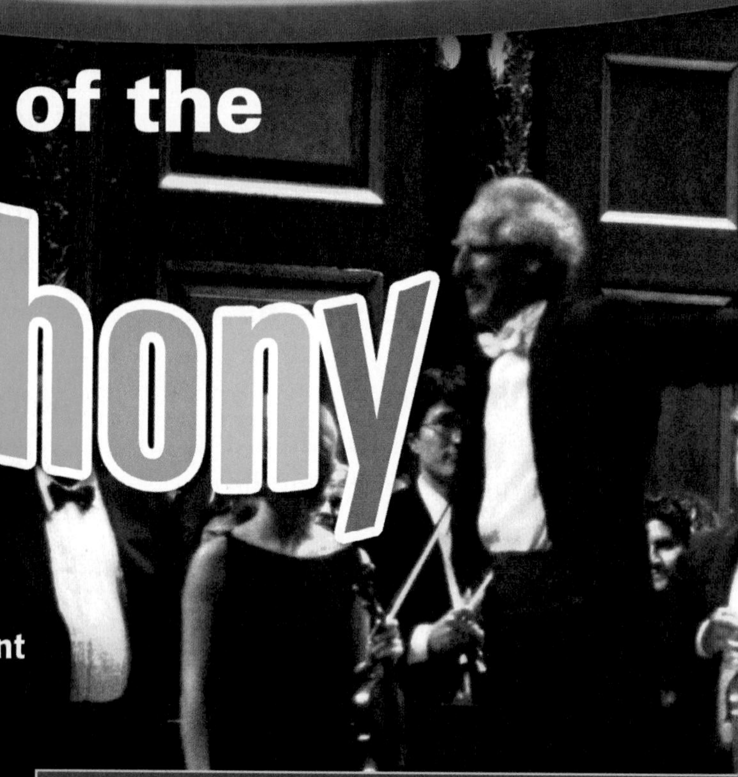

The Boston Philharmonic is a popular symphony orchestra. The orchestra has four instrument families— woodwinds, strings, brass, and percussion.

The musicians sometimes practice four times a week before a performance.

The Boston Philharmonic plays at Jordan Hall. Ticket prices are based on how close the seats are to the orchestra.

Boston Philharmonic

Instrument Family	Number of Musicians
Percussion	6
Brass	18
Woodwinds	21
Strings	70

Weekend Series

Seats	Ticket Price
A	$76
B	$58
C	$43
D	$29

Source: Boston Philharmonic

Standard 3NS2.1 **Find the sum or difference of two whole numbers between 0 and 10,000.**

Did You Know?
The oldest flute is over 43,000 years old.

Real-World Math

Use the information on page 118 to answer each question.

1. How many more woodwind musicians than percussion musicians are there?

2. Thirty-four of the string musicians play the violin. How many string musicians are not violinists?

3. The total number of musicians is 115. How many musicians do not play brass instuments?

4. On weeknights, the cost of a ticket in section D is $16. How much money do you save by going to the orchestra on Monday instead of Saturday?

5. Estimate the difference in the price of a ticket in section A and a ticket for a seat in section D.

6. If you paid for a ticket in section B with a $100 bill, how much change would you get?

7. How many musicians do not play brass or woodwind instruments?

8. Estimate the cost of each ticket to the nearest ten. Would it cost less to buy a ticket in section A and a ticket in section D or a ticket in section B and a ticket in section C?

3-4 Problem-Solving Skill

MAIN IDEA I will decide whether an answer to a problem is reasonable.

Standard 3MR3.1 Evaluate the reasonableness of the solution in the context of the original situation. Standard 3NS2.1 Find the sum or difference of two whole numbers between 0 and 10,000.

Kenji bought a box of 85 straws of 3 different colors.
He found that 53 straws were blue and green.
Kenji thinks that about 30 straws are pink.
Is this a reasonable answer?

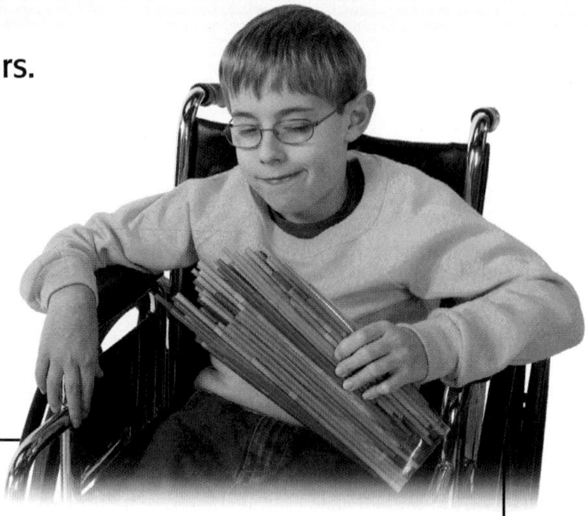

Understand	**What facts do you know?** • There are 85 straws. • There are 3 colors of straws. • There are 53 blue and green straws. **What do you need to find?** • Decide whether 30 is a reasonable amount of pink straws.
Plan	Use subtraction to find the number of pink straws. Then compare the answer to 30.
Solve	Subtract the number of blue and green straws from the total number of straws. $\begin{array}{r} 85 \\ -53 \\ \hline 32 \end{array}$ Since 32 is close to 30, it is reasonable to say that 30 of the straws are pink.
Check	Look back at the problem. Estimate by rounding. $\begin{array}{r} 85 \\ -53 \\ \hline \end{array} \begin{array}{c} \longrightarrow \\ \longrightarrow \\ \end{array} \begin{array}{r} 90 \\ -50 \\ \hline 40 \end{array}$ So, the answer makes sense for the problem.

PRACTICE the Skill

Refer to the problem on the previous page.

1. How do you know if the answer to a problem is reasonable?

2. Explain why you would ask yourself if an answer is reasonable.

3. If there are two colors of straws, and 57 are blue, about how many are green?

4. Explain why your answer to Exercise 3 is reasonable.

PRACTICE the Skill

EXTRA PRACTICE
See page R8.

Solve.

5. Is 400 a reasonable estimate for the difference in attendance on Monday and Wednesday? Explain.

County Fair Attendance	
Monday	395
Tuesday	247
Wednesday	834

6. Anson swam 28 laps last week and 24 this week. He says he needs to swim about two more weeks to swim a total of 100 laps. Is this a reasonable estimate? Explain.

7. Aubrey's class earned tokens for good behavior. The tally table shows their votes for a reward.

Reward	Tally
Extra recess	卌 |
Game time	|||
Pizza treat	卌 |||
Read aloud time	卌 卌 卌

Is it reasonable to say about half voted for a read aloud time?

8. Mrs. Kinney's class of 30 students will play a game. Each child needs 3 cubes. Alfeo says that 100 cubes will be enough for the class to play the game. Is that reasonable? Explain.

9. Mr. Gonzalez made a table of the books he has collected. He says he has more than 50 books. Is this a reasonable estimate? Explain.

Book Collection	
Mystery	13
Gardening	25
Biography	8
Fiction	15

10. Julina estimated that she needs to make 100 favors for the family reunion. Is this a reasonable estimate if 67 relatives will come on Friday and 42 will come on Saturday? Explain your reasoning.

11. **WRITING IN MATH** Explain a situation when you would determine a reasonable answer to solve the problem.

Explore

Math Activity 3-5
Subtract Three-Digit Numbers with Regrouping

MAIN IDEA

I will use models to explore regrouping in subtraction.

Standard 3NS2.1 **Find the** sum or **difference of two whole numbers between 0 and 10,000.**

Standard 3MR2.3 **Use a variety of methods, such as words, numbers, symbols,** charts, graphs, tables, **diagrams, and models, to explain mathematical reasoning.**

You Will Need:
base-ten blocks

Concepts in Motion
Animation
ca.gr3math.com

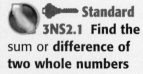

You can use models to regroup tens and hundreds.

ACTIVITY **Find 244 − 137.**

Step 1 **Model 244.**

```
  244
- 137
```

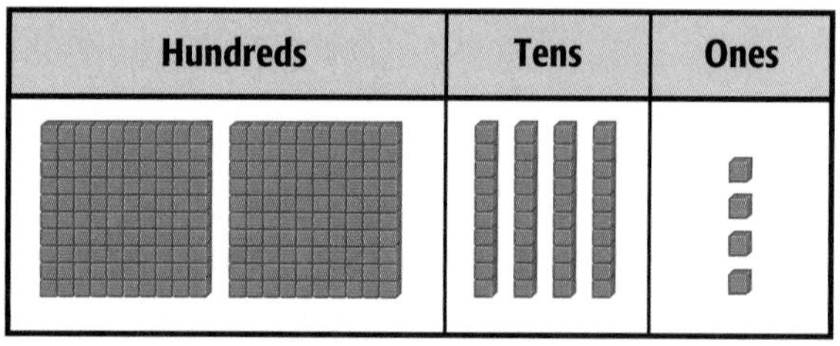

Step 2 **Subtract ones.**

```
   3 14
  2 4 4
- 1 3 7
      7
```

You cannot take 7 ones from 4 ones.
Regroup 1 ten as 10 ones.
4 ones + 10 ones = 14 ones
Subtract 14 ones − 7 ones = 7 ones

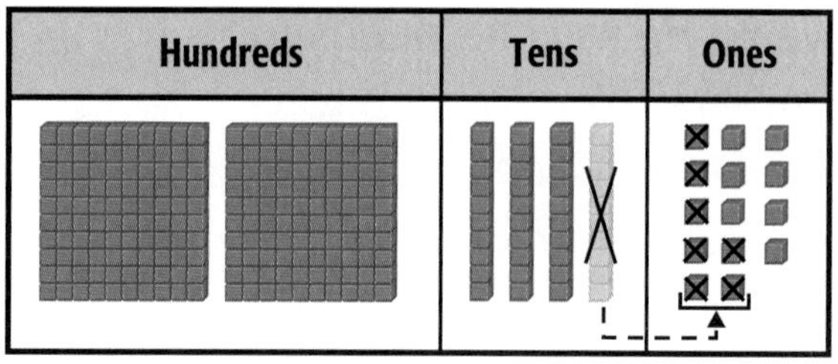

Step 3 **Subtract tens.**

```
   3 14
  2 4 4
- 1 3 7
    0 7
```

3 tens − 3 tens = 0 tens

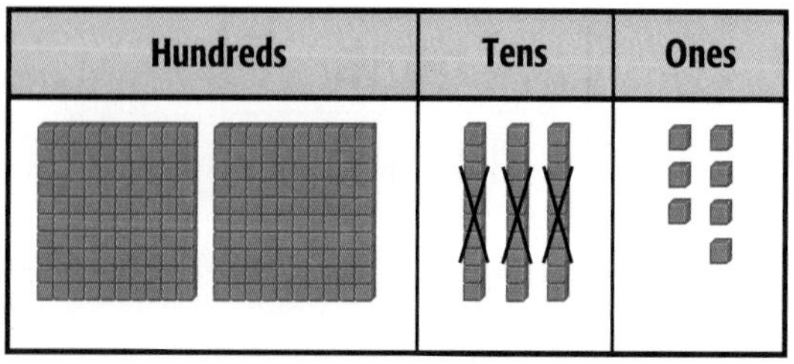

Hands-On Activity

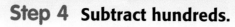

Step 4 **Subtract hundreds.**

```
  3 14
  2 4 4    2 hundreds − 1 hundred = 1 hundred
− 1 3 7
  1 0 7
```

Hundreds	Tens	Ones
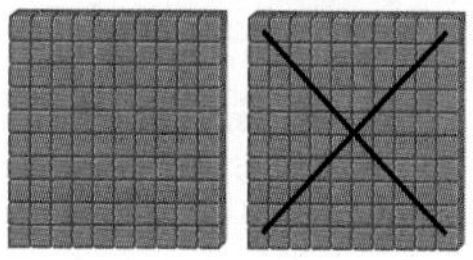		

So, 244 − 137 = 107.

Think About It

1. In Step 2, why did you regroup 1 ten as 10 ones?

2. What did you notice about the tens in Step 3 when you subtracted them?

3. Why do you sometimes have to regroup more than once?

CHECK What You Know

Subtract. Use models.

4. 181 − 93

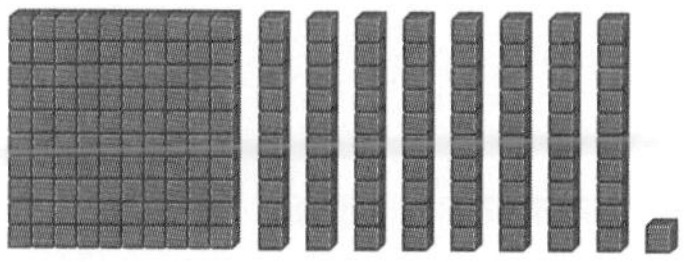

5. 322 − 148

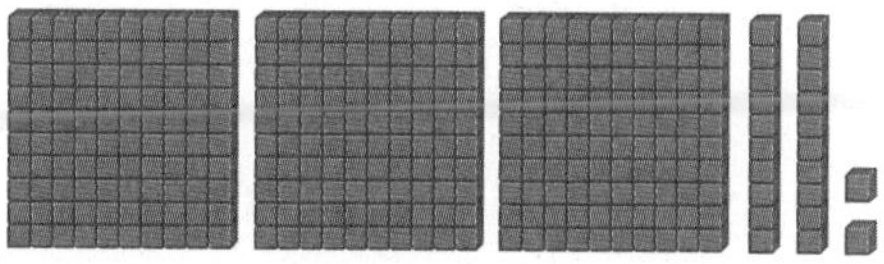

6. 342 − 179

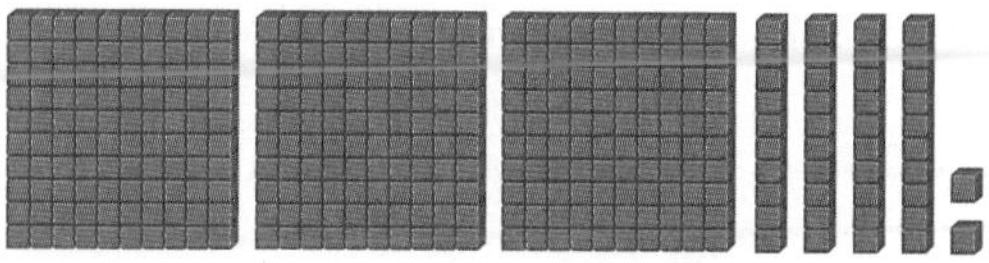

7. 212 − 123

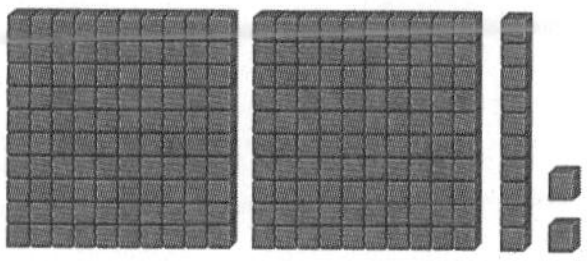

8. $\begin{array}{r} 328 \\ -\ 19 \\ \hline \end{array}$

9. $\begin{array}{r} 308 \\ -125 \\ \hline \end{array}$

10. $\begin{array}{r} 437 \\ -\ 243 \\ \hline \end{array}$

11. $\begin{array}{r} 513 \\ -\ 155 \\ \hline \end{array}$

12. WRITING IN MATH Explain when to regroup in subtraction.

3-5 Three-Digit Subtraction with Regrouping

MAIN IDEA

I will subtract three-digit numbers with regrouping.

Standard 3NS2.1 Find the sum or **difference of two whole numbers between 0 and 10,000.**

Standard 3MR3.1 Evaluate the reasonableness of the solution in the context of the original situation.

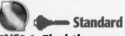

GET READY to Learn

Liseta, Will, and Alano have an assortment of construction paper. How many more sheets of paper does Will have than Liseta?

Construction Paper	
Name	**Sheets**
Liseta	79
Will	265
Alano	128

In the Explore Activity, you learned to regroup tens. Regrouping hundreds works the same way.

Real-World EXAMPLE

1 How many more sheets does Will have than Liseta?

You need to find 265 − 79.

Step 1 Subtract ones.

```
  515
  265
 − 79
    6
```

You cannot take 9 ones from 5 ones.
Regroup 1 ten as 10 ones.
5 ones + 10 ones = 15 ones.
Subtract 15 ones − 9 ones = 6 ones.

Step 2 Subtract tens.

```
  15
 1515
  265
 − 79
   86
```

You cannot take 7 tens from 5 tens.
Regroup 1 hundred as 10 tens.
5 tens + 10 tens = 15 tens.
Subtract 15 tens − 7 tens = 8 tens.

Step 3 Subtract hundreds.

```
  15
 1515
  265
 − 79
  186
```

Subtract 1 hundred − 0 hundred = 1 hundred.

So, 265 − 79 = 186.

Real-World EXAMPLE

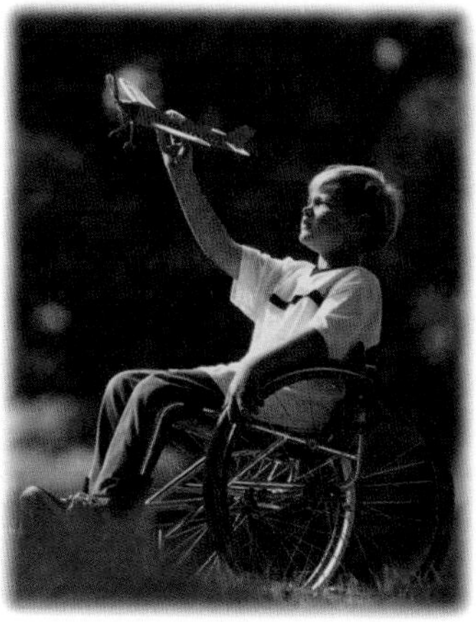

2 AIRPLANE Denzel wants to buy a new airplane model for \$5.30. He has \$7.25. How much money will he have left?

You need to find \$7.25 − \$5.30.

Step 1 Subtract cents.

```
   6 12
  $7̸.2̸5
− $5.30
    .95
```

5 pennies − 0 pennies = 5 pennies
You cannot take 3 dimes from 2 dimes.
Regroup 1 dollar as 10 dimes.
2 dimes + 10 dimes = 12 dimes
Subtract 12 dimes − 3 dimes = 9 dimes.

Step 2 Subtract dollars.

```
   6 12
  $7̸.2̸5
− $5.30
  $1.95
```

6 dollars − 5 dollars = 1 dollar
Place the dollar sign before the difference.

So, Denzel will have \$1.95 left.

Check You can check the answer by adding.

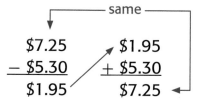

```
  $7.25          $1.95
− $5.30        + $5.30
  $1.95          $7.25
```

(same)

So, the answer is correct. ✓

Online Personal Tutor at ca.gr3math.com

CHECK What You Know

Subtract. Check your answer. See Examples 1 and 2 (pp. 124–125)

1. \$7.64 − \$1.32

2. 458 − 121

3. \$6.14 − \$4.57

4. 391 − 178

5. 542 − 167

6. 317 − 198

7. This year, the third grade raised \$342 for a dog shelter. Last year, they raised \$279. How much more money did they raise this year than last year?

8. Talk About It What happens to the tens when you have to regroup twice?

Practice and Problem Solving

EXTRA PRACTICE See page R9.

Subtract. Check your answer. See Examples 1 and 2 (pp. 124–125)

9. $6.87 − $3.53

10. $1.97 − $0.94

11. 293 − 172

12. 884 − 63

13. $8.43 − $1.87

14. $7.28 − $3.59

15. 267 − 178

16. 728 − 259

17. $1.92 − $0.83

18. $3.58 − $2.77

19. 856 − 637

20. 531 − 499

21. Greta and Mulan are eating at the Good Eats Diner. Greta buys veggies and water. Mulan buys a piece of pizza and a salad. About how much more does Mulan spend than Greta?

22. The Gateway Arch in St. Louis is 630 feet tall. The Space Needle in Seattle is 605 feet tall. How much taller is the Gateway Arch?

Good Eats Diner

Item	Cost
Pizza	$1.99
Salad	$1.95
Apple	$0.78
Veggies	$1.15
Water	$1.75
Smoothie	$2.90

Real-World PROBLEM SOLVING

Data File San Francisco's famous cable cars were invented in 1873 because horses could not pull carts up the steep hills.

23. A family of five is buying a one day pass for each person in the family. How much change will they get from three $20 bills?

24. How much money would an adult save if he or she bought a Fast Pass instead of a one day pass for one week?

Transportation

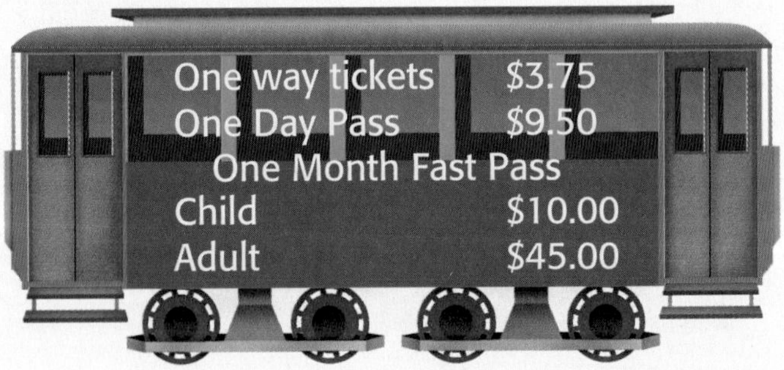

Source: sfcablecar.com

Algebra Find each missing digit.

25. 61□ − 417 = □02

26. □99 − 1□9 = 750

27. 798 − □97 = 4□1

28. 989 − 77□ = □18

H.O.T. Problems

29. **NUMBER SENSE** When Federico subtracted 308 from 785, he got 477. To check his answer he added 308 and 785. What did he do wrong?

30. **FIND THE ERROR** Odell and Liz are finding $5.66 – $3.47. Who is correct? Explain.

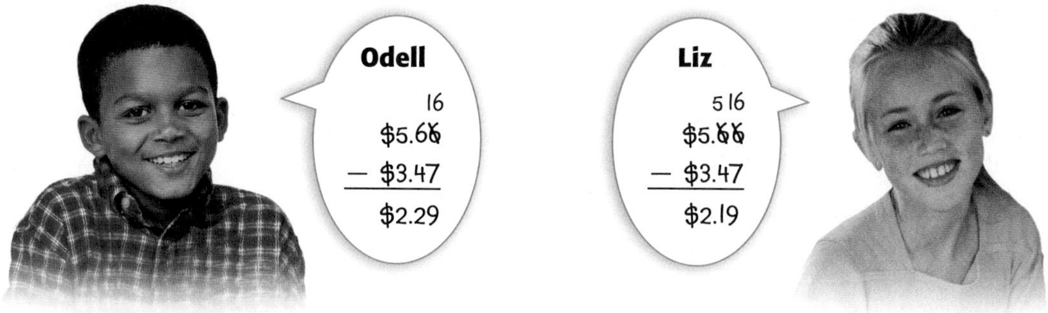

31. **WRITING IN ▶MATH** Explain what it means to check an answer for reasonableness.

Standards Practice

32 Irene wrote this pattern. **(Lesson 3-4)**

24, 26, 28, 30, __

What would be a reasonable answer for the next number?

A 28 **C** 35

B 32 **D** 40

33 Ty will hike 281 yards to get to the end of the trail. His friend is 187 yards from the end. What is the difference in the distance the boys have to walk yet? **(Lesson 3-5)**

F 94 yards **H** 106 yards

G 104 yards **J** 194 yards

Spiral Review

34. Baxter made $7.90 this week helping his dad around the house. Last week he made $8.25. Is it reasonable to say that he made at least $15 the last two weeks? Explain. **(Lesson 3-4)**

35. About how much more does the bike cost than the skates? **(Lesson 3-3)**

Write the value of the underlined digit. (Lesson 1-3)

36. 64,284 **37.** 20,002

3-6 Problem-Solving Investigation

MAIN IDEA I will choose the best strategy to solve a problem.

Standard 3MR1.1 Analyze problems by identifying relationships, distinguishing relevant from irrelevant information, sequencing and prioritizing information, and observing patterns. Standard 3NS2.1 Find the sum or difference of two whole numbers between 0 and 10,000.

P.S.I. TEAM +

MIRANDA: For a class project, my teacher needs 155 paper towel rolls. So far, Marissa collected 24, Stan collected 32, and I collected 18.

YOUR MISSION: Find out how many more cardboard rolls are needed.

Understand	You know that 155 cardboard rolls are needed. You also know that three students have already collected 24, 32, and 18 cardboard rolls. Find how many more rolls are needed.
Plan	First, add to find the number of rolls collected. Then, subtract to find the amount still needed.
Solve	$\begin{array}{r} \scriptstyle 1 \\ 24 \\ 32 \\ +\ 18 \\ \hline 74 \end{array}$ So, 74 rolls have been collected. Subtract 74 from 155 to find how many rolls are still needed. $\begin{array}{r} \scriptstyle 0\,15 \\ \cancel{1}\cancel{5}5 \\ -\ 74 \\ \hline 81 \end{array}$ So, 81 cardboard rolls are needed.
Check	Look back at the problem. You can check by adding. Since $81 + 74 = 155$, the answer is correct.

Mixed Problem Solving

EXTRA PRACTICE
See page R9.

Solve. Tell what strategy you used.

1. If 6 cans of tennis balls come in a box, how much will the box of tennis balls cost? Show your work.

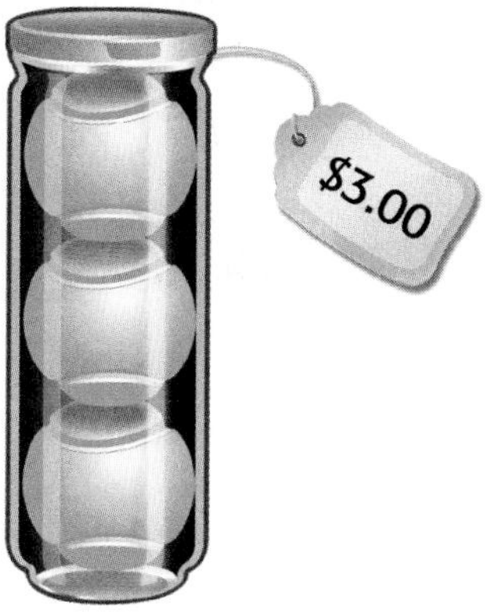

2. There are 113 people riding a train. At the first stop, 32 get off. After the second stop, there are 14 people left. How many people got off at the second stop?

3. Mr. White bought 7 daisy plants for $28. He paid with two $20 bills. How much change did he get back?

4. Mrs. Carpenter received a bill for $134 for car repairs. Is this amount an estimated amount or an exact amount? Explain your reasoning.

5. Keisha flew 1 hour and 37 minutes from San Francisco to Sacramento and then flew 3 hours and 14 minutes to Portland. About how many minutes were spent flying?

6. The library received 155 new books today. If there are now 784 books, how many were there before the new books arrived?

7. Some children took part in a penny hunt. Use the table below to tell about how many more pennies Pat found than each of his two friends.

Penny Hunt	
Cynthia	133
Pat	182
Garcia	125

8. Hale must decide what 3 different things he will buy for lunch. He wants to spend as much of his $3.00 as possible. What did he buy?

9. **WRITING IN ▶MATH** Look back at Exercise 8. Give an example of an answer that is not reasonable.

3-7 Subtract Greater Numbers

GET READY to Learn

The table shows the height of four different waterfalls. What is the difference in height between Ribbon Falls and Kalambo Falls?

Waterfalls

Name	Height (ft)
Ribbon	1,612
Angel	3,212
Yosemite	2,425
Kalambo	726

Source: factmonster.com

MAIN IDEA

I will learn to subtract three and four-digit numbers.

Standard 3NS2.1 Find the sum or **difference of two whole numbers between 0 and 10,000. Standard 3MR2.6 Make precise calculations and check the validity of the results from the context of the problem.**

In this lesson, you will subtract greater numbers.

Real-World EXAMPLE

1 MEASUREMENT **What is the height difference between Ribbon Falls and Kalambo Falls? Find 1,612 − 726.**

Step 1 Subtract ones.

```
   012
 1,612
 − 726
     6
```

You cannot take 6 ones from 2 ones.
Regroup 1 ten as 10 ones.
2 ones + 10 ones = 12 ones.
12 ones − 6 ones = 6 ones.

Step 2 Subtract tens.

```
   10
   5012
 1,612
 − 726
    86
```

You cannot take 2 tens from 0 tens.
Regroup 1 hundred as 10 tens.
0 tens + 10 tens = 10 tens.
10 tens − 2 tens = 8 tens.

Step 3 Subtract hundreds and thousands.

```
  1510
  05012
 1,612
 − 726
   886
```

You cannot take 7 hundreds from 5 hundreds.
Regroup 1 thousand as 10 hundreds.
5 hundreds + 10 hundreds = 15 hundreds.
15 hundreds − 7 hundreds = 8 hundreds.
0 thousands − 0 thousands = 0 thousands.

So, the difference in height is 886 feet.

Real-World EXAMPLE

2 BIKING The bar graph shows the length of two popular bike routes. How much longer is the bike route to San Diego?

You need to find 3,159 − 1,579.

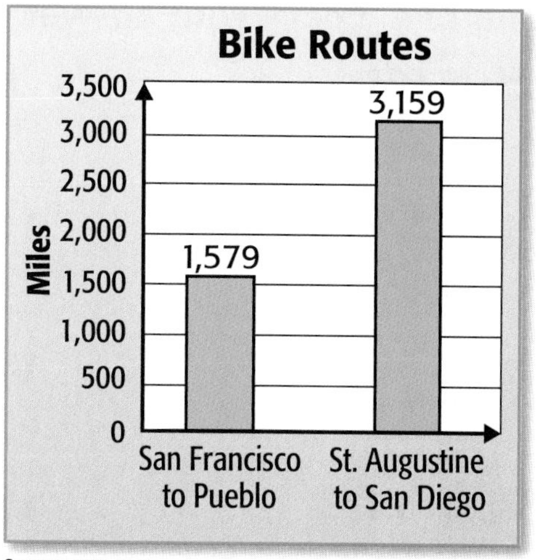

Source: *USA Today*

> **Remember**
> When subtracting whole numbers, line up the digits in the ones place.

Step 1 Subtract ones.

```
  3,159
− 1,579
      0
```

Step 2 Subtract tens.

```
   015
  3,159
− 1,579
     80
```

Step 3 Subtract hundreds and thousands.

```
   10
  2 015
  3,159
− 1,579
  1,580
```

Check Check your answer.

```
  3,159         1,580
− 1,579       + 1,579
  1,580         3,159
```

same

So, the answer is correct. ✓

So, 3,159 − 1,579 = 1,580.

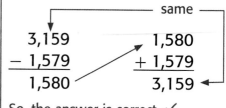

Online Personal Tutor at ca.gr3math.com

CHECK What You Know

Subtract. Check your answer. See Examples 1 and 2 (pp. 130–131)

1. $7,371 − $365

2. $3,457 − $649

3. 2,421 − 865

4. 7,234 − 6,487

5. Cell phones were invented in 1983. The TV was invented 56 years before that. What year was the TV invented?

6. Talk About It Explain the steps to find 8,422 − 5,995.

Practice and Problem Solving

EXTRA PRACTICE

See page R9.

Subtract. Check your answer. See Examples 1 and 2 (pp. 130–131)

7. 1,392 − 238

8. 3,298 − 858

9. 3,475 − 1,267

10. 3,665 − 1,643

11. \$3,421 − \$1,049

12. \$5,452 − \$1,187

13. \$4,875 − \$3,168

14. \$6,182 − \$581

15. 6,340 − 3,451

16. 5,123 − 2,736

17. \$1,856 − \$969

18. \$4,137 − \$1,562

19. Of the 2,159 pre-sold county fair tickets, only 1,947 tickets were collected at the gate. How many tickets were not collected?

20. The distance around a rectangular swimming pool is 300 yards. What are the measurements of the remaining sides?

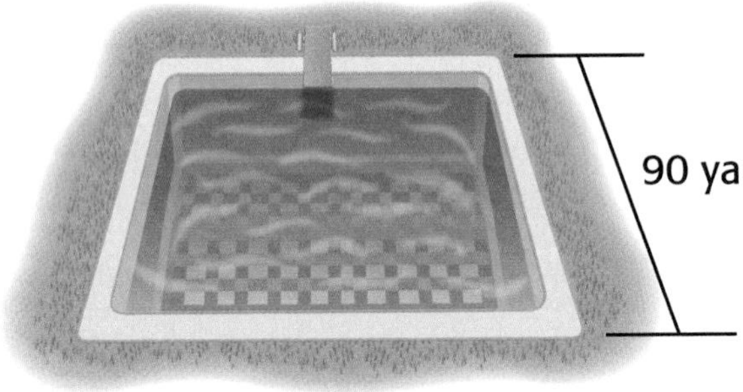

21. To earn money for a trip, band members had to sell 1,590 boxes of popcorn. So far they have sold 779 boxes. How many more boxes do they have to sell?

Algebra Compare. Write >, <, or =.

22. 1,543 − 984 ● 5,193 − 4,893

23. 2,006 − 781 ● 5,224 − 3,999

24. 8,937 − 3,038 ● 3,598 − 1,084

25. 5,070 − 2,345 ● 8,765 − 1,965

H.O.T. Problems

26. OPEN ENDED Write a real-world subtraction problem whose difference is 1,379.

27. CHALLENGE Write a subtraction problem in which the answer is 1,735.

28. WRITING IN MATH Explain how subtracting four-digit numbers is like subtracting three-digit numbers.

Game Time

Do Not Zero Out

Find Differences

Get Ready!

Players: 2 players

You will need:
one 0–5 number cube,
one blank number cube

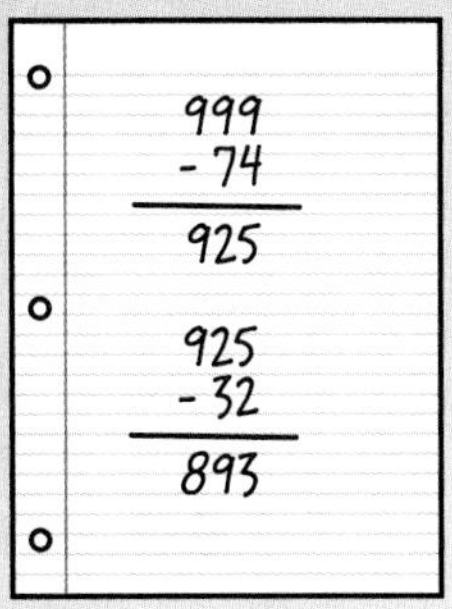

Get Set!

- Label the number cube 4–9.
- Each player writes 999 at the top of his or her paper.

Go!

- Player 1 rolls the number cubes and writes the two-digit number under 999. Subtract.
- Player 2 rolls the number cubes, makes a two-digit number, writes the number under 999 on his or her paper, and subtracts.
- Players continue, subtracting from the lowest number.
- When a player thinks the difference is as low as possible, he or she may stop. The other player may continue taking turns.
- If a player rolls a number that takes the difference below zero, the game is over. The other player wins. Otherwise, the player with the smallest difference wins.

3-8 Subtract Across Zeros

MAIN IDEA

I will learn how to subtract across zeros.

Standard 3NS2.1 Find the sum or **difference of two whole numbers between 0 and 10,000. Standard 3MR2.6 Make precise calculations and check the validity of the results from the context of the problem.**

GET READY to Learn

A large box of watermelons weighs 300 pounds. A smaller box weighs 134 pounds. What is the difference in the weights?

Sometimes before you can begin subtracting you have to regroup more than one time.

Real-World EXAMPLE — Subtract Across Zeros

1 What is the difference in the weight of the two boxes?

You need to find 300 − 134.

Step 1 Regroup.

$$\begin{array}{r} \scriptstyle 2\,10 \\ \not{3}\not{0}0 \\ -134 \\ \hline \end{array}$$

You cannot take 4 ones from 0 ones.
Regroup.
There are no tens to regroup.
Regroup 3 hundreds as 2 hundreds and 10 tens.

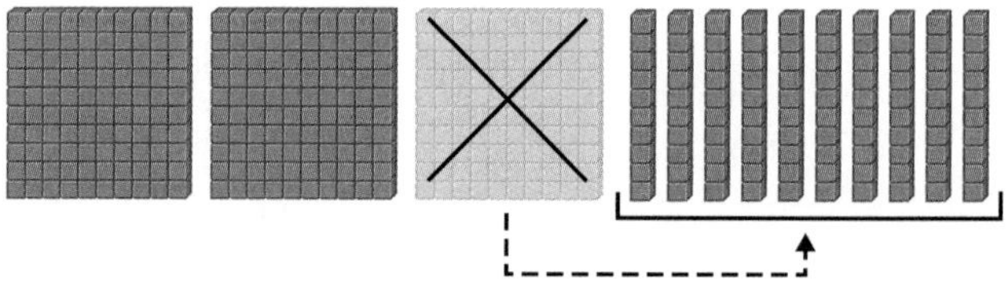

Step 2 Regroup.

$$\begin{array}{r} \scriptstyle 9 \\ \scriptstyle 2\,\not{10}\,10 \\ \not{3}\not{0}\not{0} \\ -134 \\ \hline \end{array}$$

Regroup 10 tens as 9 tens and 10 ones.

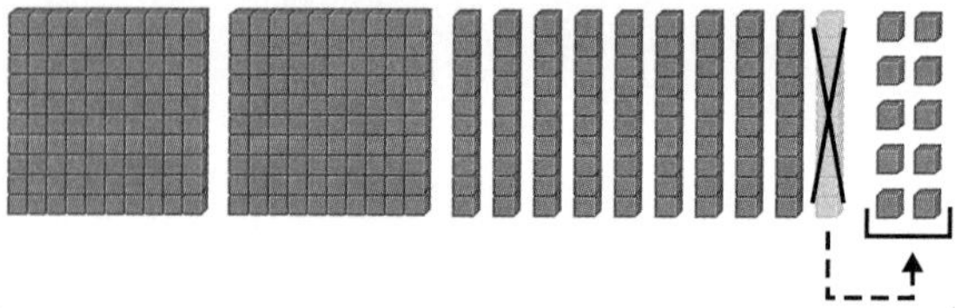

Step 3 Subtract.

$$\begin{array}{r} \scriptstyle 9 \\ \scriptstyle 2\,\not{10}\,10 \\ \not{3}\not{0}\not{0} \\ -\ 134 \\ \hline 166 \end{array}$$

Subtract the ones, tens, and hundreds.

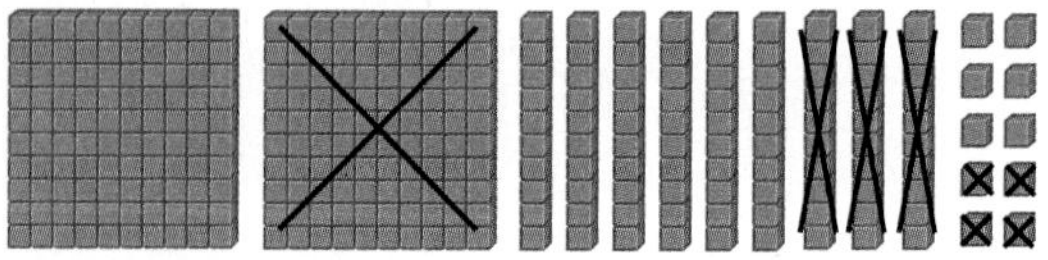

Real-World EXAMPLE — Subtract Across Zeros

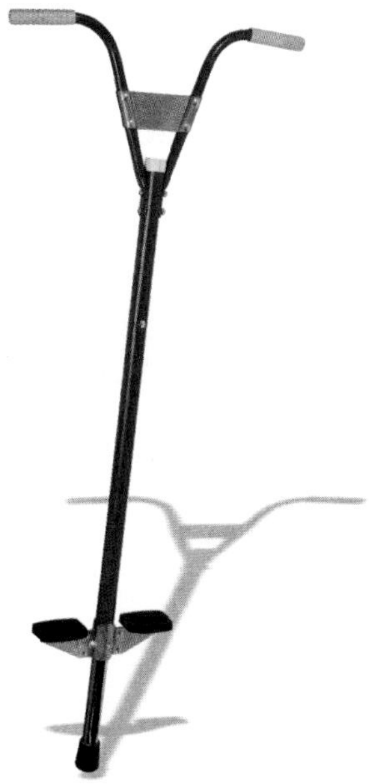

2 **TOYS Brandy made 2,000 hops on her pogo stick last week. Roque hopped 253 times. How many more hops did Brandy make?**

You need to find 2,000 − 253.

Step 1 Regroup.

```
 1 10
 2,000
− 253
```

You cannot take 3 ones from 0 ones. Regroup. There are no tens or hundreds.

Regroup 1 thousand as 10 hundreds.

Think: 2 thousands = 1 thousand + 10 hundreds

Step 2 Regroup.

```
   9
 1 10 10
 2,000
− 253
```

Regroup again.

Regroup 1 hundreds as 10 tens.

Think: 2 thousands = 1 thousand + 9 hundreds + 10 tens.

Step 3 Regroup and subtract.

```
    9  9
 1 10 10 10
 2,000
− 253
 1,747
```

Regroup 1 ten as 10 ones.

Subtract.

10 ones − 3 ones = 7 ones, 9 tens − 5 tens = 4 tens,

9 hundreds − 2 hundreds = 7 hundreds

1 thousand − 0 thousands = 1 thousand

So, Brandy hopped 1,747 times more than Roque.

Check Add up to check.

```
        same
 2,000      1,747
− 253      + 253
 1,747      2,000
```

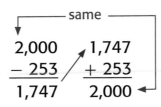

So, the answer is correct. ✓

Online Personal Tutor at ca.gr3math.com

CHECK What You Know

Subtract. Check your answer. See Examples 1 and 2 (pp. 134–135)

1. 208 − 68

2. 802 − 77

3. \$5.00 − \$3.17

4. \$33.00 − \$2.26

5. There are 200 pennies in a jar. If 27 are removed, how many are left?

6. Talk About It Explain the steps to find 503 − 366.

Practice and Problem Solving

EXTRA PRACTICE See page R10.

Estimate. Then subtract. Check for reasonableness. See Examples 1 and 2 (pp. 134–135)

7. 401 − 37

8. 902 − 84

9. 300 − 217

10. 400 − 256

11. \$500 − \$388

12. \$800 − \$685

13. \$74.00 − \$12.11

14. \$40.03 − \$2.27

15. 2,001 − 132

16. 5,006 − 1,257

17. 9,000 − 6,652

18. 6,000 − 168

19. Darnell paid for his TV set with four \$50 bills. How much did his TV set cost if he received \$42 in change?

20. A farmer picked 2,008 oranges. Of these, 32 were thrown away and 1,469 were sold. How many oranges are left?

21. Hanako would like to earn 200 points for turning her homework in on time this year. How many points does she need yet if she has 137 so far?

22. **Measurement** A playground measures 400 feet around its outside. Three sides together measure 293 feet. How many feet is the last side of the playground?

Use the bar graph for Exercises 23–25.

23. How many more 3rd graders than 4th graders are buying their lunch?

24. What is the total number of students buying their lunch?

25. The lunchroom holds 150 students at one time. Name two classes that can eat at the same time. Explain.

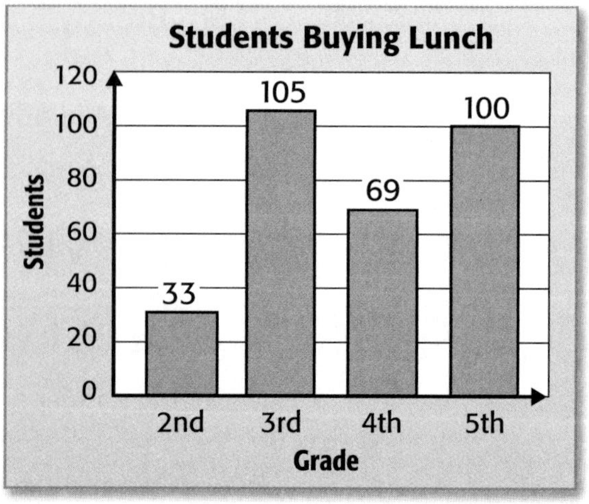

H.O.T. Problems

26. **WHICH ONE DOESN'T BELONG?** Identify the problem with the incorrect answer. Explain your reasoning.

2,017 − 1,713 = 304	8,500 − 4,764 = 4,836
1,109 − 768 = 341	5,000 − 3,574 = 1,426

27. **WRITING IN ▸MATH** Find 3,004 − 1,238. Explain the steps you follow as you find the difference.

Standards Practice

28 Which problem could be used to check 3624 − 1896 = 1728? (Lesson 3-7)

A 1896 + 1728 = ■

B 1896 − 1728 = ■

C 1896 × 1728 = ■

D 1896 ÷ 1728 = ■

29 Which number is 8 less than 2002? (Lesson 3-8)

F 1046

G 1054

H 1994

J 2044

Spiral Review

Subtract. Check your answer. (Lesson 3-7)

30. 1,951 − 563

31. 3,298 − 1,699

32. $3,679 − $2,789

33. Tyler jumped 32 inches. Grant jumped 3 feet 1 inch. Tyler said he jumped farther. Is his answer reasonable? Explain. (Lesson 3-6)

Compare. Write >, <, or =. (Lesson 1-6)

34. 475 ■ 478

35. 3,392 ■ 3,299

36. 2,381 ■ 12,000

3-9 Algebra: Expressions and Number Sentences

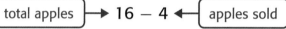

GET READY to Learn

There are 16 apples in a basket. Daniela buys 4 apples. The expression 16 − 4 tells how many apples were left.

total apples → 16 − 4 ← apples sold

MAIN IDEA

I will learn to write and simplify expressions.

Standard 3AF1.1 Represent relationships of quantities in the form of mathematical expressions, equations, and inequalities.

Standard 3AF1.3 Select appropriate operational and relational symbols to make an expression true. (e.g., if 4 _ 3 = 12, what operational symbol goes in the blank?).

New Vocabulary

expression

number sentence

An **expression** is a combination of numbers and operations. A few examples of expressions are shown.

$5 + 7 \qquad 3 + 2 + 5 \qquad 12 - 8$

A **number sentence** contains an equals sign (=), showing that two expressions are equal. A few examples are shown.

$5 + 7 = 12 \qquad 3 + 2 + 5 = 10 \qquad 12 - 8 = 4$

Real-World EXAMPLE

1 APPLES Use the information shown. Write an expression for the number of red apples and green apples.

red apples green apples

5 + 4

The expression is 5 + 4.

2 Write a number sentence to show how many apples in all are red and green.

red apples green apples

5 + 4 = 9

The number sentence is 5 + 4 = 9.

EXAMPLE Write a Number Sentence

3 Tell whether + or − makes the number sentence $4 ● 3 = 7$ true.

$4 ● 3 = 7$	$4 ● 3 = 7$
$4 - 3 = 7$	$4 + 3 = 7$
$1 = 7$	$7 = 7$
false	true

Remember

Symbols of comparison

greater than $>$
less than $<$
equals $=$

You can use $<$, $>$, or $=$ to compare expressions.

EXAMPLE Compare Expressions

4 Compare $2 + 5 ● 2 + 7$. Use $<$, $>$, or $=$.

$2 + 5 ● 2 + 7$	Write the expressions. Add 2 + 5.
$7 ● 9$	Add 2 + 7.
$7 < 9$	Compare.

So, $2 + 5 < 2 + 7$.

Online Personal Tutor at ca.gr3math.com

CHECK What You Know

Write an expression and a number sentence for each problem. Then solve. See Examples 1 and 2 (p. 138)

1. Jin wrote 3 letters today and 2 letters yesterday. How many letters in all?
2. The animal shelter had 6 puppies. They sold 3 of them. How many puppies are left?

Tell whether + or − makes each number sentence true.
See Example 3 (p. 139)

3. $9 ● 2 = 11$
4. $18 = 28 ● 10$
5. $14 ● 7 = 10 + 11$

Compare. Use $<$, $>$, or $=$. See Example 4 (p. 139)

6. $18 - 9 ● 9 - 0$
7. $18 + 20 ● 45 - 20$
8. $40 + 35 ● 40 + 45$

9. Talk About It What is the difference between an expression and a number sentence?

Practice and Problem Solving

EXTRA PRACTICE
See page R10.

Write an expression and a number sentence for each problem. Then solve. See Examples 1 and 2 (p. 138)

10. A basketball team won 11 games. A soccer team won 14 games. How many games were won in all?

11. Of the girls in a group, 14 have long hair and 9 have short hair. How many more have long hair?

12. Monisha scored 15 points Monday and 13 today. How many fewer points were made today?

13. Mick needs 4 yellow beads, 16 red, 2 white, and 14 green. How many beads are needed?

14. Cara caught 37 fish and threw 9 back. How many fish were left?

15. There are 143 goats and 291 cows. How many animals are there?

Tell whether + or − makes each number sentence true. See Example 3 (p. 139)

16. 444 ● 6 = 460 − 10

17. 74 ● 47 = 17 + 10

18. 125 − 27 = 23 ● 75

19. 345 − 126 > 217 ● 4

20. 520 ● 317 < 400 + 150

21. 715 − 617 < 25 ● 75

Compare. Use <, >, or =. See Example 4 (p. 139)

22. 16 + 12 ● 37 − 9

23. 76 − 14 ● 59 + 29

24. 204 − 21 ● 100 + 56

25. 275 + 67 ● 590 − 225

Real-World PROBLEM SOLVING

Ice Cream Use the data to write a number sentence for each phrase.

26. difference of votes for the two most favorite flavors

27. sum of votes for vanilla and cookie dough flavors

28. difference of votes for vanilla and strawberry flavors

29. sum of all the votes

H.O.T. Problems

30. CHALLENGE Use the numbers 13, 16, and 29 to write two expressions and compare them using <, >, or =.

31. WHICH ONE DOESN'T BELONG? Identify the example that is not an expression. Explain.

41 + 66	17 + 3	28 − 9 = 19	12 + 2 + 6

32. WRITING IN ▸MATH Write a real-world problem that can be solved using a subtraction number sentence.

Standards Practice

33 Jasmine's family drove 1352 miles on their vacation last year. This year they drove 1199 miles. How many fewer miles did they drive this year? **(Lesson 3-8)**

A 153 **C** 1153

B 247 **D** 2551

34 Which sign goes in the box to make the number sentence true? **(Lesson 3-9)**

79 ■ 26 = 105

F + **H** ×

G − **J** ÷

Spiral Review

Subtract. Check your answer. (Lesson 3-8)

35. 1,800 − 694 **36.** 9,009 − 1,986 **37.** $7,030 − $4,820

38. Measurement In a race, Joshua ran 206 feet and Dwayne ran 181 feet. How much farther did Joshua run than Dwayne? **(Lesson 3-7)**

39. Donna has $10. She bought a pencil and a book. She wants to buy one more thing. What is reasonable? **(Lesson 3-4)**

Round to the nearest hundred. (Lesson 1-8)

40. 729 **41.** 3,750

Compare. Write <, >, or =. (Lesson 1-6)

42. 5,384 ● 5,273 **43.** 2,039 ● 239

CHAPTER 3

Study Guide and Review

FOLDABLES™ Study Organizer **GET READY to Study**

Be sure the following Key Vocabulary words and Key Concepts are written in your Foldable.

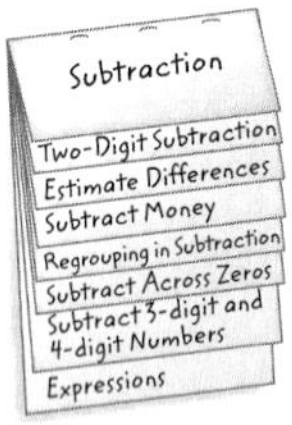

BIG Idea

- You may need to regroup to subtract. **(pp. 107–109)**

$$\begin{array}{r} \overset{3\,11}{41} \\ -27 \\ \hline 14 \end{array}$$

You cannot take 7 ones from 1 one. Regroup 1 ten as 10 ones. 1 one + 10 ones = 11 ones.

- Sometimes you have to regroup more than one time. **(pp. 124–127)**

- An **expression** is a combination of numbers and operations. **(pp. 138–140)**

  $4 - 1$ $\quad$ $5 + 12$

- A **number sentence** contains an equals sign (=), showing that two expressions are equal. **(pp. 138–140)**

  $4 - 1 = 3$ $\quad$ $5 + 12 = 17$

Key Vocabulary

difference (p. 107)
estimate (p. 110)
expression (p. 138)
number sentence (p. 138)
regroup (p. 108)
subtraction (p. 104)

Vocabulary Check

Choose the vocabulary word that completes each sentence.

1. If there are not enough ones to subtract from, you will ___?___ one ten.

2. 8 – 2 and 3 + 5 are both examples of a(n) ___?___ .

3. When you find an answer that is close to the exact answer, you ___?___ .

4. ___?___ is an operation that tells the difference when some or all is being taken away.

5. 8 – 2 = 6 is an example of a(n) ___?___ .

Math Online Vocabulary Review at ca.gr3math.com

Lesson-by-Lesson Review

3-1 Two-Digit Subtraction (pp. 107–109)

Example 1
Find 23 – 15.

Step 1 Regroup.

$$\begin{array}{r} {}^{1}\,{}^{13} \\ \not{2}\not{3} \\ -15 \\ \hline \end{array}$$

Regroup 1 ten as 10 ones.
3 ones + 10 ones = 13 ones.

Step 2 Subtract ones.

$$\begin{array}{r} {}^{1}\,{}^{13} \\ \not{2}\not{3} \\ -15 \\ \hline 8 \end{array}$$

13 ones – 5 ones = 8 ones

Step 3 Subtract tens.

$$\begin{array}{r} {}^{1}\,{}^{13} \\ \not{2}\not{3} \\ -15 \\ \hline 08 \end{array}$$

1 ten – 1 ten = 0 tens

So, 23 – 15 = 8.

Subtract. Use addition to check.

6. $\begin{array}{r} 17 \\ -4 \\ \hline \end{array}$ **7.** $\begin{array}{r} 38 \\ -6 \\ \hline \end{array}$

8. 83 – 49 **9.** 62 – 28

10. Jackie has 37 pieces of paper. She gives 14 to Sharon. How many are left for Jackie?

11. There are 18 days left in the month. If there are 31 days total, how many days have passed?

12. Mario wrote a report for extra credit. There were 25 points possible. Mario earned 19 points. How many points did he miss?

3-2 Estimate Differences (pp. 110–113)

Example 2
Estimate 679 – 325. Round to the nearest hundred.

Round each number then subtract.

$$\begin{array}{rcr} 679 & \longrightarrow & 700 \\ 325 & \longrightarrow & -300 \\ \hline & & 400 \end{array}$$

Estimate. Round to the nearest ten.

13. 94 – 55 **14.** 43 – 29

Estimate. Round to the nearest hundred.

15. 732 – 280 **16.** 668 – 325

17. A baby has about 300 bones. An adult has 206 bones. About how many more bones does a baby have?

3-3 Subtract Money (pp. 114–116)

Example 3
Find 74¢ − 58¢.

```
 6 14   Regroup.
 74¢    Subtract the ones.
−58¢    Subtract the tens.
 16¢    Place the cents sign after the answer.
```

Example 4
Find $0.74 − $0.58.

```
   6 14   Regroup.
 $0.74    Subtract the ones.
−$0.58    Subtract the tens.
 $0.16
```

Bring down the decimal point, zero, and dollar sign.

Subtract. Check your answer.

18. 73¢ − 6¢

19. $92 − $48

20. $77 − $38

21. $0.63 − $0.58

22. Denny has 50¢. If he buys a goldfish for 38¢, how much change will he receive?

23. One orange costs $0.55 at the grocery store. Maya buys two oranges. She gives the cashier $2. How much change will Maya receive?

3-4 Problem-Solving Skill: Reasonable Answers (pp. 120–121)

Example 5
Reuben's book has 96 pages. He read 47 pages today and wants to finish his book tomorrow. Is his goal reasonable?

Use estimation to check for reasonableness.

```
 96 ⟶   100   total pages
−47 ⟶  − 50   pages read today
         50   more pages to read
```

Reuben has about 50 pages to read.

Reuben can read 47 pages in one day. 47 is close to 50. So, his goal is reasonable.

Solve.

24. All 30 seats on the bus are taken. After the first stop, only 18 seats are taken. Is it reasonable to say that about 10 passengers got off? Explain.

25. Marra is saving her money to buy a bike. The bike costs $90. She saved $23 this week and $19 last week. Is it reasonable to say Marra will have enough to buy a bike after 1 more week? Explain.

3-5 Three-Digit Subtraction with Regrouping (pp. 124–127)

Example 6
A group of friends made 133 bracelets to sell at the craft fair. They sold 98. How many bracelets did they have left?

You need to find 133 – 98.

Step 1 Subtract the ones.

```
  2 13
 1 3 3
  -98
 ----
    5
```

Regroup 1 ten as 10 ones.
3 ones + 10 ones = 13 ones.
13 ones – 8 ones = 5 ones.

Step 2 Subtract the tens.

```
 0 12 13
 1  3  3
 -  9  8
 -------
    3  5
```

Regroup 1 hundred as 10 tens.
2 tens + 10 tens = 12 tens
12 tens – 9 tens = 3 tens.

So, the friends have 35 bracelets left.

Check Check the answer by adding.

```
  same
  133       35
 - 98      +98
 ----     ----
   35      133
```

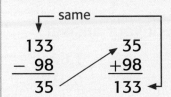

So, the answer is correct. ✓

Subtract. Check your answer.

26. 213 – 155

27. $6.33 – $4.86

28. 577 – 98

29. $4.31 – $2.52

30. 767 – 78

31. $3.33 – $2.65

32. 538 – 329

33. 875 – 677

34. 728 – 527

35. 492 – 235

36. Mandy and Zoe ate lunch at The Lunch Shop. Mandy's sandwich cost $6.20. Zoe's sandwich cost $2.32 less. How much did the sandwiches cost altogether?

37. Patsy needs to jump rope 433 times in a row to beat the school jump rope record. So far, Patsy has jumped 284 times. How many more jumps will beat the record?

38. Students are having a car wash to raise money for the drama club. Their goal is to raise $150. How much more money do they need to meet their goal?

Drama Club Car Wash	
1st hour	$23
2nd hour	$29
3rd hour	$25

3-6 Problem-Solving Investigation: Choose a Strategy (pp. 128–129)

Example 7

Students want to make 425 cards for hospital patients. The second graders have made 75 cards and the third graders have made 90 cards. How many cards still need to be made?

Find the number of cards made.

75	Second grade made
+ 90	Third grade made
165	Total made so far

Subtract to find out how many cards are still needed.

```
 3 12
 4 2 5
- 165
  260
```

So, 260 cards still need to be made.

Use any strategy to solve. Tell what strategy you used.

39. Frankie has a collection of 711 leaves. Of those leaves, he collected 126 of them this year. How many leaves were in his collection before this year?

40. The chart below shows how long it takes each child to walk to school. How much longer does Salma walk than Ernie and Kate combined?

The Walk To School	
Ernie	14 minutes
Kate	18 minutes
Salma	36 minutes

3-7 Subtract Greater Numbers (pp. 130–132)

Example 8

Find 5,236 – 2,477.

Subtract as you would with smaller numbers. Remember to regroup when needed.

```
   11 12
 4 1  2 16
 5, 2 3 6
- 2,477
  2,759
```

Subtract. Check your answer.

41. $4,246 − $1,781

42. 7,624 − 5,937

43. A farmer harvested 2,354 melons. He sold melons on the weekend at the market. How many melons are left?

Melon Sale	
Saturday	789
Sunday	677

3-8 Subtract Across Zeros (pp. 134–137)

Example 9
Find 3,000 − 588.

Step 1 Regroup the thousands.

```
  2 10
  3,000   You cannot take 8 ones from 0 ones.
−   588   There are no tens or hundreds to
          regroup. Regroup 1 thousand as
          10 hundreds.
```

Step 2 Regroup the hundreds.

```
     9
  2 10 10
  3,000   Regroup 1 hundred as 10 tens.
−   588
```

Step 3 Regroup the tens.

```
     9  9
  2 10 10 10
  3, 0  0  0   Regroup 1 ten as 10 ones.
−    5  8  8
  2, 4  1  2   Subtract.
```

Check Add up to check.

```
  3,000      2,412
−   588    +   588
  2,412      3,000
```

So, the answer is correct. ✓

Subtract. Check your answer.

44. 400 − 39

45. \$600 − \$322

46. 202 − 174

47. \$800 − \$712

48. 8,000 − 456 **49.** 4,000 − 823

50. 5,007 − 669 **51.** 3,002 − 518

52. Norma bought a doll house for \$189. She paid for the doll house with two \$100 bills. How much change should Norma receive?

53. The school sold 1,677 tickets to the choir concert. There are 3,000 seats in the auditorium. How many more tickets are available?

54. Students in Ms. Turner's class earn points for reading books. Students can use their points to buy rewards. Corina has 74 reading points. She wants to earn an extra recess. How many more points does Corina need?

Ms. Turner's Reading Rewards	
Sticker	100 points
Homework pass	200 points
Extra recess	300 points

3-9 Algebra: Expressions and Number Sentences (pp. 138–141)

The table shows the number of pies baked today.

Fresh-Baked Pies	
Apple	7
Blueberry	9
Cherry	5
Peach	8

Example 10
Write an expression for the total number of apple and peach pies.

$\underbrace{7}_{\text{apple pies}} + \underbrace{8}_{\text{peach pies}}$

Example 11
Write a number sentence to show how many pies are apple and peach.

$\underbrace{7}_{\text{apple pies}} + \underbrace{8}_{\text{peach pies}} = 15$

Example 12
Write a number sentence to show how many pies are blueberry and cherry.

$\underbrace{9}_{\text{blueberry pies}} + \underbrace{5}_{\text{cherry pies}} = 14$

Write an expression and a number sentence for each problem. Then solve.

55. There are 5 girls and 6 boys on the playground. How many children are there in all?

56. Betsy caught 8 fireflies. Three of the fireflies escaped. How many are left?

57. Stephen bought a bunch of 6 bananas. He ate 2 at lunch. How many bananas are left?

Tell whether + or – makes each number sentence true.

58. 7 ● 3 = 4

59. 5 ● 4 = 9

60. 4 ● 1 = 5

61. 14 ● 8 = 6

62. 19 ● 2 = 17

63. 15 ● 5 = 20

Compare. Use <, >, or =.

64. 6 + 10 ■ 8 + 8

65. 7 + 4 ■ 5 + 10

66. 12 – 5 ■ 32 – 26

67. 22 – 4 ■ 42 – 20

68. Tito has 6 gold coins and 2 silver coins in his collection. Mariah has 1 gold coin and 6 silver coins. Write two expressions and compare.

CHAPTER 3

Chapter Test

For Exercises 1–3, decide whether each statement is *true* or *false*.

1. An expression contains numbers and operation signs.
2. Always begin with the tens place when subtracting.
3. Sometimes before you can begin subtracting you have to regroup more than one time.

Write an expression and a number sentence for each problem. Then solve.

4. Vianca ate 2 pieces of fruit today and 3 pieces yesterday. How many pieces of fruit did she eat altogether?
5. The movie store had 8 copies of my favorite movie. Then they sold 3. How many copies do they have left?

Estimate. Round to the nearest hundred.

6. $\begin{array}{r} 632 \\ -\ 151 \\ \hline \end{array}$

7. $\begin{array}{r} 2,153 \\ -\ 679 \\ \hline \end{array}$

8. **STANDARDS PRACTICE** How much more does the black pair of ballet shoes cost than the pink pair?

Price of Ballet Shoes	
Black pair	$108
Pink pair	$91

A $9 **C** $27

B $17 **D** $117

9. A cake was cut into 40 pieces. Is it reasonable to say that there was enough cake for 32 people? Explain.

Subtract. Check your answer.

10. $\begin{array}{r} 394 \\ -\ 271 \\ \hline \end{array}$

11. $\begin{array}{r} \$9.27 \\ -\ \$4.39 \\ \hline \end{array}$

12. $\begin{array}{r} 307 \\ -\ 67 \\ \hline \end{array}$

13. $\begin{array}{r} \$8.00 \\ -\ \$2.17 \\ \hline \end{array}$

14. $5,277 − $2,568

Compare. Use <, >, or =.

15. 56 + 23 ■ 87 − 17

16. 170 − 19 ■ 121 + 30

Tell whether + or − makes each number sentence true.

17. 18 + 9 = 13 ■ 14

18. 46 ■ 5 = 58 − 7

19. **STANDARDS PRACTICE** Which sign goes in the box to make the number sentence true?

84 ■ 32 = 116

F + **H** ×

G − **J** ÷

20. **WRITING IN MATH** Explain why you should always check over your work.

California Standards Practice

Cumulative, Chapters 1–3

Standards Example

Kip has a $150 gift certificate. He bought a baseball glove for $49.50 and a baseball bat for $37.50. How much money does he have left?

A $63.00 **C** $90.00

B $87.00 **D** $237.00

Read the Question

Find how much Kip spent. Then subtract the total from the gift certificate amount.

Solve the Question

Step 1 Add.

$$\begin{array}{r} \$49.50 \\ +\ \$37.50 \\ \hline \$87.00 \end{array}$$

Bring down the decimal point and dollar sign.

Step 2 Subtract.

$$\begin{array}{r} \$150 \\ -\ \$87 \\ \hline \$63 \end{array}$$

So, Kip has $63.00 left. The answer is A.

Online Personal Tutor at ca.gr3math.com

Choose the best answer.

1 **Each year the Garden Club collects $1200. So far, the club has $958. How much more does the club need to collect?**

A $242 **C** $348

B $252 **D** $358

2 **On a car trip, Jerry counts 125 white cars. Marla counts 67 sports cars. How many more cars did Jerry count?**

F 58 **H** 68

G 62 **J** 192

3 **Last year, the theater spent $7625. This year the theater will spend $9910. How much more is the theater spending this year?**

A $2285 **C** $2325

B $2315 **D** $2395

4 **What is the best estimate of the difference rounded to the nearest hundred?**

812 − 356

F 400 **H** 475

G 450 **J** 500

5 **What is 9,000 + 400 + 50 + 2 in standard form?**

A 2549 **C** 9452

B 4925 **D** 9542

6 **A bag of apple chips at the store costs $2.39. Joe gave the clerk $5.00. How much change did he receive?**

F $1.34 **H** $2.61

G $2.19 **J** $2.42

7 **Alina has 145 stickers. Which of these equals 145?**

A 1 + 4 + 5

B 1 + 40 + 500

C 100 + 50 + 4

D 100 + 40 + 5

8 **What number makes this number sentence true?**

3 + 6 + 4 = 3 + 4 + ■

F 2 **H** 4

G 3 **J** 6

9 **Len had 6 corn muffins and 4 bran muffins. He ate 2 corn muffins and 1 bran muffin. Which number sentence describes Len's muffins?**

A (6 + 2) − (4 + 1) = 3

B (6 + 2) − (4 −1) = 5

C (6 − 2) + (4 − 1) = 7

D (6 − 2) + (4 + 1) = 9

10 **What number is missing in the pattern 12, 18, 24, 30, ___?**

F 34 **H** 38

G 36 **J** 40

CHAPTER 4

Multiplication Concepts and Facts

BIG Idea What is Multiplication?

Multiplication is an operation on two numbers to find a *product*. It can be thought of as repeated *addition*.

Example A tarantula spider is shown. Suppose there are 4 spiders. Spiders have 8 legs. So, there would be 4×8 or 32 legs in all.

What will I learn in this chapter?

- Explore the meaning of multiplication.
- Use models to multiply.
- Multiply by 2, 4, 5, 10, 0, and 1.
- Use multiplication properties and rules.
- Identify extra or missing information.

Key Vocabulary

multiply
factor
product
array
Commutative Property of Multiplication

Math Online **Student Study Tools at ca.gr3math.com**

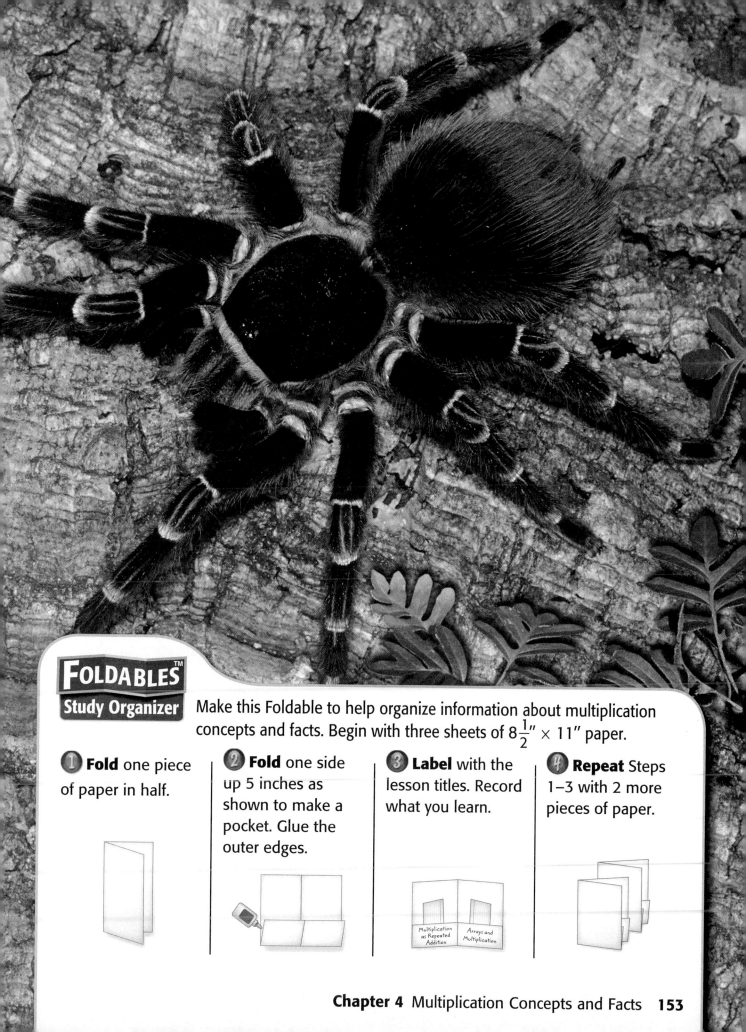

FOLDABLES™ Study Organizer

Make this Foldable to help organize information about multiplication concepts and facts. Begin with three sheets of $8\frac{1}{2}'' \times 11''$ paper.

1. **Fold** one piece of paper in half.

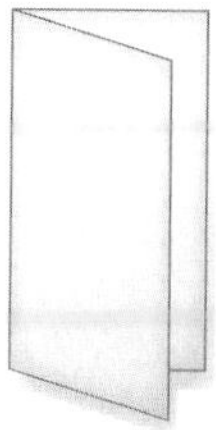

2. **Fold** one side up 5 inches as shown to make a pocket. Glue the outer edges.

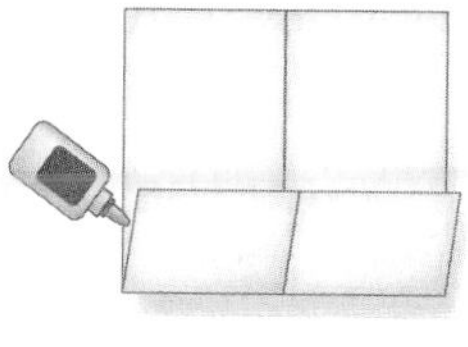

3. **Label** with the lesson titles. Record what you learn.

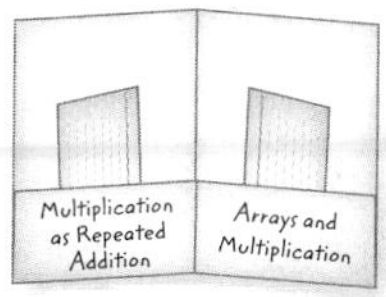

4. **Repeat** Steps 1–3 with 2 more pieces of paper.

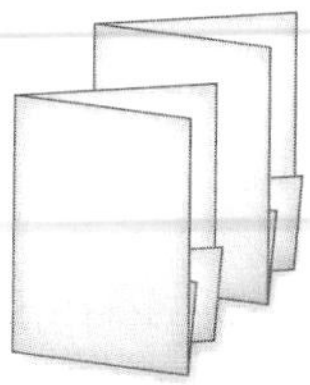

ARE YOU READY for Chapter 4?

You have two ways to check prerequisite skills for this chapter.

Option 2

Math Online Take the Chapter Readiness Quiz at ca.gr3math.com.

Option 1

Complete the Quick Check below.

QUICK Check

Find each sum. **(Lesson 2-1 and Prior grade)**

1. 2 + 2 + 2 + 2 **2.** 4 + 4 **3.** 5 + 5 + 5

4. 10 + 10 + 10 + 10 **5.** 3 + 3 + 3 **6.** 1 + 1 + 1 + 1 + 1

Copy and complete. **(Lesson 1-1)**

7. 5, 10, 15, ■, ■, 30 **8.** 2, ■, 6, 8, ■, 12 **9.** 3, 6, 9, ■, 15, ■

10. ■, 8, 12, 16, ■ **11.** ■, 20, 30, ■, 50 **12.** 6, 12, ■, 24, ■

Write an addition sentence for each picture. **(Lesson 3-9)**

13.

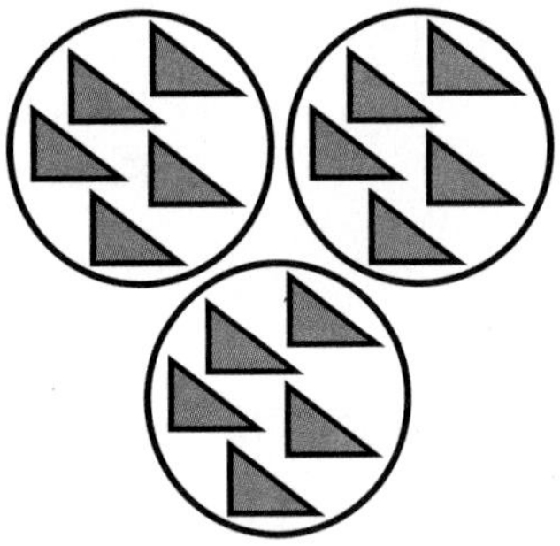

14.

15.

Solve. Use repeated addition. **(Lesson 2-1)**

16. Larisa has 2 cups with 4 crackers in each cup. How many crackers does she have in all?

17. On Monday and Tuesday Lance rode his bike around the block 3 times each day. How many times in all did he ride his bike around the block?

Explore

Math Activity for 4-1
Meaning of Multiplication

MAIN IDEA

I will use models to explore multiplication.

Standard 3MR2.3 Use a variety of methods, such as words, numbers, symbols, charts, graphs, tables, diagrams, and **models, to explain mathematical reasoning.**

Standard 3NS2.2 Memorize to automaticity the multiplication table for numbers between 1 and 10.

You Will Need
connecting cubes

Concepts in Motion
Animation
ca.gr3math.com

Multiplication is an operation on two numbers to find a *product*. It can be thought of as repeated *addition*. The sign (×) means to multiply. You can use models to explore multiplication.

ACTIVITY **Find how many are in 5 groups of 4.**

Step 1 **Show 5 groups of 4.**

Use connecting cubes to show 5 groups of 4 cubes.

There are 5 groups. There are 4 cubes in each group.

Step 2 **Find 5 groups of 4.**

Model the groups of cubes with numbers. Use repeated addition.

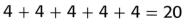

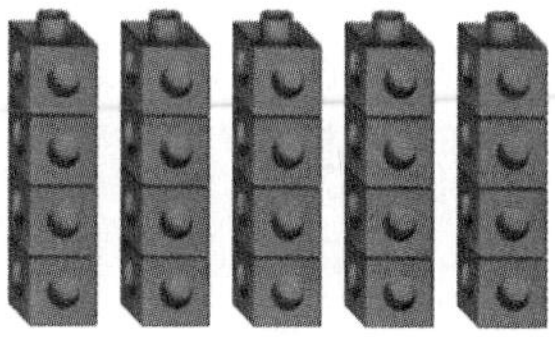

4 + 4 + 4 + 4 + 4 = 20

Hands-On Activity

Step 3 **Record the results.**

Copy the table. Record the number of groups, the number in each group, and the total.

Use connecting cubes to explore other ways to group the 20 cubes equally.

Number of Groups	Number in Each Group	Total
5	4	20

Think About It

1. How can addition help you find the total number when multiplying?

2. How did you find the total number of cubes in Step 2?

3. What do the numbers stand for in the number sentence in Step 2?

4. Explain another way to group 20 cubes equally.

CHECK What You Know

Use models to find the total number.

5. 2 groups of 3

6. 3 groups of 4

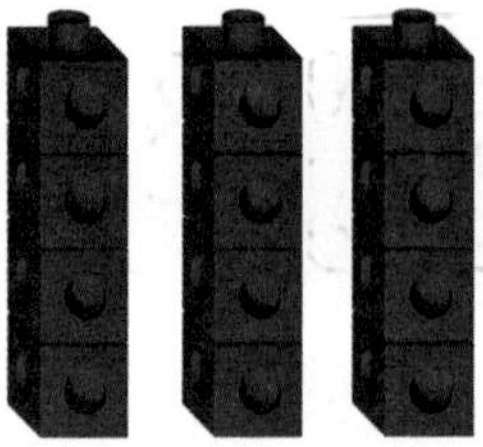

7. 1 group of 5

8. 8 groups of 2

9. 5 groups of 4

10. 4 groups of 6

11. 6 groups of 2

12. 4 groups of 5

13. 7 groups of 2

14. WRITING IN ▶MATH Explain how addition and multiplication are similar.

4-1 Multiplication as Repeated Addition

MAIN IDEA

I will relate multiplication and addition.

Standard 3NS2.2 Memorize to automaticity the multiplication table for numbers between 1 and 10.

Standard 3MR2.3 Use a variety of methods, such as words, numbers, symbols, charts, graphs, tables, diagrams, and models, to explain mathematical reasoning.

New Vocabulary

multiply
factor
product

GET READY to Learn

For Gilberto's party, his mother made 4 small pizzas. Each pizza had 6 pieces of pepperoni. How many pieces of pepperoni did Gilberto's mother use?

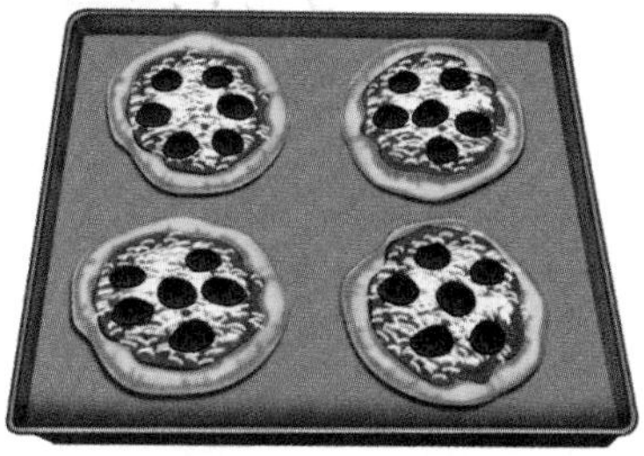

In the Explore activity, you used models to explore multiplication as repeated addition.

Real-World EXAMPLE

1 FOOD How many pieces of pepperoni did Gilberto's mother use to make 4 small pizzas?

Find how many are in 4 equal groups of 6.

One Way: Counters	Another Way: Repeated Addition
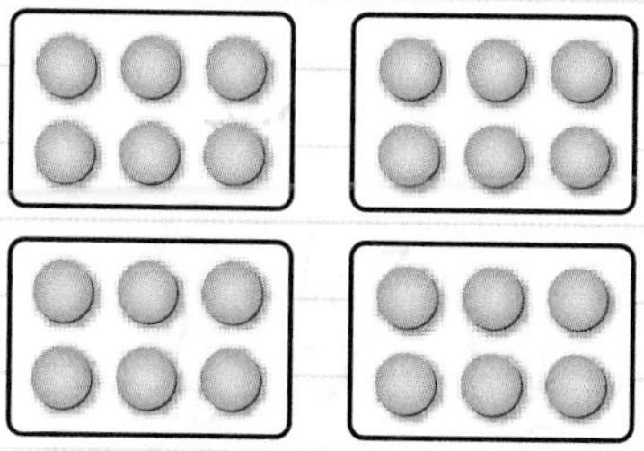 There are 4 groups. There are 6 counters in each group. This is a total of 24 counters.	Write an addition sentence to show equal groups. $6 + 6 + 6 + 6 = 24$

So, 4 equal groups of 6 are 24. Gilberto's mother used 24 pieces of pepperoni.

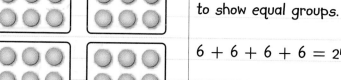

Online Personal Tutor at ca.gr3math.com

You put equal groups together to **multiply**. The numbers you multiply are **factors**. The result is the **product**.

Real-World EXAMPLE

2 **BEES A honeycomb cell has 6 sides. How many sides do 5 separate honeycomb cells have altogether?**

Find how many are in 5 equal groups of 6.

Remember

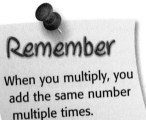

When you multiply, you add the same number multiple times.

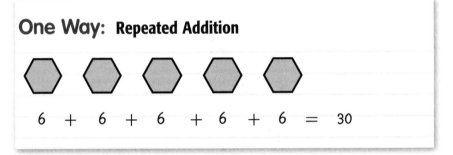

One Way: Repeated Addition

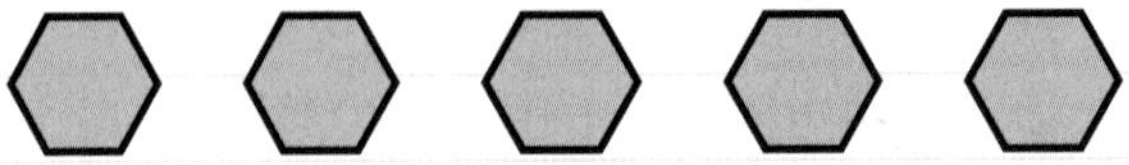

6 + 6 + 6 + 6 + 6 = 30

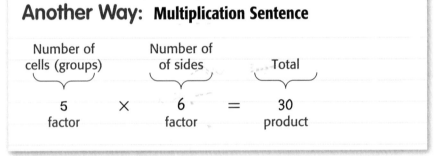

Another Way: Multiplication Sentence

Number of cells (groups)		Number of of sides		Total
5	×	6	=	30
factor		factor		product

So, there is a total of 30 sides.

CHECK What You Know

Write an addition and a multiplication sentence for each model. **See Examples 1 and 2 (pp. 157–158)**

1.

2.

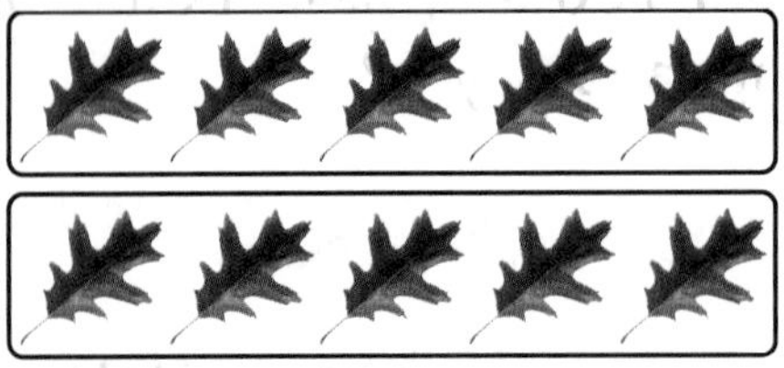

Multiply. Use repeated addition. **See Examples 1 and 2 (pp. 157–158)**

3. 2 × 6

4. 4 × 4

5. 5 × 3

6. 7 × 2

7. Marcos gives 3 friends 4 stickers each. How many stickers did he give away?

8. **Talk About It** Can a group of 5 drums be multiplied by 7? Explain.

Practice and Problem Solving

EXTRA PRACTICE
See page R10.

Write an addition and a multiplication sentence for each model. See Examples 1 and 2 (pp. 157–158)

9.

10.

11.

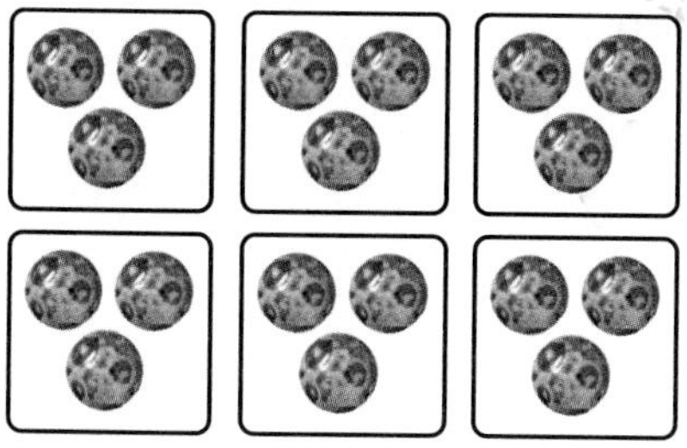

12.

13. 6 groups of 6

14. 8 groups of 4

15. 10 groups of 3

16. 7 groups of 5

17. 5 groups of 7

18. 9 groups of 4

Multiply. Use repeated addition. See Examples 1 and 2 (pp.157–158)

19. 3×5

20. 5×2

21. 3×3

22. 6×2

23. 9×2

24. 10×6

25. 5×5

26. 4×7

27. 6×4

28. Gabe bought 3 boxes of paints. Each box has 8 colors. What is the total number of paints?

29. Lena found 4 bags of buttons. Each bag has 10 buttons. How many buttons are there altogether?

30. Each boy has 5 balloons, and each girl has 3 balloons. How many balloons do they have if there are 3 boys and 6 girls?

31. A starfish has 5 legs. There are 5 starfish on the beach. If 4 of the starfish are each missing 1 leg, how many legs are there?

H.O.T. Problems

32. **OPEN ENDED** Write a real-world multiplication problem whose product is greater than 40.

33. **CHALLENGE** What is 2 more than 5 groups of 3?

34. **WRITING IN MATH** Describe a real-world situation where you would use multiplication to solve a problem.

4-2 Arrays and Multiplication

MAIN IDEA

I will use arrays to multiply.

Standard 3AF1.5 Recognize and use the Commutative and Associative **Properties of Multiplication (e.g., if 5 × 7 = 35, then what is 7 × 5?** and if 5 × 7 × 3 = 105, then what is 7 × 3 × 5?).

New Vocabulary

array

Commutative Property of Multiplication

GET READY to Learn

Roberto places party cups on a table in 3 rows of 5 cups each. How many cups are there on the table?

The cups are arranged in equal rows and equal columns. This arrangement is an **array**.

Real-World EXAMPLES Use an Array

1 **PARTY CUPS How many cups are on the table?**

To find the total number of cups, you can use addition or multiplication. There are 3 rows with 5 cups in each row.

One Way: **Add**	Another Way: **Multiply**
5 + 5 + 5 = 15	3 × 5 = 15

So, 3 equal groups of 5 cups is 15 in all.

2 **FOOD How many eggs are in a carton of eggs?**

To find the total number in the array of eggs, you can write a multiplication sentence.

2 × 6 = 12

So, 2 rows of 6 eggs is 12.

KEY CONCEPT Commutative Property

Words The **Commutative Property of Multiplication** says the order in which numbers are multiplied does not change the product.

Examples

4	×	3	=	12		3	×	4	=	12
factor		factor		product		factor		factor		product

Vocabulary Link

commute

Everyday Use to go back and forth

Math Use to change the order of factors

Real-World EXAMPLE

3 **PHOTOS One page of Elsa's photo album is shown. Write two multiplication sentences to find how many photos are on each page.**

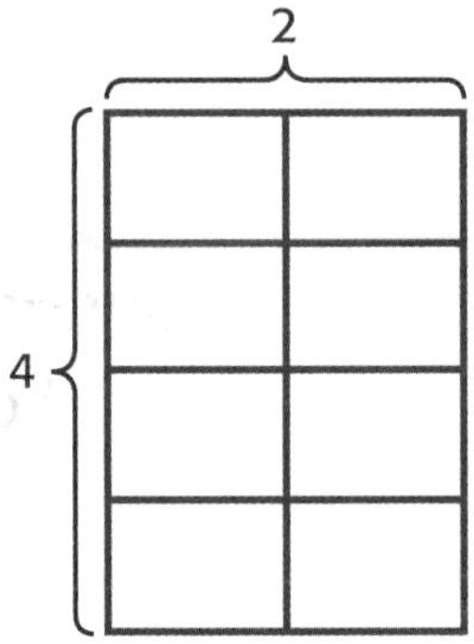

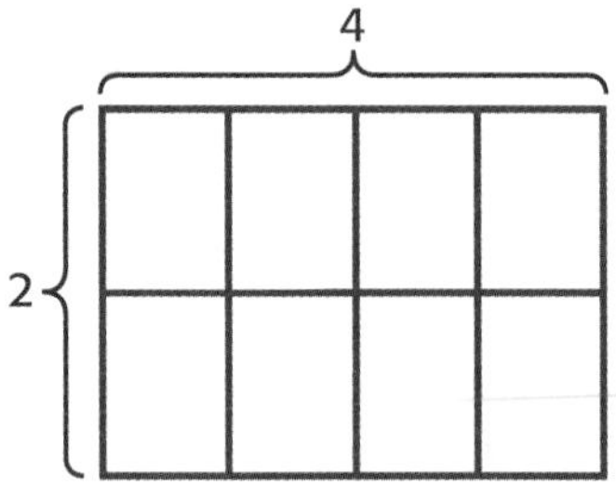

rows		number in each row		total	rows		number in each row		total
4	×	2	=	8	2	×	4	=	8

Remember

The models in Example 3 are also arrays since they have columns and rows.

Online **Personal Tutor at** ca.gr3math.com

CHECK What You Know

Write a multiplication sentence for each array. Then multiply. **See Examples 1 and 2 (p. 160)**

1. 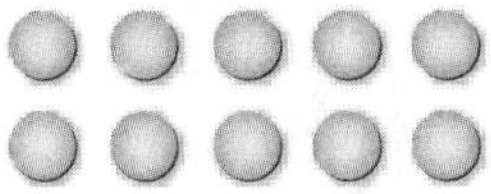

2. 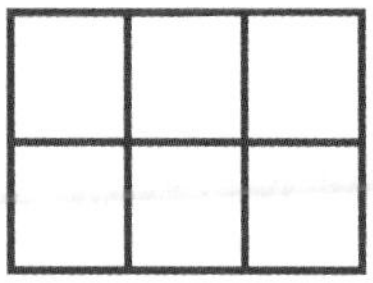

3. Write two multiplication sentences to find how many puppies there are if 5 dogs each have 2 puppies.

4. Talk About It What other operation uses the Commutative Property? Explain.

Practice and Problem Solving

EXTRA PRACTICE
See page R11.

Write a multiplication sentence for each array. Then multiply. See Examples 1 and 2 (p. 160)

5. 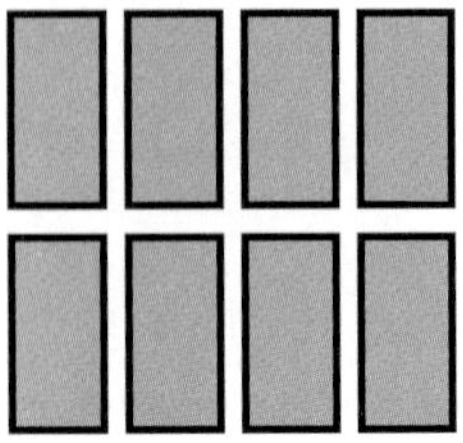

6. 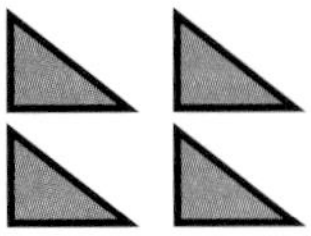

7. 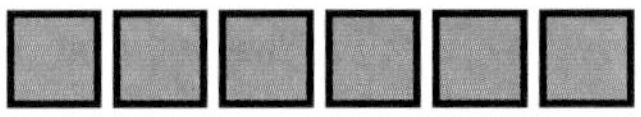

8. 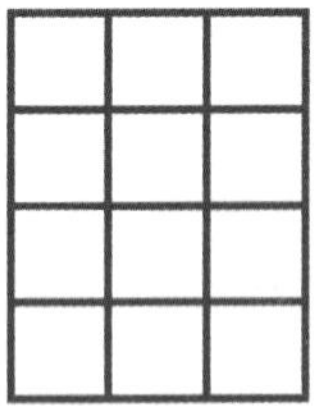

9. 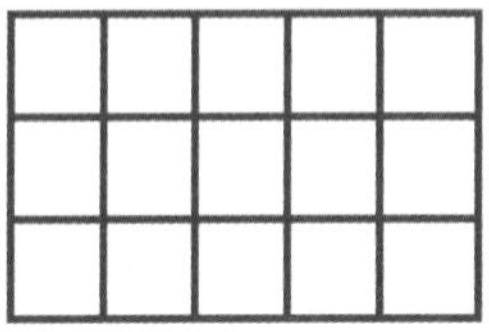

10. 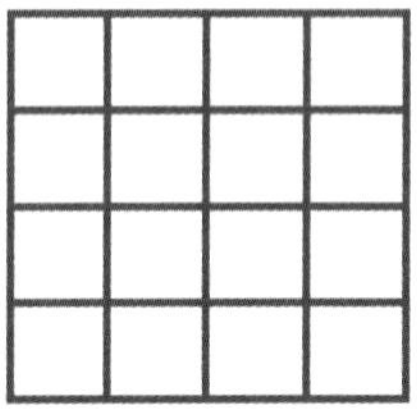

Algebra Use the Commutative Property of Multiplication to find each missing number. See Example 3 (p. 161)

11. $5 \times 2 = 10$
    $2 \times ■ = 10$

12. $3 \times 5 = 15$
    $■ \times 3 = 15$

13. $3 \times 9 = 27$
    $9 \times 3 = ■$

14. $6 \times 5 = 30$
    $5 \times ■ = 30$

15. $5 \times 8 = 40$
    $8 \times 5 = ■$

16. $4 \times 9 = 36$
    $9 \times 4 = ■$

Multiply. Use an array to help. See Examples 1 and 2 (p. 160)

17. **Geometry** Hope drew an area model. Write a multiplication sentence to represent her model.

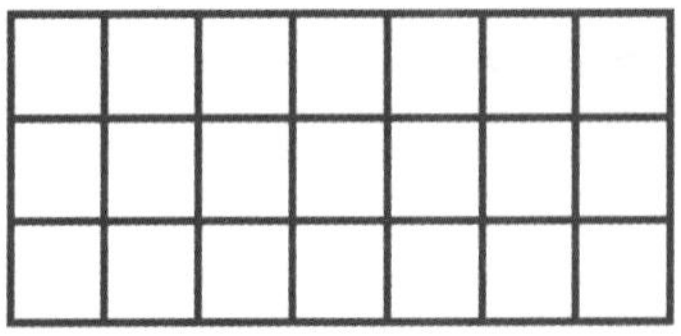

18. Adult tickets to the talent show cost $8. How much will 4 adult tickets cost?

19. Felix gives his dog 2 treats every day. How many treats does Felix's dog get in one week?

Use the Commutative Property of Multiplication to write two multiplication sentences for each situation. Then solve. See Example 3 (p. 161)

20. Estes made a 4×6 array of rocks. How many rocks does Estes have?

21. There were 4 students with 5 balloons each. How many balloons do the students have?

H.O.T. Problems

22. FIND THE ERROR Marita and Tyrone are using the numbers 3, 4, and 12 to show the Commutative Property of Multiplication. Who is correct? Explain.

Marita
$3 \times 4 = 12$
$12 \div 3 = 4$

Tyrone
$4 \times 3 = 12$
$3 \times 4 = 12$

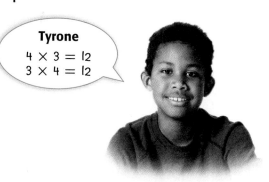

23. WRITING IN ▸MATH Describe how an array can help you find the answer to a multiplication problem.

Standards Practice

24 Which multiplication sentence is modeled below? **(Lesson 4-1)**

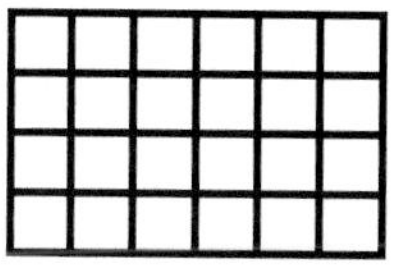

A $5 \times 7 = 35$

B $6 \times 6 = 36$

C $8 \times 3 = 24$

D $4 \times 6 = 24$

25 If $7 \times 5 = 35$, then what is 5×7? **(Lesson 4-2)**

F 30

G 35

H 40

J 45

Spiral Review

Write an addition and a multiplication sentence for each model. **(Lesson 4-1)**

26.

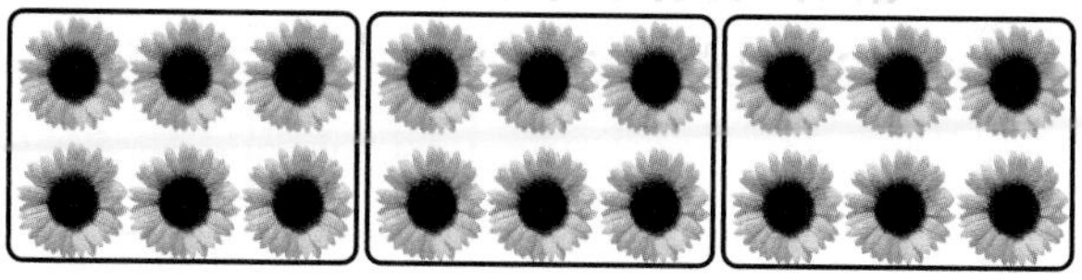

27.

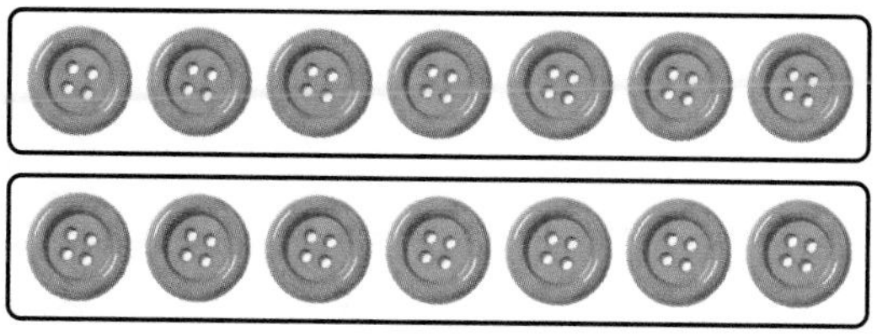

Write an expression and a number sentence for each problem. Then solve. **(Lesson 3-9)**

28. There are 24 baseballs, 17 tennis balls, and 6 footballs in a tub. How many balls are there altogether?

29. Of the 54 calculators on a shelf, 28 are not working. How many calculators are working?

4-3 Multiply by 2

MAIN IDEA

I will multiply by 2.

Standard 3NS2.2 Memorize to automaticity the multiplication table for numbers between 1 and 10.

GET READY to Learn

The students in an art class are working on an art project. They are told to work in 2 groups of 8. How many students are there in all?

There are many different ways to multiply by 2. One way is to draw a picture. Another way is to use an array.

Real-World EXAMPLE **Multiply by 2**

1 SCHOOL **How many students are there in the art class if there are 2 groups of 8?**

You need to find 2 groups of 8 or 2×8.

One Way: Draw a Picture	Another Way: Use an Array
Draw 2 groups of 8.	Show an array with 2 rows and 8 columns
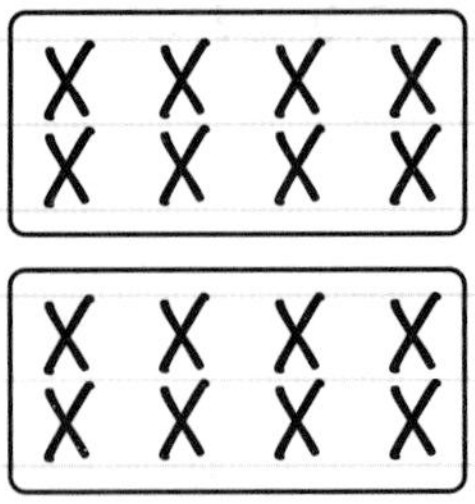	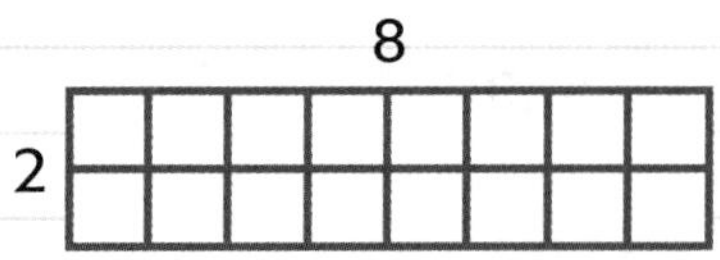
8 + 8 or 16	2 rows of 8 = 8 + 8 or 16.

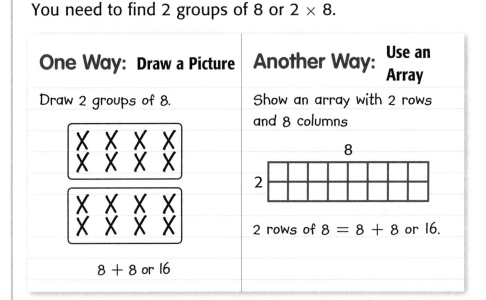

So, there are 2×8 or 16 students in all.

To multiply by 2, you can use skip counting.

Real-World EXAMPLE **Use Skip Counting**

2 **FRIENDS Sybil and her friend like to ride their bikes to the park. It is a 3-mile round trip. How many miles do they ride altogether?**

There are 2 friends. Each rides 3 miles.

To find how many miles they ride altogether, find 2 × 3.

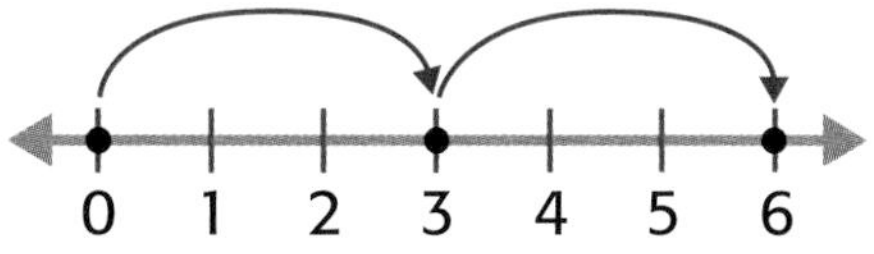

Count 2 jumps of 3.

So, Sybil and her friend ride 2 × 3, or 6 miles altogether.

Remember
You can use a number line to help you skip count.

Online **Personal Tutor at** ca.gr3math.com

CHECK What You Know

Multiply. **See Examples 1 and 2 (p. 164–165)**

1.

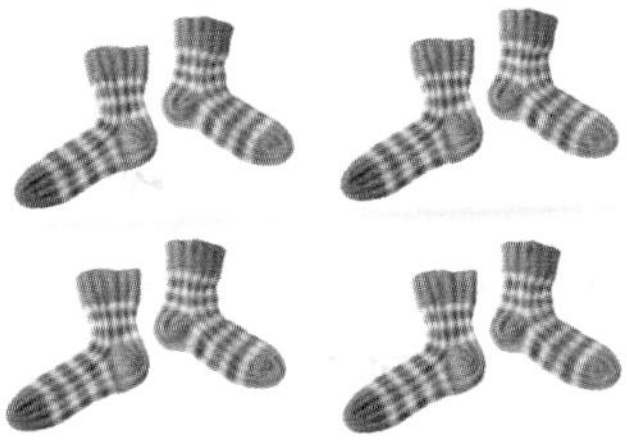

4 groups of 2

2.

2 groups of 3

3.

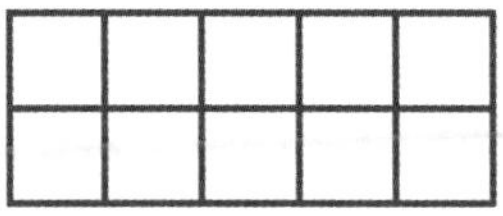

2 rows of 5

Multiply. Draw a picture or use an array. **See Example 1 (p. 164)**

4. $\begin{array}{r} 6 \\ \times 2 \\ \hline \end{array}$

5. $\begin{array}{r} 2 \\ \times 2 \\ \hline \end{array}$

6. $\begin{array}{r} 9 \\ \times 2 \\ \hline \end{array}$

7. $\begin{array}{r} 8 \\ \times 2 \\ \hline \end{array}$

8. Ten students each have 2 pieces of chalk. How many pieces of chalk are there?

9. Talk About It Explain the different strategies you can use to remember multiplication facts for 2.

Practice and Problem Solving

EXTRA PRACTICE
See page R11.

Multiply. See Examples 1 and 2 (p. 164–165)

10. 

2 groups of 3

11. 

2 groups of 6

12. 

5 groups of 2

13. 

2 rows of 2

14. 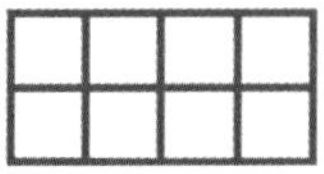

2 rows of 4

15. 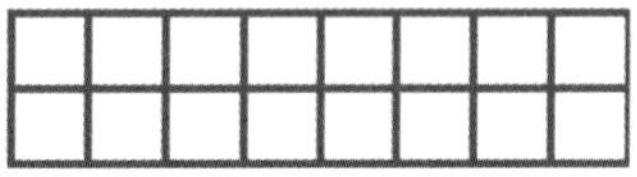

2 rows of 8

Multiply. Draw a picture or use an array. See Example 1 (p. 164)

16. $\begin{array}{r} 2 \\ \times 5 \\ \hline \end{array}$

17. $\begin{array}{r} 2 \\ \times 3 \\ \hline \end{array}$

18. $\begin{array}{r} 5 \\ \times 2 \\ \hline \end{array}$

19. $\begin{array}{r} 4 \\ \times 2 \\ \hline \end{array}$

20. 2×7

21. 2×9

22. 6×2

23. 10×2

24. 2×4

25. 2×8

26. 2×2

27. 3×2

Write a multiplication sentence for each situation.
Then solve. See Examples 1 and 2 (pp. 164–165)

28. There are 2 students. Each has 3 pencils. How many pencils are there in all?

29. There are 2 dogs. How many eyes are there in all?

30. There are 2 spiders. Each has 8 legs. How many legs are there in all?

31. There are 2 squares. How many sides are there in all?

Algebra Compare. Use >, <, or =.

32. 2×5 ■ 4×2

33. $5 + 4$ ■ 2×9

34. 7×2 ■ $7 + 7$

H.O.T. Problems

35. OPEN ENDED Write a real-world multiplication word problem whose product is between 11 and 19.

36. WRITING IN MATH Write a problem about a real-world situation in which 2 is a factor.

4 Mid-Chapter Check

Lessons 4-1 through 4-3

Write an addition and a multiplication sentence for each model. (Lesson 4-1)

1. 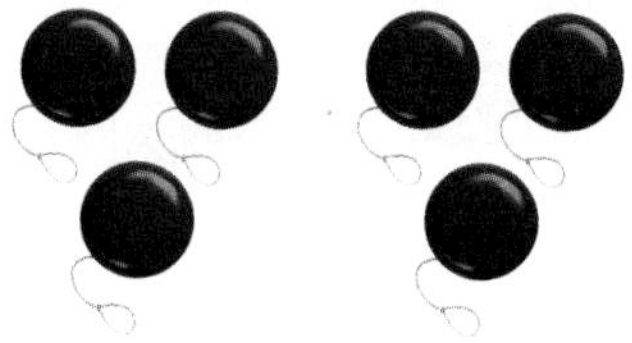

2. 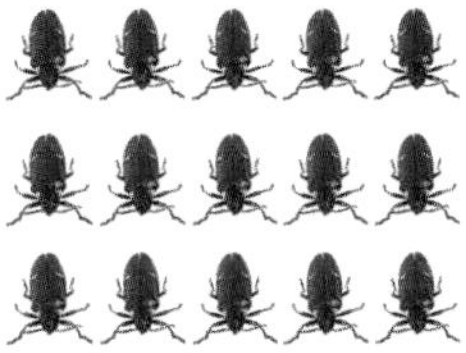

Multiply. Use repeated addition. (Lesson 4-1)

3. 3×3

4. 4×2

5. Mallory has 3 bags of shells. Each bag has 4 shells. How many shells are there in all? (Lesson 4-1)

6. **STANDARDS PRACTICE** The figure below is a model for which multiplication sentence? (Lesson 4-1)

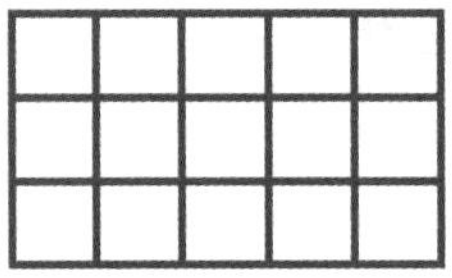

A $4 \times 5 = 20$

B $3 \times 5 = 15$

C $4 \times 5 = 9$

D $5 \times 3 = 8$

Algebra Find each missing number. (Lesson 4-2)

7. $9 \times 2 = 18$
$2 \times \square = 18$

8. $3 \times 7 = 21$
$7 \times \square = 21$

Write a multiplication sentence for each array. Then multiply. (Lesson 4-2)

9. 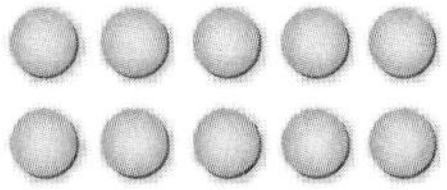

10. 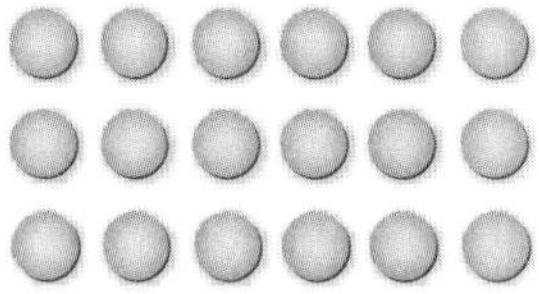

11. **STANDARDS PRACTICE** If $9 \times 4 = 36$, then what is 4×9? (Lesson 4-2)

F 28

G 32

H 36

J 40

Multiply. (Lesson 4-3)

12. $\begin{array}{r} 7 \\ \times 2 \\ \hline \end{array}$

13. $\begin{array}{r} 2 \\ \times 3 \\ \hline \end{array}$

Write a multiplication sentence for each situation. Then solve. (Lesson 4-3)

14. There are 2 elephants. How many legs in all?

15. There are 4 dogs. How many tails in all?

16. Ty is practicing his multiplication facts for 2. He has counted 9 twos. What number has Ty counted to?

17. **WRITING IN MATH** Explain how multiplication and addition are related.

4-4 Multiply by 4

MAIN IDEA

I will multiply by 4.

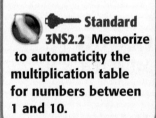

Standard 3NS2.2 Memorize to automaticity the multiplication table for numbers between 1 and 10.

GET READY to Learn

A car transport has 5 new cars. Each car has 4 wheels. How many wheels are there in all on the cars?

To multiply by 4, you can use the same strategies you used to multiply by 2.

Real-World EXAMPLE **Multiply by 4**

1 WHEELS Each car on the car transport has 4 wheels. How many wheels are there in all on the 5 new cars?

You need to find 5 groups of 4 or 5×4.

One Way: Repeated Addition

Use repeated addition to find 5×4.

$4 + 4 + 4 + 4 + 4 = 20$

Another Way: Skip Count

Count 5 jumps of 4.

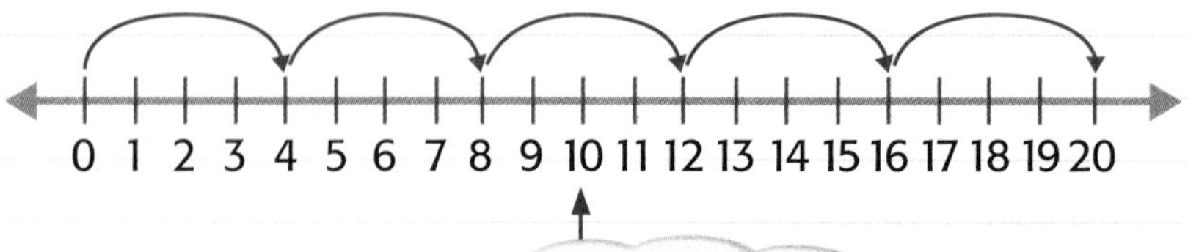

5 jumps of 4 is 20.

4, 8, 12, 16, 20

So, there are 5×4 or 20 wheels in all.

Real-World EXAMPLE Use a Number Sentence

2 **FRUIT There are 4 bunches of bananas. Each bunch has 3 bananas. How many bananas in all?**

Number of groups		Number in each group		Total
4	×	3	=	12

So, there are 12 bananas.

You can use your 2s facts to help you multiply by 4. Think about doubling the product.

Remember

To find a 4s fact, you can double a 2s fact.

Real-World EXAMPLE Double a Known Fact

3 **ORANGES A box has 4 rows of oranges. Each row has 9 oranges. How many oranges are in the box?**

You need to find 4 × 9.

4 is double of 2. So, 4 × 9 is *double* 2 × 9.

4 × 9 = 2 × 9 + 2 × 9

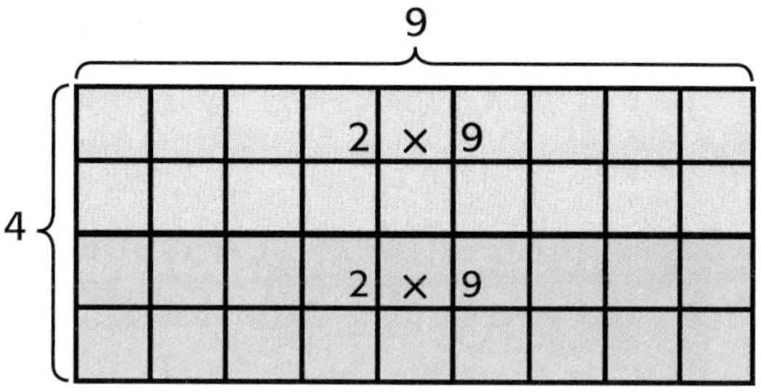

18 + 18 = 36

So, 4 × 9 = 36. There are 36 oranges in the box.

Online Personal Tutor at ca.gr3math.com

CHECK What You Know

Multiply. See Examples 1–3 (pp. 168–169)

1. 4 × 4

2. 4 × 2

3. 4 × 8

4. 6 × 4

5. 5 × 4

6. 4 × 10

7. Arleta reads 4 books. Each book has 8 chapters. How many chapters does she read in all?

8. Talk About It Explain how knowing 2 × 7 can help you find 4 × 7.

Practice and Problem Solving

EXTRA PRACTICE See page R11.

Multiply. See Examples 1–3 (pp. 168–169)

9. $\begin{array}{r} 3 \\ \times\ 4 \\ \hline \end{array}$

10. $\begin{array}{r} 4 \\ \times\ 2 \\ \hline \end{array}$

11. $\begin{array}{r} 5 \\ \times\ 4 \\ \hline \end{array}$

12. 4×6

13. 4×7

14. 5×4

15. 9×4

16. 8×4

17. 10×4

Write a multiplication sentence for each situation. Then solve. See Example 2 (p. 169)

18. Kendrick and Tyra each have an umbrella. How many umbrellas are there after 2 friends join them with their umbrellas?

19. There are 9 rows on a bus. Four children can sit in each row. If there are 48 children how many will not be able to ride the bus?

20. Write a multiplication sentence to show that 4 dimes equal 40 cents.

21. A factory packs 4 science kits in each box. They packed 7 boxes. How many kits did they pack?

H.O.T. Problems

22. OPEN ENDED Explain the strategy you would use to find 4×6. Why do you prefer this strategy?

23. FIND THE ERROR Anica and Roberta are finding 4×8. Who is correct? Explain your reasoning.

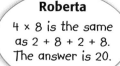

Anica
4 × 8 is the same as 2 × 8 + 2 × 8. The answer is 32.

Roberta
4 × 8 is the same as 2 + 8 + 2 + 8. The answer is 20.

24. CHALLENGE Mika bought 4 bottles of suntan lotion for \$6 each. Later the lotion went on sale for \$4 each. How many more bottles could he have bought if he waited for the sale?

25. WRITING IN ► MATH Write a real-world problem that involves multiplying by 4.

 Math Online Self-Check Quiz at ca.gr3math.com

Factor Power

Factors and Products

Get Ready!

Players: 2 players

You will need: 20 index cards, crayons, 1-inch graph paper for each player

Get Set!

Write a product of the multiplication facts you have learned so far on each card. Then shuffle.

Go!

- Player 1 turns over the top card. He or she names two factors of the product on the card.
- Player 1 then colors an array anywhere on the graph paper to match the factors.
- Player 2 checks to see if the product matches the number of squares colored in. If it is correct, Player 1 gets 1 point.
- The game continues, taking turns, until neither player can make any more arrays on their graph paper or until one player reaches 10 points after a complete round.

4-5 Problem-Solving Skill

MAIN IDEA I will decide if there is extra or missing information.

Standard 3MR1.1 **Analyze problems by** identifying relationships, **distinguishing relevant from irrelevant information,** sequencing and prioritizing information, and observing patterns. **Standard 3NS2.2 Memorize to automaticity the multiplication table for numbers between 1 and 10.**

My school's hayride will start at 6:00 P.M. There are 4 wagons that hold 9 children each. Half of the children going are girls. What is the total number of children that can ride on the 4 wagons?

Understand

What facts do you know?

- The hayride starts at 6:00 P.M.
- There are 4 wagons that hold 9 children.
- Half of the children are girls.

What do you need to find?

- Find the number of children that can ride on the 4 wagons.

Plan

Decide what facts are important to solve the question.

- the number of wagons
- the number of children each wagon holds

Extra Information

- The time of the hayride
- Half of the children are girls.

Solve

To find the total number, multiply the number of wagons by the number of children each wagon holds.

$4 \times 9 = \blacksquare$

$4 \times 9 = 36$

So, 36 children can ride on the hay wagons.

Check

Look back at the problem. Since $9 + 9 + 9 + 9 = 36$, you know the answer is correct.

ANALYZE the Skill

Refer to the problem on the previous page.

1. How did you know what information was important and what was not?

2. Suppose there are 36 children but only 3 wagons. How many children will ride on each wagon?

3. Look back to your answer for Exercise 2. How do you know that the answer is correct?

4. Draw an array to verify that your answer to Exercise 3 is correct.

PRACTICE the Skill

EXTRA PRACTICE
See page R12.

Solve. If there is missing information, tell what facts you need to solve the problem.

5. Below is a list of the items that Bert bought at a store. How much change did he get back?

Item	Cost
Pencils	$2.00
Paper	$1.00
Binder	$3.00

6. Nina is 58 inches tall. Her sister is in the first grade and is 48 inches tall. How much taller is Nina than her sister?

7. Mrs. Friedman has 2 boxes of chalk. She buys 4 more boxes with 10 pieces each. She paid $2.00 per box. How much does she spend?

8. Ten of Eduardo's baseball cards are All Star cards. His friend has twice as many cards. How many cards does Eduardo's friend have?

9. Every day for 5 days, the third grade class had 4 chicks hatch. Nine of the chicks were yellow, and the rest were brown. How many chicks hatched in all?

10. The graph below shows the number of cats and dogs at an animal shelter. How much would it cost to adopt 1 cat and 1 dog if a cat costs $35 and a dog costs $40?

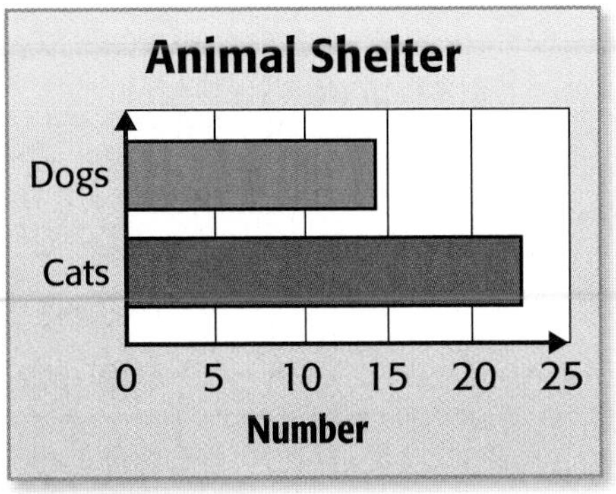

11. **WRITING IN ▶MATH** Rewrite Exercise 5 so it has enough information to solve. Then solve it.

4-6 Multiply by 5

MAIN IDEA

I will multiply by 5.

Standard 3NS2.2 Memorize to automaticity the multiplication table for numbers between 1 and 10.

GET READY to Learn

A watermelon patch has 5 rows of watermelons. Each row has 6 watermelons. How many watermelons are in the patch?

There is more than one way to multiply by 5.

Real-World EXAMPLE Multiply by 5

1 **WATERMELONS There are 5 rows and each row has 6 watermelons. How many watermelons are in the farmer's watermelon patch?**

You need to find 5×6.

One Way: Draw a Picture	**Another Way:** Use an Array
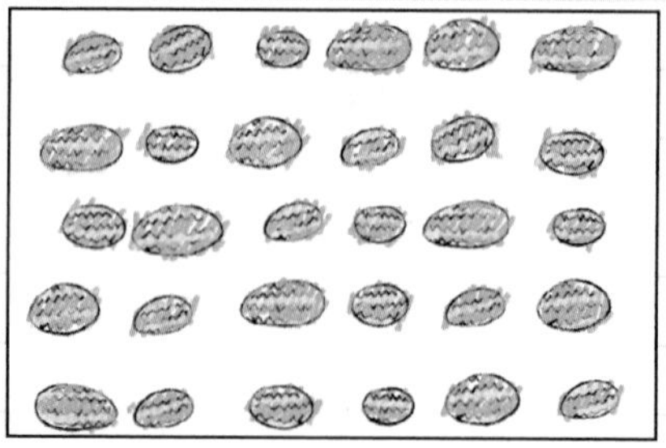	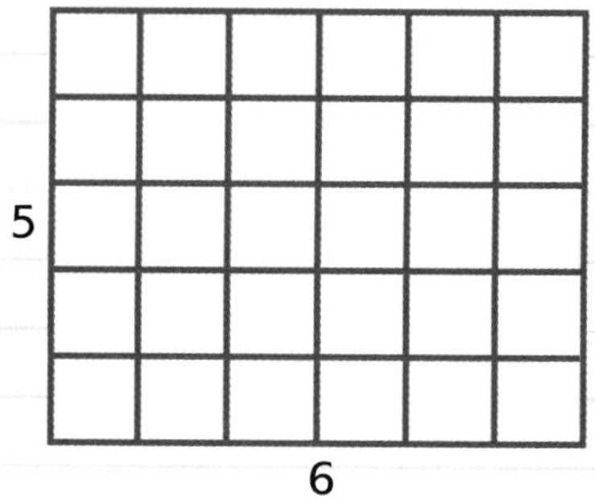
Use repeated addition. $6 + 6 + 6 + 6 + 6 = 30$ So, $5 \times 6 = 30$ watermelons.	5 rows of $6 = 5 \times 6$ or 30

You can also use skip counting to multiply by 5.

Remember

Patterns can help you multiply by five.

$5 \times 0 = \mathbf{0}$

$5 \times 1 = \mathbf{5}$

$5 \times 2 = \mathbf{10}$

$5 \times 3 = \mathbf{15}$

Notice the patterns in the products. All of the products end in 5 or 0.

Real-World EXAMPLE — Skip Count

2 **FINGERS There are 3 hands. Each hand has 5 fingers. How many fingers altogether?**

You need to find 3 groups of 5 or 3×5.

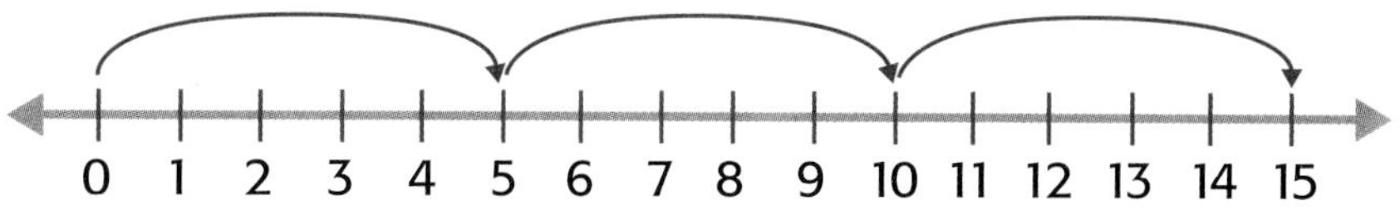

So, $3 \times 5 = 15$ fingers.

Real-World EXAMPLE — Use a Number Sentence

3 **NICKELS Jorge has 7 nickels. How much money does he have?**

You know that a nickel is 5¢. Use a multiplication sentence to find 7 × 5¢.

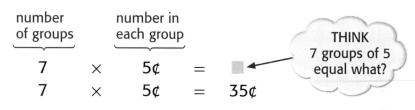

number of groups		number in each group		
7	×	5¢	=	■
7	×	5¢	=	35¢

THINK 7 groups of 5 equal what?

Online Personal Tutor at ca.gr3math.com

CHECK What You Know

Multiply. Draw a picture or use an array. See Examples 1–3 (pp. 174–175)

1. 5×4 **2.** 5×3 **3.** 6×5

Multiply. See Examples 1–3 (pp. 174–175)

4. 5×8 **5.** 5×7 **6.** 5×5

7. Kai, Lakita, and Maxwell have a box of pretzels. If each gets 5 pretzels, how many pretzels are in the box? Explain.

8. Talk About It Explain why the 5s facts might be easier to remember than most sets of facts.

Practice and Problem Solving

EXTRA PRACTICE
See page R12.

Multiply. See Examples 1–3 (pp. 174–175)

9. $\begin{array}{r} 5 \\ \times 2 \\ \hline \end{array}$

10. $\begin{array}{r} 3 \\ \times 5 \\ \hline \end{array}$

11. $\begin{array}{r} 5 \\ \times 6 \\ \hline \end{array}$

12. 7×5

13. 8×5

14. 5×10

15. 5×5

16. 5×3

17. 4×5

18. A pan of corn bread is cut into 5 rows with 4 pieces in each row. How many pieces are there in all?

19. A sunflower costs $6. Evelyn wants to buy 4. Does she have enough if she has four $5 bills? Explain.

20. Bernardo's dad paid for his new roller blades with seven $5 bills. If his dad's change was $2, how much did his roller blades cost?

21. There are 82 members in a marching band. Part of the band divides into 5 groups of 9. How many members are not divided into a group?

Real-World PROBLEM SOLVING

Data File The Golden Gate Bridge is a popular sight in San Francisco.

Golden Gate Bridge

22. The toll to travel across the bridge is $5. How much would you spend if you had to travel across the bridge 4 times a day?

23. If you buy a special pass, you can save $1 on the toll. Write a multiplication sentence to find how much you save in 5 days.

H.O.T. Problems

24. WHICH ONE DOESN'T BELONG? Identify the strategy that will not help you find the product of 5×6.

skip counting | rounding | make an array | draw a picture

25. WRITING IN MATH Can the ones-digit in the product ever end in 2 when you are multiplying by 5? Explain.

Facts Practice

Multiply.

1. $\begin{array}{r} 2 \\ \times\ 3 \\ \hline \end{array}$

2. $\begin{array}{r} 2 \\ \times\ 10 \\ \hline \end{array}$

3. $\begin{array}{r} 4 \\ \times\ 4 \\ \hline \end{array}$

4. $\begin{array}{r} 2 \\ \times\ 9 \\ \hline \end{array}$

5. $\begin{array}{r} 5 \\ \times\ 8 \\ \hline \end{array}$

6. $\begin{array}{r} 4 \\ \times\ 3 \\ \hline \end{array}$

7. $\begin{array}{r} 5 \\ \times\ 2 \\ \hline \end{array}$

8. $\begin{array}{r} 5 \\ \times\ 5 \\ \hline \end{array}$

9. $\begin{array}{r} 2 \\ \times\ 6 \\ \hline \end{array}$

10. $\begin{array}{r} 4 \\ \times\ 8 \\ \hline \end{array}$

11. $\begin{array}{r} 4 \\ \times\ 2 \\ \hline \end{array}$

12. $\begin{array}{r} 2 \\ \times\ 2 \\ \hline \end{array}$

13. $\begin{array}{r} 5 \\ \times\ 7 \\ \hline \end{array}$

14. $\begin{array}{r} 4 \\ \times\ 8 \\ \hline \end{array}$

15. $\begin{array}{r} 2 \\ \times\ 7 \\ \hline \end{array}$

16. $\begin{array}{r} 2 \\ \times\ 3 \\ \hline \end{array}$

17. $\begin{array}{r} 5 \\ \times\ 6 \\ \hline \end{array}$

18. $\begin{array}{r} 2 \\ \times\ 4 \\ \hline \end{array}$

19. $\begin{array}{r} 5 \\ \times\ 4 \\ \hline \end{array}$

20. $\begin{array}{r} 4 \\ \times\ 7 \\ \hline \end{array}$

21. 2×5

22. 5×3

23. 5×10

24. 4×9

25. 2×8

26. 4×6

27. 2×5

28. 4×7

29. 5×6

30. 5×9

31. 4×5

32. 5×4

33. 7×5

34. 4×2

35. 9×2

36. 6×5

4-7 Multiply by 10

GET READY to Learn

Walking on the beach, Oliver saw footprints. He counted 10 toes on each of the 3 sets of footprints. How many toes did he count in all?

MAIN IDEA

I will multiply by 10.

Standard 3NS2.2 Memorize to automaticity the multiplication table for numbers between 1 and 10.

To solve the problem, you need to multiply by 10.

Real-World EXAMPLE — Skip Count

1 TOES How many toes did Oliver count in all?

Find 3 × 10.

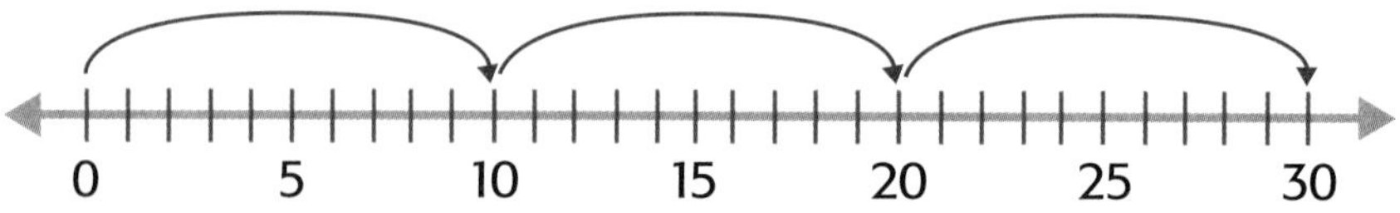

Count 3 jumps of 10. So, 3 × 10 = 30 toes.

When one of the factors in a multiplication problem is an even number, you can double a known fact.

Real-World EXAMPLE — Double a Known Fact

2 MONEY Sareeta found 9 dimes under her bed while cleaning. How much money did Sareeta find?

You need to find 9 × 10¢. 10 is the double of 5. So, 9 × 10¢ is *double* 9 × 5¢.

9 × 10¢ = 9 × 5¢ + 9 × 5¢

= 45¢ + 45¢

= 90¢

So, 9 × 10¢ = 90¢.

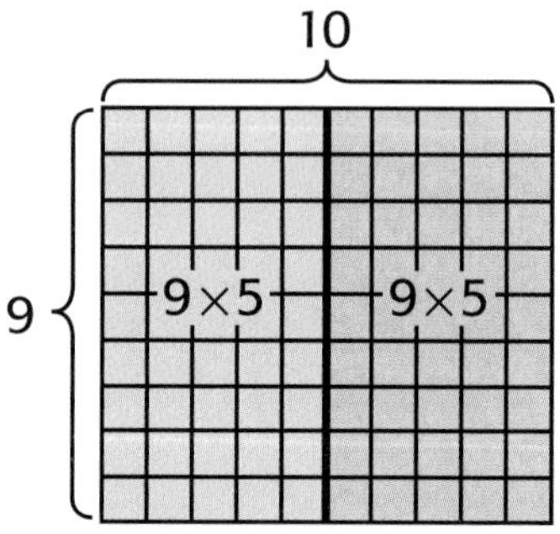

Real-World EXAMPLE Use a Number Sentence

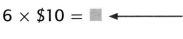

3 SCOUTS A Cub Scout troop is having a fundraiser. They sold coupon books for $10. How much money did Javier raise?

Name	Money Raised							Total
Jared	✪	✪	✪	✪	✪	✪	✪	$70
Bartolo	✪	✪	✪	✪				$40
Javier	✪	✪	✪	✪	✪	✪		■

Key ✪ = $10

To solve the problem, you need to multiply 6 by $10.

6 × $10 = ■ ← THINK How much is six $10 bills?

6 × $10 = $60

So, Javier raised $60.

Check

The model shows that 6 × 10 = 60.

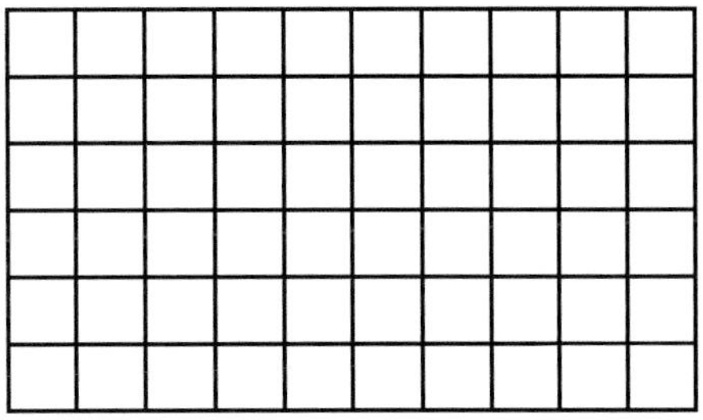

Remember

Patterns can help you multiply by 10.

10 × 1 = 10
10 × 2 = 20
10 × 3 = 30
10 × 4 = 40
10 × 5 = 50

Online **Personal Tutor at** ca.gr3math.com

CHECK What You Know

Multiply. **See Examples 1–3 (pp. 178–179)**

1. 10 × 2

2. 10 × 4

3. 10 × 7

4. 5 × 10

5. 3 × 10

6. 10 × 10

7. Mina bought a dress for $50. How many $10 bills will she need to pay for the dress?

8. Talk About It How can knowing the 5s facts help you with your 10s facts?

Practice and Problem Solving

EXTRA PRACTICE See page R12.

Multiply. See Examples 1–3 (pp. 178–179)

9. $\begin{array}{r} 10 \\ \times\ 2 \\ \hline \end{array}$

10. $\begin{array}{r} 10 \\ \times\ 6 \\ \hline \end{array}$

11. $\begin{array}{r} 10 \\ \times\ 5 \\ \hline \end{array}$

12. 10×3

13. 10×9

14. 10×10

15. 4×10

16. 10×5

17. 10×6

18. There are 10 cars. Each has 4 wheels. How many wheels are there altogether?

19. Ines has 6 packs of whistles. There are 10 whistles in each pack. How many whistles does she have altogether?

20. Measurement There are 3 feet in one yard. How many feet are in 10 yards?

21. There are 5 giraffes and 10 monkeys. How many legs are there altogether?

For Exercises 22–24, use the bar graph.

22. How much money do the children have altogether?

23. Write two expressions comparing the amount of money that Josefina has with the amount Hakeem has.

24. What is the difference in the least amount of money and the most?

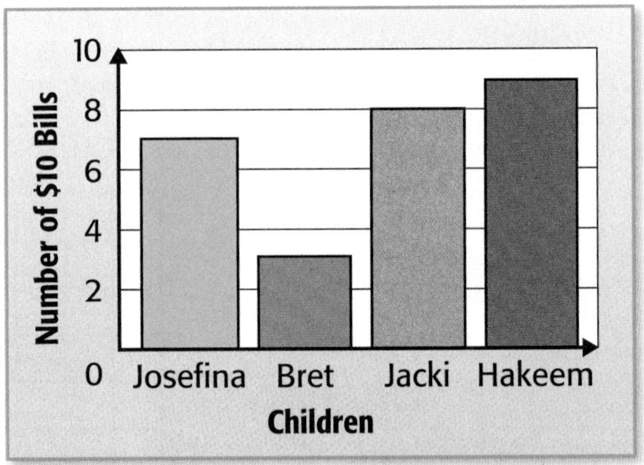

Real-World PROBLEM SOLVING

Art Some of the world's largest glass sculptures are found in the United States. Use each expression to find the length of each sculpture.

25. Fiori di Como: 5 less than 10×7.

26. Chihuly Tower: 5 more than 5×10.

27. Cobalt Blue Chandelier: 9 more than 2×10.

28. River Blue: 4 more than 10×1.

Worlds's Largest Glass Sculpture

Sculpture Name	Length (feet)
Fiori di Como, NV	
Chihuly Tower, OK	
Cobalt Blue Chandelier, WA	
River Blue, CT	

Source: *Book of World Records*

Math Online **Extra Examples at** ca.gr3math.com

H.O.T. Problems

29. WHICH ONE DOESN'T BELONG? Identify the pair of expressions that is false.

$2 \times 5 = 10 \times 1$	$4 \times 3 = 6 \times 2$	$5 \times 4 = 2 \times 10$	$10 \times 0 = 5 \times 1$

30. WRITING IN ▶MATH Explain how you know that a multiplication fact with a product of 25 cannot be a 10s fact.

Standards Practice

31 Which of the following is used to find out how many legs are on 6 chairs? **(Lesson 4-6)**

A 4×6 **C** $4 + 6$

B $4 \div 6$ **D** $6 - 4$

32 What number makes this number sentence true? **(Lesson 4-7)**

$$12 + 8 = \square \times 2$$

F 5 **H** 9

G 8 **J** 10

Spiral Review

Multiply. **(Lesson 4-6)**

33. 5×9 **34.** 7×5 **35.** 5×4

36. An adult ticket to the zoo is \$6. A child's ticket is \$4. How much would tickets cost for 2 adults and one child? **(Lesson 4-5)**

Write a multiplication sentence for each array. **(Lesson 4-2)**

37.

38.

Subtract. **(Lesson 3-8)**

39. $2{,}006 - 1998$ **40.** $5{,}002 - 2089$ **41.** $2300 - 572$

Problem Solving in Science

LOTS OF ARMS AND LEGS

Have you ever wondered why a cheetah has 4 legs instead of 3? Or why an octopus has 8 arms instead of 4? The number of arms or legs an animal has helps it hunt for food and escape from predators.

A cheetah has 4 legs that balance its body. Its legs help it run as fast as 70 miles per hour. An octopus has an unprotected body and no claws or teeth. So, 8 arms are more helpful to an octopus than only 4 or 6 arms.

ANIMAL	NUMBER OF LEGS OR ARMS
Sugar star (Sea star)	16
Ant	6
Ostrich	2
Hermit crab	10
Sea turtle	4

Standard 3AF1.1 Represent relationships of quantities in the form of mathematical expressions, equations, or inequalities.

Real-World Math

Imagine that your class is at the zoo on a field trip. Use the information on page 182 to answer each question. Write a multiplication sentence to solve. Then write an addition sentence to check.

1. Three ants are on a park bench. How many legs are there in all?
2. You see 7 ostriches. How many legs do you see altogether?
3. If you see a pack of 3 cheetahs, how many legs are there in all?
4. If there are 4 octopuses, how many octopus arms are there total?
5. You count 30 sugar star arms in the aquarium. How many sugar stars are there? Explain.
6. There are 3 sea turtles and 2 sugar stars in another aquarium. How many legs are there in all?
7. How many legs in all do 6 hermit crabs have?

Did You Know?

An octopus has 240 suction cups on each of its 8 arms.

4-8 Problem-Solving Investigation

MAIN IDEA I will choose the best strategy to solve a problem.

Standard 3MR1.1 Analyze problems by identifying relationships, distinguishing relevant and irrelevant information, sequencing and prioritizing information, and observing patterns. **Standard 3NS2.2** Memorize to automaticity the multiplication table for numbers between 1 and 10.

P.S.I. TEAM +

DENZELL: Our third grade class will make 6 holiday baskets to give away. We will fill each basket with 7 food items.

YOUR MISSION: Find how many items are needed to fill the baskets.

Understand	You know the class will make 6 baskets with 7 items each. Find out the total number of food items needed.
Plan	You can use the *draw a picture* strategy to solve this math problem.
Solve	Draw a picture to represents the situation. 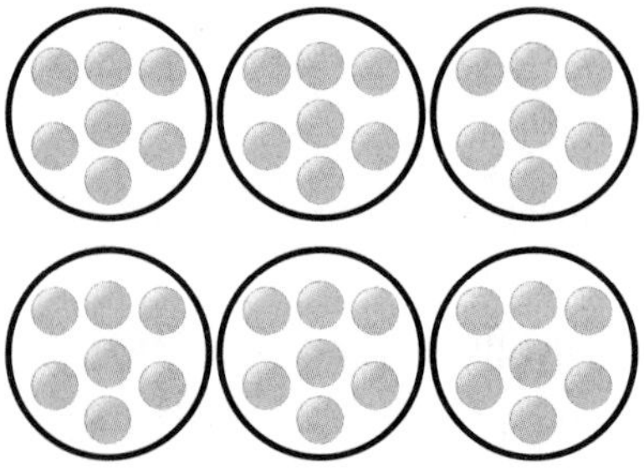 The picture shows that $6 \times 7 = 42$. So, the third grade class needs 42 food items to fill the baskets.
Check	Look back at the problem. Check by using repeated addition. $7 + 7 + 7 + 7 + 7 + 7 = 42$. So you know the answer is correct and reasonable.

Mixed Problem Solving

EXTRA PRACTICE
See page R13.

Use any strategy shown below to solve. Tell what strategy you used.

PROBLEM-SOLVING STRATEGIES
- Act it out.
- Draw a picture.
- Look for a pattern.

1. At a space museum, there are 15 large rockets, 8 space capsules, and 12 small rockets. How many rockets are there altogether?

2. George paid $5 for a movie. Is it reasonable to say he spent more money on the food than he did on the movie? Explain.

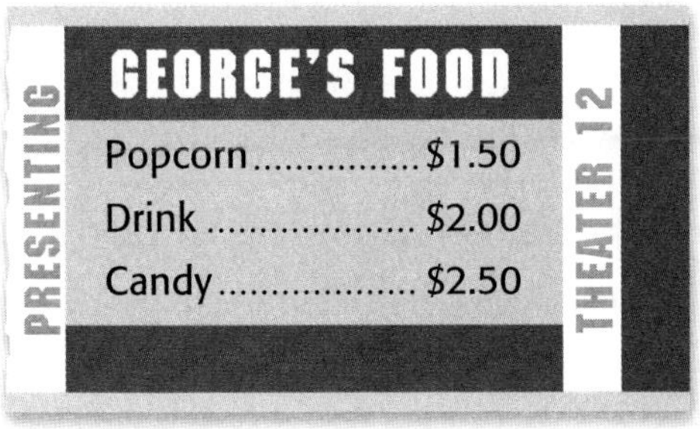
PRESENTING
GEORGE'S FOOD
Popcorn $1.50
Drink $2.00
Candy $2.50
THEATER 12

3. Jonas sells angelfish. He has 6 tanks, and each tank has 5 fish. After he sold some, he had 22 fish left. How many did he sell? How much did he make if he sold each fish for $5?

4. Mr. Trevino spent $63 on 7 berry bushes. Each bush will give 10 pints of berries. He sells each pint for $2. Find the difference in the amount of money he spent and what he makes from selling the berries?

5. Sally has a balance scale. On one side, she put 6 books. On the other side, she put 2 books and her baseball glove. The sides balanced. If each book weighs 3 ounces, how much does her glove weigh?

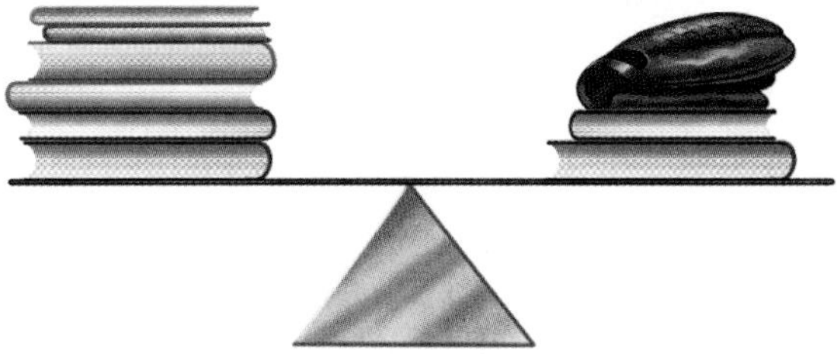

6. Grandmother picked 8 pears. Then, she picked 4 times as many apples. What is the difference in the number of apples and pears picked?

7. Two water toys cost $4 each. If you paid with a $10 bill, how much change would you receive?

8. Suki collected insects while on a nature hike. She made a pictograph to show which insects she collected. What is the total number of insects she collected?

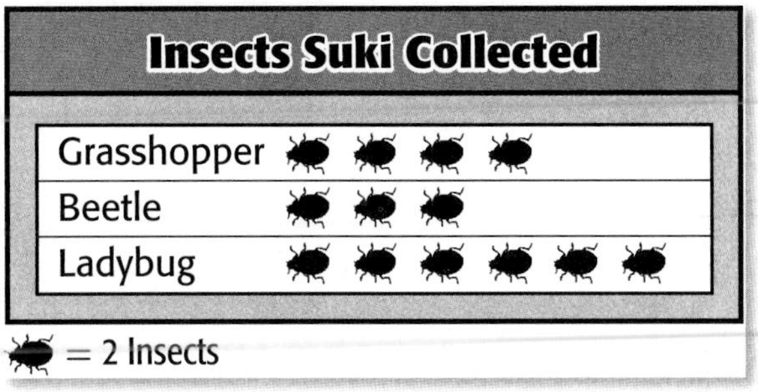
Insects Suki Collected
Grasshopper
Beetle
Ladybug
= 2 Insects

9. **WRITING IN MATH** Refer to Exercise 8. Explain how multiplication is used to find the answer.

4-9 Multiply by 0 and 1

MAIN IDEA

I will multiply by 0 and 1.

Standard 3NS2.6 Understand the special properties of 0 and 1 in multiplication and division.

New Vocabulary

Zero Property of Multiplication

Identity Property of Multiplication

GET READY to Learn

There are 4 daisies in 1 flower pot. How many daisies are there in all?

There are special properties for multiplying by 1 and 0.

KEY CONCEPT — Multiplication Properties

Words The **Identity Property of Multiplication** says that when any number is multiplied by 1, the product is that number.

Example $1 \times 4 = 4$

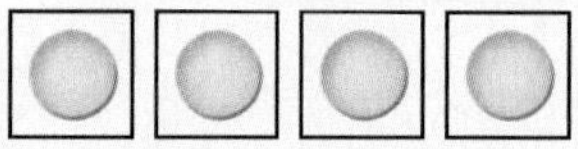

One group of 4 is 4.

Words The **Zero Property of Multiplication** says that when you multiply a number by 0, the product is zero.

Example $3 \times 0 = 0$

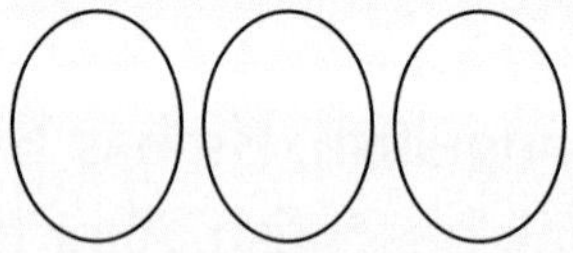

Three groups of 0 are 0.

EXAMPLE Use Properties to Multiply

1 Find 6×1. Tell what property you used.

$6 \times 1 = 6$

The product is 6. Identity Property of Multiplication.

Online **Personal Tutor at** ca.gr3math.com

CHECK What You Know

Multiply. See Example 1 (p. 186)

1. 6×0
2. 1×7
3. 5×0
4. 8×1
5. There is 1 student sitting at each of the 9 tables in the cafeteria. How many students are there altogether?
6. **Talk About It** If 100 is multiplied by 0, what will be the product? Explain your reasoning.

Practice and Problem Solving

EXTRA PRACTICE See page R13.

Multiply. See Example 1 (p. 186)

7. 7×1
8. 5×0
9. 10×1
10. 10×0
11. 3×1
12. 1×0
13. 4×0
14. 1×1
15. 8×0
16. 1×2
17. 0×1
18. 4×1
19. 9×0
20. 9×1
21. 0×2
22. 1×5

Write a multiplication sentence for each situation.

23. How many pouches does 1 kangaroo have?
24. How many legs do 8 snakes have?
25. In a fantasy story, a pirate found 3 empty treasure chests with no jewels. How many jewels were there?
26. There is only one book on the shelf. It has 90 pages. How many pages are there altogether?
27. Thomas saw a group of 8 lizards. Each lizard had one spot on its back. How many spots were there total?
28. How many legs do 15 fish have?

Algebra Find each missing number.

29. $\blacksquare \times 7 = 7$
30. $\blacksquare \times 8 = 0$
31. $6 \times \blacksquare = 0$
32. $1 \times \blacksquare = 0$
33. $\blacksquare \times 5 = 5$
34. $10 \times 0 = \blacksquare$
35. $9 \times \blacksquare = 9$
36. $\blacksquare \times 2 = 2$

H.O.T. Problems

37. OPEN ENDED Write a problem using one of the multiplication properties that you have just learned. Explain how to find the answer.

CHALLENGE Find the missing number.

38. $2{,}684 \times$ ■ $= 2{,}684$ **39.** $1{,}039 \times 1 =$ ■ **40.** $27 \times$ ■ $= 0$

41. **WRITING IN ▸MATH** Explain the Zero Property of Multiplication.

Standards Practice

42 Mrs. Smyth reads aloud to her class for 10 minutes each day. Which number sentence tells how to find the number of minutes she reads in a 5-day week? **(Lesson 4-8)**

A $10 + 5$

B 10×5

C $10 - 5$

D $10 \div 5$

43 What number can be multiplied by 3,859 to give the product 3,859? **(Lesson 4-9)**

F 0

G 1

H 2

J 10

Spiral Review

44. Elliott collected about 9 shells while at the beach every day. About how many shells did he collect over his 10-day vacation? **(Lesson 4-8)**

A survey was taken of people's favorite water activity. Use the data to answer the questions. Write a multiplication sentence. Then solve. **(Lesson 4-7)**

Favorite Water Activity

Ski	√√√√
Surf	√√
Swim	√√√√√√√√

√ = 10 votes

45. How many people enjoy surfing?

46. How many people prefer swimming?

Algebra Compare. Use >, <, or =. **(Lessons 4-3 and 4-4)**

47. 2×7 ■ 4×2 **48.** 8×5 ■ 9×2 **49.** 10×2 ■ 4×5

Facts Practice

Multiply.

1. 4×6

2. 10×5

3. 0×9

4. 2×9

5. 4×8

6. 2×3

7. 10×8

8. 0×6

9. 1×9

10. 5×5

11. 4×0

12. 2×7

13. 10×0

14. 5×3

15. 1×6

16. 2×10

17. 4×5

18. 2×2

19. 1×1

20. 5×8

21. 4×3

22. 10×1

23. 0×3

24. 4×9

25. 0×8

26. 10×7

27. 1×4

28. 2×6

29. 5×10

30. 0×7

31. 1×0

32. 10×6

33. 4×7

34. 5×6

35. 10×3

36. 2×0

37. 10×10

38. 0×10

39. 1×5

40. 0×4

CHAPTER 4

Study Guide and Review

FOLDABLES™ Study Organizer GET READY to Study

Be sure the following Key Vocabulary words and Key Concepts are written in your Foldable.

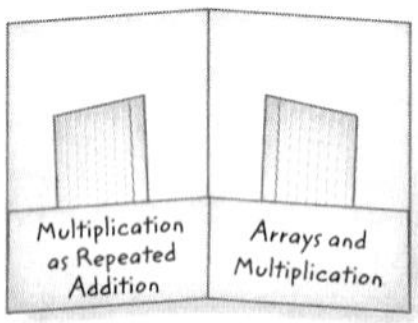

BIG Ideas

- **Use Repeated Addition to Multiply**
  3 equal groups of 5 counters **(p. 157)**

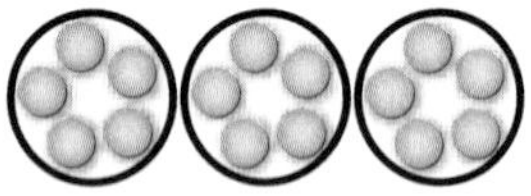

$5 + 5 + 5 = 15$

- **Use an Array to Multiply**
  2 rows of 5 **(p. 160)**

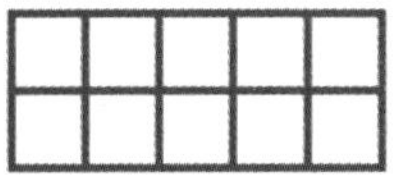

$2 \times 5 = 10$

- The **Commutative Property of Multiplication** states that the order in which numbers are multiplied does not change the product. **(p. 161)**

$3 \times 2 = 6 \qquad 2 \times 3 = 6$

- **Zero Property of Multiplication** **(p. 186)**

$2 \times 0 = 0$

- **Identity Property of Multiplication** **(p. 186)**

$1 \times 2 = 2$

Key Vocabulary

array **(p. 160)**
Commutative Property of Multiplication **(p. 161)**
factor **(p. 157)**
multiply **(p. 157)**
product **(p. 157)**

Vocabulary Check

Choose the vocabulary word that completes each sentence.

1. In $3 \times 5 = 15$, the number 15 is the ___?___.

2. The ___?___ Property of Multiplication states that the order in which numbers are multiplied does not change the product.

3. In $3 \times 5 = 15$, the number 3 is a ___?___.

4. To ___?___ is to put equal groups together.

5. A(n) ___?___ is an arrangement of equal rows and columns.

Lesson-by-Lesson Review

4-1 Multiplication as Repeated Addition (pp. 157–159)

Example 1
Write an addition sentence and a multiplication sentence to show 3 groups of 6.

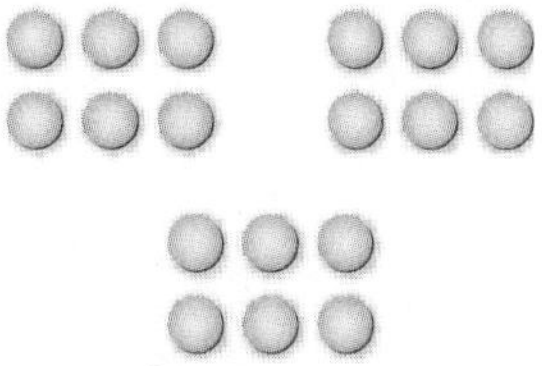

$6 + 6 + 6 = 18$

number of groups		number in each group		total
3	×	6	=	18

So, 3 equal groups of 6 are 18.

Write an addition and a multiplication sentence for each model.

6. 

7. 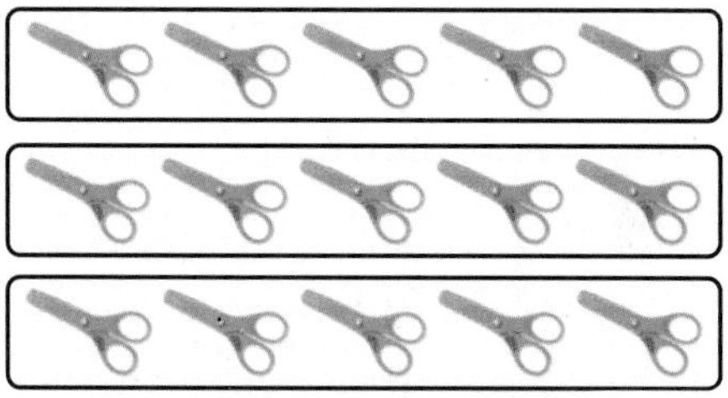

8. 

4-2 Arrays and Multiplication (pp. 160–163)

Example 2
There are 4 rows of 3 muffins. How many muffins altogether?

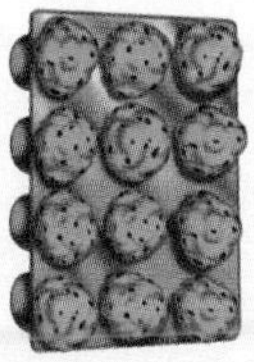

You can use addition or multiplication.

Add: $3 + 3 + 3 + 3 = 12$

Multiply: $4 \times 3 = 12$

So, 4 equal groups of 3 is 12.

Write a multiplication sentence for each array. Then multiply.

9. 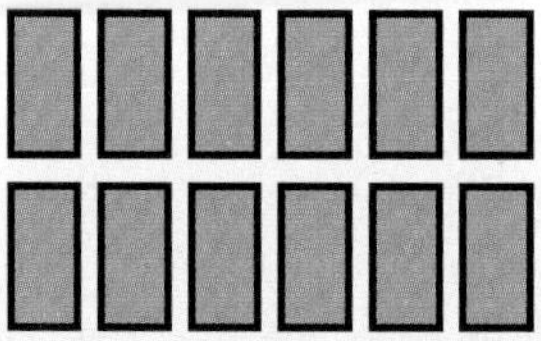

10. 

11. 

4-3 Multiply by 2 (pp. 164–166)

Example 3
How many wings are there if there are 5 butterflies?

A butterfly has 2 wings. So, you need to find 5 groups of 2 or 5×2.

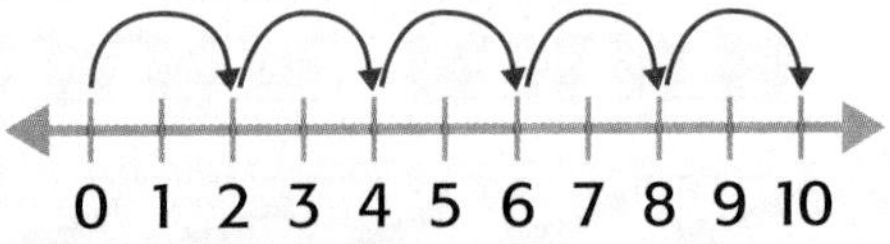

Count 5 jumps of 2

$2 + 2 + 2 + 2 + 2 = 10$

So, 5 groups of $2 = 10$.

Multiply.

12. $\begin{array}{r} 2 \\ \times 3 \\ \hline \end{array}$ **13.** $\begin{array}{r} 7 \\ \times 2 \\ \hline \end{array}$ **14.** $\begin{array}{r} 2 \\ \times 4 \\ \hline \end{array}$

Write a multiplication sentence for each situation. Then solve.

15. There are 4 birds and each has 2 legs. How many legs in all?

16. There are 7 dogs. How many ears in all?

17. Algebra Compare 5 + 3 ■ 2 × 3. Use >, <, or =.

4-4 Multiply by 4 (pp. 168–170)

Example 4
How many legs are there altogether on 6 cats?

Cats have 4 legs. So, you need to find 6 groups of 4 or 6×4.

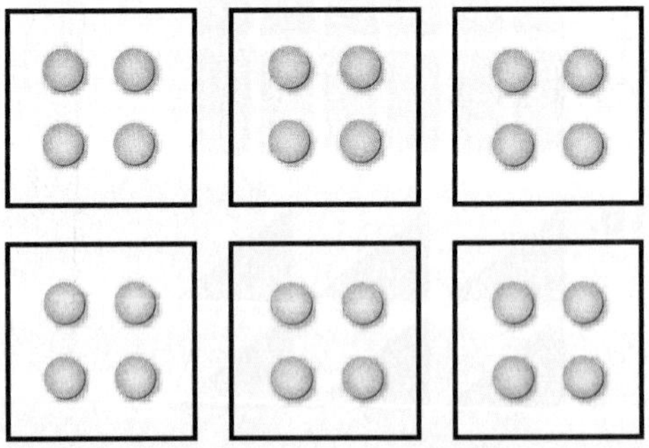

$4 + 4 + 4 + 4 + 4 + 4 = 24$

So, there are 6×4 or 24 legs.

Multiply.

18. 3×4 **19.** 4×6

20. Algebra Copy and complete the table.

Rule: Multiply by 4				
1	■	5	■	9
4	12	■	28	■

21. Write a multiplication sentence to show that 4 nickels equal 20 cents.

22. The bread factory packs 4 buns in each bag. If they packed 4 bags, how many buns did they pack?

4-5 Problem-Solving Skill: Extra or Missing Information (pp. 172–173)

Example 5
A troop leader drives 5 miles to and from the troop meeting. He leaves at 4 P.M. and gets to the meeting at 4:30 P.M. How many miles does he drive there and back?

Decide what facts are important.

- He drives 5 miles to the meeting.
- He drives 5 miles from the meeting.

Multiply to solve.

$2 \times 5 = 10$

So, he travels a total of 10 miles.

Solve. If there is missing information, tell what facts you need to solve the problem.

23. The troop ordered pizza. Each pizza was cut into 8 slices. They ate all 32 slices. How many pizzas did they order?

24. The troop left the pizza parlor at 6 P.M. Their van has 4 rows and each row holds 3 people. How many people can the van hold altogether?

4-6 Multiply by 5 (pp. 174–176)

Example 6
There are 5 rows of cars. Six cars are in each row. How many cars in all?

You need to find 5×6. Use an array.

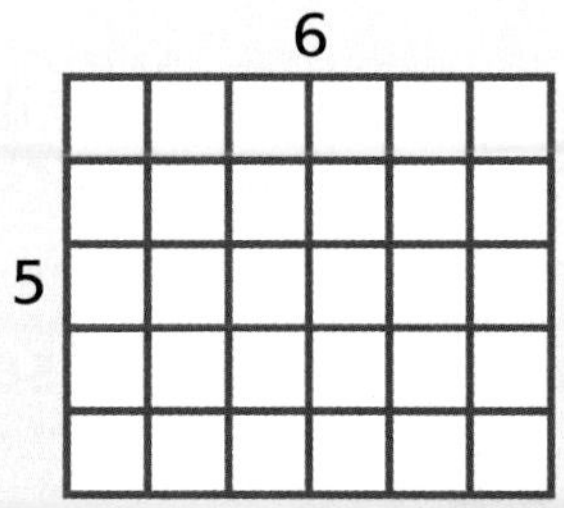

5 rows of 6 = 5×6 or 30 cars.
So, $5 \times 6 = 30$
There are 30 cars in all.

Multiply.

25. $\begin{array}{r} 5 \\ \times\ 3 \\ \hline \end{array}$

26. $\begin{array}{r} 7 \\ \times\ 5 \\ \hline \end{array}$

Algebra Find each missing number.

27. $5 \times ■ = 30$

28. $■ \times 3 = 15$

29. $9 \times ■ = 45$

30. $■ \times 5 = 25$

31. Marlena's mom paid for her new school uniform with ten $5 bills. If her mom's change was $3, how much did her uniform cost?

4-7 Multiply by 10 (pp. 178–181)

Example 7
Find 7 × 10.

7 × 10 is double 7 × 5.

$7 \times 10 = 7 \times 5 + 7 \times 5$

$= 35 + 35 = 70$

So, 7 × 10 = 70.

Multiply.

32. 10 × 3 **33.** 6 × 10

34. 10 × 5 **35.** 4 × 10

36. A book costs $10. Harvey wants to buy 6 books. Will he have enough money with five $10 bills? Explain.

4-8 Problem-Solving Strategies: Choose a Strategy (pp. 184–185)

Example 8

Bert has $25. Does he have enough to buy 6 toys for $4.95 each?

Estimate. Round $4.95 to $5.
$5 × 6 = $30

Since $25 < $30, he does not have enough money to buy the toys.

Solve.

37. A student buys a backpack for $18.67, a skateboard for $37.22, and a visor for $13.95. Estimate the cost of his purchases.

38. School lunches cost $2.75. Is $5 enough for two lunches? Explain.

4-9 Multiplying by 0 and 1 (pp. 186–188)

Example 9
Find 3 × 0.

When you multiply a number by 0, the product is 0. 3 × 0 = 0

Example 10
Find 1 × 5.

A number multiplied by 1 is that number. 1 × 5 = 5

Multiply.

39. $\begin{array}{r} 8 \\ \times 1 \\ \hline \end{array}$ **40.** $\begin{array}{r} 0 \\ \times 5 \\ \hline \end{array}$ **41.** $\begin{array}{r} 7 \\ \times 0 \\ \hline \end{array}$

Write a multiplication sentence for the situation.

42. Jade practices her violin for 1 hour, 5 days a week. How many hours does she practice?

Chapter 4 Chapter Test

For Exercises 1 and 2, tell whether each statement is *true* or *false*.

1. The Commutative Property of Multiplication says that the order in which numbers are multiplied changes the product.

2. When you multiply by a 5, you will always have either 5 or 0 in the ones place.

Write two multiplication sentences for each array.

3. 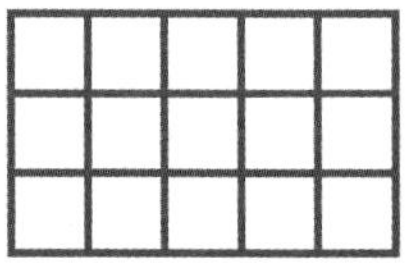

4. 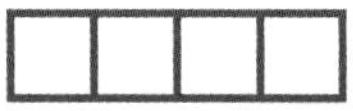

Multiply.

5. 3×2 **6.** 5×4

7. 2×6 **8.** 4×8

9. The movie theater had 6 rows. Each row had 10 people sitting in it. How many people were in the theater?

Algebra Find each missing number.

10. $5 \times ■ = 35$ **11.** $■ \times 8 = 40$

12. **STANDARDS PRACTICE** Which of the following is used to find out how many toes are on 7 people?

A 10×7 **C** $10 + 7$

B $10 \div 7$ **D** $10 - 7$

Multiply.

13. 6×5 **14.** 3×10

15. 7×5 **16.** 10×9

17. 9×1 **18.** 6×0

Solve. If there is missing information, tell what facts you need to solve.

19. Morgan buys packages of bookmarks. Each package has 30 bookmarks and cost $1.89. How many bookmarks did she get?

20. Each playground slide has 7 steps. If the playground has 3 slides, how many steps is that altogether?

21. **STANDARDS PRACTICE** What number can be multiplied by 9,250 to give the answer 9,250?

F 0 **H** 2

G 1 **J** 10

22. **WRITING IN ►MATH** Can the product ever end in 2 when you are multiplying by 10? Explain your reasoning.

4

California Standards Practice

Cumulative, Chapters 1–4

Standards Example

Tony rides his bicycle 2 miles a day. He rides 4 days a week. How many miles does Tony ride in a week?

A 4 miles　　**C** 8 miles

B 6 miles　　**D** 10 miles

Read the Question

You need to find how many miles Tony rides his bike in a week.

Solve the Question

You can draw an array to find 4×2.

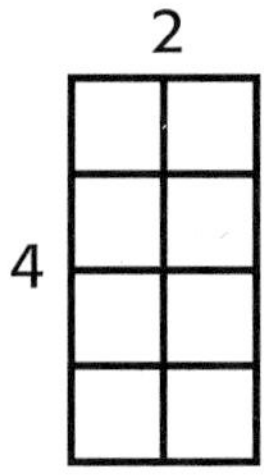

$4 \times 2 = 8$

So, Tony rides 8 miles a week.
The answer is C.

Online Personal Tutor at ca.gr3math.com

Choose the best answer.

1 **Evita swims 5 times a week for 2 hours. How many hours does Evita swim in a week?**

A 7

B 10

C 15

D 25

2 **Which number sentence is modeled by the figure below?**

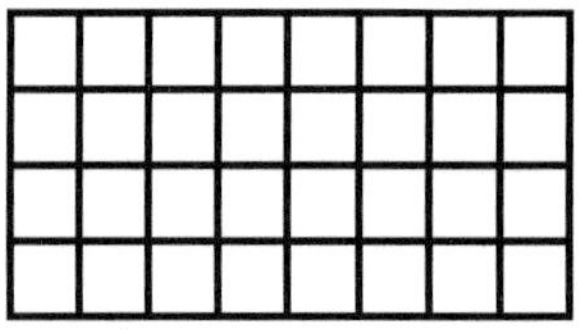

F $5 \times 8 = 40$

G $4 \times 8 = 32$

H $8 + 8 + 8 = 24$

J $3 \times 8 = 24$

3 **Which is the same as 3 × 7?**

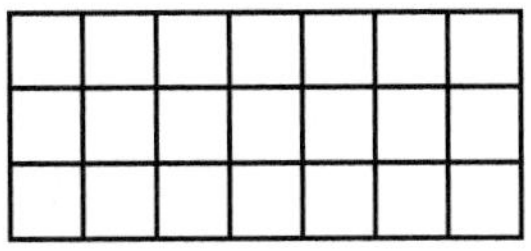

A 3 + 7

B 7 − 3

C 7 + 3

D 7 × 3

---

4 **What number would make the number sentence true?**

■ × 4 = 0

F 0

G 1

H 4

J 8

---

5 **Chua works at a car wash 6 hours a day. It takes Chua 1 hour to wash a car. Which number sentence shows how many cars he washes in a day?**

A 6 − 6 = 0

B 6 × 0 = 0

C 6 × 1 = 6

D 6 + 1 = 7

---

6 **The product of 5 and another factor is 50. What is the missing factor?**

F 45

G 10

H 9

J 5

---

7 **Tenell collected 54 shells. Janet collected 82 shells. How many more shells did Janet collect?**

A 28

B 30

C 32

D 38

---

8 **Write the number the model represents in standard form.**

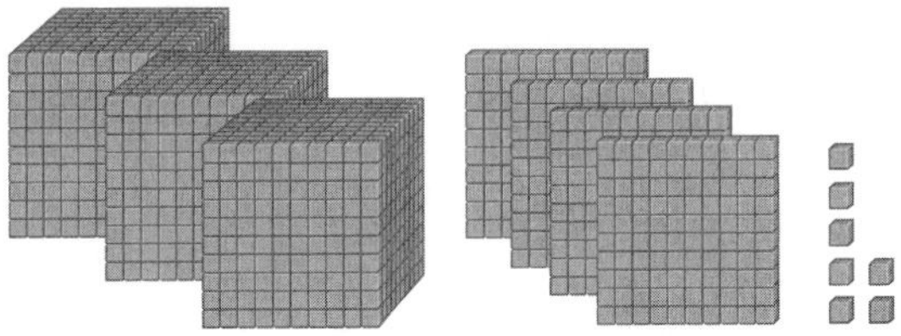

F 4370

G 3470

H 3407

J 3047

---

9 **Which set of numbers is in order from least to greatest?**

A 645, 449, 437, 345

B 449, 345, 645, 437

C 437, 449, 645, 345

D 345, 437, 449, 645

---

10 **Lynn bought an eraser for $2.25, a box of pencils for $7.32, and a notebook for $4.21. She gave the clerk $20.00. How much change should she get back?**

F $5.00

G $6.22

H $7.22

J $13.78

CHAPTER 5

More Multiplication Facts

BIG Idea When will I use multiplication?

Anytime you combine equal amounts, you use multiplication. It is useful when you buy items in a store, keep score in a game, or plant a garden.

Example Benny planted a garden. It has 3 rows with 7 vegetable plants in each row. The model shows that Benny planted 3×7 or 21 plants.

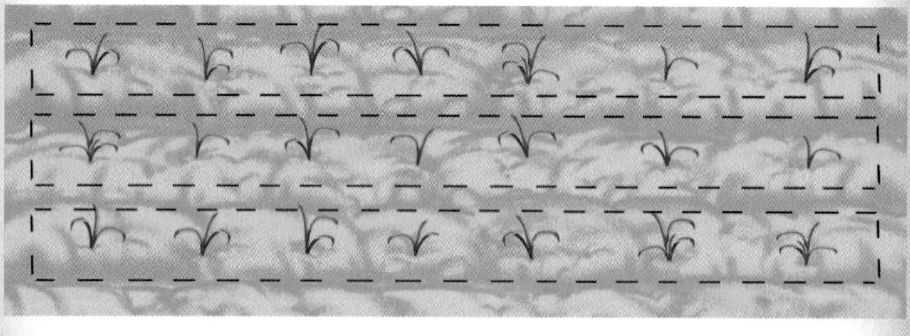

What will I learn in this chapter?

- Explore using the multiplication table.
- Multiply by 3, 6, 7, 8, and 9.
- Use properties of multiplication.
- Find a rule and extend the pattern.
- Solve problems by looking for a pattern.

Key Vocabulary

Associative Property of Multiplication

rule

Math Online **Student Study Tools at ca.gr3math.com**

FOLDABLES™
Study Organizer

Make this Foldable to help you organize information about multiplication facts. Begin with 3 sheets of $8\frac{1}{2}'' \times 11''$ paper.

1. **Fold** one sheet of paper in half as shown.

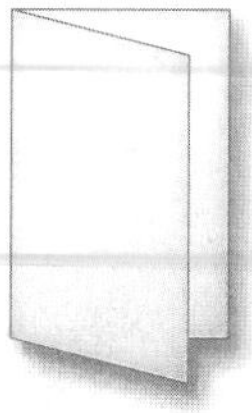

2. **Open** and fold a 2″ pocket. Glue the outside edges.

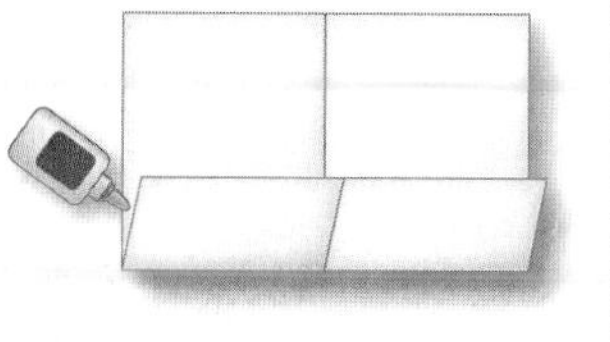

3. **Label** with the lesson titles. Write what you learn.

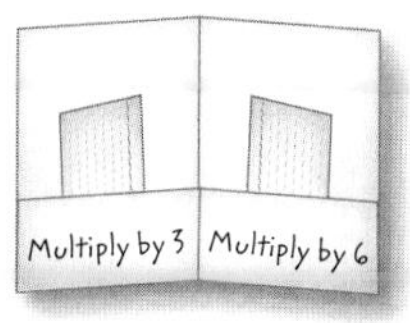

4. **Repeat** steps 1–3 with two more pieces of paper.

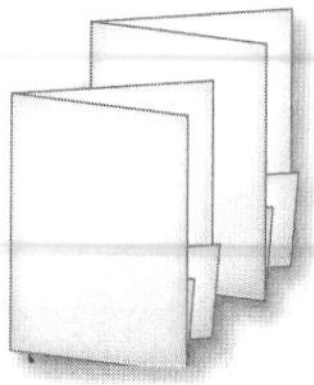

ARE YOU READY for Chapter 5?

You have two ways to check prerequisite skills for this chapter.

Option 2

Math Online Take the Chapter Readiness Quiz at ca.gr3math.com.

Option 1

Complete the Quick Check below.

QUICK Check

Write a multiplication sentence for each model. (Chapter 4)

1. 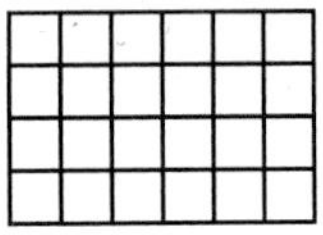

2. 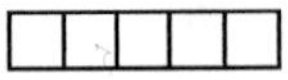

3. 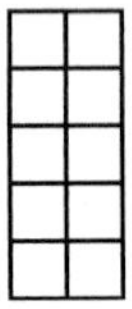

4. 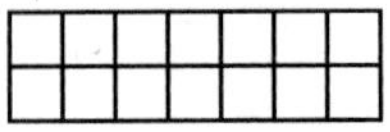

Draw an array for each fact. Write the product. (Chapter 4)

5. 5×4

6. 1×6

7. 4×7

8. 2×9

Solve. (Lessons 3-1 and 4-6)

9. Louis has 2 quarters. Yellow whistles cost 5¢ each. Louis wants to buy 8 whistles. Does he have enough money to buy 8 whistles?

10. There were 9 oak trees on each side of a street. After some trees were cut down, there were7 left. How many trees were cut down?

Identify the pattern. Then find the missing numbers. (Lesson 1-1)

11. 15, 20, 25, 30, ■, ■

12. 9, 12, 15, 18, ■, ■

13. 11, 21, 31, 41, ■, ■

14. 60, 50, 40, 30, ■, ■

Explore

Math Activity for 5-1
Multiplication Table

In Chapter 4, you learned many different strategies for finding products. Patterns you find in the multiplication table can help you remember multiplication facts.

MAIN IDEA

I will explore the multiplication table.

Standard 3NS2.2 **Memorize to automaticity the multiplication table for numbers between 1 and 10.**

Standard 3MR3.3 **Develop generalizations of the results obtained and apply them in other circumstances.**

Concepts in Motion

Animation
ca.gr3math.com

ACTIVITY **Make a Multiplication Table**

Step 1 **Find the factors.**

To find the product of two factors, find the first factor in the left column and the second factor across the top row.

factors

×	0	1	2	3	4	5	6	7	8	9	10
0											
1											
2				6							
3											
4											
5											
6											
7											
8											
9											
10											

factors

Write the product of 2 x 3 where row 2 and column 3 meet.

Step 2 **Fill in the grid.**
Write the products of the multiplication facts you know. Remember you can use the Commutative Property of Multiplication and use a known fact.

Review Vocabulary

Commutative Property of Multiplication
the order in which two numbers are multiplied does not change the product. **(Lesson 4-2)**

ACTIVITY

Hands-On Activity

Step 3 Use models.

For the products you do not know, you can use a model. For example, the array shows 3 × 4.

So, 3 × 4 = 12. Fill in the square where 3 and 4 meet with the product 12.

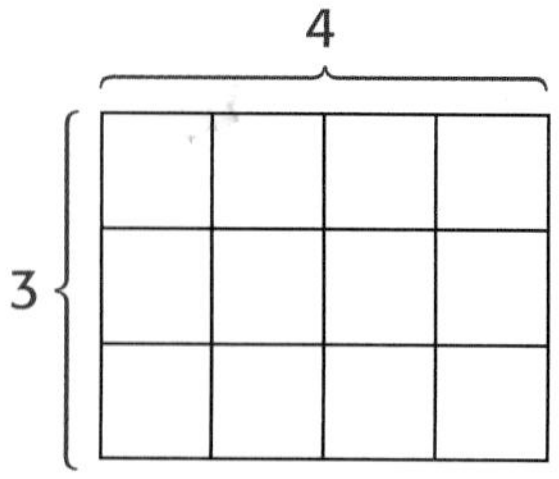

THINK ABOUT IT

1. What is the product when you multiply a number by 1? Explain.
2. What pattern do you see for row 10?
3. What do you notice about row 6 and column 6? Does it apply to all rows and columns of the same number?

CHECK What You Know

Multiply. Use the multiplication table.

4. 2×5

5. 4×0

6. 10×3

7. 5×6

Identify where each part of the multiplication table is found.

8. 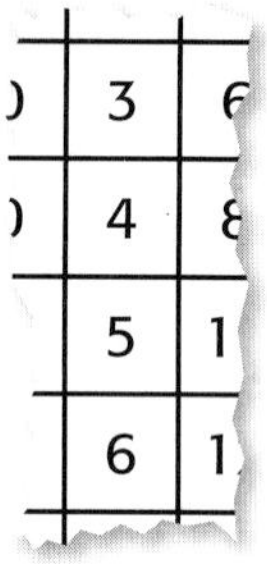

9. 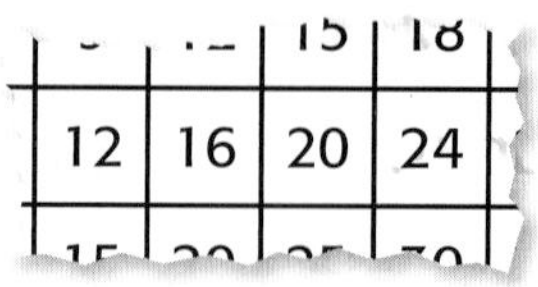

10. 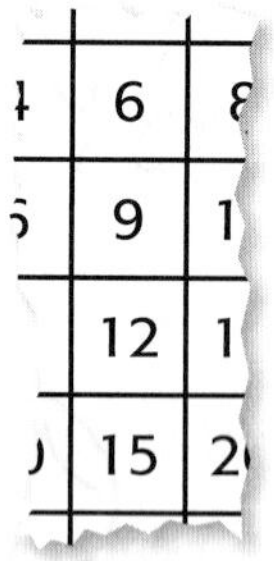

11. **WRITING IN ▶MATH** Write two other patterns you can find in the multiplication table.

5-1 Multiply by 3

MAIN IDEA

I will multiply by 3.

Standard 3NS2.2 **Memorize to automaticity the multiplication table for numbers between 1 and 10.**

Standard 3MR2.3 **Use a variety of methods, such as words, numbers, symbols, charts,** graphs, **tables, diagrams, and models, to explain mathematical reasoning.**

GET READY to Learn

In the previous activity, you explored the multiplication table.

×	0	1	2	3	4	5	6	7	8	9	10
0	0	0	0	0	0	0	0	0	0	0	0
1	0	1	2	3	4	5	6	7	8	9	10
2	0	2	4	6	8	10	12	14	16	18	20
3	0	3	6	9	12	15	18	21	24	27	30
4	0	4	8	12	16	20	24	28	32	36	40
5	0	5	10	15	20	25	30	35	40	45	50
6	0	6	12	18	24	30	36	42	48	54	60
7	0	7	14	21	28	35	42	49	56	63	70
8	0	8	16	24	32	40	48	56	64	72	80
9	0	9	18	27	36	45	54	63	72	81	90
10	0	10	20	30	40	50	60	70	80	90	100

There are different ways you can find products.

Real-World EXAMPLE Use an Array

1 PETS **There are 3 dogs. Each dog buried 4 bones in a yard. How many bones are buried in the yard?**

You can use an array to find 3 groups of 4 bones or 3×4.

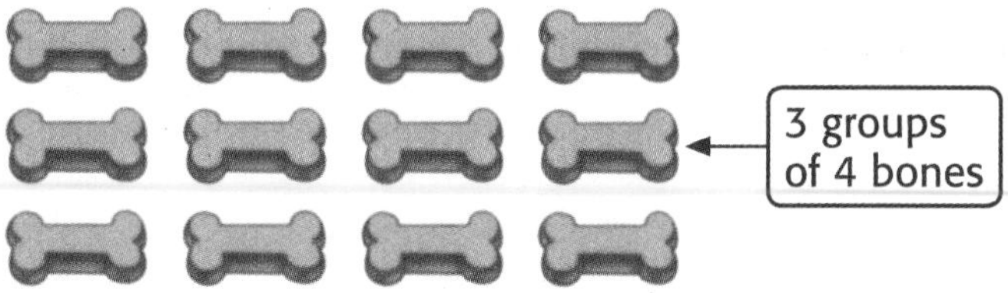

So, there are 12 bones buried in the yard.

Online Personal Tutor at ca.gr3math.com

You can draw a picture to help you solve a problem.

Remember

Ask yourself if there is a pattern that can help you find the product.

Real-World EXAMPLE **Draw a Picture**

2 GAMES **Three friends have 8 marbles each. How many marbles are there in all?**

Each friend needs a group of 8 marbles. There are 3 friends. Draw a picture to find 3×8.

$8 + 8 + 8 = 24$

So, 24 marbles are needed in all.

KEY CONCEPT — Multiplication Strategies

There are different ways to find answers for multiplication problems.

- Use models or draw a picture.
- Use repeated addition or skip count.
- Draw an array or an area model.
- Use a related multiplication fact.
- Double a know fact.

CHECK What You Know

Multiply. See Examples 1 and 2 (pp. 203–204)

1. $\begin{array}{r} 4 \\ \times 3 \\ \hline \end{array}$

2. $\begin{array}{r} 3 \\ \times 5 \\ \hline \end{array}$

3. 3×8

4. 3×9

5. The branches on a tree have leaves that grow in groups of 3. How many leaves are on 9 branches?

6. Talk About It Explain two ways to find the product 3×7.

Practice and Problem Solving

EXTRA PRACTICE See page R13.

Multiply. See Examples 1 and 2 (pp. 203–204)

7. 1×3

8. 10×3

9. 3×4

10. 5×3

11. 3×6

12. 3×9

13. 3×0

14. 8×3

15. 9×3

16. 3×7

17. 3×3

18. 6×3

19. 7×3

20. 3×4

21. 3×5

22. 3×10

Algebra **Copy and complete each table.**

23.

Rule: Multiply by 5.	
Input	Output
3	■
7	■
■	40
■	0
1	■

24.

Rule: Multiply by 4.	
Input	Output
5	■
■	28
■	40
9	■
0	■

25.

Rule: Multiply by 3.	
Input	Output
9	■
■	18
4	■
■	24
7	■

26. There are 3 students. They each put 9 books on a shelf. How many books did they place on the shelf?

27. There are 3 daisies and 3 tulips. Every flower has 9 petals. How many petals are there in all?

28. Hoshi, Joan, and Kita each had 3 snacks packed in their lunch boxes. They each ate one snack in the morning. How many snacks are left in all?

29. Benny is buying 4 packages of seeds. Each package costs $3 and contains 5 envelopes of seeds. What will be the total cost? How many envelopes will he have?

H.O.T. Problems

30. **OPEN ENDED** Look at the 3s row in a multiplication table. Describe the pattern.

31. **WRITING IN ▸MATH** Write a real-world problem in which 3 is a factor. Ask a classmate to solve. Check the answer on your multiplication table.

5-2 Multiply by 6

GET READY to Learn

There are 6 frogs sitting on a log. Each frog eats 4 flies. How many flies were eaten altogether?

MAIN IDEA

I will learn to multiply by 6.

Standard 3NS2.2 Memorize to automaticity the multiplication table for numbers between 1 and 10.
Standard 3MR2.3 Use a variety of methods, such as words, numbers, symbols, charts, graphs, tables, diagrams, **and models, to explain mathematical reasoning.**

In this lesson you will learn to multiply by 6.

Real-World EXAMPLE **Use a Model**

1 **FROGS If each frog ate 4 flies, how many flies did they eat in all?**

There are 6 frogs and each frog ate 4 flies so, the array shows 6 rows with 4 in each row.

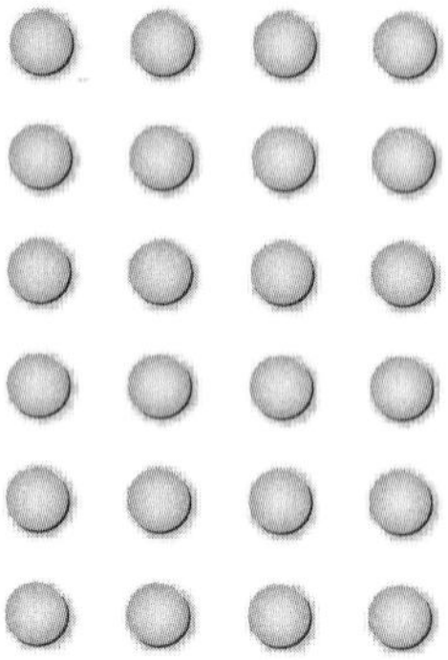

$4 + 4 + 4 + 4 + 4 + 4 = 24$

So, $6 \times 4 = 24$. The frogs ate 24 files.

Real-World EXAMPLE **Find a Missing Number**

2 **ALGEBRA Clara's jewelry box has room for 48 pairs of earrings. The box is divided into 8 rows. Each row has the same number of spaces. How many spaces are there in each row?**

To solve this problem, you can use a number sentence.

Number of rows		Number in each row		Total
8	×	■	=	48

THINK What times 8 equals 48?

Since $8 \times 6 = 48$, there are 6 spaces in each row.

You can use facts that you know to help you multiply by 6. When one of the factors is even, you can double a known fact.

Real-World EXAMPLE Double a Known Fact

3 MARCHING BAND **A band marches in 6 rows with 7 members in each row. How many members are there together?**

> **Remember**
> There are many different ways to multiply.

You can double a known fact to find 6 × 7.

Step 1 6 is the double of 3. So, 6 × 7 is the double of 3 × 7.

Step 2 6 × 7 = 3 × 7 + 3 × 7

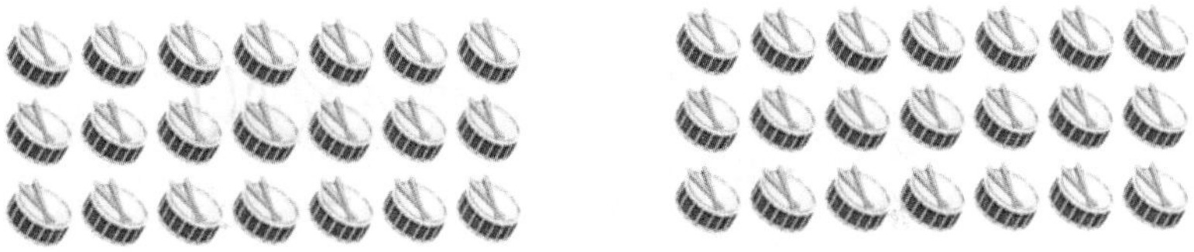

Step 3 So, 6 × 7 = 42. There are 42 members.

Check You can use an array and partial products to check.

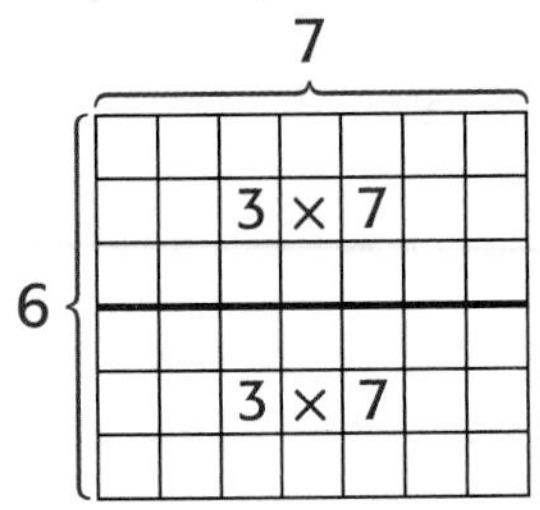

$$\begin{array}{r} 21 \\ +21 \\ \hline 42 \end{array}$$

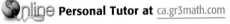

Online Personal Tutor at ca.gr3math.com

CHECK What You Know

Multiply. See Examples 1–3 (pp. 206–207)

1. $\begin{array}{r} 2 \\ \times\ 6 \\ \hline \end{array}$

2. $\begin{array}{r} 0 \\ \times\ 6 \\ \hline \end{array}$

3. $\begin{array}{r} 6 \\ \times\ 4 \\ \hline \end{array}$

4. $\begin{array}{r} 6 \\ \times\ 6 \\ \hline \end{array}$

5. 5 × 6

6. 1 × 6

7. 7 × 6

8. 6 × 9

9. Gil has 5 friends. He and each friend have 5 video games. How many video games do they have in all?

10. Talk About It Explain why the product of 8 and 3 is double the product of 4 and 3.

Practice and Problem Solving

EXTRA PRACTICE See page R14.

Multiply. See Examples 1–3 (pp. 206–207)

11. 6×2

12. 5×6

13. 4×6

14. 3×6

15. 6×6

16. 10×6

17. 6×9

18. 7×6

19. 0×6

20. 6×3

21. 8×6

22. 6×5

Algebra Find each missing factor. See Example 2 (pp. 206–207)

23. $4 \times \blacksquare = 24$

24. $\blacksquare \times 6 = 60$

25. $6 \times \blacksquare = 36$

26. $6 \times \blacksquare = 18$

Algebra Find each rule.

27.

Multiply by ■.	
Input	**Output**
2	6
3	9
4	12
5	15

28.

Multiply by ■.	
Input	**Output**
3	15
4	20
5	25
6	30

29.

Multiply by ■.	
Input	**Output**
5	20
6	24
7	28
8	32

30. Six students bought 5 pretzels each. If they gave away 6 of the pretzels, how many pretzels do they have left?

31. If Ida has 6 dimes, does she have enough money for 8 pieces of bubble gum that costs 6¢ each? Explain.

32. In 1995, the population of wild California Condors was 6. In 2005, it was 9 times that. What was the total condor population in 2005?

33. There are 7 vans driving to the park. If each holds 6 students, is there enough room for 45 students? Explain.

H.O.T. Problems

34. OPEN ENDED Use one of the multiplication strategies to explain how you would find the product 6×6.

35. WRITING IN ▸MATH Write a real-world problem that can be solved by multiplying by 6.

Standards Practice

36 Mr. Lobo buys 3 of the same item at a store. The total is \$27. What did he buy? **(Lesson 5-1)**

A

C

B

D

37 Which sign goes in the box to make the sentence true? **(Lesson 5-1)**

$3 \square 10 = 30$

F $+$ **H** $\times$

G $-$ **J** $\div$

38 Mr. Baxter bought 6 boxes of light bulbs. Each box has 4 bulbs. Which number sentence shows how to find the total number of bulbs? **(Lesson 5-2)**

A $6 - 4 = 2$

B $24 \div 6 = 4$

C $6 + 4 = 10$

D $6 \times 4 = 24$

Spiral Review

39. Henry put all the shells he collected into 3 equal groups for his friends. Each group had 7 shells. How many shells did Henry collect? **(Lesson 5-1)**

Multiply. **(Lesson 4-9)**

40. 0×9 **41.** 6×0 **42.** 8×1

43. Gina and Crystal each have 50¢. Is it reasonable to say that they have enough money to buy a box of crayons for \$1.50? Explain your reasoning. **(Lesson 3-4)**

Round to the nearest thousand. **(Lesson 1-9)**

44. 5,555 **45.** 2,009 **46.** 3,499

Add. **(Lesson 2-8)**

47. 3,748 + 1,212

48. 2,136 + 4,999

49. 2,374 + 3,158

Facts Practice

Multiply.

1. 4×9

2. 5×3

3. 6×4

4. 3×6

5. 3×2

6. 4×4

7. 2×2

8. 4×5

9. 4×6

10. 2×5

11. 2×7

12. 8×2

13. 8×3

14. 2×3

15. 6×3

16. 4×3

17. 6×5

18. 3×9

19. 6×2

20. 4×7

21. 7 × 2

22. 5 × 2

23. 6 × 6

24. 2 × 4

25. 6 × 7

26. 3 × 3

27. 5 × 6

28. 7 × 4

29. 3 × 4

30. 4 × 4

31. 7 × 3

32. 9 × 2

33. 5 × 5

34. 9 × 4

35. 2 × 6

36. 5 × 7

Three in a Row

Multiplication Facts

Get Ready!

Players: 2 players

You will need: 2 pennies
2-color counters

Get Set!

- Each player chooses a color for his or her counter.
- Make a game board like the one shown. Use the factors 2–9 and any products.

Factors

2	3	4	5	6	7	8	9

Products

20	36	12	14	30
54	45	8	24	40
28	16	27	20	32
42	15	10	21	18
6	24	12	48	35

Go!

- Player 1 places two pennies on any two factors. Then Player 1 places a counter on the product.
- Player 2 moves only one penny to a new factor. Then Player 2 places a counter on the product.
- Players take turns moving only one penny each turn and placing their counter on the corresponding product.
- The first player to get three of their counters in a row wins the game.

5-3 Problem-Solving Strategy

MAIN IDEA I will look for a pattern to solve problems.

Standard 3AF2.2 Extend and recognize a linear pattern by its rules (e.g., the number of legs on a given number of horses may be calculated by counting by 4s or by multiplying the number of horses by 4). **Standard 3MR1.1 Analyze problems by** identifying relationships, distinguishing relevant from irrelevant information, sequencing and prioritizing information, and **observing patterns.**

Christina is making a pattern with colored tiles. In the first row, she uses 2 tiles. She uses 4 tiles in the second row and 8 tiles in the third row. If she continues the pattern, how many tiles will be in the sixth row?

Understand

What facts do you know?

- There will be 2 tiles in the first row, 4 tiles in the second row, and 8 tiles in the third row.

What do you need to find?

- How many tiles will be in row six?

Plan

You can first make a table of the information. Then look for a pattern.

Solve

- First, put the information in a table.

1st	2nd	3rd	4th	5th	6th
2	4	8			

+2 +4 +8

- Look for a pattern. The numbers double.
- Once you know the pattern, you can continue it.

$$8 + 8 = 16$$
$$16 + 16 = 32$$
$$32 + 32 = 64$$

So, there will be 64 tiles in the sixth row.

Check

Look back at the problem. Complete the table using the pattern.

1st	2nd	3rd	4th	5th	6th
2	4	8	16	32	64

+2 +4 +8 +16 +32

There are 64 tiles in the sixth row. So, you know you are correct.

ANALYZE the Strategy

Refer to the problem on the previous page.

1. Why is it a good idea to put the information in a table first?

2. Explain how you identified the pattern for this problem.

3. Suppose there are 4 tiles in the first row, 8 in the second, and 16 in the third. How many tiles are in row 6?

4. Look back to Exercise 3. How do you know that your answer is correct?

PRACTICE the Strategy

EXTRA PRACTICE
See page R14.

Solve. Use the *look for a pattern* strategy.

5. A set of bowling pins is shown. If the pattern continues for 3 more rows, how many pins are there in all?

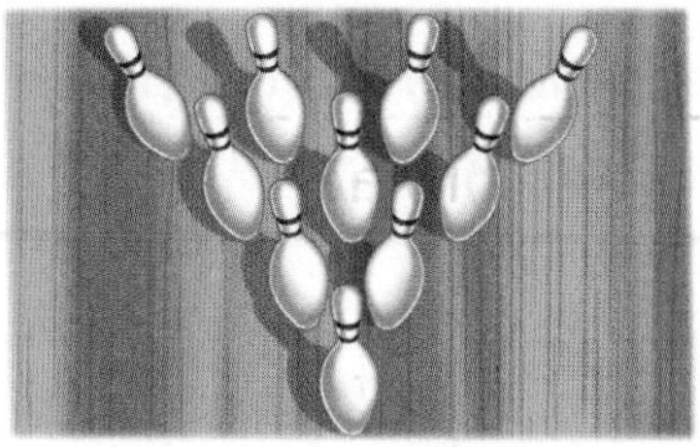

6. Yutaka is planting 24 flowers. He uses a pattern of 1 yellow daisy and then 2 red tulips. If the pattern continues, how many red tulips will he use?

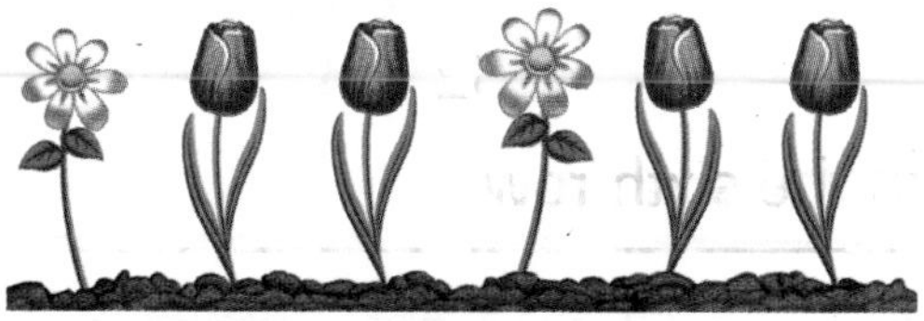

7. Gloria makes 3 hops forward and then 1 hop back. If each hop is 1 foot, how many hops does she make before she has gone 2 yards? (*Hint:* There are 3 feet in 1 yard.)

8. Howi mows lawns every other day. He earns $5 the first day. After that, he earns $1 more than the time before. If he starts mowing on the first day of the month, how much money will he earn on day 19?

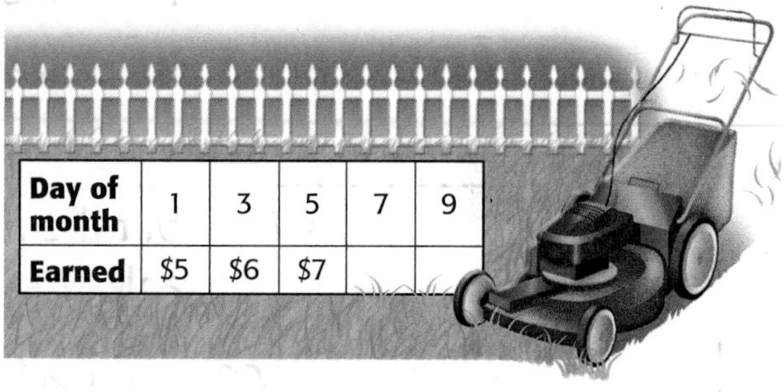

Day of month	1	3	5	7	9
Earned	$5	$6	$7		

9. Shandra is collecting cans for a recycling drive. If the pattern continues, how many cans will she collect in week 5?

Week	1	2	3	4	5
Cans	6	12	24		

10. WRITING IN ▸MATH Explain how the *look for a pattern* strategy helps you solve problems.

5-4 Multiply by 7

GET READY to Learn

A ride at an amusement park has 7 cars. Each car has 5 seats. How many people can go on the ride at the same time?

MAIN IDEA

I will learn to multiply by 7.

Standard 3NS2.2 Memorize to automaticity the multiplication table for numbers between 1 and 10.
Standard 3MR2.3 Use a variety of methods, such as words, numbers, symbols, charts, graphs, tables, **diagrams, and models, to explain mathematical reasoning.**

You can use repeated addition to multiply by 7.

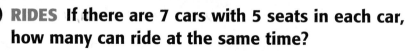

Real-World EXAMPLE Use Repeated Addition

1 RIDES If there are 7 cars with 5 seats in each car, how many can ride at the same time?

Find 7×5. Use repeated addition to count the 7 groups of 5 seats in each car. Add 5 seven times.

$$5 + 5 + 5 + 5 + 5 + 5 + 5 = 35$$

So, $7 \times 5 = 35$ people can ride at the same time.

Online **Personal Tutor at** ca.gr3math.com

To multiply by 7, you can also use a known fact.

EXAMPLE Use a Known Fact

2 Find 7 × 6.

You know $6 \times 7 = 42$.

So, $7 \times 6 = 42$. Commutative Property

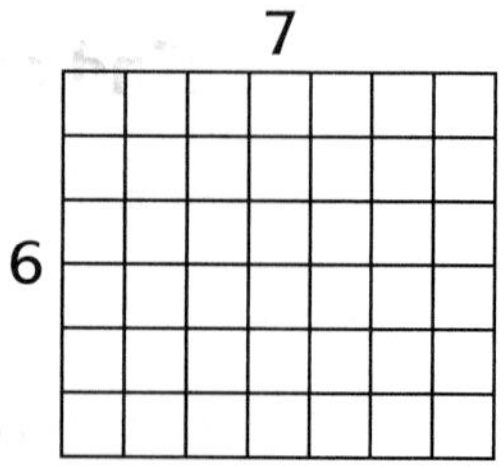

Remember

The Commutative Property of Multiplication says that the product does not change if the order of the factors changes.

Real-World EXAMPLE Use a Number Sentence

3 **QUILTS Jamila has 7 quilt squares. Each square has 3 triangles. How many triangles are there in all?**

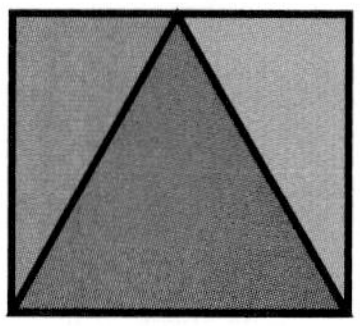

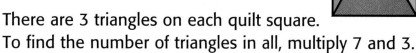

There are 3 triangles on each quilt square.
To find the number of triangles in all, multiply 7 and 3.

$7 \times 3 = \blacksquare$ 7 groups of 3 equals what?

$7 \times 3 = 21$

So, there are 21 triangles in all.

Real-World EXAMPLE Find Missing Numbers

4 **ALGEBRA A bug box has a total of 28 beetles. There are 7 different sizes of beetles. If there is an equal number of each size, how many of each size are there?**

To solve the problem, you can use a number sentence.

Different Sizes		Number of each size		Total
7	×	■	=	28 What times 7 equals 28?

The missing number is 4.

Since $7 \times 4 = 28$, there are 4 beetles of each size.

CHECK What You Know

Multiply. See Examples 1–3 (pp. 214–215)

1. $\begin{array}{r} 2 \\ \times 7 \\ \hline \end{array}$

2. $\begin{array}{r} 7 \\ \times 8 \\ \hline \end{array}$

3. 9×7

4. 7×10

Algebra Find each missing number. See Example 4 (p. 215)

5. $7 \times \blacksquare = 0$

6. $\blacksquare \times 7 = 49$

7. $7 \times \blacksquare = 70$

8. Brianna gave 7 friends 4 pencils each. How many pencils did she give them in all?

9. Talk About It Describe two different strategies for multiplying a number by 7.

Practice and Problem Solving

EXTRA PRACTICE
See page R14.

Multiply. See Examples 1–3 (pp. 214–215)

10. 3×7

11. 1×7

12. 4×7

13. 2×7

14. 0×7

15. 7×7

16. 9×7

17. 7×6

18. 7×4

19. 5×7

20. 7×8

21. 7×10

22. 7×2

23. 10×7

24. 7×9

25. 7×5

Algebra Find each missing number. See Example 4 (p. 214)

26. $4 \times ■ = 28$

27. $7 \times ■ = 49$

28. $8 \times ■ = 56$

29. $■ \times 7 = 63$

30. $■ \times 7 = 21$

31. $7 \times ■ = 42$

32. Ryan and 6 friends played basketball. They made a total of 35 baskets. If each made the same number of baskets, how many baskets did each person make?

33. **Measurement** During 9 weeks of summer vacation, Bradley spent 2 weeks at soccer camp. How many days did he not spend at camp?

34. Elian has 5 packs of rubber spiders. If each pack has 7 spiders, how many does he have in all?

35. Inez has 8 CDs. How many songs are there if each CD has 7 songs?

H.O.T. Problems

36. **NUMBER SENSE** Is 3×7 greater than 3×8? How do you know without multiplying? Explain.

37. **WHICH ONE DOESN'T BELONG?** Identify which multiplication sentence is incorrect. Explain.

$7 \times 9 = 63$ | $7 \times 7 = 48$ | $5 \times 7 = 35$ | $7 \times 0 = 0$

38. **WRITING IN ▶MATH** Explain why using a repeated addition is not the best strategy for finding a product like 7×9.

Math Online Self-Check Quiz at ca.gr3math.com

Mid-Chapter Check

CHAPTER 5

Lessons 5-1 through 5-4

Multiply. **(Lesson 5-1)**

1. 3×8

2. 3×4

3. **STANDARDS PRACTICE** Three times as many kids are having a hot lunch than a packed lunch. If there are 8 students with packed lunches, how many are having hot lunches? **(Lesson 5-1)**

A 5

B 11

C 24

D 32

Draw an array to solve. **(Lesson 5-1)**

4. 3×7

5. 3×9

Algebra Find each missing number. **(Lesson 5-2)**

6. $6 \times ■ = 42$

7. $■ \times 6 = 36$

Compare. Use >, <, or =. **(Lesson 5-2)**

8. 3×6 ■ 4×6

9. 6×8 ■ 8×6

10. Gretchen is making a sand castle. First, she makes 4 sand bricks and 1 sand tower. Next, she makes 8 bricks and 1 tower and then 12 bricks and 1 tower. If the pattern continues, how many bricks will come next? **(Lesson 5-3)**

11. Find a pattern. Complete the table. **(Lesson 5-3)**

1st	2nd	3rd	4th	5th	6th
2	7	12	■	■	■

12. Chloe's mom told her to place the biscuit dough in equal rows. She fit 7 balls of dough across the top of the baking sheet and 3 balls going down. How many biscuits can Chloe put on the sheet? **(Lesson 5-4)**

Multiply. **(Lesson 5-4)**

13. $\begin{array}{r} 7 \\ \times\ 4 \\ \hline \end{array}$

14. $\begin{array}{r} 3 \\ \times\ 7 \\ \hline \end{array}$

15. **STANDARDS PRACTICE** The school district has 6 elementary schools with 7 third grade classes in each school. How many third grade classes are there in all? **(Lesson 5-4)**

F 13

G 36

H 42

J 49

16. **WRITING IN MATH** Explain how to find 6×9 by doubling a known fact. **(Lesson 5-2)**

5-5 Multiply by 8

MAIN IDEA

I will learn to multiply by 8.

Standard 3NS2.2 Memorize to automaticity the multiplication table for numbers between 1 and 10.
Standard 3MR2.3 Use a variety of methods, such as words, numbers, symbols, charts, graphs, tables, **diagrams, and models, to explain mathematical reasoning.**

GET READY to Learn

There are 8 trees lining a street. In each tree, there are 6 birds. How many birds are there in all?

There are many ways to multiply by 8.

Real-World EXAMPLE Use an Array

1 BIRDS Find the number of birds in all if there are 6 birds in each of the 8 trees.

You need to find 8×6.

Think of each tree as a group of 6 birds.

So, $8 \times 6 = 48$ birds in all.

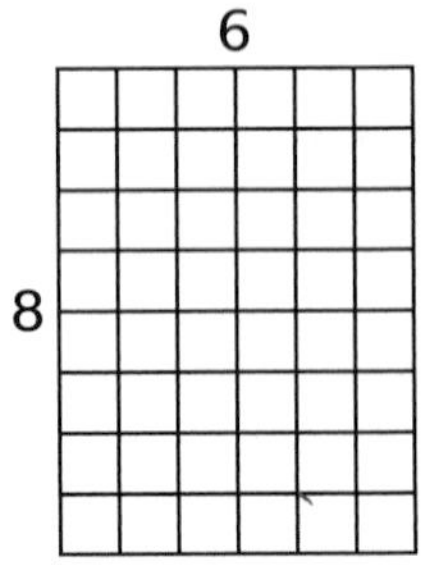

You can change the order of the factors to find a related fact.

Real-World EXAMPLE Use a Known Fact

2 BUTTONS Jaya has 8 shirts. There are 4 buttons on each shirt. How many buttons are there altogether?

Think of each shirt as a group with 4 buttons in each group. You need to find 8×4.

You know that $4 \times 8 = 32$.

So, $8 \times 4 = 32$. Commutative Property

Jaya has 32 buttons in all.

The 4s facts are helpful in remembering the 8s facts. The 8s facts are double the 4s.

Remember

When one of the factors is even, you can use the *double a known fact* strategy.

Real-World EXAMPLE **Double a Known Fact**

3 **ALLOWANCE Pearl earns $7 every week for doing her chores. How much money will she earn after 8 weeks?**

You can double a known fact to find 8 × $7.

8 is the double of 4. So, 8 × $7 is double 4 × $7.

8 × $7	=	4 × $7	+	4 × $7		
	=	$28	+	$28	=	$56

So, 8 × $7 = $56. Pearl will earn $56 after 8 weeks.

Check You can use an array and partial products to check.

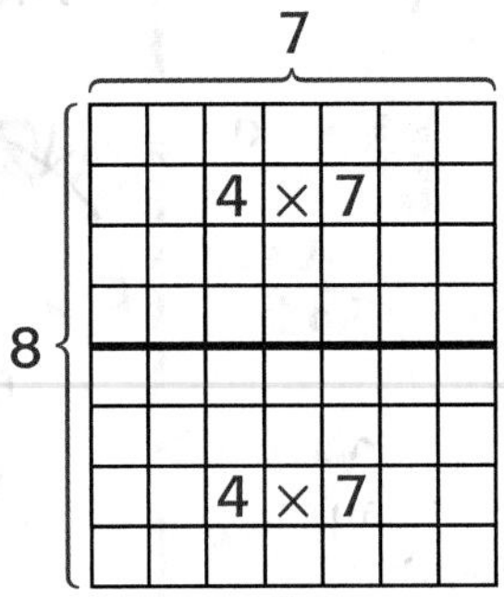

$$\begin{array}{r} 28 \\ +28 \\ \hline 56 \end{array}$$

Online Personal Tutor at ca.gr3math.com

CHECK What You Know

Multiply. See Examples 1–3 (pp. 218–219)

1. $\begin{array}{r} 8 \\ \times 2 \\ \hline \end{array}$ **2.** $\begin{array}{r} 0 \\ \times 8 \\ \hline \end{array}$ **3.** $\begin{array}{r} 4 \\ \times 8 \\ \hline \end{array}$ **4.** $\begin{array}{r} 8 \\ \times 5 \\ \hline \end{array}$

5. 8 × 1 **6.** 6 × 8 **7.** 8 × 3 **8.** 8 × 7

9. Nate buys 8 cans of dog food for $4 every week. How much does he spend in 4 weeks?

10. Talk About It If there are 4 groups of 8 students and 8 groups of 8 students, how many students are there in all? Explain.

Practice and Problem Solving

EXTRA PRACTICE
See page R15.

Multiply. **See Example 1–3 (pp. 218-219)**

11. $\begin{array}{r} 2 \\ \times\ 8 \\ \hline \end{array}$ **12.** $\begin{array}{r} 1 \\ \times\ 8 \\ \hline \end{array}$ **13.** $\begin{array}{r} 7 \\ \times\ 8 \\ \hline \end{array}$ **14.** $\begin{array}{r} 8 \\ \times\ 8 \\ \hline \end{array}$

15. $\begin{array}{r} 0 \\ \times\ 8 \\ \hline \end{array}$ **16.** $\begin{array}{r} 8 \\ \times\ 9 \\ \hline \end{array}$ **17.** $\begin{array}{r} 10 \\ \times\ 8 \\ \hline \end{array}$ **18.** $\begin{array}{r} 8 \\ \times\ 3 \\ \hline \end{array}$

19. 6×8 **20.** 5×8 **21.** 8×4 **22.** 9×8

Algebra **Find each missing number.**

23. $8 \times \blacksquare = 64$ **24.** $\blacksquare \times 8 = 40$ **25.** $8 \times \blacksquare = 56$ **26.** $8 \times \blacksquare = 80$

27. There are 3 large and 4 small spiders in a web. Each has 8 legs. How many legs are there altogether?

28. Admission to the Science Center is $8. How much would it cost a family of 5?

29. Jolon worked 5 hours the first week of the month. By the end of the month, he had worked 8 times as many hours as the first week. How many hours had he worked by the end of the month?

30. There are 9 crates, each with 8 cases of California oranges, on a delivery truck. How many cases of oranges will be left if 2 crates are delivered at the first stop?

Real-World PROBLEM SOLVING

Food A recipe for banana bread is shown. Marlo will make 8 times as much for a party.

31. How many bananas will she need?

32. Will 15 cups of flour be enough? Explain.

33. The first four times Marlo makes the recipe, she will make large loaves. The other four times she will make small loaves. How many loaves will she have in all?

34. If there are 8 teaspoons of vanilla in a bottle, how many bottles of vanilla will she need?

Banana Bread

3 bananas, mashed
$\frac{3}{4}$ cup oil
$\frac{3}{4}$ cup sugar
2 cups flour
2 teaspoons vanilla
1 teaspoon baking soda
$\frac{1}{2}$ teaspoon baking powder
$\frac{1}{2}$ cup walnuts

Stir the first four ingredients well. Mix all dry ingredients alone. Than add to liquid stirring well. Add walnuts last. Pour into prepared pans. Bake 45 minutes at 350°.

Makes 2 large or 6 small loaves

H.O.T. Problems

35. OPEN ENDED Explain a strategy that you would use to find 8×9. Why do you prefer this strategy?

36. NUMBER SENSE Explain how you can use the *double a known fact* strategy to find 8×7.

37. WRITING IN MATH Write a real-world problem that involves multiplying by 8.

Standards Practice

38 What number makes this number sentence true? **(Lesson 5-4)**

$$7 \times 5 < 4 \times \blacksquare$$

A 3

B 5

C 7

D 10

39 Which multiplication sentence is modeled below? **(Lesson 5-5)**

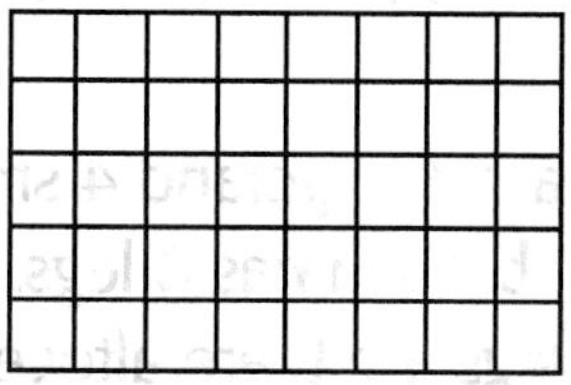

F $5 \times 8 = 40$

G $5 \times 9 = 40$

H $40 \times 8 = 5$

J $40 \times 5 = 8$

Spiral Review

Multiply. (Lesson 5-4)

40. 7×8

41. 7×7

42. 7×9

43. Algebra Martha is building shapes with straws. She uses 3 straws for a triangle and 4 straws for a square. Next, she makes a 5-sided shape. She continues this pattern. How many straws will she have used by the time she makes a 6-sided shape? **(Lessons 5-3)**

Write a multiplication sentence for each array. (Lessons 4-4 and 4-6)

44.

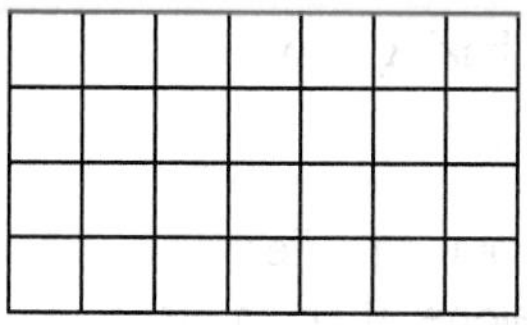

45.

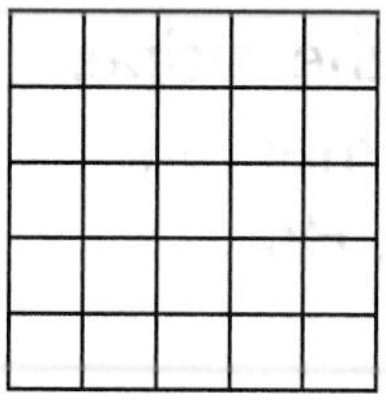

46.

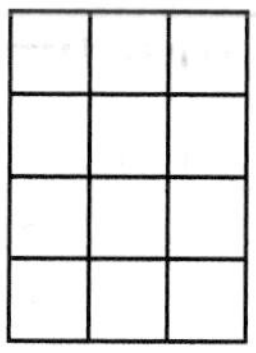

Write each number in word form. (Lesson 1-4)

47. 12,021

48. 4,910

49. 90,009

5-6 Multiply by 9

MAIN IDEA

I will learn to multiply by 9.

Standard 3NS2.2 **Memorize to automaticity the multiplication table for numbers between 1 and 10.**
Standard 3MR2.3 **Use a variety of methods, such as words, numbers, symbols,** charts, graphs, tables, **diagrams, and models, to explain mathematical reasoning.**

GET READY to Learn

There are 9 packages of hamburger buns. Each package has the same number of buns. There are 8 buns in each package. How many buns are there in all?

To multiply by 9, you can use a known fact.

Real-World EXAMPLE — Use a Known Fact

1 BUNS **How many buns are there altogether?**

To solve the problem you can use a number sentence.

Number of packages		Number in each package		Total
9	×	8	=	■

You know $8 \times 9 = 72$.

So, $9 \times 8 = 72$. There are 72 buns.

Subtracting from a known fact will help you remember your 9s facts. Multiply the smaller factor by 10 and then subtract.

Real-World EXAMPLE — Subtract from a Known Fact

2 STUDENTS **How many students are there in 9 groups with 5 students in each group?**

To find 9×5 you can subtract from a known fact.

Step 1 9×5 is 9 groups of 5. Use the known fact of 10 groups of 5. $10 \times 5 = 50$

Step 2 Subtract 1 group of 5 to get $50 - 5$ or 45.

So, $9 \times 5 = 45$ students.

You can use patterns to help remember the 9s facts. The second factor and the product in the 9s table create a pattern.

- The tens digit of the product is always 1 less than the factor that is multiplied by 9.
- The sum of the digits of the product equals 9.

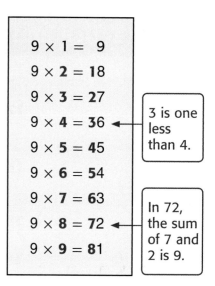

$9 \times 1 = 9$
$9 \times \mathbf{2} = \mathbf{18}$
$9 \times \mathbf{3} = \mathbf{27}$
$9 \times \mathbf{4} = \mathbf{36}$ ← 3 is one less than 4.
$9 \times \mathbf{5} = \mathbf{45}$
$9 \times \mathbf{6} = \mathbf{54}$
$9 \times \mathbf{7} = \mathbf{63}$
$9 \times \mathbf{8} = \mathbf{72}$ ← In 72, the sum of 7 and 2 is 9.
$9 \times \mathbf{9} = \mathbf{81}$

Remember

The Commutative Property of Multiplication allows you to turn the fact around to see a known fact.

Real-World EXAMPLE Use Patterns

3 MONEY **Mr. Clancy bought 9 boxes of markers. Each box cost $6. How much did he spend?**

Since the total cost is needed, multiply. Find 9 × $6.

9 × **$6** ⟶ **$5** ← THINK 6 − 1 = 5

9 × $6 = **$54** ← THINK 5 + ? = 9; 5 + 4 = 9

So, 9 × $6 = $54. Mr. Clancy spent $54.

Online **Personal Tutor at** ca.gr3math.com

CHECK What You Know

Multiply. See Examples 1–3 (pp. 222–223)

1. 9×1
2. 4×9
3. 9×2
4. 6×9
5. 0 × 9
6. 9 × 3
7. 10 × 9
8. 7 × 9
9. Lyle has 63 rocks in his collection. He places them into bags. Each bag holds 9 rocks. How many bags are there?
10. Talk About It How can patterns help you when multiplying by 9?

Practice and Problem Solving

EXTRA PRACTICE
See page R15.

Multiply. See Examples 1–3 (pp. 222–223)

11. 3×9 **12.** 9×6 **13.** 4×9 **14.** 2×9

15. 5×9 **16.** 8×9 **17.** 9×10 **18.** 9×9

19. 1×9 **20.** 7×9 **21.** 9×5 **22.** 10×9

23. 9×0 **24.** 9×3 **25.** 6×9 **26.** 9×7

ALGEBRA Find each missing factor.

27. ■ × 9 = 18 **28.** 3 × ■ = 27 **29.** 5 × ■ = 45

30. 9 × ■ = 54 **31.** 6 × ■ = 54 **32.** 9 × ■ = 72

33. Jim and Lynn have 9 marbles each. How many marbles are there in all?

34. Cecilia sold 5 books for $9 each. How much money did she get?

35. There were 4 car races on Saturday and 3 on Sunday. If there were 9 cars racing in each race, how many cars raced over the two days?

36. Phil uses 9 yards of rope for each rope ladder he makes. If he makes 4 rope ladders, how many yards of rope will he use?

H.O.T. Problems

37. NUMBER SENSE Is 9×2 the same as $3 \times 3 \times 2$? Explain.

38. FIND THE ERROR Zachary and Jacinda are finding 9×9. Who is correct? Explain.

Jacinda

If 9 × 8 = 72, then 9 × 9 must be 9 more, so 9 × 9 = 81.

Zachary

If 9 × 8 = 72, then 9 × 9 must be 8 more, so 9 × 9 = 80.

39. WRITING IN MATH Describe how the number 10 can help you to solve multiplication problems with 9 as a factor.

Math Online Self-Check Quiz at ca.gr3math.com

Standard 3NS2.2 Memorize to automaticity the multiplication table for numbers between 1 and 10.

Facts Practice

Multiply.

1. $\begin{array}{r} 4 \\ \times 6 \\ \hline \end{array}$	**2.** $\begin{array}{r} 6 \\ \times 7 \\ \hline \end{array}$	**3.** $\begin{array}{r} 3 \\ \times 9 \\ \hline \end{array}$	**4.** $\begin{array}{r} 5 \\ \times 9 \\ \hline \end{array}$
5. $\begin{array}{r} 4 \\ \times 2 \\ \hline \end{array}$	**6.** $\begin{array}{r} 9 \\ \times 5 \\ \hline \end{array}$	**7.** $\begin{array}{r} 2 \\ \times 8 \\ \hline \end{array}$	**8.** $\begin{array}{r} 9 \\ \times 6 \\ \hline \end{array}$
9. $\begin{array}{r} 8 \\ \times 9 \\ \hline \end{array}$	**10.** $\begin{array}{r} 7 \\ \times 4 \\ \hline \end{array}$	**11.** $\begin{array}{r} 8 \\ \times 3 \\ \hline \end{array}$	**12.** $\begin{array}{r} 4 \\ \times 8 \\ \hline \end{array}$
13. $\begin{array}{r} 5 \\ \times 8 \\ \hline \end{array}$	**14.** $\begin{array}{r} 5 \\ \times 3 \\ \hline \end{array}$	**15.** $\begin{array}{r} 8 \\ \times 6 \\ \hline \end{array}$	**16.** $\begin{array}{r} 3 \\ \times 3 \\ \hline \end{array}$
17. $\begin{array}{r} 4 \\ \times 5 \\ \hline \end{array}$	**18.** $\begin{array}{r} 7 \\ \times 3 \\ \hline \end{array}$	**19.** $\begin{array}{r} 2 \\ \times 7 \\ \hline \end{array}$	**20.** $\begin{array}{r} 5 \\ \times 8 \\ \hline \end{array}$
21. 6×5	**22.** 8×10	**23.** 9×8	**24.** 7×6
25. 6×6	**26.** 4×8	**27.** 8×5	**28.** 9×4
29. 6×2	**30.** 9×2	**31.** 3×7	**32.** 9×9
33. 1×1	**34.** 7×7	**35.** 5×5	**36.** 6×9

5-7 Problem-Solving Investigation

MAIN IDEA I will choose the best strategy to solve a problem.

Standard 3MR1.1 Analyze problems by identifying relationships, distinguishing relevant and irrelevant information, sequencing and prioritizing information and observing patterns. Standard 3NS2.2 Memorize to automaticity the multiplication table for numbers between 1 and 10.

P.S.I. TEAM +

ALEC: I have a goal to ride my bike 20 miles this week. Last night, I rode my bike 2 miles each way going to and from softball practice. I will ride this distance for 6 more days.

YOUR MISSION: Find if Alec will meet his goal and ride his bike 20 miles this week.

Understand	Alec wants to ride 20 miles this week. He will ride 2 miles each way to and from practice for 7 days. Find out if he will meet his goal.
Plan	Find the total miles he will ride each day and for the week. Multiply to find a total.
Solve	Alec will ride 2 miles to practice and 2 miles home, or $2 \times 2 = 4$ miles each day. 4 miles each day $\times$ 7 days $= 28$ miles So, Alec rides his bike 28 miles this week. Since 28 miles $>$ 20 miles, Alec will meet his goal.
Check	Look back at the problem. Use an array to check. $4 \times 7 = 28$. So, the answer is correct. 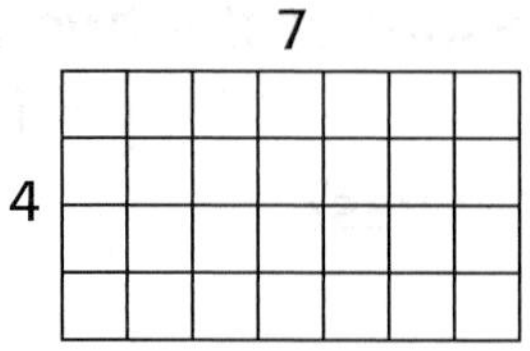

Mixed Problem Solving

EXTRA PRACTICE
See page R15.

Use any strategy shown below to solve. Tell what strategy you used.

PROBLEM-SOLVING STRATEGIES
- Act it out.
- Draw a picture.
- Look for a pattern.

1. There are 2 ladybugs. Together they have 12 spots. If one has 4 more spots than the other, how many spots do they each have?

2. **Measurement** A train travels the distances shown.

Day	Distance (miles)
Monday	75
Tuesday	■
Wednesday	200

If the train travels a total of 500 miles, how far did it travel on Tuesday?

3. **Algebra** What could be the next three numbers in the pattern?

5, 8, 11, 14, 17, ■, ■, ■

4. **Geometry** What will be the measure of the two labeled sides of the next triangle if the pattern continues?

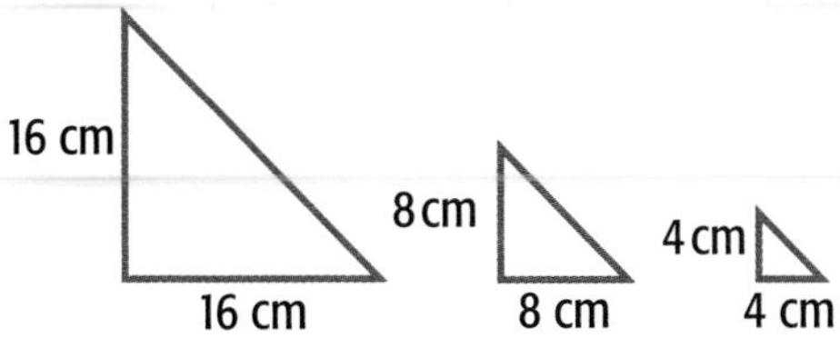

5. **Algebra** The table shows the cost of sodas at a restaurant. Identify and use the pattern to find the cost of a large soda.

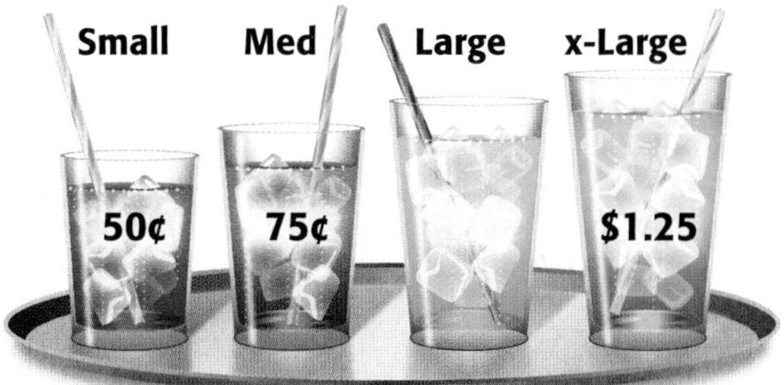

6. Carmen has $5. Darby has two times as much money as Carmen. Frank has $3 more than Carmen. What is the total in all?

7. A weaver is creating a design for a scarf. The first row has 3 hearts. The second row has 7 hearts, and the third row has 11. As she continues the pattern, how many hearts will be in the seventh row?

8. Diego, Marco, and Andrea earn money raking leaves after school. If they evenly share the money they make, how much will each get?

Money Earned Raking

Friday	$6
Saturday	$10
Sunday	$8

9. **WRITING IN MATH** Write a real-world problem that could be solved in more than one way. Explain.

5-8 Algebra: Associative Property

GET READY to Learn

Write a number sentence with three numbers and two multiplication signs to find the total number of smiley faces.

To find a product, like $2 \times 3 \times 4$, you can use properties of multiplication. The properties make multiplying easier.

KEY CONCEPT — Associative Property

Words The **Associative Property of Multiplication** states that the grouping of factors does not change the product.

Examples

$(2 \times 3) \times 4 = 6 \times 4 = 24$

$2 \times (3 \times 4) = 2 \times 12 = 24$

The parentheses tell you which factors to multiply first.

MAIN IDEA

I will identify and use the Associative Property of Multiplication.

Standard 3AF1.5

Recognize and use the commutative and **associative properties of multiplication (e.g.,** if $5 \times 7 = 35$, then what is 7×5? **and if $5 \times 7 \times 3 = 105$, then what is $7 \times 3 \times 5$?).**

New Vocabulary

Associative Property of Multiplication

EXAMPLE

1 Find $5 \times 2 \times 3$.

One Way	Another Way
$(5 \times 2) \times 3$	$5 \times (2 \times 3)$
$10 \times 3 = 30$	$5 \times 6 = 30$

So, $5 \times 2 \times 3 = 30$.

Real-World EXAMPLE

2 BOOKS Lenora reads 3 books. Each book has 6 pages. There are 2 pictures on each page. How many pictures are there altogether?

To find the total number of pictures, you can write a number sentence. You can group the easier factors.

$(3 \times 2) \times 6$ ← THINK It is easier to multiply 3 × 2.

$6 \times 6 = 36$

So, $3 \times 2 \times 6 = 36$. There were 36 pictures.

Remember

No matter how you group the factors, the product will be the same. This is the Associative Property.

Online **Personal Tutor at** ca.gr3math.com

To find missing numbers when multiplying more than two numbers, use the Associative Property of Multiplication.

Real-World EXAMPLE **Find Missing Numbers**

3 ALGEBRA Cheryl has 2 photos. Each photo shows 5 friends holding the same number of flowers. There are 30 flowers altogether. How many flowers is each person holding?

You can write a number sentence to help you find the missing number.

Number of photos		Number of friends		Flowers each is holding		Total
2	×	5	×	■	=	30

Use the Associative Property to find 2 × 5 first.

$(2 \times 5) \times ■ = 30$

$10 \times ■ = 30$ ← THINK 10 times what number equals 30?

$10 \times 3 = 30$

So, $2 \times 5 \times 3 = 30$. Each person is holding 3 flowers.

CHECK What You Know

Find each product. See Examples 1 and 2 (pp. 228–229)

1. $2 \times 4 \times 6$ **2.** $5 \times 2 \times 8$ **3.** $4 \times 1 \times 3$

Algebra Find each missing number. See Example 3 (p. 229)

4. $■ \times 2 \times 3 = 30$ **5.** $■ \times 8 \times 1 = 72$ **6.** $4 \times 2 \times ■ = 40$

7. There are 3 tables with 4 books. Each book has 2 bookmarks. Find the number of bookmarks.

8. Talk About It Explain how the Associative Property of Multiplication can help you find missing numbers.

Practice and Problem Solving

EXTRA PRACTICE See page R16.

Find each product. See Examples 1 and 2 (pp. 228–229)

9. $5 \times 2 \times 3$ **10.** $6 \times 2 \times 2$ **11.** $4 \times 5 \times 1$

12. $2 \times 4 \times 9$ **13.** $3 \times 2 \times 8$ **14.** $2 \times 7 \times 2$

Algebra Find each missing number. See Example 3 (p. 229)

15. $3 \times ■ \times 4 = 24$ **16.** $6 \times ■ \times 5 = 30$ **17.** $■ \times 3 \times 3 = 27$

18. $2 \times 5 \times ■ = 20$ **19.** $3 \times 3 \times ■ = 63$ **20.** $6 \times ■ \times 3 = 36$

Write a number sentence for each situation. Then solve. See Example 3 (p. 229)

21. Mrs. Flanagan has 2 new book stands with 3 shelves each. She put 10 books on each shelf. How many books has she set up?

22. A grocer unpacked 2 boxes of soup. Each box held 4 cartons with 10 cans of soup in each. How many cans did the grocer unpack?

For Exercises 23–25, use the table. It shows how many yards of grass Alisa needs to make baskets with decorations. How many feet of grass is needed for each? *(Hint - 1 yard = 3 feet)*

23. 2 baskets with 1 braid and 1 flower

24. 3 baskets with fringe

25. 2 baskets with 2 flowers and 2 braids

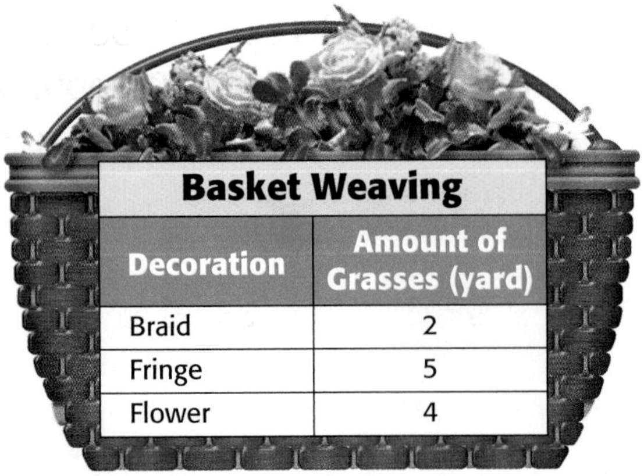

Basket Weaving

Decoration	Amount of Grasses (yard)
Braid	2
Fringe	5
Flower	4

H.O.T. Problems

26. **OPEN ENDED** Write three factors that have a product of 24.

27. **WHICH ONE DOESN'T BELONG?** Identify which of the following is not true. Explain.

$(2 \times 3) \times 3 = 2 \times (3 \times 3)$	$3 \times (1 \times 5) = (3 \times 1) \times 5$
$(4 \times 4) \times 2 = (4 \times 4) \times 4$	$6 \times (4 \times 2) = (6 \times 4) \times 2$

28. **WRITING IN ▸MATH** Explain the order in which to find $(3 \times 4) \times 2$. Explain why.

Standards Practice

29 What number makes this number sentence true? **(Lesson 5-8)**

$$(6 \times 3) \times 7 = 6 \times (\blacksquare \times 7)$$

A 3 **C** 6

B 4 **D** 7

30 There were 9 horses. Each horse ate 4 apples. Which number sentence shows how to find the number of apples in all? **(Lesson 5-6)**

F $9 + 4$ **H** 9×4

G $9 - 4$ **J** $9 \div 4$

Spiral Review

Use any strategy to solve. (Lesson 5-7)

31. **Measurement** A saltwater crocodile weighs up to 1,150 pounds. An anaconda weighs 500 pounds. Together, how much can these two animals weigh?

32. On Monday, Terrence made $3.40 selling lemonade at his stand. Tuesday he made $5.60. How much more money did he make on Tuesday than on Monday?

33. 9×6 34. 9×7 35. 9×9 36. 9×0

Compare. Use >, <, or =. (Lesson 1-4)

37. 3,839 ■ 3,973 38. 2,371 ■ 237 39. 209 ■ 290

Problem Solving in Art

Not Just a Blanket

People have been making quilts for 2,000 years. The oldest existing quilt is between 1,000 and 1,500 years old.

Quilts are made of two layers of fabric, with padding in between. Different shapes of cloth are sewn together in detailed patterns. Some quilts are very small, but others are very large. The largest quilt in the world weighs 800 pounds. It is 85 feet wide and 134 feet long. Quilts are much more than blankets. They are pieces of art!

Standard 3NS2.2 Memorize to automaticity the multiplication table for numbers between 1 and 10.

Did You Know?

Some quilts are so small they can almost fit in your hand.

Real-World Math

Use the information on page 232 and picture of the quilt above to answer each question.

1. How many feet longer is the length than the width of the largest quilt in the world?
2. How can you use repeated addition to find how many squares are in the quilt pictured?
3. Suppose you need to make a quilt that uses twice as many squares as the quilt shown. How many squares do you need to make your quilt?
4. How many squares do you need if you make 3 quilts with 9 squares each?
5. If you need to make 6 quilts with 9 squares each, how many squares do you need?
6. Each quilt square is 7 inches wide and 7 inches long. How long is the quilt?
7. A quilt is 9 squares wide and 7 squares long. How many squares are there in all?
8. You have 7 quilts. Each quilt is 3 squares long and 3 squares wide. Do you have 63 squares? Explain.

5-9 Algebra: Find a Rule

GET READY to Learn

Kathy is building 5 separate triangles with straws. The first triangle used 3 straws, and the second triangle used another 3 straws. How many straws does she need to make 5 triangles?

MAIN IDEA

I will look for a rule and extend it to solve a problem.

Standard 3AF2.1 Solve simple problems involving a functional relationship between two quantities.
Standard 3AF2.2 Extend and recognize a linear pattern by its rules

New Vocabulary

rule

The number of straws Kathy uses, follows a pattern. The pattern is called a rule. A **rule** tells you what to do to the first number to get the second.

Real-World EXAMPLE Find and Extend a Rule

1 **GEOMETRY Find the total number of straws Kathy needs to make 5 triangles.**

Step 1 Find the rule.

1 triangle = 3 straws.
$1 \times \mathbf{3} = 3$
2 triangles = 6 straws.
$2 \times \mathbf{3} = 6$
3 triangles = 9 straws.
$3 \times \mathbf{3} = 9$

The rule is to multiply the number of triangles by 3.

Rule: Multiply by 3.	
Number of Triangles	**Number of Straws**
1	3
2	6
3	9
4	■
5	■

Step 2 Extend the rule.

4 triangles = $4 \times \mathbf{3}$ or 12 straws

5 triangles = $5 \times \mathbf{3}$ or 15 straws.

So, Kathy will need 15 straws to make 5 triangles.

Real-World EXAMPLE Find and Extend a Rule

Remember

You can make a table to help you see a pattern.

2 PLANTS Mitch found one 4-leaf clover. He then found another. Now, he has 2 clovers and there are a total of 8 leaves. How many leaves will there be if he finds 5 clovers that have 4 leaves each?

Step 1 Find the rule.

Rule: Multiply by 4.	
Clover	**Leaves**
1	4
2	8
3	12
4	■
5	■

Step 2 Extend the rule.

$3 \times \mathbf{4} = 12$
$4 \times \mathbf{4} = 16$
$5 \times \mathbf{4} = 20$

So, there are 20 leaves on 5 clovers.

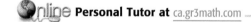

Online Personal Tutor at ca.gr3math.com

CHECK What You Know

Find and extend a rule for each table. Then copy and complete.

See Examples 1 and 2 (pp. 234–235)

1.

Rule: ■				
Input	2	3	4	5
Output	10	15	■	25

2.

Rule: ■				
Input	1	2	3	4
Output	2	4	6	■

3. There are 4 books about Japan, 6 books about China, and 8 books about Russia. If the pattern continues and the next set of books is about England, how many books will there be about England?

4. Talk About It Explain how multiplication can be used to help you extend a pattern.

Practice and Problem Solving

EXTRA PRACTICE
See page R16.

Find and extend a rule for each table. Then copy and complete.
See Examples 1 and 2 (pp. 234–235)

5.

Rule: ■	
Input	**Output**
2	16
■	8
7	56
5	40

6.

Rule: ■	
Input	**Output**
7	63
■	36
3	■
■	18

7.

Rule: ■	
Input	**Output**
3	12
■	16
6	24
9	■

8.

Rule: ■				
Input	2	4	6	8
Output	20	40	■	■

9.

Rule: ■				
Input	6	4	9	■
Output	30	20	■	35

For Exercises 10–11, find a rule. Then extend the rule to solve.
See Examples 1 and 2 (pp. 234–235)

10. The amusement park sold ride tickets in packs of 5, 10, 15, and 20 tickets. What would a pack of 5 tickets cost if 20 tickets cost $4?

11. Mrs. Glenn planted 5 flowers in the front row of her garden. The second row had 10 flowers and the third row had 15. How many flowers will be in the 5th row?

Real-World PROBLEM SOLVING

Data File Old growth redwoods are some of the world's tallest trees.

12. If a redwood grew 6 feet tall after its first year, how tall would it be after 8 years of growing at the same rate?

13. A 10-year-old tree is 40 feet tall. If it grew the same amount each year, how tall was it when it was 2 years old?

Redwoods

- A redwood tree can grow 4 to 6 feet per year.
- They can live 2,000 years.
- They can grow to over 300 feet tall.

H.O.T. Problems

14. CHALLENGE Create a table that uses a multiplication rule. Write input and output pairs.

15. WHICH ONE DOESN'T BELONG? Identify the number pair that would not be found in a table with a rule of × 6. Explain.

5 and 30 | 8 and 24 | 10 and 60 | 7 and 42

16. WRITING IN ▸MATH Explain how to find a rule when given a pattern.

Standards Practice

17 The table shows the number of crayons needed. **(Lesson 5-9)**

Crayons Needed	
Students	**Crayons**
3	15
4	20
6	30

Each student gets the same number of crayons. How many are needed for 8 students?

A 20 **C** 35

B 30 **D** 40

18 If $3 \times 7 \times 8 = 168$, then what is $7 \times 8 \times 3$? **(Lesson 5-8)**

F 75 **H** 158

G 97 **J** 168

19 One pencil costs 50¢. Two pencils cost $1.00. Three pencils cost $1.50. How much will 4 pencils cost? **(Lesson 5-9)**

A $1.75 **C** $2.50

B $2.00 **D** $2.75

Spiral Review

Algebra Find each missing number. (Lesson 5-8)

20. $4 \times 3 \times \blacksquare = 36$ **21.** $\blacksquare \times 6 \times 3 = 36$ **22.** $8 \times 5 \times \blacksquare = 80$

23. Heather has 3 assignments to turn in. Each assignment has 4 exercises. Each exercise is worth 5 points. What is the total number of points Heather can get if all of the exercises are correct? **(Lesson 5-7)**

5 Study Guide and Review

FOLDABLES™ Study Organizer GET READY to Study

Be sure the following Key Concepts and Key Vocabulary words are written in your Foldable.

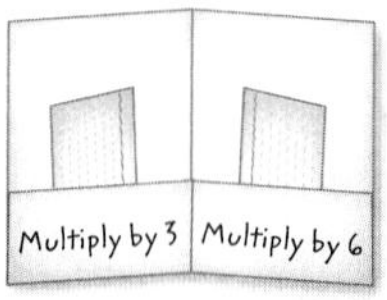

BIG Ideas

- The **Associative Property of Multiplication** states that the way that factors are grouped does not change the product. **(p. 228)**

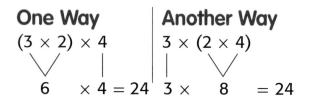

One Way	Another Way
$(3 \times 2) \times 4$	$3 \times (2 \times 4)$
$6 \times 4 = 24$	$3 \times 8 = 24$

- **Find and extend a rule (p. 234)**

Rule: Multiply by ■.	
Input	**Output**
1	4
2	8
3	12
4	16

The rule is to multiply by 4.

Key Vocabulary

Associative Property of Multiplication (p. 228)

Commutative Property of Multiplication (p. 201)

factor (p. 201)

product (p. 201)

rule (p. 234)

Vocabulary Check

1. The ___?___ Property of Multiplication states that the product does not change if the order of the factors changes.

2. A ___?___ tells you what to do to the first number to get the second.

3. The answer to a multiplication problem is called the ___?___.

4. The ___?___ Property of Multiplication states that the way that factors are grouped does not change the product.

Math Online Vocabulary Review at ca.gr3math.com

Lesson-by-Lesson Review

5-1 Multiply by 3 (pp. 203–205)

Example 1
There are 8 parrots. Each has 5 red feathers on its head. How many feathers are there in all?

There are 8 groups of 5 feathers. Use an array to find 8×5.

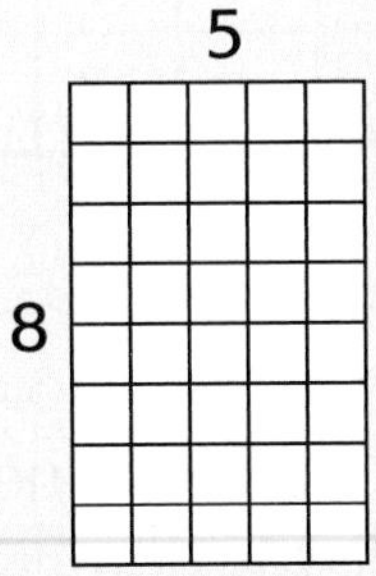

$8 \times 5 = 40$. So, there are 40 feathers.

Multiply.

5. $\begin{array}{r} 3 \\ \times 7 \\ \hline \end{array}$ **6.** $\begin{array}{r} 4 \\ \times 3 \\ \hline \end{array}$

7. $\begin{array}{r} 6 \\ \times 3 \\ \hline \end{array}$ **8.** $\begin{array}{r} 3 \\ \times 8 \\ \hline \end{array}$

Algebra Copy and complete.

9.

Rule: Multiply by 3.				
Input	7	■	2	■
Output	■	18	■	24

10. There are 4 trees with 3 rabbits sitting under each tree. How many rabbits are there after 2 rabbits hop away?

5-2 Multiply by 6 (pp. 206–209)

Example 2
Each package of yogurt has 4 cups. If Sue Ellen buys 6 packages, how many cups will she have?

Double a known fact to find 6×4.

$$\begin{aligned} 6 \times 4 &= 3 \times 4 + 3 \times 4 \\ &= 12 + 12 \\ &= 24 \end{aligned}$$

So, $6 \times 4 = 24$.

Multiply.

11. 6×5 **12.** 7×6

13. $\begin{array}{r} 6 \\ \times 4 \\ \hline \end{array}$ **14.** $\begin{array}{r} 6 \\ \times 6 \\ \hline \end{array}$

Algebra Find each missing factor.

15. $6 \times ■ = 18$ **16.** $■ \times 6 = 6$

17. Tyler and 6 friends are eating pizza. Each person gets 3 slices. How many slices of pizzas will be needed?

5-3 Problem-Solving Strategy: Look for a Pattern (pp. 212–213)

Example 3

Tate is making rows of dominoes. He lines up 3 dominoes in the first row, 5 in the second, and 7 in the third. How many dominoes will be in the 7th row if Tate continues his pattern?

Understand You know the number of dominoes in the first three rows. Find how many dominoes will be in the seventh row.

Plan Organize the data in a table and then look for and extend the pattern.

Solve

Row	1	2	3	4	5	6	7
Dominoes	3	5	7	9	11	13	15

+2 +2 +2 +2 +2 +2

$7 + 2 = 9$
$9 + 2 = 11$
$11 + 2 = 13$
$13 + 2 = 15$

So, there will be 15 dominoes in the seventh row.

Check The answer makes sense for the problem. The answer is correct.

Solve. Use the *look for a pattern* strategy.

18. The following table shows Rich's test scores. All of the scores follow a pattern. What are the last two scores he could have received?

Test	1	2	3	4	5
Score	79	84	89	■	■

19. Ravi earned \$4 allowance this week. If he continues to feed and walk his dog every day, he will earn \$2 more than the week before. What will his allowance be for week 5?

20. Lee takes care of the two family dogs. He feeds each dog 3 treats each day. How many treats does Lee give the dogs in one week?

21. Measurement Arnaldo is training for a race. The first week, he runs 2 miles. The next week he runs 5 miles. During the third week he runs 8 miles. How many weeks will it take him to reach his goal of 20 miles?

5-4 Multiply by 7 (pp. 214–216)

Example 4
William received 28 football cards from his 7 friends. Each friend gave him the same number of cards. How many cards did each friend give him?

You can use a number sentence.

7 × ■ = 28

THINK 7 times what equals 28?

Since 7 × 4 = 28, each friend gave him 4 cards.

Multiply.

22. 7 × 6 **23.** 5 × 7

24. $\begin{array}{r} 7 \\ \times 3 \\ \hline \end{array}$ **25.** $\begin{array}{r} 8 \\ \times 7 \\ \hline \end{array}$

Algebra Find each missing number.

26. 6 × ■ = 42 **27.** 7 × ■ = 28

28. ■ × 7 = 49 **29.** 8 × 7= ■

30. There are 7 flights of stairs. Each flight has 9 steps. What is the total number of steps?

5-5 Multiply by 8 (pp. 218–221)

Example 5
Jamal has 8 bags. Each bag contains 6 coins. How many coins does he have in all?

You need to find 8 groups of 6 or 8 × 6.

You know that 6 × 8 = 48.

So, 8 × 6 = 48

Jamal has 48 coins.

Multiply.

31. 8 × 3 **32.** 8 × 7

33. $\begin{array}{r} 8 \\ \times 4 \\ \hline \end{array}$ **34.** $\begin{array}{r} 8 \\ \times 5 \\ \hline \end{array}$

Compare. Use >, <, or =.

35. 7 × 8 ■ 8 × 10

36. 3 × 8 ■ 8 × 4

37. Each box contains 8 bananas. If the manager orders 9 boxes, how many bananas will arrive?

5-6 Multiply by 9 (pp. 222–224)

Example 6
Karen put her photos in a scrapbook. There are 3 on each page. When she finished, 9 pages were filled. How many photos are there?

You can subtract from a known fact.

Step 1 9×3 is 9 groups of 3. Use the known fact of 10 groups of 3. $10 \times 3 = 30$

Step 2 Subtract 1 group of 3. $30 - 3 = 27$

So, $9 \times 3 = 27$ photos.

Find each missing number.

38. $9 \times \square = 36$ **39.** $9 \times \square = 45$

40. $9 \times \square = 54$ **41.** $9 \times \square = 63$

42. Algebra Copy and complete.

Factor	3	9	■	8
Factor	9	■	9	9
Product	■	36	63	■

43. Each of Kara's dolls is worth \$9. If she sold some and made \$81, how many dolls did she sell?

5-7 Problem-Solving Investigation: Choose a Strategy (pp. 226–227)

Example 7
Gonzalo sold 9 raffle tickets today and 7 yesterday. Each costs \$5. How many more tickets does he need to sell to raise \$100?

You need to find how many more tickets he must sell to raise \$100.

$9 \times \$5 = \$45$ Today
$7 \times \$5 = \$35$ Yesterday

So, he raised \$45 + \$35 or \$80.

He still needs to raise \$100 − \$80 or \$20.

Since $4 \times \$5$ is \$20, he must sell 4 more tickets.

Solve. Tell what strategy you used.

44. To win a contest, students must read 24 books in 3 months. How many books does a student need to read each month?

45. Mrs. Larkin's students earned 4 tokens on Monday, 6 on Tuesday and 8 on Wednesday. If the pattern continues, how many will they earn on Friday?

46. Measurement It takes 3 minutes for each child to get through the lunch line. How long will it take for Ms. Toshio's last 7 students?

5-8 Algebra: Associative Property (pp. 228–231)

Example 8
There are 5 farmers. Each farmer has 4 sheep. Each sheep has 2 ears. How many ears are there altogether?

You can use the Associative Property of Multiplication to find the total number of ears.

Find the product of $4 \times 2 \times 5$.

One Way

First find 4×2.

$(4 \times 2) \times 5$

$8 \times 5 = 40$

Another Way

First find 2×5.

$4 \times (2 \times 5)$

$4 \times 10 = 40$

So, $4 \times 2 \times 5 = 40$. There are a total of 40 ears.

Find each product.

47. $7 \times (2 \times 2)$

48. $(2 \times 5) \times 3$

49. $(4 \times 2) \times 9$

50. $6 \times (2 \times 3)$

Algebra Find each missing number.

51. $3 \times (\blacksquare \times 4) = 24$

52. $(6 \times \blacksquare) \times 5 = 30$

53. Jennifer has 3 bookcases. Each one has 4 shelves. She will put 3 stuffed animals on each shelf. How many stuffed animals does Jennifer have on the three bookcases?

54. A third grade classroom has 3 rows. Each row has 10 desks. Upon each desk are 3 pencils. How many pencils are there in all?

55. There are 4 families at the fair. Each of these families has 3 children. If each of the children buys 5 ride tickets, how many tickets will the children have?

5-9 Algebra Find a Rule (pp. 234–237)

Example 9
Natasha is making bows. The first bow she made used 4 feet of ribbon. The second and third bows she made used another 4 feet of ribbon each. How many feet of ribbon does she need to make 5 bows?

Step 1 Find the rule.

Rule: Multiply by ■.	
Bow	**Ribbon (ft)**
1	4
2	8
3	12
4	■
5	■

1 bow = 4 feet of ribbon
$1 \times 4 = 4$
2 bows = 8 feet of ribbon
$2 \times 4 = 8$
3 bows = 12 feet of ribbon
$3 \times 4 = 12$

The rule is to multiply the number of bows by 4.

Step 2 Extend the rule.
$4 \times 4 = 16$
$5 \times 4 = 20$

So, Natasha will need 20 feet of ribbon to make 5 bows.

Find and extend the rule for each table. Then copy and complete.

56.

Rule: Multiply by ■.				
Input	6	4	9	■
Output	24	16	■	40

57.

Rule: Multiply by ■.				
Input	2	4	6	8
Output	10	20	■	■

58. Harada is making a necklace. She uses 2 red beads, then 1 yellow bead. Then, 2 red beads and 1 yellow bead. She continues this pattern. How many red beads will she use if she uses 24 beads?

59. Algebra Find a pattern for 2, 6, 5, 9, 8, ... Then extend it to find the next three numbers.

60. There are 20 passengers on the train. At the first stop, 2 people get off and 5 get on. At the second stop, 2 people get off and 5 get on. This pattern continues. How many stops will it be before there are 38 people on the train?

Chapter 5 Chapter Test

Multiply.

1. $\begin{array}{r} 3 \\ \times 6 \\ \hline \end{array}$

2. $\begin{array}{r} 3 \\ \times 9 \\ \hline \end{array}$

3. $\begin{array}{r} 9 \\ \times 4 \\ \hline \end{array}$

4. $\begin{array}{r} 6 \\ \times 4 \\ \hline \end{array}$

Write the rule for each table. Then copy and complete

5.

Rule: Multiply by ■.				
Input	5	6	7	8
Output	35	■	49	■

6.

Rule: Multiply by ■.				
Input	6	8	4	■
Output	48	64	■	80

Algebra Find each missing number.

7. $■ \times (2 \times 4) = 64$

8. $(■ \times 8) \times 9 = 72$

9. **STANDARDS PRACTICE** Four students are in this year's spelling bee. Each student had to pass 5 tests to be in the spelling bee. How many tests is that in all?

   A 7 **C** 12

   B 9 **D** 20

10. The soccer team scored 14 points. Each of the 7 members scored the same number of points. How many points did each member score?

11. During gym class, the teacher gave the students a number as they stood in line. She counted 1, 2, 3, 1, 2, 3, ... What number did the 22nd student get?

Multiply.

12. 9×6

13. 7×9

14. $\begin{array}{r} 8 \\ \times 8 \\ \hline \end{array}$

15. $\begin{array}{r} 8 \\ \times 3 \\ \hline \end{array}$

16. **Algebra** Copy and complete.

Rule: Multiply by 6.					
Input	3	7	■	■	1
Output	■	■	30	0	■

17. **STANDARDS PRACTICE** Mr. Thompson bought 7 of the same item at the store. He paid a total of $42. What did he buy?

   F $6 shirts **H** $35 shoes

   G $7 pants **J** $49 jacket

18. **WRITING IN MATH** If $2 \times 7 \times 4 = 56$, then what is $7 \times 4 \times 2$? Explain.

5

California Standards Practice

Cumulative, Chapters 1–5

Standards Example

On a field trip, Mrs. Kong has 8 boxes of lunches to give to students. Each box has 6 lunches. How many lunches does she have to give to students?

A 42 **C** 54

B 48 **D** 56

Read the Question

You need to find the total number of lunches Mrs. Kong has to give students.

Solve the Question

Find 8×6. You know that $6 \times 8 = 48$.
So, $8 \times 6 = 48$. Commutative Property
The answer is B.

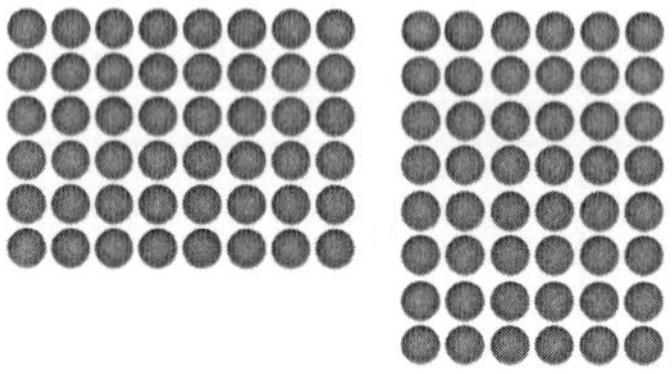

Online Personal Tutor at ca.gr3math.com

Choose the best answer.

1 **For the school play, chairs were set in 8 rows of 8 seats. How many seats are there in all?**

A 40

B 56

C 63

D 64

2 **Each package of markers has 6 markers. How many markers are in 7 packages?**

F 35

G 36

H 42

I 48

3 **What number makes this number sentence true?**

$$9 \times \blacksquare = 54$$

A 5 **C** 7

B 6 **D** 8

4 **What multiplication sentence describes the array shown.**

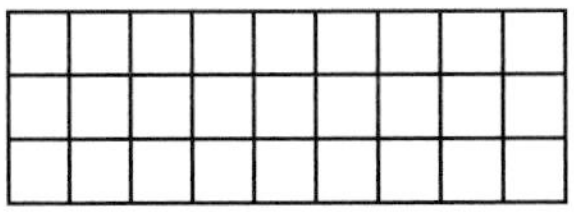

F 3×5 **H** 6×3

G 3×9 **J** 8×3

5 **If $2 \times 3 \times 7 = 42$, then what is $3 \times 2 \times 7$?**

A 35 **C** 42

B 40 **D** 52

6 **A paperback book costs \$7. How much will 4 of these books cost?**

F \$21 **H** \$28

G \$25 **J** \$35

7 **The Main Street School bought 1250 erasers. They gave out 867 to students. How many are left?**

A 383 **C** 417

B 393 **D** 483

8 **Juan bought 4 packages of juice boxes. Each package has 4 juice boxes. Which number sentence shows how to find the number of juice boxes in all?**

F $4 + 4 = \blacksquare$ **H** $4 \times 4 = \blacksquare$

G $4 - 4 = \blacksquare$ **J** $16 - 4 = \blacksquare$

9 **Which number will make the number sentence true?**

$$\blacksquare \times 3 = 0$$

A 0 **C** 3

B 1 **D** 4

10 **What is 4273 rounded to the nearest hundred?**

F 4000 **H** 4270

G 4200 **J** 4300

CHAPTER 6

Division Concepts and Facts

BIG Idea What is division?

Division is an operation with two numbers. One number tells you how many things you have. The other tells you how many equal groups to form.

Example Lonnie has 15 pennies to share among 5 friends. If Lonnie gives each friend the same number of pennies, each friend will get 15 ÷ 5 or 3 pennies.

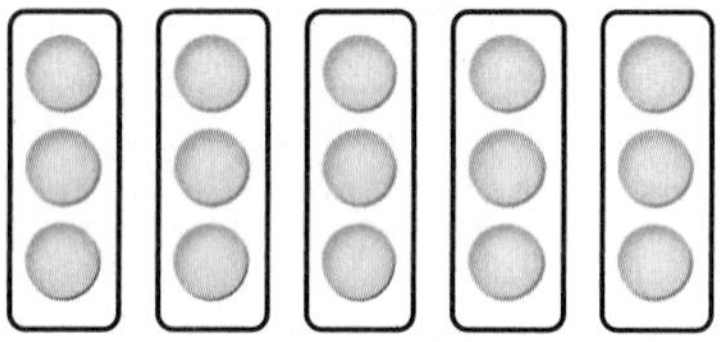

What will I learn in this chapter?

- Explore the meaning of division.
- Relate subtraction and multiplication to division.
- Divide by 2, 5, and 10.
- Use rules to divide with 0 and 1.
- To solve problems, choose an operation.

Key Vocabulary

divide
dividend
divisor
quotient

Math Online **Student Study Tools at** ca.gr3math.com

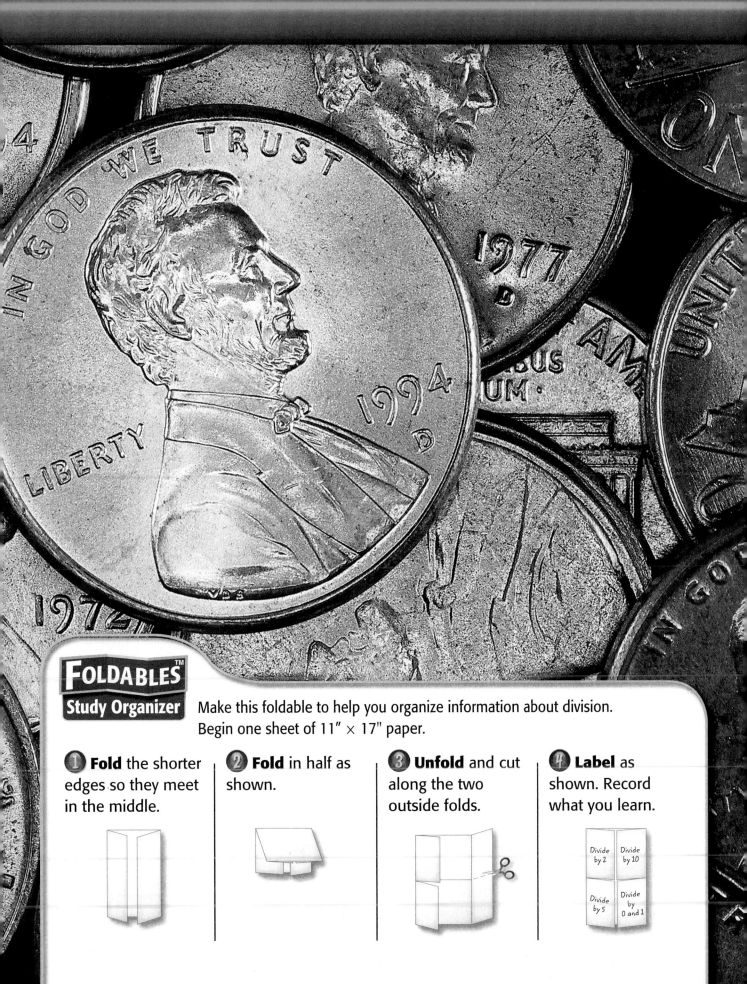

FOLDABLES™
Study Organizer

Make this foldable to help you organize information about division. Begin one sheet of 11″ × 17″ paper.

1. **Fold** the shorter edges so they meet in the middle.

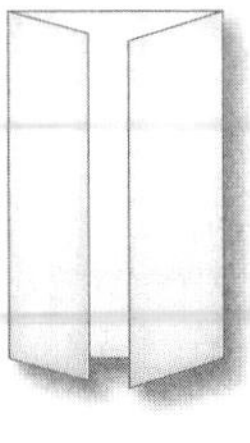

2. **Fold** in half as shown.

3. **Unfold** and cut along the two outside folds.

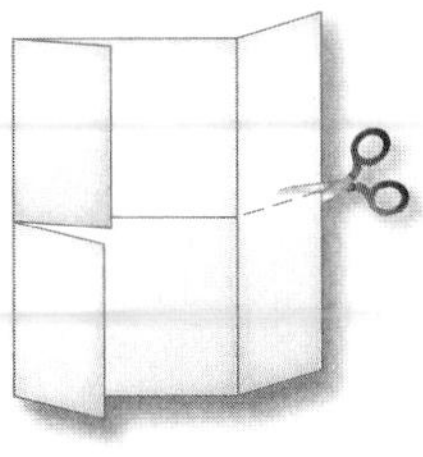

4. **Label** as shown. Record what you learn.

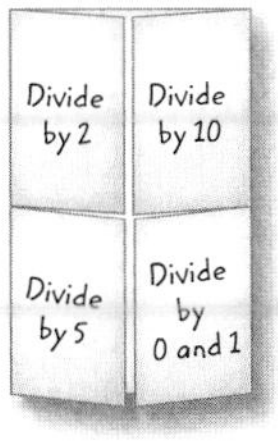

ARE YOU READY for Chapter 6?

You have two ways to check prerequisite skills for this chapter.

Option 2

Math Online Take the Chapter Readiness Quiz at ca.gr3math.com.

Option 1

Complete the Quick Check below.

QUICK Check

Subtract. **(Lesson 3-1)**

1. 14 − 7 **2.** 36 − 6 **3.** 45 − 9 **4.** 56 − 8

5. There are 18 children reading books. If 6 of them are reading mystery books, how many are reading other kinds of book?

Tell whether each pair of groups are equal. **(Lesson 3-9)**

6.

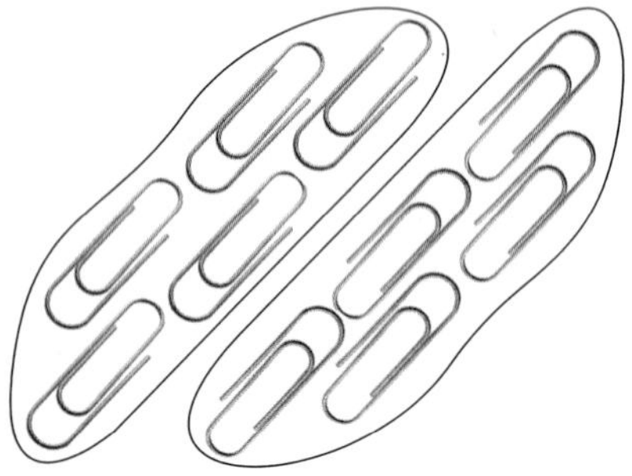

7.

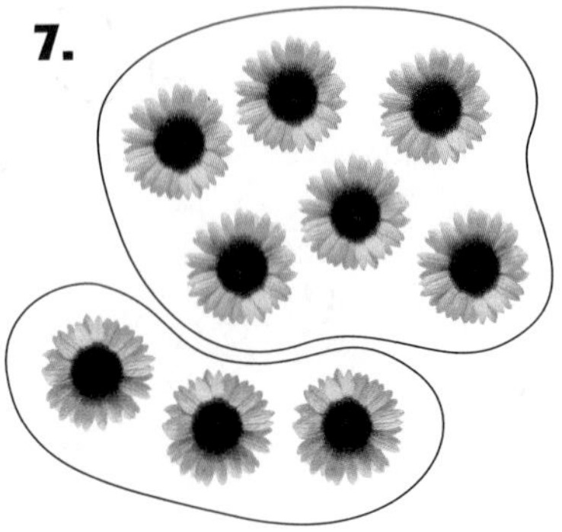

8. Camille, Diana, and Emma are sharing a box of crackers. They each get 3 crackers. How many crackers are in the box?

Multiply. **(Lessons 4-3, 4-4, 5-1, and 5-4)**

9. 2 × 4 **10.** 3 × 6 **11.** 5 × 4 **12.** 7 × 8

13. Write the multiplication sentences for the two arrays shown.

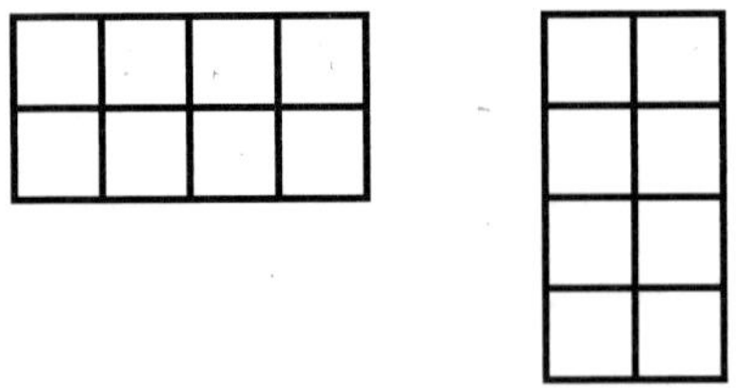

Explore

Math Activity for 6-1
Understand Division

MAIN IDEA

I will explore the meaning of division.

Standard 3MR2.3 Use a variety of methods, such as words, numbers, symbols, charts, graphs, tables, diagrams, **and models, to explain mathematical reasoning.**

Preparation for Standard 3NS2.3 Use the inverse relationship of multiplication and division to compute and check results.

You Will Need
counters
paper plates

Concepts in Motion

Animation
ca.gr3math.com

Division is an operation with two numbers. One number tells you how many things you have. The other tells you how many equal groups to form.

$10 \div 5 = 2$ ← Read ÷ as *divided by.* 10 divided by 5 is 2.

To **divide** means to separate a number into equal groups to find the number of groups or the number in each group.

ACTIVITY

1 Divide 12 counters into 3 equal groups.

Step 1 Count out 12 counters. Using paper plates, show 3 groups.

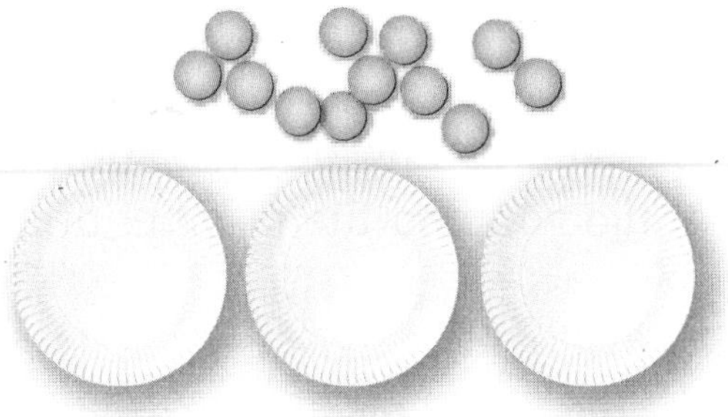

Step 2 Place counters equally among the 3 groups until all all of the counters are gone.

Step 3 Twelve counters were divided into 3 groups. There are 4 counters in each group. So, $12 \div 3 = 4$.

Hands-On Activity

ACTIVITY

2 **Group 12 counters 3 at a time. How many groups are there?**

Step 1 Count out 12 counters.

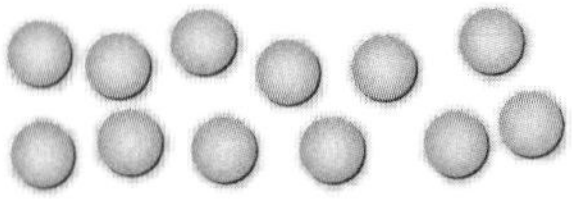

Step 2 Make equal groups of 3 until all the counters are gone.

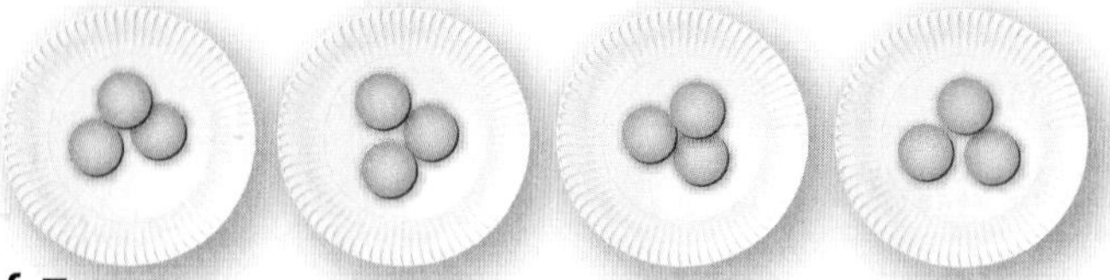

There are 4 equal groups of 3.
So, $12 \div 4 = 3$.

Think About It

1. Explain how you divided 12 counters into equal groups.

2. When you divided the counters into groups of 3, how did you find the number of equal groups?

CHECK What You Know

3. Make equal groups to find the number of counters in each group.

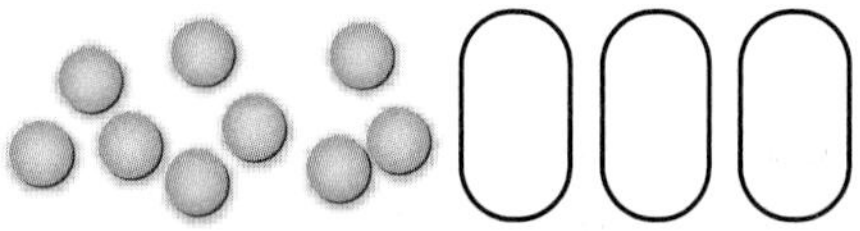

4. Find the number of equal groups of 5.

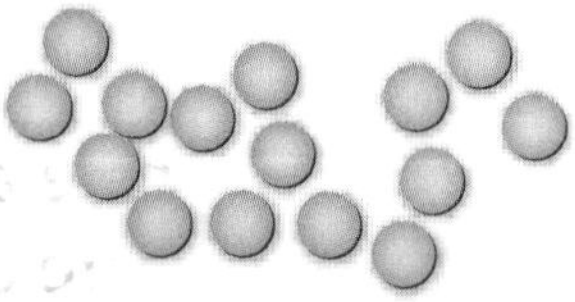

5. Copy the chart. Then use counters to help complete.

Number of Counters	Number of Equal Groups	Number in Each Group	Division Sentence
9	3	3	$9 \div 3 = 3$
14	2		
15		5	
6		3	

6. **WRITING IN ▶MATH** Can 13 counters be divided equally into groups of 3? Explain.

6-1 Relate Division to Subtraction

MAIN IDEA

I will divide using subtraction.

Standard 3MR2.3 Use a variety of methods, such as words, numbers, symbols, charts, graphs, tables, diagrams, **and models, to explain mathematical reasoning.**

Preparation for Standard 3NS2.3 Use the inverse relationship of multiplication and divisions to compute and check results.

New Vocabulary

division
divide

GET READY to Learn

There are 15 pencils in a box. Each pencil is either red, blue, or yellow. There is the same number of each color. How many pencils of each color are there?

You have used counters to model **division**. Recall that to **divide** means to separate a number into equal groups to find the number of groups or the number in each group.

Real-World EXAMPLE Use Models to Divide

1 **PENCILS How many pencils of each color are there?**
Using counters, divide 15 counters equally into 3 groups until all the counters are gone.

5 5 5

There are 5 counters in each group. So, $15 \div 3 = 5$.
There are 5 pencils of each color.

You can also divide using *repeated subtraction.* Subtract equal groups repeatedly until you get to zero.

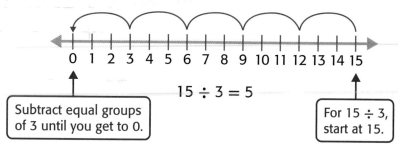

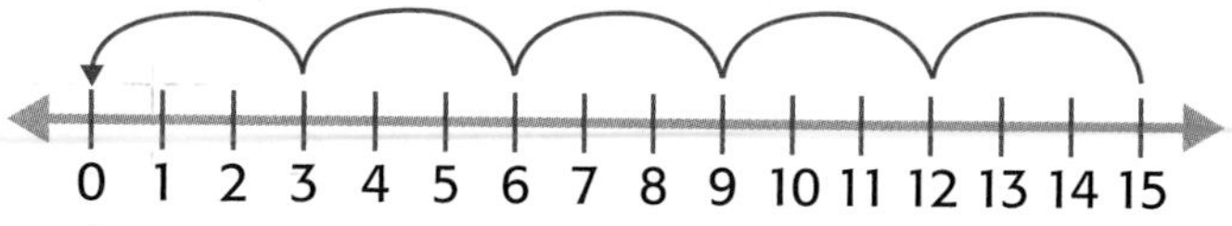

$15 \div 3 = 5$

Subtract equal groups of 3 until you get to 0.

For $15 \div 3$, start at 15.

Real-World EXAMPLE — Repeated Subtraction

2 SPORTS Nathan wants to put his 10 baseball cards in equal groups of 2. How many groups can he make?

Use repeated subtraction to find 10 ÷ 2.

One Way: Number Line	Another Way: Paper and Pencil
⑤ ④ ③ ② ① 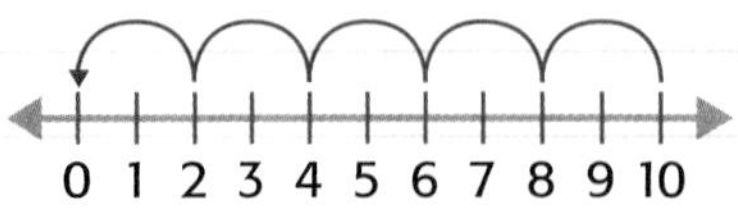	① 10 − 2 = 8 → ② 8 − 2 = 6 → ③ 6 − 2 = 4 → ④ 4 − 2 = 2 → ⑤ 2 − 2 = 0
Start at 10. Count back by 2s until you reach 0. How many times did you subtract?	Subtract groups of 2 until you reach 0. How many groups did you subtract?

So, 10 ÷ 2 = 5. Nathan will have 5 groups of cards.

Personal Tutor at ca.gr3math.com

CHECK What You Know

Divide. Use counters. See Example 1 (p. 253)

1. There are 16 flowers. Each vase has 4 flowers. How many vases?

2. There are 14 ears. Each dog has 2 ears. How many dogs are there?

Divide. Use repeated subtraction on a number line or paper and pencil. See Example 2 (p. 254)

3. 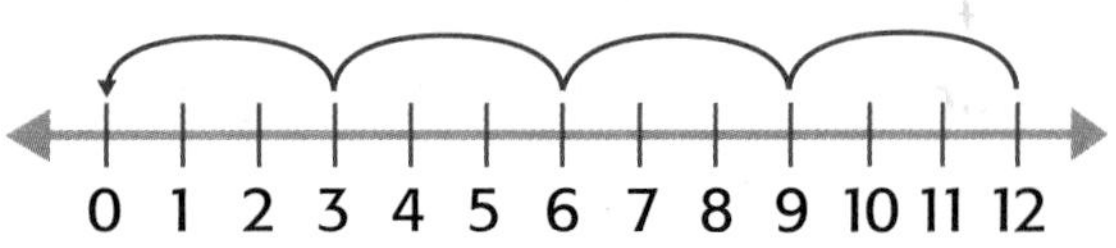
12 ÷ 3

4. 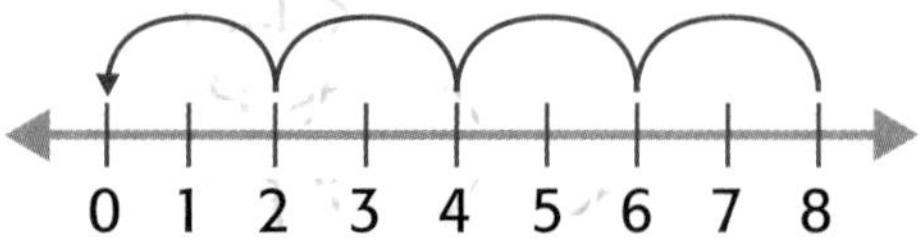
8 ÷ 2

5. 6 ÷ 2

6. 12 ÷ 6

7. 25 ÷ 5

8. There are 14 mittens. Each student wears 2 mittens. How many students are there?

9. **Talk About It** Explain how you could use a full width number line to divide 18 ÷ 9.

Math Online Extra Examples at ca.gr3math.com

Practice and Problem Solving

EXTRA PRACTICE See page R16.

Divide. Use counters. See Example 1 (p. 253)

10. There are 16 orange slices. Each orange has 8 slices. How many oranges are there?

11. **Measurement** There are 16 miles. Each trip is 2 miles. How many trips are there?

12. There are 25 marbles with 5 marbles in each bag. How many bags are there?

13. There are 12 muffins and 4 friends. How many muffins will each friend get if they get the same number of muffins?

Divide. Use repeated subtraction on a number line or paper and pencil. See Example 2 (p. 254)

14.

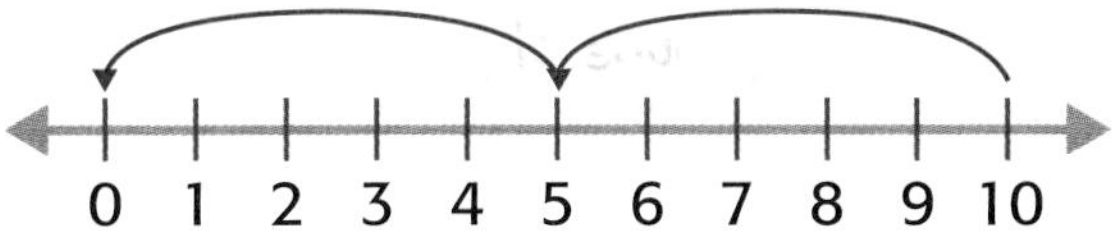

$10 \div 5$

15.

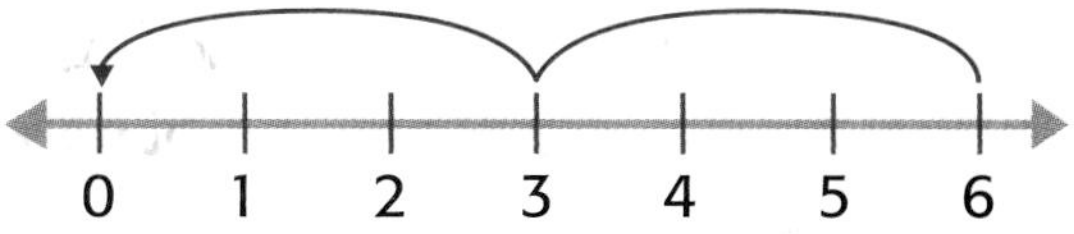

$6 \div 3$

16.

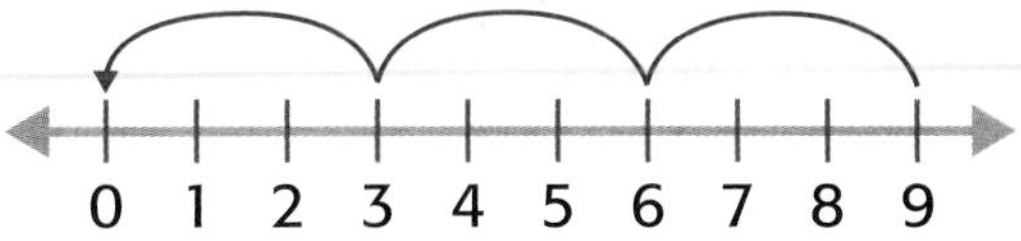

$9 \div 3$

17.

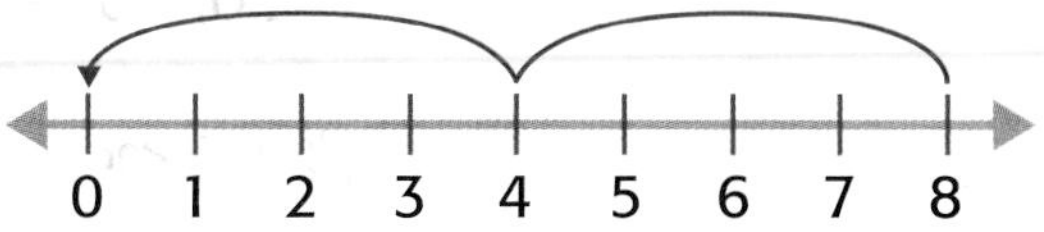

$8 \div 4$

18. $18 \div 3 = \blacksquare$

19. $12 \div 2 = \blacksquare$

20. $24 \div 6 = \blacksquare$

21. $12 \div 3 = \blacksquare$

22. $27 \div 3 = \blacksquare$

23. $28 \div 7 = \blacksquare$

24. A house has 16 windows. Each room has 4 windows. How many rooms does the house have?

25. Felecia wants to read 9 stories. If each magazine has 3 stories, how many magazines will she read?

26. There are 12 erasers in a bag. Rodrigo wants to share them equally with himself and his 2 friends. How many erasers will each person get?

27. Chester had 24 pencils. He kept 4 and shared the rest equally among his 4 brothers. How many did each brother get?

H.O.T. Problems

28. **OPEN ENDED** Write a real-world problem that could be represented by $18 \div 6$.

29. **WRITING IN ▶MATH** How is division related to subtraction?

Explore

Math Activity for 6-2

Relate Multiplication to Division

MAIN IDEA

I will relate multiplication to division.

Standard 3NS2.3 **Use the inverse relationship of multiplication and divisions to compute and check results.**

Standard 3MR2.3 **Use a variety of methods, such as words, numbers, symbols,** charts, graphs, tables, diagrams, **and models, to explain mathematical reasoning.**

You Will Need
counters

New Vocabulary

dividend
divisor
quotient

Concepts in Motion

Animation
ca.gr3math.com

You can relate multiplication to division.

ACTIVITY **Relate multiplication to division.**

Step 1 Model 21 ÷ 3.

Model 21 counters divided into 3 equal groups.

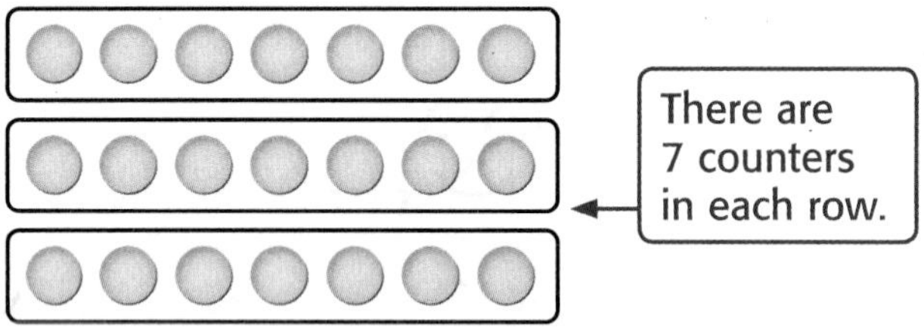
There are 7 counters in each row.

Step 2 Write a division sentence.

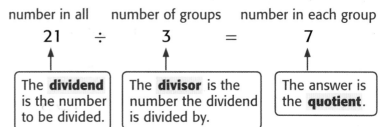

number in all		number of groups		number in each group
21	÷	3	=	7
The **dividend** is the number to be divided.		The **divisor** is the number the dividend is divided by.		The answer is the **quotient**.

Step 3 Write a multiplication sentence.

number of groups		number in each group		number in all
3	×	7	=	21

Hands-On Activity

Think About It

1. Explain how you used models to show 21 ÷ 3.

2. Explain how the array shows that 21 ÷ 3 = 7 is related to 3 × 7 = 21.

3. Explain how you would use models to show that 24 ÷ 6 = 4 is related to 6 × 4 = 24.

4. How can multiplication facts be used to divide?

CHECK What You Know

Use counters to model each problem. Then write related multiplication and division sentences to help find the quotient.

5. 12 ÷ 6
6. 18 ÷ 3
7. 25 ÷ 5
8. 15 ÷ 3
9. 16 ÷ 2
10. 24 ÷ 8

Write a related multiplication and division sentence for each picture.

11. 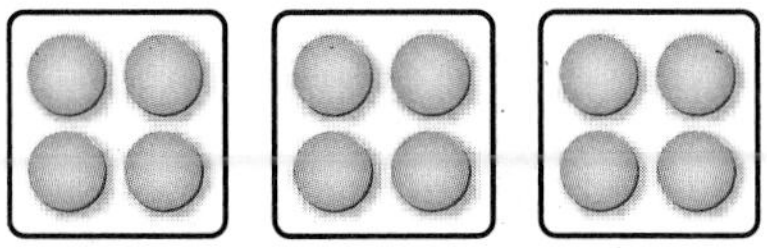

12. 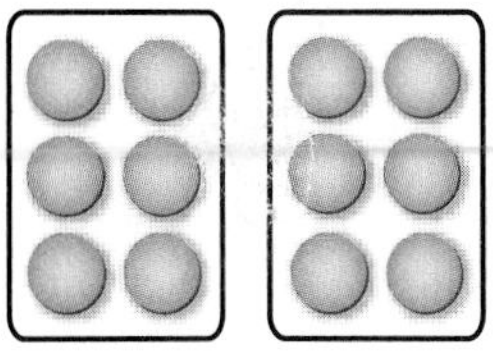

13. 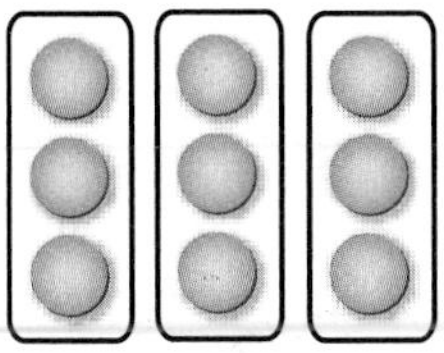

14. 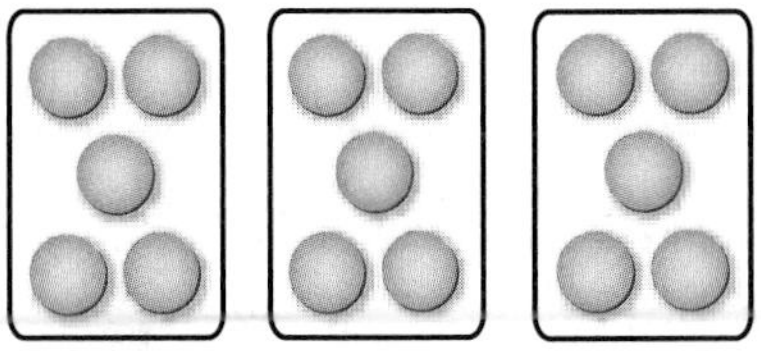

15. WRITING IN ►MATH How do you know what multiplication sentence to use to find 28 ÷ 4?

6-2 Relate Multiplication to Division

MAIN IDEA

I will divide using related multiplication facts.

Standard 3NS2.3 Use the inverse relationship of multiplication and division to compute and check results.

New Vocabulary

dividend
divisor
quotient
fact family

GET READY to Learn

A pan of blueberry muffins is shown. The pan represents an array. The array shows 3 rows of muffins with 4 muffins in each row.

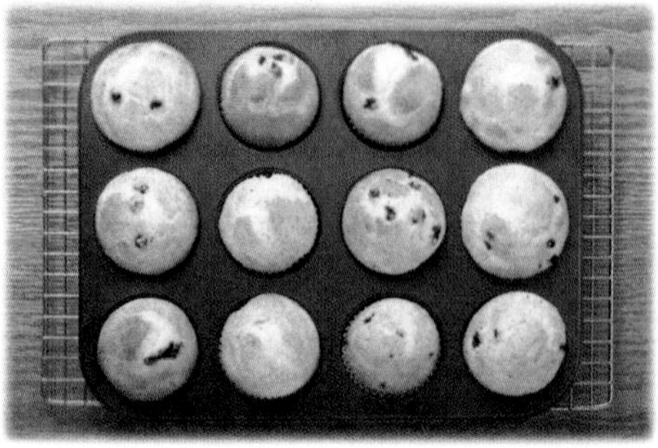

In the Explore activity, you used arrays to help you understand how multiplication and division are related.

Real-World EXAMPLE **Relate Multiplication to Division**

1 **MUFFINS Use the array of muffins to write related multiplication and division sentences.**

Multiplication

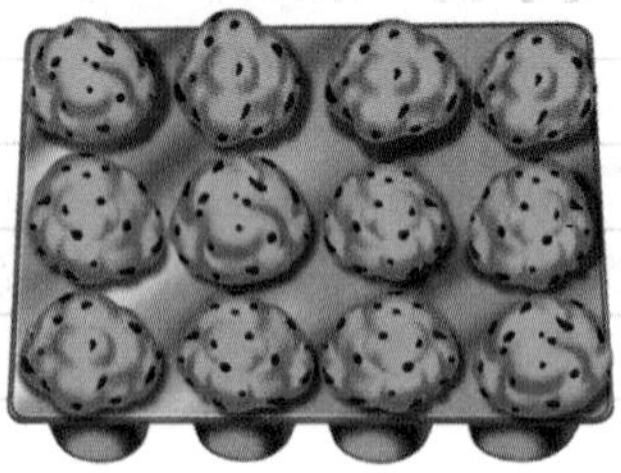

number of rows		number in each row		number in all
3	×	4	=	12
factor		factor		product

Division

number in all		number of rows		number in each row
12	÷	3	=	4
dividend		**divisor**		**quotient**

The related multiplication and division sentences are $3 \times 4 = 12$ and $12 \div 3 = 4$.

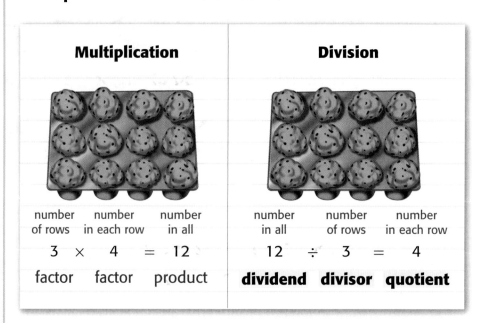

A group of related facts using the same numbers is a **fact family**.

Fact Family for 3, 4, and 12	Fact Family for 7 and 49
$3 \times 4 = 12$ $4 \times 3 = 12$ $12 \div 3 = 4$ $12 \div 4 = 3$	$7 \times 7 = 49$ $49 \div 7 = 7$

EXAMPLE Write a Fact Family

Remember

Thinking about numbers in a fact family can help you remember related facts.

2 **Use the fact family 3, 6, 18 to write four related multiplication and division sentences.**

$3 \times 6 = 18$

$6 \times 3 = 18$

$18 \div 3 = 6$

$18 \div 6 = 3$

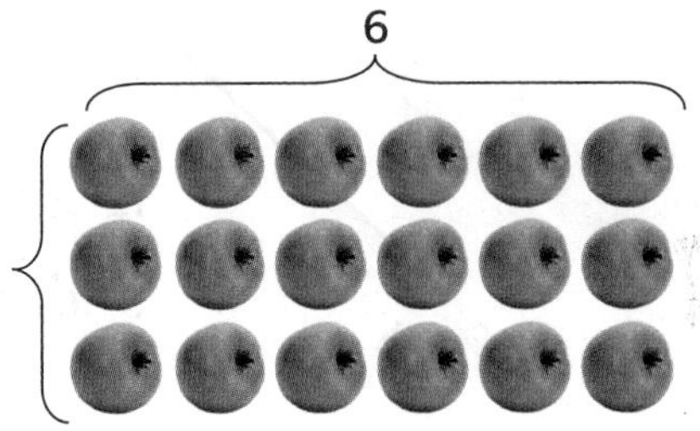

Notice each fact uses the same three numbers.

Online Personal Tutor at ca.gr3math.com

CHECK What You Know

Use the array to complete each pair of number sentences. See Example 1 (p. 258)

1. ■ $\times 5 = 15$
■ $\div 3 = 5$

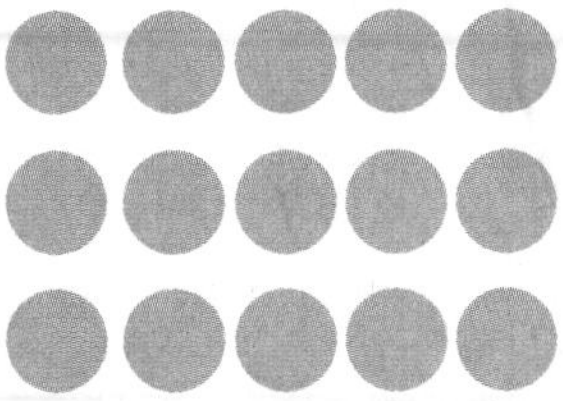

2. $4 \times$ ■ $= 24$
$24 \div$ ■ $= 6$

Write the fact family for each set of numbers. See Example 2 (p. 259)

3. 2, 6, 12 **4.** 4, 5, 20 **5.** 3, 9, 27

6. Gwen has 20 marbles and wants to divide them equally into 5 bags. How many marbles will be in each bag?

7. Talk About It Why are the product and the dividend the same in $3 \times 7 = 21$ and $21 \div 3 = 7$?

Practice and Problem Solving

EXTRA PRACTICE
See page R17.

Use the array to complete each pair of number sentences.
See Example 1 (p. 258)

8. ■ × 2 = 8
■ ÷ 4 = 2

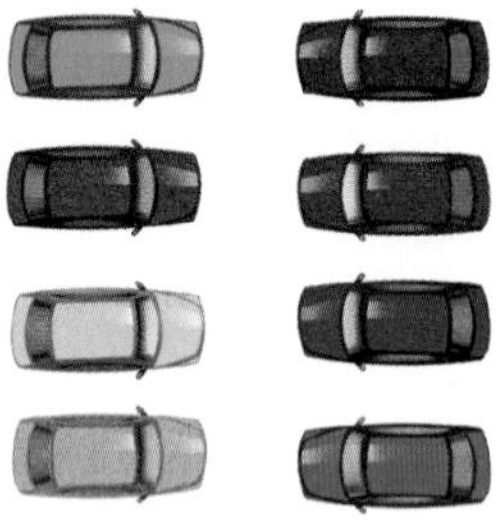

9. 2 × ■ = 4
4 ÷ ■ = 2

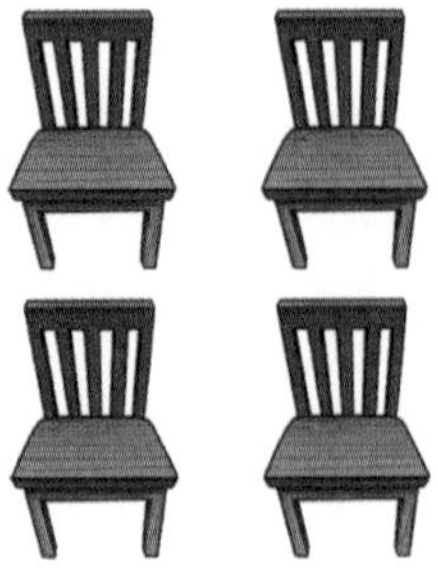

10. ■ × 7 = 14
■ ÷ 2 = 7

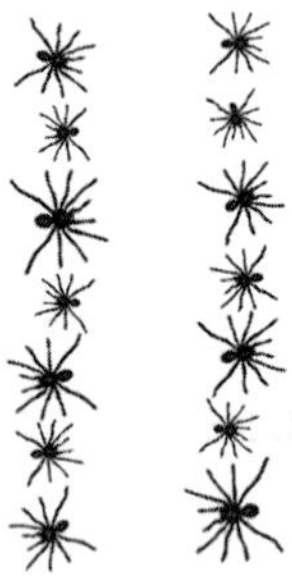

11. 4 × ■ = 20
20 ÷ ■ = 4

Write the fact family for each set of numbers. See Example 2 (p. 259)

12. 2, 3, 6

13. 2, 7, 14

14. 4, 16

15. 4, 8, 32

16. 4, 3, 12

17. 4, 7, 28

Write the set of numbers for each fact family.

18. 5 × 9 = 45
9 × 5 = 45
45 ÷ 5 = 9
45 ÷ 9 = 5

19. 7 × 2 = 14
2 × 7 = 14
14 ÷ 2 = 7
14 ÷ 7 = 2

20. 3 × 3 = 9
9 ÷ 3 = 3

21. All 5 members of the Mullin family went to the movies. Their tickets cost a total of $30. How much is each ticket?

22. The petting zoo has 21 animals. There are 7 types of animals, each with an equal number. How many animals does each type have?

23. Measurement Mr. Thomas travels 20 miles each week to and from work. If he works 5 days a week, how many miles does Mr. Thomas travel each day to go to work?

24. Stacia and her friend are each making a bracelet. They have 18 beads to share. If they use the same number of beads, how many beads will each bracelet have?

H.O.T. Problems

25. NUMBER SENSE What multiplication fact will help you find $27 \div 9$?

26. WHICH ONE DOESN'T BELONG? Identify the number sentence that does not belong. Explain.

$3 \times 6 = 18$	$18 \div 2 = 9$	$18 \div 6 = 3$	$6 \times 3 = 18$

27. WRITING IN MATH Explain how multiplication facts can help you with division facts. Give an example.

Standards Practice

28 The figure below is a model for $4 \times 6 = 24$ **(Lesson 6-2)**

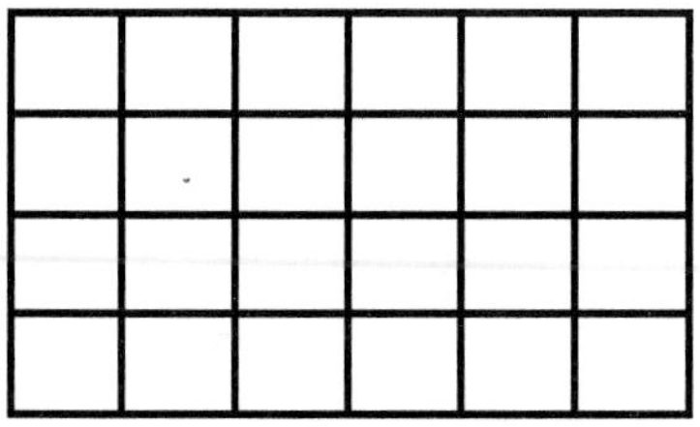

Which division sentence is modeled by the same figure?

A $6 \div 4 = 24$

B $24 \div 3 = 8$

C $24 \div 4 = 6$

D $24 \div 6 = 6$

29 Which division sentence is modeled by repeated subtraction on the number line? **(Lesson 6-1)**

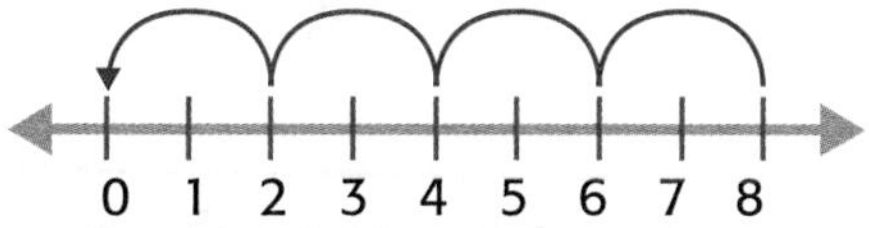

F $4 \div 2 = 8$

G $16 \div 2 = 8$

H $8 \div 2 = 4$

J $24 \div 8 = 3$

Spiral Review

Divide. Use repeated subtraction with paper and pencil. (Lesson 6-1)

30. $12 \div 4$ **31.** $18 \div 3$ **32.** $28 \div 7$ **33.** $25 \div 5$

34. Algebra Write a rule for the table. Then copy and complete. **(Lesson 5-9)**

Input	Output
7	35
2	■
4	20
■	15

35. One frog sat on a log for 29 minutes. A second frog sat for 16 minutes longer. How long did the second frog sit on the log? **(Lesson 2-2)**

6-3 Problem-Solving Skill

MAIN IDEA I will choose an operation to use to solve a problem.

Standard 3MR1.1 Analyze problems by identifying relationships, distinguishing relevant from irrelevent information, **sequencing and priortizing information, and observing patterns.** **Standard 3NS2.3 Use the inverse relationship of multiplication and division to compute and check results.**

Lakita's doctor saw patients for 5 hours today. During this time, the doctor saw 20 patients. How many patients did the doctor see each hour if she saw the same number?

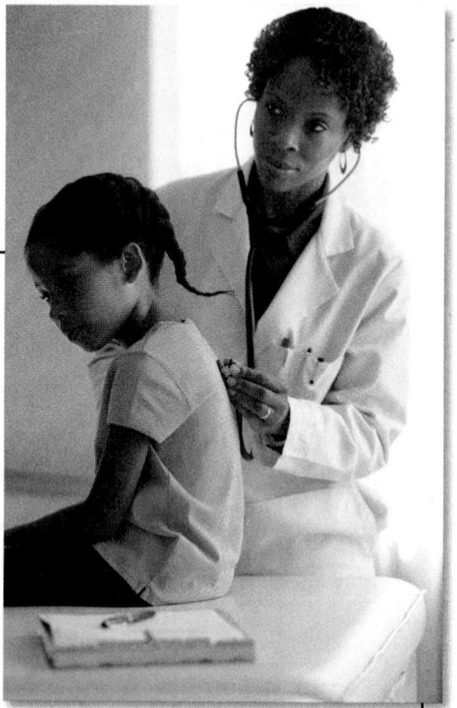

Understand

What facts do you know?

- The doctor saw patients for 5 hours.
- She saw 20 patients in all.

What do you need to find?

- The number of patients the doctor saw each hour.

Plan

There is a group of 20 patients. You need to find how many patients the doctor saw each hour in the 5 hours. Use division.

Solve

Divide $20 \div 5$.

total number of patients		number of hours		number of patients
20	÷	5	=	4

So, the doctor saw 4 patients each hour.

Check

You can use multiplication to check division.

$5 \times 4 = 20$

So, it makes sense that 4 patients would have been seen each hour.

ANALYZE the Skill

Refer to the problem on the previous page.

1. Explain why division was used to solve the problem. What other operation might you use to solve this problem?

2. Explain how the four step plan helped you solve this problem.

3. Suppose the doctor had seen the same number of patients, but in 4 hours. How many patients would have been seen each hour then?

4. Check your answer to Exercise 3. How do you know it is correct?

PRACTICE the Skill

EXTRA PRACTICE
See page R17.

Solve. Use the *choose an operation* skill.

5. Write a multiplication sentence to find how many plants are in the garden. What other operation can help you solve this problem?

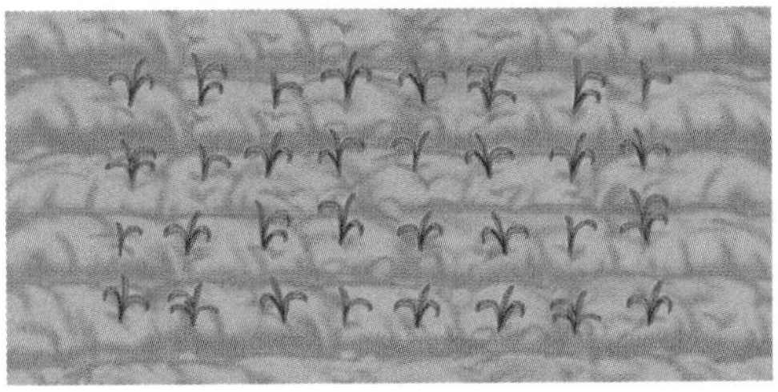

6. **Measurement** The CN Tower in Canada is 1,815 feet tall. A TV tower in North Dakota is 2,063 feet tall. How much taller is the TV tower than the CN Tower? Explain.

7. Shaun and Dean went to the park. The leaves were brown, red, and orange. They picked 7 of each color, how many leaves did they have in all?

8. It has rained 6 inches each month for the last 5 months. If it rains 6 more inches this month, what is the total rainfall?

9. Sondra and Wanda were making jewelry for the school fund raiser. They each made the amount listed. How many items were made in all?

Jewelry Made

Item	Number
Earrings	5
Pins	4
Bracelets	6

10. Kimberlee has 14 feet of string. She wants to make necklaces that are 2 feet long. How many necklaces can she make?

11. **Geometry** Jerome has a square garden. Each side is 5 yards. How many yards of fence does he need to border the garden? Explain.

12. **WRITING IN MATH** Explain how to read a problem and decide what operation to use.

6-4 Divide by 2

MAIN IDEA

I will divide by 2.

Standard 3NS2.3 Use the inverse relationship of multiplication and division to compute and check results.

Standard 3MR2.3 Use a variety of methods, such as words, numbers, symbols, charts, graphs, tables, diagrams, **and models, to explain mathematical reasoning.**

GET READY to Learn

Jose and Jenna are sharing an apple equally. If there are 8 apple slices on the plate, how many slices will each of them get?

In Lesson 6-1, you learned about the division symbol ÷. Another symbol for division is $\overline{)\ \ }$.

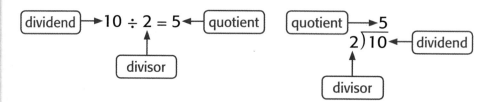

dividend → $10 \div 2 = 5$ ← quotient; divisor ↑ (2)

quotient → 5; $2\overline{)10}$ ← dividend; divisor ↑ (2)

Real-World EXAMPLE Make Equal Groups

1 FRUIT **Jose and Jenna share an apple equally. If there are 8 slices, how many slices will each of them get?**

To share equally between 2 people means to divide by 2. You can write a related fact to find $8 \div 2$ or $2\overline{)8}$.

$2 \times \blacksquare = 8$ ← You know that $2 \times 4 = 8$

So, $8 \div 2 = 4$ or $2\overline{)8}$ with quotient 4.

Each person will get 4 apple slices.

Check

The number line shows that 8 divided into equal groups of 2 is 4.

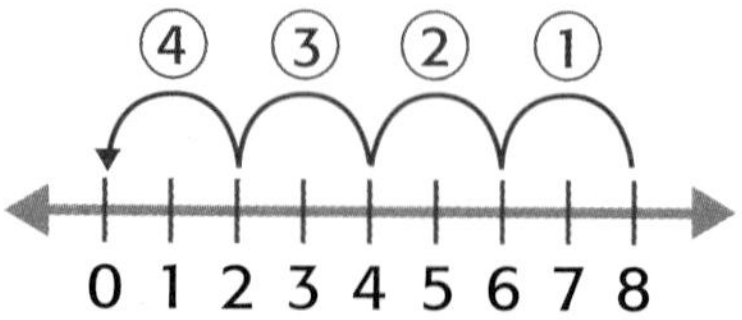

Online Personal Tutor at ca.gr3math.com

CHECK What You Know

Divide. Write a related multiplication fact. See Example 1 (p. 264)

1.

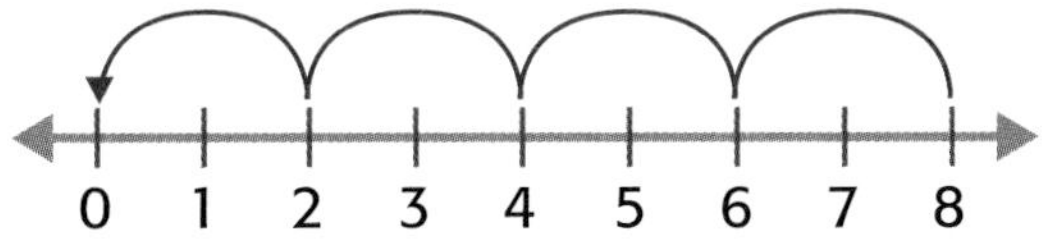

$2\overline{)8}$

2.

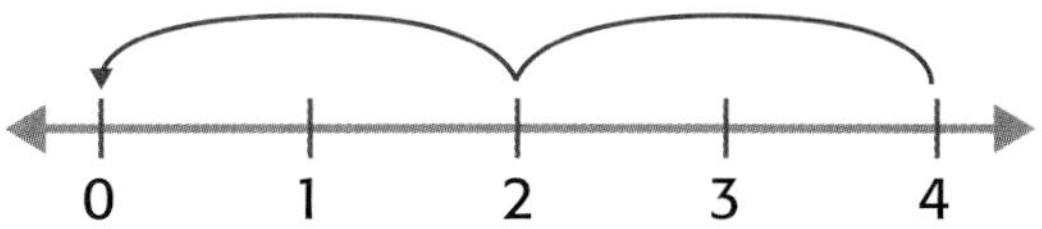

$4 \div 2$

3. $6 \div 2$

4. $14 \div 2$

5. $2\overline{)16}$

6. Vince and his sister chose an equal number of books from the library. They chose a total of 16 books. How many did each choose?

7. Talk About It What are two different ways to find $10 \div 2$?

Practice and Problem Solving

EXTRA PRACTICE See page R17.

Divide. Write a related multiplication fact. See Example 1 (p. 264)

8.

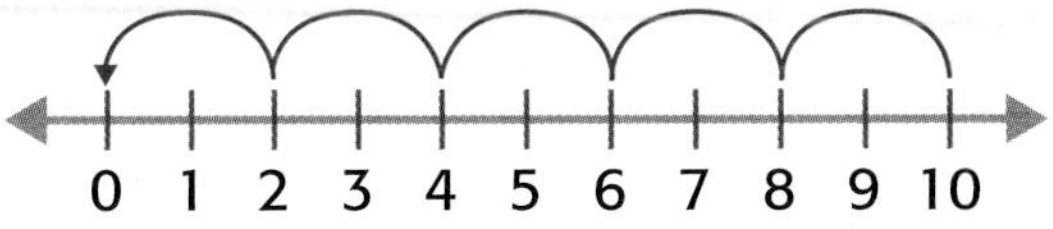

$10 \div 2$

9.

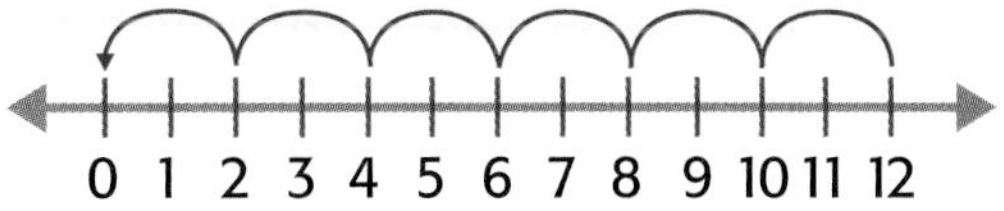

$12 \div 2$

10.

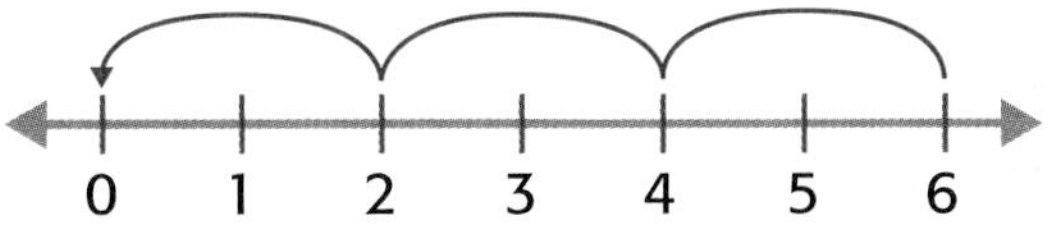

$2\overline{)6}$

11.

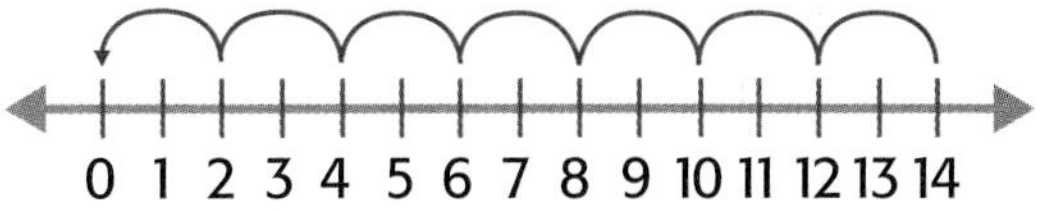

$2\overline{)14}$

12. $18 \div 2$

13. $16 \div 2$

14. $20 \div 2$

15. $2\overline{)2}$

16. $2\overline{)12}$

17. $2\overline{)10}$

18. Elan has 12 seeds to plant. He wants to plant them in groups of 2. How many groups of 2 can he plant?

19. Kyle and Al equally divide a package of 14 erasers. How many erasers will each person get?

20. Lidia shared her 16 pattern tiles equally with Pilar. Pilar then shared her tiles equally with Todd. How many tiles does each student have?

21. Each car on the Supersonic Speed ride can hold 18 people. If the seats are in groups of 2, how many groups of two are there on 3 cars?

Algebra Copy and complete each table.

22.

Rule: Divide by 2.				
In	10	■	18	14
Out	■	4	■	7

23.

Rule: Multiply by 5.				
In	7	■	6	■
Out	■	25	■	15

Real-World PROBLEM SOLVING

Data File The state marine fish of California is the garibaldi.

24. The length of a golden puffer is the length of the garibaldi divided by 2. How long is a golden puffer?

25. A mackerel's maximum life span is the maximum life span of the garibaldi divided by 2. What is the mackerel's maximum life span?

26. The garibaldi can be found at a depth of 100 feet. A shark can be found at a depth that is 100 − 50. What is this depth?

Garibaldi

Source: library.ca.gov/history

Length: 14 inches

Maximum Life Span: 18 years

Location: shallow waters, about 100 feet deep, off the Southern California coast

H.O.T. Problems

27. OPEN ENDED Write a number that when you divide it by 2 is more than 8.

Challenge Divide.

28. 36 ÷ 2 **29.** 50 ÷ 2 **30.** 42 ÷ 2

31. FIND THE ERROR Andreas and Muna are finding 8 ÷ 2. Who is correct? Explain your reasoning.

Andreas
8 ÷ 2 = 16
because
2 × 8 = 16

Muna
8 ÷ 2 = 4
because
2 × 4 = 8

32. WRITING IN MATH Can you divide 9 into equal groups of 2?

CHAPTER 6 Mid-Chapter Check

Lessons 6-1 through 6-4

Divide. Use repeated subtraction on a number line or paper and pencil.

(Lesson 6-1)

1.

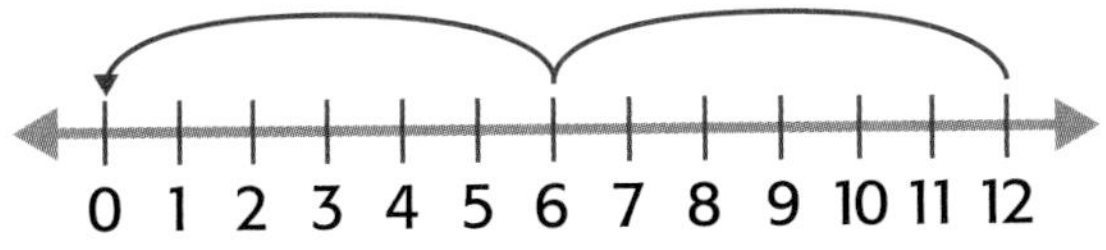

$12 \div 6$

2. $8 \div 2$

3. $16 \div 4$

4. $15 \div 3$

5. $10 \div 2$

6. Joel wants to read 3 chapters a day. His book has 18 chapters. How many days will it take for him to finish the book? **(Lesson 6-1)**

7. **STANDARDS PRACTICE** The figure shows $6 \times 3 = 18$.

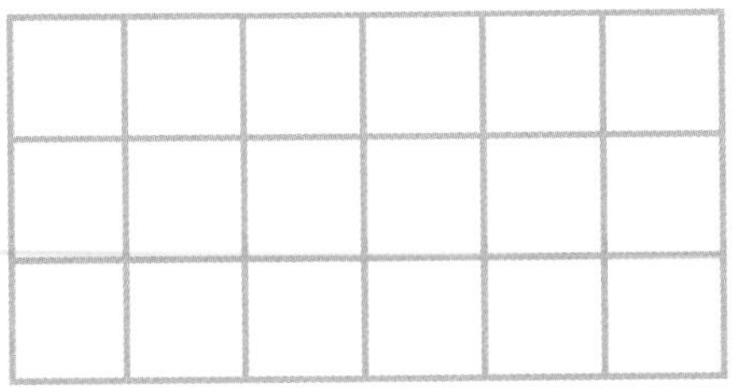

Which division sentence is modeled by the same figure? **(Lesson 6-1)**

A $6 \div 3 = 2$

B $24 \div 8 = 3$

C $18 \div 6 = 3$

D $36 \div 6 = 6$

Algebra Find each missing number.

(Lesson 6-2)

8. $16 \div ■ = 2$

9. $14 \div 2 = ■$

Complete each pair of sentences.

(Lesson 6-2)

10. $■ \times 2 = 12$
$■ \div 6 = 2$

11. $8 \times ■ = 24$
$24 \div ■ = 3$

Write the fact family for each set of numbers. **(Lesson 6-2)**

12. 5, 2, 10

13. 9, 3, 27

For Exercises 14 and 15, choose an operation. Then solve. **(Lesson 6-3)**

14. All the students in the Art Club must pay $2 each for supplies. If $20 was collected, how many students are in the club?

15. Twelve students are going on a field trip. There are 2 vans that hold the same number of students. How many students will go on each van?

16. **STANDARDS PRACTICE** Sophie divided $16 \div 2 = 8$. Which problem could she use to check her answer?

(Lesson 6-4)

F $8 - 2 = ■$

G $8 \times 2 = ■$

H $8 \div 2 = ■$

J $8 + 2 = ■$

17. **WRITING IN MATH** Can 6 roses be divided equally between 2 vases? Explain. **(Lesson 6-4)**

6-5 Divide by 5

MAIN IDEA

I will learn to divide by 5.

Standard 3NS2.3 Use the inverse relationship of multiplication and division to compute and check results.

Standard 3MR2.3 Use a variety of methods, such as words, numbers, symbols, charts, graphs, tables, diagrams, **and models, to explain mathematical reasoning.**

GET READY to Learn

A group of friends have a lemonade stand. The price of one glass of lemonade is 5¢. They earned 30¢ selling lemonade. How many glasses of lemonade did they sell?

There are different ways to divide by 5.

Real-World EXAMPLE

1 MONEY How many glasses of lemonade did the group of friends sell?

You need to find 30¢ ÷ 5¢.

One Way: Use Models

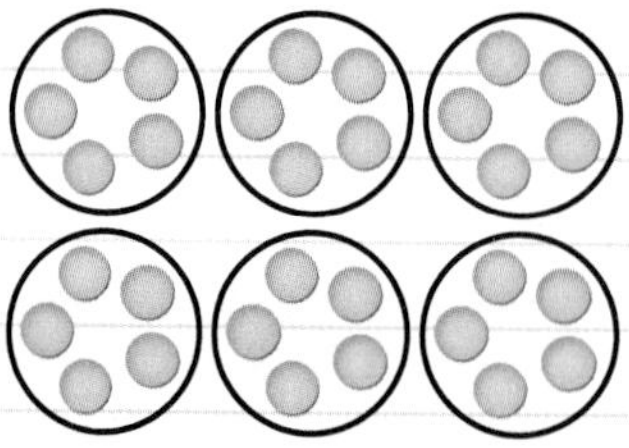

There are 30 counters and 5 counters are in each group. There are 6 equal groups.

$30¢ \div 5¢ = 6$ or $5¢\overline{)30¢}$ with quotient 6

Another Way: Repeated Subtraction

①	②	③	④	⑤	⑥
30 − 5 = 25	25 − 5 = 20	20 − 5 = 15	15 − 5 = 10	10 − 5 = 5	5 − 5 = 0

Subtract groups of 5 until you reach 0. Count the number of groups you subtracted.

$30¢ \div 5¢ = 6$ or $5¢\overline{)30¢}$ with quotient 6

So, the friends sold 6 glasses of lemonade.

You can also use related multiplication facts to divide.

Real-World EXAMPLE

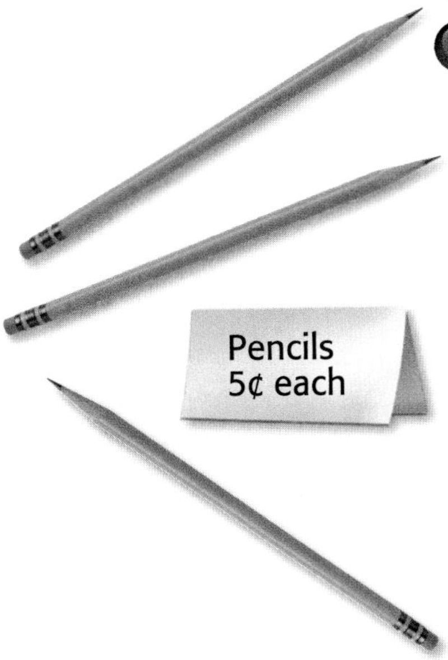

2 **MONEY The school store is selling pencils for 5¢ each. If Percy has 45¢, how many pencils can he buy with all his money?**

Write a related multiplication fact to find 45¢ ÷ 5¢.

45¢ ÷ 5¢ = ■

5¢ × ■ = 45¢ What number times 5 is 45¢?

5¢ × 9 = 45¢

So, 45¢ ÷ 5¢ = 9 or $\begin{array}{r} 9 \\ 5\text{¢}\overline{)45\text{¢}} \end{array}$. Percy can buy 9 pencils.

Check

The picture shows that 45¢ ÷ 5¢ = 9.

45¢ divided into groups of 5¢ forms 9 groups.
9 groups of 5¢ = 45¢. ✓

Online **Personal Tutor at** ca.gr3math.com

CHECK What You Know

Divide. See Examples 1 and 2 (pp. 268–269)

1. 10 ÷ 5

2. 25 ÷ 5

3. 15 ÷ 5

4. 35 ÷ 5

5. 5 ÷ 5

6. 30 ÷ 5

7. $5\overline{)20}$

8. $5\overline{)40}$

9. $5\overline{)50}$

10. **Measurement** Lucia's classroom has rows of tables that are 25 feet wide. If 5 tables are in each row, how wide is each table?

11. **Talk About It** How can you tell if a number is divisible by 5?

Practice and Problem Solving

EXTRA PRACTICE
See page R18.

Divide. See Examples 1 and 2 (pp. 268–269)

12. 20 ÷ 5 **13.** 30 ÷ 5 **14.** 45 ÷ 5 **15.** 50 ÷ 5

16. $5\overline{)5}$ **17.** $5\overline{)15}$ **18.** $5\overline{)20}$ **19.** $5\overline{)45}$

20. 30 ÷ 5 **21.** 40 ÷ 5 **22.** 5 ÷ 5 **23.** 35 ÷ 5

24. $5\overline{)40}$ **25.** $5\overline{)50}$ **26.** $5\overline{)15}$ **27.** $5\overline{)10}$

For Exercises 28–31, use the recipe for cornbread. Find how much of each is needed to make 1 loaf of cornbread.

28. cornmeal

29. flour

30. eggs

31. vanilla extract

Buttermilk Corn Bread

10 cups cornmeal	3 cups butter
5 cups flour	8 cups buttermilk
1 cup sugar	5 tsp vanilla extract
5 Tbsp baking powder	15 eggs
4 tsp salt	2 tsp baking soda

Makes: 5 loaves

32. Measurement Sally has a 35-inch piece of ribbon. If she divides the ribbon into 5 equal pieces, how many inches long will each piece be?

33. Helen is reading a book with 50 pages. If she reads 5 pages every day, how many days will it take her to finish the book?

34. Measurement Garrison has 45 minutes to do his homework. He has 9 problems left. How long can he spend on each problem if each one takes an equal amount of time?

35. Addison got 40 points on yesterday's 10-question math quiz. If each question is worth 5 points and there is no partial credit, how many questions did he miss?

Real-World PROBLEM SOLVING

Science The grizzly bear is one of the largest and most powerful animals.

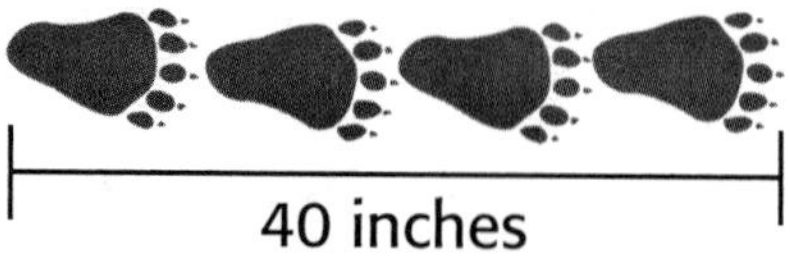

36. About how long is a foot of a grizzly bear?

37. How tall can one grizzly bear grow?

38. The grizzly runs at about a speed of 35 miles per hour. What is that divided by 5?

H.O.T. Problems

39. OPEN ENDED Write a division sentence with a quotient of 9.

40. WHICH ONE DOESN'T BELONG? Identify the division sentence that does not belong. Explain your reasoning.

$30 \div 5 = 6$	$20 \div 2 = 10$	$30 \div 6 = 5$	$35 \div 5 = 7$

41. WRITING IN ▸MATH Explain the method you would use to find $45 \div 5$ and why you prefer that method.

Standards Practice

42 This is a model for which number sentence? **(Lesson 6-5)**

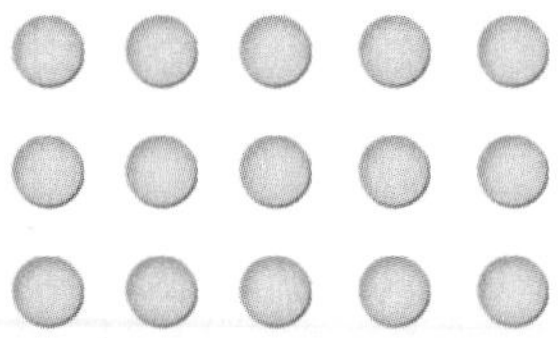

A $15 \div 3 = 5$

B $3 + 5 = 8$

C $3 + 3 + 3 + 3 + 3 = 15$

D $5 \times 5 = 25$

43 Robert solved this division problem.

$$20 \div 2 = 10$$

Which problem could he do to check his answer? **(Lesson 6-4)**

F $10 + 2 = \blacksquare$

G $10 - 2 = \blacksquare$

H $10 \times 2 = \blacksquare$

J $10 \div 2 = \blacksquare$

Spiral Review

44. Angelica had $40 to buy her mother a birthday present. She bought flowers for $16 and a new pen set for $8. How much money does she have left? **(Lesson 6-5)**

Divide. Write a related multiplication fact. (Lesson 6-4)

45. $18 \div 2$ **46.** $16 \div 2$ **47.** $2\overline{)12}$

Add. Check for reasonableness. (Lesson 2-4)

48. $\begin{array}{r} 48 \\ +\ 24 \\ \hline \end{array}$ **49.** $\begin{array}{r} 83 \\ +\ 29 \\ \hline \end{array}$ **50.** $\begin{array}{r} 954 \\ +\ 294 \\ \hline \end{array}$

Communities Within Communities

A community is a group of people who work, live, or play together. There are 9,000 public schools in California, and each school is a community. Your classroom is also a community.

Often, a class works together on an art project. A mural is an art project that many people can work on together. It is a large painting that sometimes covers an entire wall.

There are many other examples of communities. In California, there are 478 cities. Each city is a community. There are about 3 million businesses in California that also form communities. Each of the 8 million families in California is a community, too.

Did You Know?

There are more than 33 million elementary students in the United States.

Real-World Math

Use the information on page 272 to answer each question.

1. A group is painting a mural of their community. They have 14 pictures of places around their community. The mural is 7 feet wide. If they want to place the pictures evenly, how many will go on each foot?

2. There are 6 doctors and 24 patients at the local doctors' office. Each doctor saw the same number of patients. How many patients did each doctor see?

3. There are 20 students in a class. The teacher splits the class in 5 equal groups. How many students are in each group?

4. Suppose a community has 45 stores. There are 5 stores on each street. How many streets are in your community?

5. The schools in your community donate 30 boxes of clothes to the local charity. There are 10 schools. If each school donates the same number of boxes, how many boxes of clothes does each school donate?

6. There are twice as many families in California as there are in Florida. California has about 8 million families. About how many families are in Florida?

6-6 Problem-Solving Investigation

MAIN IDEA I will choose the best strategy to solve a problem.

Standard 3MR1.1 Analyze problems by identifying relationships, distinguishing relevant from irrelevent information, sequencing and priortizing information, and observing patterns. **Standard 3NS2.3 Use the inverse relationship of multiplication and division to compute and check results.**

P.S.I. TEAM +

KINAH: I want to plant a vegetable garden. I have 6 tomato plants, 5 pepper plants, and 5 zucchini plants. I want to put the plants into 4 equal rows.

YOUR MISSION: Find how many plants should be planted in each row.

Understand	Kinah has 6 tomato, 5 pepper, and 5 zucchini plants. She wants to plant them in 4 equal rows. Find how many plants to put in each row.
Plan	You need to look at how to arrange items. So, the *draw a picture* strategy is a good choice.
Solve	The picture shows 6 + 5 + 5, or 16 plants. There are 4 equal groups of 4 plants. 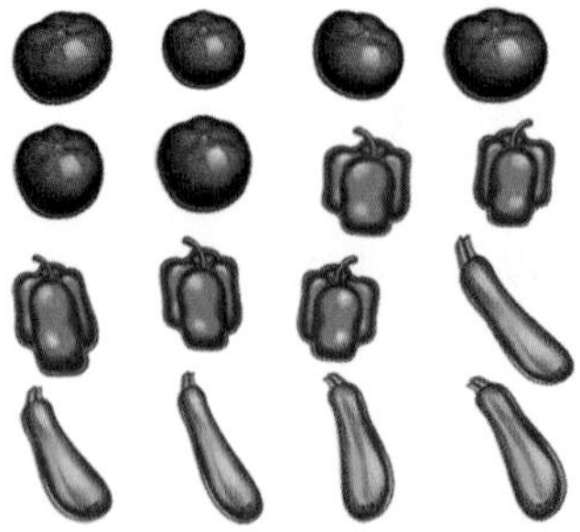 Since $16 \div 4 = 4$, Kinah needs to plant 4 plants in each row.
Check	Look back at the problem. Since $4 \times 4 = 16$, you know that the answer is correct.

Mixed Problem Solving

EXTRA PRACTICE
See page R18.

Use any strategy shown below to solve.

PROBLEM-SOLVING STRATEGIES
- Act it out.
- Draw a picture.
- Look for a pattern.

1. Mrs. Jones bought 18 cans of cat food. The cats eat the same amount each day. This amount lasts for 6 days. How many cans of food do her cats eat each day?

2. Bill catches 3 more fish than Angelo and, Eric catches 3 more fish than Bill. Bill catches 5 fish. How many fish did each person catch?

3. How much will lunch cost for 5 people if each person buys all the items on the menu?

Lunch	
Item	**Cost**
Chicken	$2
Apple	$1
Milk	$1

4. One day, 3 children played together. The next day, 5 children played together. On the third day, 7 children played together. If this pattern continues, how many children could be playing together on the sixth day?

5. Vikram bought 6 gifts at a store. His sister bought 5 gifts and their mother bought 7 gifts. How many gifts did they buy in all?

6. Latoya and Latisha are using red, blue, and yellow rubber bands to make bracelets. Each bracelet's rubber bands make the pattern red, blue, yellow, red, blue, yellow. If they make 10 bracelets how many yellow rubber bands will they use?

7. If Rita draws 15 more shapes, how many of those shapes could be triangles?

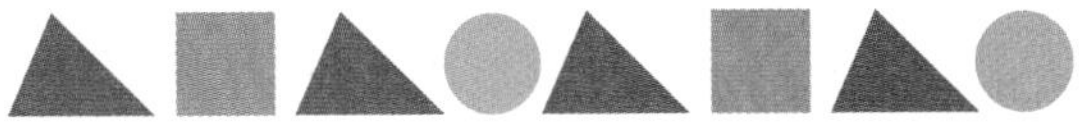

8. Marvina and Gustavo went to the grocery store. Marvina bought 5 items for $6 each. Gustavo bought 7 items for $8 each. How much did they spend in all?

9. Selena, Marcos, Jared, and Daniella each have 5 books. Selena and Jared read 4 of their books. Marcos did not read 2 of his books. Daniella read all of her books. How many books did they read in all?

10. WRITING IN ▶MATH Look back at Exercise 9. Which strategy did you use to solve it? Explain your reason for using that strategy.

6-7 Divide By 10

Main Idea

I will learn to divide by 10.

Standard 3NS2.3 Use the inverse relationship of multiplication and division to compute and check results.

Standard 3MR2.3 Use a variety of methods, such as words, numbers, symbols, charts, graphs, tables, diagrams, **and models, to explain mathematical reasoning.**

GET READY to Learn

Juice bars come 10 in a box. The third grade class needs 50 juice bars for a party treat. How many boxes will they need?

As the divisor gets larger, you will find that some methods are better than others.

Real-World EXAMPLE

1 SCHOOL How many boxes of juice bars will the third grade class need?

You need to find $50 \div 10$.

One Way: Use Repeated Subtraction

①	②	③	④	⑤
50	40	30	20	10
-10	-10	-10	-10	-10
40	30	20	10	0

Subtract groups of 10 until you reach 0. Count the number of groups you subtracted. You subtracted 10 groups five times.

Another Way: Use a Related Fact

You know that $10 \times 5 = 50$.

So, $50 \div 10 = 5$ or $10\overline{)50}$ with quotient 5.

So, $50 \div 10 = 5$. They will need 5 boxes of juice bars.

Online Personal Tutor at ca.gr3math.com

CHECK What You Know

Divide. See Example 1 (p. 276)

1. $20 \div 10$
2. $40 \div 10$
3. $10\overline{)60}$
4. $10\overline{)10}$

5. There are 40 chairs at 10 tables. Each table has an equal number of chairs. How many chairs are at each table?

6. **Talk About It** When you divide by 10, what do you notice about the quotient and dividend?

Practice and Problem Solving

EXTRA PRACTICE See page R18.

Divide. See Example 1 (p. 276)

7. $30 \div 10$
8. $50 \div 10$
9. $80 \div 10$
10. $90 \div 10$
11. $10\overline{)20}$
12. $10\overline{)70}$
13. $10\overline{)30}$
14. $10\overline{)40}$

15. A vase holds 40 flowers. There are an equal number of daisies, roses, tulips, and lilies. How many of each kind of flower are there in the vase?

16. Sam went to the car show and saw 60 cars. If he saw 10 of each kind of car, how many different kinds of cars were there?

For Exercises 17–20, use the sign shown.

HEALTH SHACK'S SNACKS

Sunflower seeds	10¢ per package
Dried fruit	10 pieces for 50¢
Juice	20¢ each
Yogurt	2 for 80¢

17. Julian spent 40¢ on sunflower seeds. How many packages did he buy?

18. How much will it cost for 20 pieces of dried fruit?

19. How much did Beth pay for 1 yogurt?

20. How much would it cost to buy 1 of everything, including 1 piece of dried fruit?

H.O.T. Problems

21. **OPEN ENDED** Use the numerals 7, 0, 8, 5 to write two 2-digit numbers that can be divided by 10.

22. **WRITING IN MATH** Explain how counting by 10s can help you find $80 \div 10$.

Standards Practice

23 Mr. Gonzales bought 30 frozen pizzas, with 5 in each box. Which number sentence shows how to find the number of boxes he bought? **(Lesson 6-5)**

A $30 - 5 = ■$

B $30 + 5 = ■$

C $30 \times 5 = ■$

D $30 \div 5 = ■$

24 Look at the number sentence below.

$$90 \div ■ = 9$$

Which number will make the number sentence true? **(Lesson 6-7)**

F 1

G 10

H 81

J 100

Spiral Review

25. Measurement On Monday, Nelson rode a horse 12 miles and Ramiro rode a horse 14 miles. If they ride the same amount 4 more days this week, how many more miles will Ramiro have ridden than Nelson? **(Lesson 6-6)**

Divide. **(Lesson 6-5)**

26. $25 \div 5$

27. $45 \div 5$

28. $50 \div 5$

29. There are 40 players attending soccer camp. Each team will have the same number of players and 1 coach. If there are 5 coaches how many players will be on each team? **(Lesson 6-5)**

Find each product. **(Lesson 5-8)**

30. $4 \times 2 \times 4$

31. $3 \times 3 \times 4$

32. $5 \times 2 \times 3$

Write a multiplication sentence for each array. **(Lesson 4-2)**

33.

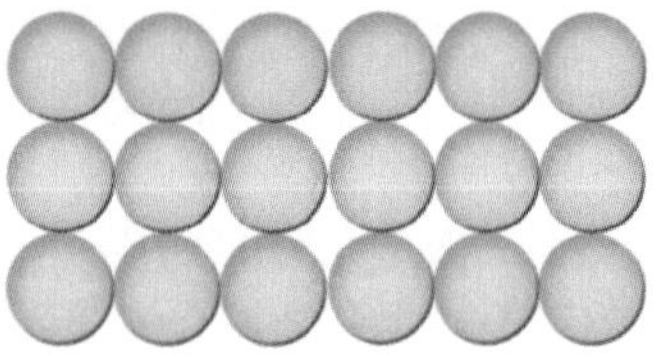

34.

35.

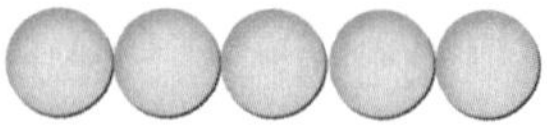

36. The table below shows Dwayne's reading pattern. If the pattern continues, how many pages will he read on Sunday? **(Lesson 1-1)**

Mon.	Tues.	Wed.	Thur.	Fri.	Sat.	Sun.
4	8	16				?

Game Time

Number Cubes

Multiply and Divide Numbers

You will need: one 0–5 number cube, one 5–10 number cube

Cube 1	Cube 2	Multiplication sentence	Division sentence
5	4	$5 \times 4 = 20$	$20 \div 5 = 4$

Get Ready!

Players: 2 players

Get Set!

Make a chart to record each roll.

Go!

- Player 1 rolls the number cubes.
- Each player writes down the numbers.
- Each player uses the two numbers in a multiplication and division sentence.
- Each player gets 1 point for each correctly written number sentence.
- The game ends when 1 player earns 50 points.

6-8 Division Properties

MAIN IDEA

I will learn to use properties about using 1 and 0 in division.

Standard 3NS2.6 Understand the special properties of 0 and 1 in division.

Standard 3NS2.3 Use the inverse relationship of multiplication and division to compute and check results.

GET READY to Learn

Suppose that you have 3 toys. The three toys will fit in 1 storage box. How many boxes will you need for the 3 toys?

There are special properties you can use when you divide.

Real-World EXAMPLE

1 TOYS How many boxes will you need for 3 toys?

You need to find $3 \div 3$ or $3\overline{)3}$. The counters represent the 3 toys. Since 3 toys fit in 1 box, make groups of 3.

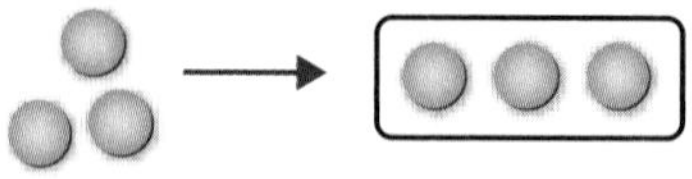

There is 1 group of 3.
So, $3 \div 3 = 1$ or $3\overline{)3}$.

KEY CONCEPT — Division Properties

Words When you divide any number (except 0) by itself, the quotient is 1.

Example $4 \div 4 = 1$.

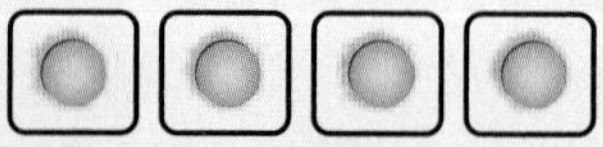

Words When you divide any number by 1, the quotient is that number.

Example $4 \div 1 = 4$

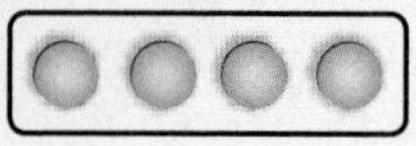

Words When you divide 0 by any number by (except 0), the quotient is 0.

Example $0 \div 4 = 0$

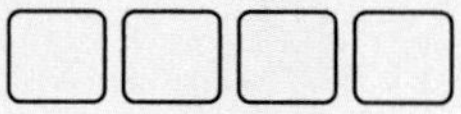

Words You cannot divide by 0.

CHECK What You Know

Divide. See Example 1 (p. 280)

1. $5 \div 1$ **2.** $0 \div 1$ **3.** $1 \div 1$ **4.** $1\overline{)9}$

5. $0 \div 7$ **6.** $10 \div 1$ **7.** $6\overline{)0}$ **8.** $7\overline{)7}$

9. If 6 people show up at the theater and there are 6 seats left, how many seats will each person get?

10. Talk About It Can you divide a number by 0? Can you divide 0 by a number other than 0? Explain.

Practice and Problem Solving

EXTRA PRACTICE See page R19.

Divide. See Example 1 (p. 280)

11. $2 \div 1$ **12.** $10 \div 10$ **13.** $0 \div 5$ **14.** $6 \div 1$

15. $0 \div 3$ **16.** $0 \div 9$ **17.** $1\overline{)4}$ **18.** $5\overline{)5}$

19. $9 \div 9$ **20.** $8 \div 1$ **21.** $6 \div 6$ **22.** $0 \div 4$

23. $1\overline{)7}$ **24.** $2\overline{)2}$ **25.** $1\overline{)10}$ **26.** $10\overline{)0}$

27. There are 35 students in Mrs. Macy's class. To play a game, each person needs 1 playing piece. How many playing pieces are needed for the class to play the game?

28. Mr. Carrington has a pack of paper with 5 different colors. If he gives 1 of each color to his students, how many pieces of paper will they each have?

29. Kari wants to give 5 friends an apple. She finds that she has no apples. How many apples can she give to her friends?

30. Marcy and her 4 friends have 5 glasses of juice. How many glasses of juice will each person get?

H.O.T. Problems

31. OPEN ENDED Write a real-world division problem in which a number is divided by itself. Ask a classmate to answer it.

32. WRITING IN ▶MATH Explain how you could divide any number someone gives you by 1 or itself.

6 Study Guide and Review

FOLDABLES™ Study Organizer GET READY to Study

Be sure the following Key Vocabulary words and Key Concepts are written in your Foldable.

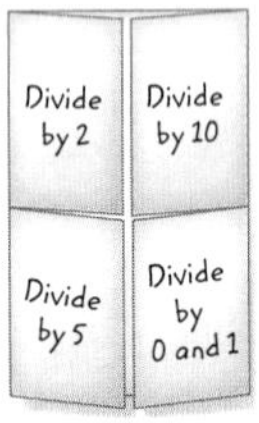

BIG Ideas

- **Division** is an operation with two numbers. One number tells you how many things you have. The other tells you how many equal groups to form.

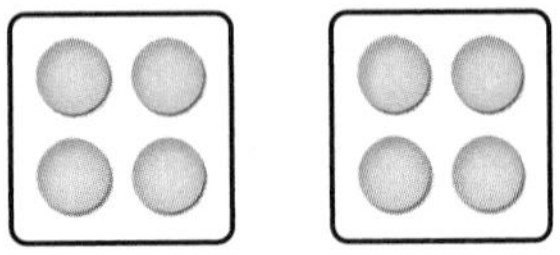

$8 \div 2 = 4$

- You can relate division to multiplication.

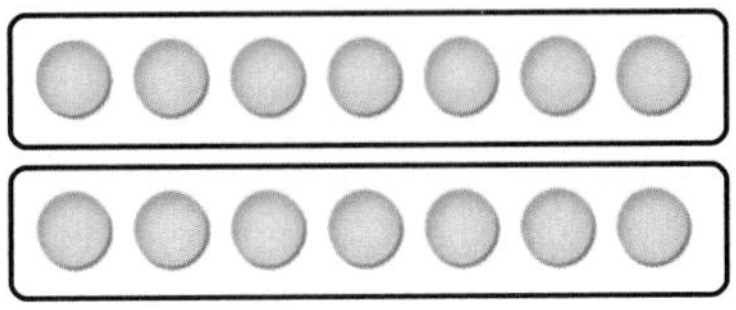

2	×	7	=	14
number of groups		number in each group		number in all

14	÷	2	=	7
number in all		number of groups		number in each group

Key Vocabulary

divide (p. 253)
dividend (p. 258)
divisor (p. 258)
fact family (p. 259)
quotient (p. 258)

Vocabulary Check

Choose the vocabulary word that completes each sentence.

1. The answer to a division problem is called the ___?___ .

2. The number to be divided is the ___?___ .

3. A ___?___ is a group of related facts using the same numbers.

4. In the sentence $36 \div 4 = 9$, 9 is the ___?___ .

5. In $42 \div 7 = 6$, the number 42 is the ___?___ .

6. The ___?___ is the number by which the dividend is divided.

Math Online Vocabulary Review at ca.gr3math.com

Lesson-by-Lesson Review

6-1 Relate Division to Subtraction (pp. 253–255)

Example 1

One Way: Number Line

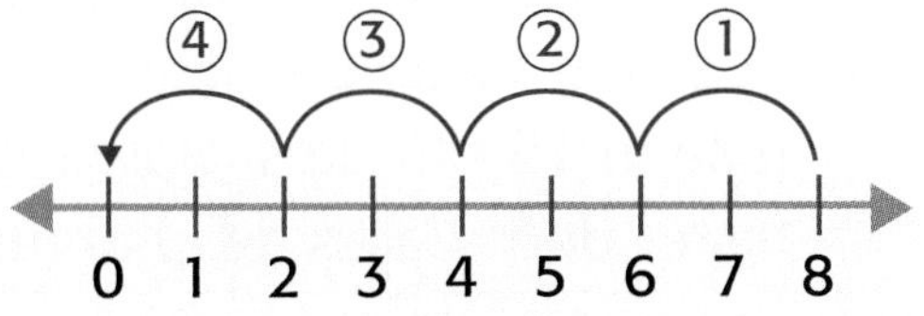

$8 \div 2$

Start at 8. Count back by 2s until you reach 0. Count how many times you subtracted. So, $8 \div 2 = 4$.

Another Way: Repeated Subtraction

①	②	③	④
8	6	4	2
-2	-2	-2	-2
6	4	2	0

So, $8 \div 2 = 4$.

Divide. Use repeated subtraction on a number line or paper and pencil.

7.

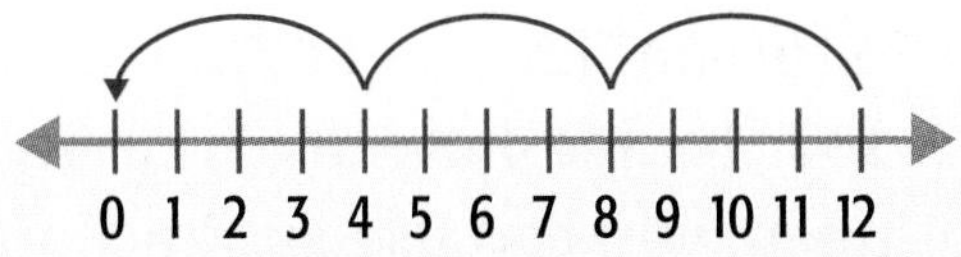

$12 \div 4$

8.

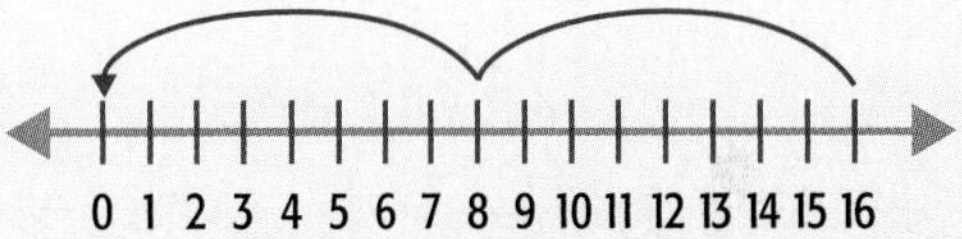

$16 \div 8$

9. $6 \div 2$ **10.** $27 \div 3$

11. Chang has 15 frogs in his pond. If he catches 3 each day, how many days will it take him to catch all of the frogs?

6-2 Relate Multiplication to Division (pp. 258–261)

Example 2
Write the fact family for 4, 2, and 8.

$4 \times 2 = 8$

$8 \div 2 = 4$

$2 \times 4 = 8$

$8 \div 4 = 2$

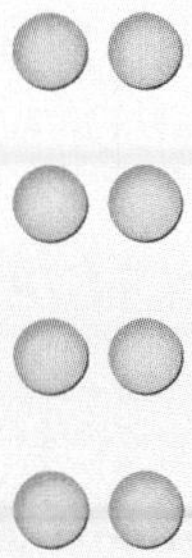

Write the fact family for each set of numbers.

12. 6, 7, 42 **13.** 8, 4, 2

14. 5, 4, 20 **15.** 4, 9, 36

16. Measurement Last week, Yon rode her bike 4 days in a row for a total of 20 miles. She rode the same number of miles each day. How many miles did she ride her bike each day?

6-3 Problem-Solving Skill: Choose an Operation (pp. 262–263)

Example 3
Alvin and Ely have $37 to build a tree house. The materials will cost $78. How much more do they need?

Alvin and Ely need $78. They have $37. To find how much more they need, you can use subtraction.

$78 – $37 = $41

So, they need $41 more.

Use addition to check subtraction.

41 + 37 = 78

So, the answer is correct.

Solve. Use the *choose an operation* strategy.

17. Caleb ran a mile in 18 minutes. To compete on the track team, he needs to be able to finish the mile in 15 minutes. How much faster does Caleb need to run?

18. The track team travels by van for competitions. Twelve people fit in a van. If there are 36 people on the team, how many vans will they need?

19. The coach has assigned 3 people to compete in each event. There are a total of 27 people. In how many events did each team member compete?

6-4 Divide by 2 (pp. 264–266)

Example 4
Marco wants to share 6 dog biscuits with his 2 dogs. How many biscuits will each dog get?

To find 6 ÷ 2 or $2\overline{)6}$, use a related fact.

2 × ■ = 6 ← You know that 2 × 3 = 6.

So, 6 ÷ 2 = 3 or $\begin{array}{r}3\\2\overline{)6}\end{array}$.
Each dog will get 3 biscuits.

Divide. Write a related multiplication fact.

20. 12 ÷ 2 **21.** 14 ÷ 2

22. 16 ÷ 2 **23.** 20 ÷ 2

24. Veronica and Koko want to equally share a piece of paper that is 14 inches long. How long will each of their pieces be?

6-5 Divide by 5 (pp. 268–271)

Example 5
Marion has 20 tadpoles. She will divide them equally between 5 fishbowls. How many tadpoles will be in each bowl?

You can use repeated subtraction to find 20 ÷ 5.

①	②	③	④
$20 - 5 = 15$	$15 - 5 = 10$	$10 - 5 = 5$	$5 - 5 = 0$

You subtracted 5 four times.
So, 20 ÷ 5 = 4 tadpoles in each.

Divide.

25. 20 ÷ 5

26. 35 ÷ 5

27. 45 ÷ 5

28. 15 ÷ 5

29. Lalo has 45 books to put in her bookcase. The bookcase has 5 shelves. If she wants to put the same number of books on each shelf, how many will there be on each shelf?

6-6 Problem-Solving Investigation (pp. 274–275)

Example 6
Mace bought 3 toys. William bought 2 more toys than Mace. How many toys did they buy?

You know that Mace bought 3 toys. Will bought 2 more than Mace. Find how many they bought together. You can act out the problem with counters.

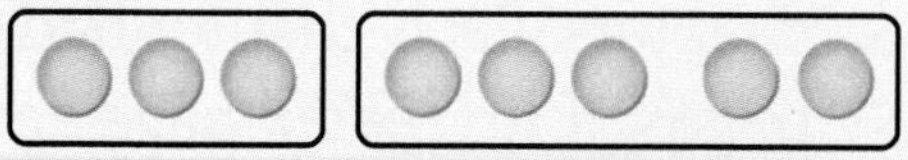

Mace Will

3 + 3 + 2 = 8

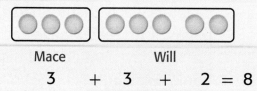

So, Mace and Will bought 8 toys.

30. One day, Maxine received 2 gifts. The next day she received 4 gifts. The third day she received 6 gifts. If the pattern continues, how many gifts will she receive on the 6th day? How many gifts did she receive altogether?

31. You need to read 5 books a month during the school year. The school year is from August to May. How many books will you read in a year?

6-7 Divide by 10 (pp. 276–278)

Example 7

Divide 50 ÷ 10.

Use repeated subtraction.

①	②	③	④	⑤
50	40	30	20	10
−10	−10	−10	−10	−10
40	30	20	10	0

Subtract groups of 10 until you reach 0. You subtracted 10 five times.
So, 50 ÷ 10 = 5.

Divide.

32. 90 ÷ 10 **33.** 80 ÷ 10

34. 70 ÷ 10 **35.** 50 ÷ 10

36. 30 ÷ 10 **37.** 100 ÷ 10

38. There are 40 baskets of grapes on store shelves. If there are 10 baskets on each shelf, how many shelves are there?

6-8 Division Properties (pp. 280–281)

Example 8
Ginger wants to give gifts to 8 friends. If she gives each friend one gift, how many gifts does Ginger need?

Use the properties of division to solve 8 ÷ 1.

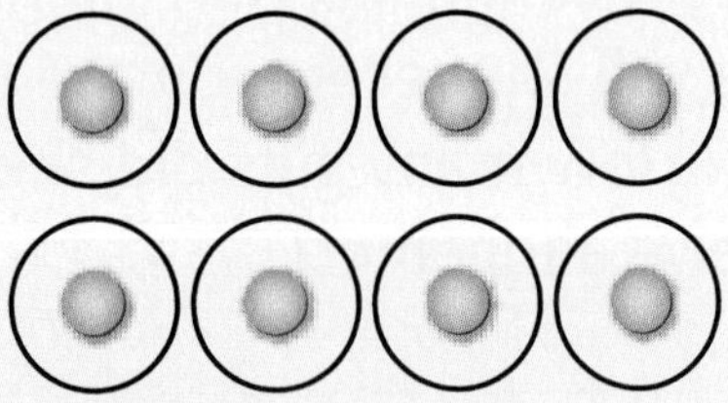

There are 8 groups of 1.
So, 8 ÷ 1 = 8.
Ginger will need 8 gifts.

Divide.

39. 5 ÷ 1 **40.** 0 ÷ 5

41. 0 ÷ 2 **42.** 10 ÷ 1

43. 10 ÷ 10 **44.** 0 ÷ 10

45. Five boys wanted to go fishing. They found 5 fishing poles in the garage. Do they have enough poles to go fishing? Explain.

46. Terrel read a book with 15 chapters. Each chapter had 10 pages. If he read a page each day for 150 days, would he finish the book? Explain.

CHAPTER 6

Chapter Test

For Exercises 1-3, tell whether each statement is *true* or *false*.

1. When you divide any number by 1, the quotient is that number.

2. In 32 ÷ 4 = 8, the 4 is the dividend.

3. Repeated subtraction can help you solve a division problem.

Divide. Write a related multiplication fact.

4. 30 ÷ 5

5. 25 ÷ 5

6. 0 ÷ 7

7. 10 ÷ 2

8. There were 28 students at the beginning of the year. Since then 4 have moved away and 3 have joined the class. How many students are there now?

9. **STANDARDS PRACTICE** During gym class 16 students were equally divided into 8 different teams. How many were on each team?

A 2

B 3

C 24

D 128

10. There are 48 students on the debate team. If 8 students from the debate team fit in each row in the room, how many rows will they need?

Divide.

11. 12 ÷ 2

12. 35 ÷ 5

13. 0 ÷ 8

14. 2 ÷ 2

15. **STANDARDS PRACTICE** Bart did this division problem.

15 ÷ 5 = 3

Which problem could he do to check his answer?

F 5 + 3

G 3 − 5

H 5 × 3

J 3 ÷ 5

Write the fact family for each set of numbers.

16. 3, 7, 21

17. 8, 4, 32

18. **Algebra** Copy and complete.

Rule: Divide by 7.	
Input	**Output**
■	6
56	■
■	10
63	■

19. **WRITING IN MATH** Nick does not understand why any number divided by 1 is that number. Explain it to Nick.

6 California Standards Practice

Cumulative, Chapters 1–6

Standards Example

Juana wants to place 15 star stickers into 3 equal rows. How many stickers will be in each row?

A 2	**C** 5
B 3	**D** 10

Read the Question

You need to find the number of star stickers that will be in each group of 5.

Solve the Question

Draw a model to help you understand the question. Show 15 star stickers in 3 equal rows.

There are 5 star stickers in each row.
So, the answer is C.

Online **Personal Tutor at** ca.gr3math.com

Choose the best answer.

1 **Daniel has 16 baseball cards. He puts the cards in piles of 8. How many piles does he make?**

A 2	**C** 6
B 4	**D** 8

2 **What number can be divided into 8 to give the answer 8?**

F 0	**H** 8
G 1	**J** 16

3 **Which number sentence relates to $35 \div 5 = 7$?**

A $35 + 5 = 40$
B $35 - 5 = 30$
C $7 \times 5 = 35$
D $7 + 5 = 12$

4 **The figure below is a model for $16 \div 2 = 8$.**

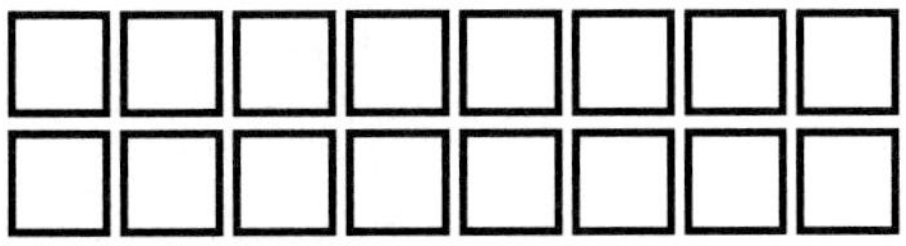

Which sentence is modeled by the same figure?

F $4 \times 4 = 16$
G $2 \times 7 = 12$
H $2 \times 8 = 16$
J $1 \times 16 = 16$

5 **Jenny has 20 beads to make bracelets. Each bracelet has 10 beads. Which number sentence shows how many bracelets Jenny can make?**

A $20 \times 10 = 200$
B $20 + 10 = 30$
C $20 - 10 = 10$
D $20 \div 10 = 2$

6 **Which set of numbers is in order from least to greatest?**

F 537, 453, 387, 345
G 345, 387, 453, 537
H 387, 537, 345, 453
J 453, 345, 537, 387

7 **Pam arranged a group of buttons in the pattern shown.**

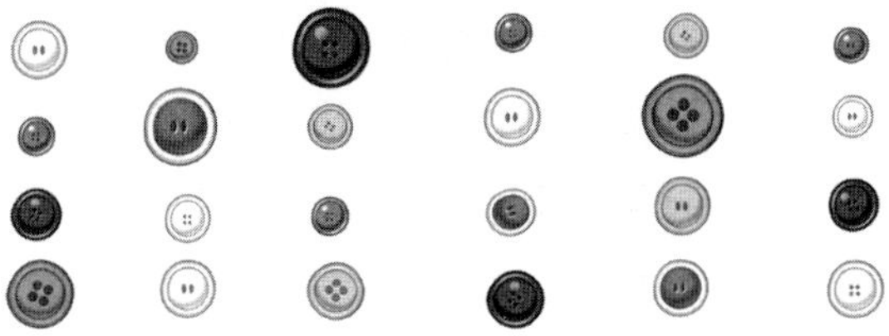

What operation best shows how she arranged them?

A $6 + 4$
B $6 \div 4$
C $4 - 6$
D 4×6

8 **Which problem could Lou do to check $60 \div 10 = 6$?**

F $10 + 6 =$ ■
G $10 - 6 =$ ■
H $10 \times 6 =$ ■
J $10 \div 6 =$ ■

9 **Parker bought these three things.**

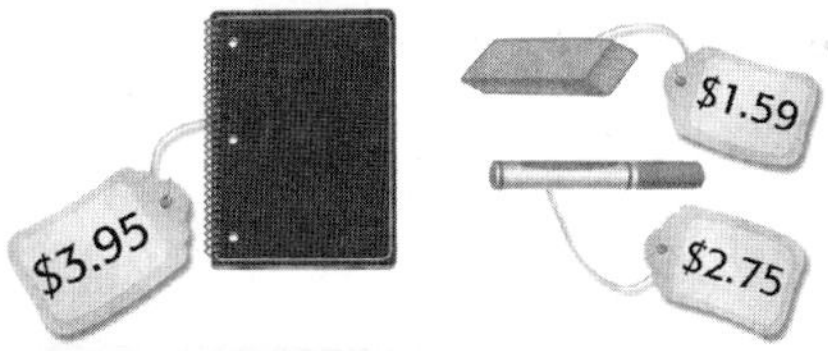

What was the total cost of these three items?

A $9.29
B $9.19
C $8.29
D $8.19

10 **Which number has a 6 in the ones place and a 6 in the thousands place?**

F 6561
G 6536
H 5636
J 4686

CHAPTER 7

More Division Facts

BIG Idea What are division facts and strategies?

Division facts and strategies will help you divide.

Example There are 16 boats on a lake. Each dock holds 8 boats. So, 16 ÷ 8 or 2 docks are needed to hold the boats.

What will I learn in this chapter?

- Use tables, arrays, and related facts to divide.
- Divide by 3, 4, 6, 7, 8, and 9.
- Find unit cost.
- Write and solve expressions and equations.
- Solve problems by making a table.

Key Vocabulary

unit cost

expression

equation

Math Online **Student Study Tools at ca.gr3math.com**

FOLDABLES™

Study Organizer

Make this Foldable to help you organize information about division facts. Begin with one piece of 11″ × 17″ paper.

1. **Fold** the sheet of paper in half.

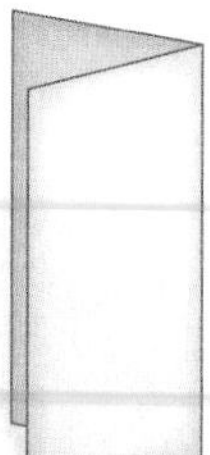

2. **Fold** the paper in half again as shown.

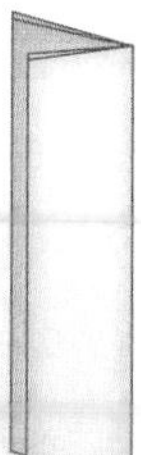

3. **Unfold** the paper and label.

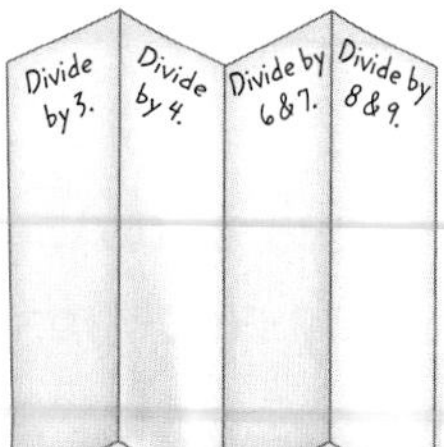

ARE YOU READY for Chapter 7?

You have two ways to check prerequisite skills for this chapter.

Option 2

Math Online Take the Chapter Readiness Quiz at ca.gr3math.com.

Option 1

Complete the Quick Check below.

QUICK Check

Write a multiplication and division sentence for each array. Lesson 6-2

1. 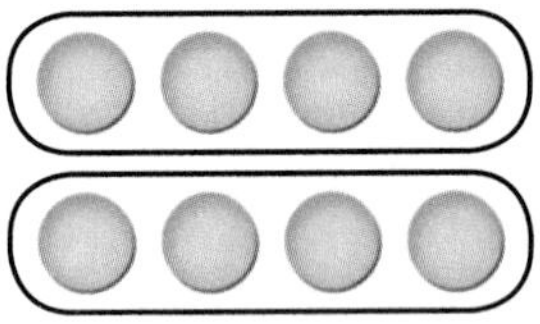

2. 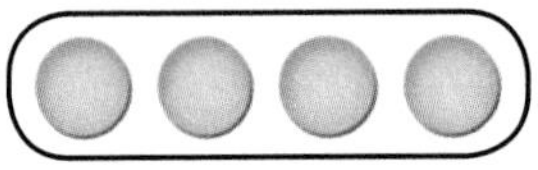

3. 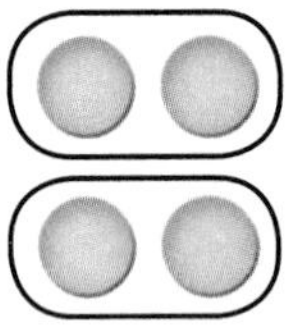

Divide. Chapter 6

4. $25 \div 5$

5. $18 \div 2$

6. $10\overline{)20}$

7. Luther and Sheila have 49 marbles. They are playing with 5 friends. Will there be enough marbles for each player to have an equal number of marbles? Explain.

Subtract. Chapter 3

8. $8 - 2$

9. $10 - 5$

10. $12 - 4$

Algebra Find each missing number. Lesson 5-4

11. $4 \times \blacksquare = 20$

12. $3 \times \blacksquare = 30$

13. $5 \times \blacksquare = 45$

14. Fidaa and Aaron each caught 8 grasshoppers. How many did they catch in all?

Explore

Math Activity for 7-1

Divide Using a Multiplication Table

The multiplication table can be used to help you divide.

MAIN IDEA

I will use the multiplication table to divide.

Standard 3NS2.3 Use the inverse relationship of multiplication and division to compute and check results.
Standard 3MR3.2 Note the method of deriving the solution and demonstrate a conceptual understanding of the derivation by solving similar problems.

You Will Need
multiplication table

Concepts in Motion
Animation
ca.gr3math.com

ACTIVITY

1 Find 40 ÷ 5.

Step 1 Find the row labeled 5. This is the divisor.

columns

rows

×	1	2	3	4	5	6	7	8	9	10
1	1	2	3	4	5	6	7	8	9	10
2	2	4	6	8	10	12	14	16	18	20
3	3	6	9	12	15	18	21	24	27	30
4	4	8	12	16	20	24	28	32	36	40
5	5	10	15	20	25	30	35	(40)	45	50
6	6	12	18	24	30	36	42	48	54	60
7	7	14	21	28	35	42	49	56	63	70
8	8	16	24	32	40	48	56	64	72	80
9	9	18	27	36	45	54	63	72	81	90
10	10	20	30	40	50	60	70	80	90	100

Step 2 Move across the row to find 40, the dividend.

Step 3 From 40, move straight up to find 8, the quotient.

So, $40 \div 5 = 8$ or $\begin{array}{r}8\\5\overline{)40}\end{array}$.

ACTIVITY

Hands-On Activity

2 **Write division sentences with a dividend of 12.**

Step 1 Find and circle 12 on the table.

×	1	2	3	4	5	6	7	8
1	1	2	3	4	5	6	7	8
2	2	4	6	8	10	(12)	14	16
3	3	6	9	(12)	15	18	21	24
4	4	8	(12)	16	20	24	28	32
5	5	10	15	20	25	30	35	40
6	6	(12)	18	24	30	36	42	48
7	7	14	21	28	35	42	49	56
8	8	16	24	32	40	48	56	64

Step 2 Copy and complete the table for the dividend 12 and all its divisors and quotients.

Divide	Divisor	Dividend	Quotient	Division Sentence	Multiplication Sentence
$12 \div 6$	6	12	2	$12 \div 6 = 2$	$2 \times 6 = 12$
$12 \div 2$	■	■	■	■	■
$12 \div 4$	■	■	■	■	■
$12 \div 3$	■	■	■	■	■

Think About It

1. Why can the multiplication table be used to divide?

2. Refer to Activity 2. Which pairs of division sentences in Step 2 are related?

CHECK What You Know

Divide. Use the multiplication table.

3. $21 \div 3$ **4.** $49 \div 7$ **5.** $36 \div 9$ **6.** $72 \div 8$

7. WRITING IN ▶MATH Explain how the multiplication table is used for division.

7-1 Divide by 3

MAIN IDEA

I will divide by 3.

Standard 3NS2.3
Use the inverse relationship of multiplication and division to compute and check results.

GET READY to Learn

Martin, Maria, and Tani have 24 markers in all. If each person has the same number of markers, how many does each person have?

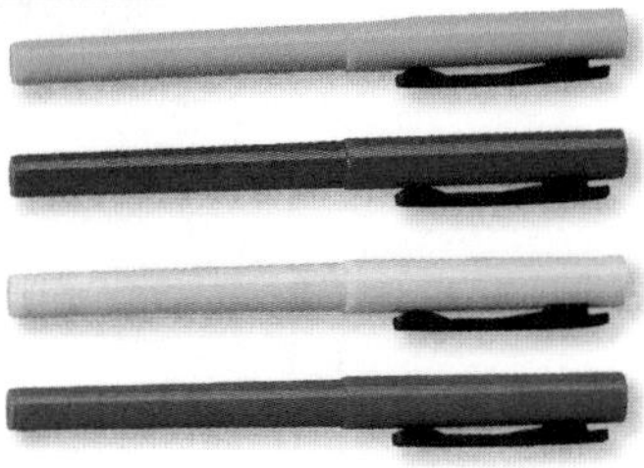

You have used the multiplication table to divide.

Real-World EXAMPLE

1 MARKERS **There are 24 markers in all. Martin, Maria, and Tani each have the same number of markers. How many markers does each person have?**

Divide a group of 24 into 3 equal groups. Find $24 \div 3$ or $3\overline{)24}$.

$24 \div 3$ or $3\overline{)24}$

24 → dividend; 3 → divisor

- Locate row 3.
- Follow row 3 to 24.
- Move straight up the column to the quotient.

×	1	2	3	4	5	6	7	8
1	1	2	3	4	5	6	7	8
2	2	4	6	8	10	12	14	16
3	3	6	9	12	15	18	21	24
4	4	8	12	16	20	24	28	32
5	5	10	15	20	25	30	35	40
6	6	12	18	24	30	36	42	48
7	7	14	21	28	35	42	49	56
8	8	16	24	32	40	48	56	64

So, $24 \div 3 = 8$ or $3\overline{)24}$ with quotient 8. Each person has 8 markers.

Check The array below shows that $24 \div 3$ is 8. ✓

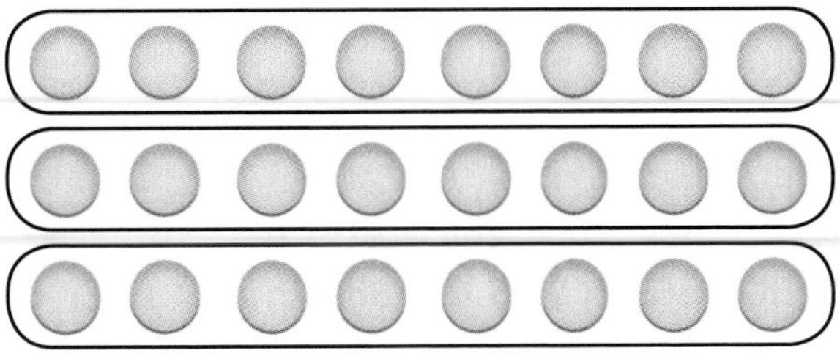

You can use related facts to help you divide.

Real-World EXAMPLE Use Related Facts

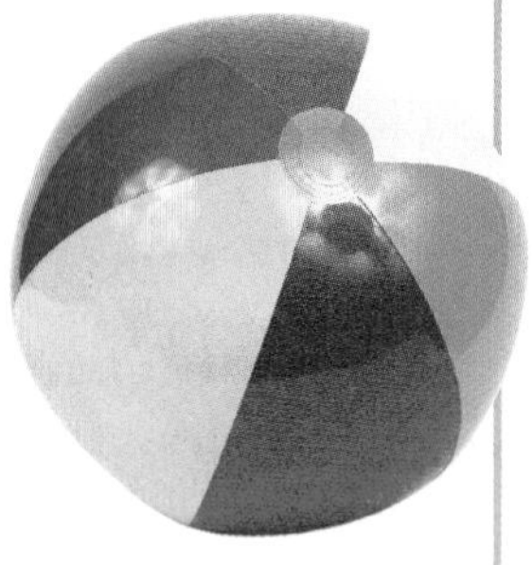

2 TRAVEL To travel to the beach, Angela and her 14 friends will divide up equally into 3 cars. How many friends will be in each car?

You need to find $15 \div 3$ or $3\overline{)15}$.

$15 \div 3 = \blacksquare$
$3 \times \blacksquare = 15$ ← THINK 3 times what number equals 15?
$3 \times 5 = 15$

So, $15 \div 3 = 5$ or $3\overline{)15}$ with quotient 5, i.e. $\begin{array}{r}5\\3\overline{)15}\end{array}$.

You can use repeated subtraction on a number line to divide.

EXAMPLE Use Repeated Subtraction

3 Find $6 \div 3$ or $3\overline{)6}$.

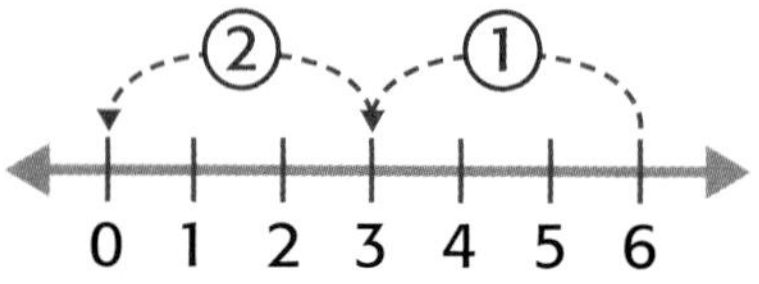

- Start at 6 and count back by 3s to 0.
- 3 was subtracted two times.

So, $6 \div 3 = 2$ or $\begin{array}{r}2\\3\overline{)6}\end{array}$.

Remember

A division sentence like $3\overline{)6}$ is read six divided by three. Always read the dividend under the symbol first.

Online Personal Tutor at ca.gr3math.com

CHECK What You Know

Divide. See Examples 1–3 (pp. 295–296)

1. $12 \div 3$
2. $18 \div 3$
3. $3\overline{)9}$
4. $3\overline{)27}$
5. Rosa spent $30 on 2 skirts and a purse. Each item costs the same. How much did each item cost?
6. Talk About It How can you use 8×3 to find $24 \div 3$?

Practice and Problem Solving

EXTRA PRACTICE See page R19.

Divide. See Examples 1–3 (pp. 295–296)

7. $15 \div 3$ **8.** $9 \div 3$ **9.** $6 \div 3$ **10.** $0 \div 3$

11. $16 \div 2$ **12.** $20 \div 10$ **13.** $3\overline{)12}$ **14.** $3\overline{)3}$

15. $3\overline{)30}$ **16.** $3\overline{)27}$ **17.** $5\overline{)25}$ **18.** $10\overline{)100}$

Algebra Copy and complete each table.

19.

Rule: Divide by 3.				
Input	24	■	30	■
Output	■	4	■	6

20.

Rule: Subtract 3.				
Input	28	■	33	■
Output	■	15	■	16

Algebra Compare. Write >, <, or =.

21. $12 \div 3$ ■ $12 + 3$ **22.** 4×10 ■ $27 \div 3$ **23.** $24 \div 3$ ■ $16 \div 2$

24. A soccer coach buys 3 new soccer balls for $21. What is the price for each ball?

25. There are 27 bananas on a counter. They will be divided equally into 3 piles. How many will be in each pile?

26. Karl is on a 3-day hike. He will hike a total of 18 miles. If he hikes the same number of miles each day, how many miles will he hike the first day?

27. Makenna placed 20 stickers in equal rows of 5. She gave away 2 stickers. Now she wants to make equal rows of 3. How many stickers will be in each row?

H.O.T. Problems

28. NUMBER SENSE Mr. Marcos buys 4 bottles of glue, 1 stapler, and 2 notebooks. Can the total amount spent be divided equally by 3? Explain why or why not.

Item	Cost
Glue	$2
Stapler	$5
Notebook	$3

29. WHICH ONE DOESN'T BELONG? Which fact does not belong with the others? Explain your reasoning.

$18 \div 3$ $3\overline{)18}$ $6 \div 3$ $6\overline{)18}$

30. WRITING IN MATH Explain how to find $18 \div 3$ in two different ways.

7-2 Divide by 4

MAIN IDEA

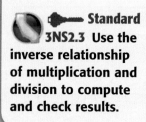

I will learn to divide by 4.

Standard 3NS2.3 Use the inverse relationship of multiplication and division to compute and check results.

GET READY to Learn

The distance around the square window in Peter's house is 24 feet. Each side has the same length. What is the length of each side?

In this lesson, you will learn different ways to divide by 4.

Real-World EXAMPLE Make Equal Groups

1 **MEASUREMENT What is the length of each side of the window?**

Divide 24 feet by the number of sides, 4.

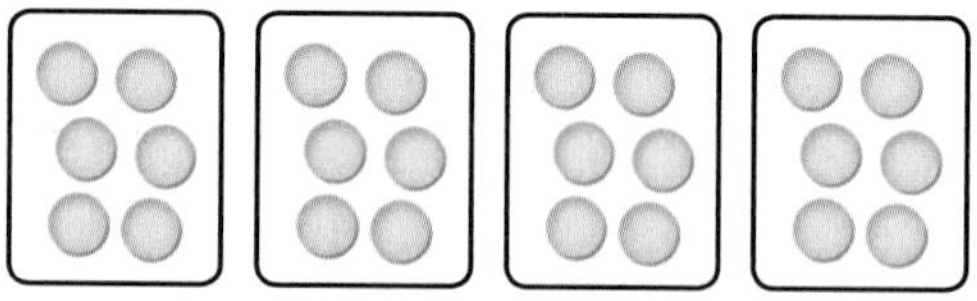

There are 24 counters divided into 4 equal groups. There are 6 counters in each group.

So, $24 \div 4 = 6$ or $\begin{array}{r}6\\4\overline{)24}\end{array}$. Each side is 6 feet long.

Real-World EXAMPLE Use Related Facts

2 **BIRDS An ostrich egg weighs 4 pounds. If the total weight of the eggs in a nest is 28 pounds, how many ostrich eggs are in the nest?**

Use a related multiplication fact to find $28 \div 4$.

$28 \div 4 = \blacksquare$

$4 \times \blacksquare = 28$ ← THINK What number times 4 equals 28?

$4 \times 7 = 28$

So, $28 \div 4 = 7$ or $\begin{array}{r}7\\4\overline{)28}\end{array}$. There are 7 eggs in the nest.

Real-World EXAMPLE — Repeated Subtraction

3 **Trey has \$20 to divide equally among 4 people. How much will each person get?**

You need to find \$20 ÷ 4 or $4\overline{)\$20}$.

①	②	③	④	⑤	
\$20	\$16	\$12	\$8	\$4	You subtracted 4 five times.
− 4	− 4	− 4	− 4	− 4	
\$16	\$12	\$ 8	\$4	\$0	

So, \$20 ÷ 4 = \$5 or $4\overline{)\$20}$ = \$5. Each person will get \$5.

Check There are 5 groups of 4 in 20. ✓

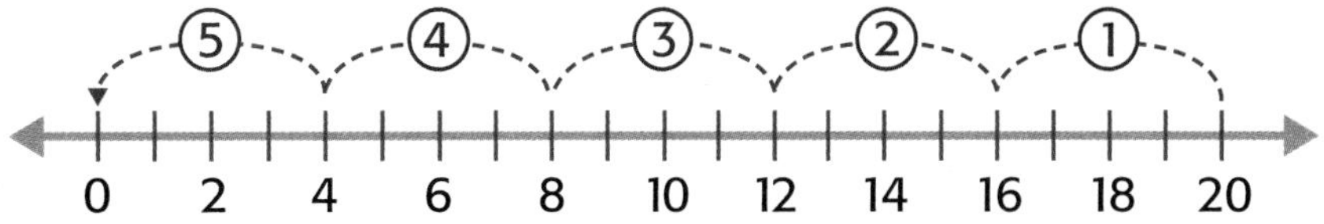

Online Personal Tutor at ca.gr3math.com

Remember

A number line can also be used for repeated subtraction.

KEY CONCEPTS — Division Strategies

There are several methods you can use to divide.

- Use models or draw an array.
- Use repeated subtraction.
- Use a related multiplication fact.
- Use the multiplication table.

CHECK What You Know

Divide. See Examples 1–3 (pp. 298–299)

1. 16 ÷ 4 **2.** 4 ÷ 4 **3.** 32 ÷ 4

4. $4\overline{)8}$ **5.** $7\overline{)28}$ **6.** $4\overline{)36}$

7. Amel has 36 quarters. If each video game machine takes 4 quarters, how many games can he play?

8. Talk About It — Without dividing, how do you know that 12 ÷ 3 is greater than 12 ÷ 4?

Practice and Problem Solving

EXTRA PRACTICE See page R19.

Divide. See Examples 1–3 (pp. 298–299)

9. $0 \div 4$ **10.** $4 \div 4$ **11.** $24 \div 4$ **12.** $36 \div 9$

13. $24 \div 6$ **14.** $20 \div 4$ **15.** $4\overline{)12}$ **16.** $4\overline{)40}$

17. $5\overline{)20}$ **18.** $3\overline{)12}$ **19.** $8\overline{)32}$ **20.** $4\overline{)28}$

Algebra Find each missing number.

21. $36 \div ■ = 4$ **22.** $■ \div 4 = 6$ **23.** $4 \times ■ = 40$ **24.** $■ \times 4 = 28$

Measurement Find the measure of the shaded part.

25.

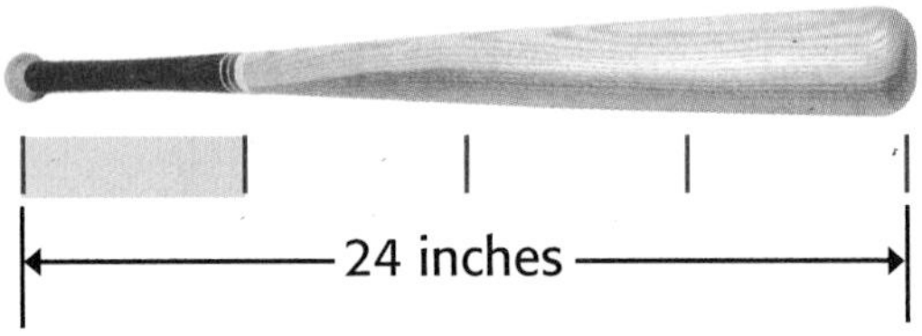

26.

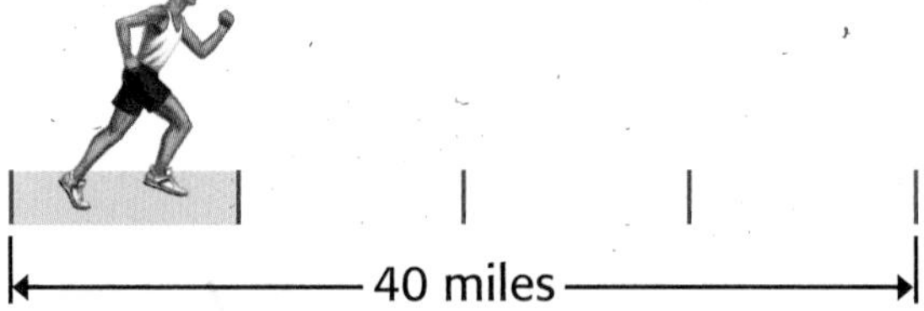

27. Greta, Clark, Emilio, and Trent will be traveling for 20 days. They are dividing the planning equally. How many days will Clark have to plan?

28. There are 36 pieces of luggage on a bus. If each person brought 4 pieces of luggage, how many people are on the trip?

29. It costs $40 for a family of 4 to ride go-carts for 1 hour. How much does it cost 1 person to ride for 2 hours?

30. There are 4 bananas, 3 apples, and 5 pears. If an equal number of fruit is placed in 4 baskets, how many pieces will be in each basket?

Roberto wants to make a pictograph from the data he collected. He will use a key where 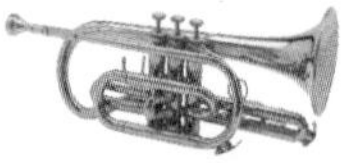 **= 4.**

31. How many symbols should he use to show the number of friends that marched in the parade? Explain your reasoning.

32. If the number of friends who watched the parade are put into groups of 4, how many groups are there?

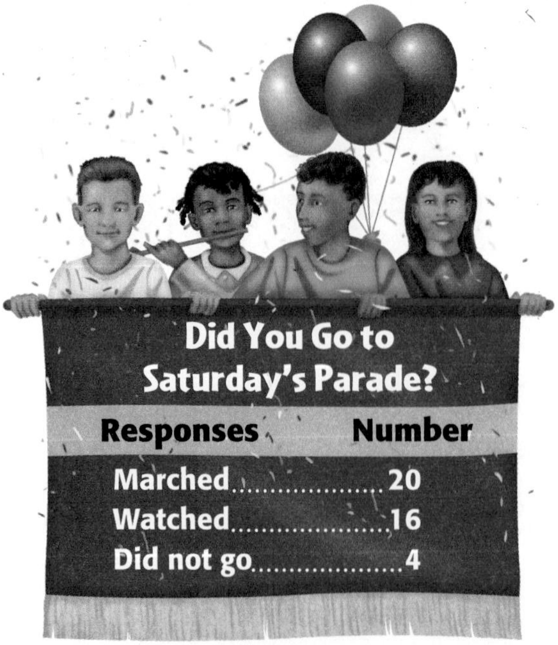

H.O.T. Problems

33. FIND THE ERROR Noelle and Brady are finding 12 ÷ 4. Who is correct? Explain your reasoning.

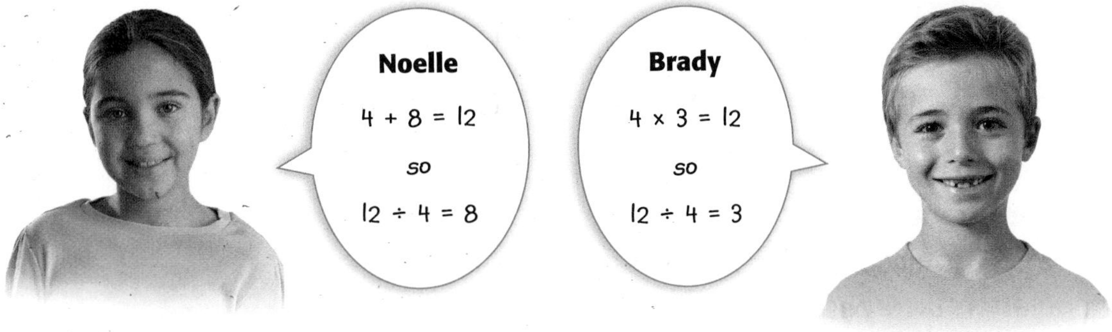

34. WRITING IN ▸MATH Write a real-world problem that uses the division fact 36 ÷ 9.

Standards Practice

35 The figure below is a model for 3 × 6 = 18. **(Lesson 7-1)**

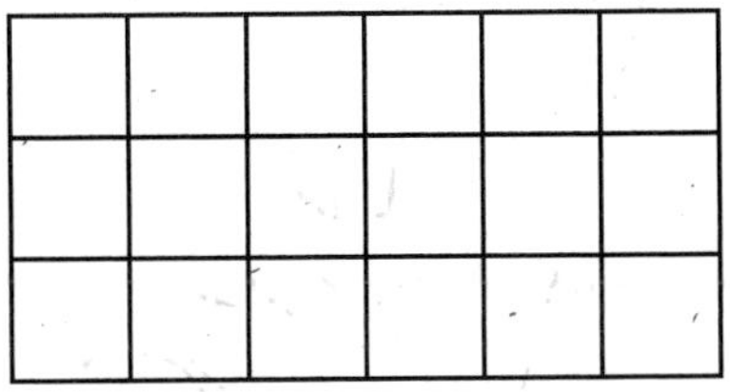

Which division sentence is modeled by the figure?

A 6 ÷ 3 = 2 **C** 18 ÷ 3 = 6

B 9 ÷ 3 = 3 **D** 21 ÷ 3 = 7

36 Which symbol goes in the box to make the number sentence true? **(Lesson 7-2)**

28 ■ 4 = 7

F +

G −

H ×

J ÷

Spiral Review

Divide. **(Lesson 7-1)**

37. 30 ÷ 3 **38.** 15 ÷ 3 **39.** 9 ÷ 3 **40.** 12 ÷ 3

41. There are 7 trucks at a rest stop. Each truck has 8 wheels. How many truck wheels are there in all? **(Lesson 5-5)**

7-3 Problem-Solving Strategy

MAIN IDEA I will solve problems by making a table.

Standard 3MR1.1 Analyze problems by identifying relationships, distinguishing relevant and irrelevant information, **sequencing and prioritizing information, and observing patterns. Standard 3AF2.2 Extend and recognize a linear pattern by its rules**

Ian plays the drum and triangle in the school band. He has to hit the drum every third beat and the triangle every fourth beat. On what two beats will Ian hit the drum and the triangle together?

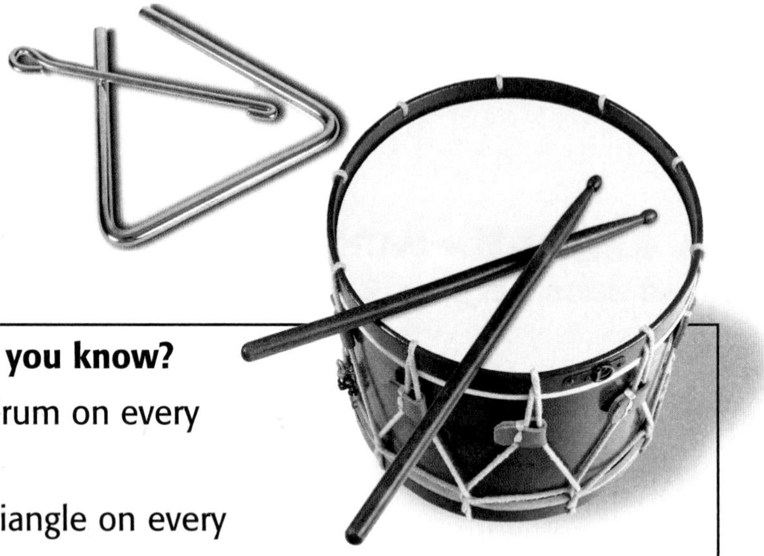

Understand

What facts do you know?

- Ian hits the drum on every third beat.
- He hits the triangle on every fourth beat.

What do you need to find?

- When Ian will hit the drum and triangle together.

Plan

Organize the information in a table. Then use the table to solve.

Solve

The table shows the beats Ian hits the drum and the beats he hits the triangle. Circle the numbers that are the same in both rows of the table.

+ 3 + 3 + 3 + 3 + 3 + 3 + 3

Drum	3	6	9	12	15	18	21	24
Triangle	4	8	12	16	20	24	28	32

+ 4 + 4 + 4 + 4 + 4 + 4 + 4

So, Ian will hit both the drum and the triangle on beats 12 and 24.

Check

Look back at the problem. Since 12 and 24 can both be evenly divided by 3 and 4, you know the answer is correct.

ANALYZE the Strategy

Refer to the problem on the previous page.

1. Describe a problem in which you use the *make a table* strategy to solve a problem.

2. Explain how you use information in a table to help solve a problem.

3. Continue the table. What will be the next beat when Ian hits the drum and the triangle together?

4. Suppose Ian hits the drum every third beat and the triangle every fifth beat. On what two beats will he hit the drum and triangle together?

PRACTICE the Strategy

EXTRA PRACTICE
See page R20.

Solve. Use the *make a table* strategy.

5. Vicky is training for a 20-lap swimming race. The table shows the laps she swims each week. If the pattern continues, how many weeks will it take to reach 20 laps a day?

Training Record	
Weeks	**Laps**
1	2
2	5
3	8

6. Mr. Rollins bought 32 books in one year. Use the information to find how many free books he received.

7. Lucas is saving his money to buy a new watch that costs $45. He has $27 saved so far. How long will it take him until he has enough money if he saves $3 a week?

8. A group of 16 people want to go to the zoo. Use the sign below to find how can they get the lowest cost for admission.

9. Jamal and his friends played a water balloon game. At station 1, each person picks up 1 water balloon. At each of the next four stations, they pick up 2 more than the time before. What is the greatest number of balloons one person can collect if none break?

10. **WRITING IN MATH** Write a problem that you could use the *make a table* strategy to solve.

7-4 Divide by 6 and 7

MAIN IDEA

I will learn to divide by 6 and 7.

Standard 3NS2.3
Use the inverse relationship of multiplication and division to compute and check results.

GET READY to Learn

Paco set each picnic table with 6 dinner plates. He used 24 plates to set the tables. How many tables did he set?

In previous lessons, you learned that arrays can help you understand how division and multiplication are related.

Real-World EXAMPLE **Use an Array**

1 **PICNIC How many tables did Paco set?**

Use an array to find $24 \div 6$ or $6\overline{)24}$. It will help you relate division and multiplication.

In the array, each table is represented by one column, which contains 6 plates. There are 4 columns. So, there will be 4 tables.

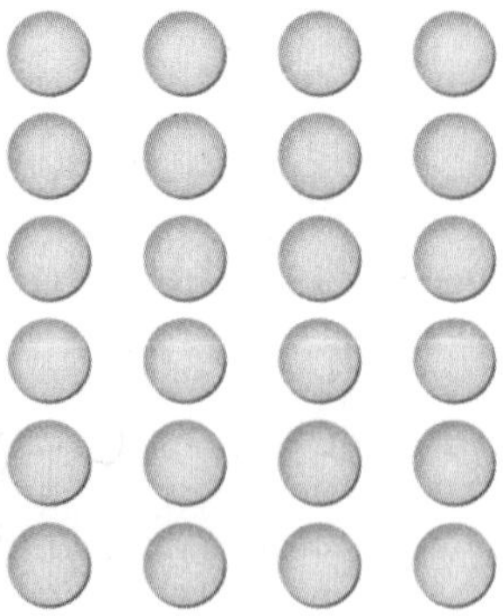

So, $24 \div 6 = 4$ or $\begin{array}{r} 4 \\ 6\overline{)24} \end{array}$.

Paco will set 4 tables.

Check

The number line below shows that $24 \div 6$ is 4. ✓

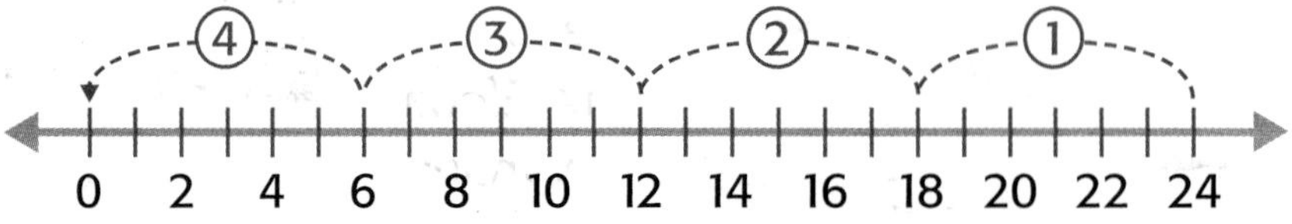

Real-World EXAMPLES

2 READING **Markel read 28 books in 7 months. She read the same number each month. How many books did she read each month?**

You want to find how many groups of 7 are in 28. Use repeated subtraction to find 28 ÷ 7.

①	②	③	④
$\begin{array}{r} 28 \\ -\ 7 \\ \hline 21 \end{array}$	$\begin{array}{r} 21 \\ -\ 7 \\ \hline 14 \end{array}$	$\begin{array}{r} 14 \\ -\ 7 \\ \hline 7 \end{array}$	$\begin{array}{r} 7 \\ -\ 7 \\ \hline 0 \end{array}$

The number 7 is subtracted four times to reach 0.

So, 28 ÷ 7 = 4. Markel read 4 books each month.

Remember

Some division strategies are more useful than others when working with large numbers.

3 TEACHING **Mr. Jeremiah has 21 papers to grade. He wants to grade the same number of papers each day for 7 days. How many papers will he grade each day?**

Use a related multiplication or division fact to find 21 ÷ 7.

21 ÷ 7 = ■

7 × ■ = 21 ← THINK 7 times what equals 21? 7 × 3 = 21

7 × 3 = 21

So, 21 ÷ 7 = 3 or $7\overline{)21}$ with quotient 3. He will grade 3 papers each day.

Online Personal Tutor at ca.gr3math.com

CHECK What You Know

Divide. See Examples 1–3 (pp. 304–305)

1. 24 ÷ 6

2. 18 ÷ 6

3. $7\overline{)35}$

4. 21 ÷ 7

5. 14 ÷ 7

6. $6\overline{)30}$

7. Measurement One kite needs a tail that measures 7 feet long. Elena has 56 feet of tail fabric. How many kite tails can she make?

8. Talk About It Are using related multiplication and division facts the same as using fact families? Explain.

Practice and Problem Solving

EXTRA PRACTICE
See page R20.

Divide. See Examples 1–3 (pp. 304–305)

9. $6 \div 6$

10. $42 \div 6$

11. $28 \div 7$

12. $70 \div 7$

13. $54 \div 6$

14. $0 \div 6$

15. $7\overline{)49}$

16. $7\overline{)63}$

17. $6\overline{)36}$

18. $6\overline{)60}$

19. $7\overline{)0}$

20. $7\overline{)42}$

Algebra Find each missing number.

21. $7 \times$ ■ $= 63$
$63 \div 7 =$ ■

22. $7 \times$ ■ $= 35$
$35 \div 7 =$ ■

23. $7 \times$ ■ $= 70$
$70 \div 7 =$ ■

Algebra Copy and complete each table.

24.

Rule: Divide by 6.				
Input	36	12	48	■
Output	■	■	■	10

25.

Rule: Divide by 7.				
Input	28	42	■	70
Output	■	■	7	■

26. A rose bush has 42 rose buds. The 7 stems of the rose bush have an equal number of buds. How many buds are on each stem?

27. The sewing club is making a quilt with 63 squares. The squares are quilted in 7 equal rows. How many quilt squares are there in each row?

28. For every tree that is cut down in California, 7 new trees are planted. If 56 new trees have been planted, how many trees were cut down?

29. There are 7 groups of 5 students and 5 groups of 7 students at the tables in the cafeteria. What is the total number of students?

H.O.T. Problems

30. **OPEN ENDED** Write two numbers that cannot be divided by 7.

31. **WHICH ONE DOESN'T BELONG?** Identify the division sentence that does not belong with the others. Explain.

$56 \div 7$ $\qquad$ $7\overline{)48}$ $\qquad$ $49 \div 7$ $\qquad$ $7\overline{)63}$

32. **WRITING IN ▶MATH** When you know that $42 \div 6 = 7$, you also know that $42 \div 7 = 6$. Explain why.

Math Online Self-Check Quiz at ca.gr3math.com

CHAPTER 7

Mid-Chapter Check

Lessons 7-1 through 7-4

Divide. (Lesson 7-1)

1. 27 ÷ 3

2. 18 ÷ 3

3. $4\overline{)12}$

4. $3\overline{)9}$

Algebra Find each missing number. (Lesson 7-1 and 7-2)

5. ■ ÷ 3 = 7

6. 15 ÷ ■ = 3

7. 24 ÷ ■ = 6

8. ■ ÷ 8 = 4

9. **STANDARDS PRACTICE** Which number will make the number sentence true? (Lesson 7-2)

40 ÷ ■ = 4

A 10

C 14

B 11

D 100

Divide. (Lesson 7-2)

10. 12 ÷ 4

11. 36 ÷ 4

12. **Measurement** On Monday, Wednesday, and Friday, Kimi runs 3 miles. On the other weekdays, she runs 2 miles. She does not run on Saturday. Sunday she runs twice as much as on Monday. How many miles does Kimi run in a week? (Lesson 7-3)

13. Samuel earns $20 for each lawn that he mows. He can mow 2 lawns in one day. How long will it take Samuel to earn $200. (Lesson 7-3)

Algebra Find each missing number. (Lesson 7-4)

14. 6 × ■ = 48
48 ÷ 6 = ■

15. 7 × ■ = 70
70 ÷ 7 = ■

16. **Algebra** Copy and complete the table. (Lesson 7-4)

Rule: Divide by 7.				
Input	28	35	42	49
Output	■	■	■	■

17. **STANDARDS PRACTICE** Adam picked 42 apples. He placed an equal number in 6 bags. How many apples were in each bag? (Lesson 7-4)

F 6

H 8

G 7

J 9

18. Horatio is placing an equal number of raisins on each muffin. He has 49 raisins, and there are 7 muffins. How many raisins will he place on each muffin? (Lesson 7-4)

19. **WRITING IN MATH** Sophia said that if she knows 36 ÷ 4 = 9, then she can find 36 ÷ 9. What is the answer to the second division problem? Explain her reasoning. (Lesson 7-2)

Problem Solving in Civics

Stars and Stripes

For more than 200 years, the American flag has been a symbol of the United States. However, it has not always looked like it does now. The first United States flag had 13 stripes and only 13 stars. George Washington wanted the stars in the flag to have 6 points. However, Betsy Ross, the maker of the first flag, chose a star with 5 points.

The American flag has changed 27 times. Today, the flag has 7 red stripes and 6 white stripes. There are 50 stars on the flag, one for each state.

Did You Know?

The world's largest flag is 550 feet long and 225 feet wide.

Standard 3NS2.3 Use the inverse relationship of multiplication and division to compute and check results.

Real-World Math

Use the information on page 308 to answer each question.

1. In 1794, the American flag had 15 stars. If there were 3 rows, how many stars were in each row?

2. In 1846, the American flag had 28 stars. There were 4 rows of stars. How many stars were in each row?

3. Suppose a flag has 7 rows of stars with 4 stars in each row. Does this flag have the same number of stars as the flag in problem 2? Explain.

4. Between 1848 and 1851, there were 30 stars on the flag. There were 6 stars in each row. How many rows were there?

5. Between 1865 and 1867, the American flag had 36 stars. How many ways can 36 stars be arranged in a rectangle?

6. A flag has 42 stars. There are 7 stars in each row. How many rows does this flag have?

7-5 Divide by 8 and 9

MAIN IDEA

I will learn to divide by 8 and 9.

Standard 3NS2.3
Use the inverse relationship of multiplication and division to compute and check results.

GET READY to Learn

The pictograph shows the number of times each student visited Lake Tahoe. If 32 students visited 2 or more times, how many symbols should be drawn in that row?

Lake Tahoe Visits

Number of Visits	Number of Students
Never	
1	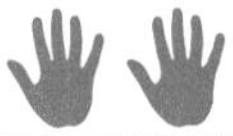
2 or more	

Each  = 8 Students

You can use either a related multiplication or division fact within a family of facts to find a quotient.

Real-World EXAMPLE Use Related Facts

1 GRAPHS **How many symbols should be drawn to show that 32 students visited Lake Tahoe 2 or more times?**

There are 32 students being divided into groups of 8. Find $32 \div 8$ or $8\overline{)32}$.

One Way: Multiplication	**Another Way:** Division
$32 \div 8 = \blacksquare$	$32 \div 8 = \blacksquare$
$8 \times \blacksquare = 32$	$32 \div \blacksquare = 8$
$8 \times 4 = 32$	$32 \div 4 = 8$
So, $32 \div 8 = 4$.	So, $32 \div 8 = 4$.

There should be 4 symbols in the row.

Remember

Think of a related fact from its family of facts to help you find the quotient.

Real-World EXAMPLE Use Related Facts

Vocabulary Link
related
Everyday Use to be connected
Math Use facts that are from the same fact family

2 **ART Adelina and 8 of her friends made 63 paper stars. They will each take home an equal number. How many paper stars will each take home?**

Find $63 \div 9$ or $9\overline{)63}$.

One Way: Multiplication	Another Way: Division
$63 \div 9 = ■$	$63 \div 9 = ■$
$9 \times ■ = 63$	$63 \div ■ = 9$
$9 \times 7 = 63$	$63 \div 7 = 9$
So, $63 \div 9 = 7$.	So, $63 \div 9 = 7$.

Real-World EXAMPLE Use Repeated Subtraction

3 **QUARTERS John collected 27 state quarters over the last 9 years. Each year he added the same number. How many quarters did he add each year?**

Use repeated subtraction to find $27 \div 9$ or $9\overline{)27}$.

①	②	③	
$\begin{array}{r} 27 \\ -\ 9 \\ \hline 18 \end{array}$	$\begin{array}{r} 18 \\ -\ 9 \\ \hline 9 \end{array}$	$\begin{array}{r} 9 \\ -\ 9 \\ \hline 0 \end{array}$	The number 9 is subtracted three times to reach zero.

So, $27 \div 9 = 3$ or $9\overline{)27}$ with quotient 3. He added 3 quarters each year.

Online Personal Tutor at ca.gr3math.com

CHECK What You Know

Divide. See Examples 1–3 (pp. 310–311)

1. $8 \div 8$ **2.** $18 \div 9$ **3.** $8\overline{)40}$

4. $64 \div 8$ **5.** $45 \div 9$ **6.** $8\overline{)48}$

7. Each art project uses 9 tiles. If there are 36 tiles, how many projects can be made?

8. Talk About It Why can multiplication help you check to see if your division is correct?

Practice and Problem Solving

EXTRA PRACTICE See page R20.

Divide. See Examples 1–3 (pp. 310–311)

9. 16 ÷ 8 **10.** 72 ÷ 8 **11.** 63 ÷ 9 **12.** 27 ÷ 9

13. 32 ÷ 8 **14.** 56 ÷ 8 **15.** 9 ÷ 9 **16.** 81 ÷ 9

17. $8\overline{)80}$ **18.** $8\overline{)32}$ **19.** $9\overline{)90}$ **20.** $9\overline{)54}$

Algebra Find the missing factor or quotient.

21. 9 × ■ = 36
36 ÷ 9 = ■

22. 8 × ■ = 40
40 ÷ 8 = ■

23. 8 × ■ = 48
48 ÷ 8 = ■

24. Trina has 24 party favors for each of the 8 guests coming to her party. How many favors will each get?

25. One baseball game has 9 innings. If 36 innings out of 54 have been played, how many games remain?

Real-World PROBLEM SOLVING

Data File Mrs. Benson's class of 9 students decided they would adopt an animal at the Oakland Zoo.

26. Which animal would cost each of the students $7 to adopt?

27. If they decided to adopt the meerkat and the squirrel monkey, how much money would each pay?

28. Which animals would cost each student more than $10 each to adopt? Explain.

H.O.T. Problems

29. OPEN ENDED Choose two facts from Exercises 9–20. Explain a strategy for remembering them.

30. WRITING IN MATH Write a real-world multiplication problem in which you would divide by 8 or 9.

Math Online Self-Check Quiz at ca.gr3math.com

Game Time

Facts Roll

Division Facts

Get Ready!

Players: 3 or more

You will need: stopwatch, number cube

Get Set!

- Choose 1 player to be the timer.

Go!

- The timer sets the stopwatch for 45 seconds.
- The timer rolls the number cube and starts the timer. The number rolled is the quotient.
- The other players write as many division facts as they can that have the same quotient as the number on the cube.
- After 45 seconds, the timer calls, "Time!".
- The player with the most correct facts wins.

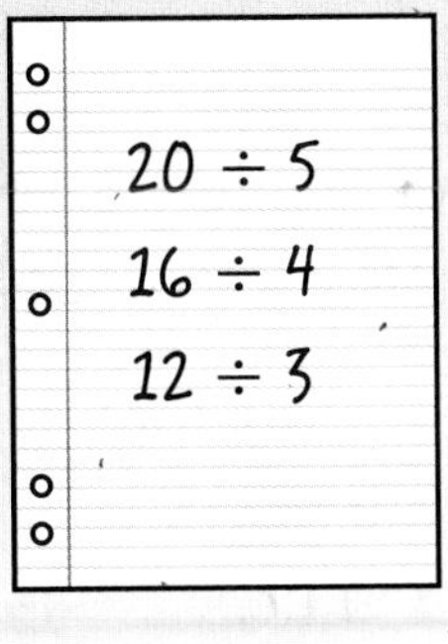

7-6 Determine Unit Cost

MAIN IDEA

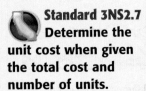

I will determine unit cost.

Standard 3NS2.7 Determine the unit cost when given the total cost and number of units.

New Vocabulary

unit cost

GET READY to Learn

Anson wants to buy one package of flower seeds. The price for 3 packages is 27¢. How much would it cost to buy only one package of seeds?

Unit cost is the price for one item (or unit). To find unit cost, you can use division.

Real-World EXAMPLE Find Unit Cost

1 MONEY How much would it cost to buy one package of flower seeds?

You need to find the cost of one package. Divide the total cost by the number of items.

total cost		number of items		cost of one
27¢	÷	3	=	■
27¢	÷	3	=	9¢

So, it costs 9¢ to buy one package of seeds.

Check

Since 9¢ × 3 = 27¢, the answer is correct. ✓

When you compare the unit cost of items, you can tell which item is a better buy.

Real-World EXAMPLE **Compare Unit Costs**

> **Remember**
> Divide to find the cost of one item.

2 **STICKERS Sean can buy a package of 6 stickers for 48¢ or he can buy a package of 7 stickers for 49¢. Which package is the better buy?**

Find the unit cost of each package. Then compare.

6 stickers for 48¢

48¢ ÷ 6 = 8¢
unit cost: 8¢ each

7 stickers for 49¢

49¢ ÷ 7 = 7¢
unit cost: 7¢ each

The unit cost of the 7-sticker package is 7¢ for each sticker. It is the better buy.

Online **Personal Tutor at** ca.gr3math.com

CHECK What You Know

Find each unit cost. See Example 1 (p. 314)

1. 3 gel pens for $6

2. 6 jumbo balls for $12

3. 4 books for $20

Find each unit cost to determine the better buy. See Example 2 (p. 315)

4. 3 jars poster paint for $15
4 jars poster paint for $16

5. 2 pounds of berries for $8
3 pounds of berries for $9

6. 9 bottles of bubbles for $18
7 bottles of bubbles for $7

7. Juanita needs 1 notebook for math class. They are 5 for $15. How much will she pay for the notebook?

8. Talk About It Why is it important to know how to find the unit cost of items?

Practice and Problem Solving

EXTRA PRACTICE
See page R21.

Find each unit cost. See Example 1 (p. 314)

9. 7 games for \$42

10. 6 burritos for \$18

11. 2 shirts for \$20

12. 1 pizza for \$9

13. 9 stickers for 72¢

14. 5 footballs for \$40

Find each unit cost to determine the better buy. See Example 2 (p. 315)

15. 3 saws for \$21
4 saws for \$24

16. 6 paint brushes for \$24
8 paint brushes for \$32

17. 2 pounds of nails for \$4
4 pounds of nails for \$12

18. 4 rolls of tape for \$4
5 rolls of tape for \$10

Algebra Complete the table. See Example 1 (p. 314)

19.

Input Total Cost	Output Unit Cost
\$56	\$8
■	\$1
\$49	\$7
■	\$6

20.

Input Total Cost	Output Unit Cost
36¢	4¢
27¢	3¢
81¢	■
■	8¢

21.

Input Total Cost	Output Unit Cost
\$24	■
\$48	\$6
\$8	■
\$40	■

22. Harry buys one of each item. What is the total cost?

SNACKS
ITEM PRICE
Popcorn 4 bags for \$8
Peanuts 3 bags for \$3
Juice 2 cups for \$8

23. If Carlos buys 6 daisies and 2 roses, how much will he spend?

FLOWERS
DAISIES
3 FOR \$3
ROSES
10
FOR
\$10

24. Kyra has \$5. She buys 2 muffins. How much change will she receive?

BAKERY
MUFFINS
6 FOR \$12

25. Yakura has \$25 to buy 5 packages of stickers. At which store should she buy them? What is her change?

Stickers

Store	Price
Card shop	4 packs for \$20
Market	3 packs for \$18

H.O.T. Problems

26. OPEN ENDED Tell about a real-world situation in which someone may need to find the unit cost of an item.

27. WHICH ONE DOESN'T BELONG? Identify the incorrect unit cost. Explain your reasoning.

4 yards for \$32 \$8 a yard	9 feet for \$81 \$9 a foot	5 pounds for \$35 \$7 a pound	8 cups for \$48 \$7 a cup

28. WRITING IN MATH Explain how to find unit cost.

Standards Practice

29 Tickets to a football game for a family of 5 cost \$45. How much does each ticket cost? **(Lesson 7-6)**

A \$5

B \$8

C \$9

D \$45

30 Which division sentence is modeled by the figure below? **(Lesson 7-5)**

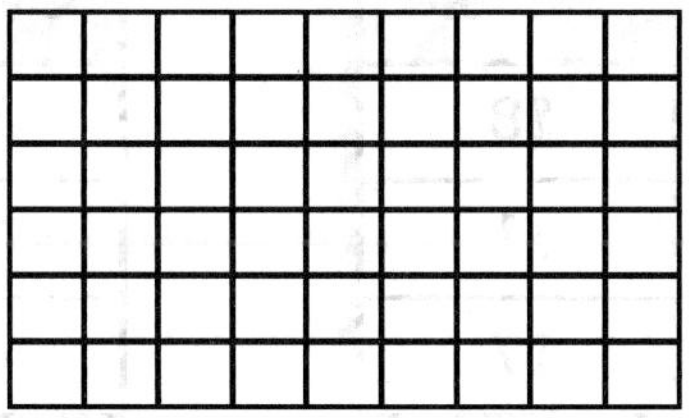

F $28 \div 7 = 4$

G $28 \div 4 = 7$

H $54 \div 8 = 9$

J $54 \div 6 = 9$

Spiral Review

Divide. **(Lesson 7-5)**

31. $56 \div 8$

32. $32 \div 8$

33. $81 \div 9$

34. There are 7 houses on a street. The houses have a total of 56 windows. How many windows does each house have? **(Lesson 7-4)**

Subtract. **(Lessons 3-5 and 3-6)**

35. $\begin{array}{r} 7{,}384 \\ -5{,}392 \\ \hline \end{array}$

36. $\begin{array}{r} 5{,}000 \\ -3{,}762 \\ \hline \end{array}$

37. $\begin{array}{r} 2{,}037 \\ -292 \\ \hline \end{array}$

38. The pet store has 115 fish in a large tank in the center of the store. There are 165 more fish in another tank in the back of the store. About how many fish does the store have altogether? **(Lesson 2-3)**

7-7 Problem-Solving Investigation

MAIN IDEA I will choose the best strategy to solve a problem.

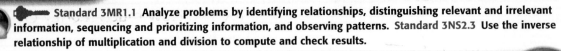

Standard 3MR1.1 **Analyze problems by identifying relationships, distinguishing relevant and irrelevant information, sequencing and prioritizing information, and observing patterns.** Standard 3NS2.3 **Use the inverse relationship of multiplication and division to compute and check results.**

P.S.I. TEAM +

SELMA: I bought 3 shorts and 2 shirts. My sister Lexie bought 4 shorts and 2 shirts.

YOUR MISSION: Find out how many different shirt and shorts combinations each girl can make.

Understand You know what each girl bought. Find out how many different shirt and shorts combinations they can each make.

Plan Organize the information in a table.

Solve Set up a table for each girl. Make a row for each pair of shorts and a column for each shirt. List the possible shirt and shorts combinations.

Selma	Shirt 1	Shirt 2
Shorts A	A1	A2
Shorts B	B1	B2
Shorts C	C1	C2

Lexie	Shirt 1	Shirt 2
Shorts A	A1	A2
Shorts B	B1	B2
Shorts C	C1	C2
Shorts D	D1	D2

Selma: 3 shorts × 2 shirts = 6 combinations

Lexie: 4 × 2 = 8

So, Lexie can make more combinations.

Check Look back at the problem. Since $3 \times 2 = 6$ and $4 \times 2 = 8$, you know that the number of clothing combinations is correct.

Mixed Problem Solving

EXTRA PRACTICE
See page R21.

Use any strategy shown below to solve. Tell what strategy you used.

PROBLEM-SOLVING STRATEGIES
- Act it out.
- Draw a picture.
- Look for a pattern.
- Make a table.

1. Bly and Danielle went to the store to buy paint for an art project. They chose 5 colors. Each bottle of paint costs $2.50. Find the total cost.

2. **Algebra** What could be the next number in the pattern?

   25, 26, 29, 30, 33, 34, ■

3. Alana's dad gave her $5 to buy seeds. Each pack of seeds costs $0.75. How many packs of seeds can Alana buy?

4. Dion and his brother have 42 bottles of water. Dion drinks 3 bottles each day, and his brother drinks 4 each day. How many days will the water last?

5. Ronnie planted 30 tomato seeds in his garden. Three out of every 5 seeds grew into plants. How many tomato plants did he have?

6. Mina spent $1.50 on popcorn and $2.10 on a soda. She had 40¢ left. How much money did she have?

7. Would it cost more to send 5 letters or 8 postcards? Explain.

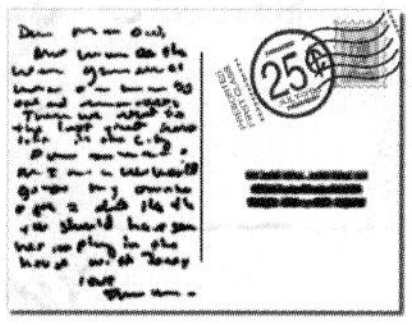

8. Coty's class has 6 more students than Shane's class. Shane's class last year had 5 more than it does this year. Shane has 24 students in his class this year. How many students are in Coty's class this year?

9. **WRITING IN ►MATH** There are 42 students going on a picnic. Each car can take 6 students. Each van can take 7 students. Would it be less expensive to take cars or vans to the picnic? Explain.

Picnic Transportation	
Vehicle	**Cost**
Car	$10
Van	$11

7-8 Algebra: Expressions and Equations

MAIN IDEA

I will use expressions and equations.

Standard 3AF1.1 **Represent relationships of quantities in the form of mathematical expressions, equations,** or inequalities.

Standard 3AF1.2 **Solve problems involving numeric equations** or inequalities.

Standard 3AF1.3 **Select appropriate operational and relational symbols to make an expression true.**

New Vocabulary

equation

GET READY to Learn

There are 5 swing sets on a street. Each swing set has 3 swings. Use numbers and an operation to show how to find the total number of swings.

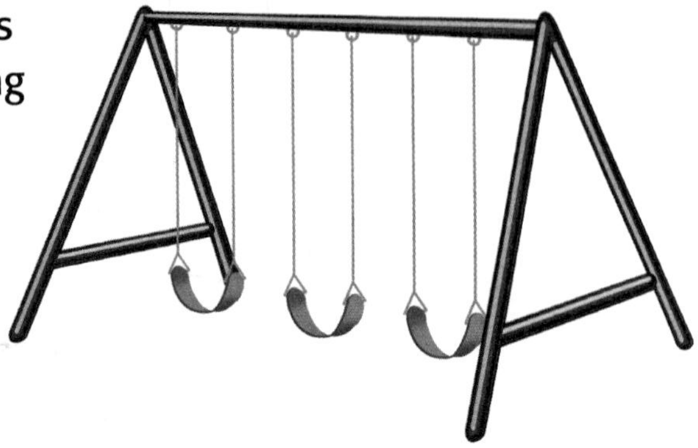

Recall that an expression is a combination of numbers and operations.

Expressions

$26 + 37$

$1 \times 2 \times 3$

$67 - 10$

Real-World EXAMPLES Write Expressions

1 **SWINGS** **Write an expression for the total number of swings.**

swing sets	groups of	swings
5	$\times$	3

The expression is 5×3.

2 **ANIMALS** **A group of dogs has a total of 36 legs. Write an expression for the number of dogs.**

total legs	equal number	legs per dog
36	$\div$	4

The expression is $36 \div 4$.

Remember

Equation begins with the word *equal*. An equation uses an equals sign.

An **equation** is a sentence like $12 \div 4 = 3$ that contains an equals sign (=), showing that two expressions are equal.

Expressions	**Equations**
$12 \div 4$	$12 \div 4 = 3$
5×3	$5 \times 3 = 15$
$2 + 1$	$2 + 1 = 3$

Real-World EXAMPLE Write Equations

3 SEASHELLS **There are 27 seashells placed in equal amounts in 3 bags. How many seashells are in each bag? Write an expression and an equation.**

total shells	divided by	3 bags	is equal to	shells in each bag
27	÷	3	=	9

The expression is $27 \div 3$. The equation is $27 \div 3 = 9$.

You can use numbers and symbols such as +, −, ×, and ÷ to make equations true.

EXAMPLES Complete Equations

4 **Choose one of the symbols +, −, ×, or ÷ to make the equation 8 ■ 4 = 32 true.**

$8 + 4 \stackrel{?}{=} 32$	$8 - 4 \stackrel{?}{=} 32$	$8 \div 4 \stackrel{?}{=} 32$	$8 \times 4 \stackrel{?}{=} 32$
$12 = 32$	$4 = 32$	$2 = 32$	$32 = 32$
false	false	false	true

So, the symbol × makes the equation true.

5 **Find a number that makes 2 + 6 = ■ × 2 true.**

$2 + 6 = ■ \times 2$
$2 + 6 = 4 \times 2$
$8 = 8$

THINK $2 + 6 = 8$
What times 2 is 8?

So, the number 4 will make the equation true.

Online Personal Tutor at ca.gr3math.com

CHECK What You Know

Write an expression and an equation for each situation.
See Examples 1–3 (pp. 320–321)

1. Brock's team had 13 baseballs. They can find only 9. How many baseballs have they lost?

2. There are 50 party favors and 10 guests. How many favors are there for each?

Choose one of the symbols +, −, ×, or ÷ to make the equation true. See Example 4 (p. 321)

3. $20 \,\blacksquare\, 8 = 3 \times 4$

4. $35 - 20 = 3 \,\blacksquare\, 5$

5. $36 \div 4 = 3 \,\blacksquare\, 3$

Algebra Find a number that makes the equation true. See Example 5 (p. 321)

6. $3 + 4 = \blacksquare \div 2$

7. $18 - \blacksquare = 6 \times 2$

8. $\blacksquare \times 5 = 23 + 7$

9. Talk About It How do you know what is the correct number in $24 - 16 = 2 \times \blacksquare$?

Practice and Problem Solving

EXTRA PRACTICE See page R21.

Write an expression and an equation for each situation.
See Examples 1–3 (pp. 320–321)

10. There are 54 new cars arranged equally in 9 rows. How many cars are in each row?

11. Seven students each ate 5 crackers. How many crackers did the students eat altogether?

12. There are 21 green frogs that are equally divided on 3 lily pads. How many frogs are on each lily pad?

13. Irena and her brother found 3 baseballs everyday for 5 days in a row. How many balls did Irena and her brother find in all?

Choose one of the symbols +, −, ×, or ÷ to make the equation true. See Example 4 (p. 321)

14. $32 \div 4 = 2 \,\blacksquare\, 4$

15. $8 \div 1 = 18 \,\blacksquare\, 10$

16. $16 \,\blacksquare\, 4 = 20 \div 5$

Algebra Find a number that makes the equation true. See Example 5 (p. 321)

17. $\blacksquare \div 8 = 35 \div 7$

18. $60 \div 10 = \blacksquare - 15$

19. $16 \div 4 = 36 \div \blacksquare$

H.O.T. Problems

20. OPEN ENDED Write a real-world word problem for the expression $40 \div 8$.

21. FIND THE ERROR Warren and Patty are choosing a symbol to make $5 \blacksquare 7 = 41 - 6$ true. Who is correct? Explain.

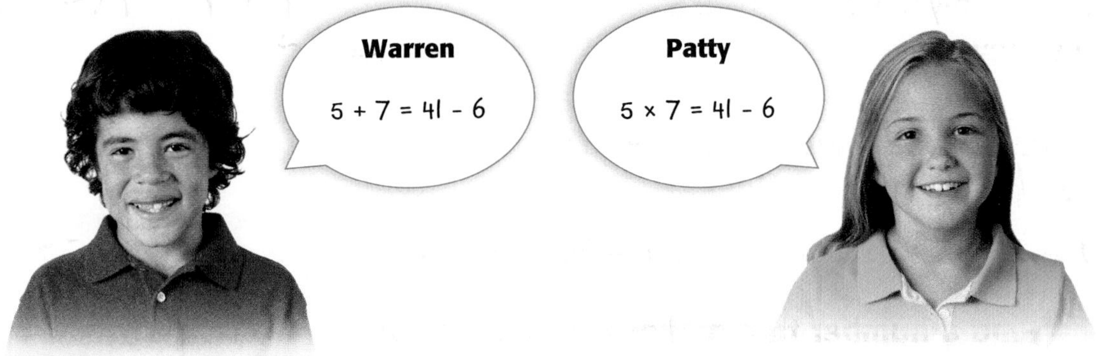

22. WRITING IN ▸MATH Write one or two sentences that describe the difference between an expression and an equation.

Standards Practice

23 Alita bought 4 shirts and 4 pants. Everything cost the same. The total cost was $64. How much did each piece of clothing cost? **(Lesson 7-5)**

A $4 **C** $12

B $8 **D** $16

24 What number will make this equation true? **(Lesson 7-8)**

$$7 \times \blacksquare = 59 + 4$$

F 3 **H** 9

G 8 **J** 10

Spiral Review

25. Cynthiana rode her bike 3 laps around the block Sunday. Monday she rode 6 laps. She made 15 laps on Thursday. With this pattern, how many laps did she ride on Wednesday? **(Lesson 7-7)**

Find each unit cost. (Lesson 7-6)

26.

27.

28.

7-9 Algebra: Translate Words to Expressions

MAIN IDEA

I will write expressions to show relationships.

Standard 3AF1.1 Represent relationships of quantities in the form of mathematical expressions, equations, or inequalities.

GET READY to Learn

Tomás has $10. Aisha has $5 more than Tomás. Write an expression that shows the amount Aisha has.

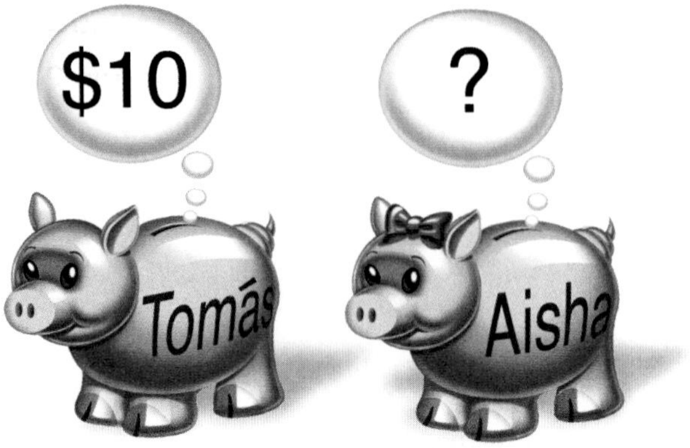

You can look for words or phrases to help you choose the operation to use when writing an expression.

Real-World EXAMPLES Write an Expression

1 MONEY Tomás has $10. Aisha has $5 more than Tomás. Write an expression to show the amount of money Aisha has.

You know that Tomás has $10. In this situation, the phrase *more than* means addition.

Words	Five dollars	more than	Tomás
Expression	$5	+	$10

2 AGE Tiffany's age minus 7 is Berto's age. Tiffany is 12. Write an expression to show Berto's age.

You know that Tiffany is 12. In this situation, the word *minus* means to subtract.

Words	Tiffany's age	minus	years
Expression	12	−	7

Real-World EXAMPLES Write an Expression

Remember

Read carefully to understand what operation you should use.

3 **VACATION** **Patricia is going on vacation for 14 days. Her friend is going for half as long. Write an expression to show how many days her friend will be on vacation.**

Patricia is going on vacation for 14 days. In this situation, the phrase *half as long* tells you to divide by two.

Words	number of days	divided by	half
Expression	14	÷	2

4 **BIKES** **At 8:00 A.M., there were 10 bicycles in the bike rack at school. By 8:30 A.M., there were 3 times as many. Write an expression for the total number of bicycles.**

The word *times* describes what is happening in the problem. It tells you to multiply.

Words	three	times as many	number of bicycles at 8:00
Expression	3	×	10

Online **Personal Tutor at** ca.gr3math.com

CHECK What You Know

Write each phrase as an expression. See Examples 1–4 (pp. 324–325)

1. 14 more than 37

2. the total of 5 rows of 6 chairs

3. half of 50

4. 3 people equally divide $24

5. Each package of muffin mix makes 8 muffins. When Taryn makes 3 packages, how many muffins will she have altogether? Write an expression.

6. Talk About It Explain how you know what operation to use when writing an expression for the phrase *total of 7 teams of 8 players each.*

Practice and Problem Solving

EXTRA PRACTICE
See page R22.

Write each phrase as an expression. See Examples 1–4 (pp. 324–325)

7. difference between 89 and 80

8. 6 groups have 6 people

9. 8 more than 45

10. the product of 8 and 4

11. 12 more than 18

12. 5 people equally divide 10 apples

13. walk 2 blocks 3 times a day

14. 7 pencils and 5 pens in a box

There are 6 pinwheels in the ground. Write an expression to tell how many there will be when there are: See Examples 1–4 (pp. 324–325)

15. 2 fewer pinwheels

16. 4 times as many pinwheels

17. half as many pinwheels

18. 10 more pinwheels

19. 3 equal groups of pinwheels

Write an expression for each situation. Then find the value of the expression to solve.

20. There were 6 groups of scouts. Each group earned 9 badges. How many badges did the scouts earn in all?

21. Mr. Lewis bought 3 flats of flowers for a total $22. How much change should he receive if he paid with two $20 bills?

Real-World PROBLEM SOLVING

Shopping There is a sale on school supplies. Write an expression for each situation.

22. the cost of 5 bottles of glue

23. the difference between the price of flashcards and a pack of pens

24. the number of notebooks for $1.00

25. the total cost of crayons, markers, and glue

BIG School Supplies Sale

Item	Price
Glue	20¢
Markers	50¢
Flashcards	$1.00
Crayons	10¢
Pens	50¢
Notebook	10¢

H.O.T. Problems

OPEN ENDED **Write one phrase for each expression.**

26. $35 \div 5$ **27.** $9 + 18$ **28.** 3×7 **29.** $36 - 12$

30. WHICH ONE DOESN'T BELONG? Identify the expression that does not use the same operation as the others. Explain.

\$25 more than \$30	total of 16 and 17	number of cats given 20 legs	the total of 12, 15, and 17

31. WRITING IN MATH Write two word phrases for the expression $18 \div 3$.

Standards Practice

32 Which sign should go in the box to make the number sentence true? **(Lesson 7-8)**

$$7 \ \square \ 5 = 35$$

A $+$

B $-$

C $\times$

D $\div$

33 Six mother ducks are in a pond. Each duck has 6 ducklings. Which equation shows how to find the total number of ducklings? **(Lesson 7-9)**

F $6 - 6 = 0$

G $6 \div 6 = 1$

H $6 + 6 = 12$

J $6 \times 6 = 36$

Spiral Review

Choose one of the symbols +, –, ×, or ÷ to make the equation true. **(Lesson 7-8)**

34. $6 \ \square \ 6 = 4 \times 3$ **35.** $4 \times 7 = 34 \ \square \ 6$ **36.** $35 - 15 = 15 \ \square \ 5$

37. Mrs. Garcia's class has 24 students. The number of students in Mr. Tran's class plus the number in Mrs. Garcia's class is 53. How many students are in Mr. Tran's class? **(Lesson 7-7)**

Algebra Compare. Use >, <, or =. **(Lesson 7-6)**

38. $3 \times 6 \ \bigcirc \ 4 \times 6$ **39.** $6 \times 8 \ \bigcirc \ 8 \times 6$ **40.** $1 \times 6 \ \bigcirc \ 6 \times 0$

7 Study Guide and Review

FOLDABLES™ Study Organizer GET READY to Study

Be sure the following Key Vocabulary words and Key Concepts are written in your Foldable.

BIG Ideas

Division Strategies (p. 299)

- There are several division strategies.

Unit Cost

- To find **unit cost**, divide the total cost by the number of items. (p. 314)

$$\underbrace{\$54}_{\text{total cost}} \div \underbrace{9}_{\text{items}} = \underbrace{\$6}_{\text{unit cost}}$$

Expressions and Equations (pp. 138, 320)

- An **expression** is a combination of numbers and operations.

$$6 \times 5$$

- An **equation** is a sentence that contains an equals sign (=), showing that two expressions are equal.

$$6 \times 5 = 30$$

Key Vocabulary

equation (p. 321)
expression (p. 320)
unit cost (p. 314)

Vocabulary Check

Choose the vocabulary word that completes each sentence.

1. The ___?___ is the cost for one item.

2. A(n) ___?___ is a combination of numbers and operations.

3. A(n) ___?___ is a mathematical sentence that contains an equals sign (=) and shows that two ___?___ are equal.

4. Six bananas cost \$1.80, so the ___?___ of one banana is \$0.30.

5. An example of a(n) ___?___ is 3 × 4.

6. 3 + 5 − 1 = 7 is an example of a(n) ___?___.

Math Online Vocabulary Review at ca.gr3math.com

Lesson-by-Lesson Review

7-1 Divide by 3 (pp. 295–297)

Example 1
There are 21 wheels. Each tricycle has 3 wheels. Find how many tricycles.

To find 21 ÷ 3, you can use a related multiplication fact.

$21 \div 3 = ■$

$3 \times ■ = 21$ ← THINK 3 times what equals 21?

$3 \times 7 = 21$

Since $21 \div 3 = 7$, there are 7 tricycles.

Divide.

7. $18 \div 3$ **8.** $24 \div 3$

9. $3\overline{)27}$ **10.** $3\overline{)9}$

Algebra Compare. Write >, <, or =.

11. $18 \div 3$ ● $18 + 3$

12. 3×10 ● $27 \div 3$

13. Carla spent $24 on 2 CDs and a poster. Each item costs the same. How much was each item?

7-2 Divide by 4 (pp. 298–301)

Example 2
A square playground measures 40 feet around its outside edge. How long is one side?

You need to find 40 ÷ 4. Make equal groups.

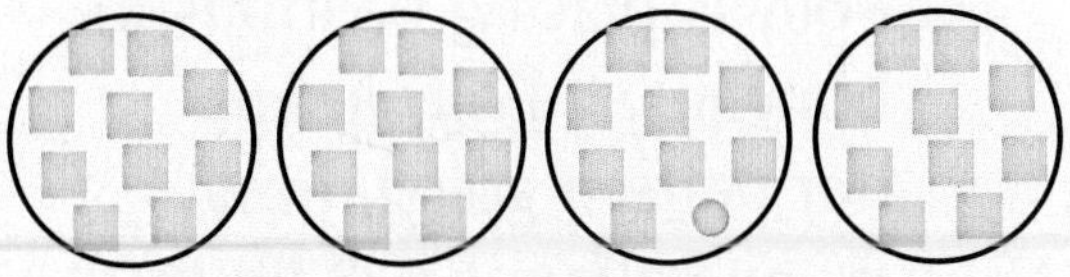

There are 10 objects in each group.

So, $40 \div 4 = 10$. Thus, each side of the playground is 10 feet.

Check
Since $4 \times 10 = 40$, you know that $40 \div 4$ is 10.

Divide.

14. $32 \div 4$ **15.** $16 \div 4$

16. $36 \div 4$ **17.** $28 \div 4$

18. There are 4 soccer teams looking for players. A total of 24 children want to play. How many children will be on each team if each has the same number of players?

19. There are 36 buttons to be sewn on 9 jackets. How many buttons will go on each jacket if they are divided equally?

Algebra Find each missing number.

20. $■ \div 4 = 5$ **21.** $■ \div 4 = 3$

7-3 Problem-Solving Strategy: Make a Table (pp. 302–303)

Example 3

At 8:00 A.M., Graham saw 24 birds sitting on a wire. At 10:00 A.M., he saw 21 birds on the wire. There were 18 birds on the wire at noon. If the pattern continues, how many birds would Graham see at 4:00 P.M.?

Understand You know the number of birds Graham saw. You need to find how many birds will be on the wire at 4:00 P.M.

Plan Make a table.

Solve The table shows a pattern. Continue the pattern.

Bird Watching	
Time	**Birds**
8:00 A.M.	24
10:00 A.M.	21
12:00 P.M.	18
2:00 P.M.	15
4:00 P.M.	12

(Time: +2, +2, +2, +2; Birds: −3, −3, −3, −3)

So, Graham will see 12 birds at 4:00 P.M.

Check Graham sees 12 birds at 4:00 P.M. Add 3 birds for each of the previous 4 hours.

$12 + \mathbf{3} = 15$
$15 + \mathbf{3} = 18$
$18 + \mathbf{3} = 21$
$21 + \mathbf{3} = 24$ ✓

Solve. Use the *make a table* strategy.

22. A toy store is having a sale. How many games will you have if you buy 6 at regular price?

23. **Measurement** Thalen rides his bike 3 days a week. He rides for 10 minutes on Mondays and twice that long on Wednesdays. On Fridays he rides three times longer than he did on Wednesdays. How many minutes does he ride in two weeks?

24. Polly is placing balloons in bunches. If Polly keeps her pattern going, how many balloons will be in the sixth bunch?

Balloon Bunches	
Bunch	**Balloons**
First	3
Second	5
Third	7

7-4 Divide by 6 and 7 (pp. 304–306)

Example 4
There are 28 students. The desks are in 7 equal rows. How many desks are in each row?

To find 28 ÷ 7 you can use a related multiplication fact.

28 ÷ 7 = ■
7 × ■ = 28 ← THINK 7 times what equals 28?
7 × 4 = 28

Since 7 × 4 = 28, 28 ÷ 7 = 4.

There are 4 desks in each row.

Divide.

25. 54 ÷ 6 **26.** 63 ÷ 7

27. 14 ÷ 7 **28.** 36 ÷ 6

Algebra Find each missing number.

29. 7 × ■ = 35
35 ÷ 7 = ■

30. 6 × ■ = 30
30 ÷ 6 = ■

31. Maggie went to dance class for 42 days without missing a day. How many 7-day weeks is that?

7-5 Divide by 8 and 9 (pp. 310–312)

Example 5
Hugo passed out 36 paper clips for an experiment. Nine people were given the same number of clips. How many paper clips did each person get?

You can find 36 ÷ 9. Use a related division fact.

36 ÷ 9 = ■
36 ÷ ■ = 9 ← THINK 36 divided by what number equals 9?
36 ÷ 4 = 9

Since 36 ÷ 9 = 4, each person got 4 clips.

Divide.

32. 81 ÷ 9 **33.** 64 ÷ 8

34. 45 ÷ 9 **35.** 48 ÷ 8

Algebra Find the missing factor or quotient.

36. 9 × ■ = 36
36 ÷ 9 = ■

37. 8 × ■ = 80
80 ÷ 8 = ■

38. There are 80 marshmallows for 8 campers. If each camper uses two marshmallows to make a s'more, how many s'mores can each camper have?

7-6 Determine Unit Cost (pp. 314–317)

Example 6

Strawberries come 8 packages per box. Each box costs $16. What would Carlota pay for one package of strawberries?

To find the cost of one package, divide the total cost by the number of items.

total cost		items		unit cost
$16	÷	8	=	■
$16	÷	8	=	$2

So, one package costs $2.

Find each unit cost.

39. 6 pencils for 48¢

40. 5 rides for $10

41. 3 paint brushes for $24

42. 2 gallons of milk for $6

Find the unit cost to determine the better buy.

43. 4 light bulbs for $12
5 light bulbs for $10

44. 3 bags of popcorn for $6
4 bags of popcorn for $12

7-7 Problem-Solving Investigation: Choose a Strategy (pp. 318–319)

Example 7

There are 146 students. Of the students, 32 take a bus home, 13 students ride home in a car, and the rest walk. How many students walk home?

Find the number of students that take a bus or ride in a car. Then subtract this amount from 146.

$$\begin{array}{r} 32 \\ +13 \\ \hline 45 \end{array} \qquad \begin{array}{r} 146 \\ -45 \\ \hline 101 \end{array}$$

So, 101 students walk to school.

Solve. Use any strategy.

45. Jamie read 5 more books than Jeremy. Yoko read twice as many books as Jamie. Yoko read 16 books. How many books did Jeremy read?

46. Of the 48 balls sold, three times as many tennis balls were sold than soccer balls. How many soccer balls were sold?

47. Benito had $20. He took out $8 and later put back $6. How much money does he have?

7-8 Algebra: Expressions and Equations (pp. 320–323)

Example 8
One baseball team has 18 baseball gloves. They will share them equally with another baseball team. How many gloves will each team get? Write an expression and an equation.

number of gloves		two teams		gloves for each team
18	÷	2	=	9

So, $18 \div 2$ is the expression and $18 \div 2 = 9$ is the equation.

Example 9
Find a number that makes $3 + 9 = 4 \times$ ■ true.

$3 + 9 = 4 \times$ ■ ←

THINK $3 + 9 = 12$
What times 4 is 12?

$3 + 9 = 4 \times \mathbf{3}$
$12 = 12$

So, the number is 3.

Example 10
Choose one of the symbols +, −, ×, or ÷ to make 9 ■ 3 = 27.

$9 + 3 = 27$
$12 = 27$
false

$9 - 3 = 27$
$6 = 27$
false

$9 \times 3 = 27$
$27 = 27$
true

$9 \div 3 = 27$
$3 = 27$
false

So, × makes the equation true.

Write an expression and an equation for each situation.

48. There are a total 35 photographs with 5 on each page of an album. How many pages are there?

49. There were 7 people at a pool when it opened. Now, there are 8 times as many people. How many people are at the pool?

50. Each of the 8 shelves at a store has 4 cases of fruit juice. How many cases are there?

51. A gymnast team won 12 trophies. Each of the 6 team members won the same number of trophies. How many trophies did each win?

Choose one of the symbols +, −, ×, or ÷ to make the equation true.

52. 25 ■ 5 = 3 + 2

53. 8 ■ 1 = 72 ÷ 9

54. 50 ÷ 10 = 30 ■ 6

Find a number that makes the equation true.

55. 63 ÷ ■ = 9 × 1

56. 14 − ■ = 100 × 0

57. ■ × 4 = 29 + 3

7-9 Algebra: Translate Words to Expressions (pp. 324–327)

Example 11

Tonya has $27 and Gabe has $13. Write an expression to show how much money they have in all.

In this situation, the words *in all* imply addition.

Words	Tonya's money	and	Gabe's money
Expression	$27	+	$13

So, $27 + $13 is the expression.

Example 12

During a softball game, 9 players will drink 18 bottles of water. They each drink the same amount of water. Write an expression to show how many bottles of water each player will drink.

In this situation, the total amount is divided equally. This means division.

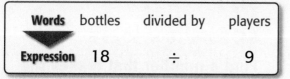

Words	bottles	divided by	players
Expression	18	÷	9

So, the expression is 18 ÷ 9.

Write each as an expression.

58. difference between 98 and 46

59. the product of 7 and 4

60. 72 people in 2 equal groups

Write two word phrases for each expression.

61. 4 × 3

62. 32 ÷ 8

63. 9 + 2

64. 20 − 6

For Exercises 65–67, use the art below. Write an expression for each situation. Then find the value of the expression.

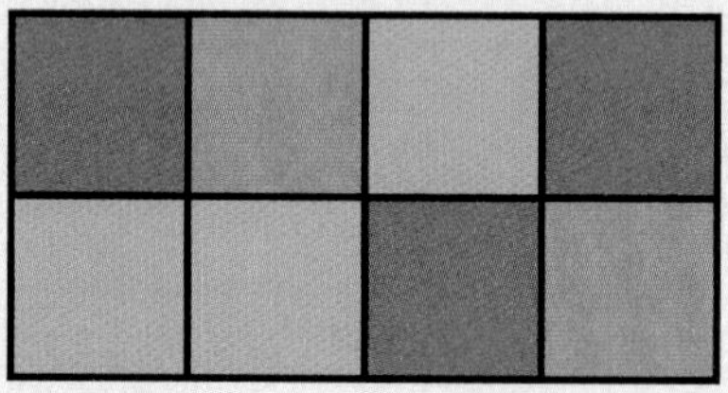

65. Three times the number of red squares.

66. What is half the total number of squares?

67. What is the total of blue and green squares?

68. Six boys were playing a game of baseball. Then 3 more groups of 6 joined them. How many boys are playing baseball now?

CHAPTER 7

Chapter Test

For Exercises 1 and 2, tell whether each statement is *true* or *false*.

1. Unit cost is the cost for one item.

2. An example of an expression is $4 \times 4 = 16$.

Divide.

3. $28 \div 4$

4. $21 \div 3$

5. $36 \div 6$

6. $42 \div 7$

7. $72 \div 8$

8. $81 \div 9$

9. **STANDARDS PRACTICE** Thomas did this division problem.

$$56 \div 7 = 8$$

Which problem could he do to check his answer?

A $56 + 7$

B 7×8

C $8 + 7$

D $7 \div 56$

10. Christopher has 64 autographed baseballs in his collection. If 8 baseballs fit on each display shelf, how many shelves will he need?

Find each unit cost.

11. 9 boxes of marker for \$36

12. 8 packages of paper for \$24

13. **STANDARDS PRACTICE** Mr. Vargas bought 9 chalkboard erasers. The total cost was \$45. How much did one eraser cost?

F \$4

G \$5

H \$36

J \$54

Make a table to solve.

14. On Monday, Martha swims 5 laps. She adds 5 laps each day, from the day before. What is the total number of laps she swims from Monday to Friday?

Write an expression and create an equation for each situation.

15. There are 9 students. Each student is wearing a sweater with 3 buttons. How many buttons are there?

16. A baker made 48 muffins. Each pan held 8 muffins. How many pans did he use?

17. **WRITING IN MATH** Write an equation that uses the expressions 18 − ■ and 10 + 2. Explain how you would decide which numbers would make it true.

CHAPTER 7

Standards Practice

Cumulative, Chapters 1–7

Standards Example

An art teacher has planned a project that uses 2 wiggle eyes for each student. They come in packages of 12. How many packages will she need to buy so that she has 84 wiggle eyes?

A 6 **C** 8

B 7 **D** 9

Read the Question

Find how many packages of wiggle eyes are needed to complete the project. Make a table.

Solve the Question

Packages	1	2	3	4	5	6	7
Eyes	12	24	36	48	60	72	84

+12 +12 +12 +12 +12 +12

So, 7 packages are needed to have 84 wiggle eyes. The answer is B.

Online Personal Tutor at ca.gr3math.com

Choose the best answer.

1 **Sue Jung collected 24 shells. She arranged them in 6 equal-size groups. How many were in each group?**

A 3 **C** 6

B 4 **D** 8

2 **Mrs. Torres divided her class of 28 students into 4 groups. Which expression describes the number of students in each group?**

F $28 + 4$

G $28 - 4$

H 28×4

J $28 \div 4$

3 **The figure below is a model for the multiplication sentence.**

$$5 \times 9 = 45$$

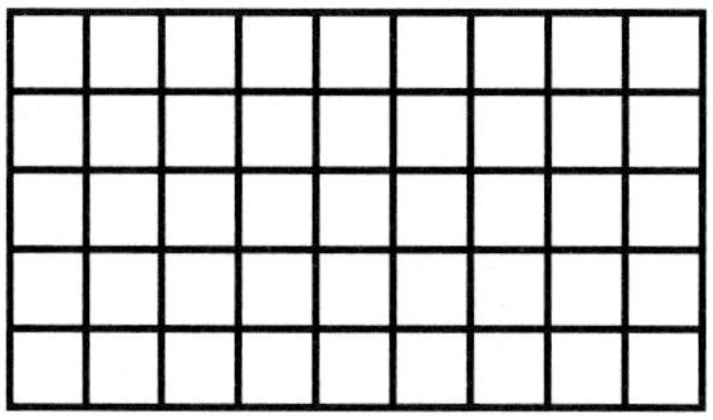

Which division sentence is modeled by the same figure?

A $36 \div 9 = 4$
B $36 \div 4 = 9$
C $45 \div 5 = 9$
D $50 \div 5 = 10$

4 **Monya bought 3 pairs of socks. Each pair of socks cost the same price. The total cost was $18. How much money did each pair of socks cost?**

F $3
G $4
H $5
J $6

5 **Brandon worked a total of 36 hours the last 4 weeks. He worked the same number of hours each week. How many hours did he work each week?**

A 3
B 6
C 8
D 9

6 **Ella placed apples in a bowl. Of the 15 apples, 5 are green. The others are red. What number makes the number sentence true?**

$$15 - 5 = \blacksquare$$

F 3
G 5
H 10
J 20

7 **Which number is 15 more than 1032?**

A 1017
B 1027
C 1047
D 1067

8 **Which sign goes in the number sentence 49 ■ 7 = 7 to make it true?**

F $+$
G $-$
H $\times$
J $\div$

9 **Which number is between 6348 and 8358?**

A 6236
B 6345
C 7143
D 8359

10 **If $3 \times 5 \times 2 = 30$, then what is $2 \times 3 \times 5$?**

F 10
G 25
H 30
J 60

CHAPTER 8

Measurement: Customary System

BIG Idea What are customary units of measurement?

Customary units for **length** are inch, foot, yard, and mile. Units for **weight** are ounce and pound. Units for **capacity** are cup, pint, quart, and gallon.

Example The table shown has the heights of three students. Each height is listed in inches.

Student Heights	
Name	**Height (in.)**
Traci	37
Marta	44
Caleb	50

What will I learn in this chapter?

- Choose appropriate measurement tools and units.
- Estimate and measure length, capacity, and weight/mass.
- Convert customary units and units of time.
- Solve problems by working backward.

Key Vocabulary

length **hour (h)**
capacity **minute (min)**
weight

Math Online **Student Study Tools at** ca.gr3math.com

FOLDABLES™ Study Organizer

Make this foldable to help you organize information about customary measurement. Begin with one sheet of 11″ × 17″ paper.

① **Fold** paper vertically in 5 equal sections. Unfold.

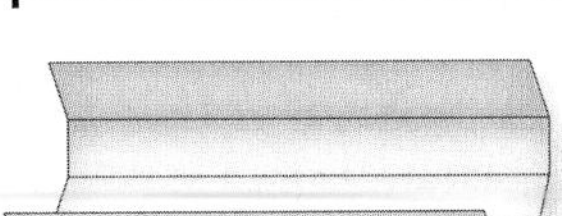

② **Fold** paper horizontally in 5 equal sections. Unfold.

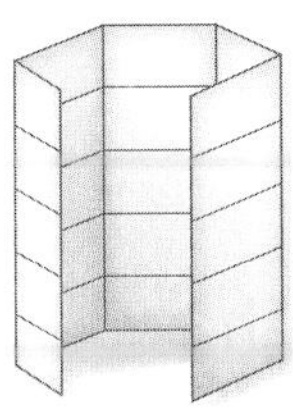

③ **Label** as shown.

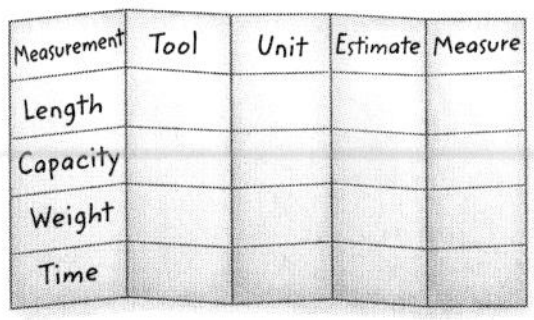

ARE YOU READY for Chapter 8?

You have two ways to check prerequisite skills for this chapter.

Option 2

Math Online Take the Chapter Readiness Quiz at ca.gr3math.com.

Option 1

Complete the Quick Check below.

QUICK Check

Identify which object is longer. **(Prior grade)**

1. 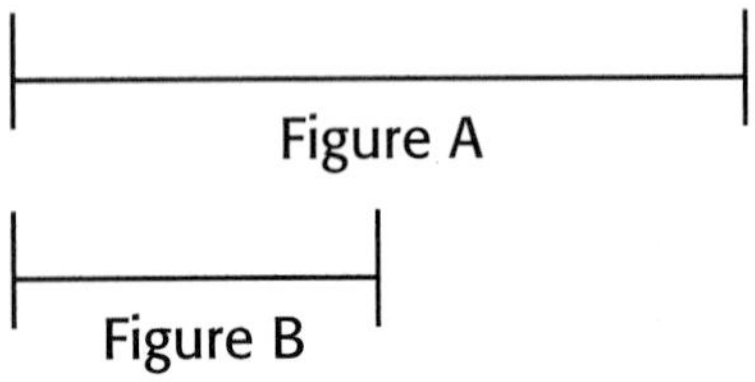

2. 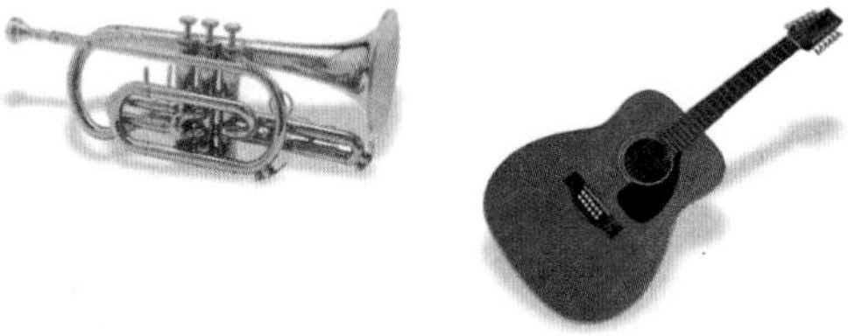

3. If Sancho walked 15 miles, and Alberto walked 15 yards, who walked farther? Explain.

Identify which object holds less. **(Prior grade)**

4. 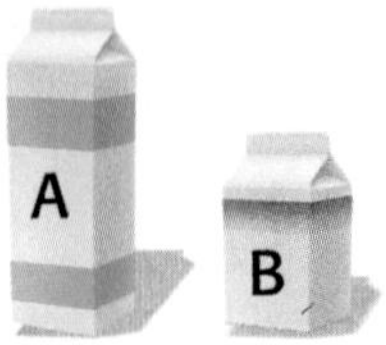

5. 

6. Consuela has two equally-sized glasses of milk. One of the glasses is full. The other is half full. Which glass is lighter?

Identify which object weighs more. **(Prior grade)**

7. 

8. 

9. Mr. Gomez is holding a hair brush and a large book. Which object weighs more?

Explore

Measurement Activity for 8-1
Length to the Nearest Inch

Length is the measure of distance between two points. You can estimate and measure length with a nonstandard unit.

MAIN IDEA

I will use models to explore length to the nearest inch.

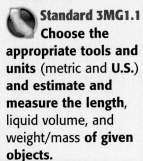

Standard 3MG1.1 Choose the appropriate tools and units (metric and **U.S.**) **and estimate and measure the length,** liquid volume, and weight/mass **of given objects.**

Standard 3MR2.3 Use a variety of methods, such as words, numbers, symbols,charts, graphs, tables, **diagrams, and models, to explain mathematical reasoning.**

You Will Need

inch ruler, small paper clips, pencil

Concepts in Motion

Animation
ca.gr3math.com

ACTIVITY

1 Estimate and measure length using a paper clip.

Step 1 Estimate

Estimate the length of a pencil in paper clips.

Step 2 Measure

Arrange paper clips end to end as shown. Count the paper clips.

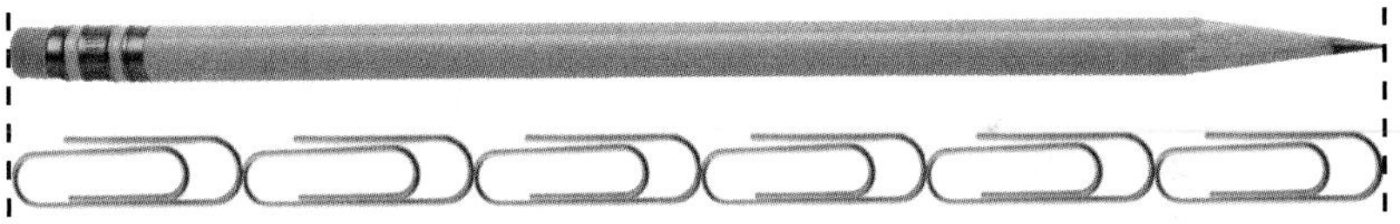

How close was your estimate to the actual length in paper clips?

Hands-On Activity

An **inch (in.)** is a standard unit of measure in the customary measurement system.

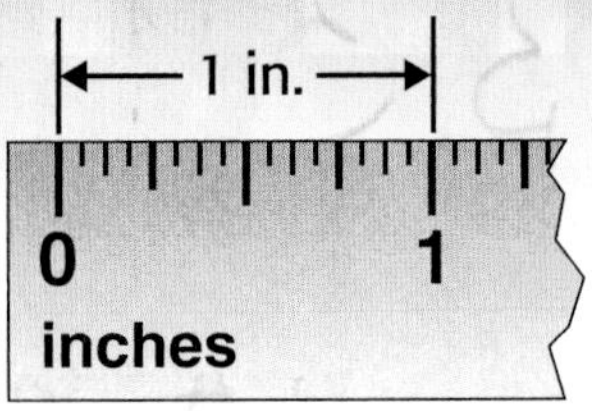

ACTIVITY

2 Estimate and measure length using a ruler.

Step 1 **Estimate**

Estimate the length of the comb in inches.

Step 2 **Measure**

Line up the comb as shown. Find the closest inch mark at the other end of the comb. How close was your estimate to the actual length?

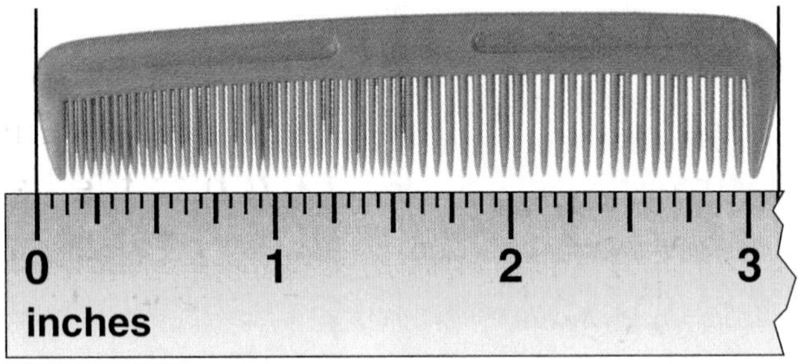

Think About It

1. In both activities, how did you estimate length?

2. Is a paper clip or a ruler more accurate for measuring? Explain.

CHECK What You Know

Estimate. Then measure each length to the nearest inch.

3.

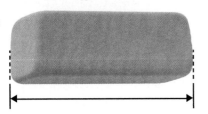

4.

5. Find objects in your classroom that measure about 1 inch, 4 inches, and 6 inches. Complete the table shown.

Measure	Object
1 inch	?
4 inches	?
6 inches	?

6. WRITING IN ▶MATH How did you decide which objects to choose?

8-1 Length to the Nearest Half Inch

GET READY to Learn

Vito has a rubber bug collection. About how long is the rubber bug shown?

MAIN IDEA

I will estimate and measure length to the nearest half inch.

Standard 3MG1.1 Choose the appropriate tools and units (metric and **U.S.) and estimate and measure the length,** liquid volume, and weight/mass **of given objects.**

New Vocabulary

length

inch (in.)

In the Explore Activity for Lesson 8-1, you measured **length** to the nearest **inch (in.)**. You can also measure length to the nearest half inch.

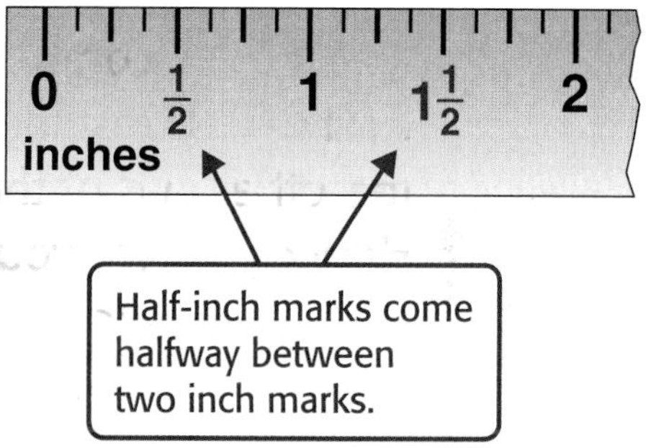
0
$\frac{1}{2}$
1
$1\frac{1}{2}$
2
inches
Half-inch marks come halfway between two inch marks.

Real-World EXAMPLE Nearest Half Inch

1 What is the length of Vito's rubber bug to the nearest half inch?

Estimate The bug is a little longer than the length of a paper clip. So, the bug is a little longer than 1 inch.

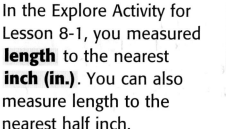

Line up one end of the bug with the 0 mark. Find the half inch mark that is closest to the other end of the bug.

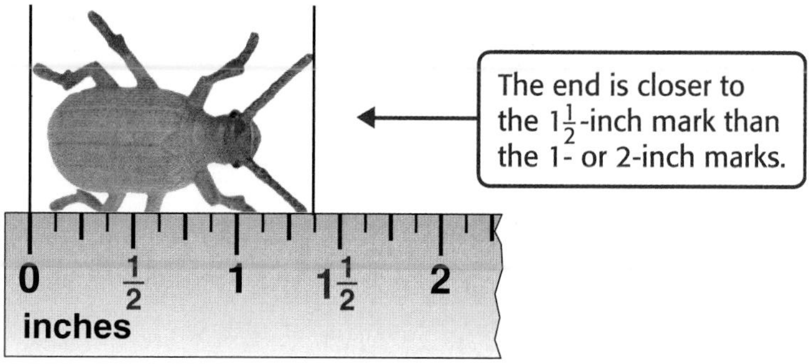
The end is closer to the $1\frac{1}{2}$-inch mark than the 1- or 2-inch marks.
0
$\frac{1}{2}$
1
$1\frac{1}{2}$
2
inches

To the nearest half inch, the bug is $1\frac{1}{2}$ inches long.

Vocabulary Link

The word *rule* comes from a Latin word meaning *straight stick.*

Sometimes when measuring to the nearest half inch, the length is a whole number.

Real-World EXAMPLE **Nearest Half Inch**

2 **What is the length of the red feather to the nearest half inch?**

Estimate The feather is a little shorter than the length of 3 paper clips. So, the feather is about 3 inches long.

Even though you are measuring to the nearest half inch, the end of the feather is closer to a whole number, 3.

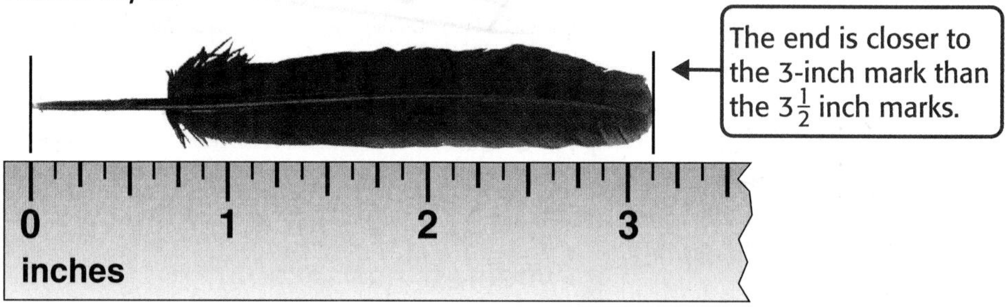

The end is closer to the 3-inch mark than the $3\frac{1}{2}$ inch marks.
0
1
2
3
inches

Remember

To measure length, line up one end of the object to be measured with the 0 mark on the ruler.

So, to the nearest half inch, the red feather is 3 inches long.

Online Personal Tutor at ca.gr3math.com

CHECK What You Know

Measure each to the nearest half inch. **See Examples 1 and 2 (pp. 343–344)**

1. 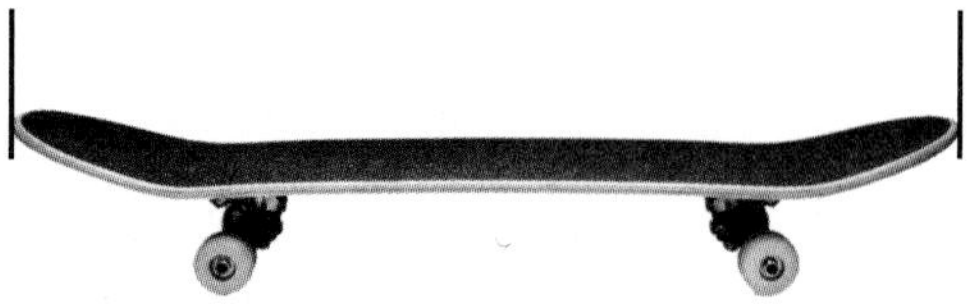

2. 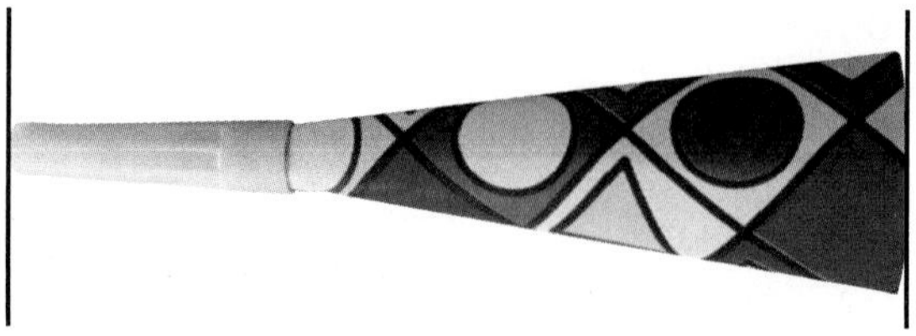

3. Curtis has a carrot that is $5\frac{1}{2}$ inches long. He cuts off $\frac{1}{2}$ inch of the carrot. How long is the carrot now?

4. Talk About It How do you know where to find the half inch mark on the ruler?

Practice and Problem Solving

EXTRA PRACTICE
See page R22.

Measure each to the nearest half inch. See Examples 1 and 2 (pp. 343-344)

5.

6.

7.

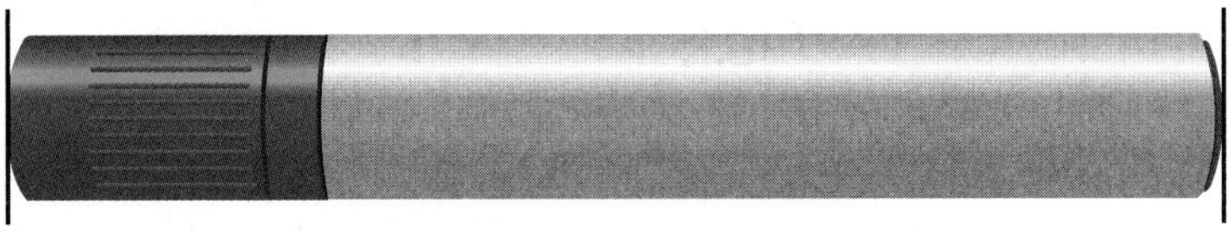

8.

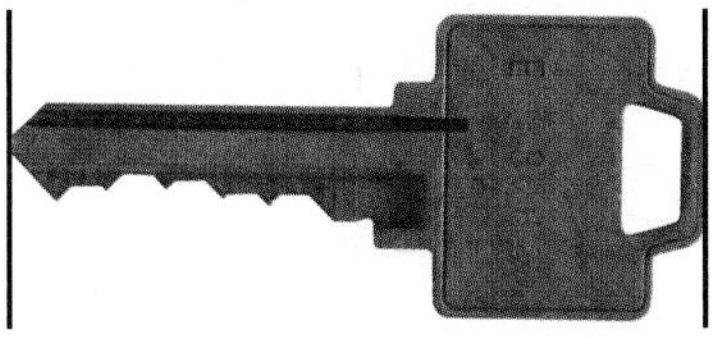

9.

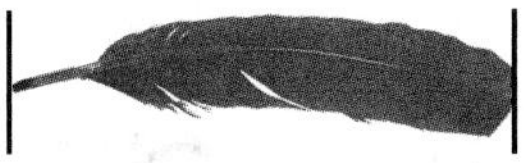

10. Ramiro needs two pieces of string. One $2\frac{1}{2}$ inches long and one 3 inches long. What is the total length of string needed?

11. Tia's hair ribbon is 10 inches long, and Amy's is $8\frac{1}{2}$ inches long. What is the difference in the lengths of the two ribbons?

12. Katie's comb is $4\frac{1}{2}$ inches long. What are the inch marks on either side of this measurement?

13. Lien's ruler is broken and starts at $2\frac{1}{2}$ inches. Can she use her ruler to draw a line that is 5 inches long? Explain?

H.O.T. Problems

14. **CHALLENGE** Explain how you could use a piece of string to measure this line.

15. **OPEN ENDED** Draw a design using straight lines. Measure the total length of all the lines.

16. **WRITING IN MATH** Explain how you would use a ruler to measure the length of the stick bug.

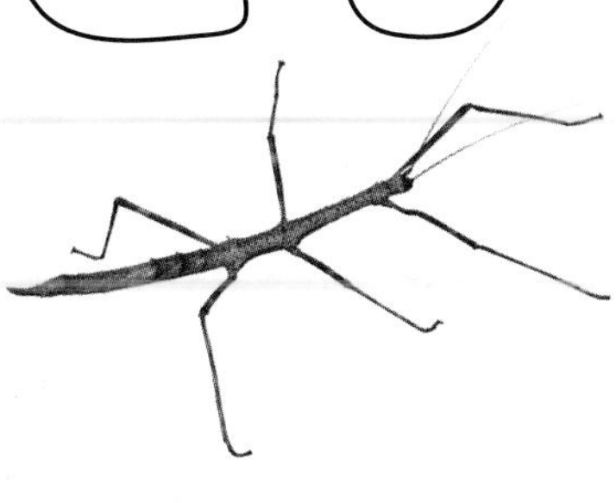

8-2 Customary Units of Length

GET READY to Learn

Patterson stood with both of his feet together and then jumped as far as he could. How far do you think he jumped?

MAIN IDEA

I will estimate, measure, and convert units of length.

Standard 3MG1.1 Choose the appropriate tools and units (metric and **U.S.**) **and estimate and measure the length,** liquid volume, and weight/mass **of given objects.**

Standard 3MG1.4 Carry out simple unit conversions within a system of measurement (e.g., centimeters and meters, hours and minutes).

New Vocabulary

foot (ft)
yard (yd)
mile (mi)

To measure longer lengths and distances, you need to use other customary units of measure.

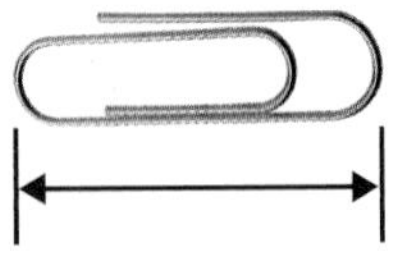

The length of a paper clip is about 1 inch long.

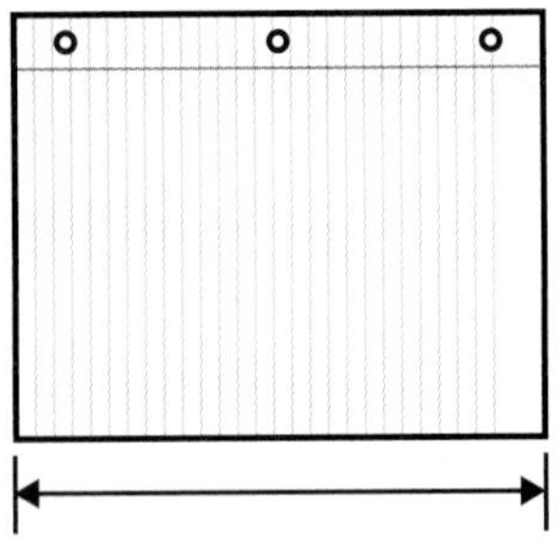

A sheet of notebook paper is about a **foot (ft)** long.

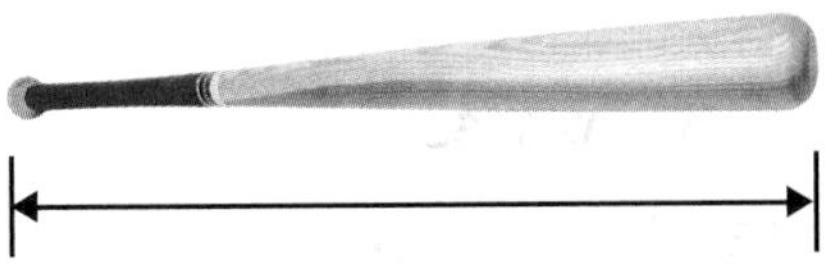

A baseball bat is about 1 **yard (yd)** long.

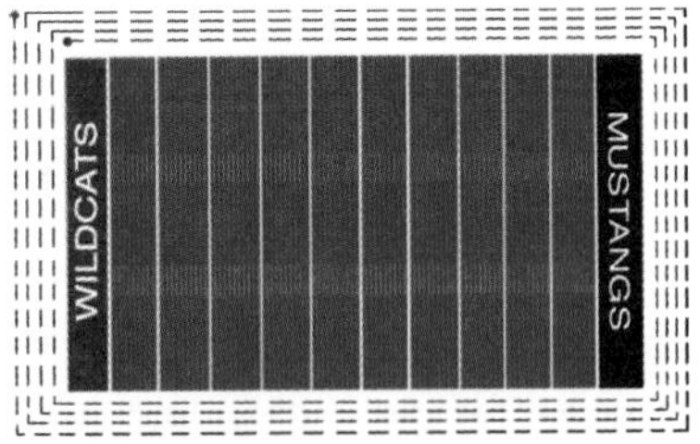

A **mile (mi)** equals 4 times around a football field.

Real-World EXAMPLE **Choose Units of Length**

1 **MEASUREMENT What unit should Patterson use to measure the distance he jumped?**

An inch is too short. A mile is too long. Even a yard is too long. The most appropriate unit to use is the foot.

You can use what you know about customary units to estimate length.

Real-World EXAMPLE — Estimate Length

2 **BOOKS Choose the best estimate for the width of your math book, 10 inches or 10 feet.**

Think about an inch and a foot.

A paper clip is 1 inch.

A ruler is 1 foot.

The width of your math book is about 10 paper clips not 10 rulers. So, the best estimate is 10 inches.

Remember

Estimating helps you check for reasonableness..

Online **Personal Tutor at** ca.gr3math.com

You can change or convert from one unit of length to another within the customary system.

Customary Units of Length
1 foot (ft) = 12 inches (in.)
1 yard (yd) = 36 inches or 3 feet
1 mile (mi) = 1,760 yards or 5,280 feet

EXAMPLES — Convert Units of Length

3 **4 feet = ■ inches**

You need to convert to a smaller unit. Add 12 four times.

1 foot = 12 inches.

$$\begin{array}{r} 12 \\ 12 \\ 12 \\ +\ 12 \\ \hline 48 \end{array}$$

$4 \times 12 = 48$

So, 4 feet = 48 inches.

4 **12 feet = ■ yards**

You need to convert to a larger unit. Use repeated subtraction or divide.

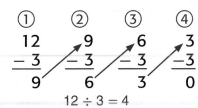

3 feet = 1 yard.

① $12 - 3 = 9$ ② $9 - 3 = 6$ ③ $6 - 3 = 3$ ④ $3 - 3 = 0$

$12 \div 3 = 4$

So, 12 feet = 4 yards.

CHECK What You Know

Choose the most appropriate unit to measure each length. Choose from *inch, foot, yard,* or *mile*. See Example 1 (p. 346)

1. height of a box of cereal

2. width of your desk

Choose the best estimate. See Example 2 (p. 347)

3. length of a cricket
1 inch or 1 foot

4. the height of a chair
3 miles or 3 feet

Convert. See Examples 3 and 4 (p. 347)

5. 1 foot = ▒ inches

6. 2 yards = ▒ feet

7. 6 feet = ▒ yards

8. Mrs. Frisk is measuring the length of of her cat. What unit should she use to measure the cat? Why?

9. Talk About It Describe a situation when it may be helpful to know how to convert units of length.

Practice and Problem Solving

EXTRA PRACTICE See page R22.

Choose the most appropriate unit to measure each length. Choose from *inch, foot, yard,* or *mile*. See Example 1 (p. 346)

10. the length of a pencil

11. the height of a boy

12. the distance between two cities

13. the length of a swing set

Choose the best estimate. See Example 2 (p. 347)

14. the length of your foot
8 inches or 8 feet

15. the width of a computer screen
16 yards or 16 inches

16. the height of a wall
11 inches or 11 feet

17. the width of a window
3 miles or 3 feet

Convert. See Examples 3 and 4 (p. 347)

18. 3 ft = ▒ in.

19. 4 ft = ▒ in.

20. 24 in. = ▒ ft

21. 48 in. = ▒ ft

22. 36 in. = ▒ yd

23. 3 yd = ▒ ft

24. A piece of rope can stretch from the front of a classroom to the back. Are there 25 miles of rope or 25 feet of rope?

25. The distance from Omar's home to school is 100 units. What is the most appropriate unit to measure, the length? Explain.

H.O.T. Problems

26. OPEN ENDED Give an example of an object that is a little longer than 1 yard.

27. WHICH ONE DOESN'T BELONG? Identify the length that does not belong. Explain your reasoning.

36 inches	3 feet	48 inches	1 yard

28. WRITING IN MATH Explain why a yardstick is a better choice than a ruler for measuring the distance around a playground.

Standards Practice

29 Melissa's ruler is broken and starts at the 2-inch mark. If she wants to draw a line that is 4 inches long, at what inch mark will she stop drawing? **(Lesson 8-1)**

A 2 inch

B $4\frac{1}{2}$ inch

C 6 inch

D 7 inch

30 Which real-life object is longer than 1 foot? **(Lesson 8-2)**

F 

G 

H 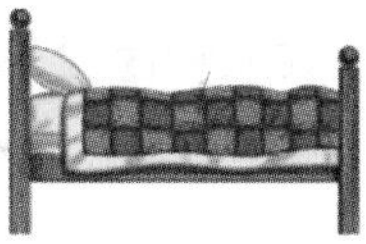

J 

Spiral Review

31. Measure the brush to the nearest half-inch. **(Lesson 8-1)**

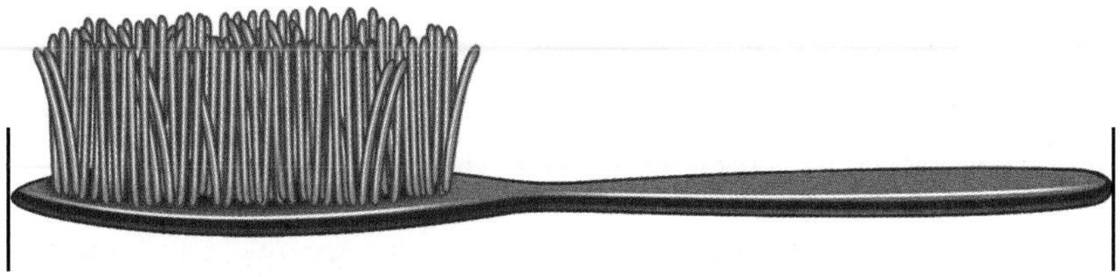

32. Write the expression that can be used to represent the phrase *5 girls have 2 braids each.* **(Lesson 7-9)**

Find each sum. Use estimation to check for reasonableness. **(Lesson 2-7)**

33. $4.22 + $1.96

34. $5.38 + $2.80

8-3 Problem-Solving Strategy

MAIN IDEA I will solve problems by working backward.

Standard 3MR1.1 Analyze problems by identifying relationships, distinguishing relevant from irrelevant information, sequencing and prioritizing information, and observing patterns. Standard 3NS2.8 Solve problems that require two or more of the skills mentioned above.

Clarissa is at a fair. She wants to play three games. The line for the second game is twice as long as the first line. The third line has 5 fewer people than the second line. There are 17 people in line for her last game. How many people are in line for the first game?

Understand	**What facts do you know?** • The second line is twice as long of the first one. • The third line has 5 fewer people than the second one. • The third line has 17 people. **What do you need to find?** • The number of people in the first line.
Plan	Work backward to find the number of people in the first line.
Solve	17 People in the third line. +5 Second line has 5 more people than third line. 22 People in the second line. $2\overline{)22}$ = 11 First line is half as long as the second one. So, there are 11 people in the first line.
Check	Look back to see if 11 people makes sense for the situation. $11 + 11 = 22$ $22 - 5 = 17$ So, the answer is correct.

ANALYZE the Strategy

Refer to the problem on the previous page.

1. Why was the *work backward* strategy the best way to solve the example?
2. If you knew how long the first line was, would you use the *work backward* strategy to solve? Explain.
3. How can you tell when to use the *work backward* strategy?
4. What would you need to do if the answer was incorrect when you checked it?

PRACTICE the Strategy

EXTRA PRACTICE
See page R23.

Solve. *Work backward.*

5. Today Mrs. Keys has 36 crayons. Yesterday she had half that amount plus 2. How many crayons did she have yesterday?
6. There are three lines. The first line is 3 times as long as the second. The second line is 4 inches longer than the third. The third line is 2 inches long. How long is the first line?
7. The table below shows Adelais' schedule. She finished at 5:00 P.M. At what time did she start her lunch?

Adelais' Schedule	
Activity	**Time**
Lunch	1 hour
Scrapbooking	3 hours

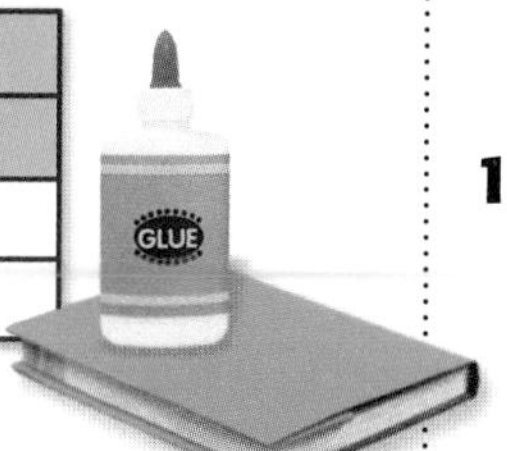

8. Dirk walked 15 miles this week. He walked twice as much Tuesday a he did on Monday. He walked 5 miles on Wednesday and 2 miles on both Thursday and Friday. How many miles did he walk on Monday?
9. The table shows the number of shapes after a pattern repeats itself five times. How many of each shape are there in the original pattern?

Pattern			
Shape	Circles	Squares	Hearts
Number	15	5	10

10. In the morning, Mr. Lawrence gave 9 pencils to students. Later, 5 of the students returned the pencils. After lunch, he handed out 5 more pencils. Now he has 15 pencils. How many did he start with?
11. Lorena played with some friends on Monday. She played with 2 times as many on Wednesday. This was 4 more than on Friday. On Friday there were 4. How many did she play with on Monday?
12. **WRITING IN MATH** Look back at Exercise 11. Explain another strategy you could use to solve the problem.

Explore

Measurement Activity for 8-4
Capacity

The amount a container can hold is called its **capacity**. The customary tools and units for capacity are shown.

ACTIVITY

1 Use tools and units to estimate and measure capacity.

Step 1 Cup and Pint

- Estimate how many cups a pint will hold.
- Use the cup to fill the pint.
- How many cups are in a pint? Record the result in a table.

Units of Capacity			
	Pint	**Quart**	**Gallon**
Cups	2	■	■
Pints		■	■
Quarts			■

Step 2 Cup, Quart, and Gallon

- Make an estimate. How many cups do you think a quart container holds? a gallon container?
- Use the cup to fill each.
- How many cups are in a quart? in a gallon? Record the results.

MAIN IDEA

I will use models to explore capacity.

Standard 3MG1.1 Choose the appropriate tools and units (metric and U.S.) **and estimate and measure the** length, **liquid volume,** and weight/mass **of given objects.**

Standard 3MR2.3 Use a variety of methods, such as words, numbers, symbols, charts, graphs, **tables, diagrams, and models, to explain mathematical reasoning.**

You Will Need
cup, pint, quart, and gallon containers; water

New Vocabulary
capacity

Concepts in Motion
Animation
ca.gr3math.com

Hands-On Activity

Step 3 **Pint, Quart, and Gallon**

- Estimate how many pints a quart and gallon holds.
- Use the pint container to fill the quart and gallon.
- How many pints are in a quart? a gallon?

Step 4 **Quart and Gallon**

- Estimate how many quarts a gallon holds.
- Use the quart container to fill the gallon container.
- How many quarts are in a gallon?

Think About It

1. How close were your estimates to the exact answers?
2. Name some containers from around the house that would be about the same size as a cup, a pint, a quart, and a gallon.
3. What happens to the number of containers needed as the capacity of the container gets larger? smaller?

CHECK What You Know

Compare. Use >, <, or =.

4. cup ● gallon
5. gallon ● pint
6. quart ● cup
7. cup ● pint
8. quart ● gallon
9. 2 cups ● pint

Copy and complete. Use your chart.

10. 1 qt = ■ pt
11. 1 gal = ■ qt
12. 2 pt = ■ qt
13. ■ c = 1 qt
14. 1 pt = ■ c
15. ■ pt = 1 gal

16. **WRITING IN MATH** How do you know that 10 gallons is equal to 40 quarts?

8-4 Customary Units of Capacity

MAIN IDEA

I will estimate, measure, and convert customary units of capacity.

Standard 3MG1.1 Choose the appropriate tools and **units** (metric and **U.S.**) and estimate and measure the length, **liquid volume**, and weight/mass **of given objects.**

Standard 3MG1.4 Carry out simple unit conversions within a system of measurement (e.g., centimeters and meters, hours and minutes).

New Vocabulary

capacity
cup (c)
pint (pt)
quart (qt)
gallon (gal)

GET READY to Learn

Armando is filling his younger sister's wading pool. How much water do you think he used to fill the pool?

The amount a container can hold is its **capacity**. The customary units of capacity are the **cup (c)**, **pint (pt)**, **quart (qt)**, and **gallon (gal)**.

Real-World EXAMPLE — Choose Units of Capacity

1 POOLS Choose the most appropriate unit Armando should use to measure the amount of water he used to fill the pool.

A cup, pint, and quart are too small. The most appropriate unit to use is the gallon.

Real-World EXAMPLE — Estimate Capacity

2 SOUP Choose the best estimate for the capacity of a soup bowl, 2 cups or 2 gallons.

Think about a cup and a gallon.

It makes sense that the capacity of a soup bowl is about 2 cups, not 2 gallons.

You can change or convert from one unit of capacity to another within the customary measurement system.

Multiply to convert to a larger unit to a smaller unit.

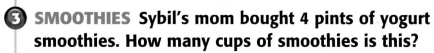

Real-World EXAMPLE **Convert to Smaller Units**

> **Remember**
> When converting a *larger* unit to a smaller unit, the number of units will be *greater*..

3 SMOOTHIES Sybil's mom bought 4 pints of yogurt smoothies. How many cups of smoothies is this?

4 pints = ■ cups

You know that there are 2 cups in 1 pint. To find the number of cups in 4 pints, multiply.

4 pints × 2 cups = 8 cups
So, 4 pints = 8 cups of smoothies.

Online **Personal Tutor at** ca.gr3math.com

Divide to convert a smaller unit to a larger unit.

Real-World EXAMPLE **Convert to Larger Units**

> **Remember**
> When converting a *smaller* unit to a larger unit, the number of units will be *less*.

4 JUICE Cesar needs to buy 8 quarts of juice. The store has only gallons. How many gallons will Cesar need?

8 quarts = ■ gallons

There are 4 quarts in 1 gallon. To find the number of gallons 8 quarts make, divide.

8 quarts ÷ 4 quarts = 2 gallons

So, 8 quarts = 2 gallons of juice.

CHECK What You Know

Choose the most appropriate unit to measure each capacity. Choose from *cup, pint, quart,* or *gallon*. See Example 1 (p. 354)

1.

2.

3.

Choose the best estimate. See Example 2 (p. 354)

4. 3c or 3 gal

5. 2 c or 2 gal

6. Megan has 12 cups of punch. How many quarts does she have?
See Examples 3 and 4 (p. 355)

7. Talk About It How do you decide which capacity unit to use?

Practice and Problem Solving

EXTRA PRACTICE See page R23.

Choose the most appropriate unit to measure each capacity. Choose from *cup, pint, quart,* or *gallon*. See Example 1 (p. 354)

8.

9.

10.

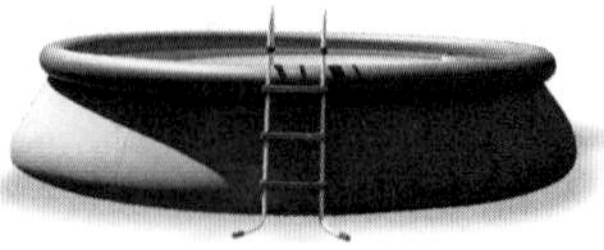

Choose the best estimate. See Example 2 (p. 354)

11. 2 qt or 2 pt

12. 5 gal or 10 qt

13. 1 pt or 6 c

14. How many gallons of water is 24 pints? See Examples 3 and 4 (p. 354)

15. Suri has 7 pints of milk. How many cups is this? See Examples 3 and 4 (p. 354)

H.O.T. Problems

16. OPEN ENDED Name 3 items from the grocery store that are measured by capacity.

17. CHALLENGE What two units of capacity does the table show?

First Unit	1	2	3	4	5	6
Second Unit	4	8	12	16	20	24

18. **WRITING IN ▸MATH** Sumey and Tina are each filling the same size pails with water. Sumey needs a pint of water. Tina needs a quart of water. Who will fill their pail first? Explain.

Standards Practice

19 Amado has 3 quarts of orange juice. How many cups does he have? **(Lesson 8-4)**

A 3 **C** 9

B 6 **D** 12

20 Fillipa has $5 in her wallet. She spent $4 on a poster and $7 on a watch. How much did Fillipa have in her wallet to begin with? **(Lesson 8-3)**

F $11 **H** $16

G $12 **J** $20

Spiral Review

Solve. Use the *work backward* strategy. **(Lesson 8-3)**

21. Mr. Lin bought a hot dog at the fair for $3 and a drink for $2. Now he has $5 left over. How much money did he start with?

Choose the best estimate. **(Lesson 8-2)**

22. the thickness of a pillow
5 inches or 5 feet

23. the length of a tennis racket
2 feet or 2 yards

24. What will be the measure of one side of the next square if the pattern continues? **(Lesson 5-7)**

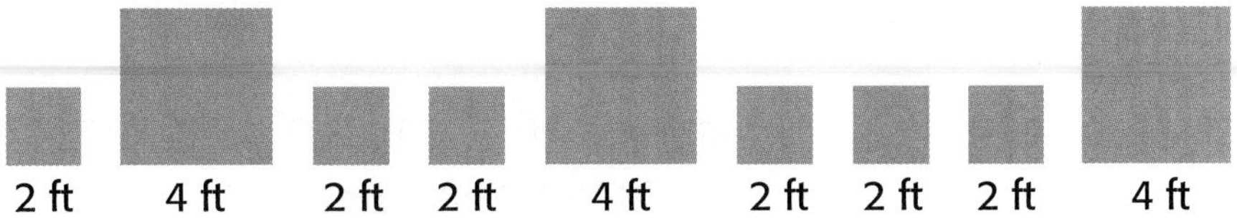

Game Time

Capacity Guess

Estimate Capacity

Get Ready!

Players: 2 or more

You will need: Measuring containers (cup, pint, quart, and gallon) that are labeled.

Unlabeled containers of different sizes and shapes.

Get Set!

Place a variety of containers on a table.

Go!

- Player 1 chooses a container.
- Player 2 guesses the capacity of the container.
- Player 1 fills the measuring container with water and then pours the water into the chosen container.
- If the capacity is incorrect, Player 1 will get to guess the capacity, and player 2 will check.
- Continue, switching roles each time.

Mid-Chapter Check

CHAPTER 8

Lessons 8-1 through 8-4

Measure each to the nearest half inch. (Lesson 8-1)

1. 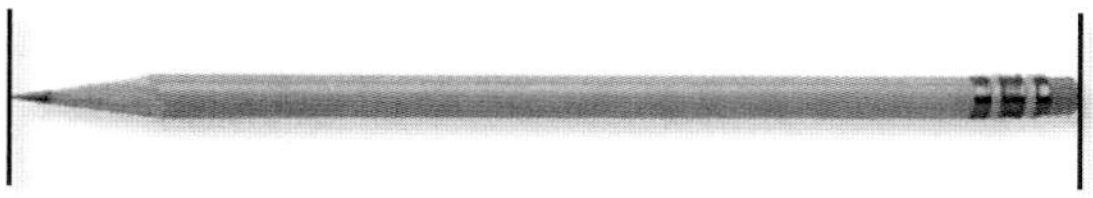

2. 

Choose the most appropriate unit to measure each length. Choose from *inch, foot, yard,* or *mile*. (Lesson 8-2)

3. height of a DVD container

4. width of your math book

5. Jillian and Sue are learning to sew. Jillian's pattern calls for 3 yards of material. Sue's pattern calls for 2 yards. How many feet do they need altogether? (Lesson 8-2)

Convert. (Lesson 8-2)

6. 3 ft = ▒ in. **7.** 5 yd = ▒ ft

8. **STANDARDS PRACTICE** Which object is longer than 1 yard? (Lesson 8-2)

A your bed **C** a toy car

B a crayon **D** a notebook

9. Some children offered to clean Ms. Dawson's garage. It took 2 days. She paid each child $4 per day. If she paid them $24 total, how many children were there? (Lesson 8-3)

Choose the the most appropriate unit to measure each capacity. Choose from *cup, pint, quart,* or *gallon*. (Lesson 8-4)

10. 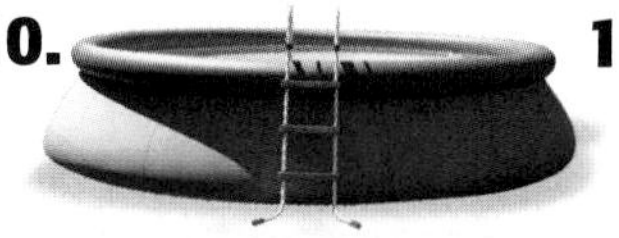 **11.** 

Choose the best estimate. (Lesson 8-4)

12. bowl of jello: 1 gal or 1 c

13. bathtub: 10 pints or 10 gallons

14. **STANDARDS PRACTICE** Which can hold more than 1 quart? (Lesson 8-4)

F milk carton **H** bathtub

G cereal bowl **J** water balloon

15. **WRITING IN MATH** If you want to measure the amount of water it would take to make an ice-rink, would you use length or capacity measurements? Explain.

8-5 Problem-Solving Investigation

MAIN IDEA I will choose the best strategy to solve a problem.

Standard 3NS2.8 Solve problems that require two or more of the skills mentioned above. Standard 3MR1.2 Determine when and how to break a problem into simpler parts.

P.S.I. TEAM +

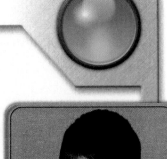

DELMAR: Morgan and I set up a lemonade stand. We sold 2 cups the first hour, 4 cups the second hour, and 6 cups the third hour. If the pattern continued, how many pints did we sell in the fourth hour?

YOUR MISSION: Find out how many pints of lemonade Delmar and Morgan sold after four hours.

Understand You know how many cups were sold and that there are 2 cups in 1 pint. Find how many pints were sold.

Plan You can organize the data in a table.

Solve The pattern is add 2 cups each hour. So, $6 + 2 = 8$ cups sold the fourth hour.

Hour	1	2	3	4
Cups	2	4	6	

+2 +2 +2

Now, change 8 cups to pints. 2 cups = 1 pint. So, divide the total number of cups by 2.

So, they sold 4 pints of lemonade.

Check Look back at the problem. Check the division using multiplication. $4 \times 2 = 8$. So, the answer is correct.

Mixed Problem Solving

Use any strategy shown below to solve. Tell what strategy you used.

PROBLEM-SOLVING STRATEGIES

- Look for a pattern.
- Choose an operation.
- Make a table.
- Work backward.

1. Brady is planning a party. He sends invitations to 3 friends from his soccer team, 5 friends from school, and 9 neighbors. Seven friends tell him they cannot come. How many friends will come to the party?

2. The pattern shown repeats seven more times. How many triangles will there be in all?

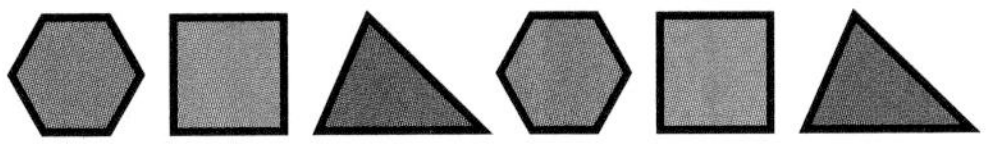

3. Muna ran 4 blocks to get to her friend's house. Then she ran twice as far to the grocery store. How many blocks was the total trip?

4. Maxwell runs 2 miles each day for a week. Jordan runs twice as much as Maxwell. At the end of 7 days, how many miles have Jordan and Maxwell run altogether?

5. Michelle bought 2 cartons of orange juice and 1 bottle of water. Carley bought a bottle of water, milk, and a soda. Who spent more money?

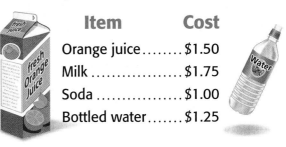

Item	Cost
Orange juice	$1.50
Milk	$1.75
Soda	$1.00
Bottled water	$1.25

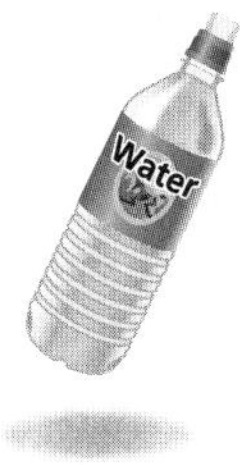

6. Cameron collected 80 rocks in the last 5 years. In the second year, he collected 23 more rocks than he did the first year. He collected 5 rocks each in his third and fourth years. His fifth year he collected 7 rocks. How many did he collect the first year?

7. A store is having a sale on fruit at half the original price. Tyson buys 4 cantaloupes, 2 mangos, and 3 apples. How much money did he spend?

Fruit Original Price

Cantaloup	$1 each
Mango	50¢ each
Apples	3 for $1

8. WRITING IN ▶MATH Look back at Exercise 4. Change the wording so that the *work backward* strategy would have to be used.

8-6 Customary Units of Weight

GET READY to Learn

Cory bought a loaf of bread. How much would one slice of bread weigh?

MAIN IDEA

I will estimate, measure, and convert customary units of weight.

Standard 3MG1.1 Choose the appropriate tools and units (metric and **U.S.**) **and estimate and measure the** length, liquid volume, and **weight**/mass **of given objects.**

Standard 3MG1.4 Carry out simple unit conversions within a system of measurement (e.g., centimeters and meters, hours and minutes).

New Vocabulary

weight
pound (lb)
ounce (oz)

A scale is often used to measure how heavy something is, or its **weight**. The customary units of weight are **ounce (oz)** and **pound (lb)**.

A golf ball weighs about 1 ounce.

A soccer ball weighs about 1 pound.

A soccer ball has about the same weight as 16 golf balls.

Customary Units of Weight
1 pound (lb) = 16 ounces (oz)

Real-World EXAMPLE — Choose Units of Weight

1 FOOD Choose the unit to use to measure the weight of a slice of bread. Write *ounce* or *pound*.

A pound is too large. The most appropriate unit to use is the ounce.

So, the slice of bread weighs about 1 ounce.

Real-World EXAMPLE — Estimate Weight

2 BOOKS Choose the best estimate for the weight of these books, 5 ounces or 5 pounds.

Think about each amount.
It makes sense that the books weigh about 5 pounds, not 5 ounces.

Online Personal Tutor at ca.gr3math.com

EXAMPLE — Convert Units of Weight

> **Remember**
> Even though two items may have the same capacity, their weight may not be the same.

3 2 pounds = ■ ounces

Convert to a smaller unit.

2 pounds = ■ ounces
1 pound = 16 ounces

Add 16 two times.

16 + 16 = 32

2 pounds = 32 ounces.

4 48 ounces = ■ pounds

Convert to a larger unit.
48 ounces = ■ pounds
16 ounces = 1 pound.

Use repeated subtraction.

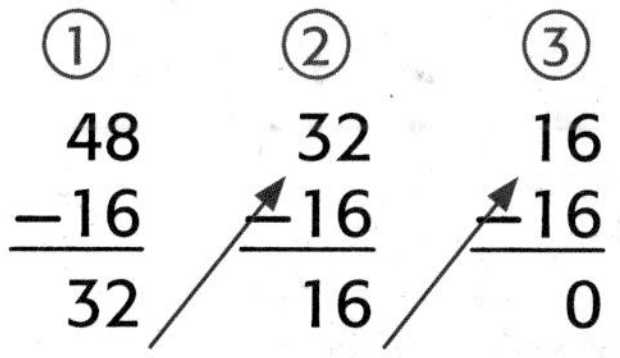

48 ounces = 3 pounds.

CHECK What You Know

Choose the most appropriate unit to measure the weight of each object. Choose from *ounce* or *pound*. See Example 1 (p. 362)

1. 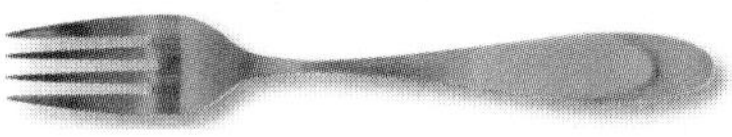

2. 

3. 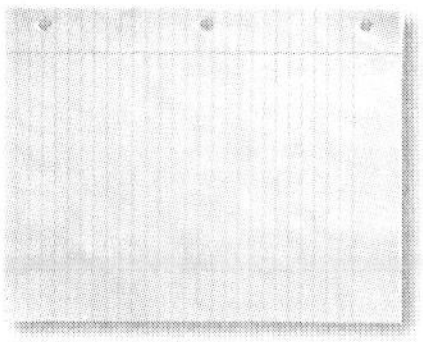

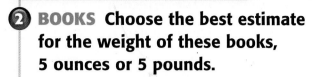

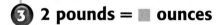

Choose the best estimate. See Example 2 (p. 363)

4.  a CD
2 oz or 2 lb

5.  a pineapple
5 oz or 5 lb

Convert. See Examples 3 and 4 (p. 363)

6. 16 oz = ■ lb

7. 32 oz = ■ lb

Practice and Problem Solving

EXTRA PRACTICE
See page R24.

Choose the unit you would use to measure the weight of each object. Choose from *ounce* or *pound*. See Example 1 (p. 362)

8.

9.

10.
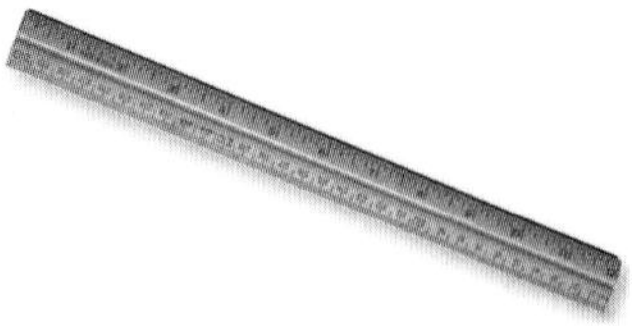

11. bag of soil

12. paper clip

13. whistle

Choose the better estimate. See Example 2 (p. 363)

14.

pair of socks
2 lb or 2 oz

15.

elephant
10,000 lb or 10,000 oz

16.

light bulb
3 lb or 3 oz

Convert. See Examples 3 and 4 (p. 363)

17. 2 lb = ▒ oz

18. 48 oz = ▒ lb

19. ▒ oz = 4 lb

20. How many ounces is 5 pounds of peanuts?

21. How many pounds is 64 ounces of bananas?

22. What is the combined weight in ounces of an ostrich egg that weighs 4 pounds and an Emperor Penguin's egg that weighs 1 pound 8 ounces?

23. One bag of grape fruit weighs 3 pounds 8 ounces. A bag of oranges weighs 2 pounds 2 ounces. What is the difference between the weights?

Real-World PROBLEM SOLVING

Data File The California condor is the largest flying bird in North America.

24. The wingspan of a condor is 9 feet long. What is the wingspan in inches?

25. The weight of a condor is 17–25 pounds. What is the weight in ounces?

Birds

Source: www.fws.gov

H.O.T. Problems

26. OPEN ENDED Name four objects that would weigh more than 1 pound.

27. CHALLENGE How many ounces are in $3\frac{1}{2}$ pounds?

28. WRITING IN ▸MATH Explain what would happen to a balance scale if a 2-pound weight was on one side, and a 24-ounce weight was on the other side.

Standards Practice

29 Mr. Mason's class has 9 students. Each student has 3 sharpened pencils and 2 unsharpened pencils. What is the total number of pencils? **(Lesson 8-5)**

A 18

B 27

C 45

D 50

30 Which of the following objects weighs more than 1 pound? **(Lesson 8-6)**

F 

H 

G 

J 

Spiral Review

31. Two different boxes of animal crackers are the same price. One box weighs 18 ounces, and the other weighs 1 pound 4 ounces. Which box is a better buy? Explain. **(Lesson 8-5)**

Convert. **(Lesson 8-4)**

32. 1 gal = ■ pint **33.** 3 pt = ■ c **34.** 8 qt = ■ gal

Algebra Write the rule for each table. Then copy and complete. **(Lesson 5-9)**

35.

Rule: ■					
Input	2	5	7	8	9
Output	20	■	70	■	■

36.

Rule: ■					
Input	6	4	3	8	9
Output	■	16	■	32	■

Lengths, Heights, and Weights Oh My!

Animals come in different shapes and sizes. For example, a ruby-throated hummingbird is $3\frac{1}{2}$ inches long and weighs less than an ounce. On the other end of the scale, a rhinoceros can weigh 2,200 pounds. A beetle is less than an inch long, but a giraffe can be more than 18 feet tall.

Animals also have different characteristics to help them live in their environments. Elephants can hold up to 3 gallons of water in their trunks. A pelican's stomach can hold up to one gallon of food at a time.

Amazing Animals

Animal	Size	Weight (lb)
zebra	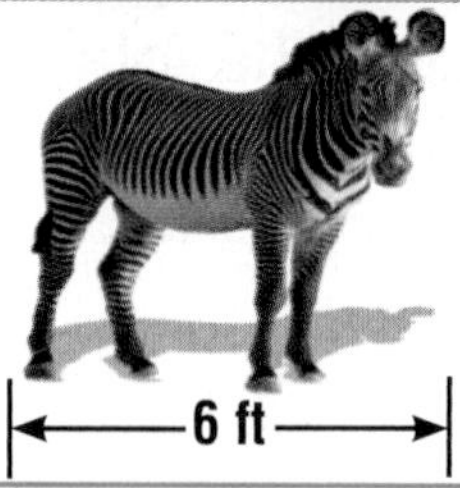	530
ostrich	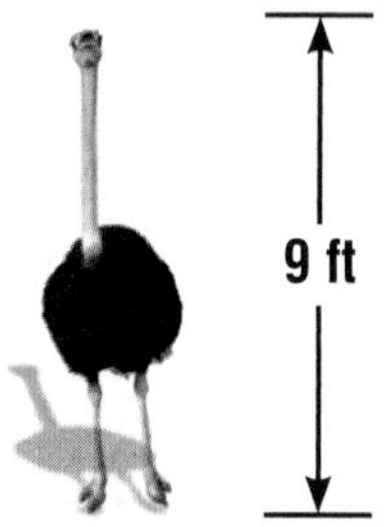	345
alligator	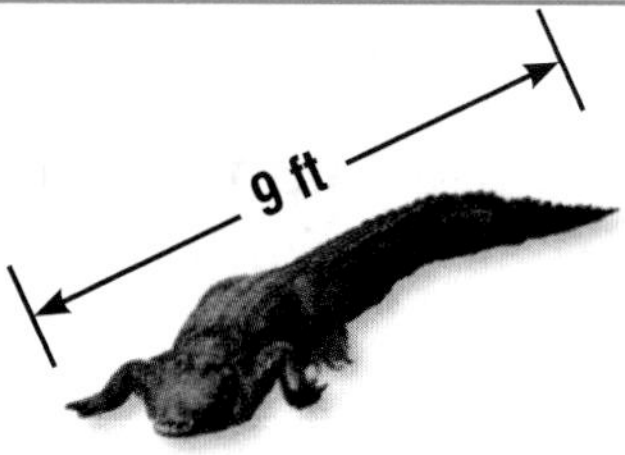	1,000
tree frog	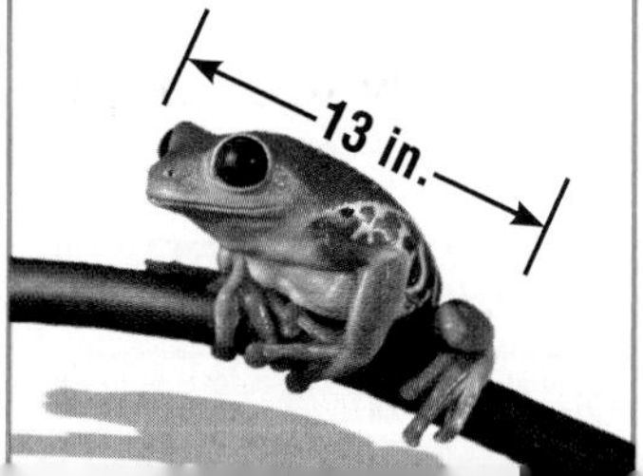	6

Standard 3MG1.4 Carry out simple unit conversions within a system of measurement (e.g., centimeters and meters, hours and minutes.)

Did You Know?

The heaviest living animal was a blue whale that weighed 389,760 pounds!

Real-World Math

Use the information on page 366 to answer each question.

1. What is the length of a ruby-throated hummingbird rounded to the nearest inch?
2. What is the most appropriate unit to measure the height of a rhinoceros?
3. How many yards tall is a giraffe?
4. About how many feet longer is an alligator than a giant tree frog?
5. How many pints of food can a pelican hold in its stomach?
6. How many more quarts of water can an elephant hold in its trunk than a pelican can hold food in its stomach?
7. How many ounces does a giant tree frog weigh?
8. An alligator is about 8 inches long when it is born. Is an adult tree frog more than twice that length? Explain how you know.

8-7 Convert Units of Time

MAIN IDEA

I will learn to convert units of time.

Standard 3MG1.4 Carry out simple unit conversions within a system of measurement (e.g., centimeters and meters, **hours and minutes**).
Standard 3AF1.4 Express simple unit conversions in symbolic form (e.g., __ inches = __ feet × 12).

New Vocabulary

hour (h)
minute (min)

GET READY to Learn

The table shows how much time Jill, Bea, Lara, and Matt exercise each day.

Name	Activity	Time
Jill	jog	15 minutes
Bea	play soccer	30 minutes
Lara	play tennis	45 minutes
Matt	bike	1 hour

As shown in the table above, two units of time are the **minute (min)** and the **hour (h)**.

Minute and Hour		
1 hour	=	60 minutes

Real-World EXAMPLE — Convert Units of Time

1 EXERCISE **How many minutes does Matt ride his bike in two days?**

The table above shows that Matt rides 1 hour each day. In two days, Matt will ride his bike 2 hours. Find the number of minutes in 2 hours.

2 hours = ■ minutes
2 hours = 60 minutes + 60 minutes ← 1 hour = 60 minutes

60 minutes

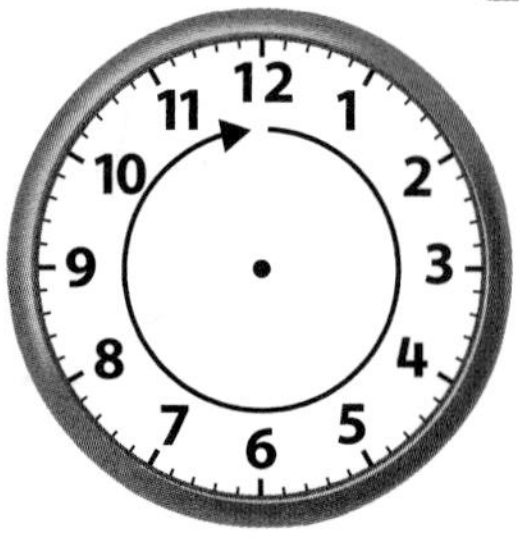

60 minutes

So, 2 hours = 120 minutes.

You can use repeated subtraction to convert units of time.

Real-World EXAMPLE Convert Units of Time

2 **CHORES** **Ashwin finished his chores in 120 minutes. How many hours is 120 minutes?**

Find 120 minutes = ■ hours.

120 minutes − 60 minutes = 60 minutes

(60 minutes: one hour)

60 minutes − 60 minutes = 0

(60 minutes: one hour)

So, Ashwin finished his chores in 2 hours.

> **Remember**
> In repeated subtraction, you subtract the same number until you reach zero.

The relationship between minutes and parts of an hour is show below.

one-quarter hour
15 minutes = $\frac{1}{4}$ hour

one-half hour
30 minutes = $\frac{1}{2}$ hour

three-quarters hour
45 minutes = $\frac{3}{4}$ hour

one hour
60 minutes = 1 hour

Real-World EXAMPLE Convert Units of Time

3 **MOVIE** **Brenda will leave for the movie theater in 30 minutes. What part of an hour is 30 minutes?**

30 minutes is $\frac{1}{2}$ of 60.

So, 30 minutes = $\frac{1}{2}$ hour.

Online **Personal Tutor at** ca.gr3math.com

CHECK What You Know

Convert. See Examples 1–3 (pp. 368–369)

1. 3 hours = ■ minutes
2. 2 half hours = ■ minutes
3. Camisha's daily baseball practice lasts 30 minutes. How many hours will she have practiced after 4 days?
4. Talk About It Explain how to use repeated subtraction to convert units of time?

Practice and Problem Solving

EXTRA PRACTICE See page R24.

Convert. See Examples 1–3 (pp. 368–369)

5. 3 hours = ■ minutes
6. 4 hours = ■ minutes
7. $\frac{1}{2}$ hour = ■ minutes
8. $\frac{1}{4}$ hour = ■ minutes
9. 60 minutes = ■ hour
10. 180 minutes = ■ hours
11. 45 minutes = ■ hour
12. 30 minutes = ■ quarter hours
13. Claudio will meet Jonas at the mall in 3 quarter hours. If it is 3:00 P.M. now, what time will it be when Claudio meets Jonas?
14. It is 6:00 P.M. in New York on the east coast. In California, it is 180 minutes earlier. What time is it in California?

Real-World PROBLEM SOLVING

Science The table shows about how long it takes for some foods to cook.

15. How many minutes does it take to bake lemon chicken?
16. About how many minutes will it take to bake the turkey?
17. How many quarter hours will it take to bake the casserole?
18. How many minutes longer do you need to cook a casserole than corn muffins?

Baking Times

Food	Time
Lemon chicken	$\frac{3}{4}$ hour
Corn muffins	$\frac{1}{4}$ hour
10 lb turkey	3 hours
Casserole	$\frac{1}{2}$ hour

H.O.T. Problems

CHALLENGE **Convert units of time.**

19. 1 day = ■ half hours

20. 3 days = ■ hours

21. **FIND THE ERROR** Hector and Martino are finding the number of minutes in 4 hours. Who is correct? Explain.

Hector
60 + 60 + 60 + 60 =
240 minutes

Martino
4 hours + 60 minutes =
64 minutes

22. **WRITING IN ▸MATH** Write a real-world problem in which you need to convert time units. Give to a classmate to complete.

Standards Practice

23 Which unit would you use to measure the weight of a watermelon? **(Lesson 8-6)**

A ounces
B inches
C pounds
D yards

24 Which answer completes the equation? **(Lesson 8-7)**

3 hours = ■ minutes

F 30
G 60
H 120
J 180

Spiral Review

Choose the best unit. Use *pound* or *ounce*. **(Lesson 8-6)**

25. toothpicks

26. watermelon

27. a lamb

28. Sandra spent $7 less on Saturday than she did on Friday. She spent $2 more on Sunday than she did on Friday. On Sunday, she spent $13. How much money did Sandra spend on Friday and Saturday? **(Lesson 8-7)**

Multiply. **(Lesson 5-4)**

29. 7 × 9

30. 7 × 7

31. 6 × 7

8 Study Guide and Review

FOLDABLES™ Study Organizer GET READY to Study

Be sure the following Key Vocabulary words and Key Concepts are written in your Foldable.

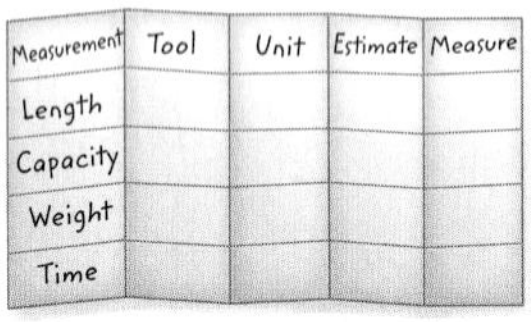

BIG Ideas

Customary Units

- The customary units of length are **inch**, **foot**, **yard**, and **mile**. (pp. 343, 346)

Units of Length
1 foot = 12 inches
1 yard = 3 feet
1 mile = 1,760 yards or 5,280 feet

- The customary units of capacity are **cup**, **pint**, **quart**, and **gallon**. (p. 354)

Units of Capacity
1 pint = 2 cups
1 quart = 2 pint
1 gallon = 4 quarts

- The customary units of weight are **ounce** and **pound**. (p. 362)

Units of Weight
16 ounces = 1 pound

Key Vocabulary

capacity (p. 354)
hour (h) (p. 368)
length (p. 343)
minute (min) (p. 368)
weight (p. 362)

Vocabulary Check

Choose the correct vocabulary word to best complete each sentence.

1. Sixty minutes is equal to one __?__ .
2. Cups, pints, quarts, and gallons are units of __?__ .
3. The amount a container can hold is its __?__ .
4. There are 60 seconds in one __?__ .
5. The units for __?__ are inches, feet, yards, and miles.
6. Ounces and pounds are units of __?__ .

Math Online Vocabulary Review at ca.gr3math.com

Lesson-by-Lesson Review

8-1 Length to the Nearest Half Inch (pp. 343–345)

Example 1
What is the length of the piece of yarn to the nearest half inch?

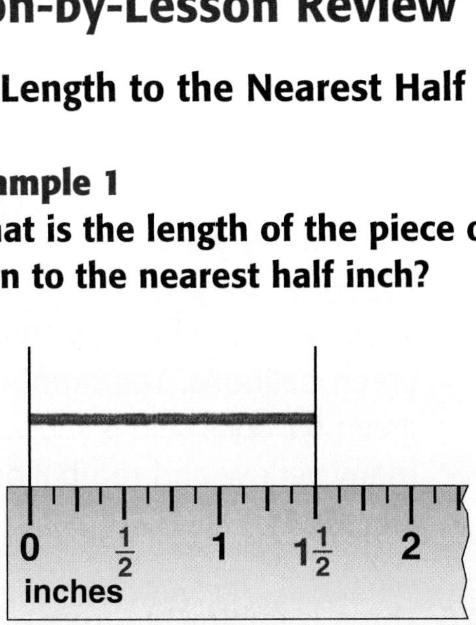

To the nearest half inch, the yarn is $1\frac{1}{2}$ inches long.

7. Measure to the nearest half inch.

8. Paul needs a piece of string that is $3\frac{1}{2}$ inches long and another one that is 4 inches longer. What is the total length of string?

8-2 Customary Units of Length (pp. 346–349)

Example 2
What unit would you use to measure the width of a door? Choose from *inch, foot, yard,* or *mile.*

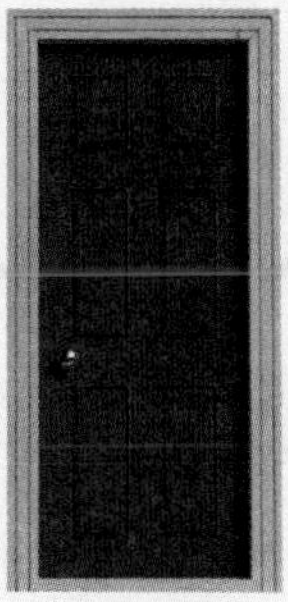

An inch and foot are too short. A mile is too long. So, a door is about 1 yard.

Choose the most appropriate unit to measure each length. Choose from *inch, foot, yard,* or *mile.*

9. the distance between cities

10. the height of a bike

Choose the best estimate.

11. the distance across a pond
8 inches or 8 yards

12. The length of your desk
24 inches or 24 feet

Convert.

13. 1 yard = ■ inches

14. ■ feet = 6 yards

8-3 Problem-Solving Strategy: Work Backward (pp. 350–351)

Example 3

On Monday, a football team practiced two hours longer than Tuesday. On Wednesday, they practiced for twice as long as Monday. They practiced 6 hours on Wednesday. How long did they practice on Monday and Tuesday?

Understand

You know the number of hours the team practiced on Wednesday.

You want to find the number of hours they practiced on Monday and Tuesday.

Plan Work backward.

Solve

$\underbrace{6}_{\text{Wednesday}} \div \underbrace{2}_{\text{half}} = \underbrace{3}_{\text{Monday}}$

$\underbrace{3}_{\text{Monday}} - \underbrace{2}_{\text{less}} = \underbrace{1}_{\text{Tuesday}}$

So, they practiced 3 hours on Monday and 1 hour on Tuesday.

Check Look back at the problem.

$1 + 2 = 3$

$2 \times 3 = 6$

So, the answer is correct.

15. A balloon store sold three times as many red balloons as yellow balloons. They sold 7 more yellow balloons than green balloons. The number of green balloons sold is shown. How many yellow and red balloons were sold?

16. Three is subtracted from a number. Next, the difference is multiplied by 2. Then, 4 is added to the product. Finally, 9 is subtracted to give a difference of 9. What is the number?

17. Chita has to be at school at the time shown. It takes her 30 minutes to get dressed and 15 minutes to eat. If her walk to school is 5 minutes long, what time does she get up?

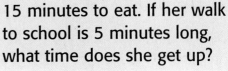

18. There are 3 dogs. The black dog is 5 pounds heavier than the brown dog. The brown dog is three times as heavy as the white dog. The white dog is 8 pounds. What is the weight of the other two dogs?

8-4 Customary Units of Capacity (pp. 354–357)

Example 4
Monica has a glass of milk. Does she have a cup or a gallon of milk?

A gallon is too large. It makes sense that she has a cup of milk.

Example 5
How many quarts is 3 gallons?

Convert 3 gallons to quarts.

1 gallon = 4 quarts
3 gallons × 4 quarts = 12 quarts

So, 3 gallons is 12 quarts.

Choose the most appropriate unit to measure each capacity. Choose from *cup, pint, quart,* or *gallon*.

19.

20.

Choose the best estimate.

21. glass of water: 1 c or 1 qt

22. bowl of soup: 1 gal or 1 c

23. How many cups are in 2 pints?

8-5 Problem-Solving Investigation: Choose a Strategy (pp. 360–361)

Example 6
Every 10 seconds, Winston can do 8 jumping jacks. How many can he do in 1 minute?

60 seconds = 1 minute.
60 seconds ÷ 10 seconds = 6

Draw a picture.

He can do 48 jumping jacks in 1 minute.

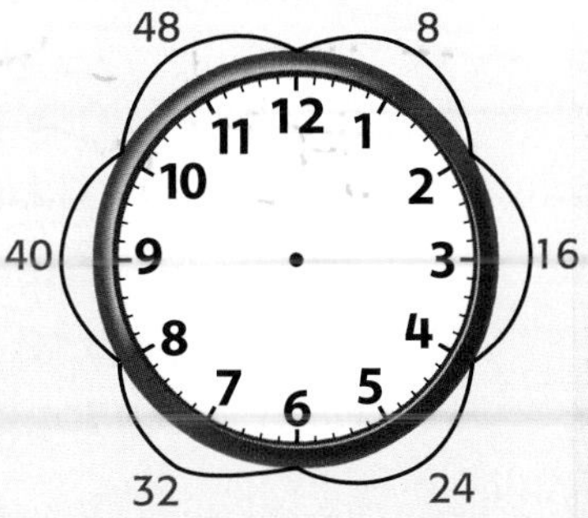

24. Claire ordered 4 gallons of punch for the party. The punch is in 16 quart containers. Does she have enough punch to serve her guests? Explain.

25. Edrick has 1 yard of fabric, 4 feet of yarn, 6 inches of ribbon, and 24 feet of thread. Place the items in order from greatest length to least.

8-6 Customary Units of Weight (pp. 362–364)

Example 7
Dawn's dad is buying sand for her sandbox. Choose the best estimate for the weight of the sand, 10 ounces or 10 pounds.

An ounce is too small of a unit to measure sand for a sandbox.

The pound is the most appropriate unit. So, Dawn's dad will buy 10 pounds of sand.

Choose the most appropriate unit to measure the weight of each object. Choose from *ounce* or *pound*.

26. dog

27. toy bear

Choose the best estimate.

28. a rhinoceros
14,000 lb or 14,000 oz

29. an empty plastic milk jug
4 oz or 4 lb

30. How many pounds are in 32 ounces?

8-7 Convert Units of Time (pp. 368–371)

Example 8
3 hours = ■ minutes.

You know 1 hour = 60 minutes. You need to find the total minutes in 3 hours.

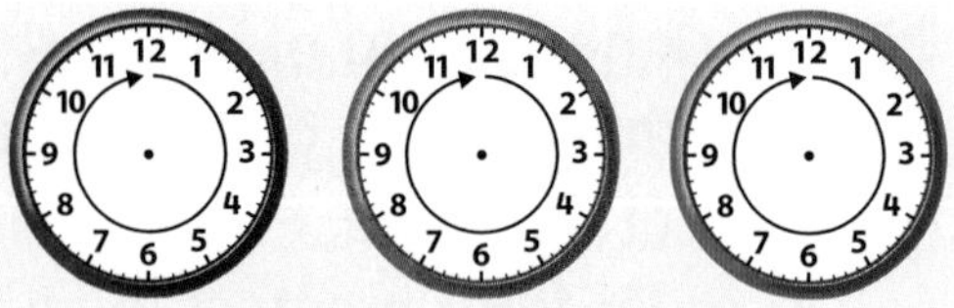

60 minutes 60 minutes 60 minutes

60 + 60 + 60 = 180 minutes

So, 3 hours = 180 minutes.

Convert.

31. 4 hours = ■ minutes

32. ■ minutes = 1 hour

33. 240 minutes = ■ hours

34. $\frac{1}{4}$ hour = ■ minutes

35. It takes Trinity 90 minutes to walk to the library and back again. Adriano takes 1 hour and 45 minutes to walk this distance. Who has a longer walk? Explain.

CHAPTER 8 Chapter Test

For Exercises 1–3, tell whether each statement is *true* or *false*.

1. There are 60 minutes in one hour.
2. When measuring how heavy something is, you measure its length.
3. The customary units of capacity are cups, pints, quarts, and gallons.

Measure to the nearest half inch.

4. 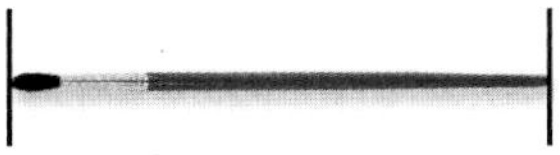
5. 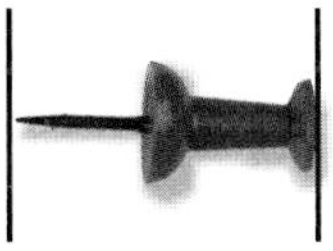
6. 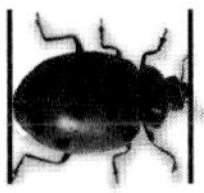
7. The circus performers take 2 hours to put on costumes. It takes twice as long to set up the tent. If the show starts at 7:00 P.M., what time do they need to start getting ready?

Convert.

8. 4 hours = ■ minutes
9. 4 quarter hours = ■ minutes
10. **STANDARDS PRACTICE** Which answer completes the equation?

    2 hours = ■ minutes

    A 60 **C** 180
    B 120 **D** 240

Choose the most appropriate unit to measure the weight of each object. Choose from *ounce* or *pound*.

11. recliner

12. pen

Convert.

13. 32 oz = ■ lb
14. 2 lb = ■ oz
15. What are the inch marks on either side of $5\frac{1}{2}$ inches?

Choose the most appropriate unit to measure the capacity of each object. Choose from *cup*, *pint*, *quart*, or *gallon*.

16. 
17. 
18. **STANDARDS PRACTICE** There are 3 feet in 1 yard. How many inches are in 4 yards?

    F 64 inches **H** 104 inches
    G 72 inches **J** 144 inches

19. **WRITING IN ▸MATH** Explain what would happen to a balance scale if the right side held 2 pounds and the left side held 48 ounces.

California Standards Practice

Cumulative, Chapters 1–8

Standards Example

The hockey team practice started at 6:30 A.M. and ended at 8:00 A.M.

What was the total amount of time that hockey practice lasted?

A 1 hour **C** 2 hours

B 1 hour 30 minutes **D** 2 hours 30 minutes

Read the Question

You need to find how long practice lasted.

Solve the Question

6:30 A.M. to 7:30 A.M. is 1 hour.

7:30 A.M. to 8:00 A.M. is 30 minutes.

So, hockey practice lasted 1 hour 30 minutes. The answer is B.

Online **Personal Tutor at** ca.gr3math.com

Choose the best answer.

1 **How many minutes are in 2 hours 30 minutes?**

A 110 minutes **C** 190 minutes

B 150 minutes **D** 210 minutes

2 **Estimate 532 + 493 to the nearest thousand.**

F 900 **H** 1000

G 925 **J** 1030

3 **Which of the following is shorter than 12 inches?**

A 

B 

C 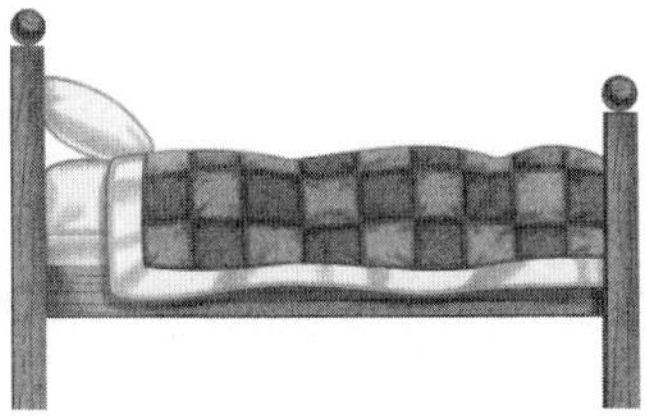

D 

4 **Which number makes 3 hours = ■ minutes true?**

F 120 H 240

G 180 J 300

5 **There are 5 ladybugs with the same number of spots. There are 40 spots total. How many spots are on each bug?**

A 3 C 8

B 5 D 10

6 **Which unit would you use to measure the weight of a dog?**

F ounces H gallons

G feet J pounds

7 **What is the length of the crayon to the nearest inch?**

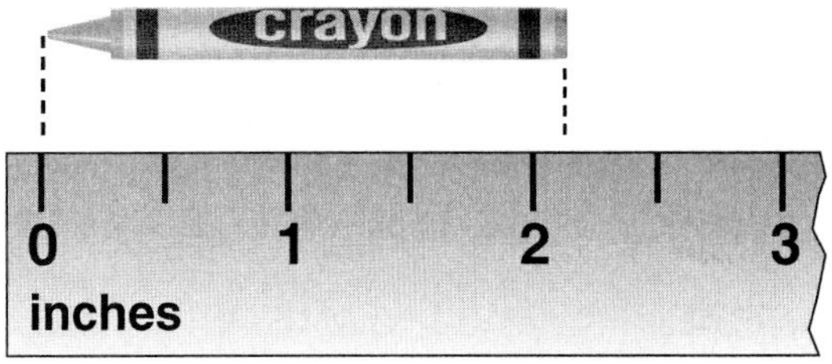

A 1 inch C $2\frac{1}{2}$ inches

B 2 inches D 3 inches

8 **Gina baby-sat 8 hours each week for 5 weeks. How many hours did she baby-sit in all?**

F 13 hours H 32 hours

G 20 hours J 40 hours

9 **Dominic has 21 stamps. He puts the stamps in 3 piles. How many stamps are in each pile?**

A 4 C 6

B 5 D 7

10 **What is 500 + 30 + 2 in standard form?**

F 532 H 3532

G 2354 J 4532

CHAPTER 9 Measurement: Metric System

BIG Idea How do metric units differ from customary units?

Metric units of measurement are used throughout the world. They are based on multiples of 10, which makes it easy to convert between units.

Example The table shows how inches compare to centimeters.

Wingspan of Butterflies		
Butterfly	**Inches**	**Centimeters**
Zebra Longwing	2	5
Tiger Swallowtail	$3\frac{1}{2}$	9
Monarch	4	10
Painted Lady	3	8

What will I learn in this chapter?

- Choose appropriate measurement tools and units.
- Estimate and measure length, capacity, and mass.
- Convert metric measurements.
- Solve problems using the *guess and check* strategy.

Key Vocabulary

meter (m)
liter (L)
mass
gram (g)

Math Online **Student Study Tools at ca.gr3math.com**

FOLDABLES™ Study Organizer

Make this Foldable to help you organize information about metric measurement. Begin with one sheet of notebook paper.

1. **Fold** a piece of paper in half, leaving a two-inch tab at the top.

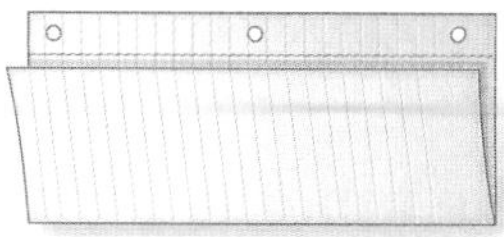

2. **Fold** the right side toward the center. Fold the left side over the right.

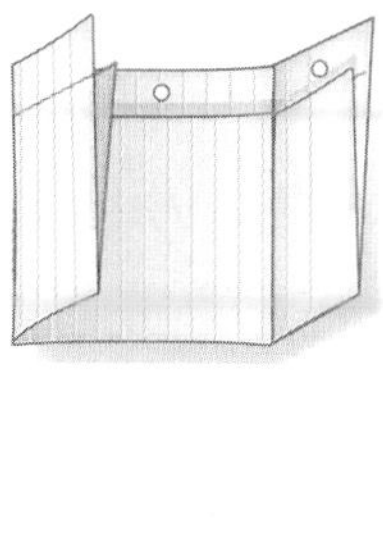

3. **Unfold** and cut along the two inside fold lines.

4. **Label** as shown. Record what you learn.

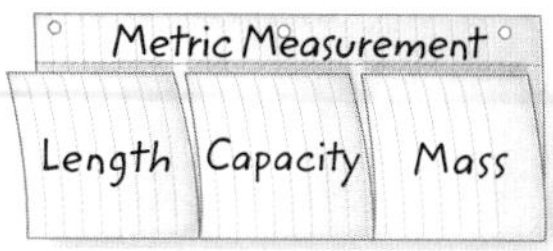

ARE YOU READY for Chapter 9?

You have two ways to check prerequisite skills for this chapter.

Option 2

Math Online Take the Chapter Readiness Quiz at ca.gr3math.com.

Option 1

Complete the Quick Check below.

QUICK Check

Tell whether each sentence means *length, capacity,* or *weight*. **(Lesson 8-2, 8-4, and 8-6)**

1. How tall is your brother?

2. How heavy is a basket?

3. How much water can a jar hold?

4. How much flour is needed for a recipe?

5. Becca needs enough dirt to fill 15 flower pots. Should she measure the dirt by length or capacity? Explain.

Identify the object that holds more. **(Lesson 8-4)**

6.

7.

Identify the object that weighs more. **(Lesson 8-6)**

8.

9.

10. Felicia has two equal-sized boxes. One is filled with books. The other is filled with feathers. Which box is heavier? Explain.

Explore

Measurement Activity for 9-1
Millimeter and Centimeter

You can use metric units to measure length. One metric unit is the **centimeter (cm)**. A centimeter is about the width of your index finger.

MAIN IDEA

I will use models to explore millimeter and centimeter.

Standard 3MG1.1 Choose the appropriate tools and units (metric and U.S.) **and estimate and measure the length,** liquid volume, and weight/mass **of given objects.**
Standard 3MR2.1 Use estimation to verify the reasonableness of calculated results.

You Will Need
centimeter ruler,
crayon, small paper clip

New Vocabulary
centimeter (cm)
millimeter (mm)

Concepts in Motion
Animation
ca.gr3math.com

ACTIVITY

1 Estimate and Measure in Centimeters

Step 1 Estimate

About how many finger widths long would you estimate the crayon to be?

Step 2 Measure

Use the width of your finger to measure the length of the crayon.

- How close was your estimate to the actual finger-width measure?

Step 3 Measure

Align the left end of the crayon with the 0 at the end of the centimeter ruler. Find the tick mark closest to the other end of the crayon.

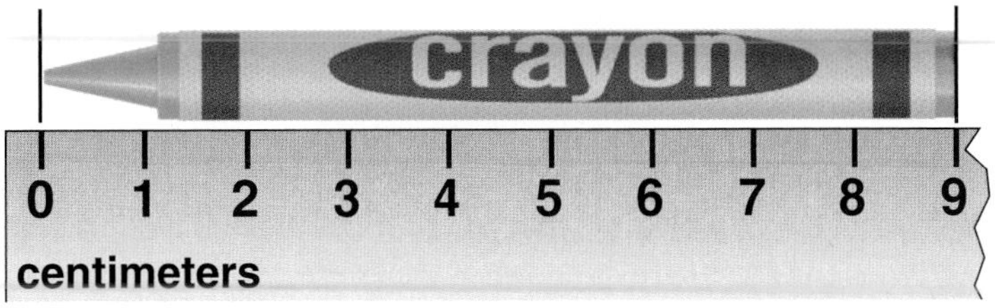

- What is the length in centimeters?
- How close was your finger-width measure to the actual number of centimeters?

Step 4 A **millimeter (mm)** is smaller than a centimeter. It is used to measure very small lengths. 1 centimeter = 10 millimeters.

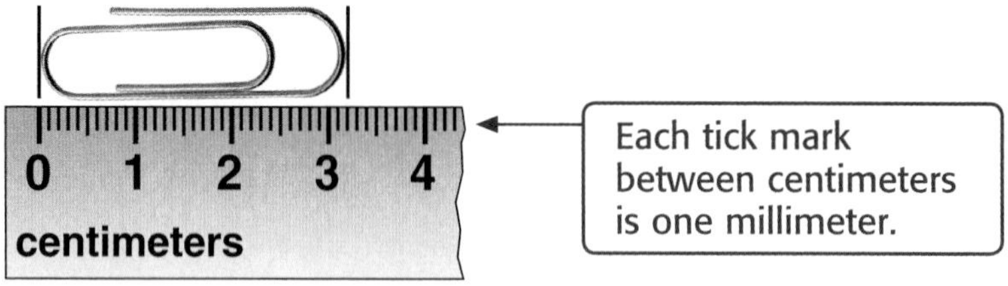
0 1 2 3 4
centimeters
Each tick mark between centimeters is one millimeter.

- How many millimeters long is the paper clip?

Think About It

1. When you compare the millimeter and centimeter measurements, which is more accurate? Explain.

CHECK What You Know

Estimate. Then measure each length to the nearest millimeter and centimeter.

2.

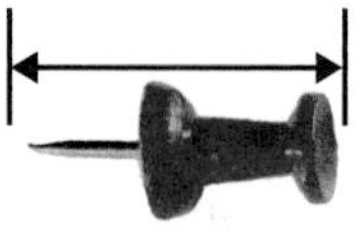

3.

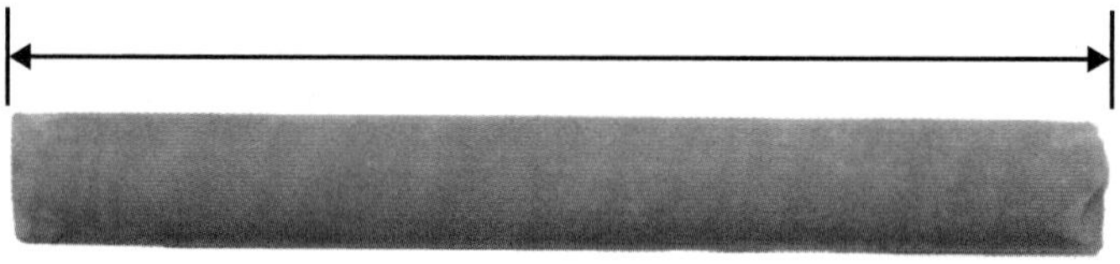

4.

LIBERTY

Choose the best estimate.

5. length of a marker
10 mm or 10 cm

6. width of your thumb
2 mm or 2 cm

7. length of your arm
30 mm or 30 cm

8. WRITING IN ▶MATH Are there more centimeters or more millimeters in something 5 centimeters long? Explain.

9-1 Metric Units of Length

MAIN IDEA

I will learn to choose the appropriate tools and units to estimate and measure metric units of length.

Standard 3MG1.1 Choose the appropriate tools and units (metric and U.S.) **and estimate and measure the length,** liquid volume, and weight/mass **of given objects.**

New Vocabulary

centimeter (cm)
millimeter (mm)
meter (m)
kilometer (km)

GET READY to Learn

Thea's sister runs high school track. If she runs one time around the track, would you measure the distance in millimeters or centimeters?

To measure short lengths, you can use the **centimeter (cm)** and **millimeter (mm)**. To measure longer lengths, use the **meter (m)** and the **kilometer (km)**.

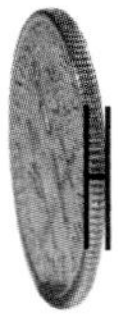

A millimeter is about the width of a dime.

A centimeter is about the width across your index finger.

1 meter

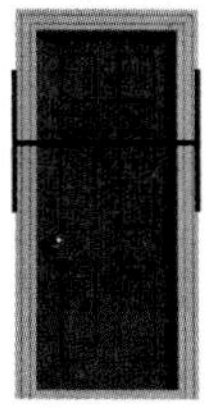

The width of a door.

It takes about 10 minutes to walk 1 kilometer.

Vocabulary Link

The prefix kilo means 1,000.

Real-World EXAMPLE — Choose Metric Units

1 SPORTS Choose the unit that should be used to find how far Thea's big sister runs around the track one time.

You need to determine whether to use *millimeter, centimeter, meter* or *kilometer*.

A millimeter and centimeter are too short. A kilometer is too long to measure one time around the track. So, use a meter.

Real-World EXAMPLE — Choose Metric Units

2 INSECTS **Carl has a bumblebee in his insect collection. Choose the unit that he should use to measure the length of the bee.**

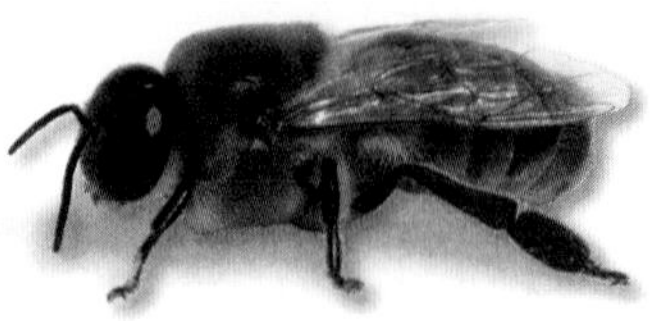

Remember

There are 100 cents in a dollar. There are 100 *cent*imeters in a meter.

You need to determine whether it is best to use *millimeter, centimeter, meter,* or *kilometer*.

A meter and kilometer are too long. A centimeter is used to measure short lengths, but it is best to use a millimeter to measure very short lengths.

So, use a millimeter.

Use what you know about meter and kilometer to make estimates.

Real-World EXAMPLE — Estimate Length

3 LONG JUMP **The world record for jumping the greatest distance in the long jump has not been broken in many years. Choose the best estimate for the distance jumped, 9 m or 9 km.**

Think about a meter and a kilometer. A meter is about the width of a door. It makes more sense that someone can jump 9 door widths.

Thus 9 m is reasonable and 9 km is not reasonable.

So, 9 meters is the best estimate.

Online Personal Tutor at ca.gr3math.com

CHECK What You Know

Choose the most appropriate unit to measure each length. Write *millimeter, centimeter, meter,* or *kilometer.* See Examples 1 and 2 (p. 385)

1. length of an ant
2. length of a car
3. length of a hiking trail
4. length of a pencil
5. Choose the best estimate for the length of a chalkboard, 5 m or 5 km. See Example 3 (p. 386)
6. Talk About It Why is it important to know both the customary and metric systems of measurement?

Practice and Problem Solving

EXTRA PRACTICE See page R24.

Choose the most appropriate unit to measure each length. Write *millimeter, centimeter, meter,* or *kilometer.* See Examples 1 and 2 (p. 385)

7. height of a flagpole
8. distance a plane travels
9. length of an insect
10. length of a crayon

Choose the best estimate. See Example 3 (p. 386)

11. width of a book
    21 cm or 21 mm
12. length of a fork
    14 km or 14 cm
13. distance you could travel on a train
    500 km or 5,000 cm
14. length of a sofa
    2 m or 20 cm

Algebra Compare. Use >, <, or =.

15. 30 cm ● 30 m
16. 4 m ● 400 cm
17. 2 m ● 3 mm

For Exercises 18 and 19, use the chart that shows the wood needed to build a fort.

18. The wood for the floor needs to be cut into 4 pieces. Two of the pieces will be 1 meter long. If the remaining wood is cut equally in half, how long will the remaining boards be?
19. The wood for the walls will be cut into 5 equal pieces. How long will each piece be in centimeters?

H.O.T. Problems

20. **MEASUREMENT** Ben is in a race that is 5 kilometers long. Jim is in a race that is 500 meters long. Whose race is longer? Explain.

21. **WRITING IN ▸MATH** Suppose you are measuring the length of an object in centimeters. What should you do if the object does not line up exactly with the centimeter mark on the ruler?

Standards Practice

22 Which of the following represents 30 minutes past 1:00? **(Lesson 8-7)**

A

C

B

D

23 Choose the best unit for measuring distance across the United States. **(Lesson 9-1)**

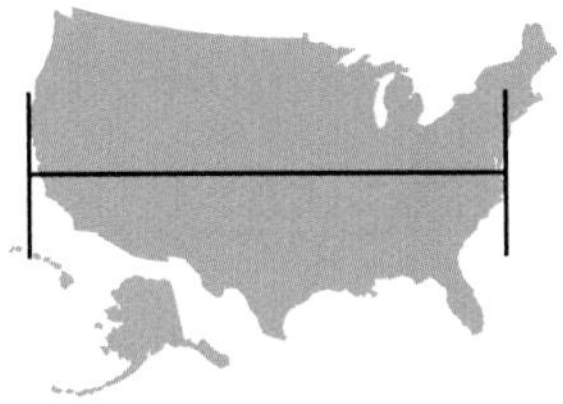

F liter

G meter

H centimeter

J kilometer

Spiral Review

Convert. **(Lesson 8-7)**

24. 45 minutes = ■ quarter hours

25. 2 quarter hours = ■ minutes

Choose the better estimate. **(Lesson 8-6)**

26. soccer ball
1 oz or 1 lb

27. piece of paper
1 oz or 1 lb

28. camera
3 oz or 3 lb

29. Kareem gave 25 football cards to Mali, 13 cards to Millie, and 14 cards to Justin. He has half of the cards he started with. How many cards did he start with? **(Lesson 8-3)**

Algebra Write an expression for each situation. **(Lesson 7-8)**

30. 4 groups with 3 bananas in each

31. 81 campers in 9 equal groups

Hit the Target

Metric Measurement

Get Ready!

Players: 2 players

You will need: game card, metric ruler, a target, and 1 square pattern block

Get Set!

Copy the game card shown.

Player's Name	Toss #1	Toss #2	Toss #3	Toss #4	Total Score

Go!

- Player 1 tosses the pattern block at the target.
- Player 2 measures the distance between the target and the pattern block to the nearest centimeter.
- Player 1 records the distance on the game card.
- Player 2 stands the same distance from the target as Player 1 and tosses the pattern block. Player 1 measures the distance.
- Move the target and toss again.
- Both players will take four turns at tossing the pattern block at the target. Add the distances of the four tosses together. The player with the lowest total wins.

9-2 Problem-Solving Strategy

MAIN IDEA I will use the *guess and check* strategy to solve problems.

Standard 3MR1.1 Analyze problems by identifying relationships, distinguishing relevant from irrelevant information, sequencing and prioritizing information, and observing patterns. **Standard 3MG1.1 Choose the appropriate tools and units (metric** and U.S.) **and estimate and measure the length,** liquid volume, and weight/mass **of given objects.**

Octavia is making 3 candles. The blue candle is 5 centimeters taller than the red and green candles. The total height of the candles is 29 centimeters. How tall is each candle?

Understand

What facts do you know?

- The total height of the candles is 29 centimeters.
- The red and green candles are the same height.
- The blue candle is 5 centimeters taller than the other two.

What do you need to find?

- The height of each candle.

Plan

You can use the *guess and check* strategy. Guess different combinations of numbers and check to see if they fit the facts in the problem.

Solve

The red and green candles are the same height. The blue one is 5 centimeters taller than the others. The total is 29.

Guess			Check
Red	**Green**	**Blue**	**Total**
10	10	15	35 no
9	9	14	32 no
8	8	13	29 yes

So, the green and the red candles are 8 centimeters each and the blue candle is 13 centimeters.

Check

Look back at the problem.
$8 + 8 + 13 = 29$ and 13 is 5 more 8.
So, the answer is correct.

ANALYZE the Strategy

Refer to the problem on the previous page.

1. How did the answer from your first guess affect your second guess?

2. Suppose the total height is still 29 centimeters. Each candle is a different height. The blue candle is 5 centimeters taller than the green candle. How tall is each candle?

3. You know 9 centimeters, 9 centimeters, and 11 centimeters is 29 centimeters. Explain why it is an incorrect answer guess.

4. Explain when you would use the guess and check strategy to solve a problem.

PRACTICE the Strategy

EXTRA PRACTICE
See page R25.

Solve. Use the *guess and check* strategy.

5. A toy store sold $67 worth of bean-bag animals. How many of each size did they sell if more large animals than small animals were sold?

6. Dylan shares 33 pineapple pieces with friends. He eats 5 pieces. His friends each have 2 more pieces than him. How many friends are there?

7. There are 30 apples in a basket. Half are red. There are 5 more green apples than yellow apples. How many of each color are there?

8. Dawnita has 8 coins. The total is $1.25. What are the coins?

9. Kira is thinking of two numbers. Their difference is 12 and their sum is 22. What are the numbers?

10. Nadia is buying her lunch today. She will buy 2 items and will spend exactly $1.20. What will she buy?

Food	Cost
Raisins	35¢
Apple	25¢
Granola bar	45¢
Grilled cheese	85¢

11. **WRITING IN MATH** Benji, Harold, and Nick have 10 pencils in all. They each have more than 1 pencil. Benji has the most pencils. Harold has the fewest pencils. How many pencils does each boy have? Explain how you would use the *guess and check* strategy to solve.

9-3 Metric Units of Capacity

MAIN IDEA

I will learn to choose the appropriate tools and units to estimate and measure metric units of capacity.

Standard 3MG1.1 Choose the appropriate tools and units (metric and U.S.) and **estimate and measure the** length, **liquid volume,** and weight/mass **of given objects.**

New Vocabulary

liter (L)

milliliter (mL)

GET READY to Learn

Himani has a pet bird. Each day, she gives it water to drink. About how much water do you think the bird drinks each day?

You have learned that capacity refers to the amount a container can hold. The metric units of capacity are the **milliliter (mL)** and **liter (L)**.

milliliter (mL)

A dropper holds about 1 mL of liquid. This is about 10 drops. Use this unit to measure containers of small capacity.

liter (L)

This water bottle holds about 1 L of liquid. Use this unit to measure larger containers of capacity.

Metric Units of Capacity
1 liter (L) = 1,000 milliliters (mL)

Real-World EXAMPLE — Choose Metric Units

1 BIRDS Choose the unit that should be used to measure the amount of water Himani's bird drinks each day.

A liter is too large. A bird would drink a small amount of water. So, the milliliter should be used.

Online **Personal Tutor at** ca.gr3math.com

Real-World EXAMPLE — Estimate Capacity

Remember
Milliliter–smaller unit.
Liter–larger unit.

2 **CHORES** **Choose the best estimate for the amount of water in the aquarium, 50 mL or 5 L.**

50 mL is a small amount. It is not reasonable. Since 5 L is a larger amount of water. 5 L is reasonable.

EXAMPLE — Compare Capacity

3 **Compare 30 mL ● 2 L. Use >, <, or =.**

30 mL ● 2 L

1 milliliter < 1 liter
Even though there are 30 milliliters, 2 liters of water is greater.

So, 30 mL < 2 L.

1 milliliter

1 liter

CHECK What You Know

Choose the most appropriate unit to measure each capacity. Write *milliliter* or *liter*. See Example 1 (p. 392)

1. bucket
2. wading pool
3. spoon

Choose the best estimate. See Example 2 (p. 393)

4.

3 mL or 3 L

5.

40 L or 4 mL

6.

50 mL or 50 L

7. Compare 500 mL ● 5 L. Use >, <, or =. See Example 3 (p. 393)

8. **Talk About It** Name two items that come in liters or milliliters.

Practice and Problem Solving

EXTRA PRACTICE
See page R25.

Choose the most appropriate unit to measure each capacity. Write *milliliter* or *liter*. See Example 1 (p. 392)

9. pot

10. juice box

11. pitcher of lemonade

12. bottle of glue

13. water bottle

14. fish tank

Choose the best estimate. See Example 2 (p. 393)

15.

250 L or 250 mL

16.

100 mL or 100 L

17.

10 mL or 10 L

18. mixing bowl
2 mL or 2 L

19. gas can
5 mL or 5 L

20. small carton of milk
200 mL or 200 L

Compare. Use >, <, or =. See Example 3 (p. 393)

21. 1 L ● 700 mL

22. 50 mL ● 2 L

23. 3,000 mL ● 3 L

24. 120 mL ● 12 L

25. 20 mL ● 1 L

26. 250 mL ● 25 L

Real-World PROBLEM SOLVING

Food A punch recipe is shown.

27. How many liters of punch will this recipe make?

28. How many liters of punch did the guests drink if there were 650 milliliters left after the party?

29. Mona made 5 liters of punch on Friday. She used seven 500-milliliters bottles of lemonade. How many milliliters of lemonade did she use?

Party Punch

3 L pineapple juice
1 L apple juice
1500 mL soda water
500 mL grape juice

Pour into a large punch bowl and chill.

H.O.T. Problems

30. OPEN ENDED Name an item that has a capacity of 1 liter.

31. WRITING IN MATH Explain how to change liters to milliliters.

Math Online Self-Check Quiz at ca.gr3math.com

CHAPTER 9

Mid-Chapter Check

Lessons 9-1 through 9-3

Choose the most appropriate unit to measure each length. Write *millimeter, centimeter, meter,* or *kilometer*. (Lesson 9-1)

1. distance driven in a car

2. length of a school bus

Choose the best estimate. (Lesson 9-1)

3. length of a window
   2 m or 2 km

4. length of a classroom
   8 km or 18 m

5. **STANDARDS PRACTICE** Choose the best unit for measuring the distance from northern California to southern California. (Lesson 9-1)

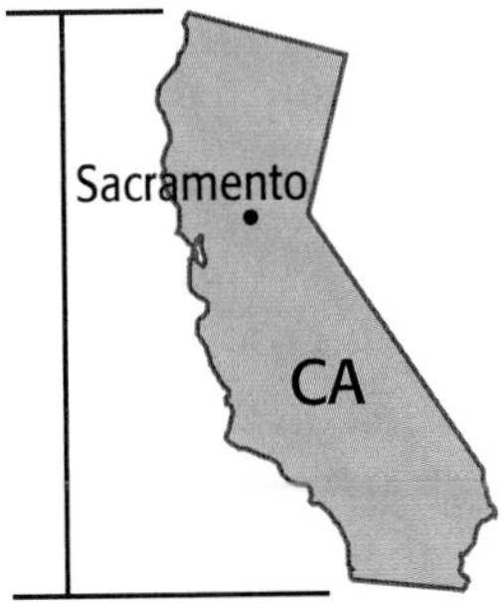

   A liter **C** centimeter
   B meter **D** kilometer

For Exercises 6 and 7, solve. Use the *guess and check* strategy. (Lesson 9-2)

6. There are 40 peppers in a basket. Half are red. There are 4 more green peppers than yellow peppers. How many of each color are there?

7. Daphne took her younger cousins to the water park. It cost her $5 to get in, and her cousins were $2 less. She spent a total of $26. How many cousins were with Daphne? (Lesson 9-2)

Choose the most appropriate unit to measure each capacity. Write *milliliter* or *liter*. (Lesson 9-3)

8. coffee cup

9. kitchen sink

10. eyedropper

Choose the best estimate. (Lesson 9-3)

11. beach pail
    3 mL or 3 L

12. aquarium
    40 L or 4 mL

13. **STANDARDS PRACTICE** Choose the best unit for measuring the amount of water in a bathtub. (Lesson 9-3)

    F millimeter **H** meter
    G milliliter **J** liter

14. **WRITING IN MATH** (Lesson 9-3) Explain how to change milliliters to liters.

9-4 Problem-Solving Investigation

MAIN IDEA I will choose the best strategy to solve a problem.

Standard 3MR2.3 Use a variety of methods, such as words, numbers, symbols, charts, graphs, **tables diagrams, and models, to explain mathematical reasoning.** Standard 3NS2.8 Solve problems that require two or more of the skills mentioned above.

P.S.I. TEAM +

CHARLIE: Ria, Marcela, and I were playing basketball. I made 3 more baskets than Marcela. Ria made 7 baskets. Marcela made one less basket than Ria.

YOUR MISSION: Find how many baskets were made in all.

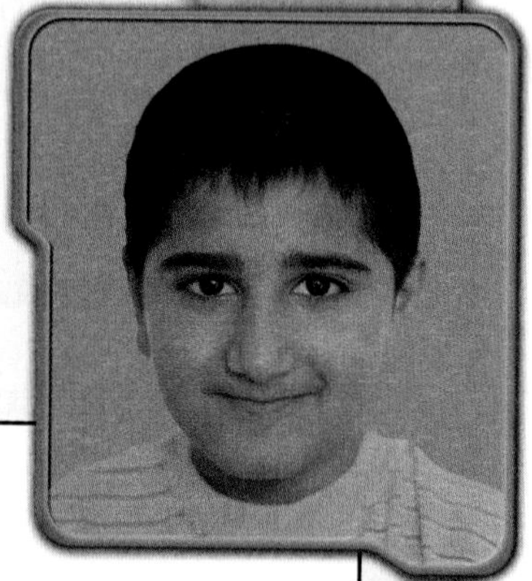

Understand

You know Charlie made 3 baskets more than Marcela. Marcela made 1 less than Ria, who made 7. Find how many baskets they made in all.

Plan

Organize the data into a table. Then solve.

Solve

The table shows the facts in the problem.

Student	Number of Baskets
Ria	7
Marcela	$7 - 1 = 6$
Charlie	$6 + 3 = 9$

$7 + 6 + 9 = 22$

So, the students made 22 baskets altogether.

Check

Look back at the problem. Draw a picture

Ria **Marcela** **Charlie**

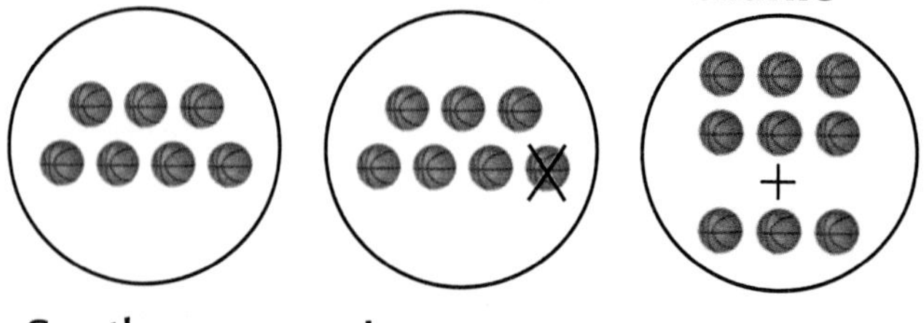

So, the answer is correct.

Mixed Problem Solving

EXTRA PRACTICE
See page R25.

Use any strategy shown below to solve. Tell what strategy you used.

PROBLEM-SOLVING STRATEGIES

- Look for a pattern.
- Make a table.
- Work backward.
- Guess and check.

1. At an amusement park, the Ghost Castle ride can hold 4 children in each car. If there are 43 children on the ride, how many cars are needed? Explain.

2. Dustin rides his bike 15 blocks home from school. Each block takes about 2 minutes. About how long will it take him to get home? Explain.

3. James needed to buy 8 ounces of sugar. How much would 8 ounces cost?

4. Sumi has 4 cups of punch left. Holly drank 3 cups, Brandon drank 2 cups, and 7 cups were spilled. How many pints of punch did Sumi have to start with?

5. Candice walked 2 kilometers in 1 hour. How long did it take her to walk 500 meters?

6. There are 36 frogs in the water. Four more are on lily pads than are on the banks of the pond. There are a total of 58 frogs. How many frogs are on lily pads and on the banks?

7. How many meters of windows are there?

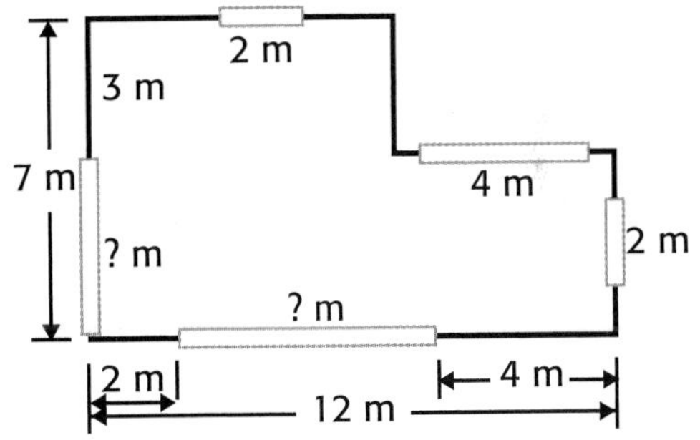

8. Mr. Corisante mowed 15 lawns in 5 days. How many days will it take him to mow 33 lawns?

9. Joey went to the playground. He played with 5 friends for 30 minutes, 7 friends for 1 hour, and 2 friends for 15 minutes. If he arrived at the park at 1:00 P.M., what time did he go home?

10. **WRITING IN MATH** Heath builds wood boxes. He has 12 pieces of wood that are each 2 meters long. Each box uses 8 pieces of wood that are 1-meter long each. How many boxes can he make? Explain your strategy.

9-5 Metric Units of Mass

MAIN IDEA

I will learn to choose the appropriate tools and units to estimate and measure metric units of mass.

Standard 3MG1.1 Choose the appropriate tools and units (metric and U.S.) **and estimate and measure the** length, liquid volume, and weight/**mass of given objects.**

New Vocabulary

mass

gram (g)

kilogram (kg)

GET READY to Learn

Virginia's dad bought a new baseball bat. What do you think is the mass of the baseball bat?

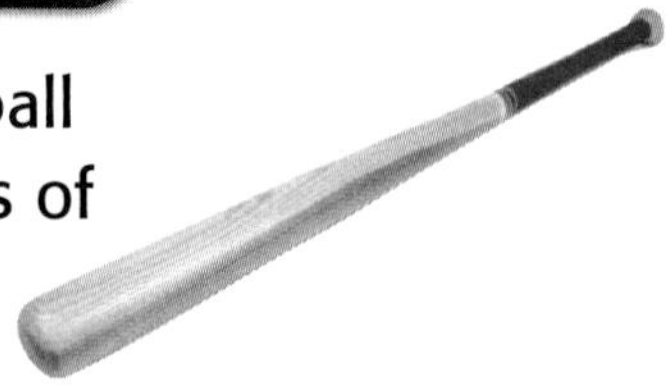

Mass is the amount of material in an object. The most common metric units used to measure the mass of an object are the **gram (g)** and **kilogram (kg)**.

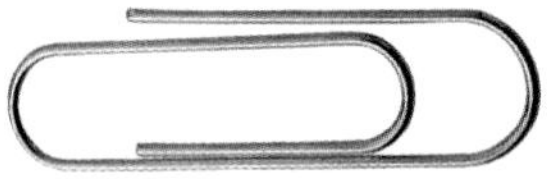

A paper clip has the mass of about 1 g.

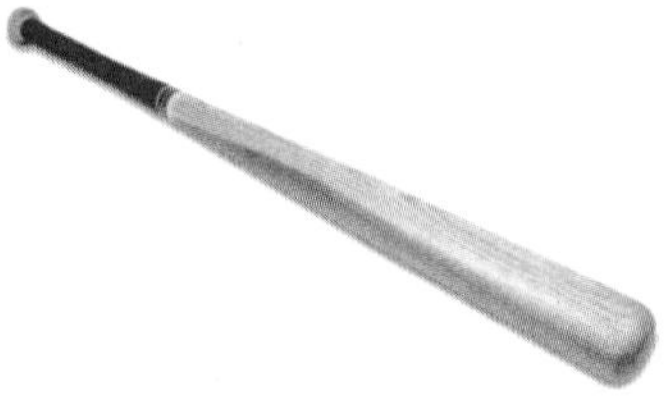

A baseball bat has the mass of about 1 kg.

=

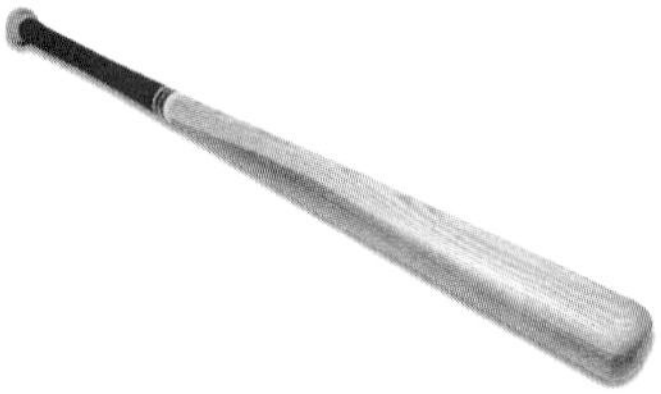

1,000 paper clips have about the same mass as one baseball bat.

Metric Units of Mass
1,000 grams (g) = 1 kilogram (kg)

Real-World EXAMPLE **Choose Units of Mass**

1 SNACKS **Choose the unit you would use to measure a pretzel.**

Pretzels are small and it would be more reasonable to measure their mass with grams.

Online **Personal Tutor at** ca.gr3math.com

Concepts in Motion

Animation
ca.gr3math.com

Hands-On Mini Activity

Materials: balance scale, 1-kilogram mass

Step 1 Choose 3 small objects. Estimate if each one is *less than, more than,* or *about* 1 kilogram. Record your estimations in a table like the one shown.

Less than 1 kilogram	1 kilogram	More than 1 kilogram

Step 2 Check your estimations using the balance scale and a 1-kilogram mass.

1. Choose one of the objects. Do you think that it is *less than, more than,* or *about* 1,000 grams? Explain.

2. Identify 2 more objects that would be about 1 gram.

You can use what you know about the gram and kilogram to estimate and compare mass.

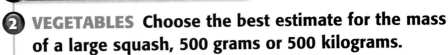

Real-World EXAMPLE Estimate Mass

2 VEGETABLES **Choose the best estimate for the mass of a large squash, 500 grams or 500 kilograms.**

Think about a gram and a kilogram.

Since a large squash does not have the same mass as 500 baseball bats, we can see that the estimate should be 500 grams. So, the best estimate is 500 g.

EXAMPLE Compare Mass

3 **Compare 9 kg ● 50 g. Use >, <, or =.**

9 kilograms ● 50 grams

9 baseball bats have a greater mass than 50 boxes of paper clips.

So, 9 kg > 50 g.

✓ CHECK What You Know

Choose the most appropriate unit to measure each mass. Write *gram* or *kilogram*. See Example 1 (p. 398)

1. toothbrush

2. orange

3. shovel

Choose the best estimate. See Example 2 (p. 399)

4.

50 g or 5 kg

5.

50 g or 5,000 g

6.

2 g or 2 kg

7. Compare 20 g ● 1 kg. Use >, <, or =. See Example 3 (p. 399)

8. Talk About It Does a large object always have a greater mass than a small object?

Practice and Problem Solving

EXTRA PRACTICE See page R26.

Choose the most appropriate unit to measure each mass. Write gram or kilogram. See Example 1 (p. 398)

9. teddy bear

10. lawn mower

11. child

12. bag of pretzels

13. pair of sunglasses

14. pencil

Choose the best estimate. See Example 2 (p. 399)

15.

15 g or 15 kg

16.

900 g or 900 kg

17.

2 g or 2 kg

18. large ball
50 g or 50 kg

19. apple
160 g or 160 kg

20. cordless phone
200 g or 200 kg

Compare. Use >, <, or =. See Example 3 (p. 399)

21. 120 g ● 12 kg

22. 5 kg ● 5,000 g

23. 350 g ● 1 kg

24. 200 g ● 2 kg

25. 1,000 g ● 2 kg

26. 25 kg ● 250 g

H.O.T. Problems

27. OPEN ENDED A bag of potatoes has a mass of about 3 kilograms. Name 2 other items that have about the same mass. Explain your reasoning.

28. WHICH ONE DOESN'T BELONG? Identify the unit that does not belong. Explain.

liters | kilograms | meters | milliliters

29. WRITING IN ▶MATH Explain how to change from kilograms to grams.

Standards Practice

30 Ellis has 3 more rocks in his rock collection than Curtis. Together they have 35 rocks. How many rocks does each boy have? (Lesson 9-4)

A Ellis has 17 and Curtis has 18.

B Ellis has 19 and Curtis has 16.

C Ellis has 20 and Curtis has 18.

D Ellis has 16 and Curtis has 19.

31 There are 1000 grams in 1 kilogram. How many grams are in 7 kilograms? (Lesson 9-5)

F 70 grams

G 700 grams

H 1,000 grams

J 7,000 grams

Spiral Review

32. The soup that Alaina is making needs 8 liters of water. She only has a 500-milliliter container. How can she use that container to measure 8 L? (Lesson 9-4)

Choose the most appropriate unit to measure each capacity. Write *milliliter* or *liter*. (Lesson 9-3)

33. gas tank in a car

34. tea cup

Estimate. Round to the nearest hundred. (Lesson 3-2)

35. $\begin{array}{r} 769 \\ -\ 389 \\ \hline \end{array}$

36. $\begin{array}{r} 5{,}257 \\ -\ 2{,}253 \\ \hline \end{array}$

37. $\begin{array}{r} 3{,}810 \\ -\ 729 \\ \hline \end{array}$

Problem Solving in Science

A Visit to the Supermarket

A supermarket is a busy place. Some people shop at a supermarket every day of the week. Today, supermarkets are as big as 20,000 square meters. That's the size of about 4 football fields!

Supermarkets sell many kinds of food, including healthy foods. Some of the healthiest foods you can buy are yogurt, broccoli, citrus fruits, nuts, oatmeal, and orange juice.

These foods come in different containers and sizes. The prices of some foods are based on size. For example, 1 kilogram of pears costs around $2. The price of a liter of soda is around $3.

Did You Know?

The world's heaviest tomato has a mass of more than 3 kilograms!

Standard 3MG1.1 **Choose the appropriate tools and units (metric and U.S.) and estimate and measure length, liquid volume, and weight/mass of given objects.**

Real-World Health

Use the information on pages 402 and 403 to answer each question.

1. What metric unit can be used to find the height of a box of oats?
2. What metric unit can be used to find how much yogurt is in each container?
3. Are there more liters of orange juice or bottled water on the shelf? Explain.
4. Each bottle of water costs $1. Which costs more, 2 liters of soda, or 2 liters of water?
5. If each apple on the shelf has a mass of 100 grams, would they weigh more or less than 1 kilogram? Explain.
6. In total, there are 3 kilograms of tomato sauce on the shelf. Each can weighs the same amount. How much does each can weigh?
7. Suppose you are making spaghetti. You need 3 cans of tomato sauce and 2 boxes of pasta. What is the total weight of your groceries in kilograms?

9-6 Metric Unit Conversions

MAIN IDEA

I will learn to convert metric units.

Standard 3AF1.4 Express simple unit conversions in symbolic form.

Standard 3MG1.4 Carry out simple unit conversions within a system of measurement.

GET READY to Learn

The jump rope is 200 centimeters long. How many meters is that?

Just like the customary system, you can also convert units in the metric system. The table below shows the relationship between metric units of length, capacity, and mass.

KEY CONCEPTS — **Metric Unit Conversions**

Length	1 meter = 100 centimeters 1 kilometer = 1,000 meters
Capacity	1 liter = 1,000 milliliters
Mass	1 kilogram = 1,000 grams

A table can be used to help you convert metric units.

Real-World EXAMPLE — **Convert Metric Units**

1 **MEASUREMENT The jump rope of yarn above is 200 centimeters long. How many meters is that?**

Use patterns to help you. You know that there are 100 centimeters in 1 meter.

Centimeters	100	200	300
Meters	1	2	3

So, there are 200 centimeters in 2 meters.

Online **Personal Tutor at** ca.gr3math.com

You can also use multiplication and division to convert units.

KEY CONCEPT — Convert

- To change from a larger unit to a smaller unit, multiply.
- To change from a smaller unit to a larger unit, divide.

Remember

To convert to smaller units, **multiply**.

To convert to larger units, **divide**.

Real-World EXAMPLES

2 **ROADTRIP** **The Jamison family will drive 4 kilometers to visit friends. How many meters is that?**

4 kilometers = ■ meters   Convert to a smaller unit.

One Way: Use a Table

Kilometer	1	2	3	4
Meter	1,000	2,000	3,000	4,000

The table shows that 4 kilometers = 4,000 meters

Another Way: Multiply

1 kilometer = 1,000 meters
So, 4 kilometers × 1,000 = 4,000 meters

3 **FOOD** **The bag of flour has a mass of 6,000 grams. How many kilograms is that?**

6,000 grams = ■ kilograms   Convert to a larger unit.

One Way: Use a Table

Grams	1,000	2,000	3,000	4,000	5,000	6,000
Kilograms	1	2	3	4	5	6

The table shows that 6,000 grams = 6 kilograms

Another Way: Divide

1,000 grams = 1 kilogram
So, 6,000 grams ÷ 1,000 = 6 kilograms

CHECK What You Know

1. The gas tank for a small tractor holds about 3 liters of gas. How many milliliters is that? See Example 1 (p. 404)

Liters	1	2	3
Milliliters	1,000	■	■

Convert each unit to a smaller unit. See Example 2 (p. 405)

2. 4 L = ■ mL
3. 7 km = ■ m
4. 3 kg = ■ g

Convert each unit to a larger unit. See Example 3 (p. 405)

5. 4,000 m = ■ km
6. 9,000 mL = ■ L
7. 1,000 g = ■ kg

8. Talk About It How is changing centimeters to meters different from changing meters to kilometers?

Practice and Problem Solving

EXTRA PRACTICE See page R26.

Copy and complete each table. See Example 1 (p. 404)

9.

Meters	4	5	6	■
Centimeters	■	■	■	700

10.

Grams	2,000	3,000	4,000	■
Kilograms	2	■	■	5

Convert each unit to a smaller unit. See Example 2 (p. 405)

11. 10 L = ■ mL
12. 4 km = ■ m
13. 11 kg = ■ g

Convert each unit to a larger unit. See Example 3 (p. 405)

14. 10,000 mL = ■ L
15. 4,000 m = ■ km
16. 8,000 g = ■ kg

17. Tommy bought 5 L of orange juice. How many milliliters is that?
18. How many meters is 300 centimeters?

Real-World PROBLEM SOLVING

Data File Trophies won by the stars in the show-biz industry have a greater mass than one would think.

19. What is the total mass of an Oscar and Emmy award in grams?
20. Find the total mass of all the awards in grams.

Data Card

H.O.T. Problems

21. FIND THE ERROR Kamilah and Len converted 9 liters to milliliters. Who is correct? Explain your reasoning.

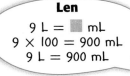

Kamilah
9 L = ■ mL
9 × 1,000 = 9,000 mL
9 L = 9,000 mL

Len
9 L = ■ mL
9 × 100 = 900 mL
9 L = 900 mL

22. WRITING IN ▶MATH Explain how changing liters to milliliters and changing kilograms to grams are alike.

Standards Practice

23 Which of the following objects does not have a mass greater than 1g? **(Lesson 9-5)**

A 

C 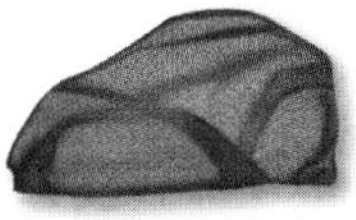

B 

D 

24 Look at the number sentence below.

1,500 cm = ■ m

Which number will make the sentence true? **(Lesson 9-6)**

F 1.5

G 15

H 150

J 15,000

Spiral Review

Write whether each object is *less than* 1 kilogram, *1 kilogram*, or *more than* 1 kilogram. **(Lesson 9-5)**

25. 

26. 

27. 

28. Geometry Mr. Viera is planting a rectangular garden. The garden measures 4 meters by 7 meters. How many meters of fence will it take to go around the area of the garden? **(Lesson 9-4)**

9 Study Guide and Review

FOLDABLES™ Study Organizer GET READY to Study

Be sure the following Key Vocabulary words and Key Concepts are written in your Foldable.

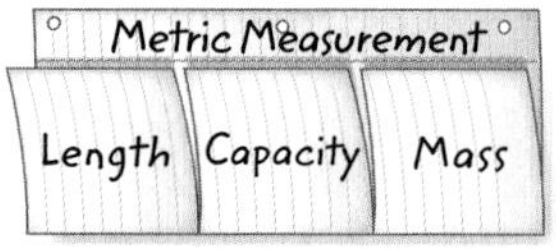

BIG Ideas

Metric Units

- The metric units of length are millimeter, centimeter, **meter**, and kilometer. (p. 385)

Metric Units of Length
10 millimeters = 1 centimeter
100 centimeters = 1 meter
1,000 meters = 1 kilometer

- The metric units of capacity are **liter** and milliliter. (p. 392)

Metric Units of Capacity
1,000 milliliters = 1 liter

- The metric units of **mass** are **gram** and kilogram. (p. 398)

Metric Units of Mass
1,000 grams = 1 kilogram

Key Vocabulary

gram (p. 398)
liter (p. 392)
mass (p. 398)
meter (p. 385)

Vocabulary Check

Choose the vocabulary word that completes each sentence.

1. 1,000 mL = 1 ____?____
2. You can use the ____?____ to measure longer lengths, such as carpet or distance across a room.
3. ____?____ is measured in grams or kilograms.
4. 2 kg = 2,000 ____?____
5. Sari made 1 ____?____ of lemonade.
6. 400 cm can be converted to 4 ________.
7. One paper clip has the mass of about 1 ____?____ and a baseball bat has the mass of about 1 kilogram.

Math Online **Vocabulary Review at** ca.gr3math.com

Lesson-by-Lesson Review

9-1 Metric Units of Length (pp. 385–388)

Example 1
Olinda will travel to another state to visit her uncle. What metric unit should be used to measure the distance she will travel?

The millimeter, centimeter, and meter are used to measure shorter lengths. The kilometer is used for long distances.

So, use the kilometer to measure the distance Olinda will travel.

Example 2
Twyla wants to know how tall the ladder is. Choose the best estimate for the height of the ladder, 2 millimeters or 2 meters.

Think about millimeter and meter.

It is best to use a millimeter to measure *very* short lengths. So, 2 millimeter is not reasonable.

A meter is used to measure longer lengths. So, 2 meters is reasonable.

Choose the most appropriate unit to measure each length. Write *millimeter, centimeter, meter,* or *kilometer*.

8. length of a dragonfly

9. length of a staple

10. length of a crosswalk

Choose the best estimate.

11. length of a football field
90 cm or 90 m

12. length of a straight pin
20 mm or 20 cm

Solve.

13. Geometry A sculpture has been made with wire shapes. There are 4 triangles, 2 squares, and 5 circles. What is the total length of wire used in meters?

Shapes in Sculpture

Shape	Length
Triangle	25 cm
Square	50 cm
Circle	1 m

9-2 Problem-Solving Strategy: Guess and Check (pp. 390–391)

Example 3
Rico is 19 years old. If you add his age, plus his two sisters ages, you get 38. His sisters are 5 years apart. How old are his sisters?

Guess			Check
Rico	**Sister 1**	**Sister 2**	**Total**
19	5	10	34 no
19	6	11	36 no
19	7	12	38 yes

So, one sister is 7 years old and the other is 12 years old.

Since 19 + 7 + 12 = 38 and 12 is 5 more than 7, the answer is correct.

Solve. Use the *guess and check* strategy.

14. Ebony completed 28 projects the last 2 months. This month, she completed 6 more than last month. How many projects did she complete this month?

15. Misty took 163 photographs. She used 15, 25, and 36 print rolls of film. How many rolls of each type of film did she use?

16. Ramón bought a popsicle for $0.30. He paid with 4 coins that were nickels and dimes. How many of each coin did he use?

9-3 Metric Units of Capacity (pp. 392–394)

Example 4
Maurice is making fruit juice. Choose the best estimate for the amount of juice he will make, 2 mL or 2 L.

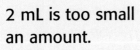

2 mL is too small an amount.

2 L is a larger amount.

So, the best estimate is 2 L.

Choose the most appropriate unit to measure each capacity. Write *milliliter* or *liter*.

17. paper cup

18. cooking pot

Choose the best estimate.

19. bottle of shampoo
200 mL or 200 L

20. bottle of liquid soap
350 mL or 350 L

Compare. Use >, <, or =.

21. 140 mL ● 14 L

22. 3,000 mL ● 3 L

9-4 Problem-Solving Investigation: Choose a Strategy (pp. 396–397)

Example 5

Ms. Martin's class has 28 students. Half of the students are 10 years old. There are 6 more nine year olds than eight year-olds. There are 4 eight year olds. How many are in each age group?

Understand

There are 28 students and half are 10 years old. There are 4 eight year olds. You need to find how many children are in each age group.

Plan Work backward to solve.

Solve 29 – 14 (half) = 14

There are 14 students who are 10 years old

14 – 4 =10

There are 10 students who are 9 years old.

So, there are 14 eight-year-olds, 14 ten-year-olds, and 10 nine-year-olds.

Check Look back at the problem.

Age	Students
10	14
9	10
8	4
Total	28

10 is 6 more than 4.

So, the answer is correct.

Use any strategy to solve.

23. Victoro has $37. His grandmother gives him $20 for his birthday. He owes his mother $15 for the money he borrowed from her. How much money does he have now?

24. Jonas has been improving his spelling test scores. He began with a 50. His third test was a 65. His sixth test was an 80. If the pattern continues, what will be the score of the ninth test?

25. Curtus and Ariel brought their rock collection to school. They have 24 rocks in all. Curtus has twice as many rocks with crystals as Ariel. Ariel has 7 rocks with crystals. How many rocks don't have crystals?

26. McKinsey needs to buy 300 cm of rope. If the store sells the rope in 1 meter sections, how many sections will she need to buy?

27. One paper clip has a mass of about 1 gram and a box of paper clips has a mass of about 1 kilogram. How many paper clips would be in the box?

9-5 Metric Units of Mass (pp. 398–401)

Example 6
Compare 250 g ● 1 kg.
Use >, <, or =.

250 g ● 1 kg

1 g

1 kg

Even though there are 250 grams, 1 kilogram is greater since 1 baseball bat has a greater mass than 250 paperclips.

So, 250 g < 1 kg.

Choose the most appropriate unit to measure each mass. Write *gram* or *kilogram*.

28. an apple **29.** a rake

Choose the best estimate.

30.

12 g or 12 kg

31.

6 g or 6 kg

Compare. Use >, <, or =.

32. 30 kg ■ 300 g

33. 150 kg ■ 15,000 g

9-6 Metric Unit Conversions (pp. 404–407)

Example 7
The bottle holds 2 liters of juice. How many milliliters is that?

Make a table and look for a pattern.

Liters	1	2	3
Milliliters	1,000	2,000	3,000

So, there are 2,000 milliliters in 2 liters.

To convert metric units, you can also multiply or divide.

34. Copy and complete the table.

Grams	1,000	2,000	3,000	■
Kilograms	1	■	■	4

Convert each unit.

35. 9 m = ■ cm **36.** 1 kg = ■ g

37. Mona's ball of yarn is 700 cm long. She wants to cut the yarn into 1 meter lengths. How many 1 meter lengths of yarn can she cut?

CHAPTER 9

Chapter Test

For Exercises 1–3, decide whether each statement is *true* or *false*.

1. The metric system of measurement is based on multiples of 10.

2. Mass is the weight of an object.

3. The metric units of capacity are called milliliter and liter.

Choose the most appropriate unit to measure each mass. Write *gram* or *kilogram*.

4. ink pen

5. eye glasses

6. How many milliliters of juice are in a 1-L bottle and $\frac{1}{2}$-L bottle?

Convert each unit to a larger unit.

7. 10,000 mL = ■ L

8. 8,000 g = ■ kg

9. **STANDARDS PRACTICE** Which number will make the sentence shown below true?

1,800 cm = ■ m

A 18

B 180

C 1,800

D 18,000

10. There are 70 grams of sugar in a bowl. How much will you have to add to make 1 kilogram of sugar?

Compare. Use >, <, or =.

11. 40 m ● 400 cm

12. 8,000 m ● 8 km

13. An auditorium can hold up to 600 people. Half of the seats are filled. There are twice as many children than adults. How many adults are there? Use the *guess and check* strategy.

Choose the best estimate.

14. small carton of juice
200 mL or 200 L

15. length of a soccer field
90 km or 90 m

16. **STANDARDS PRACTICE**
There are 1,000 grams in 1 kilogram. How many grams are in 8 kilograms?

F 80 grams

G 800 grams

H 1,000 grams

J 8,000 grams

17. **WRITING IN MATH** What is the most appropriate unit to use to measure the length of your pencil, centimeters or meters? Explain.

9 California Standards Practice

Cumulative, Chapters 1–9

Standards Example

Which is the most appropriate unit to measure the mass of a pencil?

A kilogram
B gram
C liter
D meter

Read the Question

You need to find the best metric unit of measurement for the mass of a pencil.

Solve the Question

The liter and meter do not measure mass. So, eliminate choices C and D.

Think about a gram and a kilogram. A kilogram is used to measure the mass of objects like a baseball bat.

A pencil's mass is less than one kilogram.

So, a gram is the most appropriate unit to measure the mass of a pencil. The answer is B.

Online **Personal Tutor at** ca.gr3math.com

Choose the best answer.

1 **Which is the most appropriate unit to measure the length of a shoe?**

A centimeter
B liter
C meter
D kilometer

2 **Which is most likely to be the mass of a bicycle?**

F 15 centimeters
G 15 grams
H 15 liters
J 15 kilograms

3 **What is the length of the eraser to the nearest centimeter?**

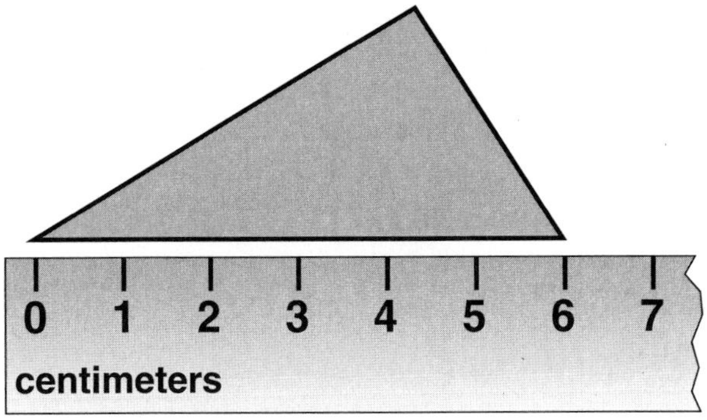

A 4 centimeters **C** 6 centimeters
B 5 centimeters **D** 7 centimeters

4 **Which is most likely to be the capacity of a cocoa mug?**

F about 10 milliliters
G about 100 milliliters
H about 2 liters
J about 5 liters

5 **Which number makes the sentence true?**

7000 grams = ■ kilograms

A 7 **C** 700
B 70 **D** 7000

6 **Which number has a 4 in the tens place and a 4 in the thousands place?**

F 4134 **H** 4364
G 4249 **J** 5443

7 **What is the sum of 33 + 237 rounded to the nearest ten?**

A 260 **C** 275
B 270 **D** 280

8 **Which sign goes in the box to make the number sentence true?**

$$54 \ ■ \ 6 = 9$$

F + **H** ×
G − **J** ÷

9 **What number makes this number sentence true?**

$$5 + 9 + 7 = 5 + 7 + ■$$

A 5 **C** 9
B 7 **D** 12

10 **The product of 6 and another factor is 42. What is the missing factor?**

F 5 **H** 8
G 7 **J** 9

CHAPTER 10

Measurement and Geometry

BIG Idea How do plane and solid figures differ?

Plane figures, or two-dimensional figures, are flat figures that have length and width. **Solid figures**, or three-dimensional figures, have length, width, and height.

Example

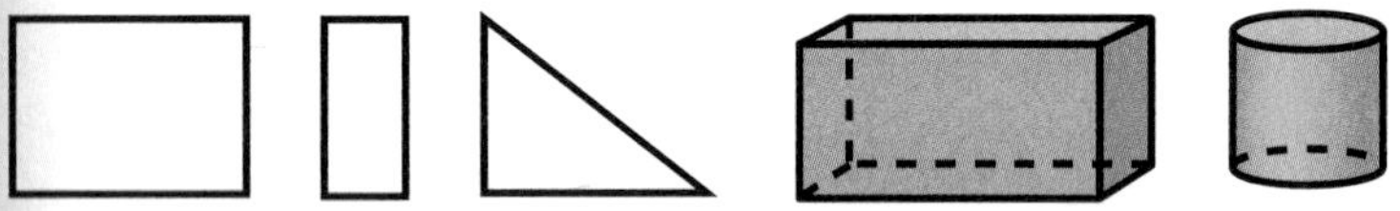

plane figures   solid figures

What will I learn in this chapter?

- Identify, describe, and classify plane and solid figures.
- Estimate and find perimeter, area, and volume.
- Identify solid figures that make up complex figures.
- Solve problems by solving a simpler problem.

Key Vocabulary

polygon
quadrilateral
perimeter
area
volume

Math Online **Student Study Tools at ca.gr3math.com**

FOLDABLES™
Study Organizer

Make this Foldable to help you organize information about plane and solid figures. Begin with one sheet of 11″ × 17″ paper.

1. **Fold** the paper so that both ends meet in the center.

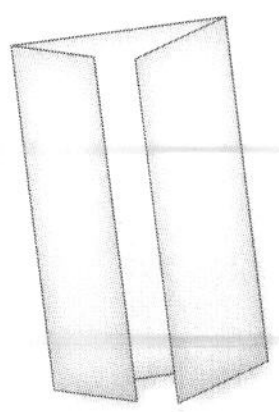

2. **Fold** twice in the opposite direction as shown.

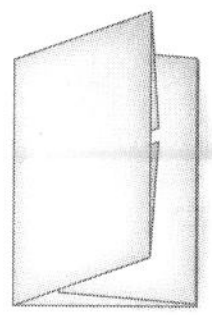

3. **Open** the paper and cut to make six flaps.

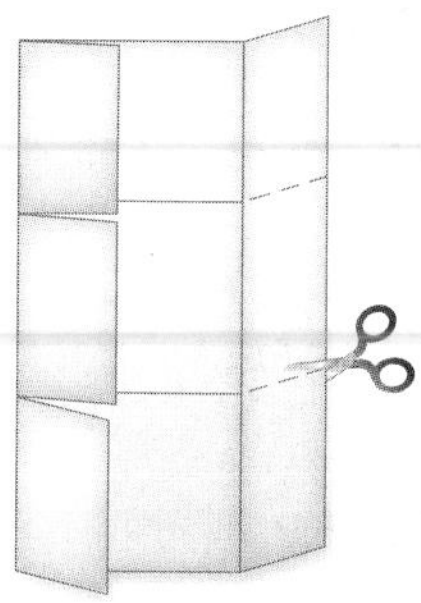

4. **Label** as shown. Record what you learn in the chapter.

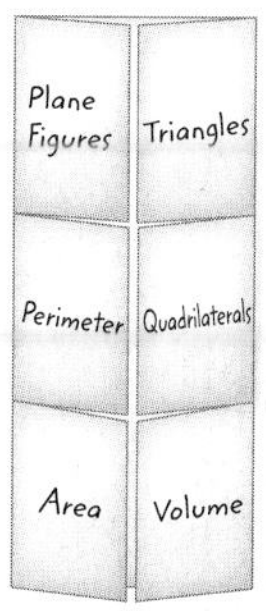

ARE YOU READY for Chapter 10?

You have two ways to check prerequisite skills for this chapter.

Option 2

Math Online Take the Chapter Readiness Quiz at ca.gr3math.com.

Option 1

Complete the Quick Check below.

QUICK Check

Identify the figure that does not belong with the other three. Explain. **(Prior grade)**

1.

figure A   figure B   figure C   figure D

2.

figure F   figure G   figure H   figure J

3. Marilyn has a box, a can of soup, and a sheet of paper. Which object does not belong with the other two? Explain.

Tell how each pair of figures differ. **(Prior grade)**

4.

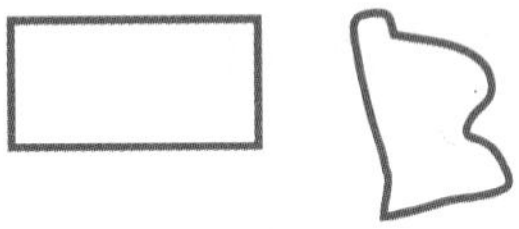

5.

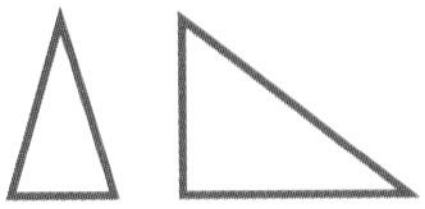

6.

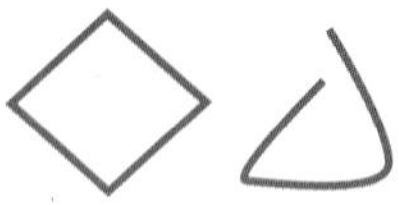

7.

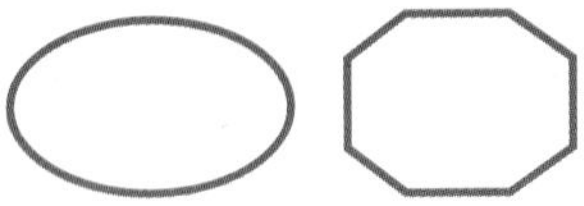

8. Jeremy and Hala each drew a different shape that has 8 sides. Draw an example of what the shapes could look like.

Find the length. **(Lesson 8-2 and 9-1)**

9.

10.

10-1 Geometry: Polygons

GET READY to Learn

Mary noticed that all stop signs are figures that have eight sides. The shape of the stop sign is a polygon.

MAIN IDEA

I will identify, describe, and classify polygons.

Standard 3MG2.1 Identify, describe, and classify polygons (including pentagons, hexagons, and octagons).

New Vocabulary

- plane figure
- polygon
- triangle
- quadrilateral
- pentagon
- hexagon
- octagon

A **plane figure** is a two-dimensional figure. A **polygon** is a closed plane figure of 3 or more line segments. Polygons can have a different number of sides and angles.

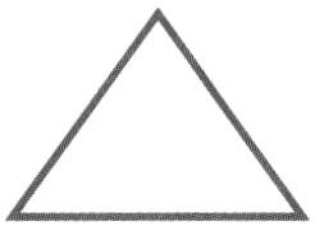

triangle
three sides
three angles

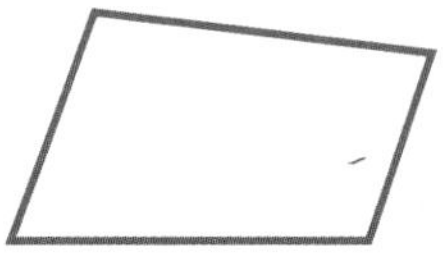

quadrilateral
four sides
four angles

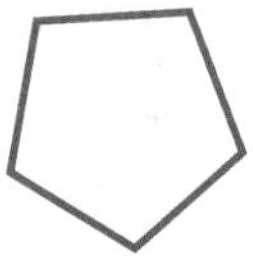

pentagon
five sides
five angles

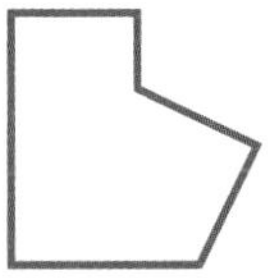

hexagon
six sides
six angles

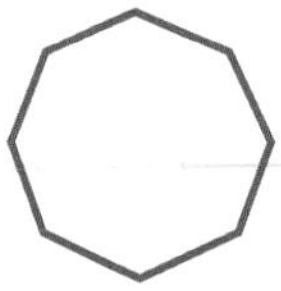

octagon
eight sides
eight angles

Real-World EXAMPLE Classify Shapes

Traffic Signs Classify the shape of each sign as a polygon.

1

There are 8 sides and 8 angles. So, it is an octagon.

2

There are 5 sides and 5 angles. So, it is a pentagon.

Online **Personal Tutor at** ca.gr3math.com

CHECK What You Know

Name each polygon. See Examples 1 and 2 (p. 419)

1. 

2. 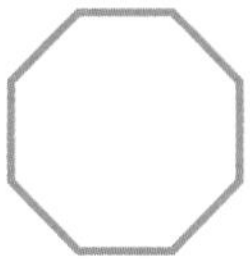

3. 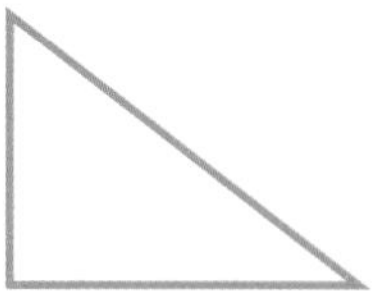

4. 

5. 

6. 

7. Bryson drew a square. Then he drew a triangle on top of it. What is the new polygon called?

8. Talk About It Explain why the shape of the tamborine at the right is not a polygon.

Practice and Problem Solving

EXTRA PRACTICE See page R26.

Name each polygon. See Examples 1 and 2 (p. 419)

9. 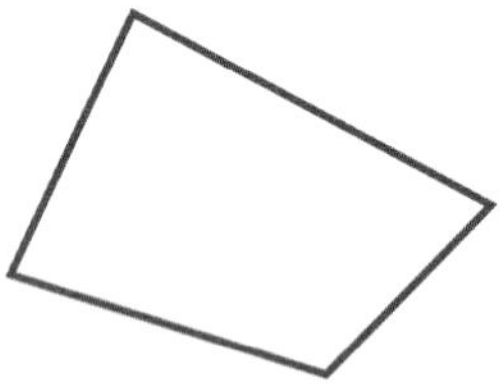

10. 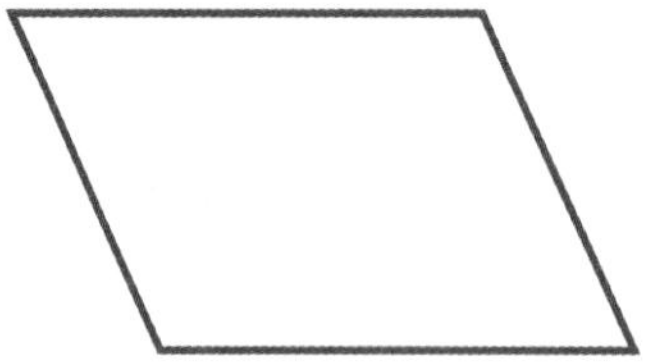

11. 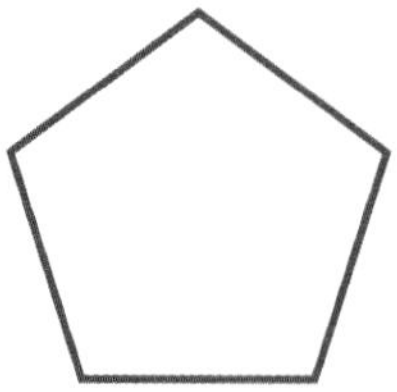

12. 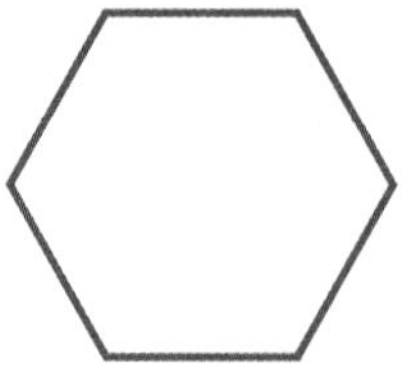

13. 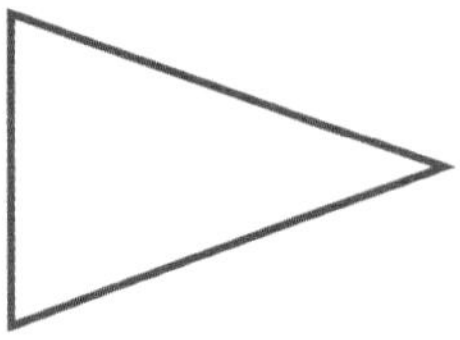

14. 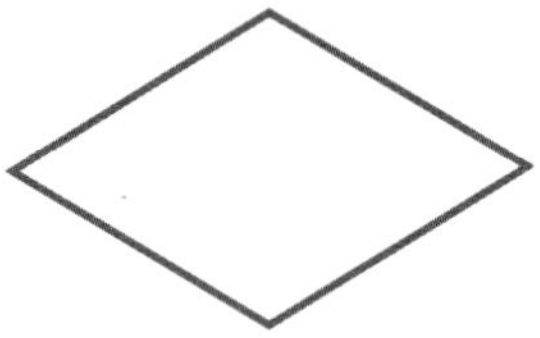

15. What is the shape of a door?

16. What three-sided polygon do you get when you fold a square in half, corner to corner?

Classify the polygons outlined in each object. See Examples 1 and 2 (p. 419)

17.

18.

19.

20. Christa draws a figure that has 5 sides. What polygon did she draw?

21. Anton's shirt has a polygon printed on it. The polygon has 6 sides. What is the name of this polygon?

Real-World PROBLEM SOLVING

Music The *triangle* is a musical instrument. It is struck with a metal rod, giving a high-pitched, ringing tone.

22. Why is this instrument called a triangle?

23. Is the shape of this instrument really a triangle? Explain your reasoning.

H.O.T. Problems

24. OPEN ENDED Draw a figure that is not a polygon. Explain why this figure is not a polygon.

25. FIND THE ERROR Jamie and Pilar are classifying the figure shown. Who is correct? Explain.

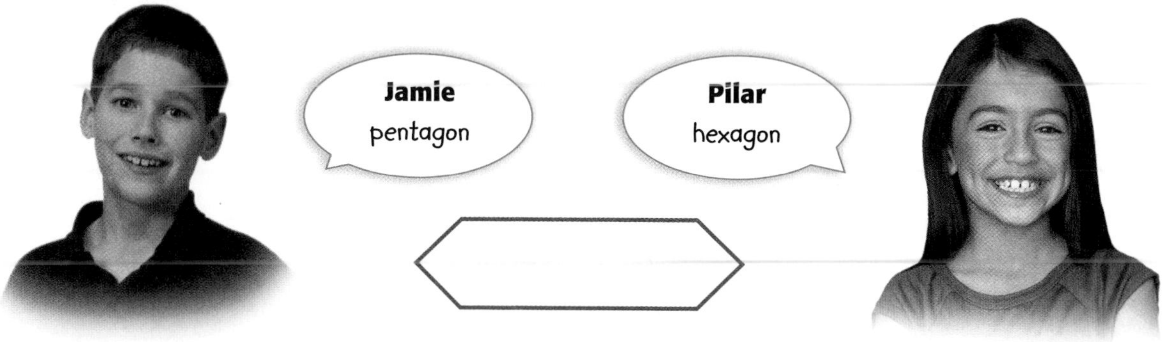

26. WRITING IN MATH Is every polygon a plane figure? Is every plane figure a polygon? Explain your answer.

10-2 Measurement: Perimeter

MAIN IDEA

I will find the perimeter of a polygon.

Standard 3MG1.3 Find the perimeter of a polygon with integer sides.

New Vocabulary

perimeter

GET READY to Learn

Hands-On Mini Activity

Perimeter is the distance around the outside of an object or shape. You can estimate and measure perimeter.

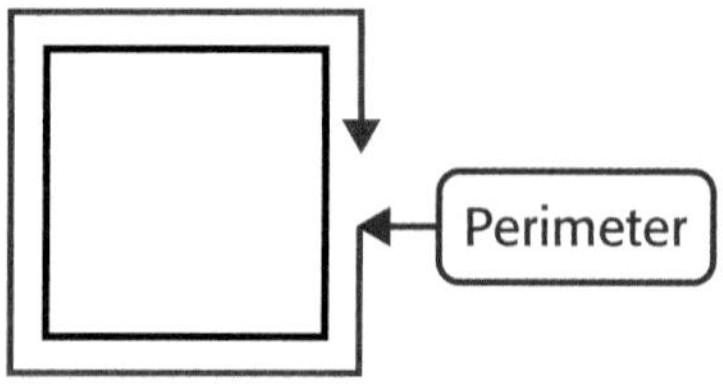

Step 1 Copy the table shown below.

Object	Estimate (cm)	Exact Measure (cm)
Math book		
Desk top		
Chalkboard eraser		

Step 2 Estimate the perimeter of your math book.

Step 3 Use a centimeter ruler to find the exact perimeter.

Step 4 Record the results. Repeat the steps for each object listed.

1. Write the number sentence for the perimeter of your math book.

2. What operation did you use to find perimeter?

KEY CONCEPT — Find Perimeter

Words The perimeter of a polygon is the sum of the side lengths.

Model

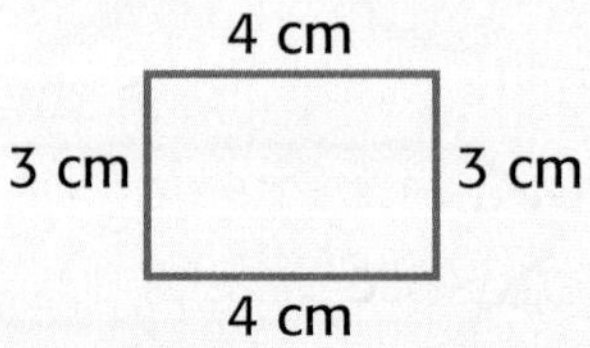

Symbols Perimeter = 3 cm + 4 cm + 3 cm + 4 cm
= 14 cm

EXAMPLES Find Perimeter

1 Find the perimeter of the triangle.

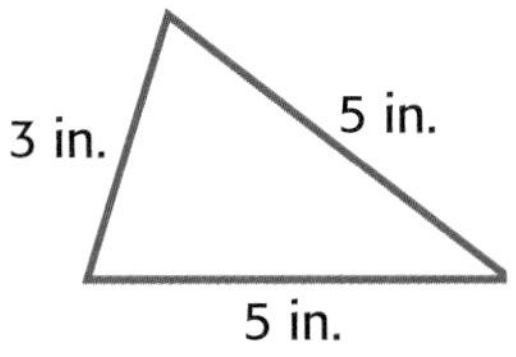

To find the perimeter, add the lengths of the sides.

5 in. + 3 in. + 5 in. = 13 inches

So, the perimeter is 13 inches.

Remember

On grid paper, think of each square as one unit.

2 Find the perimeter of the shaded quadrilateral.

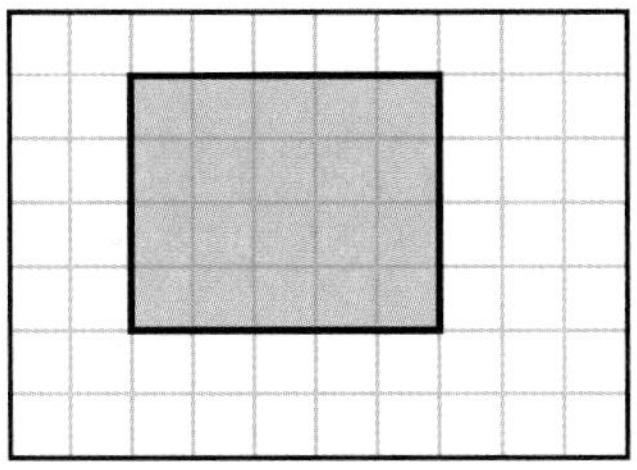

To find the perimeter add the lengths of the sides.

4 units + 5 units + 4 units + 5 units = 18 units

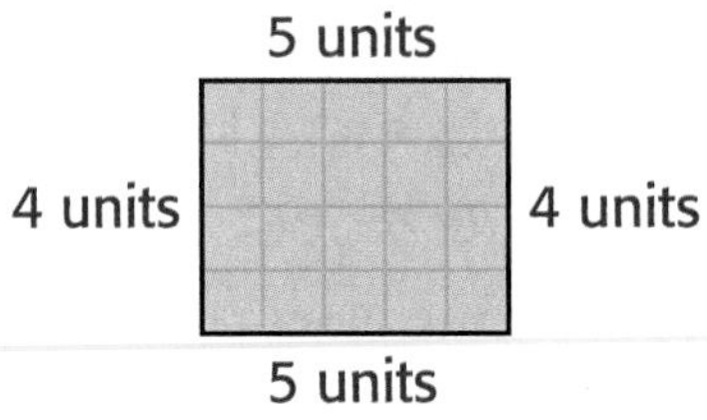

So, the perimeter is 18 units.

Online Personal Tutor at ca.gr3math.com

CHECK What You Know

Find the perimeter of each figure. See Examples 1 and 2 (p. 423)

1.

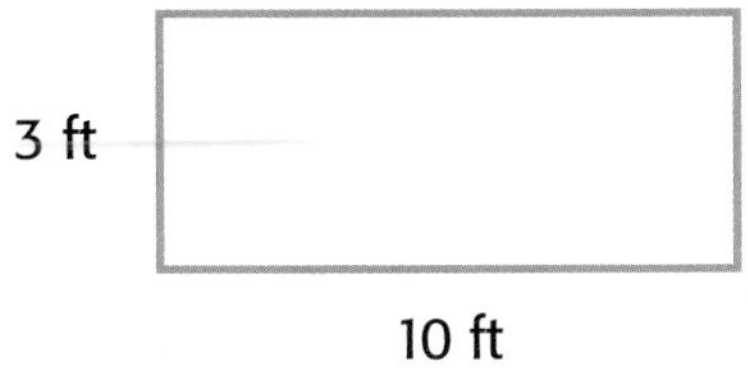

2.

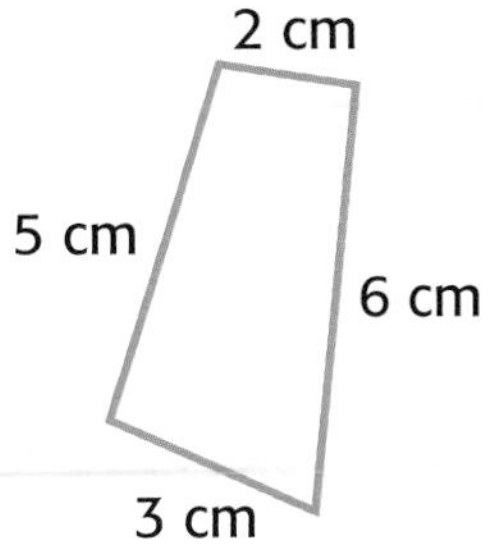

3.

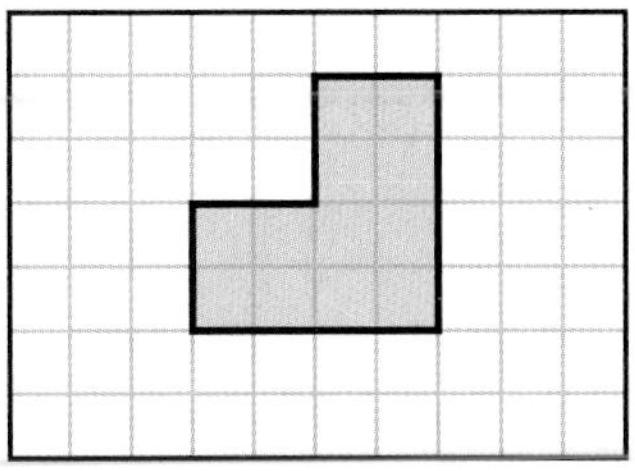

4. The front of the birdhouse at the right is shaped like a pentagon. The lengths of all of the sides are equal. What is the perimeter of the birdhouse.

5. Talk About It A triangle has three equal sides and its perimeter is 15 units. How would you find the length of each side?

Practice and Problem Solving

EXTRA PRACTICE
See page R27.

Find the perimeter of each figure. See Examples 1 and 2 (p. 423)

6.

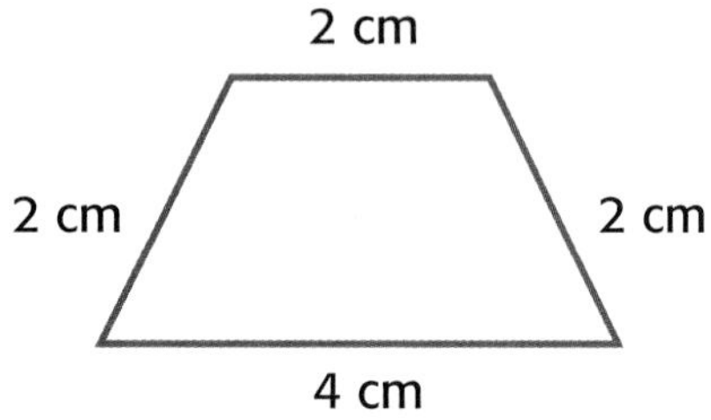

7.

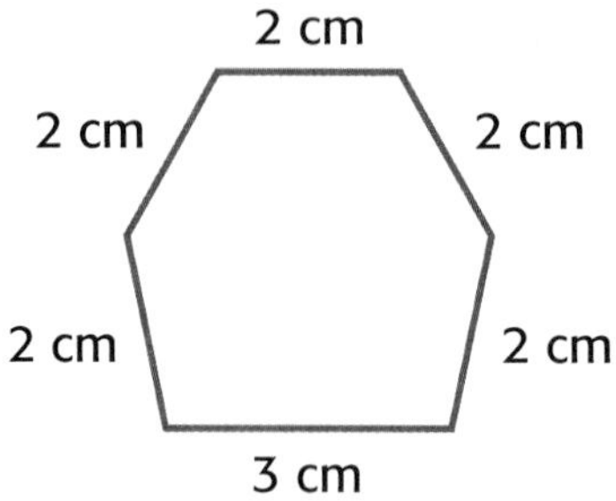

8

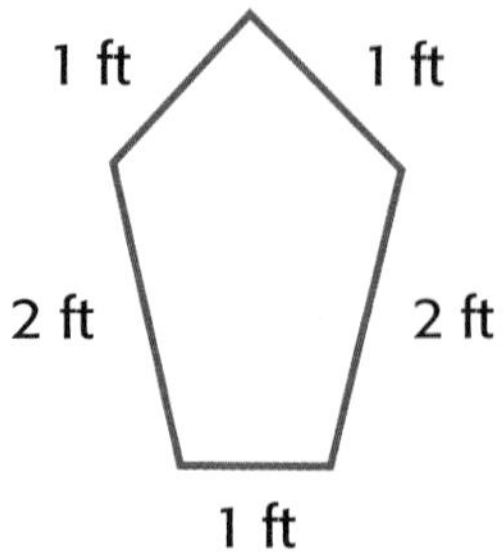

9.

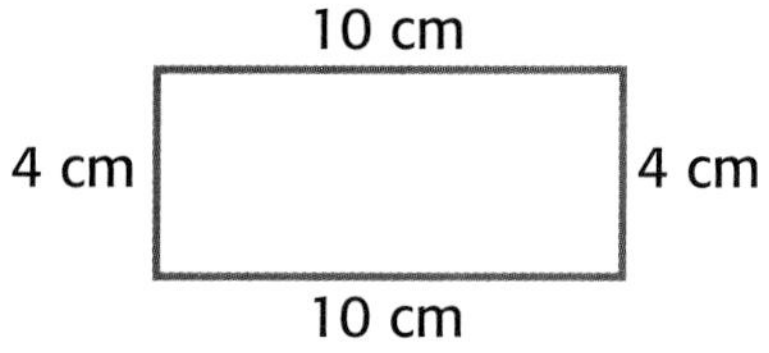

10.

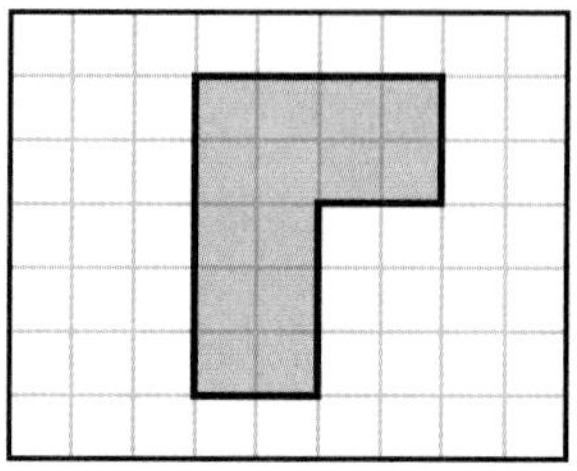

11.

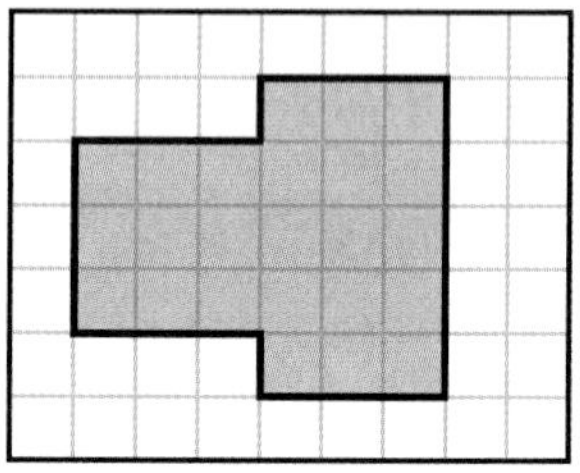

12. Algebra A fountain has a triangular water pool. The pool's perimeter is 120 feet. If one side is 40 feet and another is 50 feet, what is the length of the third side?

13. Marlo's house has a deck that is shaped like a hexagon. The sides have equal lengths. If each side of the deck is 12 feet long, what is its perimeter?

14. Murphy has two square gymnastics mats. The length of each side is 8 feet. What is the total perimeter if the mats are pushed together to make a rectangle?.

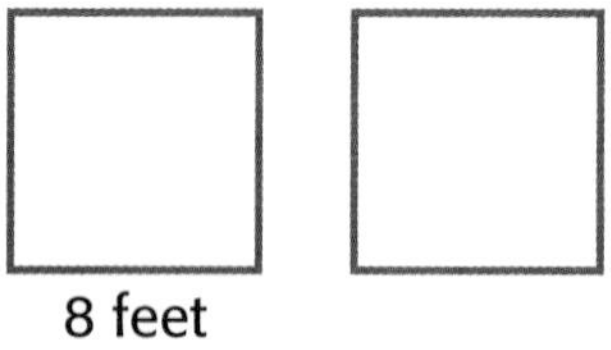

15. Algebra The pentagon shown has a perimeter of 21 feet. Find the length of the missing side.

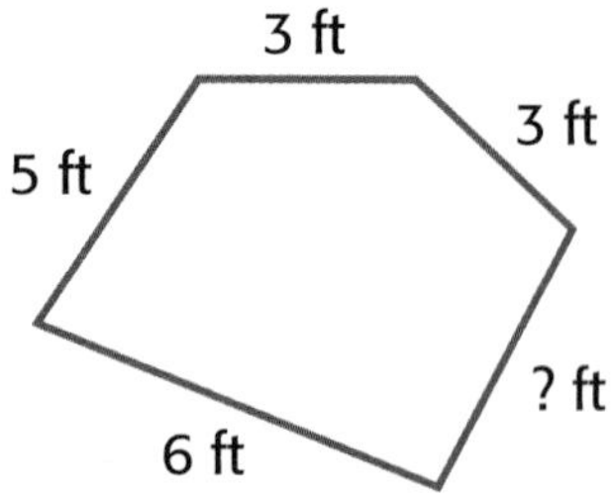

Real-World PROBLEM SOLVING

Architecture This building is called the Pentagon. It houses top military leaders for our country.

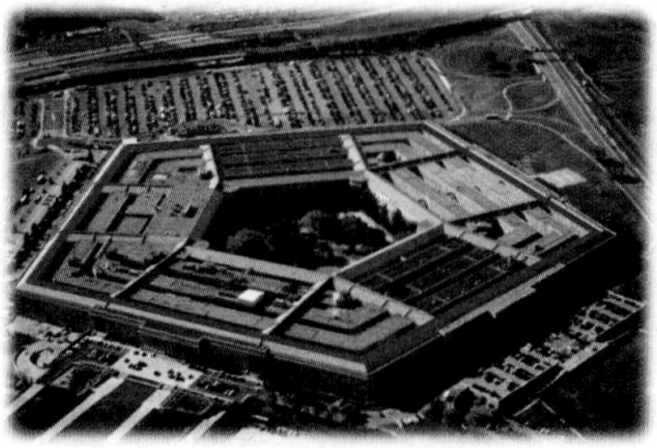

16. Why is it named the Pentagon?

17. All sides of the Pentagon have the same length. Since one side is 921 feet long, what is the perimeter of the Pentagon?

H.O.T. Problems

18. OPEN ENDED Draw and label a figure that has a perimeter of 24 inches.

19. WRITING IN ▸MATH How can you find the perimeter of a rectangle if you know the length and width?

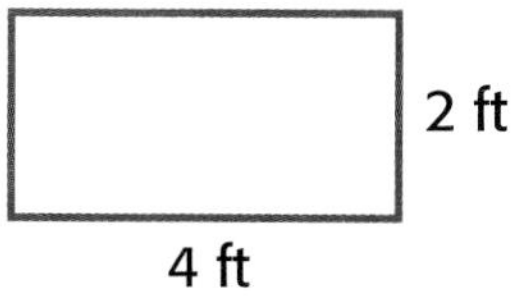

Standards Practice

20 Jeffery made a doghouse. Which figure represents the shaded area of the doghouse? **(Lesson 10-1)**

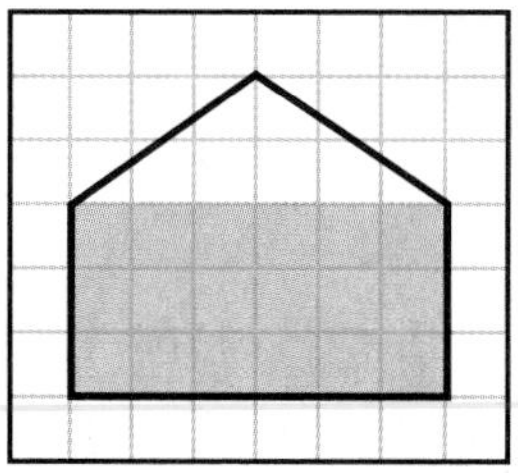

A triangle **C** pentagon
B quadrilateral **D** hexagon

21 What is the perimeter of the figure? **(Lesson 10-2)**

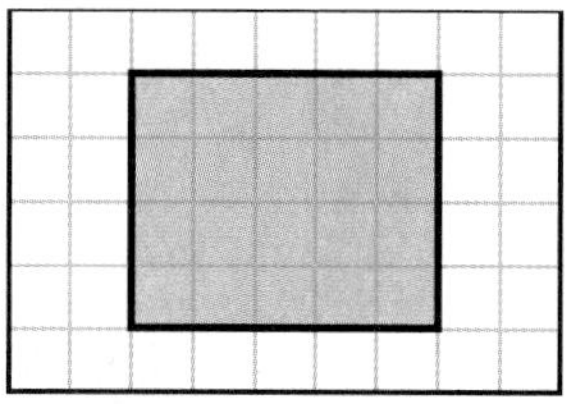

F 11 units
G 12 units
H 18 units
J 20 units

Spiral Review

Classify each polygon. (Lesson 10-1)

22.

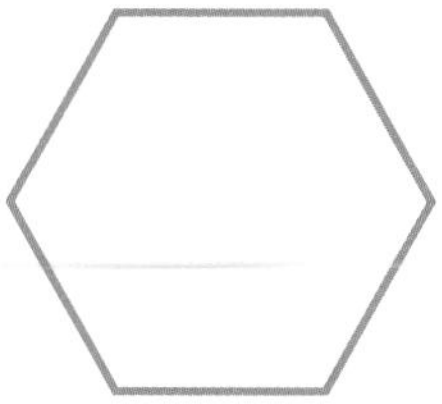

23.

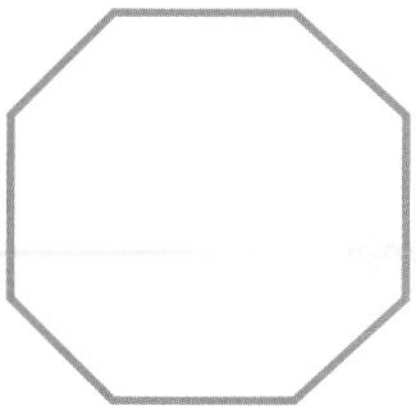

24.

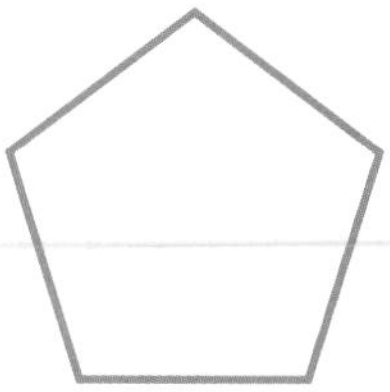

Convert. (Lesson 9-6)

25. ■ cm = 17 m

26. 23,000 m = ■ km

27. 15,000 cm = ■ m

28. Measurement Paris and Jon went to the store to buy dog food. Each 16-ounce can was $1. How much would they spend for 16 one-pound cans? **(Lesson 8-3)**

Explore

Measurement Activity for 10-3
Area

MAIN IDEA

I will estimate the area of a figure.

Standard 3MG1.2 **Estimate** or determine **the area** and volume of solid figures **by covering them with squares** or by counting the number of cubes that will fill them.
Standard 3MR2.1 **Use estimation to verify the reasonableness of calculated results.**

You Will Need
grid paper
small objects

Concepts in Motion
Animation
ca.gr3math.com

Area is the number of square units needed to cover a plane figure without overlapping. You can use grid paper to explore area.

1 square unit

ACTIVITY

1 Estimate area

Step 1 Estimate

How many square units do you think will cover the side view of the cube?

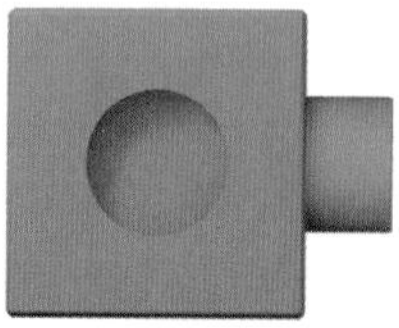

Step 2 Trace

Trace the shape of the connecting cube onto grid paper.

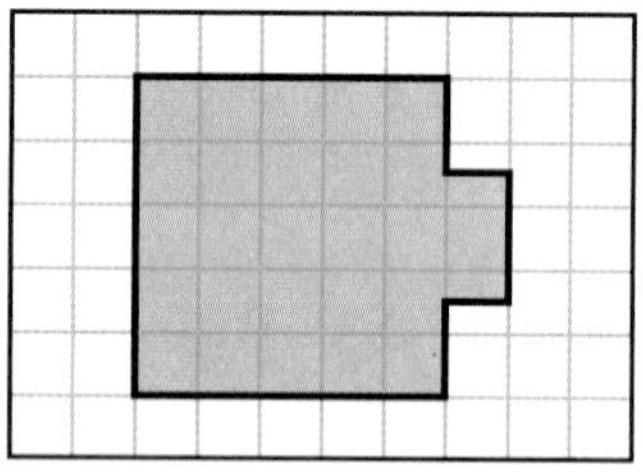

Step 3 Estimate

One whole square is 1 square unit.

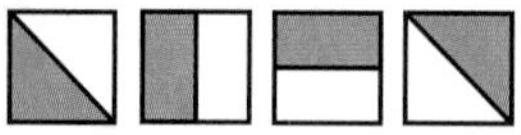
Each of these is $\frac{1}{2}$ square unit.

Each of these is more than $\frac{1}{2}$ square unit.

Count the number of whole square units. How many half-square units are there? Estimate the area. How does the estimate compare with your first estimate?

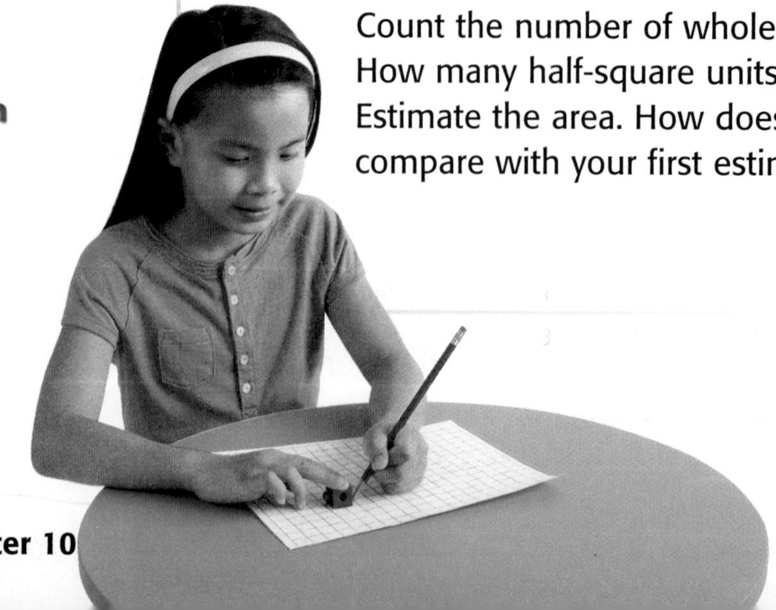

Hands-On Activity

ACTIVITY

2 Estimate area

Step 1 Draw

Draw a circle on grid paper.

Step 2 Estimate

Use what you learned in Activity 1 to estimate the area of the circle.

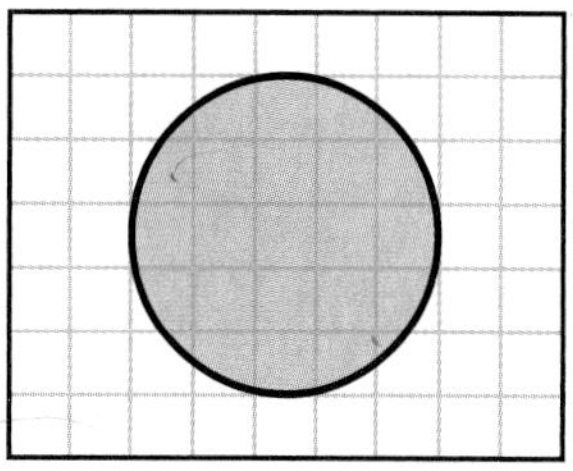

Step 3 Compare

Compare your estimate with a classmate's estimate.

Think About It

1. Is it easier to find the exact area of a rectangle on grid paper or to estimate? Explain.

2. How did you make your estimate for the area of the circle? How close is it to your friend's estimate?

CHECK What You Know

Estimate the area in square units of each figure.

3.

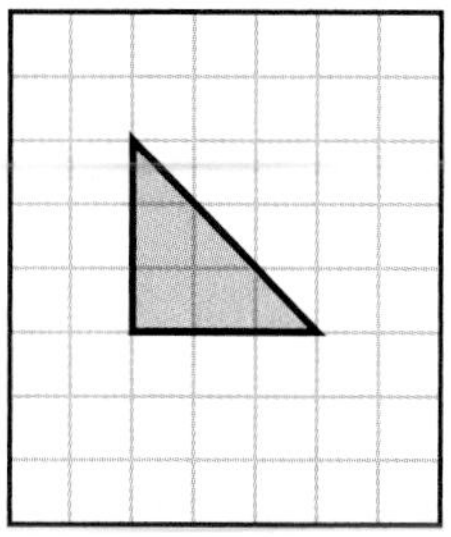

4.

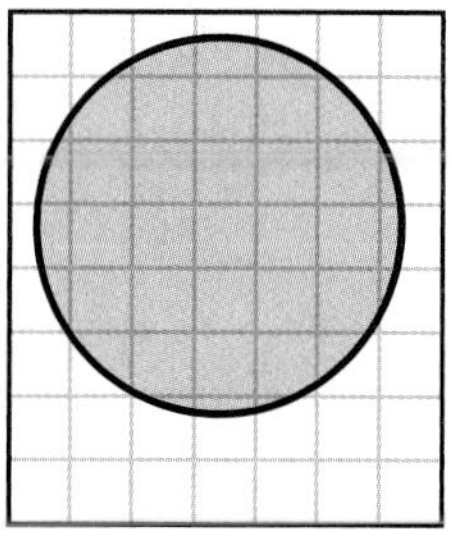

5.

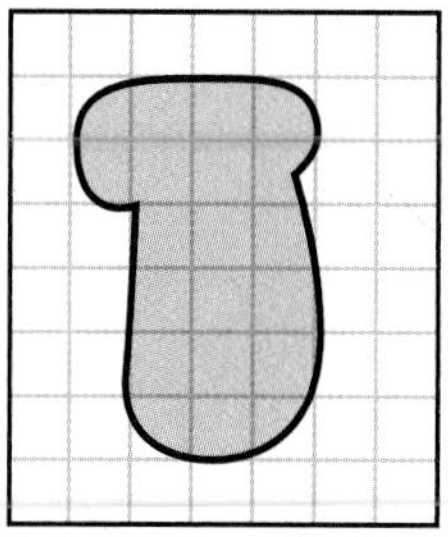

6. Make an outline of your hand with your fingers together on a piece of grid paper. Estimate the area of your hand.

7. Estimate the total area of all of the sides of a cube by tracing it on a piece of grid paper.

8. WRITING IN MATH Explain the difference between area and perimeter.

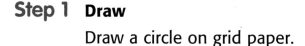

10-3 Measurement: Area

MAIN IDEA

I will detrmine area.

Standard 3MG1.2 **Estimate or determine the area** and volume of solid figures **by covering them with squares** or by counting the number of cubes that will fill them.
3MR2.1 Use estimation to verify the reasonableness of calculated results.

New Vocabulary

area

GET READY to Learn

Halley is drawing polygons on grid paper. One of the figures is shown at the right. Estimate the area of the figure.

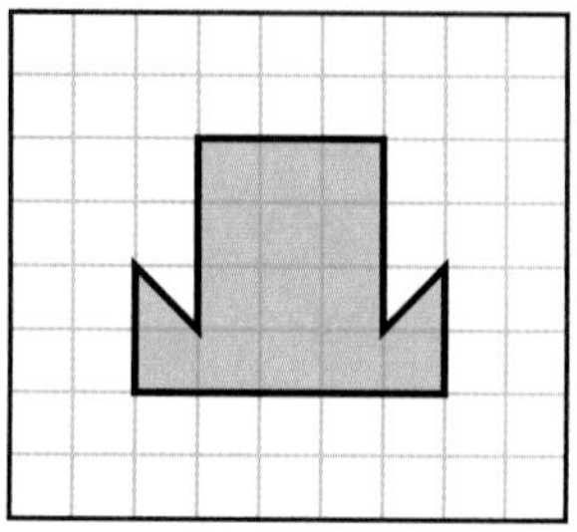

Area is the number of square units needed to cover a plane figure without overlapping. In the Explore Activity, you estimated area. You can also find the exact area of a figure.

EXAMPLES Determine Area

1 **What is the area of the figure that Halley drew?**

Count the number of whole squares. There are 14 whole squares.

There are 2 half squares. Notice that two halves equal one whole.

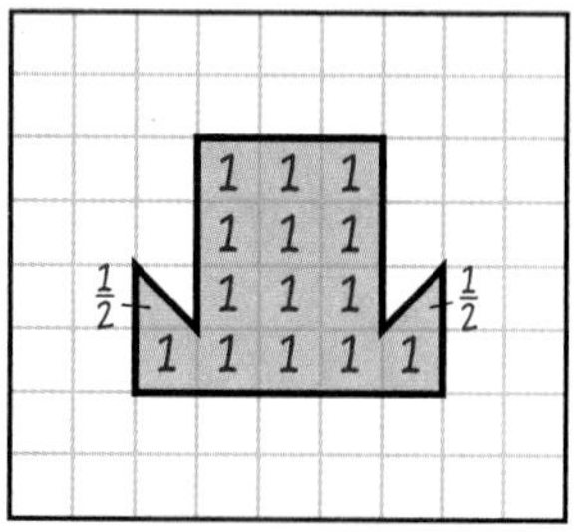

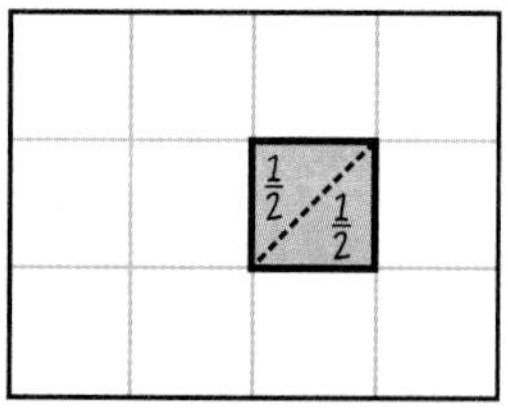

14 squares units + 1 square unit = 15 square units

So, the area is 15 square units.

2 **Find the area of the figure.**

Count the number of whole squares.

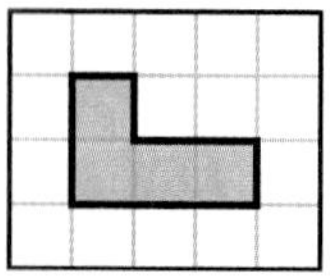

The area of this figure is 4 square units.

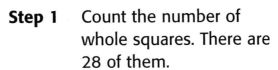

Real-World EXAMPLE — Determine Area

3 **Phillip created a tile mosaic shown at the right. What is the area of the figure?**

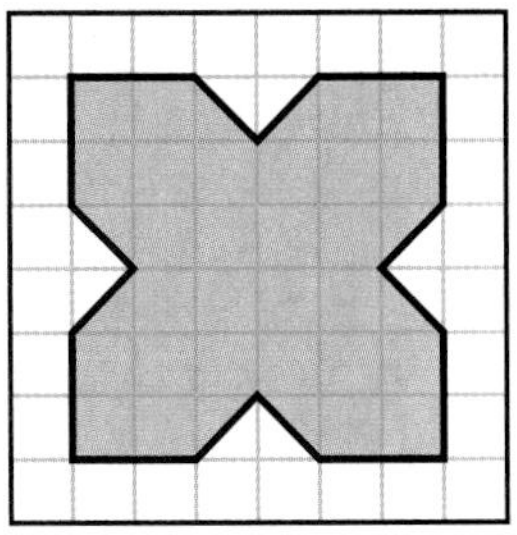

> **Remember**
> Two half squares equal one whole square.

Step 1 Count the number of whole squares. There are 28 of them.

Step 2 Count the half squares. There are 8 halves. Eight halves equal 4 whole squares.

Step 3 Add.

28 square units + 4 square units = 32 square units

So, the area of the mosaic tile is 32 square units.

Online **Personal Tutor at** ca.gr3math.com

CHECK What You Know

Find the area of each figure. See Examples 1–3 (pp. 428–429)

1.

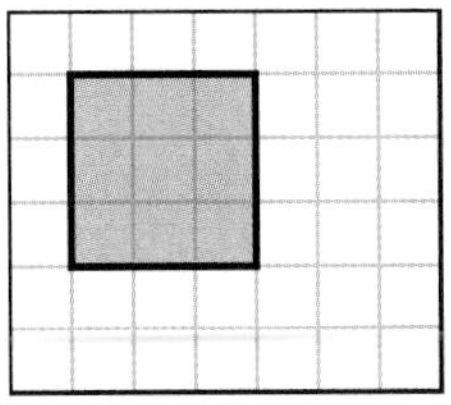

2.

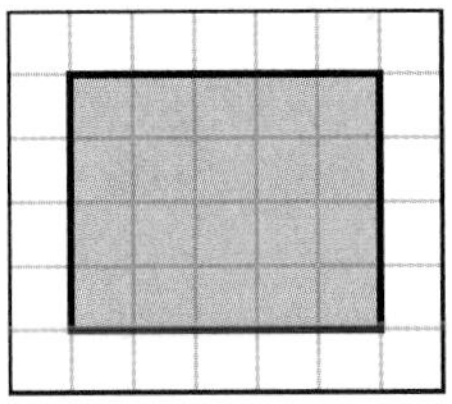

3.

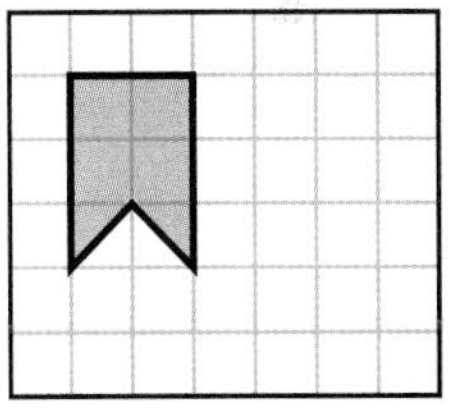

4. Denitra plans to cover a desk with decorative tiles. What is the area of the space she will cover?

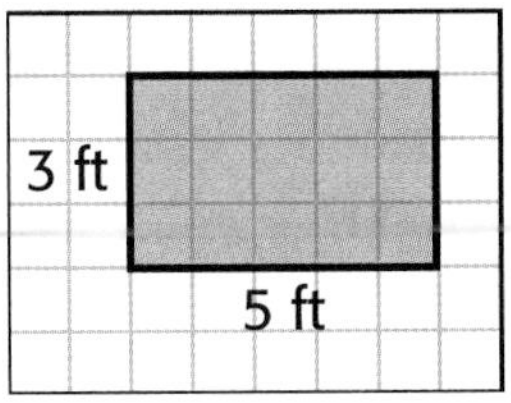

5. The frame is covered with squares of colored glass. What is the area covered by the colored glass?

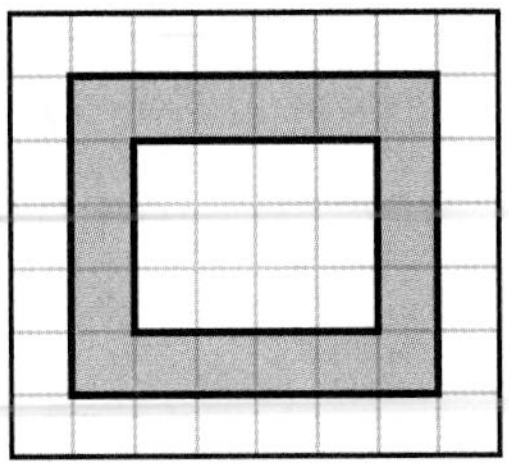

6. **Talk About It** Explain how to find the area of a rectangle.

Practice and Problem Solving

EXTRA PRACTICE
See page R27.

Find the area of each figure. See Examples 1–3 (pp. 428–429)

7. 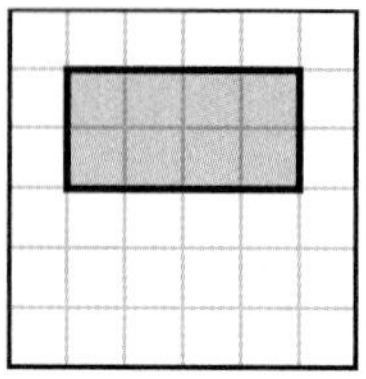

8. 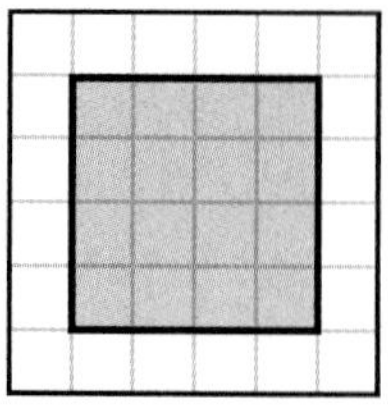

9. 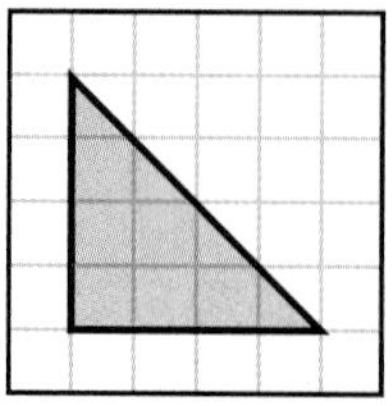

10. 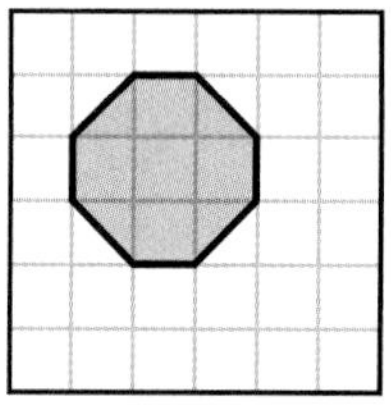

11. 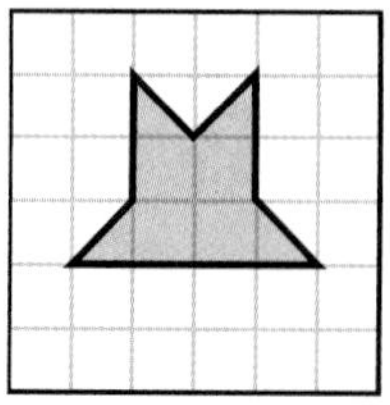

12. 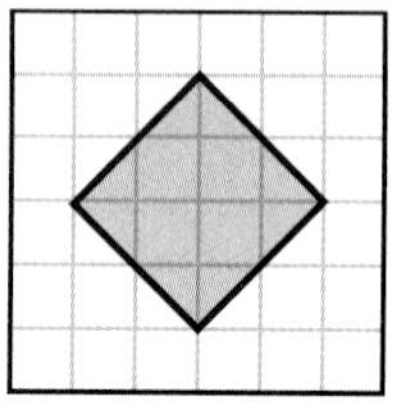

Find the area and perimeter of each figure.

13. 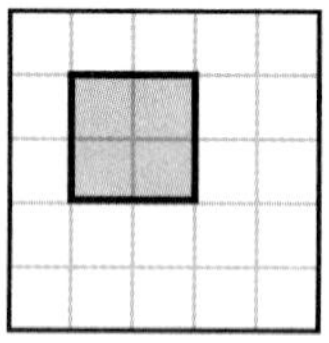

14. 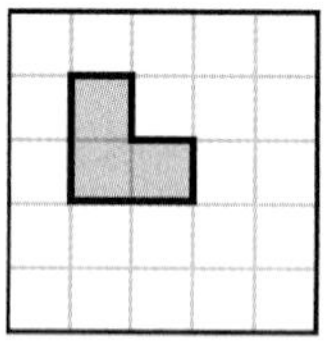

15. 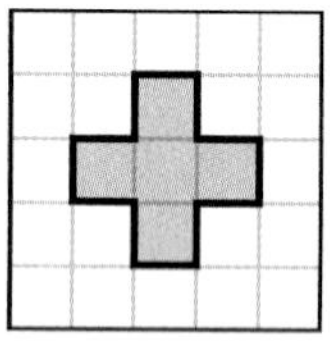

16. Diego and Luisa are helping to put new tile in a hallway. How many tiles do they need to fill the area?

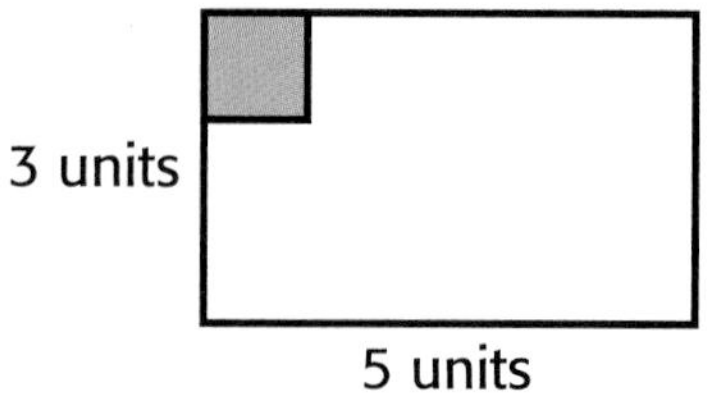

17. Elaine is finding the area of her closet. The size is shown. What is the area of her closet?

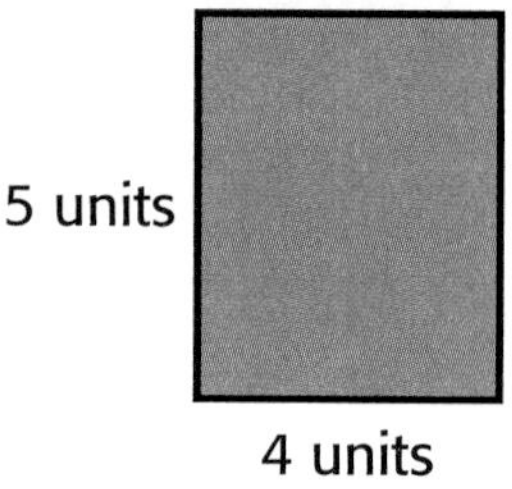

H.O.T. Problems

18. OPEN ENDED Draw two rectangles on grid paper that have different lengths and widths but the same area.

19. CHALLENGE A room is 12 units wide by 24 units long. Find the area and the perimeter of the floor of the room.

20. WRITING IN MATH Write how you would find the area of a room that is a rectangle with a length of 5 units and a width of 7 units.

Standards Practice

21 What is the perimeter of the figure? **(Lesson 10-2)**

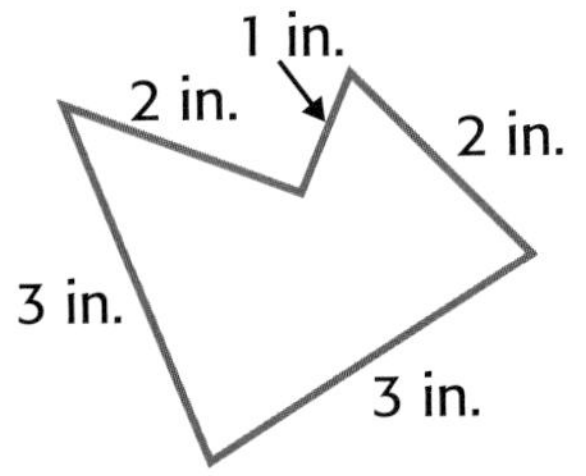

A 9 inches

B 11 inches

C 11 centimeters

D 12 inches

22 What is the area of this figure? **(Lesson 10-3)**

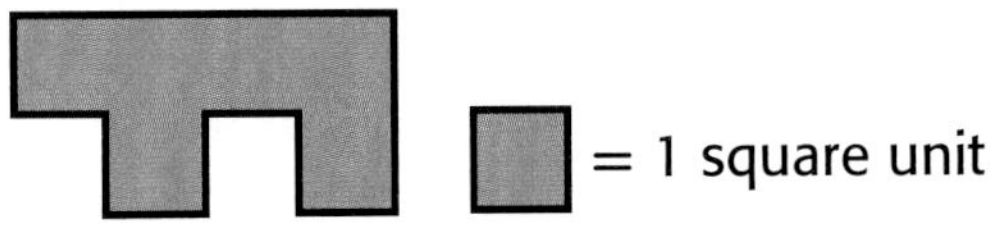

F 2 square units

G 4 square units

H 6 square units

J 8 square units

Spiral Review

Find the perimeter. (Lesson 10-2)

23.

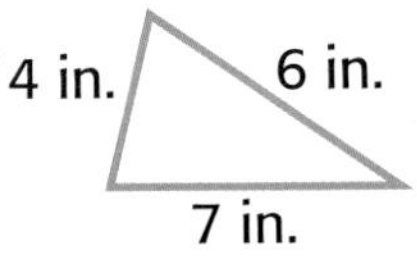

24.

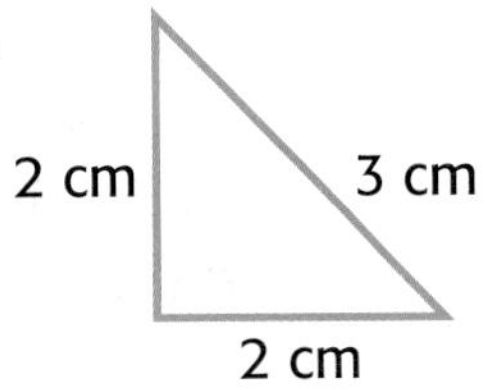

25. Classify the polygon. **(Lesson 10-1)**

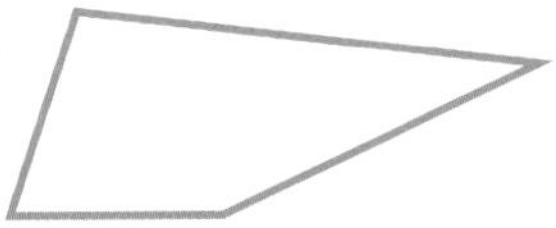

Convert each unit to a smaller unit. (Lesson 9-6)

26. 7 m = ▒ cm

27. 5 L = ▒ mL

28. 9 kg = ▒ g

29. Mandy gets ready for school at 7:00 A.M. It takes her 45 minutes to get dressed and another half hour to get to school. What time is it when she arrives at school? **(Lesson 8-7)**

Choose the most appropriate unit to measure each capacity. Choose from *cup, pint, quart,* or *gallon.* (Lesson 8-4)

30. bathtub

31. juice box

32. watering can

33. There are 32 tickets to give out equally to 8 families. How many tickets will each family get? **(Lesson 7-5)**

10-4 Problem-Solving Strategy

MAIN IDEA I will solve problems by solving a simpler problem.

Standard 3MG1.3 Find the perimeter of a polygon with integer sides. Standard 3MR1.2 Determine when and how to break a problem into simpler parts.

Julianna is placing a border around a rectangular bulletin board. The perimeter of the bulletin board is 10 feet. One side measures 2 feet. What will be the length of the border for each side?

Understand

What facts do you know?

- The bulletin board is rectangular with a perimeter of 10 feet.
- The length of one side is 2 feet.

What do you need to find?

- The length of the border for each side.

Plan

Solve a simpler problem to find the length of the border for each side.

Solve

Two sides are 2 feet long.
2 feet + 2 feet = 4 feet

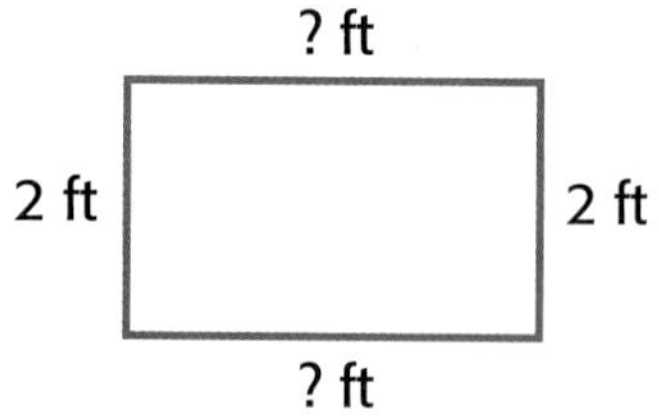

Find the total length of the other two sides.

perimeter		total of 2 sides		total of remaining sides
10 feet	−	4 feet	=	6 feet

The two unknown sides add up to 6 feet. Since both sides are the same length, divide by 2.
6 feet ÷ 2 = 3 feet

So, two pieces of border should be 2 feet long, and the other two should be 3 feet long each.

Check

Look back at the problem. Add up all of the sides.
2 feet + 2 feet + 3 feet + 3 feet = 10 feet
So, the answer is correct.

ANALYZE the Strategy

Refer to the problem on the previous page.

1. Explain how to *solve a simpler problem* strategy is helpful.

2. Suppose the perimeter of the bulletin board is still 10 feet, but the length of one side is 1 foot. Is its shape still a rectangle? Explain.

3. Explain another strategy you could have used to solve the problem.

4. A square has a perimeter of 160 inches. What is the length of each side? Write the steps you would take to solve this problem.

PRACTICE the Strategy

EXTRA PRACTICE See page R27.

Solve. Use the *solve a simpler problem* strategy.

5. During round one of a game, Cris, Nita, and Geoffrey each scored 4 points. In round two, they each scored twice as many points. Find the total number of points.

6. Percy put the photograph below in a frame. The frame is 2 inches longer and 2 inches wider than the photograph. What is the perimeter of the frame?

4 in.

6 in.

7. Paco wants to buy two gallons of milk. One gallon costs $2.25. A half-gallon costs $1.20. Should Paco buy two one-gallon jugs of milk or four half-gallon jugs to spend the least amount of money? Explain.

8. Both Duane and Suzanne followed the homework schedule shown in the table. What is the total number of hours they spent on homework?

Homework Schedule	
Day	**Time (minutes)**
Monday	45
Tuesday	30
Wednesday	15

9. There were 17 bottles, 6 mugs, and 5 glasses on a shelf. Rob used 2 bottles. Anne used 1 mug and 1 glass. How many items are left?

10. Lannetta needs to buy balloons for a party. She invited 6 friends from school, 3 friends from soccer, and 2 cousins. How many balloons will she need to buy if everyone at the party gets two?

11. **WRITING IN MATH** Explain when you would use the *solve a simpler problem* strategy.

10-5 Triangles and Angles

MAIN IDEA

I will identify and classify different triangles and compare angles.

Standard 3MG2.2 Identify attributes of triangles (e.g., two equal sides for the isosceles triangle, three equal sides for the equilateral triangle, right angle for the right triangle). **Standard 3MG2.4 Identify right angles in geometric figures and determine whether other angles are greater or less than a right angle.**

New Vocabulary

equilateral triangle
isosceles triangle
scalene triangle
right triangle

GET READY to Learn

The house in the picture is called an A-frame house because it has a shape that looks like an A. The front of an A-frame house also resembles a triangle.

Triangles have names based on the lengths of their sides.

KEY CONCEPT — Identify Triangles by its Sides

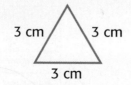

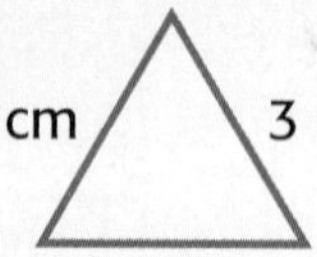

equilateral triangle
A triangle with three sides of equal length.

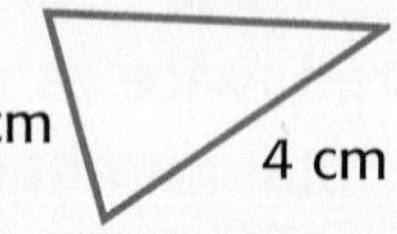

isosceles triangle
A triangle with at least two sides of equal length.

scalene triangle
A triangle with no equal sides.

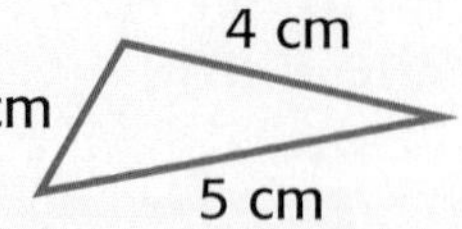

Real-World EXAMPLES — Identify a Triangle

Identify each triangle.

1

This triangle has two sides of equal length. It is an isoceles triangle.

2

No sides have equal length. It is a scalene triangle.

> **Remember**
> A right angle makes the corner of a square.

Triangles can also have names based on their angles.

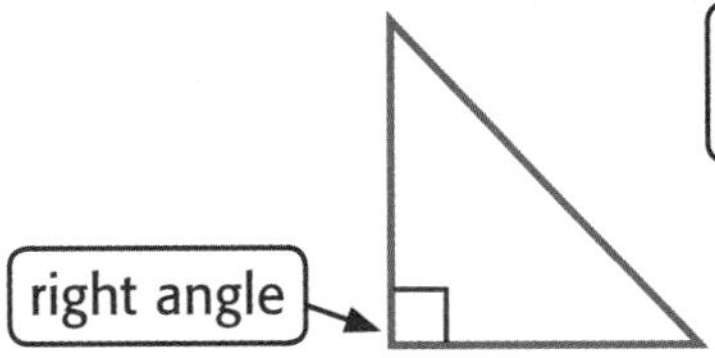

right triangle
A triangle with one right angle.

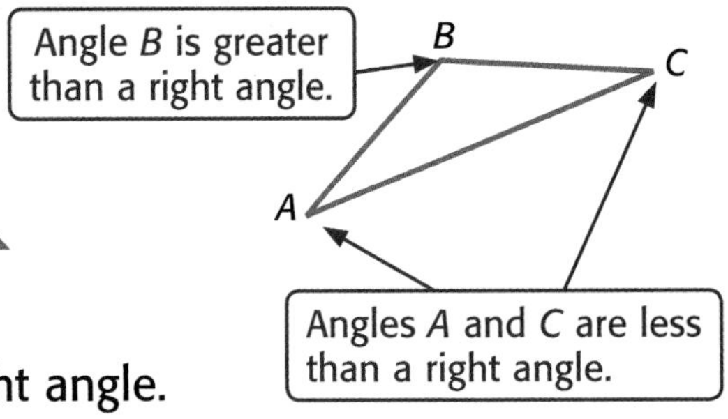

Real-World EXAMPLE **Identify Angles**

3 **TENTS Identify the triangle. Tell whether each angle is a *right angle, less than* a right angle, or *greater than* a right angle.**

This triangle has two sides that are equal. So, it is an isosceles triangle. Every angle is less than a right angle.

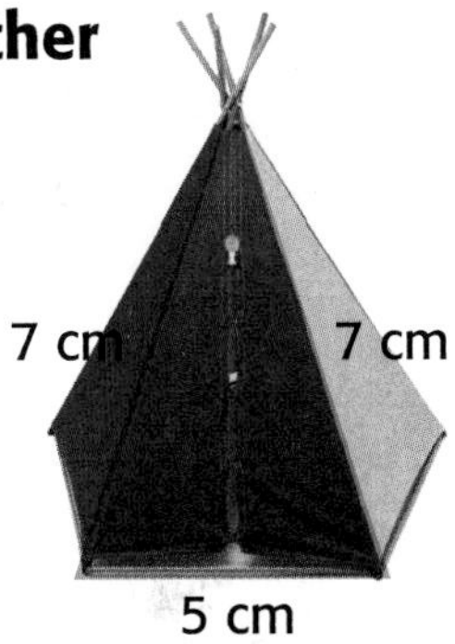

Online Personal Tutor at ca.gr3math.com

CHECK What You Know

Identify each triangle. Write *equilateral, isosceles,* or *scalene.*
See Example 1 and 2 (p. 434)

1.

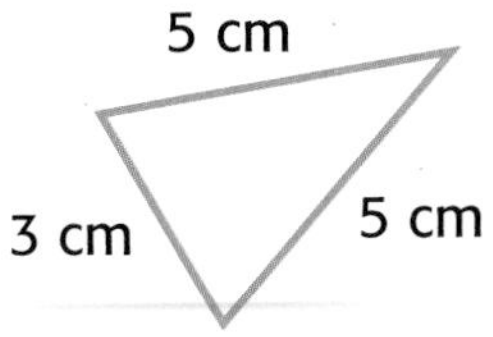

2.

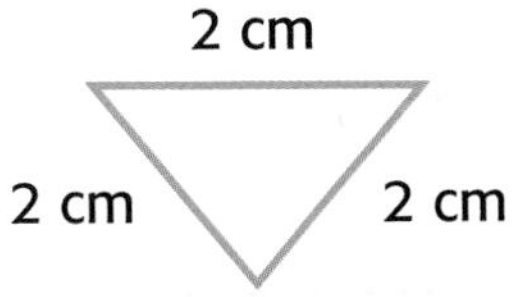

3.

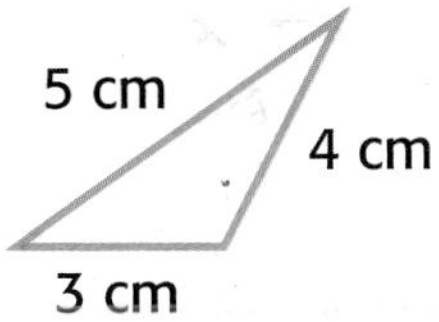

Identify each triangle. Tell whether each angle shown is a *right angle, less than* a right angle, or *greater than* a right angle. See Example 3 (p. 435)

4.

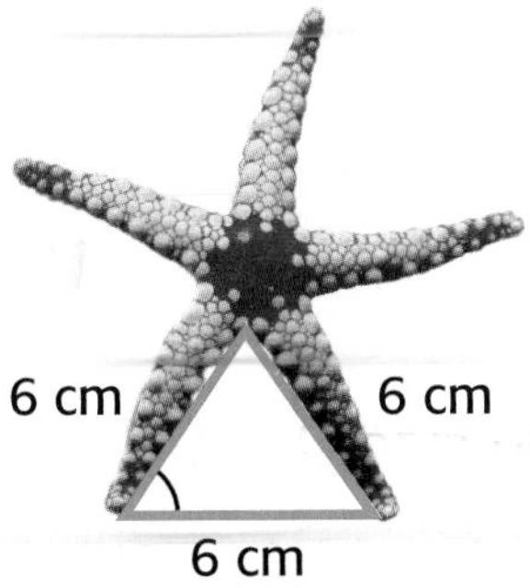

5.

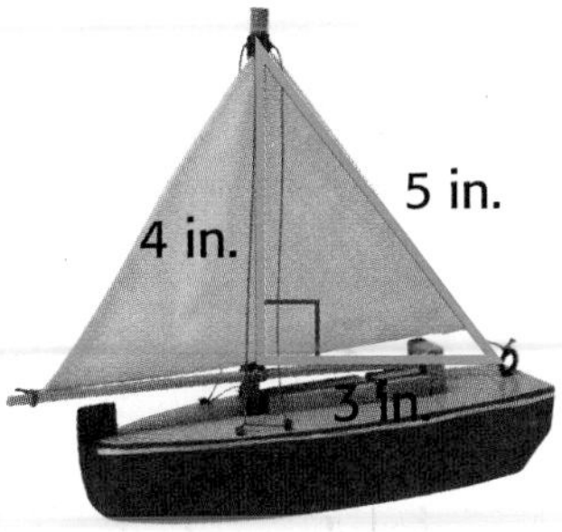

6.

7. Talk About It Can a triangle have two right angles? Explain.

Practice and Problem Solving

EXTRA PRACTICE See page R28.

Identify each triangle. Write *equilateral, isosceles,* or *scalene.*

See Examples 1 and 2 (p. 434)

8.

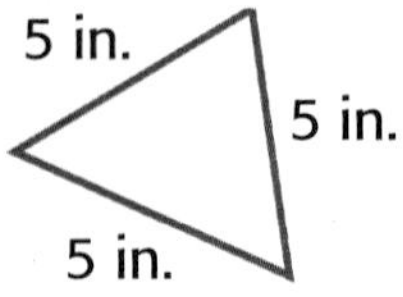

9

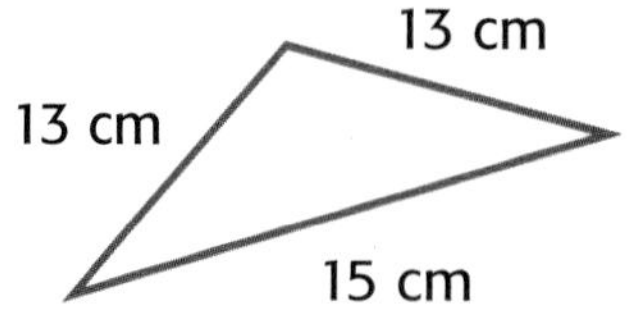

10.

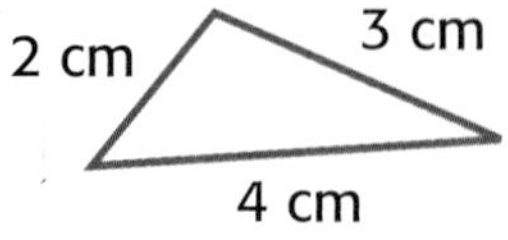

11.

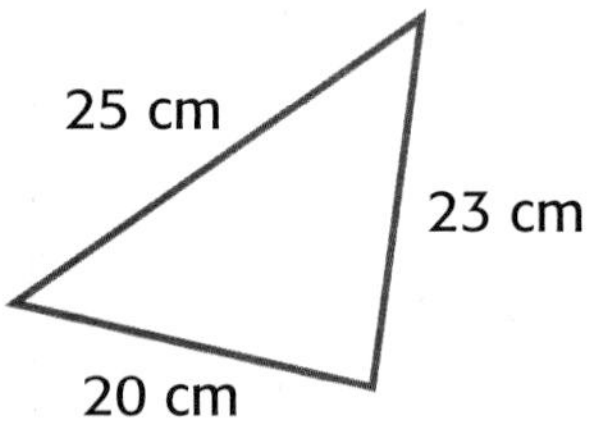

12.

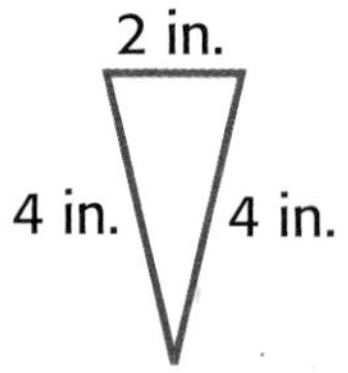

13.

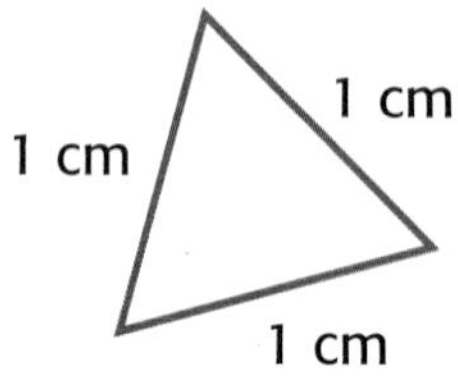

Identify each triangle. Tell whether each angle shown is a *right angle, less than* a right angle, or *greater than* a right angle. See Example 3 (p. 435)

14.

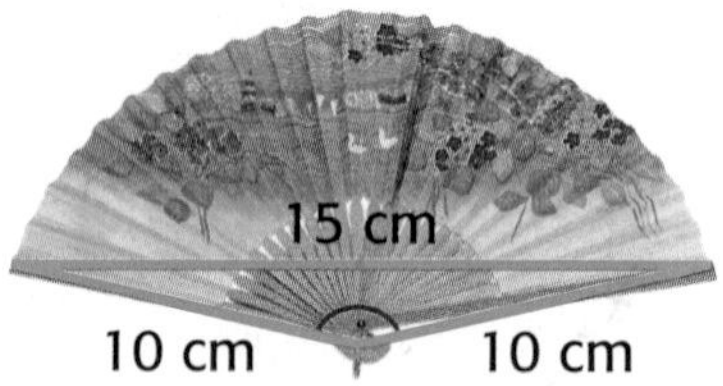

15.

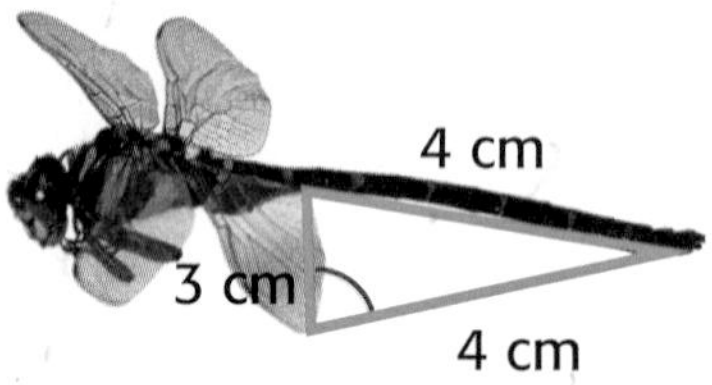

16.

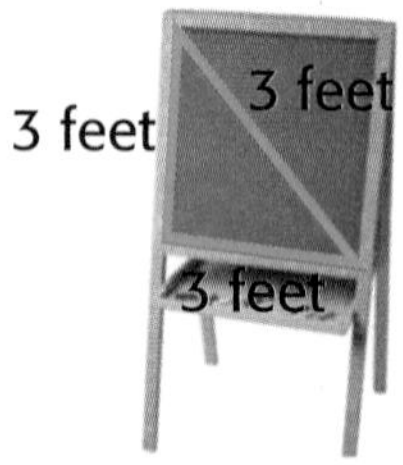

17. Draw a scalene triangle with one right angle.

18. Draw an isosceles triangle.

H.O.T. Problems

REASONING **Tell if the angle made by the hands of the clock is a *right angle, less than* a right angle, or *greater than* a right angle.**

19.

20.

21.

22. **WRITING IN ▸MATH** Describe an equilateral triangle.

Math Online Self-Check Quiz at ca.gr3math.com

CHAPTER 10 Mid-Chapter Check

Lessons 10-1 through 10-5

Classify each polygon (Lesson 10-1)

1. 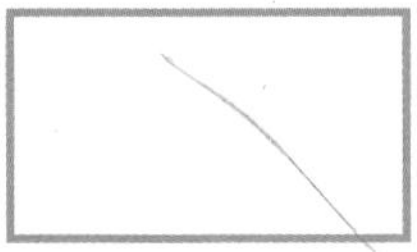

2. 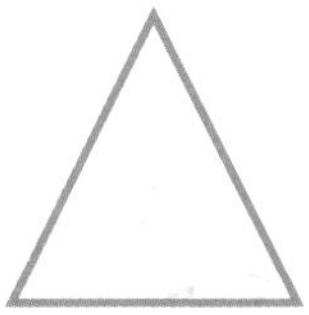

3. **STANDARDS PRACTICE** Which geometric figure best describes the sign shown below? (Lesson 10-1)

A octagon

B pentagon

C hexagon

D square

Find each perimeter. (Lesson 10-2)

4. 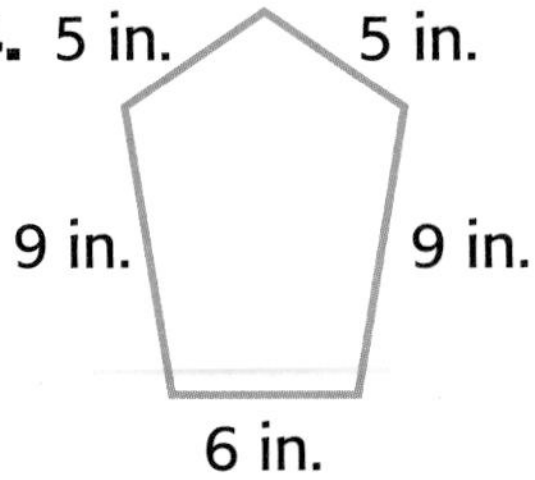

5. 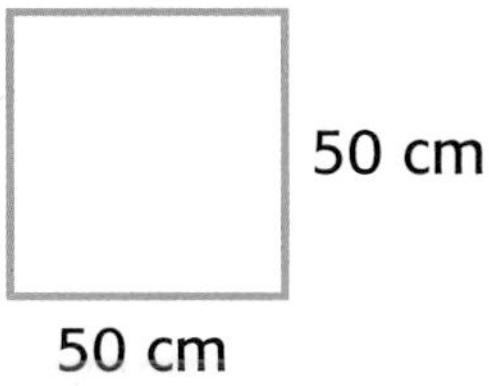

6. **STANDARDS PRACTICE** What is the perimeter? (Lesson 10-2)

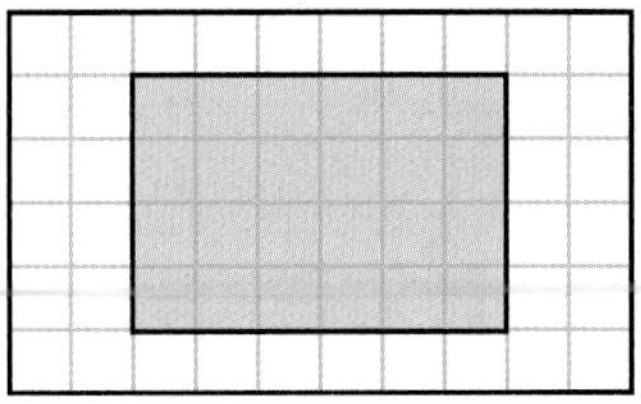

F 18 inches

G 19 inches

H 22 inches

J 25 inches

7. Find the area of the figure. (Lesson 10-3)

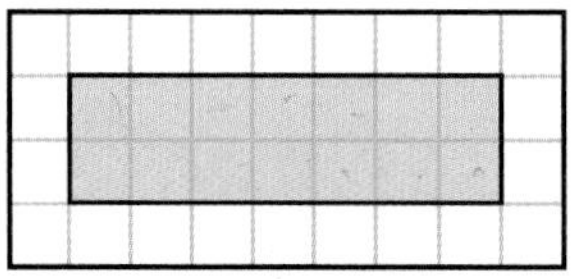

8. The length and width of a sandbox is 6 feet. Draw a picture of the sandbox on grid paper. Then find its area and perimeter. (Lesson 10-3)

9. Three friends were playing a basketball game. Lance won by 15 points. Cortez had 10 points more than George. If George had 20 points, how many points did Lance and Cortez have? (Lesson 10-4)

Identify. Write *equilateral, isosceles,* or *scalene.* (Lesson 10-5)

10. 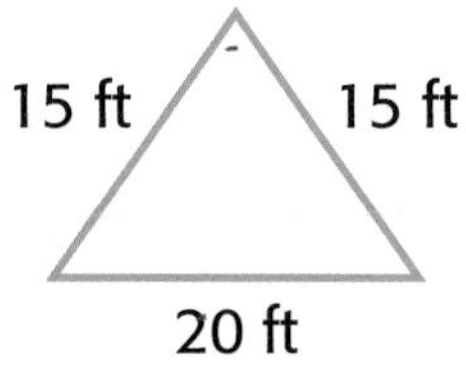

11. 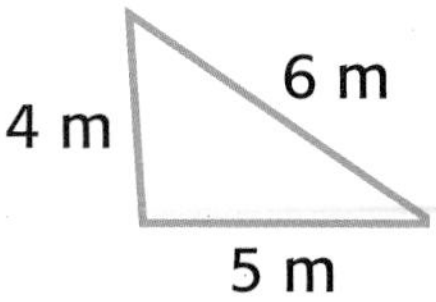

12. Tell whether the angle shown is a *right angle, less than* a right angle, or *greater than* a right angle. (Lesson 10-5)

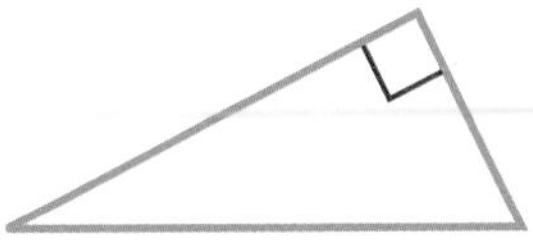

13. **WRITING IN MATH** Describe an isosceles triangle in words.

10-6 Geometry: Quadrilaterals

MAIN IDEA

I will identify, describe, and classify different quadrilaterals.

Standard 3MG2.3 **Identify attributes of quadrilaterals** (e.g., parallel sides for the parallelogram, right angles for the rectangle, equal sides and right angles for the square).

Standard 3MG2.4 **Identify right angles in geometric figures or in appropriate objects and determine whether other angles are greater or less than a right angle.**

New Vocabulary

- parallel
- rectangle
- square
- parallelogram

GET READY to Learn

Teachers often write on a chalkboard. What shape is the board? How do you know?

Some quadrilaterals have **parallel** sides which means that the sides are the same distance apart.

KEY CONCEPT — Types of Quadrilaterals

rectangle	• opposite sides have the same length and are parallel • has 4 right angles	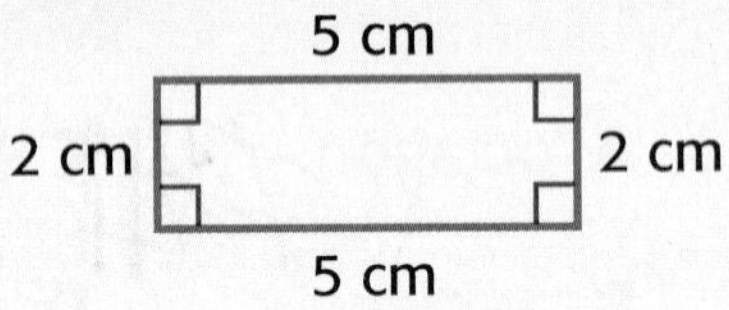
square	• 4 sides are the same length • opposites sides are parallel • has 4 right angles	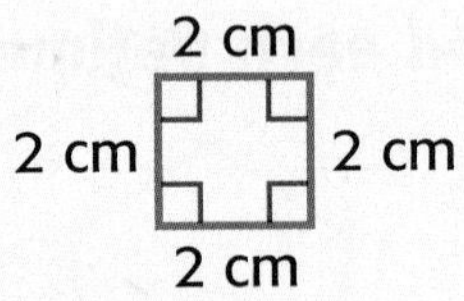
parallelogram	• opposite sides are the same length and are parallel	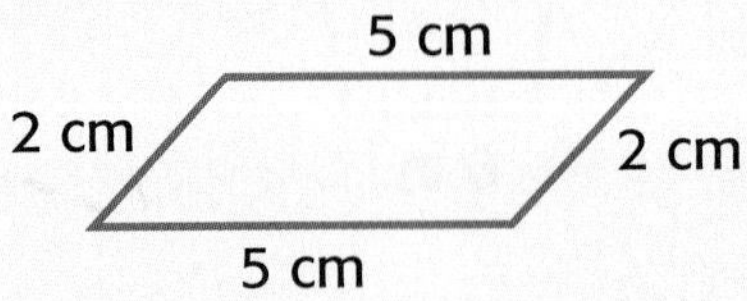

EXAMPLE Identify Quadrilaterals

1 **Identify each quadrilateral.**

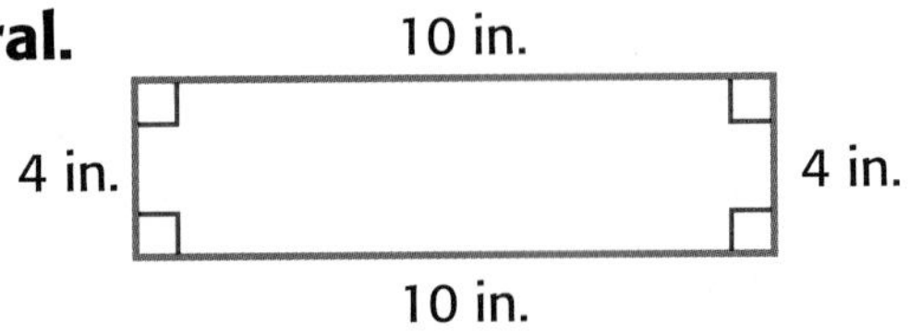

The quadrilateral has 4 right angles, opposite sides that are equal, and opposite sides that are parallel. So, it is a rectangle.

Angles in a quadrilateral can be right angles, less than a right angle, or greater than a right angle.

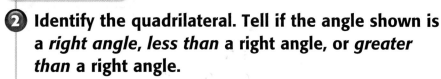

EXAMPLE Identify Angles

2 Identify the quadrilateral. Tell if the angle shown is a *right angle, less than* a right angle, or *greater than* a right angle.

This quadrilateral has opposite sides that are the same length and are parallel.

So, it is a parallelogram.

This angle is greater than a right angle.

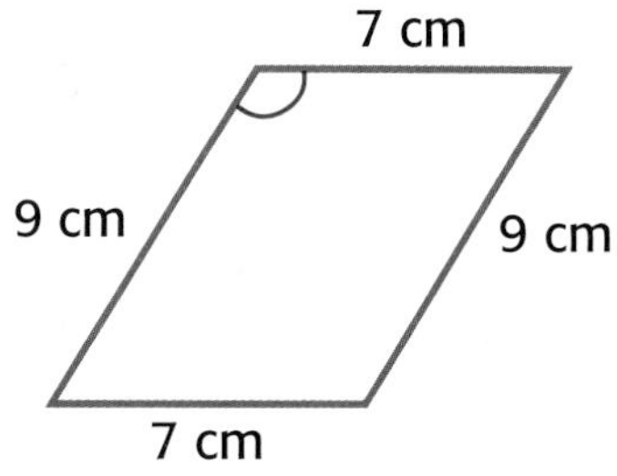

Online **Personal Tutor at** ca.gr3math.com

CHECK What You Know

Identify each quadrilateral. **See Example 1 (p. 438)**

1.

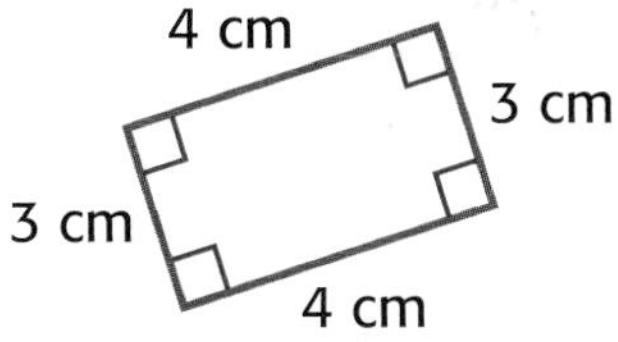

2.

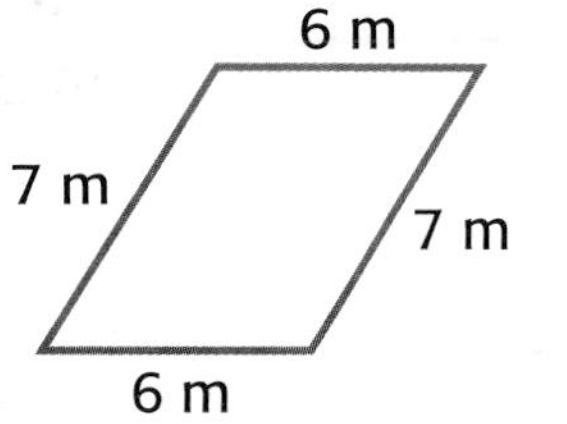

3.

Identify each quadrilateral. Tell if the angle shown is a *right angle, less than* a right angle, or *greater than* a right angle. **See Example 2 (p. 439)**

4.

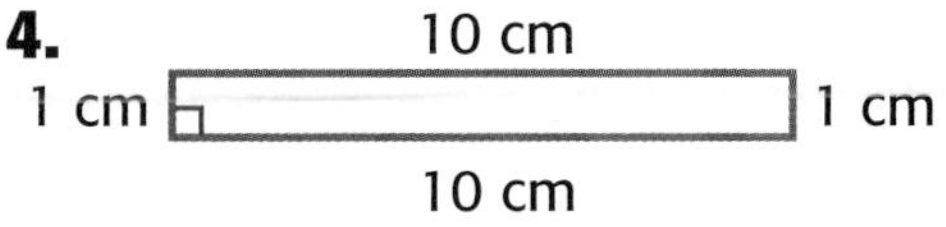

5.

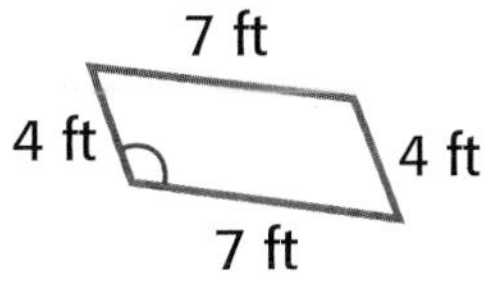

6.

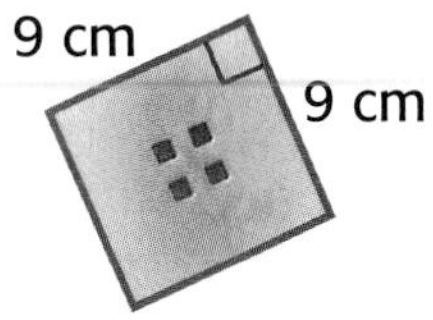

7. Kaila is thinking of a quadrilateral. Its opposite sides are parallel and the same length. There are 4 right angles. Which quadrilateral is Kaila thinking of?

8. Talk About It Describe how a rectangle is like a square. Describe how they are different.

Practice and Problem Solving

EXTRA PRACTICE
See page R28.

Identify each quadrilateral. See Example 1 (p. 438)

9.
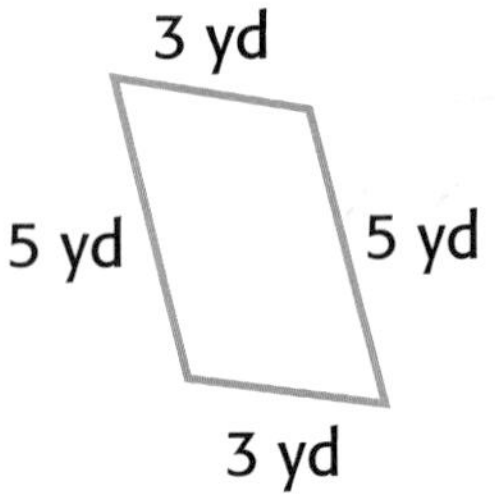

10.
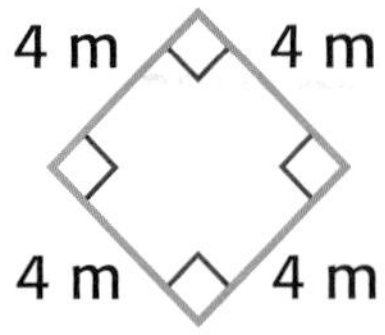

11.
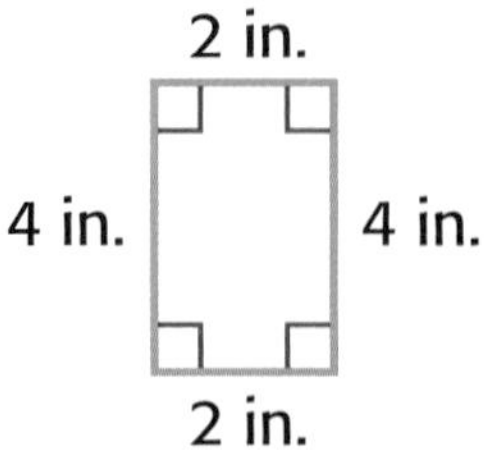

12.
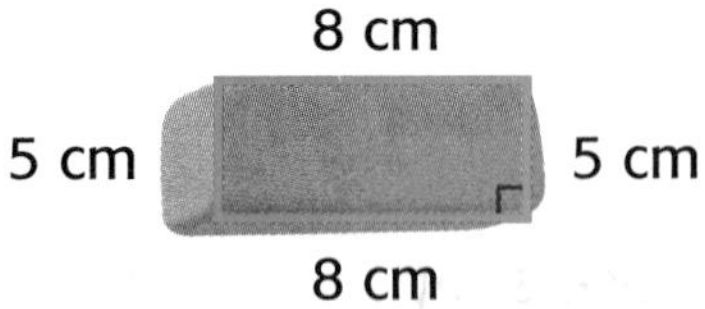

13.
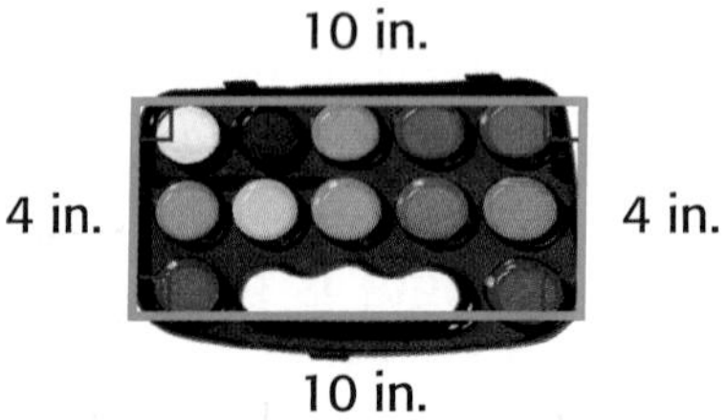

14.
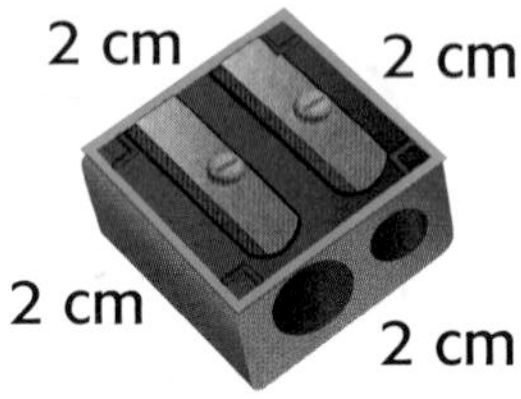

Identify each quadrilateral. Tell if the angle shown is a *right angle*, *less than* a right angle, or *greater than* a right angle. See Example 2 (p. 439)

15.
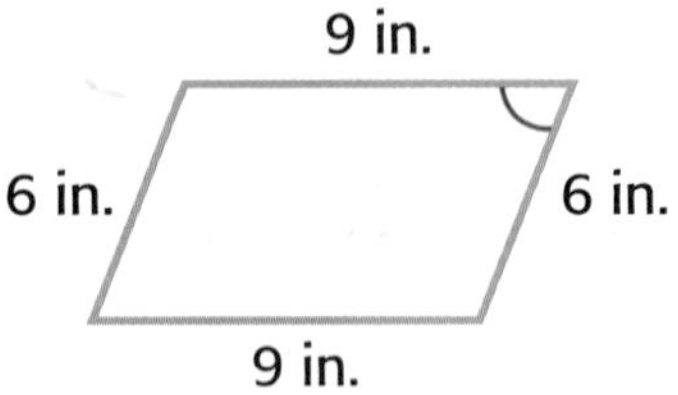

16.
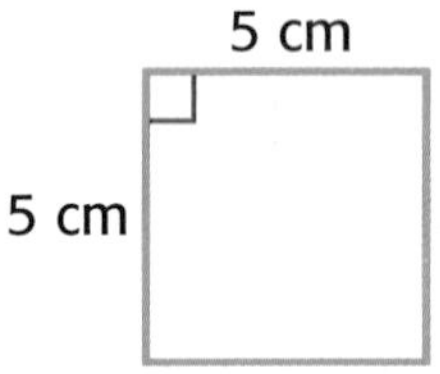

17.
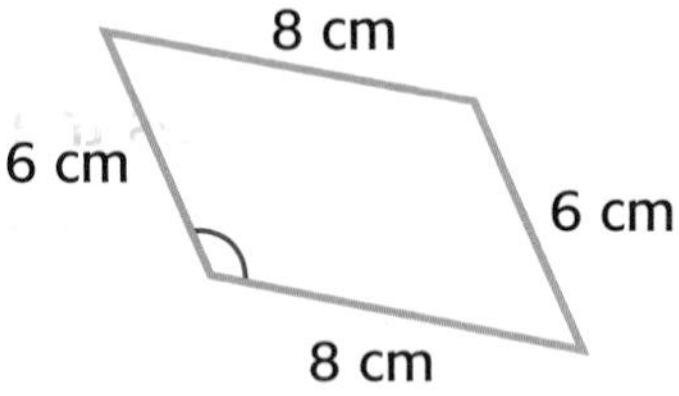

18.
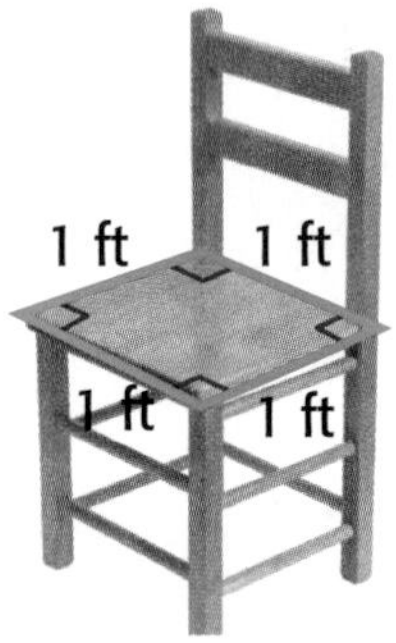

19.
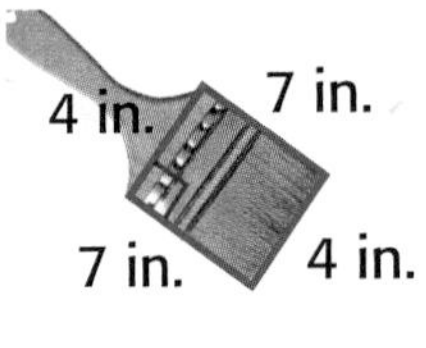

20.

Identify each quadrilateral described.

21. This figure has opposite sides that are parallel and 4 right angles. Two sides are longer than the other sides.

22. This figure has two pairs of parallel sides of the same length and no right angles.

23. Mrs. Samson measured a rug. Each side is 6 feet long. All of the corners are right angles. What is the shape of the rug?

24. Look at the previous exercise. If Mrs. Samson put 2 rugs side by side, what shape would the rug be now?

H.O.T. Problems

25. OPEN ENDED Draw and identify a quadrilateral that has 4 sides with 2 angles that are more than right angles.

CHALLENGE Look around and find an object for each shape.

26. square **27.** rectangle **28.** parallelogram

29. WRITING IN ▸MATH Describe how a parallelogram and a square are alike and how they are different.

Standards Practice

30 An equilateral triangle MUST have **(Lesson 10-5)**

A 4 sides the same length.

B 3 sides the same length.

C 2 sides the same length.

D No sides the same length.

31 Which of these shapes appears to be a rectangle? **(Lesson 10-6)**

F
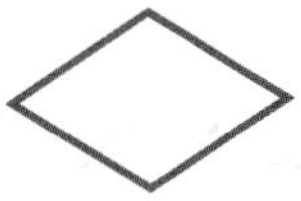

H

G

J

Spiral Review

Identify each triangle. Write *equilateral, isosceles,* or *scalene.* **(Lesson 10-5)**

33.
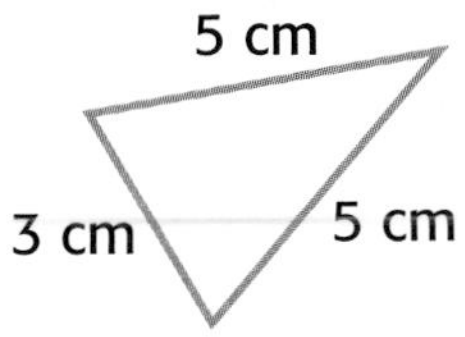

34.
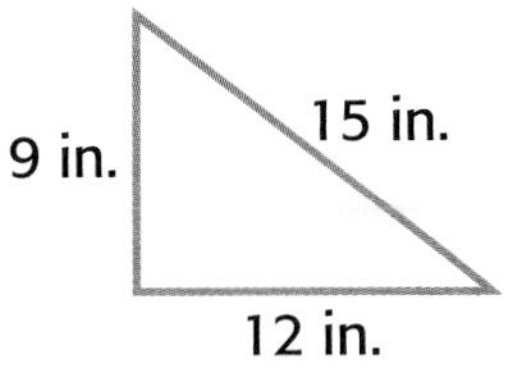

35.
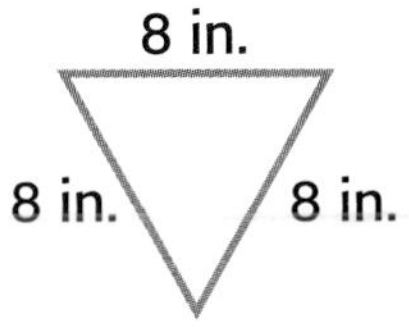

36. Benito's father is laying a new tile floor. Each tile is in the shape of a hexagon with a perimeter of 48 inches. What is the length of each of the sides of each tile? **(Lesson 10-4)**

Find each sum. **(Lesson 2-8)**

37. $\begin{array}{r} 957 \\ +\ 536 \\ \hline \end{array}$ **38.** $\begin{array}{r} \$8.27 \\ +\ \$7.99 \\ \hline \end{array}$ **39.** $\begin{array}{r} \$20.08 \\ +\ \$7.16 \\ \hline \end{array}$

40. Mrs. Garcia took her two children to the park. Each child bought a cup of lemonade for 45¢. How much did the lemonade cost in all? **(Lesson 2-3)**

10-7 Problem-Solving Investigation

MAIN IDEA I will choose the best strategy to solve a problem.

Standard 3MG1.2 **Estimate or determine the area** and volume **of solid figures by covering them with squares** or by counting the number of cubes that will fill them. Standard 3MR1.1 **Analyze problems by identifying relationships, distinguishing relevant from irrelevant information,** sequencing and prioritizing information, and observing patterns.

P.S.I. TEAM +

CASSANDRA: My family is making a sandbox. It has the shape of a rectangle with a width of 4 feet and a length of 6 feet. The plastic that goes under the sand costs $2 for each square foot.

YOUR MISSION: Determine if $50 will be enough to pay for the plastic.

Understand You know the length and width of the sandbox and the cost of the plastic per square foot. Find the total cost of the plastic.

Plan Draw a picture to help you solve the problem.

Solve The drawing shows that the area of the sandbox is 24 square feet. Multiply 24 square feet by $2 per square foot to find the total cost of the plastic.

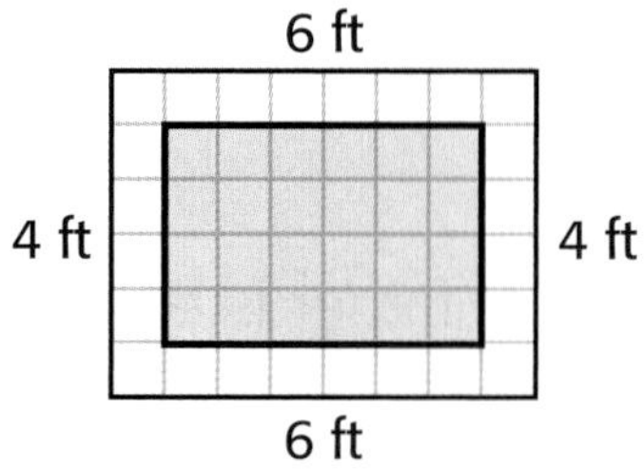

24 × $2 = $48 $48 is less than $50

So, $50 will be enough to pay for the plastic.

Check Look back at the problem. Use addition to check. $24 + $24 < $50. So, the answer is correct.

Mixed Problem Solving

EXTRA PRACTICE
See page R28.

Use any strategy shown below to solve. Tell what strategy you used.

PROBLEM-SOLVING STRATEGIES
- Choose an operation.
- Make a table.
- Guess and check.
- Work a simpler problem.

1. Min is reading a book. It has 75 pages. She reads 6 pages every day for 5 days starting on Sunday. After day 5, how many pages will she have left to read?

2. Ms. Dunn bought 6 sheets of plywood, a box of nails, and a hammer from the hardware store. How much did she spend?

3. Vic and Derrick went to the mall. They visited 14 stores on the first floor and 17 stores on the second floor. They went back to 4 of the same stores on the first floor. How many different stores did they visit?

4. Mr. Carson is measuring the length and width of his kitchen counter. Find the measurements for the missing lengths.

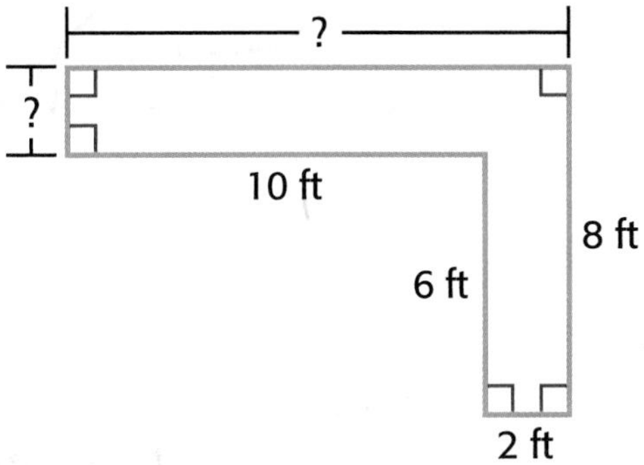

5. Three friends are fishing. Francisco caught 3 times as many fish as Haley. Haley caught 7 less fish than Petra. Petra caught 15 fish. How many did Francisco and Haley catch?

6. Angel is shooting baskets. She makes a basket every 6th shot. If she makes a total of 9 baskets, how many shots did she take?

7. Samantha and Edward need to pick 25 tomatoes from their garden. How many more tomatoes do they need to pick?

Vegetables Picked	
Samantha	**Edward**
18 tomatoes	13 peppers 2 cucumbers 4 tomatoes

8. WRITING IN MATH Three students drew a parallelogram. Each drew a different shape. Tell which shape each drew and explain why they are all parallelograms.

10-8 Geometry: Solid Figures

MAIN IDEA

I will identify, describe, and classify solid figures.

Standard 3MG2.5 Identify, describe, and classify common three-dimensional geometric objects (e.g., cube, rectangular solid, sphere, prism, pyramid, cone, cylinder).

New Vocabulary

- cube
- rectangular solid
- cone
- pyramid
- cylinder
- sphere

GET READY to Learn

We see all these objects around us everyday. They are not plane figures. They are solid figures.

A **solid figure** is a three-dimensional figure that has length, width, and height.

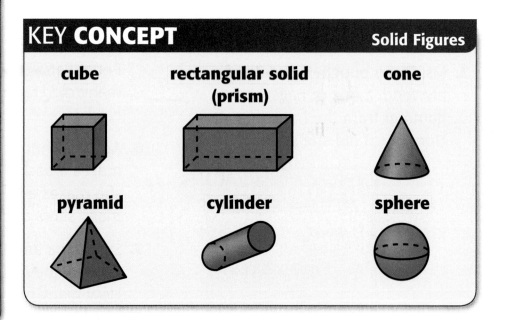

KEY CONCEPT — Solid Figures

cube

rectangular solid (prism)

cone

pyramid

cylinder

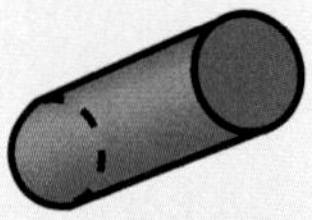

sphere

EXAMPLES Identify Solid Figures

Identify each solid figure.

1

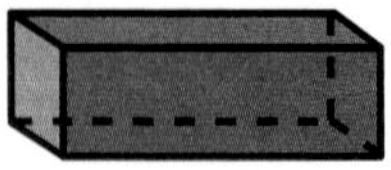

The figure is a rectangular solid.

2

A soup can looks like a cylinder.

Online Personal Tutor at ca.gr3math.com

CHECK What You Know

Identify each solid figure. See Examples 1 and 2 (p. 444)

1. 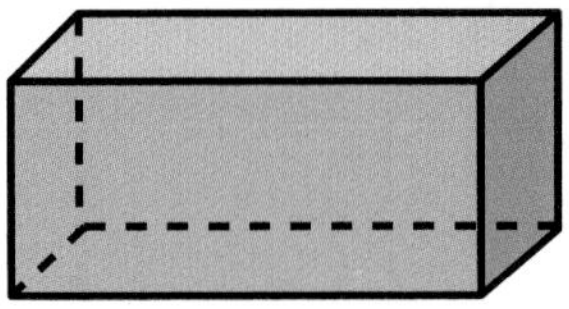

2. 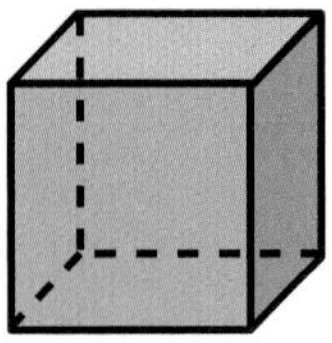

3. 

4. Carra and Ling are playing the drums. What solid figure do the drums represent?

5. What plane figure can be found on the drums?

6. Talk About It How are the solid figures of a cone and cylinder different? How are they alike?

Practice and Problem Solving

EXTRA PRACTICE See page R29.

Identify each solid figure. See Examples 1 and 2 (p. 444)

7. 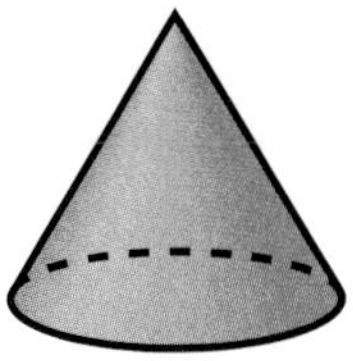

8. 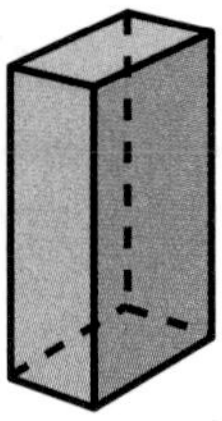

9. 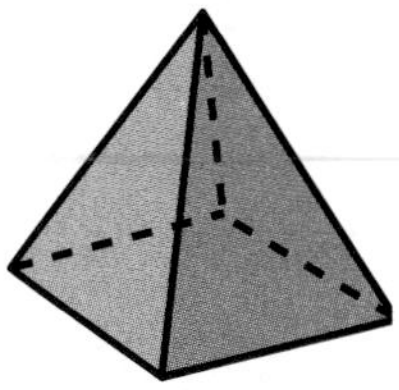

10. 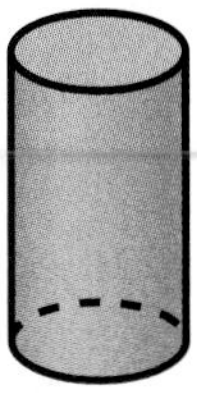

11. 

12. 

13. 

14. 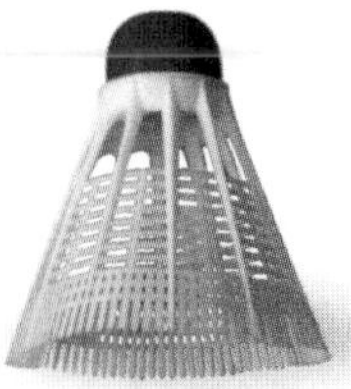

15. 

16. Taye bought a box of cereal. What solid figure is a box of cereal?

17. Max threw his basketball through the hoop. What solid figure is a basketball?

H.O.T. Problems

18. OPEN ENDED Name three real-world objects that resemble a cylinder.

REASONING **Find the total area of all of the sides of each figure.**

19. 

20. 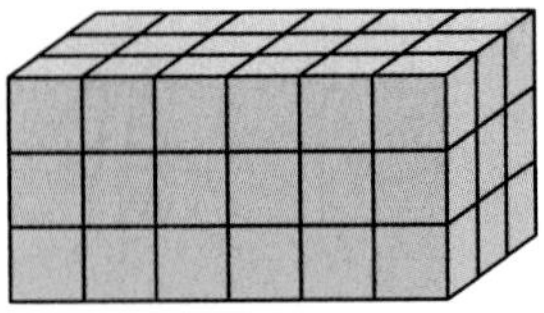

21. WRITING IN ▶MATH What do a cube, and a rectangular solid have in common?

Standards Practice

22 A room is in the shape of a rectangle. Two walls measure 10 feet each and another wall measures 6 feet. What is the length of the other wall? **(Lesson 10-7)**

A 6 feet　　**C** 10 feet

B 8 feet　　**D** 12 feet

23 Which of these is a cylinder? **(Lesson 10-8)**

F 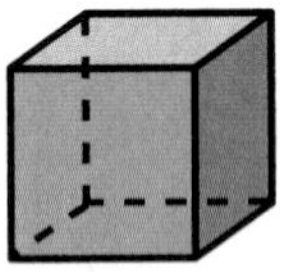

H 

G 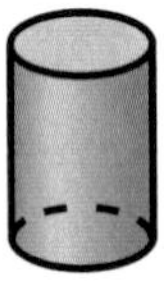

J 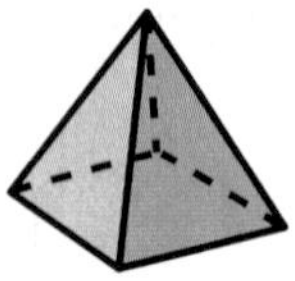

Spiral Review

Solve. **(Lesson 10-7)**

24. By the end of the game, the Wildcats had doubled their score, and the Cheetahs had increased their score by three points. What was the total number of points scored by the end of the game?

Inning	1	2	3	4	5	6	7	8	9
Wildcats	1	2	1						
Cheetahs	1	0	1						

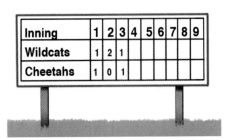

Identify each quadrilateral. **(Lesson 10-6)**

25. 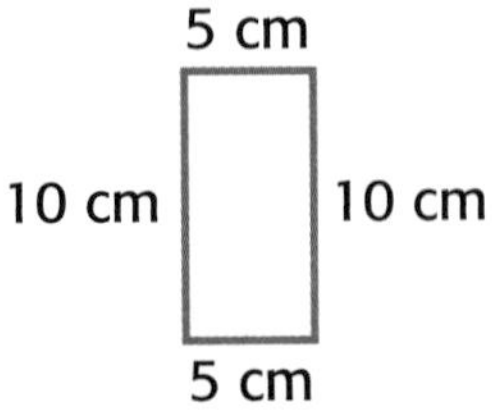

26. 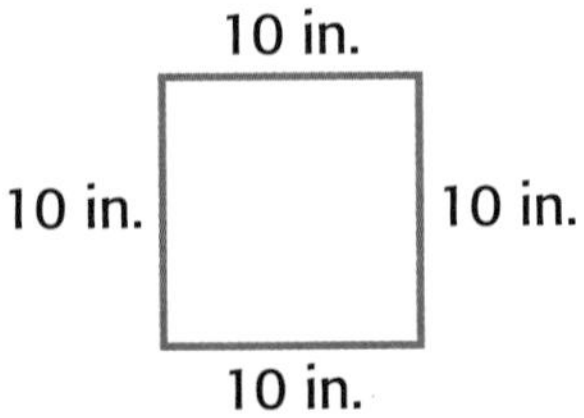

27. 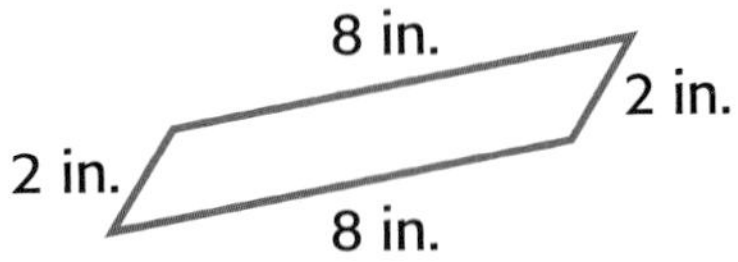

Guess the Shape

Identify Solid Figures

Get Ready!

Players: 2 players

You will need:
objects in the shape of solid figures, a shoe box

Get Set!

- Cut a hole in the box large enough for a hand to fit into it.
- Place the shapes into the box.

Go!

- Player 1 puts his or her hand in the box and chooses a figure without removing it.
- Player 1 names the figure and then removes it. If correct, he or she receives one point. If not correct, he or she places the figure back in the box.
- Player 2 takes a turn.
- Play continues until all shapes are gone.
- The player with the most points wins.

10-9 Complex Solid Figures

MAIN IDEA

I will identify common solid objects that make more complex solid objects.

Standard 3MG2.6 Identify common solid objects that are the components needed to make a more complex solid object.
3MR1.2 Determine when and how to break a problem into simpler parts.

GET READY to Learn

The snowman is made up of three different solid figures. What figures are used to make the snowman?

Many real-world objects are made by combining two or more solid figures.

Real-World EXAMPLES Complex Solid Figures

1 SNOWMAN What solid figures make the body, hat, and nose of the snowman above?

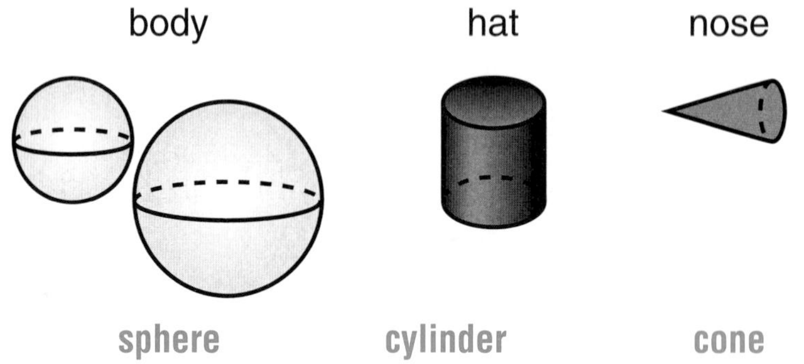

So, the snowman is made of spheres, a cylinder, and a cone.

2 TABLES What solid figures make the table?

The table legs are cylinders. The table top is a cylinder.

So, the table is made of cylinders.

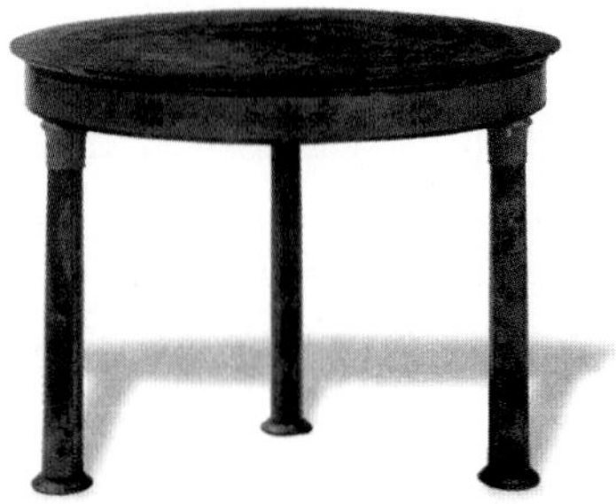

Online Personal Tutor at ca.gr3math.com

CHECK What You Know

Identify the figures that make each complex solid. See Examples 1 and 2 (p. 448)

1. 

2. 

3. 

4. Talk About It Name complex shapes you see in your classroom.

Practice and Problem Solving

Identify the figures that make each complex solid.
See Examples 1 and 2 (p. 448)

5. 

6. 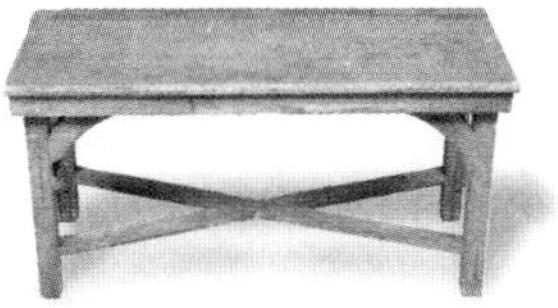

7. 

8. 

9. 

10. 

11. Celeste saw a barn and silo. Name two solid figures that were combined to make the barn and silo.

12. A play set is made of many different solid figures. Name two figures that make up this play set.

H.O.T. Problems

13. **OPEN ENDED** Give an example of a real-world object that is made up of complex solids.

14. **WRITING IN MATH** Write a description of a complex shape. Have a classmate figure out what the shape is.

GARDENS UNDER GLASS

There are three large gardens close to the United States Capitol building in Washington D.C. The Botanic Garden is right across the street. It has more than 4,000 kinds of plants. It also includes a conservatory.

This conservatory is amazing! It is made mostly of glass and aluminum. The conservatory is divided into 10 rooms.

Did You Know?

The Jungle Room is over 80 feet high and has a walkway that is 96 feet long!

Standard 3MG2.1 **Identify, describe, and classify polygons (including pentagons, hexagons, and octagons).**

Real-World Math

Use the diagram below to answer each question.

1. What is the shape of the east and west galleries?
2. Which room appears to have the greater perimeter, the Meditation Garden or the East Gallery?
3. The Jungle room has a perimeter of 384 feet. How much greater is the perimeter of the Jungle Room than a room with a perimeter of 84 feet?
4. Suppose the Oasis room was cut in half diagonally. What kind of triangles would this create?
5. What is the shape of the Meditation Garden and Children's Garden? What do you notice about these two rooms?

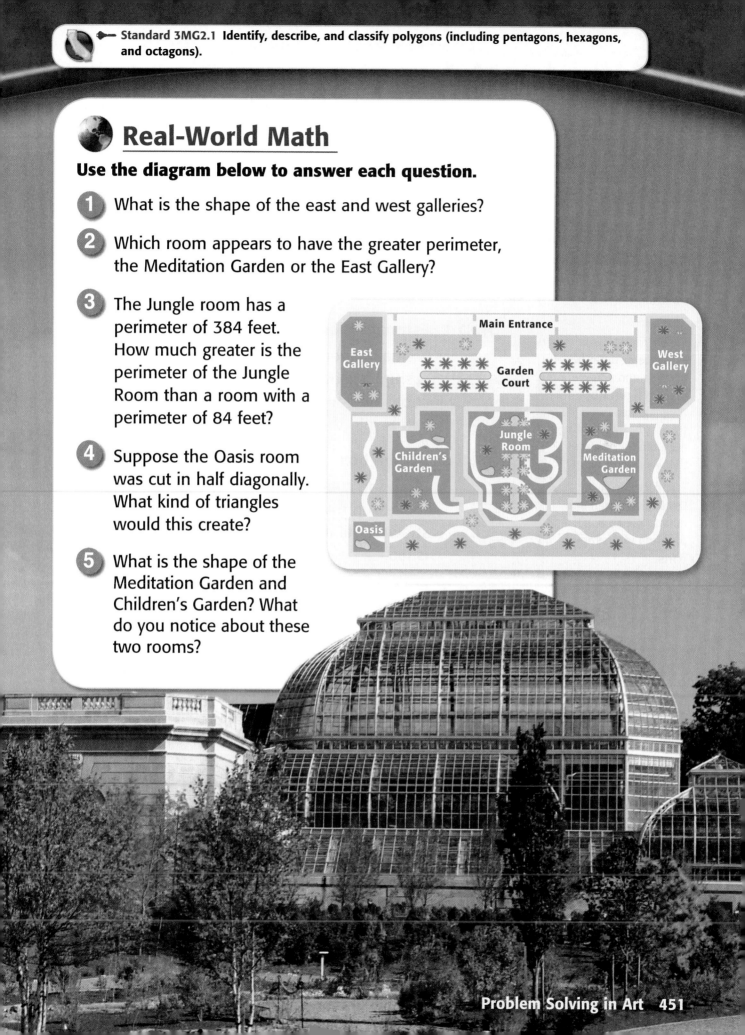

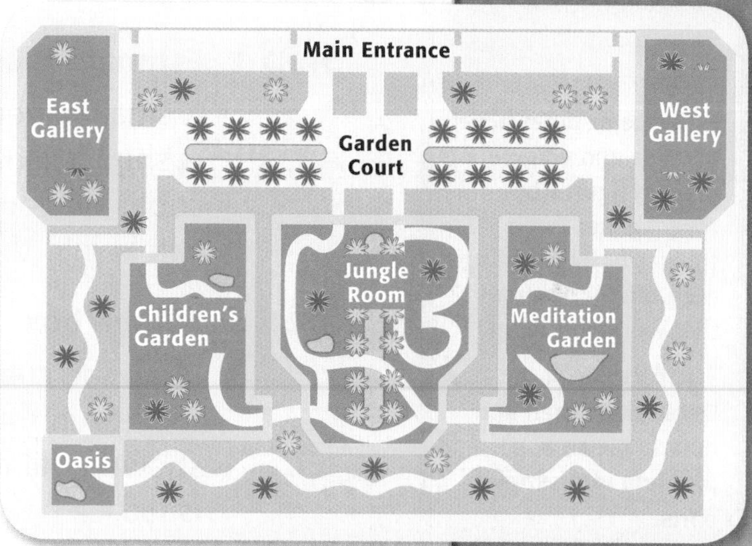

Explore

Measurement Activity for 10-10

Volume

MAIN IDEA

I will estimate volume.

Standard 3MG1.2 **Estimate or determine** the area and **volume of solid figures** by covering them with squares or **by counting the number of cubes that would fill them.**

Standard 3MR1.2 **Determine when and how to break a problem into simpler parts.**

You Will Need
cubes
small containers

New Vocabulary
volume
cubic unit

Concepts in Motion
Animation
ca.gr3math.com

Volume is the number of cubic units needed to fill a solid figure. Volume is measured in **cubic units**.

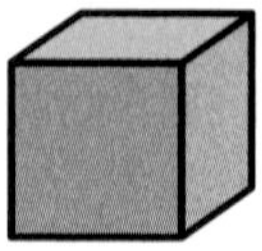

ACTIVITY

1 Estimate and determine volume.

Step 1 **Estimate the volume.**
A small paper clip box is shown. How many cubes do you think will fit into the box?

Step 2 **Fill the box.**
Place the cubes in the box in rows as shown until it is full.

Step 3 **Find the volume.**
Remove the cubes. Count to find how many filled the box. This is the volume. Compare this to your estimate.

Hands-On Activity

ACTIVITY

2 Estimate and determine volume.

Step 1 **Estimate the volume.**
Estimate the volume of the figure.

Step 2 **Build the solid.**
Use cubes to build the solid.

Step 3 **Find the volume.**
Count the number of cubes it took to build this solid. How does the actual volume compare to your estimate?

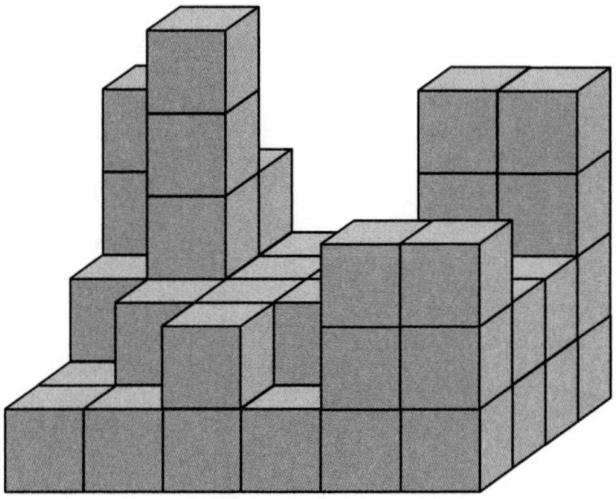

Think About It

1. Do solid figures with the same volume always have the same shape? Explain.
2. Can you use the same number of cubes to make different figures that have different volumes? Explain.
3. Do you think you can find the exact volume of a round object using cubes? Explain.

CHECK What You Know

Estimate the volume of each solid figure. Then use unit cubes to build the figure and find its exact volume.

4.

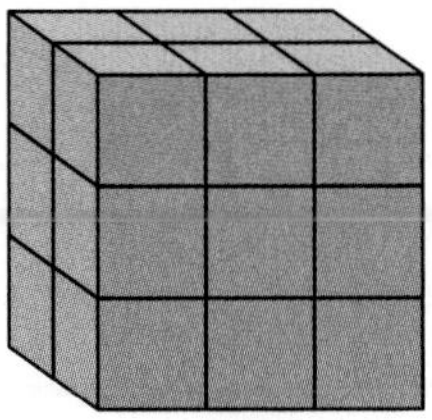

5.

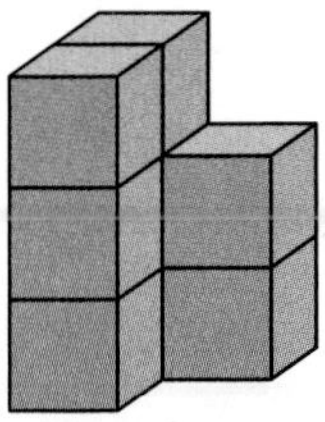

6.

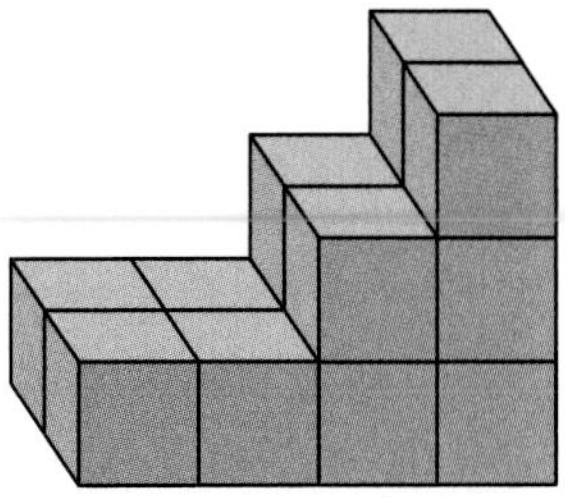

Build two different solid figures that have the same volume. Use unit cubes.

7. 12 cubic units **8.** 26 cubic units **9.** 30 cubic units

10. WRITING IN ►MATH Explain how objects that are different shapes and different sizes can have the same volume.

10-10 Measurement: Volume

MAIN IDEA

I will determine the volume of solid figures.

Standard 3MG1.2 Estimate or determine the area and **volume of solid figures** by covering them with squares or **by counting the number of cubes that would fill them.**

New Vocabulary

volume

cubic unit

GET READY to Learn

Jerome just finished cleaning his fish's aquarium. Now, he has to fill it back up with water. He is trying to determine how many cubic units of water will fill up the fish tank.

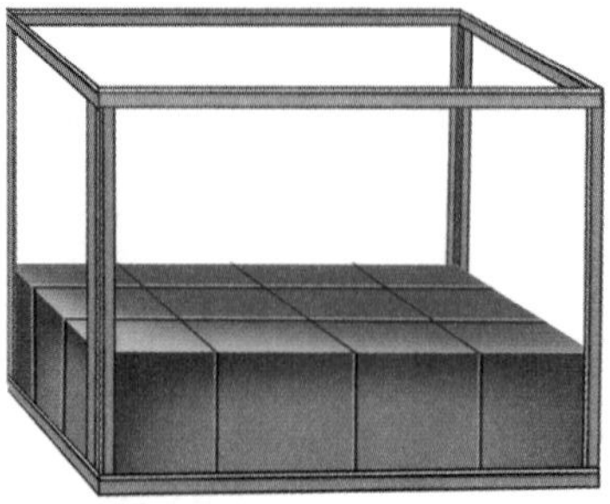

Volume is the number of unit cubes a solid figure holds. Volume is measured in **cubic units**.

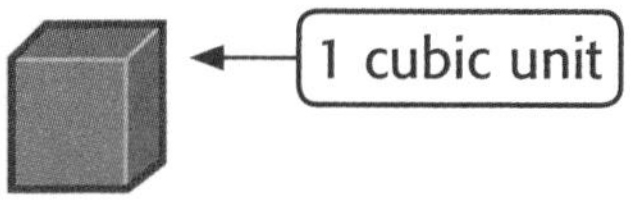

To find the volume of a solid figure, you can count the number of unit cubes needed to fill the solid.

Real-World EXAMPLE Find Volume

1. WATER **How many cubic units of water does the fish tank hold?**

There are 12 cubic units on each layer.

The aquarium will hold 3 layers of 12 cubic units. Add to find how many cubic units are needed.

12 + 12 + 12 = 36.

So, the aquarium holds 36 cubic units.

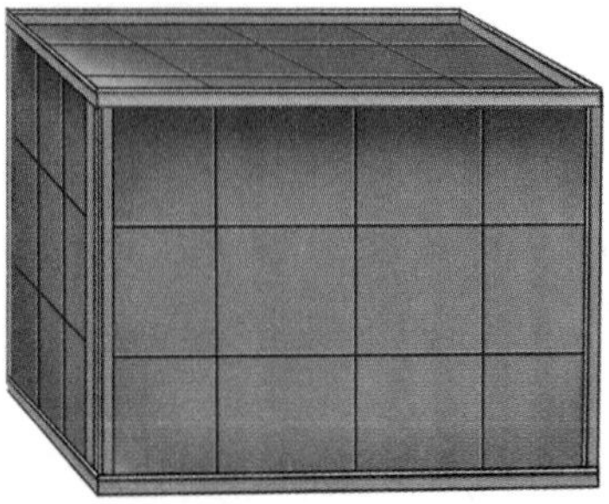

You can use what you know about volume to estimate the number of cubes that will fill a solid.

EXAMPLE **Find Volume**

2 Estimate the volume.

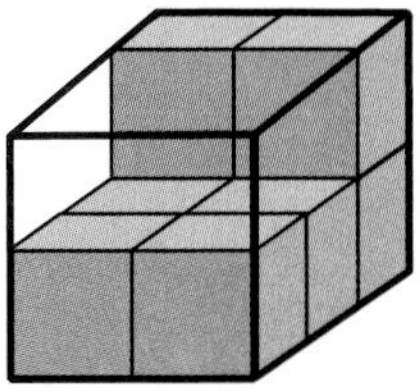

The bottom layer of the figure has a volume of 6 cubic units. The box has two layers.

So, the volume of the box is 12 cubic units.

Online **Personal Tutor at** ca.gr3math.com

CHECK What You Know

Find the volume of each solid figure. See Example 1 (p. 454)

1. 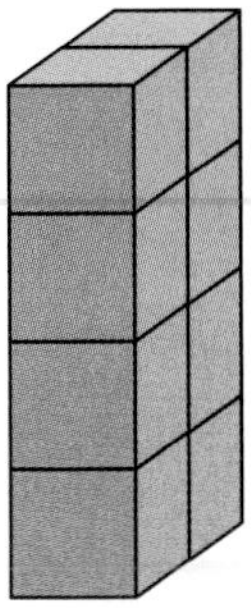

2. 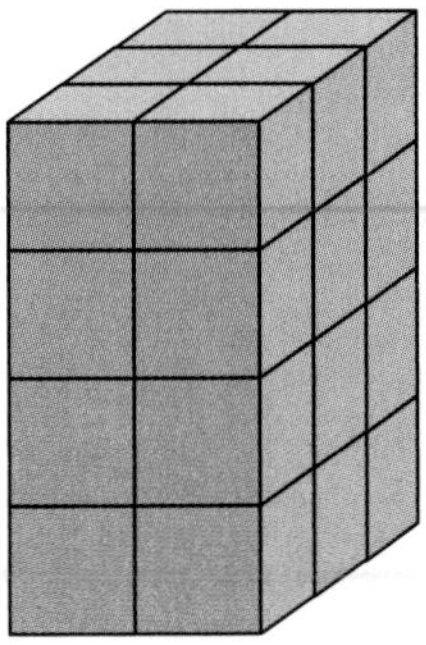

3. 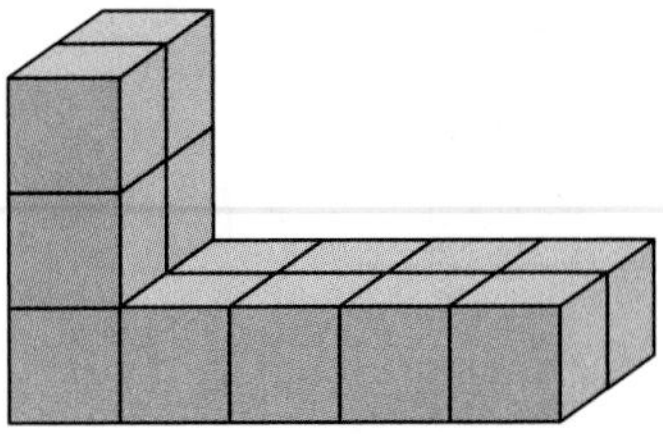

Estimate the volume. See Example 2 (p. 455)

4. 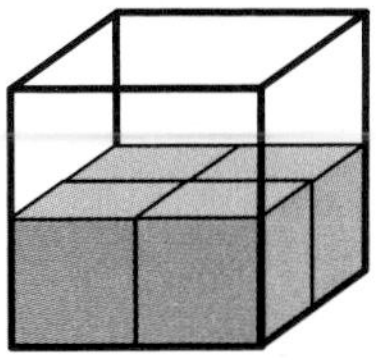

5. 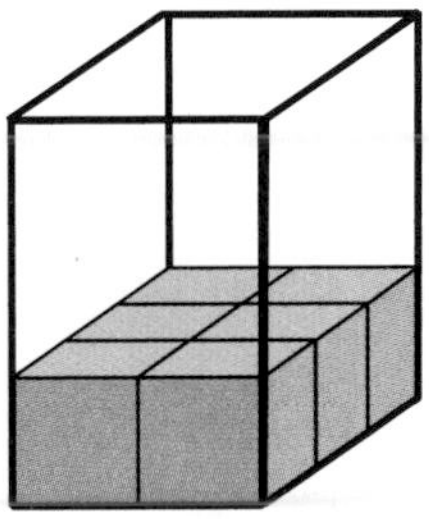

6. 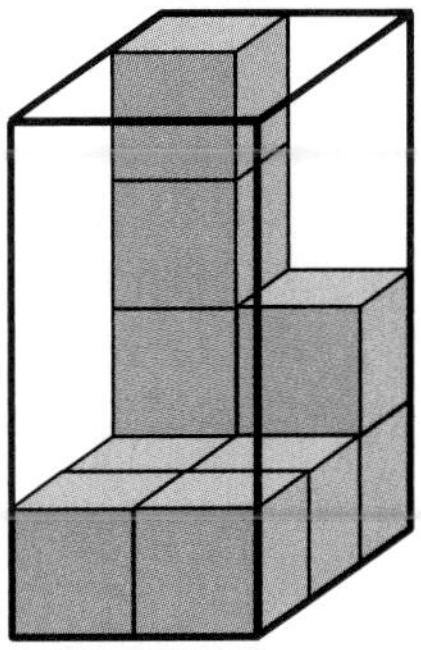

7. This gift has a volume of 16 cubic units. The length is 4 units, and the width is 2 units. What is the height of the gift? Use models if needed.

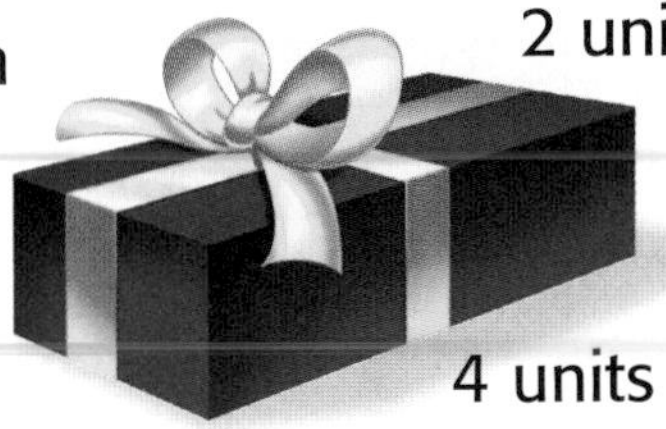

8. Talk About It If you know the volume of a solid figure, do you know its dimensions?

Practice and Problem Solving

EXTRA PRACTICE
See page R29.

Find the volume of each solid figure. See Example 1 (p. 454)

9.

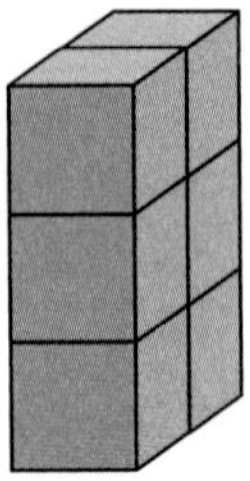

10.

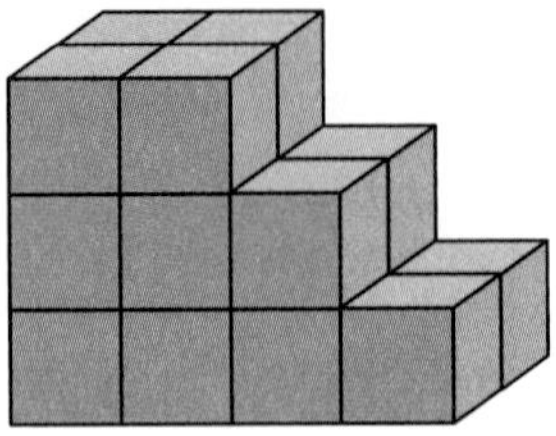

11.

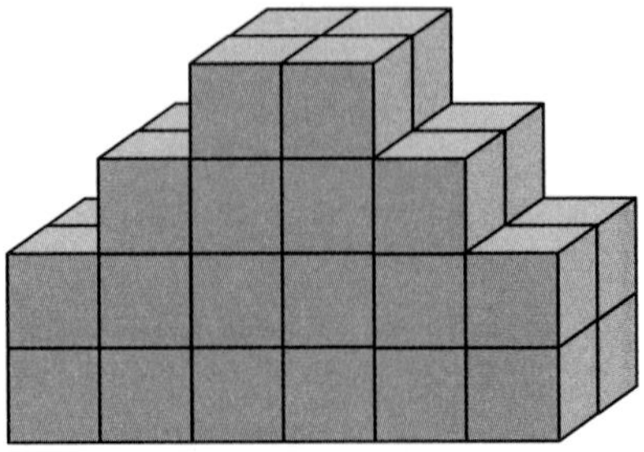

Estimate the volume. See Example 2 (p. 455)

12.

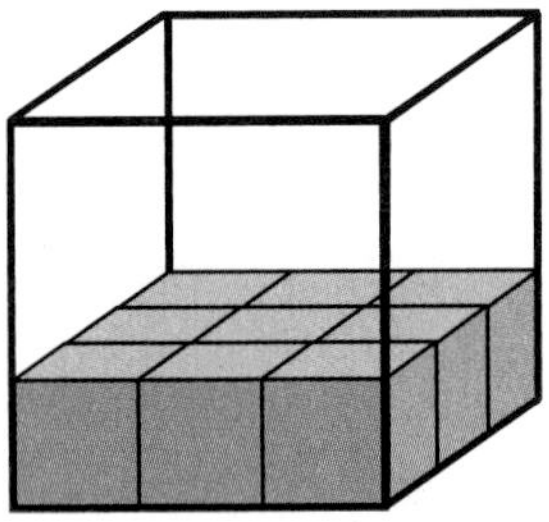

13.

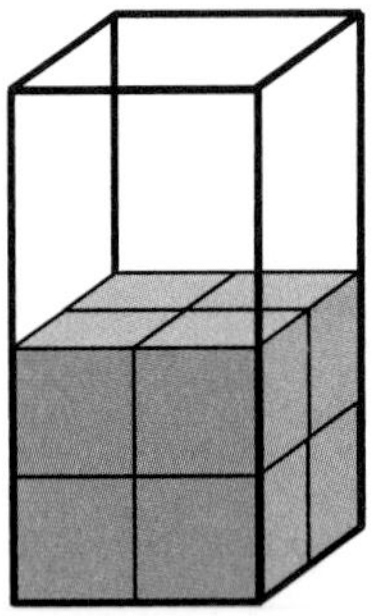

14.

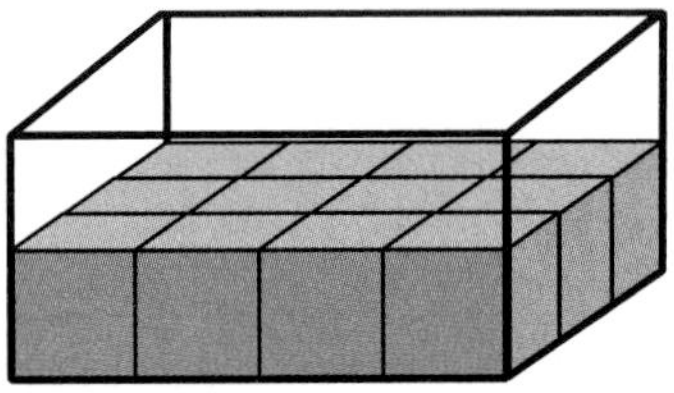

15.

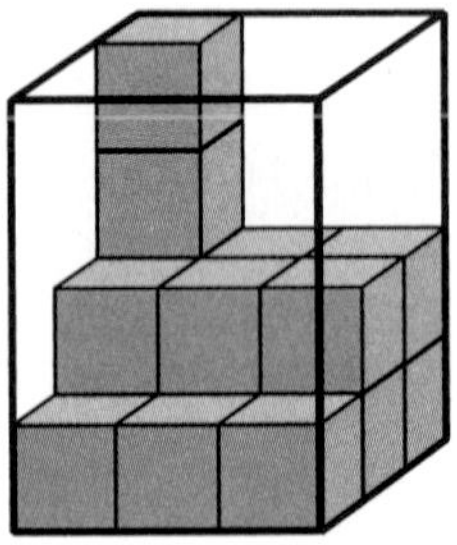

16.

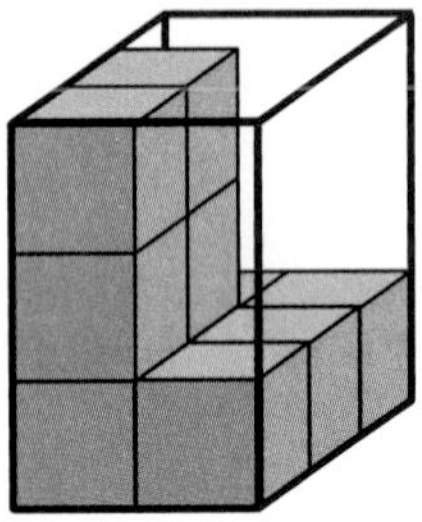

17.

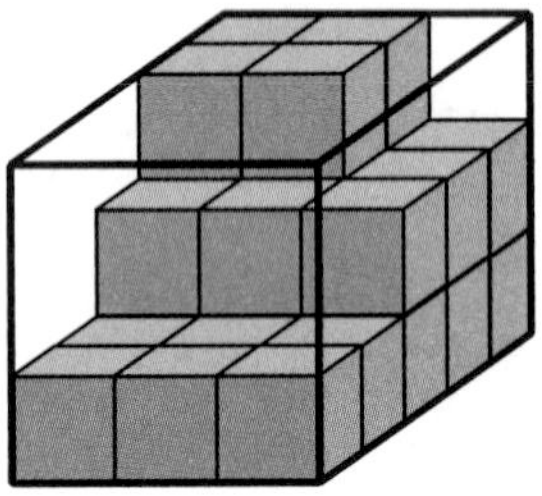

Solve. Use models.

18. Sara wants to know the volume of her music box. She filled it with cubes. It was 6 units long, 5 units high, and 4 units wide. What is the volume of Sara's music box?

19. A book is 8 units long, 6 units wide, and 1 unit high. Use a model to find the volume.

Copy and complete. Use unit cubes.

	Volume			
	Length	Width	Height	Units
20.	5	2	■	20
21.	2	6	3	■
22.	4	■	2	32

H.O.T. Problems

23. FIND THE ERROR Hunter and Jessica are making solid figures that have a volume of 6 cubic units. Whose figure is correct? Explain.

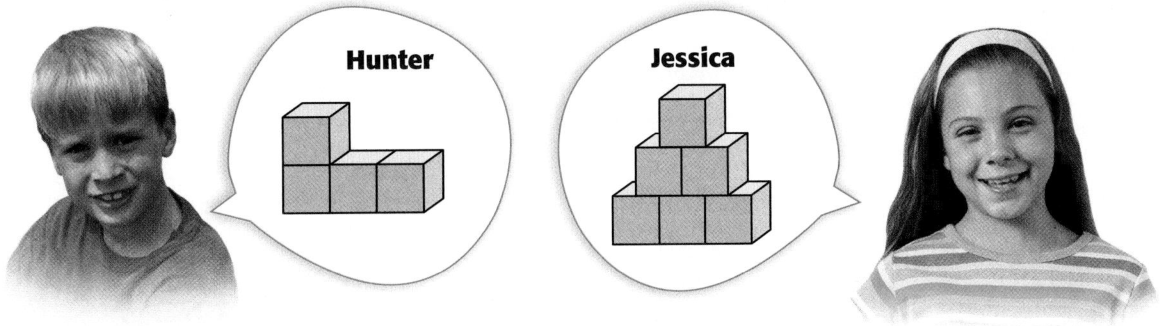

24. **WRITING IN ▸MATH** How are area and volume different?

Standards Practice

25 Which shapes make up this complex solid? **(Lesson 10-9)**

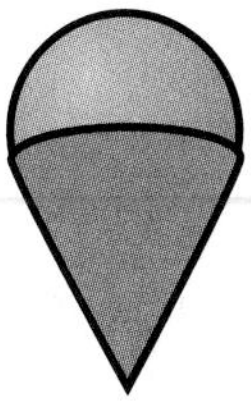

A triangle and circle

B cone and circle

C sphere and cone

D triangle, circle, and oval

26 Which of the figures below has a volume of less than 7 cubic units? **(Lesson 10-10)**

F 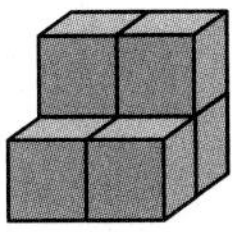

H 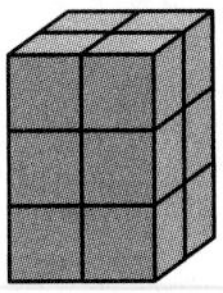

G 

J 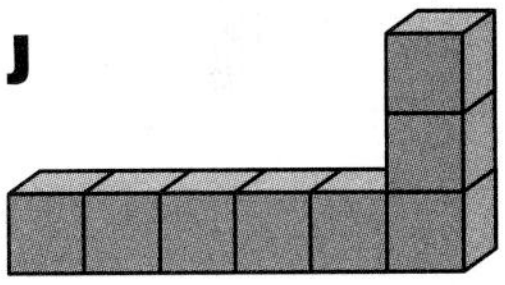

Spiral Review

27. Identify the figures that make the complex solid. **(Lesson 10-9)**

28. Identify the solid figure. **(Lesson 10-8)**

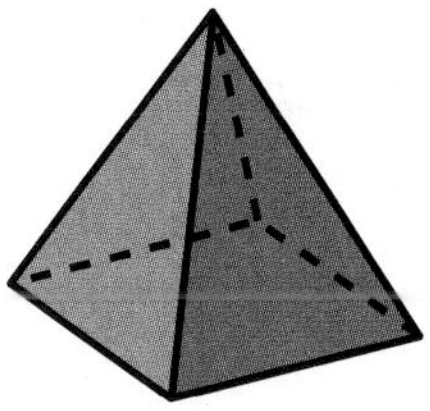

Choose one of the symbols +, −, × or ÷ to make the equation true. **(Lesson 7-8)**

29. $18 - 9 = 3$ ■ 6

30. $25 \div 5 = 10$ ■ 5

31. 3 ■ $3 = 81 \div 9$

Study Guide and Review

FOLDABLES™ Study Organizer GET READY to Study

Be sure the following Key Vocabulary words and Key Concepts are written in your Foldable.

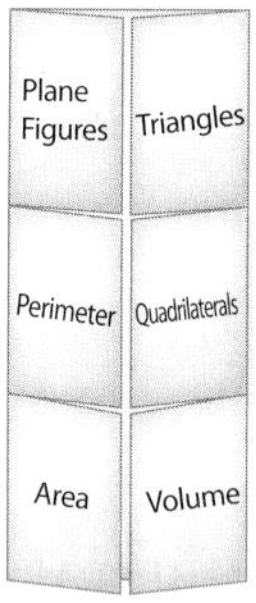

BIG Ideas

- A **polygon** is a closed plane figure that has three or more line segments. (p. 419)
- **Perimeter** is the distance around an object. (p. 422)

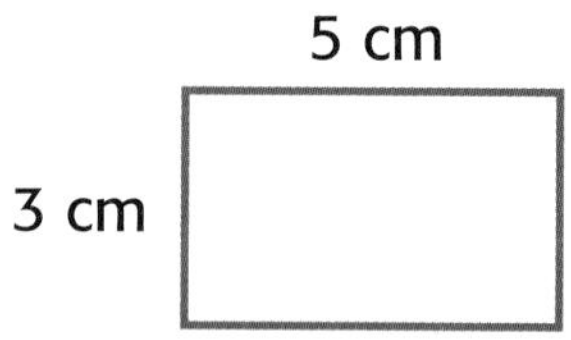

Perimeter = 5 + 5 + 3 + 3 or 16 cm.

- The **area** is the number of square units needed to cover a plane figure without overlapping. (p. 428)
- A **solid figure** is a figure that has length, width, and height. (p. 444)
- **Volume** is the number of unit cubes needed to fill a solid figure. (p. 454)

Key Vocabulary

area (p. 428)
perimeter (p. 422)
polygon (p. 419)
quadrilateral (p. 419)
solid figure (p. 444)
volume (p. 454)

Vocabulary Check

Choose the vocabulary word that completes each sentence.

1. The ___?___ of a polygon is the distance around its outside.

2. A closed plane figure with three or more line segments is called a ___?___.

3. A ___?___ is a four-sided polygon.

4. A cone is an example of a ___?___.

5. ___?___ is measured in cubic units.

6. If you wanted to put carpet in your bedroom, you would need to find the ___?___ of your bedroom floor.

Math Online Vocabulary Review at ca.gr3math.com

Lesson-by-Lesson Review

10-1 Geometry: Polygons (pp. 419–421)

Example 1
Name the polygon.

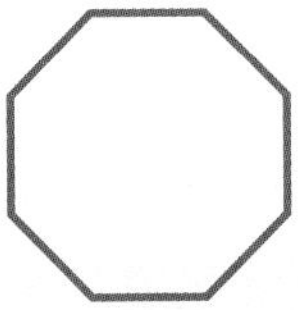

The figure has 8 sides and 8 angles. It is an octagon.

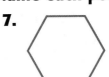

Name each polygon.

7. 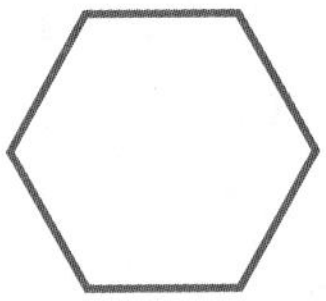

8. 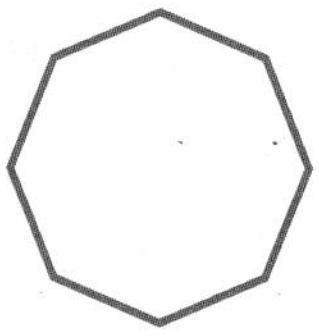

9. 

10. 

10-2 Measurement: Perimeter (pp. 422–425)

Example 2
Find the perimeter of the triangle.

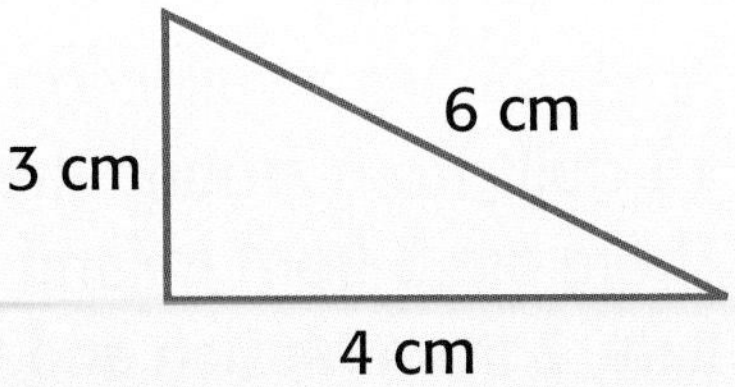

To find the perimeter add the length of the sides.

6 cm + 3 cm + 4 cm = 13 cm

So, the perimeter of this triangle is 13 centimeters

Find the perimeter of each figure.

11. 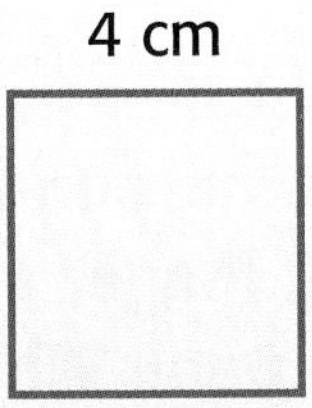

12. 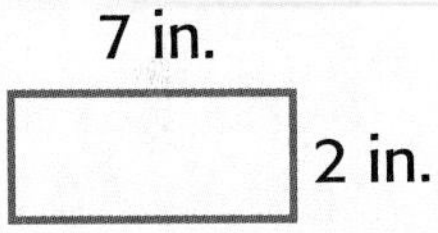

13. 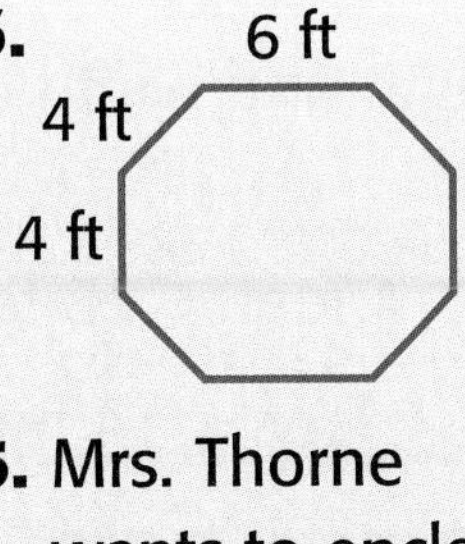

14. 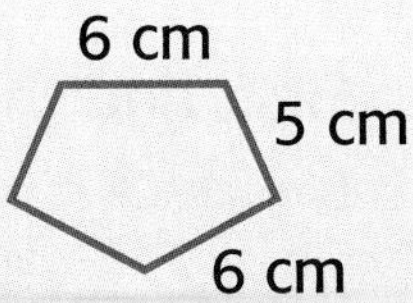

15. Mrs. Thorne wants to enclose part of her backyard. What is the perimeter of the area?

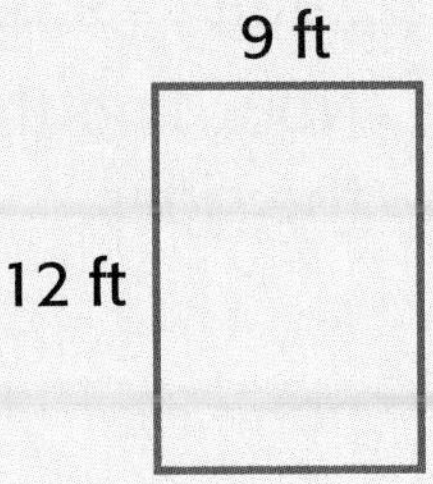

10-3 Measurement: Area (pp. 428–431)

Example 3
What is the area of the figure?

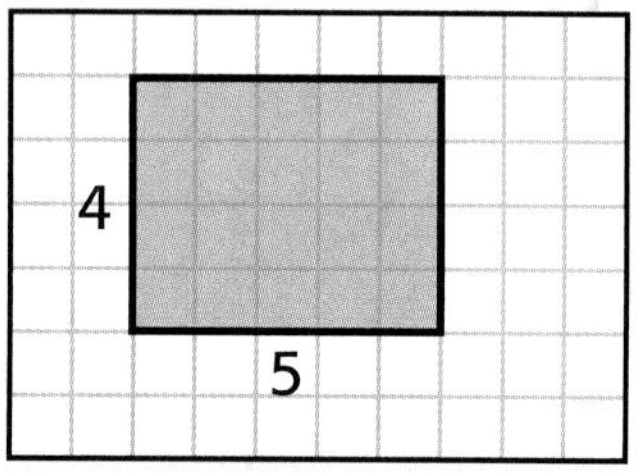

Count the number of squares the figure covers.

The figure covers 20 squares.

So, the area is 20 square units.

Find the area of each figure.

16.

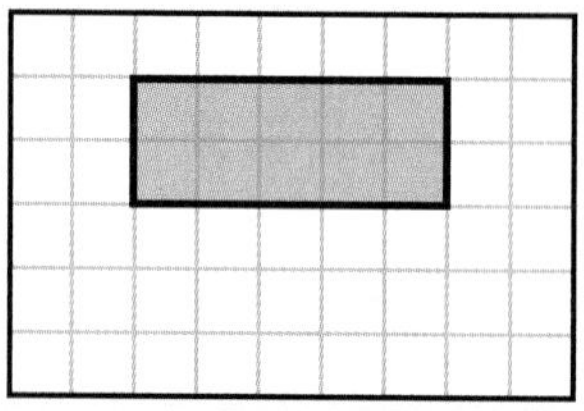

17.

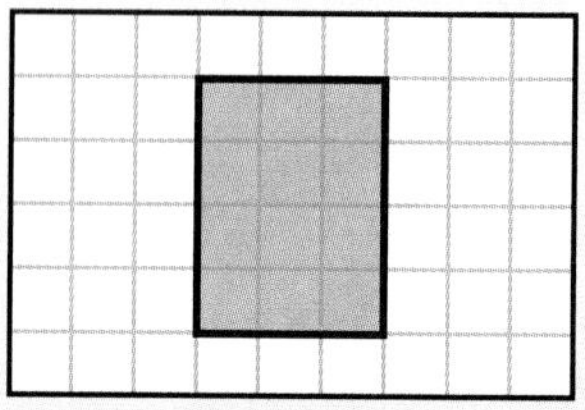

10-4 Problem-Solving Strategy: Solve a Simpler Problem (pp. 432–433)

Example 4
Berta has a pool that measures 14 feet by 10 feet. It is surrounded by a deck that is 4 feet longer and 4 feet wider than the pool. What is the perimeter of the deck?

First, find the length and width of the deck.

Length: 14 feet + 4 feet = 18 feet

Width: 10 feet + 4 feet = 14 feet

Now, find the perimeter by adding the sides.

So, 14 + 14 + 18 + 18 = 64. The perimeter of the deck is 64 feet.

Solve. Use the *solve a simpler problem* strategy.

18. Amanda has a collection of 14 dolls from around the world. There are 3 from Ireland, 2 from Italy, 2 from Mexico and the rest are from the Americas. How many are from the Americas?

19. Kiki walks her dog for 20 minutes each morning and 25 minutes each afternoon. On Saturday, she walks the dog 5 minutes less in the morning and 10 minutes longer in the afternoon. How long does she walk the dog on Saturday?

10-5 Triangles and Angles (pp. 434–436)

Example 5
Identify the triangle. Tell if the angle shown is a *right angle, less than* a right angle, or *greater than* a right angle.

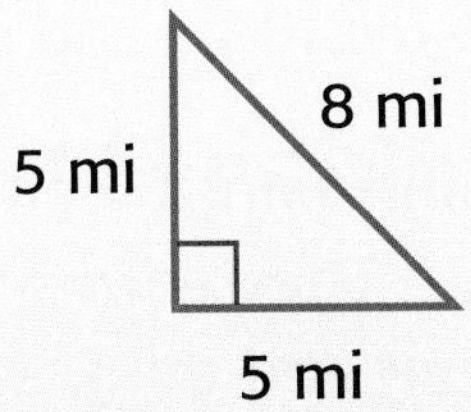

Two sides are equal. So, the triangle is isosceles.

The angle forms a square corner. So, the angle is a right angle.

Identify each triangle. Write *equilateral, isosceles,* or *scalene.*

20.

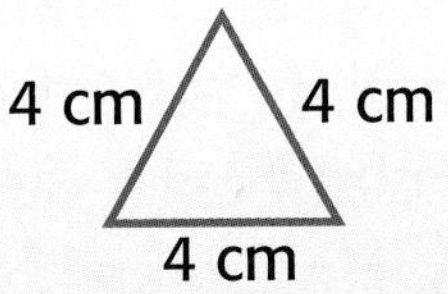

21.

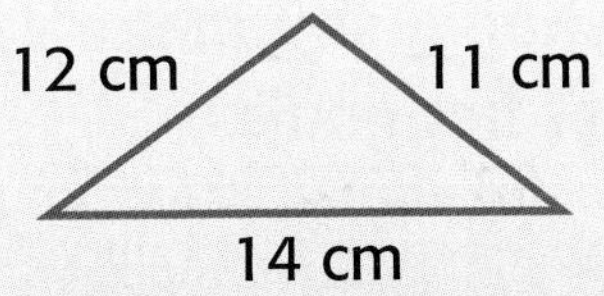

22. Identify the triangle. Tell whether the angle is a *right angle, less than* a right angle, or *greater than* a right angle.

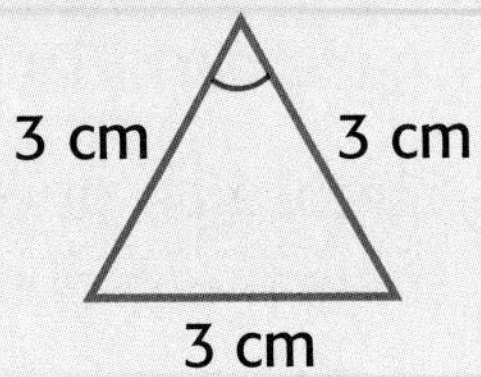

10-6 Quadrilaterals (pp. 438–441)

Example 6
Identify the quadrilateral. Tell if each angle shown is a *right angle, less than* a right angle, or *greater than* a right angle.

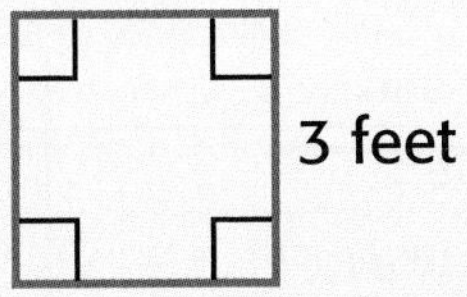

The quadrilateral has 4 right angles, 4 equal sides, and its opposite sides are parallel. So, it is a square.

Identify each quadrilateral. Tell if the angle marked is *a right angle, less than* a right angle, or *greater than* a right angle.

23.

24.

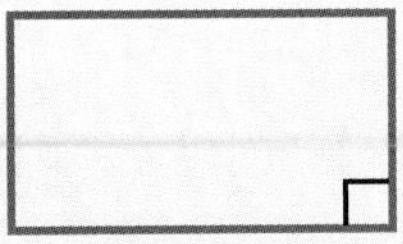

25.

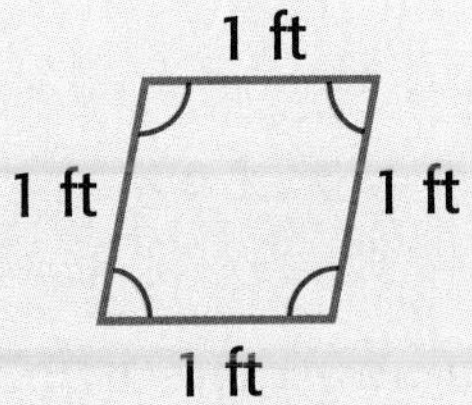

10-7 Problem-Solving Investigation: Choose a Strategy (pp. 442–443)

Example 7

Kiwi's goal is to make 42 bracelets. She has already made 7 bracelets. She plans on making an equal number of bracelets each day for the next 5 days. How many bracelets should she make each day to meet her goal?

Understand You know how many bracelets Kiwi wants to make, and how many she has already made. Find how many bracelets need to be made each day.

Plan Choose an operation to solve the problem.

Solve First, subtract the number of bracelets already made from 42.

$42 - 7 = 35$

Then divide by the number of days.

$35 \div 5 = 7$.

She needs to make 7 bracelets each day.

Check Work backward to check.

$5 \times 7 = 35$

and $35 + 7 = 42$.

The solution is correct.

Solve.

26. Ricco scored 5 points higher than Bruno on the spelling test. Leroy scored 76, which was 2 points lower than Bruno. How many points did Ricco and Bruno score?

27. Jada and James went to the movies. They each ordered a popcorn and drink. James paid for all the items. If he gave the cashier $20, how much change should he receive?

Item	Cost
Popcorn	$4
Drink	$3

28. A group of dancers wants to stomp on every 24th beat of the song. On which beats will they stomp in the first 120 beats of the song?

29. Tarie bought 3 items from the school store. She spent $1.50. What 3 items did she buy?

Item	Cost
Pencil	10¢
Pen	25¢
Eraser	35¢
Notebook paper	95¢
Bookmark	45¢
Pencil sharpener	85¢

10-8 Geometry: Solid Figures (pp. 444–446)

Example 8
Identify the solid figure.

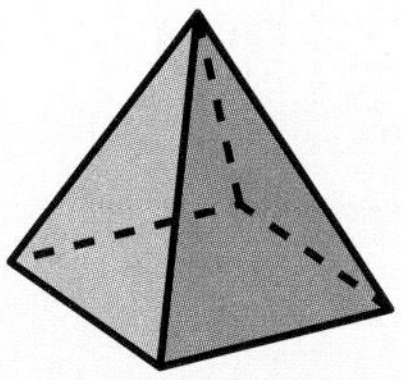

The figure is a square pyramid. The base gives the solid figure its name.

Identify each solid figure.

30. 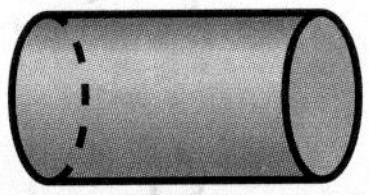

31. 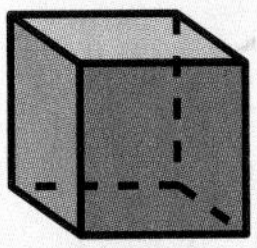

32. 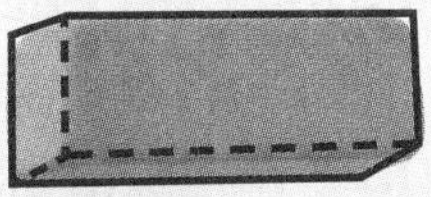

33. 

34. Scott and Trent are playing basketball. What type of a solid figure is a basketball?

10-9 Complex Solid Figures (pp. 448–449)

Example 9
Identify the figures used to make the complex solid shown below.

The ice cream cone is made of a cone and a sphere.

Identify each solid figure.

35. 

36. 

37. Michelle and her sister are playing in their tree house. Identify 2 solid figures that could be used to make a tree house.

10-10 Measurement: Volume (pp. 454–457)

Example 10
Find the volume of the solid figure shown below.

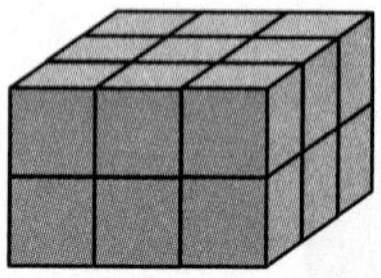

There are 9 cubic units on each layer. There are 2 layers of cubic units. Add the cubic units to find the volume.

$9 + 9 = 18$

The volume of the solid figure is 18 cubic units.

Example 11
Estimate the volume of the solid figure.

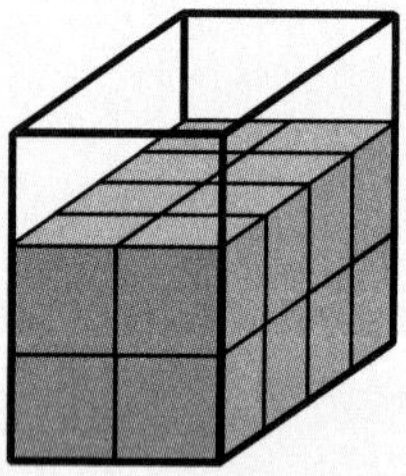

The bottom layer of the figure is 4 units by 2 units. Its volume is about 8 cubic units.
There will be 3 layers.

$8 + 8 + 8$ or 24

So, the volume is 24 cubic units.

Find the volume of each solid figure.

38. 

39. 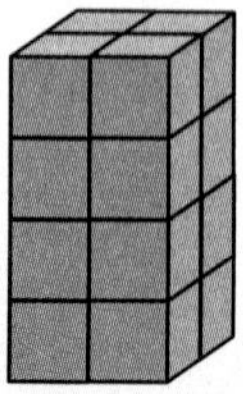

40. 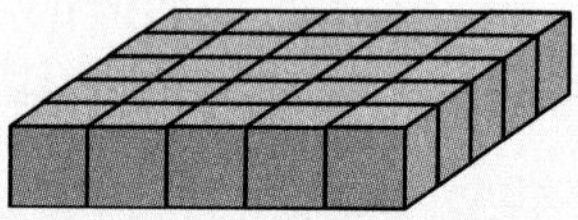

Estimate the volume.

41. 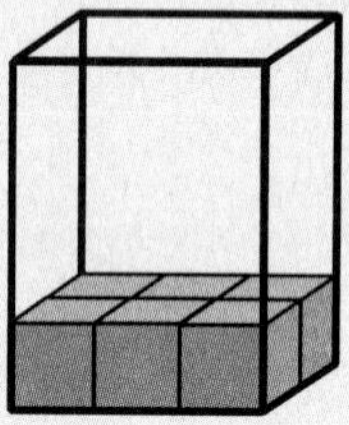

42. 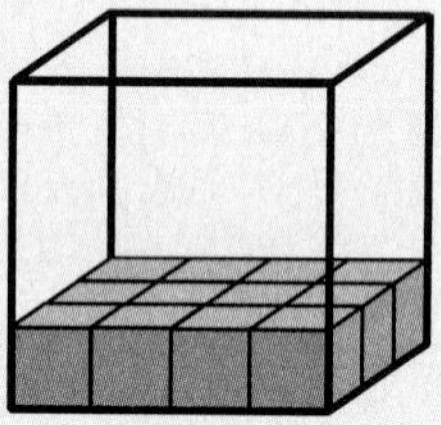

Solve. Use unit cubes.

43. Theresa wants to find the volume of her pencil box. She fills it with cubes. It is 7 cubes long, 5 cubes high, and 3 cubes wide. What is the volume of Theresa's pencil box?

44. Mark made a rectangular solid with a volume of 24 cubic units. If its width is 4 units and its height is 2 units, what is it's length?

CHAPTER 10

Chapter Test

Classify each polygon.

1. 

2. 

3. **STANDARDS PRACTICE** Nick bought the home base shown. Which geometric figure best represents the home base?

A triangle
B quadrilateral
C pentagon
D hexagon

Find the perimeter of each figure.

4. 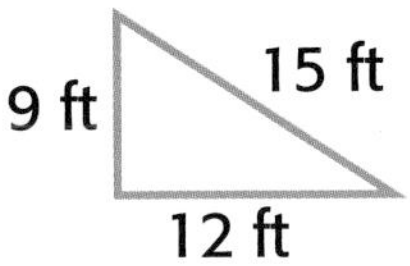

5. 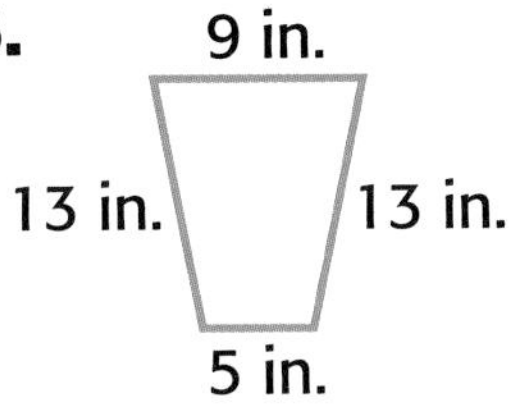

6. The diagram shows the shape of a room. What is the area?

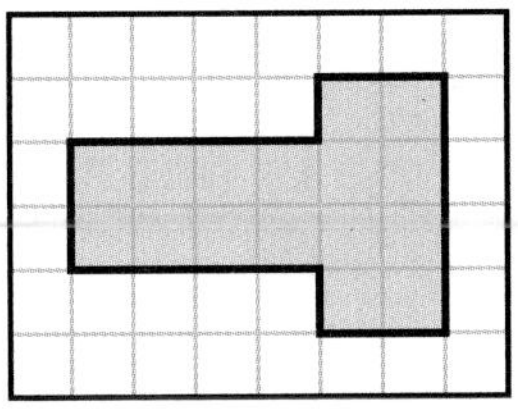

7. Gabriella walks 7 blocks to her friend's house, 3 blocks to the library, and then 5 blocks to the post office. If she takes the same path home, how many blocks will she walk in all?

Identify the triangle. Tell if the angle shown is a *right angle, less than,* or *greater than* a right angle.

8. 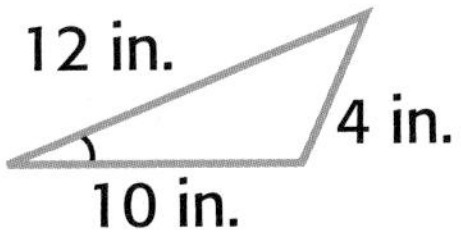

9. 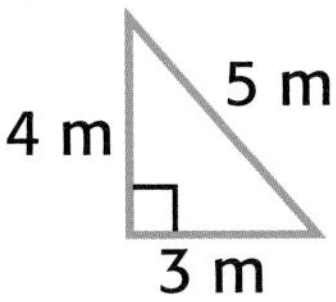

10. Collin is flying a kite. What type of polygon is this kite?

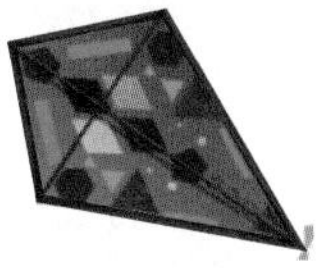

11. **STANDARDS PRACTICE** Which figure contains a sphere and a cone?

F 

H 

G 

J 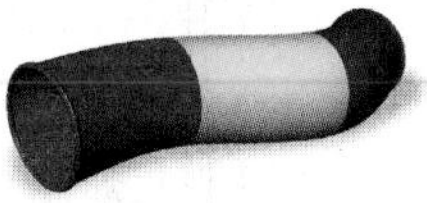

Estimate the volume of each solid figure. Then find the volume.

12. 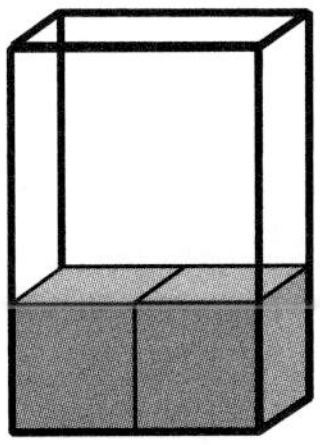

13. 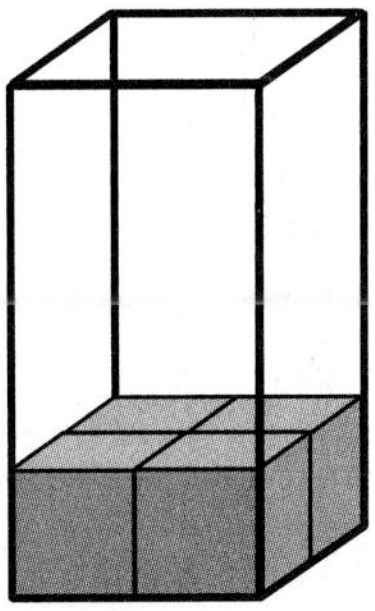

14. **WRITING IN ▸MATH** Can you find the perimeter of your desk if you know the measure of the length and width? Explain your reasoning.

CHAPTER 10

California Standards Practice

Cumulative, Chapters 1–10

Standards Example

Beth drew a shape that has 8 sides and 8 angles. What shape did she draw?

A right triangle

B trapezoid

C pentagon

D octagon

Read the Question

You need to use the description to identify the shape.

Solve the Question

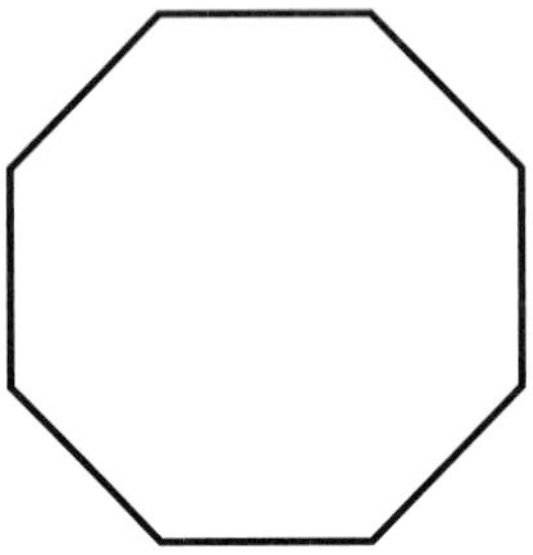

The shape has 8 sides and 8 angles.

So, the shape is an octagon.

So, the answer is D.

Online Personal Tutor at ca.gr3math.com

Choose the best answer.

1 **Which shape is a pentagon?**

A 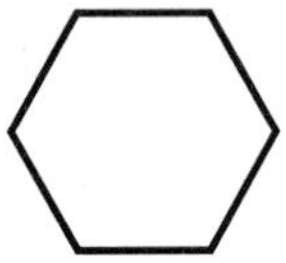

B 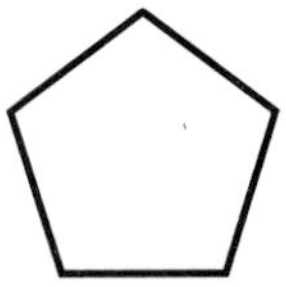

C 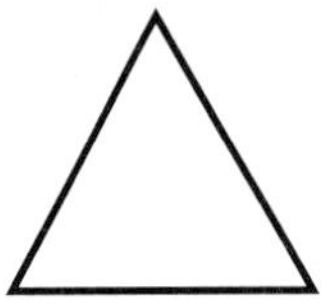

D 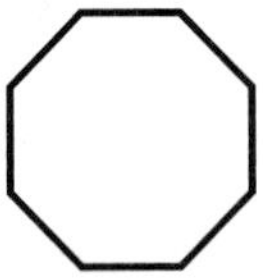

2 **Which shape is not a parallelogram?**

F 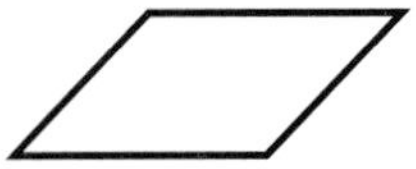

G 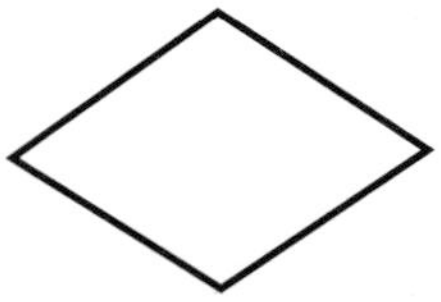

H 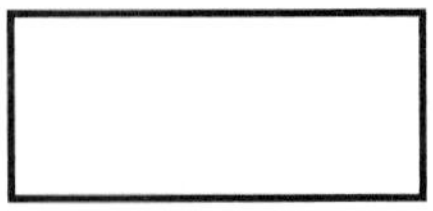

J 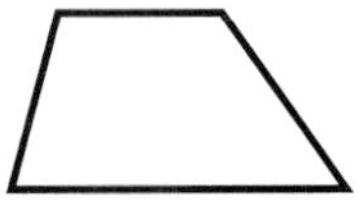

More California Standards Practice
For practice by standard, see pages CA1–CA39.

3 **What is the perimeter of a house that measures 34 feet long and 24 feet wide?**

A 58 feet
B 82 feet
C 92 feet
D 116 feet

4 **What is the best estimate for the volume of the figure below?**

F 11 cubic units
G 30 cubic units
H 36 cubic units
J 40 cubic units

5 **A rectangular horse stable has a perimeter of 176 feet. If one side measures 63 feet, what is the length of the other 3 walls?**

A 25 feet, 25 feet, and 25 feet
B 25 feet, 25 feet, and 63 feet
C 25 feet, 63 feet, and 63 feet
D 63 feet, 63 feet, and 63 feet

6 **Which object looks like a sphere?**

F 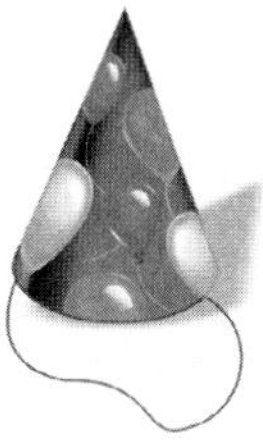

H 

G 

J 

7 **Soccer practice starts at 4:00 P.M. and ends 90 minutes later. What time does soccer practice end?**

A 5:00 P.M.
B 5:30 P.M.
C 6:00 P.M.
D 6:30 P.M.

8 **What is the area of a rectangle that is 4 units long and 3 units wide?**

F 7 square units
G 8 square units
H 12 square units
J 15 square units

CHAPTER 11 Statistics: Data, Graphs, and Probability

BIG Idea What is Data?

Data is information collected from a survey or experiment.

Example The **line plot** shows the number of floors in some of the tallest buildings in Los Angeles.

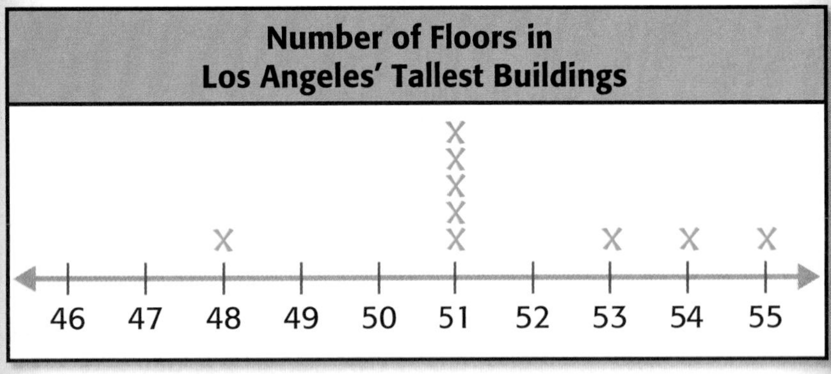

What will I learn in this chapter?

- Collect, organize, record, and display data.
- Display and read data in a bar graph and line plot.
- Identify whether events are certain, likely, unlikely, or impossible.
- Record outcomes and predict future events.
- Solve problems by making a list.

Key Vocabulary

tally chart **line plot**
bar graph **probability**

Math Online **Student Study Tools at ca.gr3math.com**

FOLDABLES™ Study Organizer

Make this Foldable to help you organize information about data, graphs, and probability. Begin with one sheet of $8\frac{1}{2}'' \times 11''$ paper.

1. **Fold** one sheet of paper into three equal sections.

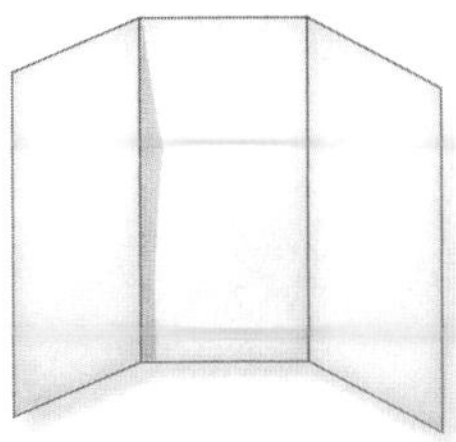

2. **Fold** a 2-inch pocket along the long edge. Glue the outside edges.

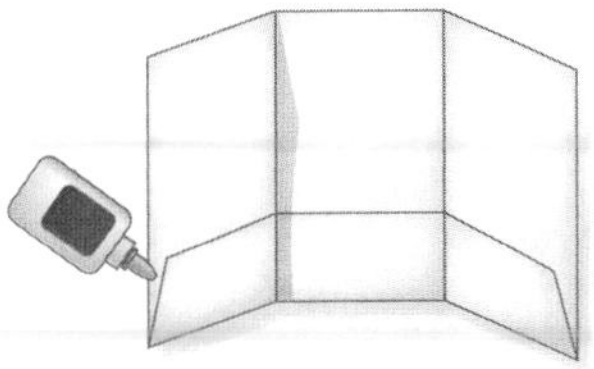

3. **Label** each pocket as shown. Record what you learn on index cards.

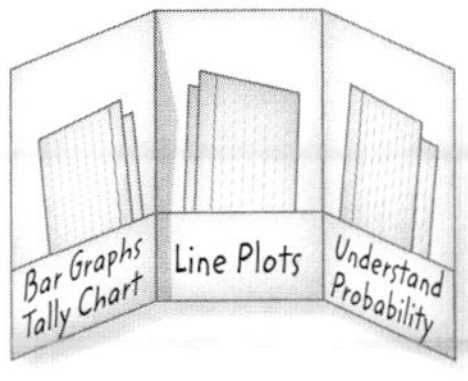

ARE YOU READY for Chapter 11?

You have two ways to check prerequisite skills for this chapter.

Option 2

Math Online Take the Chapter Readiness Quiz at ca.gr3math.com.

Option 1

Complete the Quick Check below.

QUICK Check

Refer to the pictograph. **(Prior grade)**

1. How many students said they like summer?
2. How many more students said they like winter than fall?
3. How many students said they like spring or winter?
4. What is the total number of students?

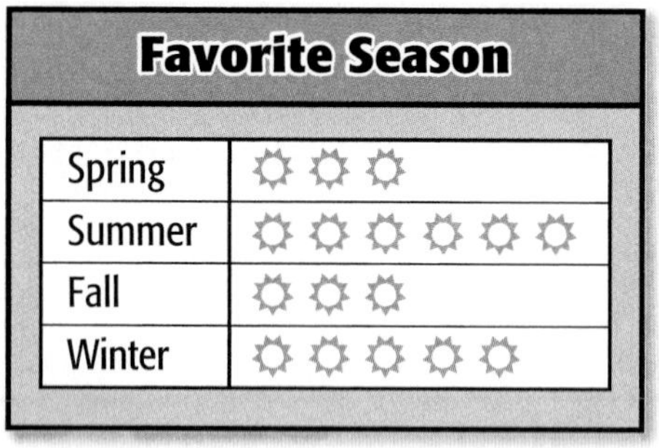

☼ = 2 Students

Find each sum. **(Lesson 2-1)**

5. $\begin{array}{r} 3 \\ 2 \\ 5 \\ +\ 6 \\ \hline \end{array}$

6. $\begin{array}{r} 8 \\ 7 \\ 4 \\ +\ 1 \\ \hline \end{array}$

7. $\begin{array}{r} 5 \\ 6 \\ 9 \\ +\ 2 \\ \hline \end{array}$

Identify the color each spinner is likely to land on. **(Prior grade)**

8.

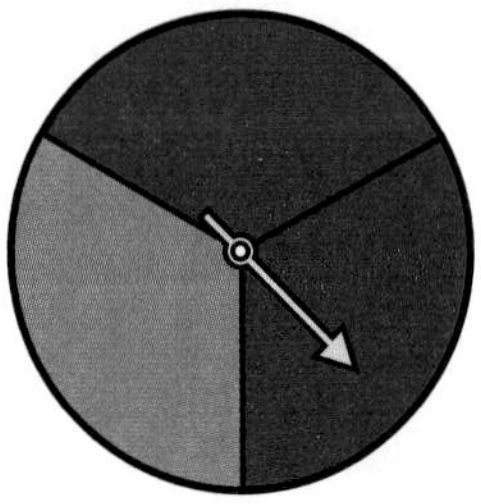

9.

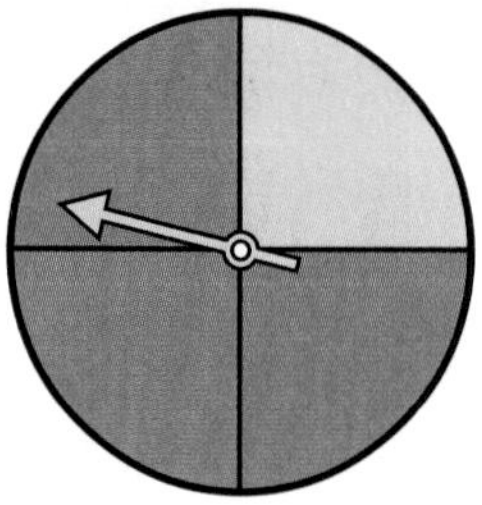

10.

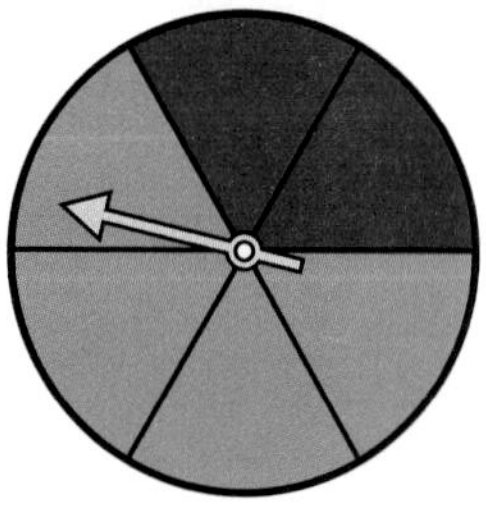

Explore

Graphing Activity for 11-1
Make a Bar Graph

MAIN IDEA

I will explore how to make a bar graph.

Preparation for Standard 3SDAP1.3 Summarize and display the results of probability experiments in a clear and organized way (e.g., use a bar graph or line plot).
Standard 3MR3.3 Develop generalizations of the results obtained and apply them in other circumstances.

You Will Need
grid paper;
colored pencils

New Vocabulary
- tally chart
- bar graph
- scale

Concepts in Motion
Animation
ca.gr3math.com

A **tally chart** is a table that organizes data using tally marks. Data displayed in a tally chart can also be displayed in a bar graph.

A **bar graph** is a graph that uses bars to show data by using bars of different lengths and heights.

How Many Pets Do You Have?	
Pets	**Tally**
0	𝍸
1	𝍸 𝍸 𝍷
2	𝍷𝍷𝍷
3	𝍷𝍷𝍷𝍷
4 or more	𝍷𝍷

ACTIVITY Make a Bar Graph

Step 1 **Draw and label.**

- Draw a rectangle. Separate it into equal rows.
- Label the side and bottom of the graph to describe the information.
- Give the graph a title.

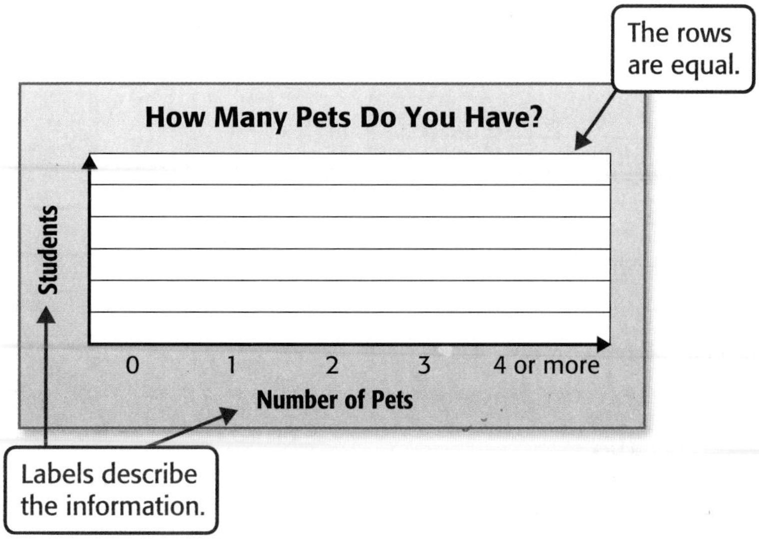

Step 2 **Choose a scale.**

Write a scale on the side of the graph. A **scale** is a set of numbers that represent the data.

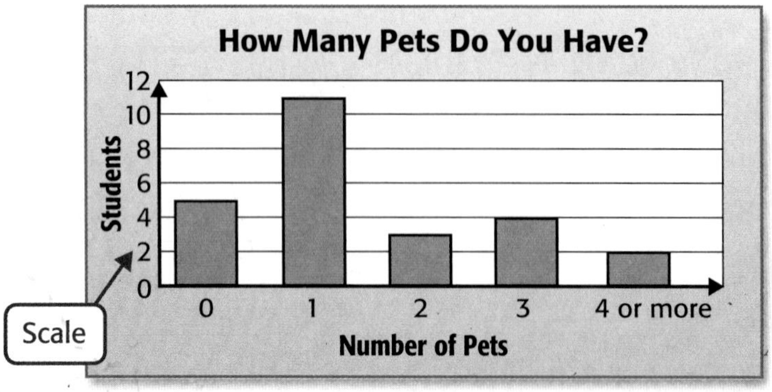

Step 3 **Draw the bars.**

Draw vertical bars to match each number from your data.

Think About It

1. How would you decide what scale to use?
2. Why do you think the scale counts by 2?
3. Why do some bars stop between two numbers or two lines?

CHECK What You Know

Display each set of data in a bar graph.

4.

Favorite Meal	
Meal	**Tally**
Breakfast	||||
Lunch	卌 卌 ||
Dinner	卌 卌 卌

5.

Favorite Fruit	
Fruit	**Tally**
Apple	卌 卌 卌 |
Orange	卌 卌
Banana	卌 |||

6. **WRITING IN ▸MATH** Refer to Step 2. Explain how the bar graph will change when you change its scale.

11-1 Bar Graphs

GET READY to Learn

Desmond asked his friends to name their favorite summer sport. He recorded the data that he collected in a tally chart.

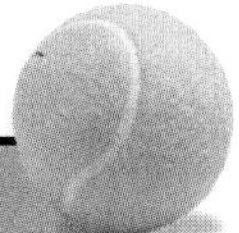

Favorite Summer Sports		
Sport	**Tally**	**Number**
Tennis	||||	4
Swimming	~~||||~~ ~~||||~~	10
Baseball	~~||||~~ ||	7
Biking	~~||||~~ |	6

MAIN IDEA

I will learn to make and read bar graphs.

Preparation for Standard

3SDAP1.3 Summarize and display the results of probability experiments in a clear and organized way (e.g., use a bar graph or line plot).

New Vocabulary

survey
tally chart
bar graph

A **survey** is a way of collecting data by asking a question. You can take data from a **tally chart** and make a **bar graph**.

Real-World EXAMPLE Make a Bar Graph.

1 SPORTS **Make a vertical bar graph to display the results of Desmond's survey.**

In a *vertical* bar graph, the bars go from the bottom up. It includes a title, labels, a scale, and bars. There is a space between each bar.

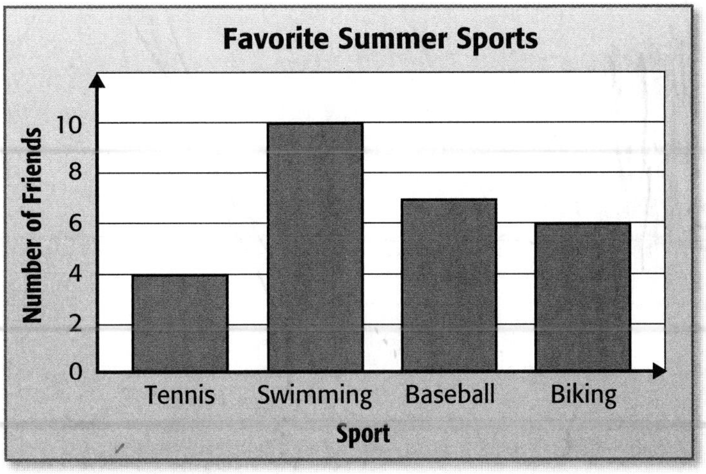

Vocabulary Link

The word *graph* comes from a Greek word meaning *to write*.

Real-World EXAMPLE Read a Bar Graph

2 ANIMALS The bar graph shows how long some animals sleep. Which two animals sleep the most?

In a *horizontal* bar graph, the bars go from left to right.

> **Remember**
> On a bar graph, there is a space between each bar.

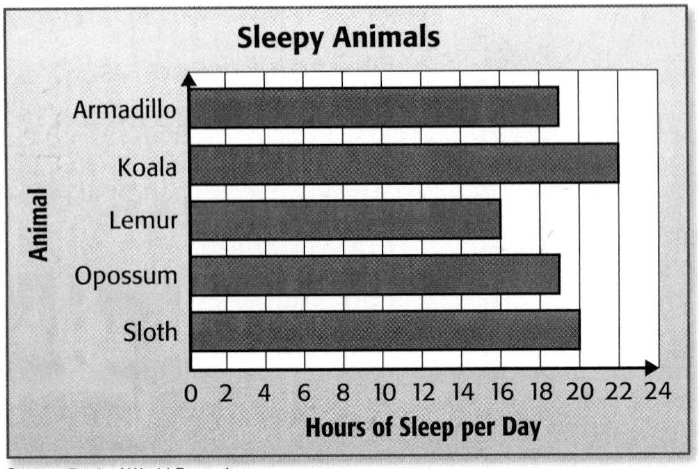

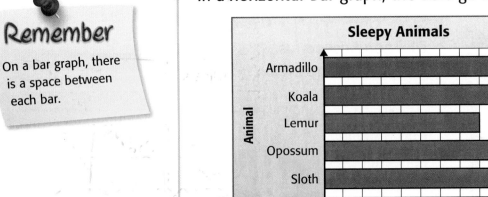

Source: *Book of World Records*

The lengths of the bars for the sloth and the koala are the longest. So, the sloth and the koala sleep the most.

Online Personal Tutor at ca.gr3math.com

CHECK What You Know

1. **Display the data below in a vertical bar graph.** See Example 1 (p. 473)

Favorite Birds to Watch	
Bird	**Tally**
Cardinal	卌 |||
Robin	||||
Goldfinch	卌 ||||

2. **Display the data below in a horizontal bar graph.** See Example 2 (p. 474)

Animal Life Spans	
Animal	**Time (years)**
Lion	10
Hamster	2
Kangaroo	5
Rabbit	7

Source: *Time for Kids Almanac*

For Exercises 3 and 4, refer to Example 2. See Example 2 (p. 474)

3. Which animal sleeps the most?

4. Name one animal that sleeps three hours longer than the lemur?

5. Talk About It How are vertical and horizontal bar graphs alike? How are they different?

EXTRA PRACTICE See page R30.

Display the data below in a vertical bar graph. See Example 1 (p. 473)

6.

Width of Birds' Nests	
Bird	**Width (ft)**
Bald eagle	8
Blue heron	5
Monk parakeet	3
Stork	6

Source: *Book of World Records*

Display the data below in a horizontal bar graph. See Example 2 (p. 474)

7.

World Series Wins	
Team	**Wins**
Cardinals	𝍸 ||||
Giants	𝍸
Yankees	𝍸 𝍸 𝍸 𝍸 𝍸 |
Dodgers	𝍸 |

Source: *Book of World Records*

For Exercises 8–15, refer to the graphs.

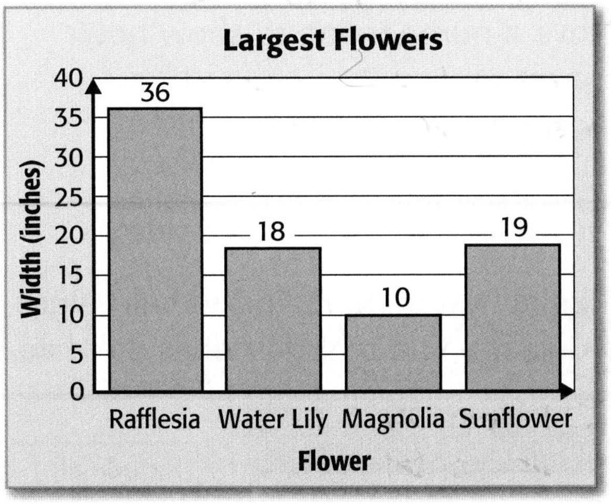

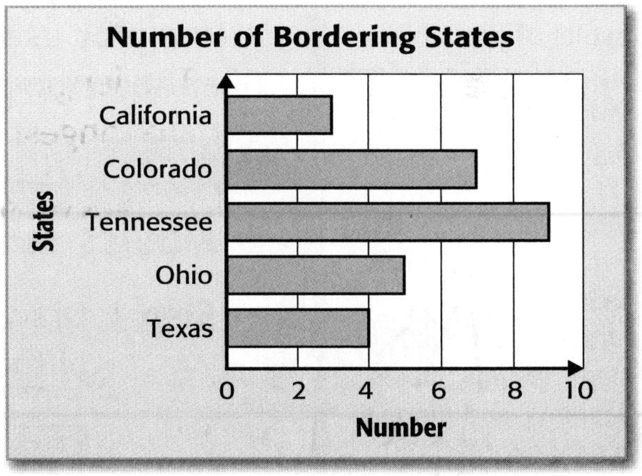

8. How wide is the largest flower?

9. Which two flowers are closest in size?

10. What is the difference between the largest and the smallest flower?

11. Which flower is half the size of the largest flower?

12. How many states border Tennessee?

13. How many more states border Ohio than California?

14. Which states have 5 or less states bordering them?

15. Which state has the least number of bordering states?

H.O.T. Problems

16. OPEN ENDED Give an example of a set of data that can be displayed in a bar graph. Make this bar graph.

17. WRITING IN ▸MATH Why are a title and labels needed?

11-2 Line Plots

GET READY to Learn

Antoine surveyed his friends to find out how often they went to a movie theater. The table shows the results.

Movies Per Month			
Zack 0	Carla 1	Grace 2	Ivan 1
Ricardo 1	Nina 2	Betty 0	Tama 1
Latisha 2	Kelley 1	Gabe 4	Ademo 1
David 0	Judie 1	Drew 1	Lauren 3

POP CORN
POP CORN

MAIN IDEA

I will learn how to make and read line plots.

Standard Preparation for 3SDAP1.3 Summarize and display the results of probability experiments in a clear and organized way (e.g., use a bar graph or a line plot). Standard 3MR2.3 Use a variety of methods, such as words, numbers, symbols, charts, **graphs,** tables, diagrams, and models, **to explain mathematical reasoning.**

New Vocabulary

line plot

A **line plot** uses Xs above a number line to show how often something happens.

Real-World EXAMPLE Make a Line Plot

1 MOVIES Make a line plot for the survey results.

Step 1 Draw and label a number line. Include all values of the data. Give it a title that describes the data.

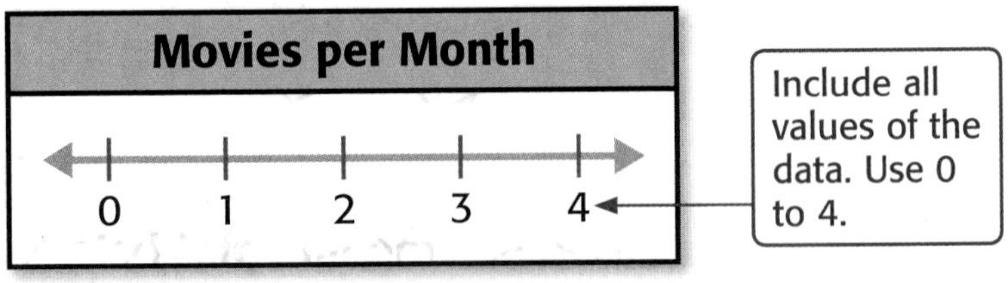
Movies per Month
0
1
2
3
4
Include all values of the data. Use 0 to 4.

Step 2 Draw an X above the number for each response.

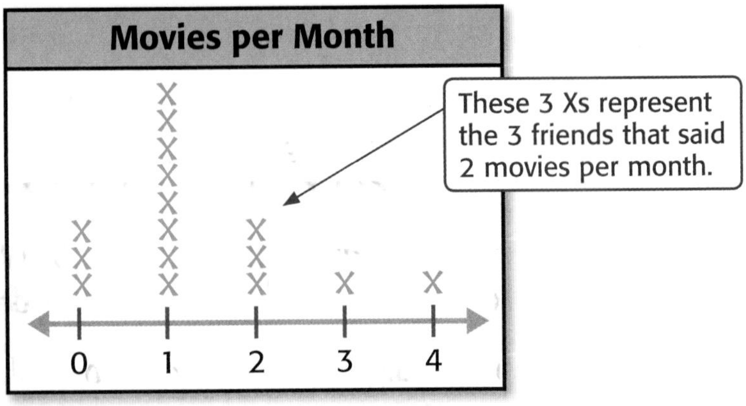
Movies per Month
These 3 Xs represent the 3 friends that said 2 movies per month.
0
1
2
3
4

Remember

Start with the least number and end with the greatest number you need when numbering a line plot.

Real-World EXAMPLE Read a Line Plot

2 MOVIES Use Antoine's line plot to find how often most students went to the movies.

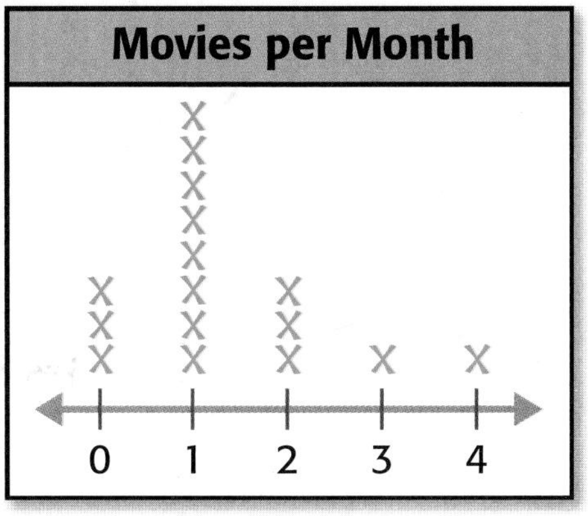

The most Xs are above number 1. Antoine can see that most of his friends went to the movies 1 time per month.

Online Personal Tutor at ca.gr3math.com

CHECK What You Know

Display each set of data in a line plot. See Example 1 (p. 476)

1.

Third-Grade Shoe Size			
Jose 2	Ana 4	Julia 8	Martin 3
Lin 6	Tanya 5	Ronaldo 3	Cheye 4
William 4	Cole 5	Nat 4	Gabriel 5

2.

Weekly Time Spent on Homework

Time (hours)	Tally
8	III
9	~~IIII~~ I
10	~~IIII~~
11	~~IIII~~ III

For Exercises 3 and 4, use the line plot below. See Example 2 (p. 477)

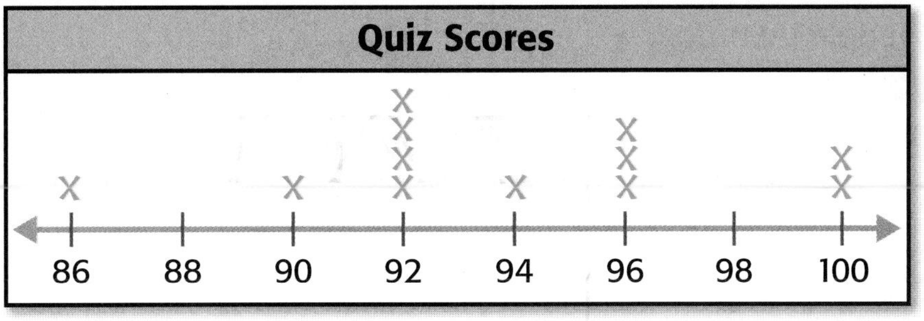

3. How many student's quiz scores are recorded? Explain.

4. What is one conclusion you can draw from this line plot? Explain.

5. Talk About It Does a tally table or a line plot make it easier to see how often numbers happen in a set of data? Explain.

Practice and Problem Solving

EXTRA PRACTICE See page R30.

Display each set of data in a line plot. See Example 1 (p. 476)

6.

Chores Per Week				
Layla 1	Ciro 4	Nikita 3	Pat 2	Pilar 3
Hao 2	Rico 5	Sugi 2	Jerome 4	Pia 3
Alvin 2	Flor 6	Paz 3	Rashid 1	Trey 2
Ayana 3	Jim 5	Maxine 4	Ellis 3	Nate 3

7.

Rollercoaster Rides				
Yu 1	Barry 3	Rogelio 2	Matt 3	Anshi 0
Nick 1	Jen 6	Karrie 0	Anshi 3	Vic 3
Charlie 0	Terry 3	Kato 1	Eric 1	Stu 2
Irene 0	Sandra 3	Paul 2	Macy 0	Hannah 1

8.

Hours of TV Watched	
Hours of TV	**Students**
0	ǀ
1	ǀǀǀǀ
2	
3	ǀǀ
4	ǀ
5	ǀǀ

9.

Number of Siblings	
Siblings	**Students**
0	卌 ǀǀ
1	卌
2	卌 ǀǀǀǀ
3	ǀǀǀ
4	ǀǀ
5 or more	ǀǀ

For Exercises 10–13, use the line plot below. See Example 2 (p. 477)

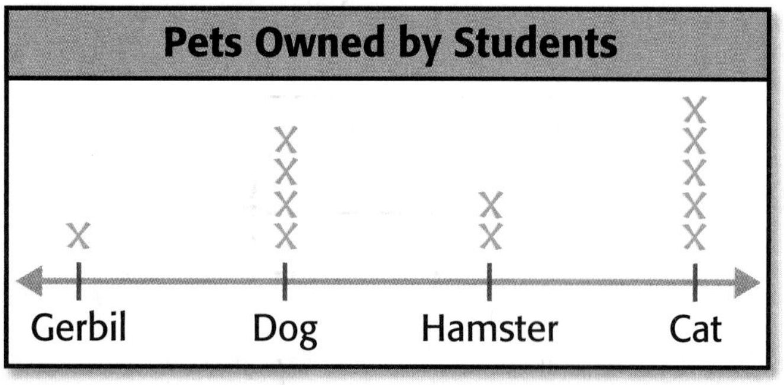

10. What do the Xs stand for on this line plot?

11. Which animal is owned by the most students?

12. Do more people own dogs or hamsters?

13. What conclusion could you draw?

H.O.T. Problems

14. **OPEN ENDED** Give an example of a set of data that is not best displayed in a line plot. Explain.

15. **WRITING IN MATH** Explain how a tally chart and a line plot are alike and different.

Standards Practice

16 Which statement about the data below is true? **(Lesson 11-2)**

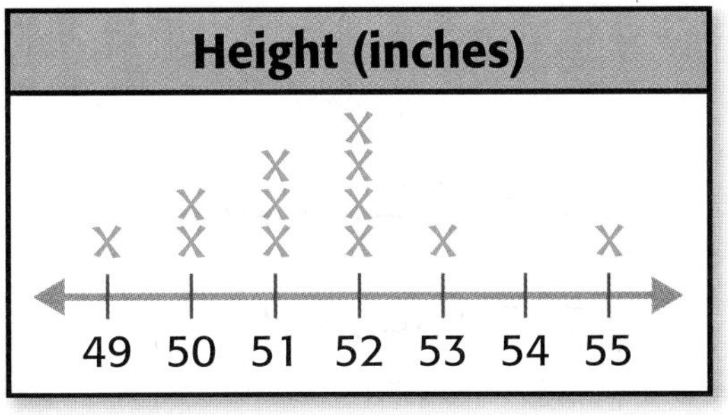

A All members are 55 inches.

B Half of the team members are 52 inches or greater.

C Most members are 51 inches.

D No one is 49 inches tall.

17 Which shapes make up this object? **(Lesson 10-9)**

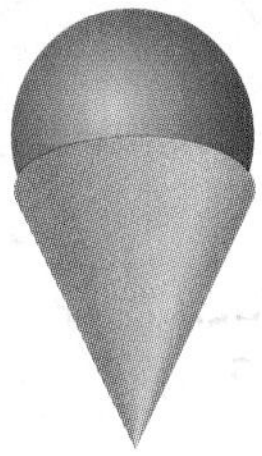

F cylinder and cube

G sphere and cone

H triangle and circle

J rectangle and triangle

Spiral Review

Display each set of data in a vertical bar graph. **(Lesson 11-1)**

18.

Orchestra Instruments	
Instrument	**Tally**
Brass	||||
Woodwind	𝍸
Strings	𝍸
Percussion	𝍸 ||

19.

Favorite After-School Snack	
Snack	**Tally**
Apple	|||
Granola Bar	||
Smoothie	𝍸 |||
Yogurt	𝍸

Find the volume of each figure. **(Lesson 10-10)**

20.

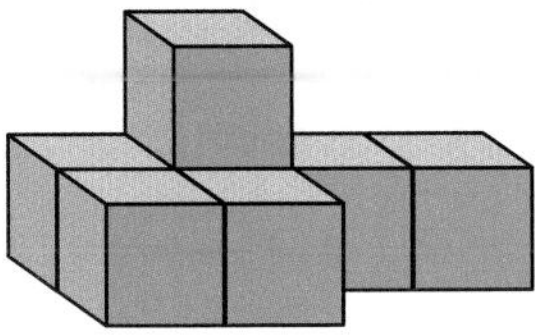

21.

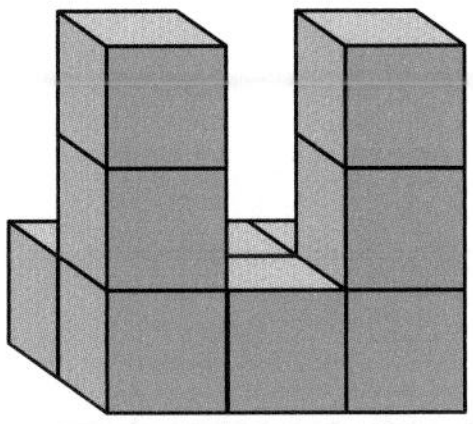

22.

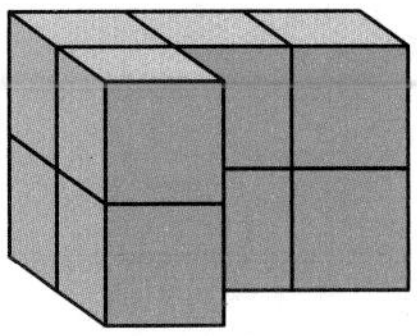

23. Admission to an amusement park is $25.95. Bus fare is $2.50 for one way. Find the total cost for Kali and her friend for admission and bus fare to and from the park. **(Lessons 2-6 and 2-3)**

11-3 Problem-Solving Strategy

MAIN IDEA I will solve problems by making an organized list.

Standard 3MR1.1 Analyze problems by identifying relationships, distinguishing relevant from irrelevant information, sequencing and prioritizing information, and observing patterns. **Standard 3SDAP1.2 Record the possible outcomes for a simple event (e.g., tossing a coin) and systematically keep track of the outcomes** when the event is repeated many times.

Kia, Karl, and Carrie are lining up to come in from recess. They are deciding the order they should line up. How many different ways can they line up?

Understand

What facts do you know?

- There are three students.

What do you need to find?

- Find how many different ways they can line up.

Plan

Arrange the different ways in an organized list. Then use the list to solve the problem.

Solve

- Start with Kia. Create different combinations with her first.
- Repeat this method of making a list with each of of the other students being first.
- Count all the different combinations.

Possible Ways to Line Up

	First	Second	Third
1.	Kia	Karl	Carrie
2.	Kia	Carrie	Karl
3.	Karl	Carrie	Kia
4.	Karl	Kia	Carrie
5.	Carrie	Karl	Kia
6.	Carrie	Kia	Karl

There are 6 possible ways for the students to line up.

Check

Look back at the problem. None of the ways repeat. So, the answer makes sense.

ANALYZE the Strategy

Refer to the problem on the previous page.

1. Explain why the make a list strategy was helpful in solving this problem.
2. Explain how to organize all of the combinations in a table.
3. If there were four students, what is the number of combinations?
4. How do you know your answer to Exercise 3 is correct?

PRACTICE the Strategy

EXTRA PRACTICE
See page R30.

Solve. Use the *make a list* strategy.

5. Aleta has black pants and tan pants. She also has a striped shirt, a plaid shirt, and a flowered shirt. How many different outfits can Aleta make?
6. Garcia orders one scoop each of vanilla, chocolate, and strawberry. In how many different ways can his ice cream cone be made?
7. How many lunches can Malia make if she chooses one main item and one side item from the menu shown?

8. Koko will make a fan out of three different colors of paper. How many color combinations can Koko make if he uses blue,red, and green?
9. List all the possible sandwiches that can be made using one type of bread, meat, and cheese.

10. How many different three-digit numbers can be made using the numbers 5, 7, and 8 exactly once?
11. There are some coins in a jar. The sum of the coins is 13¢. What are the possible coin combinations Amanda could have.
12. **WRITING IN ▸MATH** Give an example of a problem for which you would use the *make a list* to solve.

Chapter 11 Mid-Chapter Check

Lessons 11-1 through 11-3

1. Make a horizontal bar graph. **(Lesson 11-1)**

Weekend Activities	
Activity	**Time (hours)**
Swim	2
Shop	4
TV	5
Jog	3

Use the graph. **(Lesson 11-1)**

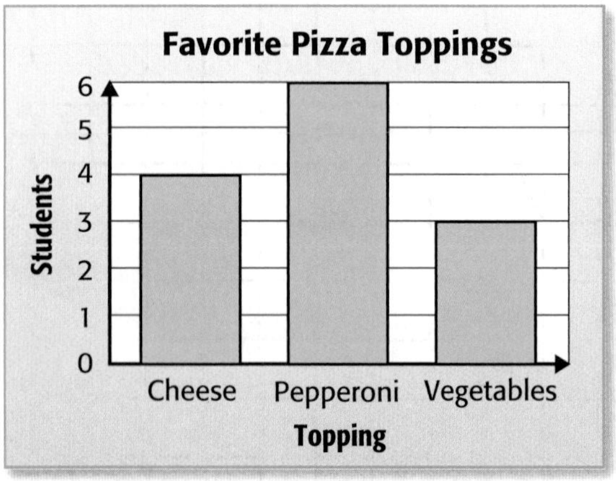

2. How many more students like pepperoni than cheese?

3. Find the total number of students.

4. Use the line plot. What is the difference between the most and least number of students in a classroom?

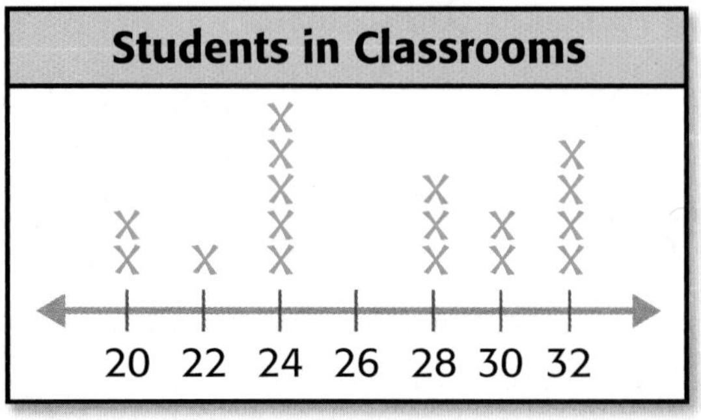

5. **STANDARDS PRACTICE** Which statement is true? **(Lesson 11-2)**

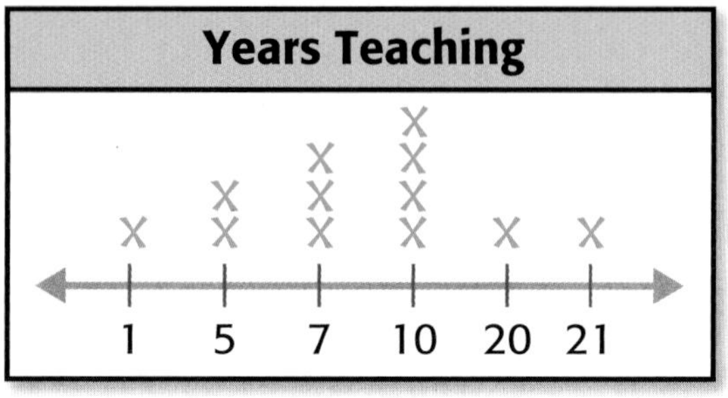

A All teachers have been teaching 10 years, except one.

B All have taught 7 years or more.

C Most of the teachers have taught 7 years or more.

D No one has taught 21 years.

6. Display the data in a line plot. **(Lesson 11-2)**

Favorite Place to Read a Book	
Place	**Students**
Bed	𝍸 ||||
Outside	|||
School	𝍸 |||
Library	||||

7. **WRITING IN MATH** Explain the difference between a line plot and a bar graph.

Catch Me If You Can!

Make a Graph

Get Ready!

Players: 2 players

You will need: 2 spinners, grid paper

Get Set!

- Divide one spinner into 3 equal parts. Label the parts 1, 2, and 4.
- Divide the other spinner into 4 equal parts. Label the parts 1, 2, 3, and 5.
- Make the game board shown.

Catch Me If You Can

1	**2**	**3**	**4**	**5**	**6**	**8**	**10**	**12**	**20**

Products

Go!

- Player 1 spins each spinner and finds the product of the two numbers.
- Player 1 then colors in one square on the graph paper above the product.
- Player 2 takes a turn.
- The game continues, taking turns, until one bar reaches the top.

11-4 Identify Probability

GET READY to Learn

Avery has a bag of 8 wristbands. Only one wristband is blue. Dana picks a wristband without looking. How likely is it that Dana will pick a blue wristband?

MAIN IDEA

I will tell whether events are certain, likely, unlikely, or impossible.

Standard 3SDAP1.1 Identify whether common events are certain, likely, unlikely, or improbable.

New Vocabulary

probability

You can use words to describe probability.

KEY CONCEPT — **Probability**

Words **Probability** describes how likely it is that an event will happen.

Examples

Certain to choose a marble.

Likely to choose red.

Unlikely to choose green.

Impossible to choose yellow.

Real-World EXAMPLES — **Describe Probability**

1 How likely is it that Dana will pick blue?

There is only 1 blue wristband out of a total of 8. So, it is *unlikely* that Dana will pick a blue wristband.

2 How likely is it that Dana will pick green?

There are 7 green wristbands out of a total of 8. So, it is *likely* that a green one will be picked.

Real-World EXAMPLES Describe Probability

3 **SPINNERS Andrea spins the spinner. How likely is it that the she will spin a multiple of 3?**

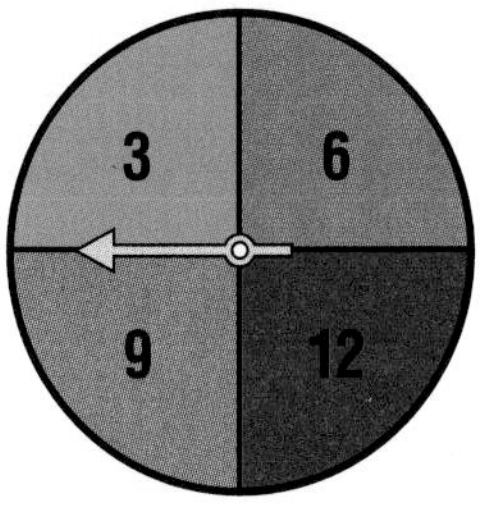

The numbers 3, 6, 9, and 12 are all multiples of 3. So, it is *certain* that Andrea will spin a multiple of 3.

4 **GAMES Paul and Yasmin are playing a card game. Yasmin needs to draw a 4 to win. The cards shown will be shuffled and placed facedown on a table. How likely is it that Yasmin will draw a 4?**

There are no 4s. The probability that Yasmin will draw a 4 is *impossible*.

Online Personal Tutor at ca.gr3math.com

CHECK What You Know

Describe the probability of landing on each color. Write *certain, likely, unlikely,* or *impossible.* See Examples 1–4 (pp. 484–485)

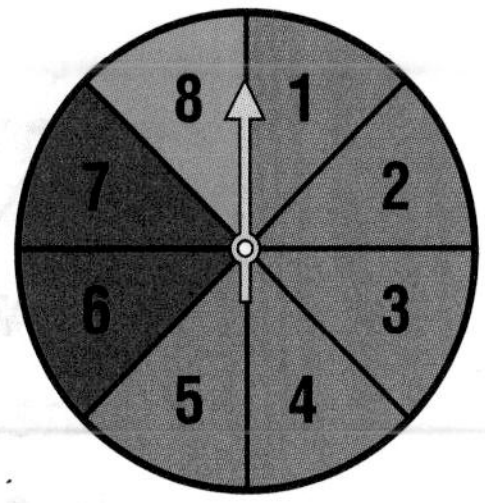

1. green

2. blue

3. yellow

4. blue, red, or green

5. Jamila is playing a game. She uses a number cube labeled 1, 2, 3, 4, 5, and 6. Describe the probability that she will roll a 7.

6. Talk About It Explain the difference between an event that is *certain* and an event that is *likely.*

Practice and Problem Solving

EXTRA PRACTICE
See page R31.

Describe the probability of choosing each color. Write *certain, likely, unlikely,* or *impossible.*

See Examples 1–4 (pp. 484–485)

7. purple

8. green

9. white

10. blue or green

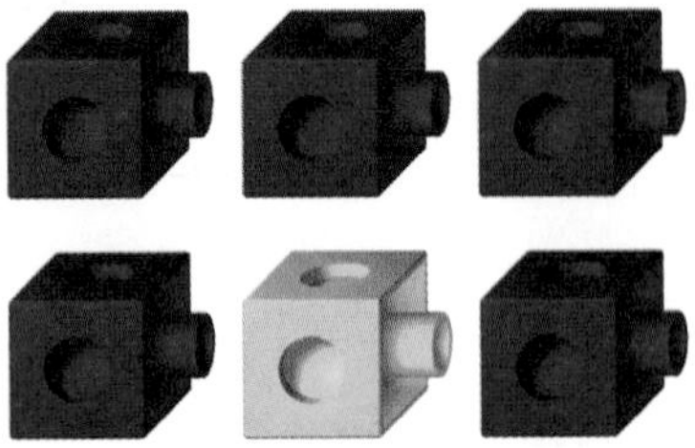

11. yellow

12. green

13. red

14. blue

Describe a bag of marbles that represents each statement.

15. Choosing a red marble is *impossible*.

16. Choosing a red marble is *certain*.

17. There are 7 letter tiles in a bag. Five of the tiles are labeled S. One tile is labeled R, and the other is M. Describe the probability of choosing the letter S.

18. Francis asks Dan to choose a marble from a bag of 10 marbles. What is the probability of choosing the color blue if one is blue?

Real-World PROBLEM SOLVING

Data File California's state colors are blue and gold. Blue is for the sky and gold is for the metal, once found in the state's hills.

19. What color is the spinner *likely* to land on?

20. Is the spinner *likely* or *unlikely* to land on gold?

21. How could you change the spinner so that it was *certain* to land on blue?

State Colors

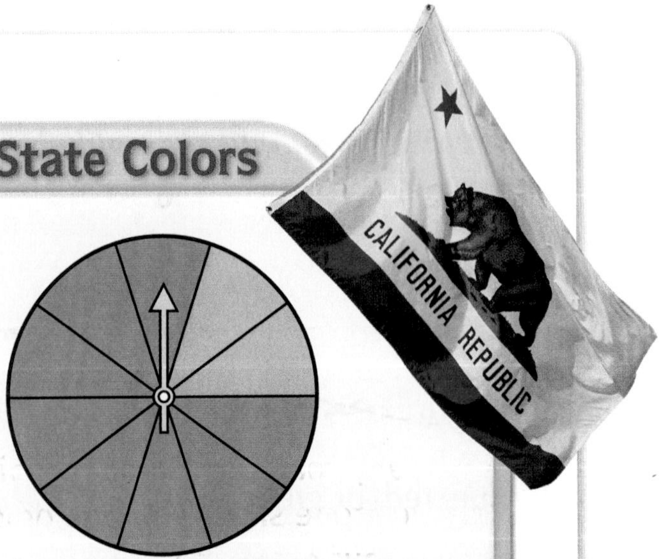

H.O.T. Problems

22. FIND THE ERROR Janice and Gus are spinning a spinner. The spinner is evenly divided into 4 sections. The colors are red, yellow, green, and blue. Who is correct? Explain.

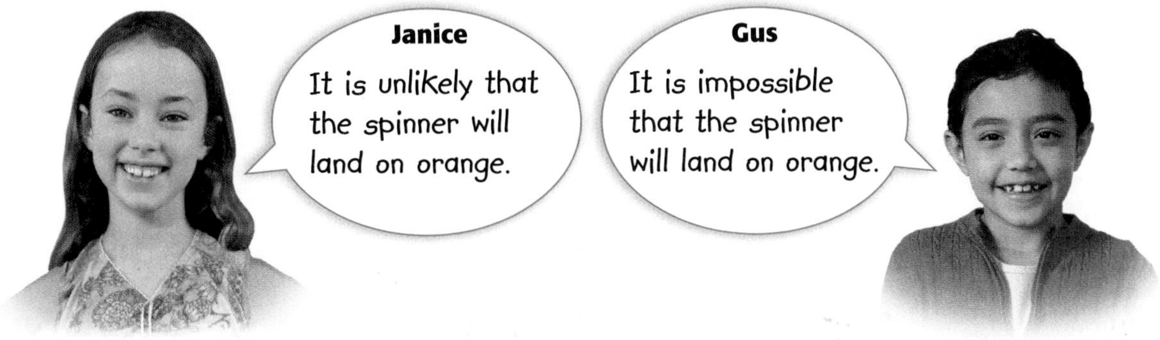
Janice
It is unlikely that the spinner will land on orange.
Gus
It is impossible that the spinner will land on orange.

23. WRITING IN ▶MATH Describe the probability of the following event. Explain.

A cow can fly like a bird.

Standards Practice

24 How many shirt-pant outfits are possible? **(Lesson 11-3)**

A 2 **C** 6

B 4 **D** 8

25 Lina has 7 cubes in a bag.

She closes her eyes and picks one cube. Describe the probability that she picks a green cube. **(Lesson 11-4)**

F certain **H** unlikely

G likely **J** impossible

Spiral Review

26. How many snack and drink combinations are possible if one snack and one drink is chosen? Explain your reasoning. **(Lesson 11-3)**

Cold Snacks
Juice bar
Ice cream cone
Pudding bar
Cold Drinks
Smoothie
Ice water
Ice tea

27. Make a line plot for the data: **(Lesson 11-2)**
5, 7, 2, 1, 5, 2, 8, 9, 3, 5, 7, 3, 9, 7, 2, 10, 4, 4, 3

EGGS!

When you go to the grocery store, what do the eggs look like? Most of them are usually white and about $1\frac{1}{2}$ inches long. Did you know that eggs come in all sorts of colors, sizes, and shapes? Most birds that lay white eggs, like kingfishers and woodpeckers, lay their eggs in dark holes. Birds that lay their eggs in open areas without a nest are colored like the soil. This keeps predators from finding them.

Did You Know?

Some birds lay their eggs in the nests of other birds so that the other birds will hatch them.

Real-World Math

For Exercises 1–4, describe the probability of each situation. Write *certain*, *likely*, *unlikely*, or *impossible*.

1. An emperor penguin egg is larger than a robin egg.
2. A hummingbird laid an egg the same length as an emu egg.
3. Tomorrow, an elephant bird will lay an egg.
4. An egg that is colored like the soil was laid on the ground.
5. Why would a bird that lays more eggs at a time have a greater probability of not becoming extinct than a bird that only lays one egg at a time?

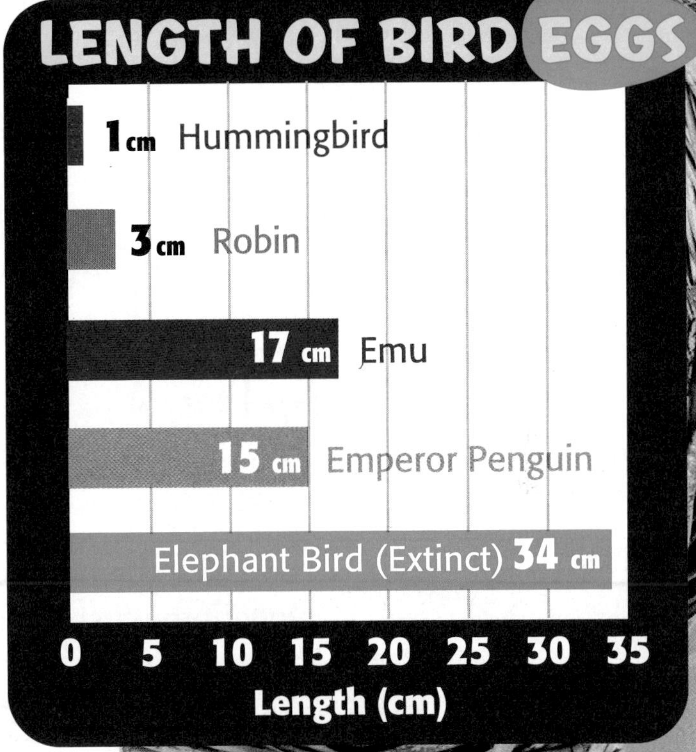

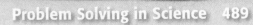

11-5 Problem-Solving Investigation

MAIN IDEA I will choose the best strategy to solve a problem.

Standard 3MR1.1 Analyze problems by identifying relationships, distinguishing relevant from irrelevant information, sequencing and prioritizing information, and observing patterns. Standard 3NS2.1 Find the sum or difference of two whole numbers between 0 and 10,000.

P.S.I. TEAM +

ELAN: My school is having a book swap. The first day, 8 books were brought to school. The second day, 12 books came. Yesterday, my friends brought 16 books.

YOUR MISSION: Suppose the pattern continues. Find the total number of books after 7 days.

Understand You know the number of books brought the first three days. Find the total number of books after 7 days.

Plan Use the *make a table* strategy. Find and extend the pattern to solve the problem.

Solve The pattern is to add 4 books each day. To find the total, add the number of books from each day.

Day	1	2	3	4	5	6	7
Books	8	12	16	20	24	28	32

+4 +4 +4 +4 +4 +4

$8 + 12 = 20$ $\quad 20 + 16 = 36$ $\quad 36 + 20 = 56$ $\quad 56 + 24 = 80$ $\quad 80 + 28 = 108$ $\quad 108 + 32 = 140$

So, the total number of books is 140.

Check Look back at the problem. The answer makes sense for the facts given in the problem.

Mixed Problem Solving

EXTRA PRACTICE
See page R31.

Use any strategy shown below to solve. Tell what strategy you used.

PROBLEM-SOLVING STRATEGIES

- Draw a picture.
- Look for a pattern.
- Act it out.
- Make a table.
- Work backward.
- Make an organized list.

1. Horatio has 40 comic books. He keeps 10 comic books for himself and divides the rest equally among his 5 friends. How many comic books does each friend get?

2. Five girls signed up for a table tennis tournament. Each girl has to play each of the other girls one time. How many games will the girls play in all? Show your work.

3. Two teams scored a total of 20 points. The Bears scored 6 more points than the Seahawks. How many points did each team score?

4. Suppose you add 35 to a number then subtract 10. The result is 26. What was the original number?

5. The graph shows the number of people in each car that drove by Niguel's house. What is the total number of people who drove by?

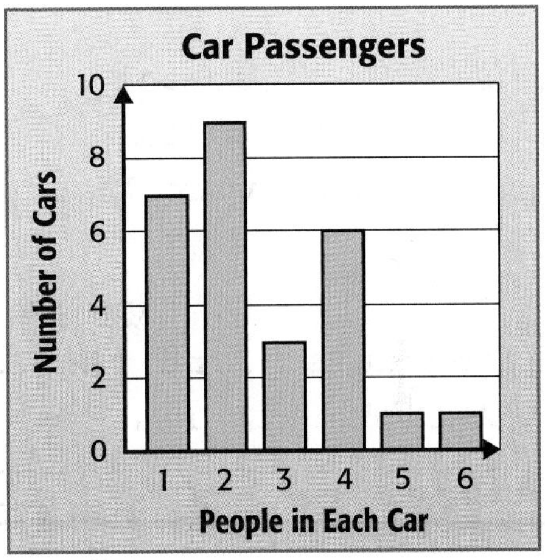

6. Mrs. Bryce bought 3 bundles of yarn, each 50 feet long. She used 27 feet of the blue yarn, 19 feet of the red yarn, and 38 feet of the yellow. What is the total length of yarn remaining?

7. The window in Jody's room is 4 feet wide by 5 feet high. The perimeter of her brother's window is twice as much. What could be the measurements of her brother's window?

8. **WRITING IN ▶MATH** There are 48 oranges in a box and half as many grapefruit. To find the total number of pieces of fruit, would you use the *make a table* strategy? Explain.

Explore

Probability Activity for 11-6
Outcomes

MAIN IDEA

I will record results from probability experiments.

Standard 3SDAP1.2 **Record the possible outcomes for a single event (e.g., tossing a coin) and systematically keep track of the outcomes when the event is repeated many times.**

Standard 3MR2.2 **Apply strategies and results from simpler problems to more complex problems.**

You Will Need

a two-color counter, 0–5 number cube

New Vocabulary

outcomes

equally likely

Concepts in Motion

Animation

ca.gr3math.com

Suppose you toss a two-color counter. There are two possible **outcomes**, or results. Since the two outcomes have the same probability of happening, we say that the outcomes are **equally likely**.

ACTIVITY

1 Toss a Counter

Step 1 **Record results.**

Make a table like the one shown. Take turns tossing a counter 50 times. Record each outcome.

Counter-Toss Experiment		
Outcome	Tally	Number
Red		
Yellow		

Step 2 **Summarize results.**

- How many times did the counter land on red?
- How many times did it land on yellow?
- Are the outcomes of this experiment equally likely? Explain.

ACTIVITY

Hands-On Activity

2 Toss a Number Cube

Step 1 Record results.

Toss a number cube 50 times. Record the outcomes on a table like the one shown.

Number Cube Experiment		
Outcome	**Tally**	**Number**
0		
1		
2		
3		
4		
5		

Step 2 Display results.

Display the results in a bar graph and a line plot.

Step 3 Summarize results.

Are the outcomes of this experiment equally likely? Explain.

CHECK What You Know

Conduct each probability experiment described below.

Toss a coin 50 times. Record the results in a tally table.

Coin Experiment		
Outcome	**Tally**	**Number**
Heads		
Tails		

1. How many possible outcomes are there?

2. Would you say that it is equally likely that the coin lands on heads or tails? Explain.

Spin an equally divided 4-color spinner 50 times. Record the results on a line plot.

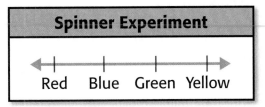

Spinner Experiment

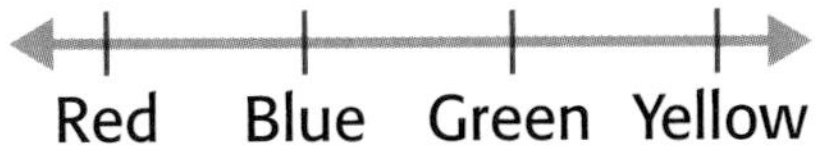

3. What color did the spinner land on the most?

4. Were the results for this experiment the same as the results from the coin experiment? Explain.

5. WRITING IN ▸MATH If you repeated the coin experiment, would the results be the same or similar? Explain your reasoning.

11-6 Make Predictions

MAIN IDEA

I will learn to use the results of probability experiments to predict future events.

Standard 3SDAP1.4 Use the results of probability experiments to predict future events (e.g., use a line plot to predict the temperature forecast for the next day).

Standard 3MR3.3 Develop generalizations of the results obtained and apply them in other circumstances.

New Vocabulary

prediction

GET READY to Learn

Cole picked one cube from a bag, recorded its color and repeated his experiment. The tally table shows his results. Suppose Cole picks one more cube. What color do you think he will pick? Explain.

Cubes in a Bag		
Outcome	**Tally**	**Total**
Purple	𝍷𝍷𝍷	3
Green	𝍸 𝍸	10
Red	𝍷𝍷	2

You can use the results from an experiment to make **predictions** about what is likely to happen next.

EXAMPLE Make a Prediction

1 **Cole displayed the results in a bar graph and in a line plot. Predict the next color he will pick.**

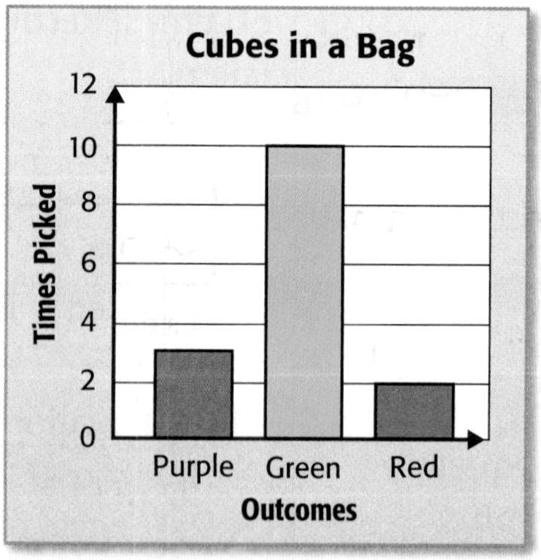

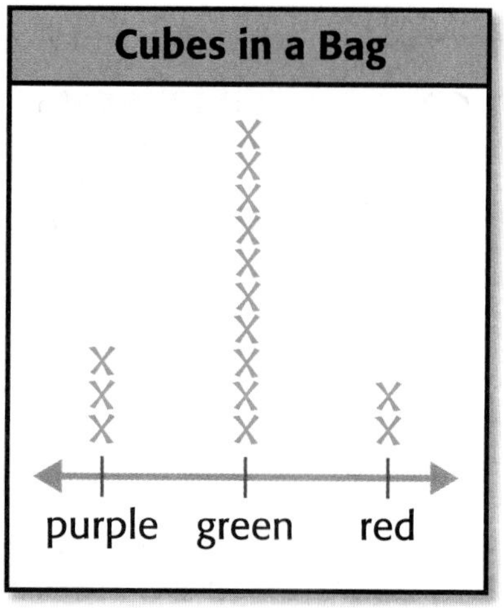

Green cubes were picked more often than red or blue cubes. So, green is more likely to be picked than any other color.

Online Personal Tutor at ca.gr3math.com

Hands-On Mini Activity

Step 1 Make a spinner and a tally chart like the ones shown.

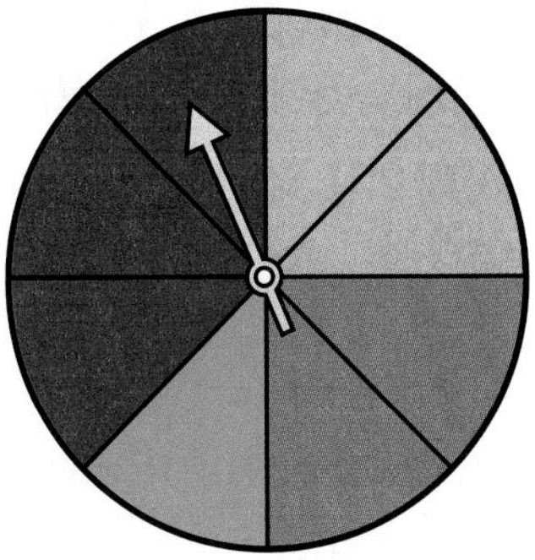

Step 2 Perform an experiment. Spin the spinner 50 times. Record the result.

Step 3 Graph the results on a bar graph or line plot.

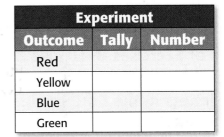

Remember

In order to make reliable predictions, probability experiments need to be performed many times.

1. Use the results to make a prediction for your next spin.
2. What kinds of things do you look for when making predictions?
3. What information from your graph or line plot helped you make your predictions?

Experiment		
Outcome	**Tally**	**Number**
Red		
Yellow		
Blue		
Green		

CHECK What You Know

For Exercises 1–3, use the tally table. It shows the results of choosing a marble from a bag 50 times and then replacing it each time. See Example 1 (p. 494)

Pick a Marble		
Outcome	**Tally**	**Total**
Yellow	卌 卌 卌 卌 卌 |	26
Orange	||||	4
Green	卌 卌	10
Blue	卌 卌	10

1. What color is likely to be chosen next? Why?
2. What two colors are equally likely to be picked? Explain.
3. Is it reasonable to predict that twice as many marbles are yellow than any other colors? Why?
4. **Talk About It** There are 28 students. Of the students, 18 are girls. If the students put their names in a bag, do you think a boy's or girl's name will be picked first? Explain.

Practice and Problem Solving

EXTRA PRACTICE
See page R31.

For Exercises 5–7, use the line plot. It shows the results from rolling a number cube labeled 1, 2, 3, 4, 5, and 6. See Example 1 (p. 494)

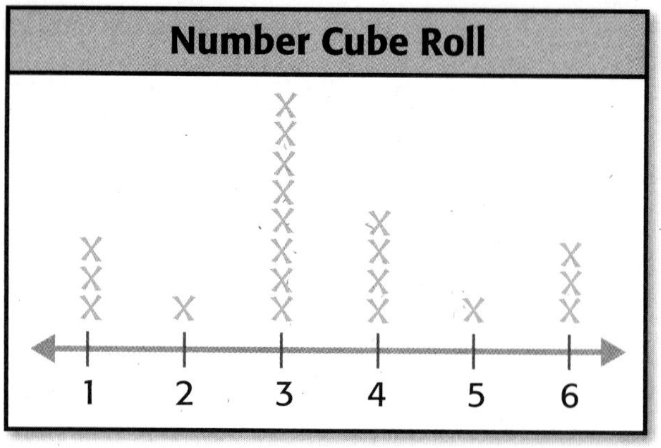

5. How many times did Sari roll the cube?

6. Which numbers have been rolled so far?

7. What number do you predict Sari would roll next? Why?

For Exercises 8–10, use the bar graph. It shows the number of letters in the third grade spelling words. See Example 1 (p. 494)

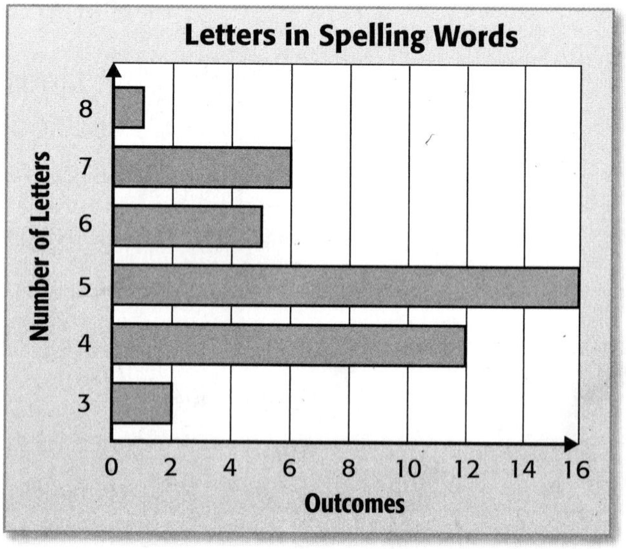

8. Explain whether it is *likely* or *unlikely* that an 8-letter word will be on the next spelling list.

9. How many letters do most of the spelling words have?

10. Predict the number of letters most of the words will have on the next spelling list.

Real-World PROBLEM SOLVING

Weather In order to closely predict the weather each day, weather forecasters use data that has been gathered for a long period of time.

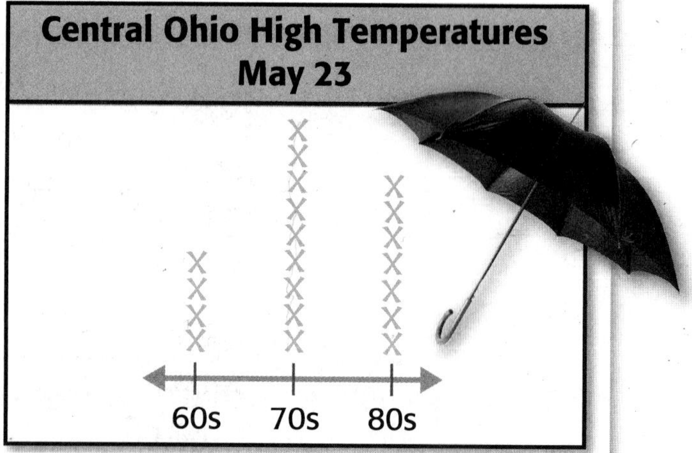

Source: almanac4kids.com/weather

11. How many years does this data cover?

12. Predict a *likely* temperature for May 23 next year in central Ohio? Explain.

13. Predict an *unlikely* temperature for May 23 next year? Explain.

H.O.T. Problems

14. **CHALLENGE** Use the table that shows the results from spinning a spinner. Draw a spinner that could have produced these outcomes. Explain your decision for the spinner you drew.

Spinner Results		
Outcomes	**Tally**	**Total**
Orange	𝍸 𝍸 |||	13
Red	||||	4
Green	|||	3

15. **WRITING IN MATH** Explain how graphs and line plots can be used to make predictions.

Standards Practice

16 Nora had $5. She bought 3 boxes of colored pencils. Each box cost $1.25. What amount of money did she have then? **(Lesson 11-5)**

A $1.25 **C** $3.75

B $2.00 **D** $4.00

17 A triangle has a perimeter of 25 inches. One side measures 10 inches and another side measures 8 inches. Find the length of the third side. **(Lesson 10-2)**

F 5 **J** 7

G 6 **H** 8

18 What color is the spinner most likely to land on next time? **(Lesson 11-6)**

Color Spin		
Outcomes	**Tally**	**Number**
Red	|||	3
Blue	𝍸 𝍸 𝍸	15
Green	||	2
Yellow	𝍸	5

A red **C** green

B blue **D** yellow

Spiral Review

19. Wesley bought 4 bags of beads. Each bag has 155 beads. If he gave away 111 beads, how many did he have left? **(Lesson 11-5)**

Describe the probability of choosing each color(s). Write *certain, likely, unlikely,* or *impossible*. **(Lesson 11-4)**

20. red **21.** green

22. yellow **23.** red, green, and blue

Study Guide and Review

FOLDABLES™ Study Organizer GET READY to Study

Be sure the following Key Vocabulary words and Key Concepts are written in your Foldable.

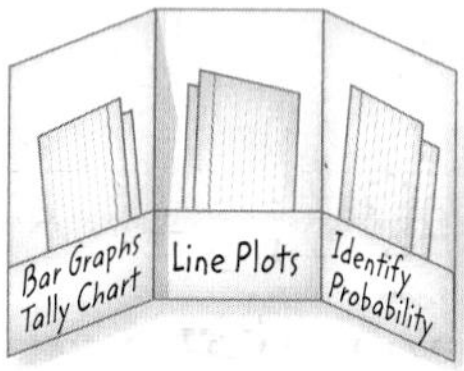

BIG Ideas

Record Data (p. 471)

- There are different ways to record and organize data. Two ways are to use a **tally chart** and a table.

Display Data (p. 471)

- A **bar graph** uses bars to show data.
- A **line plot** uses a number line to show how often something happens.

Probability (p. 484)

Probability describes how likely it is that an event will happen.

- *Certain* to choose a marble.
- *Likely* to choose a red.
- *Unlikely* to choose green.
- *Impossible* to choose blue.

Key Vocabulary

bar graph (p. 471)
line plot (p. 476)
probability (p. 484)
tally chart (p. 471)

Vocabulary Check

Choose the vocabulary word that completes each sentence.

1. In a vertical ___?___, the bars go from the bottom up.
2. A ___?___ uses a number line to show how often something happens.
3. ___?___ describes how likely it is that an event will happen.
4. A ___?___ organizes data using tally marks.
5. In a horizontal ___?___, the bars go from left to right.
6. A ___?___ can be used when recording results from a survey.

Lesson-by-Lesson Review

11-1 Bar Graphs (pp. 473–475)

Example 1
The vertical bar graph shows campers favorite activity. What activity do campers prefer most?

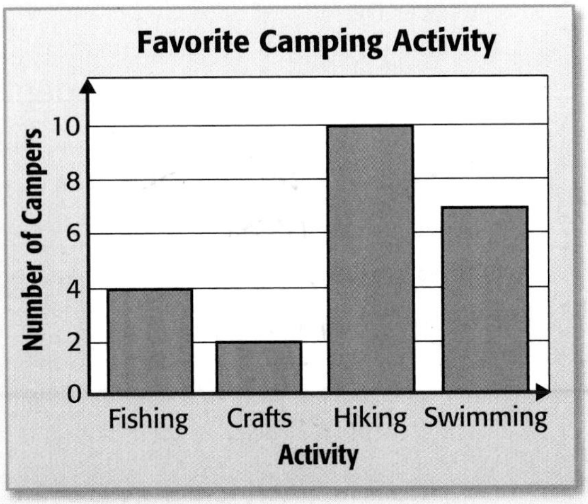

The tallest bar is hiking. So, campers prefer hiking.

7. Display the data in a horizontal bar graph.

Location of Birds' Nests	
Tree	7
Roof	3
Bush	4
Porch swing	1

8. Display the data in a vertical bar graph.

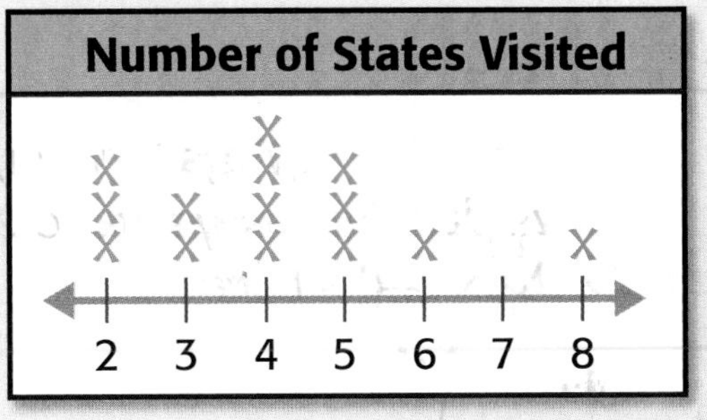

11-2 Line Plots (pp. 476–479)

Example 2
The number of homeruns scored this season are shown below. Display this set of data in a line plot.

3, 6, 1, 2, 2, 4, 3, 1, 1, 3, 2, 2, 2

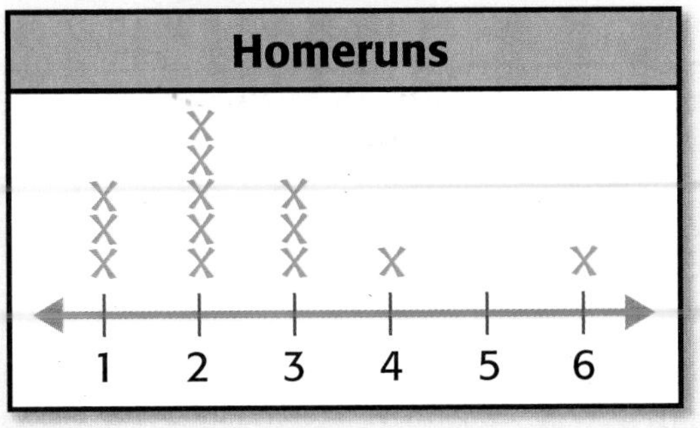

9. The ages of the members of a swim team are shown. Display this set of data in a line plot.

10, 10, 6, 7, 12, 8, 7, 7, 10, 7, 8, 10, 9, 9, 9, 8, 10, 9, 10

10. How many members are there?

11. Write an expression comparing the number of members who are 6 and 8.

12. How many swimmers are 10 years or older?

11-3 Problem-Solving Strategy: Make an Organized List (pp. 480–481)

Example 3
Julie has bologna and turkey. She also has cheddar, provolone, and swiss cheese. How many different sandwiches can she make with one meat and one cheese?

Meat		Cheese
Bologna	–	cheddar
Bologna	–	provolone
Bologna	–	Swiss
Turkey	–	cheddar
Turkey	–	provolone
Turkey	–	Swiss

Julie can make 6 different sandwiches.

Solve. Use the *make an organized list* strategy.

13. There are some coins in a jar. They add up to 29¢. How many coin combinations could there be?

14. Mr. Parsons asked his students to make as many different 4-digit number arrangements they could using the numbers 4, 3, 2, and 1. How many arrangements can be made?

11-4 Understand Probability (pp. 484–487)

Example 4
Andrew spins the spinner shown. How likely is it that the he will spin a multiple of 4?

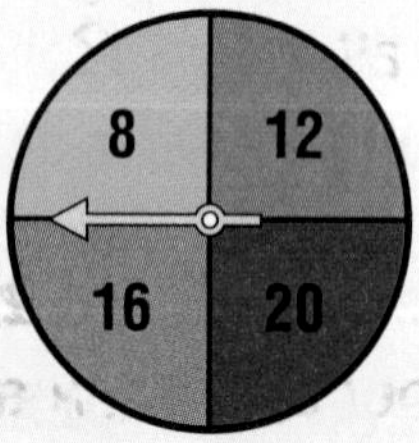

The numbers 8, 12, 16, and 20 are all multiples of 4, so it is *certain* that Andrew will spin a multiple of 4.

Describe the probability of the spinner landing on each number. Write *certain, likely, unlikely,* or *impossible*.

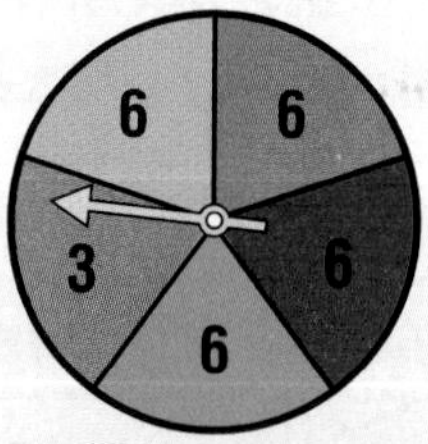

15. four

16. six

17. three

18. multiple of 3

11-5 Problem-Solving Investigation: Choose a Strategy (pp. 490–491)

Example 5
Ashley has 20 stuffed animals. She will keep 5 and divide the rest equally among 3 friends. How many stuffed animals does each friend get?

Understand Ashley has 20 stuffed animals. She will keep 5 and divide the rest equally among her 3 friends. Find how many each friend gets.

Plan Subtract and divide to solve the problem.

Solve Find how many stuffed animals she has to give away.

20	Total
− 5	Number Ashley keeps
15	Number to divide equally

Then, divide to find how many each gets.

$15 \div 3 = 5$

So, each gets 5 animals.

Check Look back at the problem. Check by multiplying and adding. $5 \times 3 = 5$ and $15 + 5 = 20$. So, the answer is correct.

Use any strategy to solve.

19. Two teams scored 40 points. Team A scored 8 fewer points than Team B. How many points did each team score?

20. Marsha has the money shown. Will she have enough money to buy an eraser for 35¢ and a note pad for $1.25? Explain.

21. There are 35 members in a marching band. When marching, there are 5 members in each row. The first and fifth person in each row has a gold star on their hat. How many gold stars are there altogether?

22. Suppose you add 25 to a number and then subtract 14. The result is 48. What was the original number?

11-6 Make Predictions (pp. 494–497)

Example 6
The results from rolling a six-sided number cube 14 times are shown in the line plot. Predict the next number to be rolled.

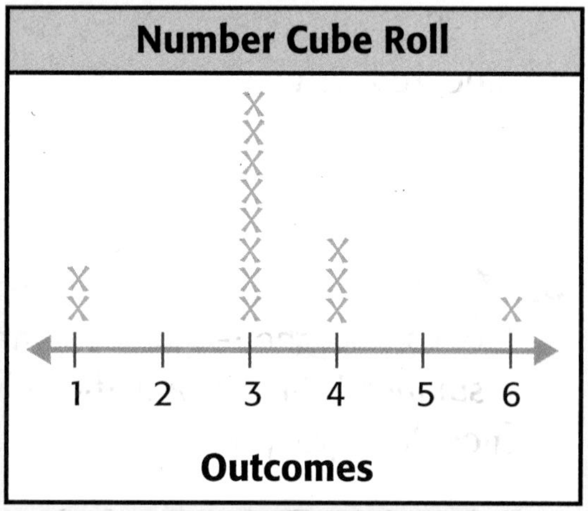

The next roll is likely to be a 3.

Example 7
The results from picking letter tiles 20 times is shown. What letter is least likely to be picked next?

Letter Pick	
Letter	**Tally**
A	||||
B	|
C	𝍸 |||
D	𝍸 ||

It is least likely that the letter B would be picked next.

A four-color spinner is divided into four equal parts. The tally chart shows the results from spinning the spinner 50 times.

Spinner Results	
Color	**Tally**
Yellow	||
Blue	𝍸 𝍸 𝍸 𝍸 𝍸 |||
Green	𝍸 𝍸
Red	𝍸 𝍸

23. What color is the spinner most likely to land on next? Why?

24. What two colors is the spinner equally likely to land on? Explain.

25. Is it reasonable to say that half of the colors on the spinner are blue? Explain.

The results from choosing a marble from a bag 50 times is shown.

Marble Pick	
red 28	green 10
blue 12	yellow 0

26. What color marble is most likely to be picked next?

27. What two colors are equally likely to be chosen?

Chapter 11 Chapter Test

1. Display the data in a horizontal bar graph.

Pick a Marble	
Outcome	**Tally**
Yellow	卌 卌 卌 |
Orange	卌 |||
Green	卌 卌 ||
Blue	卌 |||

2. **STANDARDS PRACTICE** The line plot shows the number of ribbons each gymnast earned. Find the total ribbons earned?

Gymnast Ribbons

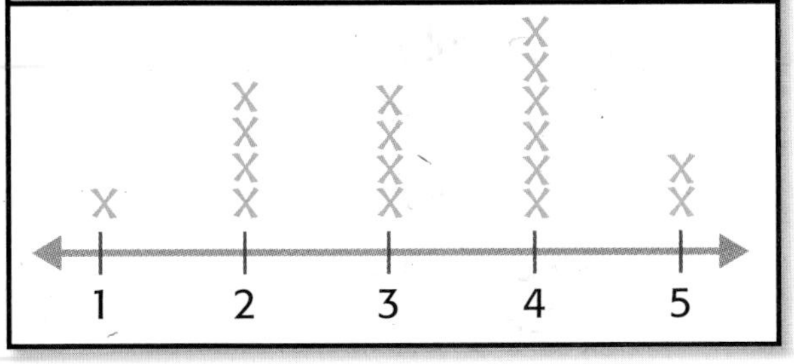

A 5
B 17
C 55
D 65

3. How many different color combinations can be made by spinning each spinner?

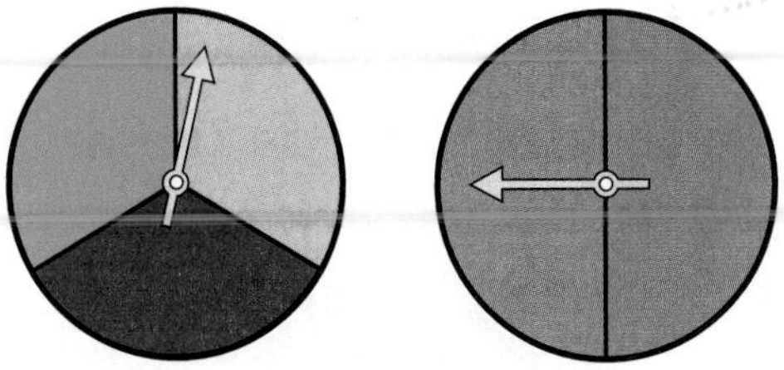

Describe the probability of each outcome. Write *certain, likely, unlikely,* or *impossible.*

4. blue
5. purple
6. green
7. blue, red, or green

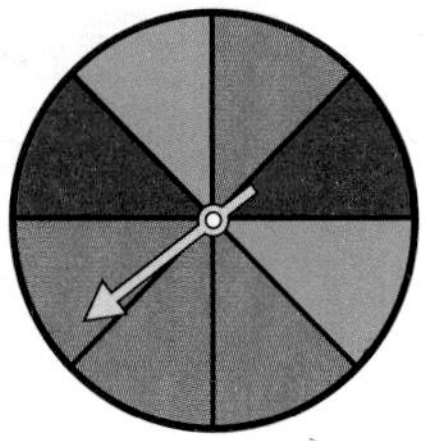

8. **STANDARDS PRACTICE** The table shows the results of spinning a spinner. What color is the spinner most likely to land on?

Color Spin	
Outcomes	**Number**
Red	15
Blue	40
Green	5
Yellow	3

F red
G blue
H green
J yellow

9. **WRITING IN MATH** What does a tally chart of results from an experiment tell you about the probability of each possible outcome?

11 California Standards Practice

Cumulative, Chapters 1–11

Standards Example

How many students checked out more than 4 books?

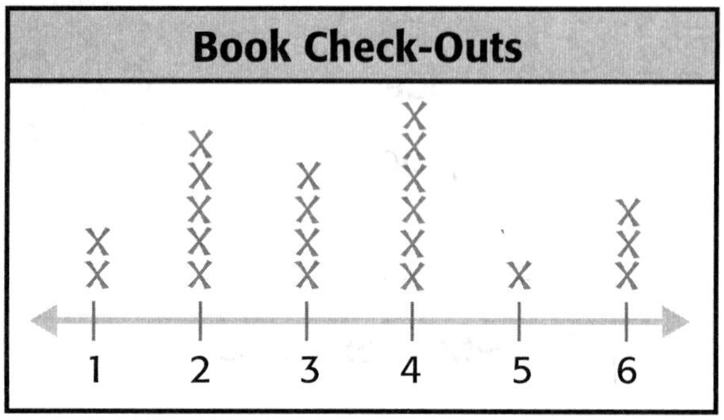

A 4 **C** 10

B 7 **D** 23

Read the Question

You need to find out how many students checked out more than 4 books.

Solve the Question

More than 4 means 5 and 6. Use the line plot and count the number of Xs above 5 and 6.

So, 1 + 3 or 4 students checked out more than 4 books.
The answer is A.

Online **Personal Tutor at** ca.gr3math.com

Choose the best answer.

1 **Which is most likely to be the mass of a basketball?**

A 1 gram **C** 1 kilogram

B 1 centimeter **D** 1 meter

2 **Which event is certain to happen?**

F Earth will rotate on its axis.

G It will never rain on Tuesdays.

H It will rain every Tuesday.

J It will stop snowing on Earth.

3 **What conclusion can you draw from the line plot?**

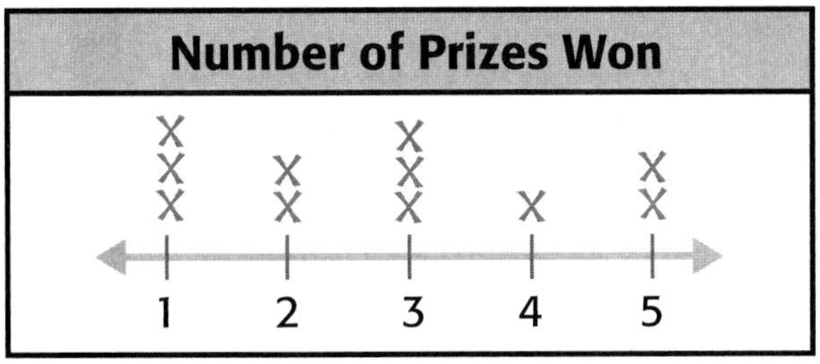

A Most students won 4 or more prizes.

B Most students won 1 to 3 prizes.

C More students won 5 prizes.

D Only 6 students won more than 4 prizes.

4 **Chiyo has a bag of marbles. She has 3 red marbles, 2 blue marbles, 4 green marbles, and 6 black marbles. Which color marble will she most likely pull from the bag?**

F green **H** black

G blue **J** red

5 **Chris and Brianna are making sand castles at the beach. What unit is most appropriate to measure the capacity of a sand pail?**

A gram **C** pint

B cup **D** gallon

6 **Jan spun the spinner once. On which color is the spinner most likely to land?**

F green

G red

H blue

J yellow

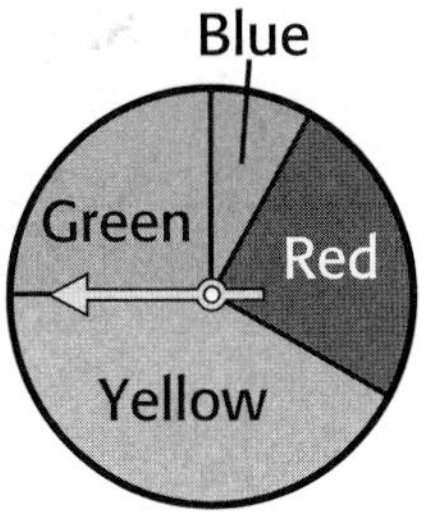

7 **Which object is a cone?**

A

C

B

D

8 **Which number is 100 more than 2354?**

F 2254 **H** 2454

G 2364 **J** 3354

9 **Dennis buys 3 packages of paper. Each package cost the same price. The total was $24. How much did each package cost?**

A $6 **C** $8

B $7 **D** $9

CHAPTER 12

Fractions

BIG Idea What is a Fraction?

A **fraction** is a number that names part of a whole.

Example The fruit plate shown has 4 equal sections. Each section is *one-fourth* or *one of four* sections.

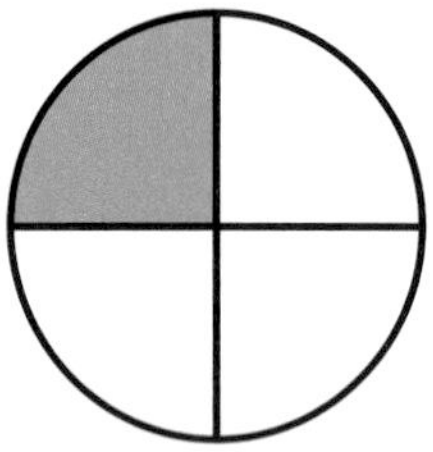

or

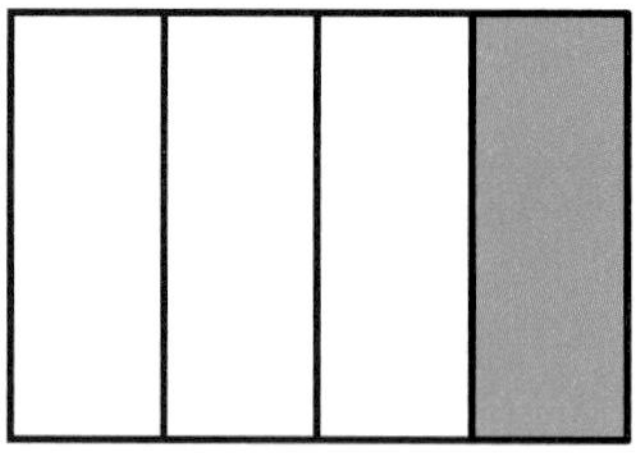

What will I learn in this chapter?

- Identify, read, and write fractions.
- Find equivalent fractions.
- Compare fractions.
- Add and subtract like fractions.
- Solve problems by drawing pictures.

Key Vocabulary

fraction
numerator
denominator
equivalent fractions
like fractions

Math Online **Student Study Tools at** ca.gr3math.com

FOLDABLES™ Study Organizer

Make this Foldable to help you organize information about fractions. Begin with 3 sheets of $8\frac{1}{2}$" × 11" paper.

1. **Stack** the paper so that each sheet is one inch higher than the other.

2. **Fold** the sheets upward so that all of the layers are the same distance apart.

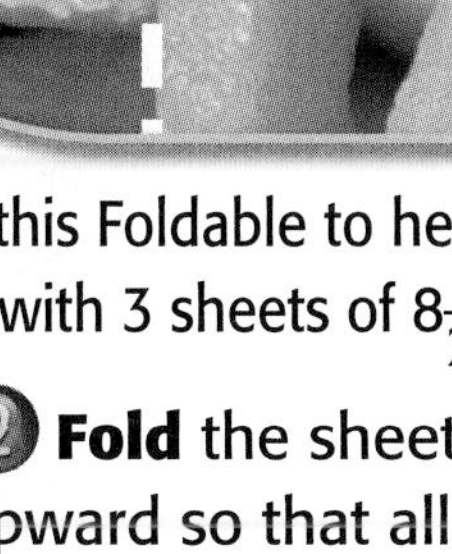

3. **Crease** well. Then open and glue together as shown.

4. **Label** as shown. Record what you learn.

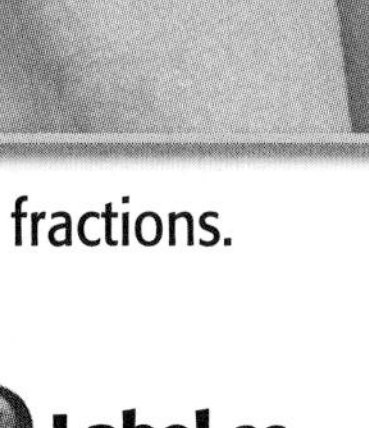

ARE YOU READY for Chapter 12?

You have two ways to check prerequisite skills for this chapter.

Option 2

Math Online Take the Chapter Readiness Quiz at ca.gr3math.com.

Option 1

Complete the Quick Check below.

QUICK Check

Write the number of parts. Then tell whether each figure shows *equal* or *not equal* parts. **(Prior grade)**

1. 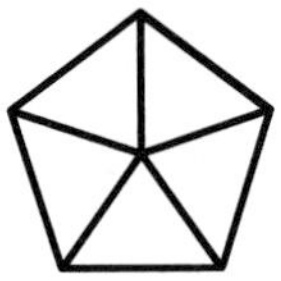

2. 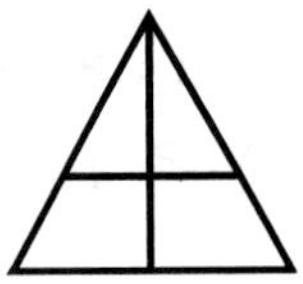

3. 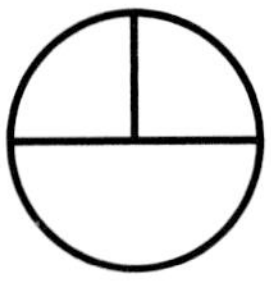

4. 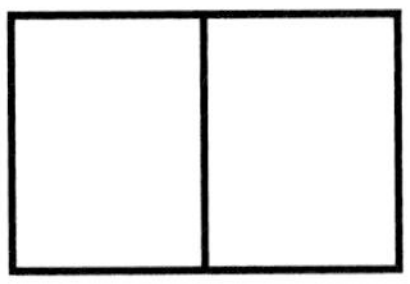

5. Draw a circle that is divided into 6 equal parts.

Tell the number of equal parts. Write *halves, thirds,* or *fourths.* **(Prior grade)**

6. 

7. 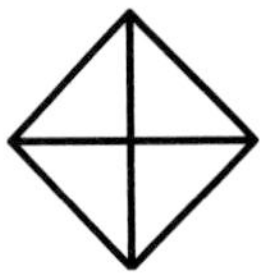

8. 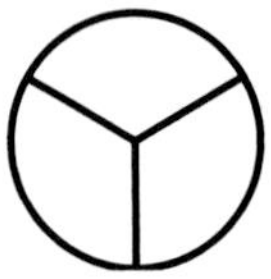

9. 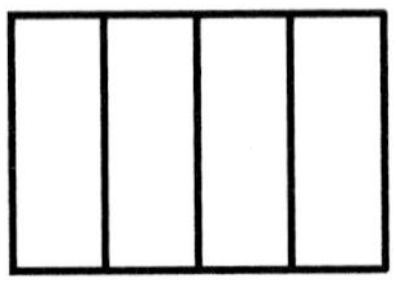

10. Jacob draws a figure and divides it into fifths. What could his figure look like?

Add or subtract. **(Lesson 2-1)**

11. 1 + 5 **12.** 6 + 4 **13.** 5 + 3 **14.** 5 + 7

15. 7 − 2 **16.** 6 − 5 **17.** 8 + 3 **18.** 8 − 1

19. There are 9 books on a desk. A student takes 4 of the books. How many are left on the desk?

12-1 Parts of a Whole

GET READY to Learn

This spinner has 5 equal sections. The sections are red, orange, purple, yellow, and green. What fraction of the spinner is red?

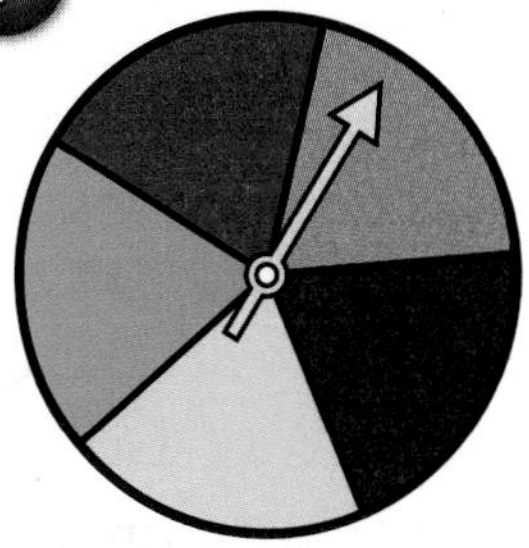

MAIN IDEA

I will read and write fractions for part of a whole.

Preparation for Standard 3NS3.1 **Compare fractions represented by drawings or concrete materials to show equivalency** and to add and subtract simple fractions in context.

New Vocabulary

- fraction
- numerator
- denominator

A **fraction** is a number that names part of a whole. You can use a fraction to tell what part of the spinner is red.

Real-World EXAMPLE — Write and Read Fractions

1 **SPINNERS** **What fraction of the spinner is red?**

One Way: Models

The spinner above represents one whole. There are 5 equal parts. A whole can be divided into 5 equal parts, or fifths.

Another Way: Paper and Pencil

The spinner has 5 equal parts. One part is red.

$\frac{1}{5}$ ← part that is red; ← total number of equal parts

Write $\frac{1}{5}$

Read one-fifth

So, one fifth or $\frac{1}{5}$ of the spinner is red.

In a fraction, the **numerator** tells the number of equal parts. The **denominator** tells the total number of equal parts in all.

$\frac{1}{5}$ ← numerator; ← denominator

Remember

The bottom number (denominator) is the total number of equal parts. The top number (numerator) is the number of shaded parts.

EXAMPLE Write and Read Fractions

2 What fraction of the figure is green?

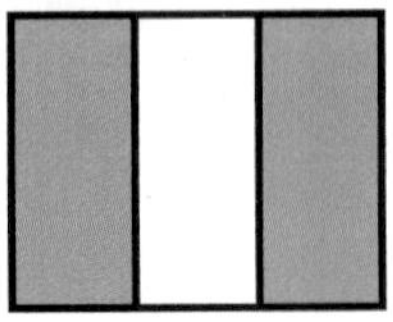

$\frac{2}{3}$ ← parts that are green / ← total number of equal parts

Write $\frac{2}{3}$

Read two-thirds

Two-thirds or $\frac{2}{3}$ of the figure are green.

Online Personal Tutor at ca.gr3math.com

Sometimes a part of a whole cannot easily be named by a fraction because the parts are not equal.

Real-World EXAMPLE

3 SPINNER A spinner is shown. What fraction of the spinner is labeled with a 2?

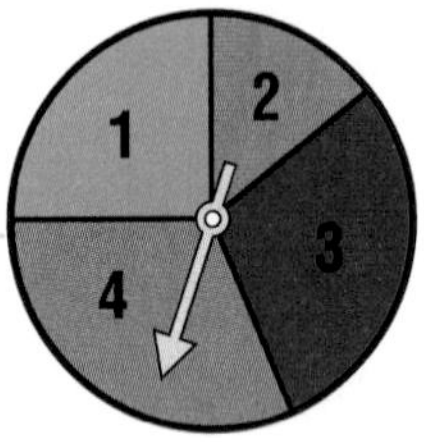

There are 4 parts. But, the parts are not equal. So, you cannot easily write a fraction.

CHECK What You Know

Write the fraction for the part that is yellow. Then write the fraction for the part that is *not* yellow. Label your answers. See Examples 1–3 (pp. 509–510)

1. 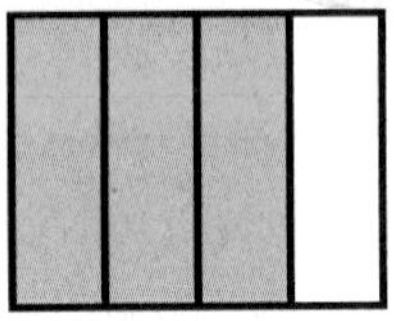

2. 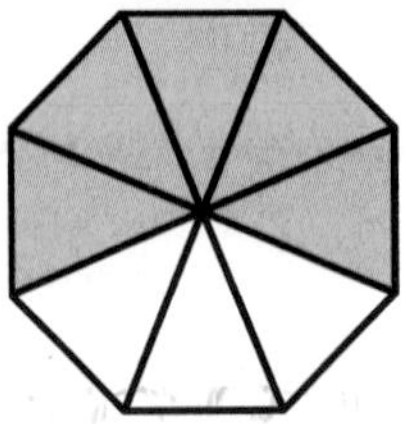

3. 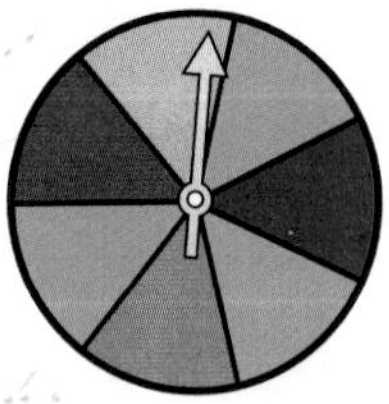

4. What fraction of the pizza has cheese only?

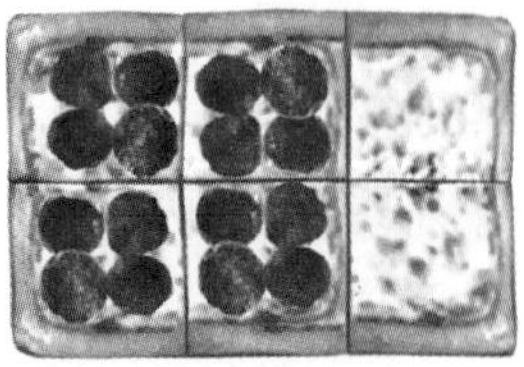

5. Talk About It What is a fraction? How does a fraction describe the shaded part of a whole?

Practice and Problem Solving

EXTRA PRACTICE
See page R32.

Write the fraction for the part that is blue. Then write the fraction for the part that is *not* blue. Label your answers. See Examples 1–3 (pp. 509–510)

6. 

7. 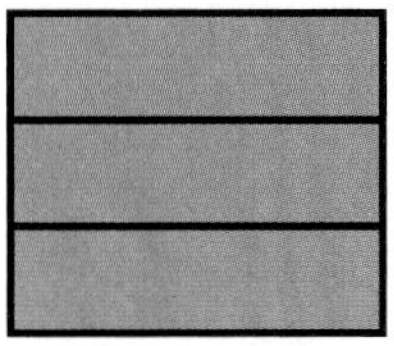

8. 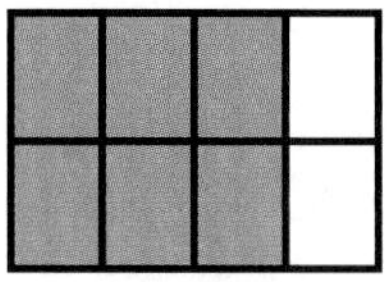

9. 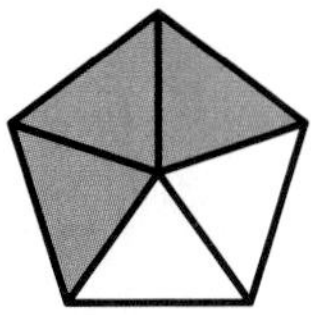

10. 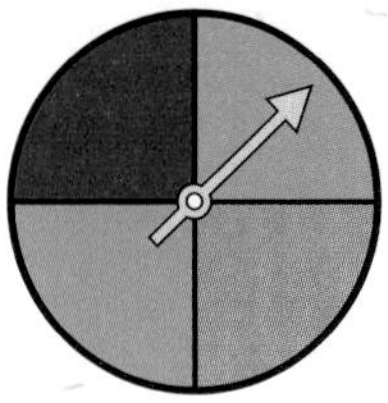

11. 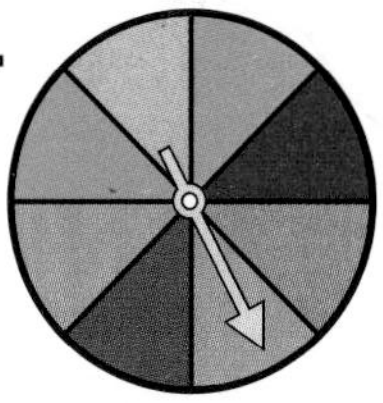

12. What fraction of the honeycomb has bees?

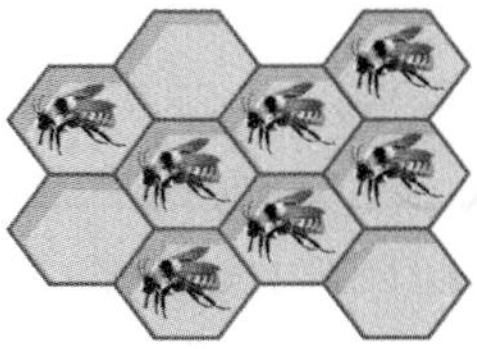

13. What fraction of the pizza has pepperoni?

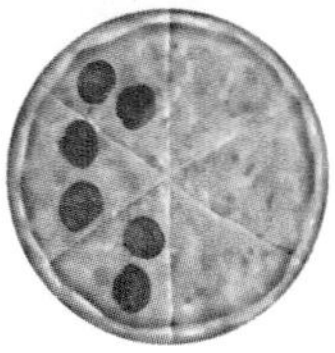

Draw a picture for each fraction. Shade the fraction.

14. $\frac{2}{5}$ **15.** $\frac{1}{7}$ **16.** three-eighths **17.** two-halves

Real-World PROBLEM SOLVING

Art The primary colors are red, blue, and yellow. The secondary colors are green, orange, and violet.

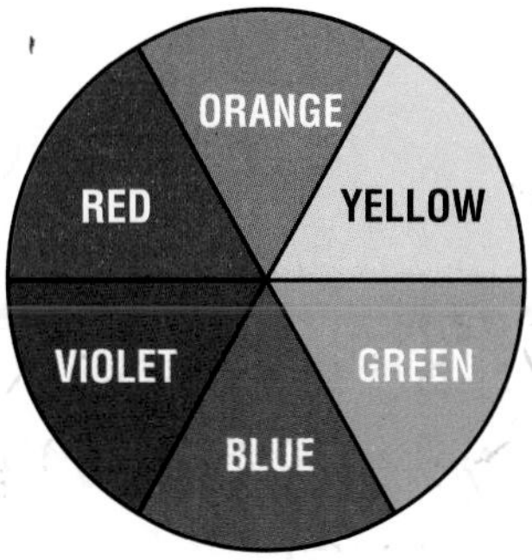

18. What fraction of the primary and secondary colors is red?

19. What fraction is blue or orange?

20. What fraction is not violet?

H.O.T. Problems

21. OPEN ENDED Draw a picture for which you cannot easily write a fraction to describe the shaded parts of the whole. Explain your thinking.

22. WRITING IN MATH What fraction names the point on the number line? Explain your reasoning.

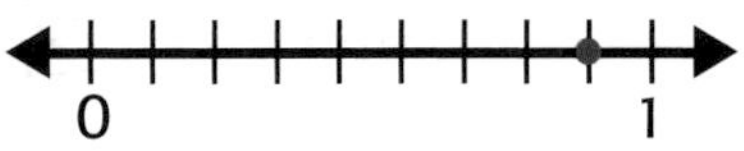

12-2 Problem-Solving Investigation

MAIN IDEA I will choose the best strategy to solve a problem.

Standard 3MR2.3 Use a variety of methods, such as words, numbers, symbols, charts, graphs, tables, diagrams, and models, to explain mathematical reasoning. **Standard 3NS2.1** Find the sum or difference of two whole numbers between 0 and 10,000.

P.S.I. TEAM +

CARLOTA: Last night, I played a board game. On one turn, I rolled two number cubes. The sum of the numbers was 9. The difference was 3.

YOUR MISSION: Find the two numbers Carlota rolled.

Understand Carlota rolled two number cubes. The sum of the numbers was 9. The difference was 3. Find the two numbers rolled.

Plan Make a table to show all of the possible rolls and their sums.

Solve The table shows that to get a sum of 9, Carlota must have rolled 5 and 4 or 6 and 3.

6 + 3 = **9**
5 + 4 = **9**

Find the difference.

6 − 3 = **3**
5 − 4 = 1

Since 6 + 3 = 9 and 6 − 3 = 3, Carlota must have rolled 6 and 3.

+	0	1	2	3	4	5	6
0	0	1	2	3	4	5	6
1	1	2	3	4	5	6	7
2	2	3	4	5	6	7	8
3	3	4	5	6	7	8	9
4	4	5	6	7	8	9	10
5	5	6	7	8	9	10	11
6	6	7	8	9	10	11	12

Check Look back at the problem. Since 3 + 6 = 9 and 6 − 3 = 3, you know that the answer is correct.

Mixed Problem Solving

EXTRA PRACTICE
See page R32.

Use any strategy shown below to solve. Tell what strategy you used.

PROBLEM-SOLVING STRATEGIES

- Draw a picture.
- Look for a pattern.
- Guess and check.
- Make a table.
- Work backward.

1. **Measurement** Candace practices soccer 35 minutes each day. She finished soccer practice at 5:30 P.M. What time did she begin?

2. A family of 4 goes bowling. What is the total cost if each person rents a ball and shoes and plays two games?

3. **Measurement** A moose weighs about 1,300 pounds. A cougar weighs about 250 pounds. How much more does the moose weigh than the cougar?

4. Emil is drawing the pattern shown. He has room for 25 shapes. How many squares will he draw in all?

5. Pablo, Annie, and Terrance each have a pet. One has a cat. One has a turtle, and another has a dog. Annie and Pablo have a pet with fur. Annie's pet gets baths. Who has the turtle?

6. Suppose you buy the items shown for lunch. If you pay with a $10 bill, how much change will you receive?

7. **Algebra** There are two numbers whose sum is 8 and quotient is 3. Find the numbers.

8. Gavin's parents took Gavin and 2 of his friends to the zoo. How much money did they pay for admission and parking?

9. Alejandro paid $140 for the cable, phone, and Internet bills. The cable bill was $62. The phone bill was $59. How much was the Internet bill?

10. **WRITING IN MATH** A frozen yogurt cake has 4 layers. One layer is strawberry, another is vanilla, and the other layers are peach. What fraction of the cake is peach? Explain.

Explore

Math Activity for 12-3

Equivalent Fractions

MAIN IDEA

I will use models to explore equivalent fractions.

Standard 3NS3.1 Compare fractions represented by drawings or concrete materials to show equivalency and to add and subtract simple fractions in context.

Standard 3MR2.3 Use a variety of methods, such as words, numbers, symbols, charts, graphs, tables, **diagrams, and models, to explain mathematical reasoning.**

You Will Need
fraction models

Concepts in Motion

Animation
ca.gr3math.com

Fraction models can help you find fractions that name the same number, or **equivalent fractions**.

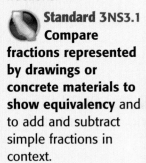

ACTIVITY **Find two fractions equivalent to $\frac{1}{2}$.**

Step 1 **Model $\frac{1}{2}$.**

Start with 1 whole and the $\frac{1}{2}$-fraction piece.

Step 2 **Find one fraction equivalent to $\frac{1}{2}$.**

Use $\frac{1}{4}$-fraction pieces to equal the length of the $\frac{1}{2}$-fraction piece. Count the number of $\frac{1}{4}$-fraction pieces. So, $\frac{1}{2} = \frac{2}{4}$.

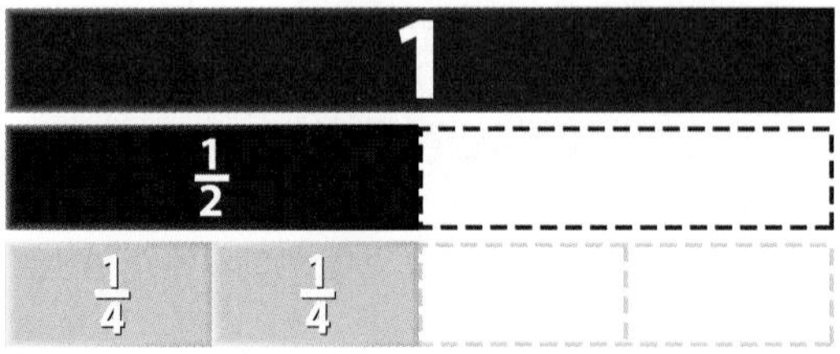

Step 3 **Find another fraction equivalent to $\frac{1}{2}$.**

Use $\frac{1}{8}$-fraction pieces to equal the length of the $\frac{1}{2}$-fraction piece. Count the number of $\frac{1}{8}$-fraction pieces. So, $\frac{1}{2} = \frac{4}{8}$.

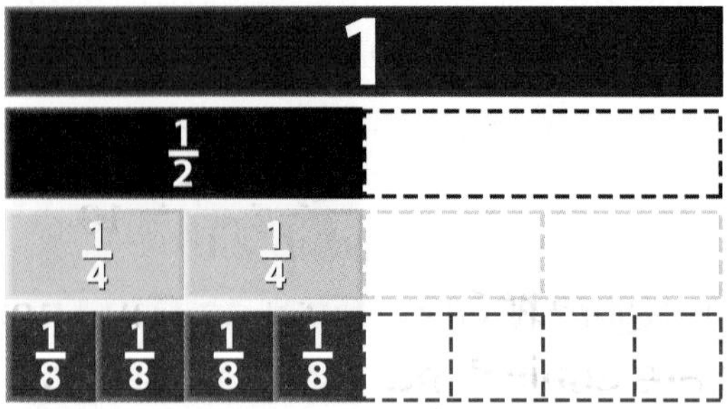

Think About It

1. How many of the $\frac{1}{4}$-fraction pieces are equal to the length of the $\frac{1}{2}$-fraction piece?
2. How many of the $\frac{1}{8}$-fraction pieces are equal to the length of the $\frac{1}{2}$-fraction piece?
3. Write two fractions that name the same amount as $\frac{1}{2}$.
4. Copy and complete $\frac{1}{2} = \frac{\blacksquare}{4} = \frac{\blacksquare}{8}$.

CHECK What You Know

5. Use fraction models to find two fractions that are equivalent to $\frac{1}{3}$.

Use models to complete the equivalent fractions.

6. $\frac{1}{4}$ = How many $\frac{1}{8}$?

   $\frac{1}{4} = \frac{\blacksquare}{8}$

7. $\frac{1}{5}$ = How many $\frac{1}{10}$?

   $\frac{2}{5} = \frac{\blacksquare}{10}$

8. $\frac{1}{3}$ = How many $\frac{1}{6}$?

   $\frac{1}{3} = \frac{\blacksquare}{6}$

9. $\frac{1}{6}$ $\frac{1}{6}$ = How many $\frac{1}{12}$?

   $\frac{2}{6} = \frac{\blacksquare}{12}$

Use fraction models to determine whether each pair of fractions is equivalent or not equivalent. Write *yes* or *no*.

10. $\frac{1}{2}$ and $\frac{3}{6}$
11. $\frac{1}{4}$ and $\frac{2}{4}$
12. $\frac{3}{4}$ and $\frac{6}{8}$
13. $\frac{3}{3}$ and $\frac{6}{6}$
14. $\frac{3}{5}$ and $\frac{5}{10}$
15. $\frac{2}{3}$ and $\frac{4}{6}$
16. **WRITING IN ▸MATH** How do you know whether two fractions are equivalent? Explain how you know whether two fractions are not equivalent.

12-3 Find Equivalent Fractions

GET READY to Learn

Kwan has a bookshelf. One of the 3 shelves has books. Kwan says that $\frac{1}{3}$ of the shelves have books. What other fractions name the same number as $\frac{1}{3}$?

MAIN IDEA

I will find equivalent fractions.

Standard 3NS3.1 Compare fractions represented by drawings or concrete materials to show equivalency and to add and subtract simple fractions in context (e.g., $\frac{1}{2}$ of a pizza is the same amount as $\frac{2}{4}$ of another pizza that is the same size; show that $\frac{3}{8}$ is larger than $\frac{1}{4}$).

New Vocabulary

equivalent fractions

Vocabulary Link

Prefixes The prefix *equi-* means equal.

Two or more different fractions that name the same amount or part of a whole are called **equivalent fractions**.

EXAMPLE Find Equivalent Fractions

1 Complete $\frac{1}{3} = \frac{\blacksquare}{6}$ to find equivalent fractions.

One Way: Fraction Models

Think about the number of equal parts in fraction modeles.

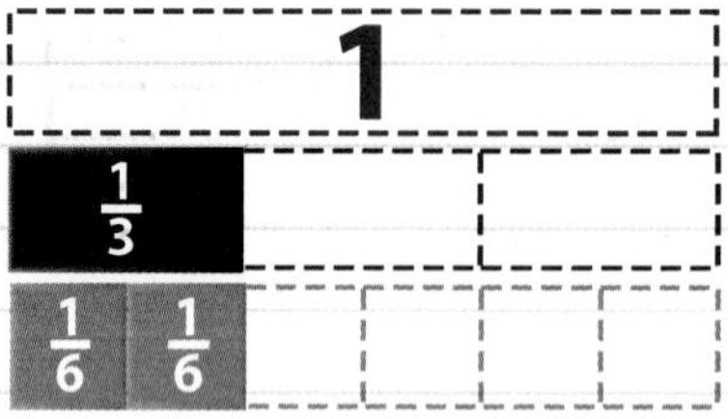

There are 2 sixths in $\frac{1}{3}$.

So, $\frac{1}{3} = \frac{2}{6}$.

Another Way: Picture

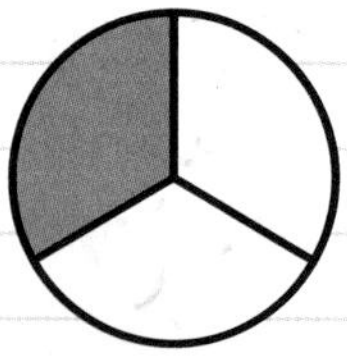

The circle is divided into thirds. One part is shaded.

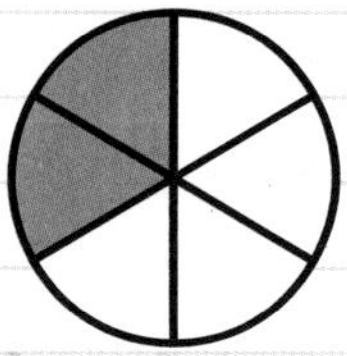

Another equal circle is divided into sixths. The same part is shaded.

There are 2 sixths in $\frac{1}{3}$.

So, $\frac{1}{3} = \frac{2}{6}$.

Online Personal Tutor at ca.gr3math.com

CHECK What You Know

Complete each number sentence to find equivalent fractions. See Example 1 (p. 516)

1.

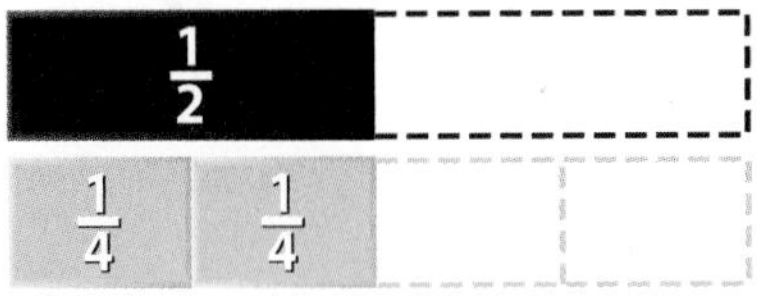

$\frac{1}{2} = \frac{■}{4}$

2.

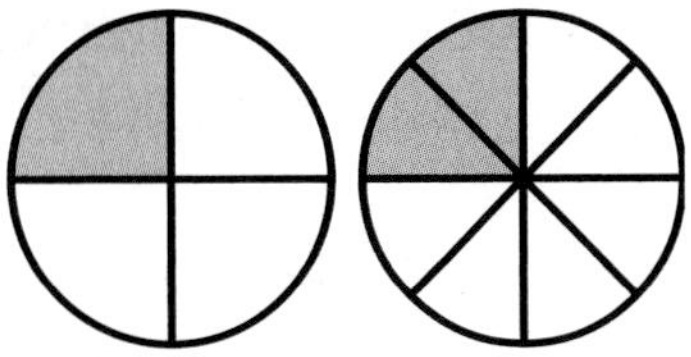

$\frac{■}{4} = \frac{2}{8}$

3.

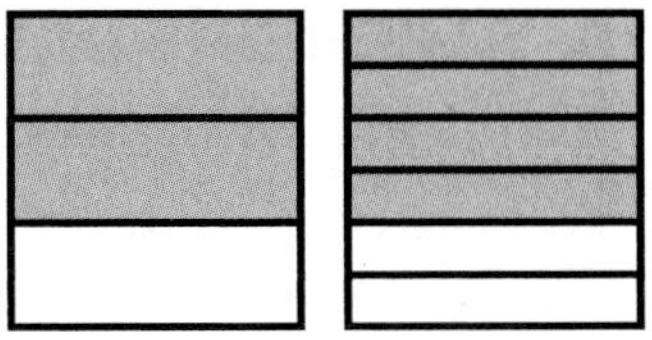

$\frac{■}{3} = \frac{■}{6}$

4. Two-fifths of an apple pie is eaten. Write another fraction that names $\frac{2}{5}$.

5. Talk About It What pattern do you see in the fractions $\frac{1}{2} = \frac{2}{4} = \frac{4}{8}$?

Practice and Problem Solving

EXTRA PRACTICE See page R32.

Complete each number sentence to find equivalent fractions. See Example 1 (p. 516)

6.

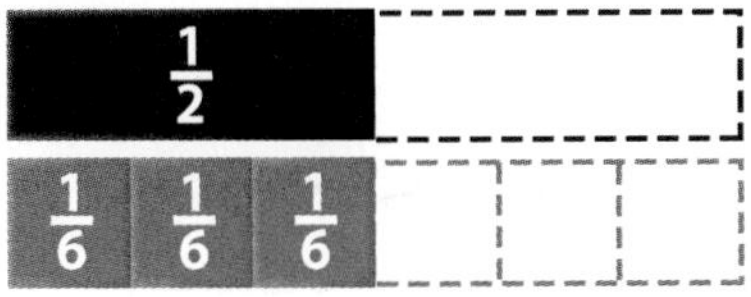

$\frac{1}{2} = \frac{■}{6}$

7.

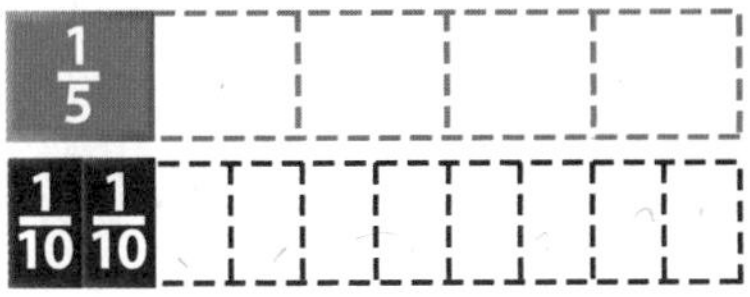

$\frac{1}{5} = \frac{■}{10}$

8.

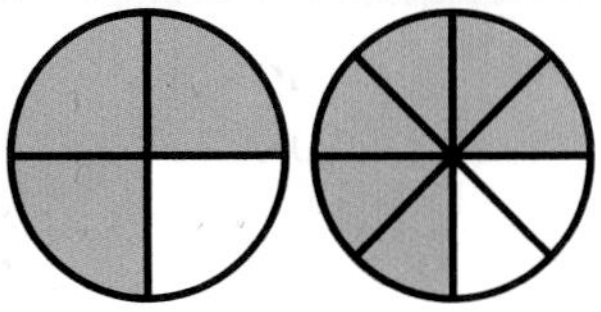

$\frac{■}{4} = \frac{6}{8}$

9.

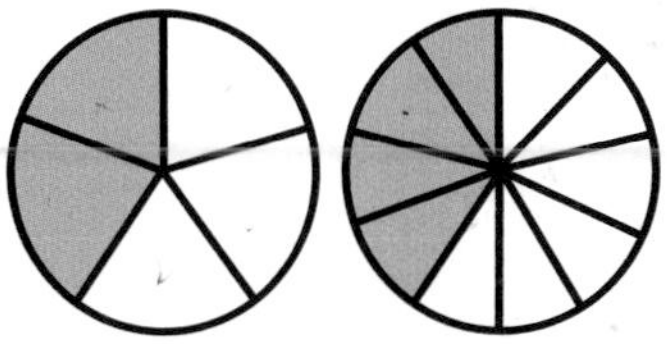

$\frac{■}{5} = \frac{4}{10}$

10.

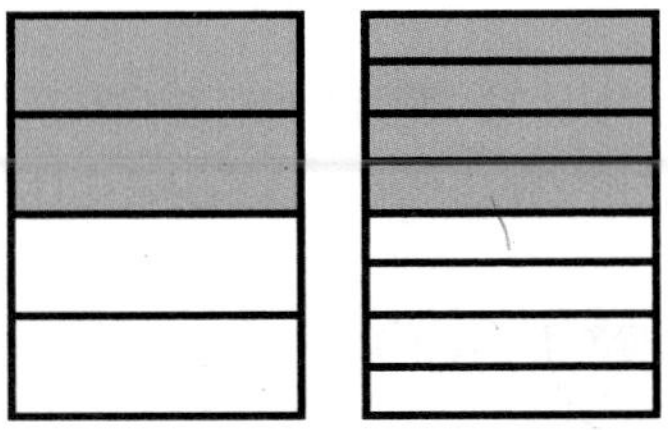

$\frac{■}{4} = \frac{■}{8}$

11.

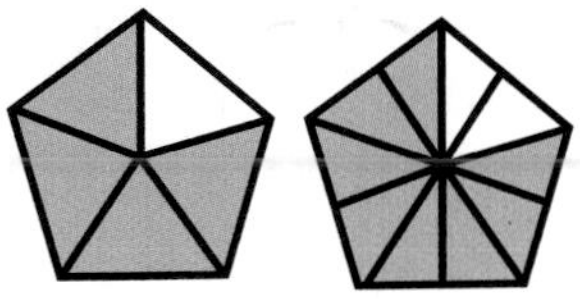

$\frac{■}{5} = \frac{■}{10}$

Algebra Find each missing value.

12. $\frac{1}{2} = \frac{■}{8}$

13. $\frac{2}{3} = \frac{■}{12}$

14. $\frac{3}{■} = \frac{6}{8}$

15. $\frac{4}{■} = \frac{8}{10}$

Write another fraction that names each fraction.

16. One-sixth of a game spinner is red.

17. Amy read two-thirds of a book.

H.O.T. Problems

18. OPEN ENDED Give an example of two fractions that are not equivalent. Draw a picture to support your answer.

19. WHICH ONE DOESN'T BELONG? Which fraction does not belong with the other three? Explain your reasoning.

$\frac{4}{8}$ $\frac{1}{2}$ $\frac{5}{10}$ $\frac{3}{5}$

20. WRITING IN ▸MATH Explain how you would find a fraction equivalent to $\frac{1}{2}$.

Standards Practice

21 What fraction of the figure is shaded? **(Lesson 12-1)**

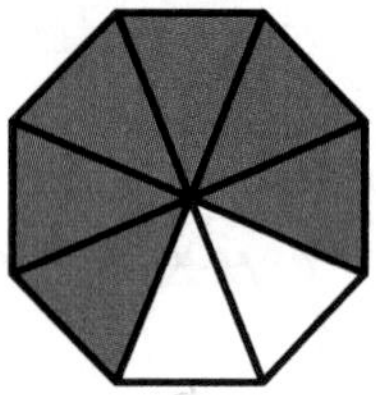

A $\frac{1}{8}$

B $\frac{5}{8}$

C $\frac{6}{8}$

D $\frac{5}{6}$

22 Which figure is equivalent to $\frac{2}{3}$? **(Lesson 12-3)**

F

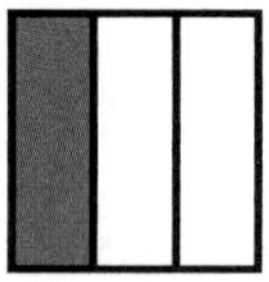

H

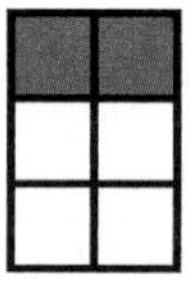

G

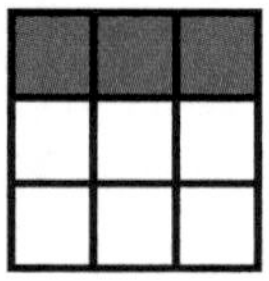

J

Spiral Review

23. One-fifth of 30 students own a scooter. How many students do not own a scooter? Use the *draw a picture* strategy. **(Lesson 12-2)**

Write the fraction for the part that is yellow. Then write the fraction for the part that is not yellow. (Lesson 12-1)

24.

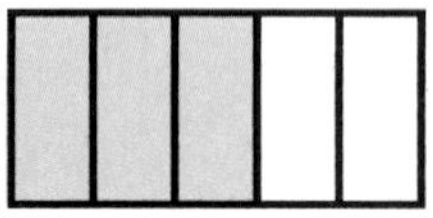

25.

26.

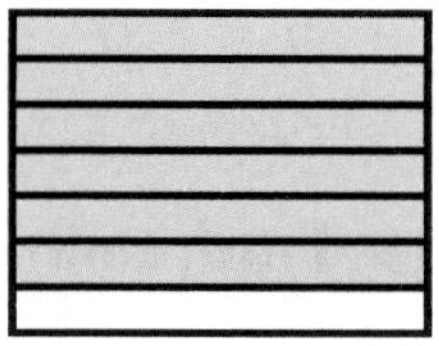

27. Geometry If the perimeter of the figure at the right is 23 cm, what is the length of x? **(Lesson 10-2)**

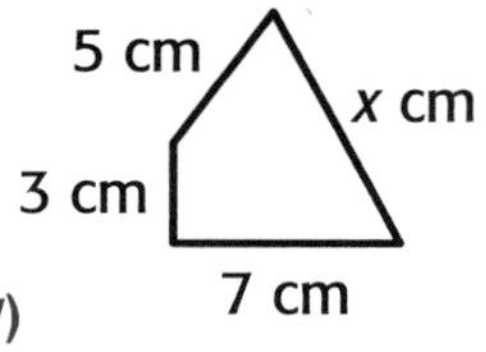

28. Measurement How many seconds are in 2 minutes? **(Lesson 8-7)**

Game Time

Fraction Concentration

Find Equivalent Fractions

You will need: 10 index cards

$\frac{1}{2}$	$\frac{1}{3}$	$\frac{1}{4}$	$\frac{1}{5}$
$\frac{3}{4}$	$\frac{2}{5}$	$\frac{2}{3}$	$\frac{3}{9}$
$\frac{4}{5}$	$\frac{4}{8}$	$\frac{4}{10}$	$\frac{2}{12}$
$\frac{1}{6}$	$\frac{6}{10}$	$\frac{2}{8}$	$\frac{3}{5}$
$\frac{2}{10}$	$\frac{8}{10}$	$\frac{4}{6}$	$\frac{6}{8}$

Get Ready!

Players: 2 players

Get Set!

Cut each index card in half. Then label as shown.

Go!

- Shuffle the cards. Then spread out the cards face-down.
- Player 1 turns over any two of the cards.
- If the fractions are equivalent, Player 1 keeps the cards and continues his or her turn.
- If the fractions are not equivalent, the cards are turned over and Player 2 takes a turn.
- Continue playing until all fractions matches are made. The player with the most cards wins.

12-4 Problem-Solving Strategy

MAIN IDEA I will draw a picture to solve problems.

Standard 3MR1.1 Analyze problems by identifying relationships, distinguishing relevant from irrelevant information, sequencing and prioritizing information, and observing patterns. Standard 3NS3.1 Compare fractions represented by drawings or concrete materials to show equivalency and to add and subtract simple fractions in context.

Ana and her brother have 8 insects in a jar. One-half of the insects are beetles. One is a firefly, and the rest are crickets. How many of the insects are crickets?

Understand

What facts do you know?

- There are 8 insects.
- One is a firefly.
- One-half are beetles.
- The rest are crickets.

What do you need to find?

- Find how many of the insects are crickets.

Plan

You can draw a picture to solve the problem.

Solve

- First draw a figure that is divided into 8 equal parts. This shows 8 insects.

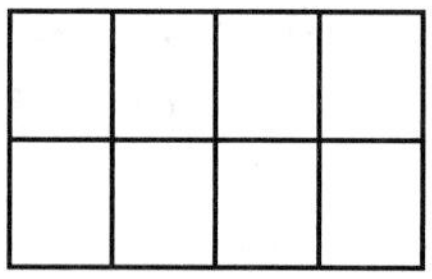

- To show the beetles, shade $\frac{1}{2}$ of the figure. Shade 1 part to show the firefly.

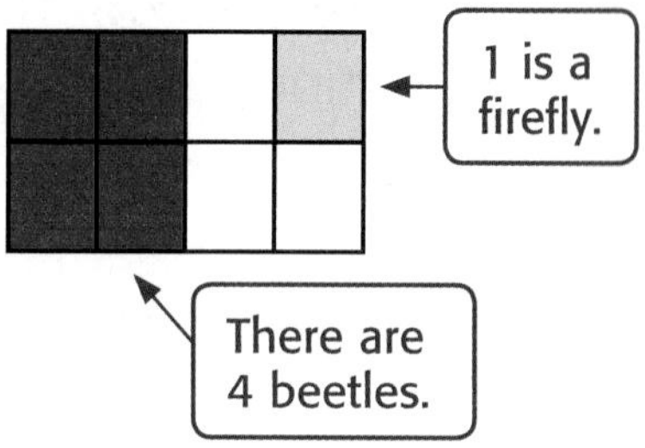
1 is a firefly.
There are 4 beetles.

- There are 3 parts not shaded. This is the number of crickets.

So, 3 of the insects are crickets.

Check

Look back at the problem.
4 beetles + 1 firefly + 3 crickets = 8 insects.
There are 8 insects. So, the answer is correct.

ANALYZE the Strategy

Refer to the problem on the previous page.

1. Explain why the figure was divided into 8 equal parts.

2. Explain why 4 of the 8 boxes were shaded to show the number of beetles.

3. Suppose Ana had 10 insects. How many of the insects would be crickets?

4. Look back to Exercise 3. Check your answer. How do you know that it is correct? Show your work.

PRACTICE the Strategy

EXTRA PRACTICE
See page R33.

Solve. Use the *draw a picture* strategy.

5. There are 12 books. One-third of the books are Mia's. Two belong to Basilio. The others belong to Tyrone. How many belong to Tyrone?

6. Mill Park is 5 miles directly east of Bear Cabin. Nature museum is 5 miles directly south of Bear Cabin. Glacier Lake is 5 miles directly west of Mill Park. Is this possible? Explain.

7. Lola and Olivia each have an equal-size piece of pizza. The table shows how much of each piece Lola and Olivia ate. Who ate more?

Lola	Olivia
$\frac{1}{2}$	$\frac{3}{4}$

8. Berta rides the elevator 3 floors up from her home to meet her friend Seki. They then go down 7 floors, where they meet Tamera. How many floors is Berta from her home?

9. There are 36 houses on a street. The table shows what fraction of the houses have a dog or cat. How many of the houses have a dog?

Dogs	Cats
$\frac{3}{4}$	$\frac{1}{4}$

10. Four students are standing in a lunch line. Tariq is ahead of Kendra. Domingo is behind Kendra. Tariq is behind Ben. In what order are the students standing?

11. Allison is playing jacks. She tosses 10 jacks on the floor. She then picks up $\frac{2}{5}$ of them. How many jacks are left on the floor?

12. **WRITING IN MATH** Explain what it means to draw a picture to solve a problem. How is a picture helpful in solving a problem?

12-5 Compare Fractions

MAIN IDEA

I will compare fractions.

Standard 3NS3.1 Compare fractions represented by drawings or concrete materials to show equivalency and to add and subtract simple fractions in context (e.g., $\frac{1}{2}$ of a pizza is the same amount as $\frac{2}{4}$ of another pizza that is the same size; show that $\frac{3}{8}$ is larger than $\frac{1}{4}$).

GET READY to Learn

Hands-On Mini Activity

Arrange the fraction models shown from longest to shortest.

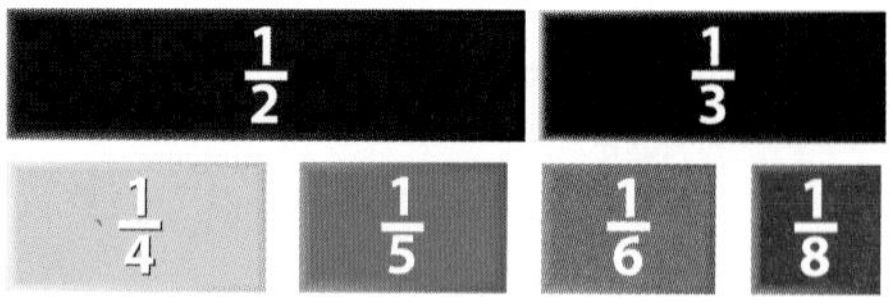

1. Which fraction model is the longest? How many parts make a whole?

2. Which is the shortest? How many parts make a whole?

3. *True* or *false*: As each piece gets smaller, the denominator gets larger.

4. *True* or *false*: If two fractions have the same numerator, the fraction with the greater denominator is less than the other.

You can compare fractions to see which fraction **is greater than (>)**, which fraction **is less than (<)**, or if they are equivalent.

Review Vocabulary

is greater than (>) symbol to show that the first number is greater than the second; Example: 5 > 6

is less than (<) symbol to show that the first number is less than the second; Example: 3 < 8

(Lesson 1-4)

EXAMPLE Compare Fractions

1 **Compare $\frac{5}{8}$ and $\frac{3}{8}$.**

One Way: Fraction Models

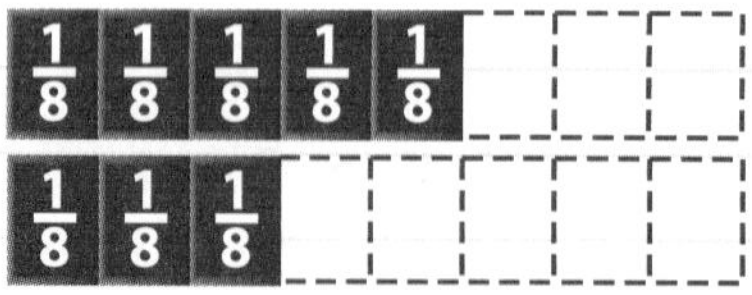

$\frac{5}{8}$ is greater than $\frac{3}{8}$.

So, $\frac{5}{8} > \frac{3}{8}$ or $\frac{3}{8} < \frac{5}{8}$.

Another Way: Number Line

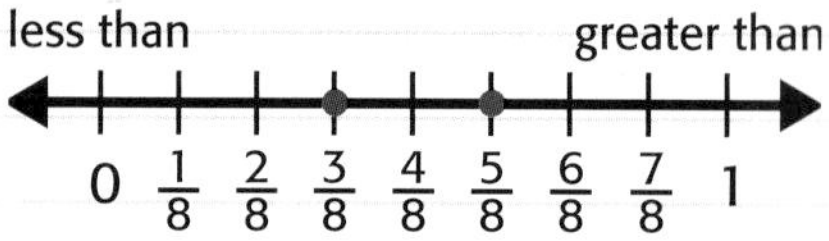

$\frac{5}{8}$ is to the right of $\frac{3}{8}$.

So, $\frac{5}{8} > \frac{3}{8}$ or $\frac{3}{8} < \frac{5}{8}$.

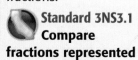

You can compare fractions with different denominators.

Real-World EXAMPLE Compare Fractions

2 FOOD Keri and Arturo each have a mini pizza that are the same size. Keri ate $\frac{1}{2}$ of her pizza. Arturo ate $\frac{3}{4}$ of his pizza. Who ate less?

You need to compare $\frac{1}{2}$ and $\frac{3}{4}$.

Remember

When you compare fractions, be sure the wholes are the same size.

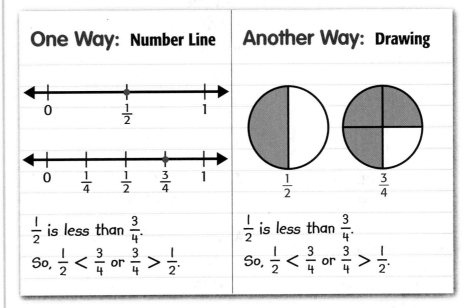

One Way: Number Line

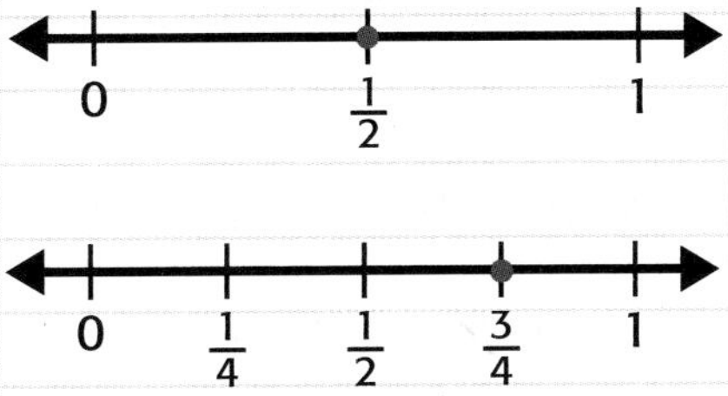

$\frac{1}{2}$ is less than $\frac{3}{4}$.

So, $\frac{1}{2} < \frac{3}{4}$ or $\frac{3}{4} > \frac{1}{2}$.

Another Way: Drawing

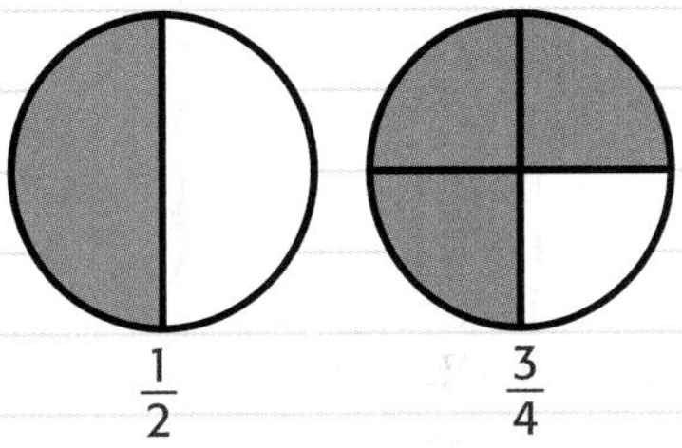

$\frac{1}{2}$ is less than $\frac{3}{4}$.

So, $\frac{1}{2} < \frac{3}{4}$ or $\frac{3}{4} > \frac{1}{2}$.

So, Keri ate less pizza than Arturo.

Online **Personal Tutor at** ca.gr3math.com

CHECK What You Know

Compare. Write >, <, or =. **See Examples 1 and 2 (pp. 522–523)**

1.

$\frac{4}{5}$ ● $\frac{3}{5}$

2.

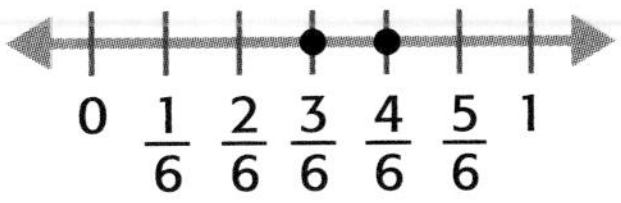

$\frac{3}{6}$ ● $\frac{4}{6}$

3.

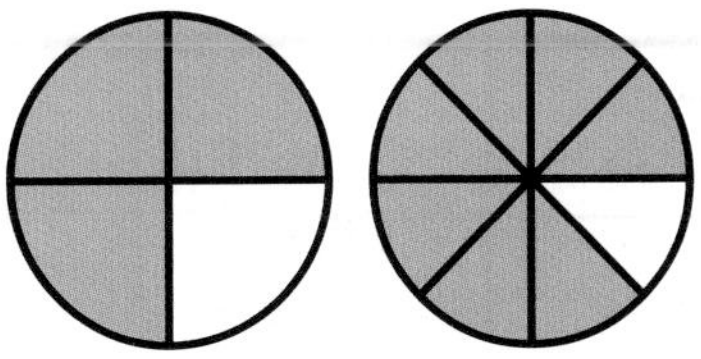

$\frac{3}{4}$ ● $\frac{7}{8}$

4. Camila read $\frac{2}{4}$ of a book. Tyree read $\frac{2}{8}$ of the same book. Who read more?

5. Talk About It Tell how you know that $\frac{1}{4}$ is less than $\frac{3}{4}$.

Practice and Problem Solving

EXTRA PRACTICE
See page R33.

Compare. Write >, <, or =. See Examples 1 and 2 (pp. 522–523)

6.
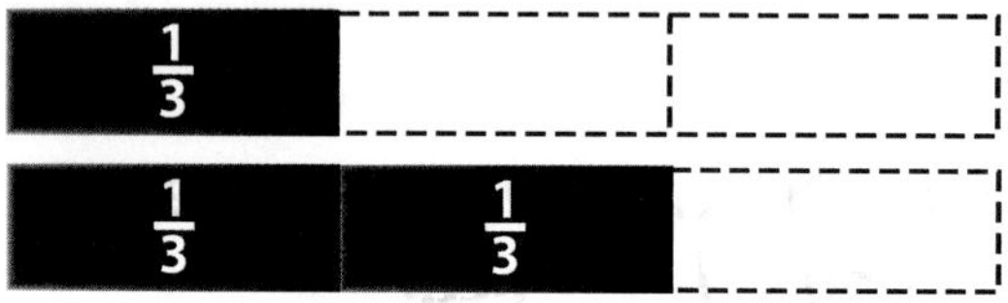

$\frac{1}{3}$ ● $\frac{2}{3}$

7.
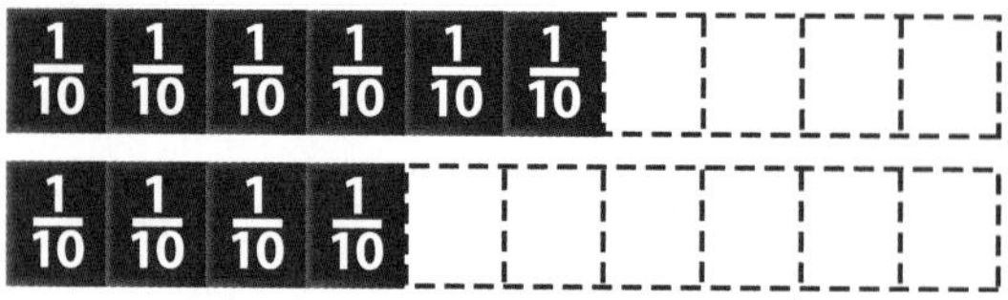

$\frac{6}{10}$ ● $\frac{4}{10}$

8.
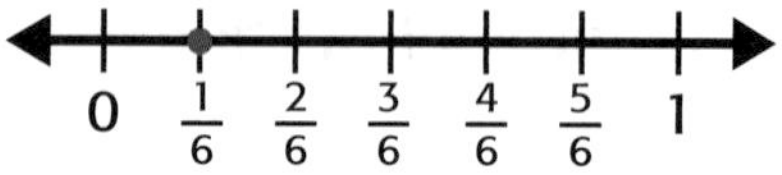

$\frac{1}{3}$ ● $\frac{1}{6}$

9.
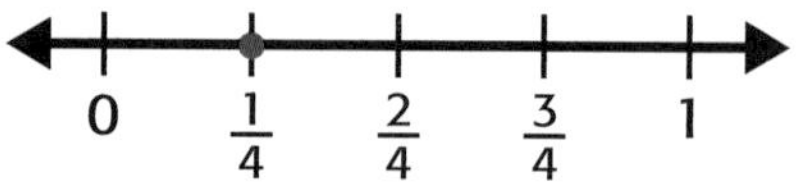

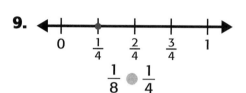

$\frac{1}{8}$ ● $\frac{1}{4}$

10.
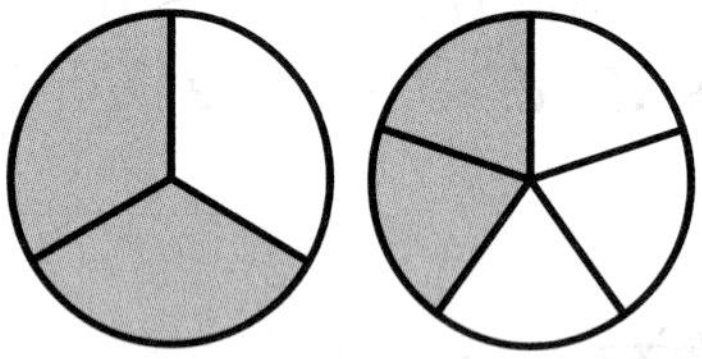

$\frac{2}{3}$ ● $\frac{2}{5}$

11.
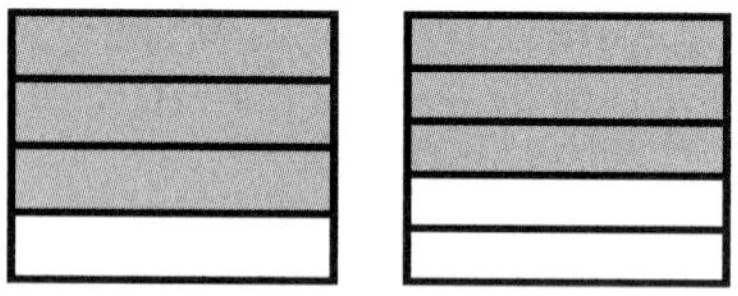

$\frac{3}{4}$ ● $\frac{3}{5}$

Compare. Write >, <, or =. Use fraction models, a number line, or a drawing if needed.

12. $\frac{5}{8}$ ● $\frac{7}{8}$

13. $\frac{5}{6}$ ● $\frac{3}{6}$

14. $\frac{4}{8}$ ● $\frac{3}{6}$

15. $\frac{4}{5}$ ● $\frac{6}{10}$

16. Of the kids at camp, $\frac{5}{8}$ are boys and $\frac{3}{8}$ are girls. Are there more boys or girls? Explain.

17. Measurement Which is greater, $\frac{3}{8}$ of an inch or $\frac{1}{2}$ of an inch?

H.O.T. Problems

18. NUMBER SENSE Is $\frac{1}{4}$ of the smaller waffle the same as $\frac{1}{4}$ of the larger waffle? Explain.

19. OPEN ENDED Write a real-world math problem where you need to compare two fractions.

20. WRITING IN MATH Two sandwiches are the same size. One is cut into 4 pieces. The other is cut into 8 pieces. How do you know which has the smaller pieces?

Math Online **Extra Examples at** ca.gr3math.com

CHAPTER 12

Mid-Chapter Check

Lessons 12-1 through 12-5

Write the fraction for the part that is green. Then write the fraction for the part that is *not* green. Label your answers. (Lesson 12-1)

1. 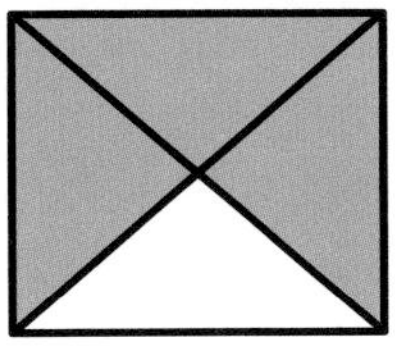

2. 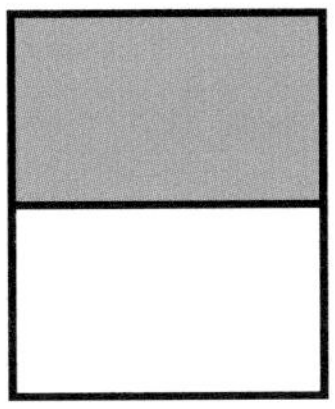

Draw a picture for each fraction. Shade the fraction (Lesson 12-1)

3. $\frac{1}{6}$

4. $\frac{3}{5}$

5. A cake is divided equally into 8 pieces. If two pieces are eaten, what fraction of the cake is left? (Lesson 12-1)

6. **STANDARDS PRACTICE** What fraction of the figure is shaded? (Lesson 12-1)

A $\frac{1}{2}$

B $\frac{5}{9}$

C $\frac{5}{8}$

D $\frac{3}{8}$

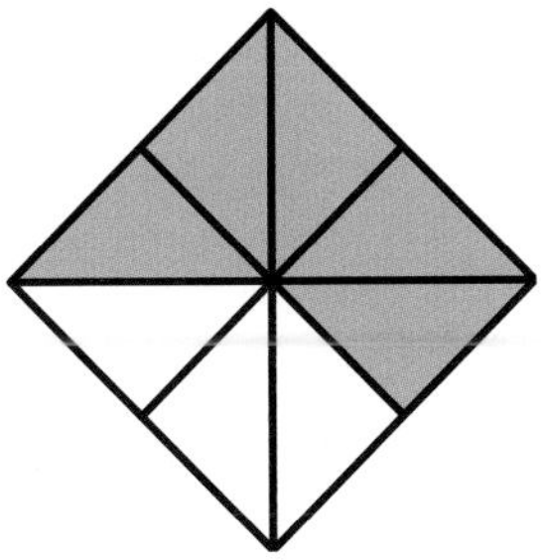

7. Hayden has 6 pets. One-third of the animals are cats. One is a hamster, and the rest are turtles. How many are turtles? (Lesson 12-2)

Complete each number sentence to find equivalent fractions. (Lesson 12-3)

8. $\frac{\blacksquare}{6} = \frac{2}{12}$

9. $\frac{3}{4} = \frac{\blacksquare}{8}$

10. Write an equivalent fraction for $\frac{2}{6}$. (Lesson 12-3)

11. Clem is thinking of two numbers. The sum of the numbers is 8. The product is 15. What are the numbers? (Lesson 12-4)

Compare. Write >, <, or =. (Lesson 12-5)

12. $\frac{4}{6} \bullet \frac{7}{8}$

13. $\frac{2}{4} \bullet \frac{1}{2}$

14. **STANDARDS PRACTICE** What figure shows more than $\frac{1}{2}$? (Lesson 12-5)

F 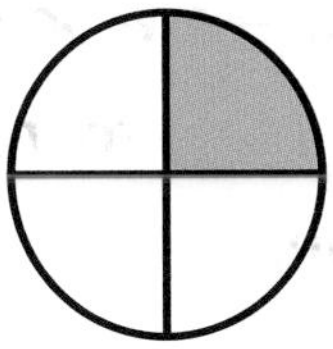

H 

G 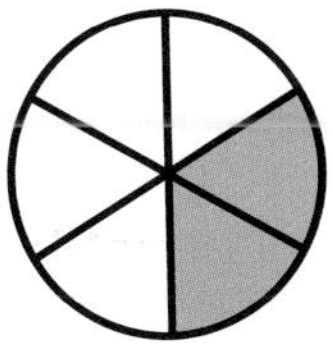

J 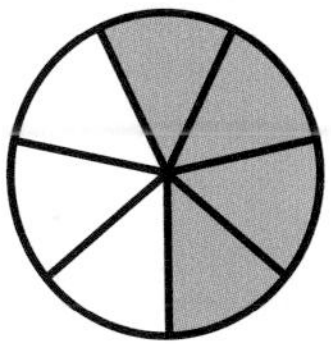

15. **WRITING IN MATH** A figure is divided into 12 equal parts. Six parts are shaded. Is more than one-half of the figure shaded? Explain. (Lesson 12-5)

Explore

Math Activity for 12-6
Add Like Fractions

Two fractions, such as $\frac{2}{5}$ and $\frac{1}{5}$, are called **like fractions** because they have the same denominator. Fraction models can be used to explore adding like fractions.

MAIN IDEA

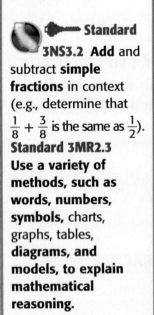

I will use models to add like fractions.

Standard 3NS3.2 Add and subtract **simple fractions** in context (e.g., determine that $\frac{1}{8} + \frac{3}{8}$ is the same as $\frac{1}{2}$).

Standard 3MR2.3 Use a variety of methods, such as words, numbers, symbols, charts, graphs, tables, **diagrams, and models, to explain mathematical reasoning.**

You Will Need
fraction models

New Vocabulary

like fractions

Concepts in Motion

Animation
ca.gr3math.com

ACTIVITY

1. **Find $\frac{2}{5} + \frac{1}{5}$.**

Step 1 **Model $\frac{2}{5}$.**
Use two $\frac{1}{5}$-fraction pieces to show $\frac{2}{5}$.

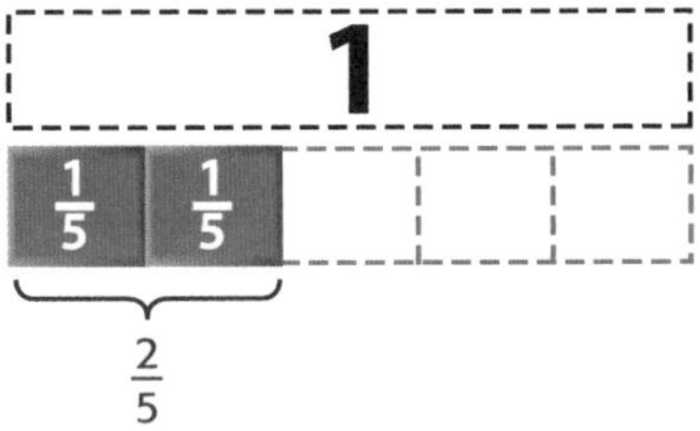

Step 2 **Model $\frac{1}{5}$.**
Use one $\frac{1}{5}$-fraction piece to show $\frac{1}{5}$.

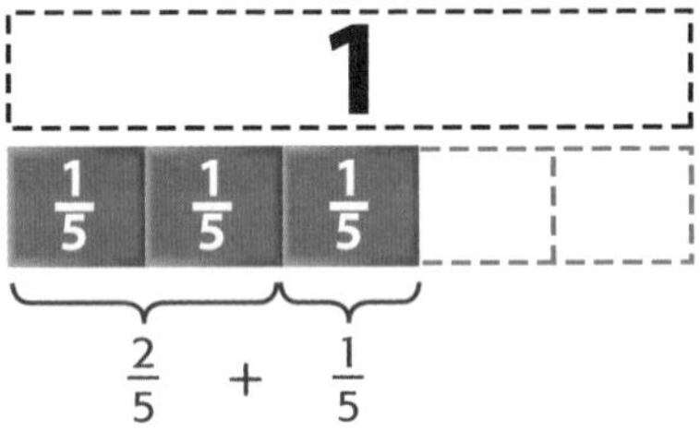

Step 3 **Add.**
Count the total number of $\frac{1}{5}$-fraction pieces. So, $\frac{2}{5} + \frac{1}{5} = \frac{3}{5}$.

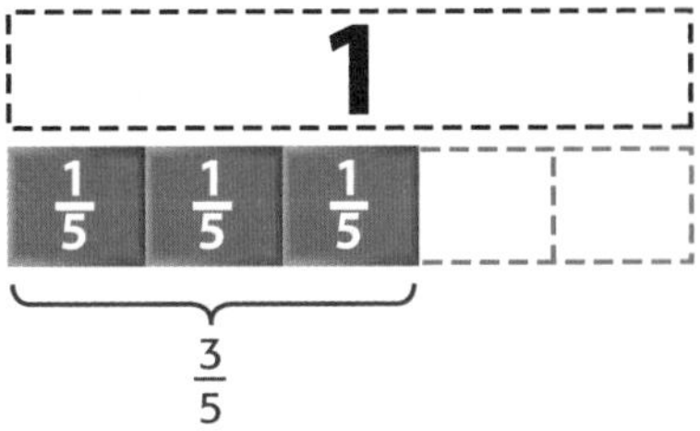

Hands-On Activity

ACTIVITY

2 **Find $\frac{3}{8} + \frac{4}{8}$.**

Step 1 **Model $\frac{3}{8}$.**

Start with 1 whole.

Use three $\frac{1}{8}$-fraction pieces to show $\frac{3}{8}$.

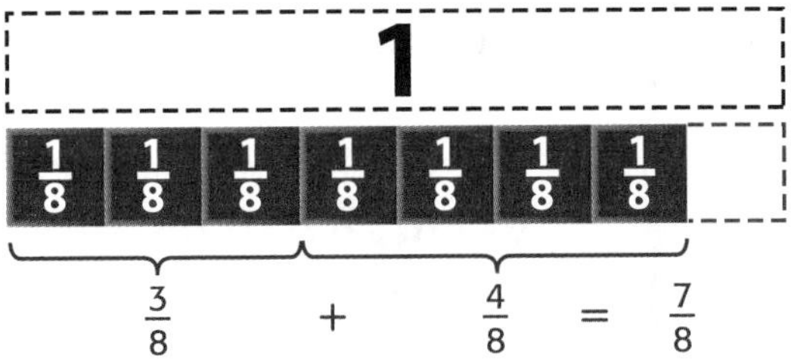

Step 2 **Model $\frac{4}{8}$.**

Use four $\frac{1}{8}$-fraction pieces to show $\frac{4}{8}$.

Step 3 **Add.**

Count the total number of $\frac{1}{8}$-fraction pieces.

So, $\frac{3}{8} + \frac{4}{8} = \frac{7}{8}$.

Think About It

1. How did you use fraction models to show the addends?

2. How did you find each sum?

CHECK What You Know

Add.

3.

$\frac{2}{6} + \frac{3}{6}$

4.

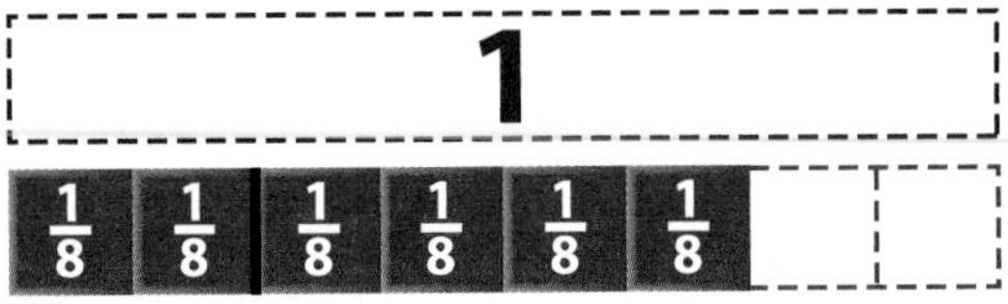

$\frac{2}{8} + \frac{4}{8}$

5. **WRITING IN ►MATH** Look at the numerators and the denominators in each exercise above. Can you find each sum without using fraction models? Explain.

12-6 Add Like Fractions

MAIN IDEA

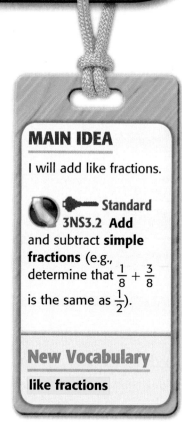

I will add like fractions.

Standard 3NS3.2 Add and subtract **simple fractions** (e.g., determine that $\frac{1}{8} + \frac{3}{8}$ is the same as $\frac{1}{2}$).

New Vocabulary

like fractions

GET READY to Learn

Tamera planted beans in $\frac{1}{5}$ of the garden. Her sister Cecelia planted carrots in $\frac{3}{5}$ of the garden. What fraction of the garden did they plant with vegetables?

To add two **like fractions** such as $\frac{1}{5}$ and $\frac{3}{5}$, you add the numerators the same way you add whole numbers. You keep the same denominator.

Real-World EXAMPLE Add Fractions

1 GARDENS **What fraction of the garden did Tamera and Cecelia plant with vegetables?**

One Way: Models

$\frac{1}{5} + \frac{3}{5} = \frac{4}{5}$

Another Way: Paper and Pencil

$\frac{1}{5} + \frac{3}{5} =$

$\frac{1+3}{5} =$ ← Add the numerators.

$\frac{4}{5}$ ← Use the same denominator.

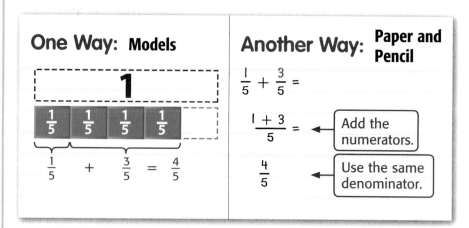

So, they planted $\frac{4}{5}$ of the garden with vegetables.

Real-World EXAMPLE — Add Like Fractions

2 **WEATHER** **A local weather report showed the rainfall for Wednesday and Thursday. How much rain fell in these two days?**

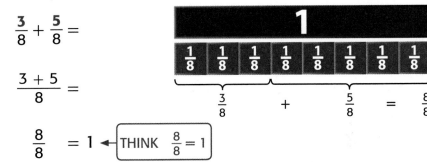

You need to find $\frac{3}{8} + \frac{5}{8}$.

$\frac{3}{8} + \frac{5}{8} =$

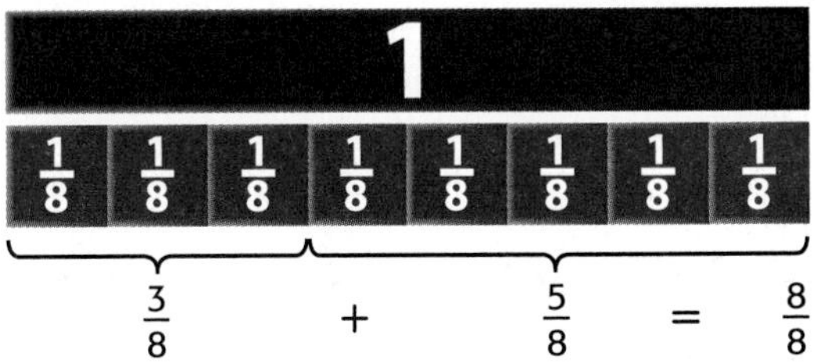

$\frac{3 + 5}{8} =$

$\frac{8}{8} = 1$ ← THINK $\frac{8}{8} = 1$

So, $\frac{8}{8}$ or 1 inch of rain fell in the two days.

Remember

If a fraction has the same numerator and denominator, write the fraction as 1.

$\frac{8}{8} = 1$

Online **Personal Tutor at** ca.gr3math.com

KEY CONCEPT — Add Like Fractions

Words To add fractions with the same denominator, add the numerator and keep the same denominator.

Example $\frac{5}{7} + \frac{1}{7} = \frac{5 + 1}{7} = \frac{6}{7}$

CHECK What You Know

Add. Use fraction models if needed. See Examples 1 and 2 (pp. 528–529)

1. $\frac{1}{8} + \frac{2}{8}$

2. $\frac{1}{10} + \frac{2}{10}$

3. $\frac{5}{12} + \frac{2}{12}$

4. $\frac{1}{6} + \frac{5}{6}$

5. Alister uses $\frac{1}{3}$ cup of cereal to make one batch of party mix. How much cereal will he use to make 2 batches?

6. Talk About It Describe the numerator and denominator of a fraction that can be written as 1.

Practice and Problem Solving

EXTRA PRACTICE
See page R33.

Add. Use fraction models if needed. See Examples 1 and 2 (pp. 528–529)

7. $\frac{1}{8} + \frac{4}{8}$ **8.** $\frac{1}{6} + \frac{4}{6}$ **9.** $\frac{1}{4} + \frac{3}{4}$ **10.** $\frac{2}{3} + \frac{1}{3}$

11. $\frac{1}{3} + \frac{1}{3}$ **12.** $\frac{2}{5} + \frac{2}{5}$ **13.** $\frac{1}{7} + \frac{4}{7}$ **14.** $\frac{3}{9} + \frac{2}{9}$

15. $\frac{2}{9} + \frac{7}{9}$ **16.** $\frac{4}{10} + \frac{6}{10}$ **17.** $\frac{2}{10} + \frac{7}{10}$ **18.** $\frac{7}{12} + \frac{4}{12}$

19. Becky paints $\frac{2}{5}$ of a wall. Her dad paints $\frac{1}{5}$ of the wall. How much of the wall did they paint in all?

20. A recipe uses $\frac{1}{4}$ cup of cheese. How many cups of cheese would you use if you doubled the recipe?

21. Write an addition sentence that can be used to find what fraction of the weekdays had sunshine or rain.

22. What is the total length of the turtle?

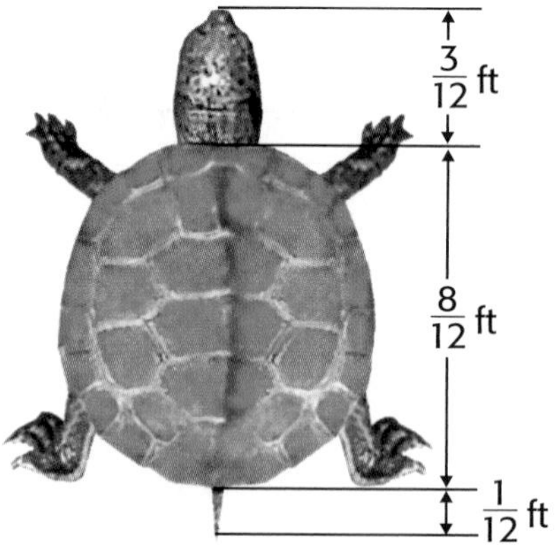

23. Steven has $\frac{3}{10}$ of one dollar. Peter has $\frac{6}{10}$ of one dollar. Together, what part of one dollar do they have?

Algebra Find the value of *x*.

24. $\frac{3}{8} + \frac{x}{8} = \frac{5}{8}$ **25.** $\frac{x}{7} + \frac{2}{7} = \frac{6}{7}$ **26.** $\frac{5}{6} + x = 1$

Real-World PROBLEM SOLVING

Data File The state bird of California is the valley quail.

27. How much would two of the smallest quails weigh?

28. Find the total weight of two of the largest quails.

Valley Quail

Size:
9–10 inches

Weight:
smallest: $\frac{1}{4}$ pound
largest: $\frac{1}{2}$ pound

Source: Enchanted Learning

H.O.T. Problems

29. FIND THE ERROR Ajay and Eva are adding fractions. Who is correct? Explain your reasoning.

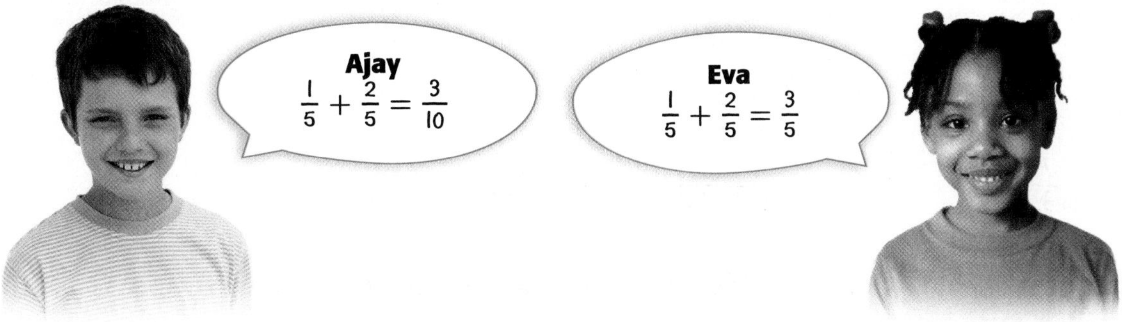

30. WRITING IN ▸MATH Explain how to find $\frac{2}{9} + \frac{4}{9}$.

Standards Practice

31 Which fraction is more than $\frac{5}{8}$? **(Lesson 12-5)**

A $\frac{3}{8}$

B $\frac{2}{4}$

C $\frac{1}{2}$

D $\frac{3}{4}$

32 A pie was divided into eighths. Kelly ate $\frac{1}{8}$ of the pie. Malik ate $\frac{2}{8}$ of the pie. How much of the pie did they eat? **(Lesson 12-6)**

F $\frac{1}{8}$

G $\frac{3}{8}$

H $\frac{1}{2}$

J $\frac{5}{8}$

Spiral Review

Compare. Write >, <, or =. Use models if needed. (Lesson 12-5)

33. $\frac{1}{4}$ ● $\frac{3}{4}$

34. $\frac{1}{3}$ ● $\frac{1}{2}$

35. $\frac{2}{3}$ ● $\frac{3}{5}$

36. Gus bought a package of baseball cards for $4.95. He paid with a $10 bill. How much change did he receive? **(Lesson 12-4)**

Find an equivalent fraction for each fraction. (Lesson 12-3)

37. $\frac{1}{2}$

38. $\frac{2}{3}$

39. $\frac{3}{5}$

40. Measurement It takes Stefanie $\frac{1}{2}$ hour to get to school. How many minutes is this? **(Lesson 8-7)**

The BUZZ on Insects

Insects have been around for 250 million years…long before the dinosaurs. Today, there are over 800,000 known species of insects! These species represent $\frac{1}{12}$ of all the animal species on Earth.

Insects have different size and shape but they all have four things in common. Insects have
- three body parts,
- six jointed legs,
- two antennae, and
- an outside skeleton.

Real-World Math

Use the information on page 532 and 533 to solve each question.

1. How many more beetle species are there on Earth than fly species?
2. What is the total number of fly, bug, and dragonfly species on Earth?
3. Of Earth's animals species, $\frac{1}{12}$ are insects. What part are not insects? Draw a model to show your work.
4. What part of all animals on Earth are not beetles?
5. There are about 859,000 species of insects on Earth. How many of these species are not bee and ant species?
6. What fraction of the insects shown are longer than $\frac{1}{2}$-inch?
7. Suppose you put one lady beetle in front of another. Which insect would have this same length?

Six Spotted Green Tiger Beetle
$\frac{5}{8}$-inch

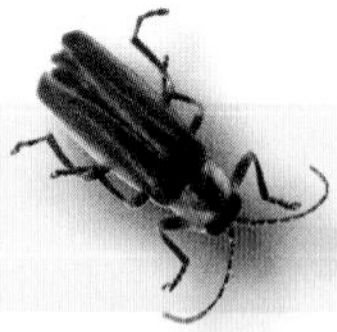

Firefly
$\frac{3}{4}$-inch

Honey Bee
$\frac{4}{8}$-inch

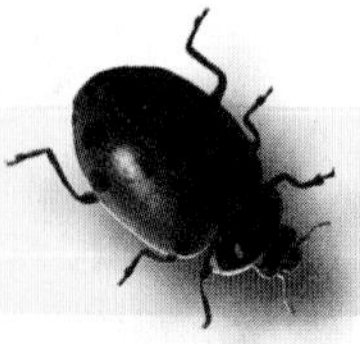

Lady Beetle
$\frac{3}{8}$-inch

House Fly
$\frac{1}{2}$-inch

Standard 3NS3.2 **Add and subtract simple fractions** (e.g., determine that $\frac{1}{8} + \frac{3}{8}$ is the same as $\frac{1}{2}$).

That's a lot of Insects!

Insect	Number of Species
Beetle	350,000
Butterfly & Moth	170,000
Fly	120,000
Bee & Ant	110,000
Bug	82,000
Grasshopper	20,000
Dragonfly	5,000

Source: Enchanted Learning

Did You Know?

Of all the animals on Earth, $\frac{1}{4}$ are beetles.

Explore

Math Activity for 12-7
Subtract Like Fractions

You can also use fraction models to help you understand how to subtract like fractions.

MAIN IDEA

I will use models to subtract like fractions.

Standard 3NS3.2 Add and **subtract simple fractions** (e.g., determine that $\frac{1}{8} + \frac{3}{8}$ is the same as $\frac{1}{2}$).

Standard 3MR2.3 **Use a variety of methods, such as words, numbers, symbols,** charts, graphs, tables, **diagrams, and models, to explain mathematical reasoning.**

You Will Need
fraction models

ACTIVITY

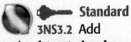

1 Find $\frac{5}{6} - \frac{2}{6}$.

Step 1 Model $\frac{5}{6}$.

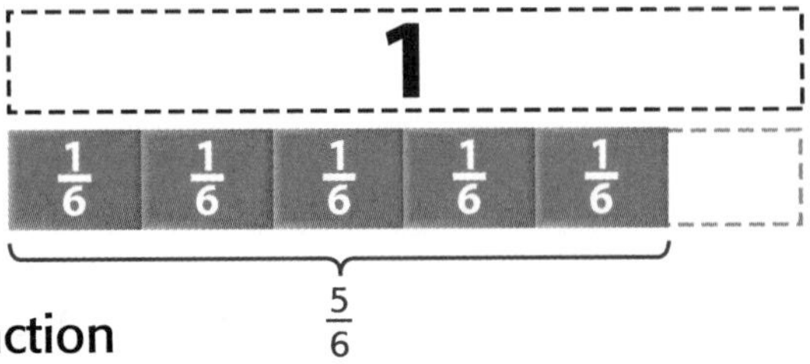

Use five $\frac{1}{6}$-fraction pieces to show $\frac{5}{6}$.

Step 2 Subtract $\frac{2}{6}$.

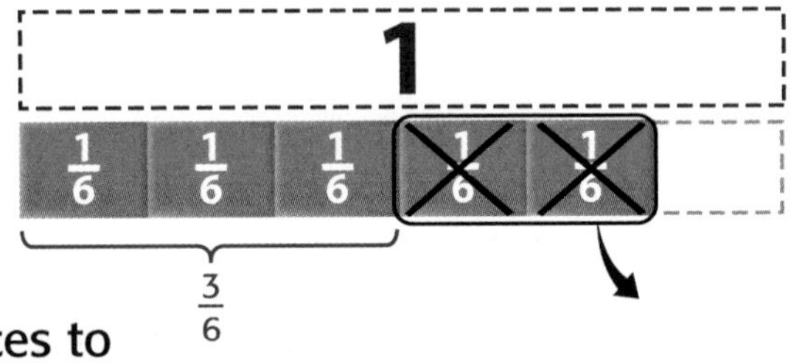

Remove two $\frac{1}{6}$-fraction pieces to show the subtraction of $\frac{2}{6}$. Count the fraction pieces left.

So, $\frac{5}{6} - \frac{2}{6} = \frac{3}{6}$.

Concepts in Motion
Animation
ca.gr3math.com

ACTIVITY

2 **Find $\frac{7}{12} - \frac{3}{12}$.**

Step 1 **Model $\frac{7}{12}$.**

Use seven $\frac{1}{12}$-fraction pieces to show $\frac{7}{12}$.

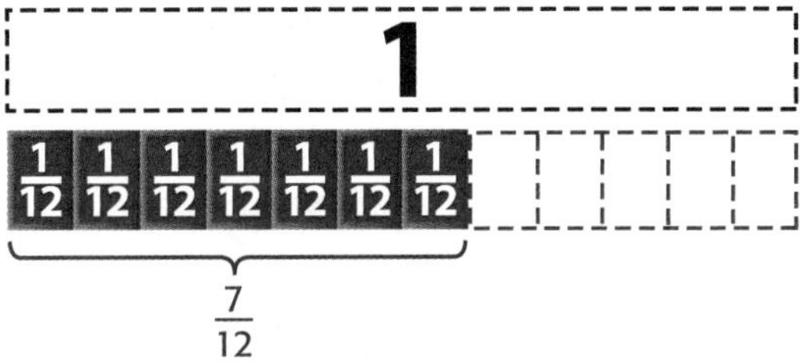

Step 2 **Subtract $\frac{3}{12}$.**

Remove three $\frac{1}{12}$-fraction pieces. Count the fraction pieces left.

So, $\frac{7}{12} - \frac{3}{12} = \frac{4}{12}$.

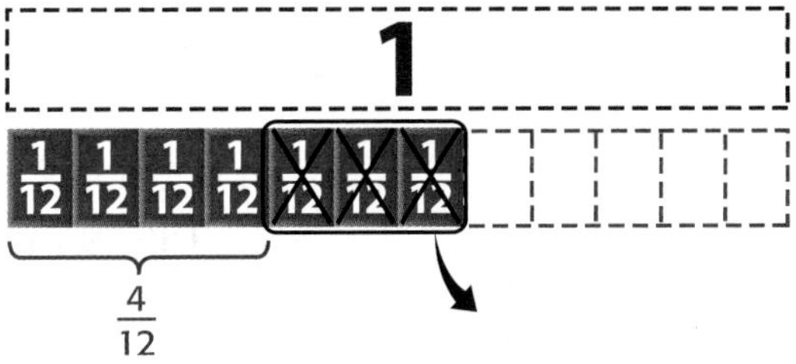

Think About It

1. How did you use fraction models to show $\frac{7}{12}$?

2. What did you do to find the difference?

CHECK What You Know

Write the subtraction sentence for each model. Then subtract.

3.

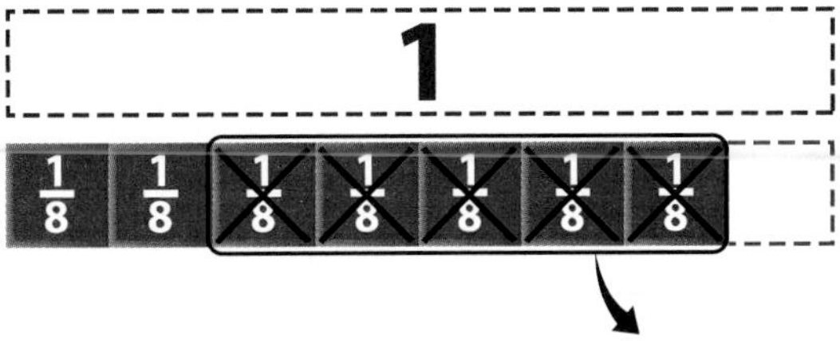

4.

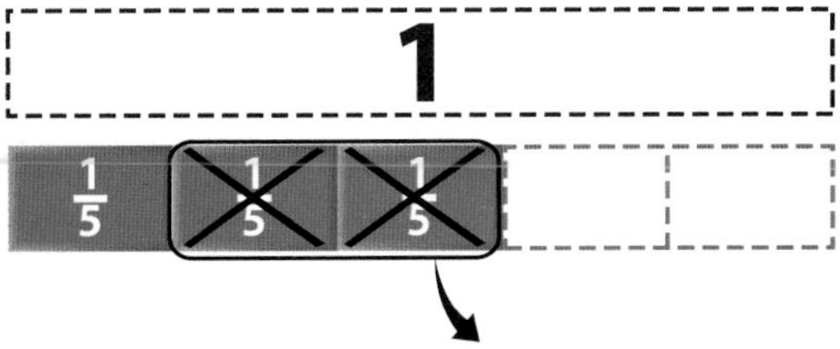

5. $\frac{5}{6} - \frac{1}{6}$

6. $\frac{8}{9} - \frac{7}{9}$

7. $\frac{4}{4} - \frac{2}{4}$

8. **WRITING IN MATH** Look at the numerators and the denominators in each exercise. What do you notice about the difference?

12-7 Subtract Like Fractions

MAIN IDEA

I will subtract like fractions.

Standard 3NS3.2 Add and **subtract simple fractions** (e.g., determine that $\frac{1}{8} + \frac{3}{8}$ is the same as $\frac{1}{2}$).

GET READY to Learn

To make a pitcher of lemonade, Vanessa needs $\frac{2}{4}$ cup of lemonade mix. She has $\frac{3}{4}$ cup of mix. How much mix will be left after making one pitcher of lemonade?

Subtracting fractions is like adding fractions. The difference is that you subtract the numerators instead of adding them. Keep the same denominator.

Real-World EXAMPLE **Subtract Like Fractions**

1 **MEASUREMENT** **How much mix will Vanessa have after making one pitcher of lemonade?**

You need to find $\frac{3}{4} - \frac{2}{4}$.

One Way: Models

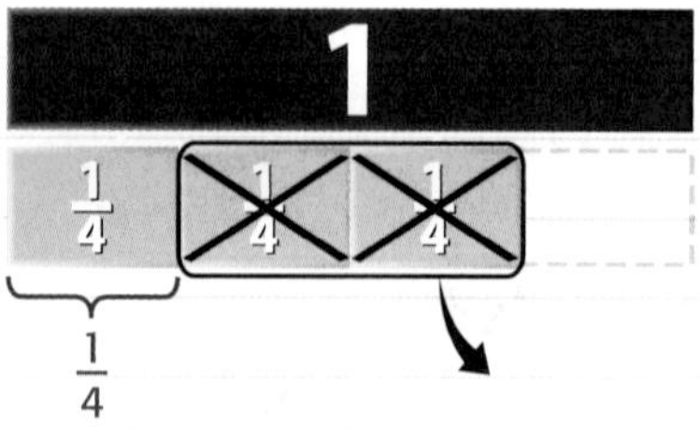

Another Way: Paper and Pencil

$\frac{3}{4} - \frac{2}{4} =$ ← Subtract the numerators.

$\frac{3-2}{4} =$ ← Use the same denominator.

$\frac{1}{4}$

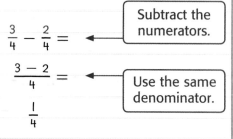

So, Vanessa will have $\frac{1}{4}$ cup of lemonade mix left.

Real-World EXAMPLE — Subtract Like Fractions

Remember

When subtracting a fraction from 1, write 1 as a fraction.

2 **SCIENCE** **About $\frac{9}{10}$ of an iceberg is below water. Subtract $1 - \frac{9}{10}$ to find what part of the iceberg is above water.**

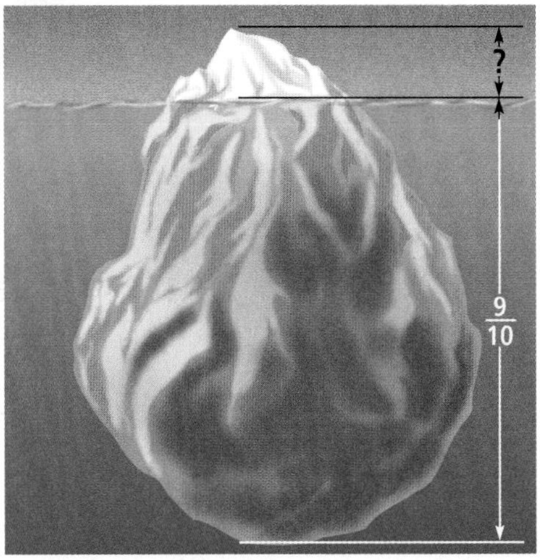

Find $1 - \frac{9}{10}$.

$1 - \frac{9}{10}$

THINK $1 = \frac{10}{10}$

$$\frac{10}{10} - \frac{9}{10} = \frac{10 - 9}{10}$$

$$= \frac{1}{10}$$

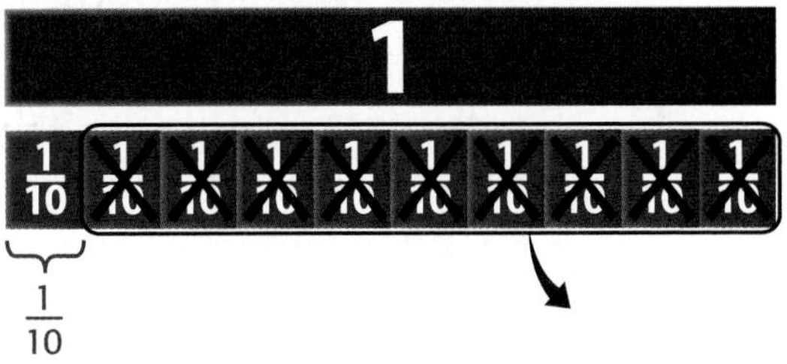

So, $\frac{1}{10}$ of the iceberg is above water.

Online Personal Tutor at ca.gr3math.com

KEY CONCEPT — Subtract Like Fractions

Words	To subtract fractions with the same denominator, subtract the numerators and use the same denominator.
Example	$\frac{6}{8} - \frac{1}{8} = \frac{6 - 1}{8} = \frac{5}{8}$

CHECK What You Know

Subtract. Use fraction models if needed. See Examples 1 and 2 (pp. 536–537)

1. $\frac{5}{6} - \frac{4}{6}$

2. $\frac{7}{8} - \frac{3}{8}$

3. $\frac{6}{9} - \frac{4}{9}$

4. $\frac{1}{3} - \frac{1}{3}$

5. Inez has 1 cup of juice. She drinks $\frac{3}{4}$ cup. How much juice is left?

6. Talk About It: To find $1 - \frac{7}{8}$, why do you write 1 as $\frac{8}{8}$?

Practice and Problem Solving

EXTRA PRACTICE
See page R34.

Subtract. Use fraction models if needed. See Examples 1 and 2 (pp. 536–537)

7. $\frac{2}{3} - \frac{1}{3}$ **8.** $\frac{4}{5} - \frac{1}{5}$ **9.** $\frac{4}{6} - \frac{3}{6}$ **10.** $\frac{6}{8} - \frac{5}{8}$

11. $\frac{1}{2} - \frac{1}{2}$ **12.** $\frac{5}{6} - \frac{5}{6}$ **13.** $\frac{7}{8} - \frac{2}{8}$ **14.** $\frac{8}{9} - \frac{2}{9}$

15. $\frac{7}{10} - \frac{3}{10}$ **16.** $\frac{9}{12} - \frac{5}{12}$ **17.** $1 - \frac{1}{5}$ **18.** $1 - \frac{7}{9}$

19. There is $\frac{3}{5}$ of a pan of lasagna. A family eats $\frac{1}{5}$ of the lasagna. What fraction of the lasagna is left?

20. A box is divided into 10 equal sections. If $\frac{7}{10}$ of the sections are filled, what fraction is not filled?

21. The fish is 1 inch long. Write a subtraction expression you can use to find the length of the fish's tail.

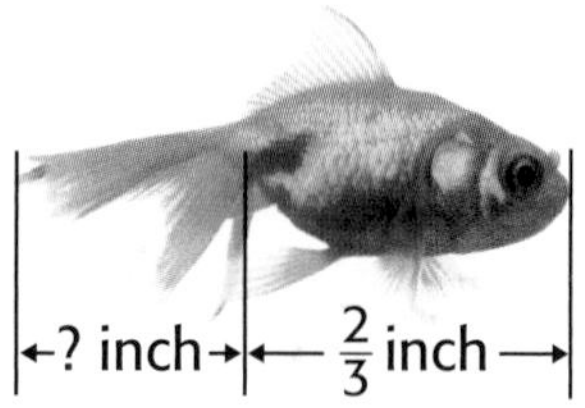

22. A pizza shop cuts a pizza into eighths. They sell $\frac{3}{8}$ of the slices to one customer and $\frac{1}{8}$ to another customer. What fraction of the pizza is left?

Algebra Find the value of *x*.

23. $\frac{4}{5} - \frac{x}{5} = \frac{1}{5}$ **24.** $\frac{x}{8} - \frac{1}{8} = \frac{6}{8}$ **25.** $1 - x = \frac{2}{5}$

H.O.T. Problems

26. OPEN ENDED Write a real-world word problem that contains subtraction of fractions.

27. FIND THE ERROR Elisa and Maurice are finding $1 - \frac{3}{3}$. Who is correct? Explain.

28. WRITING IN MATH Write about two ways you may use subtraction of fractions each day.

Math Online Extra Examples at ca.gr3math.com

Standards Practice

29 Find $\frac{4}{12} + \frac{1}{12}$. **(Lesson 12-6)**

A $\frac{5}{24}$

B $\frac{3}{12}$

C $\frac{4}{12}$

D $\frac{5}{12}$

30 A pizza is cut into ten equal slices. Mora and Adriana each eat $\frac{2}{10}$ of the pizza. How much of the pizza is left? **(Lesson 12-7)**

F $\frac{3}{10}$

G $\frac{4}{10}$

H $\frac{6}{10}$

J $\frac{8}{10}$

Spiral Review

Add. Use fraction models if needed. **(Lesson 12-6)**

31. $\frac{1}{5} + \frac{2}{5}$

32. $\frac{3}{8} + \frac{5}{8}$

33. $\frac{1}{12} + \frac{3}{12}$

34. A dessert recipe uses $\frac{2}{3}$ cup of berries and $\frac{3}{4}$ cup of grapes. Which is the greater amount, the berries or the grapes? **(Lesson 12-5)**

Geometry Identify the triangles shown. **(Lesson 10-5)**

35.

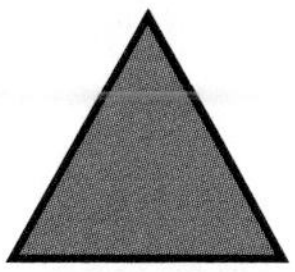

36.

37.

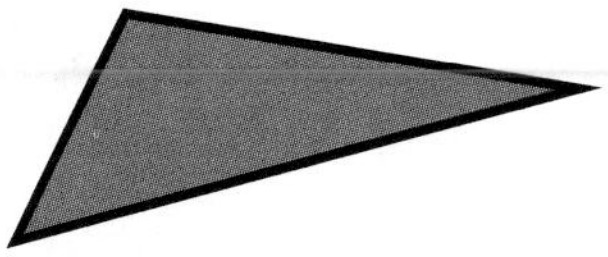

38. Measurement How many centimeters are in 2 meters? **(Lesson 9-1)**

Measurement Choose the most appropriate unit to measure each length. Choose from *inch, foot, yard,* or *mile*. **(Lesson 8-2)**

39. height of a box of crayons

40. length of a football field

Divide. **(Lesson 7-5)**

41. $18 \div 9$

42. $64 \div 8$

43. $63 \div 9$

CHAPTER 12 Study Guide and Review

FOLDABLES Study Organizer GET READY to Study

Be sure the following Key Concepts words and Key Vocabulary are written in your Foldable.

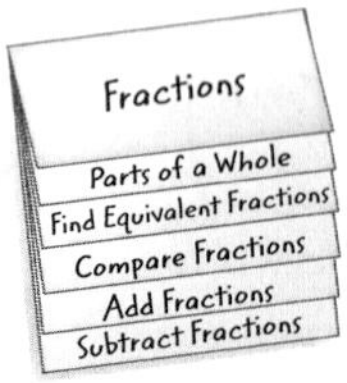

BIG Ideas

- A **fraction** names part of a whole. (p. 509)

$\frac{2}{3}$ ← numerator (2), ← denominator (3)

- **Equivalent fractions** name the same number. (p. 516)

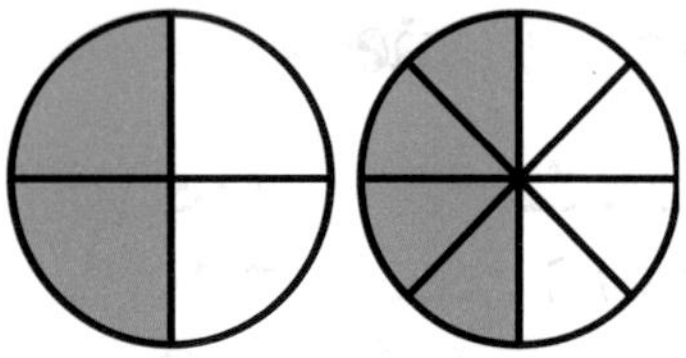

$\frac{1}{2} = \frac{4}{8}$

Add and Subtract Like Fractions

- To add like fractions, add the numerators. Keep the same denominator. (p. 528)

$$\frac{3}{8} + \frac{2}{8} = \frac{3+2}{8} = \frac{5}{8}$$

- To subtract like fractions, subtract the numerators. Keep the same denominator. (p. 536)

$$\frac{7}{9} - \frac{4}{9} = \frac{7-4}{9} = \frac{3}{9}$$

Key Vocabulary

denominator (p. 509)
equivalent fraction (p. 516)
fraction (p. 509)
like fractions (p. 526)
numerator (p. 509)

Vocabulary Check

Choose the vocabulary word that completes each sentence.

1. The number $\frac{1}{2}$ is a(n) ___?___.

2. In the fraction $\frac{1}{5}$, the 5 is called the ___?___.

3. In the fraction $\frac{3}{4}$, the 3 is called the ___?___.

4. The fractions $\frac{1}{3}$ and $\frac{2}{6}$ are ___?___ fractions.

5. To add fractions, add the ___?___ and use the same ___?___.

6. A ___?___ is a number that names part of a whole.

7. The fractions $\frac{1}{4}$ and $\frac{3}{4}$ are ___?___ because they have the same denominator.

Math Online **Vocabulary Review at** ca.gr3math.com

Lesson-by-Lesson Review

12-1 Parts of a Whole (pp. 509–511)

Example 1
What fraction of the figure is blue.

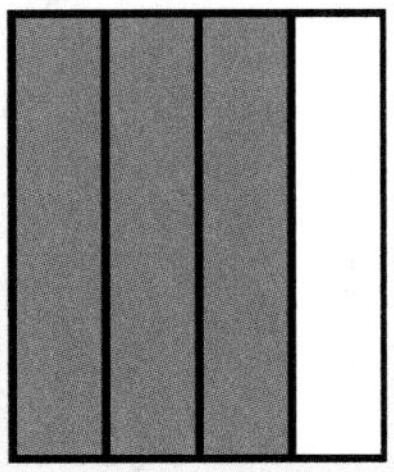

$\frac{3}{4}$ ← numerator / ← denominator

Write $\frac{3}{4}$

Read three-fourths

So, three-fourths or $\frac{3}{4}$ is blue.

Write the fraction for the part that is blue. Then write the fraction for the part that is *not* blue.

8. 

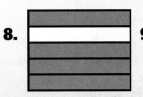

9. 

Draw a picture for each fraction. Shade the fraction.

10. $\frac{2}{3}$

11. $\frac{3}{8}$

12-2 Problem-Solving Investigation: Choose a Strategy (pp. 512–513)

Example 2
Zane saves $6 each month in coins. How long will it take him to save $48 in coins?

To solve the problem, you can use the *guess and check* strategy.

$6 × 7 = $42 no
$6 × 9 = $54 no
$6 × 8 = $48 yes

It will take Zane 8 months to save $48.

12. Sodas cost $2. Salads cost $4. Yukio buys 1 soda and 1 salad. Dyani orders 1 soda and 2 salads. How much money is spent in all?

13. Mr. Janis drove 7 hours each day for 2 days. Then he drove 4 hours each day for 2 days. How many hours did he drive in all?

14. Paloma needs 5 wall tiles for each mural she makes. She has 15 tiles. How many murals did she make?

Study Guide and Review

12-3 Equivalent Fractions (pp. 516–518)

Example 3

Complete $\frac{2}{3} = \frac{\blacksquare}{6}$.

One Way: Fraction Models

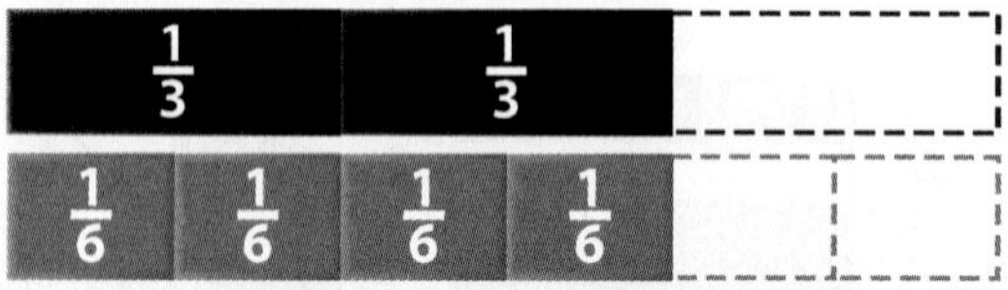
1/3
1/3
1/6
1/6
1/6
1/6

Another Way: Picture

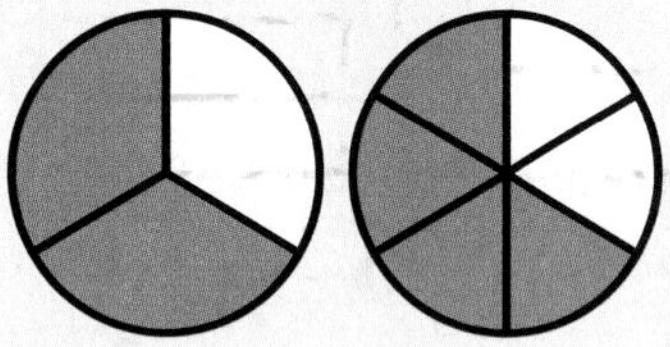

There are 4 sixths in $\frac{2}{3}$. So, $\frac{2}{3} = \frac{4}{6}$.

Complete each number sentence to find equivalent fractions.

15. $\frac{1}{2} = \frac{\blacksquare}{4}$

16. $\frac{2}{2} = \frac{\blacksquare}{6}$

17. $\frac{1}{3} = \frac{\blacksquare}{6}$

18. $\frac{3}{5} = \frac{\blacksquare}{10}$

Algebra Find the value of *x*.

19. $\frac{2}{3} = \frac{x}{12}$

20. $\frac{5}{x} = \frac{10}{12}$

Write another fraction that names each fraction.

21. Jordan put extra cheese on $\frac{1}{5}$ of a pizza.

22. Four-fifths of the quilt squares are red.

12-4 Problem-Solving Strategy: Draw a Picture (pp. 520–521)

Example 4

There are 12 trucks. One-third are red. Two are blue. The rest are green. How many trucks are green?

Divide a figure into 12 equal parts. Shade $\frac{1}{3}$ to show the red trucks and 2 parts to show the blue trucks.

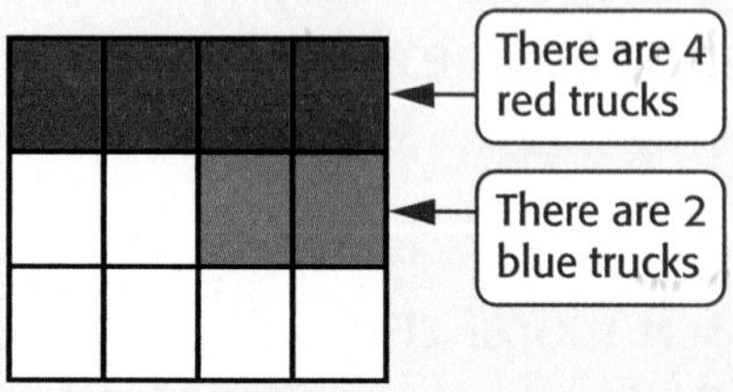
There are 4 red trucks
There are 2 blue trucks

There are 6 parts left. So, 6 are green.

23. A music CD tower can hold 16 CDs. One-half of the slots are filled with CDs. How many CDs are in the CD tower?

24. A boat ride has 15 boats. The boats are yellow, purple, and orange. One-fifth are yellow. Five are purple. How many of the boats are orange?

25. Raini and Ruben are playing tic-tac-toe. Raini has Xs in one-third of the squares. Ruben has Os in 2 of the squares. How many squares are empty?

12-5 Compare Fractions (pp. 522–524)

Example 5

Compare $\frac{2}{3}$ and $\frac{3}{5}$.

One Way: Fraction Models

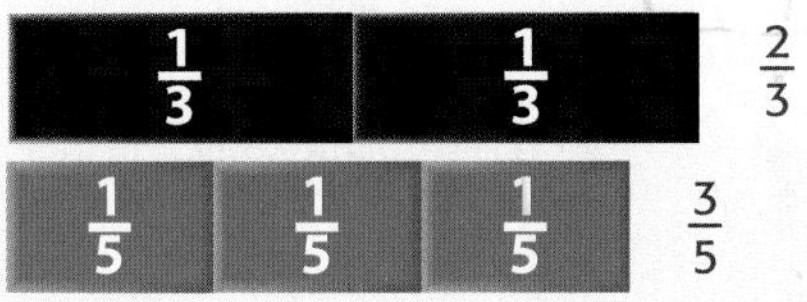

Another Way: Picture

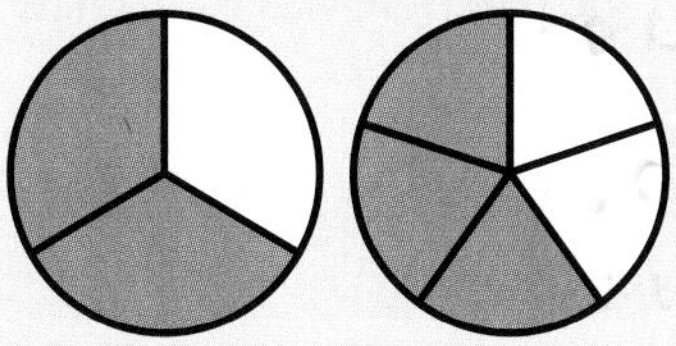

$\frac{2}{3}$ is greater than $\frac{3}{5}$. So, $\frac{2}{3} > \frac{3}{5}$.

Compare. Write >, <, or =.

26.

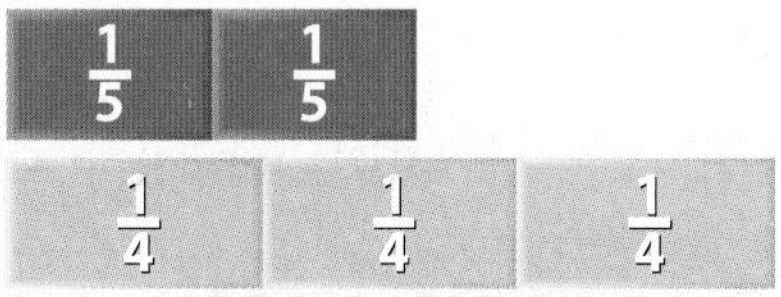

$\frac{2}{5} \bigcirc \frac{3}{4}$

27.

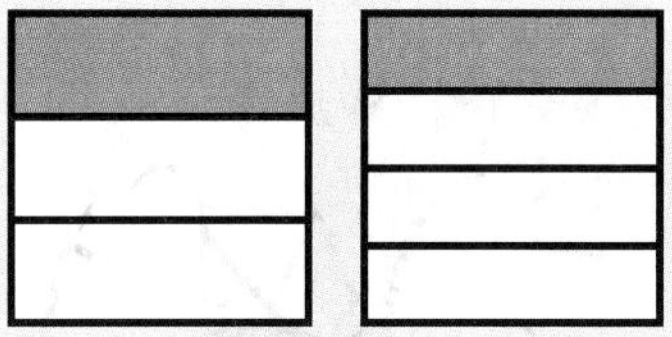

$\frac{1}{3} \bigcirc \frac{1}{4}$

28. Kiyo walks $\frac{1}{4}$ mile. Santos walks $\frac{3}{8}$ mile. Who walks farther?

12-6 Add Like Fractions (pp. 528–531)

Example 6

Add $\frac{3}{8} + \frac{1}{8}$.

One Way: Use Fraction Models

$\frac{3}{8} + \frac{1}{8} = \frac{4}{8}$

Another Way: Paper and Pencil

$$\frac{3}{8} + \frac{1}{8} = \frac{3+1}{8}$$

$$= \frac{4}{8}$$

Add. Use fraction models if needed.

29. $\frac{3}{6} + \frac{1}{6}$

30. $\frac{3}{7} + \frac{1}{7}$

31. $\frac{5}{9} + \frac{2}{9}$

32. $\frac{8}{12} + \frac{2}{12}$

33. Marissa has $\frac{1}{4}$ of a treasure map. Mika also has $\frac{1}{4}$ of the map. What fraction of the map do they have together?

34. A wall is $\frac{1}{3}$ brick and $\frac{1}{3}$ stone. What part of the wall is *not* brick or stone?

12-7 Subtract Like Fractions (pp. 536-539)

Example 7

Find $\frac{4}{8} - \frac{3}{8}$.

You can use fraction models or paper and pencil.

One Way: Fraction Models

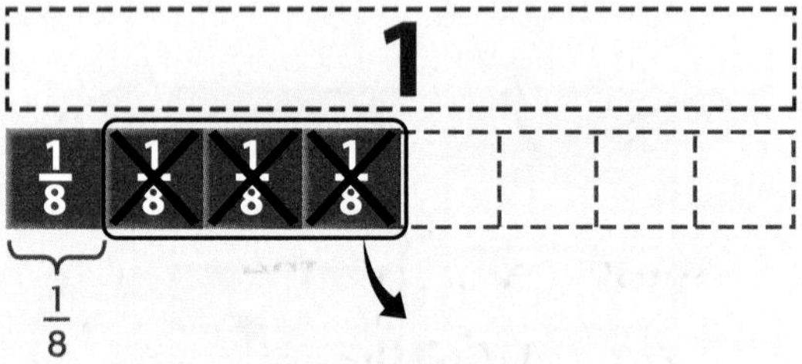

$$\frac{4}{8} - \frac{3}{8} = \frac{1}{8}$$

Another Way: Paper and Pencil

$$\frac{4}{8} - \frac{3}{8} = \frac{4-3}{8}$$

$$= \frac{1}{8}$$

So, $\frac{4}{8} - \frac{3}{8} = \frac{1}{8}$.

Example 8

Eduardo bought an apple. He has eaten $\frac{3}{5}$ of the apple for lunch. What part has not been eaten?

You need to find $1 - \frac{3}{5}$.

$1 - \frac{3}{5}$ Think $1 = \frac{5}{5}$.

↓

$\frac{5}{5} - \frac{3}{5} = \frac{2}{5}$ Now you can subtract.

So, $\frac{2}{5}$ of the apple has not been eaten.

Subtract.

35. $\frac{3}{5} - \frac{1}{5}$

36. $\frac{4}{7} - \frac{1}{7}$

37. $\frac{5}{9} - \frac{3}{9}$

38. $\frac{7}{8} - \frac{3}{8}$

39. $\frac{8}{10} - \frac{2}{10}$

40. $\frac{9}{12} - \frac{7}{12}$

41. Dante had $\frac{4}{5}$ of one dollar. The table shows the fraction he gave away. What fraction of one dollar did he keep?

Money Dante Gave Away	
Krista	$\frac{2}{5}$
Carter	$\frac{1}{5}$

42. Natalie has $\frac{5}{8}$ yard of ribbon. She uses $\frac{4}{8}$ yard to make a bracelet. How much of the ribbon was not used?

43. The tail of a squirrel is about $\frac{1}{2}$ of the length of its entire body. What fraction does the squirrel's body represent?

CHAPTER 12

Chapter Test

For Exercises 1 and 2, tell whether each statement is *true* or *false*.

1. The numerator is the top number in a fraction.

2. The fractions $\frac{3}{5}$ and $\frac{5}{10}$ are equivalent fractions.

Find an equivalent fraction for each fraction.

3. $\frac{1}{4}$

4. $\frac{3}{5}$

5. What fraction of the spinner is purple?

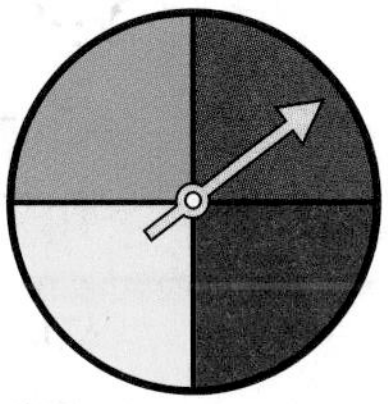

6. There are 2 groups of 5 students and 2 groups of 7 students. How many students are there in all?

7. **STANDARDS PRACTICE** Which fractional part of a square below is equal to $\frac{3}{4}$?

A

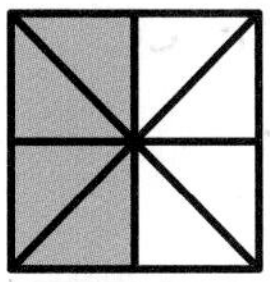

C

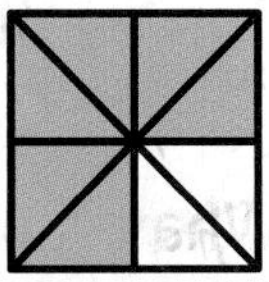

B

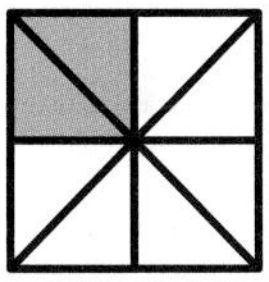

D

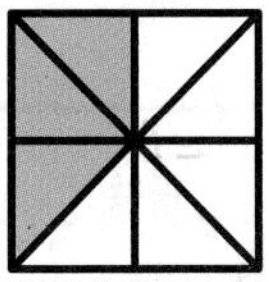

8. Of the fish in an aquarium, $\frac{8}{12}$ are orange and $\frac{4}{12}$ are striped. Are more fish orange or striped?

Add.

9. $\frac{1}{6} + \frac{3}{6}$

10. $\frac{1}{4} + \frac{2}{4}$

11. **STANDARDS PRACTICE** A sandwich is divided into eighths.

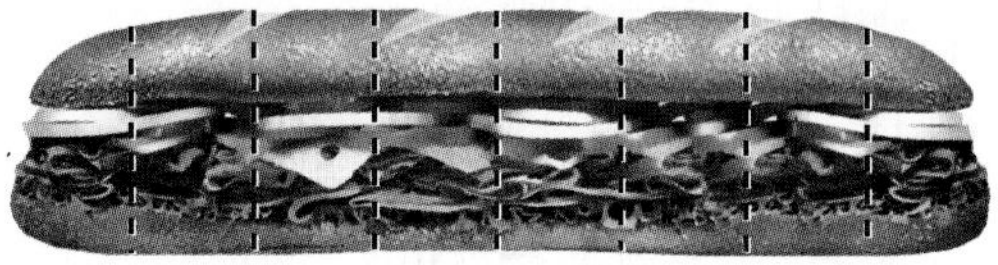

Antonio ate $\frac{3}{8}$ of the sandwich. Mandy and Anita each ate $\frac{1}{8}$ of the sandwich. How much was left?

F $\frac{3}{8}$

G $\frac{4}{8}$

H $\frac{5}{8}$

J $\frac{6}{8}$

Subtract.

12. $\frac{4}{8} - \frac{3}{8}$

13. $\frac{5}{10} - \frac{3}{10}$

14. Use the table. How much longer does Tomas practice piano than oboe?

Instrument	Time (hour)
oboe	$\frac{1}{8}$
piano	$\frac{5}{8}$

15. **WRITING IN ▸MATH** There are 9 students. One-third of them are carrying a backpack. How many are not carrying a backpack? Explain your answer. Include a picture.

12 California Standards Practice

Cumulative, Chapters 1–12

Standards Example

A container is divided into fifths. Andy fills $\frac{1}{5}$ of the container with peanuts, $\frac{2}{5}$ with popcorn, and $\frac{1}{5}$ with pretzels. What fraction of the container is empty?

A $\frac{1}{5}$ **C** $\frac{3}{5}$

B $\frac{2}{5}$ **D** $\frac{4}{5}$

Read the Question

Find the fraction of the container that is empty.

Solve the Question

Draw a picture to solve the problem.

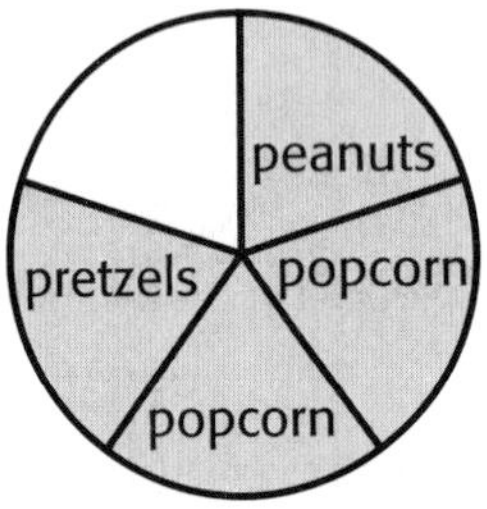

$\frac{1}{5}$ peanuts
$\frac{2}{5}$ popcorn
$\frac{1}{5}$ pretzels

$\frac{1}{5} + \frac{2}{5} + \frac{1}{5} = \frac{4}{5}$

So, $\frac{4}{5}$ of the container is filled and $\frac{1}{5}$ of the container is empty.

The answer is A.

Online Personal Tutor at ca.gr3math.com

Choose the best answer.

1 **If $\frac{3}{5}$ of a wheel of cheese has been eaten, what fraction of the cheese has not been eaten?**

A $\frac{1}{4}$ **C** $\frac{2}{5}$

B $\frac{3}{8}$ **D** $\frac{2}{4}$

2 **Miguel divided a piece of paper into 9 equal rectangles. He shaded $\frac{2}{3}$ of the paper. How many rectangles are shaded?**

F 3 **H** 6

G 5 **J** 8

More California Standards Practice
For practice by standard, see pages CA1–CA39.

Choose the best answer.

3 **Which fraction represents the same part of the whole as $\frac{5}{25}$?**

A $\frac{1}{6}$

B $\frac{1}{5}$

C $\frac{1}{3}$

D $\frac{1}{2}$

---

4 **Judie had $8000 in her savings account. She spent $4537 on a used car. How much does she have left in her savings account?**

F $3463

G $3467

H $4363

J $5473

---

5 **A play area has a width of 9 feet and a length of 7 feet. What is the perimeter of the play area?**

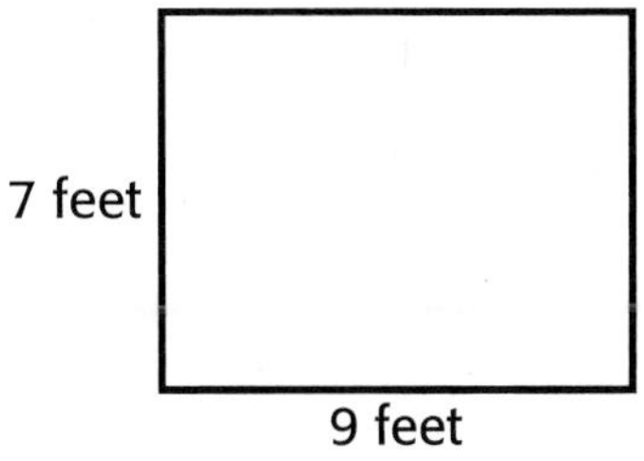

A 11 feet

B 16 feet

C 32 feet

D 58 feet

---

6 **There are 1000 meters in 1 kilometer. How many meters are in 7 kilometers?**

F 70 meters

G 1000 meters

H 2000 meters

J 7000 meters

7 **What is the fraction for the part that is shaded?**

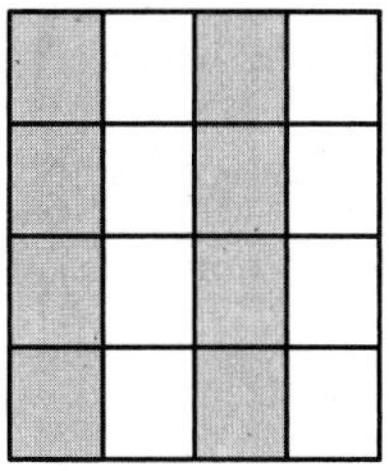

A $\frac{8}{16}$

B $\frac{3}{5}$

C $\frac{8}{12}$

D $\frac{16}{8}$

---

8 **If $6 \times 5 \times 7 = 210$, then what is $7 \times 6 \times 5$?**

F 210

G 310

H 500

J 800

---

9 **A humpback whale weighs 2558 pounds. What is the weight rounded to the nearest hundred?**

A 2530

B 2540

C 2600

D 3000

---

10 **What number makes this number sentence true?**

$$28 + 2 = 6 \times \square$$

F 4

G 5

H 8

J 10

CHAPTER 13

Fractions and Decimals

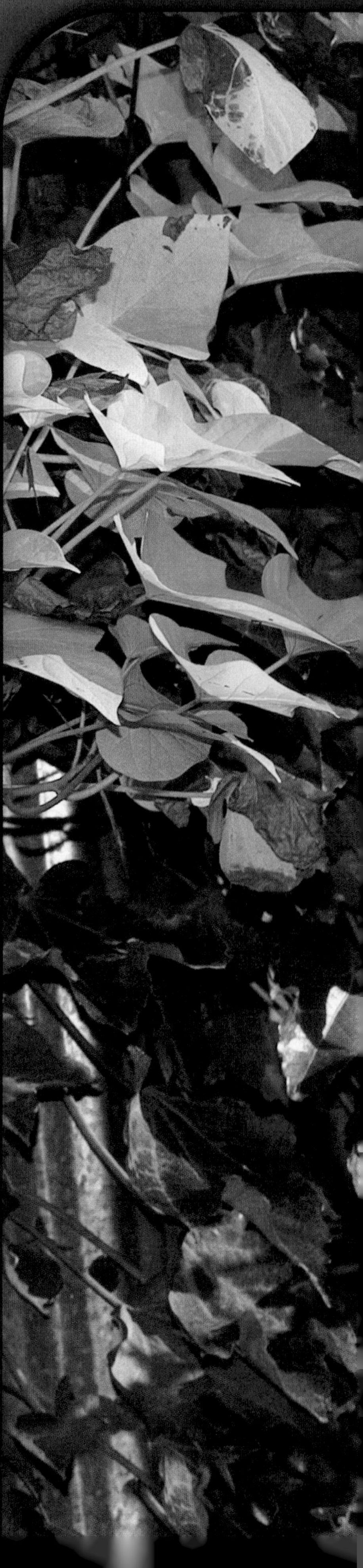

BIG Idea **How are fractions and decimals alike?**

Fractions and decimals both describe parts of a whole.

Example Adriana uses a rain gauge to measure the amount of rainfall in inches. It shows 0.1, one-tenth.

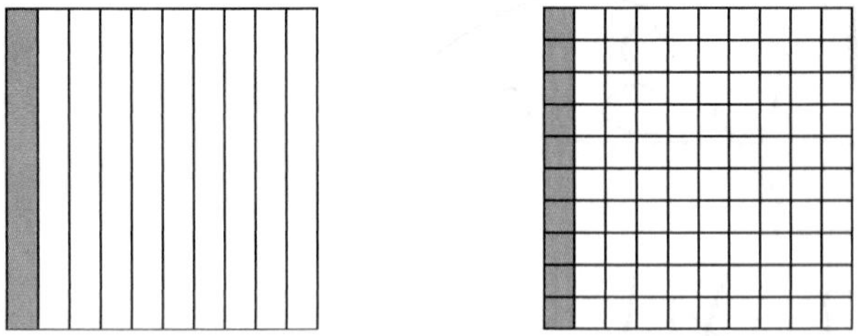

$\frac{1}{10} = 0.1$

What will I learn in this chapter?

- Understand tenths and hundredths.
- Relate fractions and decimals to money.
- Solve problems by acting them out.

Key Vocabulary

decimal
decimal point
tenths
hundredths

Math Online **Student Study Tools at ca.gr3math.com**

FOLDABLES™ Study Organizer

Make this Foldable to help you organize information about fractions and decimals. Begin with one sheet of $8\frac{1}{2}'' \times 11''$ paper.

1. **Fold** the end of the paper to meet in the middle.

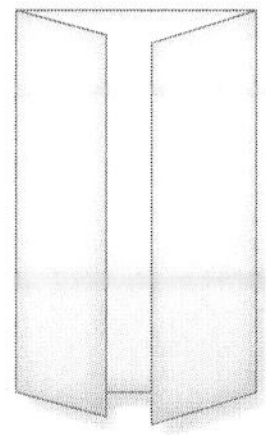

2. **Fold** again in half as shown.

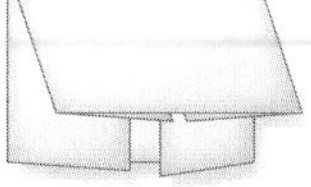

3. **Unfold** and cut along the two inside folds as shown.

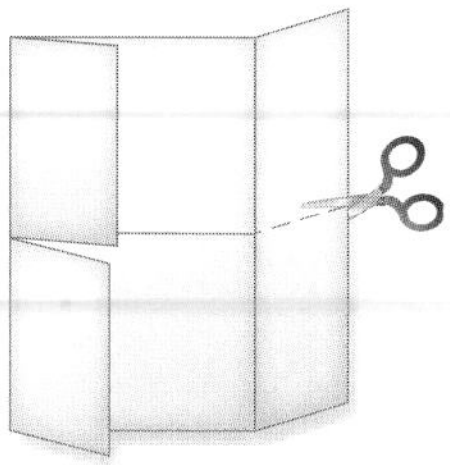

4. **Label**. Record what you learn.

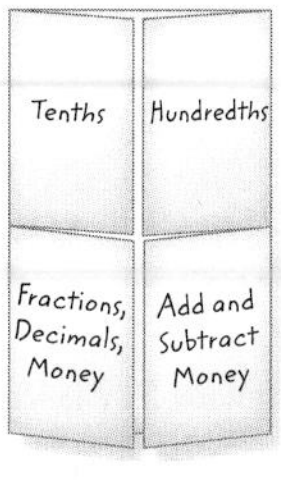

ARE YOU READY for Chapter 13?

You have two ways to check prerequisite skills for this chapter.

Option 2

Math Online Take the Chapter Readiness Quiz at ca.gr3math.com.

Option 1

Complete the Quick Check below.

QUICK Check

Write the fraction for the part that is shaded. **(Lesson 12-1)**

1. 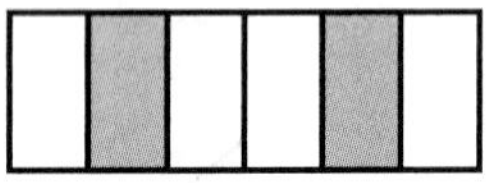

2. 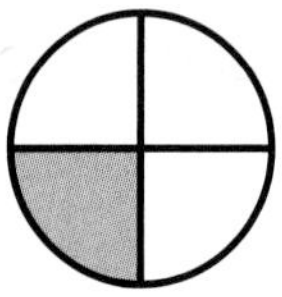

3. 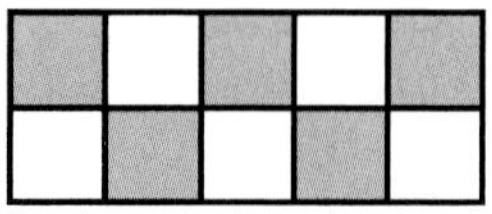

4. Three of 5 trees are oak trees. What fraction of the trees are not oak trees?

Write each fraction using numbers. **(Lesson 12-1)**

5. three-fourths

6. two-tenths

7. one-half

8. Alan will sing 3 verses of a song. The song has 7 verses. Write the fraction for the part of the song that he will sing in words and in numbers.

Write the amount of money shown. Use a cent sign then a dollar sign and decimal point. **(Lesson 2-3)**

9. 

10. 

11. 

12. Write 25¢ using a decimal point.

Explore

Math Activity for 13-1
Fractions and Decimals

A **decimal** is a number that uses place value and a **decimal point** to show part of a whole. You can use models to show how fractions and decimals are related.

MAIN IDEA

I will relate fractions to decimals.

Standard 3NS3.4 Know and understand that fractions and decimals are two different representations of the same concept (e.g., 50 cents is $\frac{1}{2}$ of a dollar, 75 cents is $\frac{3}{4}$ of a dollar).

Standard 3MR3.2 Note the method of deriving the solution and demonstrate a conceptual understanding of the derivation by solving similar problems.

You Will Need

grid paper
colored pencils

New Vocabulary

decimal
decimal point

Concepts in Motion

Animation
ca.gr3math.com

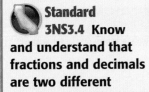

ACTIVITY Explore Fractions and Decimals

Step 1 Make a Model

Make a grid that is divided into 10 equal parts or columns. Shade 3 parts.

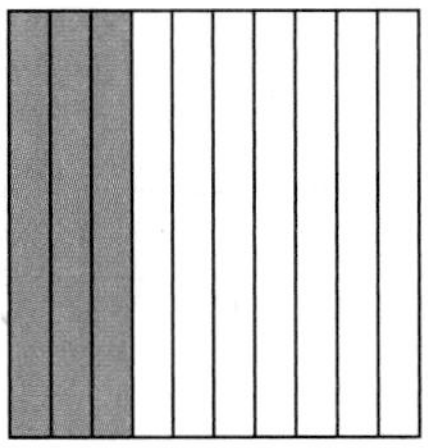

Step 2 Write a Fraction and Decimal

Write the fraction for the shaded part of the grid. Copy and complete the place value chart.

$\frac{\square \text{ shaded part}}{\square \text{ parts in all}}$

Hundreds	Tens	Ones	Tenths
		0.	

decimal point

Step 3 Make Another Model

Make a grid that is divided into 10 rows and 10 columns. Shade 30 of the 100 parts.

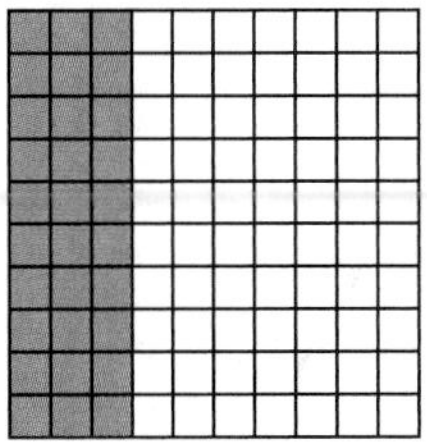

Step 4 Write a Fraction and a Decimal

Write the fraction for the shaded part. Copy and complete the place value chart.

$\frac{\square \text{ shaded part}}{\square \text{ parts in all}}$

Hundreds	Tens	Ones	Tenths	Hundredths
		0.		

Think About It

1. In Step 1, how many tenths are shaded in the grid?
2. In Step 3, how many hundredths are shaded in the grid?
3. How do you write in words the shaded part of the grids?
4. Do $\frac{3}{10}$ and $\frac{30}{100}$ name the same number? How do you know?

CHECK What You Know

Write a fraction and a decimal for each shaded part.

5. 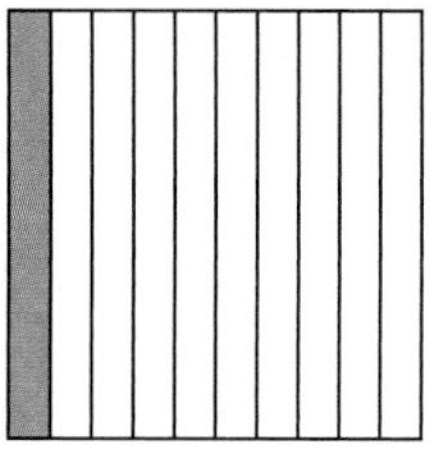

6. 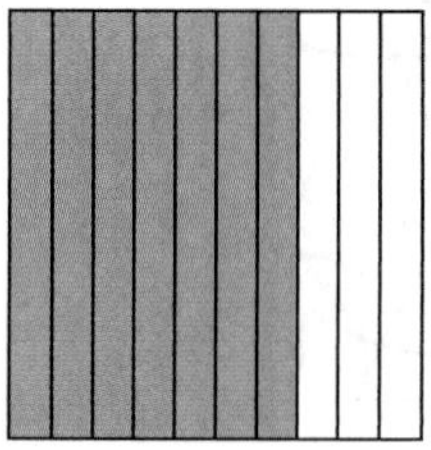

7. 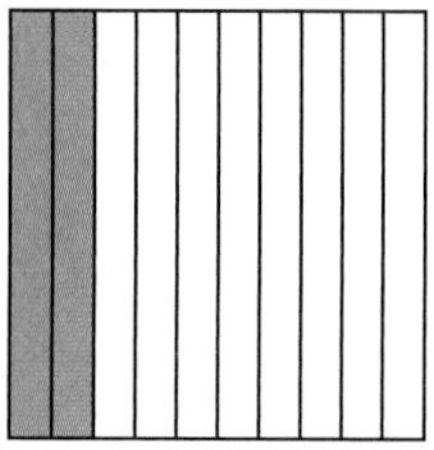

8. 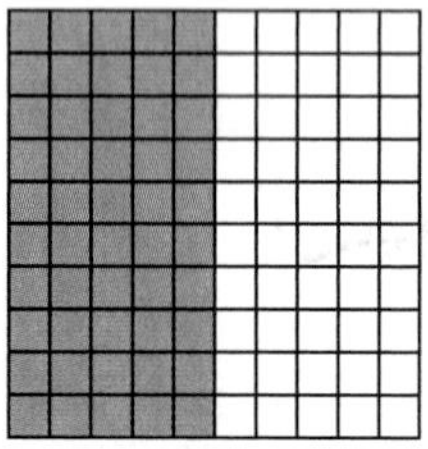

9. 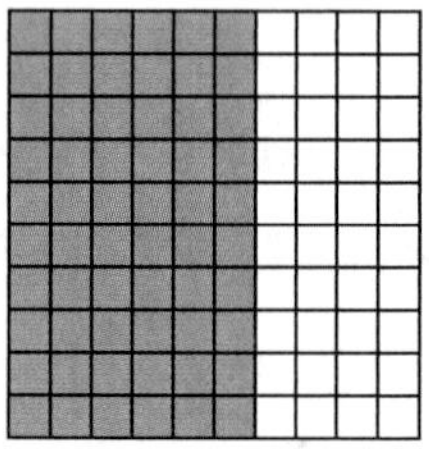

10. 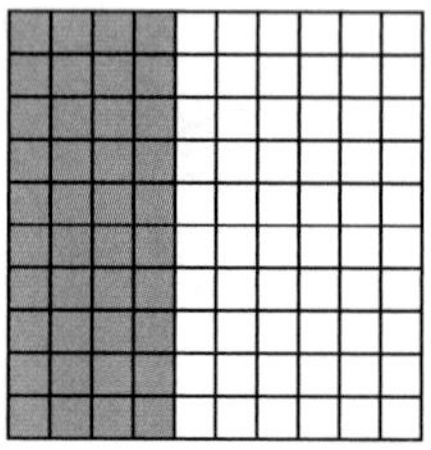

Model each fraction. Then write the fraction as a decimal.

11. $\frac{15}{100}$ **12.** $\frac{5}{10}$ **13.** $\frac{7}{10}$

Model each decimal. Then write each decimal as a fraction.

14. 0.25 **15.** 0.80 **16.** 0.4

17. WRITING IN MATH Describe how fractions are like decimals and how they are different from decimals.

13-1 Tenths

GET READY to Learn

Alfredo's mother made a blanket using pieces of old cloth. What part of the blanket is blue?

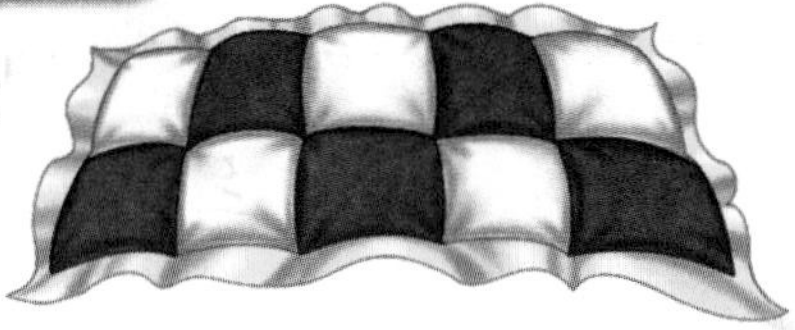

MAIN IDEA

I will learn the meaning of tenths.

Standard 3NS3.4 Know and understand that fractions and decimals are two different representations of the same concept (e.g., 50 cents is $\frac{1}{2}$ of a dollar, 75 cents is $\frac{3}{4}$ of a dollar).

New Vocabulary

decimal
decimal point
tenths

Recall that a **decimal** is a number that uses place value and a **decimal point** to show part of a whole. Everything to the right of the decimal point is *part of a whole*. A **tenth** is one of ten equal parts.

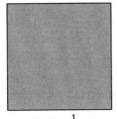

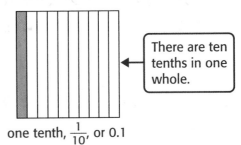

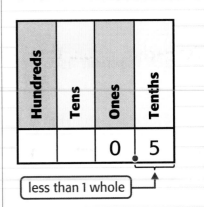

one whole, $\frac{1}{1}$, or 1.0

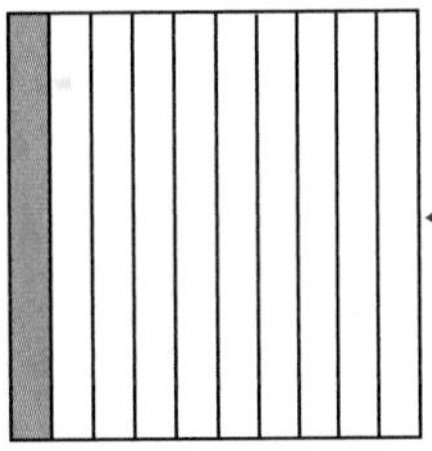

There are ten tenths in one whole.

one tenth, $\frac{1}{10}$, or 0.1

Real-World EXAMPLE — Write Tenths

1 **SEWING What part of the blanket is blue?**

One Way: Fraction

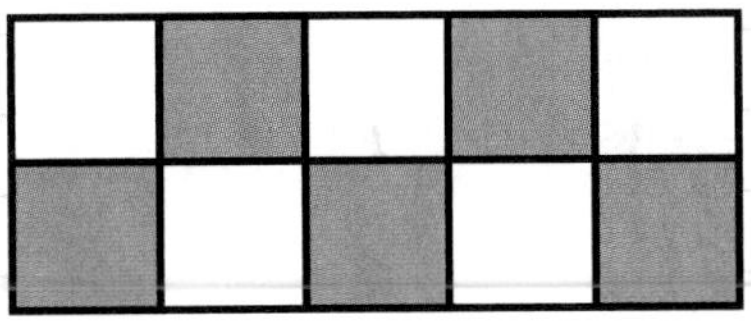

Write $\frac{5}{10}$ ← blue parts / ← parts in all

Read five-tenths

Another Way: Decimal

Hundreds	Tens	Ones	Tenths
		0	. 5

less than 1 whole

So, $\frac{5}{10}$ or 0.5 of the blanket is blue.

Remember

To read a decimal, read the digits to the right of the decimal point as a whole number. Then say its place value. Example: 0.7 is read *seven-tenths*.

You can write a fraction as a decimal and a decimal as a fraction.

EXAMPLES Write Fractions and Decimals

2 Write $\frac{4}{10}$ as a decimal.

$\frac{4}{10}$ is written as 0.4.

Hundreds	Tens	Ones	Tenths
		0.	4

So, $\frac{4}{10} = 0.4$.

3 Write 0.8 as a fraction.

0.8 is eight-tenths.

Hundreds	Tens	Ones	Tenths
		0.	8

So, $0.8 = \frac{8}{10}$.

Online Personal Tutor at ca.gr3math.com

CHECK What You Know

Write a fraction and a decimal for the part that is shaded. See Example 1 (p. 553)

1. 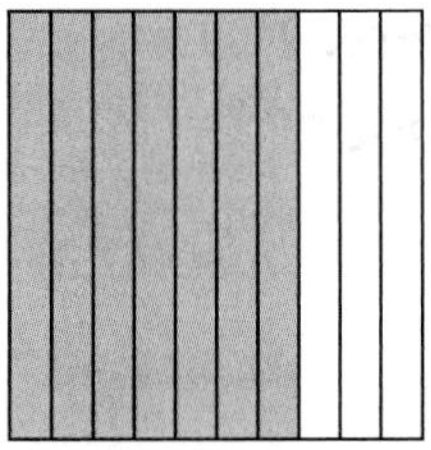

2. 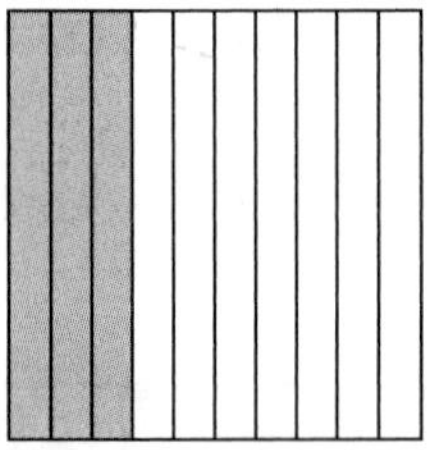

3. 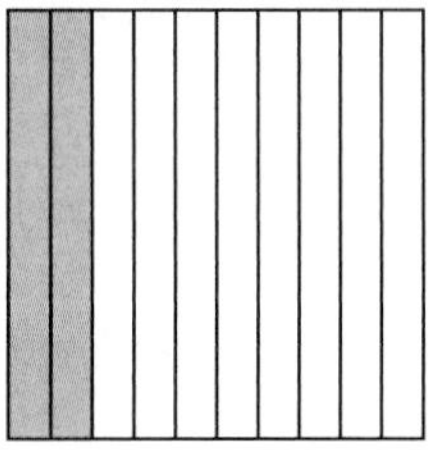

Write each fraction as a decimal. See Example 2 (p. 554)

4. $\frac{7}{10}$

5. $\frac{1}{10}$

6. $\frac{2}{10}$

Write each decimal as a fraction. See Example 3 (p. 554)

7. 0.5

8. 0.9

9. 0.4

10. There are six-tenths of pizza left. What is the decimal for this amount?

11. Talk About It What is the number 0.7 in word form? What does the amount mean?

Practice and Problem Solving

EXTRA PRACTICE
See page R34.

Write a fraction and a decimal for the part that is shaded. See Example 1 (p. 553)

12.
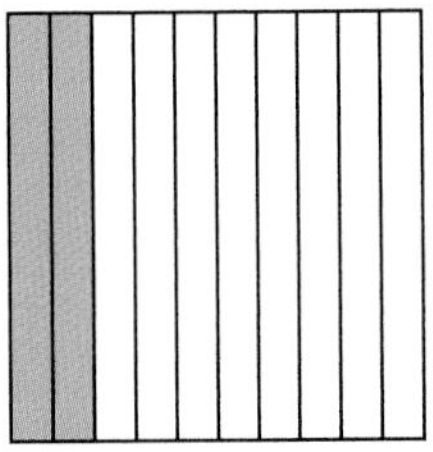

13.
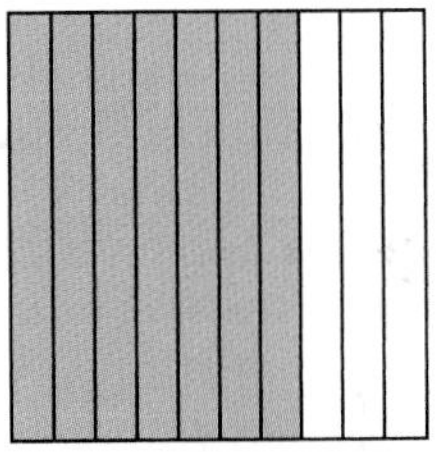

14.
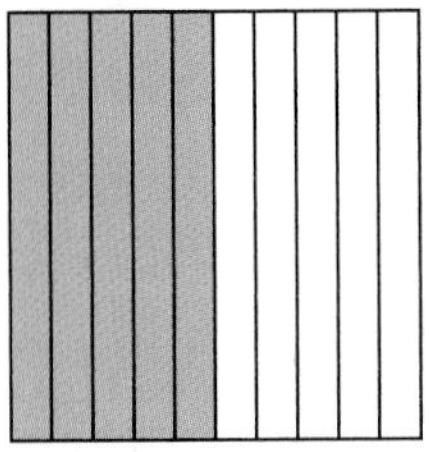

15.
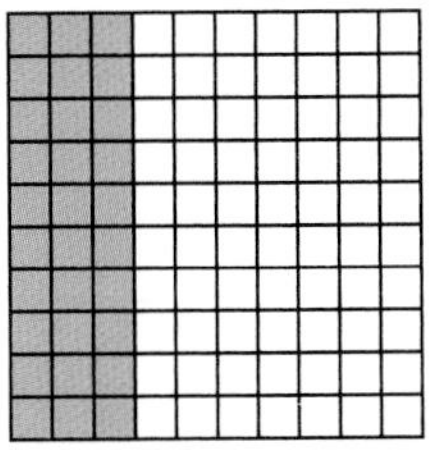

16.
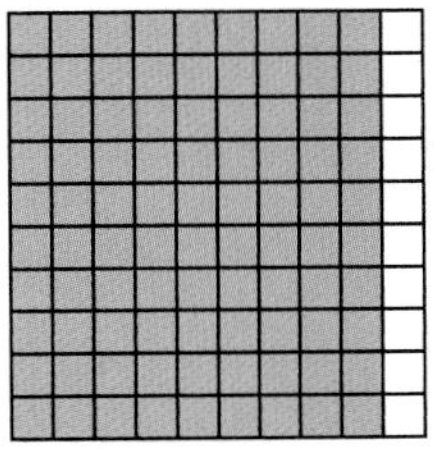

17.
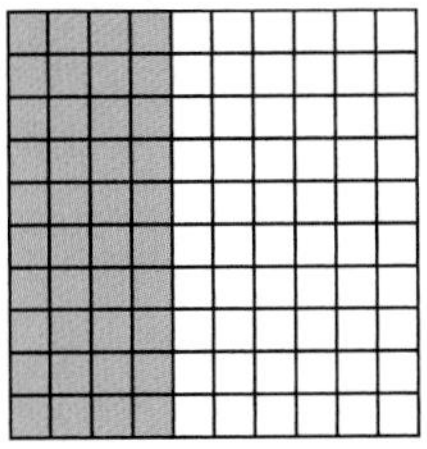

Write each fraction as a decimal. See Example 2 (p. 554)

18. $\frac{2}{10}$

19. $\frac{6}{10}$

20. $\frac{9}{10}$

21. $\frac{3}{10}$

22. eight-tenths

23. five-tenths

Write each decimal as a fraction. See Example 3 (p. 554)

24. 0.4

25. 0.9

26. 0.5

27. 0.8

28. six-tenths

29. three-tenths

30. Four out of 10 chess players are girls. What part of the group are boys? Write as a decimal.

31. Estella needs five-tenths of a cup of flour. Write the amount of flour needed as a fraction.

Real-World PROBLEM SOLVING

Data File Rainfall is measured in tenths and hundredths of an inch.

32. Write Redding's rainfall as a fraction.

33. Write the rainfall for Raywood Flats and Shasta Dam as fractions. What is the difference?

Weather

City	Average Rainfall July–Aug. (in.)
Palomar Mountains	$\frac{2}{10}$
Redding	0.2
Raywood Flats	0.5
Shasta Dam	0.3
Eureka	0.4

H.O.T. Problems

34. OPEN ENDED Write any number in the tenths place as a decimal and as a fraction. Explain the meaning of the number.

35. NUMBER SENSE Is the number 0.3 greater than or less than 1? Explain how you know.

36. WRITING IN ▶MATH Write about a real-world situation where you see tenths written as decimals.

Standards Practice

37 Lian shaded $\frac{3}{10}$ of this figure then erased $\frac{1}{10}$. Which fraction represents the shaded part? **(Lesson 12-7)**

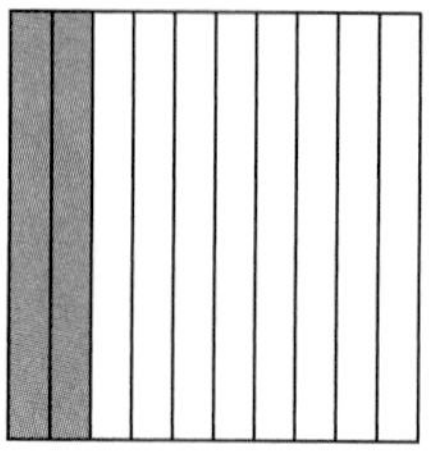

A $\frac{2}{100}$

B $\frac{3}{100}$

C $\frac{2}{10}$

D $\frac{3}{10}$

38 Dena shaded $\frac{9}{10}$ of the figure. Which decimal equals $\frac{9}{10}$? **(Lesson 13-1)**

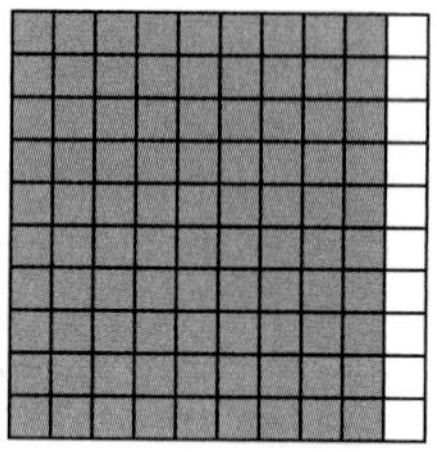

F 10.59

G 9.5

H 5.09

J 0.9

Spiral Review

Subtract. **(Lesson 12-7)**

39. $\frac{5}{9} - \frac{3}{9}$

40. $\frac{7}{8} - \frac{4}{8}$

41. $\frac{8}{12} - \frac{8}{12}$

Add. **(Lesson 12-6)**

42. $\frac{2}{7} + \frac{3}{7}$

43. $\frac{15}{24} + \frac{9}{24}$

44. $\frac{13}{19} + \frac{1}{19}$

45. Edmund and Leon are planning to help cut the grass. Leon says he will cut $\frac{1}{2}$ of the grass. Edmund says he will cut $\frac{4}{8}$ of the grass. Who will cut more? Explain. **(Lesson 12-5)**

46. Algebra Find the missing value in $\frac{5}{7} = \frac{10}{\blacksquare}$. **(Lesson 12-3)**

Game Time

Fractoes and Decimoes

Match Fractions and Decimals

Get Ready!

Players: 2–3 players

You will need: Fractoes and Decimoes resource master.

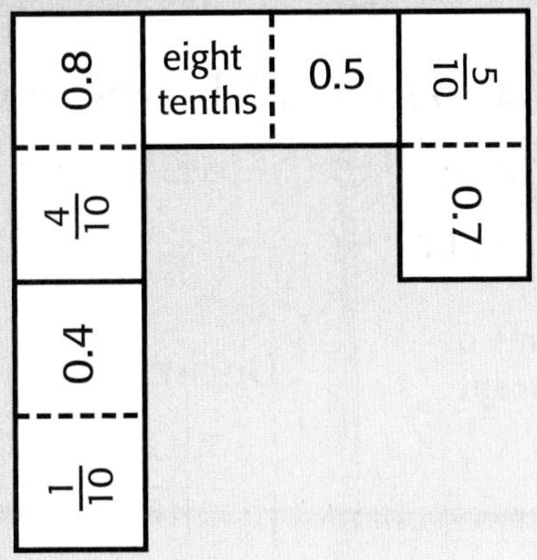

Get Set!

Cut apart the Fractoes and Decimoes tiles.

Go!

- Place the tiles spread out on a table face down.
- Each player chooses five tiles and holds them so the other players cannot see them.
- The first player chooses a tile from his or her hand and places it on the table. A new tile is then chosen.
- The next player places one tile from his or her hand that matches one of the ends of the tiles on the table. A new tile is then chosen.
- If a player is unable to make a match, a new tile must be chosen until a match is made.
- Play continues until one player has placed all his or her tiles and wins the game.

13-2 Hundredths

GET READY to Learn

Mr. Rivera's class took a survey of 100 people to find out their favorite food. What part of the group favors spaghetti?

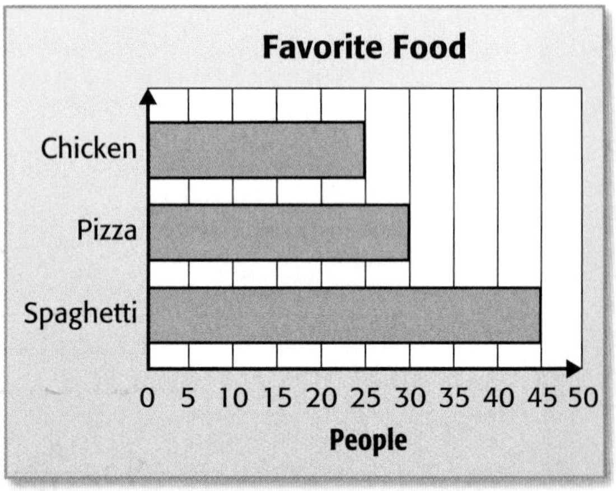

MAIN IDEA

I will learn the meaning of hundredths.

Standard 3NS3.4 Know and understand that fractions and decimals are two different representations of the same concept (e.g., 50 cents is $\frac{1}{2}$ of a dollar, 75 cents is $\frac{3}{4}$ of a dollar).

New Vocabulary

hundredths

Decimals can also be written in **hundredths**.

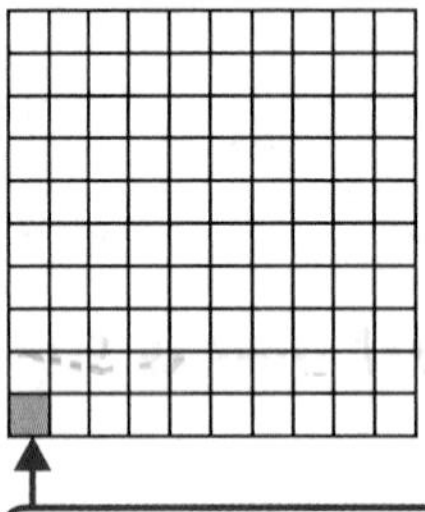

One hundredth. There are 100 hundredths in one whole.

Hundreds	Tens	Ones	Tenths	Hundredths
		0.	0	1

No tenths.

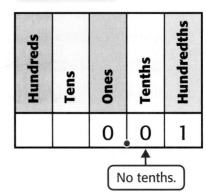

Real-World EXAMPLE

1 **FOOD What part of the group favors spaghetti?**
Out of the 100 students, 45 students favor spaghetti.

One Way: Fraction

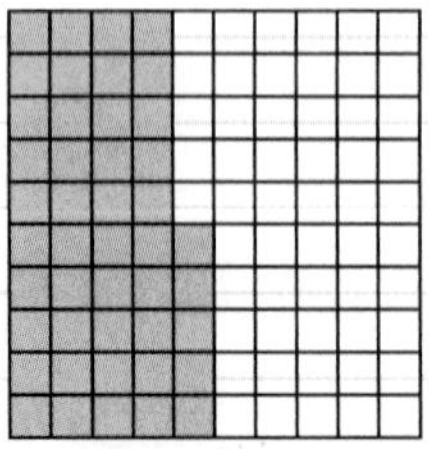

$\frac{45}{100}$ forty-five hundredths

Another Way: Decimal

Hundreds	Tens	Ones	Tenths	Hundredths
		0.	4	5

0.45 forty-five hundredths

Fractions can be written as decimals and decimals can be written as fractions.

EXAMPLE

Remember

Place value names to the right of the decimal point end in *ths*. Example: *tenths*, *hundredths*.

2 Write $\frac{48}{100}$ as a decimal.

$\frac{48}{100}$ is written as 0.48.

Hundreds	Tens	Ones	Tenths	Hundredths
		0.	4	8

So, $\frac{48}{100} = 0.48$.

3 Write 0.75 as a fraction.

0.75 is seventy-five hundredths.

Hundreds	Tens	Ones	Tenths	Hundredths
		0.	7	5

So, $0.75 = \frac{75}{100}$.

Online **Personal Tutor at** ca.gr3math.com

CHECK What You Know

Write a fraction and a decimal for the part that is shaded.
See Example 1 (p. 558)

1. 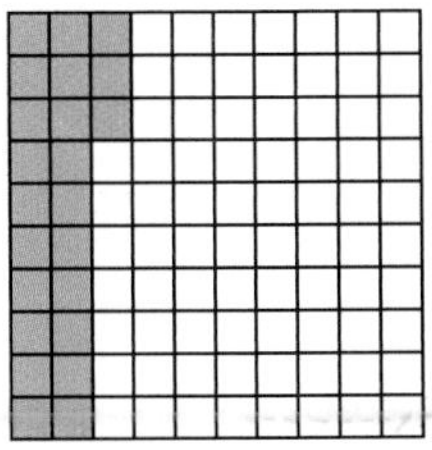

2. 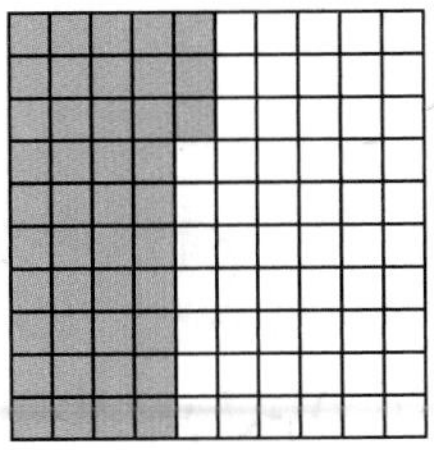

3. 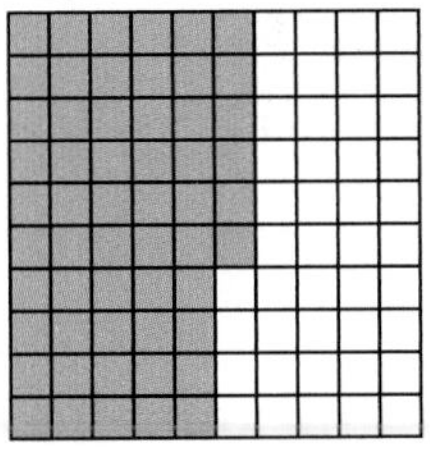

Write each fraction as a decimal. See Example 2 (p. 559)

4. $\frac{56}{100}$ **5.** $\frac{25}{100}$ **6.** $\frac{86}{100}$

Write each decimal as a fraction. See Example 3 (p. 559)

7. 0.85 **8.** 0.34 **9.** 0.19

10. Andre is reading a book. It has 100 pages. He has read 54 pages. Write the fraction and decimal for the amount that he has read.

11. Talk About It Where have you seen a decimal in the hundredths used everyday?

Practice and Problem Solving

EXTRA PRACTICE See page R34.

Write a fraction and a decimal for the part that is shaded.
See Example 1 (p. 558)

12. 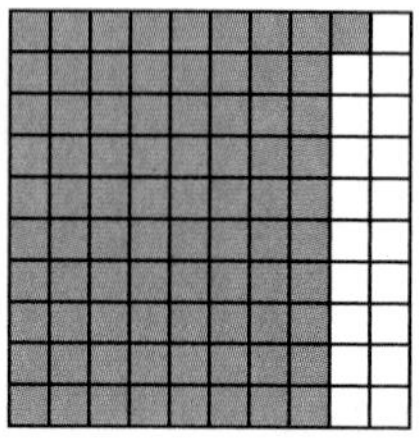

13. 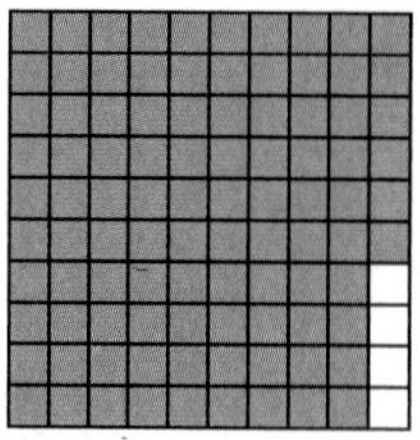

14. 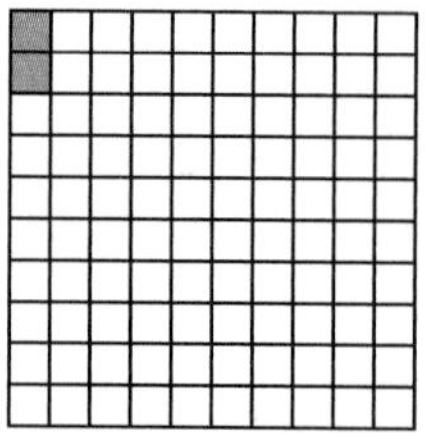

15. 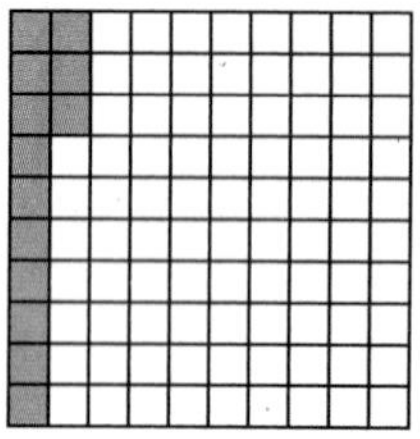

16. 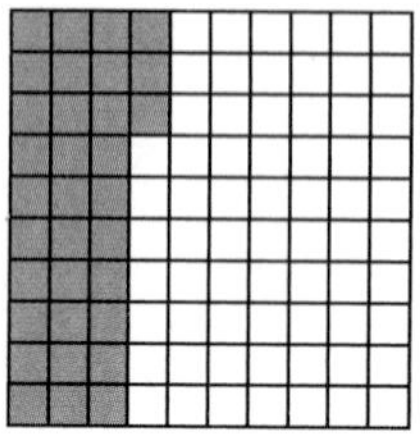

17. 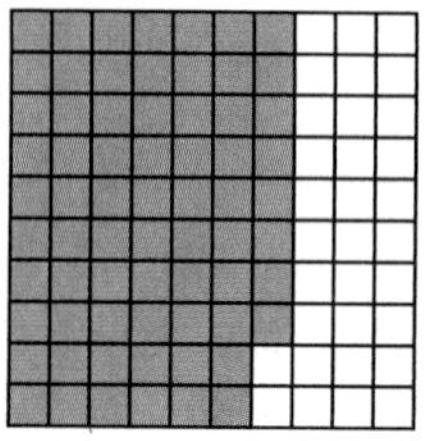

Write each fraction as a decimal. See Example 2 (p. 559)

18. $\frac{23}{100}$ **19.** $\frac{27}{100}$ **20.** $\frac{14}{100}$

21. $\frac{10}{100}$ **22.** $\frac{73}{100}$ **23.** $\frac{91}{100}$

Write each decimal as a fraction. See Example 3 (p. 559)

24. 0.58 **25.** 0.24 **26.** 0.05

27. 0.49 **28.** 0.55 **29.** 0.30

For Exercises 30 and 31, write a fraction and a decimal.

30. Moira has a box of 100 crackers. She eats 15 crackers. What part of the crackers did she not eat?

31. Yolanda read 100 books. Of these, 35 are fiction. What part of the books are not fiction?

H.O.T. Problems

32. OPEN ENDED Write a decimal with 9 in the hundredths place.

33. WHICH ONE DOESN'T BELONG? Which of these numbers does not belong? Explain.

$\frac{4}{10}$ $\frac{25}{100}$ 0.36 0.58

34. WRITING IN MATH Explain why 0.38 contains 3 tenths and 8 hundredths.

CHAPTER 13

Mid-Chapter Check

Lessons 13-1 through 13-2

Write a fraction and a decimal for the part that is shaded. (Lessons 13-1 and 13-2)

1. 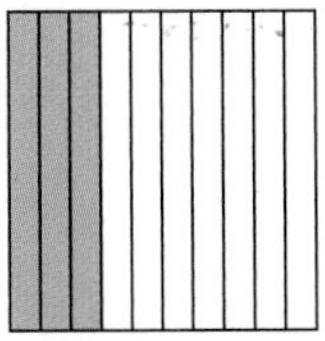

2. 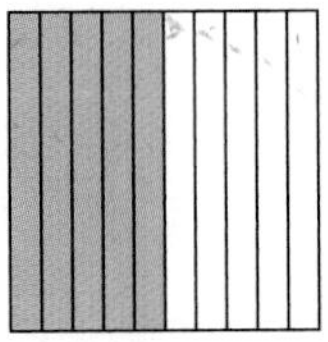

3. 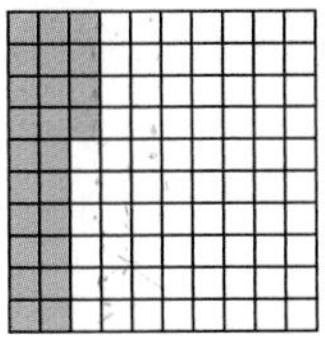

4. 

Write each fraction as a decimal.
(Lesson 13-1)

5. Anne has $\frac{2}{10}$ of a dollar.

6. Rhonda ate $\frac{7}{10}$ of a bag of fruit snacks.

Write each decimal as a fraction.
(Lesson 13-1)

7. 0.1

8. 0.8

9. **STANDARDS PRACTICE** Which decimal equals $\frac{4}{10}$? (Lesson 13-1)

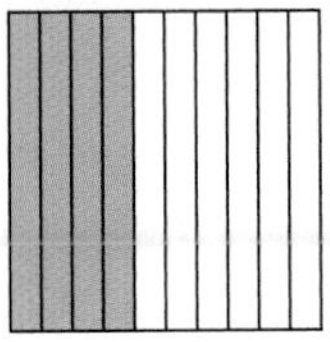

A 10.4

B 5.4

C 0.4

D 0.04

Write each fraction as a decimal.
(Lesson 13-2)

10. $\frac{37}{100}$

11. $\frac{10}{100}$

Write each decimal as a fraction.
(Lesson 13-2)

12. 0.94

13. 0.43

14. **STANDARDS PRACTICE**
Burt shaded $\frac{4}{100}$ of a figure then erased $\frac{1}{100}$. Which fraction equals the amount left shaded? (Lesson 13-2)

F $\frac{3}{100}$

G $\frac{2}{100}$

H $\frac{3}{10}$

J $\frac{2}{10}$

15. Jean played 20 CDs. She played half of them in the car, and the rest in her room. How many tenths did she play in her room? Explain.
(Lesson 13-1)

16. Three friends have 5 toads each. If 2 friends give away 2 toads each, how many are left? (Lesson 13-2)

17. Arlo counts 100 vehicles in a parking lot. What decimal represents the other vehicles? (Lesson 13-2)

Parking Lot Vehicles	
Type	**Amount**
Car	65
Mini-van	30
Other	■

18. **WRITING IN MATH** Is the number 0.5 greater than or less than 1? Explain how you know.
(Lesson 13-1)

Problem Solving in Science

CONTINENTS

The land masses of Earth are continents. There are seven continents. The continents make up about $\frac{3}{10}$ of Earth's surface. The rest of Earth's surface, about $\frac{7}{10}$, is water.

The seven continents on Earth are Africa, Antarctica, Asia, Australia, Europe, North America, and South America. The table shows the amount of Earth's land that each continent covers.

Earth's Land Area

Continent	Land Area
Africa	0.2
Antarctica	0.09
Asia	0.3
Australia	0.05
Europe	0.07
North America	0.17
South America	0.12

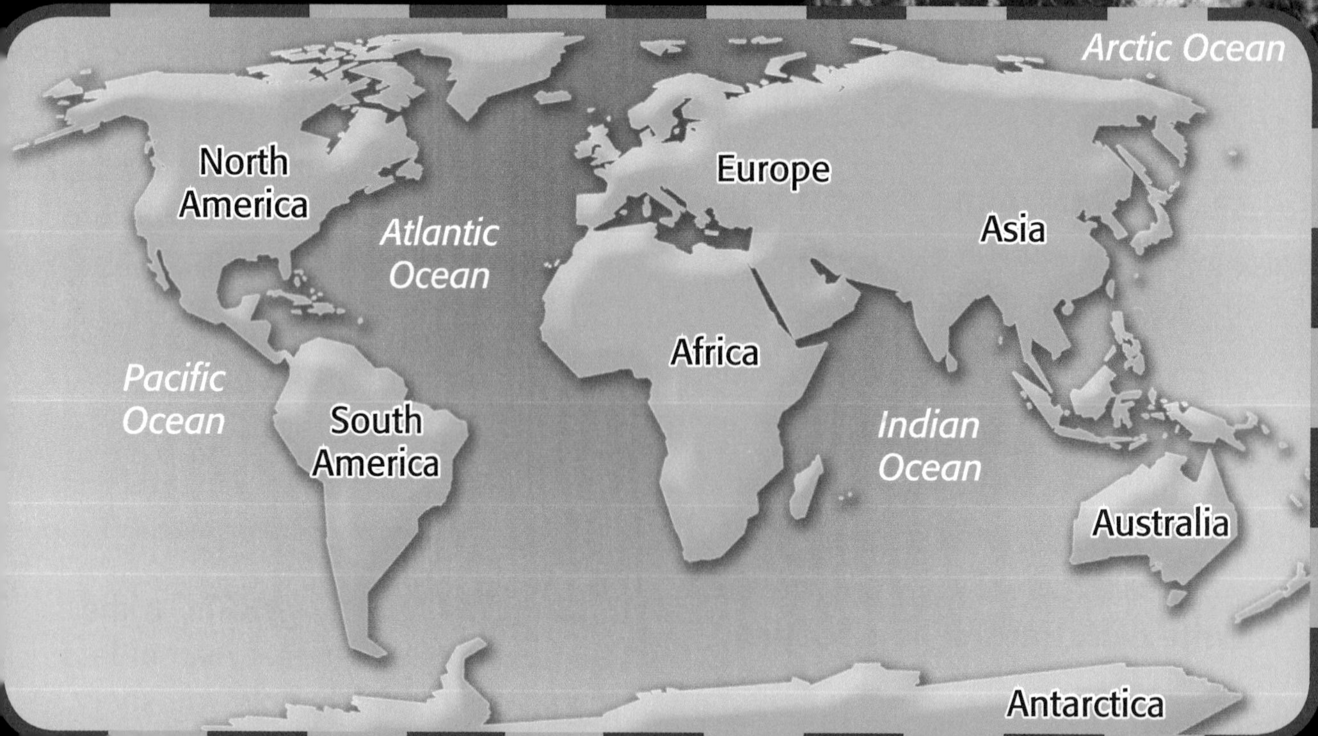

Standard 3NS3.4 Know and understand that fractions and decimals are two different representations of the same concept.

Did You Know?

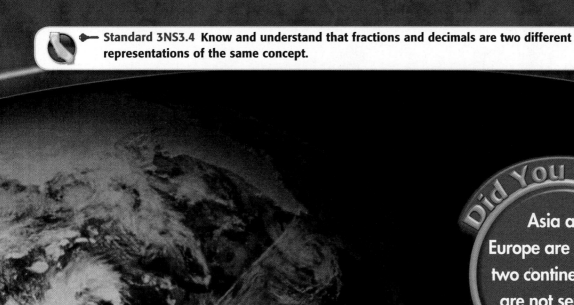

Asia and Europe are the only two continents that are not separate land masses.

Real-World Math

Use the information on page 562 to answer each problem.

1. Write a decimal that shows how much of Earth is water.
2. Copy and complete the tenths model to show what part of Earth is land. Then, write the decimal.

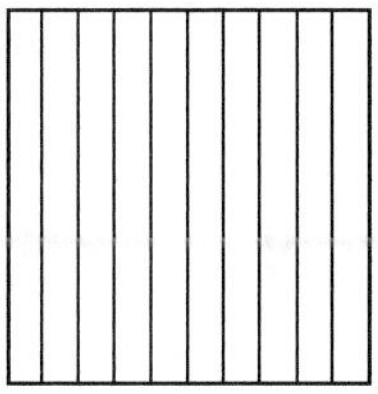

3. Name the continents whose land area is written in tenths. Change those decimals to fractions.
4. Which continent covers the greatest area? Tell how you know.
5. Which continent's land area has a 2 in the hundredths place?
6. Write the decimal that represents the total land area for the continent of North America in words.
7. Name the continents whose land areas are written with a decimal that have no tenths. Write those decimals as fractions.
8. If you added all the decimals from the table together, what would they add up to? Explain.

13-3 Problem-Solving Strategy

MAIN IDEA I will solve problems by acting them out.

Standard 3MR2.3 Use a variety of methods, such as words, numbers, symbols, charts, graphs, tables, **diagrams, and models, to explain mathematical reasoning. Standard 3NS3.4 Know and understand that fractions and decimals are two different representations of the same concept** (e.g., 50 cents is $\frac{1}{2}$ of a dollar, 75 cents is $\frac{3}{4}$ of a dollar).

Five students are throwing paper balls into a basket. They line up in order from tallest to shortest. Adriana is taller than Bryce, but she is shorter than Jenelle. Delmar is shorter than Evan, but taller than Jenelle. In what order are they lined up?

Understand

What facts do you know?

- Adriana is taller than Bryce.
- Adriana is shorter than Jenelle.
- Delmar is shorter than Evan.
- Delmar is taller than Jenelle.
- The students line up from tallest to shortest.

What do you need to find?

- The order in which they line up.

Plan

Act out the problem using 5 students.

Solve

Use the facts in the problem to arrange the students. Work with the facts that make sense first.

	tallest				shortest
Adriana is taller than Bryce.	A	B			
Adriana is shorter than Jenelle.	J	A	B		
Delmar is taller than Jenelle.	D	J	A	B	
Delmar is shorter than Evan.	E	D	J	A	B

So, the order is Evan, Delmar, Jenelle, Adrianna, and Bryce.

Check

Look back at the problem. The answer makes sense for the facts given in the problem.

ANALYZE the Strategy

Refer to the problem on the previous page.

1. Would the results have been the same if any of the facts were missing? Explain.

2. Explain why this strategy is a good choice for this kind of problem.

3. Could you use this strategy if 5 students are not available to act it out? Explain.

4. Could you use another strategy to solve this problem? Explain.

PRACTICE the Strategy

EXTRA PRACTICE
See page R35.

Solve. Use the *act it out* strategy.

5. Skylar has 8 baseball cards now. Her sister gave her 4 cards and took 2 from her. How many baseball cards did Skylar have to begin with?

6. The length of a football field is 100 yards. Alonso ran 20 yards in one play and another 40 yards for the next play. Write the total number of yards Alonso ran as a fraction and a decimal.

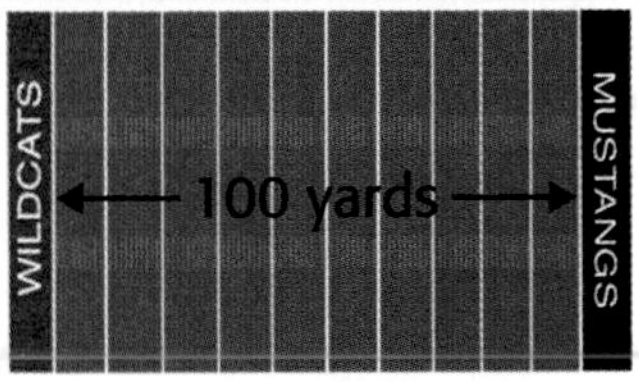

7. An empty bus picks up 5 people at the first stop. At the second stop, 4 people get on and 2 people get off. At the third stop, 5 people get on. At the last stop 1 person gets on and 4 people get off. How many passengers are now on the bus?

8. One face of a cube is shown. All six faces look the same. What fraction of the cube is blue?

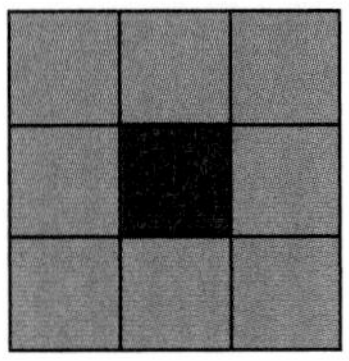

9. Alfonso and Alisa go to a park to play basketball, feed the ducks, and have a picnic. How many different ways can they order what they want to do at the park?

10. There was a total of 10 fish in three different tanks. Four-tenths of the fish were sold by noon. Each tank had a different number of fish. What fraction of fish was left in each tank?

11. **WRITING IN MATH** Look back at Exercise 10. Explain how you solved the problem by using the *act it out* strategy.

Explore

Math Activity for 13-4
Fractions, Decimals, and Money

You can use what you know about money to understand fractions and decimals.

MAIN IDEA

I will relate money to fractions and decimals.

Standard 3NS3.4 Know and understand that fractions and decimals are two different representations of the same concept.

Standard 3MR2.4 Express the solution clearly and logically by using the appropriate mathematical notation and terms and clear language; support solutions with evidence in both verbal and symbolic work.

You Will Need
play money

Concepts in Motion
Animation
ca.gr3math.com

ACTIVITY Explore Parts of a Dollar

Step 1 Count coins.

- Count out enough pennies to make one dollar. Recall that 100 pennies = 1 dollar.
- Take 1 penny from the pile.
- How much money is 1 penny in cents?
- How do you write 1¢ as a fraction?
- How do you write 1¢ as a decimal?

Coin	Amount in Cents	Fraction of a Dollar	Amount as a Decimal
Penny	1¢	$\frac{1}{100}$	$0.01
Nickel			
Dime			
Quarter			
Half-Dollar			

Step 2 Complete the table.

Copy the table shown. Repeat Step 1 for each coin listed. Record your answers on your table.

Step 3 Model fractions.

The model shows that 1¢ is $\frac{1}{100}$ of a dollar. Model the fraction of a dollar for 5¢, 10¢, 25¢, and 50¢.

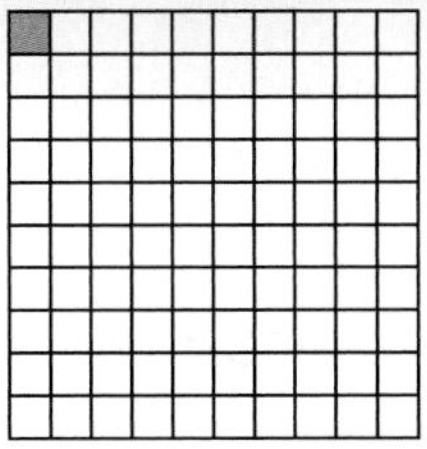

Hands-On Activity

Think About It

1. Write a fraction for the part of a dollar that is 7 pennies.
2. Use graph paper to model the fraction in Exercise 1.
3. Make a model to show 50¢.

CHECK What You Know

4. Copy and complete the table. What patterns do you notice?

Coins	Fraction of a Dollar	Amount as a Decimal	How Many Make $1.00?
Penny			
Nickel			
Dime	$\frac{10}{100}$		
Quarter			
Half-Dollar		$0.50	

Model each amount. Then write as a fraction and a decimal.

5. 47¢ 6. 26¢ 7. 87¢

Write each fraction as cents and as a decimal.

8. $\frac{22}{100}$ 9. $\frac{34}{100}$ 10. $\frac{75}{100}$

11. WRITING IN ▶MATH You have 2 nickels. Explain how you know what that amount is in decimal form.

13-4 Decimals and Money

GET READY to Learn

On Monday, Jamil paid 75¢ or \$0.75 for a can of orange juice. What part of a dollar is 75¢?

MAIN IDEA

I will relate money to fractions and decimals.

Standard 3NS3.4 Know and understand that fractions and decimals are two different representations of the same concept (e.g., 50 cents is $\frac{1}{2}$ of a dollar, 75 cents is $\frac{3}{4}$ of a dollar).

In the Explore Activity, you related fractions and decimals. In this lesson, you will look at specific parts of a dollar.

KEY CONCEPT — Fractions, Decimals, and Money

Money	Words	Numbers
	*one cent* one hundredth of a dollar	1¢ or \$0.01 $\frac{1}{100}$
	*five cents* five hundredths of a dollar	5¢ or \$0.05 $\frac{5}{100}$
	*ten cents* ten hundredths of a dollar	10¢ or \$0.10 $\frac{10}{100}$
	*twenty-five cents* twenty-five hundredths of a dollar	25¢ or \$0.25 $\frac{25}{100}$
	*fifty cents* fifty hundredths of a dollar	50¢ or \$0.50 $\frac{50}{100}$
	*one hundred cents* one hundred hundredths of a dollar	100¢ or \$1.00 $\frac{100}{100}$

You can write amounts of money as part of a dollar.

Real-World EXAMPLES

1 **MONEY Jamil spent 75¢ on a can of orange juice. What part of a dollar is 75¢?**

Write 75¢ as a fraction.

You know that 75¢ can be written as \$0.75 or $\frac{75}{100}$.

$$\frac{75}{100} = \frac{3}{4}$$

So, 75¢ is $\frac{3}{4}$ of a dollar.

Remember

There are 100 pennies in one dollar.

2 **MONEY Yoshi found 2 dimes on the counter. What part of a dollar is 20¢?**

Write 20¢ as a fraction.

You know that 20¢ can be written as \$0.20 or $\frac{20}{100}$.

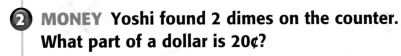

$$\frac{20}{100} = \frac{2}{10} = \frac{1}{5}$$

So, 20¢ is $\frac{2}{10}$ or $\frac{1}{5}$ of a dollar.

3 **MONEY Belinda bought an apple for 50¢. What part of a dollar is 50¢?**

Write 50¢ as a fraction.

You know that 50¢ can be written as \$0.50 or $\frac{50}{100}$.

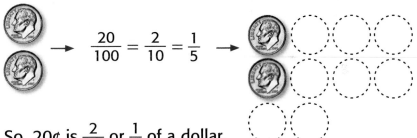

$$\frac{50}{100} = \frac{1}{2}$$

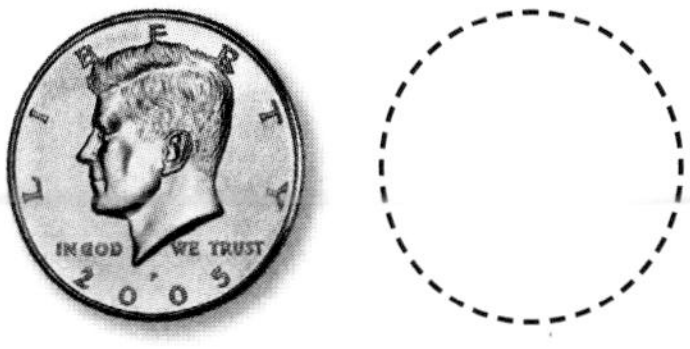

So, 50¢ is $\frac{1}{2}$ of a dollar.

Online Personal Tutor at ca.gr3math.com

CHECK What You Know

Write the part of a dollar each amount represents. See Examples 1–3 (p. 569)

1. 

2. 

3. 

4. 

5. Raymond has 9 dimes and 5 pennies. He wants to buy something that costs $1.00. What part of a dollar does he still need?

6. **Talk About It** Six dimes is $0.60. How can you use $\frac{6}{10} = \frac{\blacksquare}{5}$ to find the part of a dollar for 60¢

Practice and Problem Solving

EXTRA PRACTICE See page R35.

Write the part of a dollar each amount represents. See Examples 1–3 (p. 569)

7. 

8. 

9. 

10. 

11. 

12. 

13. Cierra saves $\frac{3}{4}$ of every dollar she earns. If she earns $5, how much will she save?

14. Mel spent $\frac{7}{10}$ of a dollar on a pen. He gave the clerk $\frac{3}{4}$ of a dollar. How much change did he receive?

H.O.T. Problems

15. OPEN ENDED Explain how you could represent the decimal 0.6 as money.

16. WHICH ONE DOESN'T BELONG? Identify the form that does not name the part of a dollar for 75¢.

seventy-five hundredths	2 quarters and 2 dimes	$0.75	$\frac{75}{100}$

17. WRITING IN ▶MATH Compare money written as a fraction and money written as a decimal. How are they alike? How are they different?

Standards Practice

18 Lorenzo shaded $\frac{1}{100}$ of the figure. Which decimal equals $\frac{1}{100}$? **(Lesson 13-2)**

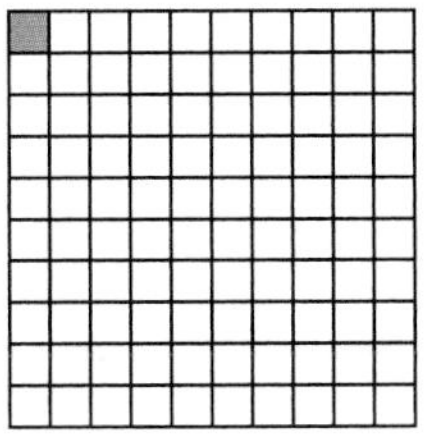

A 1.0

B 0.100

C 0.1

D 0.01

19 How would you write 3 dollars and 45 cents in decimal form? **(Lesson 13-4)**

F 345

G $34.5

H $3.45

J $0.345

Spiral Review

20. In line, Enrique said he could not see over Brent's head. Lydia is not last but is taller than Enrique. What is the order of the line if Halley is not first and can't see over anyone? **(Lesson 13-3)**

Write each decimal as a fraction. **(Lesson 13-2)**

21. 0.82 **22.** 0.47 **23.** 0.07

24. If Alek takes a pair of jeans, a pair of shorts, a pair of dress pants, and 3 different T-shirts, how many outfits will he have for his vacation? **(Lesson 7-3)**

13-5 Problem-Solving Investigation

MAIN IDEA I will choose the best strategy to solve a problem.

Standard 3MR1.2 Determine when and how to break a problem into simpler parts. Standard 3NS3.3 Solve problems involving addition, subtraction, multiplication, and division of money amounts in decimal notation and multiply and divide money amounts in decimal notation by using whole-number multipliers and divisors.

P.S.I. TEAM +

JANE: I planted 30 tomato seeds in my garden. Three out of every 5 seeds grew into tomato plants.

YOUR MISSION: Find how many seeds grew into tomato plants.

Understand

You know 30 seeds were planted and that 3 out of every 5 seeds grew. into tomato plants. Find out how many seeds grew into tomato plants.

Plan

You can *draw a picture* to help solve the problem. Use tallies to represent the seeds.

Solve

Put the tallies in groups of 5 until there are 30 tallies.

Three of each group became plants.

3 + 3 + 3 + 3 + 3 + 3

So, $6 \times 3 = 18$ seeds grew into tomato plants.

Check

Look back at the problem.

$3 + 3 + 3 + 3 + 3 + 3 = 18$

So, the answer is correct.

Math Online Extra Examples at ca.gr3math.com

Mixed Problem Solving

EXTRA PRACTICE
See page R35.

Use any strategy shown below to solve. Tell what strategy you used.

PROBLEM-SOLVING STRATEGIES
- *Guess and check.*
- *Work a simpler problem.*
- *Make an organized list.*
- *Draw a picture.*
- *Act it out.*

1. Darius has 17 apples in a basket. He wants to share them with 3 of his friends. How many will each friend get if each one has the same amount? How many will be left?

2. Two boys and a girl share $80. The girl gets twice as much money as each of the boys. How much money do each of the children get?

3. How many more sticks of butter need to be added to the right side to balance the scale?

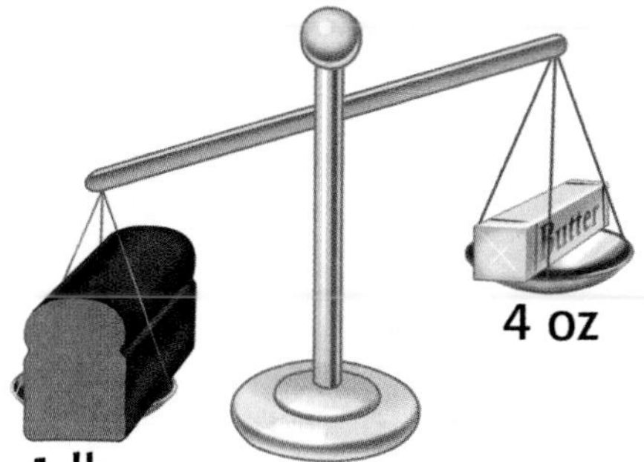

4. Suni earned an allowance of $2.00. She also took care of her baby sister for $1.50. She spent $1.75 on a snack and drink. How much money does she have left?

5. Sei played marbles with her friends and lost some. She now has 25 marbles. She lost 3 to Hakeem, 6 to Mavis, 1 to Mikayla and 4 to Ramous. How many marbles did she have to start with?

6. Josie has one folder of each color red, green, and blue. How many different ways can she order them?

7. Jocelyn and Maska want to install a fence around their garden. How many feet of fence will they need?

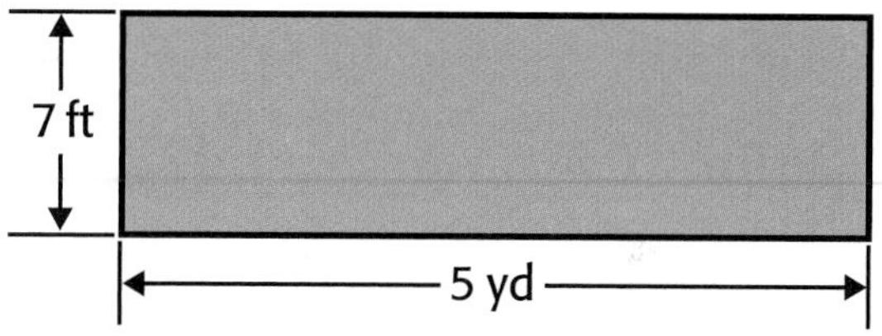

8. Morris has 15 nickels and 2 dimes. Will he be able to buy a toy that costs $0.98? Explain.

9. A man walks 2 kilometers to a store. He walks 30 meters while in the store and then walks back home. How many meters does he walk in all?

10. WRITING IN ►MATH When you add 8 to a number, subtract 10 from the sum, and double the difference, you get 44. What is the number? Explain.

13 Study Guide and Review

FOLDABLES™ Study Organizer GET READY to Study

Be sure the following Key Vocabulary words and Key Concepts are written in your Foldable.

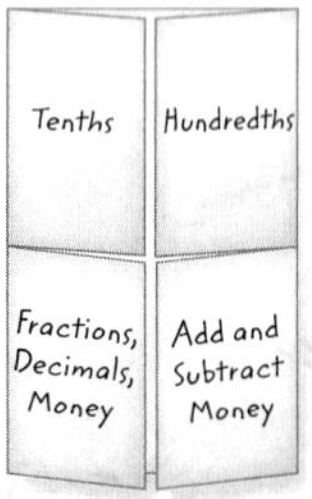

BIG Ideas

- A **tenth** is one of ten equal parts. (p. 553)

Write: 0.5

Read: five-tenths

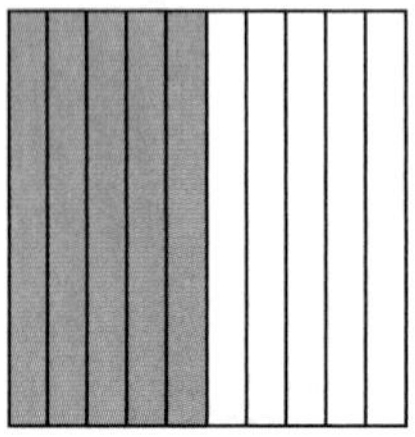

- A **hundredth** is one of one hundred equal parts. (p. 558)

Write: 0.45

Read: forty-five hundredths

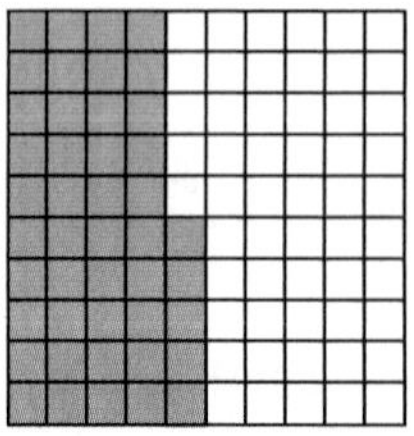

Fractions, Decimals, and Money (p. 568)

$25¢ = \frac{25}{100} = \frac{1}{4}$ of a dollar

$50¢ = \frac{50}{100} = \frac{1}{2}$ of a dollar

Key Vocabulary

decimal (p. 553)
decimal point (p. 553)
hundredths (p. 558)
tenths (p. 553)

Vocabulary Check

Choose the vocabulary word that completes each sentence.

1. In 6.31, the 3 is in the ___?___ place.
2. When adding money, you line up the ___?___ .
3. In 3.47, the 7 is in the ___?___ place.
4. The tenths place is to the right of the ___?___ .
5. $\frac{76}{100}$ reads as seventy-six ___?___ .
6. A dime is one-___?___ of a dollar.
7. The number 5.2 is a ___?___ .
8. One quarter is 25 ___?___ of a dollar.

Lesson-by-Lesson Review

13-1 Tenths (pp. 553–556)

Example 1
What part of the figure is shaded? Write as a fraction and decimal.

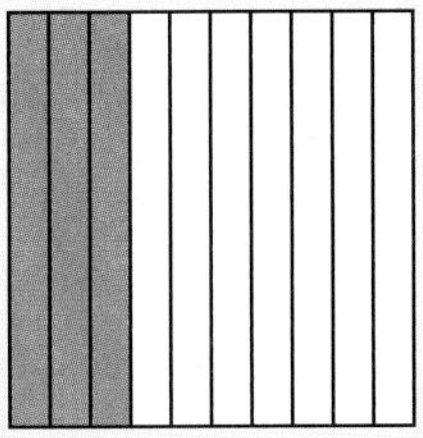

Fraction: $\frac{3}{10}$

Decimal: 0.3

So, $\frac{3}{10}$ or 0.3 of the figure is shaded.

Write a fraction and decimal for the part that is shaded.

9. 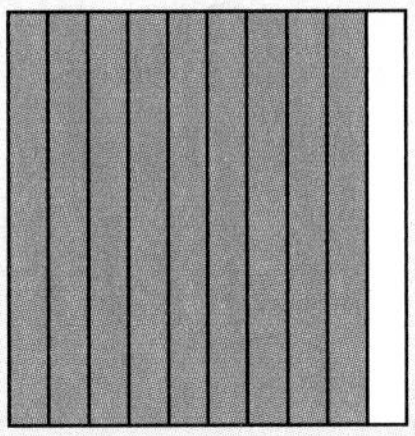 **10.** 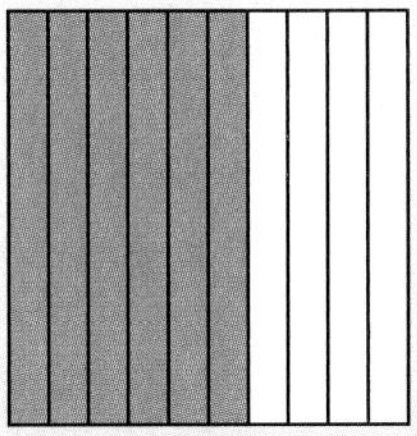

Write each fraction as a decimal.

11. $\frac{2}{10}$ **12.** $\frac{9}{10}$

Write each decimal as a fraction.

13. 0.8 **14.** 0.2

15. Dorian ate 0.5 of a banana and gave away the rest. How much of the banana did he give away?

13-2 Hundredths (pp. 558–560)

Example 2
The table shows how 100 students answered the question, "How do you help at school?" What part of the group answered recycle?

Helping Hands	
Follow the rules	55
Pick up litter	26
Recycle	19

Fraction: $\frac{19}{100}$ **Decimal:** 0.19

So, $\frac{19}{100}$ or 0.19 students said recycle.

Write a fraction and a decimal for the part that is shaded.

16. 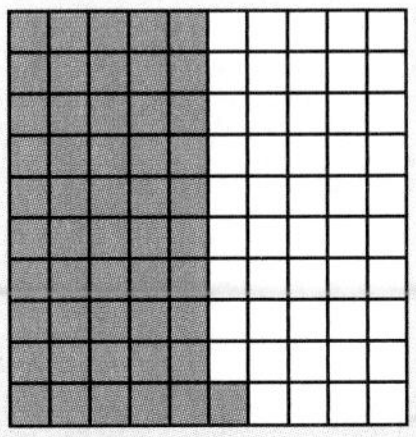 **17.** 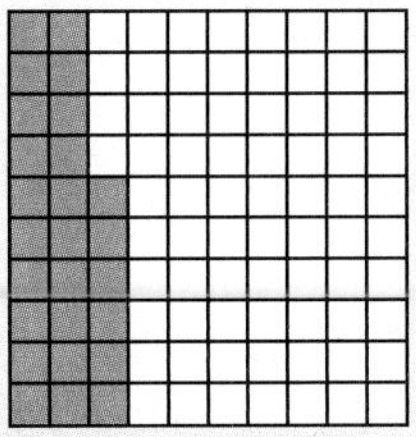

Write each fraction as a decimal.

18. $\frac{37}{100}$ **19.** $\frac{14}{100}$

Write each decimal as a fraction.

20. 0.03 **21.** 0.18

13-3 Problem-Solving Strategy: Act it Out (pp. 564–565)

Example 3

Kiki is making a necklace. She strings 3 red beads then 1 green bead, 3 red beads then 1 green bead. She continues this pattern until she has used 36 beads. How many red beads did she use?

Understand Kiki used 36 beads. She strings red and green beads in a pattern. Find how many red beads she used.

Plan Act out the pattern with connecting cubes.

Solve First, place 3 red cubes and 1 green cube in a row.

Continue until you have used 36 cubes.

Count the number of red cubes by 3s.

$9 \times 3 = 27$

So, Kiki used 27 red beads.

Check Look back at the problem. Check by dividing.
$27 \div 3 = 9$
So, the answer is correct.

Solve. Use the *act it out* strategy.

22. Six basketball players took the same number of practice shots. They took 54 shots in all. How many shots did each player take?

23. A quilt has 10 rows with 10 squares in each row. Each row has 4 blue squares. What decimal represents the total number of blue squares in the whole blanket?

24. Lance buys 3 two-pound bags and one $\frac{1}{2}$-pound bag of ice. Jill buys three $\frac{1}{2}$-pound bags of ice. How much more will Lance spend?

Ice			
Size (lb)	$\frac{1}{2}$	1	2
Price	$0.50	$1	$2

25. Lonzo gave 10 apple slices to his friends. He gave 0.3 to Pat, 0.2 to Sue, 0.1 to Kurt, and the rest to Oliver. How much of the apple slices did Oliver get? Write as a decimal and a fraction.

13-4 Decimals and Money (pp. 568–571)

Example 4
Shing bought a goldfish for 25¢. What part of a dollar is 25¢?

Write 25¢ as a fraction.

You know that 25¢ can be written as \$0.25 or $\frac{25}{100}$.

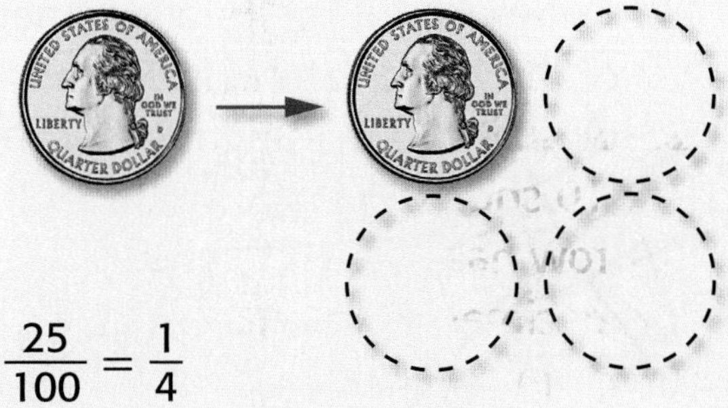

$\frac{25}{100} = \frac{1}{4}$

So, 25¢ is $\frac{1}{4}$ of a dollar.

Example 5
A store sells stickers for 40¢ each. What part of a dollar is 40¢?

Write 40¢ as a fraction.

You know that 40¢ can be written as \$0.40 or $\frac{40}{100}$.

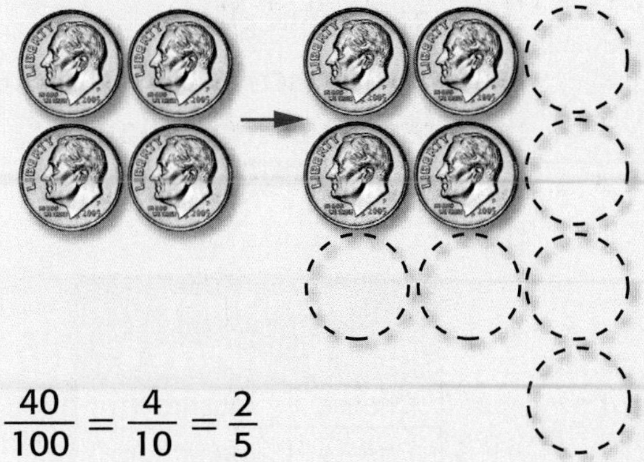

$\frac{40}{100} = \frac{4}{10} = \frac{2}{5}$

So, 40¢ is $\frac{4}{10}$ or $\frac{2}{5}$ of a dollar.

Write the part of a dollar each amount represents.

26.

27.

28.

29. Sherman wants to buy 2 tickets for a ride at the fair. The tickets cost \$1.00. If he still needs \$0.22, what part of a dollar does he have? Write it as a fraction.

30. A keychain costs \$1.75. Syreeta and Tionna will share the cost of the keychain. The table shows how much money they each have. What part of a dollar do they still need?

Coins	Q	D	N	P
Syreeta	0	1	5	17
Tionna	2	4	0	1

13-5 Problem-Solving Investigation: Choose a Strategy (pp. 572–573)

Example 6
Marquez has six coins that total \$0.75. There is at least one quarter, one dime, and one nickel. What are the other three coins?

Understand

You know the number of coins and their total value. Find the other three coins.

Plan *Guess and check* to solve.

Solve Find the value of the three coins you know.

\$0.25 + \$0.10 + \$0.05 = \$0.40

Then, find the difference between the total value of the six coins and the value of the three coins.

\$0.75 – \$0.40 = \$0.35

Guess and check to find the three coins that add to \$0.35.

Guess			Check
dime	dime	nickel	\$0.25 no
quarter	dime	dime	\$0.45 no
quarter	nickel	nickel	\$0.35 yes

So, 1 quarter and 2 nickels.

Check Look back at the problem. The answer makes sense for the situation.

Use any strategy to solve.

31. **Measurement** Russ wakes up at 7:30. If he gets to school at 8:45, how many quarter hours does it take him to get dressed, eat, and walk to school?

32. **Geometry** If the total perimeter of the quadrilateral is 71 cm, what is the missing measure?

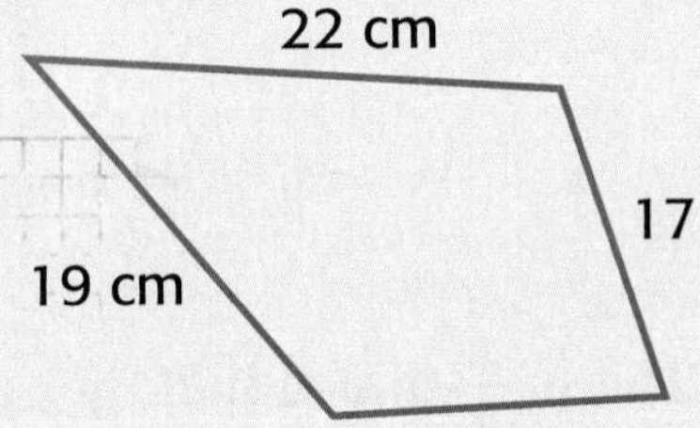

33. Kareem gave 25 football cards to Cindy, 13 to Millie, and 14 to Braden. Kareem now has half the cards he started with. How many cards did he start with?

34. Two pizzas are cut into four slices each. The table shows the topping on each slice. What are the possible combinations choosing one slice from each pizza?

Pizza Slices

Pizza A	Pizza B
Cheese	Mushroom
Cheese	Mushroom
Sausage	Pepperoni
Sausage	Pepperoni

CHAPTER 13 Chapter Test

For Exercises 1–3, tell whether each statement is *true* or *false*.

1. One cent is one hundredth of a dollar.
2. You must always line up the decimal point when you add money.
3. One place to the right of the decimal point is hundredths place.

Write a fraction and a decimal for the part that is shaded.

4. 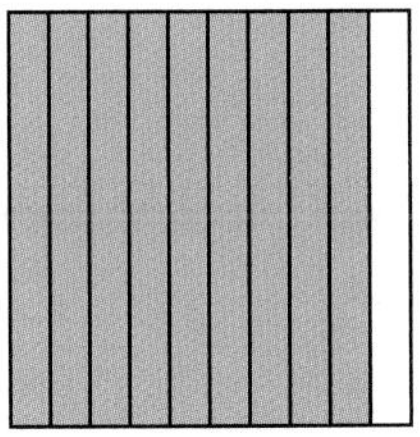

5. 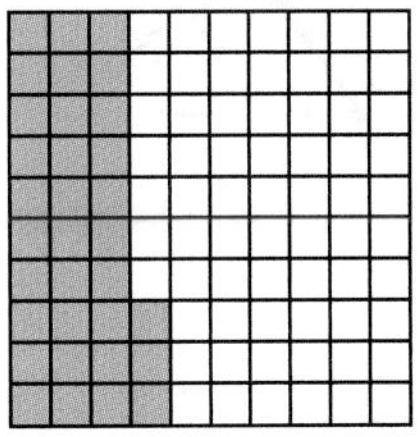

6. Minda wants to share her 17 dolls with her three friends. Will she be able to share them equally? Explain.

Write the part of a dollar each amount represents.

7. 3 quarters
8. 2 pennies

Write each decimal as a fraction.

9. 0.08
10. 0.18

11. **STANDARDS PRACTICE** How would you write 2 dollars and 95 cents in decimal form?

A \$0.295 **C** \$29.5

B \$295 **D** \$2.95

12. At the beginning of the school year, the 3rd grade class had 29 students. Four students moved away and 6 new students moved in. How many students were in the 3rd grade class at the end of the year?

Write each amount as a fraction and a decimal.

13. 2 dimes, 6 pennies
14. 1 quarter, 3 nickels

Write each fraction as a decimal.

15. $\frac{3}{10}$
16. $\frac{97}{100}$

17. **STANDARDS PRACTICE** What is the total cost of these 4 items?

F \$1.519 **H** \$15.20

G \$151.9 **I** \$.1519

18. **WRITING IN ▸MATH** Is \$2.39 greater than \$5? Explain your reasoning.

CHAPTER 13

California Standards Practice

Cumulative, Chapters 1–13

Standards Example

Amalia owns a rule book for board games and card games. Of the set of 10 rules, 7 are rules for board games. Which decimal shows the number of rules for board games?

A 0.07 **C** 0.77

B 0.7 **D** 7.0

Read the Question

Find the decimal for 7 out of 10 games.

Solve the Question

Write 7 out of 10 as a fraction.

7 out of 10 $= \frac{7}{10}$

Write the fraction as a decimal.

$\frac{7}{10} = 0.7$

So, 0.7 of the game rules are board games. The answer is B.

Online **Personal Tutor at** ca.gr3math.com

Choose the best answer.

1 **What decimal does the model below show?**

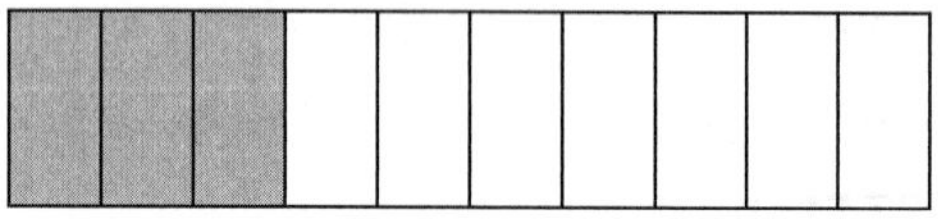

A 3 **C** 0.3

B 0.33 **D** 0.03

2 **Which fraction is equal to 0.5?**

F $\frac{1}{2}$

G $\frac{5}{12}$

H $\frac{1}{5}$

J $\frac{5}{100}$

More California Standards Practice
For practice by standard, see pages CA1–CA33.

3 How do you write twenty-seven hundredths as a decimal?

A 2700 **C** 2.7

B 27 **D** 0.27

---

4 Ava placed her money shown below on the table.

How much money does she have?

F \$0.55 **H** \$0.75

G \$0.65 **J** \$0.85

---

5 Bailey gave the clerk \$5 to pay for these items shown.

How much change will she receive?

A \$2.11 **C** \$3.00

B \$2.89 **D** \$7.89

---

6 Which shows $\frac{9}{100}$ as a decimal?

F 0.90 **H** 0.19

G 0.49 **J** 0.09

---

7 Which fraction equals $\frac{1}{2}$?

A $\frac{2}{4}$

B $\frac{4}{10}$

C $\frac{2}{6}$

D $\frac{1}{4}$

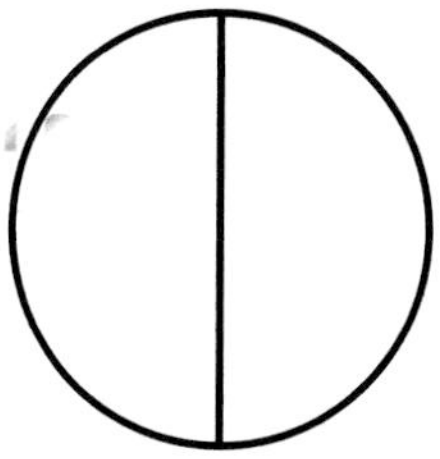

---

8 Which object looks like a cone?

F 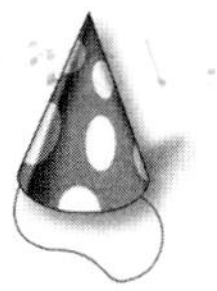

H 

G 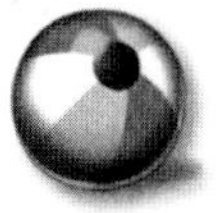

J 

---

9 Which number sentence relates to $45 \div 5 = 9$?

A $45 - 5 = 40$ **C** $9 + 5 = 14$

B $9 \times 5 = 45$ **D** $45 + 5 = 50$

---

10 Last year a bike shop had bike sales of \$2355. For the first 6 months of this year, the bike sales are \$975. How much more does the shop need to sell to reach last year's sales?

F \$1380 **H** \$2620

G \$2480 **J** \$3330

CHAPTER 14 Multiply by One-Digit Numbers

BIG Idea How do I multiply greater numbers?

Models can be used to multiply larger numbers.

Example If 2 prairie dogs each dig 13 holes, there will be 2 × 13 or 26 holes.

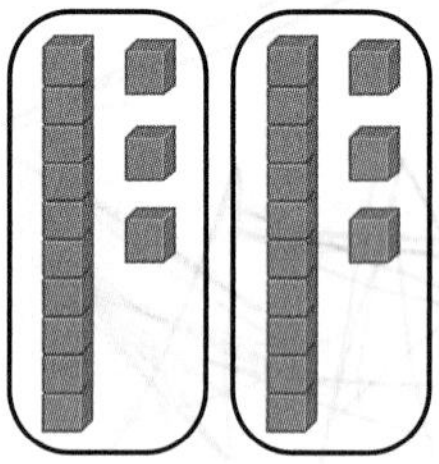
2 groups of 13

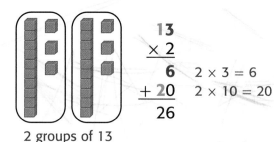

$$\begin{array}{rl} 13 & \\ \times\ 2 & \\ \hline 6 & 2 \times 3 = 6 \\ +\ 20 & 2 \times 10 = 20 \\ \hline 26 & \end{array}$$

What will I learn in this chapter?

- Multiply multi-digit numbers.
- Estimate products.
- Multiply money.
- Solve problems by using logical reasoning.

Key Vocabulary

multiples
factors
product
estimate
round

Math Online **Student Study Tools at** ca.gr3math.com

FOLDABLES™ Study Organizer

Make this Foldable to organize information about multiplying by a one-digit number. Begin with one sheet of 11″ × 17″ paper.

1. **Fold** the sheet of paper into thirds as shown.

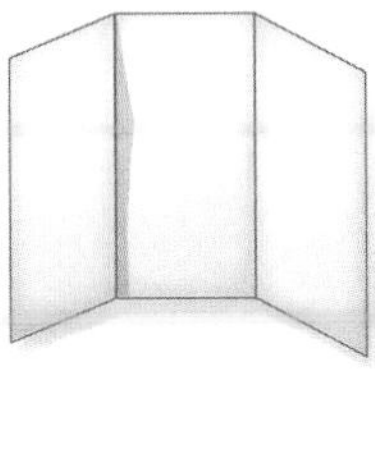

2. **Fold** the bottom edge up two inches and crease well.

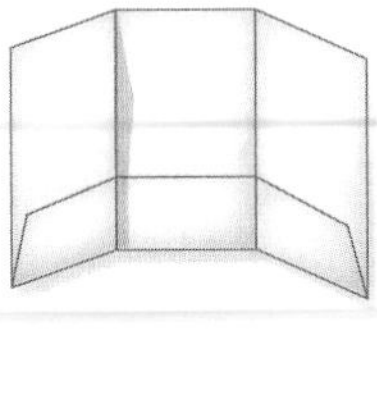

3. **Glue** the outer edges to create three pockets.

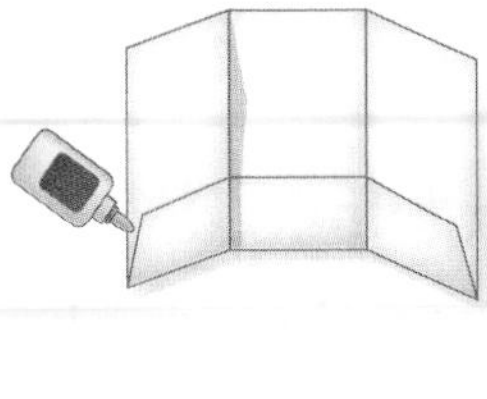

4. **Label** as shown. Record what you learn on index cards.

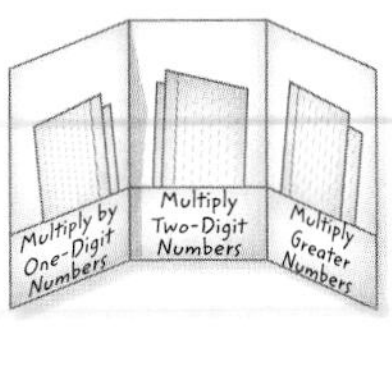

ARE YOU READY for Chapter 14?

You have two ways to check prerequisite skills for this chapter.

Option 2

Math Online Take the Chapter Readiness Quiz at ca.gr3math.com.

Option 1

Complete the Quick Check below.

QUICK Check

Write a multiplication sentence for each array. Then multiply. (Lesson 4-2)

1. 

2. 

3. 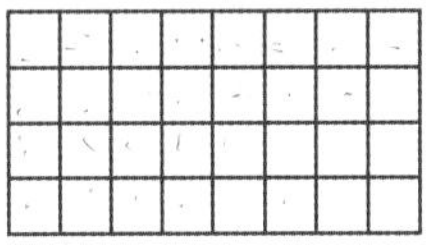

Multiply. (Chapters 4 and 5)

4. $\begin{array}{r} 4 \\ \times\ 7 \\ \hline \end{array}$

5. $\begin{array}{r} 5 \\ \times\ 6 \\ \hline \end{array}$

6. $\begin{array}{r} 9 \\ \times\ 2 \\ \hline \end{array}$

7. 5×5

8. 9×1

9. 10×8

10. There are 2 space shuttles docked at the station. If each shuttle has 5 astronauts, how many astronauts are there altogether?

11. For every pound of play clay Reynaldo makes, he needs 6 cups of flour. How many cups of flour does he need to make 6 pounds of play clay?

Round to the nearest ten. (Lesson 1-8)

12. 78

13. 53

14. 49

Round to the nearest hundred.

15. 125

16. 111

17. 199

14-1 Multiply Multiples of 10, 100, and 1,000

MAIN IDEA

I will multiply multiples of 10, 100, and 1,000.

Standard 3NS2.4 Solve simple problems involving multiplication of multidigit numbers by one-digit numbers (3,671 × 3 = ___). Standard 3MR2.2 Apply strategies and results from simpler problems to more complex problems.

New Vocabulary

multiple

GET READY to Learn

Four multiplication sentences are modeled below. Notice the pattern of zeros. Describe this pattern.

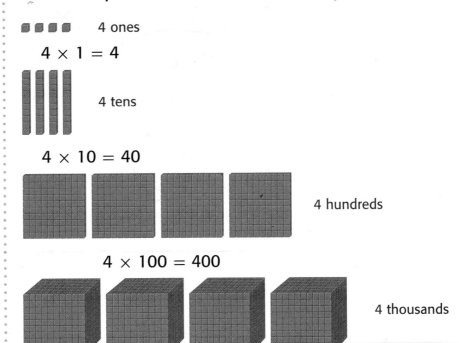

4 ones

$4 \times 1 = 4$

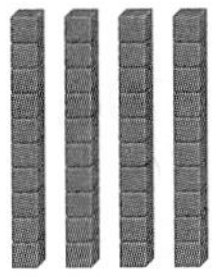
4 tens

$4 \times 10 = 40$

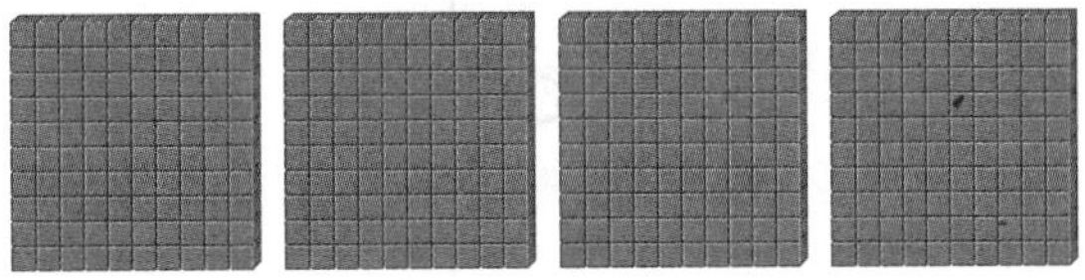
4 hundreds

$4 \times 100 = 400$

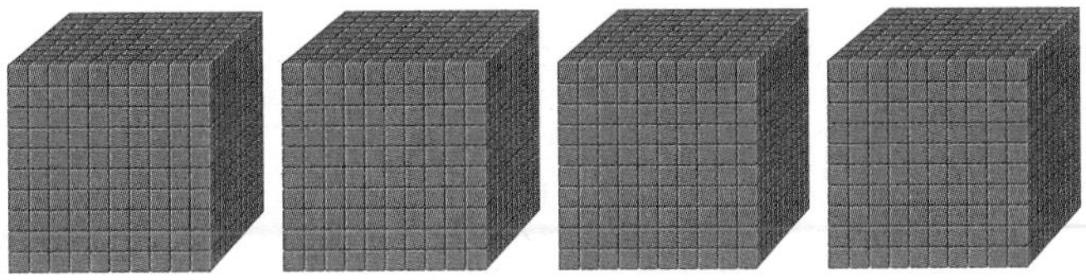
4 thousands

$4 \times 1{,}000 = 4{,}000$

You can use basic facts and patterns of zeros to help you multiply a number mentally by 10, 100, and 1,000.

Real-World EXAMPLE

1 ART **Ernie buys 7 boxes of straws for a project. Each box has 100 straws. How many straws does he have?**

Find 7 × 100. Use basic facts and patterns of zeros.

$7 \times 1 = 7$	7 × 1 one = 7 ones
$7 \times 10 = 70$	7 × 1 ten = 7 tens
$7 \times 100 = 700$	7 × 1 hundred = 7 hundred

So, Ernie has 700 straws.

You can also multiply a number mentally by multiples of 10, 100, and 1,000. A **multiple** is the product of a given number and any other whole number.

20 is a multiple of 10.

200 is a multiple of 100.

2,000 is a multiple of 1,000.

Remember

To multiply by multiples of 10, find the product of the basic fact then place the zeros.

Real-World EXAMPLE

2 **CRAFT** **Bags of 3,000 craft beads are on sale. Ellie bought 5 bags. How many beads did Ellie buy?**

You need to find $5 \times 3{,}000$.

$5 \times 3 = 15$	5×3 ones $= 15$ ones
$5 \times 30 = 150$	5×3 tens $= 15$ tens
$5 \times 300 = 1{,}500$	5×3 hundreds $= 15$ hundreds
$5 \times 3{,}000 = 15{,}000$	5×3 thousands $= 15$ thousands

So, $5 \times 3{,}000 = 15{,}000$. Ellie bought 15,000 beads.

Online **Personal Tutor at** ca.gr3math.com

When the basic fact has a zero in it, you still need to add all the other zeros.

Real-World EXAMPLE

3 **TRAFFIC** **A busy intersection has 5,000 vehicles pass through each day. How many vehicles will pass through in 4 days?**

You need to find $4 \times 5{,}000$.

$4 \times 5 = 20$ ← THINK Sometimes the basic fact has a zero.

$4 \times 50 = 200$

$4 \times 500 = 2{,}000$

$4 \times 5{,}000 = 20{,}000$

So, $4 \times 5{,}000 = 20{,}000$. About 20,000 vehicles will pass through in 4 days.

Math Online **Extra Examples at** ca.gr3math.com

CHECK What You Know

Multiply. Use basic facts and patterns. See Examples 1–3 (p. 585)

1. $3 \times 1 = \blacksquare$
$3 \times 10 = \blacksquare$
$3 \times 100 = \blacksquare$
$3 \times 1{,}000 = \blacksquare$

2. $7 \times 4 = \blacksquare$
$7 \times 40 = \blacksquare$
$7 \times 400 = \blacksquare$
$7 \times 4{,}000 = \blacksquare$

3. $5 \times 6 = \blacksquare$
$5 \times 60 = \blacksquare$
$5 \times 600 = \blacksquare$
$5 \times 6{,}000 = \blacksquare$

4. 4×90

5. $4 \times 4{,}000$

6. 500×8

7. Hunter's Pizza Shop sold 3,000 pizzas each month for 6 months. Find the total number of sold.

8. Talk About It Explain the pattern of zeros that you see when you multiply by 10, 100, or 1,000.

Practice and Problem Solving

EXTRA PRACTICE See page R36.

Multiply. Use basic facts and patterns. See Examples 1–3 (pp. 585–586)

9. $2 \times 1 = \blacksquare$
$2 \times 10 = \blacksquare$
$2 \times 100 = \blacksquare$
$2 \times 1{,}000 = \blacksquare$

10. $6 \times 4 = \blacksquare$
$6 \times 40 = \blacksquare$
$6 \times 400 = \blacksquare$
$6 \times 4{,}000 = \blacksquare$

11. $7 \times 8 = \blacksquare$
$7 \times 80 = \blacksquare$
$7 \times 800 = \blacksquare$
$7 \times 8{,}000 = \blacksquare$

12. 5×50

13. 30×8

14. 4×30

15. 900×7

16. 600×90

17. 60×80

18. Demont's album has 20 pages, and 6 trading cards are on each page. How many cards all?

19. There are 100 houses. Each house has 10 windows. How many windows are there in all?

20. Carmen sold 200 flats of flowers each day for 9 days. Each flat holds 4 flowers. How many flowers did she sell?

21. Carlita has 3 boxes of teddy bears. Each box holds 20 bears. She sells each bear for $4. How much money did she earn?

H.O.T. Problems

22. OPEN ENDED Write a multiplication sentence that uses a multiple of 10 and has a product of 24,000.

23. WRITING IN ▸MATH Write a real-world problem that involves multiplying by a multiple of 10.

14-2 Problem-Solving Strategy

MAIN IDEA I will solve problems by using logical reasoning.

Standard 3MR2.3 Use a variety of methods, such as words, numbers, symbols, charts, graphs, tables, diagrams, and models, to explain mathematical reasoning. **Standard 3NS2.1 Find the sum or difference of two whole numbers between 0 and 10,000.**

Three friends all have on different shirts. Hallie's shirt is white. Jimar's shirt is not green. Lina's shirt is not red. What is the color of each of their shirts?

Understand

What facts do you know?

- Hallie has on a white shirt.
- Jimar's shirt is not green.
- Lina's shirt is not red.

What do you need to find?

- The color of each person's shirt.

Plan

Make a table to show what you know. Then use logical reasoning to find the color of each person's shirt.

Solve

Hallie is wearing white. So, write yes by her name under white. Place an X in all the rest of the white column and the other colors for Hallie.

	White	Red	Green
Hallie	yes	X	X
Lina	X	X	yes
Jimar	X	yes	X

Lina's shirt is not red and can not be white, so it is green. The color that is left is red. Jimar's shirt must be red.

So, Hallie is wearing white, Lina is wearing green, and Jimar is wearing red.

Check

Look back at the problem. The answer makes sense for the facts given. So, the answer is correct.

ANALYZE the Strategy

Refer to the problem on the previous page.

1. Explain how making a table helped in solving the problem.

2. What does it mean to use logical reasoning?

3. If the colors of shirts changed how would the problem be different? How would it be the same?

4. How would the results be different if Lina's shirt was not green?

PRACTICE the Strategy

EXTRA PRACTICE
See page R36.

Solve. Use logical reasoning.

5. Marilee places her math book next to her reading book and language book. Her language book is next to her science book, which is next to her history book. What is a possible order?

6. Emerson, Thi, Joyce, and Shenice each have a different pet. Emerson has a cat. Thi does not have a dog or a fish. Joyce does not have a bird or a fish. What pet does each person have?

7. Paloma, Daniel, and Pirro each play a different sport. According to the information in the table what sport does each student play?

Sports Students Play

Student	Sport
Paloma	soccer
Pirro	not basketball
Daniel	not soccer or football

8. Larrisa, Jo, and Cali went to lunch. They each ordered something different. Larrisa does not like hamburgers. Jo and Cali do not like salad. Who ordered the salad?

9. Three friends want to buy the game shown below. Cletus has 5 quarters and 6 dimes. Alma has 6 quarters and 8 dimes. Deshawn has 5 coins. If they will receive 10 cents in change, what coins does Deshawn have?

10. **WRITING IN MATH** Write two sentences describing how you would use logical reasoning to help solve a real-world situation.

14-3 Estimate Products

MAIN IDEA

I will estimate products.

Standard 3NS2.4 Solve simple problems involving multiplication of multidigit numbers by one-digit numbers (3,671 × 3 = __).
Standard 3MR2.1 Use estimation to verify the reasonableness of calculated results.

GET READY to Learn

Each of the 26 schools in Fair City sends 6 of their best spellers to the city spelling bee. About how many students go to the spelling bee?

When you do not need an exact answer, you can estimate. One way to estimate is to round.

Review Vocabulary

estimate
An estimate indicates *about* how much;
Example:
3 × 42 → 3 × 40
(Lesson 2-3)

Real-World EXAMPLE — Estimate by Rounding

1 SCHOOL About how many students go to the spelling bee?

Estimate 6 × 26 by rounding to the nearest ten.

Step 1 Round the factor, that is greater than 10, to the nearest ten.

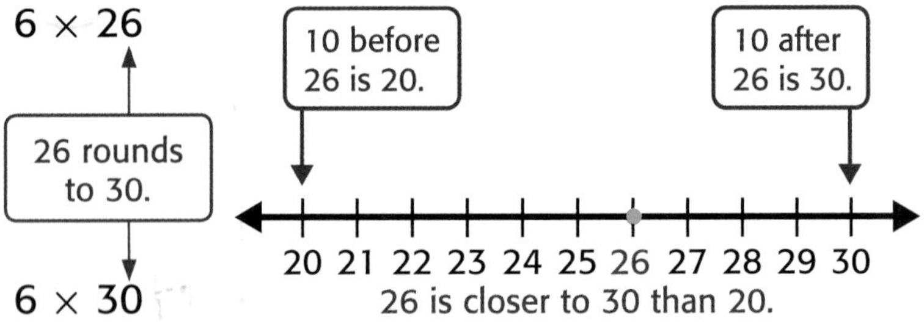

Step 2 Multiply mentally.

6 × 30 = 180

So, about 180 spellers go to the spelling bee.

Online Personal Tutor at ca.gr3math.com

Real-World EXAMPLE — Estimate by Rounding

Remember

Round the factor that is greater than 10.

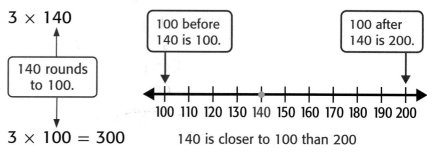

2 **PLAYS There are 140 students. Each student can invite 3 people to a play. About how many people can be invited?**

Estimate 3 × 140 by rounding to the nearest hundred.

3 × 140

140 rounds to 100.

3 × 100 = 300

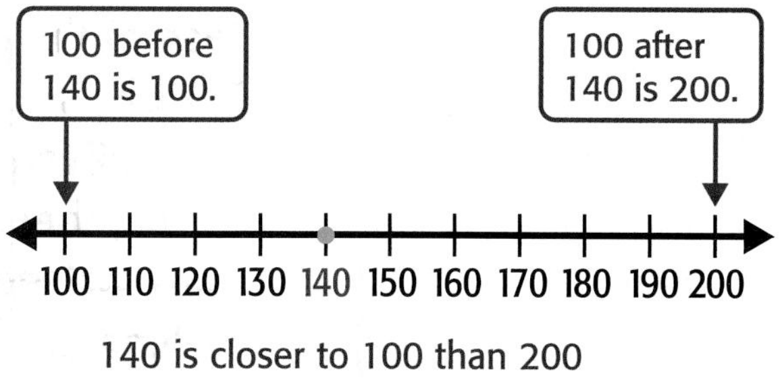

100 before 140 is 100.
100 after 140 is 200.
100 110 120 130 140 150 160 170 180 190 200
140 is closer to 100 than 200

You can use estimation to verify reasonableness.

Real-World EXAMPLE — Verify Reasonableness

3 **SCHOOL BUS A school bus holds about 52 students. Will 4 buses be enough to transport 175 students?**

Estimate 4 × 52. Then compare to 175 .

4 × 52 Round 52 to 50.

4 × 50 = 200 Multiply mentally.

The buses can hold about 200 students. 200 > 175. So, 4 buses will be enough to transport the 175 students.

CHECK What You Know

Estimate. Round to the nearest ten. **See Example 1 (p. 590)**

1. 47 × 4

2. 51 × 8

3. 58 × 2

Estimate. Round to the nearest hundred. **See Example 2 (p. 591)**

4. 315 × 3

5. 189 × 5

6. 150 × 6

7. **Measurement** Janet spends 5 hours each week in math class. Is her estimate reasonable if each class is 55 minutes long? **See Example 3 (p. 591).**

8. Talk About It Will estimating 878 × 9, to the nearest hundred be greater than the actual product? Explain.

Practice and Problem Solving

EXTRA PRACTICE
See page R36.

Estimate. Round to the nearest ten. See Example 1 (p. 590)

9. 27×4

10. 17×6

11. 36×3

12. 28×8

13. 32×5

14. 43×4

Estimate. Round to the nearest hundred. See Example 2 (p. 591)

15. 180×9

16. 197×6

17. 306×3

18. 271×4

19. 290×7

20. 114×8

21. Hiking burns about 288 Calories each hour. About how many Calories can be burned if someone hikes 3 days a week for an hour?

23. Carisa uses 27 sheets of paper for a book she makes. About how many sheets would she need if she makes 8 books?

24. Hector studies about 3 hours each day. Is it reasonable to estimate that is equal to about 100 hours in 4 weeks? Explain.

22. A restaurant keeps track of the paper goods it uses for one day. Is it reasonable to estimate 2,500 napkins, cups, and bags are used in one week? Explain.

Daily Paper Use

H.O.T. Problems

25. FIND THE ERROR Libby and Alvar are estimating 458×4. Who is correct? Explain.

Libby

458×4
$\downarrow \quad \downarrow$
$400 \times 4 = 1{,}600$

Alvar

458×4
$\downarrow \quad \downarrow$
$500 \times 4 = 2{,}000$

26. WRITING IN MATH Explain how you would estimate 77×6.

CHAPTER 14 Mid-Chapter Check

Lessons 14-1 through 14-3

Multiply. Use basic facts and patterns.
(Lesson 14-1)

1. $4 \times 6 = ■$
$4 \times 60 = ■$
$4 \times 600 = ■$
$4 \times 6{,}000 = ■$

2. $8 \times 4 = ■$
$8 \times 40 = ■$
$8 \times 400 = ■$
$8 \times 4{,}000 = ■$

Multiply. Use mental math.

3. 2×60

4. $3 \times 3{,}000$

5. **STANDARDS PRACTICE** What number makes this number sentence true? **(Lesson 14-1)**

$6 \times ■ = 48{,}000$

A 80

B 800

C 8,000

D 80,000

Solve. Use logical reasoning. **(Lesson 14-2)**

6. Robert, Aiden, and Ramon like different kinds of books. Ramon does not like mysteries, Aiden does not like science fiction or sports stories, and Robert loves science fiction. What kind of book does each boy like?

7. Taran lives down the street from Roger. Dakota lives next door to Roger. Regina lives in between Taran and Dakota. What order do the kids live in on the block? **(Lesson 14-2)**

Estimate. Round to the nearest ten. **(Lesson 14-3)**

8. $\begin{array}{r} 78 \\ \times\ 8 \\ \hline \end{array}$

9. $\begin{array}{r} 23 \\ \times\ 2 \\ \hline \end{array}$

10. Mrs. Henry plans to teach 2 math chapters each week. About how many chapters does she plan to teach in 22 weeks? **(Lesson 14-3)**

Estimate. Round to the nearest hundred. **(Lesson 14-3)**

11. $\begin{array}{r} 173 \\ \times\ 5 \\ \hline \end{array}$

12. $\begin{array}{r} 168 \\ \times\ 6 \\ \hline \end{array}$

13. A third grade class has 122 students. Each student needs 4 folders. About how many folders do the third graders need? **(Lesson 14-3)**

14. **STANDARDS PRACTICE** Kisho made a quilt out of squares by putting the squares in 6 equal rows of 11 squares each. About how many squares did Kisho use? **(Lesson 14-3)**

F 40

G 50

H 60

J 70

15. **WRITING IN MATH** Explain the steps in estimating the product of 88×3 by rounding to the nearest ten. **(Lesson 14-3)**

14-4 Multiply by a One-Digit Number

MAIN IDEA

I will multiply two-digit numbers by a one-digit number with no regrouping.

Standard 3NS2.4 Solve simple problems involving multiplication of multidigit numbers by one-digit numbers (3,671 × 3 = ___).

New Vocabulary

partial products

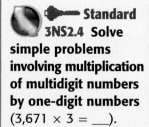

GET READY to Learn

Ken and his two brothers each have 13 marbles. How many marbles do they have in all.

You can use what you know about multiplying smaller numbers to find products like 3 × 13.

Real-World EXAMPLE — Use a Model

1 MARBLES Ken and his two brothers each have 13 marbles. How many marbles do they have in all?

The array shows 3 × 13. Break the grid into parts.

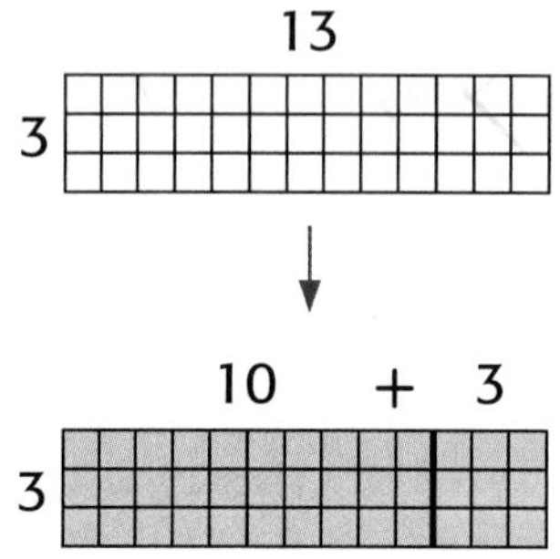

The orange shaded part shows 3 × 10.

The blue shaded part shows 3 × 3.

Find the product of each part, or the **partial products**. Then add the partial products.

$3 \times 10 = 30$
$3 \times 3 = 9$

$30 + 9 = 39$

So, $3 \times 13 = 39$

So, Ken and his brothers have 39 marbles in all.

Online Personal Tutor at ca.gr3math.com

You can also use an area model to find a product. Area models do not have grid lines but you can still break the rectangle into parts to find the product.

Real-World EXAMPLE Use a Model

2 **BOOKS A library has 2 shelves. Each shelf holds 23 books. How many books will fit on the 2 shelves?**

Find the product of 2 and 23.

Estimate $2 \times 23 \longrightarrow 2 \times 20 = 40$

Think of 23 as 20 + 3.

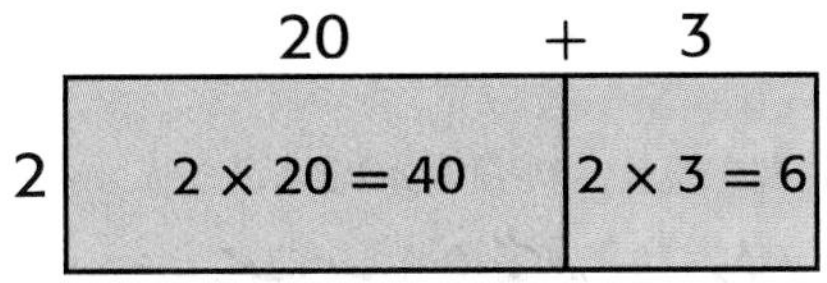

$$\begin{array}{r} 23 \\ \times\ 2 \\ \hline 6 \\ +40 \\ \hline 46 \end{array}$$

So, 46 books will fit on the shelves.

You can also multiply by a one-digit number without models.

Remember
You can also use base-ten models to help you multiply by one-digit numbers.

EXAMPLE Use Paper and Pencil

3 **Find 3 × 32.**

Multiply the ones. Then multiply the tens.

Step 1 Multiply ones.

$$\begin{array}{r} 32 \\ \times\ 3 \\ \hline 6 \end{array} \longleftarrow \boxed{3 \times 2 \text{ ones} = 6 \text{ ones}}$$

Step 2 Multiply tens.

$$\begin{array}{r} 32 \\ \times\ 3 \\ \hline 96 \end{array} \longleftarrow \boxed{3 \times 3 \text{ tens} = 9 \text{ tens}}$$

Check

The model shows that 3 × 32 = 96. ✓

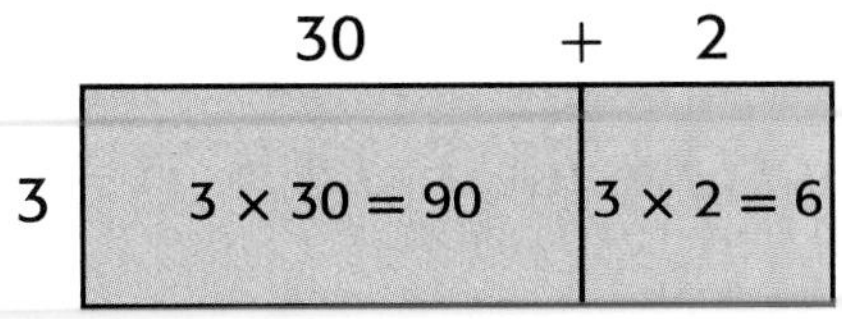

$$\begin{array}{r} 32 \\ \times\ 3 \\ \hline 6 \\ +90 \\ \hline 96 \end{array}$$

3 × 2 = 6
3 × 30 90

CHECK What You Know

Multiply. Use estimation to check. See Examples 1 and 2 (pp. 594–595)

1. 4×22

2. 3×21

3. 5×11

4. 12×4

5. 41×2

6. 32×3

7. A classroom has 23 desks. Each desk has 3 books on it. How many books are on the desks?

8. Talk About It Explain how area models help you multiply.

Practice and Problem Solving

EXTRA PRACTICE See page R37.

Multiply. Use estimation to check. See Examples 1 and 2 (pp. 594–595)

9. 21×4

10. 32×2

11. 44×2

12. 13×3

13. 12×4

14. 20×3

15. 43×2

16. 33×3

17. 2×23

18. 2×33

19. 2×22

20. 2×14

21. There are 21 bags of bagels with 4 bagels in each. If the scouts ate all but 9, how many did they eat?

22. Measurement Fran cut 4 pieces of yarn that measured 15 inches each. How many feet of yarn did she use?

Real-World PROBLEM SOLVING

School The table shows the number of classes and students in grades 3, 4, and 5.

Fair Street School Student Count

Grade	Number of Classes	Students per Class
3	3	23
4	4	22
5	2	31

23. Write an expression for the total number of students in the fourth grade.

24. How many more students are in grade 4 than grade 3?

25. Write an expression that compares the total number of students in the 3rd grade and 5th grade. Use < or >.

26. How many students are in all of the grades?

H.O.T. Problems

27. OPEN ENDED Write a number that when multiplied by 3 is one less than 100.

28. WRITING IN ►MATH Is the product of 3 and 32 the same as the product of 32 and 3? Explain your reasoning.

Standards Practice

29 Kome made a large mat out of carpet squares by putting the squares in 3 equal rows of 21 squares each. How many squares did Kome use? **(Lesson 14-4)**

A 42　　**C** 63

B 62　　**D** 84

30 Which product would be a reasonable estimate for this number sentence? **(Lesson 14-3)**

$82 \times 9 = ■$

F 70

G 700

H 720

J 810

Spiral Review

Estimate. Round to the nearest hundred. (Lesson 14-3)

31. 125×8

32. 233×4

33. 158×3

34. A number has two digits. The first digit is odd. The difference of the digits is 2 and their sum is 12. What is the number? **(Lesson 14-2)**

Multiply. Use basic facts and patterns. (Lesson 14-1)

35. $5 \times 300 = ■$

36. $8 \times 9{,}000 = ■$

37. $400 \times 60 = ■$

Write the part of a dollar represented. (Lesson 13-4)

38.

39.

40.

41. Mr. Harris bought a tie for $12 and a pair of shoes for $26. He paid with a $50 bill. What is his change? **(Lesson 3-2)**

14-5 Problem-Solving Investigation

MAIN IDEA I will choose the best strategy to solve a problem.

Standard 3MR1.1 **Analyze problems by identifying relationships, distinguishing relevant from irrelevant information, sequencing** and prioritizing information, and observing patterns. Standard 3NS2.4 **Solve simple problems involving multiplication of multi digit numbers by one-digit numbers** (3,671 × 3 = __).

P.S.I. TEAM +

RYDELL: I need to fill 3 pitchers and 2 punch bowls with punch. It takes 11 cans of punch to fill one pitcher and 24 cans of punch to fill the punch bowl.

YOUR MISSION: Find how many cans of punch are needed in all.

Understand	It takes 11 cans to fill one pitcher. It takes 24 cans of punch to fill one punch bowl. Find how many cans of punch are needed in all.
Plan	Solve a simpler problem. Solve for each part of the problem then add.
Solve	1 pitcher = 11 cans of punch. So, it takes 11 × 3 or 33 cans to fill 3 pitchers. 1 punch bowl = 24 cans. So, it takes 24 × 2 or 48 cans to fill 2 bowls. Now find the total. 33 + 48 = 81 So, 81 cans of punch are needed in all.
Check	Look back at the problem. Use addition to check. bowl + bowl + pitcher + pitcher + pitcher 24 + 24 + 11 + 11 + 11 = 81 So, the answer is correct.

Mixed Problem Solving

EXTRA PRACTICE
See page R37.

Use any strategy shown below to solve. Tell what strategy you used.

PROBLEM-SOLVING STRATEGIES
- Work a simpler problem.
- Make an organized list.
- Draw a picture.
- Act it out.
- Use logical reasoning.

1. Theo and Freda collected tin cans for recycling. Theo collected 3 times as many as Freda. The total number collected by their class was 500 cans. Theo and Freda collected $\frac{1}{5}$ of that. How many cans did they each collect?

2. **Measurement** A log is shown. Suppose a piece that measures 11 inches is cut off. How many 5-inch pieces can be made from the part of the log that is left?

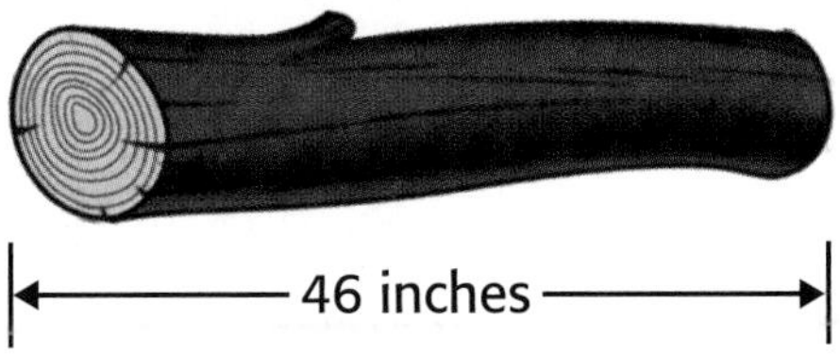

3. **Measurement** Constance places 6 books on one side of a scale. To balance the scale, Eli places 2 books and his baseball glove on the other side. If each book weighs 3 ounces, how much does Eli's baseball glove weigh?

4. Sofia, Paulita, and Adrian are playing a game. Sofia has 88 points. Paulita has 26 points more than Sofia. Adrian wins with 50 points more than Paulita. How many points does each person have?

5. Benato and Juanna are playing a game with one 0–5 number cube and one 5–10 number cube. Each cube is rolled twice. The total of their rolls is 25. What could be the other three numbers rolled if one was a 5?

6. Logan, Rodolfo, Engracia, and Mazo were waiting for the bus. Logan was next to Engracia, who was not next to Mazo. Mazo was next to Rodolfo, but not next to Logan. In what order were they standing?

7. Martino wants to exchange 75 pennies for coins of greater value. If he gets 8 coins in exchange, what could be the coins he receives?

8. **WRITING IN MATH** Alexa ran the distances shown. She ran 2 miles more than the total of these on Sunday. Explain how to find how many miles she ran for the four days.

Day	Distance Ran
Monday	4 miles
Thursday	6 miles
Saturday	8 miles

Explore

Math Activity for 14-6

Multiplication with Regrouping

MAIN IDEA

I will use models to explore multiplication with regrouping.

Standard 3NS2.4 Solve simple problems involving multiplication of multidigit numbers by one-digit numbers (3,671 × 3 = ___).
Standard 3MR2.2 Apply strategies and results from simpler problems to more complex problems.

You Will Need
base-ten blocks

Concepts in Motion
Animation
ca.gr3math.com

You sometimes need to regroup when adding. Regrouping is also sometimes used when multiplying.

ACTIVITY **Multiply 2 × 16.**

Step 1 **Model 2 × 16.**
Model 2 groups of 16.
Use 1 ten and 6 ones in each group.

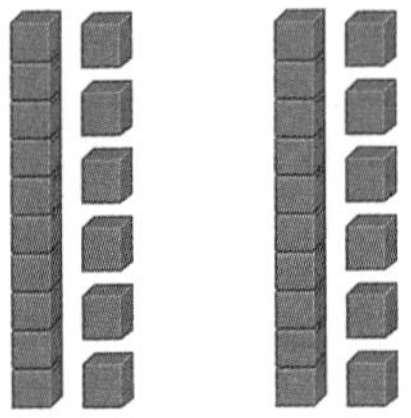

2 groups of 16

$$\begin{array}{r} 16 \\ \times\ 2 \\ \hline \end{array}$$

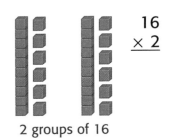

Step 2 **Combine the models.**
Combine the ones.
Combine the tens.

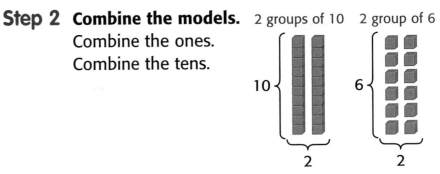

2 groups of 10   2 group of 6

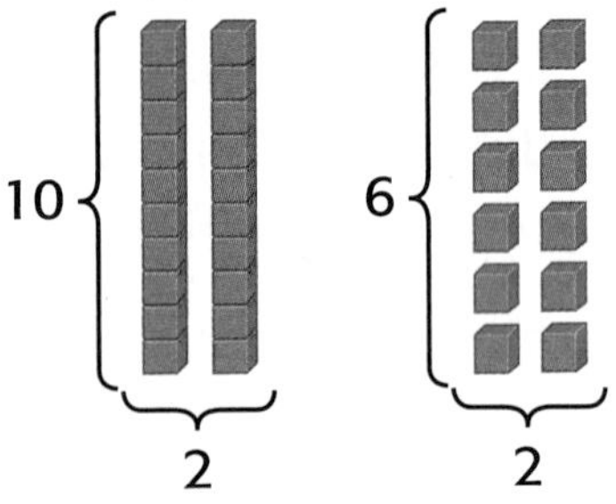

Step 3 **Regroup.**
Regroup 12 ones as 1 ten and 2 ones.

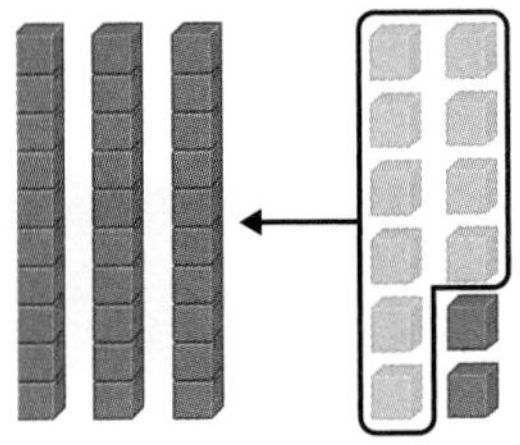

12 ones = 1 ten, 2 ones

Step 4 **Add the partial products.**

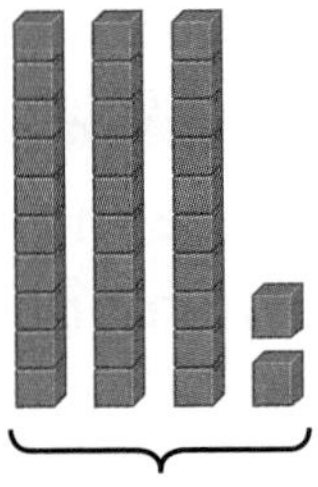

30 + 2

$$\begin{array}{r} 30 \\ +\ 2 \\ \hline 32 \end{array}$$

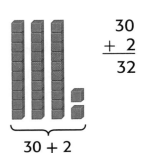

So, 2 × 16 = 32.

Think About It

Hands-On Activity

1. How did you model each factor?

2. Why did you regroup?

3. How did the number of tens and ones change after you regrouped?

4. Will you always have to regroup in multiplication? Explain.

5. If you have 4 groups of 16, what would be the product?

CHECK What You Know

Write a multiplication expression for each model. Then multiply.

6. 

7. 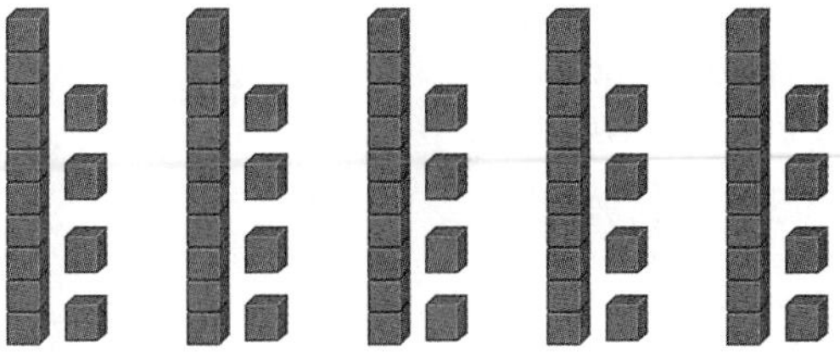

8. 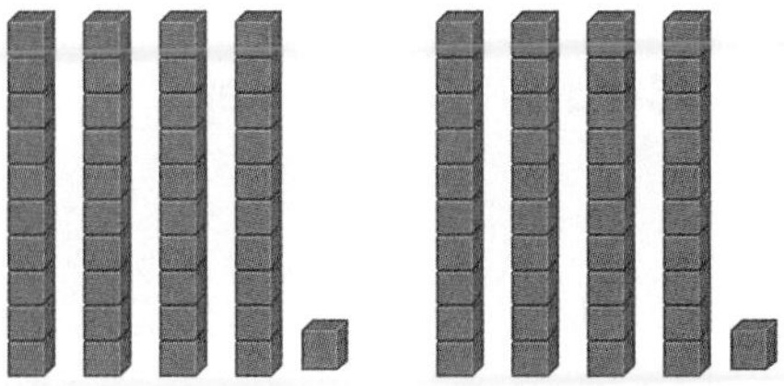

9. 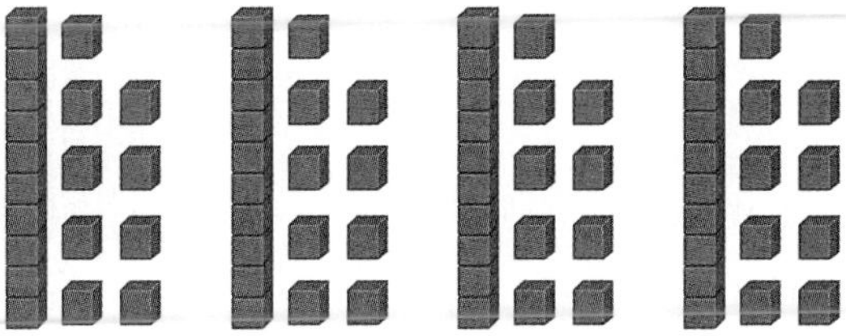

Multiply. Use base-ten models.

10. 5 × 18 **11.** 12 × 6 **12.** 4 × 24 **13.** 17 × 3

14. WRITING IN MATH Explain why knowing how to estimate is useful when multiplying larger numbers.

14-6 Multiply Two-Digit Numbers

GET READY to Learn

A new apartment building will have 5 floors with 13 apartments on each floor. How many new apartments will there be to rent once the building is built?

MAIN IDEA

I will multiply a two-digit number by a one-digit number with regrouping.

Standard 3NS2.4 Solve simple problems involving multiplication of multidigit numbers by one-digit numbers (3,671 × 3 = ___). **Standard 3MR2.1 Use estimation to verify the reasonableness of calculated results.**

You can connect multiplication models to paper and pencil.

Real-World EXAMPLE **Multiply with Regrouping**

1 **BUILDINGS How many new apartments will there be to rent once the building is built?**

Use models to help you find the product of 5 × 13.

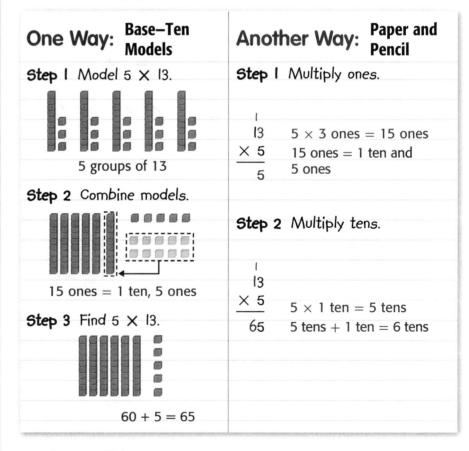

One Way: Base–Ten Models

Step 1 Model 5 × 13.

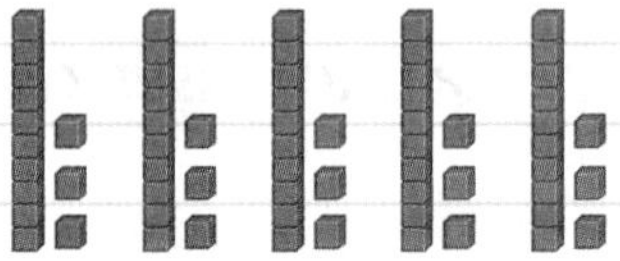

5 groups of 13

Step 2 Combine models.

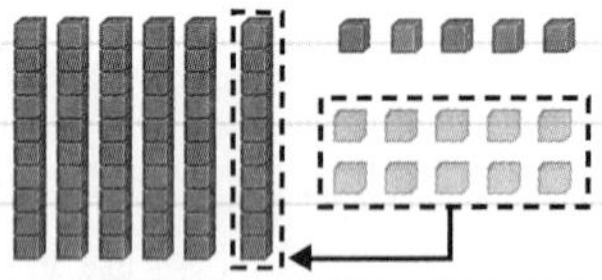

15 ones = 1 ten, 5 ones

Step 3 Find 5 × 13.

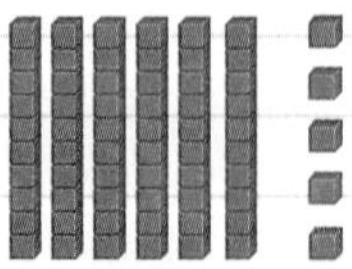

60 + 5 = 65

Another Way: Paper and Pencil

Step 1 Multiply ones.

$$\begin{array}{r} {}^{1}\\ 13 \\ \times\ 5 \\ \hline 5 \end{array}$$

5 × 3 ones = 15 ones
15 ones = 1 ten and 5 ones

Step 2 Multiply tens.

$$\begin{array}{r} {}^{1}\\ 13 \\ \times\ 5 \\ \hline 65 \end{array}$$

5 × 1 ten = 5 tens
5 tens + 1 ten = 6 tens

So, there will be 65 new apartments to rent.

Real-World EXAMPLE

2 REPTILES A female desert tortoise can lay as many as 8 eggs at one time. How many eggs could 12 female desert tortoises lay?

Find 8×12. **Estimate** $8 \times 12 \longrightarrow 8 \times 10 = 80$

Step 1 Multiply ones.

$$\begin{array}{r} {}^{1}\\ 12 \\ \times\ 8 \\ \hline 6 \end{array} \quad 8 \times 2 \text{ ones} = 16 \text{ ones}$$

Step 2 Multiply tens.

$$\begin{array}{r} {}^{1}\\ 12 \\ \times\ 8 \\ \hline 96 \end{array} \quad \begin{array}{l} 8 \times 1 \text{ ten} = 8 \text{ tens} \\ 8 \text{ tens} + 1 \text{ ten} = 9 \text{ tens} \end{array}$$

Remember

Do not multiply the regrouped tens again, add them once the tens are multiplied.

The area model shows that 8×12 is 96.

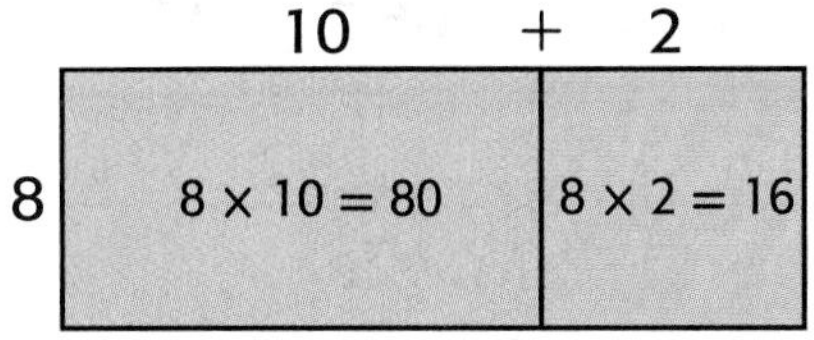

$$\begin{array}{r} 12 \\ \times\ 8 \\ \hline 16 \\ +80 \\ \hline 96 \end{array}$$

Multiply ones.
Multiply tens.
Add partial products.

So, 12 female tortoises could lay 96 eggs.

Check for Reasonableness

80 is close to 96, so the answer is reasonable. ✓

Online Personal Tutor at ca.gr3math.com

CHECK What You Know

Multiply. Use models if needed. **See Examples 1 and 2 (pp. 602–603)**

1. $\begin{array}{r} 13 \\ \times 4 \\ \hline \end{array}$

2. $\begin{array}{r} 27 \\ \times 3 \\ \hline \end{array}$

3. $\begin{array}{r} 13 \\ \times 8 \\ \hline \end{array}$

4. A construction crew finished 14 miles of highway in 1 week. At this rate, how many miles could they finish in 4 weeks?

5. Talk About It What is the greatest number of ones that could be in the ones column without having to regroup? Explain.

Practice and Problem Solving

EXTRA PRACTICE
See page R37.

Multiply. Use models if needed. **See Examples 1 and 2 (pp. 602–603)**

6. 46×2

7. 17×4

8. 53×2

9. 92×3

10. 13×6

11. 18×9

12. 15×4

13. 12×5

14. 18×8

15. 14×9

16. 28×4

17. 31×8

18. Measurement A stick insect can measure 22 inches in length. How many inches long would 3 stick insects measure?

19. Measurement A gecko can grow close to 35 centimeters in length. How many centimeters would 4 geckos measure?

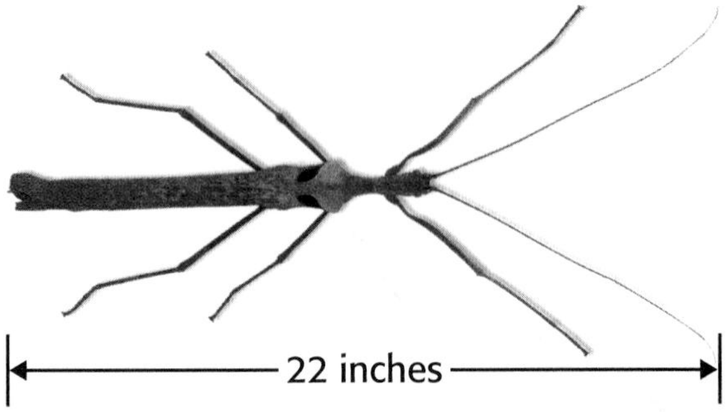

20. It is suggested to eat 5 servings of grains each day. How many servings is this in a 31-day month?

21. The American flag has 13 stripes. How many stripes would there be on 8 American flags?

Real-World PROBLEM SOLVING

Data File Both California and the 49ers experienced great changes during the Gold Rush.

22. How far could a 49er travel in a 30-day month if he traveled 12 hours a day?

23. How many hours did a 49er spend looking for gold in 2 weeks?

24. How many new houses were built in 1 week?

Gold Rush

California Gold Rush Facts
• The 49ers traveled for 6 months in their wagons at a speed of about 2 miles per hour to reach California.
• A miner would spend up to 10 hours a day digging and panning for gold.
• As a result of the Gold Rush, San Francisco grew from a few hundred people to so many people that they needed to build 30 houses a day.

Source: www.pbs.org

H.O.T. Problems

25. **OPEN ENDED** Write a multiplication sentence whose product is less than 52.

26. **NUMBER SENSE** Without multiplying, how do you know that 21 × 3 is greater than 60?

27. **WHICH ONE DOESN'T BELONG?** Identify the multiplication expression that does not belong. Explain.

3 × 33	4 × 23	5 × 15	7 × 18

28. **WRITING IN ▸MATH** Describe the steps you would take for multiplying 76 × 4.

Standards Practice

29 On Thursday, 132 people visited the library. Three times as many people visited over the weekend. How many people visited over the weekend? **(Lesson 14-4)**

A 264 **C** 375

B 300 **D** 396

30 Lee's Pizza Shop puts 75 pepperoni slices on every pizza. If someone buys 6 pizzas, how many pepperoni slices would there be altogether? **(Lesson 14-6)**

F 150 **H** 420

G 300 **J** 450

Spiral Review

31. Milo's grandmother is making 3 baby quilts. Each quilt's squares will be sewn in an array of 8 rows with 4 squares in each row. How many squares will she need to cut out? **(Lesson 14-5)**

Estimate. Round to the nearest hundred. (Lesson 14-4)

32. $\begin{array}{r} 225 \\ \times\ 5 \\ \hline \end{array}$

33. $\begin{array}{r} 168 \\ \times\ 8 \\ \hline \end{array}$

34. $\begin{array}{r} 177 \\ \times\ 9 \\ \hline \end{array}$

Geometry Identify each triangle. Write *equilateral, isosceles,* or *scalene.* (Lesson 10-5)

35. 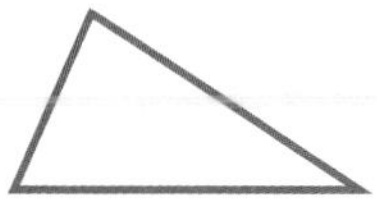

36. 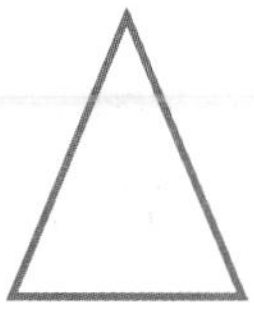

37. 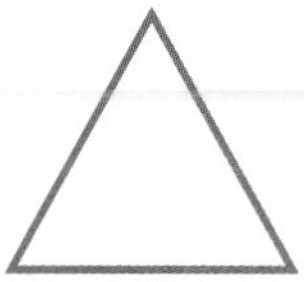

14-7 Multiply Greater Numbers

GET READY to Learn

Griffen is reading a book about pencil making. He learns about a machine that makes 132 pencils a minute. How many pencils are made in 5 minutes?

MAIN IDEA

I will multiply three and four-digit numbers by a one-digit number with regrouping.

Standard 3NS2.4 Solve simple problems involving multiplication of multidigit numbers by one-digit numbers (3,671 × 3 = ___).
Standard 3MR2.1 Use estimation to verify the reasonableness of calculated results.

You have learned how to multiply two-digit numbers. Use what you know to multiply larger numbers.

Real-World EXAMPLE

1 PENCILS How many pencils are made in 5 minutes?

Find 5 × 132. **Estimate** 5 × 132 ⟶ 5 × 100 = 500

Step 1 Multiply ones.

$$\begin{array}{r} {\scriptstyle 1} \\ 132 \\ \times\ 5 \\ \hline 0 \end{array}$$

5 × 2 ones = 10 ones

Step 2 Multiply tens.

$$\begin{array}{r} {\scriptstyle 11} \\ 132 \\ \times\ 5 \\ \hline 60 \end{array}$$

5 × 3 tens = 15 tens
Add the regrouped amount. 15 + 1 = 16 tens

Step 3 Multiply hundreds.

$$\begin{array}{r} {\scriptstyle 11} \\ 132 \\ \times\ 5 \\ \hline 660 \end{array}$$

5 × 1 hundred = 5 hundreds
Add the regrouped amount. 5 + 1 = 6 hundreds

So, 660 pencils are made in 5 minutes.

Check for Reasonableness

Since 660 is close to 500, the answer is reasonable. ✓

Real-World EXAMPLE

2 **DUCKS A duck eats about 1,960 grams of food in 1 week. How much would it eat in 4 weeks.**

Find 1,960 × 4.

Step 1 Multiply ones.

$$\begin{array}{r} 1{,}960 \\ \times \quad 4 \\ \hline 0 \end{array}$$

4 × 0 one = 0 ones

Step 2 Multiply tens.

$$\begin{array}{r} {\scriptstyle 2} \quad \\ 1{,}960 \\ \times \quad 4 \\ \hline 40 \end{array}$$

4 × 6 tens = 24 tens

Step 3 Multiply hundreds.

$$\begin{array}{r} {\scriptstyle 3\ 2} \quad \\ 1{,}960 \\ \times \quad 4 \\ \hline 840 \end{array}$$

4 × 9 hundreds = 36 hundreds
Add the regrouped amount.
36 hundreds + 2 hundreds = 38 hundreds

Step 4 Multiply thousands.

$$\begin{array}{r} {\scriptstyle 3\ 2} \quad \\ 1{,}960 \\ \times \quad 4 \\ \hline 7{,}840 \end{array}$$

4 × 1 thousand = 4 thousands
Add the regrouped amount.
4 thousands + 3 thousands = 7 thousands

So, 1,960 × 4 = 7,840.

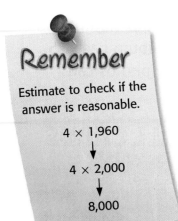

> **Remember**
> Estimate to check if the answer is reasonable.
> 4 × 1,960
> ↓
> 4 × 2,000
> ↓
> 8,000

Online **Personal Tutor at** ca.gr3math.com

CHECK What You Know

Multiply. See Examples 1 and 2 (pp. 606–607)

1. $\begin{array}{r} 125 \\ \times 5 \\ \hline \end{array}$

2. $\begin{array}{r} 248 \\ \times 3 \\ \hline \end{array}$

3. $\begin{array}{r} 1{,}276 \\ \times \quad 4 \\ \hline \end{array}$

4. $\begin{array}{r} 1{,}342 \\ \times \quad 7 \\ \hline \end{array}$

5. If there are 365 days in one year, how many days are in 3 years?

6. **Talk About It** How is multiplying a three-digit number with regrouping similar to multiplying a two-digit number with regrouping?

EXTRA PRACTICE See page R38.

Multiply. See Examples 1 and 2 (pp. 606–607)

7. 518×2

8. 222×5

9. 159×3

10. 293×7

11. $1,042 \times 8$

12. $1,513 \times 9$

13. $2,278 \times 3$

14. $3,150 \times 6$

15. 170 × 4

16. 821 × 4

17. 1,122 × 9

18. 1,189 × 5

Algebra Copy and complete each table.

19.

Rule: Multiply by 6.	
Input	**Output**
112	■
821	■
145	■

20.

Rule: Multiply by 4.	
Input	**Output**
38	■
29	■
417	■

21.

Rule: Multiply by ■.	
Input	**Output**
60	120
17	■
75	■

22. Measurement A jet is 232 feet long. What is the length if 7 jets were lined up nose to tail?

23. Each page of a photo album holds 6 pictures. If the album has 125 pages, how many photos can it hold?

Use the table and the following information.

Tanner and Talli bought boxes of baseball cards. Tanner bought 3 boxes and Talli bought 5 boxes.

BASEBALL CARDS

large box	small box
1,324	520

24. What is the greatest number of cards Talli could have bought?

25. What is the least number of cards Talli could have bought?

26. Is it possible for Tanner to have bought more cards than Talli? Explain.

H.O.T. Problems

27. OPEN ENDED Write a multiplication problem in which you multiply a four-digit number by 5 and regroup two times.

28. WRITING IN MATH Is the product of a two-digit number and a one-digit number always a three-digit number? Explain.

 Math Online Self-Check Quiz at ca.gr3math.com

Game Time

High and Low

Find a Product

Get Ready!

Players: 2 or more

You will need:
number cube, game sheet

Get Set!

Label a number cube 1–6.
Make 2 game sheets.

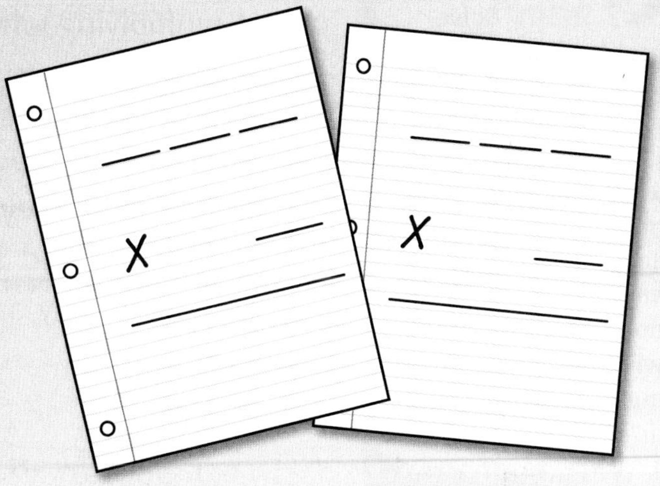

Go!

- Decide if the product goal for the game is HIGH or LOW.
- Player 1 rolls the number cube, and records the number in any of the factor spaces on the game sheet.
- Player 2 rolls the number cube and records the number in any of the factor spaces on their game sheet.
- Play continues until all players have filled in the factor spaces.
- Each player then find the products of his or her factors.
- The winner is the player with the greatest or least product, depending on the goal.

14-8 Multiply Money

MAIN IDEA

I will learn to multiply money.

Standard 3NS3.3 Solve problems involving addition, subtraction, **multiplication,** and division **of money amounts in decimal notation and multiply** and divide **money amounts in decimal notation by using whole-number multipliers** and divisors.

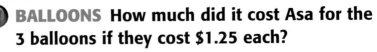

GET READY to Learn

The school carnival is selling balloons for $1.25 each. Asa bought 3 balloons for his friends. How much did Asa spend on the balloons?

To multiply dollars and cents, use what you already know about multiplying whole numbers.

Real-World EXAMPLE Multiply Money

1 **BALLOONS How much did it cost Asa for the 3 balloons if they cost $1.25 each?**

You need to find $1.25 × 3.

Step 1 Multiply ones.

$$\begin{array}{r} {}^{1} \\ \$1.25 \\ \times \quad 3 \\ \hline 5 \end{array} \qquad 3 \times 5 \text{ ones} = 15 \text{ ones.}$$

Step 2 Multiply tens.

$$\begin{array}{r} {}^{1} \\ \$1.25 \\ \times \quad 3 \\ \hline 75 \end{array} \qquad \begin{array}{l} 3 \times 2 \text{ tens} = 6 \text{ tens.} \\ \text{Add the regrouped ten. } 6 + 1 = 7 \end{array}$$

Step 3 Multiply hundreds.

$$\begin{array}{r} {}^{1} \\ \$1.25 \\ \times \quad 3 \\ \hline 3\ 75 \end{array} \qquad 3 \times 1 \text{ hundred} = 3 \text{ hundreds.}$$

Step 4 Write the dollar sign and decimal point.

$$\begin{array}{r} \$1.25 \\ \times \quad 3 \\ \hline \$3.75 \end{array} \qquad \text{Place the decimal point and dollar sign.}$$

So, Asa spent $3.75 on balloons.

Real-World EXAMPLE Zeros in Products

2 **TICKETS Tickets for rides and games at the carnival cost $0.75 each. Shantell buys 8 tickets. How much money did Shantell spend on tickets?**

You need to find 8 × $0.75.

Estimate 8 × $0.75 ⟶ 8 × $1.00 = $8.00

Step 1 Multiply ones.

$$\begin{array}{r} {\scriptstyle 4} \\ \$0.75 \\ \times\quad 8 \\ \hline 0 \end{array}$$

8 × 5 ones = 40 ones.

Step 2 Multiply tens.

$$\begin{array}{r} {\scriptstyle 4} \\ \$0.75 \\ \times\quad 8 \\ \hline 600 \end{array}$$

8 × 7 tens = 56 tens.
Add the 4 regrouped tens. 56 + 4 = 60 tens

Step 3 Write the dollar sign and decimal point.

$$\begin{array}{r} \$0.75 \\ \times\quad 8 \\ \hline \$6.00 \end{array}$$

Place the decimal point and dollar sign.

So, Shantell spent $6.00 on tickets.

Check for Reasonableness

$6.00 is close to $8.00, so the answer is reasonable. ✓

Remember
In money, there are 2 places to the right of the decimal point. Sometimes they are zeros.

Online Personal Tutor at ca.gr3math.com

CHECK What You Know

Multiply. See Examples 1 and 2 (pp. 610–611)

1. $$\begin{array}{r} \$4.10 \\ \times\quad 8 \\ \hline \end{array}$$

2. $$\begin{array}{r} \$2.15 \\ \times\quad 4 \\ \hline \end{array}$$

3. $$\begin{array}{r} \$0.23 \\ \times\quad 9 \\ \hline \end{array}$$

4. $2.13 × 9

5. $0.42 × 8

6. $14.62 × 3

7. Clowns are selling glow-in-the-dark light sticks for $4.95 each. How much would 6 light sticks cost?

8. **Talk About It** When you multiply money, how do you know where to place the decimal point?

Practice and Problem Solving

EXTRA PRACTICE See page R38.

Multiply. See Examples 1 and 2 (pp. 610–611)

9. $\begin{array}{r} \$2.25 \\ \times \quad 6 \\ \hline \end{array}$

10. $\begin{array}{r} \$1.45 \\ \times \quad 3 \\ \hline \end{array}$

11. $\begin{array}{r} \$4.21 \\ \times \quad 7 \\ \hline \end{array}$

12. $\begin{array}{r} \$0.68 \\ \times \quad 4 \\ \hline \end{array}$

13. $\begin{array}{r} \$0.94 \\ \times \quad 8 \\ \hline \end{array}$

14. $\begin{array}{r} \$0.86 \\ \times \quad 7 \\ \hline \end{array}$

15. 4 × \$6.14

16. 6 × \$9.55

17. 9 × \$0.62

18. Stella can buy 6 greeting cards for \$1.15 each. Or, she can buy 5 cards for \$1.25 each. Which cards have a better price? Explain.

19. Mr. Dimas pays \$51.25 each month for his phone bill. He has \$976 in the bank. How much money will he have left after he pays 3 phone bills?

For Exercises 20–23, use the menu.

20. What is the cost of 5 burgers?

21. What is the cost of 5 drinks and 2 desserts?

22. What is the total cost for 5 dinners, 5 beverages, and 5 desserts?

23. What is the cost of 3 salads and 6 brownies?

Carnival Cafe

Dinner	burger salad sandwich	\$2.75 each
Beverages	lemonade milk water	\$1.25 each
Dessert	ice cream brownie	\$1.50 each

Real-World PROBLEM SOLVING

Money The Denver Mint is one of four places in the U.S. where money is made.

24. How many coins can be produced in 5 minutes?

25. How much money does the mint produce in 1 week?

26. How much money are the nickels in the mosaic worth?

Denver Mint Fun Facts
• Machines can produce 850 coins per minute.
• Every 24 hours, \$112 million worth of coins are produced.
• Part of an eagle mosaic in the floor is made with 88 nickels.

Source: The Denver Mint

H.O.T. Problems

27. NUMBER SENSE When multiplying money in decimal notation, why is it important to keep zeros in the products even if there are no cents?

28. WHICH ONE DOESN'T BELONG? Identify the incorrect solution. Explain your reasoning.

1 4	1	3 4	2
$5.27	$1.33	$1.68	$5.05
× 6	× 6	× 5	× 5
$31.62	$698	$8.40	$25.25

29. WRITING IN ▸MATH Write a real-world problem about a situation that uses multiplication of money with regrouping.

Standards Practice

30 What number can be multiplied by 4,573 to give the answer 9,146? **(Lesson 14-7)**

$$4,573 \times \blacksquare = 9,146$$

A 1

B 2

C 3

D 5

31 Mrs. Beal bought 5 books. Each book cost $5.25. What was the total cost? **(Lesson 14-8)**

F $15.50

G $25.25

H $26.25

J $75.20

Spiral Review

Multiply. **(Lessons 14-6 and 14-7)**

32. 125 × 4

33. 158 × 5

34. 2,513 × 3

35. 26 × 3

36. 91 × 5

37. 106 × 2

38. Shilo bought 4 balls of yarn for $2.55 and 2 balls of yarn for $3.75. How much did she receive in change if she paid with a $20 bill? **(Lesson 13-6)**

Problem Solving in Art

STAMP COLLECTING

The U.S. government began issuing stamps in 1847. People began saving and collecting them. During the Civil War, unused Union stamps were actually used as money. At first, small engraving and printing companies produced stamps for the government. Many of the same images—American leaders and symbols—appeared on stamps.

In 1924, a new era of stamp making began in response to collectors' great interest in stamps. Stamp makers began producing colorful, exotic stamps with a wide variety of subjects and many different colors of ink. Today, you can see everything from comic-book characters to your favorite musicians on stamps.

Real-World Math

Use the stamps on page 615 to answer each question.

1. What was the original cost of seven Elvis stamps? Write the answer in dollars.
2. About how much did nine 24¢ stamps cost in dollars?
3. Find the original cost of 52 Air Mail stamps.
4. If 24 Lincoln stamps were on a page, what is the total value of the page of stamps?
5. If 78 stamp collectors each have one of each of the five stamps, how many stamps are there altogether?
6. Suppose the First Man on the Moon stamp was issued in rolls of 500 stamps each and 3,000 stamps each. What was the value of each roll of stamps?
7. Suppose Elvis stamps were issued in booklets of 18 stamps each. What was the value of a booklet of Elvis stamps?

Standard 3NS2.4 **Solve simple problems involving multiplication of miltidigit numbers by one-digit numbers (3,671 x 3 = _____).**

Did You Know?

The most valuable U.S. stamp was sold for $930,000.

14 Study Guide and Review

FOLDABLES Study Organizer GET READY to Study

Be sure the following Key Vocabulary words and Key Concepts are written in your Foldable.

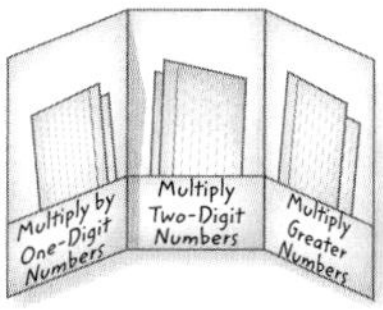

BIG Ideas

Multiply by Multiples of 10, 100, and 1,000 (p. 585)

Use basic facts and patterns.

$3 \times 8 = 24$	3×8 ones
$3 \times 80 = 240$	3×8 tens
$3 \times 800 = 2{,}400$	3×8 hundreds
$3 \times 8{,}000 = 24{,}000$	3×8 thousands

Estimate

- You can **estimate** a product by rounding. (p. 590)

3×115 — 115 rounds to 100.

↓

$3 \times 100 = 300$

Multiply by One-Digit Numbers (p. 594)

$$\begin{array}{r} {}^{1}\\ 36 \\ \times\ 2 \\ \hline 72 \end{array} \qquad \begin{array}{r} {}^{2\,1}\\ 173 \\ \times\ \ 4 \\ \hline 692 \end{array}$$

Key Vocabulary

estimate (p. 590)
factors (p. 585)
multiples (p. 586)
product (p. 585)
round (p. 590)

Vocabulary Check

Choose the vocabulary word that completes each sentence.

1. A(n) ___?___ is the product of a given number and any other whole number.
2. ___?___ are numbers that are multiplied together to get a product.
3. When you find an answer that is close to the exact answer you ___?___.
4. One way to estimate is to ___?___.
5. 36, 45, 54, and 63 are ___?___ of 9.
6. In 70×6, the number 420 is the ___?___.

Math Online Vocabulary Review at ca.gr3math.com

Lesson-by-Lesson Review

14-1 Multiply Multiples of 10, 100, and 1000 (pp. 585–587)

Example 1
Each student needs 200 felt squares. There are 4 students. What is the total number of felt squares needed?

You need to find 4×200. Use a basic fact and patterns of zeroes.

$4 \times 2 = 8$
$4 \times 20 = 80$ 4×2 tens
$4 \times 200 = 800$ 4×2 hundreds

So, $4 \times 200 = 800$ felt squares.

Multiply. Use basic facts and patterns.

7. $3 \times 1 = \blacksquare$
$3 \times 10 = \blacksquare$
$3 \times 100 = \blacksquare$
$3 \times 1{,}000 = \blacksquare$

8. $7 \times 4 = \blacksquare$
$7 \times 40 = \blacksquare$
$7 \times 400 = \blacksquare$
$7 \times 4{,}000 = \blacksquare$

9. 8×50

10. 5×70

11. There are 120 crayons in each box. The teacher dumped all 7 boxes into an art tub. How many crayons are in the tub?

14-2 Problem-Solving Strategy: Use Logical Reasoning (pp. 588–589)

Example 2
Heather has 3 people in her family. Angela does not have 4 or 7 people. Joyce does not have 5 or 7 people. How many people are in each family?
Use a table and logical reasoning.

Girl	3	4	5	7
Heather	yes	✗	✗	✗
Angela	✗	✗	yes	✗
Joyce	✗	yes	✗	✗
Joanna	✗	✗	✗	yes

So, Heather has 3 family members, Angela has 5, Joyce has 4, and Joanna has 7.

Solve. Use logical reasoning.

12. The girls' softball team wants to buy new uniforms for $495. There are 20 girls. How much does each uniform cost?

13. Suppose you meet 5 friends and all of you shook hands with each other when you met. How many handshakes would there be?

14. Jodi planted sunflower seeds in 10 rows. If there were 25 seeds in each row, how many seeds were planted?

Study Guide and Review

14-3 Estimate Products (pp. 590–592)

Example 3
Bena's mom spent 4 days baking for the craft fair. If she made 120 baked goods each day, about how many things did she bake in 4 days?

Estimate 4 × 120 by rounding to the nearest hundred.

4 × 120

120 rounds to 100.

4 × 100 = 400   Multiply mentally.

Estimate. Round to the nearest ten.

15. 37 × 4   **16.** 27 × 6

17. 38 × 8   **18.** 42 × 5

Multiply.

19. 190 × 9   **20.** 187 × 6

21. 371 × 4   **22.** 490 × 7

23. There are 4 different types of cereal stacked in rows of 21 boxes each. About how many boxes of cereal are there altogether?

14-4 Multiply by a One-Digit Number (pp. 594–597)

Example 4
If 2 men caught 24 fish each, how many fish is that altogether?

Find 2 × 24.

Step 1 Multiply ones.

$$\begin{array}{r} 24 \\ \times\ 2 \\ \hline 48 \end{array}$$ 2 × 4 ones = 8 ones

Step 2 Multiply tens.

$$\begin{array}{r} 24 \\ \times\ 2 \\ \hline 48 \end{array}$$ 2 × 2 tens = 4 tens

So, 48 fish were caught.

Multiply. Use estimation to check.

24. $\begin{array}{r} 41 \\ \times\ 2 \\ \hline \end{array}$ **25.** $\begin{array}{r} 22 \\ \times\ 2 \\ \hline \end{array}$

26. 2 × 34   **27.** 6 × 11

28. Measurement Two triangles have a perimeter of 44 centimeters each. What is the total perimeter of the two triangles?

29. When the new office building opens, there will be 32 new desks for each of the 3 floors. How many new desks will need to be ordered?

14-5 Problem-Solving Investigation: Choose the Best Strategy (pp. 598–599)

Example 5

Lorena earned $70 each week for 7 weeks. She spent $125 and saved the rest. How much money was she able to save?

First, find $70 × 7.

$$\begin{array}{r} \$70 \\ \times\ \ 7 \\ \hline \$490 \end{array}$$ Lorena earned $490.

Then subtract.

$$\begin{array}{r} {}^{8\,10} \\ \$490 \\ -\$125 \\ \hline \$365 \end{array}$$

$490 earned
$125 spent
$365 saved

So, Lorena saved $365.

30. **Measurement** Each day you run 15 miles. In two weeks, how many miles will you have run?

31. A book has 300 pages. A second book has 3 times as many pages. How many pages are in both books?

32. It takes Alvin's dad about 5 hours to drive to his aunt's house. If he drives about 62 miles each hour, about how many miles does Alvin live from his aunt?

14-6 Multiply Two-Digit Numbers (pp. 602–605)

Example 6

Eight boys have 12 baseballs each. How many baseballs altogether?

Find 8 × 12.

Step 1
Multiply ones.

$$\begin{array}{r} {}^{1} \\ 12 \\ \times\ 8 \\ \hline 6 \end{array}$$

Step 2
Multiply tens.

$$\begin{array}{r} {}^{1} \\ 12 \\ \times\ 8 \\ \hline 96 \end{array}$$

So, 96 baseballs

Multiply. Use models if needed.

33. $\begin{array}{r} 46 \\ \times\ 2 \\ \hline \end{array}$

34. $\begin{array}{r} 17 \\ \times\ 4 \\ \hline \end{array}$

35. $\begin{array}{r} 35 \\ \times\ 2 \\ \hline \end{array}$

36. $\begin{array}{r} 29 \\ \times\ 3 \\ \hline \end{array}$

37. Akashi drew a 12-inch chalk line down his driveway. He made 8 more end to end. How long was Akashi's chalk line?

14-7 Multiply Greater Numbers (pp. 606-608)

Example 7

Find 6 × 112.

Step 1 Multiply ones.

```
   1
  112
×   6   2 × 6 ones = 12 ones
    2   12 ones = 1 ten and 2 ones
```

Step 2 Multiply the tens.

```
   1
  112
×   6   6 × 1 tens = 6 tens
   72   6 tens + 1 ten = 7 tens
```

Step 3 Multiply the hundreds.

```
   1
  112
×   6   6 × 1 hundred = 6 hundreds
  672
```

Multiply.

38. 418 × 2

39. 272 × 5

40. 1,042 × 8

41. 1,313 × 9

42. The first 2,525 people who came to the game received 4 coupons for free beverages. How many coupons did they give away?

14-8 Multiply Money (pp. 610–613)

Example 8

Each pencil costs $2.25. What is the total cost for 4 pencils?

Find $2.25 × 4.

```
  1 2
 $2.25
 ×   4
 $9.00  Place the decimal point and $.
```

The total cost is $9.00.

Multiply.

43. $3.25 × 6

44. $2.45 × 3

45. $7.14 × 3

46. $8.77 × 4

47. Algebra Copy and complete.

Rule: Multiply by 5.	
Input	**Output**
■	$20.00
$4.15	■
■	$30.00

Chapter Test

For Exercises 1–3, tell whether each statement is *true* or *false.*

1. When you write money as a decimal, there are two places to the right of the decimal point. Sometimes they are zeros.

2. You do not need to add any regrouped tens after multiplying the tens.

3. When an exact answer is not needed, you can estimate to find an answer that is close to the exact answer.

Multiply.

4. $\$1.15 \times 4$

5. $\$0.43 \times 9$

6. 270×3

7. 421×2

8. **STANDARDS PRACTICE** Mrs. Malone bought 7 magazines. Each one cost $6.25. What was the total cost?

   A $42.45 **C** $43.50

   B $42.75 **D** $43.75

Estimate. Round to the nearest ten.

9. 42×6

10. 75×4

11. **Algebra** Copy and complete.

Rule: Multiply by 6.	
Input	**Output**
251	■
332	■
469	■
102	■

12. Jen and Tom each collected $75 for a fund-raiser. They want to raise $250 altogether. How much more does each of them need to collect if they each raise the same amount?

Estimate. Round to the nearest hundred.

13. 289×5

14. 350×6

15. There are 7 months in a year that have 31 days. About how many days is that altogether?

16. **STANDARDS PRACTICE** What number can be multiplied by 3,573 to give the answer 7,146?

    3,573 × ■ = 7,146

    F 2 **H** 7

    G 8 **J** 6

17. **WRITING IN MATH** Explain why it is important to estimate the answer before finding the exact answer.

14 California Standards Practice

Cumulative, Chapters 1–14

Standards Example

Emiko reads 45 pages a day for 8 days. How many pages does she read in the 8 days?

A 320 pages **C** 360 pages

B 352 pages **D** 400 pages

Read the Question

Emiko reads 45 pages each day for 8 days. To find how many pages she reads in 8 days, multiply 45 × 8.

Solve the Question

$$\begin{array}{r} ^{4} \\ 45 \\ \times\ 8 \\ \hline \mathbf{0} \end{array}$$

Multiply the ones.
8 × 5 = 40 ones.

$$\begin{array}{r} ^{4} \\ 45 \\ \times\ 8 \\ \hline \mathbf{360} \end{array}$$

Multiply the tens.
8 × 4 = 32
32 + 4 = 36

So, Emiko reads 360 pages in 8 days. The answer is C.

Online Personal Tutor at ca.gr3math.com

Choose the best answer.

1 **Silas spent 24 days at camp. He hiked 3 miles each day. How many miles did he hike in all?**

A 72 miles **C** 27 miles

B 60 miles **D** 8 miles

2 **Ashanti collected $125. Anna collected 3 times as much. How much money did Anna collect?**

F $128 **H** $375

G $275 **J** $500

3 **If tomatoes cost $2.49 a pound, how much do 4 pounds cost?**

A $2.53 **C** $9.96

B $7.47 **D** $10.00

4 **Daisy emptied her change bag.**

How much money does she have?

F $1.30 **H** $1.90

G $1.75 **J** $2.05

5 **How many feet are in 4 yards?**

A 12 feet **C** 16 feet

B 15 feet **D** 48 feet

6 **Trent's bookcase has 6 shelves. Each shelf holds 14 books. About how many books does Trent have in his bookcase?**

F 20 **H** 100

G 60 **J** 120

7 **What decimal does the model show?**

A 7 **C** 0.7

B 0.77 **D** 0.07

8 **Melody has 30 shells. Brenda owns 10 times as many as Melody. How many shells does Brenda have?**

F 40 **H** 400

G 300 **J** 3000

9 **If a gallon of gasoline costs $3.04, how much will 9 gallons cost?**

A $3.13 **C** $30.13

B $27.36 **D** $36.36

10 **Which expression describes the array shown below?**

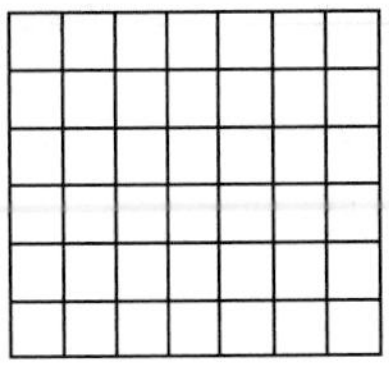

F 8×6 **H** 7×6

G 7×8 **J** 6×6

CHAPTER 15

Divide by One-Digit Numbers

BIG Idea How do I divide by one-digit numbers?

Models can help you divide by one-digit numbers.

Example There are 38 painters who paint the Golden Gate Bridge on an on-going basis. If the painters work in groups of 2, there will be 38 ÷ 2 or 19 painters in each group.

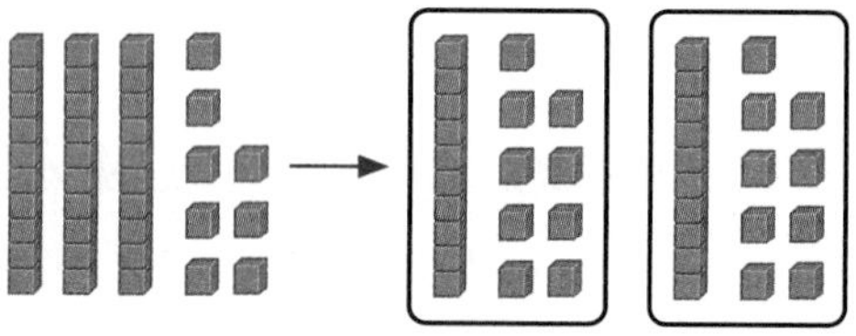

What will I learn in this chapter?

- Divide two- and three-digit numbers by a one-digit number.
- Divide money.
- Estimate quotients.
- Solve problems by working backward.

Key Vocabulary

dividend

divisor

quotient

unit cost

Math Online **Student Study Tools at ca.gr3math.com**

FOLDABLES™ Study Organizer

Make this Foldable to organize information about dividing by one-digit numbers. Begin with two sheets of $8\frac{1}{2}'' \times 11''$ paper.

1. **Stack** the paper so that one is higher than the other.

2. **Fold** upward aligning the edges as shown.

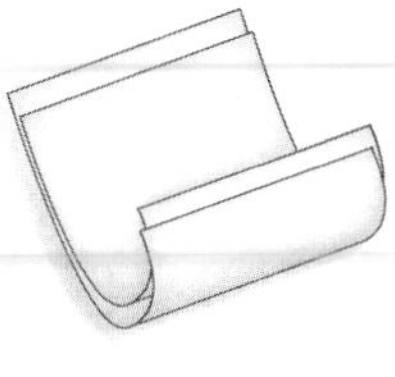

3. **Crease.** Then open and glue together along the creases.

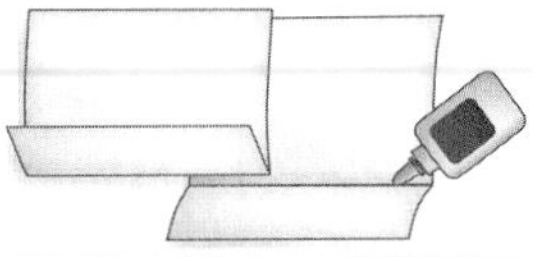

4. **Label** as shown. Record what you learn.

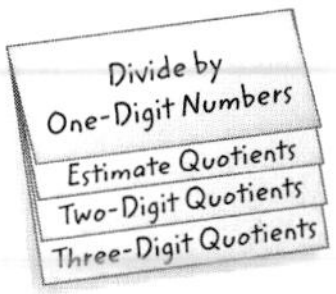

ARE YOU READY for Chapter 15?

You have two ways to check prerequisite skills for this chapter.

Option 2

Math Online Take the Chapter Readiness Quiz at ca.gr3math.com.

Option 1

Complete the Quick Check below.

QUICK Check

Divide. **(Chapters 6 and 7)**

1. $9 \div 3 =$ **2.** $15 \div 5 =$ **3.** $3\overline{)27}$ **4.** $6\overline{)42}$

Write a division sentence for each model. Then solve.

5.

6.

Round to the nearest ten. **(Lesson 1-8)**

7. 24 **8.** 55 **9.** 11 **10.** 97

Round to the nearest hundred. **(Lesson 1-8)**

11. 895 **12.** 423 **13.** 349 **14.** 110

15. There are 26 adult sea lions and 33 young sea lions on a pier. About how many sea lions are there in all?

Subtract. **(Lesson 3-1)**

16. $\begin{array}{r} 66 \\ -\ 4 \\ \hline \end{array}$ **17.** $\begin{array}{r} 42 \\ -\ 8 \\ \hline \end{array}$ **18.** $\begin{array}{r} 78 \\ -\ 35 \\ \hline \end{array}$ **19.** $\begin{array}{r} 34 \\ -\ 27 \\ \hline \end{array}$

20. There are 42 cars in the mall parking lot. Thirteen cars drive away. How many cars are left?

15-1 Divide Multiples of 10, 100, and 1,000

MAIN IDEA

I will learn to divide multiples of 10, 100, and 1,000.

Standard 3NS2.5 Solve division problems in which a multidigit number is evenly divided by a one-digit number (135 ÷ 5 = __).

GET READY to Learn

Hands-On Mini Activity

The models show how basic facts and patterns of zeros can be used to find a quotient like 800 ÷ 4.

8 ÷ 4 = 2

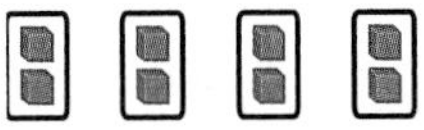

80 ÷ 4 = 20

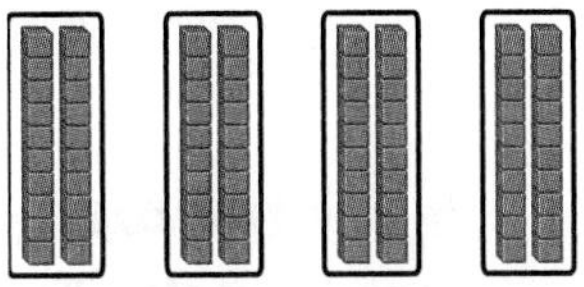

800 ÷ 4 = 200

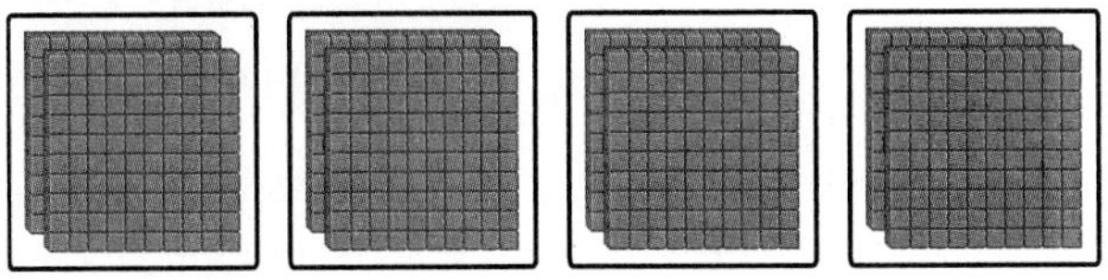

1. Why were the 8 tens divided into 4 equal groups?
2. What do you notice about the zeros in the dividend and quotient?

Review Vocabulary

dividend a number that is divided by another number; **(Lesson 6-2)**

divisor the number by which another number is divided; **(Lesson 6-2)**

quotient the answer to a division problem; **(Lesson 6-2)**

Real-World EXAMPLE Use Models to Divide

1 Use models to find 120 ÷ 3.

Step 1 Show 120 as 12 tens.

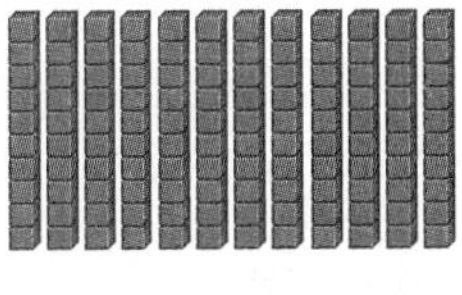

Step 2 Divide the 12 tens into 3 equal groups.

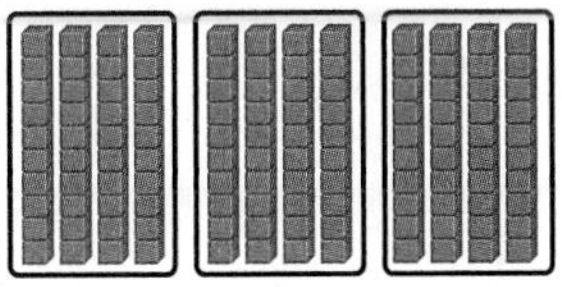

40 40 40

120 ÷ 3 = 40

dividend divisor quotient

Use basic facts and patterns to divide multiples of 10, 100, and 1,000.

Real-World EXAMPLES Divide Multiples

2 **A factory packed 1,500 balls equally in 3 boxes. How many balls are in each box?**

Find 1,500 ÷ 3. Use basic facts and patterns.

15 ÷ 3 = 5	15 ones ÷ 3 = 5 ones
150 ÷ 3 = 50	15 tens ÷ 3 = 5 tens
1,500 ÷ 3 = 500	15 hundreds ÷ 3 = 5 hundreds

So, there are 500 rubber balls in each box.

3 **How many balls are in each box if 3,600 are packed equally in 4 boxes?**

Find 3,600 ÷ 4.

36 ÷ 4 = 9	Use the basic fact
360 ÷ 4 = 90	Use the pattern of zeros
3,600 ÷ 4 = 900	

There are 900 balls in each box.

Online Personal Tutor at ca.gr3math.com

CHECK What You Know

Use basic facts and patterns of zeros to find each quotient. See Examples 1–3 (pp. 627–628)

1. 16 ÷ 4 = ■
160 ÷ 4 = ■
1,600 ÷ 4 = ■

2. 28 ÷ 7 = ■
280 ÷ 7 = ■
2,800 ÷ 7 = ■

3. 40 ÷ 5 = ■
400 ÷ 5 = ■
4,000 ÷ 5 = ■

Divide. Use patterns. See Examples 2 and 3 (p. 628)

4. 270 ÷ 3 =

5. 360 ÷ 6 =

6. 5,400 ÷ 9 =

7. Five classes collected an equal number of cans for recycling. They collected 500 cans in all. How many did each class collect?

8. Talk About It Explain what happens to the pattern of zeros in the quotient when the dividend has zeros in it.

Practice and Problem Solving

EXTRA PRACTICE
See page R38.

Use basic facts and patterns of zeros to find each quotient. See Examples 1–3 (pp. 627–628)

9. 7 ÷ 7 = ■
70 ÷ 7 = ■
700 ÷ 7 = ■
7,000 ÷ 7 = ■

10. 6 ÷ 2 = ■
60 ÷ 2 = ■
600 ÷ 2 = ■
6,000 ÷ 2 = ■

11. 9 ÷ 3 = ■
90 ÷ 3 = ■
900 ÷ 3 = ■
9,000 ÷ 3 = ■

12. 12 ÷ 2 = ■
120 ÷ 2 = ■
1,200 ÷ 2 = ■

13. 45 ÷ 9 = ■
450 ÷ 9 = ■
4,500 ÷ 9 = ■

14. 42 ÷ 7 = ■
420 ÷ 7 = ■
4,200 ÷ 7 = ■

Divide. Use patterns. See Examples 2 and 3 (p. 628)

15. 160 ÷ 8

16. 320 ÷ 8

17. 720 ÷ 9

18. 1,500 ÷ 5

19. 3,000 ÷ 6

20. 2,700 ÷ 9

21. Hoshi knew that his 4 friends had 360 marbles in all. If each friend had the same amount of marbles, how many did each have?

22. **Measurement** The area of a rectangle is 120 square units. If there are 6 rows of square units, how many square units are in each row?

23. There are 4,000 acres of land for sale. Five people want to buy an equal number of acres. How many acres will each person get?

24. A pencil factory boxes 7,200 pencils in 1 hour. If 8 pencils are put into each box, how many boxes are filled in 2 hours?

H.O.T. Problems

25. **FIND THE ERROR** Leroy and Brian are finding 30,000 ÷ 5. Who is correct? Explain your reasoning.

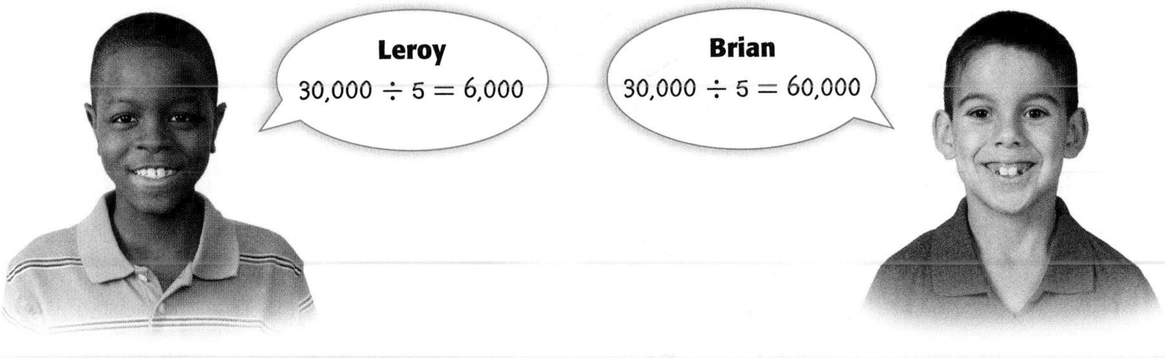

26. **WRITING IN ▸MATH** Explain what it means to look for patterns of zeros when dividing multiples of 10, 100, or 1,000.

15-2 Estimate Quotients

MAIN IDEA

I will estimate quotients.

Standard 3NS2.5 Solve division problems in which a multidigit number is evenly divided by a one-digit number (135 ÷ 5 = __).
Standard 3MR2.1 Use estimation to verify the reasonableness of calculated results.

GET READY to Learn

In the White House, there are 451 prints and drawings. If 5 prints or drawings are in each room except one, about how many rooms have art?

Sometimes an exact answer is not needed. Instead, you can estimate. Rounding can be used to estimate.

Real-World EXAMPLE Estimate by Rounding

1 SOCIAL STUDIES **There are 451 prints and drawings. If 5 prints or drawings are in each room, about how many rooms will have art?**

You need to estimate 451 ÷ 5 or $5\overline{)451}$.

Step 1 Round 451 to the nearest ten that has a basic fact you can use.

451 ÷ 5 → 450 ÷ 5

Step 2 Write the basic fact you will use to divide.

45 ÷ 5 = 9

Step 3 Use the basic fact and patterns to divide.

45 ÷ 5 = 9
450 ÷ 5 = **90**

So, 451 ÷ 5 is about 90.
About 90 rooms will have 5 pieces of art.

You can also estimate the quotient of a multi-digit number and a one-digit number.

Remember

There are 2 ways to show a division problem. $7\overline{)490}$ or $490 \div 7$

Real-World EXAMPLE

2 CARS A car factory completed 1,386 cars in 6 days. About how many cars were completed each day?

You need to estimate $1,386 \div 6$ or $6\overline{)1,386}$.

Step 1 Round 1,386 to the nearest hundred that has a basic fact you can use.

$1,386 \div 6 \longrightarrow 1,200 \div 6$

Step 2 Write the basic fact you will use to divide.

$12 \div 6 = 2$

Step 3 Divide.

Use the basic fact and patterns to divide.

$12 \div 6 = 2$

$1,2\mathbf{00} \div 6 = 2\mathbf{00}$

So, $1,386 \div 6$ is about 200.
About 200 cars were completed each day.

Online **Personal Tutor at** ca.gr3math.com

CHECK What You Know

Estimate by rounding. **See Examples 1 and 2 (pp. 630–631)**

1. $83 \div 8$

2. $175 \div 9$

3. $7\overline{)493}$

4. $1,750 \div 3$

5. $6\overline{)5,970}$

6. $4,330 \div 8$

7. For a fund-raiser, a third grade class must sell 221 kites in 7 days. About how many kites need to be sold each day?

8. Talk About It How is rounding three- and four-digit dividends different than rounding two-digit dividends?

Practice and Problem Solving

EXTRA PRACTICE See page R39.

Estimate by rounding. See Examples 1 and 2 (pp. 630–631)

9. $318 \div 4$ **10.** $869 \div 9$ **11.** $9\overline{)622}$ **12.** $5\overline{)289}$

13. $148 \div 3$ **14.** $285 \div 5$ **15.** $6\overline{)591}$ **16.** $5\overline{)453}$

17. $7{,}559 \div 4$ **18.** $8{,}401 \div 8$ **19.** $3\overline{)9{,}003}$ **20.** $9\overline{)7{,}164}$

21. $2{,}054 \div 3$ **22.** $3{,}964 \div 5$ **23.** $9\overline{)8{,}742}$ **24.** $9\overline{)9{,}183}$

25. A school has 8 rooms. The principal orders 240 desks. About how many desks will go in each classroom?

26. Six schools shared 1,776 magazines. About how many magazines did each get?

For Exercises 27–29, use the table.

27. About how long did it take Suko to walk 1 mile?

28. Which two walkers walked about the same time per minute? Explain your reasoning.

29. Which walker walked the slowest? Explain.

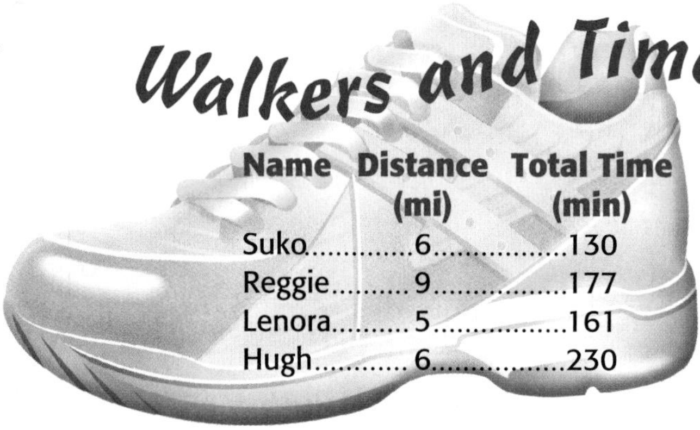

Walkers and Times

Name	Distance (mi)	Total Time (min)
Suko	6	130
Reggie	9	177
Lenora	5	161
Hugh	6	230

Real-World PROBLEM SOLVING

Civics A few facts about the White House are shown.

- 132 rooms on its 6 levels
- 412 doors and 147 windows
- 5 chefs who can serve 140 guests at one time

30. If there are the same number of rooms on each level, about how many rooms would there be on each level?

31. Estimate how many doors and windows there would be on each level if they were each equally divided among the 6 floors.

H.O.T. Problems

32. OPEN ENDED Write a real-world word problem with a quotient between 30 and 40. Ask a classmate to solve.

33. WHICH ONE DOESN'T BELONG? Identify the incorrect estimated quotient. Explain your reasoning.

$342 \div 9 = 40$ | $718 \div 8 = 80$ | $649 \div 8 = 80$ | $125 \div 2 = 60$

34. WRITING IN ▸MATH Describe the steps to take when estimating the quotient for $5{,}861 \div 7$.

Standards Practice

35 $3600 \div 6 =$ ■ **(Lesson 15-1)**

A 6

B 60

C 600

D 6,000

36 On Game Day, the 1,167 students at Enzo's school were divided into equal groups for the 6 different games. About how many students were in each group? **(Lesson 15-2)**

F 20 **H** 200

G 30 **J** 300

Spiral Review

Use basic facts and patterns of zeros to find each quotient. (Lesson 15-1)

37. $300 \div 6 =$ ■ **38.** $2{,}400 \div 4 =$ ■ **39.** $490 \div 7 =$ ■

40. While at the baseball game, Mr. Wayne bought 2 hotdogs for himself and 2 for each of his 3 children. How much did he spend if each hotdog was $2.25? **(Lesson 14-7)**

41. 272×3 **42.** $\$1.08 \times 7$ **43.** $1{,}302 \times 6$

Add the fractions. (Lesson 12-6)

44.

$\frac{1}{4}$-pound $\frac{3}{4}$-pound

45.

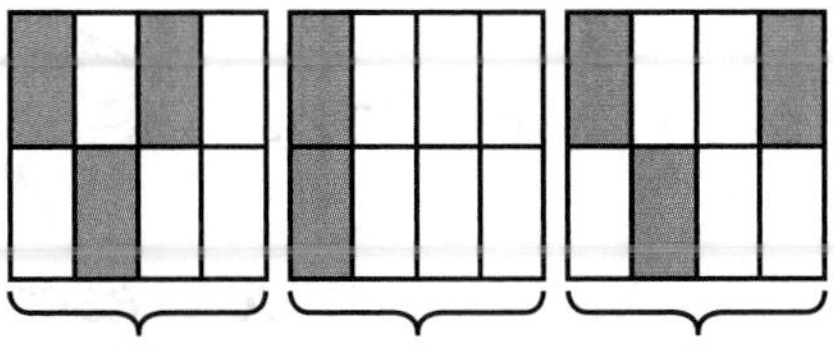

$\frac{3}{8}$ $\frac{2}{8}$ $\frac{3}{8}$

Explore

Math Activity for 15-3
Division

Base-ten blocks can help you understand dividing a two-digit number by a one-digit number.

MAIN IDEA

I will use models to explore division of greater numbers.

Standard 3NS2.5 Solve division problems in which a multidigit number is evenly divided by a one-digit number ($135 \div 5 =$ __).

Standard 3MR2.3 Use a variety of methods, such as words, numbers, symbols, graphs, **diagrams, and models, to explain mathematical reasoning.**

You Will Need
base-ten blocks

Concepts in Motion
Animation
ca.gr3math.com

ACTIVITY

Find 42 ÷ 3.

Step 1 **Model 42 ÷ 3.**
Show 42 as 4 tens and 2 ones.
Show 3 groups.

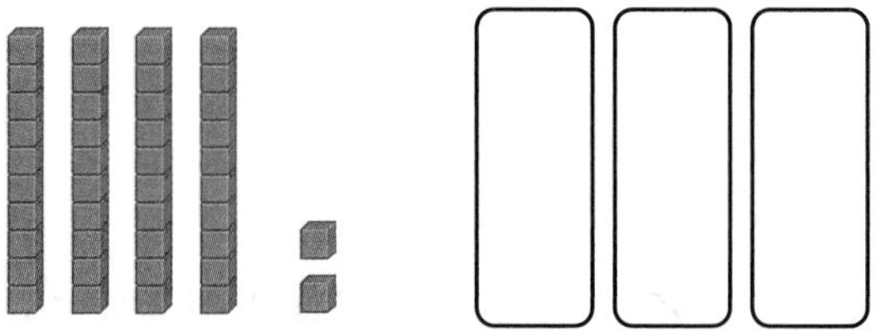

Step 2 **Divide tens.**
Divide the tens equally among each group.

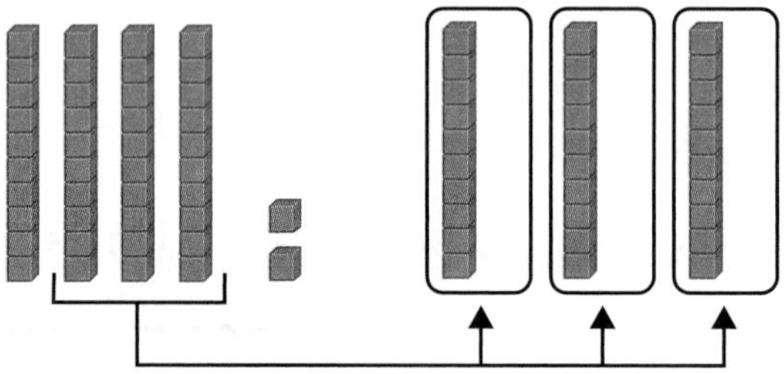

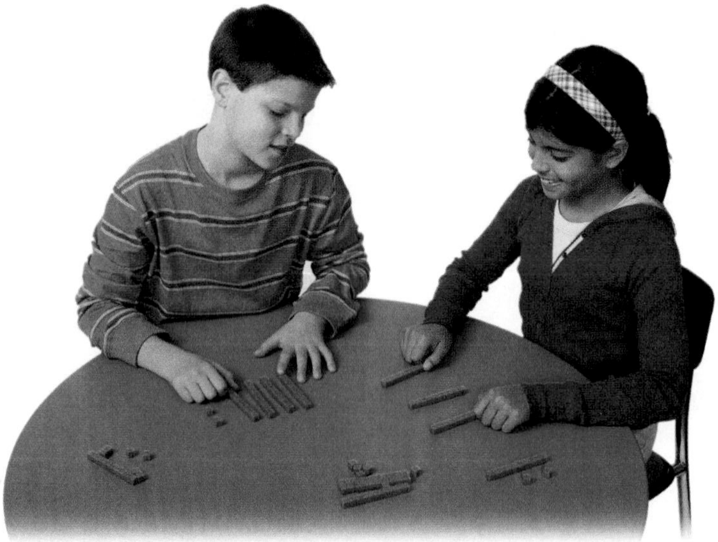

Step 3 Regroup.

Regroup the remaining 1 ten and 2 ones as 12 ones.

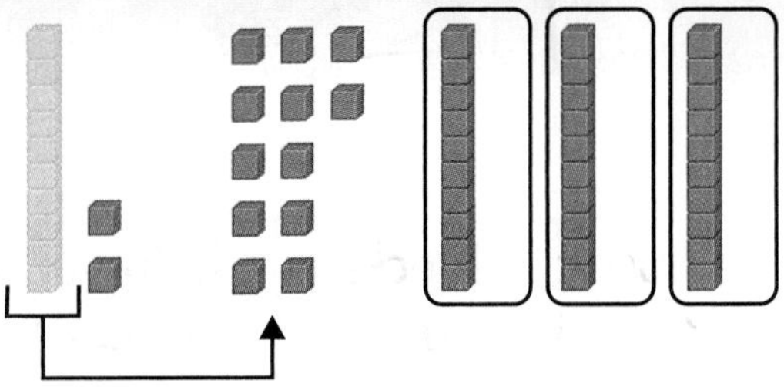

Step 4 Divide ones.

Divide the ones equally among each group. Count the number in each group.

So, 42 ÷ 3 = 14 or $\begin{array}{r}14\\3\overline{)43}\end{array}$.

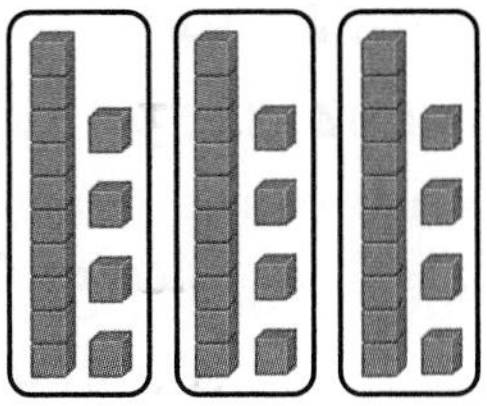

Think About It

1. How did you model the dividend and the divisor?
2. Why did you need to regroup 1 ten?
3. What did you do with the ones after regrouping the ten?

CHECK What You Know

Divide. Use models.

4. 36 ÷ 2

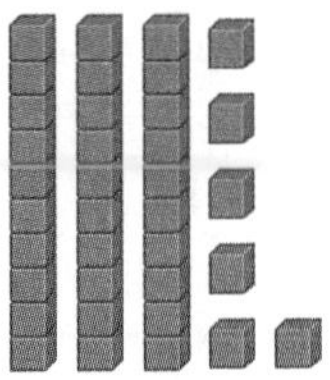

5. 48 ÷ 4

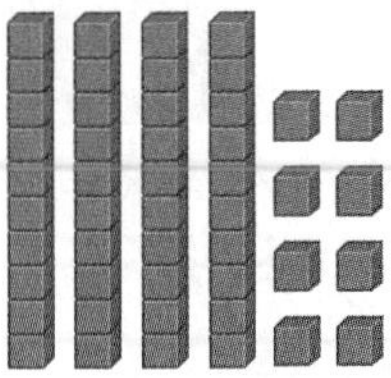

6. 75 ÷ 5

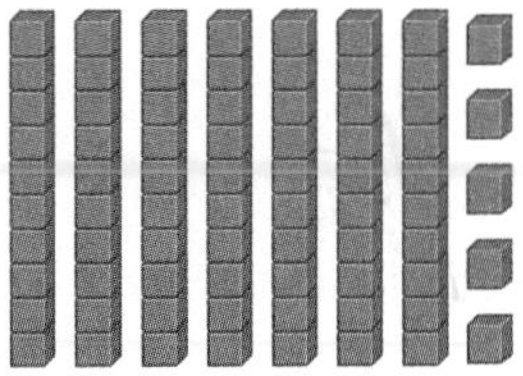

7. $4\overline{)68}$

8. $2\overline{)76}$

9. $4\overline{)56}$

10. WRITING IN ▶MATH Why should you use the models with the greatest place value when you begin to divide?

15-3 Two-Digit Quotients

MAIN IDEA

I will divide a two-digit number by a one-digit number.

Standard 3NS2.5 Solve division problems in which a multidigit number is evenly divided by a one-digit number ($135 \div 5 = \_$)

Standard 3NS2.3 Use the inverse relationship of multiplication and division to compute and check results.

GET READY to Learn

Alina made 64 ounces of lemonade for her hike. She wants to divide the lemonade equally into 4 water bottles. How many ounces will be in each water bottle?

You have used models to divide a two-digit number by a one-digit number. You can use paper and pencil.

Real-World EXAMPLE

1 **MEASUREMENT How many ounces of lemonade will be in each water bottle? Find 64 ÷ 4.**

Step 1 Model 64. Show 4 groups.

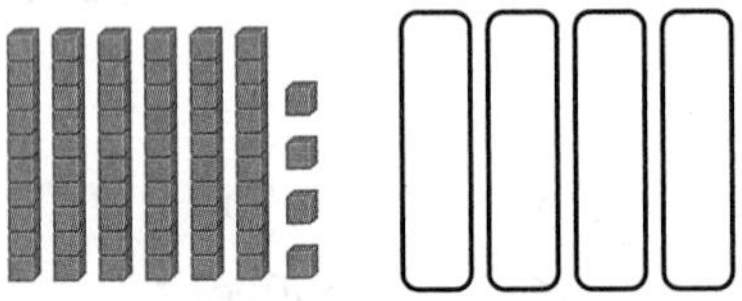

$4\overline{)64}$ ← dividend (■ ← quotient; 4 ↑ divisor)

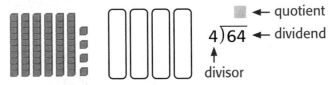

Step 2 Divide the tens.

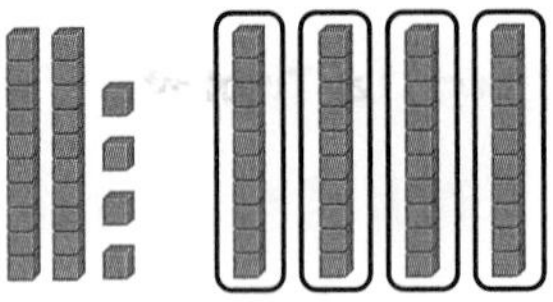

$$\begin{array}{r} 1 \\ 4\overline{)64} \\ -\mathbf{4} \\ \hline \mathbf{2} \end{array}$$

1 ten in each group
4 tens used
2 tens left

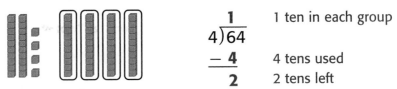

Step 3 Regroup and divide the ones.

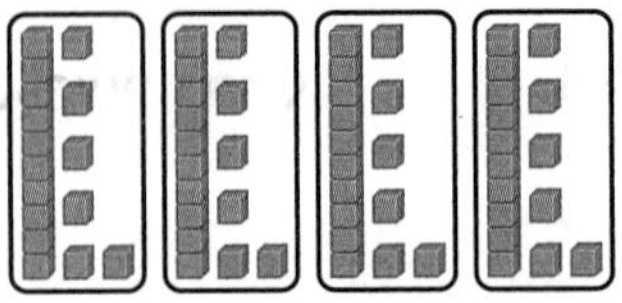

$$\begin{array}{r} 16 \\ 4\overline{)64} \\ -4\downarrow \\ \hline 24 \\ -\mathbf{24} \\ \hline \mathbf{0} \end{array}$$

6 ones in each group
24 ones used
0 ones left

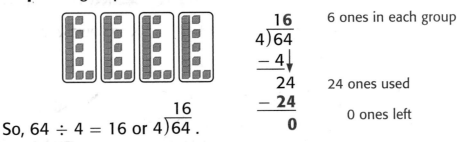

So, $64 \div 4 = 16$ or $4\overline{)64}$ with quotient 16.

Real-World EXAMPLE

2 Measurement Alina and her family want to hike 60 miles in 5 weeks. How many miles will they need to hike each week?

Find 60 ÷ 5.

Remember

Keep dividing until the remainder is smaller than the divisor and no other digits can be brought down.

Step 1 Decide if there are enough tens to divide.

$5\overline{)60}$ — 6 > 5 There are enough tens.

Step 2 Divide the tens.

$$\begin{array}{r} 1 \\ 5\overline{)60} \\ -\,5 \\ \hline 1 \end{array}$$

Divide 6 tens by 5 groups.
Write 1 in the tens place.

Multiply. 1 × 5 tens = 5 tens

Subtract. 5 tens from 6 tens
Compare 1 < 5.

Step 3 Divide the ones.

$$\begin{array}{r} 12 \\ 5\overline{)60} \\ -\,5\downarrow \\ \hline 10 \\ -\,10 \\ \hline 0 \end{array}$$

Bring down the ones.
Divide 10 ones by 5 groups.
Write 2 in the ones place.

Multiply. 2 × 5 ones = 10 ones

Subtract. 10 ones from 10 ones.
Compare 0 < 5

Check Multiply the quotient by the divisor.

$$\begin{array}{rl} {}^{1} & \\ 12 & \text{quotient} \\ \times\ 5 & \text{divisor} \\ \hline 60 & \text{dividend} \end{array}$$

The answer is correct. ✓

Online Personal Tutor at ca.gr3math.com

CHECK What You Know

Divide. Use models if needed. Check your answer. **See Examples 1 and 2 (pp. 636–637)**

1. 96 ÷ 3

2. 52 ÷ 4

3. $2\overline{)28}$

4. Lourdes has 84 flowers. She is going to put 4 flowers in each vase. How many vases will she need?

5. Talk About It Explain how to check the quotient of 65 ÷ 5 by multiplication.

Practice and Problem Solving

EXTRA PRACTICE
See page R39.

Divide. Use models if needed. Check your answer.

See Examples 1 and 2 (pp. 636–637)

6. $88 \div 8$ **7.** $84 \div 7$ **8.** $3\overline{)45}$ **9.** $3\overline{)63}$

10. $91 \div 7$ **11.** $81 \div 3$ **12.** $5\overline{)80}$ **13.** $4\overline{)52}$

14. $78 \div 6$ **15.** $86 \div 2$ **16.** $5\overline{)65}$ **17.** $9\overline{)99}$

Algebra **Copy and complete the table.**

18.

Rule: Divide by 4.	
Input	Output
84	■
92	■
■	19
96	■

19.

Rule: Divide by 7.	
Input	Output
■	9
98	■
70	■
77	■

20.

Rule: Divide by 3.	
Input	Output
51	■
87	■
■	24
33	■

21. Carmela's aunt is making a quilt. It has 98 squares in 7 rows. How many squares are in each row?

22. Measurement Pancho climbed a lighthouse tower that was 93 feet tall. How many yards is that? (*Hint:* 3 ft = 1 yd)

23. Tamika is dividing 96 oatmeal bars into boxes. She wants to put 4 oatmeal bars in each box. How many boxes will she need?

24. Measurement Over the next $1\frac{1}{2}$ hours, Ivan needs to move the water sprinkler every 5 minutes. How many times will he move it during that time? (*Hint:* 60 min = 1 hr and 30 min = $\frac{1}{2}$ hr)

H.O.T. Problems

25. OPEN ENDED Write a real-world division problem whose quotient is 42.

26. NUMBER SENSE How can you tell which is greater without dividing: $77 \div 7$ or $84 \div 7$.

27. WRITING IN ▸MATH How do you find the dividend in a problem if you know the quotient and the divisor? Write a problem to illustrate your answer.

CHAPTER 15

Mid-Chapter Check

Lessons 15-1 through 15-3

Use basic facts and patterns of zeros to find each quotient. **(Lesson 15-1)**

1. $21 \div 7 = ■$
$210 \div 7 = ■$
$2,100 \div 7 = ■$

2. $20 \div 4 = ■$
$200 \div 4 = ■$
$2,000 \div 4 = ■$

Divide. Use patterns. **(Lesson 15-1)**

3. $240 \div 8$

4. $360 \div 6$

5. **STANDARDS PRACTICE** A school football stadium has room for 5,600 people. The stadium is divided evenly into 8 sections. How many people will each section hold? **(Lesson 15-1)**

A 7

B 70

C 700

D 7,000

Estimate by rounding. **(Lesson 15-2)**

6. $76 \div 8$

7. $273 \div 9$

8. $3,721 \div 4$

9. $3,002 \div 7$

10. Rusty bought 274 berries to make fruit cups. This picture shows the number of berries in one fruit cup. About how many fruit cups can he make? **(Lesson 15-2)**

11. Natalie needs 6 dozen muffins for the bake sale. If each mix makes 8 muffins, about how many mixes does she need to make? **(Lesson 15-2)**

Divide. Check your answer. **(Lesson 15-3)**

12. $69 \div 3$

13. $76 \div 4$

14. Lester's dog ate 48 bones in 4 weeks. If the dog ate the same amount each week, how many bones does Lester's dog eat in one week?

15. **Algebra** Copy and complete the table. **(Lesson 15-3)**

Rule: Divide by 3.	
Input	**Output**
63	■
75	■
■	24
33	■

16. **STANDARDS PRACTICE** If 96 students are divided into equal groups of 6, how many students are there in each group? **(Lesson 15-3)**

F 16

G 31

H 42

J 576

17. **WRITING IN MATH** Explain the steps you would take to divide 287 by 7.

15-4 Problem-Solving Strategy

MAIN IDEA I will work backward to solve problems.

Standard 3MR1.2 Determine when and how to break a problem into simpler parts. Standard 3NS2.1 Find the sum or difference of two whole numbers between 0 and 10,000.

Frannie put some money in the bank to start a savings account. Last month she put in enough money to double that amount. Today, she put in more money and the total amount doubled, again. Now she has $20. How much money did Frannie start with?

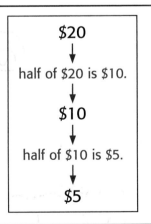

Understand	**What facts do you know?** • The money doubled two times. • The total amount at the end is $20. **What do you need to find?** • The amount of money Frannie started with.
Plan	Work backward from what you know, $20, to find the amount Frannie started with.
Solve	• Start with $20. • Find the number that was doubled. • Since the amount was doubled two times, find half of $10. $20 ↓ half of $20 is $10. ↓ $10 ↓ half of $10 is $5. ↓ $5 So, the amount of money Frannie started with was $5.
Check	Look back at the problem. When you double $5, the result is $5 × 2 or $10. When you double $10, the result is $10 × 2 or $20. So, the answer is correct.

ANALYZE the Strategy

Refer to the problem on the previous page.

1. Explain how the *work backward* strategy helped to solve the problem.
2. Explain when to use the *work backward* strategy.
3. Suppose Frannie ended up with $36 after the amount doubled two times. How much did she start with?
4. How would you check your answer in Exercise 3?

PRACTICE the Strategy

EXTRA PRACTICE
See page R39.

Solve. Use the *work backward* strategy to solve.

5. It took Geraldo one hour to eat lunch. Then he worked at a store for 3 hours. If he finished at 5:00 P.M., what time did he start eating lunch?
6. Flora, Alonso, and Luz went fishing. Find how many fish each caught.

Fish Caught

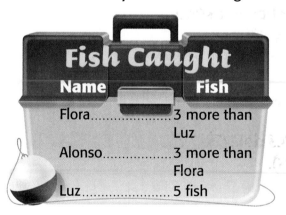

Name	Fish
Flora	3 more than Luz
Alonso	3 more than Flora
Luz	5 fish

7. Mariah celebrated her birthday in March, 4 months after joining the swim team. Two months after joining the team, she swam in her first swim meet. What month did she swim in her first meet?
8. The table shows the starting times of the three movies at the mall.

Movie	Starting Times		
Finding Freddie	NOON	3:00 P.M.	6:00 P.M.
Eating Oranges	2:00 P.M.	3:30 P.M.	5:00 P.M.
Running Races	2:30 P.M.	5:00 P.M.	7:30 P.M.

Whitney and her brother saw a movie that lasted 2 hours. It took 30 minutes to get home. They got home at 5:00 P.M. Which movie did they see? What was the starting time?

9. Mr. Rockwell gave 9 students one pencil each. That afternoon, he gave 5 more students one pencil each. Now he has 15 pencils. How many pencils did he start with?
10. **WRITING IN ▸MATH** Write a real-world problem in which the *work backward* strategy must be used to solve.

15-5 Three-Digit Quotients

MAIN IDEA

I will divide three-digit numbers by one-digit numbers.

Standard 3NS2.5 Solve division problems in which a multidigit number is evenly divided by a one-digit number ($135 \div 5 = \_\_$).

Standard 3NS2.3 Use the inverse relationship of multiplication and **division to compute and check results.**

GET READY to Learn

Kiley walked 354 steps to the Statue of Liberty's crown. She stopped halfway up to rest. How many steps did she walk before she rested?

Dividing 3-digit numbers is like dividing two-digit numbers.

Real-World EXAMPLE

1 STEPS Divide 354 ÷ 2 to find how many steps Kiley walked before she rested?

Step 1 Divide hundreds.
3 > 2. So, there are enough hundreds.

$$\begin{array}{r} 1 \\ 2\overline{)354} \\ -2 \\ \hline 1 \end{array}$$

Divide. 3 ÷ 2
Multiply. 2 × 1 = 2
Subtract. 3 − 2 = 1
Compare. 1 < 2

Step 2 Regroup.
Regroup 1 hundred as 10 tens. Bring down the 5 tens.

$$\begin{array}{r} 1 \\ 2\overline{)354} \\ -2\downarrow \\ \hline 15 \end{array}$$

Step 3 Divide tens.
Regroup the remaining ten as 10 ones. Bring down the ones.

$$\begin{array}{r} 17 \\ 2\overline{)354} \\ -2 \\ \hline 15 \\ -14\downarrow \\ \hline 14 \end{array}$$

Divide. 15 ÷ 2
Multiply. 2 × 7 = 14
Subtract. 15 − 14 = 1
Compare. 1 < 2

Step 4 Divide the ones.

$$\begin{array}{r} 177 \\ 2\overline{)354} \\ -2 \\ \hline 15 \\ -14 \\ \hline 14 \\ -14 \\ \hline 0 \end{array}$$

Divide. 14 ÷ 2 = 7
Multiply. 2 × 7 = 14
Subtract. 14 − 14 = 0
Compare. 0 < 2

Sometimes there is not enough to divide in the first digit to the left. Then, you need to divide the first two digits.

Real-World EXAMPLE

2 **CAMP There are 328 students going to 4 different camps. The students are equally divided among the camps. How many students will be at each camp?**

Divide 328 ÷ 4.

Step 1 Divide the hundreds.

$4\overline{)328}$ There are not enough hundreds to divide. Regroup the 3 hundreds as 30 tens.

$4\overline{)\mathbf{32}8}$ 32 > 4 Place the first digit in the tens place.

Step 2 Divide the tens.

$$\begin{array}{r} \mathbf{8} \\ 4\overline{)\mathbf{32}8} \\ -\mathbf{32} \\ \hline \mathbf{0} \end{array}$$

Divide. 32 ÷ 4 = 8
Multiply. 4 × 8 = 32
Subtract. 32 − 32 = 0
Compare. 0 < 4

Step 3 Divide the ones.

$$\begin{array}{r} 8\mathbf{2} \\ 4\overline{)32\mathbf{8}} \\ -32\downarrow \\ \hline 0\mathbf{8} \\ -\mathbf{8} \\ \hline \mathbf{0} \end{array}$$

Bring down the ones.
Divide. 8 ÷ 4 = 2
Multiply. 4 × 2 = 8
Subtract. 8 − 8 = 0
Compare. 0 < 4

Check Multiply to check

82	quotient
× 4	divisor
328	dividend

So, the answer is correct. ✔

So, 328 ÷ 4 = 82.

Online **Personal Tutor at** ca.gr3math.com

> **Remember**
> If the first digit of the dividend is not large enough to divide, then divide the first *two* digits.

CHECK What You Know

Divide. Check your answers. **See Examples 1 and 2 (pp. 642–643)**

1. 288 ÷ 2

2. $5\overline{)580}$

3. $9\overline{)153}$

4. There are 186 empty milk cartons in a summer camp kitchen. The cook puts the cartons in bags. How many bags will he use if he puts 6 cartons in each bag?

5. Talk About It Explain what is similar about the way you divide a 3-digit number by a one-digit number, and a two-digit number by a one-digit number.

Practice and Problem Solving

EXTRA PRACTICE See page R40.

Divide. Check your answers. See Examples 1 and 2 (pp. 642–643)

6. $650 \div 5$ **7.** $632 \div 2$ **8.** $4\overline{)644}$ **9.** $3\overline{)342}$

10. $847 \div 7$ **11.** $625 \div 5$ **12.** $3\overline{)384}$ **13.** $5\overline{)740}$

14. $7\overline{)168}$ **15.** $5\overline{)130}$ **16.** $141 \div 3$ **17.** $198 \div 6$

18. There is a total of 256 pieces of pizza. If each pizza has 8 slices, how many pizzas are there?

19. Sonny bought 7 strings of lights. If there is a total of 168 lights, how many lights are on each string?

20. **Geometry** A building has 168 windows. Each side has the same number of windows. How many windows are on each of the four sides?

21. **Measurement** An equilateral triangle has a perimeter of 819 centimeters. What is the length of 2 sides?

For Exercises 22–25, use the table. Find the number of boxes of each.

22. crayons

23. gel pens

24. chalk

25. pencils

School Store

Item	Total	Number in each box	Boxes
Chalk	864	6	■
Pencils	780	5	■
Crayons	576	8	■
Gel pens	312	8	■

H.O.T. Problems

26. **FIND THE ERROR** Neil and Hilary are finding $368 \div 8$. Who is correct? Explain.

Neil

$$\begin{array}{r} 46 \\ 8\overline{)368} \\ -\,32 \\ \hline 48 \\ -\,48 \\ \hline 0 \end{array}$$

Hilary

$$\begin{array}{r} 458 \\ 8\overline{)368} \\ -\,32 \\ \hline 48 \\ -\,48 \\ \hline 0 \end{array}$$

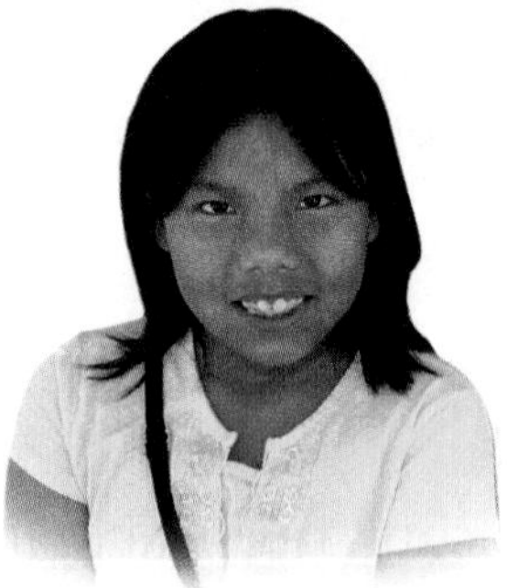

27. **WRITING IN MATH** Explain where to put the first digit in a quotient.

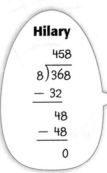

 Math Online Self-Check Quiz at ca.gr3math.com

Game Time

That's Close!

Estimate Quotients

Get Ready!

Players: 2 players

You will need: 1 blank number cube, calculator

Get Set!

Label a cube 1–6.

Go!

- Player 1 rolls the number cube. The number will be the tens digit in the dividend. Both players record the digit.
- Player 1 rolls the number cube, again. This number will be the ones digit in the dividend. Both players record the digit in the ones position.
- Player 2 rolls the number cube for the divisor.
- Each player estimates the quotient.
- Use a calculator to find the actual quotient. The player whose estimate is closest earns 1 point.
- Continue reversing rolls until one player earns 10 points.

Problem Solving in Science

Roller Coaster Physics

When the Millennium Force opened at Cedar Point Amusement Park in Ohio in 2000, it broke 10 world records for roller coasters. This roller coaster takes its riders 310 feet into the air and twists them into two 122 degree turns. In 2005, the Millennium Force was voted the best steel roller coaster in the world in a survey of roller coaster fans.

A ride on a roller coaster is an incredible thrill. Did you ever think about how roller coasters work? The train of the roller coaster is pulled up the lift hill along the track with a steel cable. At the top of the hill, the energy of the train plunges the cars down the first downward slope. This energy carries the train up the second hill. As the train goes up and down the hills, this energy conversion continues.

Millennium Force FACTS

Ride capacity	108 people per ride
Time capacity	1,620 people per hour
Lift height	310 feet
Track length	6,600 feet
Vertical drop	3,600 inches
Second hill height	169 feet
Third hill height	182 feet

Source: rcdb.com

Standard 3NS2.5 **Solve division problems in which a multidigit number is evenly divided by a one-digit number (135 ÷ 5 = ___).**

Did You Know?

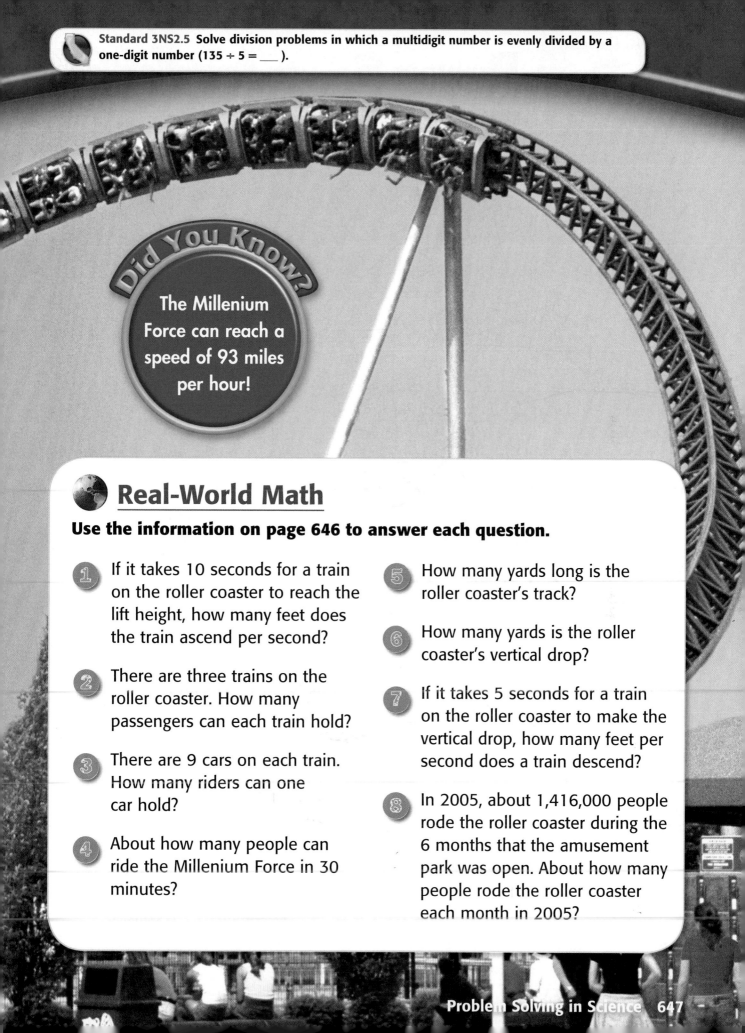

The Millenium Force can reach a speed of 93 miles per hour!

Real-World Math

Use the information on page 646 to answer each question.

1. If it takes 10 seconds for a train on the roller coaster to reach the lift height, how many feet does the train ascend per second?

2. There are three trains on the roller coaster. How many passengers can each train hold?

3. There are 9 cars on each train. How many riders can one car hold?

4. About how many people can ride the Millenium Force in 30 minutes?

5. How many yards long is the roller coaster's track?

6. How many yards is the roller coaster's vertical drop?

7. If it takes 5 seconds for a train on the roller coaster to make the vertical drop, how many feet per second does a train descend?

8. In 2005, about 1,416,000 people rode the roller coaster during the 6 months that the amusement park was open. About how many people rode the roller coaster each month in 2005?

15-6 Problem-Solving Investigation

MAIN IDEA I will choose the best strategy to solve a problem.

Standard 3MR1.1 Analyze problems by identifying relationships, distinguishing relevant from irrelevant information, sequencing and prioritizing information, and observing patterns. Standard 3NS2.5 Solve division problems in which a multidigit number is evenly divided by a one-digit number (135 ÷ 5 = __).

P.S.I. TEAM +

JULIO: A community pool is in the shape of a circle. It measures 80 feet across. A square fence is going to be placed around the pool.

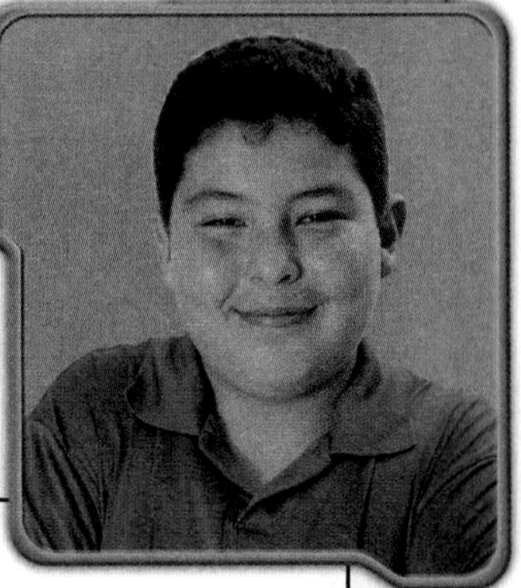

YOUR MISSION: Find if 340 feet of fencing is enough to go around the pool.

Understand The pool is a circle. It measures 80 feet across. A square fence will be put around the pool. You have 340 feet of fencing. You need to know if 340 feet of fencing is enough.

Plan Divide 340 by 4 to find the length of each side of the fence. Make a drawing to compare the length of the fence to the pool.

Solve

$$\begin{array}{r} 85 \\ 4\overline{)340} \\ -\underline{32} \\ 20 \\ -\underline{20} \\ 0 \end{array}$$

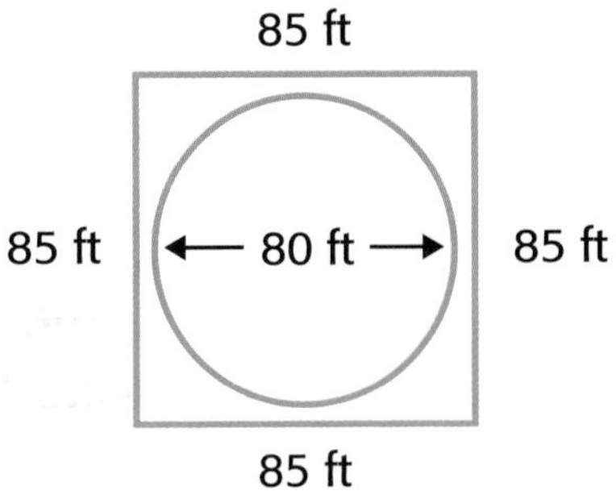

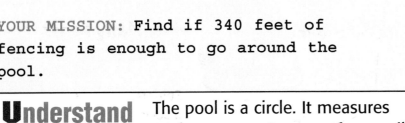

340 feet of fence is enough to make a square that is 85 feet on each side. 80 feet is smaller than 85 feet. So, 340 feet of fencing is enough.

Look Back Look back at the problem. Check the answer by multiplying. $85 \times 4 = 340$. So, the answer is correct.

Mixed Problem Solving

EXTRA PRACTICE
See page R40.

Use any strategy shown below to solve. Tell what strategy you used.

PROBLEM-SOLVING STRATEGIES
- Make an organized list.
- Draw a picture.
- Act it out.
- Use logical reasoning.
- Work backward.

1. There are 136 guests coming to the party. Should 5, 6, or 8 guests be seated at each table so that each table is full and the same number of guests are at each table? Explain.

2. A potato-sack race will be held inside a rectangular area that is 50 meters long and 40 meters wide. The teacher gave Donna a piece of rope that was 200 meters long and told her to make the rectangle. How much of the rope will be left over?

3. Izzie and her family buy the items shown. They want to make 4 equal payments to pay for the items. If they already paid $100, how much will each payment be?

Computer Items	
Item	**Cost**
Computer	$676
Printer	$177
Software	$ 99

4. The third grade class went on a one-day trip to state park. They arrived at 12:45 P.M. after driving for 3 hours and 15 minutes. At what time did they leave?

5. At a zoo, Exhibit One has 3 spiders and 4 camels. Exhibit Two has 3 insects and 10 birds. What is the difference in the number of legs in Exhibit One and Two?

How Many Legs?

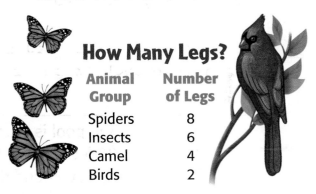

Animal Group	Number of Legs
Spiders	8
Insects	6
Camel	4
Birds	2

6. There are 1,440 minutes in one day. What is the total number of minutes in one week?

7. The tables show finishing times for walkers in a 7-mile race. Who walked faster per mile? Explain.

7-Mile Race	
Walker	**Time (min)**
Janice	133
Gilbert	154

8. WRITING IN ▸MATH How many 8-ounce packages of dog bones are in a box that weighs 200 ounces? Explain the strategy you found was most helpful in solving this problem.

15-7 Divide Money

MAIN IDEA

I will divide amounts of money.

Standard 3NS3.3 Solve problems involving addition, subtraction, multiplication, and **division of money amounts in decimal notation** and multiply **and divide money amounts in decimal notation by using whole-number** multipliers and **divisors.**
Standard 3NS2.7 Determine the unit cost when given the total cost and number of units.

GET READY to Learn

Blair and 2 friends bought a pumpkin for \$8.82. They split the cost equally. How much did each girl pay?

To divide money amounts, divide the same way you divide whole numbers.

Real-World EXAMPLE

1 PUMPKINS **How much did each pay for the pumpkin?**

You need to find \$8.82 ÷ 3.

Estimate \$8.82 ÷ 3 ⟶ \$9.00 ÷ 3 = \$3.00

Step 1 Divide the dollars.

$$\begin{array}{r} 2 \\ 3\overline{)\$8.82} \\ -6 \\ \hline 2 \end{array}$$

Divide. 8 ÷ 3
Multiply. 3 × 2 dollars
Subtract. 8 − 6 = 2
Compare. 2 < 3

Step 2 Divide the dimes.

$$\begin{array}{r} 29 \\ 3\overline{)\$8.82} \\ -6 \\ \hline 28 \\ -27 \\ \hline 01 \end{array}$$

Divide. 28 ÷ 3
Multiply. 3 × 9 dimes
Subtract. 28 − 27 = 1
Compare. 1 < 3

Step 3 Divide the pennies.

$$\begin{array}{r} \$2.94 \\ 3\overline{)\$8.82} \\ -6 \\ \hline 28 \\ -27 \\ \hline 12 \\ -12 \\ \hline 0 \end{array}$$

Place the decimal point and dollar sign.
Divide. 12 ÷ 3 = 4
Multiply. 3 × 4 pennies
Subtract. 12 − 12 = 0
Compare. 0 < 3

Check

\$2.94 is close to the estimate of \$3.00. So, the answer is reasonable.

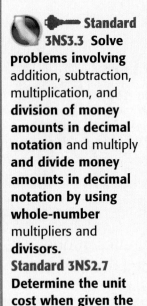

Since \$2.94 × 3 = \$8.82, the answer is correct. ✓

Sometimes, a quotient is less than $1.

EXAMPLE Quotients Less Than $1.00

2 **Divide $2.75 ÷ 5.**

Estimate $2.75 ÷ 5 ⟶ $3.00 ÷ 5 = $0.60

Step 1 Decide if there are enough dollars to divide.

```
5)$2.75
```

There are not enough dollars since 2 < 5.

Step 2 Divide the dollars as 20 dimes.

```
      5
5)$2.75
 - 25↓
     25
```

Step 3 Divide the pennies.

```
  $0.55
5)$2.75
 - 25↓
    025
   - 25
      0
```

Add the dollar sign and decimal point. Add a zero to show 0 dollars.

Check

The estimate of $0.60 is close to $0.55. So, the answer is reasonable. Since $0.55 × 5 = $2.75, the answer is correct. ✓

Online Personal Tutor at ca.gr3math.com

Remember

Be careful to place the first digit of the quotient over the correct digit in the dividend.

```
Example    9
         4)364
```

You can divide to find the unit cost.

Review Vocabulary

unit cost the price for one item (or unit). **(Lesson 7–6)**

Real-World EXAMPLE Find Unit Cost

3 **PAINT** **Dion paid $6.55 for 5 bottles of model paint. How much did each bottle cost?**

Find the unit cost. Divide $6.55 ÷ 5.

```
  $1.31
5)$6.55
 - 5
   15
  - 15
      5
    - 5
      0
```

Check

Since $1.31 × 5 = $6.55, the answer is correct. ✓

So, $6.55 ÷ 5 = $1.31. Each bottle costs $1.31.

CHECK What You Know

Divide. Check your answer. See Examples 1 and 2 (pp. 650–651)

1. $8.50 ÷ 5 **2.** $3.50 ÷ 2 **3.** $3\overline{)\$3.39}$

Find the unit cost. See Example 3 (p. 651)

4.

5.

6.

7. How much does one apple cost if 5 apples cost $4.55?

8. Talk About It Is $7.59 the same as $759? Explain.

Practice and Problem Solving

EXTRA PRACTICE See page R40.

Divide. Check your answer. See Examples 1 and 2 (pp. 650–651)

9. $3.30 ÷ 3 **10.** $4.14 ÷ 2 **11.** $3\overline{)\$6.81}$

12. $4\overline{)\$2.28}$ **13.** $5\overline{)\$4.60}$ **14.** $6.72 ÷ 6

Find the unit cost. See Example 3 (p. 651)

15.

16.

17.

Real-World PROBLEM SOLVING

Whale Watching The Pacific Ocean is the home of the gray whale. Whale watching cruises allow people to view them as they migrate.

18. Kendall bought 3 of one item and spent $8.85. What did she buy?

19. Guy bought 2 cameras for $7.20. How much did each one cost?

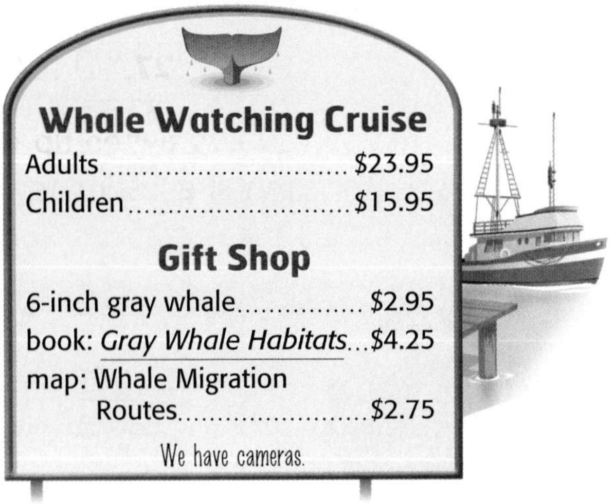

H.O.T. Problems

20. OPEN ENDED Write a real-world problem in which the unit cost of an item needs to be found.

21. NUMBER SENSE Without dividing, how do you know that the quotient of $2.87 ÷ 7 is a two-digit number?

22. WRITING IN ▶MATH Why can you use multiplication to check division?

Standards Practice

23 Kimberly read 132 pages of her new book in 4 days. If she read the same number of pages each day, how many pages were read each day? **(Lesson 15-6)**

A 20 **C** 30

B 23 **D** 33

24 Mrs. Baker spent $64 on 4 new sets of dishes. How much money did each set cost? **(Lesson 15-7)**

F $11

G $16

H $18

J $24

Spiral Review

25. There are 60 families living in an apartment building. Half of the families have 4 people. Seven of the families have 3 people. The rest of the families have 5 people. How many people live in the apartment building? **(Lesson 15-6)**

Divide. Check your answers. **(Lesson 15-5)**

26. 650 ÷ 2 **27.** $4\overline{)464}$ **28.** 189 ÷ 9

29. There were 434 runners signed up for the race, but only 79 crossed the finish line. Estimate by rounding how many did not finish the race. **(Lesson 3-7; 3-3)**

Subtract. **(Lesson 3-6)**

30. 607 − 349 **31.** 800 − 725 **32.** $300 − $244

Algebra Find the missing numbers. **(Lesson 1-1)**

33. 175, 225, ___, 325, ___, ___ **34.** 520, 490, ___, 430, 400, ___, ___

15 Study Guide and Review

FOLDABLES™ Study Organizer GET READY to Study

Be sure the following Key Vocabulary words and Key Concepts are written in your Foldable.

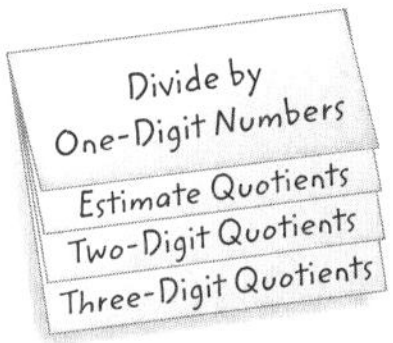

BIG Ideas

Divide by Multiples of 10, 100, and 1,000 **(p. 627)**

Use basic facts and patterns.

$21 \div 7 = 3$	21 ones ÷ 3
$210 \div 7 = 30$	21 tens ÷ 3
$2{,}100 \div 7 = 300$	21 hundreds ÷ 3

Estimate Quotients **(p. 630)**

- Use rounding to estimate quotients.

$$4\overline{)165} \longrightarrow 4\overline{)160}$$

$$160 \div 4 = 40$$

Divide Two- and Three-Digit Numbers **(p. 636)**

```
   19          123
 4)76        6)738
  -4          -6
   36          13
  -36         -12
    0           18
               -18
                 0
```

Key Vocabulary

dividend **(p. 627)**
divisor **(p. 627)**
quotient **(p. 627)**
unit cost **(p. 650)**

Vocabulary Check

Choose the vocabulary word that completes each sentence.

1. A number that is divided by another number is called the ___?___ .
2. The answer to a division problem is called the ___?___ .
3. The price for one item is called the ___?___ .
4. In the division problem $7\overline{)490}$, 490 is called the ___?___ and 7 is the ___?___ .
5. The ___?___ of 65 ÷ 5 is 13.
6. The number by which another number is divided is called the ___?___ .

 Math Online **Vocabulary Review at** ca.gr3math.com

Lesson-by-Lesson Review

15-1 Divide Multiples of 10, 100, and 1,000 (pp. 627–629)

Example 1
There are 1,600 stickers in 4 packs. How many stickers are in each pack?

Find 1,600 ÷ 4.

Use basic facts and patterns.

16 ÷ 4 = 4	16 ones ÷ 4 = 4 ones
160 ÷ 4 = 40	16 tens ÷ 4 = 4 tens
1,600 ÷ 4 = 400	16 hundreds ÷ 4 = 4 hundreds

So, there are 400 stickers in each pack.

Use basic facts and patterns of zeros to find each quotient.

7. 16 ÷ 2 = ■
160 ÷ 2 = ■
1,600 ÷ 2 = ■

8. 36 × 9 = ■
360 × 9 = ■
3,600 × 9 = ■

9. 42 ÷ 6 = ■
420 ÷ 6 = ■
4,200 ÷ 6 = ■

10. 49 ÷ 7 = ■
490 × 7 = ■
4,900 × 7 = ■

11. Lonny measured the perimeter of his square desk top. It was 1,200 millimeters. How long is

15-2 Estimate Quotients (pp. 630–633)

Example 2
There were 351 juice pops sold at five snack booths. About how many juice pops did each booth sell?

Estimate 351 ÷ 5.

Step 1 Round 351 ÷ 5 to 350 ÷ 5.

Step 2 Write the basic fact.
35 ÷ 5 = 7

Step 3 Divide. 350 ÷ 5 = 70

So, 351 ÷ 5 is about 70.

Estimate by rounding.

12. 238 ÷ 4 **13.** 82 ÷ 8

14. $7\overline{)652}$ **15.** $6\overline{)289}$

16. 75 ÷ 4 **17.** 84 ÷ 8

18. $4\overline{)89}$ **19.** $9\overline{)716}$

20. Arthur and Allan collected 988 pennies in a penny drive. About how many pennies will each boy turn in if they turn in an equal amount?

15-3 Two-Digit Quotients (pp. 636–638)

Example 3
Divide 77 ÷ 7.

Step 1 Decide if there are enough tens to divide.

$7\overline{)77}$ 7 = 7 There are enough tens.

Step 2 Divide the tens.

$$\begin{array}{r} 1 \\ 7\overline{)77} \\ -7 \\ \hline 0 \end{array}$$

Divide 7 tens by 7.
Multiply 1 × 7 tens = 7 tens
Subtract. 7 − 7 tens = 0 tens
Compare 0 < 7.

Step 3 Divide the ones.

$$\begin{array}{r} 11 \\ 7\overline{)77} \\ -7\downarrow \\ \hline 7 \\ -\ 7 \\ \hline 0 \end{array}$$

Divide 7 ones by 7.
Multiply. 7 × 1 ones = 7 ones
Subtract. 7 ones − 7 ones = 0 ones.
Compare. 0 < 7

Divide. Check your answer.

21. 99 ÷ 9 **22.** 84 ÷ 4

23. $3\overline{)45}$ **24.** $3\overline{)63}$

Algebra Copy and complete.

25.

Rule: Divide by 4.	
Input	**Output**
84	■
56	■
■	18

26. There are 64 people at the mall. An equal number of people shop at 4 different stores. How many people shop at each store?

15-4 Problem-Solving Strategy: Work Backward (pp. 640–641)

Example 4
Bernardo lives 5 minutes from a library. He walks to the library and returns home by 2:15 P.M. If he is at the library 25 minutes, what time did he leave for the library?

Work backward.

2:15 – 25 minutes = 1:50

1:50 – 10 minutes = 1:40

So, Bernardo left for the library at 1:40 P.M.

Solve.

27. Leanne gave 4 apples away. She now has 5 apples. How many apples did she have to start with?

28. Maria has 40 recipe books in her collection. She will keep 10 books for herself and divide the rest equally among 5 friends. How many recipe books does each friend get?

15-5 Three-Digit Quotients (pp. 642–644)

Example 5
Divide 164 ÷ 2.

Step 1 Divide the hundreds.

$2\overline{)164}$ $2 > 1$ hundred. There are not enough hundreds to divide.

$2\overline{)164}$ $2 < 16$ tens

Step 2 Divide the tens.

```
   8
2)164
 -16
   0
```

Divide. 16 tens ÷ 2 = 8 tens

Multiply. 2 × 8 tens = 16 tens

Subtract. 16 tens – 16 tens = 0 tens

Compare. 0 < 2

Step 3 Divide the ones.

```
   82
2)164
 -16↓
   04
  - 4
    0
```

Divide. 4 ones ÷ 2 = 2 ones

Multiply. 2 ones × 2 = 4 ones

Subtract. 4 ones – 4 ones = 0

Compare. 0 = 0

Check

Multiply to check.

```
  82
× 2
 164
```

The answer is correct. ✓

Divide. Check your answers.

29. 450 ÷ 5 **30.** 525 ÷ 5

31. 987 ÷ 7 **32.** 120 ÷ 3

33. 579 ÷ 3 **34.** 856 ÷ 4

35. There are 108 third grade students in the local elementary school. The principal has hired 3 third grade teachers. How many students will be in each teacher's class?

36. Algebra Copy and complete.

Rule: Divide by 6.	
Input	**Output**
684	■
426	■
■	123
336	■

37. The table lists how many raisins were found in each box of cereal and the number of people who shared the box. Which box gave each person the most raisins?

Cereal Box	Number of raisins	Number of people
A	675	5
B	455	7
C	757	8

15-6 Problem-Solving Investigation: Choose the Best Strategy (pp. 648–649)

Example 6
To sew a new dress, Dorene needs 5 yards of fabric. Will she have enough fabric if she bought 16 feet of one type of fabric and 5 feet of another kind?

First add to find the number of feet then divide to find how many yards.

16 feet + 5 feet = 21 feet.

You know 3 feet = 1 yard. Divide.

$21 \div 3 = 7$

Since she has 7 yards, Dorene will have enough fabric.

Solve using the best strategy.

38. Ginger receives 5 stars for every A, 3 stars for every B, and 1 star for every C. Calculate how many stars she will receive.

Subject	Grade
Social Studies	C
Math	A
Reading	A
Writing	B
Spelling	C
Science	B

39. The train travels 924 miles in one trip. It travels 168 miles one day and 252 miles the next. How many miles are left to travel?

15-7 Divide Money (pp. 650–653)

Example 7
Mrs. Garcia bought 3 equally-priced plants. How much did she pay for each plant if she spent $8.64?

Divide $8.64 ÷ 3.

```
    $2.88
3)$8.64    Place the dollar sign and
  −6       decimal point directly above.
   26
  −24
    24
   −24
     0
```

So, each plant costs $2.88.

Divide. Check your answer.

40. $6.14 ÷ 2 **41.** $3.72 ÷ 4

42. $6.12 ÷ 6 **43.** $5.25 ÷ 5

Find the unit cost.

44.

45. Sheree bought a new set of juice glasses for her mom. There were 8 glasses in the box. She paid $6.40 for the box. What is the unit cost for each glass?

CHAPTER 15

Chapter Test

For Exercises 1-3, tell whether each statement is *true* or *false*.

1. To divide money, divide the same way you divide whole numbers.

2. Dividing three-digit numbers is similar to dividing two-digit numbers.

3. A dividend is the answer in a division problem.

Divide. Check your answer.

4. $3\overline{)\$6.81}$ **5.** $4\overline{)\$9.84}$

6. $3\overline{)342}$ **7.** $632 \div 2$

8. Misty buys 5 bags of pebbles to put in the planter. If there was a total of 565 pebbles, how many pebbles were in each bag?

9. Thomas buys the items listed in the table. He had $4.67 left over. How much money did he start with?

Item	Price
Book	$3.75
Dozen Pencils	$0.89

10. **STANDARDS PRACTICE** Which number completes this pattern.

$$18 \div 6 = 3$$
$$180 \div 6 = ■$$
$$1{,}800 \div 6 = 300$$

A 3,000   **C** 30

B 300   **D** 3

Find the unit cost.

11.

12.

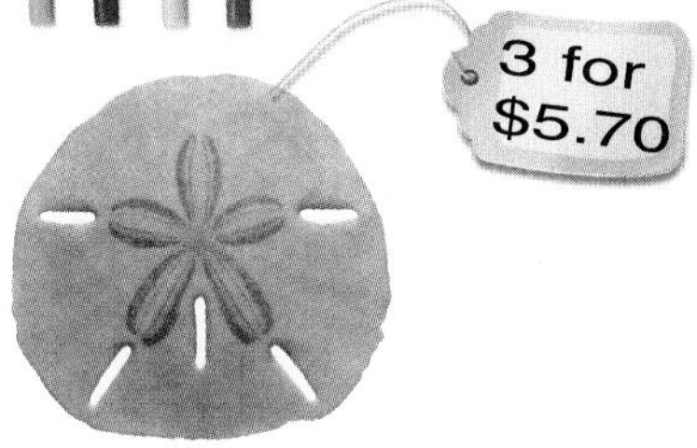

13. Larissa and Ben need $34 to attend the state fair. How much does it cost for each child?

14. **Algebra** Copy and complete the table.

Rule: Divide by 7.	
Input	**Output**
■	7
434	■
70	■
147	■

15. **STANDARDS PRACTICE** How much does 1 milk cost if 6 milks are $7.50?

F $1.50   **H** $1.00

G $1.25   **J** $0.75

16. **WRITING IN MATH** Explain how to check $248 \div 2 = 124$.

CHAPTER 15

California Standards Practice

Cumulative, Chapters 1–15

Standards Example

At a science fair, 128 students entered a project. There were an equal number of projects for 4 different categories. How many projects were in each category?

A 32 **C** 43

B 34 **D** 46

Read the Question

To find the number of projects in each of 4 categories, divide 128 by 4.

Solve the Question

Divide the hundreds, tens, then ones.

$$\begin{array}{r} 32 \\ 4\overline{)128} \\ -\ 12 \\ \hline 08 \\ -\ 8 \\ \hline 0 \end{array}$$

So, 32 science projects were in each category. The answer is A.

Online Personal Tutor at ca.gr3math.com

Choose the best answer.

1 **Jan's mystery book has 275 pages. She wants to read the book in 5 days. How many pages will she read each day?**

A 45 **C** 65

B 55 **D** 75

2 **What number will make each number sentence true?**

$$8 \div 2 = \blacksquare$$
$$80 \div 20 = \blacksquare$$
$$800 \div 200 = \blacksquare$$

F 2 **H** 6

G 4 **J** 8

3 Enrique did this division problem.

$426 \div 6 = 71$

Which problem could he do to check his answer?

A $71 \div 6 =$ ■

B 426 - 71 = ■

C $6 + 426 =$ ■

D $71 \times 6 =$ ■

---

4 Over the weekend 1450 people saw a new movie. That is five times more people than last weekend. How many people saw the movie last weekend?

F 210 **H** 1445

G 290 **J** 7250

---

5 Gilberto bought 4 balloons for his younger brother. He paid $0.64. How much did each balloon cost?

A $0.11 **C** $0.24

B $0.16 **D** $1.60

---

6 Mrs. Park spent $99 on 9 rose bushes. All of the bushes cost the same amount. How much did each plant cost?

F $8 **H** $11

G $9 **J** $12

---

7 Which expression describes the array shown below?

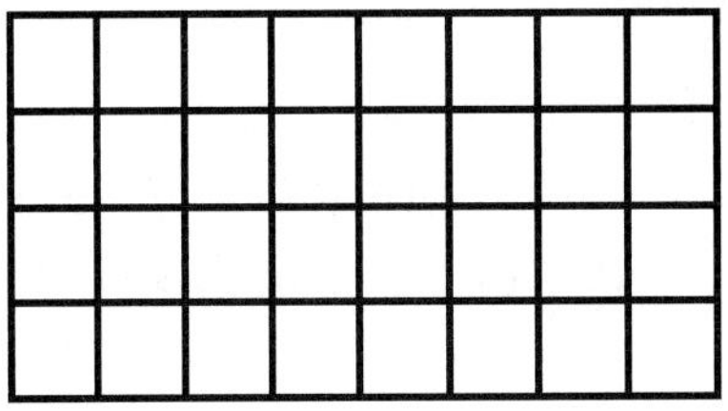

A 4×8 **C** 8×9

B 6×7 **D** 7×7

---

8 Asher earned $54 selling his old toys. He sold each toy for $3. How many toys did he sell?

F 6 **H** 18

G 9 **J** 27

---

9 Which shape is a hexagon?

A 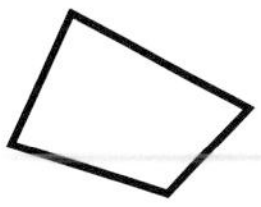

C 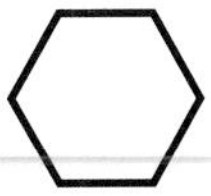

B 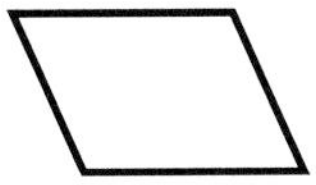

D 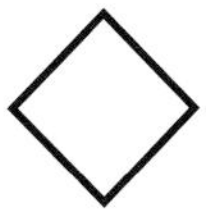

---

10 What number makes this number sentence true?

$3 + 8 + 9 = 8 + 9 +$ ■

F 3 **H** 9

G 8 **J** 20

Standards Review

Throughout the school year, you may be required to take several tests, and you may have many questions about them. Here are some answers to help you get ready.

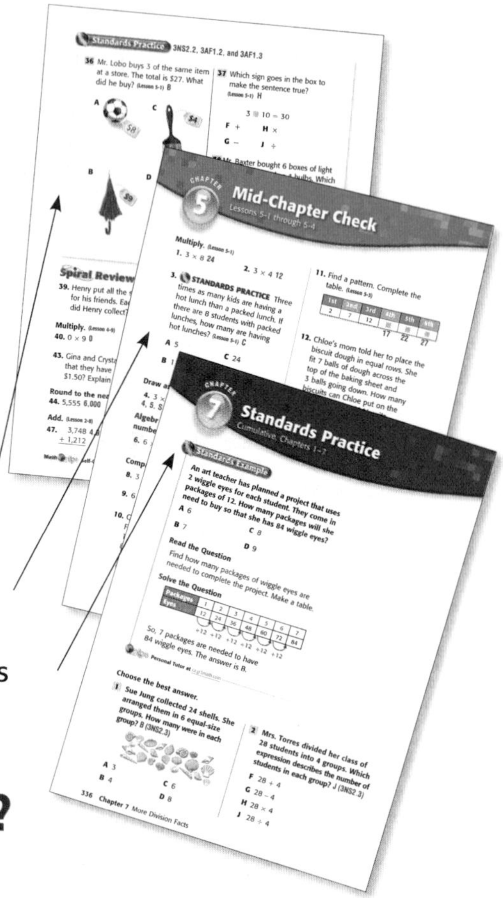

How Should I Study?

The good news is that you've been studying all along—a little bit every day. Here are some of the ways your textbook has been preparing you.

- **Every Day** Each lesson had practice questions that cover the California standards.
- **Every Week** The Mid-Chapter Check and Chapter Test had several practice questions.
- **Every Month** The California Standards Practice pages at the end of each chapter had even more questions similar to those on tests.

Are There Other Ways to Review?

Absolutely! The following pages contain even more practice for each California Standard.

Tips for Success CA1

Multiple-Choice Questions. CA2

Practice by Standard. CA4–CA33

Tips for SUCCESS

Before the Test

- Go to bed early the night before the test. You will think more clearly after a good night's rest.
- Become familiar with common measurement units and when they should be used.
- Think positively.

During the Test

- Read each problem carefully. Underline key words and think about different ways to solve the problem.
- Watch for key words like *not.* Also look for order words like *least, greatest, first,* and *last.*
- Answer questions you are sure about first. If you do not know the answer to a question, skip it and go back to that question later.
- Check your answer to make sure it is reasonable.
- Make sure that the number of the question on the answer sheet matches the number of the question on which you are working in your test booklet.

Whatever you do...

- Don't try to do it all in your head. If no figure is provided, draw one.
- Don't rush. Try to work at a steady pace.
- Don't give up. Some problems may seem hard to you, but you may be able to figure out what to do if you read each question carefully or try another strategy.

Multiple-Choice Questions

Incomplete shading
(A) (B) (C) (D)

Too light shading
(A) (B) (C) (D)

Correct shading
(A) (B) (C) (D)

In multiple-choice questions you are asked to choose the best answer from four possible answers.

To record a multiple-choice answer, you will be asked to shade in a bubble that is a circle. Always make sure that your shading is dark enough and completely covers the bubble.

Standards Example

1 The table shows the price of cheese per pound at a local farmers' market.

Amount (lb)	Price
1	$ 5
2	$10
3	$15

If the price increases at the same rate, how much would you pay for 5 pounds of cheese?

A $35 **B** $25 **C** $20 **D** $15

STRATEGY

Patterns Can you find a pattern to solve the problem?

Read the Problem Carefully You know the price of cheese per pound in dollars. Find how much you will pay if you buy 5 pounds of cheese.

Solve the Problem Look for a pattern. One pound of cheese costs $5. Two pounds cost $10. Three pounds cost $15. So, for each pound of cheese, the price increases by $5.

Extend the pattern to find the price of five pounds of cheese.

4 pounds ⟶ $15 + $5 or $20
5 pounds ⟶ $20 + $5 or $25

So, 5 pounds of cheese will cost $25.

The correct choice is B.

Standards Example

STRATEGY

Elimination Can you eliminate any of the choices?

2 The figure below represents the fraction $\frac{3}{10}$.

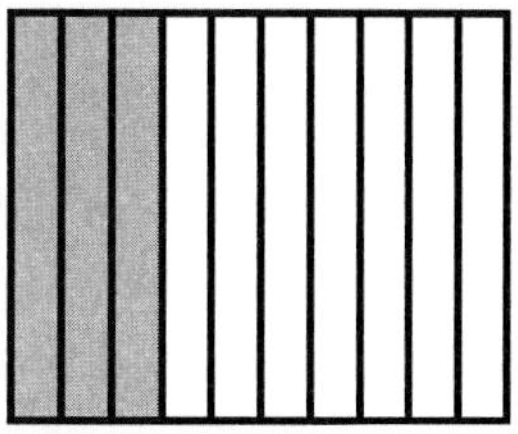

Which decimal is equal to $\frac{3}{10}$?

F 3.0 **G** 0.33 **H** 0.3 **J** 0.03

Read the Problem Carefully Find which decimal is equal to $\frac{3}{10}$.

Solve the Problem Since $\frac{3}{10}$ is less than one, 3.0 can be eliminated as one of the choices. Next, since $\frac{3}{10}$ is read *three-tenths*, you can eliminate 0.03, because it is read *three-hundredths*. Since 0.33 has a number in the hundredths place, it is not equal to $\frac{3}{10}$.

The correct choice is H.

Standards Example

3 Jeanette spent a total of $64 on four shirts. If each shirt was the same price, how much did she pay for each shirt?

A $12 **B** $16 **C** $60 **D** $256

Read the Problem Carefully You know the total cost and that each shirt costs the same. Find the cost of each shirt.

STRATEGY

Work Backward Can you work backward from the total to find the unit cost?

Solve the Problem Divide the total price by the number of items.

$64 \div 4 = 16$.
So, each shirt costs $16.

The correct choice is B.

Practice by Standard: Number Sense

Standard Set 1.0: Students understand the place value of whole numbers.

DIRECTIONS
Choose the best answer.

QUICK Practice	QUICK Review
1 How is five thousand forty-one written in standard form? **(3NS1.1)** **A** 5401 **B** 5410 **C** 5014 **D** 5041	**STRATEGY** Write the digits of the number in a place-value chart. How would you read each number in the answer choices? For more help with writing numbers in standard form, see page 25.
2 Which set of numbers is in order from least to greatest? **(3NS1.2)** **F** 211, 256, 308, 347 **G** 211, 308, 347, 256 **H** 308, 211, 347, 256 **J** 347, 308, 256, 211	**STRATEGY** Compare the digits in each place value to write the number from least to greatest. Which is the smallest number? Which is the greatest number? For more help with ordering whole numbers, see page 38.
3 Which number has a 5 in the hundreds place and a 1 in the ones place? **(3NS1.3)** **A** 1565 **B** 5516 **C** 5615 **D** 6551	**READING HINT** The *ones* place is the right most digit. The *hundreds* place is the third digit from the right. Find the number that has a 1 in the ones place and a 5 in the hundreds place. For more help with identifying place value, see page 24.

QUICK Practice

4 Gina has 329 stickers in her collection. Which of these is the same as 329? **(3NS1.5)**

F 300 + 200 + 90

G 300 + 20 + 9

H 3 + 20 + 900

J 3 + 2 + 9

QUICK Review

STRATEGY Write each number as the sum of the place value positions.

How many hundreds are there in 329? How many tens? How many ones?

For more help with writing numbers in expanded notation, see page 25.

5 The highest point in California is Mt. Whitney. It has an elevation of 4418 meters. What is this elevation rounded to the nearest hundred? **(3NS1.4)**

A 4000 **C** 4410

B 4400 **D** 4420

STRATEGY Think of the hundred that is closest to the number 4418.

What hundred is closest to 4418?

For more help with rounding whole numbers, see page 44.

6 Which digit is in the hundreds place in the number 8312? **(3NS1.3)**

F 1 **H** 3

G 2 **J** 8

READING HINT The *hundreds* digit is the third digit from the right.

The number has a ones, tens, hundreds, and thousands digit. Which is the hundreds digit?

For more help with identifying place value, see page 24.

7 How is three thousand one hundred ninety-five written in standard form? **(3NS1.1)**

A 3195 **C** 3109

B 3159 **D** 3105

STRATEGY Write the digits of the number in the appropriate places.

How would you read each number in the answer choices?

For more help with writing numbers in standard form, see page 25

Practice on Your Own

Standard Set 1.0

8 Which digit in 1594 is in the tens place? **(3NS1.3)**

F 1 **H** 5

G 4 **J** 9

9 The four high scores on a video game are shown in the table.

Video Game Scores
5679
5880
5103
5334

Which of the following shows the high scores in order from highest to lowest? **(3NS1.2)**

A 5103, 5334, 5679, 5880

B 5880, 5334, 5679, 5103

C 5880, 5679, 5334, 5103

D 5880, 5679, 5103, 5334

10 Which number has a 7 in the thousands place and a 3 in the tens place? **(3NS1.3)**

F 7335 **H** 7357

G 7353 **J** 7513

11 There are 528 students. Which of these is the same as 528? **(3NS1.5)**

A 500 + 200 + 80

B 500 + 20 + 8

C 5 + 20 + 800

D 5 + 2 + 8

12 Which digit is in the tens place in the number 3452? **(3NS1.3)**

F 2 **H** 4

G 3 **J** 5

13 What is 7139 rounded to the nearest thousand? **(3NS1.4)**

A 6000 **C** 8000

B 7000 **D** 9000

14 The boys basketball team scored a total of 745 points this season. Which of these is the same as 745? **(3NS1.5)**

F 700 + 400 + 50

G 7 + 40 + 500

H 700 + 40 + 5

J 7 + 4 + 5

15 How is nine thousand eighty-one written in standard form? **(3NS1.1)**

A 9081

B 9018

C 9801

D 9810

16 Which digit is in the hundreds place in the number 9781? **(3NS1.3)**

F 9 **H** 7

G 8 **J** 1

Practice by Standard: Number Sense

Standard Set 2.0: Students calculate and solve problems involving addition, subtraction, multiplication, and division.

DIRECTIONS
Choose the best answer.

QUICK Practice	QUICK Review
1 4000 − 1256 = **(3NS2.1)** **A** 2744 **B** 2734 **C** 2646 **D** 2644	**STRATEGY** Use borrowing to subtract the numbers. How can you regroup from larger place values to subtract the numbers? For more help with subtracting whole numbers, see page 135.
2 There are 8 teams in a volleyball tournament. Each team has 12 players. How many players are there altogether? **(3NS2.4)** **F** 4 **H** 84 **G** 20 **J** 96	**READING HINT** Read the problem carefully to see which operation is needed. What operation can be used to perform repeated addition? For more help with solving multiplication problems, see page 157.
3 Abe did this division problem. 420 ÷ 21 = 20 Which problem could he do to check his answer? **(3NS2.3)** **A** 21 + 20 = ■ **B** 21 − 20 = ■ **C** 21 × 20 = ■ **D** 21 ÷ 20 = ■	**STRATEGY** What operation can be used to "undo" division? Division and ________ are inverse operations. For more help with using inverse relationships, see page 258.

QUICK Practice

4 At a teacher conference, 228 teachers were divided evenly into groups of 6. How many groups of teachers were there? **(3NS2.5)**

F 38 **H** 116
G 42 **J** 222

5 What number can be multiplied by 8012 to give the answer 8012? **(3NS2.6)**

A 0 **C** 2
B 1 **D** 10

6 Mrs. Chan bought 5 picture frames. All of the picture frames were the same price. The total cost was $80. How much money did each picture frame cost? **(3NS2.7)**

F $400 **H** $16
G $18 **J** $12

7 Which number is 83 more than 3268? **(3NS2.1)**

A 3351 **C** 3471
B 3466 **D** 3586

QUICK Review

READING HINT Read the problem carefully to see which operation is needed.

Divide the number of teachers by the size of each group to find the total number of groups.

For more help with solving division problems, see page 642.

STRATEGY Use the properties of 0 and 1 to solve the problem.

What is the result when you multiply a number by 1?

For more help with using the properties of 0 and 1, see page 186.

READING HINT Read the problem carefully to see which operation is needed.

This problem can be solved by dividing $80 by 5.

For more help with determining unit cost, see page 650.

STRATEGY Use addition to find the number.

What is the result when you add 8 to 3268?

For more help with finding the sum of two whole numbers, see page 92.

Practice on Your Own

Standard Set 2.0

8 7 × 9 = **(3NS2.2)**

F 56 **H** 61

G 59 **J** 63

9 Look at the number sentence below.

28 + ■ = 61

Which number will make the number sentence true? **(3NS2.1)**

A 23 **C** 31

B 27 **D** 33

10 The figure below is a model for the multiplication sentence.

5 × 9 = 45

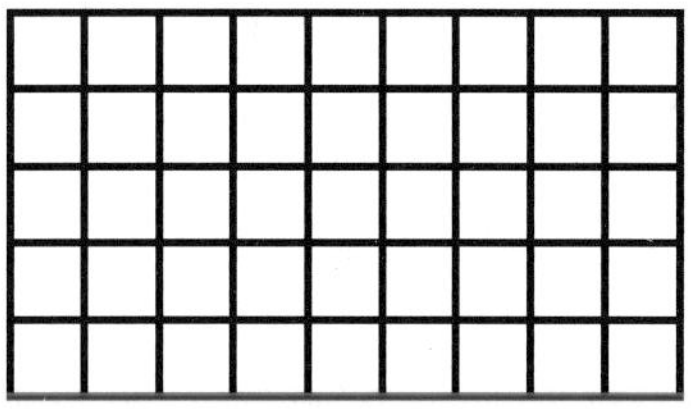

Which division sentence is modeled by the figure? **(3NS2.3)**

F 36 ÷ 4 = 9 **H** 42 ÷ 7 = 6

G 45 ÷ 5 = 9 **J** 45 ÷ 9 = 4

11 What number can be added to 456 to give the answer 456? **(3NS2.6)**

A 0 **C** 10

B 1 **D** 456

12 On Thursday, 325 people visited the park. Four times as many people visited on Friday than on Thursday. How many people visited the park on Friday? **(3NS2.4)**

F 1200

G 1250

H 1300

J 1325

13 The third graders went on a field trip in 4 vans. Each van held 14 students. How many students went on the field trip? **(3NS2.4)**

A 56 **C** 48

B 52 **D** 44

14 Roberto had \$20. He paid \$5 for admission to the carnival. While there, he bought \$6 worth of ride tickets. How much money did Roberto have left for food? **(3NS2.8)**

F \$8 **H** \$10

G \$9 **J** \$11

15 Mikayla did this subtraction problem.

1856 − 1524 = 332

Which problem could she do to check her answer? **(3NS2.3)**

A 332 + 1524 = ■

B 1524 − 332 = ■

C 332 × 1524 = ■

D 1524 ÷ 332 = ■

Practice by Standard: Number Sense

Standard Set 3.0: Students understand the relationship between whole numbers, simple fractions, and decimals.

DIRECTIONS
Choose the best answer.

QUICK Practice

1 The rectangle shows $\frac{1}{5}$ shaded.

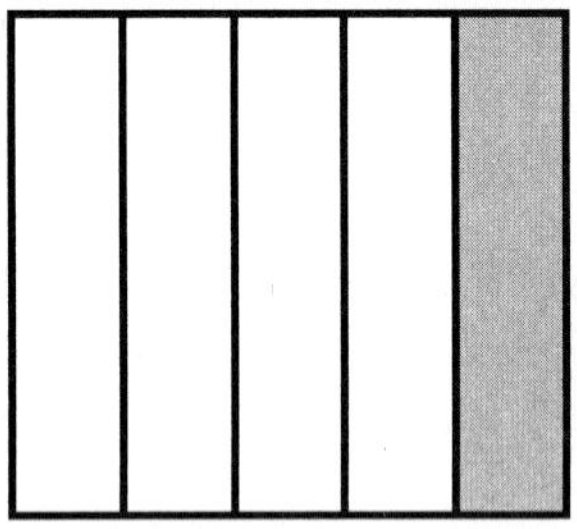

Which shaded part of a rectangle below is equal to $\frac{1}{5}$? **(3NS3.1)**

A  $= \frac{2}{8}$

B 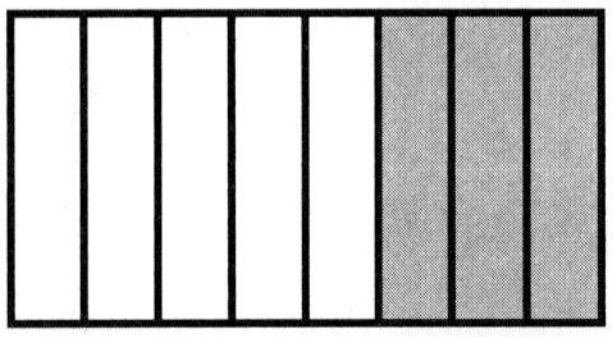 $= \frac{3}{8}$

C 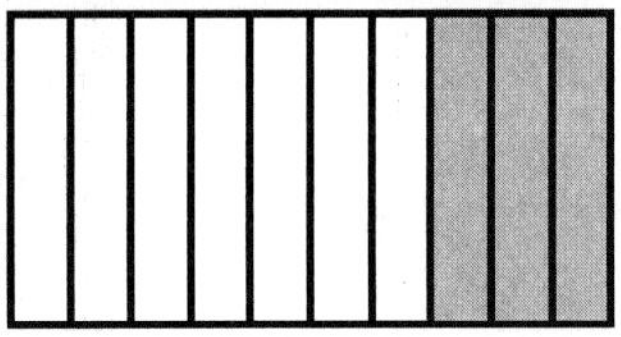 $= \frac{3}{10}$

D 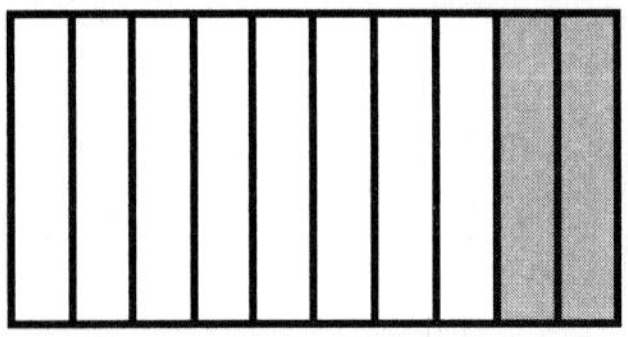 $= \frac{2}{10}$

QUICK Review

STRATEGY Find a fraction that is equivalent to one-fifth.

Which fraction names the same part of a whole as $\frac{1}{5}$?

$\frac{1}{5}$ ← numerator / ← denominator

For more help with equivalent fractions, see page 516.

QUICK Practice

QUICK Review

2 $\frac{1}{6} + \frac{4}{6} =$ **(3NS3.2)**

F $\frac{5}{6}$

G $\frac{2}{3}$

H $\frac{1}{2}$

J $\frac{5}{12}$

STRATEGY To add fractions with the same denominator, add the numerators and keep the old denominator.

Sketch a rectangle and divide it into 6 equal parts. Shade 1 part. Then shade 4 more parts. How much of the rectangle is shaded?

For more help with adding fractions, see page 528.

3 Jenny has $20 to buy a CD that costs $12.38. How much change should she receive? **(3NS3.3)**

A $8.62

B $8.52

C $7.62

D $7.52

READING HINT The amount of change received back is the difference between the starting amount and the cost of the item.

Write $20 as $20.00. Then use regrouping to find $20.00 – $12.38.

For more help with subtracting money amounts, see page 114.

4 Ravi shaded $\frac{3}{10}$ of the figure.

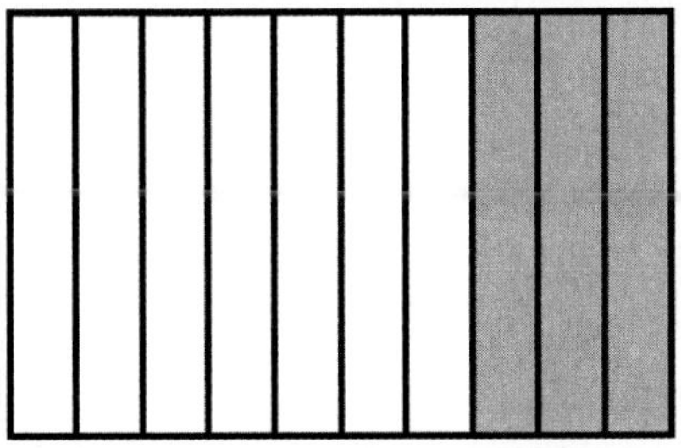

Which decimal equals $\frac{3}{10}$? **(3NS3.4)**

F 0.31

G 0.30

H 0.10

J 0.03

STRATEGY Find the decimal that is equivalent to $\frac{3}{10}$.

How would you read the fraction $\frac{3}{10}$? Which decimal reads the same way?

For more help with understanding the equivalence between fractions and decimals, see page 553.

Practice on Your Own

Standard Set 3.0

5 A pizza was divided into eighths. Marco ate $\frac{2}{8}$ of the pizza. Peggy ate $\frac{2}{8}$ of the pizza. Derek ate $\frac{3}{8}$ of the pizza. How much of the pizza was left? **(3NS3.2)**

A $\frac{1}{8}$ **C** $\frac{3}{8}$

B $\frac{2}{8}$ **D** $\frac{4}{8}$

6 Dina compared the prices of two book bags. The table below shows the prices.

Cost of Book Bags	
Brand	**Cost**
A	$14.73
B	$12.96

How much more does Brand A cost than Brand B? **(3NS3.3)**

F $1.67

G $1.73

H $1.77

J $1.83

7 $\frac{2}{8} + \frac{5}{8} = \square$ **(3NS3.2)**

A $\frac{3}{16}$ **C** $\frac{7}{16}$

B $\frac{3}{8}$ **D** $\frac{7}{8}$

8 Juan bought the three items listed in the table below.

Item	Cost
Swim Goggles	$8.75
Raft	$5.60
Beach Ball	$3.29

What was the total cost of these three items? **(3NS3.3)**

F $17.64

G $16.82

H $14.35

J $14.11

9 $\frac{2}{8} + \frac{3}{8} = \square$ **(3NS3.2)**

A $\frac{1}{8}$ **C** $\frac{4}{8}$

B $\frac{3}{8}$ **D** $\frac{5}{8}$

10 Raven has $10 to buy lunch. Her lunch total comes to $6.53. How much change should she receive? **(3NS3.3)**

F $3.37

G $3.47

H $4.37

J $4.47

11 Which decimal equals $\frac{7}{10}$? **(3NS3.4)**

A 0.07

B 0.17

C 0.7

D 0.710

Practice by Standard: Algebra and Functions

Standard Set 1.0: Students select appropriate symbols, operations, and properties to represent, describe, simplify, and solve simple number relationships.

DIRECTIONS
Choose the best answer.

QUICK Practice	QUICK Review
1 Nia bought 48 apples packed equally into 6 bags. Which number sentence shows how to find the number of apples in each bag? **(3AF1.1)** **A** $48 \times 6 = ■$ **C** $48 - 6 = ■$ **B** $48 \div 6 = ■$ **D** $48 + 6 = ■$	**READING HINT** Read the problem statement carefully to see which operation is needed to solve it. You know the total number of apples and the number of bags. Which operation will tell you how many apples are in each bag? For more help with modeling situations with number sentences, see page 320.
2 Which number makes this number sentence true? **(3AF1.2)** $7 + 5 = ■ \times 3$ **F** 1 **H** 3 **G** 2 **J** 4	**STRATEGY** Find the value of each side of the equals sign. Substitute each answer choice into the box. Then, multiply to see if the product is the same as 7 + 5. For more help with solving number sentences, see page 138.
3 Which symbol goes in the box to make the number sentence true? **(3AF1.3)** $12 ■ 5 = 60$ **A** + **C** × **B** − **D** ÷	**STRATEGY** Ue what you know about operational symbols. Substitute each symbol into the box. Then, check to see if a true number sentence is formed. For more help with selecting appropriate symbols, see page 320.

QUICK Practice	QUICK Review
4 Which of the following is used to find the number of feet in 7 yards? **(3AF1.4)** **F** $7 - 3$ **G** $7 + 3$ **H** 7×3 **J** $7 \div 3$	**READING HINT** There are 3 feet in 1 yard. Multiply the number of yards by the number of feet per yard to find the total number of feet. For more help with expressing simple unit conversions, see page 346.
5 If $9 \times 15 \times 6 = 810$, then what is $15 \times 6 \times 9$? **(3AF1.5)** **A** 135 **B** 340 **C** 770 **D** 810	**STRATEGY** Use the Commutative Property of Multiplication. If you change the order that numbers are multiplied, is there any change to the product? For more help with using the Commutative Property of Multiplication, see page 160.
6 Which value makes this number sentence true? **(3AF1.2)** $8 \times 9 < \blacksquare \times 4$ **F** 19 **G** 18 **H** 17 **J** 16	**STRATEGY** Use properties to help you multiply each number by 4. Then compare to 8×9. $19 \times 4 = (10 + 9) \times 4$ $18 \times 4 = (10 + 8) \times 4$ $17 \times 4 = (10 + 7) \times 4$ $16 \times 4 = (10 + 6) \times 4$ For more help with multiplication properties, see page 594.

Practice on Your Own

7 The choir is set up in 3 rows with 12 singers in each row. Which number sentence shows how to find the total number of singers in the choir? **(3AF1.1)**

A $12 \times 3 = \square$

B $12 \div 3 = \square$

C $12 - 3 = \square$

D $12 + 3 = \square$

8 Which of the following is used to find out how many inches there are in 8 feet? **(3AF1.4)**

F $12 - 8$

G $12 + 8$

H $12 \div 8$

J 12×8

9 Which sign goes in the box to make the number sentence true? **(3AF1.3)**

$$49 \;\square\; 7 = 7$$

A $+$

B $-$

C $\times$

D $\div$

10 There are 15 students in Robbie's gym class. Suppose 2 students move away. Which number sentence could be used to represent how many students will be left? **(3AF1.1)**

F $15 + 2 = \square$

G $15 \times 2 = \square$

H $15 - 2 = \square$

J $15 \div 2 = \square$

11 If $4 \times (3 \times 12) = 144$, then what is $(4 \times 3) \times 12$? **(3AF1.5)**

A 12

B 96

C 144

D 168

12 There are nine more people than 83 in the cafeteria right now. Which number sentence could be used to represent the number of people in the cafeteria? **(3AF1.1)**

F $83 + 9$

G $83 - 9$

H 83×9

J $83 \div 9$

13 Which sign goes in the box to make the number sentence true? **(3AF1.3)**

$$88 \;\square\; 11 = 99$$

A $+$

B $-$

C $\times$

D $\div$

14 There are 27 third graders and 24 fourth graders on the playground. Which number sentence shows how to find how many more third graders there are? **(3AF1.1)**

F $27 \times 24 = \square$

G $27 \div 24 = \square$

H $27 - 24 = \square$

J $27 + 24 = \square$

Practice by Standard: Algebra and Functions

Standard Set 2.0: Students represent simple functional relationships.

DIRECTIONS
Choose the best answer.

QUICK Practice

1 At the school bookstore, each notebook costs $0.59. Two notebooks cost $1.18 and three cost $1.77. If the price of each notebook remains the same, how much would 4 notebooks cost? **(3AF2.1)**

A $2.25 **C** $2.36

B $2.31 **D** $2.48

2 The table shows the number of crayons given to students in an art class.

Crayons	
Students	**Crayons**
1	8
2	16
3	24

Each student gets the same number of crayons. How many crayons are needed for 5 students? **(3AF2.2)**

F 32 **H** 44

G 40 **J** 48

QUICK Review

STRATEGY Add the cost of 1 notebook to the given cost of 3 notebooks to find the cost of 4 notebooks.

You can solve this problem by finding the sum of $1.77 and $0.59.

For more help with solving problems involving functional relationships, see page 234.

STRATEGY Look for a pattern in the table. Then extend the pattern.

How many crayons are needed for each student? How many crayons would be needed for 5 students?

For more help with recognizing and extending patterns, see page 234.

QUICK Practice

3 If cashews cost $3.79 per pound, how much would 3 pounds of cashews cost? **(3AF2.1)**

A $9.42 **C** $10.96
B $10.35 **D** $11.37

QUICK Review

STRATEGY Multiply the cost of 1 pound of cashews by 3 to find the cost of 3 pounds.

You can solve this problem by finding the product of $3.79 and 3.

For more help with solving problems involving functional relationships, see page 234.

4 The table shows the number of computers needed for the students in a computer class.

Computer Class	
Students	**Computers**
2	1
4	2
6	3

If there are the same number of students at each computer, how many computers will be needed for a class of 12 students? **(3AF2.2)**

F 5 **H** 8
G 6 **J** 10

STRATEGY Look for a pattern in the table. Then extend the pattern.

How many students are seated at each computer? How many computers would be needed for 12 students?

For more help with recognizing patterns, see page 212. For more help with extending linear patterns, see page 234.

5 If a taxi charges $0.65 per mile, how much would a 5-mile taxi ride cost? **(3AF2.1)**

A $2.75
B $3.25
C $4.15
D $5.65

STRATEGY Use multiplication to find the total cost.

You can solve this problem by finding the product of $0.65 and 5.

For more help with solving problems involving functional relationships, see page 234.

Practice on Your Own

Standard Set 2.0

6 At the school cafeteria, one carton of milk costs $0.45. Two cartons of milk cost $0.90. Three cartons of milk cost $1.35. If the price of each carton remains the same, how much would 6 cartons of milk cost? **(3AF2.1)**

F $2.55

G $2.70

H $2.85

J $2.90

7 If pears cost $0.85 per pound at a farmer's market, how much would 4 pounds of pears cost? **(3AF2.1)**

A $3.25

B $3.40

C $3.80

D $3.95

8 The table shows the number of ride tickets needed for students at a carnival.

Ride Tickets	
Number of Students	**Number of Tickets**
1	10
2	20
3	30

If each student gets the same number of ride tickets, how many tickets are needed for 8 students? **(3AF2.2)**

F 60

G 70

H 80

J 90

9 If an electrician charges $35 per hour to work on your home, how much would a 3-hour job cost? **(3AF2.1)**

A $70

B $85

C $100

D $105

10 Ana collects stickers in a book. The table shows the total number of stickers on different numbers of pages.

Sticker Collection	
Pages	**Stickers**
1	15
2	30
3	45

If each page has the same number of stickers, how many stickers are there total on 8 pages? **(3AF2.2)**

F 120

G 135

H 150

J 180

11 Nate's heart beats 75 times each minute. How many times will his heart beat in 7 minutes? **(3AF2.1)**

A 475

B 515

C 525

D 595

Practice by Standard: Measurement and Geometry

Standard Set 1.0: Students choose and use appropriate units and measurement tools to quantify the properties of objects.

DIRECTIONS
Choose the best answer.

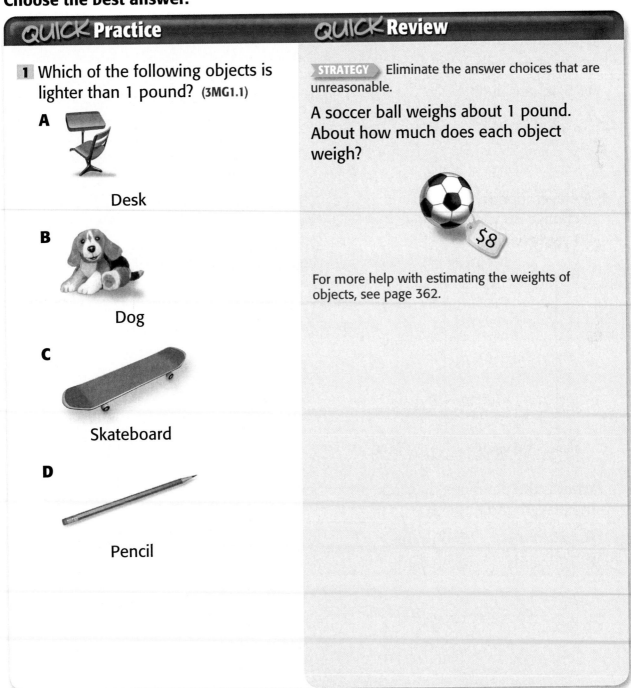

QUICK Practice

1 Which of the following objects is lighter than 1 pound? **(3MG1.1)**

A

Desk

B

Dog

C

Skateboard

D

Pencil

QUICK Review

STRATEGY Eliminate the answer choices that are unreasonable.

A soccer ball weighs about 1 pound. About how much does each object weigh?

For more help with estimating the weights of objects, see page 362.

QUICK Practice

2 What is the area of this figure? (3MG1.2)

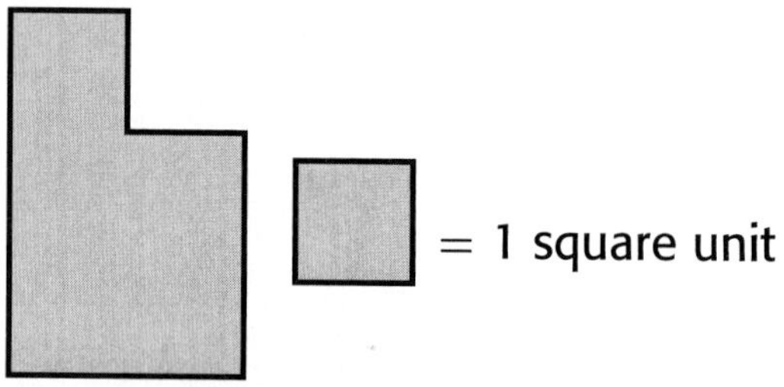

F 3 square units
G 4 square units
H 5 square units
J 6 square units

QUICK Review

READING HINT The *area* of a figure is the amount of space that it covers.

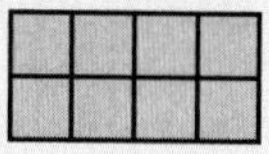

How many square units would it take to completely cover the figure?

For more help with finding the area of a figure, see page 428.

3 A playground is shaped like a rectangle 30 yards long and 20 yards wide.

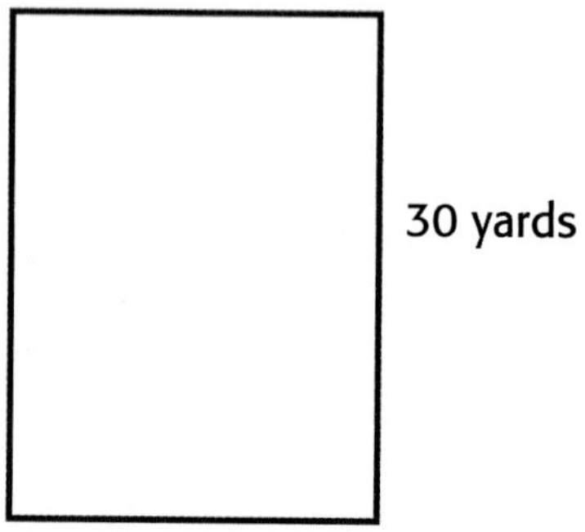

What is the perimeter, in yards, of the playground? (3MG1.3)

A 120 yards **C** 60 yards
B 100 yards **D** 50 yards

READING HINT The *perimeter* is the distance around the outside of a figure.

What are the lengths of the 4 sides? What is the sum of these lengths?

For more help with finding the perimeter of a figure, see page 422.

Practice on Your Own

Standard Set 1.0

4 What is the perimeter of the figure? **(3MG1.3)**

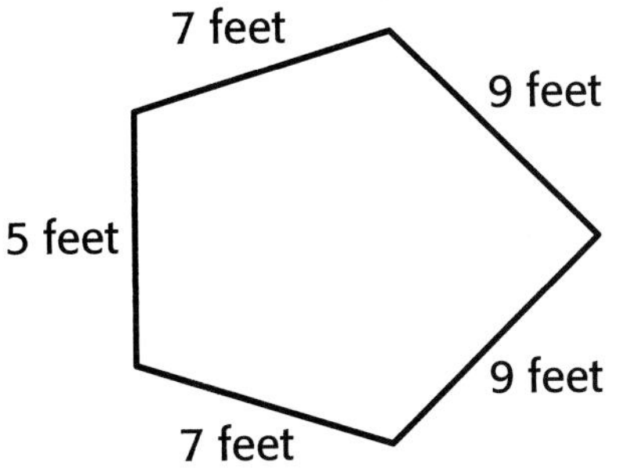

F 37 feet

G 39 feet

H 43 feet

J 47 feet

5 There are 60 minutes in each hour. How many minutes are there in a 7-hour school day? **(3MG1.4)**

A 360 minutes

B 380 minutes

C 420 minutes

D 440 minutes

6 The square below has 3-centimeter sides. What is the area of the square? **(3MG1.2)**

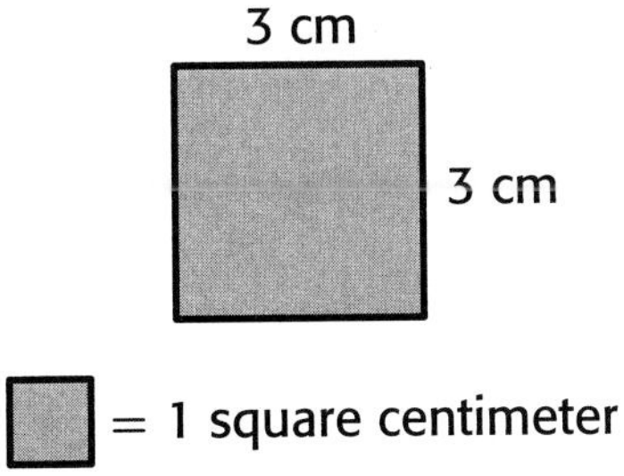

F 3 square centimeters

G 6 square centimeters

H 7 square centimeters

J 9 square centimeters

7 What is the volume of the figure below? **(3MG1.2)**

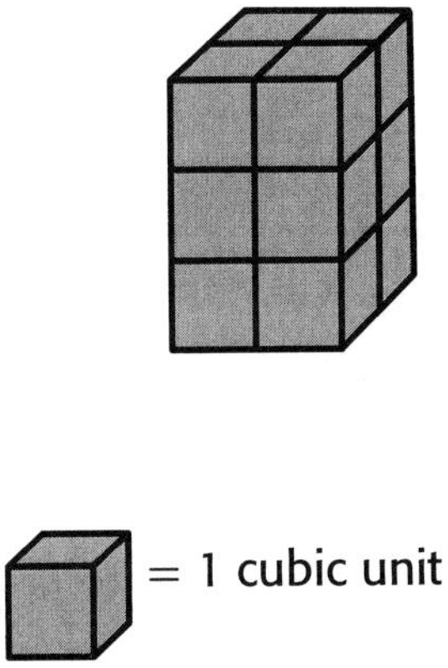

A 6 cubic units

B 8 cubic units

C 10 cubic units

D 12 cubic units

8 Edgar's backyard has the size and shape shown below. It is shaped like a rectangle.

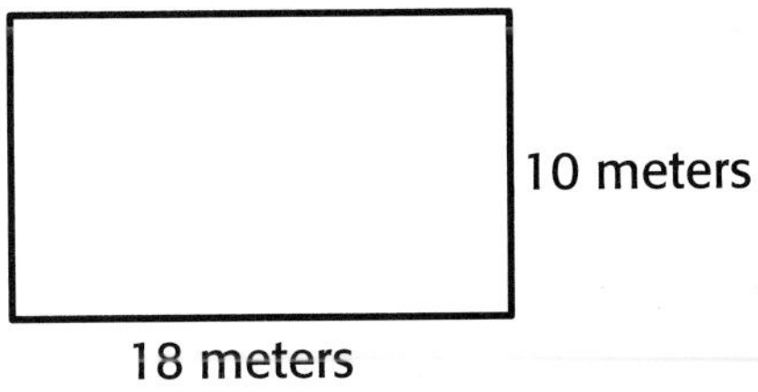

Edgar wants to place fencing around the perimeter of the yard. How much fencing is needed? **(3MG1.3)**

F 28 meters

G 56 meters

H 72 meters

J 80 meters

Practice by Standard: Measurement and Geometry

Standard Set 2.0: Students describe and compare the attributes of plane and solid geometric figures and use their understanding to show relationships and solve problems.

DIRECTIONS
Choose the best answer.

QUICK Practice

1 Which of these is a pentagon?
(3MG2.1)

A

C

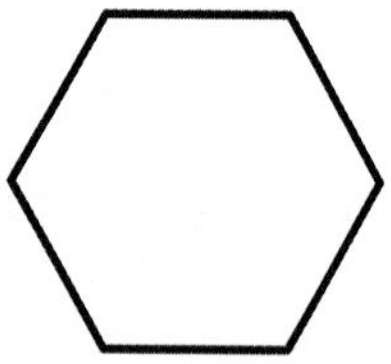

B

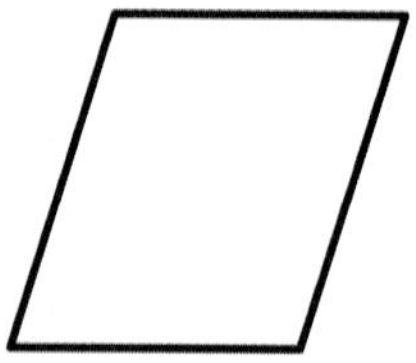

D

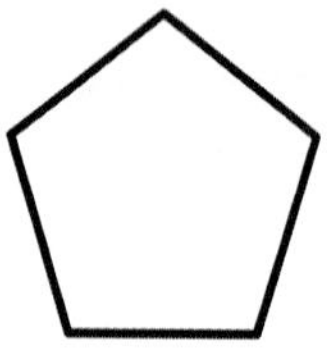

QUICK Review

READING HINT A pentagon is a figure with 5 sides?

Which figure has 5 sides?

For more help with identifying polygons, see page 419.

2 An equilateral triangle MUST have
(3MG2.2)

F no sides that are the same length.

G 2 sides that are the same length.

H 3 sides that are the same length.

J 4 sides that are the same length.

STRATEGY Eliminate answer choices that are unreasonable.

How would you describe the sides of an equilateral triangle? Which answer choice matches this description?

For more help with identifying the attributes of triangles, see page 434.

QUICK Practice

3 How many equal sides are there in a square? **(3MG2.3)**

A 4

B 3

C 2

D none

QUICK Review

STRATEGY Eliminate choices first that you know are not correct.

Draw a square on your paper. How many equal sides does it have?

For more help with identifying the attributes of quadrilaterals, see page 438.

4 Which object is shaped like a cone? **(3MG2.5)**

F

H

G

J

STRATEGY Eliminate answer choices that are not shaped like a cone.

What does a cone look like? Which object is shaped like this?

For more help with identifying three-dimensional figures, see page 444.

5 How many equal sides must a triangle have to be isosceles? **(3MG2.2)**

A none

B 1

C 2

D 3

STRATEGY Eliminate answer choices that do not match the definition of an isosceles triangle.

How would you describe the sides of an isosceles triangle? Which answer choice matches this description?

For more help with identifying the attributes of triangles, see page 434.

Practice on Your Own

Standard Set 2.0

6 Look at the angles in the figure below.

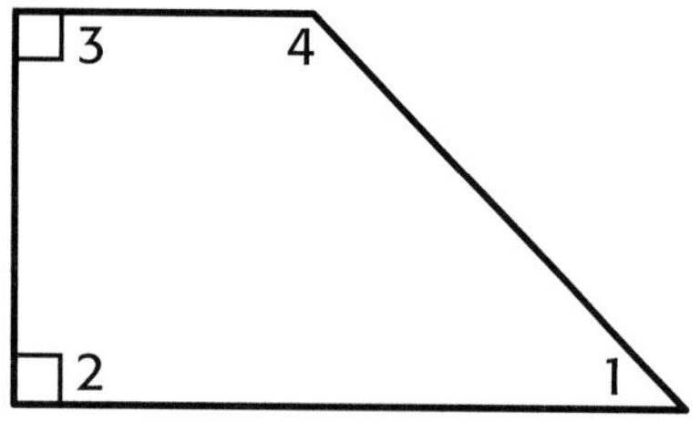

Which angle has a measure that is greater than the measure of a right angle? **(3MG2.4)**

F angle 1   **H** angle 3

G angle 2   **J** angle 4

7 Which shapes make up this solid object? **(3MG2.6)**

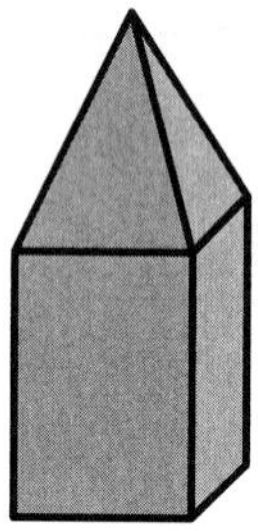

A prism and cone

B prism and pyramid

C pyramid and cone

D prism and cube

8 A rectangle MUST have **(3MG2.3)**

F five sides.

G four equal sides.

H three equal sides.

J four right angles.

9 One side of a parallelogram is 15 inches long. Another side of the parallelogram is 10 inches long. What are the lengths of the other two sides of the parallelogram? **(3MG2.3)**

A 10 inches and 15 inches

B 10 inches and 10 inches

C 15 inches and 15 inches

D 11 inches and 13 inches

10 Which of these is an octagon? **(3MG2.1)**

F

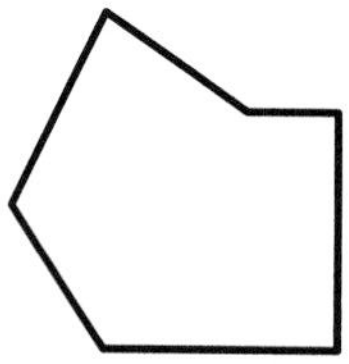

H

G

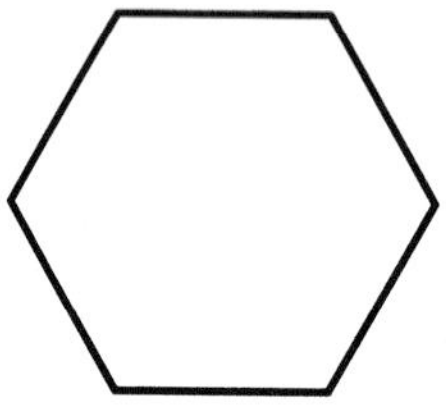

J

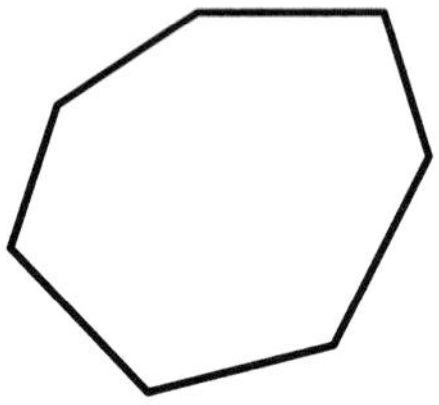

11 How many right angles does a right triangle have? **(3MG2.2)**

A 0   **C** 2

B 1   **D** 3

12 A hexagon has how many sides? **(3MG2.1)**

F four

G five

H six

J eight

Practice by Standard: Statistics, Data Analysis, and Probability

Standard Set 1.0: Students conduct simple probability experiments by determining the number of possible outcomes and make simple predictions.

DIRECTIONS
Choose the best answer.

QUICK Practice

1 Missy rolled a number cube 12 times and recorded the results. The cube landed on an odd number 5 times, an even number 7 times, and a number greater than two 8 times. Which tally chart shows these results?
(3SDAP1.2)

A

Roll Results	
Odd Number	𝍸 ||
Even Number	𝍸
Greater than 2	𝍸 |||

B

Roll Results	
Odd Number	𝍸
Even Number	𝍸 ||
Greater than 2	𝍸 |||

C

Roll Results	
Odd Number	𝍸 |
Even Number	𝍸 |
Greater than 2	𝍸 ||

D

Roll Results	
Odd Number	||||
Even Number	𝍸 |
Greater than 2	𝍸 |||

QUICK Review

STRATEGY Eliminate answer choices that do not show the correct tallies.

Which chart has 5 tally marks for an odd number, 7 tally marks for an even number, and 8 tally marks for a number greater than two?

For more help with recording the outcomes of an experiment systematically, see page 473.

QUICK Practice

2 Andy has 1 penny, 3 nickels, 5 dimes, and 4 quarters. He closes his eyes and picks one coin without looking. Is it certain, likely, unlikely, or impossible that he will pick a penny? **(3SDAP1.1)**

F certain **H** unlikely
G likely **J** impossible

QUICK Review

READING HINT An event is *certain* if it will always happen and *impossible* if it will never happen. Otherwise it is either *likely* or *unlikely*.

How many coins are in the piggy bank? How many of them are pennies? How many of them are not pennies?

For more help with determining the likelihood of an event, see page 484.

3 Rex spun a spinner 9 times. It landed on red 3 times, green twice, and blue 4 times. Which bar graph shows these results? **(3SDAP1.3)**

A

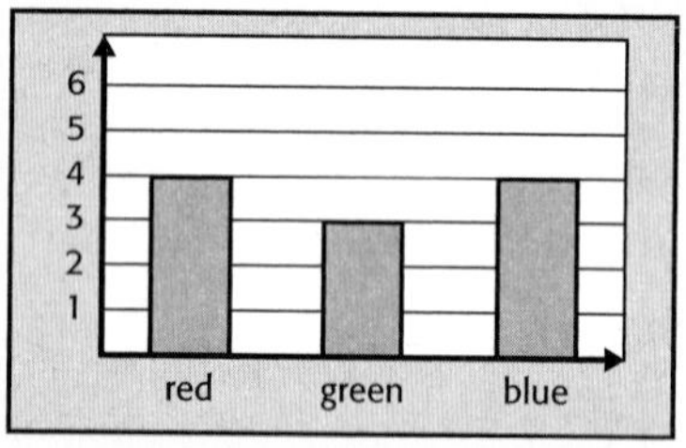

B

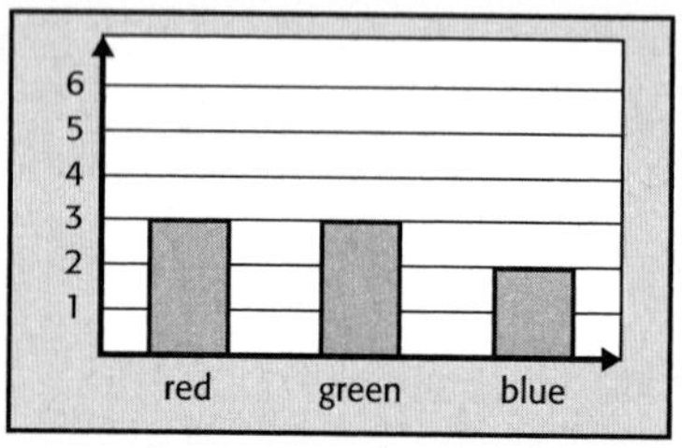

C

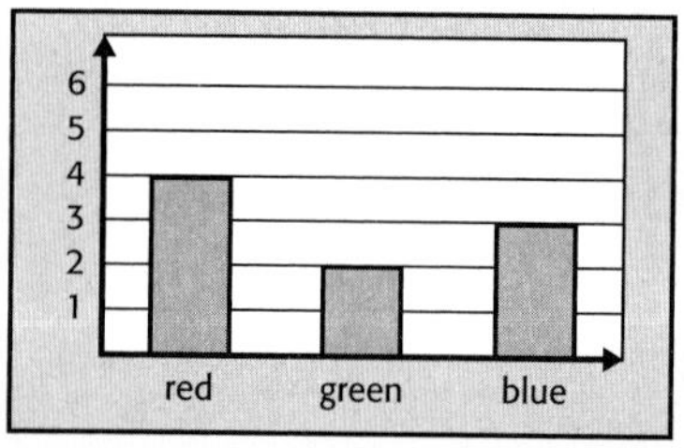

D

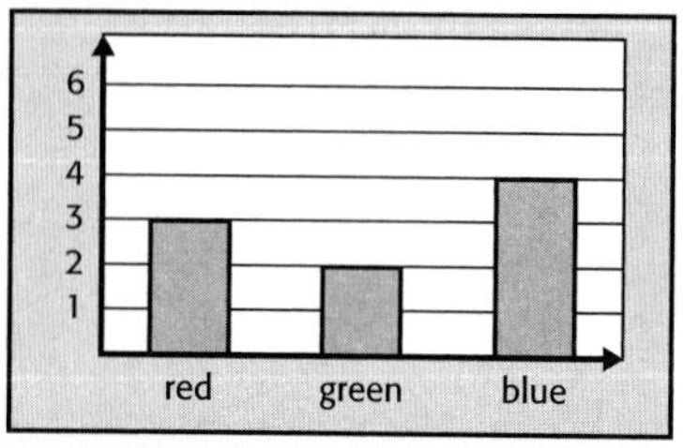

STRATEGY Eliminate answer choices that do not show the correct number for each spin.

Which bar graph shows the correct number of spins for each color?

Recall that there are many ways to display data.

<table>
<tr><th colspan="2">Color Spin</th></tr>
<tr><th>Color</th><th>Tally</th></tr>
<tr><td>Red</td><td>|||</td></tr>
<tr><td>Green</td><td>||</td></tr>
<tr><td>Blue</td><td>||||</td></tr>
</table>

For more help with displaying the results of an experiment, see page 492.

Practice on Your Own

Standard Set 1.0

4 The tally chart shows the weights of the fish that Josie caught on a week-long fishing trip.

Weight (lb)	Tally
1	||
2	𝍸
3	||||
4	||
5	|

Which graph shows these results? **(3SDAP1.3)**

F

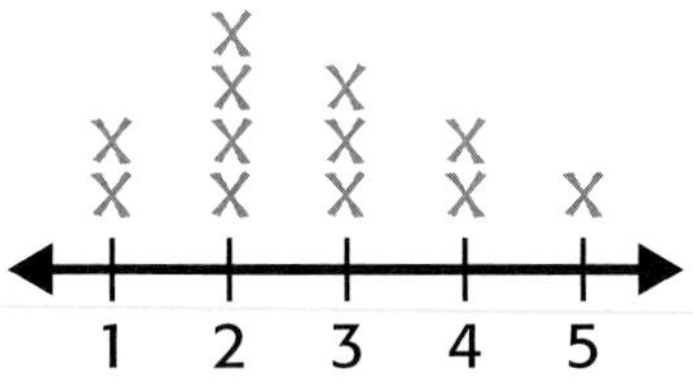

G

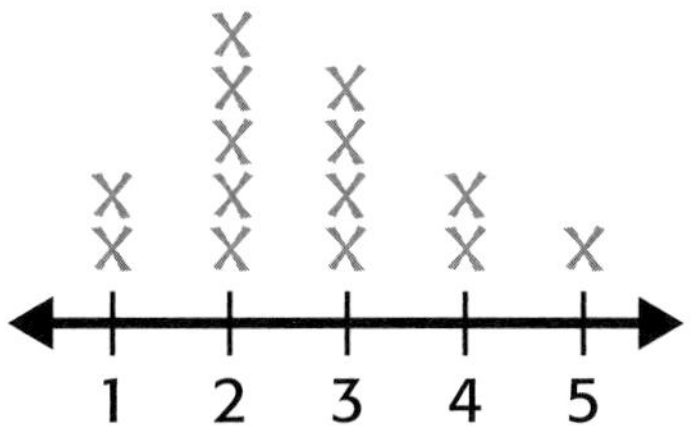

H

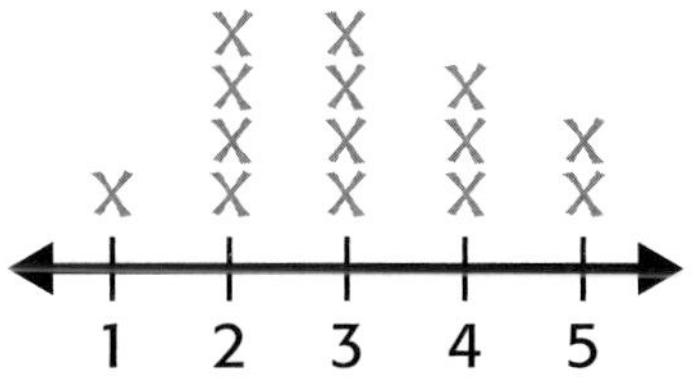

J

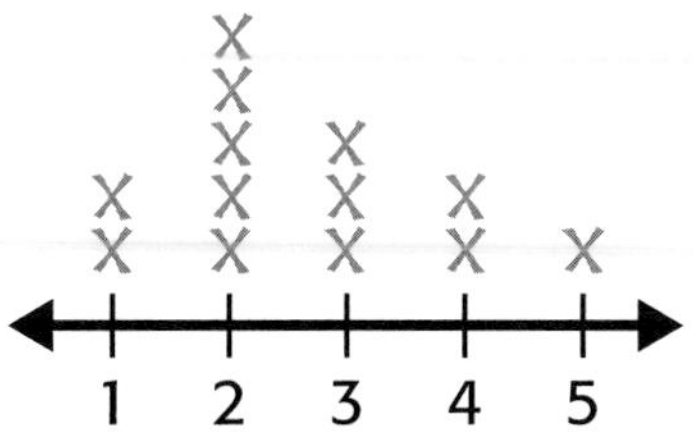

5 At a carnival game, there are 20 rubber ducks floating on the water. On the bottom of 15 of the ducks, there is a black dot. On the other 5 ducks there is no dot. Players pick a duck and win a prize if it has a dot on the bottom. Is it certain, likely, unlikely, or impossible that a player will win a prize? **(3SDAP1.1)**

A certain
B likely
C unlikely
D impossible

6 To play a math game, players take turns selecting a chip from a bag. They note the color and return the chip to the bag. The tally chart shows how many times each color has been selected after 30 turns.

Color	Tally
Black	𝍸 |||
White	𝍸
Purple	||||
Green	|||

Which color chip will the next player most likely select? **(3SDAP1.4)**

F black
G white
H purple
J green

7 Refer to the tally chart in Exercise 6. Is it certain, likely, unlikely, or impossible that the next player will select an orange chip? **(3SDAP1.4)**

A certain
B likely
C unlikely
D impossible

Practice by Standard: Mathematical Reasoning

Standard Set 1.0: Students make decisions about how to approach problems.

DIRECTIONS
Choose the best answer.

QUICK Practice

1 During the first four days of vacation, Carlo found 3, 5, 7, and 9 seashells. Suppose this pattern continues. How many seashells will he find on the fifth day? **(3MR1.1)**

A 9 **C** 11
B 10 **D** 13

QUICK Review

STRATEGY Look for a pattern in the problem statement. Set up a table.

How many more shells does Carlo find each day?

For more help with observing and extending patterns, see page 17.

QUICK Practice

2 Mira is creating a picture frame with a 10-inch by 12-inch board. The perimeter is 44 inches. She wants to cut out a 2-inch square 2 inches long from each corner. What will the new perimeter be? **(3MR1.2)**

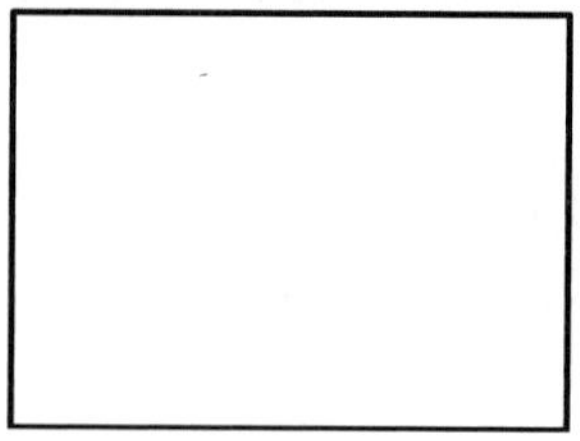

$P = 44$ inches

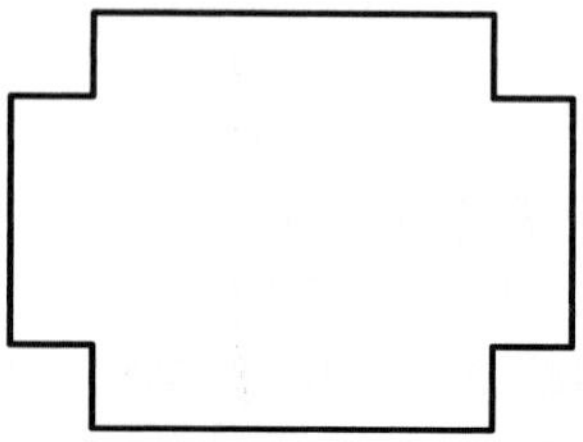

$P = ?$

F 48 inches **H** 40 inches
G 44 inches **J** 32 inches

QUICK Review

STRATEGY Break the problem into simpler parts. What happens in each corner of the frame?

How is the perimeter changed when one corner is removed? How will it change when all four corners are removed?

For more help with breaking a problem into simpler parts, see page 432.

Practice on Your Own

Standard Set 1.0

3 At the bookstore at Josey's school, one folder costs $0.20. Two folders cost $0.40. Three folders cost $0.60. Josey wants to buy 10 folders. If the price of each folder remains the same, how much would 10 folders cost? **(3MR1.1)**

A $2.00

B $2.10

C $2.20

D $2.40

4 Reggie collects baseball cards. He keeps them in a binder. The table shows the total number of cards for different numbers of pages.

Baseball Card Collection

Pages	Cards
1	12
2	24
3	36
4	48
5	60
6	?
7	84
8	96
9	108

If each page has the same number of baseball cards, how many cards total are there on 6 pages? **(3MR1.1)**

F 64

G 68

H 70

J 72

5 What is the area of the figure below? **(3MR1.2)**

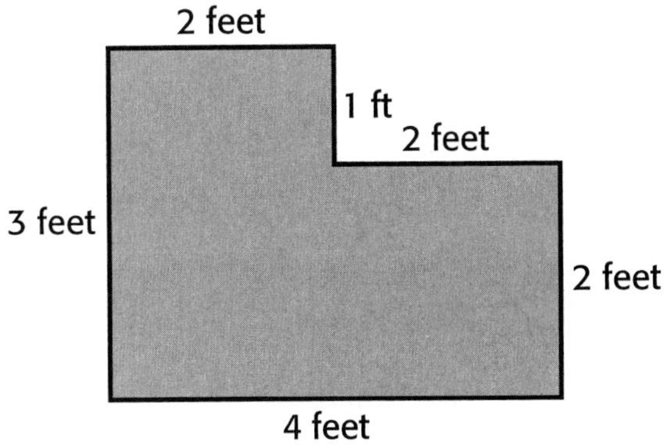

= 1 square foot

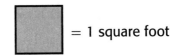

A 8 square feet

B 10 square feet

C 11 square feet

D 12 square feet

6 Elio bought 6 packages of hot dog buns for a party. There are 8 buns in each package. They sell for $1.59 per package. How much did Elio spend on hot dog buns? **(3MR1.1)**

F $12.72

G $10.56

H $9.54

J $9.28

7 A gift shop sells one candle for $4, two candles for $8, and three candles for $12. Danielle wants to buy nine candles. If the price of each candle remains the same, how much would nine candles cost? **(3MR1.1)**

A $16

B $32

C $36

D $40

Practice by Standard: Mathematical Reasoning

Standard Set 2.0: Students use strategies, skills, and concepts in finding solutions.

DIRECTIONS
Choose the best answer.

QUICK Practice

1 The table shows the number of fans at the Badgers' first four soccer games. Estimate the total number of people for these four games. **(3MR2.1)**

Badgers Soccer	
Game	**People**
1	79
2	83
3	82
4	78

A 250 **C** 300
B 280 **D** 320

2 To ride a roller coaster, you must be at least 48 inches tall. Which of the following shows the heights of people who cannot ride the roller coaster? **(3MR2.3)**

F height = 48
G height + 1 = 48
H height > 48
J height < 48

QUICK Review

STRATEGY Use rounding to estimate the solution.

Each number is close to 80. You can estimate the total number of people by finding 4 × 80.

For more help with estimating solutions, see page 70.

READING HINT The phrase *at least* means greater than or equal to.

Can you ride the roller coaster if you are 48 inches tall? Can you ride the roller coaster if you are taller than 48 inches?

For more help with using numbers and symbols to represent mathematical reasoning, see pages 138 and 320.

Practice on Your Own

Standard Set 2.0

3 The sum of the angles of a triangle is 180°. Look at the triangle below. What is the measure of the missing angle? **(3MR2.6)**

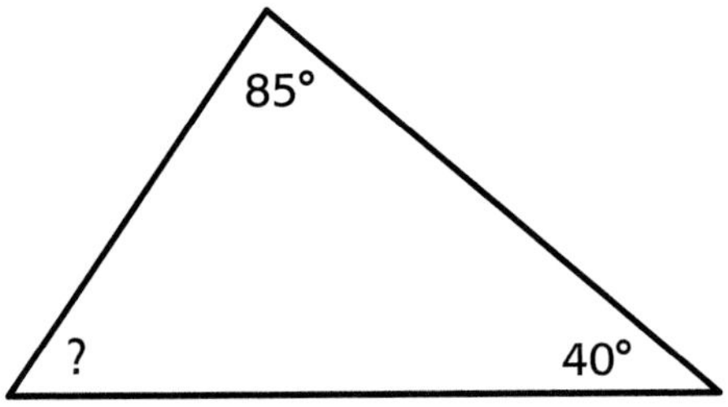

A 45°

B 55°

C 65°

D 75°

4 Melisa estimates how far a wheel will roll in one turn by multiplying the diameter of the wheel by 3. About how far would a 20-inch bicycle wheel in one turn? **(3MR2.2)**

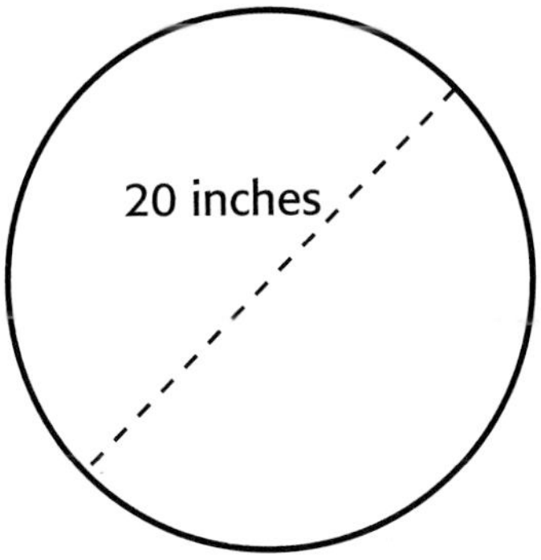

F 20 inches

G 40 inches

H 60 inches

J 80 inches

5 The third graders are raising money for a charity. The table shows how much has been raised during the first 4 months.

Fundraiser	
Month	**Money Raised**
1	$322
2	$409
3	$353
4	$328

How much money has been raised so far? Round your answer to the nearest $10. **(3MR2.5)**

A $1380

B $1400

C $1410

D $1450

6 There are 140 students in 5 classrooms. Each room has the same number of students in it. How could you find how many students are in each classroom? **(3MR2.4)**

F Add 5 to 140.

G Subtract 5 from 140.

H Multiply 140 by 5.

J Divide 140 by 5.

7 Gerald has four bags of bagels. Each bag has 16 bagels. How could you find the total number of bagels in the four bags? **(3MR2.4)**

A Add 4 and 16.

B Subtract 4 from 16.

C Multiply 4 by 16.

J Divide 16 by 4.

California Standards Review

Practice by Standard: Mathematical Reasoning

Standard Set 3.0: Students move beyond a particular problem by generalizing to other situations.

DIRECTIONS
Choose the best answer.

QUICK Practice

1 The table shows how many players and winners there were at a carnival game the first 3 days.

Dart Game	
Players	**Winners**
80	20
60	15
100	■
120	30

Suppose there were 100 players. How many winners can you expect? **(3MR3.1)**

A 15 **C** 25
B 20 **D** 30

QUICK Review

STRATEGY Look for a common fraction of winners to players during the first 3 days. Then choose the most reasonable answer.

What fraction of the players were winners during each of the first 3 days? What would be an equivalent fraction of 100 players?

For more help with evaluating the reasonableness of a solution, see page 120.

QUICK Practice

2 Irena wrote the following pattern.

1 1 1
1 2 2 1
1 3 3 3 1
1 4 4 4 4 1

What is the next line in the pattern? **(3MR3.2)**

F 1 5 5 1 **H** 1 5 5 5 5 1
G 1 5 5 5 1 **J** 1 5 5 5 5 5 1

QUICK Review

STRATEGY Look for a pattern and predict the next number.

What happens to the numbers between the first and last digits?

For more help with extending patterns, see page 212.

Practice on Your Own

Standard Set 3.0

3 Leo uses the method shown below to find the areas of squares with different side lengths.

Side Length (units)	Method	Area (square units)
1	1 × 1	1
2	2 × 2	4
3	3 × 3	9
4	4 × 4	16
5	5 × 5	25
6	6 × 6	36

What is the area of the square shown below? **(3MR3.2)**

12 meters

12 meters

A 156 square meters

B 144 square meters

C 132 square meters

D 96 square meters

4 Refer to Exercise 3. How could you use Leo's method to find the area of a square with a side length of 15 inches? **(3MR3.2)**

F Find 15 + 15.

G Find 15 − 140.

H Find 15 × 15.

J Find 15 ÷ 15.

5 The table shows how many days it has rained over the past 4 months.

Month	Rainy Days
April	13
May	12
June	10
July	9

Which is the most reasonable number of rainy days to expect for the month of August? **(3MR3.1)**

A 15

B 13

C 8

D 5

6 Tasha has kept track of the amount of savings over the last few months.

Tasha's Savings	
Months	**Total Savings**
1	$35
2	$70
3	$105
4	$140

Suppose Tasha continues to save the same amount each month. How much will she have saved after 7 months? **(3MR3.3)**

F $245

G $254

H $280

J $315

Looking Ahead

to the Grade 4 Standards

Let's Look Ahead!

1 Algebra: Function Tables (+, −) 664
2 Algebra: Function Tables (×, ÷) 668
3 Ordered Pairs 672
4 Geometry: Congruent Figures 676
5 Geometry: Symmetry 678

Looking Ahead 1

Algebra: Function Tables (+, −)

MAIN IDEA

I will use addition and subtraction to complete function tables.

Preparation for Standard 4AF1.5 Understand that an equation such a y = 3x + 5 is a prescription for determining a second number when a first number is given.

New Vocabulary

function

variable

GET READY to Learn

The table shows the amount of money four children each have saved. If each child receives $5 to add to their savings, how much money will each child have?

Savings Accounts	
Name	**Amount ($)**
Lorena	25
Nina	23
Shelly	22
Trey	21

The amount each child will have depends on the amount they each will receive. A relationship where one quantity depends upon another quantity is a **function**.

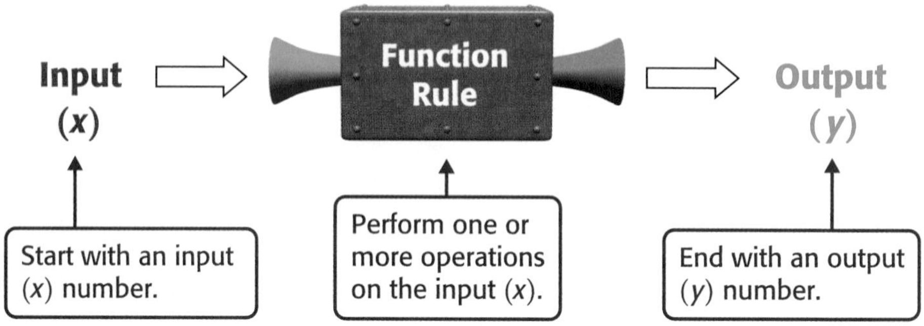

Input
(x)
Function Rule
Output
(y)
Start with an input (x) number.
Perform one or more operations on the input (x).
End with an output (y) number.

A letter such as *x* or *y* that represents an unknown number is called a **variable**. The input number (*x*), output number (*y*), and function rule can be shown in a table.

Real-World EXAMPLE

1 **MONEY Make a function table to find how much money each child will have in savings after receiving $5.**

Rule: Add $5.		
Input (*x*)	***x* + $5**	**Output (*y*)**
$25	$25 + $5	$30
$23	$23 + $5	$28
$22	$22 + $5	$27
$21	$21 + $5	$26

EXAMPLE Complete a Function Table (+)

2 **Use the rule to complete the function table.**

The input numbers are 2, 3, 4, and 5.

The rule is $x + 3$ or add 3.

Rule: $x + 3$	
Input (x)	**Output (y)**
2	■
3	■
4	■
5	■

Start with each input (x) number. Apply the rule to find the output (y) number.

Rule: $x + 3$		
Input (x)	**$x + 3$**	**Output (y)**
2	$2 + 3$	5
3	$3 + 3$	6
4	$4 + 3$	7
5	$5 + 3$	8

Remember

To check your answer, reverse the operation of your function and see if it works out.

$5 - 3 = 2$
$6 - 3 = 3$
$7 - 3 = 4$
$8 - 3 = 5$

You can use subtraction to complete a function table.

EXAMPLE Complete a Function Table (–)

3 **Use the rule to complete the function table.**

The input numbers are 20, 21, 22, and 23.

The rule is $x - 2$ or subtract 2.

Rule: $x - 2$	
Input (x)	**Output (y)**
20	■
21	■
22	■
23	■

Start with each input (x) number. Apply the rule to find the output (y) number.

Rule: $x - 2$		
Input (x)	**$x - 2$**	**Output (y)**
20	$20 - 2$	18
21	$21 - 2$	19
22	$22 - 2$	20
23	$23 - 2$	21

CHECK What You Know

Copy and complete each function table. See Examples 1–3 (pp. 664–665)

1.

Rule: $x + 4$	
Input (x)	Output (y)
1	■
2	■
3	■
4	■

2.

Rule: $x - 7$	
Input (x)	Output (y)
15	■
14	■
13	■
12	■

For Exercises 3 and 4, use the following information.

Alicia is four years older than her pet turtle.

3. Make a function table to find how old Alicia will be when her pet turtle is 3, 4, 5, and 6 years old.

4. Write the function rule.

5. Talk About It How do function tables show patterns?

Practice and Problem Solving

Copy and complete each function table. See Examples 1–3 (pp. 664–665)

6.

Rule: $x + 2$	
Input (x)	Output (y)
3	■
4	■
5	■
6	■

7.

Rule: $x + 6$	
Input (x)	Output (y)
1	■
3	■
5	■
7	■

8.

Rule: $x - 9$	
Input (x)	Output (y)
17	■
18	■
19	■
20	■

9.

Rule: $x - 4$	
Input (x)	Output (y)
15	■
12	■
9	■
6	■

Find the rule for each function table.

10.

Rule: ■	
Input (x)	Output (y)
2	7
4	9
6	11
8	13

11.

Rule: ■	
Input (x)	Output (y)
44	33
33	22
22	11
11	0

Make a function table for each situation. Write the function rule.

12. Pasqual and his friends will each get $7 for allowance. How much money will each child have if they already have $1, $2, $3, and $4?

13. A store orders 3 more boxes of strawberries than oranges. How many boxes of oranges will the store order if they order 8, 9, 10, and 11 boxes of strawberries?

14. Caroline is reading a book that has 122 pages. If she reads 25 pages every day, how many pages will she have left to read after 1, 2, 3, and 4 days?

15. Every week, Mr. Montoya pays $3 to send a package. He began with $30. How much money will he have after 4 weeks?

H.O.T. Problems

16. OPEN ENDED Make a function table for the rule add 5.

17. FIND THE ERROR Dai and Lonzo are making a function table for $y = x + 9$. Who is correct? Explain your reasoning.

Dai

x	7	5	6
y	16	13	15

Lonzo

x	8	10	15
y	17	19	24

18. WRITING IN ▶MATH Write a real-world problem that would result in the function table to the right. What is the function rule?

Rule: ■			
Input (x)	250	251	252
Output (y)	260	261	262

Algebra: Function Tables (×, ÷)

Looking Ahead 2

GET READY to Learn

Christine's neighbor owns a farm. On the farm, one of the pigs is 5 feet long. Christine made a table to convert 5 feet to inches. What pattern do you see in the input and output numbers?

Change Feet to Inches	
Feet Input (x)	Inches Output (y)
1	12
2	24
3	36
4	48
5	■

MAIN IDEA

I will use multiplication and division to complete function tables.

Preparation for Grade 4 Standard AF1.5 Understand that an equation such as $y = 3x + 5$ is a prescription for determining a second number when a first number is given.

Function rules can also involve multiplication or division.

EXAMPLE

1 MEASUREMENT **Make a function table to find the length of the pig if it is 5 feet long.**

There are 12 inches in one foot. To find the output values (y), multiply each input value (x) by 12.

Change Feet to Inches		
Input (x)	Rule: $x \times 12$	Output (y)
1	1×12	12
2	2×12	24
3	3×12	36
4	4×12	48
5	5×12	60

There are 60 inches in 5 feet. So the length of the pig in inches is 60 inches.

Multiplication can be used to complete function tables.

EXAMPLE Complete a Function Table (×)

2 Use the rule to complete the function table.

Rule: $x \times 4$	
Input (x)	Output (y)
1	■
2	■
3	■
4	■

The input numbers are 1, 2, 3, and 4.

The rule is $x \times 4$ or multiply by 4.

Start with each input (x) number. Apply the rule to find the output (y) number.

Rule: $x \times 4$		
Input (x)	$x \times 4$	Output (y)
1	1×4	4
2	2×4	8
3	3×4	12
4	4×4	16

Remember

x is the input number and y is the output number.

Division can also be used to complete function tables.

EXAMPLE Complete a Function Table (÷)

3 Use the rule to complete the function table.

Rule: $x \div 3$	
Input (x)	Output (y)
27	■
24	■
21	■
18	■

The input numbers are 27, 24, 21, and 18.

The rule is $x \div 3$ or divide by 3.

Start with each input (x) number. Apply the rule to find the output (y) number.

Rule: $x \div 3$		
Input (x)	$x \div 3$	Output (y)
27	$27 \div 3$	9
24	$24 \div 3$	8
21	$21 \div 3$	7
18	$18 \div 3$	6

CHECK What You Know

Copy and complete each function table. See Examples 1–3 (pp. 668–669)

1.

Rule: $x \times 3$	
Input (x)	Output (y)
5	■
6	■
7	■
8	■

2.

Rule: $x \div 2$	
Input (x)	Output (y)
8	■
10	■
12	■
14	■

3. A butterfly has 2 wings. Make a function table to show the total number of wings for 4, 5, 6, and 7 butterflies.

4. Talk About It Can you look only at the input numbers in a function table to determine the function rule? Explain.

Practice and Problem Solving

Copy and complete each function table. See Examples 1–3 (pp. 668–669)

5.

Rule: $x \div 5$	
Input (x)	Output (y)
10	■
50	■
70	■
100	■

6.

Rule: $x \times 6$	
Input (x)	Output (y)
5	■
6	■
7	■
8	■

7.

Rule: $x \times 8$	
Input (x)	Output (y)
2	■
4	■
6	■
8	■

8.

Rule: $x \div 9$	
Input (x)	Output (y)
18	■
27	■
36	■
45	■

Make a function table for each situation. Write the rule.

9. The price for admission to a zoo is \$7. How many tickets can you buy for \$63, \$56, \$49, and \$42?

10. Each box holds 12 water bottles. How many boxes are there if there are 60, 48, 36, or 24 bottles?

11. Rama bought 6 bags of chips. He spent \$12. How many bags of chips would he have bought if he spent \$14, \$16, \$18, and \$20?

12. Dorian and her friends went to the movies. Each ticket cost \$5. How much would they spend if there were 2, 3, 4, or 5 friends?

Find the rule for each function table.

13.

Rule: ■	
Input (x)	Output (y)
27	9
21	7
15	5
9	3

14.

Rule: ■	
Input (x)	Output (y)
72	12
54	9
36	6
18	3

15.

Rule: ■	
Input (x)	Output (y)
12	24
13	26
14	28
15	30

16.

Rule: ■	
Input (x)	Output (y)
6	24
7	28
8	32
9	36

H.O.T. Problems

17. OPEN ENDED Name two pairs of input and output values for the function rule $2x = y$.

18. CHALLENGE Look at the function table shown. What is the function rule?

Input (x)	15	25	40	50
Output (y)	4	6	9	11

19. NUMBER SENSE In the function rule $x + 3$, the output value is 8. How can you determine the value of x?

20. WRITING IN ►MATH Write a real-world math problem where using a function table for multiplication or division will help you solve the problem.

Ordered Pairs

Looking Ahead 3

MAIN IDEA

I will read and locate points on a grid.

Preparation for Grade 4 Standard MG2.1 Draw the points corresponding to linear relationships on graph paper.

New Vocabulary

coordinate grid
ordered pair

GET READY to Learn

A map of a zoo is shown. From the entrance, the zebras are located 2 units right and 6 units up. This can be written as (2, 6). Where are the giraffes located?

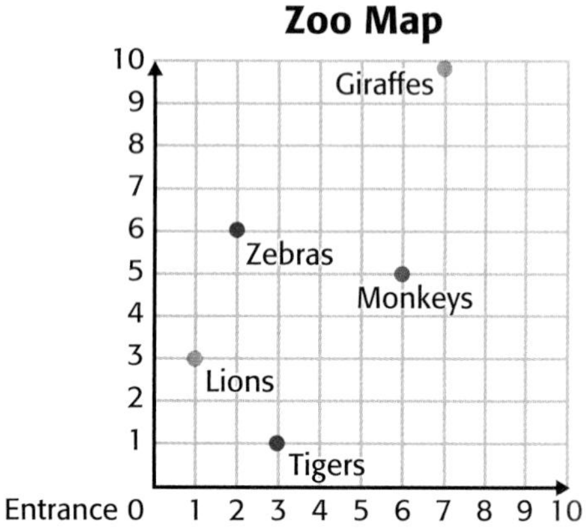

The map is an example of a **coordinate grid**. An **ordered pair** like (2, 6) names a location on the grid.

Real-World EXAMPLE **Write an Ordered Pair**

1 MAPS **Write the ordered pair for the location of the giraffes.**

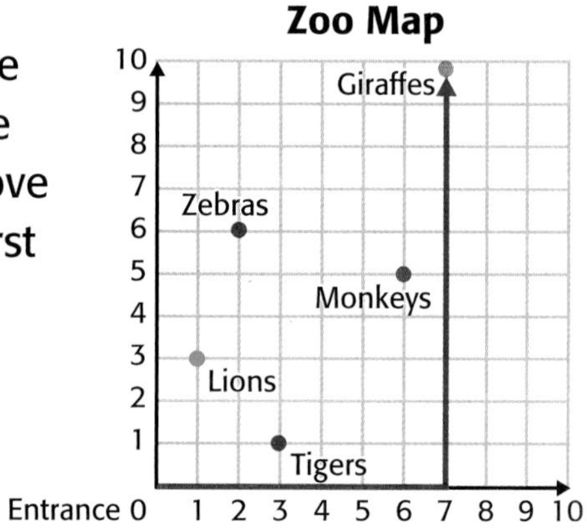

Step 1 Start at (0, 0). Move right 7 spaces since the giraffes are above the 7. This is the first number of the ordered pair.

Step 2 Move up until you reach the giraffes. The second number in the ordered pair is 10.

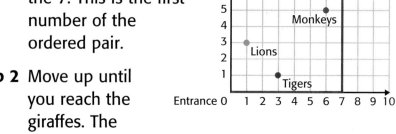

So, the ordered pair is (7, 10).

Real-World EXAMPLE **Locate a Coordinate**

2 **SCHOOL A map of Mrs. Jamison's classroom is shown. What is located at (7, 3)?**

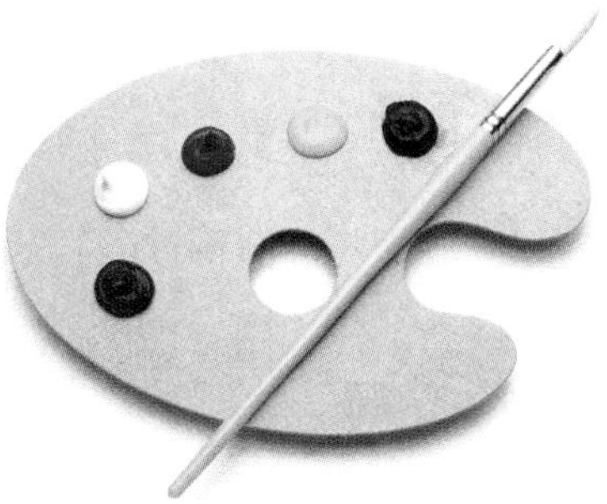

Mrs. Jamison's Classroom

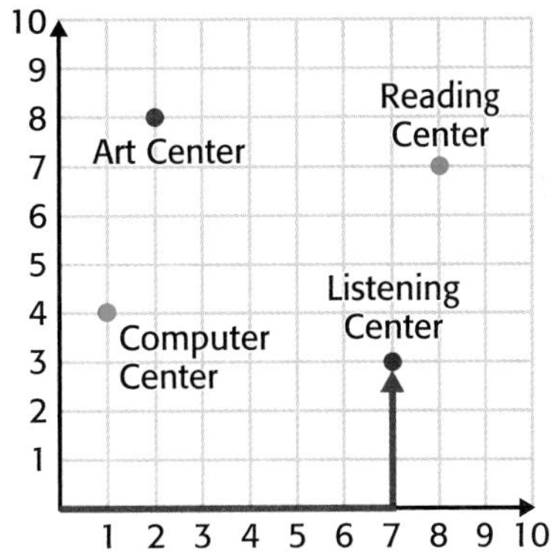

Start at (0, 0). Move 7 spaces to the right. Then, move 3 spaces up. The Art Center is at (7, 3).

Real-World EXAMPLE **Draw Points**

Remember

The first number tells you how many spaces to move right. The second number tells you how many spaces to move up.

3 **ALGEBRA Elki spends \$2 each day on lunch. The function table shows how much he spends after 1, 2, 3, and 4 days. Graph the ordered pairs (*x*, *y*) on a coordinate grid.**

Rule: $x \times 2$		
Input (*x*)	Output (*y*)	(*x*, *y*)
1	2	(1, 2)
2	4	(2, 4)
3	6	(3, 6)
4	8	(4, 8)

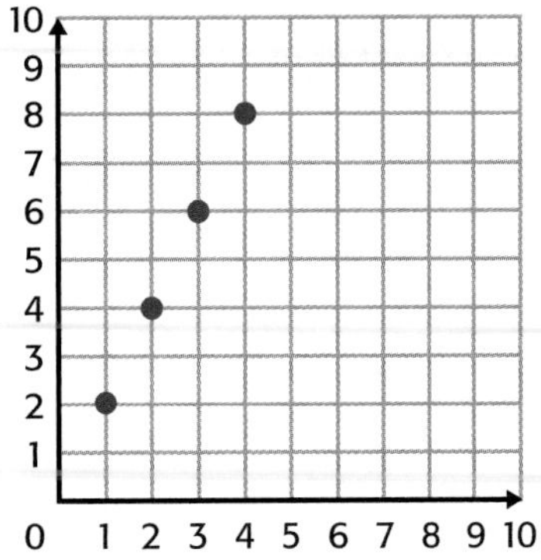

CHECK What You Know

Write the ordered pair for the location of each item on the coordinate grid. See Example 1 (p. 672)

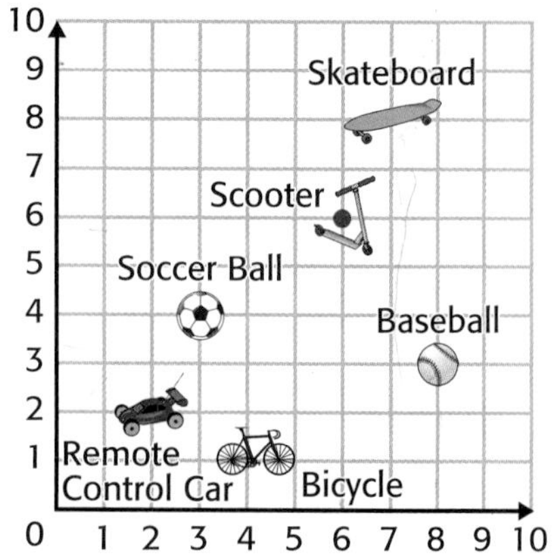

1. soccer ball

2. skateboard

3. baseball

4. scooter

Name the toy at each location. See Example 2 (p. 673)

5. (4, 1)

6. (6, 6)

7. (2, 2)

8. (8, 3)

Algebra Copy and complete each function table. Then graph the points. See Example 3 (p. 673)

9.

Rule: $x + 1$		
Input (x)	Output (y)	(x, y)
3	4	(3, 4)
4	5	(4, 5)
5	6	(5, 6)
6		(6,)

10.

Rule: $x \div 2$		
Input (x)	Output (y)	(x, y)
2	1	(2, 1)
4	2	(4, 2)
6	3	(6, 3)
8		(8,)

11. Refer to the grid in Exercises 1–8. If each grid line shows 5 feet, how far is the game from the scooter?

12. Talk About It Explain how to locate (0, 2) on a grid.

Practice and Problem Solving

Write the ordered pair for the location of each item on the coordinate grid. See Example 1 (p. 672)

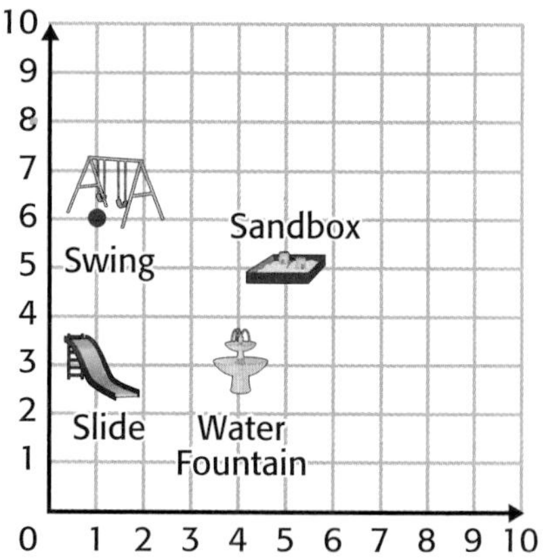

13. swing

14. slide

15. water fountain

16. sandbox

Name the place at each location.

See Example 2 (p. 673)

17. (1, 3) **18.** (4, 1)

19. (5, 5) **20.** (3, 1)

21. (4, 3) **22.** (2, 4)

Grocery Store

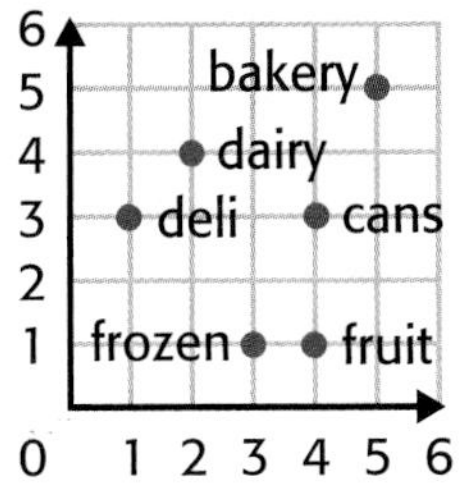

Algebra Copy and complete each function table. Then graph the points. See Example 3 (p. 673)

23.

Rule: $x + 3$		
Input (x)	Output (y)	(x, y)
2	5	(2, 5)
3	6	(3, 6)
4	7	(4, 7)
5	■	(5, ■)

24.

Rule: $x - 4$		
Input (x)	Output (y)	(x, y)
10	6	(10, 6)
8	4	(8, 4)
6	2	(6, 2)
4	■	(4, ■)

25.

Rule: $x \times 3$		
Input (x)	Output (y)	(x, y)
0	0	(0, 0)
1	3	(1, 3)
2	6	(2, 6)
3	■	(3, ■)

26.

Rule: $x \div 1$		
Input (x)	Output (y)	(x, y)
8	8	(8, 8)
6	6	(6, 6)
4	4	(4, 4)
2	■	(2, ■)

H.O.T. Problems

27. FIND THE ERROR Keith and Suzanne are describing the location of (2, 3). Who is correct? Explain.

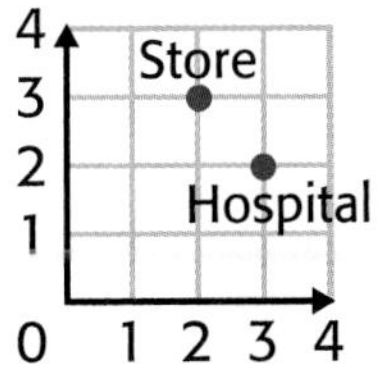

28. WRITING IN ►MATH Does the ordered pair (1, 3) give the same location as (3, 1)? Explain.

Geometry: Congruent Figures

GET READY to Learn

The surfaces of the two soccer balls are made up of hexagons and pentagons. What do you notice about the hexagons?

MAIN IDEA

I will identify congruent figures.

Preparation for Grade 4 MG3.3 Identify congruent figures.

New Vocabulary

congruent

Figures that have the same size and same shape are **congruent**.

EXAMPLES Identify Congruent Figures

Tell whether the figures in each pair are congruent.

1

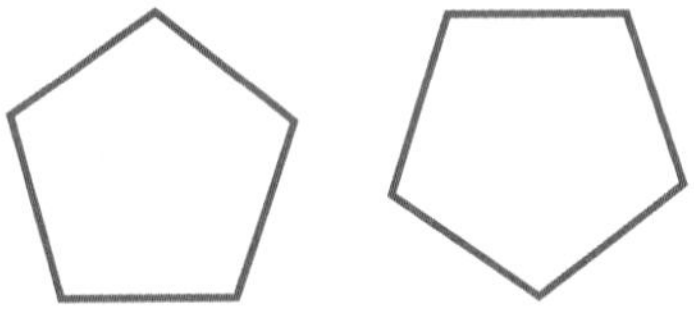

The figures have the same size and shape. So, they are congruent.

2

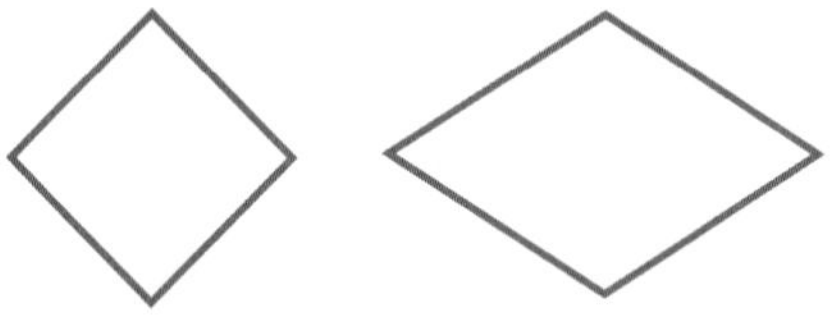

The figures are not the same size or shape. So, they are not congruent.

CHECK What You Know

Tell whether each pair of figures is congruent. Write *yes* or *no*. See Examples 1 and 2 (p. 676)

1.

2.

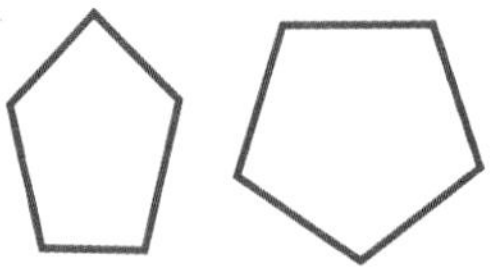

3.

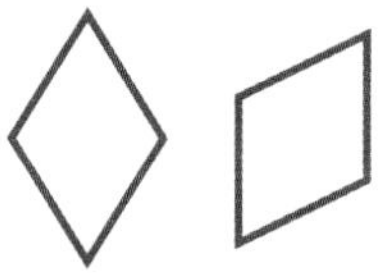

4. One rectangle is 6 inches by 12 inches. Another rectangle is 6 inches by 12 inches. Are the rectangles congruent? Explain.

5. Talk About It Can a rectangle and a trapezoid be congruent? Explain your reasoning.

Practice and Problem Solving

Tell whether the figures in each pair are congruent. Write *yes* or *no*. See Examples 1 and 2 (p. 676)

6. 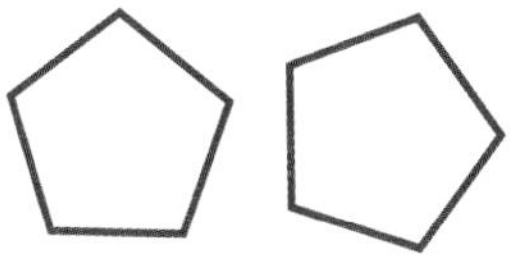

7. 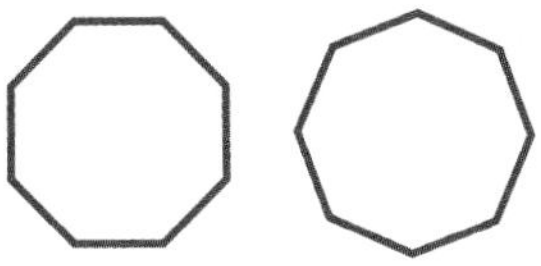

8. 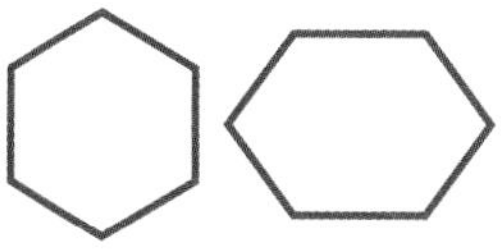

9. 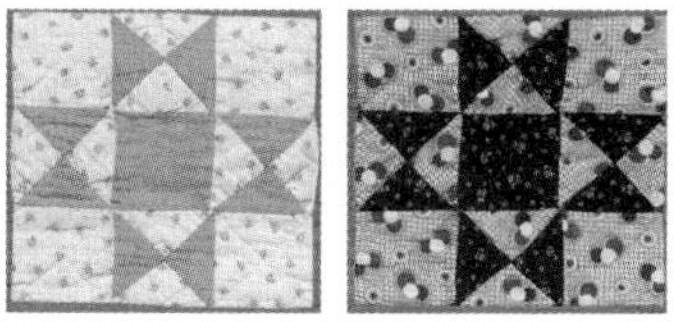

10. 

11. 

12. One pool measures 16 feet by 12 feet. Another pool measures 12 feet by 6 feet. Are the pools congruent shapes? Explain.

13. All of the rectangular doors in Ani's house are the same size. Ani says they are congruent. Is she correct? Explain.

Measurement **Solve.**

14. A rectangle has two sides that measure 3 feet and 5 feet. What are the measurements of the other two sides?

15. One side of a square is 9 feet long. What is the perimeter of the square? Explain how you know.

H.O.T. Problems

16. **OPEN ENDED** Draw two triangles that are not congruent.

17. **WHICH ONE DOESN'T BELONG?** Which figure is not congruent to the others? Explain.

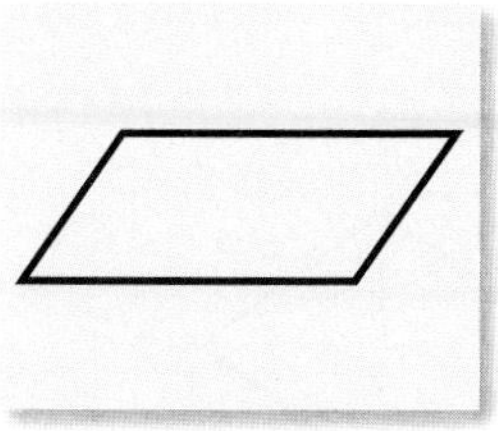

figure A

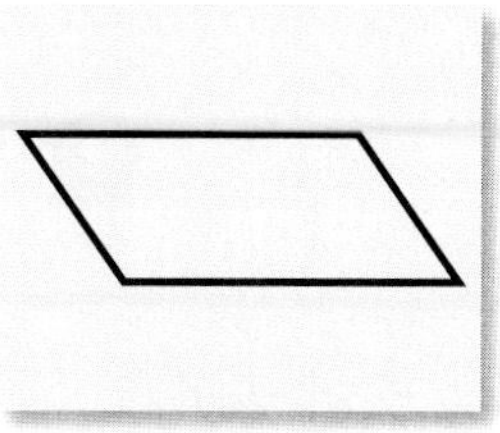

figure B

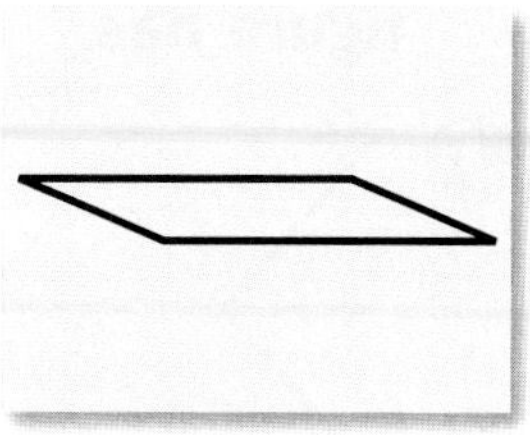

figure C

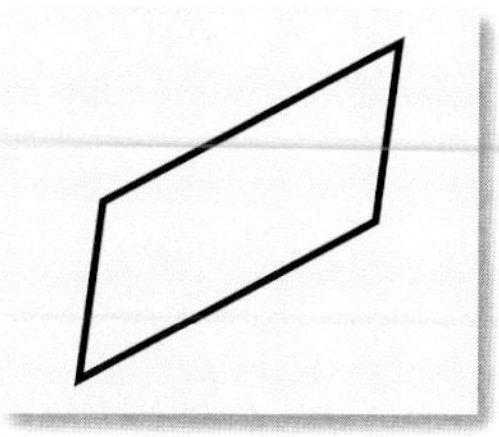

figure D

18. **WRITING IN ▸MATH** Do figures have to be in the same position to be congruent? Explain. Draw a picture to support your answer.

Looking Ahead 5

Geometry: Symmetry

GET READY to Learn

A kite is designed with balance to help it fly better. Its balance comes from the sides being exactly the same.

Some figures like the kite are exact matches when cut in half. This is called **symmetry**. In the kite above, the dashed line is called the **line of symmetry**.

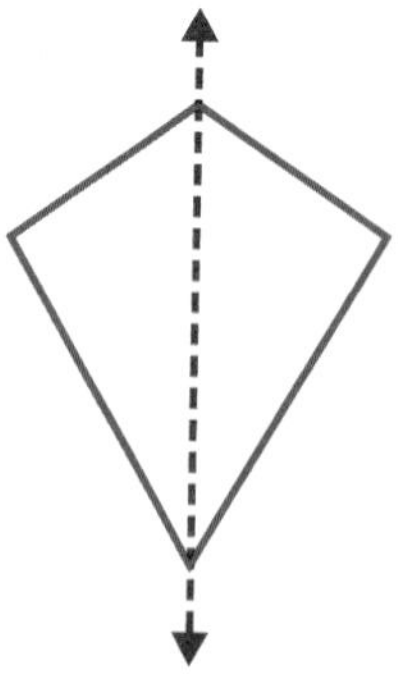

1 line of symmetry
line symmetry

no lines of symmetry

MAIN IDEA

I will identify types of symmetry in figures.

Preparation for Grade 4 Standard MG3.4 **Identify figures that have bilateral** and rotational **symmetry.**

New Vocabulary

symmetry

line of symmetry

EXAMPLES

Tell whether each figure has line symmetry. Write *yes* or *no*. If yes, tell how many lines of symmetry the figure has.

1

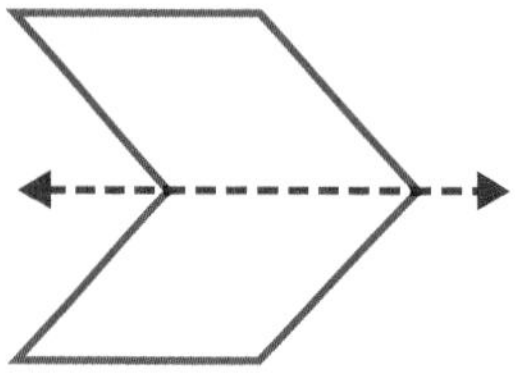

Yes; the figure has one line of symmetry.

2

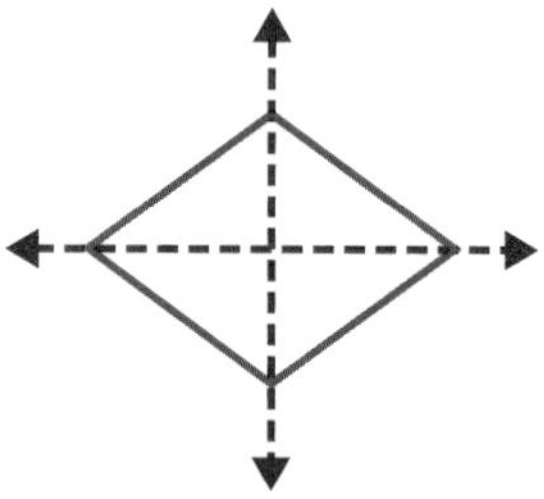

Yes; the figure has 2 lines of symmetry.

CHECK What You Know

Tell whether each figure has line symmetry. Write *yes* or *no*. If yes, tell how many lines of symmetry the figure has.

See Examples 1 and 2 (p. 678)

1. 

2. 

3. 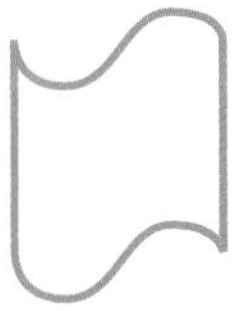

4. Draw the letter T, and draw any lines of symmetry

5. Talk About It: Draw 3 examples of objects that show symmetry.

Practice and Problem Solving

Tell whether each figure has line symmetry. Write *yes* or *no*. If yes, tell how many lines of symmetry the figure has.

See Examples 1 and 2 (p. 678)

6. 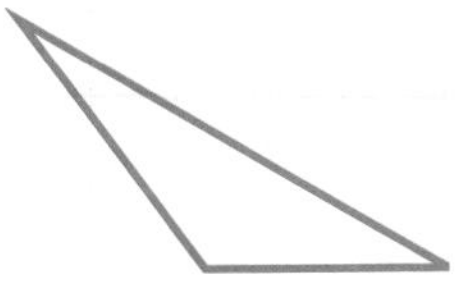

7. 

8. 

9. 

10. 

11. 

12. Name three letters that have line symmetry.

13. Name three numbers that have line symmetry.

H.O.T. Problems

14. OPEN ENDED Draw a picture of half of a shape that shows symmetry. Have a classmate draw the other half.

15 CHALLENGE Look at this picture. How would you test this object to make sure that it shows symmetry?

16. WRITING IN ►MATH Can a shape have more than one line of symmetry? Explain.

Student Handbook

Built-In Workbooks

Extra Practice **R2**

Facts Practice **R41**

Reference

English-Spanish Glossary **R49**

Photo Credits **R69**

Index **R70**

Measurement Conversions
and Multiplication Facts . . . . **Inside Back Cover**

How to Use the Student Handbook

A Student Handbook is the additional skill and reference material found at the end of books. The Student Handbook can help answer these questions.

What If I Need More Practice?

You, or your teacher, may decide that working through some additional problems would be helpful. The **Extra Practice** section provides these problems for each lesson so you have ample opportunity to practice new skills.

What If I Forget a Vocabulary Word?

The **English-Spanish Glossary** provides a list of important, or difficult, words used throughout the textbook. It provides a definition in English and Spanish as well as the page number(s) where the word can be found.

What If I Need to Find Something Quickly?

The **Index** alphabetically lists the subjects covered throughout the entire textbook and the pages on which each subject can be found.

What If I Forget Measurement Conversions or Multiplication Facts?

Inside the back cover of your math book is a list of measurement conversions that are used in the book. You will also find a multiplication table inside the back cover.

Extra Practice

Lesson 1-1

Pages 17–19

Identify a pattern. Then find the missing numbers.

1. 9, 12, 15, ■, 21, 24

2. 26, 31, ■, 41, 46, 51

3. 77, 71, 65, ■, 53, 47

4. 11, 15, ■, 23, 27, 31

5. 99, ■, 85, 78, 71, ■

6. 55, ■ 45, ■, 35, 30

7. 20, ■, 60, 80, ■

8. 86, 94, 102, ■, 118, ■

9. 700, 600, ■, 400, ■, 200

10. 85, ■, ■, 112, 121, 130

Lesson 1-2

Pages 20–21

Solve. Use the *four-step plan.*

1. Maria ate 7 grapes and 5 strawberries. How many pieces of fruit did she eat?

2. There were 22 people at the park. 7 people left. How many people were at the park then?

3. John has 18 more toy airplanes than Soto does. Soto has 13 toy airplanes. How many toy airplanes does John have?

4. During a treasure hunt, Megan walked 12 yards left, 6 yards forward, and 7 yards left. How many yards did Megan walk altogether?

Lesson 1-3

Pages 24–27

Write the place of the underlined digit. Then write the value of the digit.

1. $7\underline{0}6$

2. $2{,}\underline{4}32$

3. $5{,}68\underline{2}$

4. $\underline{6}{,}734$

5. $8{,}\underline{0}98$

6. $\underline{3}{,}365$

Write each number in expanded form and word form.

7. 4,371

8. 2,988

9. 5,654

10. 7,702

11. 6,520

12. 8,906

Lesson 1-4

Pages 28–30

Write the place of each underlined digit. Then write its value.

1. 4,322 **2.** 80,761 **3.** 3,000

4. 67,023 **5.** 51,089 **6.** 27,055

Write each number in expanded form and word form.

7. 8,954 **8.** 14,523 **9.** 81,306

10. 27,621 **11.** 9,909 **12.** 50,345

Lesson 1-5

Pages 32–33

Use the *four-step plan* to solve each problem.

1. Tony has 7 games, Allison has 9 games, and Jarrod has 12 games. They each bought 3 more games. How many does each child have now?

2. Carlos jogged for 30 minutes today. Tomorrow he plans to jog 3 times as long as he did today. How long does he plan to jog tomorrow?

3. Gina bought a sweater for $14. She paid with a $20 bill. How much change did Gina get?

4. Sara picked 48 cherries. She ate 9 cherries. Her sister ate 12 cherries. How many cherries are left?

Lesson 1-6

Pages 34–37

Compare. Write >, <, or =.

1. 77 ● 67 **2.** $45 ● $54 **3.** 610 ● 610

4. 234 ● 342 **5.** 404 ● 440 **6.** 908 ● 889

7. 56 ● 65 **8.** 3,576 ● 3,567 **9.** 222 ● 232

10. 45 ● 450 **11.** 57 ● 57 **12.** 787 ● 878

Lesson 1-7

Pages 38–41

Order the numbers from least to the greatest.

1. 888; 8,008; 81
2. 46; 49; 43
3. 678; 768; 5,667
4. 1,790; 1,978; 1,843
5. 3,438; 896; 2,122
6. 1,222; 2,221; 1,022

Order the numbers from greatest to the least.

7. 765; 7,650; 79
8. 999; 3,221; 4,000
9. 368; 386; 833
10. 2,567; 2,982; 2,199
11. 4,235; 4,325; 3,443
12. 616; 6,116; 6,611

Lesson 1-8

Pages 44–46

Round to the nearest ten.

1. 68
2. 23
3. 84
4. 233
5. 397
6. 408
7. 1,656
8. 2,492

Round to the nearest hundred.

9. 231
10. 778
11. 645
12. 1,282
13. 442
14. 581
15. 4,774
16. 987

Lesson 1-9

Pages 48–51

Round to the nearest thousand.

1. 3,810
2. 1,221
3. 5,989
4. 8,297
5. 3,099
6. 6,572
7. 1,100
8. 2,667
9. 1,589
10. 4,088
11. 7,476
12. 2,821

Lesson 2-1

Pages 65–67

Find each sum. Identify the property.

1. $8 + 0 = ■$

2. $7 + 3 = ■$
$3 + 7 = ■$

3. $(4 + 5) + 3 = ■$
$4 + (5 + 3) = ■$

4. $0 + 5 = ■$

5. $6 + 5 = ■$
$5 + 6 = ■$

6. $9 + (4 + 3) = ■$
$(9 + 4) + 3 = ■$

7. $16 + 4 = ■$
$4 + 16 = ■$

8. $9 + 12 = ■$
$12 + 9 = ■$

9. $(6 + 2) + 4 = ■$
$6 + (2 + 4) = ■$

Find each missing number. Identify the property.

10. $0 + 7 = 7 + ■$

11. $6 + (3 + 5) = (6 + ■) + 5$

12. $8 + 4 = ■ + 8$

13. $5 + ■ = 7 + ■$

14. $(9 + 3) + 4 = ■ + (3 + 4)$

15. $■ + 0 = 5 + ■$

Lesson 2-2

Pages 68–69

Tell whether an estimate or an exact answer is needed. Then solve.

1. How many sandwiches can be made with 3 loaves of bread that have 18 slices each?

2. Carmen walked 12 blocks forward and 25 blocks to the left. How many blocks did she walk in all?

3. A box of cookies costs \$1.85. Milk costs \$2.10. About how much will 2 boxes of cookies and milk cost?

4. Maya has 90 beads. She uses about 25 beads to make a necklace. Does she have enough beads to make 4 necklaces?

Lesson 2-3

Pages 70–73

Estimate each sum using rounding.

1. $\begin{array}{r} 22 \\ +\,41 \\ \hline \end{array}$

2. $\begin{array}{r} 58 \\ +\,39 \\ \hline \end{array}$

3. $\begin{array}{r} 67 \\ +\,23 \\ \hline \end{array}$

4. \$2.89 + \$1. 33

5. \$4.72 + \$3.28

6. 280 + 34

7. $\begin{array}{r} 38 \\ +\,21 \\ \hline \end{array}$

8. $\begin{array}{r} 45 \\ +\,33 \\ \hline \end{array}$

9. $\begin{array}{r} 52 \\ +\,12 \\ \hline \end{array}$

10. 24 + 51

11. 38 + 29

12. \$0.83 + \$0.17

Lesson 2-4

Pages 74–76

Add. Check for reasonableness.

1. $\begin{array}{r} 36 \\ +\ 8 \\ \hline \end{array}$
2. $\begin{array}{r} 24 \\ +\ 5 \\ \hline \end{array}$
3. $\begin{array}{r} 53 \\ +\ 7 \\ \hline \end{array}$
4. $\begin{array}{r} 48 \\ +\ 7 \\ \hline \end{array}$
5. $\begin{array}{r} 36 \\ +\ 15 \\ \hline \end{array}$
6. $\begin{array}{r} 43 \\ +\ 32 \\ \hline \end{array}$
7. $\begin{array}{r} 64 \\ +\ 29 \\ \hline \end{array}$
8. $\begin{array}{r} 54 \\ +\ 34 \\ \hline \end{array}$
9. $\begin{array}{r} 33 \\ +\ 5 \\ \hline \end{array}$
10. 46 + 4
11. 67 + 8
12. 41 + 7

Lesson 2-5

Pages 78–81

Add. Use estimation to check for reasonableness.

1. $\begin{array}{r} \$4.10 \\ +\ \$1.80 \\ \hline \end{array}$
2. $\begin{array}{r} \$2.70 \\ +\ \$3.50 \\ \hline \end{array}$
3. $\begin{array}{r} \$5.90 \\ +\ \$2.60 \\ \hline \end{array}$
4. $\begin{array}{r} \$0.38 \\ +\ \$0.23 \\ \hline \end{array}$
5. $\begin{array}{r} \$0.52 \\ +\ \$0.23 \\ \hline \end{array}$
6. $\begin{array}{r} \$0.47 \\ +\ \$0.34 \\ \hline \end{array}$
7. $\begin{array}{r} \$0.81 \\ +\ \$0.13 \\ \hline \end{array}$
8. $\begin{array}{r} \$0.35 \\ +\ \$0.48 \\ \hline \end{array}$
9. $\begin{array}{r} \$0.35 \\ +\ \$0.08 \\ \hline \end{array}$
10. \$4.30 + \$2.70
11. \$0.28 + \$0.55
12. \$0.32 + \$0.16

Lesson 2-6

Pages 84–85

Use the four-step plan to solve each problem.

1. Tony jogs about 28 miles each week. Does he jog more than 110 miles each month? Explain.
2. Terry made 4 dozen muffins. Rob made 35 muffins. How many muffins did Terry and Rob make altogether?
3. Oranges cost 3 for \$0.75. Apples cost 4 for \$1.25. Peter bought 17 pieces of fruit for \$4.75. How many oranges and apples did he buy?
4. There are 28 windows on the first floor of a library. There are 34 windows on the second floor. About how many windows are there in the library?

Lesson 2-7

Pages 88–90

Find each sum. Use estimation to check for reasonableness.

1. 35 + 46

2. 53 + 38

3. \$124 + \$49

4. 237 + 57

5. \$4.25 + \$2.72

6. 436 + 288

7. \$7.19 + \$2.55

8. 409 + 354

9. 73 + 236

10. 174 + 349

11. \$3.84 + \$5.67

12. 439 + 211

13. \$5.63 + \$3.98

14. 277 + 562

15. \$4.78 + \$3.35

Lesson 2-8

Pages 92–95

Find each sum. Use estimation to check for reasonableness.

1. 298 + 367

2. 245 + 107

3. \$366 + \$523

4. 648 + 751

5. 1,988 + 3,766

6. \$13.75 + \$8.17

7. 4,543 + 2,376

8. \$26.40 + \$37.65

9. 3,905 + 4,227

10. 3,465 + 5,555

11. 2,988 + 2,675

12. 6,042 + 2,309

13. \$19.91 + \$26.85

14. 4,768 + 2,644

15. 1,548 + 5,673

Lesson 3-1

Pages 107–109

Subtract. Check your answer.

1. 38 − 9

2. 55 − 8

3. 73 − 7

4. 92 − 5

5. 46 − 18

6. 37 − 21

7. 84 − 36

8. 54 − 27

9. 45 − 9

10. 93 − 25

11. 68 − 34

12. 72 − 19

13. 53 − 29

14. 85 − 72

15. 59 − 28

Lesson 3-2

Pages 110–113

Estimate. Round to the nearest ten.

1. $73 - 28$

2. $86 - 58$

3. $243 - $89

4. 92 − 34

5. $137 − $48

6. $0.81 − $0.47

Estimate. Round to the nearest hundred.

7. $698 − $322

8. 781 − 273

9. 542 − 386

10. 291 − 77

11. $362 − $125

12. 976 − 529

Lesson 3-3

Pages 114–116

Subtract. Check your answer.

1. $76 − $24

2. $38 − $19

3. $0.63 − $0.47

4. $6.80 − $2.30

5. $33 − $25

6. $8.07 − $2.56

7. $58 − $39

8. $92 − $66

9. $6.76 − $5.90

10. $5.12 − $2.85

11. $78 − $39

12. $7.45 − $6.75

Lesson 3-4

Pages 120–121

Solve. Check for reasonableness.

1. Julie had a pizza party for 7 of her friends. She ordered 4 large pizzas. Each pizza was cut into 10 slices. Is it reasonable to say that each person got at least 6 slices of pizza? Explain.

2. Joey bought a notebook for $2.25 and paint set for $4.95. He paid for them with two $5 bills. Is it reasonable to say that Joey has enough money to buy a set of paintbrushes for $1.95? Explain.

3. At soccer camp, there are 220 drinks in coolers. There are 3 kinds of drinks. There are 64 bottles of water and 78 bottles of sports drinks. Is it reasonable to say that there are 115 bottles of juice?

4. Juan walks to and from school every day. His school is 9 blocks from his house. Is it reasonable to say that Juan walks about 150 blocks to and from school every week?

Lesson 3-5

Pages 124–127

Subtract. Check your answer.

1. 267 − 154

2. 498 − 207

3. \$6.34 − \$3.21

4. 867 − 89

5. \$5.76 − \$2.83

6. 755 − 448

7. \$2.34 − \$0.97

8. 923 − 542

9. \$7.44 − \$4.52

10. \$3.53 − \$0.86

11. 824 − 619

12. 563 − 227

Lesson 3-6

Pages 128–129

Solve. Tell what strategy you used.

1. There were 123 people in line to ride a roller-coaster. 48 people got on the roller-coaster for the next ride. How many people were left in line?

2. Jesse bought a baseball bat for \$16.75 and a baseball for \$5.30. He paid for them with a \$20 bill and a \$10 bill. How much change did he get back?

3. Mei collected 240 shells at the beach. 128 of the shells were spiral-shaped. The rest were scallop-shaped. About how many scallop-shaped shells did Mei collect?

4. Jim had 583 baseball cards. He gave 212 of his cards to his brother. How many baseball cards does Jim have left?

Lesson 3-7

Pages 130–132

Subtract. Check your answer.

1. 306 − 87

2. 703 − 405

3. 500 − 376

4. 205 − 56

5. 600 − 248

6. \$308 − \$221

7. 407 − 99

8. \$903 − \$775

9. 700 − 456

10. 902 − 543

11. \$507 − \$489

12. 807 − 256

Lesson 3-8

Pages 134–137

Subtract. Check your answer.

1. 2,453 − 1,231

2. 5,691 − 207

3. \$8,732 − \$6,215

4. 4,863 − 3,788

5. 7,239 − 908

6. 9,000 − 3,455

7. \$4,091 − \$1,637

8. 2,472 − 848

9. 3,643 − 1,784

10. \$7,208 − \$3,495

11. 5,064 − 2,659

12. \$7,000 − \$4,833

Lesson 3-9

Pages 138–141

Write an expression and a number sentence for each problem. Then solve.

1. There are 47 cats and 29 dogs in the animal shelter. How many more cats than dogs are there?

2. Gina had \$78.50 in her savings account. She deposited \$15 into her account. How much does Gina have in her savings account?

3. Alberto picked 86 apples. His mother used 49 of the apples to make pies. How many apples are left?

4. There are 116 girls in the park playing soccer and softball. 72 of the girls are playing softball. How many girls are playing soccer?

Lesson 4-1

Pages 157–159

Write an addition and a multiplication sentence for each model.

1.

2.

3. 7 groups of 4

4. 4 groups of 8

5. 2 groups of 10

6. 3 groups of 9

7. 5 groups of 5

8. 3 groups of 6

Lesson 4-2

Pages 16[illegible]–163

Write a multiplication sentence for each array. Then multiply.

1. 

2. 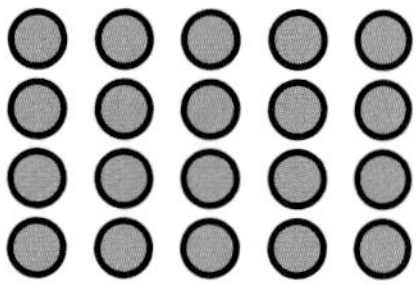

3. 

Use the Commutative Property of Multiplication to find each missing number.

4. $4 \times 5 = 20$
$\blacksquare \times 4 = 20$

5. $4 \times 9 = 36$
$9 \times \blacksquare = 36$

6. $5 \times 7 = 35$
$7 \times 5 = \blacksquare$

Lesson 4-3

Pages 164–166

Multiply.

1. 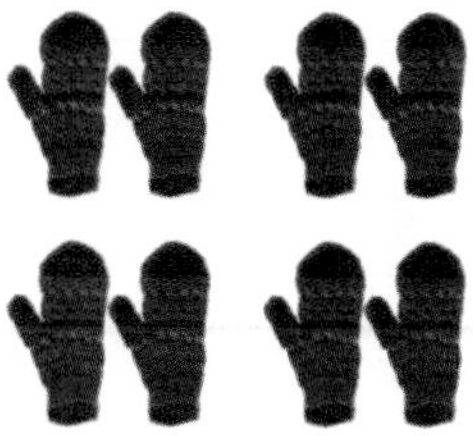

4 groups of 2

2. 

2 groups of 7

3. 

2 groups of 8

4. 2×6

5. 8×2

6. 9×2

7. 10×2

8. 5×2

9. 2×4

10. 2×2

11. 2×3

Lesson 4-4

Pages 168–170

Multiply.

1. 4×3

2. 4×6

3. 5×4

4. 10×4

5. 8×4

6. 4×7

7. 9×4

8. 1×4

9. 6×4

10. 4×0

11. 7×4

12. 4×8

13. 3×4

14. 4×9

Extra Practice

Lesson 4-5

Pages 172–173

Solve. If there is missing information, tell what facts you need to solve the problem.

1. A vegetable garden has 4 rows of corn. There are 7 corn plants in each row. There are 5 rows of tomato plants next to the corn. How many corn plants are there?
2. Tony bought 5 boxes of crayons. There were 8 crayons in each box. Each box of crayons cost $2. How many crayons did Tony buy?
3. Zina played soccer for 30 minutes. Then she played basketball. How many minutes did Zina play sports?
4. Mark wants to buy a CD-player that costs $45. He has saved $20. How many hours will he have to work before he has enough money for the CD-player?

Lesson 4-6

Pages 174–176

Multiply.

1. 2×5
2. 5×5
3. 5×6
4. 9×5
5. 8×5
6. 10×5
7. 5×1
8. 5×7
9. 5×8
10. 10×5
11. 5×0
12. 5×9
13. 6×5
14. 7×5

Lesson 4-7

Pages 178–181

Multiply.

1. 10×2
2. 10×5
3. 10×1
4. 10×7
5. 10×6
6. 10×9
7. 10×4
8. 10×8
9. 5×10
10. 10×7
11. 10×4
12. 3×10
13. 10×9
14. 8×10

Lesson 4-8

Pages 184–185

Use any strategy to solve. Tell what strategy you used.

1. Tennis balls are on sale for $3 a can or 4 cans for $10. If you buy 4 cans of tennis balls, how much will you save on each can?
2. Sara collected 3 colors of fall leaves to make a collage. She collected 9 orange leaves and 7 yellow leaves. How many red leaves did she collect?
3. There are about 18 soccer players on each team. There are 6 soccer teams in the league. About how many soccer players are in the league?
4. There are 7 spiders in a display at the zoo. Each spider has 8 legs. Each spider also has 2 body segments. How many spider legs are there altogether?

Lesson 4-9

Pages 186–188

Multiply.

1. 9×0
2. 10×1
3. 8×1
4. 0×6
5. 0×8
6. 1×5
7. 10×0
8. 7×1
9. 5×0
10. 0×4
11. 1×9
12. 0×7
13. 1×6
14. 3×0

Lesson 5-1

Pages 203–205

Multiply.

1. 7×3
2. 3×8
3. 6×3
4. 5×3
5. 10×3
6. 1×3
7. 0×3
8. 9×3
9. 8×3
10. 3×2
11. 3×7
12. 4×3
13. 3×9
14. 3×0

Lesson 5-2

Pages 206–209

Multiply.

1. $\begin{array}{r} 6 \\ \times\ 2 \\ \hline \end{array}$
2. $\begin{array}{r} 3 \\ \times\ 6 \\ \hline \end{array}$
3. $\begin{array}{r} 5 \\ \times\ 6 \\ \hline \end{array}$
4. $\begin{array}{r} 6 \\ \times\ 9 \\ \hline \end{array}$
5. $\begin{array}{r} 1 \\ \times\ 6 \\ \hline \end{array}$
6. $\begin{array}{r} 7 \\ \times\ 6 \\ \hline \end{array}$
7. $\begin{array}{r} 10 \\ \times\ 6 \\ \hline \end{array}$
8. $\begin{array}{r} 6 \\ \times\ 8 \\ \hline \end{array}$
9. 4×6
10. 0×6
11. 6×7
12. 6×8
13. 5×6
14. 6×6

Lesson 5-3

Pages 212–213

Solve. Use the *look for a pattern* strategy.

1. An oak tree was 3 feet tall at the end of the first year it was planted. By the end of the third year, it was 9 feet tall. If the tree grows 3 feet each year, how tall will the tree be at the end of the 5th year?
2. Carlos is making a castle. For each tower, he uses 6 triangle blocks and 8 square blocks. If Carlos makes 4 towers on his castle, how many more square blocks than triangle blocks will he use?
3. Suki ran one lap on a track in 84 seconds. The next week, she ran the same lap in 81 seconds. If she continues to decrease her time by 3 seconds how many seconds will it take her to run the lap on the 4th week?
4. The dancers in a play are arranged by height. The first student is 50 inches tall, the second student is 47 inches tall, the third student is 52 inches tall, and the fourth student is 49 inches tall. If the pattern continues, how tall is the fifth student?

Lesson 5-4

Pages 214–216

Multiply.

1. $\begin{array}{r} 4 \\ \times\ 7 \\ \hline \end{array}$
2. $\begin{array}{r} 6 \\ \times\ 7 \\ \hline \end{array}$
3. $\begin{array}{r} 7 \\ \times\ 7 \\ \hline \end{array}$
4. $\begin{array}{r} 1 \\ \times\ 7 \\ \hline \end{array}$
5. $\begin{array}{r} 7 \\ \times\ 9 \\ \hline \end{array}$
6. $\begin{array}{r} 10 \\ \times\ 7 \\ \hline \end{array}$
7. $\begin{array}{r} 5 \\ \times\ 7 \\ \hline \end{array}$
8. $\begin{array}{r} 7 \\ \times\ 8 \\ \hline \end{array}$
9. 2×7
10. 7×6
11. 0×7
12. 7×10
13. 9×7
14. 7×3

Lesson 5-5
Pages 218–221

Multiply.

1. $\begin{array}{r} 8 \\ \times\ 3 \\ \hline \end{array}$ **2.** $\begin{array}{r} 8 \\ \times\ 1 \\ \hline \end{array}$ **3.** $\begin{array}{r} 7 \\ \times\ 8 \\ \hline \end{array}$ **4.** $\begin{array}{r} 8 \\ \times\ 5 \\ \hline \end{array}$

5. $\begin{array}{r} 8 \\ \times\ 0 \\ \hline \end{array}$ **6.** $\begin{array}{r} 10 \\ \times\ 8 \\ \hline \end{array}$ **7.** $\begin{array}{r} 8 \\ \times\ 6 \\ \hline \end{array}$ **8.** $\begin{array}{r} 9 \\ \times\ 8 \\ \hline \end{array}$

9. 2×8 **10.** 8×4 **11.** 8×7

12. 8×9 **13.** 5×8 **14.** 8×10

Lesson 5-6
Pages 222–224

Multiply.

1. $\begin{array}{r} 9 \\ \times\ 4 \\ \hline \end{array}$ **2.** $\begin{array}{r} 3 \\ \times\ 9 \\ \hline \end{array}$ **3.** $\begin{array}{r} 9 \\ \times\ 0 \\ \hline \end{array}$ **4.** $\begin{array}{r} 5 \\ \times\ 9 \\ \hline \end{array}$

5. $\begin{array}{r} 7 \\ \times\ 9 \\ \hline \end{array}$ **6.** $\begin{array}{r} 9 \\ \times\ 9 \\ \hline \end{array}$ **7.** $\begin{array}{r} 9 \\ \times\ 8 \\ \hline \end{array}$ **8.** $\begin{array}{r} 10 \\ \times\ 9 \\ \hline \end{array}$

9. 6×9 **10.** 9×2 **11.** 0×9

12. 7×9 **13.** 1×9 **14.** 9×5

Lesson 5-7
Pages 226–227

Use any strategy to solve. Tell what strategy you used.

1. Rita made 6 paintings. Luis made 3 times as many paintings as Rita and 4 more paintings than Tara did. How many paintings did Luis and Tara make?

2. In 1 week there are 7 days. In 2 weeks there are 14 days. There are 21 days in 3 weeks. How many days are in 4 and 5 weeks?

3. Freddie has 6 cats and 3 dogs. Each cat eats 4 ounces of food each day. How many ounces of food do Freddie's cats and dogs eat altogether?

4. Ivan unpacked16 bunches of grapes at the grocery store. He unpacked 13 bunches of bananas. How many bunches of fruit did Ivan unpack?

Lesson 5-8

Pages 228–231

Find each product.

1. $2 \times (4 \times 3)$ **2.** $(4 \times 5) \times 1$ **3.** $(4 \times 2) \times 6$

4. $3 \times (3 \times 3)$ **5.** $(2 \times 4) \times 7$ **6.** $5 \times (9 \times 1)$

Find each missing number.

7. $2 \times (\blacksquare \times 3) = 18$ **8.** $(5 \times \blacksquare) \times 7 = 70$ **9.** $8 \times (2 \times \blacksquare) = 48$

10. $5 \times (\blacksquare \times 2) = 40$ **11.** $(6 \times 1) \times \blacksquare = 54$ **12.** $5 \times (2 \times \blacksquare) = 20$

Lesson 5-9

Pages 234–237

Find and extend the rule for each table. Then copy and complete.

1.

Rule: ■	
Input	Output
4	20
6	■
8	40
9	■

2.

Rule: ■	
Input	Output
3	21
■	28
5	■
6	42

3.

Rule: ■	
Input	Output
4	■
■	20
6	24
7	28

Lesson 6-1

Pages 253–255

Divide. Use counters.

1. $12 \div 3$ **2.** $9 \div 3$ **3.** $16 \div 2$

4. $15 \div 5$ **5.** $24 \div 4$ **6.** $10 \div 2$

Divide. Use repeated subtraction on a number line or paper and pencil.

7. $21 \div 3$ **8.** $16 \div 4$ **9.** $8 \div 1$

10. $14 \div 2$ **11.** $20 \div 5$ **12.** $27 \div 9$

13. $18 \div 9$ **14.** $24 \div 3$ **15.** $12 \div 6$

Lesson 6-2

Pages 258–261

Draw an array to complete each pair of number sentences.

1. $2 \times 3 = \blacksquare$
$6 \div \blacksquare = 2$

2. $1 \times \blacksquare = 7$
$7 \div 7 = \blacksquare$

3. $4 \times \blacksquare = 16$
$\blacksquare \div 4 = 4$

4. $\blacksquare \times 4 = 12$
$12 \div \blacksquare = 3$

5. $5 \times 4 = \blacksquare$
$20 \div 4 = \blacksquare$

6. $8 \times \blacksquare = 24$
$24 \div \blacksquare = 3$

Write the fact family for each set of numbers.

7. 2, 4, 8
8. 3, 7, 21
9. 1, 5, 5
10. 2, 9, 18
11. 4, 3, 12
12. 4, 5, 20

Lesson 6-3

Pages 262–263

Solve. Use the *choose the operation* skill.

1. Sung made 3 sets of frozen lemon treats and 2 sets of frozen cherry treats. There made 25 treats altogether. How many treats were in each set?
2. Jaime ordered 4 pizzas for himself and 5 of his friends. Each pizza had 6 slices. How many slices of pizza did each boy have?
3. Each mother duck has 4 ducklings. There are 4 mother ducks. How many ducklings are there?
4. Mrs. Diaz has five rows of peppers in her garden. There are 30 pepper plants in all. How many pepper plants are in each row?

Lesson 6-4

Pages 264–266

Divide.

1. $18 \div 2$
2. $12 \div 2$
3. $8 \div 2$
4. $24 \div 2$
5. $14 \div 2$
6. $30 \div 2$
7. $10 \div 2$
8. $22 \div 2$
9. $28 \div 2$

Divide. Write a related multiplication fact.

10. $16 \div 2$
11. $20 \div 2$
12. $28 \div 2$
13. $60 \div 2$
14. $44 \div 2$
15. $50 \div 2$

Lesson 6-5

Pages 268–271

Divide.

1. $35 \div 5$
2. $20 \div 5$
3. $55 \div 5$
4. $40 \div 5$
5. $25 \div 5$
6. $45 \div 5$

Copy and complete each table.

7.

Rule: – 5	
Input	Output
45	■
35	■
20	■
■	10

8.

Rule: ÷ 5	
Input	Output
50	■
30	■
■	4
■	1

9.

Rule: × 5	
Input	Output
9	■
8	■
6	■
■	15

Lesson 6-6

Pages 274–275

Use any strategy to solve. Tell what strategy you used.

1. Mike jogged for 15 minutes on Monday. He jogged twice as long on Tuesday. How long did Mike jog on Tuesday?
2. Jose had 18 baseball cards. He gave 4 to his sister. He bought 7 more. How many baseball cards does Jose have now?
3. Wanda is putting 4 colored candles in each of the cupcakes she made. She puts the candles in the order blue, green, red, green. If Wanda make 12 cupcakes, how many green candles will she use?
4. The Jackson family has $35 to spend for dinner. There are 2 adults and 3 children in the family. If they divide the money evenly, how much will each person spend on dinner?

Lesson 6-7

Pages 276–278

Divide.

1. $40 \div 10$
2. $110 \div 10$
3. $70 \div 10$
4. $120 \div 10$
5. $100 \div 10$
6. $180 \div 10$

Solve. Find the missing number.

7. ■ $\div 10 = 6$
8. $200 \div 10 =$ ■
9. ■ $\div 10 = 9$
10. $80 \div 10 =$ ■
11. ■ $\div 14 = 10$
12. ■ $\div 10 = 50$

Lesson 6-8

Pages 280–281

Divide.

1. $9 \div 1$ **2.** $0 \div 6$ **3.** $10 \div 10$ **4.** $8 \div 1$

5. $5 \div 5$ **6.** $4 \div 1$ **7.** $0 \div 8$ **8.** $2 \div 1$

9. $10\overline{)0}$ **10.** $8\overline{)0}$ **11.** $9\overline{)9}$ **12.** $1\overline{)7}$

13. $2\overline{)2}$ **14.** $1\overline{)1}$ **15.** $4\overline{)0}$ **16.** $1\overline{)5}$

Lesson 7-1

Pages 295–297

Divide.

1. $9 \div 3$ **2.** $12 \div 3$ **3.** $0 \div 3$

4. $15 \div 3$ **5.** $3 \div 3$ **6.** $21 \div 3$

7. $3\overline{)24}$ **8.** $3\overline{)6}$ **9.** $3\overline{)30}$

Compare. Write >, <, or =.

10. $15 \div 3$ ■ $15 - 3$ **11.** $12 \div 2$ ■ $18 \div 3$ **12.** $21 \div 3$ ■ $3 + 3$

Lesson 7-2

Pages 298–301

Divide.

1. $16 \div 4$ **2.** $8 \div 4$ **3.** $20 \div 4$

4. $24 \div 4$ **5.** $0 \div 4$ **6.** $32 \div 4$

7. $4\overline{)12}$ **8.** $4\overline{)28}$ **9.** $4\overline{)40}$

Find each missing number.

10. $20 \div$ ■ $= 4$ **11.** ■ $\div 4 = 10$ **12.** $4 \times$ ■ $= 28$

Lesson 7-3

Pages 302–303

Solve. Use the *make a table* strategy.

1. Diego is picking lemons and oranges. For every 2 lemons he picks, he picks 4 oranges. When Diego has picked 6 lemons, how many oranges will he have picked?

2. Scott earns $4 per hour doing yard work. He works 2 hours a day. How many days will it take him to earn $32?

3. Jared is putting cans of food on a shelf. He can fit 6 large cans on each shelf. How many cans could he fit on 4 shelves?

4. Colored markers are on sale at a store for $0.20 each or a set of 6 for $1. How much would you save if you bought 5 sets of colored markers instead of the number of individual markers?

Lesson 7-4

Pages 304–306

Divide.

1. $12 \div 6$ **2.** $28 \div 7$ **3.** $24 \div 6$

4. $35 \div 7$ **5.** $0 \div 7$ **6.** $21 \div 7$

7. $42 \div 6$ **8.** $30 \div 6$ **9.** $36 \div 6$

10. $6\overline{)6}$ **11.** $7\overline{)14}$ **12.** $6\overline{)18}$

13. $7\overline{)63}$ **14.** $6\overline{)48}$ **15.** $7\overline{)56}$

Lesson 7-5

Pages 310–312

Divide.

1. $32 \div 8$ **2.** $27 \div 9$ **3.** $45 \div 9$

4. $40 \div 8$ **5.** $24 \div 8$ **6.** $36 \div 9$

7. $0 \div 9$ **8.** $16 \div 8$ **9.** $63 \div 9$

10. $9\overline{)27}$ **11.** $9\overline{)81}$ **12.** $8\overline{)80}$

13. $9\overline{)72}$ **14.** $8\overline{)64}$ **15.** $9\overline{)54}$

Lesson 7-6

Pages 314–317

Find each unit cost.

1. 7 notebooks for \$21
2. 6 sandwiches for \$24
3. 9 movie tickets for \$45
4. 9 CDs for \$63

Find each unit cost to determine the better buy.

5. 2 dozen cupcakes for \$8
   4 dozen cupcakes for \$20
6. 5 paint sets for \$35
   6 paint sets for \$36
7. 6 bags of popcorn for \$12
   3 bags of popcorn for \$9
8. 4 books for \$28
   7 books for \$21

Lesson 7-7

Pages 318–319

Use any strategy to solve. Tell what strategy you used.

1. A swim team has 9 members. 5 members of the team each swam 3 laps. The other members each swam twice as many laps as the first 5. How many laps did the team members swim altogether?
2. A camp leader packed 8 sandwiches and 6 apples in each picnic basket. She packed 36 apples altogether. How many sandwiches did she pack? How many picnic baskets did she use?
3. At a flower shop, roses cost 6 for \$5, and tulips cost 9 for \$4. How much more would it cost to buy 24 roses than 36 tulips?
4. Rick is making a square pen for his turtle. Each side of the pen will be 3 feet long. Rick will use 4 posts for each foot of the pen. How many posts will he need?

Lesson 7-8

Pages 320–323

Choose one of the symbols +, −, ×, or ÷ to make the equation true.

1. $24 \div 6 = 8 \, \blacksquare \, 2$
2. $12 \, \blacksquare \, 7 = 25 \div 5$
3. $27 \div 3 = 3 \, \blacksquare \, 3$
4. $4 \times 5 = 5 \, \blacksquare \, 15$
5. $22 \, \blacksquare \, 5 = 9 \times 3$
6. $16 - 10 = 18 \, \blacksquare \, 3$

Find a number that makes the equation true.

7. $4 \times \blacksquare = 36 - 4$
8. $25 \div 5 = \blacksquare - 4$
9. $4 \times 10 = \blacksquare \times 5$
10. $20 - 6 = \blacksquare \times 2$
11. $12 + 3 = 3 \times \blacksquare$
12. $20 + 7 = 9 \times \blacksquare$

Lesson 7-9

Pages 324–327

Write each phrase as an expression.

1. the product of 7 and 4
2. 24 pens divided among 4 people
3. 5 groups of 8 people each
4. 9 more than 16
5. difference between 30 and 6
6. 8 less than 23
7. 22 and 10 more
8. 4 times as many as 5

Lesson 8-1

Pages 343–345

Measure each to the nearest half inch.

1. 
2. 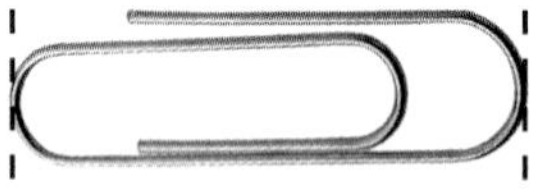

Lesson 8-2

Pages 346–349

Choose the most appropriate unit to measure each length. Choose from *inch, foot, yard,* or *mile*.

1. the length of a bicycle
2. The distance from Texas to Georgia
3. the width of a book
4. The length of a truck

Convert.

5. 5 yd = ■ ft
6. 48 in. = ■ ft
7. 18 ft = ■ yd
8. 2 yd = ■ in.
9. 24 ft = ■ in.
10. 24 ft = ■ yd

Lesson 8-3

Pages 350–351

Solve. Use the *work backward* strategy.

1. Jenna began a star map on Monday night. On Tuesday, she mapped 12 stars. On Wednesday night, she mapped 14 more stars. By then, she had mapped 33 stars in all. How many stars did she map on Monday?

2. Gustavo walked his dog for an hour. Next, he played at the park for 2 hours. Then, he did chores for 2 hours. He finished at 3:00 in the afternoon. At what time did he start walking his dog?

3. Petra ate some strawberries for breakfast. She ate 3 times as many strawberries for lunch. She ate 20 strawberries in all that day. How many strawberries did she eat for breakfast?

4. Sam added 8 shells to his collection. His sister gave him 9 shells. Sam found 5 more shells. Now he has 43 shells. How many shells did he have at first?

Lesson 8-4

Pages 354–357

Choose the most appropriate unit to measure each capacity. Use *cup, pint, quart,* or *gallon*.

1. dog dish

2. milk bottle

3. cocoa

Convert.

4. 8 pt = ■ c
5. 3 gal = ■ qt
6. 2 qt = ■ c
7. 1 gal = ■ c
8. 3 qt = ■ pt
9. 16 qt = ■ gal

Lesson 8-5

Pages 360–361

Use any strategy to solve. Tell what strategy you used.

1. Louis stopped working at 5:00. He pulled weeds for 2 hours, and he took a $\frac{1}{2}$-hour break. He raked leaves for $1\frac{1}{2}$ hours. What time did he start working?

2. Mei has 7 green marbles, 8 blue marbles, and 3 times as many red marbles as green ones. How many marbles does she have altogether?

Lesson 8-6

Pages 362–365

Choose the most appropriate unit to measure the weight of each object. Use *ounce* or *pound*.

1. a tennis ball
2. a tiger
3. a cell phone
4. a pencil
5. a television
6. a shovel

Convert.

7. 5 lb = ■ oz
8. 32 oz = ■ lb
9. 64 oz = ■ lb

Lesson 8-7

Pages 368–371

Convert.

1. 2 hours = ■ quarter hours
2. 240 minutes = ■ hours
3. 6 quarter hours = ■ minutes
4. 180 minutes = ■ $\frac{1}{2}$ hours
5. 5 hours = ■ $\frac{1}{2}$ hours
6. 12 quarter hours = ■ hours
7. $\frac{3}{4}$ hour = ■ minutes
8. 120 minutes = ■ quarter hours
9. 10 quarter hours = ■ $\frac{1}{2}$ hours
10. 7 hours = ■ $\frac{1}{2}$ hours

Lesson 9-1

Pages 385–388

Choose the most appropriate unit to measure each length. Write *millimeter, centimeter, meter,* or *kilometer*.

1. length of a crayon
2. length of a rake
3. length of a soccer field
4. Length of an ocean shoreline

Choose the best estimate.

5. length of an alligator
2 m or 2 cm

6. length of a pencil
13 km or 13 cm

7. width of California
1,240 cm or 1,240 km

8. length of a jet
62 km or 62 m

Lesson 9-2

Pages 390–391

Solve. Use the *guess and check* strategy.

1. Sara made 8 putts at the miniature golf course. Each putt was about 50 centimeters long. About how many meters was the total length of all the putts?
2. Each car on an amusement park ride holds 15 people. There are 20 cars on the ride. How many people can the ride hold?
3. David practiced playing his violin for $4\frac{1}{2}$ hours during 1 week. He practiced the same number of minutes from Monday through Friday. He practiced twice as long on Saturday and Sunday. How long did he practice each day?
4. There are 12 dog pens in an animal shelter. Each pen can hold about 6 large dogs or 10 small dogs. Is there enough room for 90 small dogs and 20 large dogs?

Lesson 9-3

Pages 392–394

Choose the most appropriate unit to measure each capacity. Write *milliliter* or *liter*.

1. a washing machine
2. a test tube
3. a drinking glass
4. a shark aquarium
5. a watering can
6. a juice box

Choose the best estimate.

7. bathroom sink
   8 mL or 8 L
8. tablespoon
   15 mL or 15 L
9. large bottle of soda
   2 mL or 2 L

Lesson 9-4

Pages 396–397

Use any strategy to solve. Tell what strategy you used.

1. Kiri picks 500 grams of blueberries every $\frac{1}{2}$ hour. How long will it take her to pick 3 kilograms of blueberries?
2. Ana is 120 centimeters tall. Her father is 2 meters tall. How much taller is her father than Ana?
3. Deanna walked 7 blocks to get to school. She took a different route on the way home that was 3 times as many blocks. How many blocks did Deanna walk that day?
4. Potatoes cost $1.25 for 3 kilograms at the grocery store. How much will 12 kilograms of potatoes cost?

Lesson 9-5
Pages 398–401

Choose the most appropriate unit to measure each mass. Write *gram* or *kilogram*.

1. a bowling ball
2. a grasshopper
3. a wheelbarrow
4. a golf ball
5. a bag of pretzels
6. A piece of chalk

Compare. Use >, <, or =.

7. 9,000 g ■ 9 kg
8. 5 kg ■ 50 g
9. 2 g ■ 26 kg
10. 500 g ■ 5 kg
11. 18,000 g ■ 7 kg
12. 1 kg ■ 1,000 g

Lesson 9-6
Pages 404–407

Convert each unit to a smaller unit.

1. 6 L = ■ mL
2. 7 kg = ■ g
3. 13 m = ■ cm

Convert each unit to a larger unit.

4. 14,000 g = ■ kg
5. 26,000 mL = ■ L
6. 10,000 g = ■ kg

Compare. Use >, <, or =.

7. 2,200 mL ■ 20 L
8. 50,000 g ■ 5 kg
9. 28 m ■ 3 km

Lesson 10-1
Pages 419–421

Classify each polygon.

1.
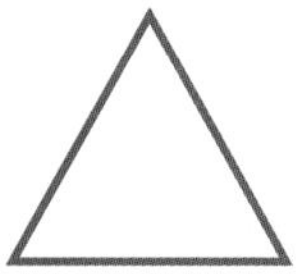

2.
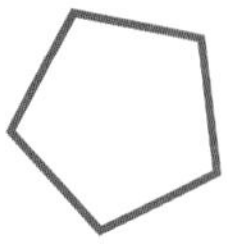

3.
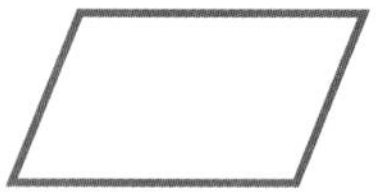

4.
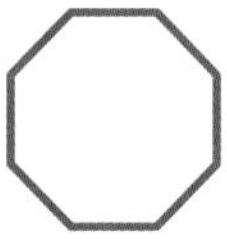

5.

6.
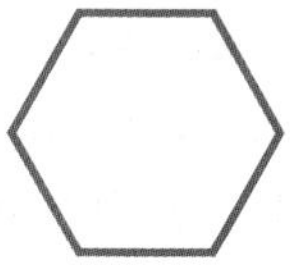

Lesson 10-2

Pages 422–425

Find the perimeter of each figure.

1. 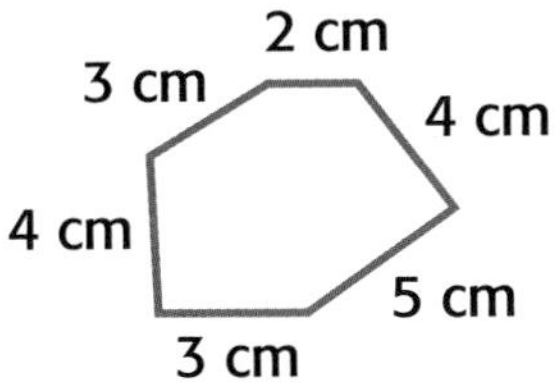

2. 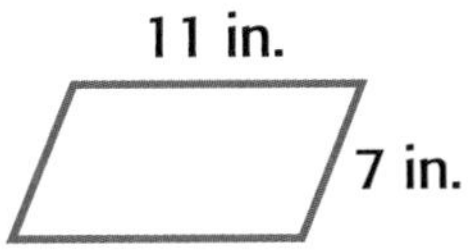

3. 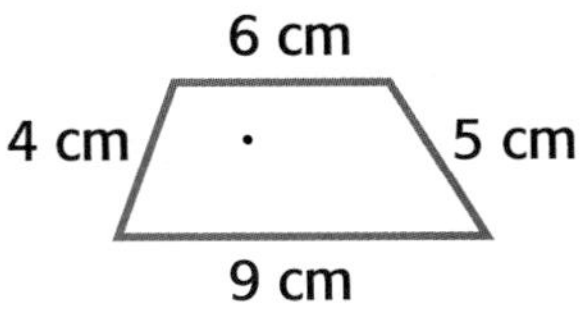

4. 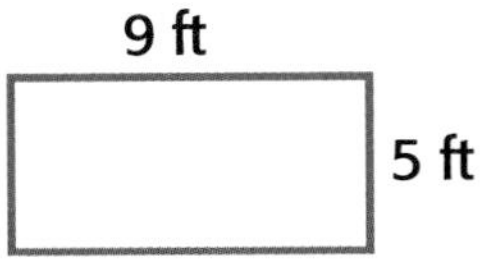

5. 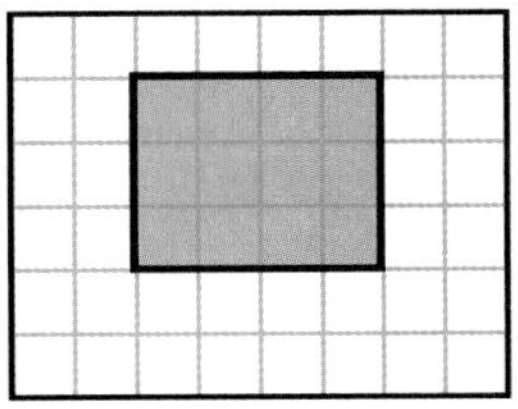

6. 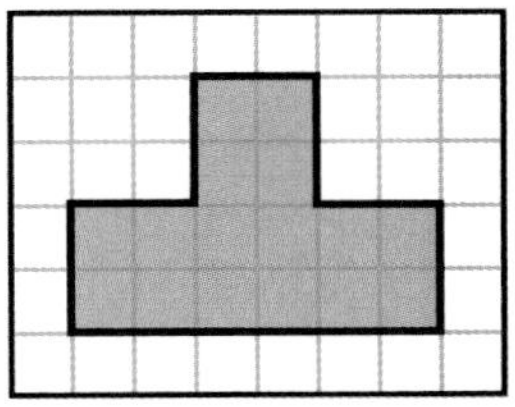

Lesson 10-3

Pages 428–431

Find the area of each figure.

1. 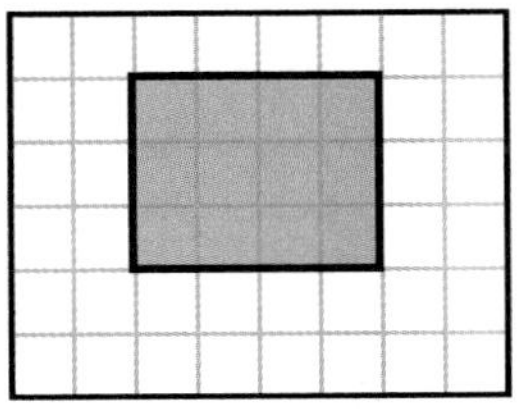

2. 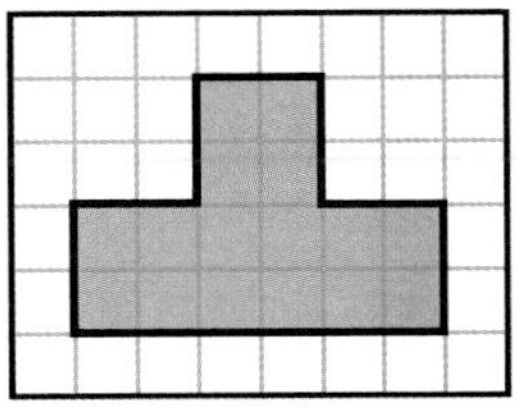

3. 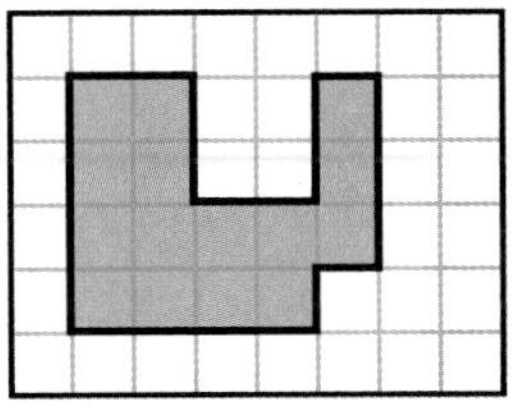

4. 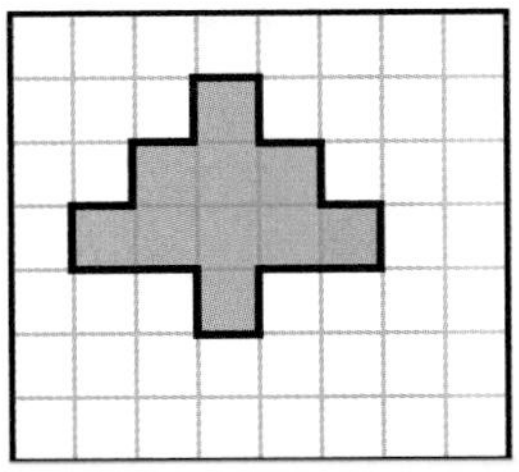

5. 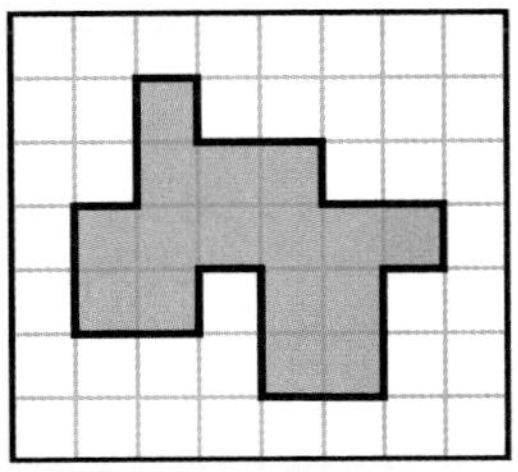

6. 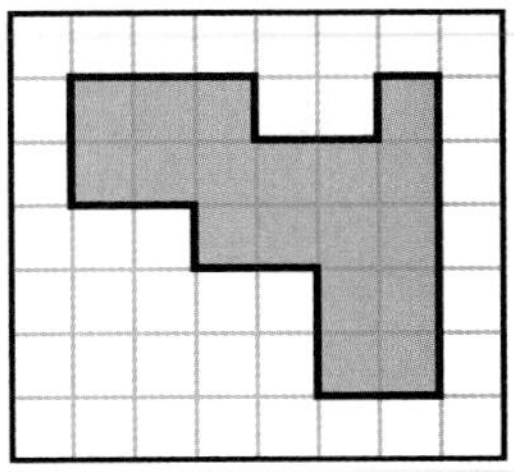

Lesson 10-4

Pages 432–433

Solve. Use the *solve a simpler problem* strategy.

1. A chess board is a square with eight squares on each side. Each player begins with a playing piece on each square in the two rows closest to him or her. How many pieces are in a chess set?

2. There are 16 peaches, 8 plums, and 24 carrot sticks in the refrigerator. Toni took out 2 peaches, 3 plums, and 10 carrot sticks. Ali took out 2 plums, 8 carrot sticks, and one peach. How many of each is left?

Lesson 10-5

Pages 434–436

Identify each triangle. Tell whether each angle shown is a *right* angle, *less than* a right angle, or *greater than* a right angle.

1. 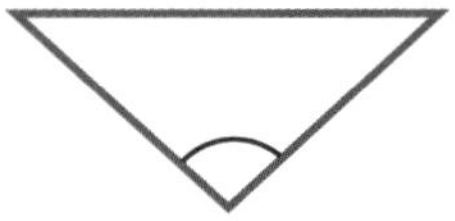
2. 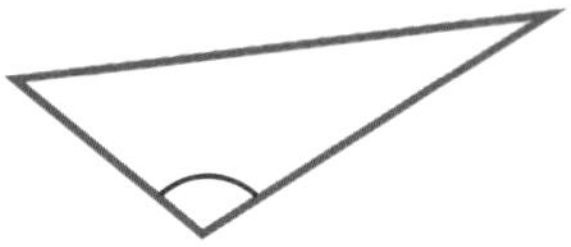
3. 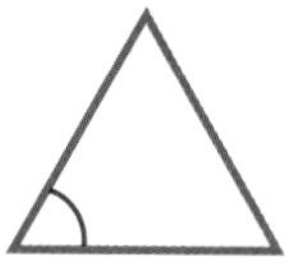
4. 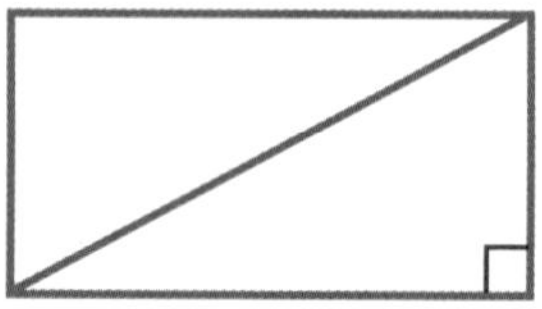
5. 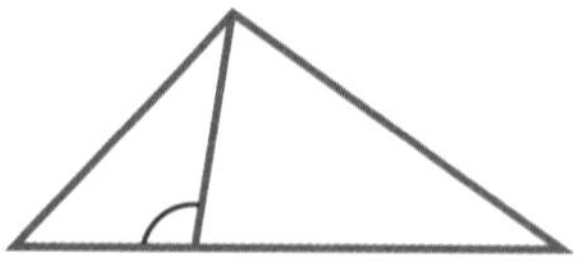
6. 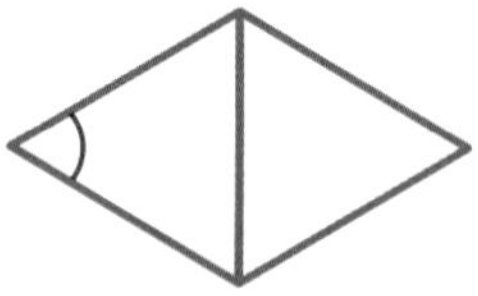

Lesson 10-6

Pages 438–441

Identify each quadrilateral. Tell if the angle shown is a *right* angle, *less than* a right angle, or *greater than* a right angle.

1. 
2. 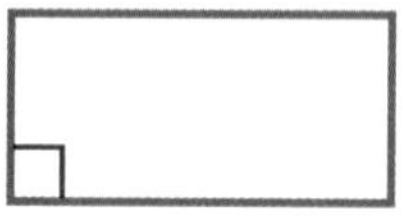
3. 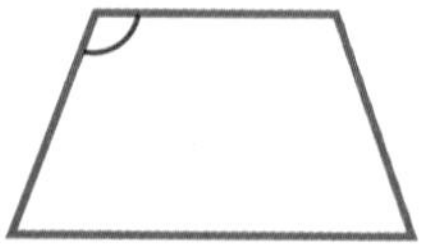
4. 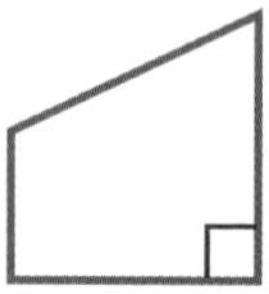
5. 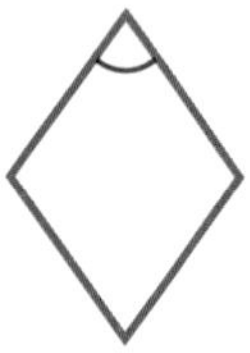
6. 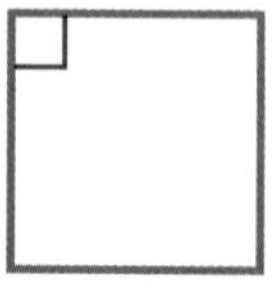

Lesson 10-7

Pages 442–443

Use any strategy to solve. Tell what strategy you used.

1. A mall has 3 levels. Each level has 15 stores. Each store has 4 windows. How many windows are in the mall?
2. Carmen and Rob played 60 games of checkers. Rob won twice as many games as Carmen did. How many games did each person win?
3. For every \$5 that Henry saves, his dad gives him \$3 to save. When Henry has saved \$100, how much will he have in all?
4. Stella bought 12 stickers and 4 posters. The stickers cost 3 for \$0.25. The posters cost 2 for \$6. How much did Stella spend?

Lesson 10-8

Pages 444–446

Identify each solid figure.

1. 

2. 

3. 

4. 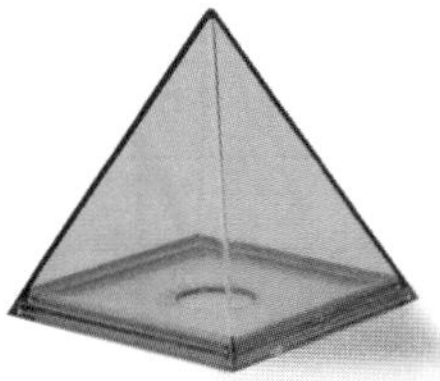

Lesson 10-9

Pages 448–449

Identify the figures that make each complex solid.

1. 

2. 

Lesson 10-10

Pages 454–457

Find the volume of each solid figure.

1. 

2. 

3. 

4. 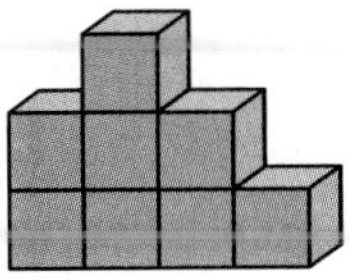

5. 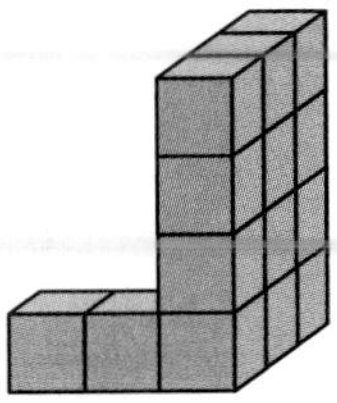

6. 

Lesson 11-1

Pages 473–475

1. Display the data below in a vertical bar graph.

Average Length of Adult Male Animals	
Animal	**Length (ft)**
Alligator	11
Hippopotamus	15
Otter	3
Tiger	9

Source: Smithsonian National Zoo

2. Display the data below in a horizontal bar graph.

Most Popular Pets	
Animal	**Length**
Bird	𝍸 𝍷𝍷
Cat	𝍸 𝍸 𝍸 𝍷
Dog	𝍸 𝍸 𝍸 𝍸 𝍸
Snake	𝍷𝍷

Lesson 11-2

Pages 476–479

Display each set of data in a line plot.

1.

Books Read in One Week	
Number of Books	**Students**
0	0
1	4
2	9
3	5
4	4
5	2

2.

Hours Spent on the Computer on the Weekend	
Hours	**Students**
0	6
1	5
2	8
3	2
4	4
5	0

Lesson 11-3

Pages 480–481

Solve. Use the *make a list* strategy.

1. Marta's pocket has coins in it that add up to 15¢. How many combinations of coins could there be in her pocket?

2. Nita has a white scarf, a blue scarf, and a pink scarf. She also has purple mittens, pink mittens, and green mittens. How many combinations of scarves and mittens can Nita make?

Lesson 11-4

Pages 484–487

Describe the probability of landing on each number or color. Write *certain, likely, unlikely,* or *impossible*.

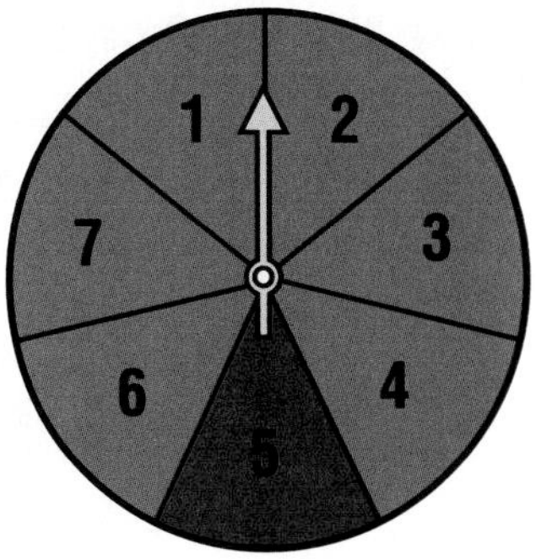

1. a number that is less than 5.
2. a number that is between 0 and 8.
3. an odd number.
4. a number that is less than 2.
5. orange
6. red
7. blue
8. not yellow

Lesson 11-5

Pages 490–491

Use any strategy to solve. Tell what strategy you used.

1. Four teams in a tournament have to play every other team once. The top two teams then play each other. How many games will the top two teams play?
2. Hugo has 8 baseballs. He gave 3 baseballs to each of his 5 brothers. He gave 4 baseballs to his sister. How many baseballs did Hugo have at first?
3. Shani is making a bracelet. She will use 3 different colored beads. She can choose from a blue, green, yellow, purple, and pink bead. How many different combinations could she choose?
4. The perimeter of a rectangular yard is 24 feet. What are the possible lengths of the sides in whole units?

Lesson 11-6

Pages 494–497

For Exercises 1–4, use the line plot. It shows the results from spinning a spinner with 6 colors.

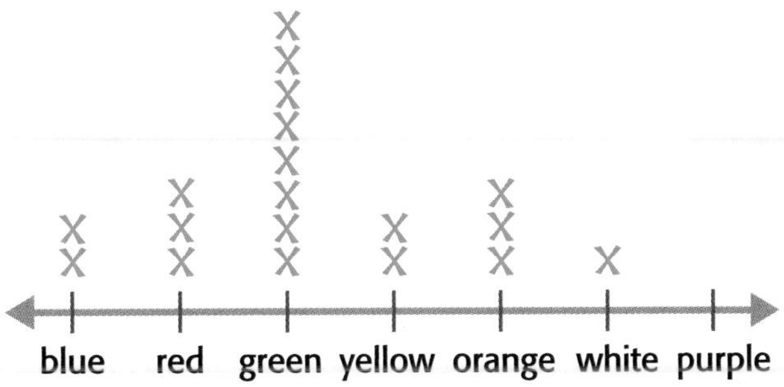

1. How many times did Miguel spin the spinner?
2. Which colors would it be reasonable to say are on the spinner?
3. What color do you think the spinner will land on next?

Lesson 12-1

Pages 509–511

Write the fraction for the part that is blue. Then write the fraction for the part that is *not* blue. Label your answers.

1. 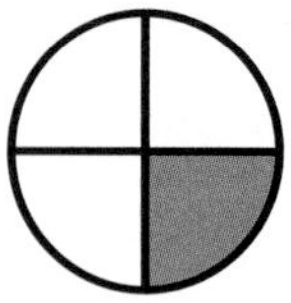

2. 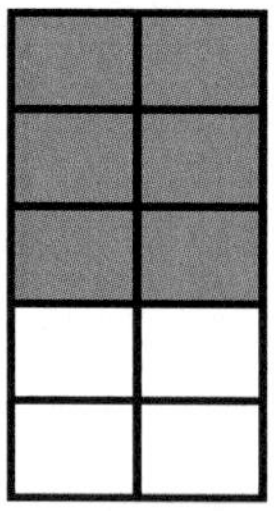

3. 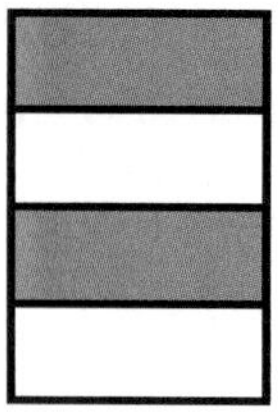

4. 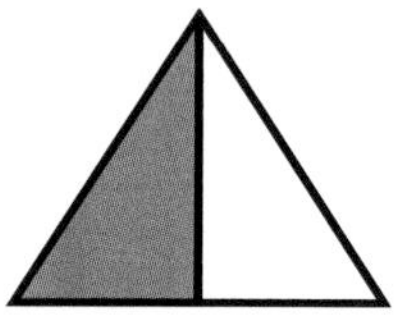

5. 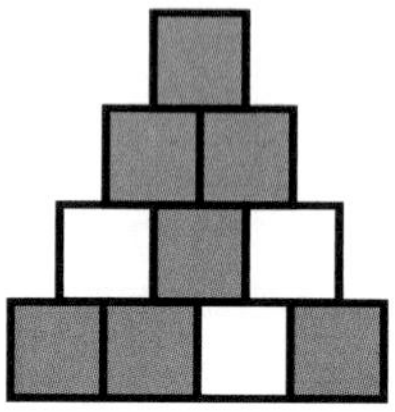

6. 

Lesson 12-2

Pages 512–513

Use any strategy to solve. Tell what strategy you used.

1. Josh rolled two number cubes at once. The sum of the numbers was 10. The difference was 2. What two numbers did Josh roll?

2. Lille bought a salad for $1.75 and a bowl of soup for $1.50. She has $2.25 left. How much did she have before she bought lunch?

3. For every blue headband Kitty has, she has 3 white ones and 2 red ones. Kitty has 3 blue headbands. How many white and red headbands does she have?

4. Alex delivered 26 papers on one block. He delivered half as many on another block. How many papers did Alex deliver?

Lesson 12-3

Pages 516–518

Complete each number sentence to find equivalent fractions.

1. 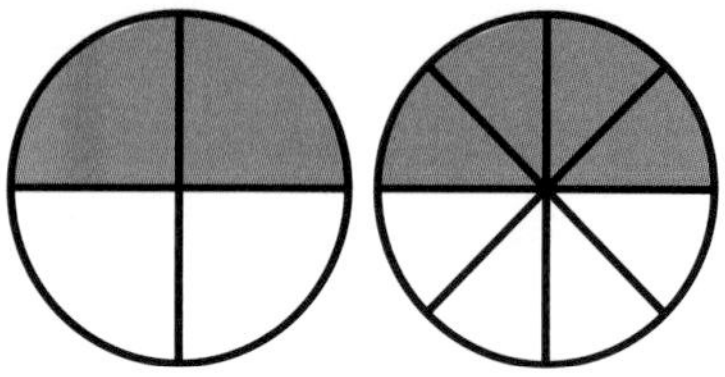

$\frac{2}{4} = \frac{\blacksquare}{8}$

2. 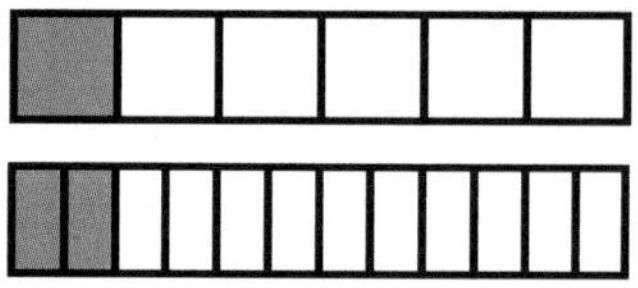

$\frac{1}{6} = \frac{\blacksquare}{12}$

3. 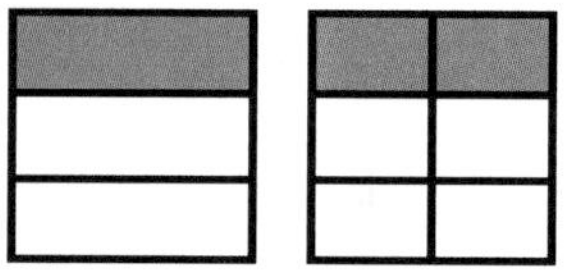

$\frac{\blacksquare}{3} = \frac{\blacksquare}{6}$

Find each missing value.

4. $\frac{2}{3} = \frac{\blacksquare}{12}$

5. $\frac{3}{5} = \frac{\blacksquare}{10}$

6. $\frac{2}{6} = \frac{\blacksquare}{3}$

Lesson 12-4

Pages 520–521

Solve. Use the *draw a picture* strategy.

1. John and Ben played 8 games of checkers. John won 2 more games than Ben did. What fraction of the games did each boy win?

2. Alisha sliced a pizza into 10 pieces. She ate $\frac{3}{5}$ of the pizza. How many slices are left?

3. Carli practiced dancing for $\frac{3}{6}$ of an hour. Lauren practiced for $\frac{3}{4}$ of an hour. Who practiced longer?

4. There were 24 cherries in a bowl. Tara took $\frac{1}{4}$ of them. Yuri took $\frac{1}{8}$ of them. How many cherries were left in the bowl?

Lesson 12-5

Pages 522–524

Compare. Write >, <, or =.

1. 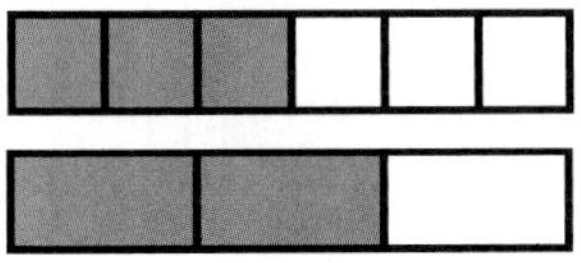

$\frac{3}{6}$ ● $\frac{2}{3}$

2. 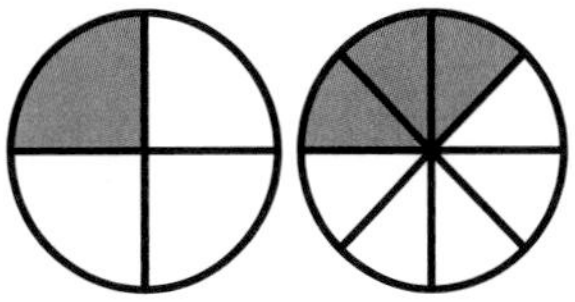

$\frac{1}{4}$ ● $\frac{3}{8}$

3. 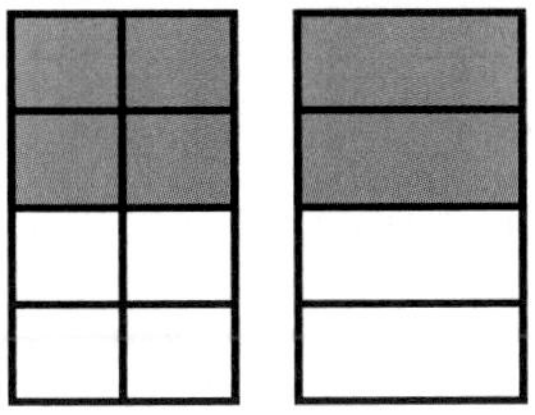

$\frac{4}{8}$ ● $\frac{1}{2}$

4. 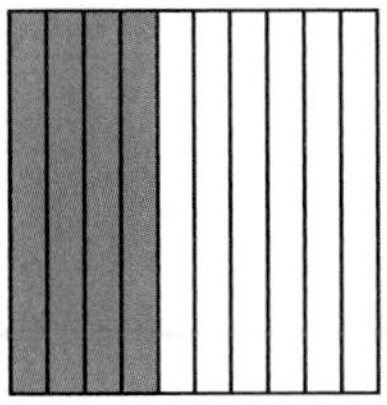

$\frac{2}{6}$ ● $\frac{1}{5}$

Compare. Write >, <, or =. Use fraction models, a number line, or a drawing if needed.

5. $\frac{1}{5}$ ● $\frac{1}{8}$

6. $\frac{3}{5}$ ● $\frac{4}{5}$

7. $\frac{4}{10}$ ● $\frac{2}{5}$

Lesson 12-6

Pages 528–531

Add. Use fraction models if needed.

1. $\frac{2}{4} + \frac{1}{4}$

2. $\frac{3}{6} + \frac{2}{6}$

3. $\frac{5}{10} + \frac{3}{10}$

4. $\frac{3}{12} + \frac{4}{12}$

5. $\frac{3}{9} + \frac{5}{9}$

6. $\frac{2}{7} + \frac{3}{7}$

7. $\frac{3}{4} + \frac{1}{4}$

8. $\frac{3}{5} + \frac{1}{5}$

9. $\frac{5}{8} + \frac{2}{8}$

Lesson 12-7

Pages 536–539

Subtract. Use fraction models if needed.

1. $\frac{5}{8} - \frac{2}{8}$

2. $\frac{7}{12} - \frac{4}{12}$

3. $\frac{5}{10} - \frac{2}{10}$

4. $1 - \frac{2}{5}$

5. $\frac{4}{6} - \frac{3}{6}$

6. $\frac{1}{4} - \frac{1}{4}$

7. $\frac{7}{8} - \frac{5}{8}$

8. $\frac{8}{9} - \frac{4}{9}$

9. $\frac{3}{7} - \frac{2}{7}$

Lesson 13-1

Pages 553–556

Write a fraction and a decimal for the part that is shaded.

1.
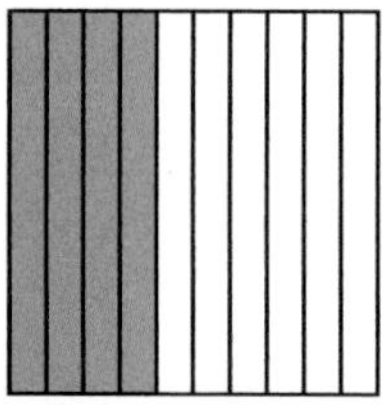

2.
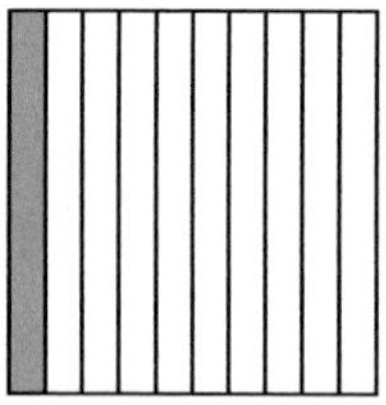

3.
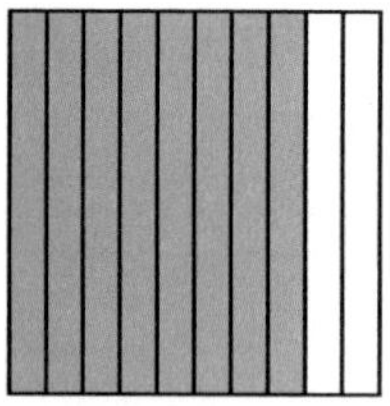

4.
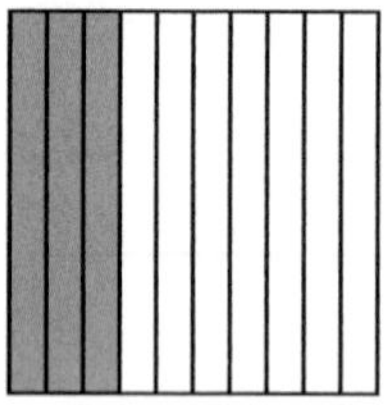

5.
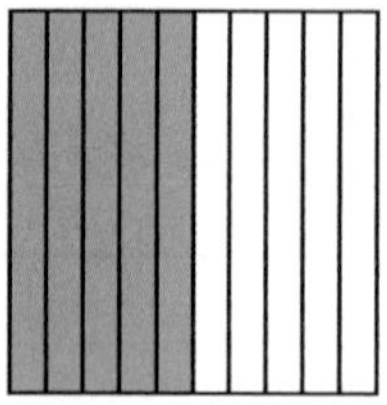

6.
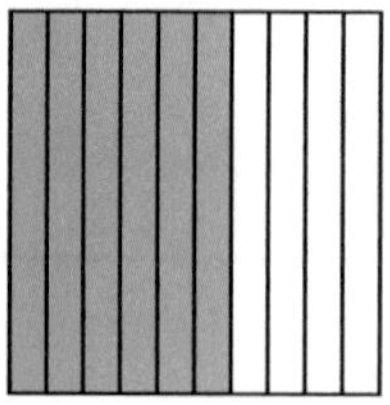

Lesson 13-2

Pages 558–560

Write each fraction as a decimal.

1. $\frac{18}{100}$

2. $\frac{36}{100}$

3. $\frac{88}{100}$

4. $\frac{20}{100}$

5. $\frac{48}{100}$

6. $\frac{57}{100}$

Write each decimal as a fraction.

7. 0.45

8. 0.10

9. 0.75

10. 0.14

11. 0.54

12. 0.23

13. 0.37

14. 0.98

15. 0.42

Lesson 13-3

Pages 564–565

Solve. Use the *act it out* strategy.

1. Freddie ate 0.3 of a pizza. Tim ate 0.5 of the pizza. How much of the pizza is left?

2. Janet made 2 out of every 5 basketball shots she took. She made 12 shots. How many shots did she take?

3. Elena is halfway up a flight of stairs. Karen is one-third of the way up the stairs. There are 12 stairs in all. Which stair is each girl on?

4. There are 10 birds in a pond. 0.2 of them are swans. 0.4 of them are ducks. The rest are geese. How many geese are there?

Lesson 13-4

Pages 568–571

Write the part of a dollar each amount represents.

1. 18¢ **2.** 40¢ **3.** 72¢

4. 85¢ **5.** 64¢ **6.** 55¢

7. 75¢ **8.** 14¢ **9.** 48¢

10. 57¢ **11.** 6¢ **12.** 30¢

Lesson 13-5

Pages 572–573

Use any strategy to solve. Tell what strategy you used.

1. Rafi has 8 nickels, 3 dimes, and 2 quarters. Does he have enough to buy a beach ball that costs $1.25? Explain.

2. Sonya made a batch of 22 brownies. She will give an equal number to each of 5 friends. How many brownies will each friend get? How many will be left over?

3. A waiting room has 6 rows of seats. There are 10 seats in each row. There are people sitting in half of the seats. How many seats are empty?

4. Sam is shorter than Rory. Ben is taller than Lee. Rory is shorter than Lee. Name the boys from tallest to shortest.

Lesson 14-1

Pages 585–587

Multiply. Use basic facts and patterns.

1. $3 \times 7 = \blacksquare$
$3 \times 70 = \blacksquare$
$3 \times 700 = \blacksquare$
$3 \times 7{,}000 = \blacksquare$

2. $5 \times 9 = \blacksquare$
$5 \times 90 = \blacksquare$
$5 \times 900 = \blacksquare$
$5 \times 9{,}000 = \blacksquare$

3. $8 \times 6 = \blacksquare$
$8 \times 60 = \blacksquare$
$8 \times 600 = \blacksquare$
$8 \times 6{,}000 = \blacksquare$

4. $9 \times 4 = \blacksquare$
$9 \times 40 = \blacksquare$
$9 \times 400 = \blacksquare$
$9 \times 4{,}000 = \blacksquare$

5. $7 \times 7 = \blacksquare$
$7 \times 70 = \blacksquare$
$7 \times 700 = \blacksquare$
$7 \times 7{,}000 = \blacksquare$

6. $6 \times 5 = \blacksquare$
$6 \times 50 = \blacksquare$
$6 \times 500 = \blacksquare$
$6 \times 5{,}000 = \blacksquare$

Lesson 14-2

Pages 588–589

Solve. Use *logical reasoning*.

1. Four friends have different types of pets. Tina has a cat. Suni does not have a turtle. Ed does not have a dog. Mark does not have a dog or a snake. What type of pet does each person have?

2. Cameron got on the elevator and rode down 5 floors. Then she rode up 7 floors. She rode down 6 floors and got off on the 10th floor. What floor did she start on?

3. Curtis and Anna have change that has the same value. The value is under $1. Curtis has 7 coins. Anna has 4 coins. What two possible combinations could they have?

4. A baby stacked 4 different shapes. The rectangle is on top. A triangle is on top of a square. A circle is not at the bottom. What is the order of the shapes from top to bottom?

Lesson 14-3

Pages 590–592

Estimate. Round to the nearest ten.

1. 28×5

2. 42×4

3. 37×7

Estimate. Round to the nearest hundred.

4. 170×6

5. 210×8

6. 390×5

7. 289×3

8. 113×9

9. 274×6

Lesson 14-4

Pages 594–597

Multiply. Use estimation to check.

1. $\begin{array}{r} 26 \\ \times 3 \\ \hline \end{array}$

2. $\begin{array}{r} 312 \\ \times\ 4 \\ \hline \end{array}$

3. $\begin{array}{r} 432 \\ \times\ 3 \\ \hline \end{array}$

4. $\begin{array}{r} 2,321 \\ \times\quad 4 \\ \hline \end{array}$

5. $\begin{array}{r} 3,443 \\ \times\quad 2 \\ \hline \end{array}$

6. $\begin{array}{r} 4,200 \\ \times\quad 4 \\ \hline \end{array}$

7. 2×34

8. 2×241

9. 3×28

10. $3 \times 3,100$

11. 2×432

12. $3 \times 1,221$

Lesson 14-5

Pages 598–599

Use any strategy to solve. Tell what strategy you used.

1. Diana put 7 plums on one side of a scale. To balance the scale, she put 4 plums and 1 apple on the other side of the scale. Each plum weighs 2 ounces. How much does the apple weigh?

2. Troy, Andre, and Ana gathered 450 acorns. Troy gathered 5 times as many acorns as Ana did. Andre gathered 3 times as many as Ana did. How many acorns did each one collect?

3. Ms. McCoy has 3 pitchers of tea. Each pitcher holds 1 gallon of tea. How many cups of tea can she fill will with the pitchers?

4. Alicia, Katie, and Megan each play a sport. Megan does not play soccer, Katie does not play basketball or tennis, and Alicia plays basketball. Which sport does each girl play?

Lesson 14-6

Pages 602–605

Multiply. Use models if needed.

1. $\begin{array}{r} 29 \\ \times 5 \\ \hline \end{array}$

2. $\begin{array}{r} 33 \\ \times 6 \\ \hline \end{array}$

3. $\begin{array}{r} 51 \\ \times 9 \\ \hline \end{array}$

4. $\begin{array}{r} 205 \\ \times\ 4 \\ \hline \end{array}$

5. $\begin{array}{r} 113 \\ \times\ 8 \\ \hline \end{array}$

6. $\begin{array}{r} 223 \\ \times\ 5 \\ \hline \end{array}$

7. $\begin{array}{r} 532 \\ \times\ 3 \\ \hline \end{array}$

8. $\begin{array}{r} 1,204 \\ \times\quad 7 \\ \hline \end{array}$

9. $\begin{array}{r} 1,023 \\ \times\quad 4 \\ \hline \end{array}$

Lesson 14-7

Pages 606–608

Multiply.

1. 214×2 **2.** 128×3 **3.** 405×8

4. 160×4 **5.** 391×7 **6.** 286×3

7. 622×3 **8.** 153×5 **9.** 112×9

10. 203×8 **11.** $1{,}089 \times 3$ **12.** 393×5

Lesson 14-8

Pages 610–613

Multiply.

1. $\$1.25 \times 5$ **2.** $\$2.17 \times 4$ **3.** $\$4.68 \times 2$

4. $\$1.82 \times 6$ **5.** $\$3.44 \times 3$ **6.** $\$0.84 \times 6$

7. $5 \times \$6.22$ **8.** $7 \times \$3.08$ **9.** $4 \times \$5.06$

10. $6 \times \$2.71$ **11.** $8 \times \$5.34$ **12.** $6 \times \$4.12$

Lesson 15-1

Pages 627–629

Use basic facts and patterns of zeros to find each quotient.

1. $8 \div 2 =$ ■
$80 \div 2 =$ ■
$800 \div 2 =$ ■
$8{,}000 \div 2 =$ ■

2. $6 \div 1 =$ ■
$60 \div 1 =$ ■
$600 \div 1 =$ ■
$6{,}000 \div 1 =$ ■

3. $15 \div 3 =$ ■
$150 \div 3 =$ ■
$1{,}500 \div 3 =$ ■

4. $24 \div 3 =$ ■
$240 \div 3 =$ ■
$2{,}400 \div 3 =$ ■

5. $36 \div 6 =$ ■
$360 \div 6 =$ ■
$3{,}600 \div 6 =$ ■

6. $63 \div 9 =$ ■
$630 \div 9 =$ ■
$6{,}300 \div 9 =$ ■

Divide. Use patterns.

7. $490 \div 7$ **8.** $300 \div 5$ **9.** $270 \div 3$ **10.** $350 \div 7$

11. $480 \div 6$ **12.** $810 \div 9$ **13.** $2{,}500 \div 5$ **14.** $2{,}800 \div 7$

Lesson 15-2

Pages 630–633

Estimate by rounding.

1. 251 ÷ 6
2. 348 ÷ 7
3. 647 ÷ 9
4. 310 ÷ 5
5. 807 ÷ 9
6. 492 ÷ 8
7. 277 ÷ 4
8. 558 ÷ 8
9. 7,231 ÷ 7
10. 2,245 ÷ 5
11. 4,138 ÷ 7
12. 8,077 ÷ 9

Compare. Use > or <.

13. 492 ÷ 7 ■ 646 ÷ 8
14. 334 ÷ 4 ■ 534 ÷ 9

Lesson 15-3

Pages 636–638

Divide. Use models if needed. Check your answer.

1. 66 ÷ 6
2. 70 ÷ 5
3. 72 ÷ 2
4. 52 ÷ 4
5. 84 ÷ 2
6. 91 ÷ 7
7. 60 ÷ 5
8. 88 ÷ 8
9. 98 ÷ 7
10. 65 ÷ 5
11. 85 ÷ 5
12. 90 ÷ 6

Lesson 15-4

Pages 640–641

Solve. Use the *work backward* strategy to solve.

1. Tara played at the park for $1\frac{1}{2}$ hours. She ate lunch for $\frac{1}{2}$ hour. Then she spent $\frac{1}{2}$ hour walking home. She got home at 6:30. What time did she get to the park?
2. Jamal received 9 CDs for his birthday. Then, he bought 7 more CDs. Now, he has 37 CDs. How many CDs did he have before his birthday?
3. Ms. McCoy packed 6 coolers with equal numbers of juice and water bottles. She packed 36 bottles of juice altogether. How many bottles of juice and water did she pack in each cooler?
4. Tom had some money in his piggy bank. Last week he put twice as much money in his bank as he already had. This week he put 3 times as much in as he did last week. Now he has $27 in his bank. How much did he start with?

Lesson 15-5

Pages 642–644

Divide. Check your answers.

1. 180 ÷ 5 **2.** 492 ÷ 4 **3.** 294 ÷ 7

4. 366 ÷ 3 **5.** 342 ÷ 6 **6.** 440 ÷ 5

7. 666 ÷ 9 **8.** 861 ÷ 7 **9.** 750 ÷ 2

10. 678 ÷ 3 **11.** 567 ÷ 7 **12.** 744 ÷ 6

Lesson 15-6

Pages 648–649

Use any strategy to solve. Tell what strategy you used.

1. A box contains 8 individual packages of 12 crackers each. How many crackers are in 3 boxes?

2. The temperature was 34 degrees at 5:00 P.M. The temperature fell 4 degrees every hour for the next 5 hours. What was the temperature at 10:00 P.M.?

3. There are 448 markers in a box to be shared by 56 students. Will each student get 7, 8, or 9 markers?

4. Dan's yard is 35 feet long and 20 feet wide. He has 135 feet of fencing. How much will be left after he fences his yard?

Lesson 15-7

Pages 650–653

Divide. Check your answer.

1. \$6.30 ÷ 2 **2.** \$8.46 ÷ 3 **3.** \$9.63 ÷ 3

4. \$5.90 ÷ 5 **5.** \$7.83 ÷ 9 **6.** \$4.75 ÷ 5

7. \$9.24 ÷ 4 **8.** \$6.24 ÷ 8 **9.** \$9.12 ÷ 3

10. \$9.30 ÷ 5 **11.** \$8.72 ÷ 4 **12.** \$9.17 ÷ 7

Find the unit cost.

13. 2 yoyos for \$4.48 **14.** 5 sunflowers for \$8.40 **15.** 4 markers for \$3.80

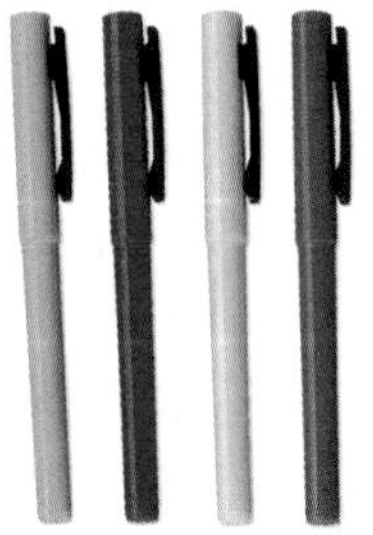

Addition

1. $\begin{array}{r} 6 \\ +\ 3 \\ \hline \end{array}$

2. $\begin{array}{r} 1 \\ +\ 9 \\ \hline \end{array}$

3. $\begin{array}{r} 2 \\ +\ 5 \\ \hline \end{array}$

4. $\begin{array}{r} 0 \\ +\ 10 \\ \hline \end{array}$

5. $\begin{array}{r} 1 \\ +\ 7 \\ \hline \end{array}$

6. $\begin{array}{r} 3 \\ +\ 7 \\ \hline \end{array}$

7. $\begin{array}{r} 3 \\ +\ 9 \\ \hline \end{array}$

8. $\begin{array}{r} 9 \\ +\ 9 \\ \hline \end{array}$

9. $\begin{array}{r} 5 \\ +\ 3 \\ \hline \end{array}$

10. $\begin{array}{r} 2 \\ +\ 10 \\ \hline \end{array}$

11. $\begin{array}{r} 4 \\ +\ 1 \\ \hline \end{array}$

12. $\begin{array}{r} 6 \\ +\ 7 \\ \hline \end{array}$

13. $\begin{array}{r} 9 \\ +\ 5 \\ \hline \end{array}$

14. $\begin{array}{r} 8 \\ +\ 1 \\ \hline \end{array}$

15. $\begin{array}{r} 4 \\ +\ 4 \\ \hline \end{array}$

16. $\begin{array}{r} 3 \\ +\ 8 \\ \hline \end{array}$

17. $\begin{array}{r} 10 \\ +\ 10 \\ \hline \end{array}$

18. $\begin{array}{r} 4 \\ +\ 3 \\ \hline \end{array}$

19. $\begin{array}{r} 7 \\ +\ 2 \\ \hline \end{array}$

20. $\begin{array}{r} 6 \\ +\ 0 \\ \hline \end{array}$

21. $5 + 1$

22. $4 + 6$

23. $3 + 3$

24. $8 + 7$

25. $2 + 6$

26. $0 + 5$

27. $10 + 4$

28. $9 + 8$

29. $7 + 7$

30. $8 + 5$

31. $9 + 10$

32. $3 + 2$

33. $10 + 8$

34. $1 + 6$

35. $8 + 10$

36. $5 + 5$

37. $2 + 2$

38. $7 + 9$

39. $10 + 5$

40. $8 + 6$

Addition

1. $\begin{array}{r} 2 \\ +\,4 \\ \hline \end{array}$	**2.** $\begin{array}{r} 6 \\ +\,6 \\ \hline \end{array}$	**3.** $\begin{array}{r} 1 \\ +\,8 \\ \hline \end{array}$	**4.** $\begin{array}{r} 9 \\ +\,7 \\ \hline \end{array}$
5. $\begin{array}{r} 3 \\ +\,5 \\ \hline \end{array}$	**6.** $\begin{array}{r} 4 \\ +\,9 \\ \hline \end{array}$	**7.** $\begin{array}{r} 7 \\ +\,6 \\ \hline \end{array}$	**8.** $\begin{array}{r} 10 \\ +\,1 \\ \hline \end{array}$
9. $\begin{array}{r} 7 \\ +\,0 \\ \hline \end{array}$	**10.** $\begin{array}{r} 2 \\ +\,9 \\ \hline \end{array}$	**11.** $\begin{array}{r} 3 \\ +\,4 \\ \hline \end{array}$	**12.** $\begin{array}{r} 6 \\ +\,4 \\ \hline \end{array}$
13. $\begin{array}{r} 5 \\ +\,8 \\ \hline \end{array}$	**14.** $\begin{array}{r} 1 \\ +\,4 \\ \hline \end{array}$	**15.** $\begin{array}{r} 2 \\ +\,7 \\ \hline \end{array}$	**16.** $\begin{array}{r} 9 \\ +\,3 \\ \hline \end{array}$
17. $\begin{array}{r} 5 \\ +\,7 \\ \hline \end{array}$	**18.** $\begin{array}{r} 9 \\ +\,0 \\ \hline \end{array}$	**19.** $\begin{array}{r} 10 \\ +\,6 \\ \hline \end{array}$	**20.** $\begin{array}{r} 8 \\ +\,8 \\ \hline \end{array}$
21. 5 + 4	**22.** 1 + 3	**23.** 6 + 5	**24.** 1 + 2
25. 10 + 3	**26.** 8 + 3	**27.** 4 + 7	**28.** 0 + 8
29. 6 + 8	**30.** 1 + 5	**31.** 3 + 6	**32.** 7 + 3
33. 0 + 4	**34.** 5 + 2	**35.** 7 + 8	**36.** 9 + 6
37. 0 + 3	**38.** 8 + 4	**39.** 10 + 7	**40.** 8 + 9

Subtraction

1. $3 - 2$

2. $19 - 10$

3. $13 - 4$

4. $9 - 7$

5. $15 - 5$

6. $5 - 5$

7. $16 - 8$

8. $7 - 5$

9. $6 - 1$

10. $18 - 10$

11. $9 - 6$

12. $17 - 9$

13. $8 - 4$

14. $9 - 1$

15. $20 - 10$

16. $14 - 6$

17. $11 - 3$

18. $4 - 3$

19. $12 - 7$

20. $10 - 8$

21. 7 − 6

22. 19 − 9

23. 16 − 7

24. 9 − 4

25. 17 − 7

26. 11 − 5

27. 6 − 6

28. 8 − 1

29. 5 − 0

30. 15 − 8

31. 10 − 6

32. 14 − 9

33. 12 − 5

34. 10 − 0

35. 9 − 8

36. 6 − 5

37. 7 − 0

38. 8 − 6

39. 14 − 7

40. 12 − 6

Subtraction

Facts Practice

1. $\begin{array}{r} 4 \\ -2 \\ \hline \end{array}$ 2. $\begin{array}{r} 11 \\ -2 \\ \hline \end{array}$ 3. $\begin{array}{r} 8 \\ -0 \\ \hline \end{array}$ 4. $\begin{array}{r} 12 \\ -9 \\ \hline \end{array}$

5. $\begin{array}{r} 10 \\ -5 \\ \hline \end{array}$ 6. $\begin{array}{r} 8 \\ -3 \\ \hline \end{array}$ 7. $\begin{array}{r} 13 \\ -6 \\ \hline \end{array}$ 8. $\begin{array}{r} 5 \\ -1 \\ \hline \end{array}$

9. $\begin{array}{r} 12 \\ -3 \\ \hline \end{array}$ 10. $\begin{array}{r} 7 \\ -1 \\ \hline \end{array}$ 11. $\begin{array}{r} 10 \\ -9 \\ \hline \end{array}$ 12. $\begin{array}{r} 6 \\ -4 \\ \hline \end{array}$

13. $\begin{array}{r} 10 \\ -1 \\ \hline \end{array}$ 14. $\begin{array}{r} 14 \\ -5 \\ \hline \end{array}$ 15. $\begin{array}{r} 7 \\ -7 \\ \hline \end{array}$ 16. $\begin{array}{r} 5 \\ -2 \\ \hline \end{array}$

17. $\begin{array}{r} 15 \\ -9 \\ \hline \end{array}$ 18. $\begin{array}{r} 8 \\ -2 \\ \hline \end{array}$ 19. $\begin{array}{r} 6 \\ -3 \\ \hline \end{array}$ 20. $\begin{array}{r} 13 \\ -9 \\ \hline \end{array}$

21. 7 − 2 22. 17 − 8 23. 10 − 3 24. 6 − 2

25. 13 − 7 26. 15 − 6 27. 8 − 5 28. 5 − 3

29. 11 − 4 30. 9 − 0 31. 12 − 8 32. 10 − 7

33. 13 − 5 34. 7 − 3 35. 10 − 4 36. 6 − 0

37. 10 − 2 38. 18 − 9 39. 14 − 7 40. 16 − 9

Multiplication

1. $\begin{array}{r} 1 \\ \times\ 1 \\ \hline \end{array}$

2. $\begin{array}{r} 10 \\ \times\ 2 \\ \hline \end{array}$

3. $\begin{array}{r} 5 \\ \times\ 5 \\ \hline \end{array}$

4. $\begin{array}{r} 8 \\ \times\ 6 \\ \hline \end{array}$

5. $\begin{array}{r} 7 \\ \times\ 4 \\ \hline \end{array}$

6. $\begin{array}{r} 3 \\ \times\ 0 \\ \hline \end{array}$

7. $\begin{array}{r} 9 \\ \times\ 8 \\ \hline \end{array}$

8. $\begin{array}{r} 5 \\ \times\ 2 \\ \hline \end{array}$

9. $\begin{array}{r} 8 \\ \times\ 1 \\ \hline \end{array}$

10. $\begin{array}{r} 6 \\ \times\ 5 \\ \hline \end{array}$

11. $\begin{array}{r} 7 \\ \times\ 2 \\ \hline \end{array}$

12. $\begin{array}{r} 9 \\ \times\ 3 \\ \hline \end{array}$

13. $\begin{array}{r} 5 \\ \times\ 9 \\ \hline \end{array}$

14. $\begin{array}{r} 6 \\ \times\ 10 \\ \hline \end{array}$

15. $\begin{array}{r} 7 \\ \times\ 7 \\ \hline \end{array}$

16. $\begin{array}{r} 0 \\ \times\ 6 \\ \hline \end{array}$

17. $\begin{array}{r} 4 \\ \times\ 2 \\ \hline \end{array}$

18. $\begin{array}{r} 2 \\ \times\ 9 \\ \hline \end{array}$

19. $\begin{array}{r} 10 \\ \times\ 0 \\ \hline \end{array}$

20. $\begin{array}{r} 7 \\ \times\ 5 \\ \hline \end{array}$

21. 1×9

22. 3×6

23. 4×8

24. 5×10

25. 2×3

26. 10×8

27. 7×0

28. 6×4

29. 4×10

30. 6×2

31. 0×4

32. 4×4

33. 1×0

34. 7×6

35. 9×4

36. 3×5

37. 8×0

38. 10×7

39. 8×7

40. 7×3

Facts Practice

Multiplication

1. $\begin{array}{r} 2 \\ \times\ 2 \\ \hline \end{array}$

2. $\begin{array}{r} 4 \\ \times\ 3 \\ \hline \end{array}$

3. $\begin{array}{r} 5 \\ \times\ 8 \\ \hline \end{array}$

4. $\begin{array}{r} 4 \\ \times\ 0 \\ \hline \end{array}$

5. $\begin{array}{r} 8 \\ \times\ 8 \\ \hline \end{array}$

6. $\begin{array}{r} 7 \\ \times\ 8 \\ \hline \end{array}$

7. $\begin{array}{r} 9 \\ \times\ 7 \\ \hline \end{array}$

8. $\begin{array}{r} 1 \\ \times\ 6 \\ \hline \end{array}$

9. $\begin{array}{r} 4 \\ \times\ 10 \\ \hline \end{array}$

10. $\begin{array}{r} 6 \\ \times\ 8 \\ \hline \end{array}$

11. $\begin{array}{r} 5 \\ \times\ 3 \\ \hline \end{array}$

12. $\begin{array}{r} 0 \\ \times\ 2 \\ \hline \end{array}$

13. $\begin{array}{r} 9 \\ \times\ 9 \\ \hline \end{array}$

14. $\begin{array}{r} 5 \\ \times\ 1 \\ \hline \end{array}$

15. $\begin{array}{r} 8 \\ \times\ 3 \\ \hline \end{array}$

16. $\begin{array}{r} 5 \\ \times\ 7 \\ \hline \end{array}$

17. $\begin{array}{r} 0 \\ \times\ 5 \\ \hline \end{array}$

18. $\begin{array}{r} 6 \\ \times\ 3 \\ \hline \end{array}$

19. $\begin{array}{r} 10 \\ \times\ 1 \\ \hline \end{array}$

20. $\begin{array}{r} 9 \\ \times\ 6 \\ \hline \end{array}$

21. 4×7

22. 3×1

23. 2×8

24. 6×7

25. 8×4

26. 3×3

27. 6×0

28. 2×5

29. 5×6

30. 4×6

31. 3×9

32. 7×10

33. 9×2

34. 4×1

35. 0×10

36. 4×5

37. 1×7

38. 8×9

39. 6×6

40. 10×9

Division

1. $4\overline{)16}$ **2.** $10\overline{)50}$ **3.** $1\overline{)1}$ **4.** $6\overline{)48}$

5. $3\overline{)0}$ **6.** $7\overline{)56}$ **7.** $9\overline{)27}$ **8.** $5\overline{)25}$

9. $9\overline{)90}$ **10.** $6\overline{)36}$ **11.** $2\overline{)14}$ **12.** $4\overline{)32}$

13. $1\overline{)5}$ **14.** $8\overline{)72}$ **15.** $3\overline{)15}$ **16.** $7\overline{)0}$

17. $10\overline{)70}$ **18.** $2\overline{)18}$ **19.** $8\overline{)64}$ **20.** $1\overline{)8}$

21. $12 \div 4$ **22.** $10 \div 2$ **23.** $45 \div 9$ **24.** $36 \div 9$

25. $60 \div 10$ **26.** $10 \div 1$ **27.** $42 \div 7$ **28.** $9 \div 3$

29. $8 \div 8$ **30.** $81 \div 9$ **31.** $36 \div 6$ **32.** $20 \div 4$

33. $10 \div 5$ **34.** $54 \div 9$ **35.** $8 \div 2$ **36.** $49 \div 7$

37. $4 \div 1$ **38.** $40 \div 8$ **39.** $0 \div 6$ **40.** $100 \div 10$

Division

1. $5\overline{)5}$	**2.** $10\overline{)20}$	**3.** $7\overline{)28}$	**4.** $9\overline{)18}$
5. $21\overline{)3}$	**6.** $6\overline{)60}$	**7.** $5\overline{)0}$	**8.** $8\overline{)56}$
9. $4\overline{)24}$	**10.** $10\overline{)30}$	**11.** $5\overline{)45}$	**12.** $1\overline{)3}$
13. $8\overline{)80}$	**14.** $10\overline{)0}$	**15.** $2\overline{)2}$	**16.** $5\overline{)30}$
17. $2\overline{)20}$	**18.** $6\overline{)18}$	**19.** $3\overline{)27}$	**20.** $5\overline{)35}$
21. $16 \div 2$	**22.** $72 \div 9$	**23.** $3 \div 3$	**24.** $48 \div 8$
25. $9 \div 1$	**26.** $12 \div 3$	**27.** $8 \div 4$	**28.** $2 \div 1$
29. $40 \div 4$	**30.** $28 \div 9$	**31.** $0 \div 9$	**32.** $6 \div 2$
33. $54 \div 6$	**34.** $63 \div 7$	**35.** $4 \div 36$	**36.** $15 \div 5$
37. $32 \div 8$	**38.** $36 \div 4$	**39.** $6 \div 3$	**40.** $35 \div 7$

Glossary/Glosario

Math Online A mathematics multilingual glossary is available at www.ca.gr3math.com/multilingual_glossary. The glossary includes the following languages.

Arabic	Cantonese	Korean	Tagalog
Bengali	English	Russian	Urdu
Brazilian Portuguese	Haitian Creole	Spanish	Vietnamese
	Hmong		

Cómo usar el glosario en español:

1. Busca el término en inglés que desces encontrar.
2. El término en español, junto con la definición, se encuentran en la columna de la derecha.

English

A

addend (p. 65) Any numbers being added together.

add (adding, addition) (p. 65) An operation on two or more *addends* that results in a *sum*.

$$9 + 3 = 12$$

angle (p. 419) A figure that is formed by two *rays* with the same *endpoint*.

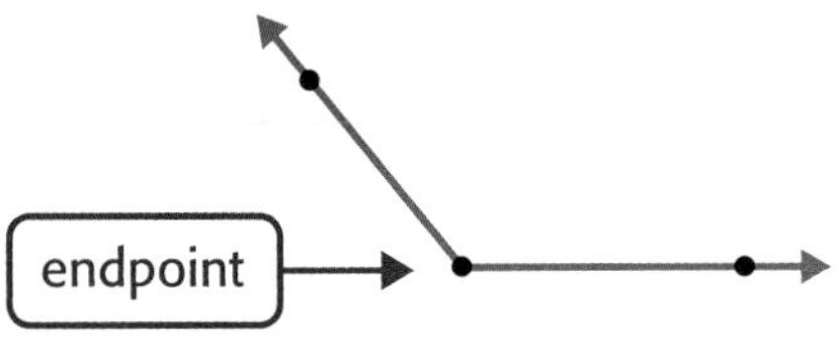

area (p. 428) The number of *square units* needed to cover the inside of a region or plane figure.

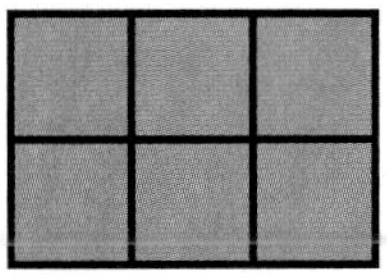

area = 6 square units

array (p. 160) Objects or symbols displayed in rows of the same length and columns of the same length.

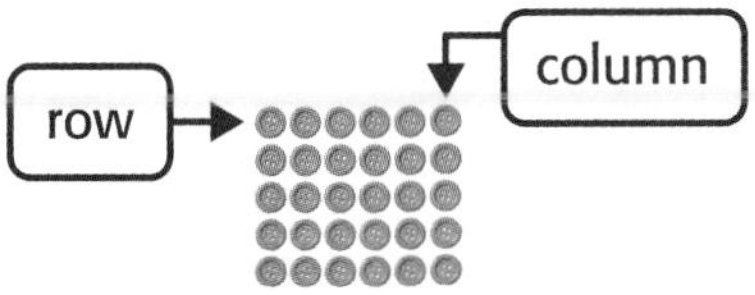

Español

sumando Cualquier número que se le suma a otro.

suma (sumar) Operación que se realiza en dos o más *sumandos* y que resulta en una *suma*.

$$9 + 3 = 12$$

ángulo Figura formada por dos *rayos* con el mismo *extremo*.

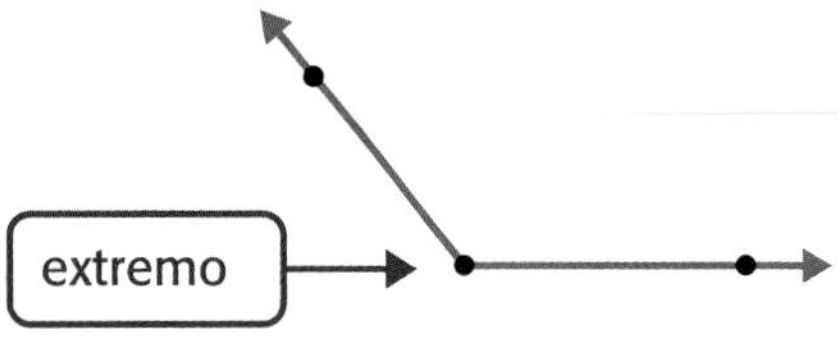

área Número de *unidades cuadradas* necesarias para cubrir el interior de una región o figura plana.

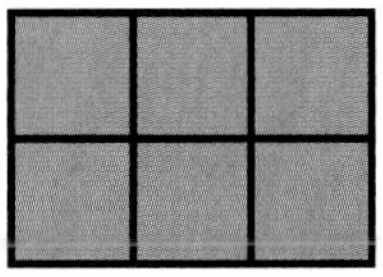

área = 6 unidades cuadradas

arreglo Objetos o símbolos representados en filas de la misma longitud y columnas de la misma longitud.

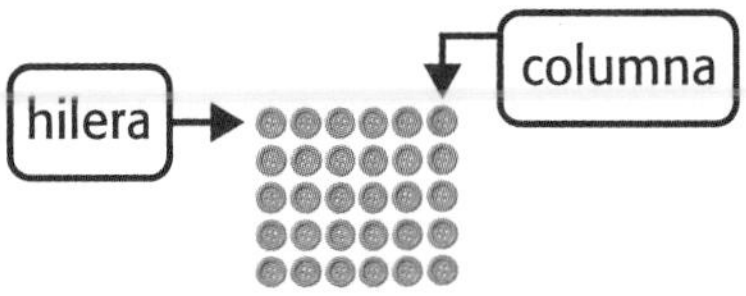

Associative Property of Addition (p. 65) The property which states that the grouping of the *addends* does not change the *sum*.

$(4 + 5) + 2 = 4 + (5 + 2)$

propiedad asociativa de la adición Propiedad que establece que la agrupación de los *sumandos* no altera la *suma*.

$(4 + 5) + 2 = 4 + (5 + 2)$

Associative Property of Multiplication (p. 228) The property which states that the grouping of the factors does not change the *product*.

$3 \times (6 \times 2) = (3 \times 6) \times 2$

propiedad asociativa de la multiplicación Propiedad que establece que la agrupación de los factores no altera el *producto*.

$3 \times (6 \times 2) = (3 \times 6) \times 2$

B

bar graph (p. 471) A graph that compares *data* by using bars of different lengths or heights to show the values.

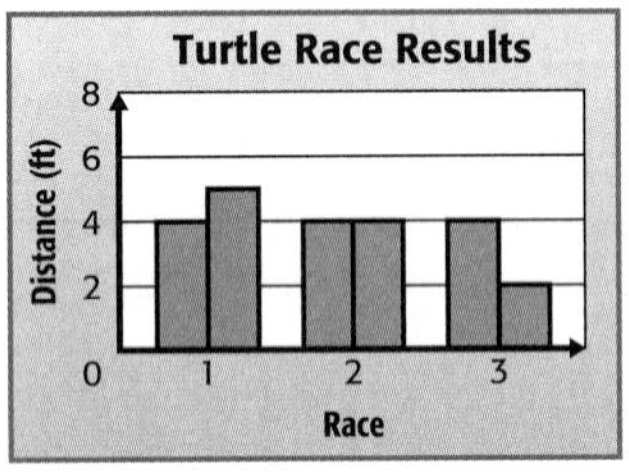

gráfica de barras Gráfica que compara los datos usando barras de distintas longitudes o alturas para mostrar los valores.

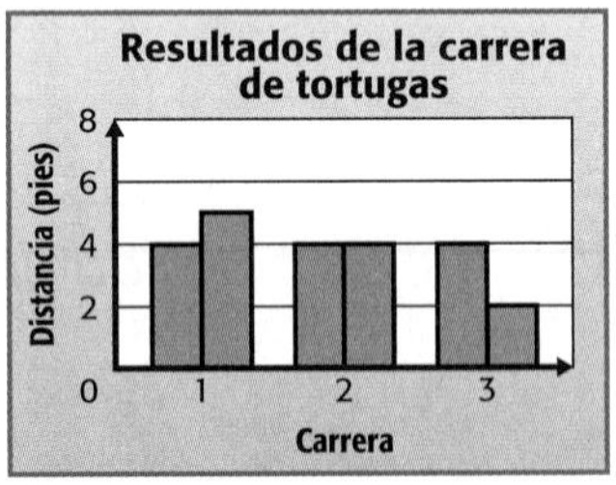

C

capacity (p. 354) The amount a container can hold, measured in units of dry or liquid measure.

capacidad Cantidad que puede contener un envase, medida en unidades liquídas o secas.

centimeter (cm) (p. 385) A *metric unit* for measuring *length and height.*

100 centimeters = 1 meter

centímetro (cm) *Unidad métrica* para medir de longitud y altura.

100 centímetros = 1 metro

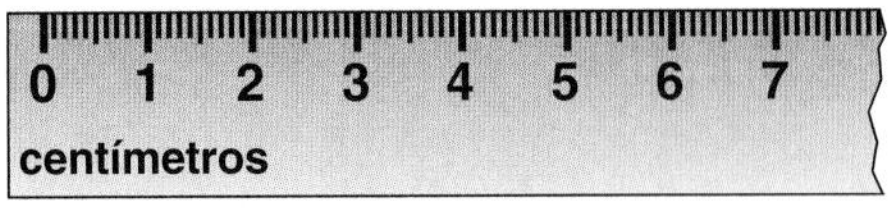

Commutative Property of Addition (p. 65) The property that states that the order in which two numbers are added does not change the *sum*.

$12 + 15 = 15 + 12$

Commutative Property of Multiplication (p. 161) The property that states that the order in which two numbers are multiplied does not change the *product*.

$7 \times 2 = 2 \times 7$

cone (p. 444) A *3-dimensional figure* with a curved surface and a circular *base* which comes to a point called the *vertex*.

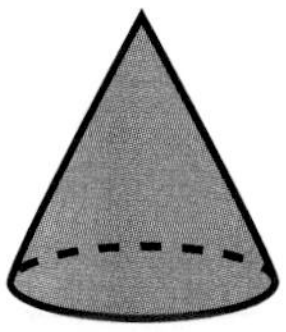

cube (p. 444) A *3-dimensional* figure with six faces that are congruent.

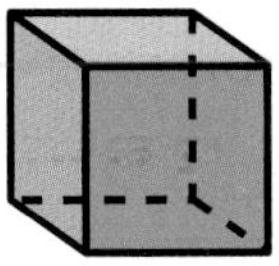

cubic unit (p. 454) A unit for measuring *volume*, such as a cubic inch or a cubic centimeter.

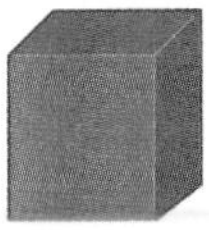

cup (c) (p. 354) A customary unit for measuring *capacity*.

1 cup = 8 ounces
16 cups = 1 gallon

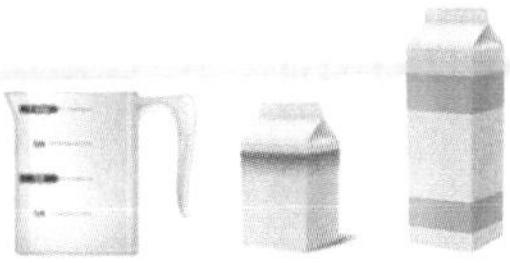

propiedad conmutativa de la adición Propiedad que establece que el orden en el cual se suman dos o más números no altera la *suma*.

$12 + 15 = 15 + 12$

propiedad conmutativa de la multiplicación Propiedad que establece que el orden en el cual se multiplican dos o más números no altera el *producto*.

$7 \times 2 = 2 \times 7$

cono *Figura tridimensional* con una superficie curva y una la *base* circular que terminan en un punto llamado *vértice*.

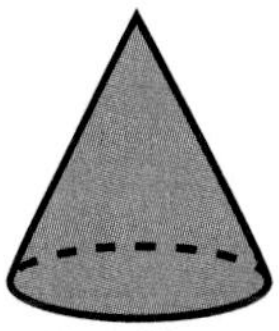

cubo Figura *tridimensional* con seis caras cuadradas *congruentes*.

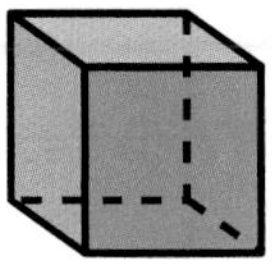

unidad cúbica Unidad para medir *volumen*, como la pulgada cúbica o el centímetro cúbico.

taza (c) Unidad inglesa de *capacidad*.

1 taza = 8 onzas
16 tazas = 1 galón

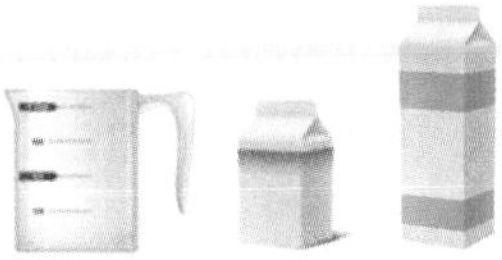

customary system (p. 346) The measurement system that includes units such as foot, pound, quart, and degrees Fahrenheit. Also called *standard measurement.*

sistema inglés Sistema de medición que incluye unidades como el pie, la libra, el cuarto de galón y los grados Fahrenheit. También llamado *medición estándar*.

cylinder (p. 444) A *3-dimensional figure* having two circular *bases* and a curved surface connecting the two *bases*.

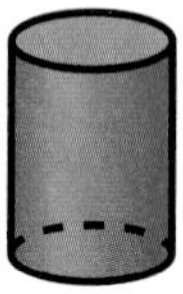

cilindro *Figura tridimensional* que tiene dos *bases* circulares y una superficie curva que une las dos *bases*.

D

data (p. 468) Numbers or symbols sometimes collected from a *survey* or experiment to show information. Datum is singular; data is plural.

datos Números o símbolos, algunas veces recolectados de una *encuesta* o un experimento, para mostrar información.

decimal (p. 553) A number with one or more digits to the right of the decimal point, such as 8.37 or 0.05.

número decimal Número con uno o más dígitos a la derecha del punto decimal, como 8.37 ó 0.05.

decimal point (p. 78) A period separating the ones and the *tenths* in a decimal number.

0.8 or $3.77

punto decimal Punto que separa las unidades de las *décimas* en un número decimal.

0.8 ó $3.77

denominator (p. 509) The bottom number in a *fraction*.

In $\frac{5}{6}$, 6 is the denominator.

denominador El número inferior en una *fracción*.

En $\frac{5}{6}$, 6 es el denominador.

difference (p. 110) The answer to a *subtraction* problem.

diferencia Respuesta a un problema de *resta*.

digit (p. 24) A symbol used to write numbers. The ten digits are 0, 1, 2, 3, 4, 5, 6, 7, 8, and 9.

dígito Símbolo que se usa para escribir números. Los diez dígitos son 0, 1, 2, 3, 4, 5, 6, 7, 8 y 9.

divide (division) (p. 251) To separate into equal groups.

dividend (p. 256) A number that is being divided.

3)9 9 is the dividend

divisor (p. 256) The number by which the dividend is being divided.

3)19 3 is the divisor

dollar ($) (p. 78) one dollar = 100¢ or 100 cents. Also written as $1.00.

front

back

E

edge (p. 444) The line segment where two faces of a solid figure meet.

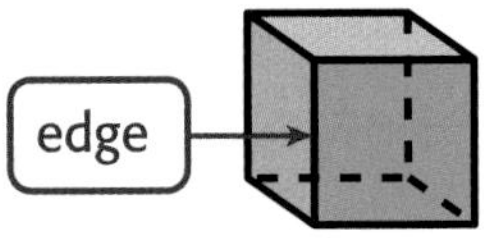

equally likely (p. 492) Having the same chance of occurring.

In a coin toss, you are equally likely to flip heads or tails.

equals sign (=) (p. 34) A symbol of equality.

dividir (división) Separar en grupos iguales.

dividendo El número que se divide.

3)9 9 es el dividendo

divisor Número entre el cual se divide el dividendo.

3)19 3 es el divisor

dólar ($) Un dólar = 100¢ ó 100 centavos. También se escribe como $1.00.

frente

revés

arista Segmento de recta donde concurren dos caras de una figura sólida.

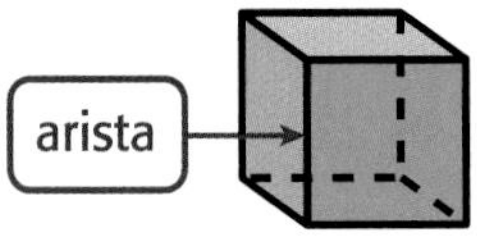

equiprobable Que tienen la misma posibilidad de ocurrir.

Al lanzar una moneda, tienes la misma posibilidad de que caiga cara o escudo.

signo de igualdad (=) Símbolo que muestra igualdad.

equation (p. 321) A sentence that contains an equals sign (=) showing that two *expressions* are equal.

$5 + 7 = 2$

ecuación Expresión que contiene un signo de igualdad y que muestra que dos expresiones son iquales.

$5 + 7 = 2$

equilateral triangle (p. 434) A *triangle* with three *sides* of the same *length.*

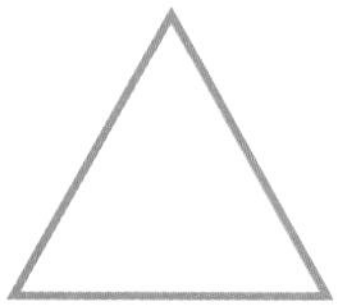

triángulo equilátero *Triángulo* con tres *lados* de la misma *longitud.*

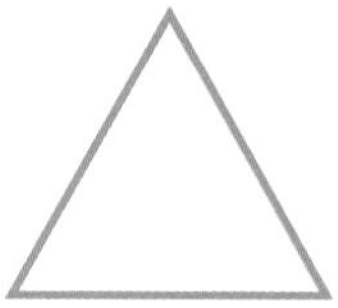

equivalent fractions (p. 516) *Fractions* that have the same value.

$\frac{2}{4} = \frac{1}{2}$

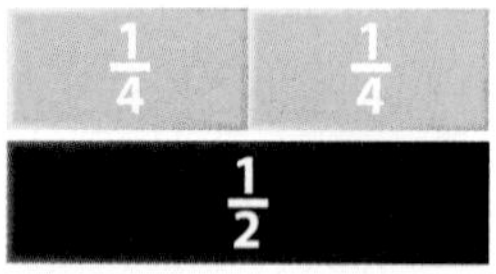

fracciones equivalentes *Fracciones* que tienen el mismo valor.

$\frac{2}{4}$ y $\frac{1}{2}$

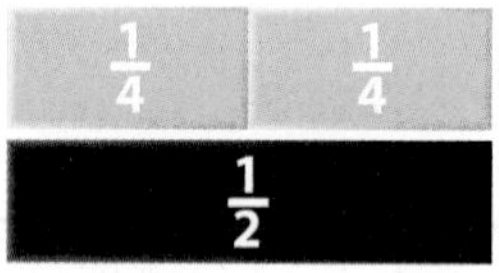

estimate (p. 70) A number close to an exact value. An estimate indicates *about* how much.

47 + 22 is about 70.

estimación Número cercano a un valor exacto. Una estimación indica aproximadamente cuánto.

47 + 22 es aproximadamente 70.

event (p. 492) A set of *outcomes* in a *probability* experiment.

evento Conjunto de *resultados* de un experimento *probabilístico*.

expanded form/expanded notation (p. 25) The representation of a number as a sum that shows the value of each digit.

536 is written as 500 + 30 + 6.

forma desarrollada/notación desarrollada Representación de un número como suma que muestra el valor de cada dígito.

536 se escribe como 500 + 30 + 6.

expression (p. 138) A combination of numbers and operations.

$5 + 7$

expresión Combinación de números y símbolos.

$5 + 7$

face (p. 444) The flat part of a 3-dimensional figure.

A square is a face of a cube.

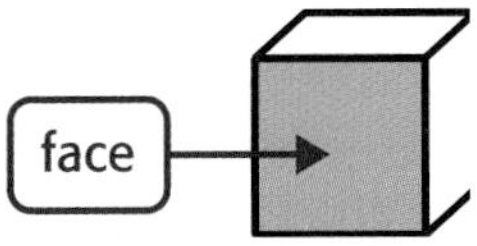

fact family (p. 259) A group of *related facts* using the same numbers.

$5 + 3 = 8$	$5 \times 3 = 15$
$3 + 5 = 8$	$3 \times 5 = 15$
$8 - 3 = 5$	$15 \div 5 = 3$
$8 - 5 = 3$	$15 \div 3 = 5$

factor (p. 158) A number that divides a whole number evenly. Also a number that is multiplied by another number.

foot (ft) (p. 346) A *customary unit* for measuring *length*. Plural is feet.

1 foot = 12 inches

fraction (p. 509) A number that represents part of a whole or part of a set.

$\frac{1}{2}, \frac{1}{3}, \frac{1}{4}, \frac{3}{4}$

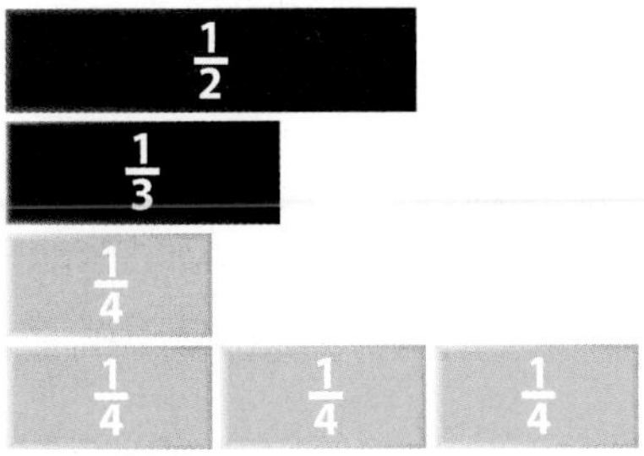

frequency (p. 476) The number of times a result occurs or something happens in a set amount of time or collection of data.

cara La parte llana de una figura tridimensional.

Un cuadrado es una cara de un cubo.

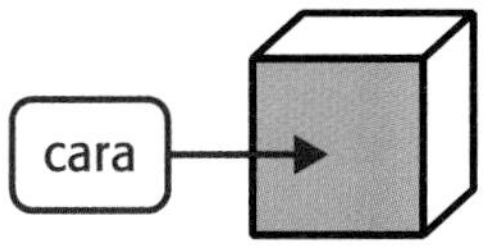

familia de operaciones Grupo de *operaciones relacionadas* que usan los mismos números.

$5 + 3 = 8$	$5 \times 3 = 15$
$3 + 5 = 8$	$3 \times 5 = 15$
$8 - 3 = 5$	$15 \div 5 = 3$
$8 - 5 = 3$	$15 \div 3 = 5$

factor Número que divide exactamente a otro número entero. También es un número multiplicado por otro número.

pie (pie) *Unidad inglesa* para medir *longitud*.

1 pie = 12 pulgadas

fracción Número que representa parte de un todo o parte de un conjunto.

$\frac{1}{2}, \frac{1}{3}, \frac{1}{4}, \frac{3}{4}$

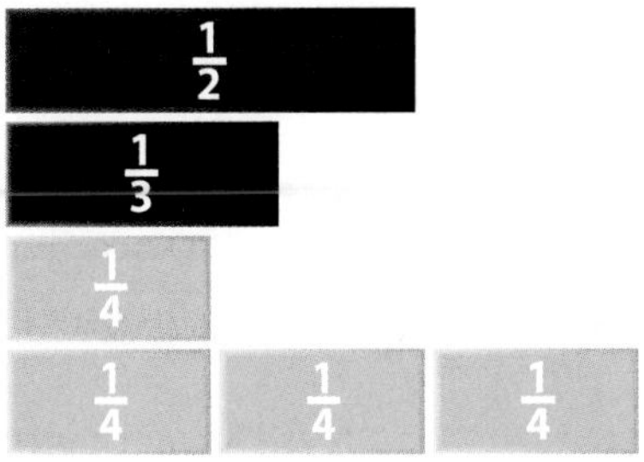

frecuencia El número de veces que ocurre un resultado o sucede algo en un período de tiempo dado o en una colección de datos.

function (p. 234) A relationship in which one quantity depends upon another quantity.

función Relación en que una cantidad depende de otra cantidad.

G

gallon (gal) (p. 354) A *customary unit* for measuring *capacity* for liquids.

1 gallon = 4 quarts

galón (gal) *Unidad de medida inglesa* para medir la *capacidad* líquida.

1 galón = 4 cuartos de galón

gram (g) (p. 398) A *metric unit* for measuring *mass*.

gramo (g) *Unidad métrica* para medir la *masa*.

graph (p. 471) An organized drawing that shows sets of data and how they are related to each other. Also a type of chart.

a bar graph

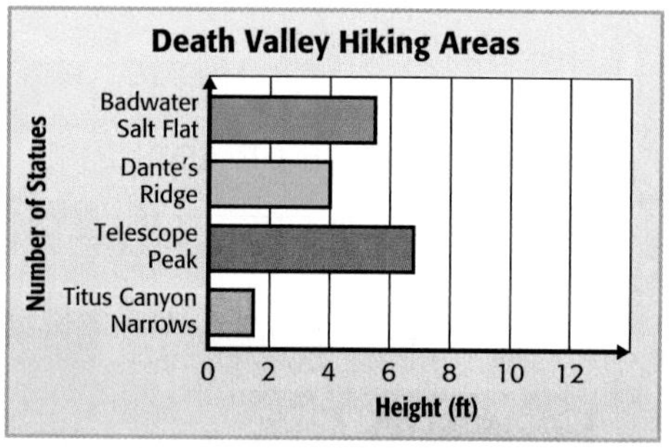

gráfica Dibujo organizado que muestra conjuntos de datos y cómo se relacionan. También, un tipo de diagrama.

una gráfica de barras

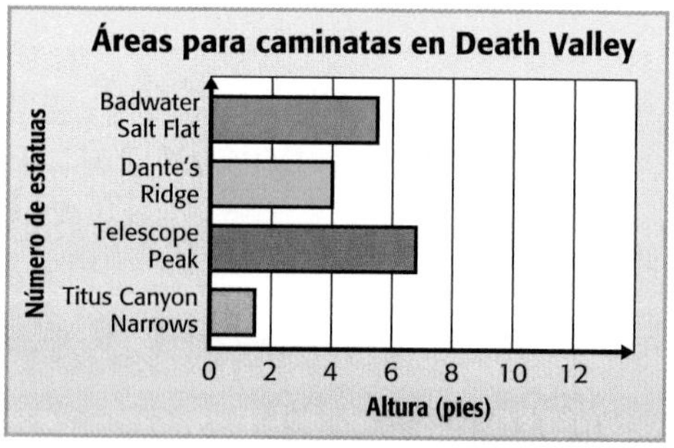

H

hexagon (p. 419) A *polygon* with six *sides* and six *angles*.

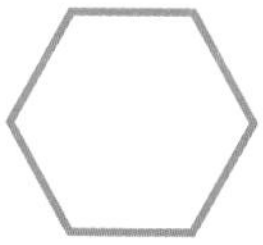

hexágono *Polígono* con seis *lados* y seis *ángulos*.

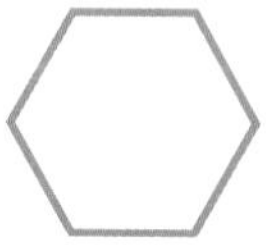

hour (h) (p. 368) A unit of time equal to 60 *minutes*.

1 hour = 60 minutes

hundredth (p. 558) A place value position. One of one hundred equal parts. In the number 0.05, the number 5 is in the hundredths place.

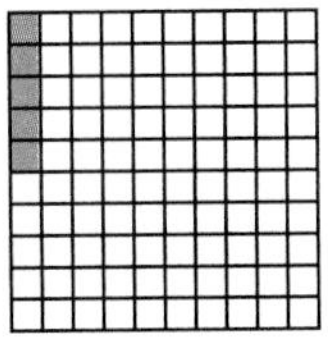

I

Identity Property of Addition (p. 65) If you add zero to a number, the sum is the same as the given number.

$3 + 0 = 3$ or $0 + 3 = 3$

Identity Property of Multiplication (p. 186) If you multiply a number by 1, the product is the same as the given number.

$8 \times 1 = 8 = 8 \times 1$

impossible (p. 484) An event that cannot happen. It has a probability of zero.

It is impossible to choose red.

inch (in.) (p. 343) A *customary unit* for measuring *length*. Plural is inches.

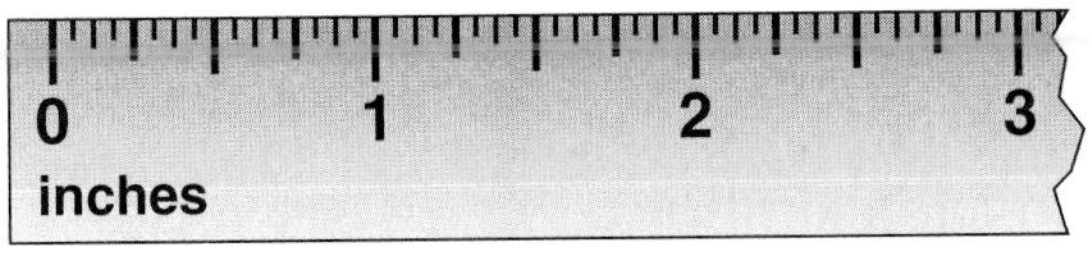

hora (h) Unidad de tiempo igual a 60 *minutos*.

1 hora = 60 minutos

centésima Valor de posición. Una de cien partes iguales.
En el número 0.05, 5 está en el lugar de las centésimas.

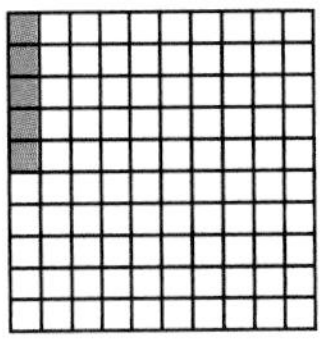

propiedad de identidad de la suma Si sumas cero a un número, la suma es igual al número dado.

$3 + 0 = 3$ ó $0 + 3 = 3$

propiedad de identidad de la multiplicación Si multiplicas un número por 1, el producto es igual al número dado.

$8 \times 1 = 8 = 1 \times 8$

imposible Evento que no puede suceder, el cual tiene probabilidad cero.

Es imposible elegir rojo.

pulgada (pulg) *Unidad inglesa* para medir la *longitud*.

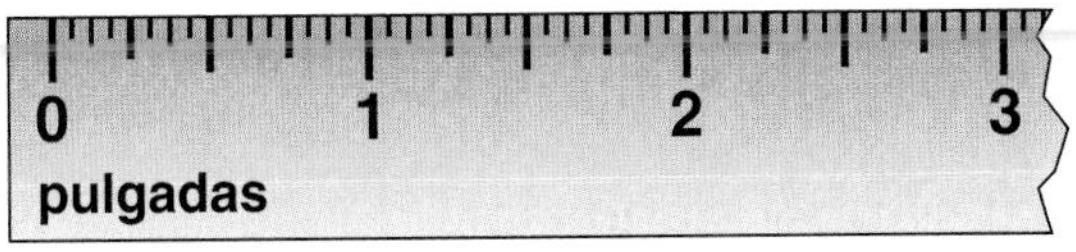

inequality (p. 34) A number sentence that uses $<$ (less than) or $>$ (greater than).

desigualdad Expresión numérica que usa $<$ (menor que) $>$ (mayor que).

inverse operation (p. 107) Operations that undo each other.
Addition and subtraction are inverse or opposite operations.
Multiplication and division are also inverse operations.

operación inversa Operaciones que se anulan entre sí.
La suma y la resta son operaciones inversas u opuestas.
La multiplicación y la división también son operaciones inversas.

is greater than $>$ (p. 34) An inequality relationship showing that the value on the left of the symbol is greater than the value on the right.

$5 > 3$ 5 is greater than 3

es mayor que $>$ Relación de desigualdad que muestra que el valor a la izquierda del símbolo es mayor que el valor a la derecha.

$5 > 3$ 5 es mayor que 3

is less than $<$ (p. 34) The value on the left side of the symbol is smaller than the value on the right side.

$4 < 7$ 4 is less than 7

es menor que $<$ El valor a la izquierda del símbolo es más pequeño que el valor a la derecha.

$4 < 7$ 4 es menor que 7

isosceles triangle (p. 434) A *triangle* with 2 *sides* of the same *length.*

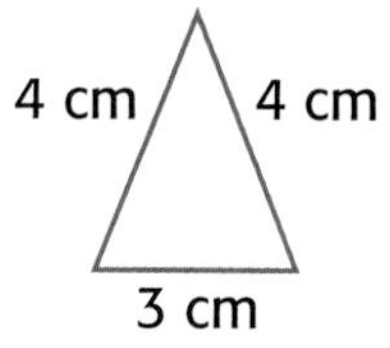

triángulo isósceles *Triángulo* con 2 *lados* del mismo largo.

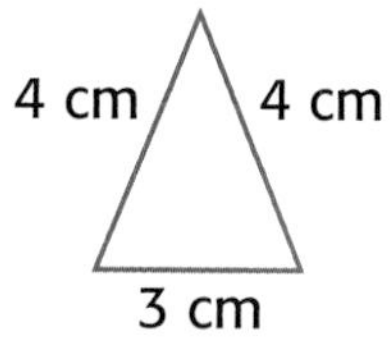

K

key (p. 179) Tells what or how many each symbol stands for.

clave Indica qué significa o cuánto vale cada símbolo.

kilogram (kg) (p. 398) A *metric unit* for measuring *mass*.

kilogramo (kg) *Unidad métrica* para medir la *masa*.

kilometer (km) (p. 385) A *metric unit* for measuring *length*.

kilómetro (km) *Unidad métrica* para medir la *longitud*.

L

length (p. 343) Measurement of the distance between two points.

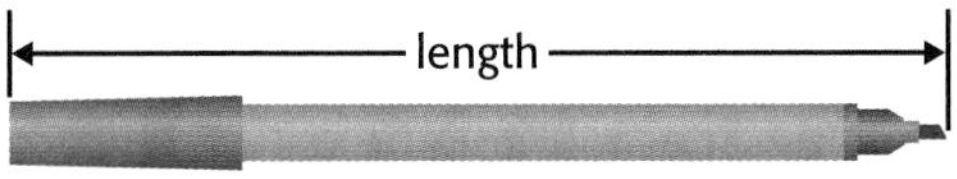

longitud Medida de la distancia entre dos puntos.

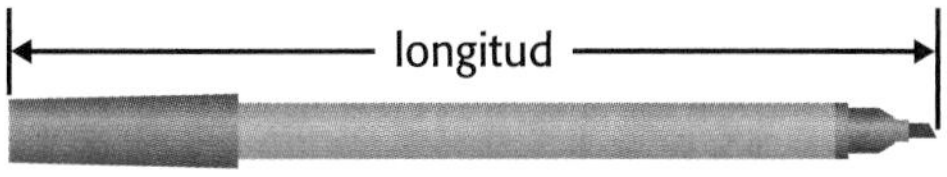

likely (p. 484) An event that will probably happen.
It is likely you will choose a red tile.

posible Evento que probablemente sucederá.
Es posible que elijas un cubo rojo.

line plot (p. 476) A graph that uses columns of Xs above a *number line* to show frequency of data.

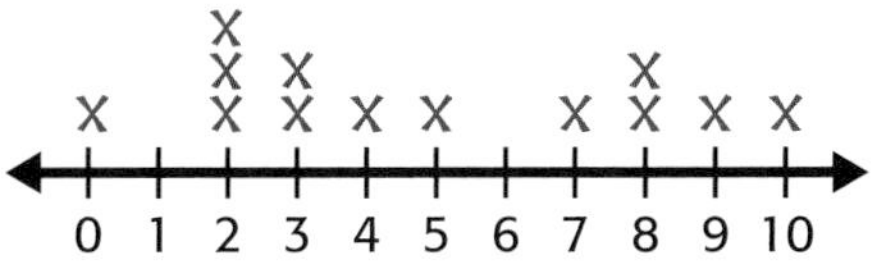

esquema lineal Gráfica que usa columnas de X sobre una *recta numérica* para representar frecuencias de datos

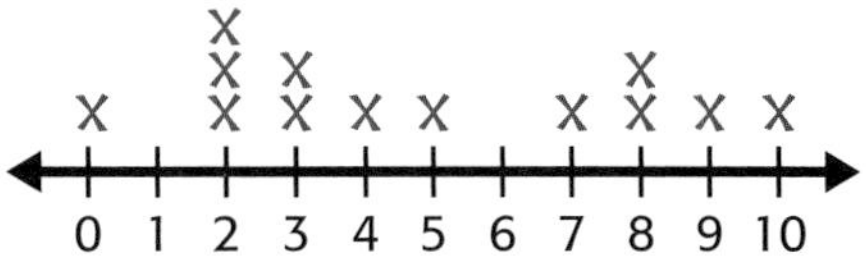

liter (L) (p. 392) A *metric unit* for measuring *volume* or *capacity*.
1 liter = 1,000 milliliters

litro (L) *Unidad métrica* para medir *volumen* o *capacidad*.
1 litro = 1000 mililitros

M

mass (p. 398) The amount of matter in an object. Two examples of units of *mass* would be gram and kilogram.

masa Cantidad de materia de un cuerpo. Dos ejemplos de unidades de medida son el gramo y el kilogramo.

meter (m) (p. 385) A *metric unit* for measuring *length*.
1 meter = 100 centimeters

metro (m) *Unidad métrica* para medir la *longitud*.
1 metro = 100 centímetros

metric system (SI) (p. 385) The measurement system based on powers of 10 that includes units such as meter, gram, and liter.

mile (mi) (p. 346) A *customary unit* of measure for distance.
1 mile = 5,280 feet

milliliter (mL) (p. 392) A *metric unit* used for measuring *capacity*.
1,000 milliliters = 1 liter

millimeter (mm) (p. 385) A *metric unit* used for measuring *length*.
1,000 millimeters = 1 meter

minute (min) (p. 368) A unit used to measure time.
1 minute = 60 seconds

multiplication (p. 155) An operation on two numbers to find their product. It can be thought of as repeated *addition*.

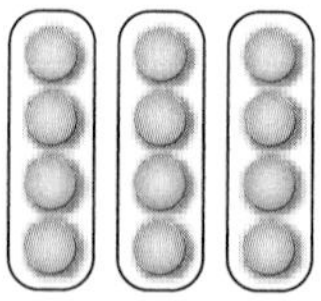

$3 \times 4 = 12$
$4 + 4 + 4 + 4 = 12$

multiply (p. 158) To find the product of 2 or more numbers.

N

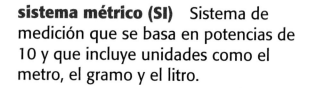

number sentence (p. 138) An expression using numbers and the = sign, or the < or > sign.
$5 + 4 = 9; 8 > 5$

sistema métrico (SI) Sistema de medición que se basa en potencias de 10 y que incluye unidades como el metro, el gramo y el litro.

milla (mi) *Unidad inglesa* para medir la distancia.
1 milla = 5,280 pies

mililitro (ml) *Unidad métrica* para medir la *capacidad*.
1,000 mililitros = 1 litro

milímetro (mm) *Unidad métrica* que se usa para medir la *longitud*.
1,000 milímetros = 1 metro

minuto (min) Unidad que se usa para medir el tiempo.
1 minuto = 60 segundos

multiplicación Operación en dos números para hallar su producto. Se puede considerar una suma repetida.

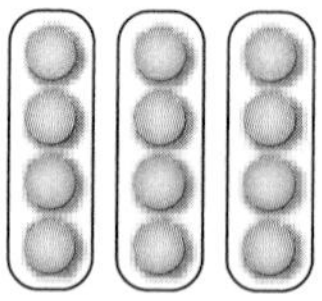

$3 \times 4 = 12$
$4 + 4 + 4 + 4 = 12$

multiplicar (multiplicación) Calcular el producto de 2 o más números.

expresión numérico Expresión que usa números y el signo = o los signos < o >.

$5 + 4 = 9; 8 > 5$

numerator (p. 509) The number above the bar in a *fraction*; the part of the fraction that tells how many of the equal parts are being used.

numerador Número que está encima de la barra de *fracción*; la parte de la fracción que indica cuántas partes iguales se están usando.

O

octagon (p. 419) A *polygon* with eight *sides*.

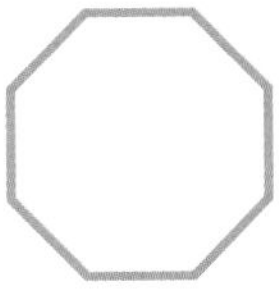

octágono *Polígono* de ocho *lados*.

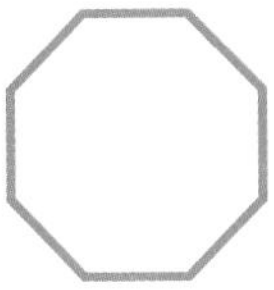

operation (p. 104) A mathematical process such as addition (+), subtraction (–), multiplication (×), and division (÷).

operación Proceso matemático como la suma (+), la resta (–), la multiplicación (×), y la división.

ounce (oz) ounces (p. 362) A *customary unit* for measuring *weight or capacity*.

onza (oz) *Unidad inglesa* para medir *peso* o *capacidad*.

outcome (p. 492) A possible result of an experiment.

resultado Resultado posible de un experimento.

P

parallel (p. 438) Lines that are the same distance apart. Parallel lines do not meet.

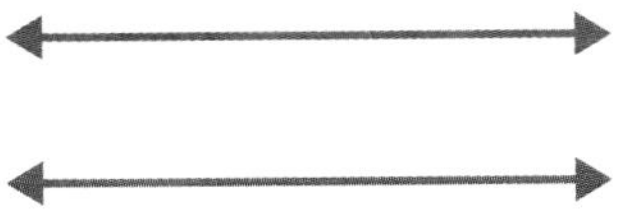

rectas paralelas Rectas separadas por la misma distancia. Las rectas paralelas no se intersecan.

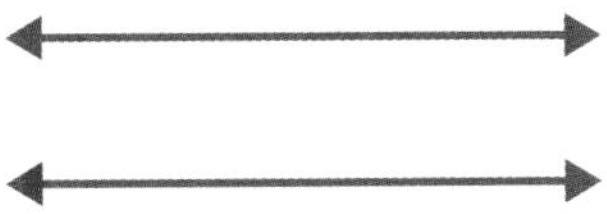

parallelogram (p. 438) A quadrilateral with four sides in which each pair of opposite sides are parallel and equal in length.

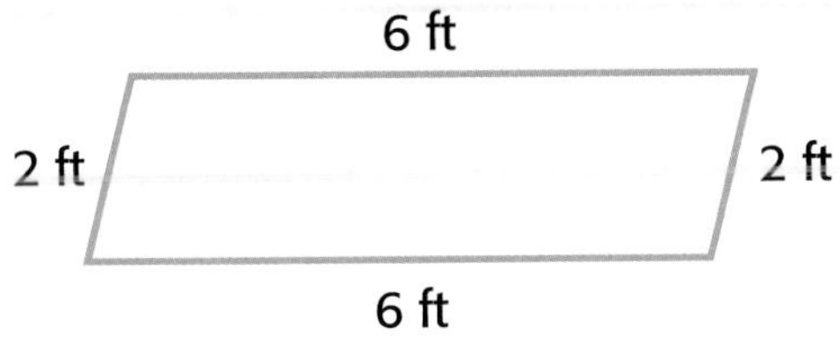

paralelogramo Cuadrilátero con cuatro lados en el cual cada par de lados opuestos son paralelos y de la misma longitud.

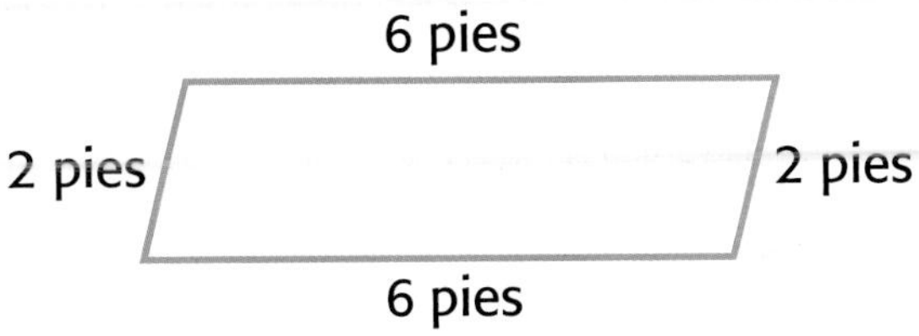

pattern (p. 17) A sequence of numbers, figures, or symbols that follows a rule or design.

2, 4, 6, 8, 10

patrón Sucesión de números, figuras o símbolos que sigue una regla o un diseño.

2, 4, 6, 8, 10

pentagon (p. 419) A *polygon* with five *sides*.

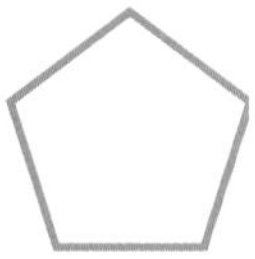

pentágono *Polígono* de cinco *lados*.

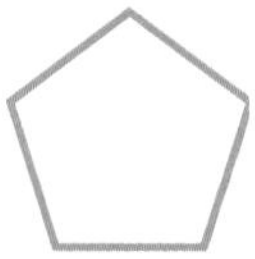

perimeter (p. 422) The *distance* around a shape or region.

perímetro *Distancia* alrededor de una figura o región.

pictograph (p. 300) A graph that compares *data* by using picture symbols.

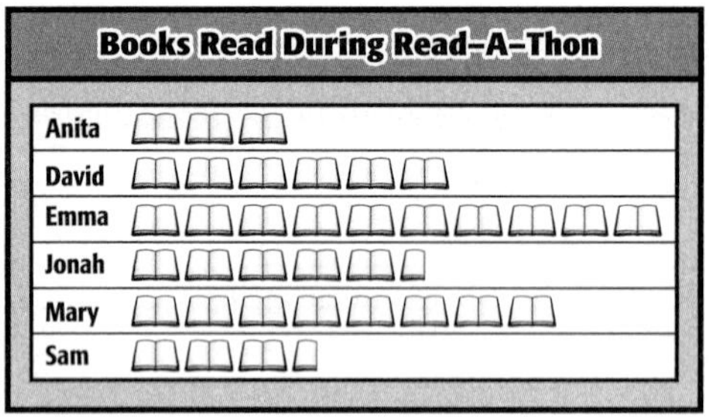

pictograma Gráfica que compara *datos* usando figuras.

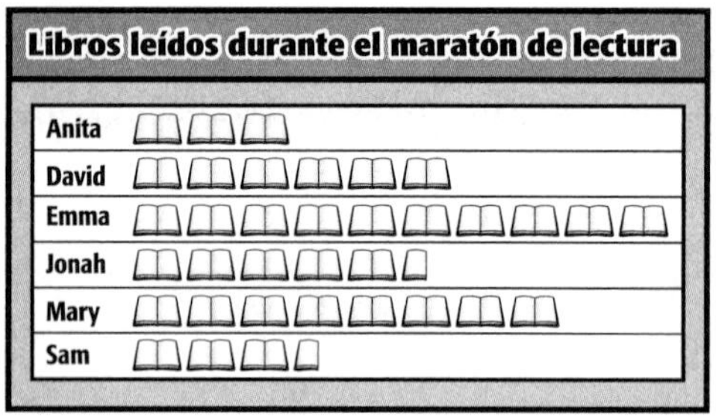

pint (pt) (p. 354) A *customary unit* for measuring *capacity*.

1 pint = 2 cups

pinta (pt) *Unidad inglesa* para medir la *capacidad*.

1 pinta = 2 tazas

place value (p. 24) The value given to a *digit* by its place in a number.

valor de posición El valor de un *dígito* según su lugar en el número.

plane figure (p. 419) A 2-*dimensional figure* that lies entirely within one *plane* such as a triangle or square.

figura plana *Figura bidimensional* que yace completamente en un *plano*, como un triángulo o un cuadrado.

point (p. 553) An exact location in space. Also refers to a decimal place.

punto Ubicación exacta en el espacio. También se refiere a un lugar decimal.

polygon (p. 419) A closed plane figure formed using line segments that meet only at their endpoints.

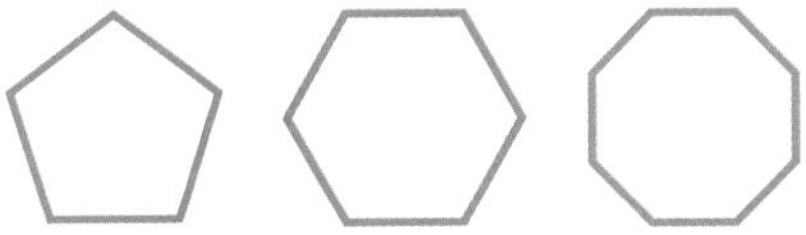

pound (lb) (p. 362) A *customary unit* for measuring *weight.*

1 pound = 16 ounces.

prediction (p. 494) Something you think will happen such as a specific outcome of an experiment.

prism (p. 444) A 3-*dimensional figure* with two parallel, congruent polygons as bases and parallelograms for faces.

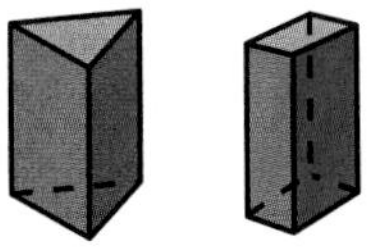

probability (p. 484) The chance that an event will happen.

product (p. 158) The answer to a multiplication problem.

polígono Figura plana cerrada formada por segmentos de recta que sólo concurren en sus extremos.

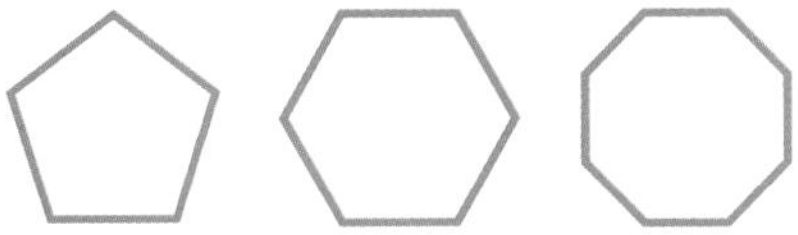

libra (lb) *Unidad inglesa* para medir el *peso* o *masa*.

1 libra = 16 onzas

predicción Algo que crees que sucederá, como un resultado específico de un experimento.

prisma *Figura tridimensional* con dos polígonos paralelos y congruentes como bases y paralelogramos como caras.

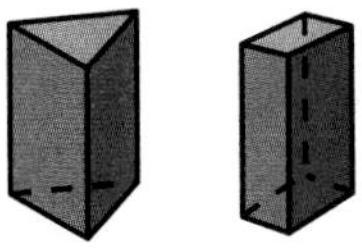

probabilidad La posibilidad de que ocurra un evento.

producto Respuesta a un problema de multiplicación.

Q

quadrilateral (p. 419) A shape that has 4 sides and 4 angles.
square, rectangle, and parallelogram

cuadrilátero Figura con 4 lados y 4 ángulos.
cuadrado, rectángulo y paralelogramo

quart (qt) (p. 354) A *customary unit* for measuring *capacity*.

1 quart = 4 cups

cuarto de galón (ct) *Unidad inglesa* de galón para mdir la *capacidad*.

1 cuarto de galón = 4 tazas

quotient (p. 256) The answer to a *division problem*.

15 ÷ 3 = 5 ← 5 is the quotient

cociente Respuesta a un *problema de división*.

15 ÷ 3 = 5 ← 5 es el cociente

R

rectangle (p. 438) A *quadrilateral* with four *right angles*; opposite *sides* are equal length and *parallel*.

rectángulo *Cuadrilátero* con cuatro *ángulos rectos*; los *lados* opuestos son de igual longitud y *paralelos*.

rectangular solid (p. 444) A 3-*dimensional figure* with six faces that are rectangles.

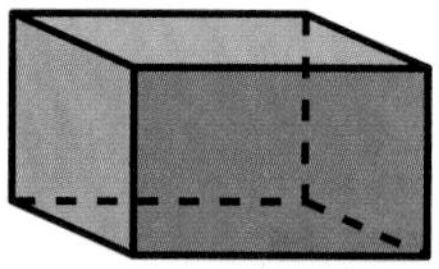

sólido rectangular *Figura tridimensional* con seis caras rectangulares.

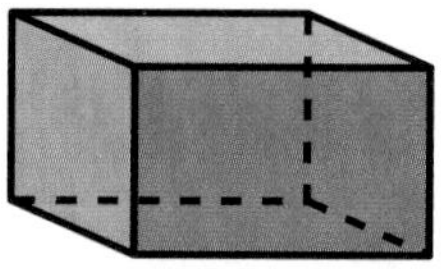

regroup (p. 74) To use place value to exchange equal amounts when renaming a number.

reagrupar Usar el valor de posición para intercambiar cantidades iguales cuando se convierte un número.

related fact(s) (p. 259) Basic facts using the same numbers. Sometimes called a fact family.

4 + 1 = 5	5 × 6 = 30
1 + 4 = 5	6 × 5 = 30
5 − 4 = 1	30 ÷ 5 = 6
5 − 1 = 4	30 ÷ 6 = 5

operación (u operaciones relacionada(s) Operaciones básicas que usan los mismos números. A veces llamadas familia de operaciones.

4 + 1 = 5	5 × 6 = 30
1 + 4 = 5	6 × 5 = 30
5 − 4 = 1	30 ÷ 5 = 6
5 − 1 = 4	30 ÷ 6 = 5

rhombus (p. 438) A *parallelogram* with four *sides* of the same *length*.

right angle (p. 438) An *angle* of a square corner (90°).

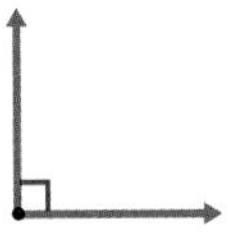

right triangle (p. 435) A *triangle* with one *right angle*.

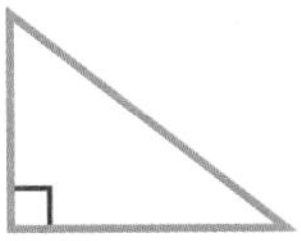

round (p. 44) To change the *value* of a number to one that is easier to work with. To find the nearest value of a number based on a given place value. 27 rounded to the nearest 10 is 30.

rombo *Paralelogramo* con cuatro *lados* del mismo *largo*.

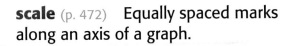

ángulo recto *Ángulo* que se forma en una esquina cuadrada (90°).

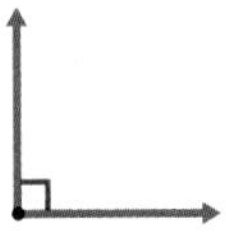

triángulo rectángulo *Triángulo* con un *ángulo recto*.

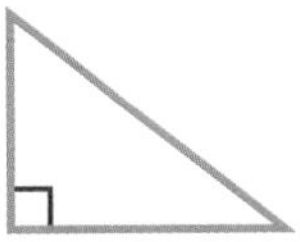

redondear Cambiar el *valor* de un número por uno con el que es más fácil trabajar. Calcular el valor más cercano de un número en base a un valor de posición dado.
27 redondeado a la décima más cercana es 30.

S

scale (p. 472) Equally spaced marks along an axis of a graph.

scalene triangle (p. 434) A *triangle* with no *congruent sides*.

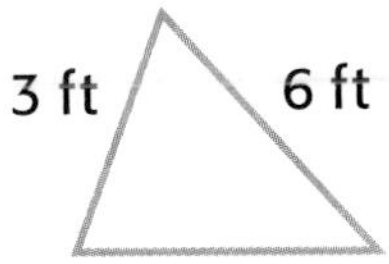

simplest form (p. 516) A fraction in which the numerator and the denominator have no common factor greater than 1.
$\frac{3}{5}$ is the simplest form of $\frac{6}{10}$.

escala Marcas igualmente separadas a lo largo del eje de una gráfica.

triángulo escaleno *Triángulo* sin lados *congruentes*.

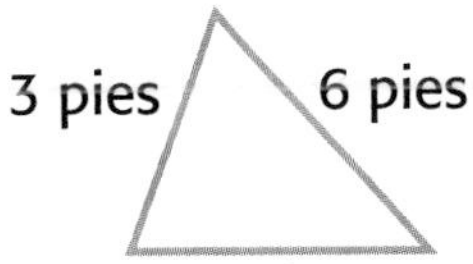

forma reducida Fracción en que el numerador y el denominador no tienen un factor común mayor que 1.

$\frac{3}{5}$ es la forma reducida de $\frac{6}{10}$.

skip count (p. 165) To count forward or backward by a given number or in intervals of a number.
3, 6, 9, 12 ...

solid figure (p. 444) A solid figure having the three dimensions: length, width, and height.

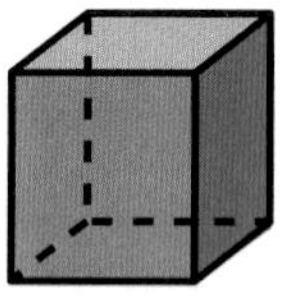

sphere (p. 444) A *3-dimensional figure* that has the shape of a round ball.

square (p. 438) A quadrilateral with four *congruent sides* and 4 right angles.

standard form/standard notation (p. 25) The usual way of writing a number that shows only its *digits*, no words.

537 89 1,642

standard units (p. 342) Measuring units from the customary or metric system.

subtraction (subtract) (p. 104) An operation that tells the difference, when some or all are taken away.

$9 - 4 = 5$

sum (p. 65) The answer to an addition problem.

$8 + 5 = 13$

conteo salteado Contar hacia adelante o hacia atrás por un número dado o en intervalos de un número.
Ejemplo: 3, 6, 9, 12, ...

figura sólida Figura sólida tridimensional: largo, ancho y alto.

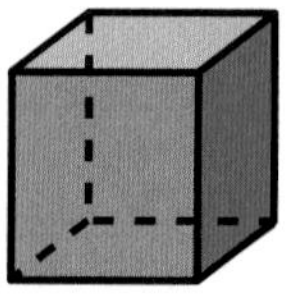

esfera *Figura tridimensional* con forma de pelota redonda.

cuadrado Rectángulo con cuatro *lados congruentes*.

forma estándar/notación estándar La manera habitual de escribir un número que sólo muestra sus *dígitos*, sin palabras.

537 89 1642

unidades estándar Unidades de medida del sistema inglés o del métrico.

resta (restar) Operación que indica la diferencia cuando se elimina algo o todo.

$9 - 4 = 5$

suma Respuesta a un problema de suma.

$8 + 5 = 13$

survey (p. 473) A method of collecting data.

T

table (p. 476) A way to organize and display data with rows and columns.

tally chart (p. 471) A way to keep track of data using tally marks to record the results.

What is Your Favorite Color?	
Color	**Tally**
Blue	~~IIII~~ III
Green	IIII

tally mark(s) (p. 471) A mark made to keep track and display data recorded from a survey.

tenth (p. 553) One of ten equal parts or $\frac{1}{10}$.

thousand(s) (p. 24) A place value of a number.
In 1,253, the **1** is in the thousands place.

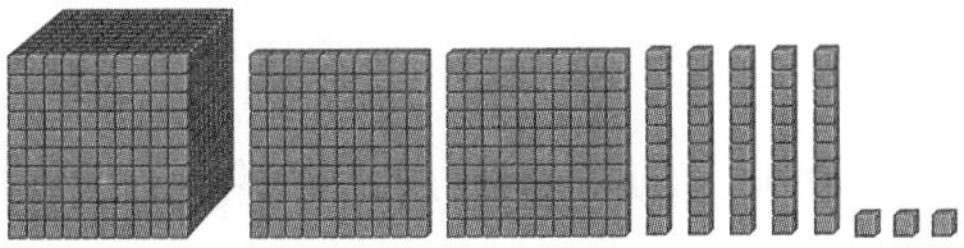

3-dimensional figure (p. 444) A solid figure that has *length*, *width*, and *height*.

triangle (p. 419) A *polygon* with three sides and three angles.

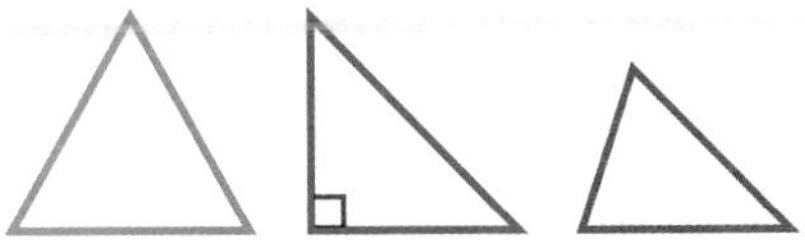

encuesta Un método para reunir datos.

tabla Manera de organizar y representar datos con filas y columnas.

tabla de conteo Una manera de llevar la cuenta de los datos usando marcas de conteo para anotar los resultados.

¿Cuál es tu color favorito?	
Color	**Conteo**
Azul	~~IIII~~ III
Verde	IIII

marcas(s) de conteo Marca hecha para llevar la cuenta y presentar datos reunidos con una encuesta.

décima Una de diez partes iguales ó $\frac{1}{10}$.

millares Valor de posición de un número.
En 1,253, el **1** está en el lugar de las unidades de millar.

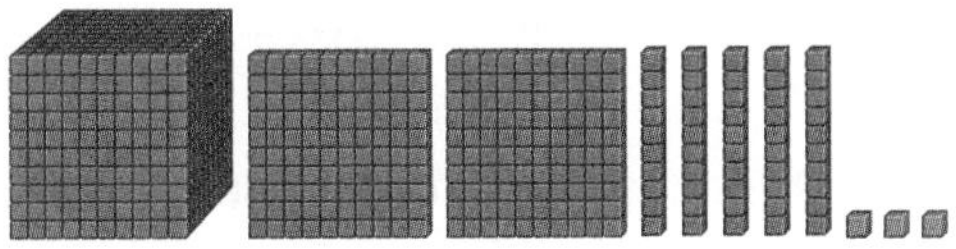

figura tridimensional Figura sólida que tiene *largo*, *ancho* y *alto.*

triángulo *Polígono* con tres lados y tres ángulos.

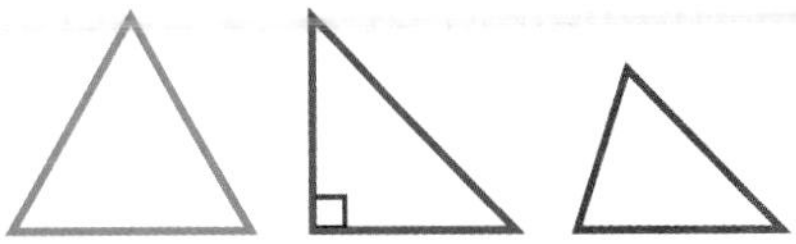

2-dimensional figure (p. 419) The outline of a shape, such as a triangle, square, or rectangle, which has only *length*, *width*, and *area*. Also called a plane figure.

figura bidimensional El contorno de una figura, como un triángulo, un cuadrado o un rectángulo, que sólo tiene *largo*, *ancho* y *área*. También se llama figura plana.

U

unit cost (p. 314) The price of a single piece or item.

costo unitario El precio de una sola pieza o artículo.

unlikely (p. 484) An event that will probably *not* happen.

It is unlikely you will choose a yellow tile.

improbable Evento que probablemente *no* sucederá.

Es improbable que elijas una baldosa amarilla.

V

volume (p. 454) The number of cubic units needed to fill a *3-dimensional figure* or solid figure.

volumen Número de unidades cúbicas necesarias para llenar una *figura tridimensional* o sólida.

W

weight (p. 362) A measurement that tells how heavy an object is.

peso Medida que indica la pesadez de un cuerpo.

whole number (p. 22) The numbers 0, 1, 2, 3, 4 ...

número entero Los números 0, 1, 2, 3, 4 ...

Y

yard (yd) (p. 346) A *customary unit* for measuring *length*.

1 yard = 3 feet or 36 inches

yarda (yd) *Medida inglesa* para medir la *longitud*.

1 yarda = 3 pies eo 36 pulgadas

Z

Zero Property of Multiplication (p. 186) The property that states any number multiplied by zero is zero.

$0 \times 5 = 0 \qquad 5 \times 0 = 0$

propiedad del producto nulo de la multiplicación Propiedad que establece que cualquier número multiplicado por cero es igual a cero.

$0 \times 5 = 0 \qquad 5 \times 0 = 0$

Acknowledgements

Unless otherwise credited, all currency courtesy of the US Mint.
iv Doug Martin; **v** (br)Courtesy Dinah Zike, (others)Doug Martin; **vi** (l to r t to b)Courtesy Cheryl Avalos, Courtesy William Bokesh, Courtesy Patty Brown, Courtesy David Chamberlain, Courtesy Eppie Chung, Courtesy Lisa Cirrincione, Courtesy Carol Cronk, Courtesy Ilene Foster, Courtesy Grant Fraser; **vii** (l to r, t to b)Courtesy Suzanne Freire, Courtesy Beth Holguin, Courtesy Donna Kopenski, Courtesy Kelly Mack, Courtesy Juvenal Martinez, Courtesy John McGuire, Courtesy Donald Price, Courtesy Kasey St. James, Courtesy Art Wayman, Courtesy Beverly Wells, Courtesy Frances Whitney; **x** Arthur Morris/CORBIS; **xii–xv** CORBIS; **xvi–xvii** Brandon D. Cole/CORBIS; **xviii–xix** Michael Hagedorn/zefa/CORBIS; **xx** PETE OXFORD/Minden Pictures; **xxii–xxiii** CORBIS; **xxiv–xxv** Joeseph Sohm-Visions of America/Getty Images; **xxvi–xxvii** Walter Bibikow/Getty Images; **1** Kennan Ward/CORBIS; **2** AgeFotostock/SuperStock; **3** Greg Probst/Panoramic Images; **4** F. Lukasseck/Masterfile; **5** (t)David Kommel, (b)Discovery Comm/Panoramic Images; **6** Robert Holmes/CORBIS; **7** Arthur Morris/CORBIS; **8** VStock/Alamy Images; **9** Walter Bibikow/Getty Images; **10** (t)Craig Lovell/CORBIS, (c)2006 Photos To Go/Index Open, (b)Getty Images **11** Tony Hertz/CORBIS; **12** AgeFotostock/SuperStock; **13** Richard Cummins/CORBIS; **14–15** Getty Images; **17** S. Wanke/PhotoLink/Getty Images; **20** Nature Picture Library/Alamy Images; **22** Ed-Imaging; **24** Image Source/Getty Images; **27** Ed-Imaging; **28** John Giustina/Getty Images; **32** CORBIS; **40** (l to r)Siede Preis/Getty Images, C Squared Studios/Getty Images, Getty Images, G.K. & Vikki Hart/Getty Images, G.K. & Vikki Hart/Getty Images, G.K. & Vikki Hart/Getty Images; **41** Ed-Imaging; **42–43** CORBIS; **44** Bob Torrez/PhotoEdit; **47** Ed-Imaging; **49** David Crausby/Alamy Images; **51** (l to r)Jupiterimages, Getty Images, Preis/Getty Images, Ryan McVay/Getty Images; **62–63** Joe McBride/Getty Images; **66** Getty Images; **68** Lori Adamski Peek/Getty Images; **73** Ed-Imaging; **75** Akira Matoba/SuperStock; **77** (l)CORBIS, (r)The McGraw-Hill Companies; **79** (t to r t to b)Getty Images, Siede Preis/Getty Images, C Squared Studios/Getty Images, Getty Images, The McGraw-Hill Companies; **81** (l)Getty Images, (r)Ryan McVay/Getty Images; **82–83** CORBIS; **84** Marilyn Conway/Getty Images; **86** Ed-Imaging; **88** David De Lossy/Getty Images; **89** Comstock Images/Alamy Images; **91** Ed-Imaging; **92** Tim Jones/Getty Images; **93** Michael Newman/PhotoEdit; **95** (l to r t to b)Ed-Imaging, Stockbyte/Getty Images, Siede Preis/Getty Images, 2006 Photos To Go/Index Open, photos.com/Jupiterimages; **102** (l)Getty Images, (r)photos.com/Jupiterimages; **104 110** Getty Images; **113** (l to r, t to b)Richard Hutchings/Digital Light Source, Getty Images, CORBIS, The McGraw-Hill Companies, 2006 Photos To Go/Index Open, Getty Images; **118–119** (bkgd)Culliganphoto/Alamy Images, (inset)courtesy of New England Conservatory; **120** Ed-Imaging; **124** David Young-Wolff/PhotoEdit; **125** (l)Michael Pole/CORBIS, (r)Getty Images; **127** (tl)Getty Images, (tr)Comstock Images, (bl)2006 Photos To Go/Index Open, (br)CORBIS; **128** PunchStock; **133** Ed-Imaging; **135** Siede Preis/Getty Images; **146** Jupiterimages; **152–153** BRIAN P. KENNEY/Animals Animals; **155** Ed-Imaging; **158** (t)Siede Preis/Getty Images, (b)IT Stock Free/SuperStock; **159** (cw from top)Stockbyte, Getty Images, Getty Images, The McGraw-Hill Companies; **163** (tl)Ed-Imaging, (tr)Getty Images, (bl)Ryan McVay/Getty Images, (bc br)The McGraw-Hill Companies; **164** BananaStock/Alamy Images; **165** (l)Brand X Pictures/PunchStock, (r)Stockdisc/PunchStock; **166** (tl)Getty Images, (tr)CORBIS; **167** Siede Preis/Getty Images; **170–171** Ed-Imaging; **172** Chip Henderson/Index Stock; **176** CORBIS; **180** Ellen McKnight/Alamy Images; **181** The McGraw-Hill Companies; **182–183** Jeffrey L. Rotman/CORBIS; **184** image100 Ltd; **191** (tl)The McGraw-Hill Companies, (tr)Siede Preis/Getty Images, (b)Getty Images; **198–199** Michael Newman/PhotoEdit; **203** Stockdisc/Getty Images; **211–212** Ed-Imaging; **214** CORBIS; **215** Thomas J Peterson/Getty Images; **216** Ryan McVay/Getty Images; **219** G.K. Vikki Hart/Getty Images; **224** (l)BananaStock/Alamy Images, (r)Getty Images; **226** Ed-Imaging; **229** C Squared Studios/Getty Images; **232–233** (bkgd)John Warden/SuperStock, (inset)Museum of Fine Arts, Houston, Texas, USA, The Bayou Bend Collection/Bridgeman Art Library; **234** Ed-Imaging; **236** J. A. Kraulis/Masterfile ; **248–249** CORBIS; **250** (l)C Squared Studios/Getty Images, (r)Getty Images; **251** Ed-Imaging; **253** The McGraw-Hill Companies; **254** Don Smetzer/PhotoEdit; **256** Ed-Imaging; **258** David Young-Wolff/PhotoEdit; **262** Jose Luis Pelaez, Inc /Jupiterimages; **266** (t)Brandon D. Cole/CORBIS, (bl)BananaStock/Alamy Images, (br)Richard Hutchings/Digital Light Source; **269** Getty Images; **272–273** (bkgd)David Young Wolff/PhotoEdit, (inset)Jim West/The Image Works; **274** Ed-Imaging; **275** Stockdisc/PunchStock; **279** Ed-Imaging; **280** 2006 Photos To Go; **281** Jupiterimages; **290–291** Index Stock; **293** Ed-Imaging; **295** CORBIS; **296** 2006 Photos To Go; **301** (l)Blend Images/Alamy Images, (r)Ed-Imaging; **302** (tl)Ingram Publishing/SuperStock, (tr)C Squared Studios/Getty Images; **308–309** (bkgd)CORBIS, (inset)Dennis Hallinan/Alamy Images; **313** Ed-Imaging; **315** 2006 Photos To Go; **318** Ed-Imaging; **321** Getty Images; **322** 2006 Photos To Go; **323** Ed-Imaging; **338–339** Getty Images; **340** (l to r, t to b)Getty Images, C Squared Studios/Getty Images, Jupiterimages, photos.com/Jupiterimages, Jeremy Woodhouse/Getty Images, The McGraw-Hill Companies, C Squared Studios/Getty Images, Siede Preis/Getty Images; **341** (t)PhotoLink/Getty Images, (c)C Squared Studios/Getty Images, (b)Ed-Imaging; **342** (l)PhotoObjects/Jupiterimages, (r)Getty Images; **343** Jupiterimages; **344** (t)Brand X Pictures/PunchStock, (bl)Image Source, (br)Stockbyte/PictureQuest; **345** (l to r, t to b) PhotoObjects/Jupiterimages, The McGraw-Hill Companies, Max Delson/istockphoto, Jackie DesJarlais/istockphoto, Creatas/SuperStock, The McGraw-Hill Companies, Gerry Ellis/Minden Pictures; **346** (t)Ed-Imaging, (b)C Squared Studios/Getty Images; **347** C Squared Studios/Getty Images; **350** Doug Menuez/Getty Images; **351** The McGraw-Hill Companies; **354** (t)Nick Daly/Getty Images, (b)Amy Etra/PhotoEdit; **356** (l to r, t to b)Spencer Grant/PhotoEdit, comstock.com/Comstock, D. Hurst/Alamy Images, Hirdes/f1online/Alamy Images, Ton Kinsbergen/Beateworks/CORBIS, Jupiterimages, Getty Images, CORBIS, 2006 Photos To Go, GK & Vikki Hart/Getty Images, Brian Leatart/Jupiterimages; **358** Ed-Imaging; **359** (l)CORBIS, (r)Jupiterimages; **360** Ed-Imaging; **362** C Squared Studios/Getty Images; **363** (l to r, t to b) Ryan McVay/Photodisc/Getty Images, Photodisc/Getty Images, Siede Preis/Photodisc/Getty Images, Getty Images, 2006 Photos to Go/Index Open; **364** (tl)Ryan McVay/Getty Images, (tc)Getty Images, (tr)Burke/Triolo/Brand X Pictures/Jupiterimages, (cl)C Squared Studios/Getty Images, (c)Getty Images, (cr)Photodisc Collection/Getty Images, (b)John Cancalosi/Peter Arnold, Inc.; **366–367** (bkgd)Michael Hagedorn/zefa/CORBIS, (t to b)D. Robert & Lorri Franz/CORBIS, RAOUL SLATER/WWI/Peter Arnold, Inc., Punchstock, Michael Durham/Minden Pictures; **371** Ed-Imaging; **373** (t)C Squared Studios/Getty Images, (b)Dorling Kindersley/Getty Images; **374** Getty Images; **376** (l)G.K. Vikki Hart/Getty Images, (r)Getty Images; **377** (cw from top)CORBIS, image100/SuperStock, Photos to Go/Index Open, Jupiterimages, Getty Images, David Toase/Getty Images, Jupiterimages; **380–381** CORBIS; **382** (l to r, t to b)Ingram Publishing/SuperStock, The McGraw-Hill Companies, C Squared Studios/Getty Images, C Squared Studios/Getty Images, CORBIS, Getty Images, CORBIS, Getty Images, Getty Images; **384** (t)C Squared Studios/Getty Images, (cl)CORBIS, (cr)The McGraw-Hill Companies, (b)CORBIS; **385** (cw from top)Michael Wong/CORBIS, Ed-Imaging, CORBIS, Dorling Kindersley/Getty Images, Comstock/Jupiterimages; **386** Dorling Kindersley/Getty Images; **389–390** Ed-Imaging; **392** DK Limited/CORBIS; **393** (tl)Adrianna Williams/zefa/CORBIS, (tr)Amon/PhotoCuisine/CORBIS, (bl)photos.com/Jupiterimages, (bc)Didier Robcis/CORBIS, (br)The McGraw-Hill Companies; **394** (tl)Mick Broughton/Alamy Images, (tc)Comstock Images/Alamy Images, (tr)Jupiterimages; **396** Geoff du Feu/Alamy Images; **398** (l)CORBIS, (r)Getty Images; **399** CORBIS; **400** (tl)Jupiterimages, (tc)CORBIS, (tr)DK Limited/CORBIS, (bl)CORBIS, (bc)Michael Newman/PhotoEdit, (br)Ed-Imaging; **402–403** Ciaran Griffi/Stockbyte Platinum/Getty Images; **407** (tl tr)Ed-Imaging, (cl)The McGraw-Hill Companies, (cr)C Squared Studios/Getty Images, (b)Siede Preis/Getty Images; **409** (l)C Squared Studios/Getty Images, (r)Creatas/PunchStock; **410** (l)Adrianna Williams/zefa/CORBIS, (r)Amon/PhotoCuisine/CORBIS; **412** (l)CORBIS, C Squared Studios/Getty Images, (r)G.K. Vikki Hart/Getty Images; **414** Getty Images; **416–417** Index Stock; **419** (t)Ryan McVay/Getty Images, (bl)Getty Images, (br)CORBIS; **420** (tl)Hank Shiffman/Big Stock Photo, (tc)Dynamicgraphics/InMagine Images, (tr)AgeFotostock/SuperStock, (b)Photos to Go; **421** (tl)2006 Photos To Go, (tc)Comstock Images/Alamy Images, (tr)2006 Photos to Go, (c)Digital Vision Ltd./SuperStock, (bl)Ed-Imaging, (br)Brad Wilson/Getty Images; **423** Brand X Pictures/PunchStock; **424** Hisham F. Ibrahim/Getty Images; **426** Ed-Imaging; **432** PunchStock; **433** Getty Images **434** (t)Paul Thompson/Jupiterimages, (bl)Stockbyte/PictureQuest, (br)photos.com/Jupiterimages; **435** (t)2006 Photos To Go, (bl)Ian Cartwright/Getty Images, (bc)C Squared Studios/Getty Images, (br)Getty Images; **436** (l)photos.com/Jupiterimages, (c)Creatas/PunchStock, (r)2006 Photos To Go; **437** Ryan McVay/Getty Images; **438** Photos to Go; **439** (t)Dynamic Graphics/Jupterimages, (b)The McGraw-Hill Companies; **440** (tl)Getty Images, (tr)photos.com/Jupiterimages, (bl)photos.com/Jupiterimages, (bc)C Squared Studios/Getty Images, (br)Siede Preis/Getty Images; **442** Ed-Imaging; **444** (tl)Stockbyte Platinum/Alamy Images, (tr)Michael Newman/PhotoEdit, (bl)Klaus Hackenberg/zefa/CORBIS, (br)The McGraw-Hill Companies; **445** (l to r, t to b)Getty Images, C Squared Studios/Photodisc/Getty Images, CORBIS, Ryan McVay/Getty Images, HomeStudio/Shutterstock, CORBIS, Hemera Technologies/Jupiterimages; **447** Ed-imaging; **448** Peter Harholdt/SuperStock; **449** (tl)Getty Images, (tc)Siede Preis/Getty Images, (tr)Gibson & Smith/Jupiterimages, (cl)George Doyle/Stockdisc/Getty Images, (c)photos.com/Jupiterimages, (cr)2000 Photos To Go, (b)Comstock/Jupiterimages; **450–451** Michael Ventura/Folio Inc.; **452** (br)Ed-imaging, (others)The McGraw-Hill Companies; **457** (l)Getty Images, (r)Ed-Imaging; **459** (l)photos.com/Jupiterimages, (r)C Squared Studios/Getty Images; **463** (t)Getty Images, (bl)Brian Leatart /Jupiterimages, (br)Getty Images; **468–469** Getty Images; **473** (l)CORBIS, (r)Getty Images; **474** Pete Oxford/Minden Pictures **476** 2006 Photos To Go; **480 484** Ed-Imaging; **486** Joseph Sohm/CORBIS **487** (l)PunchStock, (r)Ed-Imaging; **488–489** (bkgd)Frans Lanting/CORBIS, (inset)Siede Preis/Getty Images; **490** CORBIS; **492** Ed-Imaging; **496** Getty Images; **505** (cw from top)The McGraw-Hill Companies/Ken Karp, Getty Images, Steve Cole/Getty Images, Ryan McVay/Getty Images; **506–507** Ed-Imaging; **511** C Squared Studios/Getty Images; **512** CORBIS; **519** Ed-Imaging; **520** CORBIS; **521** Getty Images; **526** Ed-Imaging; **530** Art Wolfe/Getty Images; **531** (l)Stockdisc/PunchStock, (r)Ross Whitaker/Getty Images; **532–533** (bkgd)CORBIS, (l to r)John T. Fowler/Alamy Images, CORBIS, Dorling Kindersley/Getty Images, Getty Images, James Cotier/Getty Images; **534 536** Ed-Imaging; **538** (t)G.K. Vikki Hart/Getty Images, (bl)Creatas/PictureQuest, (br)Stockdisc/PunchStock; **548–549** Ed-Imaging; **555** Getty Images; **557** Ed-Imaging; **562–563** PunchStock; **564** digitalvision/Punchstock; **566** Ed-Imaging; **569** Stockdisc/PunchStock; **572** PunchStock; **573** The McGraw-Hill Companies **576** Ryan McVay/Getty Images; **579** (cw from top)Getty Images, 2006 Photos To Go/Index Open, photos.com/Jupiterimages, 2006 Photos To Go/Index Open; **582–583** Jeff Vanuga/CORBIS; **586** Stockdisc Classic/Alamy Images; **592** (l)Getty Images, (r)Ed-Imaging; **594** The McGraw-Hill Companies; **598** PunchStock; **602** David Young-Wolff/PhotoEdit; **604** (l)Hemera Technologies/Jupiterimages, (r)Cre8tive Studios/Alamy Images; **606** CORBIS; **607** Getty Images, **609** Ed-imaging, **611** 2006 Photos To Go/Index Open; **614–615** (bkgd) Sergio Delle Vedove/Alamy Images **615** (tl)The British Library/HIP/The Image Works, (tc)Sygma/CORBIS, (tr br)The Granger Collection, New York, (bl)PictureArts/NewsCom; **624–625** Henryk T. Kaiser/IndexStock; **628** CORBIS; **629** Ed-Imaging; **630** Joeseph Sohm-Visions of America/Getty Images; **633** (l)Stockdisc/PunchStock, (r)Getty Images; **634** Ed-Imaging; **636** CORBIS; **639** 2006 Photos to Go/Index Open, **640** Steve Smith/SuperStock; **642** Bill Ross/CORBIS; **644** (l)CORBIS, (r)Jeff Greenberg/Photo Edit; **645** (t)The McGraw-Hill Companies, (b)Ed-Imaging; **646–647** Joel A. Rogers; **648** David Young-Wolff/PhotoEdit; **650** Myrleen Ferguson Cate/PhotoEdit; **658** David Toase/Getty Images; **659** (t)CORBIS, (b)Siede Preis/Getty Images; **CA1** Ed-Imaging; **662–663** Tim Fuller; **666** Stockdisc/PunchStock; **667** Ed-Imaging; **668** G.K. & Vikki Hart/Getty Images; **670** Stockbyte; **673** 2006 Photos To Go/Index Open; **675** (l)Comstock, (r)Ed-Imaging; **676** Ryan McVay/Getty Images; **677** (l) David Spindel/SuperStock, (c)Getty Images, (r)2006 Photos to Go/Index Open **678** C Squared Studios/Getty Images; **679** (cl c) Getty Images, (cr)C Squared Studios/Getty Images, (b)Brand X Pictures/PunchStock; **R10** Stockdisc/PunchStock; **R11** (bl bc)Jupiterimages, (br)The McGraw-Hill Companies; **R22** (tl)Getty Images, (cr)C Squared Studios/Getty Images; **R23** (tl)Comstock Images/Alamy Images, (r)Jupiterimages; **R29** (tl cr)Jupiterimages, (cl)Getty Images, (bl)Creative Studios/Alamy Images, (br)David J. Green/Alamy Images, (tr)Ryan McVay/Getty Images; **R40** (l)Siede Preis/Getty Images, (c)C Squared Studios/Getty Images, (r)CORBIS; **R53** Michael Houghton/StudiOhio.

McGraw-Hill would like to acknowledge the artists and agencies who contributed to illustrating this program: **Cover** Ron Berg represented by Mendola Artists; Argosy Publishing; Keith Batcheller, Shawn McKelvey, Tony Randazzo represented by AA Reps. Inc.

Index

A

Act It Out, 185, 227, 275, 319, 564–565, 573, 576, 599, 649, R35

Activities
- *Add Fractions*, 526–527
- *Area*, 426–427
- *Capacity*, 352–353
- *Divide Using a Multiplication Table*, 293–294
- *Division*, 634–635
- *Equivalent Fractions*, 514–515
- *Fractions and Decimals*, 551–552
- *Fractions, Decimals, and Money*, 566–567
- *Length to the Nearest Inch*, 341–342
- *Make a Bar Graph*, 471–472
- *Millimeter and Centimeter*, 383–384
- *Multiplication Table*, 201–202
- *Multiplication with Regrouping*, 600–601
- *Place Value*, 22–23
- *Probability*, 492–493
- *Relate Multiplication to Division*, 256–257
- *Subtract Fractions*, 534–535
- *Subtract Three-Digit Numbers with Regrouping*, 122–123
- *Understand Division*, 251–252
- *Volume*, 452–453

Addition, 62–81, 84–100, R5–R7, R41, R42
- Associative Property of Addition, 65–67, 96, 97
- Commutative Property of Addition, 65–67, 96, 97
- Estimation, 70–73, 90, 94, 96, 97, R6, R7
- Fractions, 526–531, 543, R53
- Identity Property of Addition, 65–67, 96, 97
- Money, 78–81, 89, 90, 94, 99, R5–R7
- Multi-digit, 74–76, 86–95, 98–100
- Regrouping, 74–76, 86–95, 98–100
- Repeated addition, 155–159, 167, 191, 206–209, 214–216

Algebra, 6, 7, 36, 67, 73, 76, 90, 132, 138–141, 148, 162, 166, 187, 205, 206, 208, 215–217, 220, 224, 228–231, 234–237, 239, 244, 245, 254, 261, 267, 287, 292, 297, 300, 306, 307, 312, 316, 319, 320–327, 329, 331, 333, 334, 497, 517, 525, 530, 538, 556, 596, 608, 638, 653, 664–675, R3, R5, R11, R16, R17, R18, R19, R21
- Equations, 320–323, 328, 333, 702
- Expressions, 138–141, 148, 320–328, 333, 334, R10, R22
- Function rules, 6, 7, 208, 234–238, 244, 664–671
- Function tables, 208, 234–237, 244, 316, 664–666, 668–671, R16, R18
- Functions, 6, 7, 208, 234–237, 244
- Missing factors, 216, 224, 229, 241
- Ordered pairs, 672–675
- Writing equations, 320–323, 333
- Writing expressions, 320–327, 333, 334

Angles, 419–421, 434–436, 461, R28
- Greater than a right angle, 435, 436, 461, R28
- Less than a right angle, 435, 436, 461, R28
- Right angles, 435, 436, 438–441, 461, R28

Area, 426–431, 460, R27
- Estimating, 426, 427
- Square units, 426–431, 460

Arrays, 160–167, 174, 191, 201–205, 207, 218, 219, 222, 238–239, 257, 260, 282, 295, 304, R11, R17

Assessment
- Chapter Test, 59, 101, 149, 195, 245, 287, 335, 377, 413, 465, 503, 545, 579, 621, 659
- Formative, 31, 77, 117, 167, 217, 267, 307, 359, 395, 437, 482, 482, 525, 561, 593, 639
- Mid-Chapter Check, 31, 77, 117, 167, 217, 267, 307, 359, 395, 437, 482, 525, 561, 593, 639
- Spiral Review, 27, 37, 51, 73, 81, 95, 113, 127, 137, 141 163, 181, 188, 209, 221, 231, 237, 261, 271, 278, 301, 317, 323, 327, 349, 365, 371, 388, 401, 407, 425, 431, 441, 446, 457, 479, 487, 497, 518, 531, 539, 556, 571, 597, 605, 613, 633, 653
- Standards Practice, 27, 31, 37, 41, 51, 59, 60–61, 73, 77, 81, 95, 101, 102–103, 113, 117, 127, 137, 141, 149, 150–151, 163, 167, 181, 188, 195, 196–197, 209, 217, 221, 231, 237, 245, 246–247, 261, 267, 271, 278, 287, 288–289, 301, 307, 317, 323, 327, 335, 336–337, 349, 357, 359, 365, 371, 377, 378–379, 388, 395, 401, 407, 413, 414–415, 425, 431, 437, 441, 446, 457, 465, 466–467, 479, 482, 487, 497, 503, 504–505, 518, 525, 531, 539, 545, 546–547, 556, 561, 571, 579, 580–581, 593, 597, 605, 613, 621, 622–623, 633, 639, 653, 659–661
- Study Guide and Review, 52–58, 96–100, 142–148, 190–194, 238–244, 282–286, 328–334, 372–376, 408–412, 458–464, 498–502, 540–543, 574–578, 616–620, 654–658
- Summative Assessment,

59, 60–61, 101, 102–103, 149, 150–151, 195, 196–197, 245, 246–247, 287, 288–289, 335, 336–337, 377, 378–379, 413, 414–415, 465, 466–467, 503, 504–505, 545, 546–547, 579, 580–581, 621, 622–623, 659, 660–661

Associative Property of Addition, 65–67, 96, 97

Associative Property of Multiplication, 228–231, 238, 243

B

Bar graphs, 12, 13, 471–475, 482, 483, 493, 495, 496, 499

C

Capacity, 338–340, 352–358, 375, 392–395, 404–407, 410, R23, R25
- Cups, 352–358, 375, R23
- Estimating, 358, 393, 394
- Gallons, 352–358, 375, R23
- Liters, 392–394, 404–407, 410, R25
- Milliliters, 392–394, 404–407, 410, R25
- Pints, 352–358, 375, R23
- Quarts, 352–358, 375, R23

Centimeters, 8, 9, 383–389, 404–407, 409, R24

Challenge H.O.T. Problems, 27, 51, 81, 90, 95, 109, 132, 141, 159, 170, 188, 237, 266, 357, 365, 371, 431, 436, 441, 497, 644, 671, 679

Chapter Test, 59, 101, 149, 195, 245, 287, 335, 377, 413, 465, 503, 545, 579, 621, 659

Choose an Operation, 84, 85, 99, 262, 263, 284, 361, 397, 443

Commutative Property of Addition, 65–67, 96, 97

Commutative Property of Multiplication, 161–163, 201, 202, 214, 215, 223, R11

Comparing
- Fractions, 522–524, 543, 714
- Measures, 353
- Numbers, 4, 5, 34–37, 56, R3

Complex solid figures, 448, 449, 463, R29

Cones, 10, 11, 444–446, 448

Congruent figures, 676, 677

Converting measures, 348, 349, 354–357, 363–365, 368–371, 373, 375, 376, 388, 404–407, 412, R22, R23, R24, R26

Cross-Curricular Connections,
- *The Buzz on Insects*, 532–533
- *Communities Within Communities*, 272–273
- *Continents*, 562–563
- *Eggs!*, 488–489
- *Gardens under Glass*, 450–451
- *Lengths, Heights, and Weights, Oh My!*, 366–367
- *Lots of Arms and Legs*, 182–183
- *The Mighty Mississippi*, 42–43
- *Not Just a Blanket*, 232–233
- *Roller Coaster Physics*, 646–647
- *The Sounds of the Symphony*, 118–119
- *Stamp Collecting*, 614–615
- *Stars and Stripes*, 308–309
- *A Visit to the Supermarket*, 402–403
- *A Walk in the Park*, 82–83

Cubes, 10, 11, 444–446

Cubic units, 452–457, 464

Cups, 352–358, 375, R23

Customary system, 8, 9, 40, 341–349, 352–358, 362–365, 372–376, R22–R24
- Cups, 352–358, 375, R23
- Gallons, 352–358, 375, R23
- Half inch, 343–345
- Inches, 8, 9, 341–349, 373
- Ounces, 362–365, 376, R24
- Pints, 352–358, 375, R23
- Pounds, 362–365, 376, R24
- Quarts, 352–358, 375, R23
- Yards, 346–349, 373, R22

Cylinders, 10, 11, 444–449

D

Data, 468–483, 492–502, R30
- Analysis, 12, 13
- Bar graphs, 12, 13, 471–475, 482, 483, 493, 495, 496, 499, R30
- Collecting, 12, 13
- Displays, 471–483, 492–497
- Graphing, 471–481, 483, 493, 495–497, 499
- Line plot, 468, 476–479, 482, 493, 495, 496, 498, R30, R31
- Pictographs, 12, 13
- Predictions, 494–497, 502
- Recording, 492, 493
- Surveys, 473–475
- Tally chart, 12, 13, 471–475, 494–497

Data File, 30, 76, 112, 126, 176, 236, 266, 312, 364, 406, 445, 486, 530, 555, 596, 604

Decimals, 548–563, 566–571, 574–578
- Decimal points (.), 78
- Fraction equivalence, 548–563, 566–571, 574
- Hundredths, 558–560, 574, 575
- Money, 566–571, 574, 577
- Place value, 553–556, 558–561, 574, 575
- Tenths, 553–556, 574, 575

Denominator, 509–511

Digits, 14–16, 22–31, R2

Divide a number by itself, 280, 281

Division, 248–273, 276–279, 282–334, 624–639, 642–645, 650–661, R16–R20, R39–R40, R47, R48
- As repeated subtraction, 253–257, 268–271, 276–278, 282, 283
- By 0, 280, 281
- By 2, 264–266, 284
- By 3, 295–297, 329
- By 4, 298–301, 329
- By 5, 268–271, 285
- By 6, 304–306, 331
- By 7, 304–306, 331
- By 8, 310–312, 331

By 9, 310–312, 331
By 10, 276–278, 286
By 1-digit numbers, 624–626
By multiples of 10, 627–629, 655
By multiples of 100, 627–629, 655
By multiples of 1,000, 627–629, 655
Divide a number by itself, 280, 281
Dividend, 257
Division-multiplication relationship, 253–267, 272, 273, 276–278, 282–289, 296, 298–301, 305, 310–312, 328, R17
Divisor, 257
Estimating, 630–633, 645, 654, 655
Facts, 248–273, 276–279, 282–334, R16–R20, R47–R48
Functions, 668–671
Money, 650–653, 658, R40
Patterns, 627–629, R38
Properties, 280, 281, 286
Quotient, 257
Regrouping, 634–648
Repeated subtraction, 253–257, 268–271, 276–278, 282, 283, 296, 299, 305, 311, 328, R16
Three-digit quotients, 642–644, 657
Two-digit quotients, 636–638, 656
Unit cost, 314–317, 328, 332, 651–653, R21, R40

Doubling (multiplication facts), 169, 178–181, 207, 219, 239

Draw a Picture, 185, 227, 275, 319, 512–513, 521, 541, 573, 599, 649

E

Equal to (=), 4, 5, 34–37, 56, 522–524, R3, R33

Equations, 320–323, 328, 333, R21
Writing equations, 320–323, 333

Equilateral triangles, 434–436, 461

Equivalent fractions, 514–519, 542, R32

Estimation, 71–73, 590–593, 618, 630–633, 645, 654, 655
Addition, 70–73, 90, 94, 96, 97, R5, R6
Area, 426, 427
Capacity, 358, 393, 394
Division, 630–633, 645, 654, 655, R39
Front-end estimation, 71–73, 592
Length, 341–343, 383, 384
Mass, 399–401
Multiplication, 590–592, 618, R37
Subtraction, 110–113, 143, R8
Volume, 455–457, 464
Weight, 363

Estimation or Exact Answer, 68, 69, 85, 97, 129, R5

Expanded form, 4, 5, 24–31, 37, 54, R3

Expressions, 138–141, 148, 320–328, 333, 334, 691, 703
Writing expressions, 320–327, 333, 334

Extra or Missing Information, 172, 173, 193, R12

F

Fact family, 259–261, 282, R17

Factors, 158, 159, 171, 201, 202

Facts
Addition, R41, R42
Division, 248–273, 276–279, 282–334, R16–R20, R47–R48
Doubling (multiplication), 169, 178–181, 207, 219, 239
Fact family, 259–261, 282
Fast Facts, 177, 210, 225
Multiplication, 152–171, 174–181, 186–189, 191–194, 198–247, R11–R16
Subtraction, R43–R44

Find the Error H.O.T. Problems, 24, 27, 41, 73, 95, 113, 127, 163, 170, 266, 27, 41, 301, 323, 371, 407, 421, 457, 487, 531, 538, 629, 644, 667, 675

Foldables, 15, 52, 63, 105, 142, 153, 190, 199, 238, 249, 282, 291, 328, 339, 372, 381, 408, 417, 458, 469, 498, 507, 540, 549, 574, 583, 616, 625, 654

Foot (feet), 346–349, 373, R22

Formative Assessment, 31, 77, 117, 167, 217, 267, 307, 359, 395, 437, 482, 482, 525, 593, 639

Four-Step Plan, 2, 3, 20, 21, 32, 33, 53, 66, 85, 129, 185, 227, 275, 319, 361, 397, 443, 491, 521, 573, 599, 649, R2, R3, R6

Fractions, 506–563, 566–571, 574–578, R32–R34
Addition, 526–531, 543, R33
Comparing, 522–524, 543, R33
Denominator, 509–511
Fraction-decimal equivalence, 548–563, 566–571, 574, 715
Money, R35
Numerator, 509–511
Parts of a whole, 509–511
Subtracting, 534–539, 544, R34

Front-end estimation, 71–73, 592

Function rules, 6, 7, 208, 234–238, 244, 664–671

Function tables, 208, 234–237, 244, 316, 664–666, 668–671, R16, R18

Functions, 6, 7, 208, 234–237, 244, 668–671
Division, 668–671
Multiplication, 668–671
Subtraction, 664–667

G

Gallons, 352–358, 375, R23

Game Time,
Capacity Guess, 358
Catch Me If You Can, 483
Do Not Zero Out, 133
Factor Power, 171

Fraction Concentration, 519
Fractoes and Decimoes, 557
High and Low, 609
Hit the Target, 389
How Low Can You Go?, 91
Number Cubes, 279
Quotient Roll, 313
Round Numbers, 47
That's Close!, 645
Three in a Row, 211
What's the Shape?, 447

Geometry, 10, 11, 416–441, 444–446, 676–679, R26
Angles, 419–421, 434–436
Closed figures, 419–421
Complex solid figures, 448, 449, 463, R29
Cones, 10, 11, 444–449
Congruent figures, 676, 677
Cubes, 10, 11, 444–446
Cylinders, 10, 11, 444–449
Edges, R29
Equilateral triangles, 434–436, 461
Faces, R29
Hexagons, 419–421, 676, 677
Isosceles triangles, 434–436, 461
Octagons, 419–421
Open figures, 419–421
Parallel lines, 438–441, 461
Parallelograms, 438–441, 461
Pentagons, 419–421, 676, 677
Plane figures, 416–421, R26
Polygons, 419–421, 447, 459, R26
Pyramids, 10, 11, 444–446
Quadrilaterals, 419–421, 438–441, 461, R27
Rectangles, 10, 11, 438–441
Rectangular prisms, 10, 11, 444–446
Rhombus, 438–441, 461
Right angles, 435, 436, 438–441, 461, R27
Scalene triangles, 434–436
Sides, 10, 11, 419–421, 434–436, 438–441
Solid figures, 416–418, 444–446, 448, 449, 463, R29
Spheres, 10, 11, 444–446, 448, 449
Squares, 10, 11, 438–441
Symmetry, 678, 679
Three-dimensional figures, 10, 11, 416–418
Trapezoids, 438–441, 461
Triangles, 10, 11, 419–421, 434–436, 461, R28
Two-dimensional figures, 10, 11, 416–421
Vertex, R28

Grams, 398–401, 404–407, 411, R26

Graphing, 471–481, 483, 493, 495–497, 499
Bar, 12, 13, 471–475, 482, 483, 493, 495, 496, 499
Coordinate grids, 672–675
Line plot, 468, 476–479, 482, 493, 495, 496, 498, R30, R31
Ordered pairs, 672–675
Pictographs, 12, 13
Scale, 471, 472

Greater than (>), 4, 5, 34–37, 56, 522–524, R3, R33

Greater than a right angle, 435, 436, 461, R28

Guess and Check, 390, 391, 397, 410, 443, 491, 521, 573, R25

H

Hexagons, 419–421, 676–677

Horizontal bar graph, 474, 475, 482, 499, R30

H.O.T Problems,
Challenge, 27, 51, 81, 90, 95, 109, 132, 141, 159, 170, 188, 237, 266, 357, 365, 371, 431, 436, 441, 497, 644, 671, 679
Find the Error, 24, 27, 41, 73, 95, 113, 127, 163, 170, 266, 27, 41, 301, 323, 371, 407, 421, 457, 487, 531, 538, 629, 644, 667, 675
Number Sense, 19, 41, 51, 109, 127, , 216, 221, 224, 261, 277, 297, 365, 431, 457, 524, 556, 605, 613, 653, 671
Open Ended, 19, 30, 37, 46, 67, 73, 76, 90, 116, 132, 159, 166, 170, 188, 205, 209, 221, 231, 255, 271, 277, 281, 297, 306, 312, 317, 323, 327, 345, 349, 357, 365, 394, 401, 421, 425, 431, 441, 446, 449, 457, 475, 478, 487, 511, 518, 524, 538, 556, 560, 571, 587, 597, 605, 608, 633, 638, 653, 667, 671, 675, 677, 679
Reasoning, 436, 446, 511
Which One Doesn't Belong? 37, 51, 81, 137, 141, 176, 181, 216, 231, 237, 261, 271, 297, 306, 317, 327, 349, 401, 518, 560, 571, 605, 613, 633, 677, 216, 231, 237

Hundreds chart, 17–19, 24–30, 35, 38, 56, 57

I

Identity Property of Addition, 65–67, 96, 97

Identity Property of Multiplication, 186–188, 202

Inches, 8, 9, 341–349, 373, R22

Isosceles triangles, 434–436, 461

K

Key Concepts, 49, 65, 204, 228, 280, 299, 362, 405, 422, 434, 444, 484, 529, 537, 568

Kilograms, 398–401, 404–407, 411, R26

Kilometers, 385–388, 404–407, 409, R24

L

Length, 338–349, 373, 383–388, 404–407, 409, R22
Centimeters, 8, 9, 383–389, 404–407, 409, R24
Estimating, 341–343, 383, 384
Foot (feet), 346–349, 373, R22
Half inch, 343–345
Inches, 8, 9, 341–349, 373, R22

Kilometers, 385–388, 404–407, 409, R24
Meters, 385–388, 404–407, 409, R24
Miles, 346–349, 373, R24
Millimeters, 383–388, 404–407, 409, 705
Yards, 346–349, 373, R24

Less than (<), 4, 5, 34–37, 56, 522–524, R3, R33

Less than a right angle, 435, 436, 461, R28

Line plot, 468, 476–479, 482, 493, 495, 496, 498, R30, R31

Line symmetry, 678, 679

Lines of symmetry, 678, 679

Liters, 392–394, 404–407, 410, R25

Look for a Pattern, 185, 212–213, 227, 240, 275, 319, 361, 397, 521, R14

M

Make a Table, 302, 303, 319, 330, 335, 361, 397, 443, 491, 521, R20

Make an Organized List, 480, 481, 491, 500, 573, 599, 649, R30

Making predictions, 494–497, 502

Mass, 398–401, 404–407, 411, R26
Estimating, 399–401
Grams, 398–401, 404–407, 411, R26
Kilograms, 398–401, 404–407, 411, R26

Measurement, 8, 9, 338–349, 352–358, 362–365, 372–376, 380–389, 392–395, 398–401, 404–418, 422–433, 437, 454–457, R22–R26
Area, 426–431, 460, R27
Centimeters, 8, 9, 383–389, 404–407, 409, R24
Comparing measures, 353
Cubic units, 452–457, 464
Cups, 352–358, 375, R23
Customary system, 8, 9, 40, 341–349, 352–358, 362–365, 372–376, R22–R26
Foot (feet), 346–349, 373
Gallons, 352–358, 375, 704
Grams, 398–401, 404–407, 411, R26
Half inch, 343–345
Hours, 368–371, 376
Inches, 8, 9, 341–349, 373
Kilograms, 398–401, 404–407, 411, R26
Kilometers, 385–388, 404–407, 409, R24
Liters, 392–394, 404–407, 410, R25
Mass, 398–401, 404–407, 411, R26
Meters, 385–388, 404–407, 409, R24
Metric system, 8, 9, 380–389, 392–395, 398–401, 404–413, R24–R26
Miles, 346–349, 373, R22
Milliliters, 392–394, 404–407, 410, R25
Millimeters, 383–388, 404–407, 409, R24
Minutes, 368–371, 376
Perimeter, 422–425, 431, 459, R27
Pints, 352–358, 375, R23
Pounds, 362–365, 376, R24
Quarts, 352–358, 375, R23
Square units, 426–431, 460
Time, 368–371, 376
Weight, 338–340, 362–365, 376, R24
Yards, 346–349, 373, R22

Meters, 385–388, 404–407, 409, R24

Metric system, 8, 9, 380–389, 392–395, 398–401, 404–413, R24–R26
Centimeters, 8, 9, 383–389, 404–407, 409, R24
Grams, 398–401, 404–407, 411, R26
Kilograms, 398–401, 404–407, 411, R26
Kilometers, 385–388, 404–407, 409, R24
Liters, 392–394, 404–407, 410, R25
Meters, 385–388, 404–407, 409, R24
Milliliters, 392–394, 404–407, 410, R25
Millimeters, 383–388, 404–407, 409, R24

Mid-Chapter Check, 31, 77, 117, 167, 217, 267, 307, 359, 395, 437, 482, 525, 561, 593, 639

Miles, 346–349, 373, R22

Milliliters, 392–394, 404–407, 410, R25

Millimeters, 383–388, 404–407, 409, R24

Missing factors, 216, 224, 229, 241

Money, 78–81, 566–571, 574, 577
Addition, 78–81, 89, 90, 94, 99, R5–R7
Cent sign (¢), 78–81
Decimal notation, 566–571, 574, 577
Division, 650–653, 658, R40
Dollar sign ($), 78–81
Estimating, R6, R7
Fractions, R35
Multiplication, 610–613, 620, R38
Rounding, R5
Subtraction, 114–117, 144, R8, R9, R10

Multi-digit addition, 74–76, 86–95, 98–100

Multi-digit multiplication, 602–608, 619, 620, R36–R38

Multi-digit subtraction, 107–116, 122–127, 130–137, 143, 146, 147

Multiples, 201, 202, 585–587

Multiplication, 152–171, 174–181, 186–194, 198–247, 582–613, 616–620, R10–R16, R36, R37, R38, R45, R46
Arrays, 160–167, 174, 191, 201–205, 207, 218, 219, 222, 238, 239, 257, 260, 282, 295, 304, R11, R17
Associative Property of Multiplication, 228–231, 238, 243
By 0, 186–188
By 1, 186–188
By 2, 164–167, 192
By 3, 203–209, 239
By 4, 168–170, 192

By 5, 174–176, 195
By 6, 206–209, 239
By 7, 214–216, 241
By 8, 218–221, 241
By 9, 222–224, 242
By 10, 178–181, 194
By 1-digit numbers, 582–584, 594–597, 618
By multiples of 10, 585–587, 617
By multiples of 100, 585–587, 617
By multiples of 1,000, 585–587, 617
Commutative Property of Multiplication, 161–163, 201, 202, 214, 215, 223, R11
Division-multiplication relationship, 253–267, 272–273, 276–278, 282–289, 296, 298–301, 305, 310–312, 328
Doubling (Facts), 169, 178–181, 207, 219, 239
Estimation, 590–592, 618, R37
Factors, 158, 159, 171, 201, 202
Facts, 152–171, 174–181, 186–189, 191–194, 198–247, R11–R15
Functions, 668–671
Identity Property of Multiplication, 186–188, 202
Money, 610–613, 620, R38
Multidigit, 602–608, 619, 620, R36, R38
Number sentence, 158, 159, 175, 179, 204, 206, 230, 241, 257
Of two-digit numbers, 602–605
Patterns, 202, 223, 234–237, 585–587, 617, R36
Products, 158, 159, 171, 201, 202
Properties, 201, 202, 214, 215, 223, 228–231, 238, 243
Regrouping, 600–608
Repeated addition, 155–159, 167, 191, 206–209, 214–216
Skip counting, 17–19, 165–170, 175, 178, 203–205
Table, 201–205, 293–297
Use a known fact, 214, 218, 219, 222, 238, 241, 242
Writing multiplication sentences, 204, 206, 230, 241
Zero Property of Multiplication, 186–188

N

Number lines, 44–46, 48–51, 56, 110–113, 165, 299, 304, 523, 590, 591
Division, 299, 304
Fractions, 523

Number patterns, 17–19, 31, 53, 202, 223, 234–237

Number properties, 161–163, 186–188, 201, 202, 214, 215, 223, 228–231, 238, 243, R5
Associative Property of Addition, 65–67, 96, 97
Associative Property of Multiplication, 228–231, 238, 243
Commutative Property of Addition, 65–67, 96, 97
Commutative Property of Multiplication, 161–163, 201, 202, 214, 215, 223, R11
Division Properties, 280, 281, 286
Identity Property of Addition, 65–67, 96, 97
Identity Property of Multiplication, 186–188, 202
Multiplication, 201, 202, 214, 215, 223, 228–231, 238, 243
Zero Property of Multiplication, 186–188

Number Sense H.O.T. Problems, 19, 41, 51, 109, 127, 216, 221, 224, 261, 277, 297, 365, 431, 457, 524, 556, 605, 613, 653, 671

Number sentences, 6, 7, 138–141, 148, 158, 159, 175, 179, 204, 206, 230, 241, 257, R10, R11
Multiplication, 158, 159, 175, 179, 204, 206, 230, 241, 257

Numbers
Comparing, 4, 5, 34–37, 56, R3
Digits, 14–16, 22–31, 683, R2, R3
Expanded notation, 4, 5, 24–31, 37, 54, R2–R3
Hundreds, 4, 5, 14, 15, 22–30
Hundreds chart, 17–19, 24–30, 35, 38, 56, 57
Hundredths, 558–560, 574, 575
Ordering, 4, 5, 38–41, 57, R4
Standard notation, 24–31, 37, 54
Word notation, 24–31, 37, 54, R2, R3

Numerator, 509–511

O

Octagons, 419–421

Online Personal Tutor, 18, 25, 28, 45, 49, 66, 70, 75, 78, 88, 108, 111, 114, 125, 131, 135, 139, 157, 161, 165, 175, 186, 203, 207, 214, 218, 222, 228, 234, 254, 259, 264, 269, 276, 280, 296, 299, 305, 311, 315, 325, 343, 347, 355, 363, 369, 386, 392, 399, 420, 423, 435, 438, 444, 448, 455, 466, 474, 476, 485, 494, 504, 510, 516, 523, 529, 537, 554, 559, 569, 580, 586, 591, 607, 622, 628, 631, 637, 643, 651, 660

Open Ended H.O.T. Problems, 19, 30, 37, 46, 67, 73, 76, 90, 116, 132, 159, 166, 170, 188, 205, 209, 221, 231, 255, 271, 277, 281, 297, 306, 312, 317, 323, 327, 345, 349, 357, 365, 394, 401, 421, 425, 431, 441, 446, 449, 457, 475, 478, 487, 511, 518, 524, 538, 556, 560, 571, 587, 597, 605, 608, 633, 638, 653, 667, 671, 675, 677

Open figures, 419–421

Operation properties, 65–67, 73, 96, 97

Ordered pairs, 672–675

Ordering numbers, 4, 5, 38–41, 57, R4

Ounces, 362–365, 376, R24

P

Parallel lines, 438–441, 461

Parallelograms, 438–441, 461

Partial sums, 75, 76

Parts of a whole, 509–511, 541

Patterns, 627–629, R2
- Division, 627–629, R38
- Multiplication, 202, 223, 234–237, 585–587, 617
- Number, 17–19, 31, 53, 202, 223, 234–237

Pennies, 568–571, 577

Pentagons, 419–421, 676, 677

Perimeter, 422–425, 431, 459

Pints, 352–358, 375, R23

Place value, 4, 5, 14–16, 22–31, 37, 54, R2, R3
- Chart, 24–30, 35, 38, 56, 57
- Decimals, 553–556, 558–561, 574, 575
- Decimal point (.), 78
- Hundreds, 4, 5, 14, 15, 22–30
- Hundreds chart, 17–19, 24–30, 35, 38, 56, 57
- Hundredths, 558–560, 574, 575
- Ones, 4, 5, 14–16, 22–30
- Tens 4, 5, 14–16, 22–30
- Ten thousands, 28–30
- Tenths, 553–556, 574, 575
- Thousands, 28–30

Plane figures, 416–421, R26, R28
- Circles, 10, 11
- Closed figures, 419–421
- Congruent figures, 676, 677
- Equilateral triangles, 434–436, 461
- Hexagons, 419–421, 676, 677
- Isosceles triangles, 434–436, 461
- Open figures, 419–421
- Parallelograms, 438–441, 461
- Pentagons, 419–421, 676, 677
- Polygons, 419–421, 447, 459, R26
- Quadrilaterals, 419–421, 438–441, 461, R28
- Rectangles, 10, 11, 438–441, 461
- Rhombus, 438–441, 461
- Scalene triangles, 434–436, 461
- Squares, 10, 11, 438–441, 461
- Trapezoids, 438–441, 461
- Triangles, 10, 11, 419–421, 434–436, 461, R28
- *What's the Shape?* Game, 447

Polygons, 419–421, 447, 459, R26

Possible outcomes, 480, 481, 492, 493, 500, 520, 521

Predictions, 494–497, 502

Probability, 12, 13, 484–487, 492, 493, 500, R31
- Certain, 484–487, 500, R31
- Combinations, 480, 481, 492, 493, 500
- Equally likely, 492, 493
- Impossible, 484–487, 500, R31
- Likely, 484–487, 500, R31
- Possible outcomes, 480, 481, 492, 493, 500, 520, 521
- Unlikely, 484–487, 500, R31

Problem Solving in Art,
- *Eggs!*, 488–489
- *Not Just a Blanket*, 232–233
- *Stamp Collecting*, 614–615

Problem Solving in Music,
- *The Sounds of the Symphony*, 118–119

Problem Solving in Science,
- *The Buzz on Insects*, 532–533
- *Continents*, 562–563
- *Lengths, Heights, and Weights, Oh My!*, 366–367
- *Lots of Arms and Legs*, 182–183
- *Roller Coaster Physics*, 646–647
- *A Visit to the Supermarket*, 402–403

Problem Solving in Social Studies,
- *Communities Within Communities*, 272–273
- *Gardens under Glass*, 450–451
- *The Mighty Mississippi*, 42–43
- *Stars and Stripes*, 308–309
- *A Walk in the Park*, 82–83

Problem-Solving Investigation, 32, 33, 55, 84, 85, 99, 128, 129, 145, 184, 185, 194, 226, 227, 274, 275, 285, 318, 319, 332, 360, 361, 375, 396, 397, 411, 442, 443, 462, 490, 491, 501, 520, 521, 542, 572, 573, 578, 598, 599, 619, 648, 649, 658

Problem-Solving Skills and Strategies,
- *Act It Out*, 185, 227, 275, 319, 564, 565, 573, 576, 599, 649, R35
- *Choose an Operation*, 84, 85, 99, 262, 263, 284, 361, 397, 443
- *Draw a Picture*, 185, 227, 275, 319, 512, 513, 521, 541, 573, 599, 649
- Estimation or Exact Answer, 68, 69, 85, 97, 129, R5
- Extra or Missing Information, 172, 173, 193, R12
- *Four-Step Plan*, 2, 3, 20, 21, 32, 33, 53, 66, 85, 129, 185, 227, 275, 319, 361, 397, 443, 491, 521, 573, 599, 649, R2, R3
- *Guess and Check*, 390, 391, 397, 410, 443, 491, 521, 573, R25
- *Look for a Pattern*, 185, 212, 213, 227, 240, 275, 319, 361, 397, 521, R14
- *Make an Organized List*, 480, 481, 491, 500, 573, 599, 649, R30
- *Make a Table*, 302, 303, 319, 330, 335, 361, 397, 443, 491, 521, R20
- Reasonable Answers, 120, 121, 129, 144
- *Use Logical Reasoning*, 588, 589, 599, 617, 649, R36
- *Solve a Simpler Problem*, 432, 433, 443, 460, 491, 573, 599, R27
- *Work Backward*, 350, 351, 361, 374, 397, 491, 521, 640, 641, 649, 656, R23, R39

Products, 158, 159, 171, 201, 202

Properties of numbers, 65–67, 73, 96, 97, 161–163, 186–188,

201, 202, 214, 215, 223, 228–231, 238, 243, 280, 281, 286, R11
Associative Property of Addition, 65–67, 96, 97
Associative Property of Multiplication, 228–231, 238, 243
Commutative Property of Addition, 65–67, 96, 97
Commutative Property of Multiplication, 161–163, 201, 202, 214, 215, 223, R11
Division Properties, 280, 281, 286
Identity Property of Addition, 65–67, 96, 97
Identity Property of Multiplication, 186–188, 202
Multiplication, 201, 202, 214, 215, 223, 228–231, 238, 243
Zero Property of Multiplication, 186–188

Pyramids, 10, 11, 444–446

Q

Quadrilaterals, 419–421, 438–441, 461, R28
Parallelograms, 438–441, 461
Rectangles, 10, 11, 438–441
Rhombus, 438–441, 461
Squares, 10, 11, 438–441
Trapezoids, 438–441, 461

Quarts, 352–358, 375, R23

R

Real-World Math, 183, 233, 273, 367, 403, 451, 532, 533, 562, 563

Real-World Problem Solving, 30, 40, 46, 76, 80, 109, 112, 126, 139, 176, 180, 220, 236, 266, 270, 364, 370, 394, 421, 424, 445, 496, 511, 596, 612

Reasonable Answers, 120, 121, 129, 144

Reasoning H.O.T. Problems, 436, 446, 511

Recording data, 492, 493

Rectangles, 10, 11, 438–441, 461

Rectangular prisms, 10, 11, 444–446

Regrouping, 634–639
Addition, 74–76, 86–95, 98–100
Division, 634–648
Multiplication, 600–608
Subtraction, 108, 109, 122–127, 134–137

Relationship symbols, 4, 5, 34–37, 56, 522–524, R3, R33
Equal to (=), 4, 5, 34–37, 56, 522–524, R3, R33
Greater than (>), 4, 5, 34–37, 56, 522–524, R3, R33
Less than (<), 4, 5, 34–37, 56, 522–524, R3, R33

Repeated addition, 155–159, 167, 191, 206–209, 214–216

Repeated subtraction, 253–257, 268–271, 276–278, 282, 283, 296, 299, 305, 311, 328, R16

Rhombus, 438–441, 461

Right angles, 435–436, 438–441, 461, R28

Rounding, 44–51, 57, 58, 70–73, 92, 97, 110–113, 143, 590–592, 618, 630–633, 645, 654, 655, R5, R8, R36, R39
Nearest 10, 44–46, 57
Nearest 100, 44–46, 57
Nearest 1,000, 48–51, 58

S

Scalene triangles, 434–436, 461

Sides, 10, 11, 419–421, 434–436, 438–441

Skip counting, 17–19, 165–170, 175, 178, 203–205

Solid figures, 416–418, 444–446, 448, 449, 463, R29
Complex solid figures, 448, 449, 463, R29
Cones, 10, 11, 444–446, 448, 449
Cubes, 10, 11, 444–446
Cylinders, 10, 11, 444–446, 448, 449
Pyramids, 10, 11, 444–446
Rectangular prisms, 10, 11, 444–446
Spheres, 10, 11, 444–446, 448, 449

Solve a Simpler Problem, 432, 433, 443, 460, 491, 573, 599, R27

Spheres, 10, 11, 444–446, 448, 449

Spiral Review, 27, 37, 51, 73, 81, 95, 113, 127, 137, 141 163, 181, 188, 209, 221, 231, 237, 261, 271, 278, 301, 317, 323, 327, 349, 365, 371, 388, 401, 407, 425, 431, 441, 446, 457, 479, 487, 497, 518, 531, 539, 556, 571, 597, 605, 613, 633, 653

Square units, 426–431, 460

Squares, 10, 11, 438–441, 461

Standard form, 24–31, 37, 54

Standards Practice, 27, 31, 37, 41, 51, 59, 60–61, 73, 77, 81, 95, 101, 102–103, 113, 117, 127, 137, 141, 149, 150–151, 163, 167, 181, 188, 195, 196–197, 209, 217, 221, 231, 237, 245, 246–247, 261, 267, 271, 278, 287, 288–289, 301, 307, 317, 323, 327, 335, 336–337, 349, 357, 359, 365, 371, 377, 378–379, 388, 395, 401, 407, 413, 414–415, 425, 431, 437, 441, 446, 457, 465, 466–467, 479, 482, 487, 497, 503, 504–505, 518, 525, 531, 539, 545, 546–547, 556, 561, 571, 579, 580–581, 593, 597, 605, 613, 621, 622–623, 633, 639, 653, 659, 660–661

Study Guide and Review, 52–58, 96–100, 142–148, 190–194, 238–244, 282–286, 328–334, 372–376, 408–412, 458–464, 498–502, 540–543, 574–578, 616–620, 654–658

Subtraction, 104–117, 122–127, 130–148, R7–R10, R43, R44

Across zeros, 134–137, 147
Estimation, 110–113, 143, R8
Facts, R43, R44
Fractions, 534–539, 544, R34
Functions, 664–667
Money, 114–117, 144, R8, R9, R10
Multidigit, 107–116, 122–127, 130–137, 143, 146, 147
Regrouping, 108, 109, 122–127, 134–137
Repeated subtraction, 253–257, 268–271, 276–278, 282, 283, 296, 299, 305, 311, 328, R16
Three-digit, 122–127
Two-digit, 107–117, 143

Summative Assessment, 59, 60–61, 101, 102–103, 149, 150–151, 195, 196–197, 245, 246–247, 287, 288–289, 335, 336–337, 377, 378–379, 413, 414–415, 465, 466–467, 503, 504–505, 545, 546–547, 579, 580–581, 621, 622–623, 659, 660–661

Surveys, 473–475

Symmetry, 678, 679
Lines of symmetry, 678, 679
Line symmetry, 678, 679

T

Talk About It, 18, 26, 29, 36, 39, 45, 50, 67, 71, 75, 111, 115, 125, 139, 158, 161, 165, 169, 175, 179, 187, 204, 215, 219, 230, 235, 254, 259, 269, 281, 299, 305, 311, 315, 322, 325, 348, 355, 363, 369, 387, 393, 420, 423, 435, 439, 449, 455, 474, 477, 485, 495, 510, 517, 523, 529, 537, 554, 559, 570, 587, 596, 607, 611, 628, 631, 643, 666, 670, 676, 679

Tally chart, 12, 13, 471–475, 494–497

Think About It, 23, 123, 156, 202, 252, 257, 294, 353, 384, 427, 453, 472, 493, 515, 527, 535, 552, 567, 601, 635

Three-dimensional figures, 10, 11, 416–418

Time, 368–371, 376
Hours, 368–371, 376
Minutes, 368–371, 376

Trapezoids, 438–441, 461

Triangles, 10, 11, 419–421, 434–436, 461, 708
Equilateral, 434–436, 461
Isosceles, 434–436, 461
Scalene, 434–436, 461

Two-dimensional figures, 10, 11, 416–421

U

Unit cost, 314–317, 328, 332, 651–653, R21, R40

Use a known fact, 214, 218, 219, 222, 238, 241, 242

Use Logical Reasoning, 588, 589, 599, 617, 649, R36

V

Vertical bar graph, 473–475, 482, 483, 499, R30

Volume, 452–457, 464, R29
Cubic units, 452–457, 464
Estimating, 455–457, 464

W

Weight, 338–340, 362–365, 376, R24
Estimating, 363
Grams, 398–401, 404–407, 411, R26
Kilograms, 398–401, 404–407, 411, R26
Mass, 398–401, 404–407, 411
Ounces, 362–365, 376, R24
Pounds, 362–365, 376, R24

Which One Doesn't Belong? H.O.T. Problems, 37, 51, 137, 141, 176, 181, 216, 231, 237, 261, 271, 297, 306, 317, 327, 349, 401, 518, 560, 571, 605, 613, 633, 677

Word form, 24–31, 37, 54, R2, R3

Work Backward, 350, 351, 361, 374, 397, 491, 521, 640, 641, 649, 656, R23, R39

Writing equations, 320–323, 333

Writing expressions, 320–327, 333, 334

Writing in Math, 3, 5, 7, 9, 11, 13, 19, 21, 23, 27, 30, 31, 37, 41, 46, 59, 51, 67, 69, 73, 76, 77, 81, 87, 95, 109, 116, 117, 121, 123, 127, 129, 132, 137, 141, 149, 156, 159, 163, 166, 167, 170, 173, 176, 181, 185, 188, 195, 202, 205, 209, 213, 216, 217, 221, 224, 227, 231, 237, 245, 252, 255, 257, 261, 263, 266, 267, 271, 275, 277, 281, 287, 294, 297, 301, 303, 306, 307, 312, 317, 319, 323, 327, 335, 345, 349, 351, 353, 357, 359, 361, 365, 371, 377, 384, 388, 391, 394, 395, 397, 401, 407, 413, 421, 425, 427, 431, 433, 436, 441, 443, 446, 449, 453, 457, 465, 472, 475, 478, 481, 482, 487, 491, 493, 497, 503, 511, 513, 515, 518, 521, 524, 525, 527, 531, 535, 538, 545, 552, 556, 560, 561, 565, 567, 571, 579, 587, 589, 593, 597, 601, 605, 608, 613, 621, 629, 633, 635, 638, 641, 644, 653, 659, 667, 671, 675, 677, 679

Writing multiplication sentences, 204, 206, 230, 241

Writing numbers, 4, 5, 24–31, 37, 54, R2, R3
Expanded form, 4, 5, 24–31, 37, 54, R3, R4
Standard form, 24–31, 37, 54
Word form, 24–31, 37, 54, R2, R3

Y

Yards, 346–349, 373, R22

Z

Zero Property of Multiplication, 186–188

Measurement Conversions

	Metric	Customary
Length	1 kilometer (km) = 1,000 meters (m) 1 meter = 100 centimeters (cm)	1 mile (mi) = 1,760 yards (yd) 1 mile = 5,280 feet (ft) 1 yard = 3 feet 1 foot = 12 inches (in.)
Volume and Capacity	1 liter (L) = 1,000 milliliters (mL)	1 gallon (gal) = 4 quarts (qt) 1 gallon = 128 ounces (oz) 1 quart = 2 pints (pt) 1 pint = 2 cups (c) 1 cup = 8 ounces
Weight and Mass	1 kilogram (kg) = 1,000 grams (g)	1 pound (lb) = 16 ounces (oz)

Time	1 year (yr) = 365 days (d) 1 year = 12 months (mo) 1 year = 52 weeks (wk) 1 week = 7 days 1 day = 24 hours (h) 1 hour = 60 minutes (min) 1 minute = 60 seconds (s)

Multiplication Table

×	1	2	3	4	5	6	7	8	9	10
1	1	2	3	4	5	6	7	8	9	10
2	2	4	6	8	10	12	14	16	18	20
3	3	6	9	12	15	18	21	24	27	30
4	4	8	12	16	20	24	28	32	36	40
5	5	10	15	20	25	30	35	40	45	50
6	6	12	18	24	30	36	42	48	54	60
7	7	14	21	28	35	42	49	56	63	70
8	8	16	24	32	40	48	56	64	72	80
9	9	18	27	36	45	54	63	72	81	90
10	10	20	30	40	50	60	70	80	90	100

KEYBOARD MUSICIANSHIP

KEYBOARD MUSICIANSHIP

by Guy Duckworth

Professor of Music,
University of Colorado

THE FREE PRESS, NEW YORK • COLLIER-MACMILLAN LIMITED, LONDON

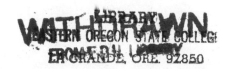

A Division of The Macmillan Company
Printed in the United States of America

The Free Press
A Division of The Macmillan Company
866 Third Avenue, New York, New York 10022

Collier-Macmillan Canada Ltd., Toronto, Ontario

Library of Congress Catalog Card Number: 79-132080

printing number 1 2 3 4 5 6 7 8 9 10

To Joeon, my wife;
Mary, my assistant; Don, Gail and Peter.

CONTENTS

PREFACE ix

INTRODUCTION 1

BLACK KEYS
Playing by ear 3
Improvising 6
Reading 11

UNIT ONE 15

Section 1. TETRACHORDS
Major 17
Modal 46

Section 2. PENTACHORDS 68
Major 72
Modal 83
Repertoire—Pentachords 95
Pieces for Duets Op. 149, A. Diabelli
Scherzo, C Major 96
Andante Cantabile, D Major 98
Allegro, C Major 100
Hongroise, F Major 102
Alla Turca, A Minor 104

UNIT TWO 107

Section 1. HAND POSITION CHANGE—LIMITED RANGE 109
Major 111
Modal 121
Repertoire—Hand Position Change
Prelude, G Major , H. Purcell 131
Andante Grazioso, Theme from K331, W. Mozart 132
Eccossaise, G Major, L. Van Beethoven 133

Section 2. STRETCHES—LIMITED RANGE 134
Major 136
Modal 146
Repertoire—Stretches
Eccossaise, D. Major, F Schubert 157
Menuet Duet from Sonatina 11 for four hands B♭ Major, W. Mozart 158

Section 3. CROSSES—LIMITED RANGE 162
Major 164
Modal 173

Repertoire—Crosses
Sonatine, for four hands, B♭ Major, D. G. Turk 178
Reigen Mit Zwei Zwischenspielen for four hands, G. B. Turk 180
Eccossaise, C Major, J. Haydn 182

Section 4. REPERTOIRE—LIMITED RANGE
Minuet, G. Major, J. C. Bach 183
Minuet, G Major, G. Telemann 184
Minuet, B Minor, G. Handel 185
Minuet, D Minor, L. Mozart 186
Trumpet Piece, L. Mozart 187
Landler—J. C. Bach 188
The Hunt, D. G. Turk 189
Eccossaise, F. Schubert 189
Polonaise (Duet) for four hands, A. Diabelli 190
Andante, (Duet) E Major for four hands, A. Diabelli 194

UNIT THREE 197

Section 1. CROSSES UNLIMITED RANGE-SCALE PLAYING 199
Repertoire—Crosses on Steps
Allegro (Duet) for four hands, D. G. Turk 208
Courante, F. Major, F. Handel 212

Section 2. CROSSES—UNLIMITED RANGE—ARPEGGIO PLAYING 214
Repertoire—Crosses on Skips
Eccossaise, E♭ Major, L. Van Beethoven 218
Chopin (from Carnival Op. 9) R. Schumann 218
Prelude, G. Major, D. Scarlatti 220

Section 3. CONTRACTIONS—UNLIMITED RANGE 221
Repertoire—Contractions
Prelude, J. S. Bach 225
Landler, L. van Beethoven 227

Section 4. REPEATED NOTES—UNLIMITED RANGE 228
Repertoire—Repeated Notes
Sarabande, D Major, G. Handel 232
Waltz, G Major, F. Schubert 233
Waltz, G Major, C. von Weber 233

Section 5. REPERTOIRE—UNLIMITED RANGE
Rondeau, D. Major, J. P. Rameau 234
Little Prelude, C Major J. S. Bach 236
La Charolaise, F. Couperin 239
Allemande, B Minor, L. van Beethoven 240
Entree, L. Mozart 242
Turkish March, L. van Beethoven 243
Waltz Op. 33, F. Schubert 244
Etude Op. 25 #9, F. Chopin 245
Prelude Op. 28 #15, F. Chopin 245
Allegretto, C Minor, F. Schubert 246
Waltz Op. 39 #15 (Duet) for four hands, J. Brahms 248
Allemande, G Major, C. M. von Weber 250

Section 6. RESOURCE MATERIALS 251
Verse for Improvising 251
Keyboard Sequences 256
Scale Playing 258
Arpeggio Playing 261

PREFACE

KEYBOARD MUSICIANSHIP is designed primarily for music majors whose performance medium is different from a keyboard instrument. An adult beginner, under teacher guidance for learning the music elements, however, can benefit from use of the text.

The non-piano major may be a beginner or a student with little to considerable experience. Whatever the case this text provides him with the keyboard skills he needs as a music educator. In the institutions where the piano major is expected to have a broad keyboard background, in addition to his repertoire performance, this text is also useful.

KEYBOARD MUSICIANSHIP contains music largely based upon folk material. This material is set by the author into piano pieces which expose the student to both traditional and contemporary harmonic practices. In addition to folk material, a repertoire is included from keyboard literature of the Baroque, Classic and Romantic periods of music.

All keyboard skills expected of the music major including scale and arpeggio playing are developed in the text, thereby affording a maximum number of transfers for his learnings. Additional applications of concepts and skills are easily found in public school music texts.

READING

Over two hundred compositions in solo and ensemble which include all key centers, all modes, and individual hand independence.

IMPROVISING

Opportunity for 1) completing musical patterns which expose traditional and contemporary sounds while reading and 2) applying these same patterns to improvisations.

TRANSPOSING

All compositions written so as to develop gradual technical competence and keyboard topographical knowledge thus realistically facilitating this skill.

HARMONIZING

Obligatory harmonization of folk material in traditional idioms even though the author has set much of the material using contemporary harmonic practices.

The premise for the organization of the text is based upon the need for the student to build as quickly as possible a *technical skill* that allows him to play easily and musically. The author feels this is accomplished by:

1. Developing a thorough knowledge of keyboard topography.
2. Relating the concepts of musical elements to their control at the keyboard.

Beginning with the black keys and moving quickly to the complete eight note scale of all major keys and the five additional modes which share the same key signatures—Dorian, Phrygian, Lydian, Mixo-lydian and Aeolian—the student learns the sounds and feel of the formal scales he should know as a musician. He does this by dividing the scales between two hands in tetrachords. To provide musical interest studies and improvisations are written and designed for duet performance.

To facilitate the performance of these scales with one hand, compositions in solo and duet first appear in pentachords—the first five pitches of a scale. Then compositions exposing the sixth and seventh pitches of the scales follow the pentachord material by relating this wider but limited range of pitches to 1) fingering concepts and 2) musical concepts regarding melody and form. Changing hand position between phrases and stretching, crossing, and contracting within phrases organize this subsequent material.

G. D.

INTRODUCTION

BLACK KEYS

In this introductory section to the piano, the student plays only on the black keys using both hands. Sometimes he plays in solo, sometimes in ensemble. He plays by ear, improvises and reads.

PLAYING BY EAR

MERRILY WE ROLL ALONG

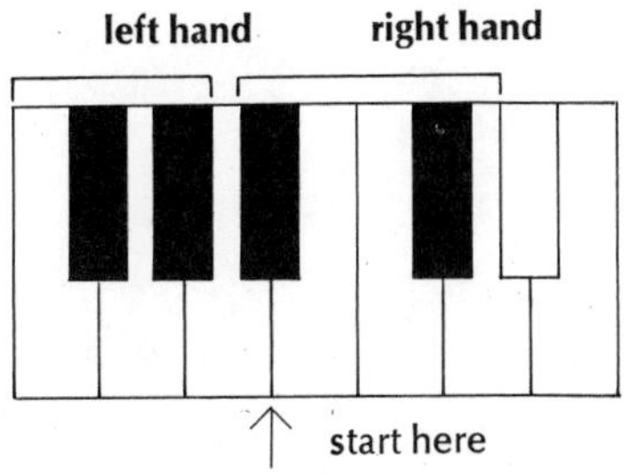
left hand
right hand
start here

American

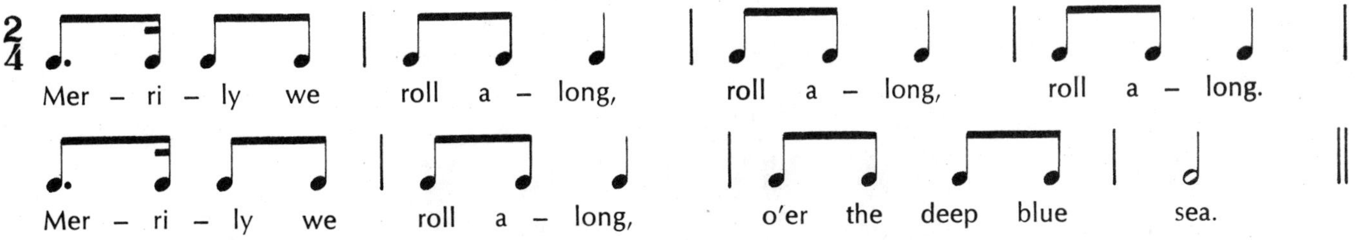
Mer – ri – ly we roll a – long, roll a – long, roll a – long.
Mer – ri – ly we roll a – long, o'er the deep blue sea.

THE FARMER IN THE DELL

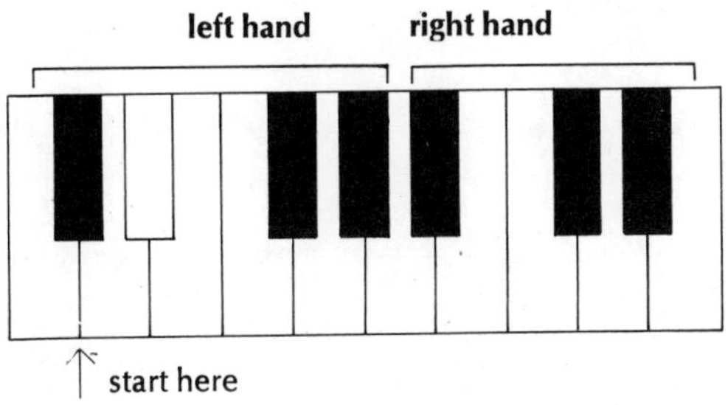
left hand
right hand
start here

Traditional

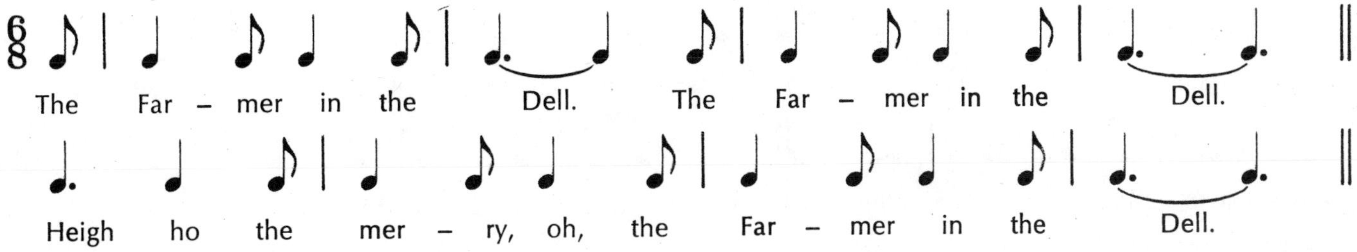
The Far – mer in the Dell. The Far – mer in the Dell.
Heigh ho the mer – ry, oh, the Far – mer in the Dell.

OLD MacDONALD

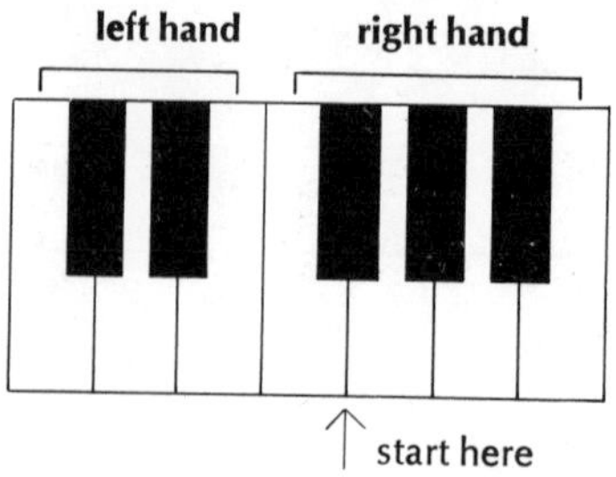
left hand
right hand
start here

American

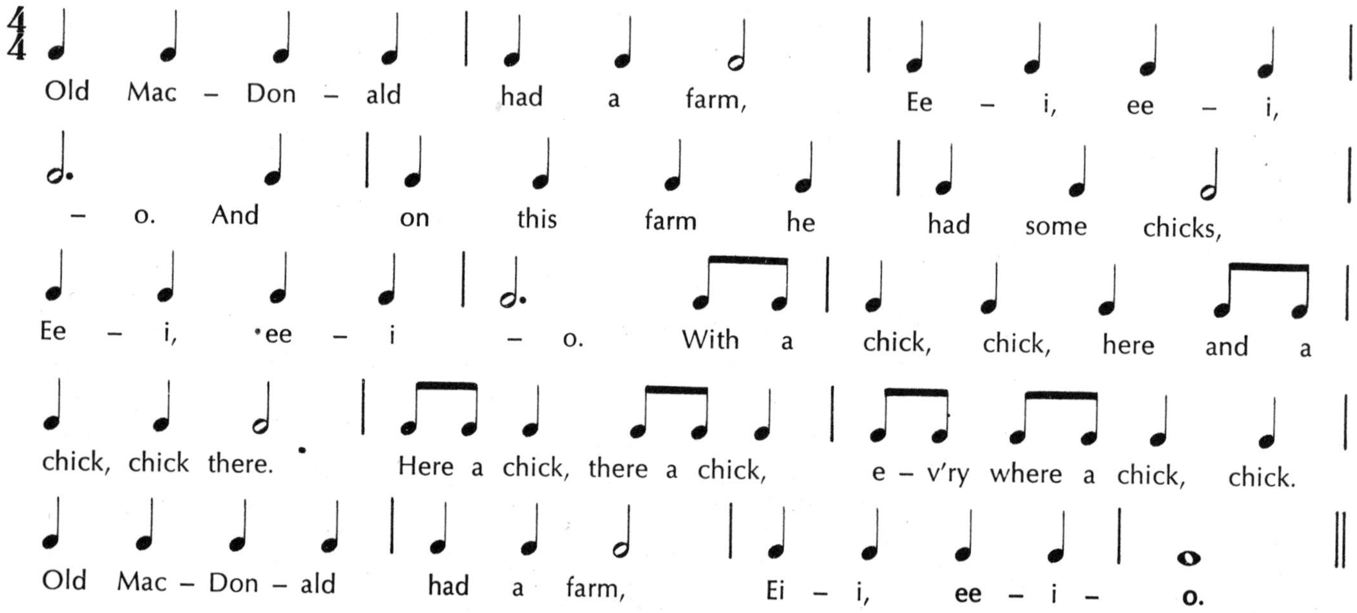
Old Mac – Don – ald had a farm, Ee – i, ee – i,
– o. And on this farm he had some chicks,
Ee – i, ee – i – o. With a chick, chick, here and a
chick, chick there. Here a chick, there a chick, e – v'ry where a chick, chick.
Old Mac – Don – ald had a farm, Ei – i, ee – i – o.

AULD LANG SYNE

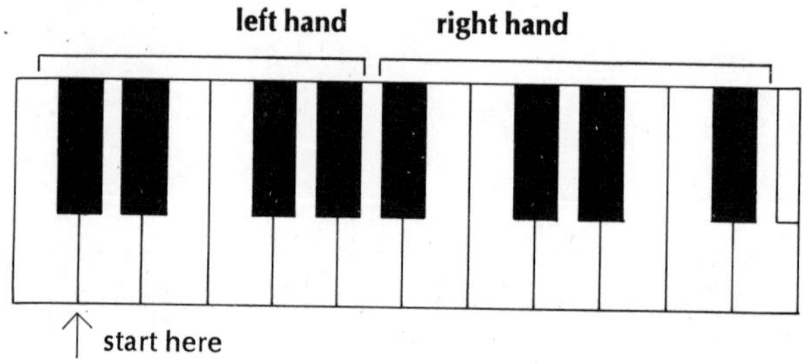
left hand
right hand
start here

Scottish

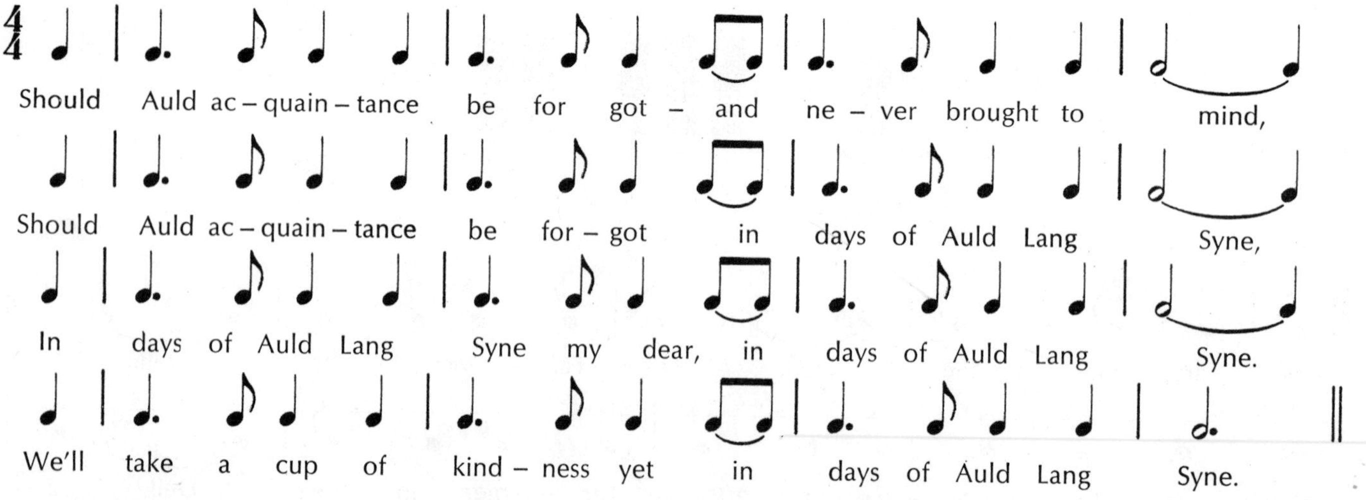
Should Auld ac – quain – tance be for got – and ne – ver brought to mind,
Should Auld ac – quain – tance be for – got in days of Auld Lang Syne,
In days of Auld Lang Syne my dear, in days of Auld Lang Syne.
We'll take a cup of kind – ness yet in days of Auld Lang Syne.

NOBODY KNOWS THE TROUBLE I'VE SEEN

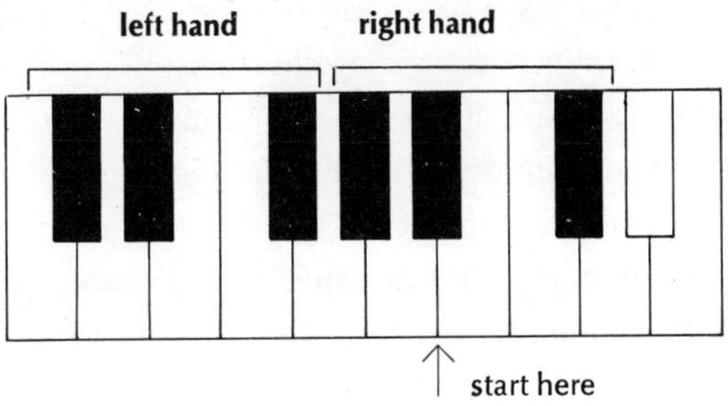
left hand
right hand
start here

Spiritual

No – bo – dy knows the troub – le I've seen No – bo – dy knows my sor – row.
No – bo – dy knows the troub – le I've seen. Glo – ry Hal – le lu – lia.

IMPROVISING

The following canons are to be improvised. The canon form is maintained more through rhythm than melody. In studying these canons it is best first to tap the patterns in unison to learn the note values and gain a conception of the dynamics and phrasings. After the rhythms can be tapped perfectly in unison, improvisations should be done with everyone starting from the beginning at the same time establishing thereby the starting pitch of each phrase. At which time the group is ready to begin to improvise in canon.

The directions for improvising in canon are the following. Each part starts at the beginning of the canon and completes the canon. Part 2 enters when Part 1 arrives at the number "2" in the score. Part 3 enters when Part 1 arrives at the number "3," and so forth.

TWO-PART CANON

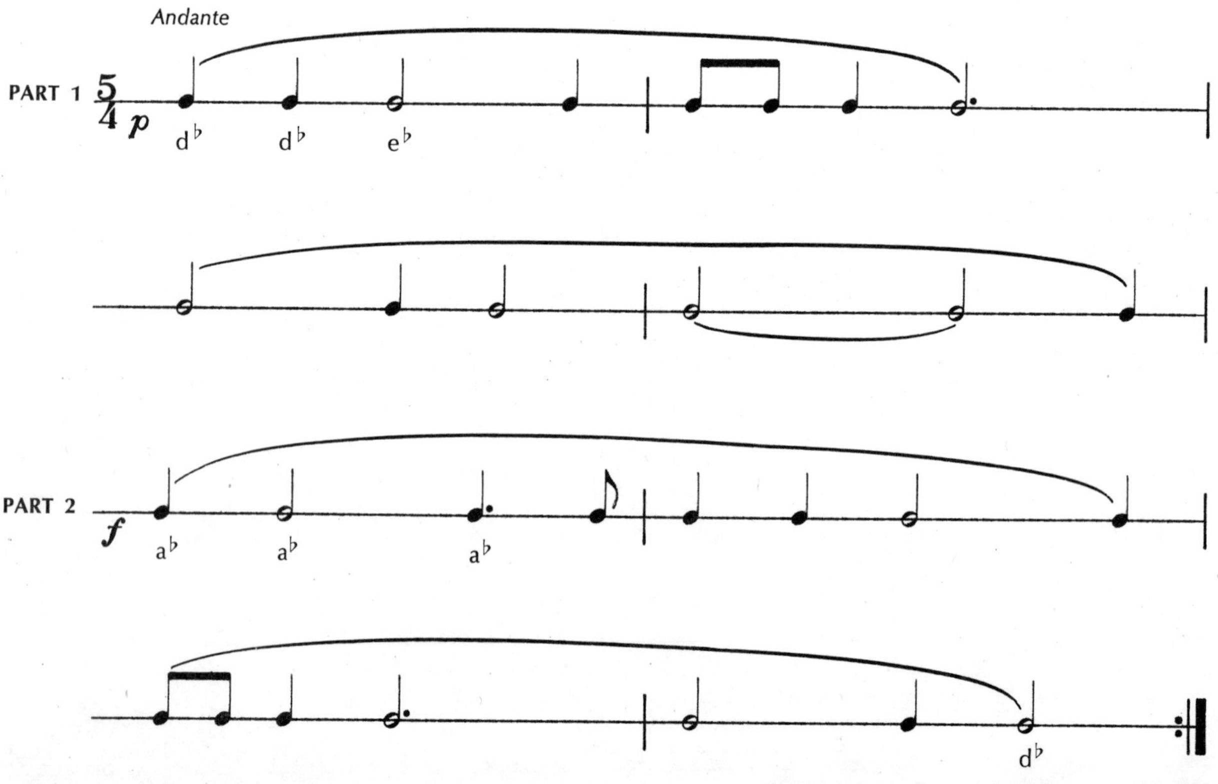

THREE-PART CANON WITH OSTINATO

2

PARTS 1 AND 2

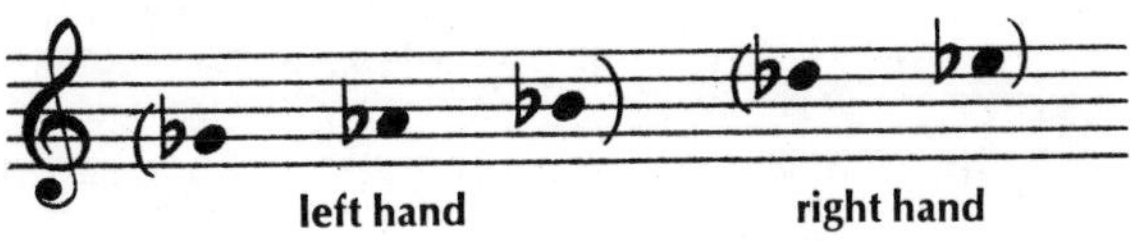

PART 3

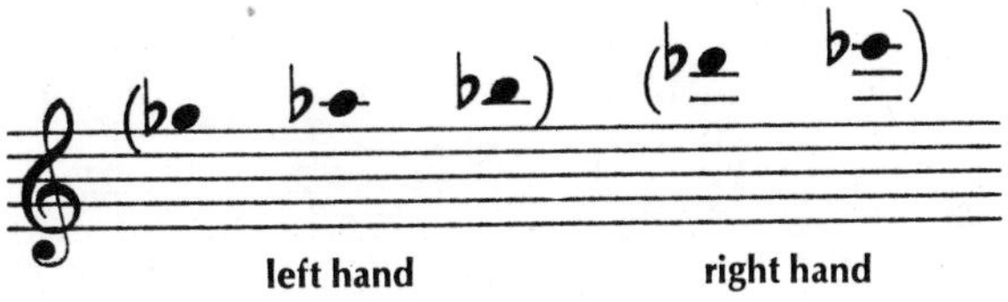

OSTINATO (optional)

Moderato

Two measure introduction with ostinato (optional)

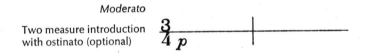

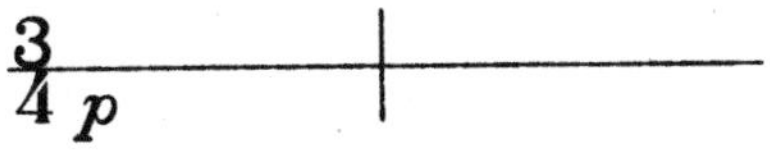

PART 1

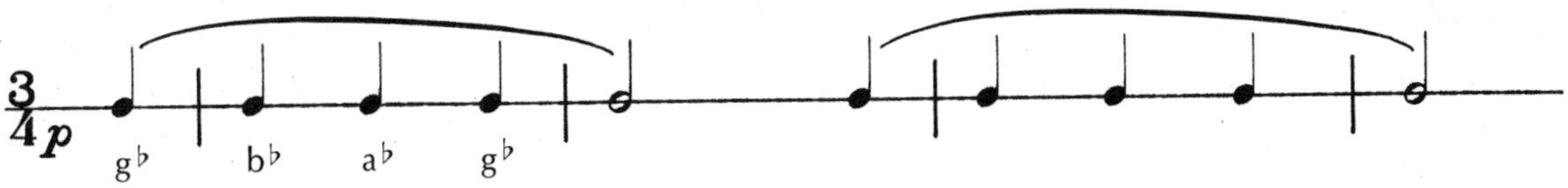

PART 2

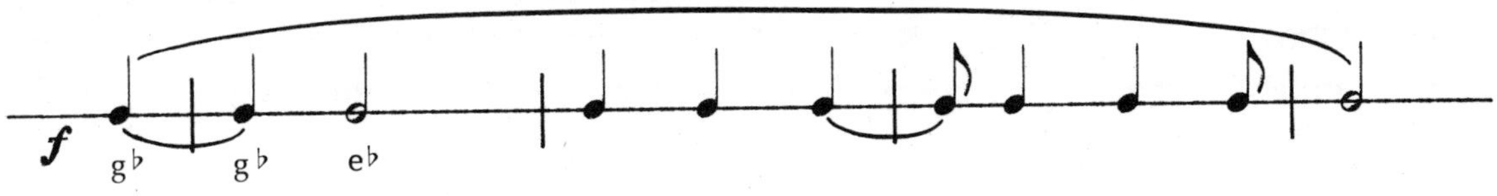

PART 3

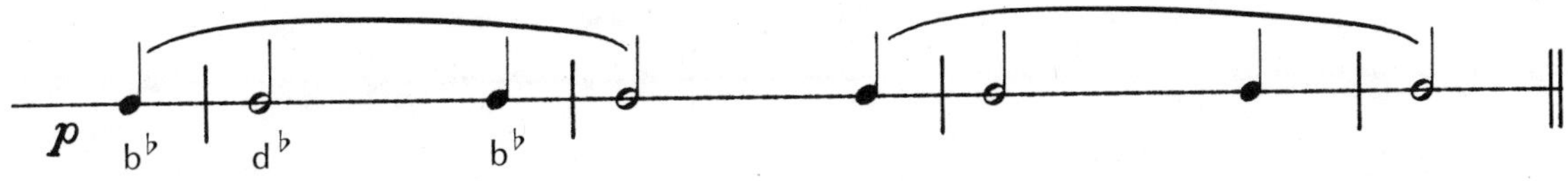

FOUR-PART CANON

3

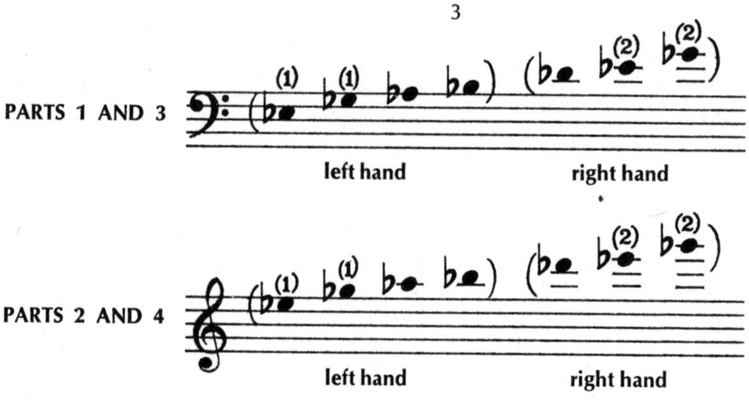

FOUR-PART CANON WITH OSTINATO

4

PARTS 1 AND 3

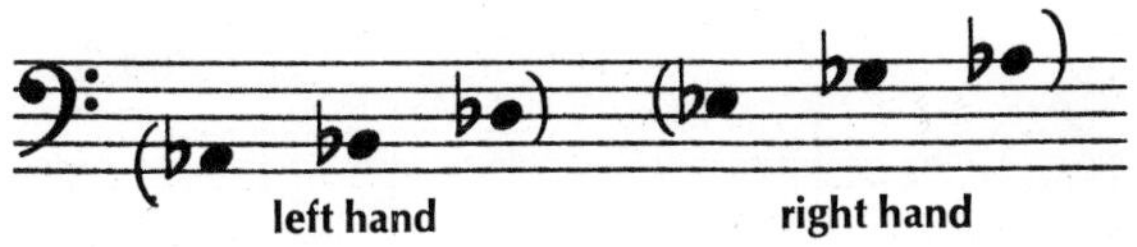

PARTS 2 AND 4

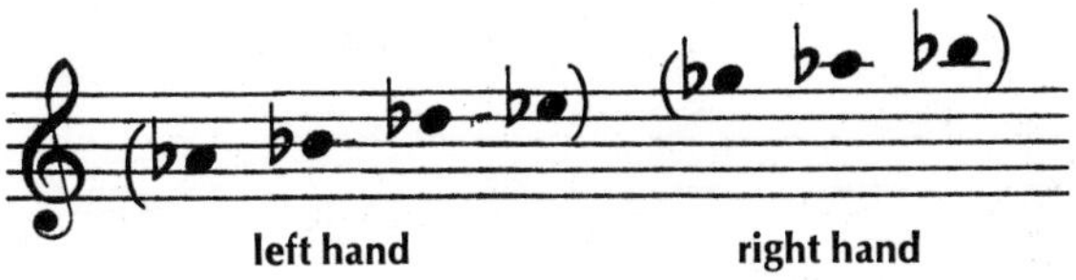

OSTINATO (optional)

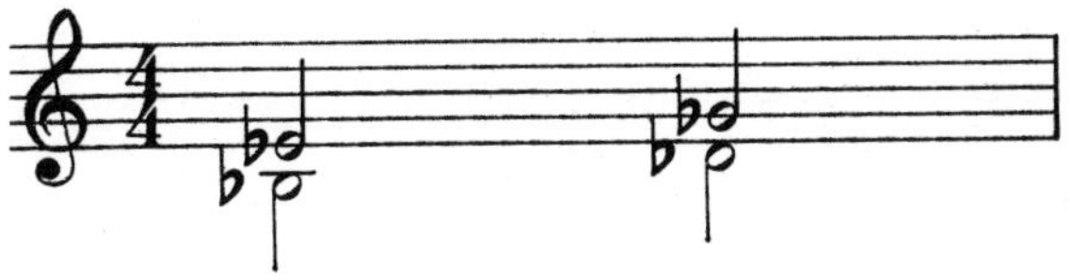

Lento

Two measure introduction
with ostinato (optional)

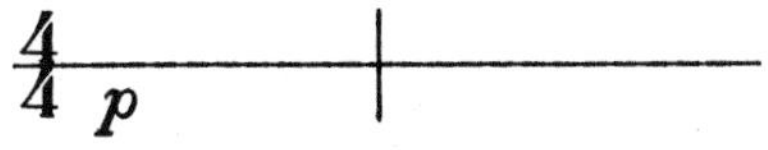

PART 1

PART 2

PART 3

PART 4

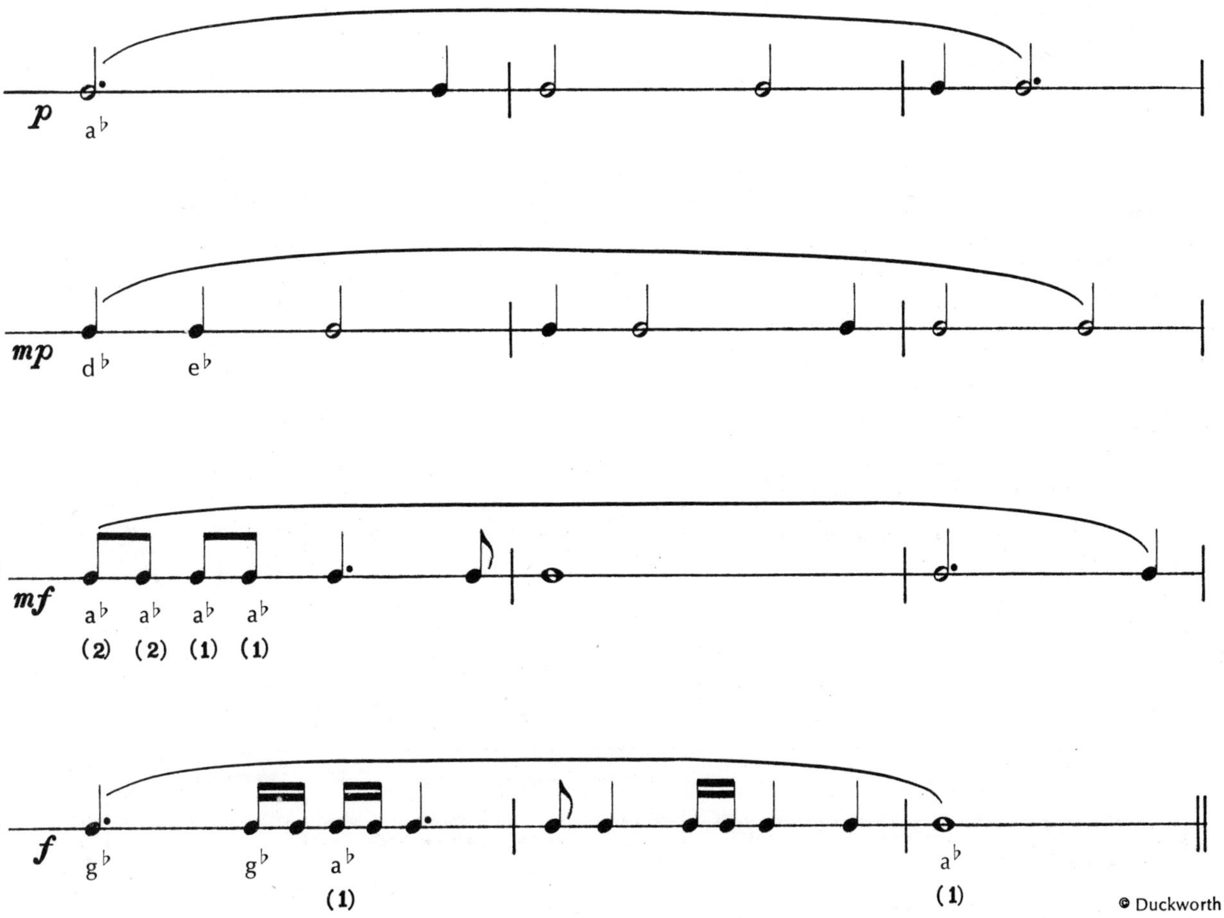

THREE-PART CANON WITH OSTINATO

5

PARTS 1 AND 3

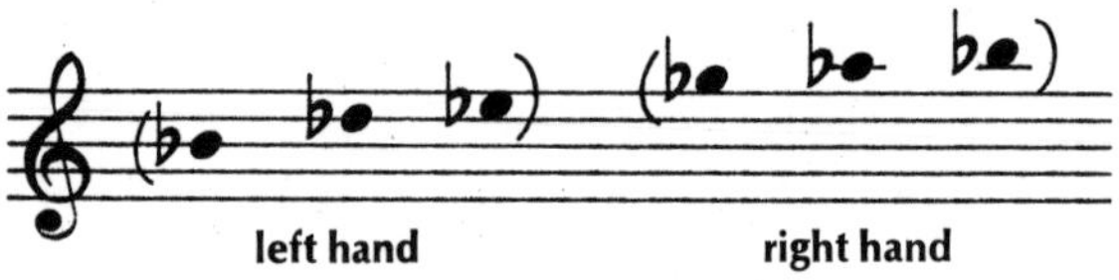

PART 2

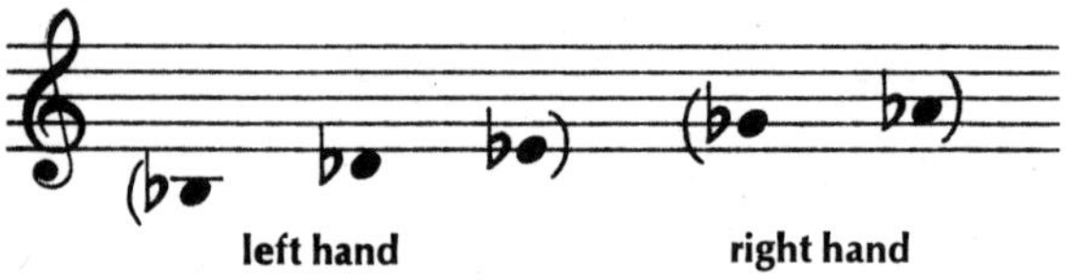

OSTINATO (optional)

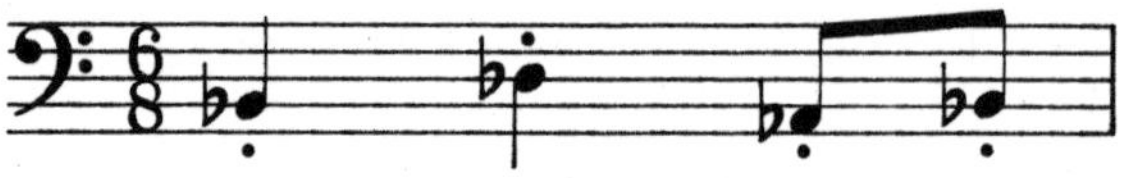

Moderato

Two measure introduction
with ostinato (optional)

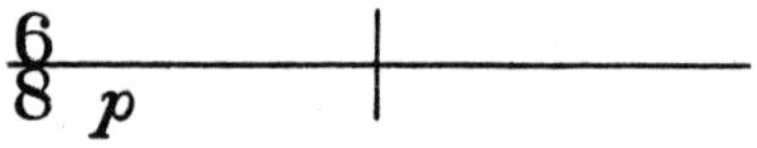

PART 1

PART 2

PART 3

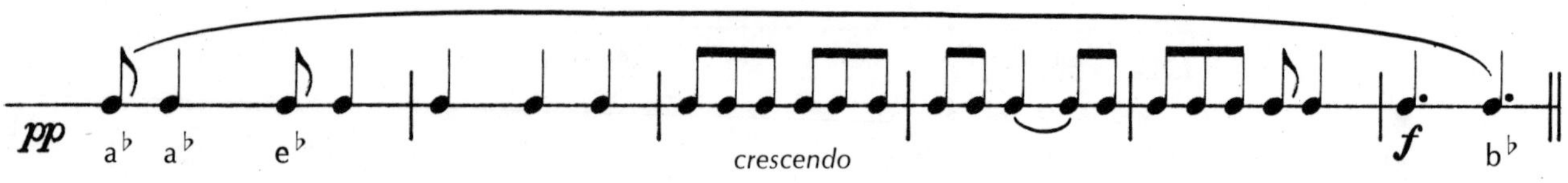

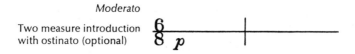

READING

The following melodies are to be read. After each is played with reasonable accuracy, counter melodies can be improvised and basses added for accompaniments, introductions and endings.

FOUR IN A BOAT

Appalachian Mountain Song

*A second performer can play in duet with the person(s) reading this song by improvising a counter melody to these rhythmic patterns. Use two hands playing 8va higher than melody on black keys.

A third performer can provide a bass for this melody. In addition, an introduction and ending to the song can be supplied by this person. Select from the following intervals the appropriate fifth to play on the first and third beats of each measure. An introduction and ending to this song might be played by alternating these fifths. Play with two hands.

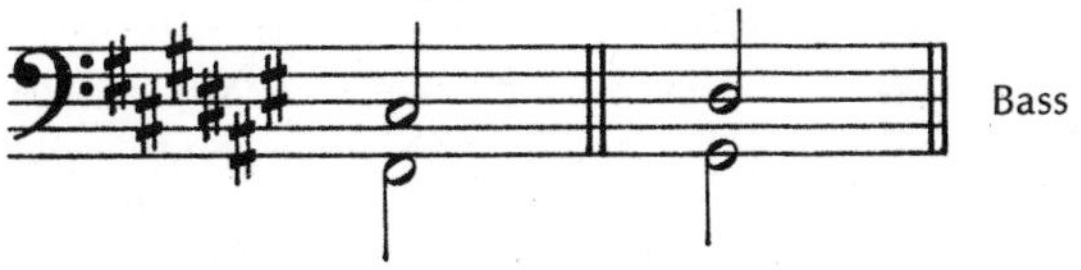

FRENCH FOLK SONG

*Using two hands play 8va higher than melody on black keys.

Free ostinato

To form an ostinato the performer is free to arrange these pitches in any order with any rhythmic patterns he wishes. The placement of the ostinato in the meter depends upon the rhythmic pattern chosen. The ostinato can be used as an introduction and ending to the song. Two hands can be used.

PRETTY SARO

Kentucky Folk Song

Improvised Counter Melody*

Down in some lone val – ley in a lone - some place, Where the
wild birds do whis – tle and their notes do in – crease; Fare
– well pret – ty Sa – ro, I bid you a – dieu. But I'll
dream of pret– ty Sa – ro where ev – er I go.

*Using two hands play 8va higher than melody on black keys.

Bass

Select from the following intervals appropriate ones to play on the first beat of each measure. Use the intervals for supplying an introduction and ending to this song. Use two hands.

UNIT ONE

TETRACHORDS

The following compositions are written by the author for duet performance. When the part is melodic, pitch range and fingering clues are indicated following the title. The melody is always divided between two hands, usually in tetrachords. When the part is accompaniment it is written so as to explore exclusively root position triads. All major and modal scales are presented.*

The teacher might find these duets beneficial for clarifying scale organizations discovered in the pentachord section of the text—Section 2. In which case, the student skips to Section 2 and refers back to this material to clarify the scales he encounters there.

TETRACHORDS—MAJOR

The tetrachords in the following chart should be practiced and key signatures memorized.

TETRACHORDS

Chant letter names of the notes as you practice the tetrachords.

Sharp Keys

C Major

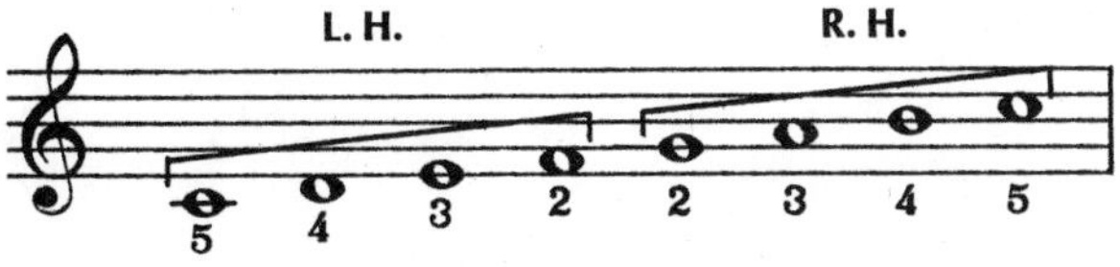

G Major

D Major

Flat Keys

G♭ Major

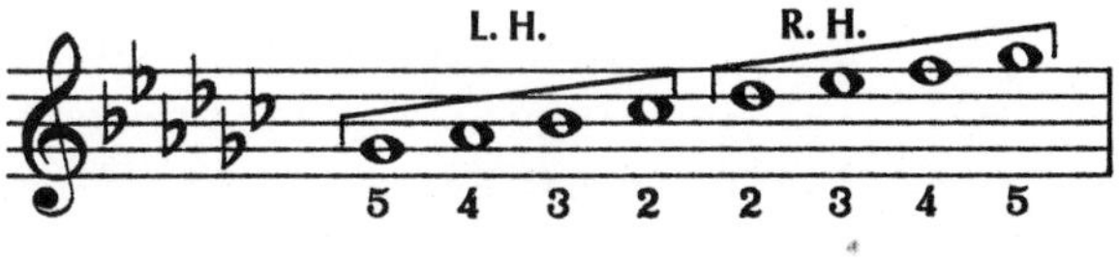

D♭ Major

A♭ Major

*Although the major scale is also the Ionian Mode the author henceforth has chosen to separate it from the other modes so as to establish a point of relativity for determining key signatures for the remaining modes. For some examples:
What is the relative major (key signature) of D Dorian? C major.
What is the relative major of F# Dorian? E major.

A Major

E Major

B Major

F# Major

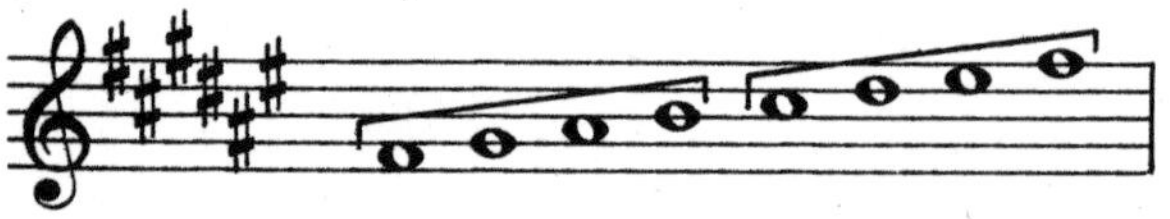

E♭ Major

B♭ Major

F Major

C Major

READING

Each of the duets is written in a different major key. Twelve keys are presented. The melodic part of each duet, which sometimes appears in secondo as well as primo parts, is exclusively for student performance designated "Student" in the score. Since this part is written for two hands, each hand usually covers a tetrachord position. There will be situations where the thumb of either hand will be needed. In these cases the fingering is indicated. It is advisable to play the melodic part alone before playing it with its accompanying part.

Inasmuch as the accompaniment part of the duets, designated "Teacher," uses only the root position of triads in various patterns and counter melodies are in pentachord positions, the beginning student can eventually learn this part. At first, however, the teacher or student with keyboard experience should play this portion of the composition.

TRANSPOSING

Each composition should be transposed to as many key centers as possible so as to facilitate the ability to think within any key. No limitation should be placed on the key centers selected for training this skill.

IMPROVISING

Space is provided for improvising compositions in duet in each major key. Limiting conditions for improvising are indicated by style of the composition immediately preceding; harmonic structures, phrasings, starting and closing pitches.

HARMONIZING

An harmonic structure is often indicated in the improvisation. It should be remembered that all accompaniment material utilizes only root position triads. The harmonic structures quickly move out of the primary triads. Along with his tetrachord practice, therefore, the student should construct and practice triads with both hands on each pitch of each scale. For example:

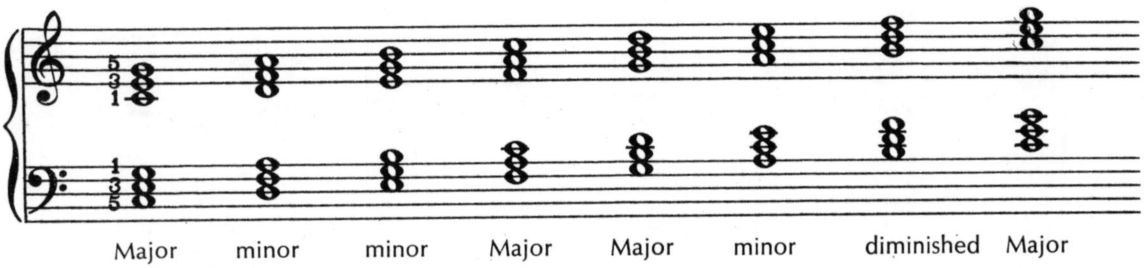

GAME

1a

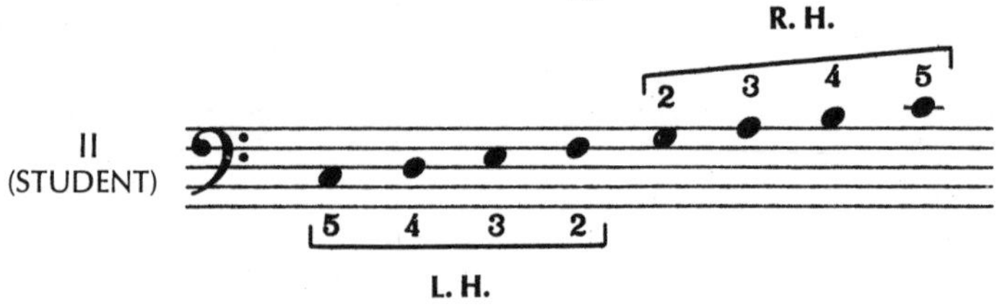

*Note: Inasmuch as melodic material is exchanged between hands rests are not provided in the staff of the hand that is not playing. Keeping the score simple in this manner allows the student to focus his complete attention on melodic contour as he reads.

IMPROVISATION

1b

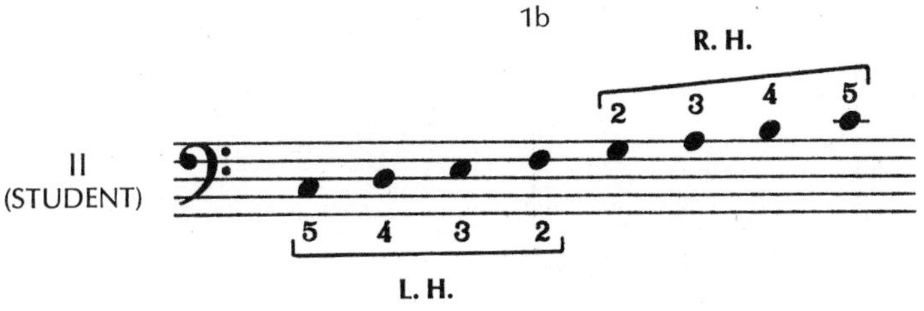

This is a two-hand improvisation. After playing the pitches indicated at the beginning of each phrase the performer is on his own for selecting the pitches he wishes to use as long as they fit into the harmonic structure indicated for the composition. The improvisation is to have a similar sound to that of Game; thus the different note values assigned to each part.

O NUIT, HEUREUSE NUIT

2a

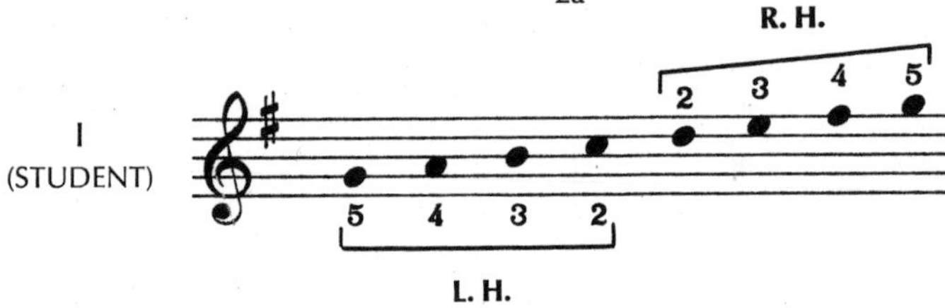

Melody by
F. A. Gevaert
1828-1908

I
II
I
II
I
II

IMPROVISATION (Duet)

*dominant of the dominant

RØGTERS SONG (Duet)

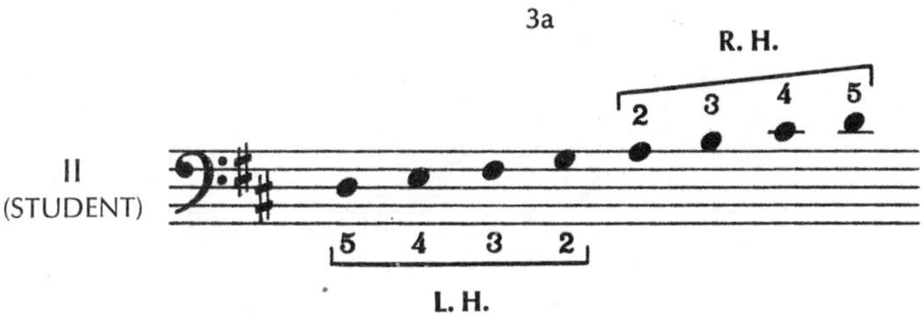

Melody by
Carl Nielson
1865-1931

*Continue rolling chords

IMPROVISATION (Duet)

*Continue rolling chords

POLONAISE (Duet)

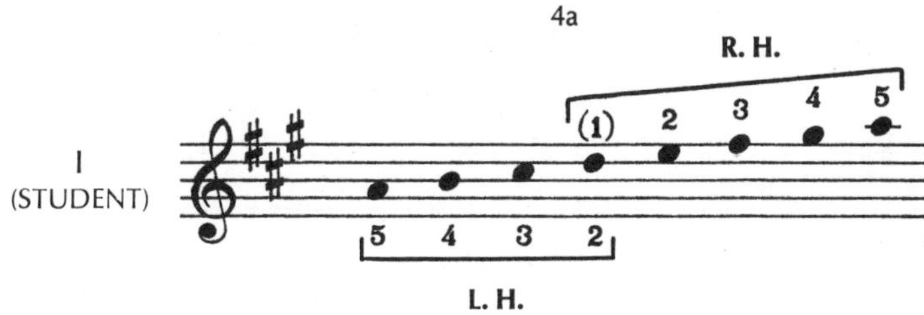

IMPROVISATION (Duet)

4b

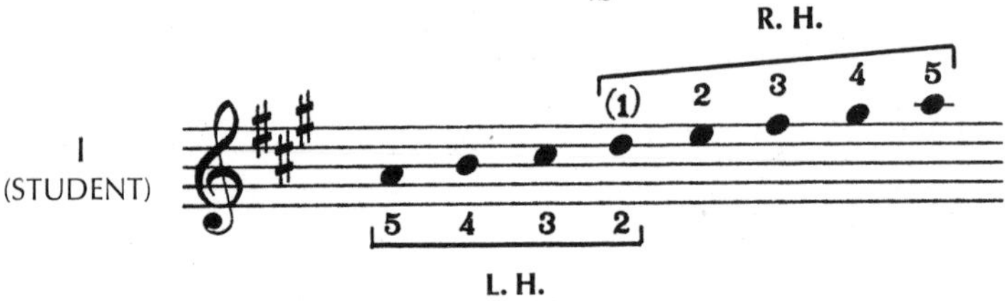

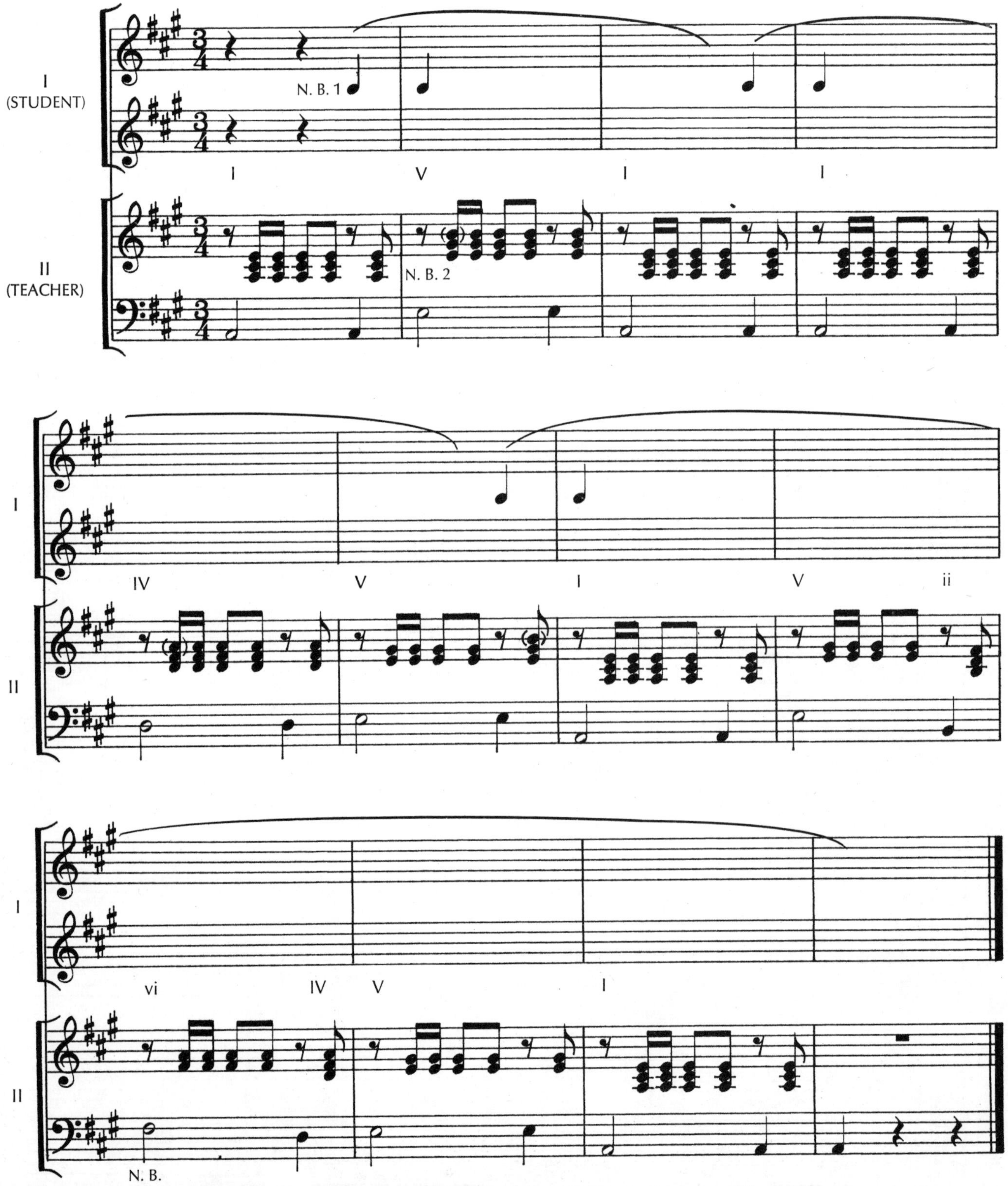

1. These quarter notes indicate the rhythmic pattern for starting each phrase while pitches for the quarter notes are to be selected by the performer.
2. Notes in parenthesis are optional to play.

SUMMER IS CUMEN IN (Duet)

5a

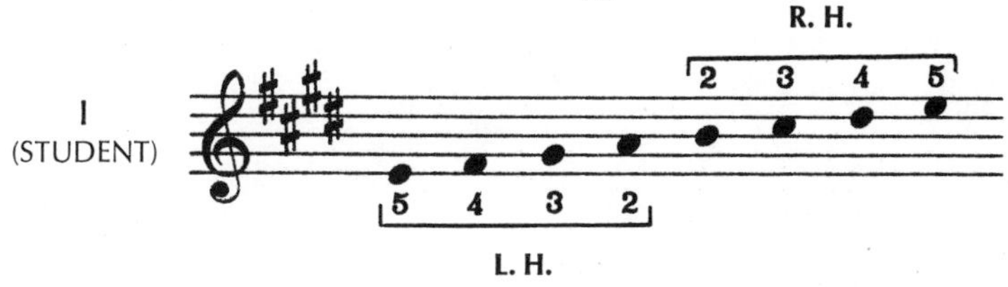

Anonymous

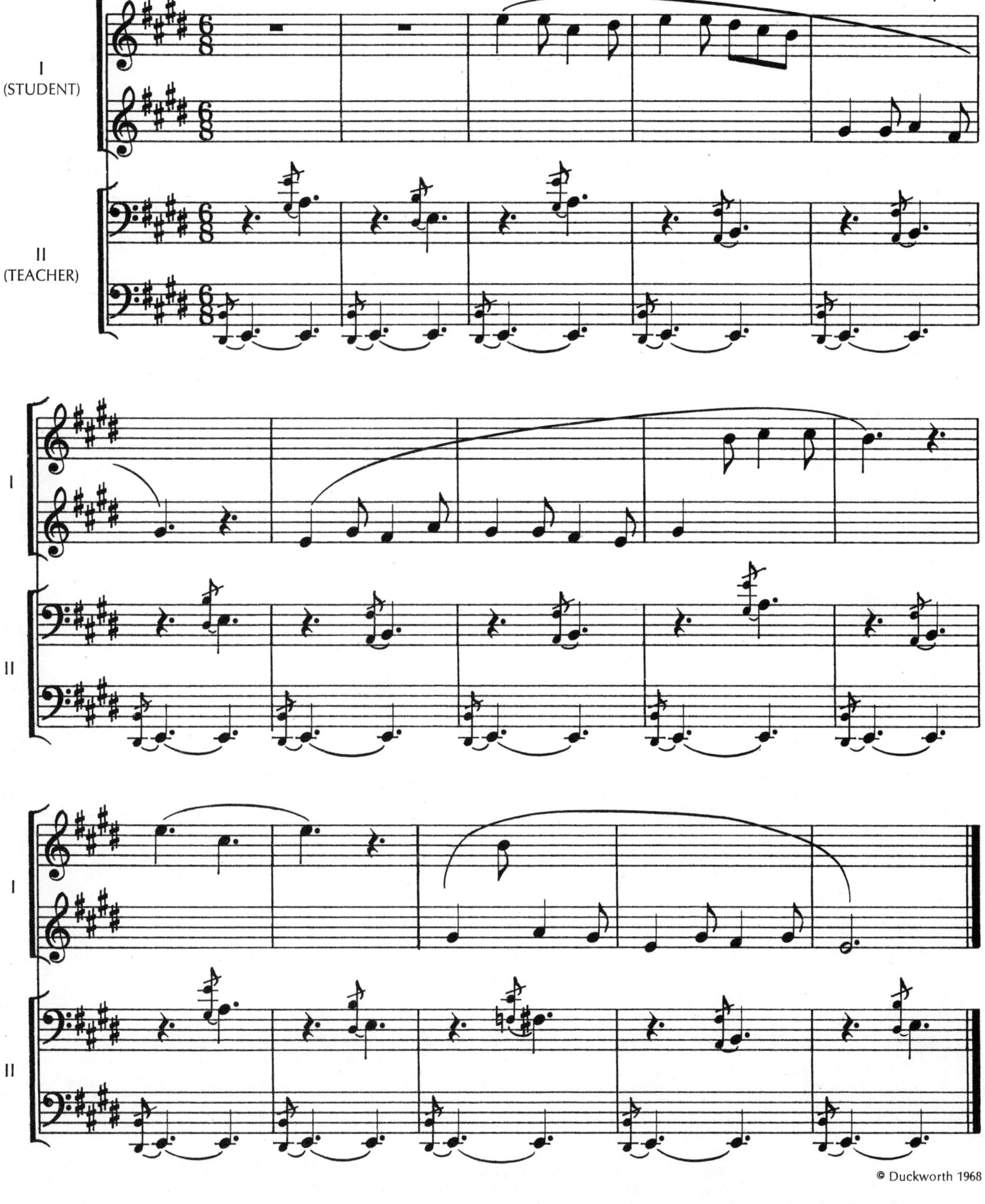

IMPROVISATION (Duet)

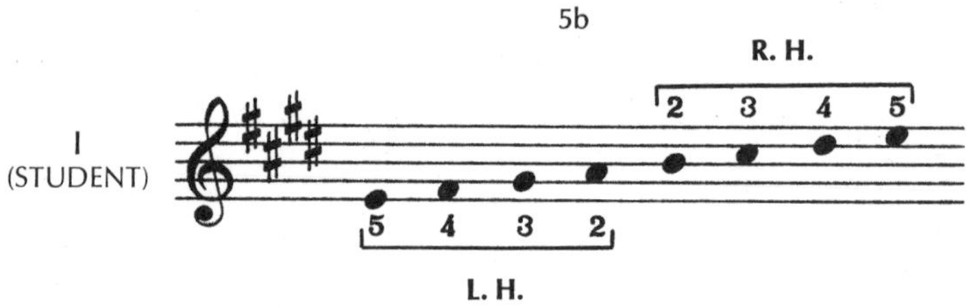

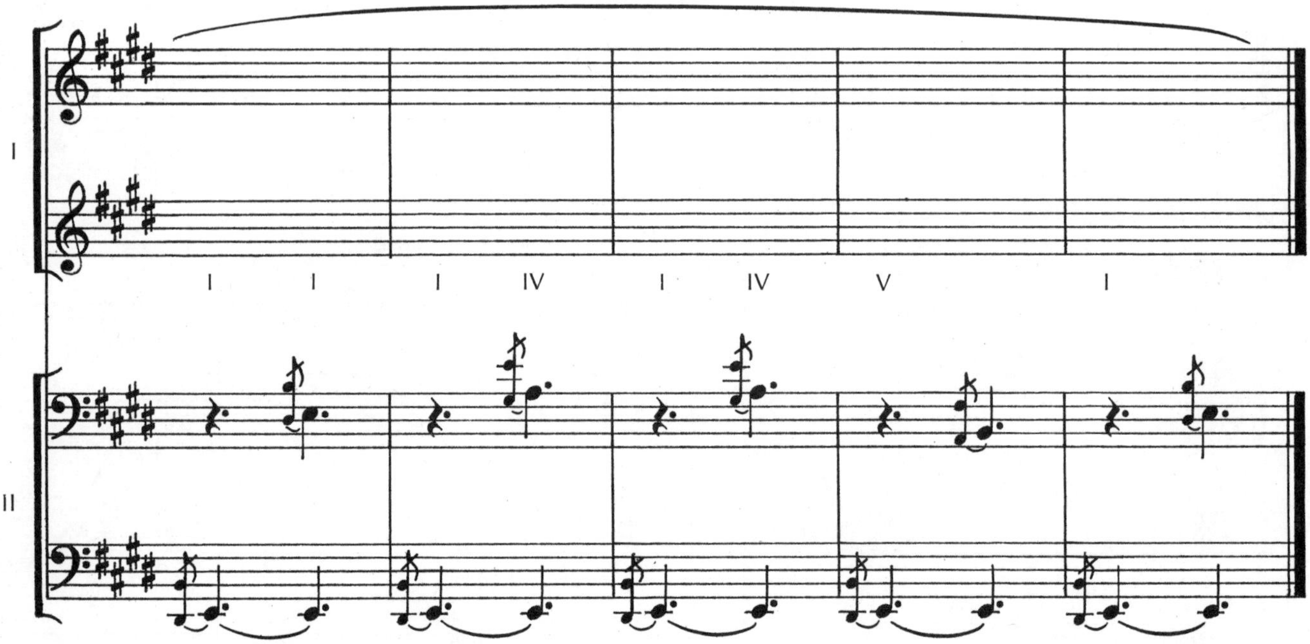

MARCH (Duet)

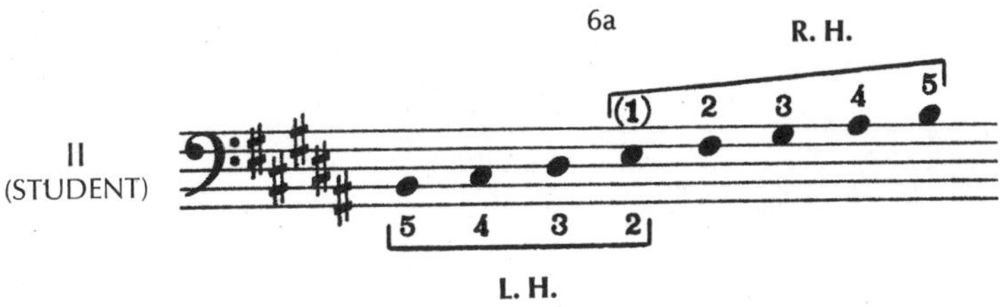

British

IMPROVISATION (Duet)

6b

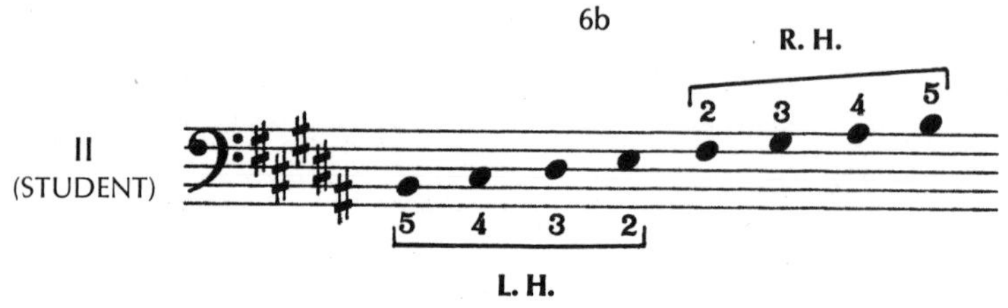

GAMES (Duet)

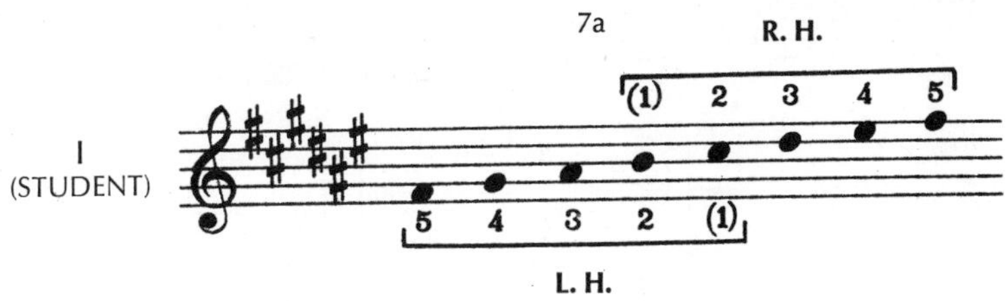
7a
R. H.
(1) 2 3 4 5
I
(STUDENT)
5 4 3 2 (1)
L. H.

Finnish
I
(STUDENT)
II
(TEACHER)

I
1
II

I
II
1

IMPROVISATION (Duet)

BELLS (Duet)

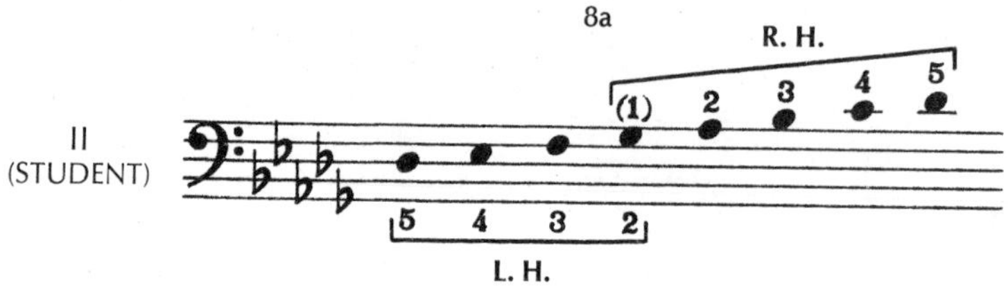

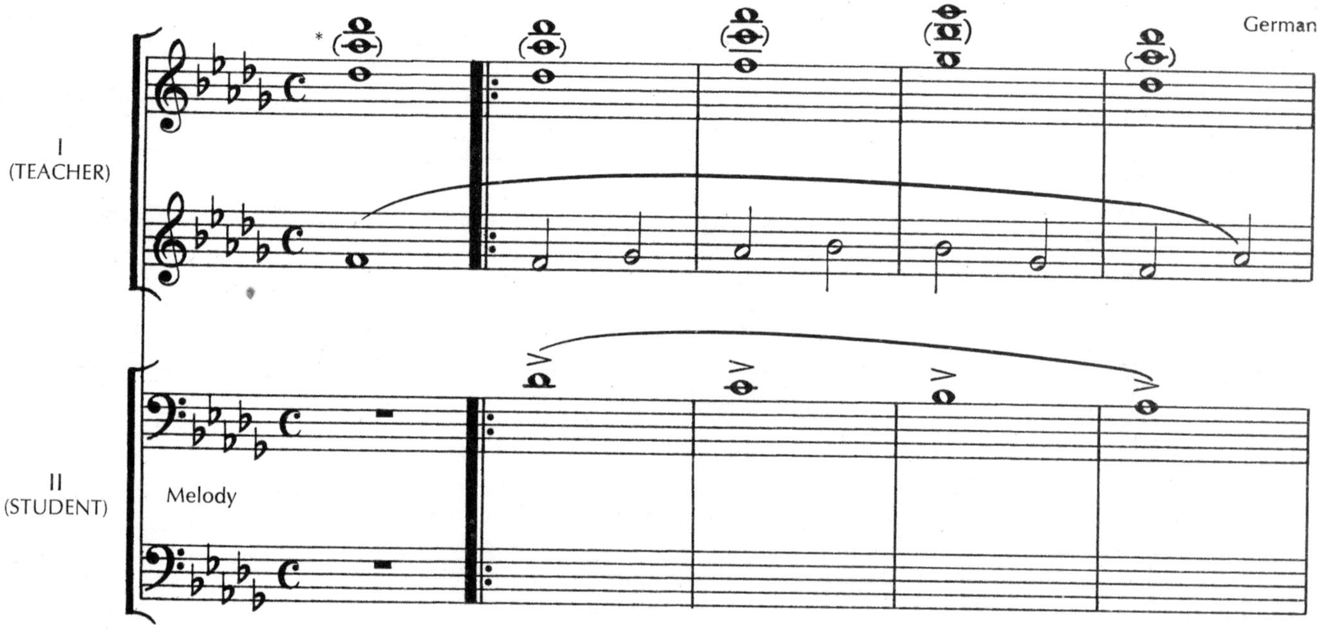

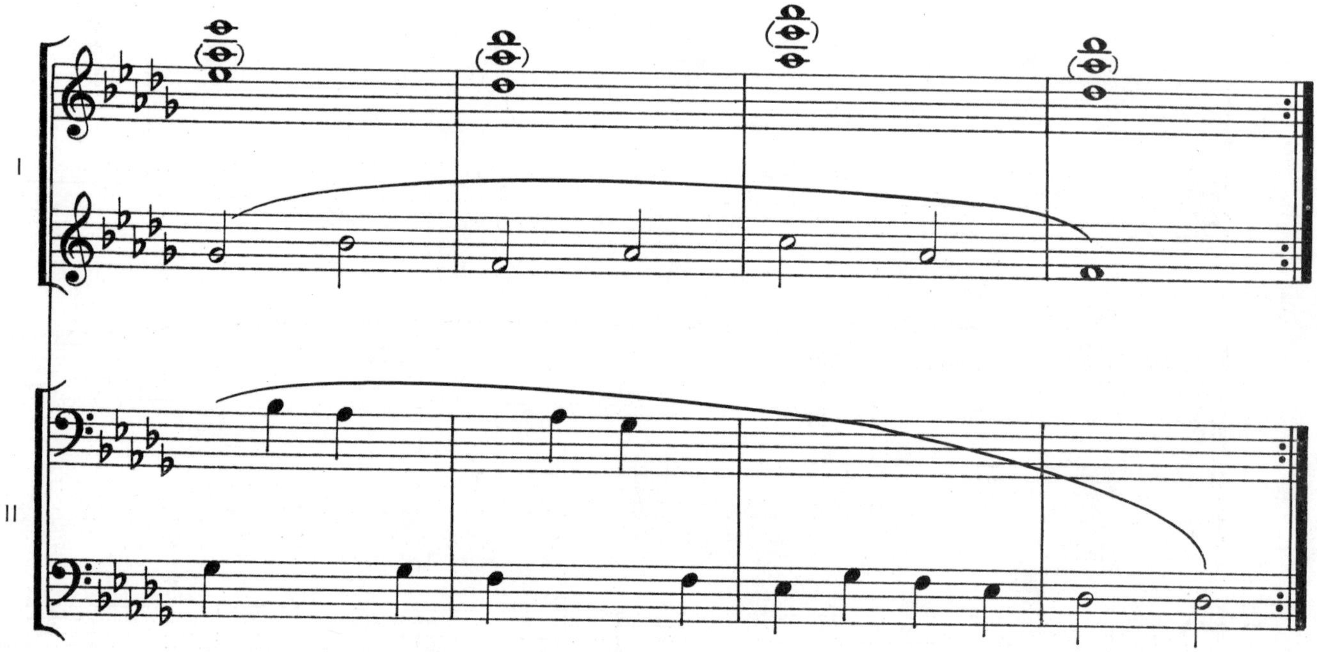

*Notes in parenthesis are optional to play

Play three times:

1. As written
2. Twice as fast
3. As written

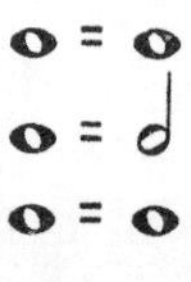

IMPROVISATION (Duet)

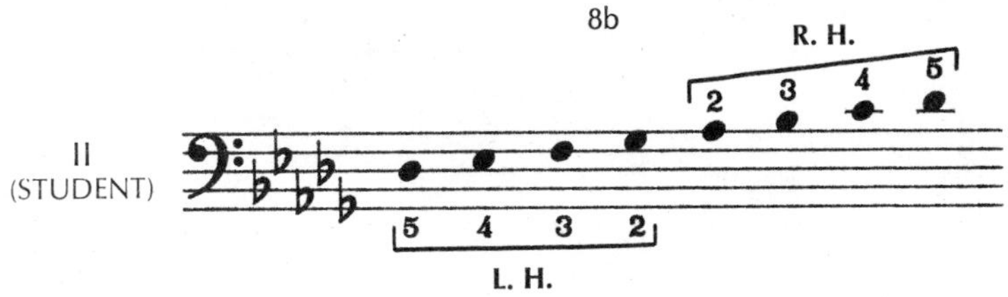

*Notes in parentheses are optional to play.

Play three times:

1. As written
2. Twice as fast
3. As written

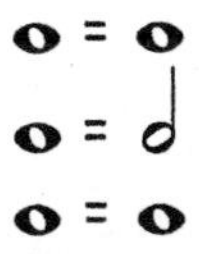

BROKEN TRIADS (Duet)

9a

British

I
II

IMPROVISATION (Duet)

9b

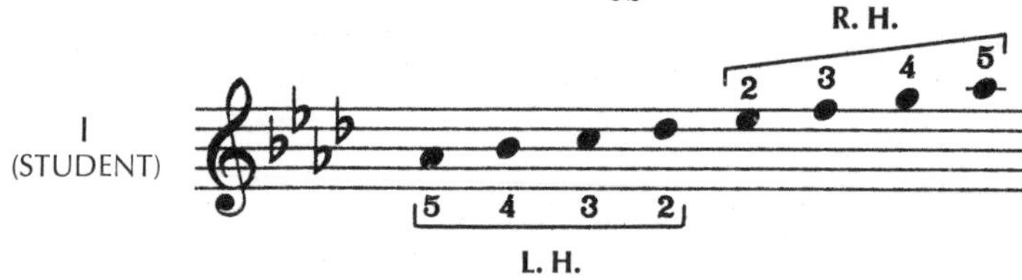

BERCEUSE (Duet)

10a

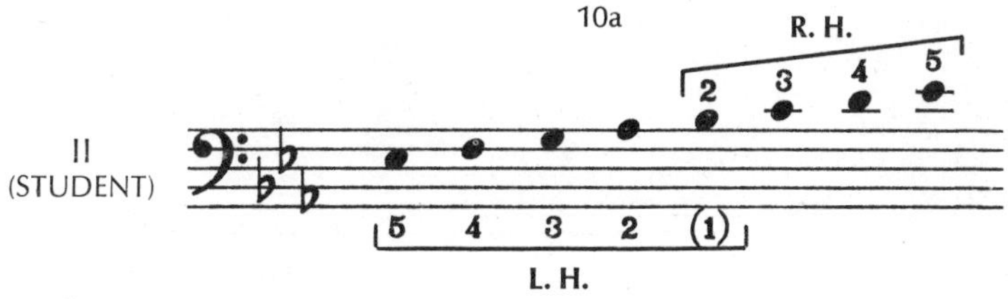

British

IMPROVISATION (Duet)

10b

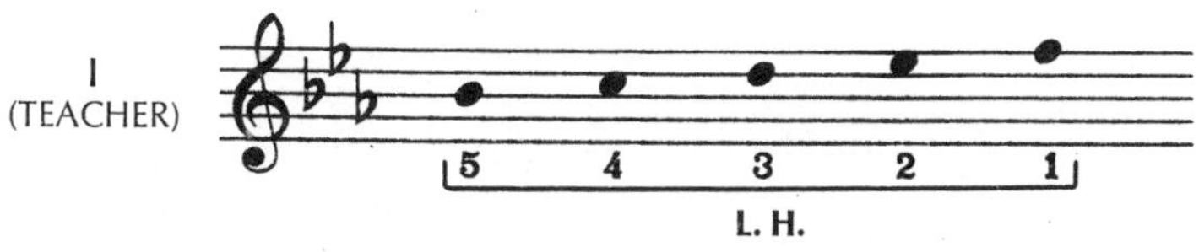

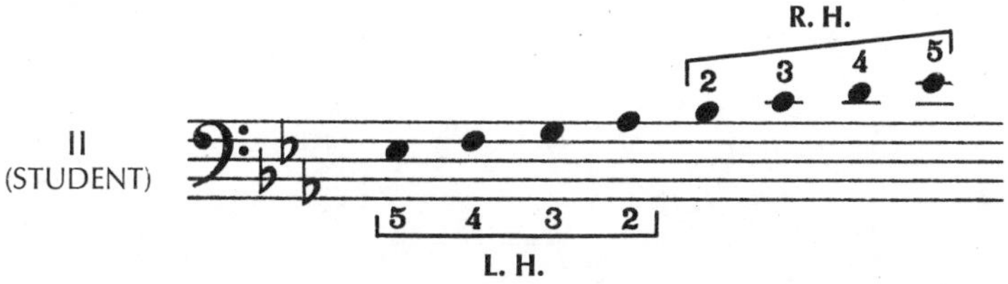

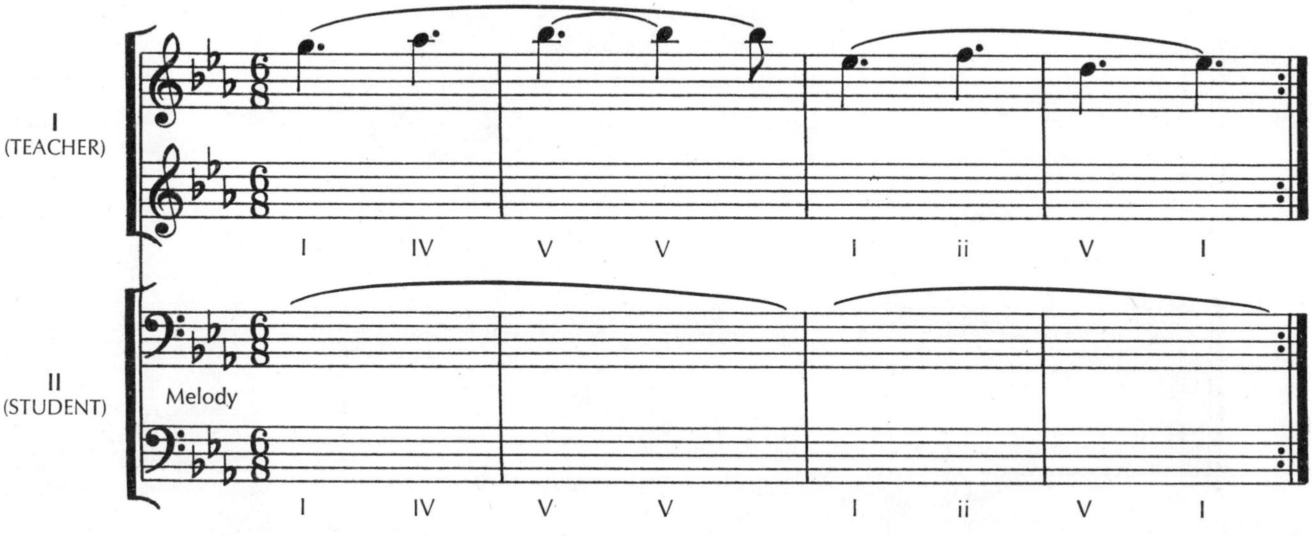

CAROL (Duet)

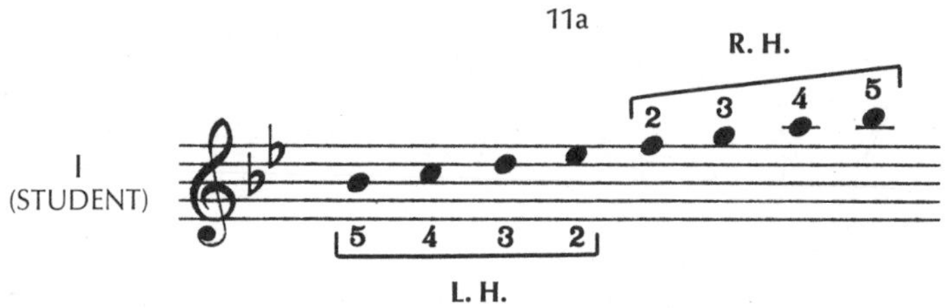
11a
R. H.
2 3 4 5
I
(STUDENT)
5 4 3 2
L. H.

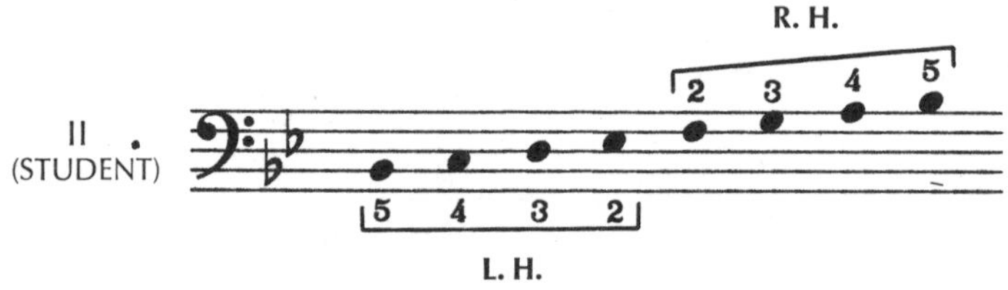
R. H.
2 3 4 5
II
(STUDENT)
5 4 3 2
L. H.

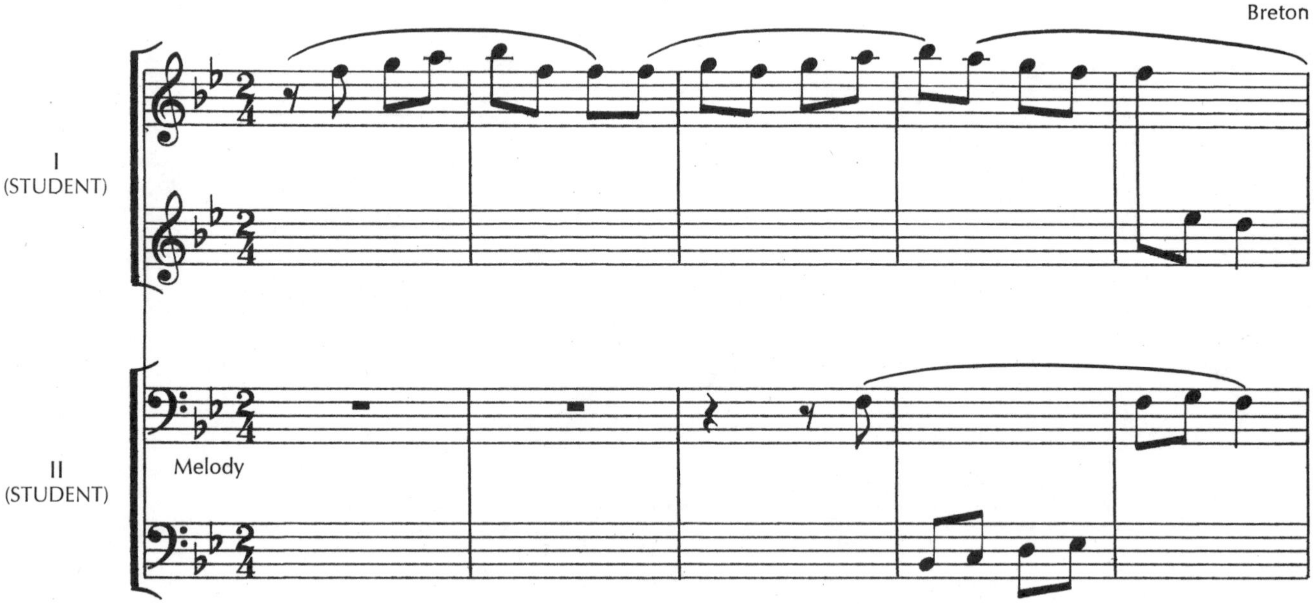
Breton
I
(STUDENT)
II
(STUDENT)
Melody

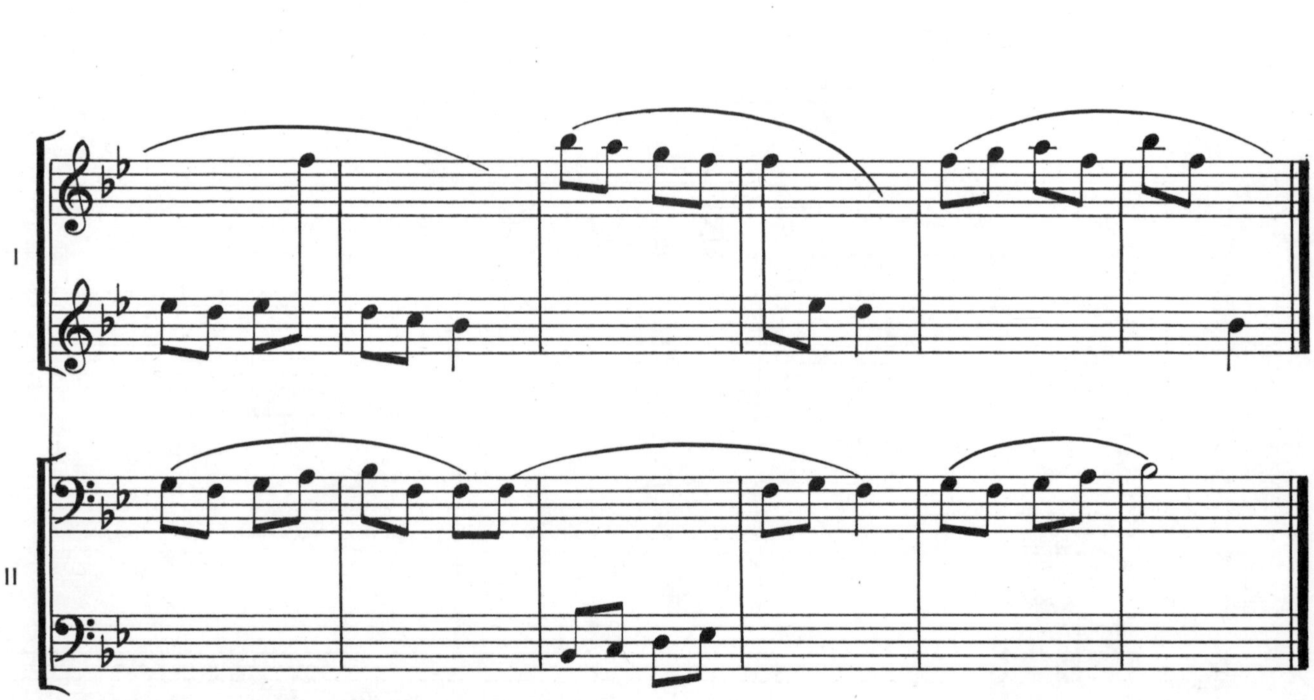
I
II

IMPROVISATION (Duet)

11b

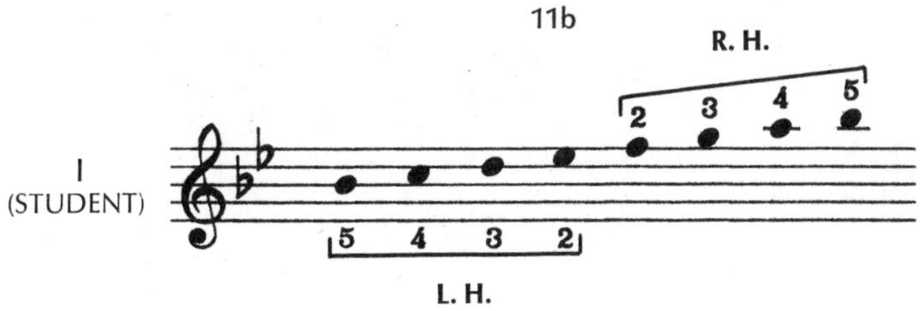

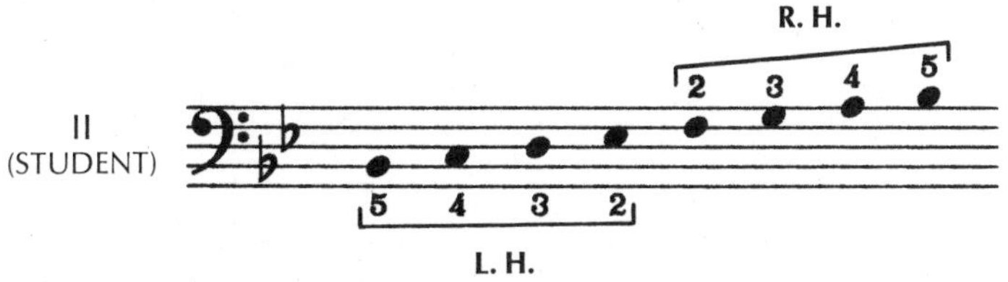

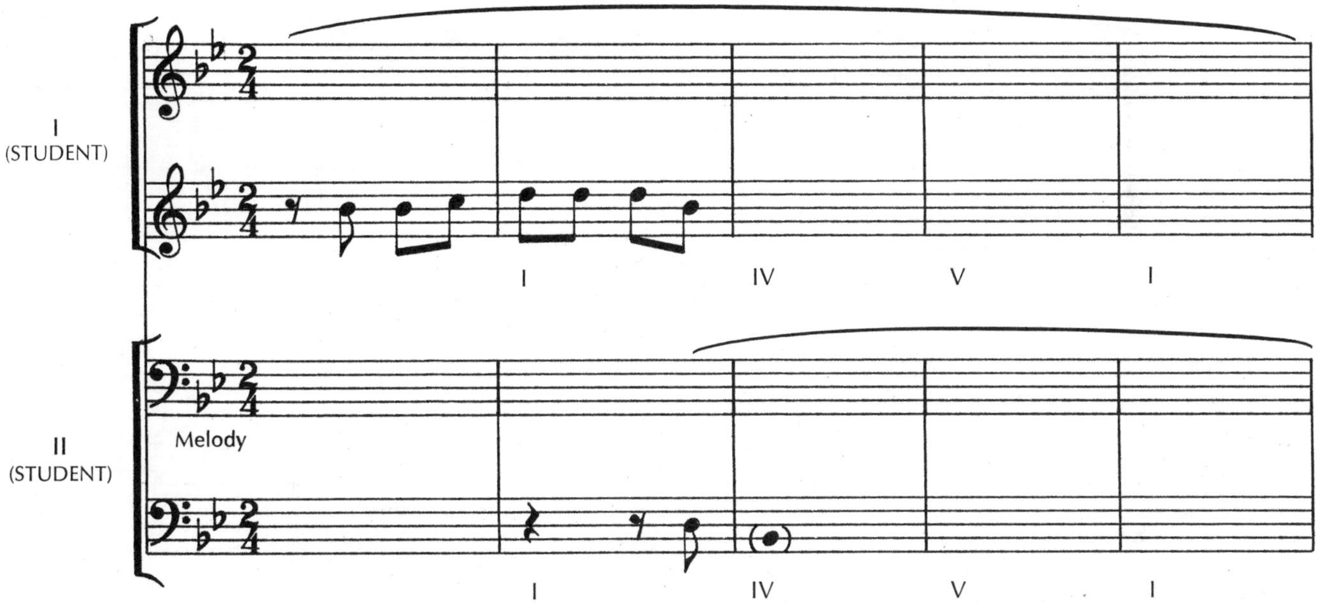

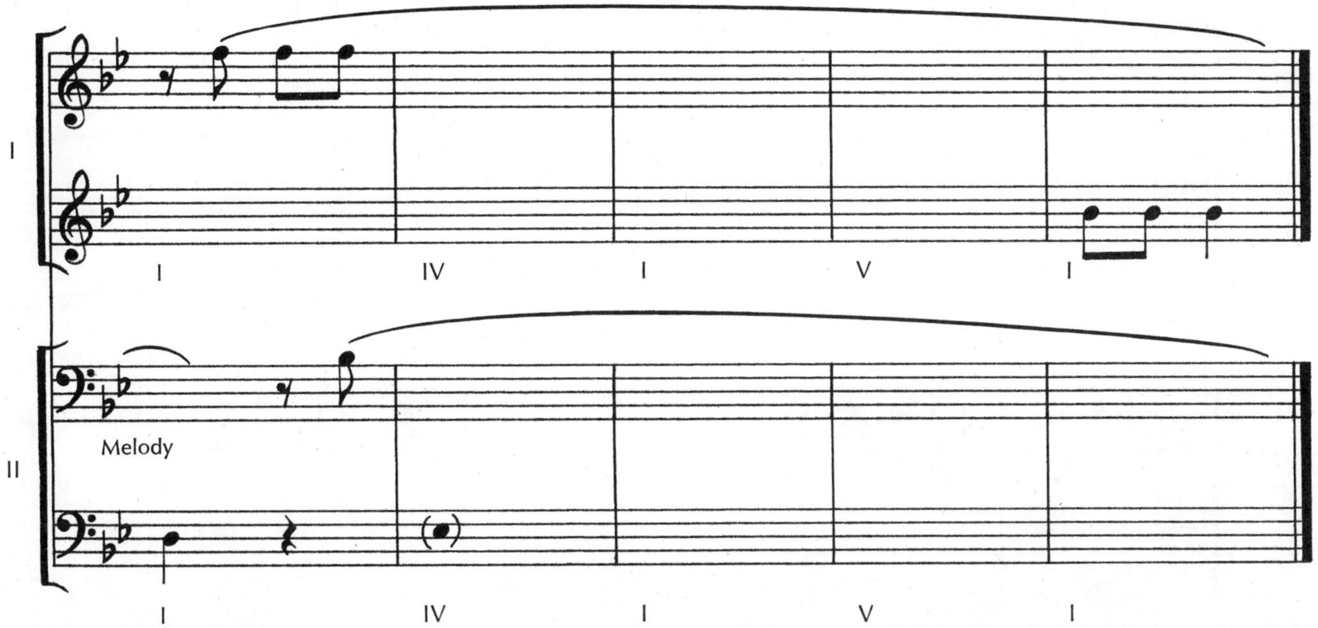

DANCE (Duet)

12a

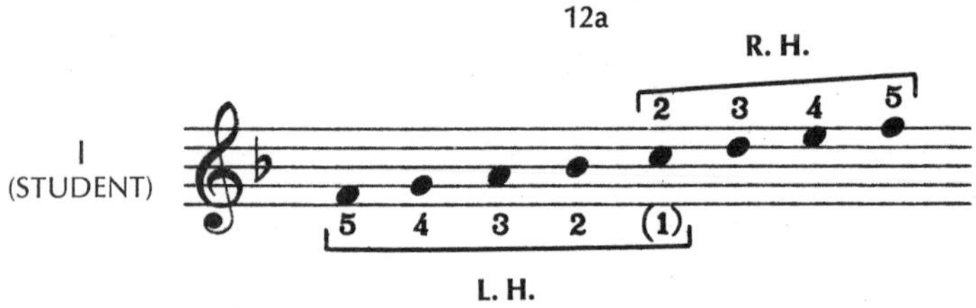

English

IMPROVISATION (Duet)

12b

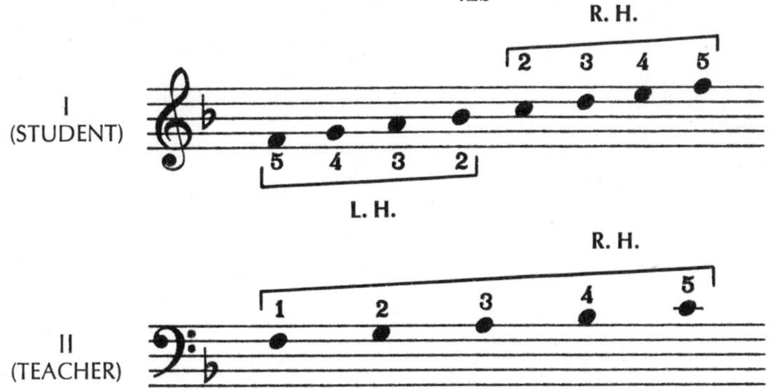

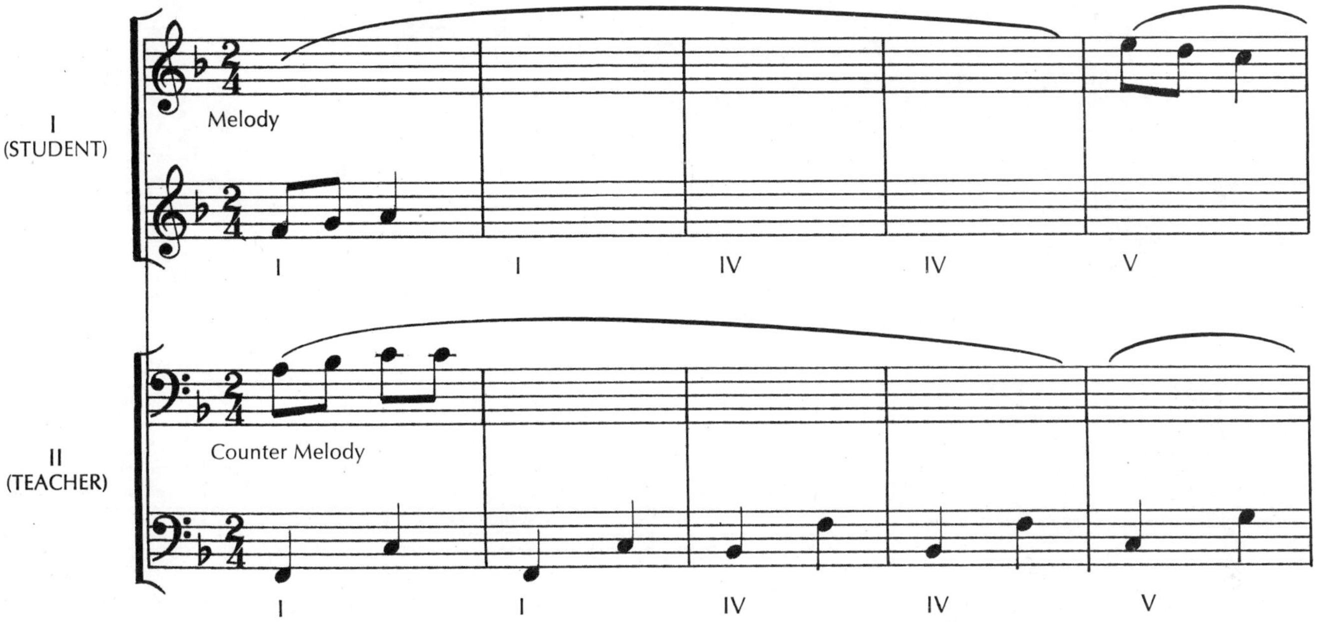

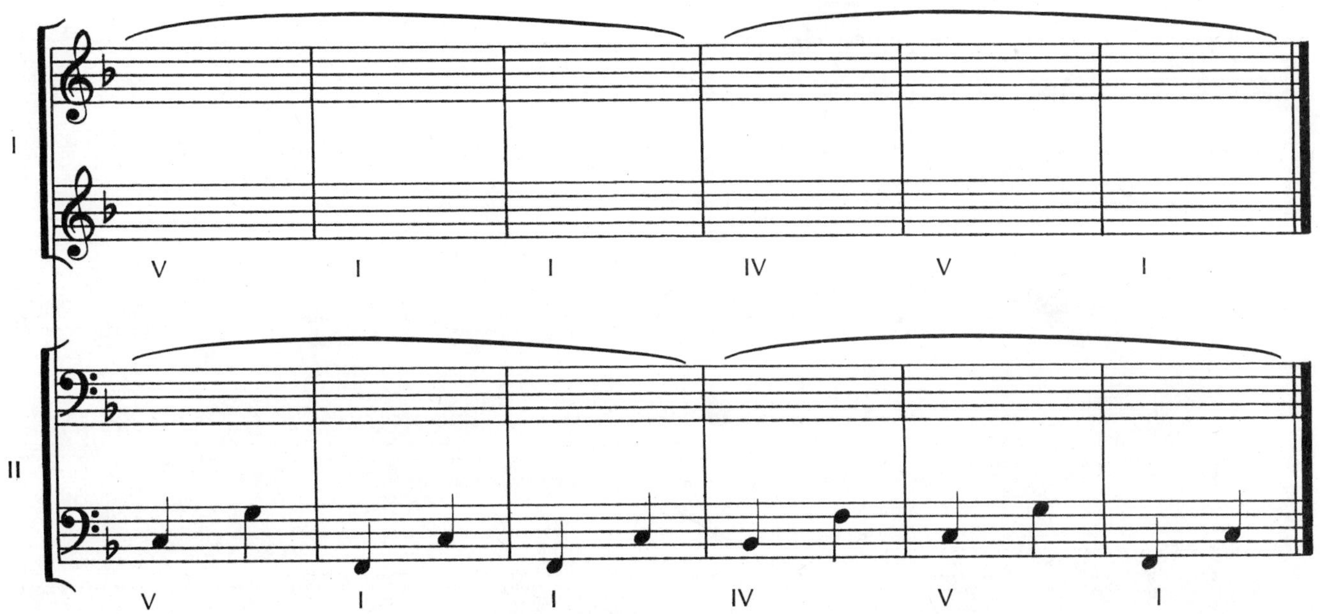

TETRACHORDS—MODAL

While the student is acquainting himself with the major scale organization he should realize that by building tetrachords on each pitch of a major scale, within a given tonality, he can find the modal scales with the same key signature.

The following chart of modal tetrachords should be practiced within all major tonalities. The brackets [ ] within the modes indicate the unique pitch which characterizes each mode.

BUILDING TETRACHORDS ON EACH PITCH OF THE MAJOR SCALE

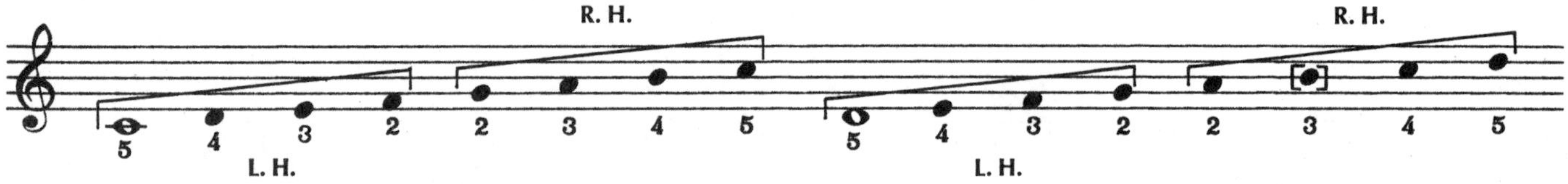

Ionian *(Major)*   Dorian *(minor mode)*

Phrygian *(minor mode)*   Lydian *(major mode)*

Mixolydian *(major mode)*   Aeolian *(Natural form of minor)*

(harmonic form of minor)   *(melodic form of minor)*

*Locrian

*No Tetrachord compositions are written in this mode since its tonic triad is diminished.

READING

There is one composition written in each mode with a key signature equivalent to C major. In addition, a composition transposed to another key center also appears for each mode.

IMPROVISING

Following the two compositions in each mode is an opportunity to improvise in the same mode.

TRANSPOSING

As with the duets in major these compositions should be transposed to an unlimited number of key centers.

HARMONIZING

In the compositions for improvising a harmonic structure is often indicated. The primary chords for the modes are not tonic, sub-dominant and dominant. On the contrary, they differ according to the mode in question and are determined by the organization of the mode. For example, since the Dorian mode is minor in character—its tonic triad is minor. Also, since the pitch in the scale which distinguishes it from the natural form of the minor scale is a raised sixth, its primary triads, in addition to its tonic, are the super tonic and sub-dominant chords, both of which include this pitch.

The primary chords are indicated with the compositions of each mode. Inasmuch as the student has constructed and practiced triads on each pitch of all major scales, he is well prepared for isolating and playing the primary triads for each mode.

D DORIAN* WITH F LYDIAN (Duet)

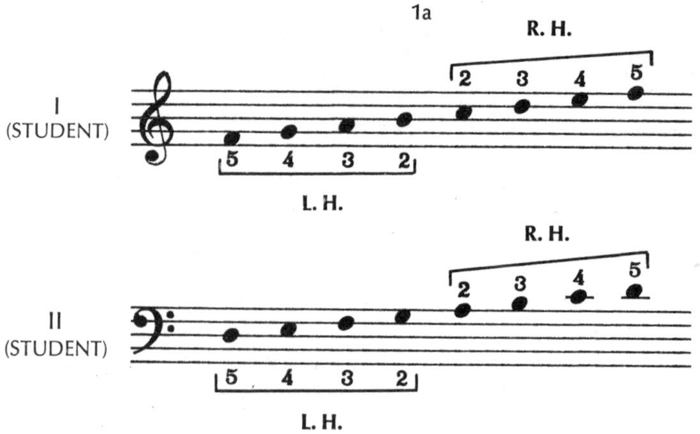

Melody by
Neithart Reunthal
C 1240

*Primary triads: i, ii, iv.

B DORIAN (Duet)

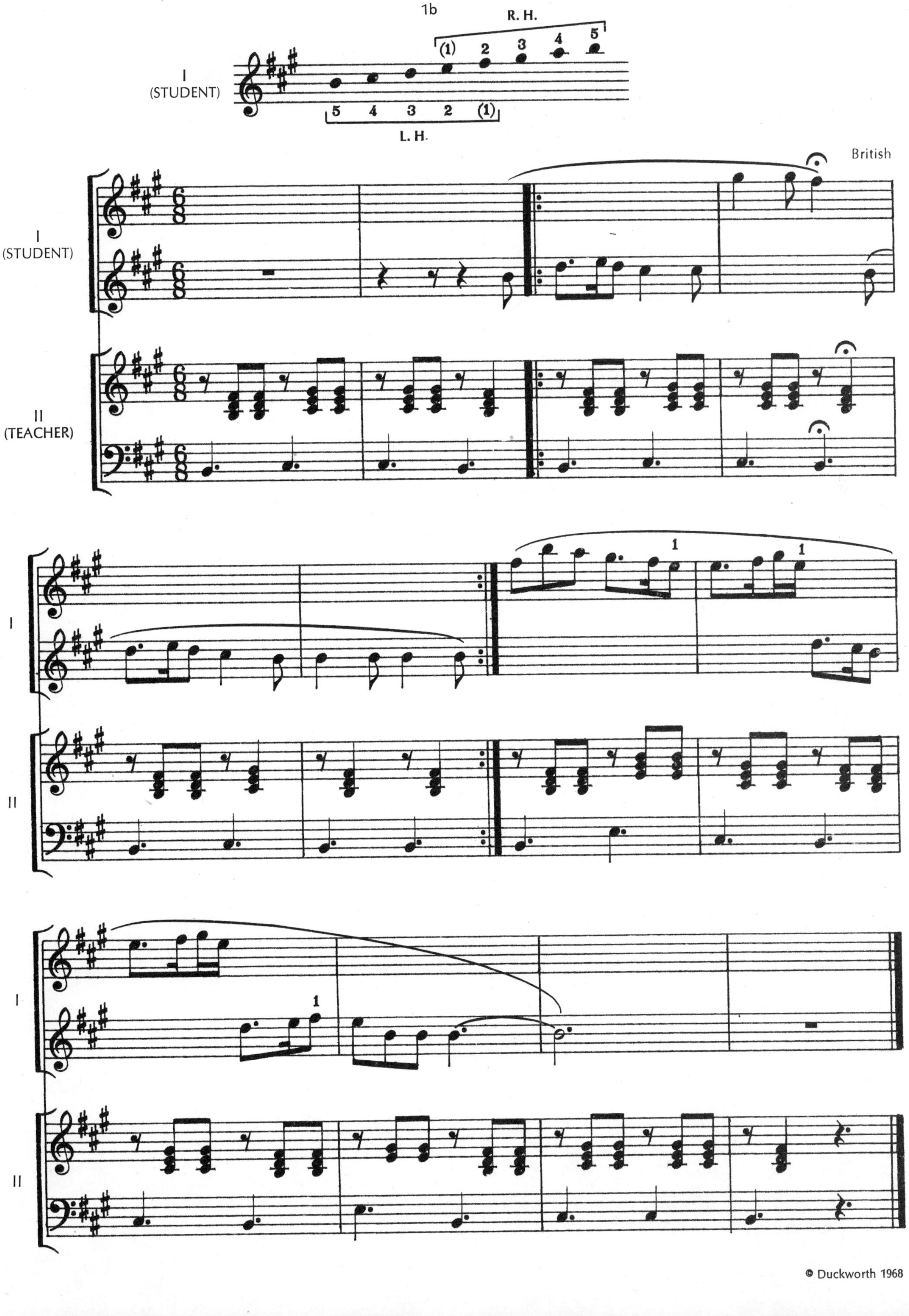

IMPROVISATION IN B DORIAN (Duet)

VOS OMNES IN E PHRYGIAN* (Duet)

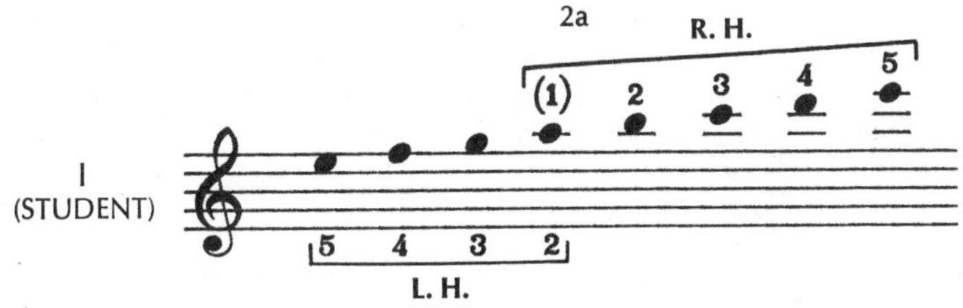

Melody by
Loyset Compere
1455-1518

*Primary triads: i, II, vii

A PHRYGIAN (Duet)

2b

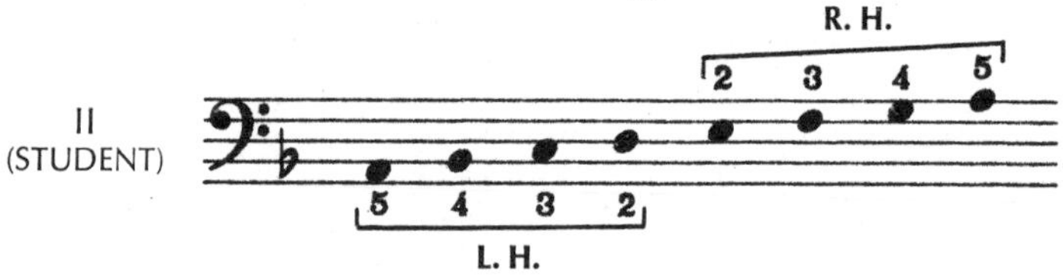

Irish

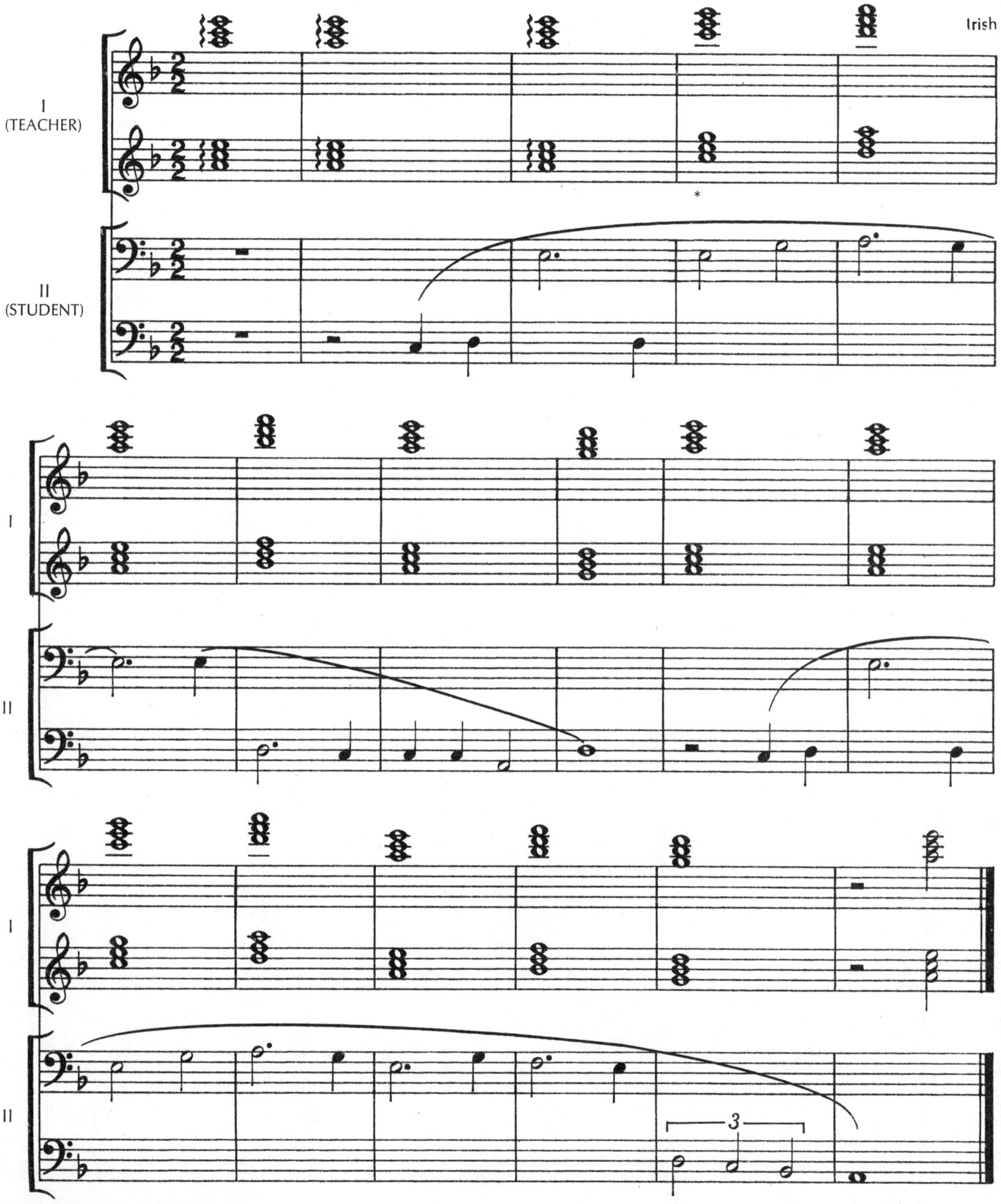

*Continue rolling chords.

IMPROVISATION IN G PHRYGIAN (Duet)

SYNCOPATION IN F LYDIAN* (Duet)

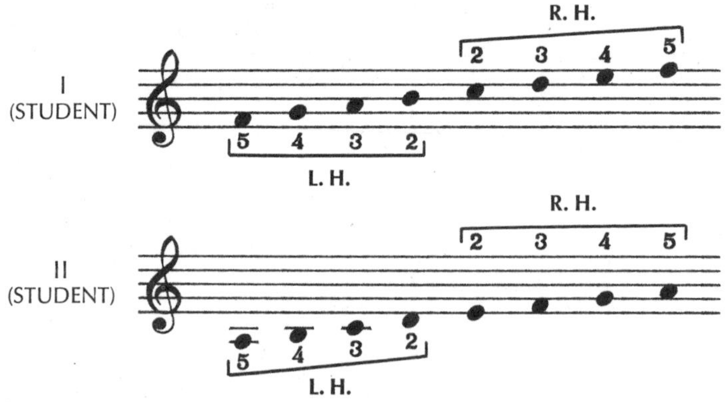

British

*Primary triads: I, II, vii.

G LYDIAN (Duet)

3b

German

IMPROVISATION IN F LYDIAN (Duet)

G MIXOLYDIAN* (Duet)

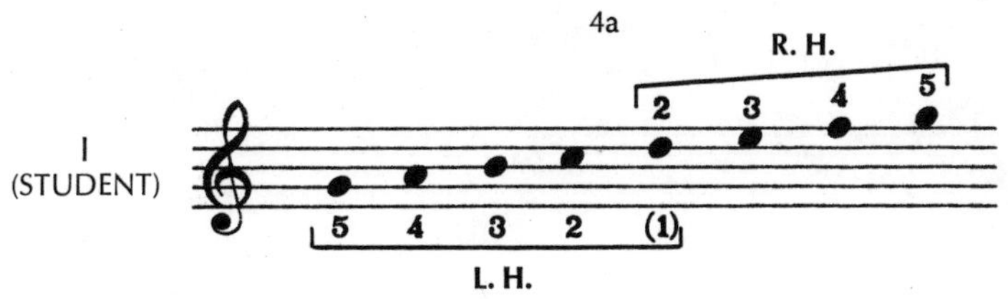

British

*Primary triads: I, v, VII

CANON IN F MIXOLYDIAN (Duet)

4b

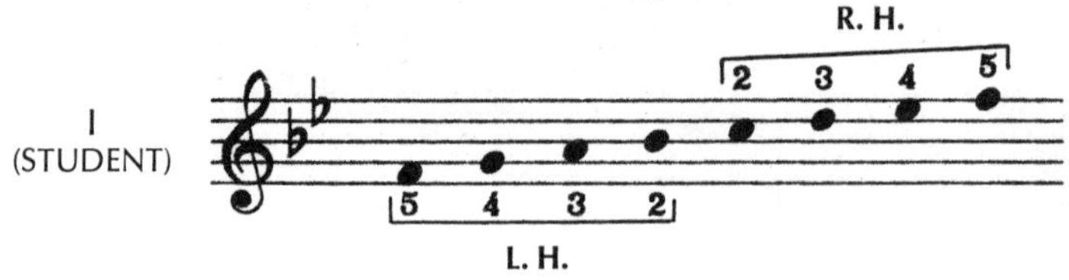

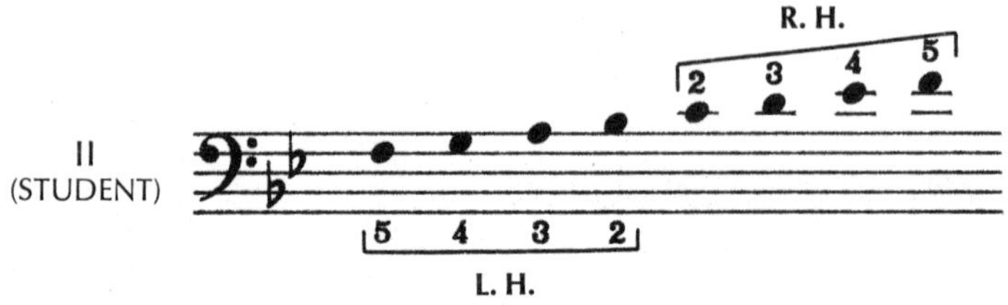

Serbian

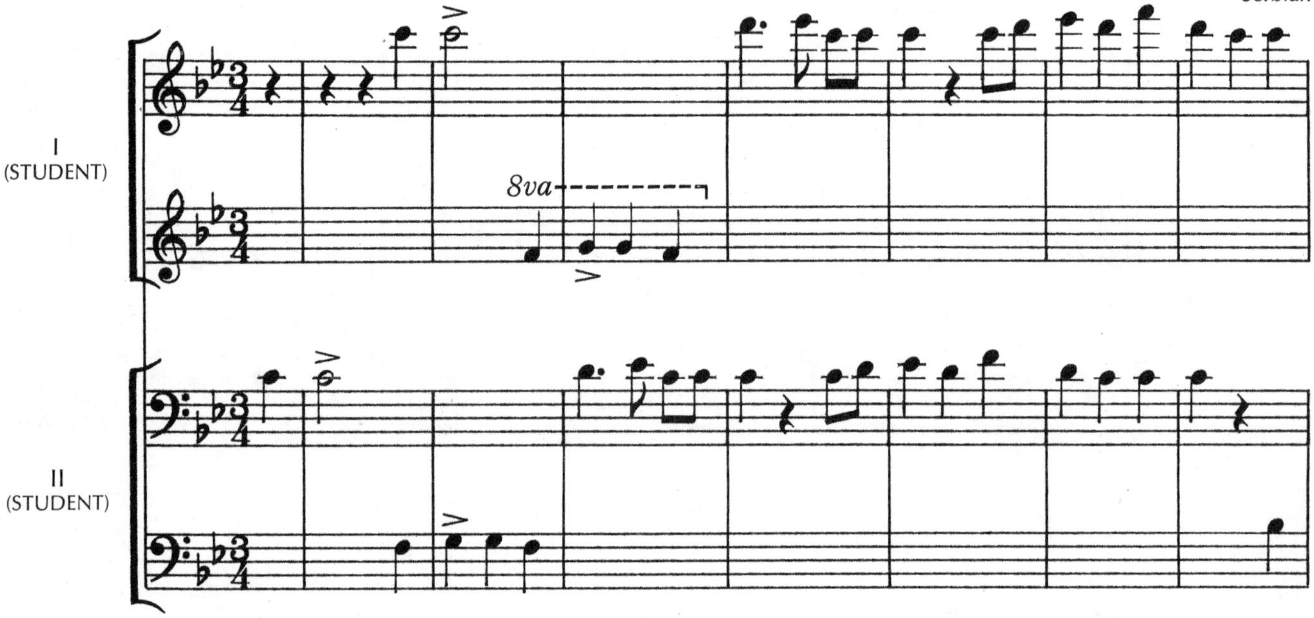

CANON IMPROVISATION IN B♭ MIXOLYDIAN (Duet)

A AEOLIAN* HORNPIPE (Duet)

*Primary triads: i, iv, v

D AEOLIAN (Duet)

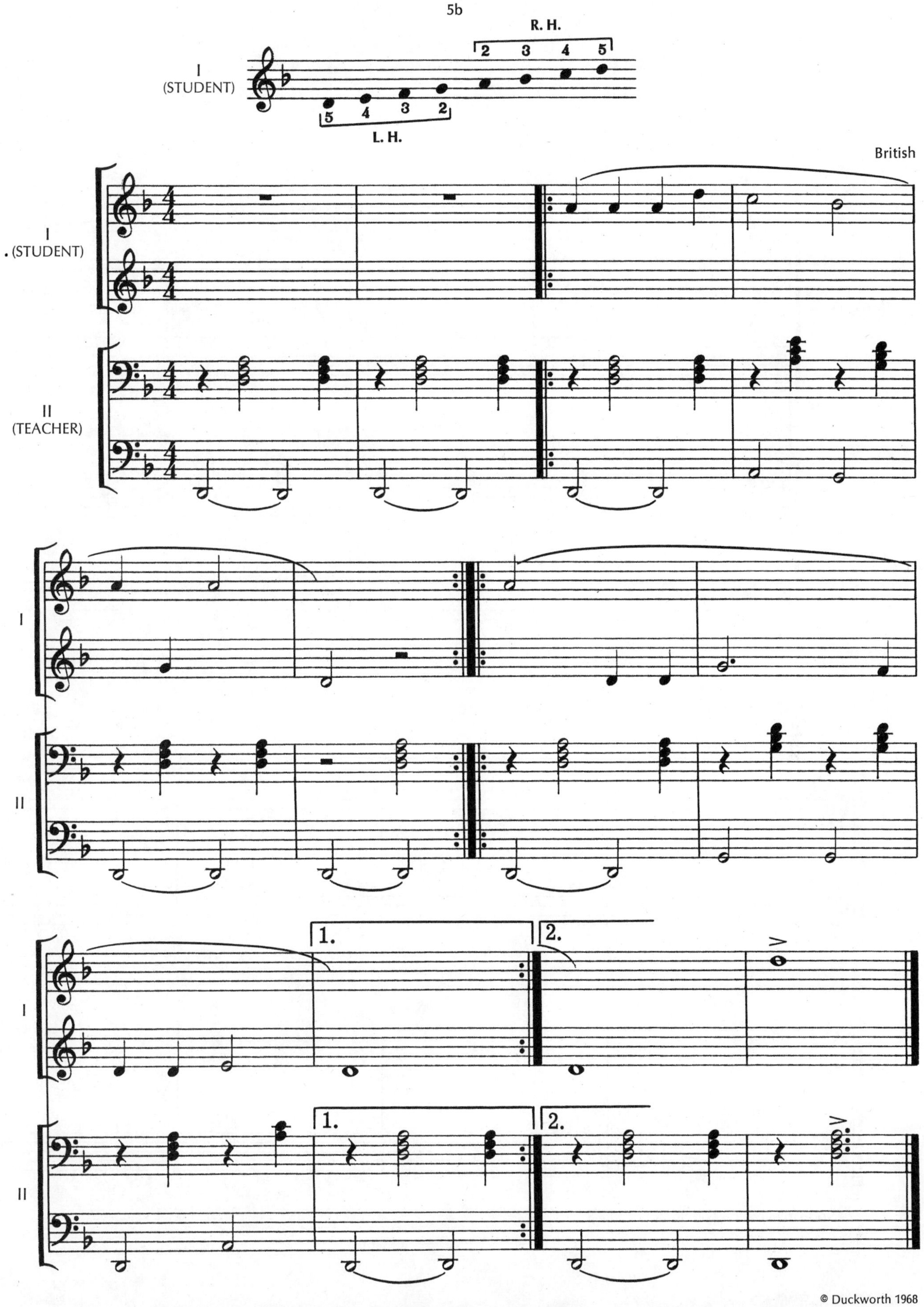

E AEOLIAN IMPROVISATION (Duet)

5c

I
(STUDENT)

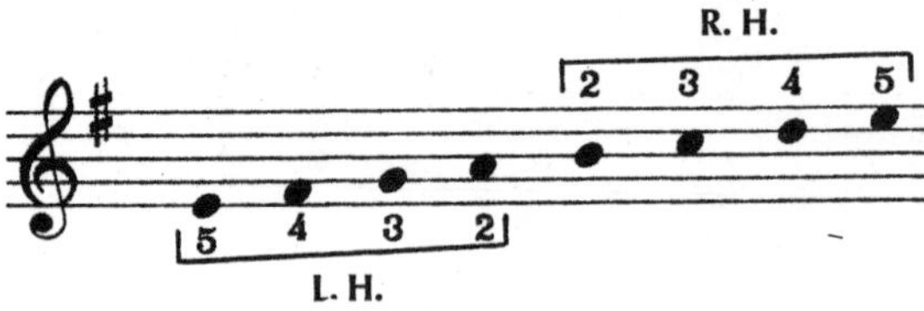

*Notes in parenthesis are optional to play

HARMONIC FORM OF A MINOR* (Duet)

6a

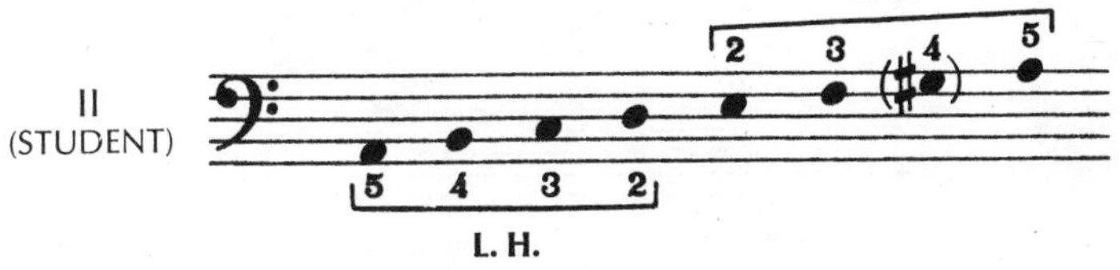

8va throughout

Scandinavian

*Primary triads: i, iv, V

IMPROVISATION IN HARMONIC FORM OF B♭ MINOR (Duet)

6b

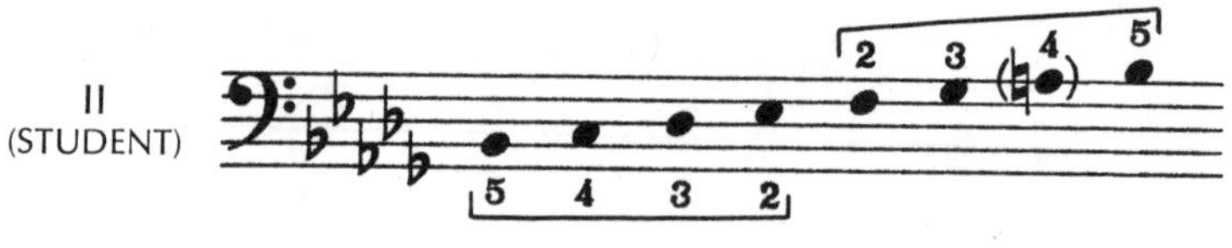

*Primary triads: i, IV (iv), V (v)

MELODIC FORM OF A MINOR (Duet)

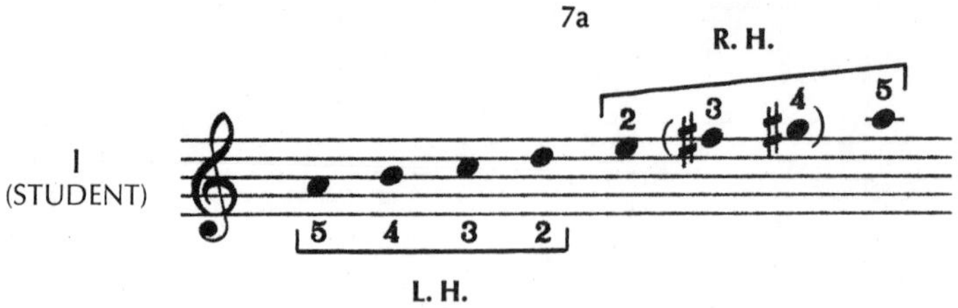

IMPROVISATION IN MELODIC FORM OF G MINOR (Duet)

7b

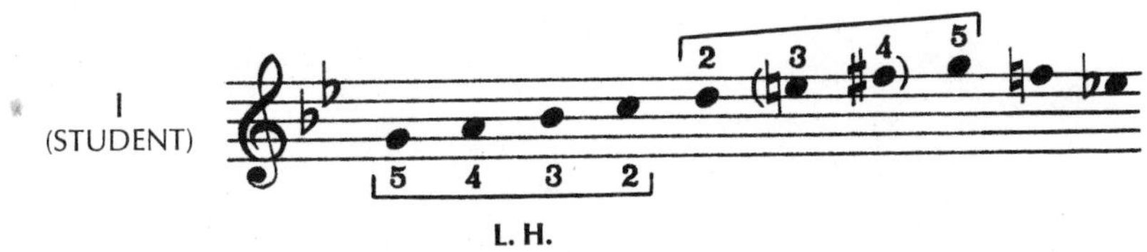

PENTACHORDS

The following compositions have a pitch range of a fifth—a pentachord. To locate the pentachords for each composition the performer investigates the range of pitches—the lows and highs—written for each hand.

Pentachords on each pitch of the major scale are practiced by using five fingers of each hand playing the five pitches of the pentachord in parallel and contrary motion. In this way the student becomes acquainted with the first five pitches of not only the major scale but of all the modes which have that same key signature. With this practice the student finds his ability to move easily on the keyboard improving rapidly. For example.

PENTACHORDS ON THE FIRST PITCH OF G MAJOR

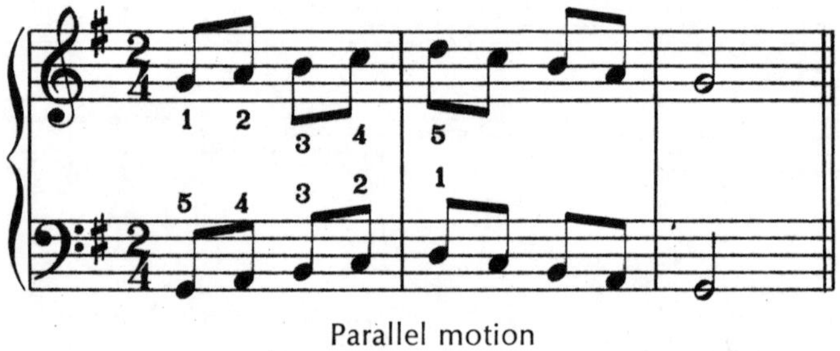

Parallel motion

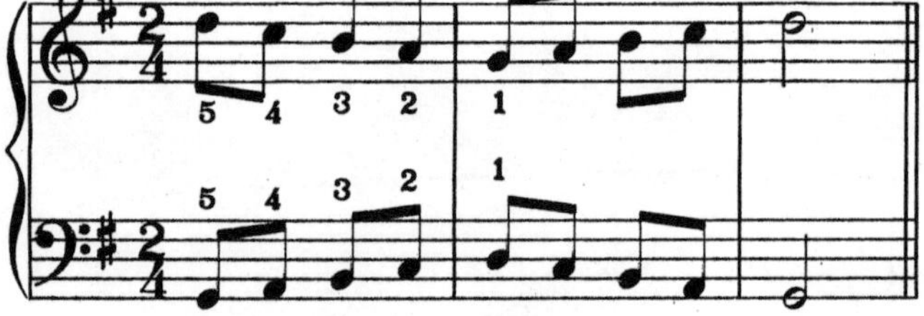

Contrary motion

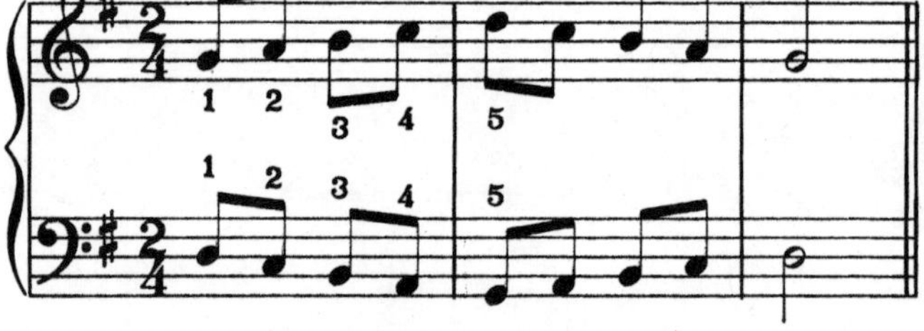

Contrary motion

This fingering remains the same no matter what the relationships are between the black-white keys. In other words, thumbs do play on black keys under these conditions.

BUILDING PENTACHORDS ON EACH PITCH OF THE MAJOR SCALE

Inasmuch as the student is getting to know the complete major scale by playing tetrachords, he is able to build pentachords on each pitch of the major scale.

The tetrachords of the scale are played first to find out what pitches and piano keys are in the scale. The pentachords are built on each of these piano keys making sure only the piano keys in that particular scale are used. The student finds his hands assuming a different "feel and look" according to the black-white key relationships in each pentachord.

G major tetrachords.

G major pentachords:

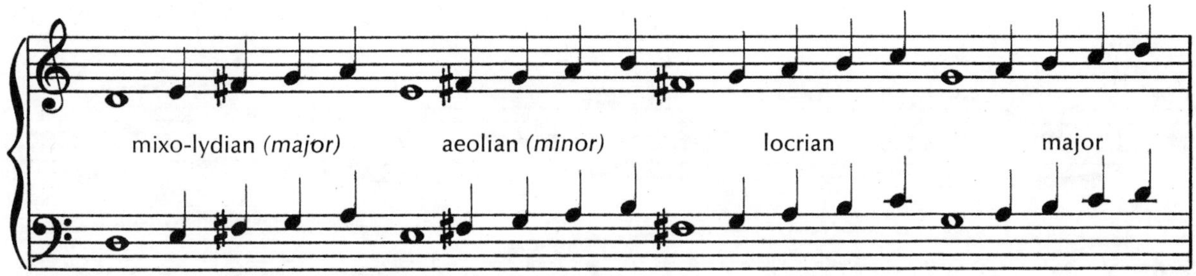

READING

The compositions in this section include all major and modal scales and are written so as to provide reading experiences in all key centers. In order to train the hands equally the melodic material is written as much for the left hand as for the right hand. It is advisable to play the melody of each composition alone before reading the complete composition.

FINGERING

The step-skip-repeat patterns are followed in this manner:

1. Move to closest fingers on steps.
2. Skip as many fingers as keys on skips.
3. Repeat fingers on repeats.

TRANSPOSING

Each composition should be transposed to as many key centers as possible so as to facilitate the ability to think within any key center. (See Harmonizing.)

IMPROVISING

Each melody has an unique setting. After the pattern is introduced the performer is expected to continue with the same pattern to complete the composition—in a sense, improvising. For example,

ACCOMPANIMENT IN LYDIAN

French

Performer continues with pattern.
simile

See piano piece number 1.

"Simile" is used in the score to indicate to the performer that he is to continue with the patterns and/or relationships indicated.

"A piacere" is used when the performer is to complete a harmonization in the style indicated, contemporary or traditional.

Each "accompaniment figure" should be isolated from its composition and utilized for settings to improvised melodies. There is poetry included in Resource Materials for this purpose. Additional use of the settings can be experienced by finding more melodies which are easily found in public school music texts. (See Harmonizing.)

HARMONIZING

In addition to reading and performing each piano piece, the major and minor melodies should be harmonized using traditional tonic-dominant harmonies. See Keyboard Sequence in Resource Materials. For example:

ACCOMPANIMENT IN LYDIAN

French

See piano piece number 1.

The student should transpose these traditional settings so as to familiarize himself with keyboard sequences in all keys. Further, these same kinds of settings should be used when improvising melodies to the verses in Resource Materials.

As soon as possible, the student should create different accompaniment patterns with the pitches of the chords he has chosen to harmonize a given melody. Using the folk song above, for an example, the following accompaniment patterns are appropriate:

1

2

3

4

ACCOMPANIMENT IN LYDIAN

1

PARALLEL AT THE OCTAVE

2

SYMMETRICAL INVERSION*

3

Melody by Fauré

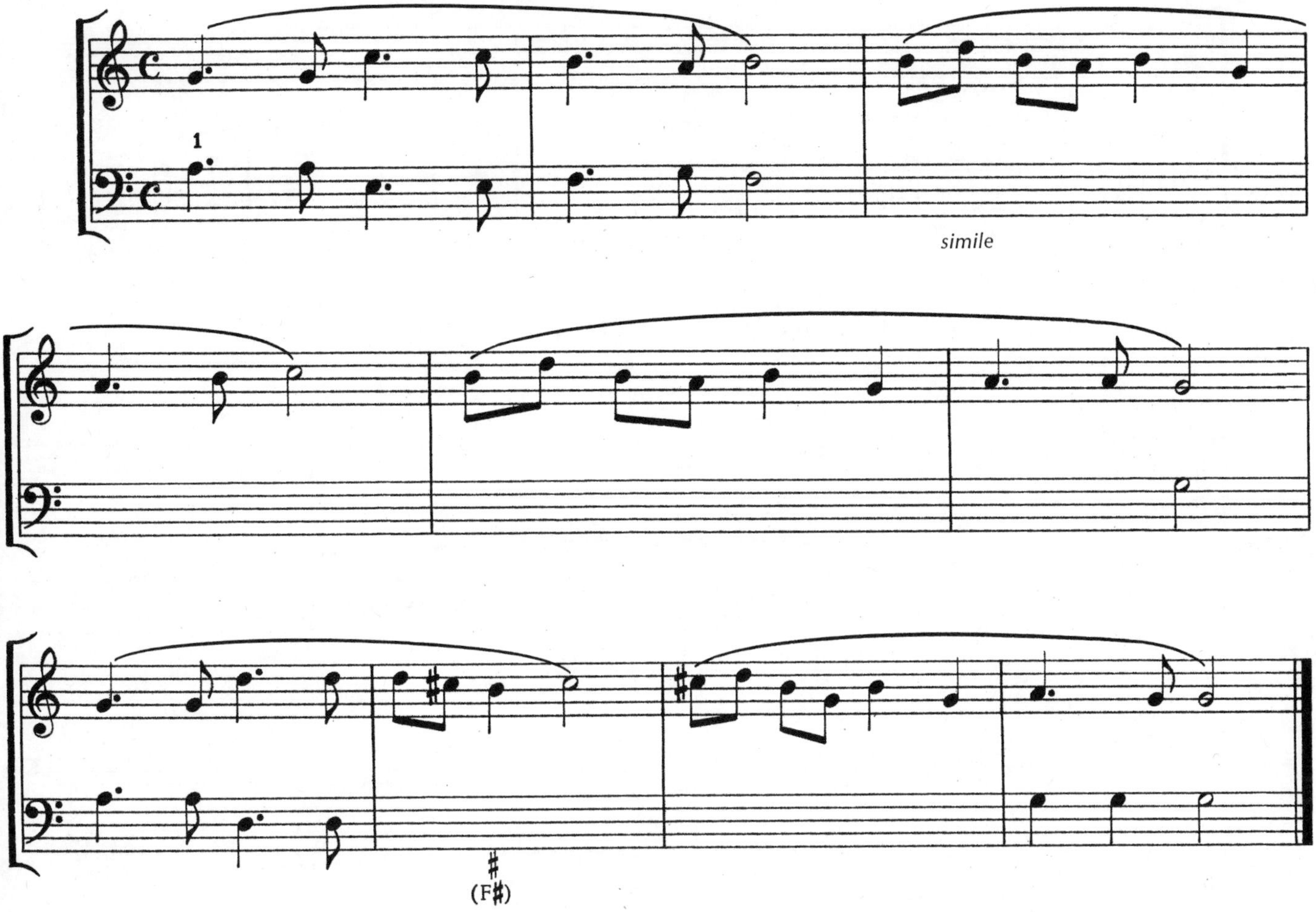

*The structure of the left hand pentachord is the same descending as is the right hand ascending.

PARALLEL AT THE FOURTH

4

Balkan

BI-TONAL

5

PARALLEL IN MAJOR THIRDS

6

PARALLEL IN AUGMENTED FIFTHS

7

IMITATION REFLECTED

8

Polish

OSTINATO

9

Polish

ACCOMPANIMENT IN FOURTHS

10

Dutch

*Revise this ostinato by starting with 

TONIC AND SUPER-TONIC

11

British

Exchange parts between hands on repeat.

LOWERED SEVENTH

12

TRIADS IN OSTINATO

13

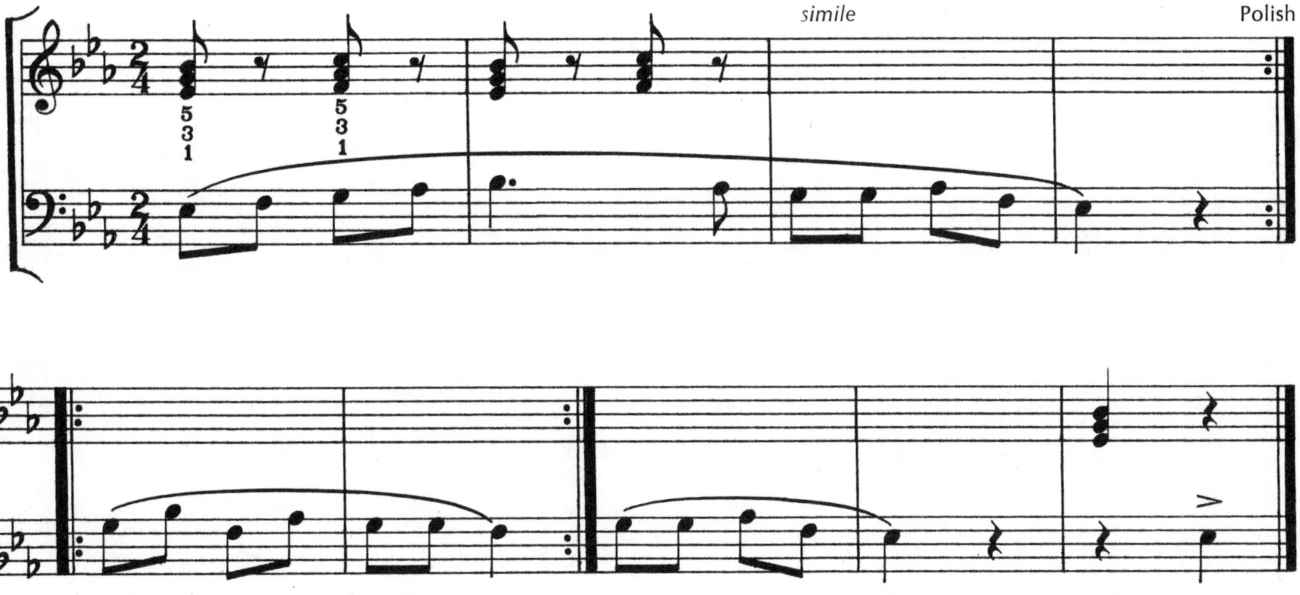

Parts may be exchanged between hands.

IMITATION EXCHANGED

14

CHANGING HAND POSITION

15

CHANGING REGISTERS

16A

16B

RHYTHMIC IMITATION

17

Polish

OSTINATO ACCOMPANIMENT IN PENTACHORDS

18

French

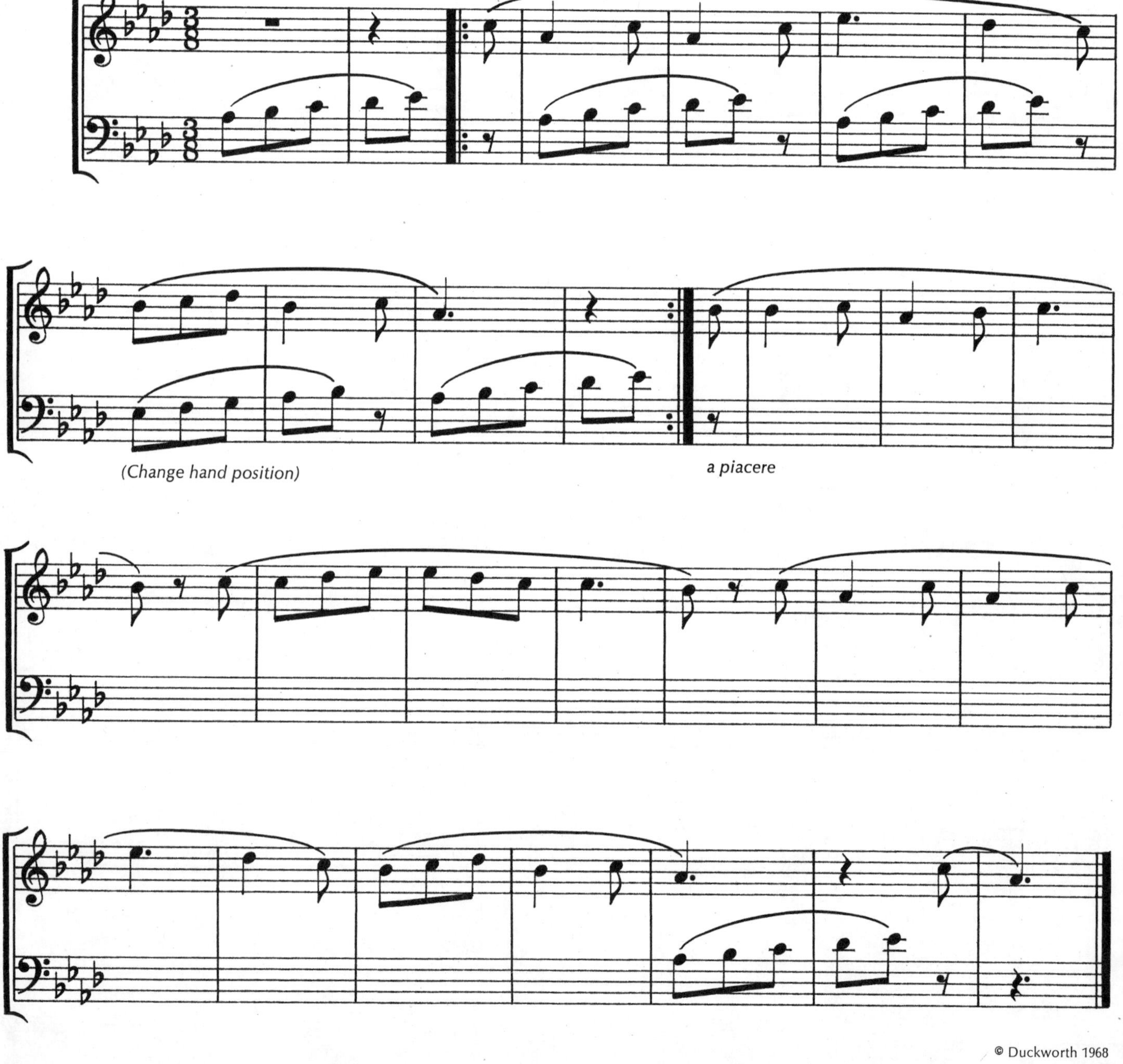

OPEN FIFTHS

19

African

R. H. 8va on repeat

PEDAL POINT

20

German

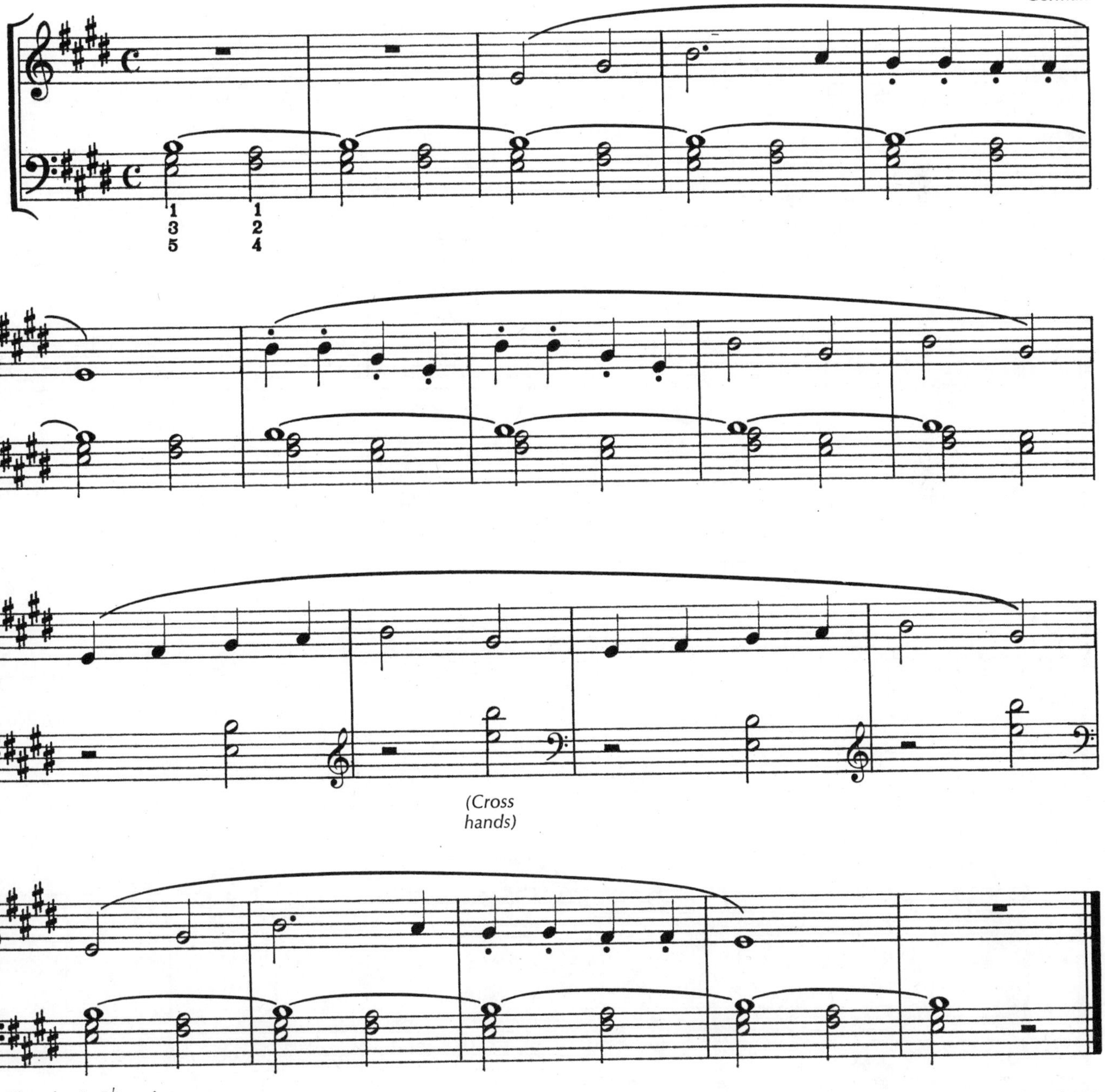

Play also in E♭ major

RHYTHMIC PATTERNS REPEATED

21

British

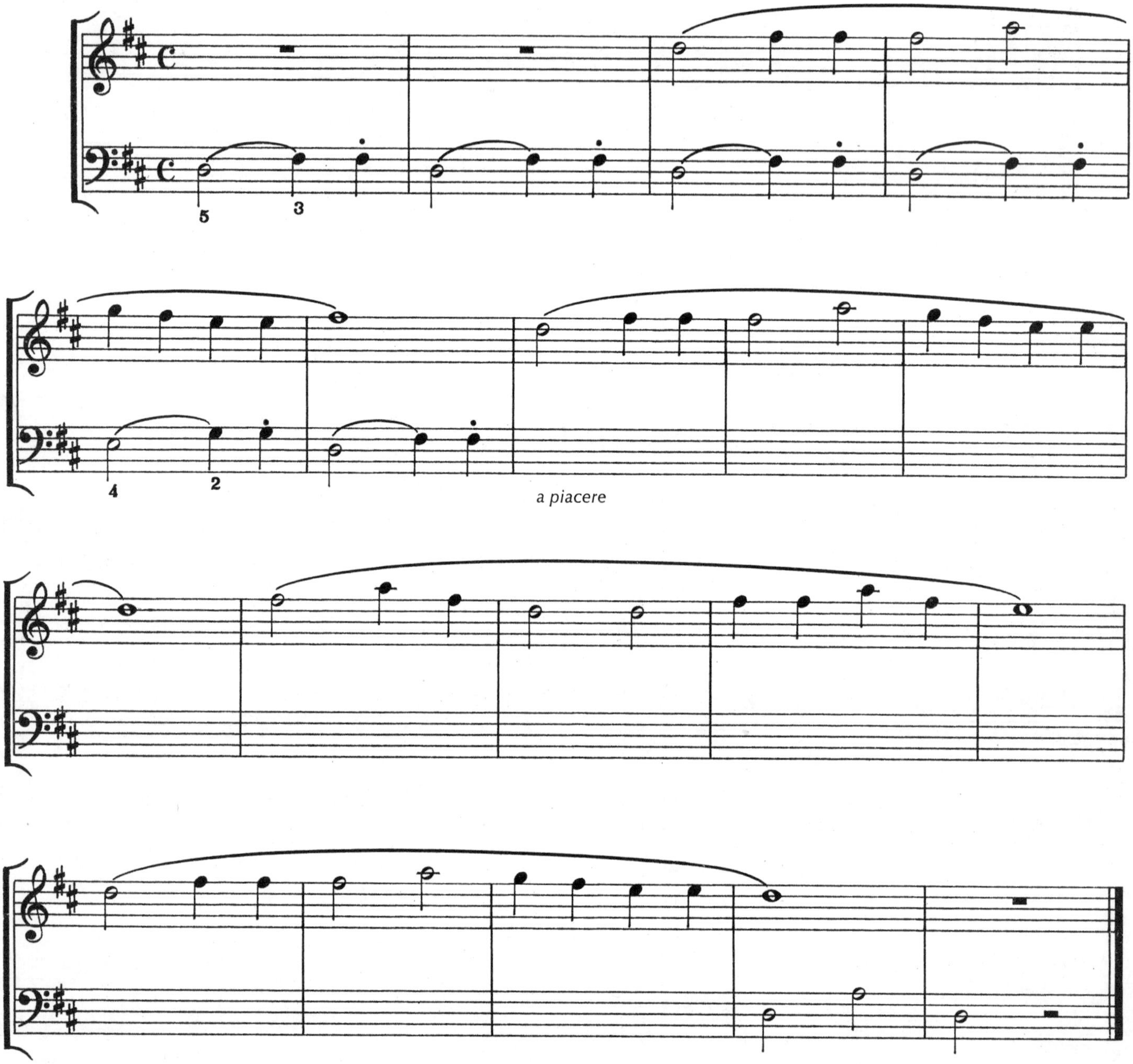

FIFTHS IN PENTATONIC

22

Hungarian

TIED NOTES

23

German

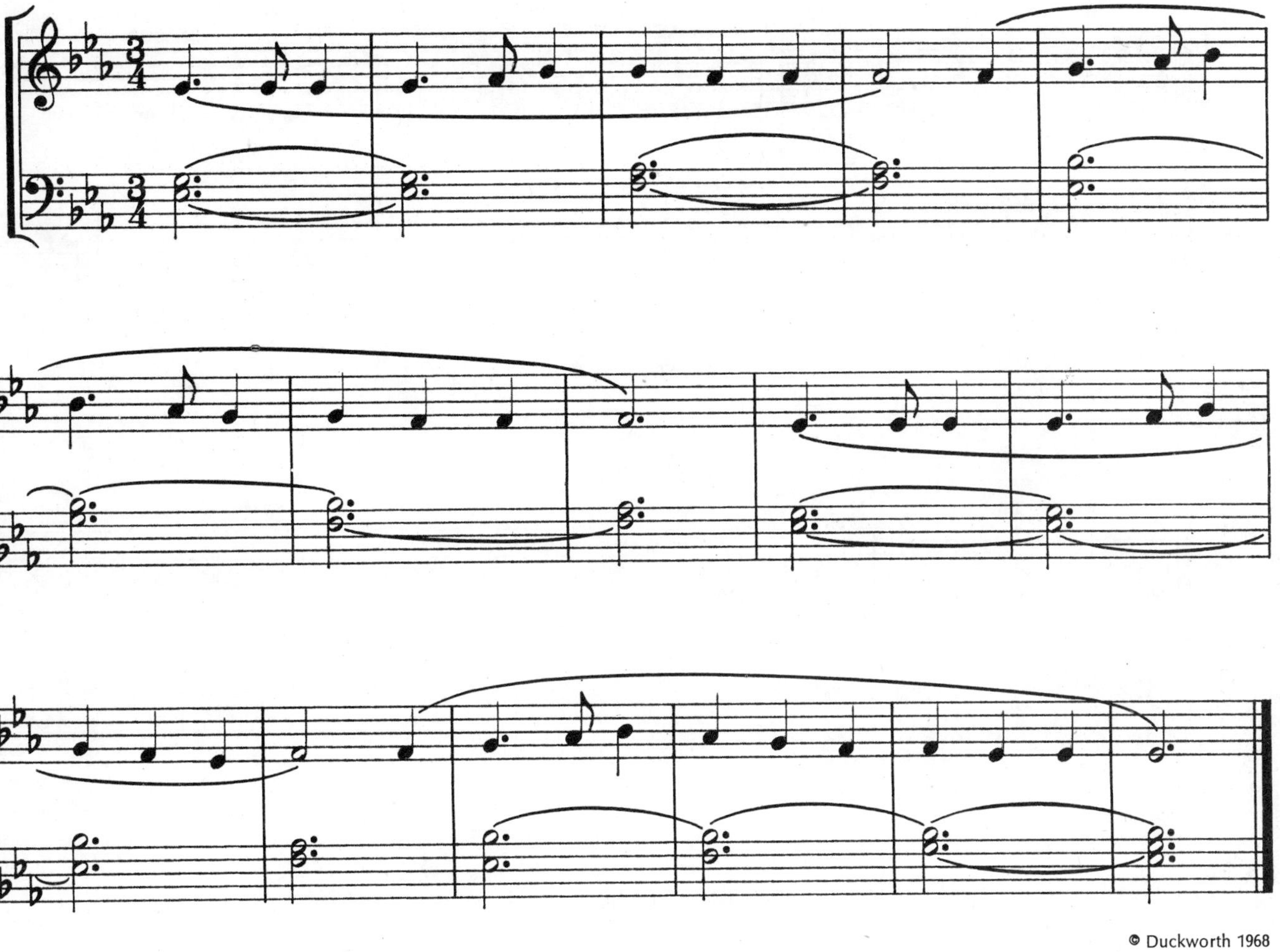

PENTACHORDS—MODAL

PHRYGIAN IN PARALLEL MOTION WITH MINOR

1

American

CONTRARY MOTION

2A

Polish

2B

Hungarian

CONTRARY MOTION AND RHYTHMIC AUGMENTATION

3

Finnish

CONTRARY MOTION

4

Hungarian

OSTINATO

5

Flemish

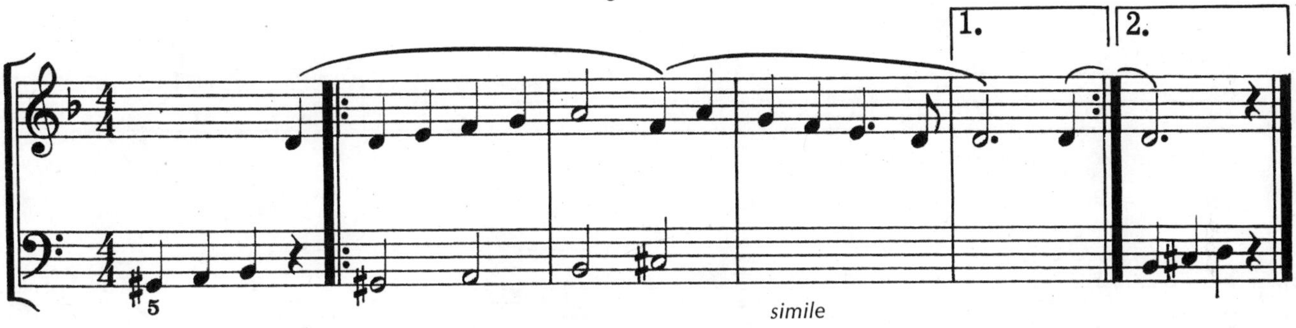

CONTRARY AND PARALLEL MOTION

6

Russian

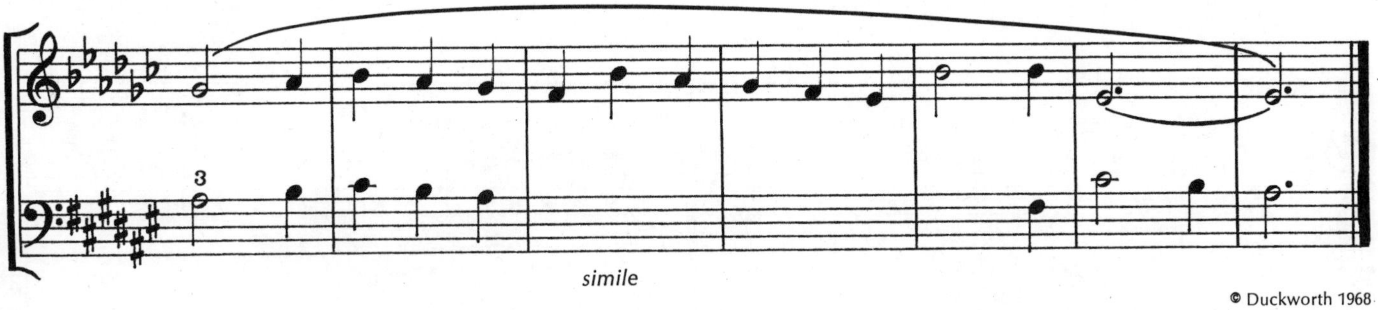

LYDIAN IN PARALLEL MOTION AT THE SIXTH

7

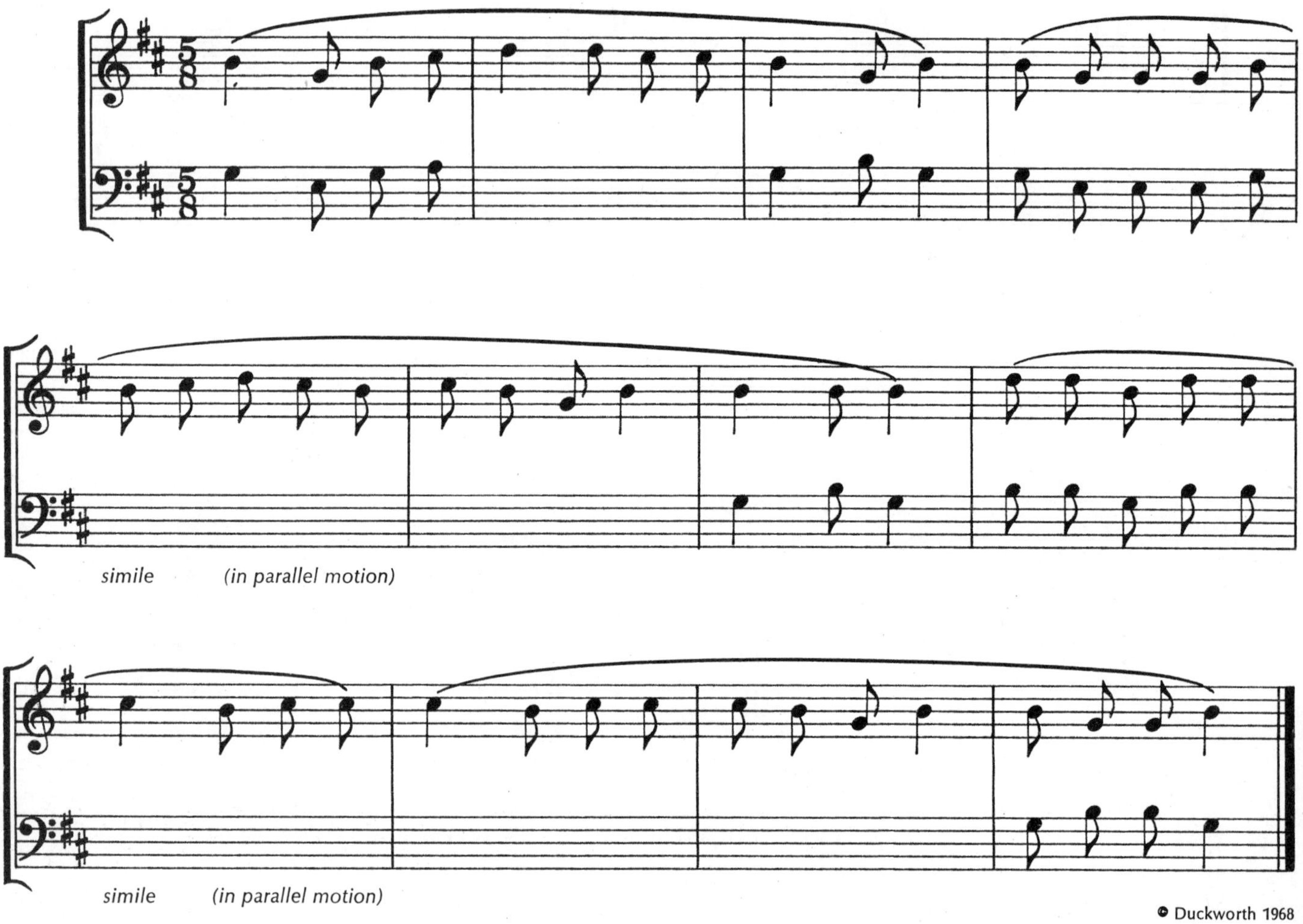

PARALLEL MOTION WITH MAJOR

8

Melody from
13th Century

CONTRARY AND PARALLEL MOTION

9

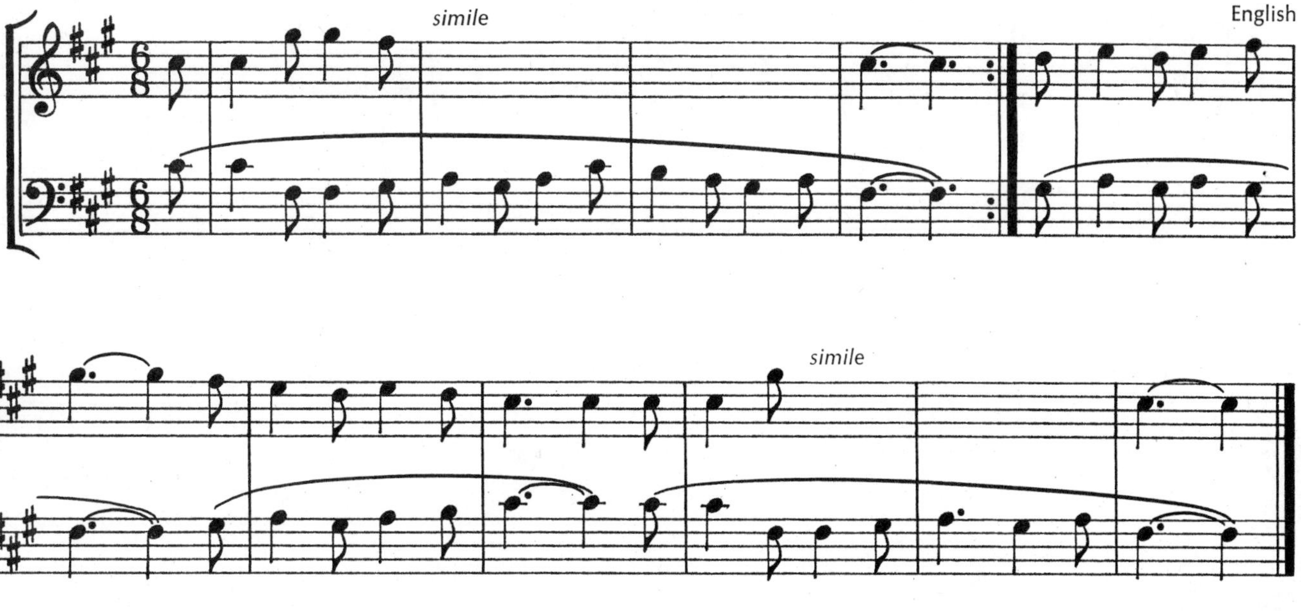

OSTINATO

10A

OSTINATO

10B

German

OSTINATO IN FIFTHS

11

Hungarian

OPEN FIFTHS

12

French

OSTINATO

13

American Indian

PHRYGIAN MODE

14

British

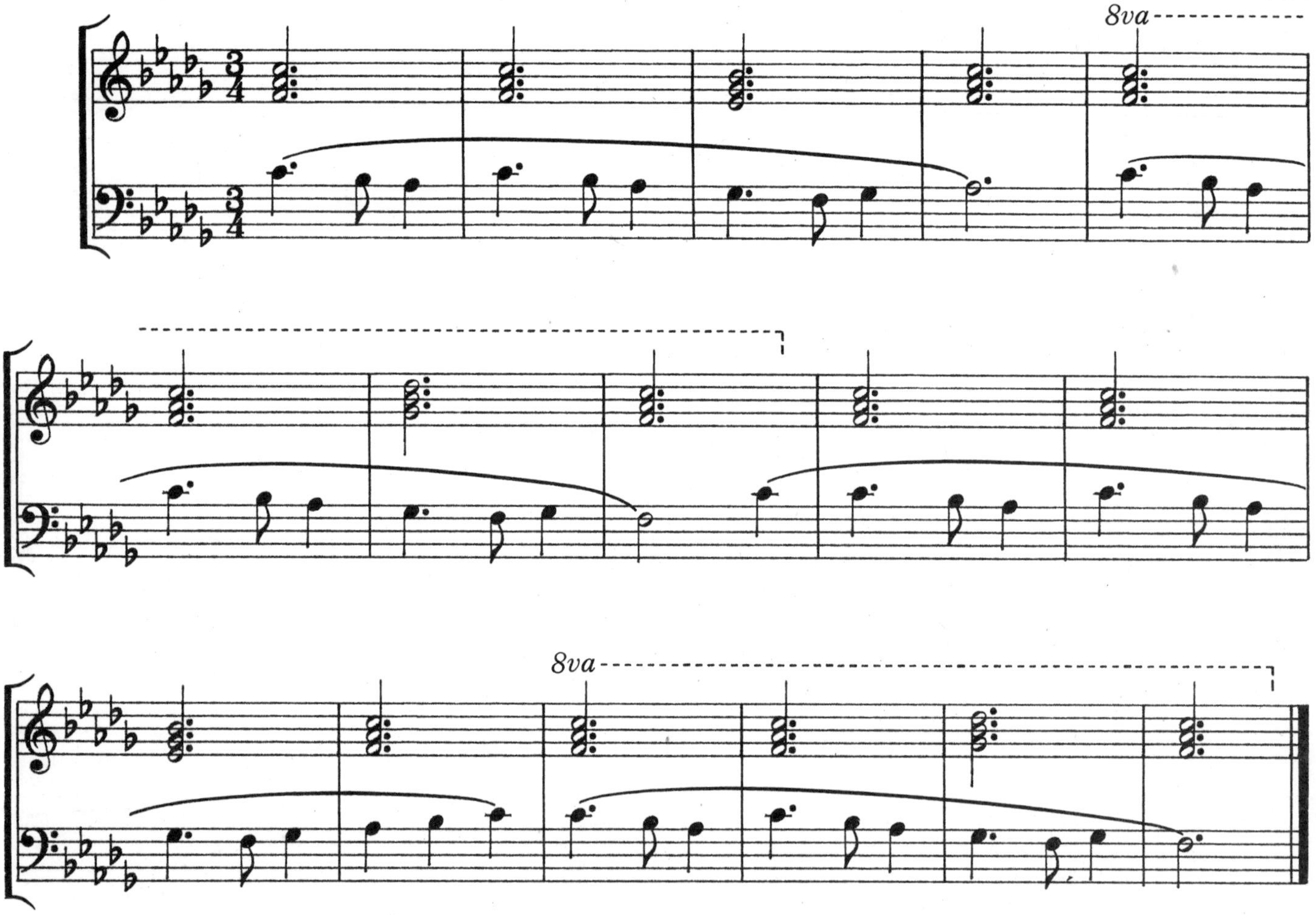

MINOR WITH LYDIAN

15

Swedish

OSTINATO IN FIFTHS

16

Hungarian

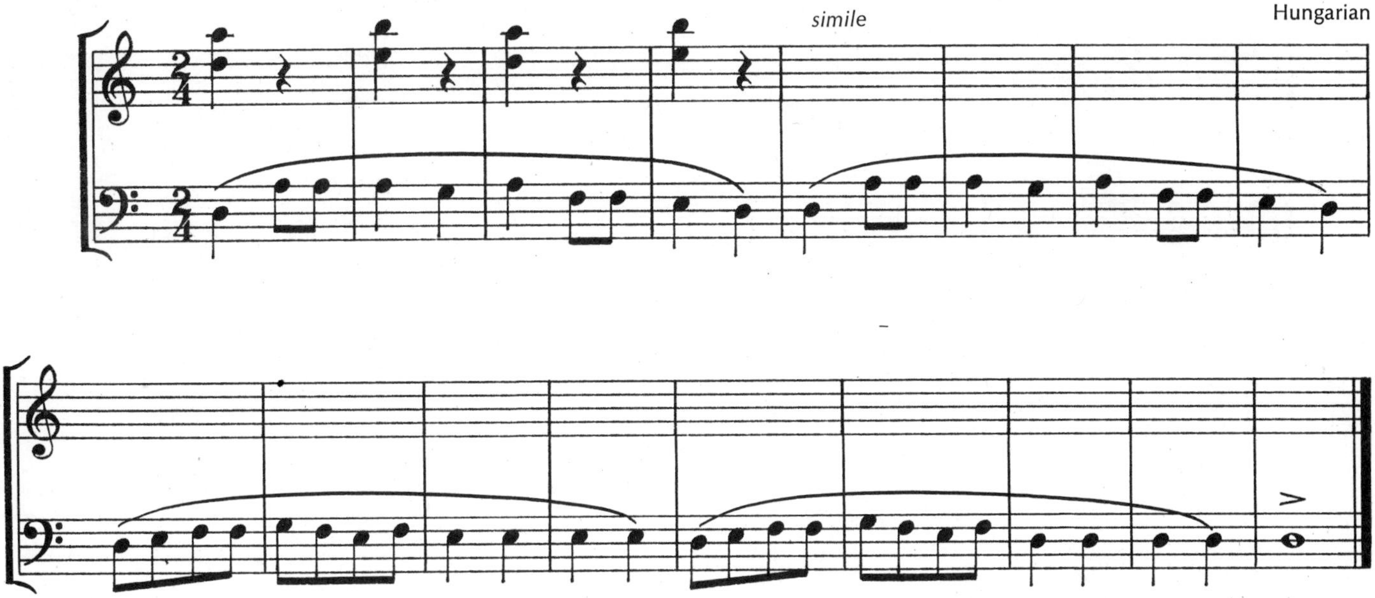

KYRIE IN PHRYGIAN

17

Melody by
ANTONIO LOTTI
C1667-1740

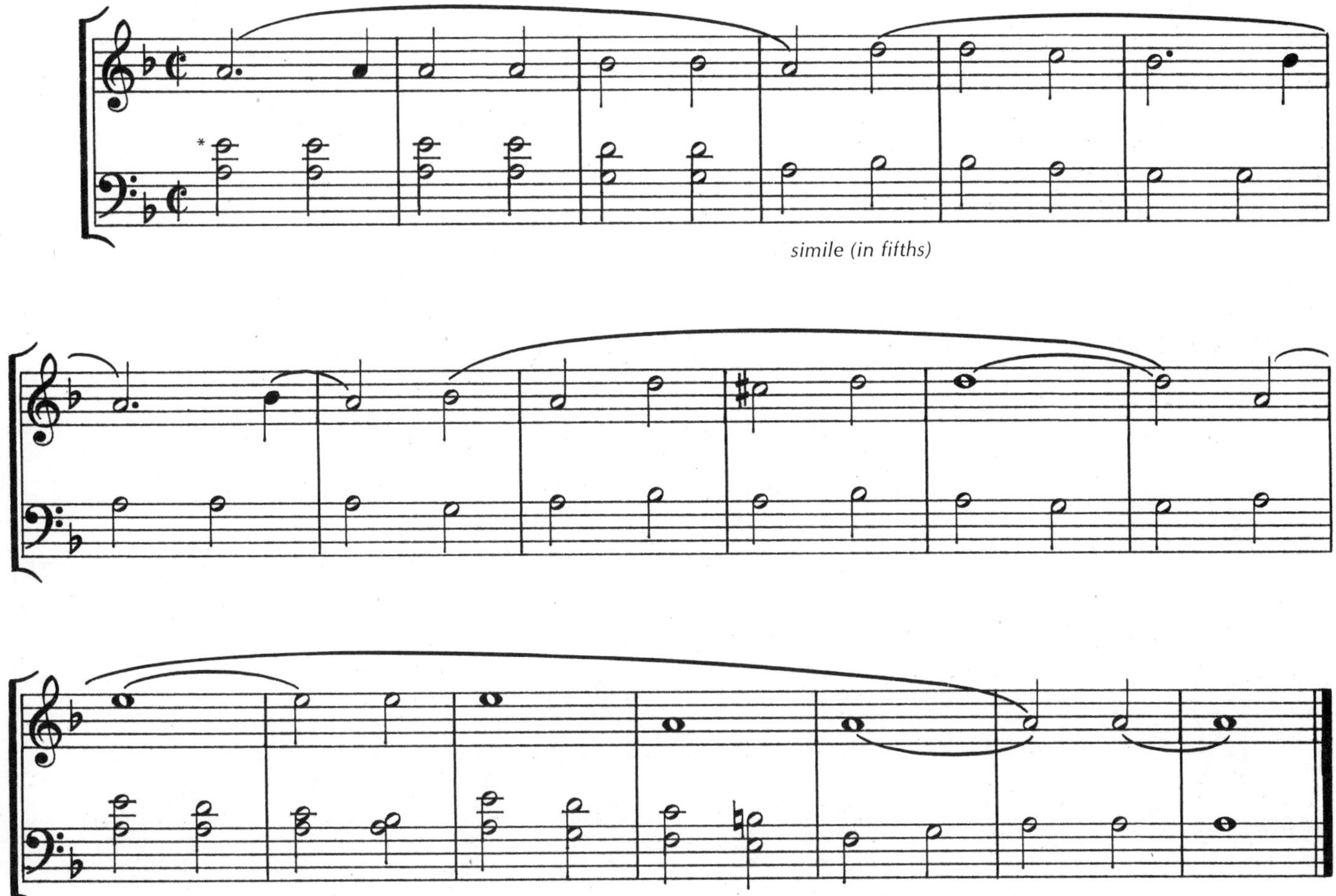

simile

*A legato pedal is useful here

IMITATION REFLECTED

18

French

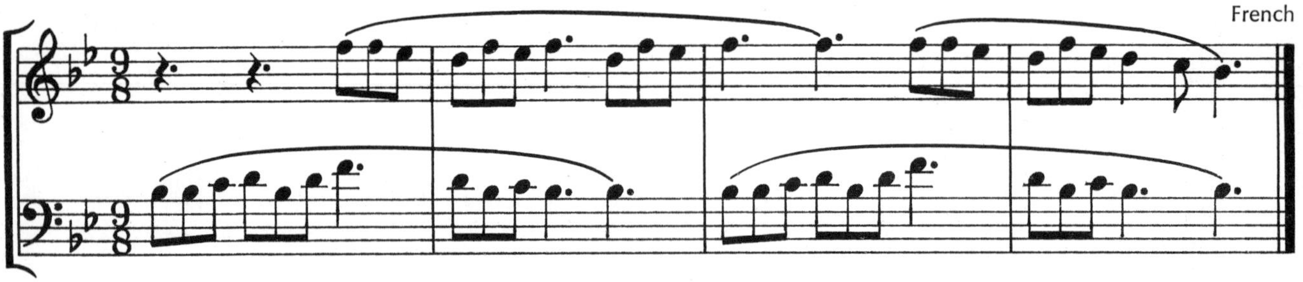

CLUSTERS IN OSTINATO

19

Hungarian

PHRYGIAN MODE

20

Russian

*Small notes are optional to play.

IMITATION IN MAJOR

21

Melody by
COUPERIN

DANCE IN DORIAN

22

Melody from
13th CENTURY

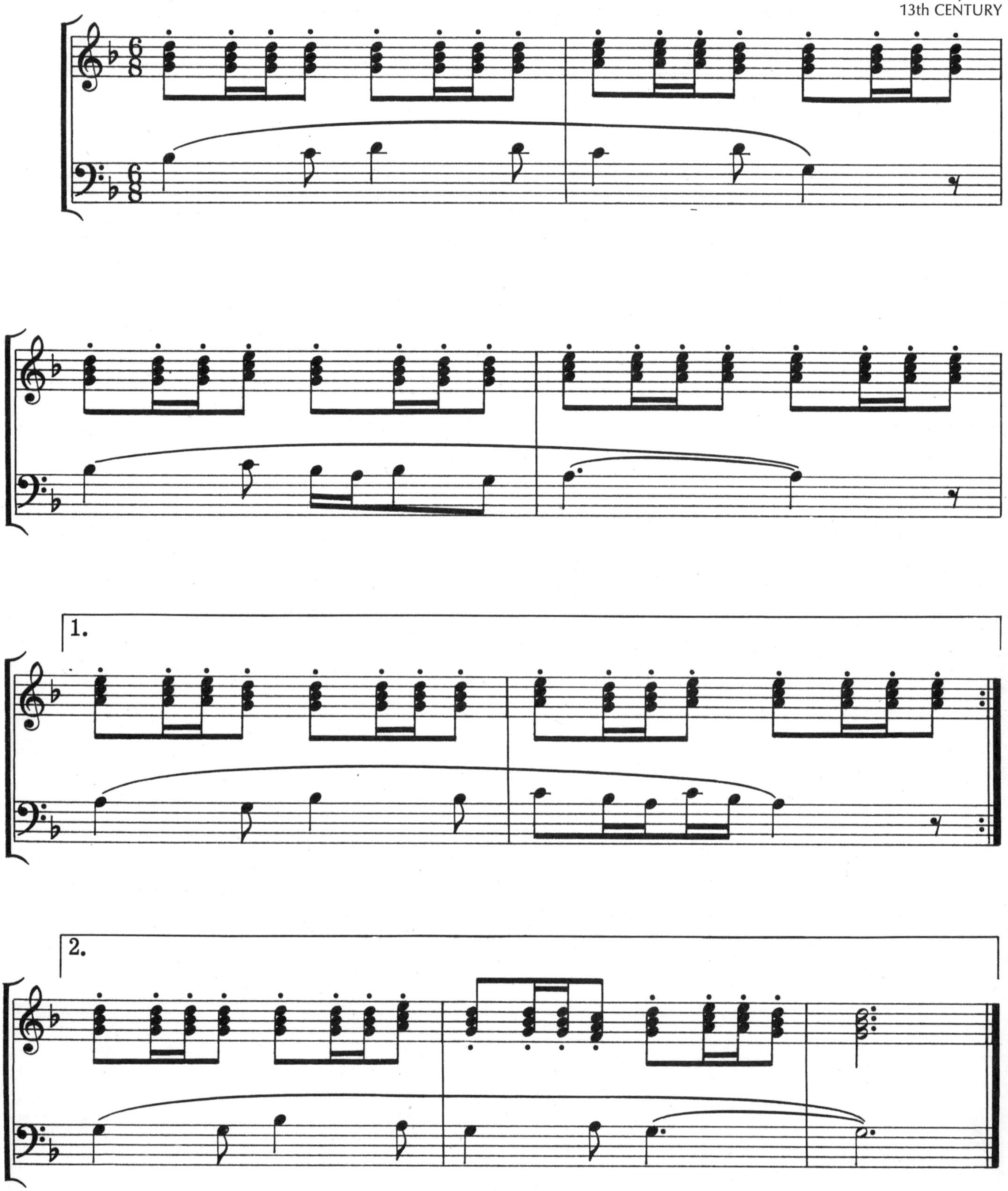

The following repertoire is selected from Anton Diabelli's *Melodious Pieces for Duet,* Op. 149. The primo part of the duets have a pitch range of a fifth for each hand. The secondo parts expose the basic, traditional harmonic sequences in their different positions. (See Resource Materials.)

Transposing these duets is another way the student can familiarize himself with pentachords as well as traditional harmonies in all keys while he works within a musical context. The accompaniment patterns Diabelli uses in the secondo parts give the student ideas for varying accompaniments of folk songs and melodic improvisations.

The beginning student may find the secondo parts too difficult at this time in his development, in which case, he should go on to Unit II, where he encounters more slowly these same keyboard sequences.

PIECES FOR DUET, OP. 149
BY ANTON DIABELLI

SCHERZO

1

SECONDO

Allegro

A. Diabelli

PIECES FOR DUET, OP. 149
BY ANTON DIABELLI

SCHERZO

1

PRIMO

Allegro

A. Diabelli

D. C. al Fine

ANDANTE CANTABILE

2

SECONDO

A. Diabelli

ANDANTE CANTABILE

2

PRIMO

A. Diabelli

ALLEGRO

3

SECONDO

A. Diabelli

ALLEGRO

3

PRIMO

A. Diabelli

HONGROISE

4

SECONDO

A. Diabelli

HONGROISE

4

PRIMO

A. Diabelli

ALLA TURCA

5

SECONDO

A. Diabelli

ALLA TURCA

5

PRIMO

Allegro

A. Diabelli

UNIT TWO

HAND POSITION CHANGE-LIMITED RANGE

The following compositions have a range of a sixth or seventh. Each phrase, however, does not exceed a range of a fifth—a pentachord.

READING

The compositions in this section again are based upon major and modal material and written so as to provide reading experiences in all key centers while emphasizing the need for changing hand positions within a composition. It is advisable to play the melody alone before reading the complete composition.

FINGERING

A change of hand position is required BETWEEN phrases in these piano pieces. Since each phrase does not exceed a range of a fifth, the pentachord is located for each hand position by investigating each phrase for its range of pitches—lows and highs. When a change of hand position is required, the finger number should be written in the score with the first note of that phrase. For example:

(Performer continues with pattern.)

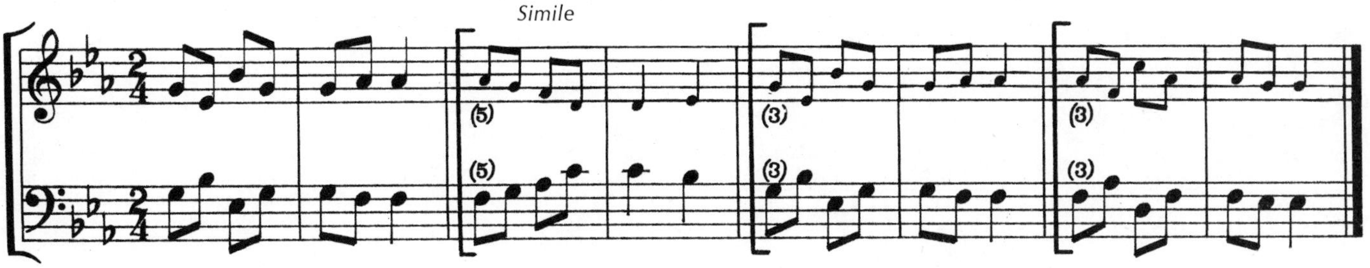

Brackets [ ] are indicated in the score of the first few compositions to show where a change of hand position is required.

TRANSPOSING

The majority of these piano pieces use all pitches of a given scale. To extend the ability of the performer to think within any key center each composition should be transposed to as many keys as possible. No limitation should be placed on the keys selected for training this ability. (See Harmonizing.)

IMPROVISING

The same improvising skills as outlined for piano pieces with pentachords continue with these compositions. (See Harmonizing.)

HARMONIZING

The piano pieces which are written in major and minor modes should be harmonized in a traditional manner. The student should also transpose these traditional settings. Further, these same kinds of settings should be used when improvising to the verse in Resource Materials.

Inasmuch as triads are inverted and sequences resulting from these inversions are utilized, the author suggests isolating the keyboard sequences in Resource Materials and playing them in all keys, major and minor modes. The beginning student should return to the secondo parts of the Diabelli duets in Unit I for further application since these parts use to a large degree these same keyboard sequences.

CONTRARY MOTION

1

Polish

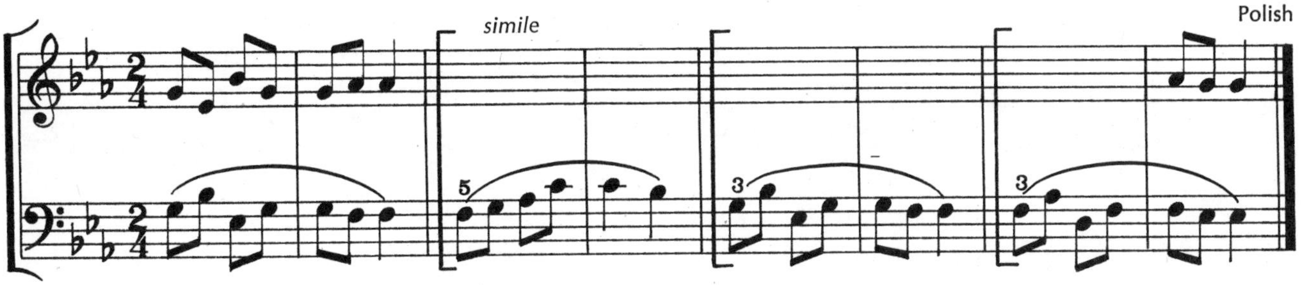

ROUND

2

French

PARALLEL AT THE THIRD AND NINTH (Duet)

3

British

I

II

Melody

I

II

THIRDS

4

British

ACCOMPANIMENT IN THIRDS

5

British

ADDED SECONDS

6

German

PENTACHORD CLUSTERS

7

Polish

HARMONIZED AT THE MEDIANT IN MAJOR

8

ACCOMPANIMENT IN RELATIVE MINOR

9

Latin

THREE SETTINGS IN CYCLES OF FIFTHS, THIRDS, SECONDS

10

A. FIFTHS

Hungarian

B. THIRDS

C. SECONDS

According to Vincent Persichetti in *Twentieth Century Harmony*, W. W. Norton, chordal relationships can be considered in three ways:

in fifths (traditional tonic-dominant harmony)
in thirds
in seconds.

An equivalency chart gives the performer an idea of these relationships.

Cycle of Fifths	I	V	II	VI	III	VII	IV
Cycle of Thirds	I	III	V	VII	II	IV	VI
Cycle of Seconds	I	II	III	IV	V	VI	VII

MUSETTE
CYCLE OF THIRDS

11

French

TRIADS

12

German

POLKA (Duet)

13

British

OSTINATO IN FOURTHS

14

French

OSTINATO IN FOURTHS

14

Dutch

*Notes in parentheses are optional to play.

HAND POSITION CHANGE—MODAL

PARALLEL MOTION AT THE SIXTH, TENTH

1

Czechoslovakian

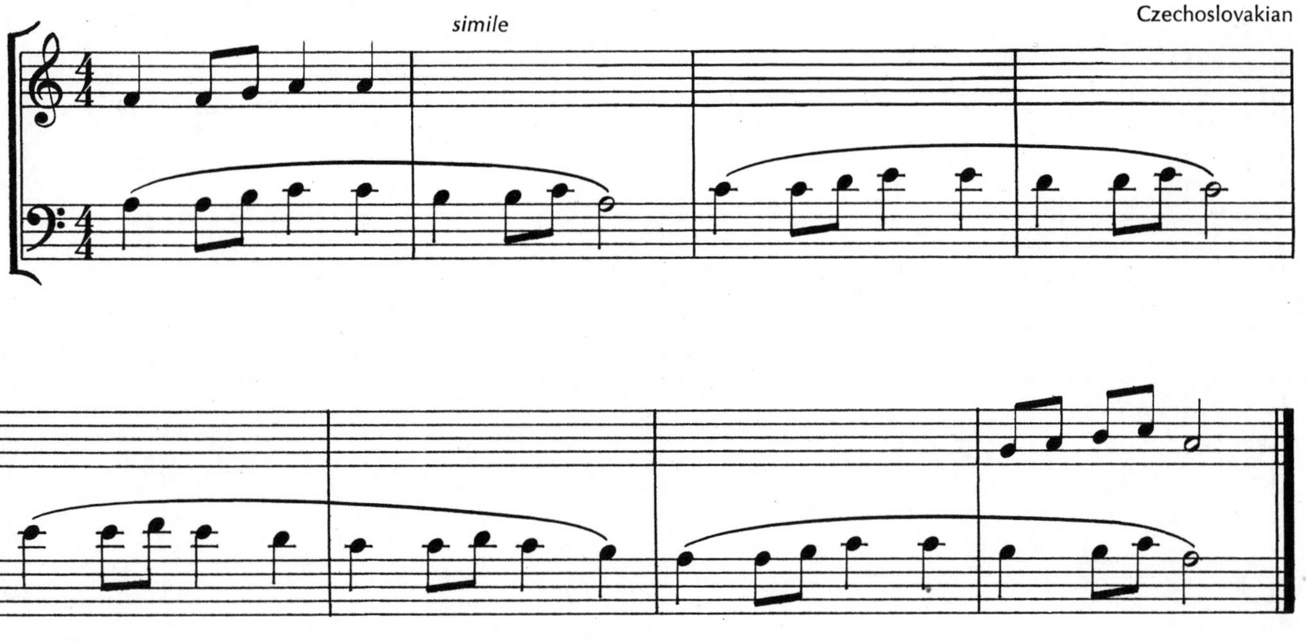

CONTRARY MOTION

2

Finnish

SYMMETRICAL INVERSION

3

French

IMITATION IN CONTRARY MOTION

4

British

MIXOLYDIAN

5

A. PARALLEL FOURTHS

Latin

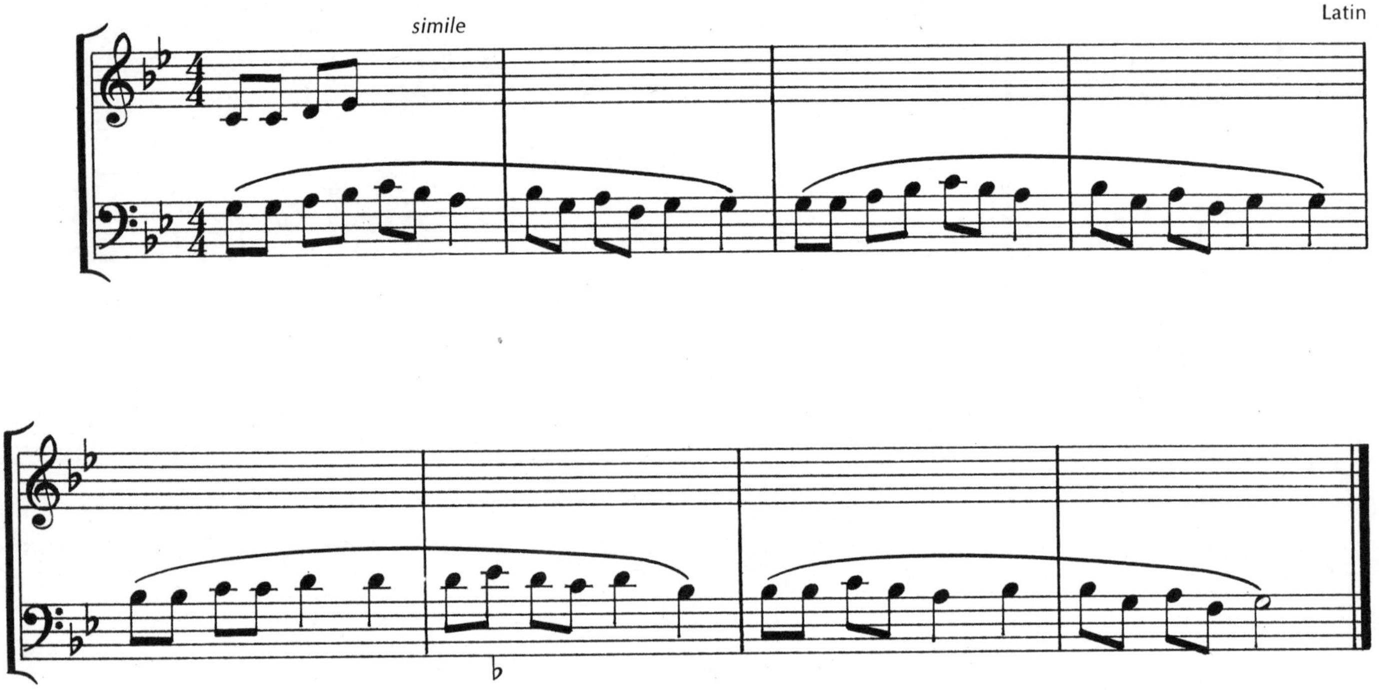

B. HARMONIZED

CYCLE OF SECONDS

6

French

INVERSIONS (Duet)

7

Polish

DORIAN ON B

8

Serbian

CHORD SEQUENCE IN SECOND INVERSION (Duet)

9

Dutch

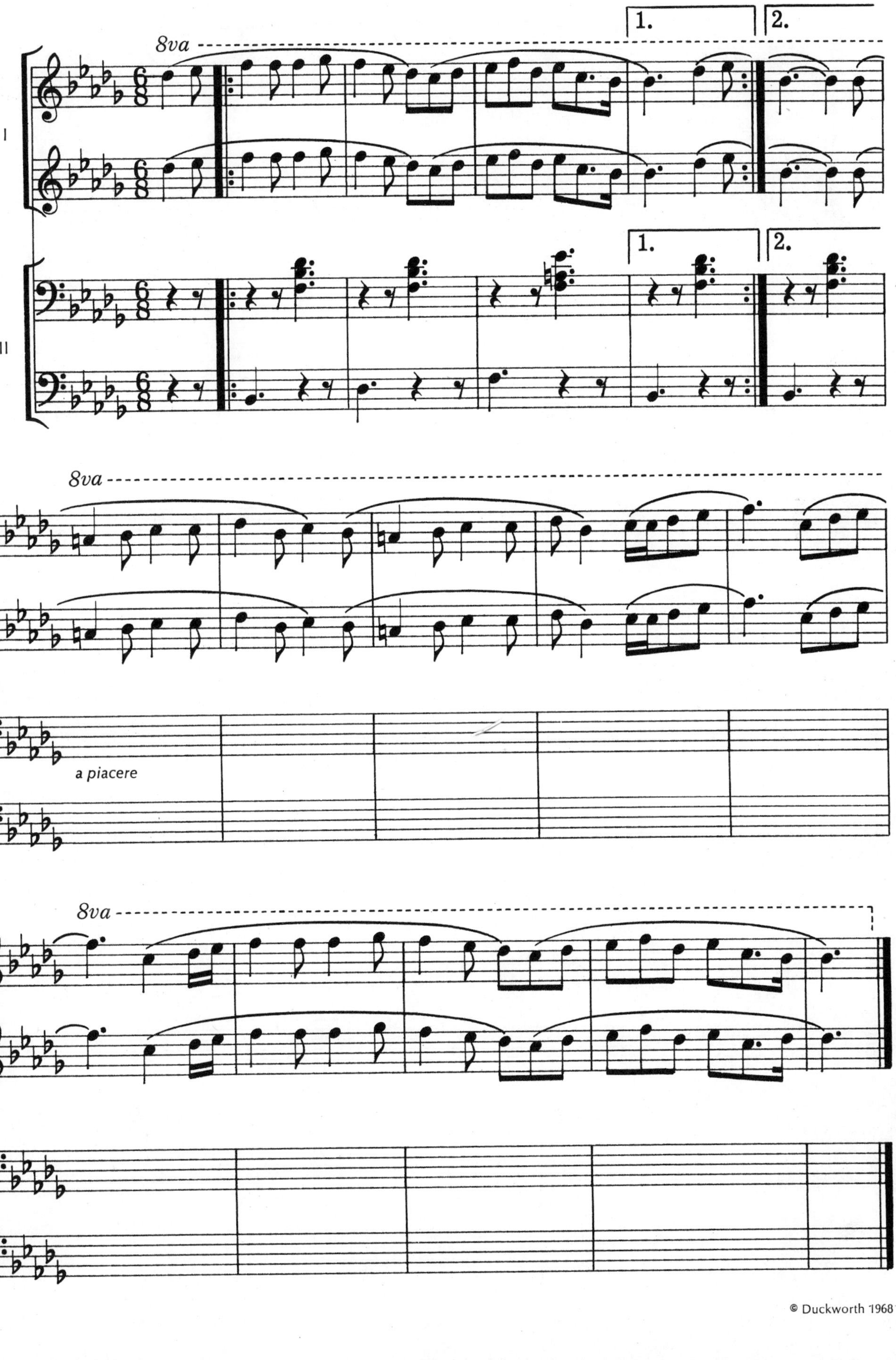

PHRYGIAN ON G

10

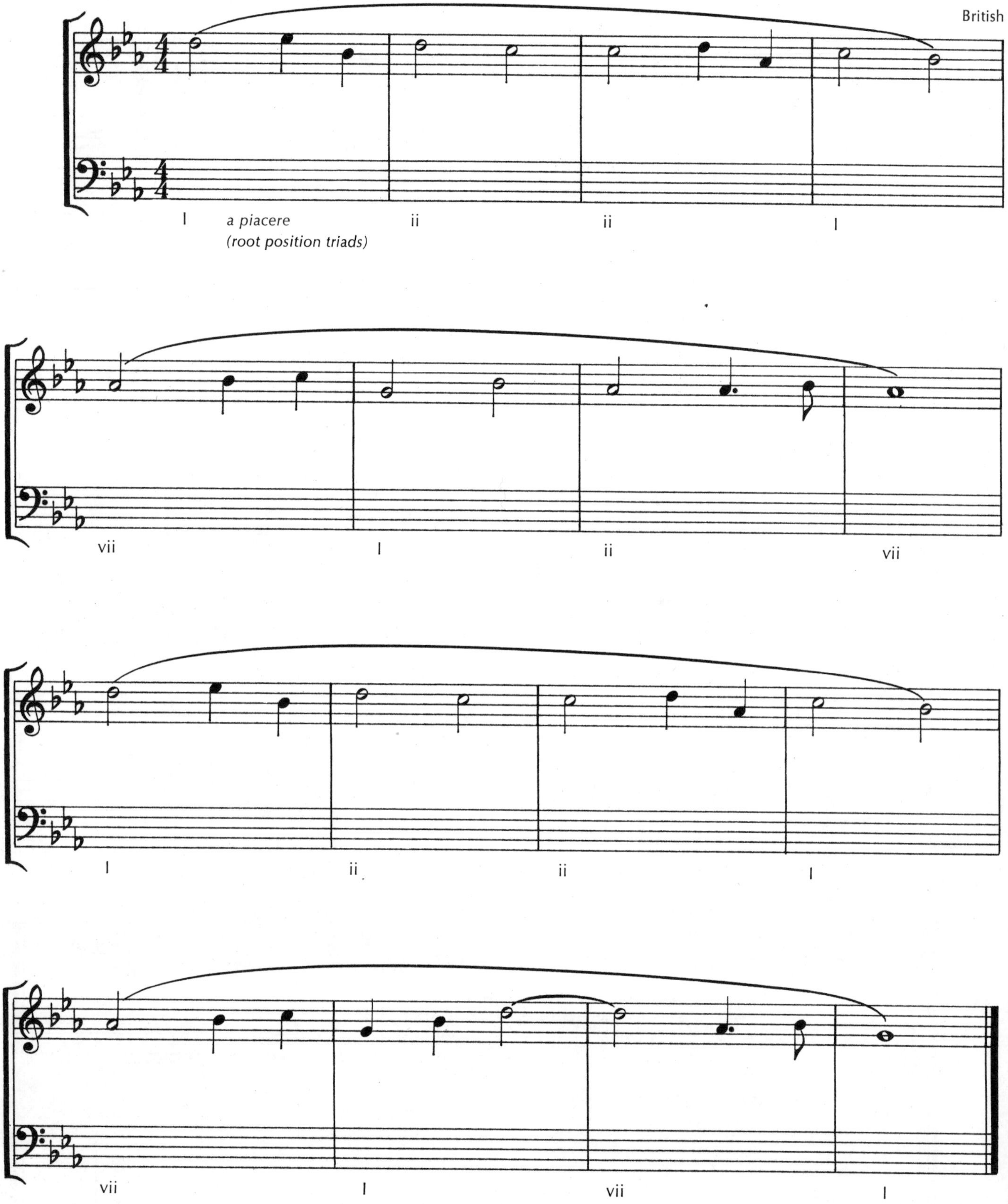

ROLLED PENTACHORDS

11

Finnish

*Roll from bottom or top of pentachord

CHORDS IN FOURTHS

12

British

*Notes in parentheses are optional to play.

PENTACHORD CLUSTERS

13

Italian

*Natural and sharp symbols refer to each pitch in the cluster.

CHORDS IN FOURTHS WITH ADDED THIRD

14

Polish

*Notes in parenthesis are optional to play.

THIRDS

15

Dutch

PRELUDE

16

H. Purcell

THEME FROM K331

17

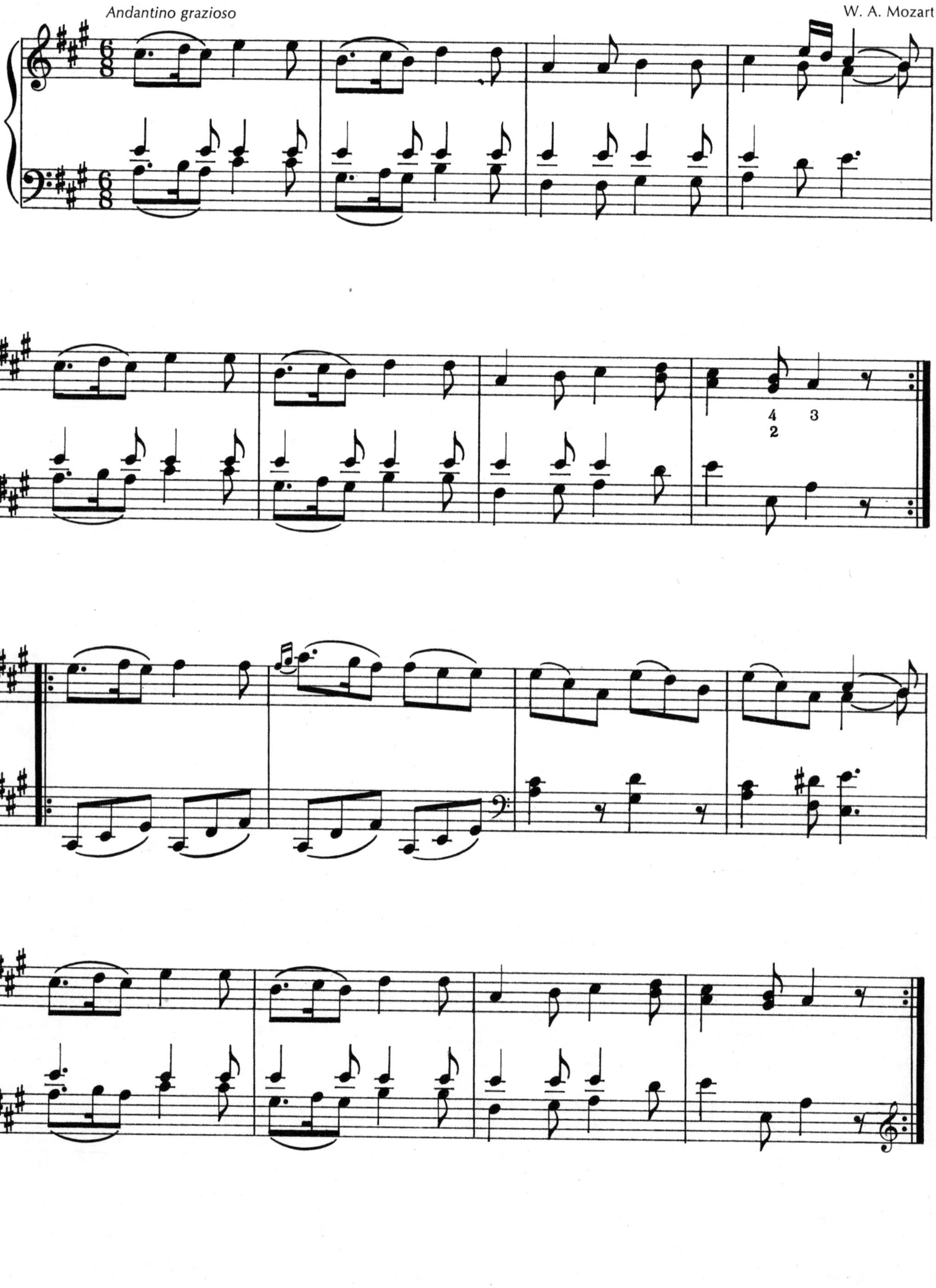

ECCOSSAISE

18

L. van Beethoven

section 2.

STRETCHES-LIMITED RANGE

The following compositions continue to have a range of a sixth or seventh. The phrases themselves can now exceed a range of a fifth. The student needs additional fingering concepts for accommodating the pitches he is now required to play WITHIN phrases.

READING

These major and modal compositions are written to provide reading experiences in all key centers while emphasizing a need for stretching the hand to secure the fingers necessary for performing the phrases in these compositions. A concentration on skip patterns WITHIN phrases is required since it is these kinds of patterns that facilitate stretches in the hand. It is advisable to play the melody alone before reading the complete composition.

FINGERING

The most ideal place in the hand to stretch from-or-to is the thumb. The next best is the second finger, with the least desirable being the fourth. A change of hand position between phrases is still required in the performance of this material.

When a skip pattern is located in which a stretch is appropriate the fingering should be written in the score. For example:

BAGPIPES

British

Brackets [ ] are indicated in the score of the first few compositions to show where a stretch is required.

TRANSPOSING

Extending the ability to think within any key center by transposing these piano pieces continues. It is important to select key centers now which approximate as much as possible the same keyboard topography as the original key center—relationship of black to white keys—so as to maintain with relative ease the same fingering on transposition. (See Harmonizing.)

IMPROVISING

The same improvising skills as outlined for piano pieces with pentachords continue with these compositions. (See Harmonizing.)

HARMONIZING

Harmonizing and transposing traditional settings of the major and minor piano pieces that are set in a contemporary or contrapuntal manner continue. Using these same settings for improvisations to the verse in Resource Materials also continues.

POLKA (Duet)

Polish

OSTINATO

2

Polish

BAGPIPES

3

British

DRONE BASS

4

French

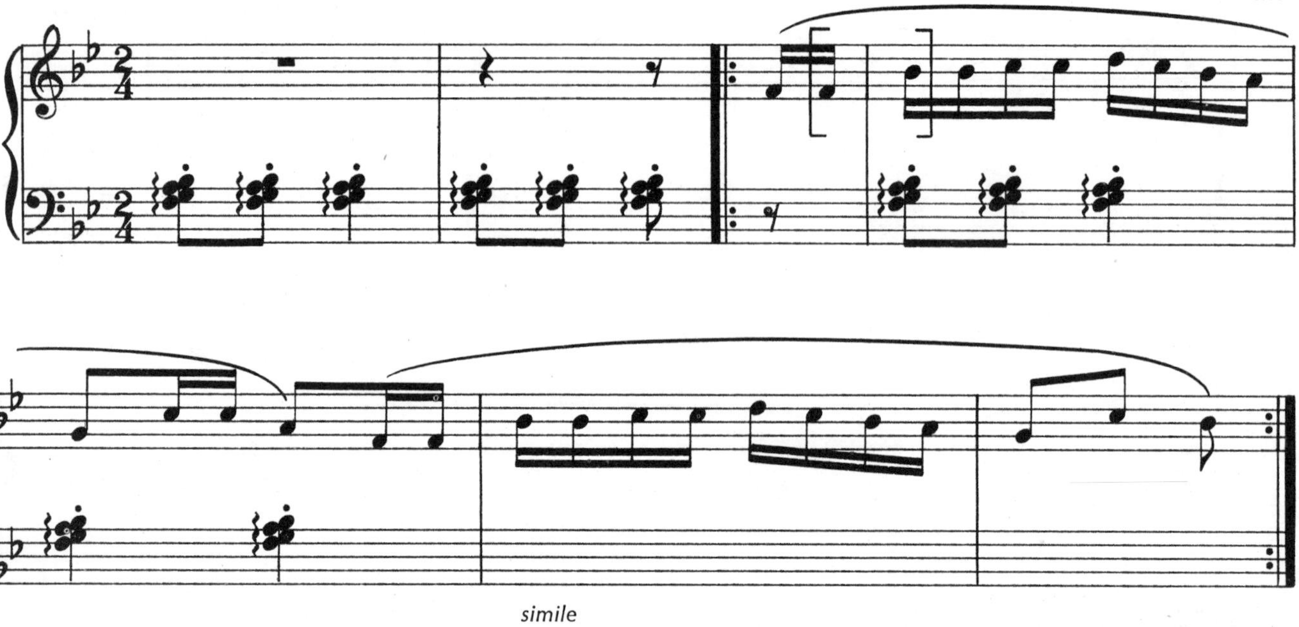

TRIADS WITH SECONDS

5

British

CHORD SEQUENCE IN ROOT POSITION

6A

British

6B

German

CHORD SEQUENCE IN FIRST INVERSION

7A

7B

CHORD SEQUENCE IN SECOND INVERSION

8A

German

8B

Swedish

8C

Canadian

TRIADS—ALL POSITIONS

9

E

German

IN PARALLEL MOTION

10

German

Melody

Fine

D. C. al Fine

IMITATION

11

Polish

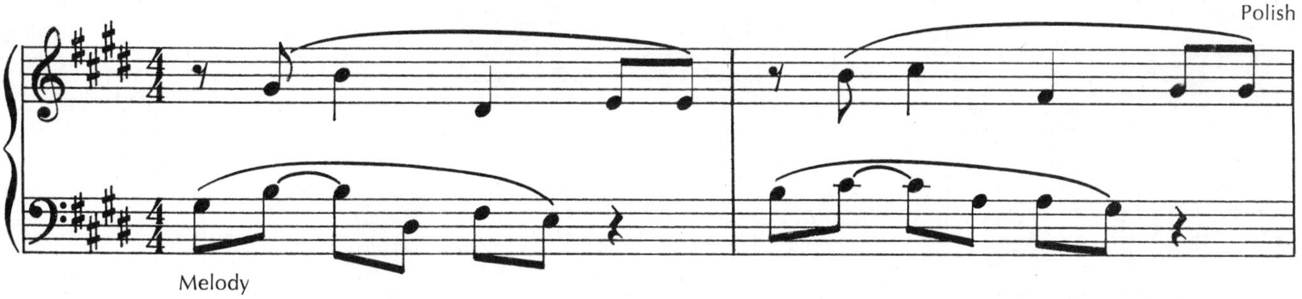

Melody

REPEATED PATTERN

12A

Slovakian

12B

French

PATTERN IN SEQUENCE

13

Polish

MELODY AND HARMONY COMBINED

14

German

OSTINATO

1

Change rhythm on repeat as suggested.

BASS LINE USING A SCALE

2

British

LOCRIAN WITH SECONDS IN INVERSIONS

3

German

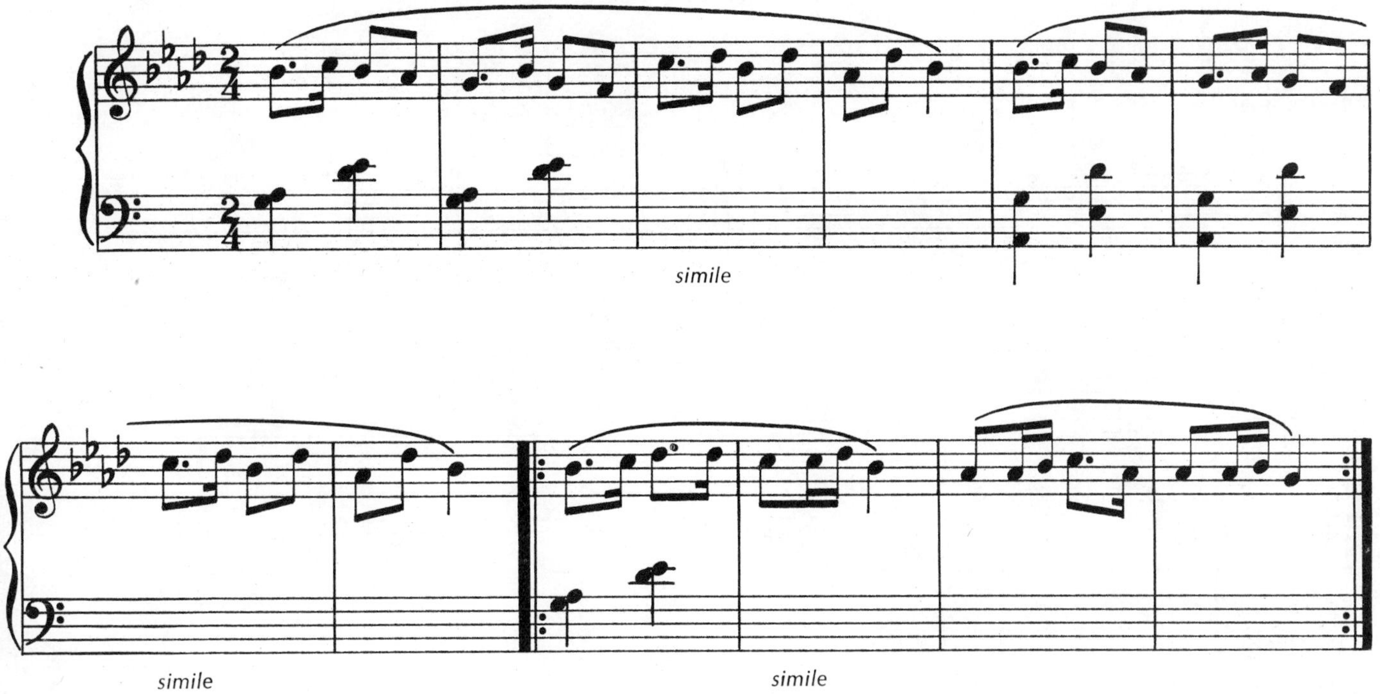

DORIAN

4

French

CHORDS IN TRIADS

5

Russian

CHORD SEQUENCE IN ROOT POSITION

6

Polish

a piacere *Repeat twice*

SECONDS

7

British

IMPROVISATION

8

Russian

SARABANDE

9

Spanish

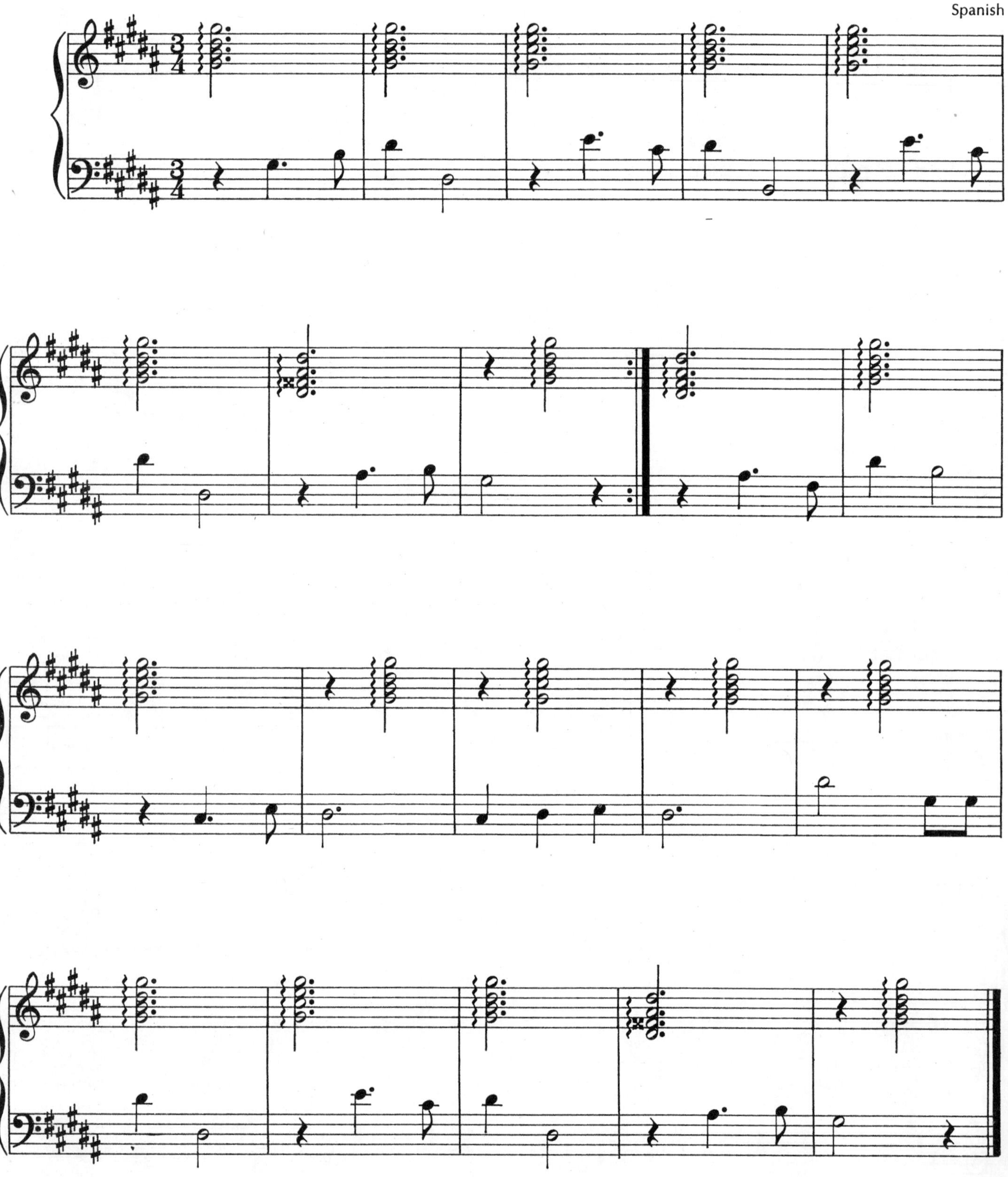

CLUSTERS

10

Latin

CHORDS IN FOURTHS

11

French

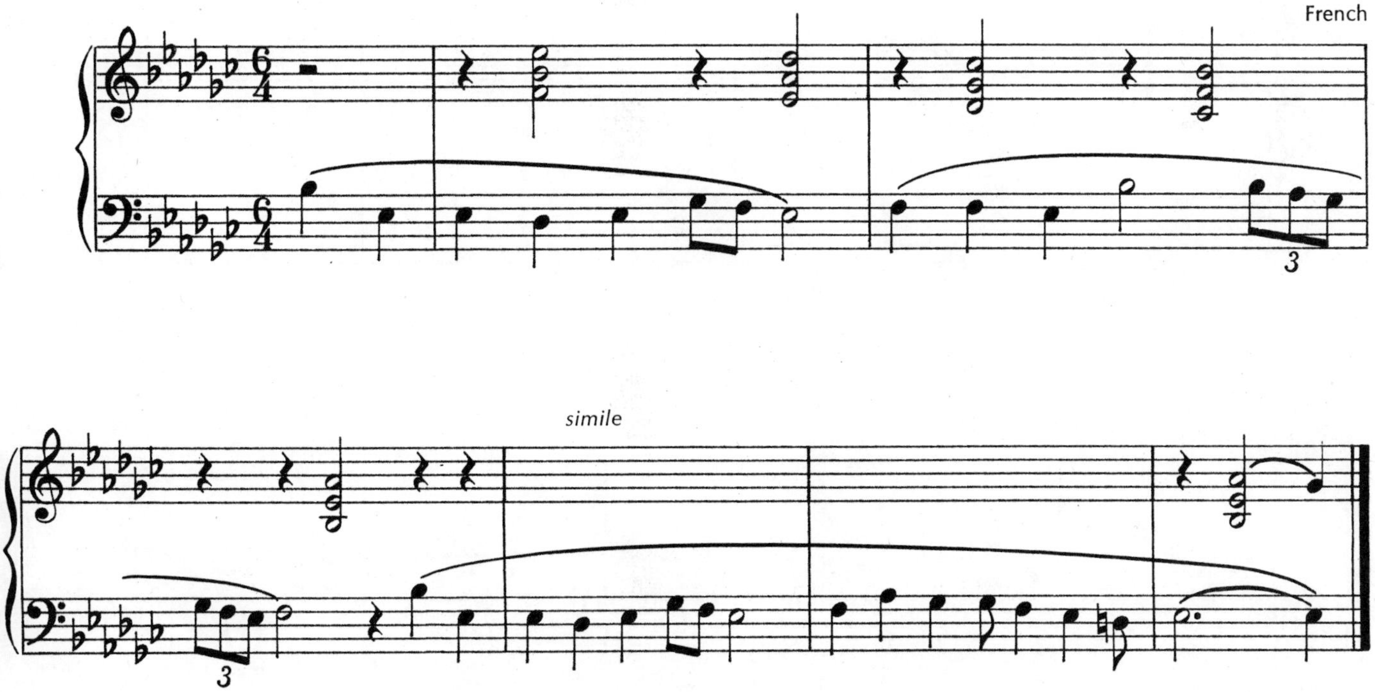

CANON

12

Greek

Play also in duet by doubling bass with two hands for the secondo part and doubling treble with two hands for the primo part.

IN CONTRARY MOTION

13

Scandinavian

CHANGING REGISTER

14

French

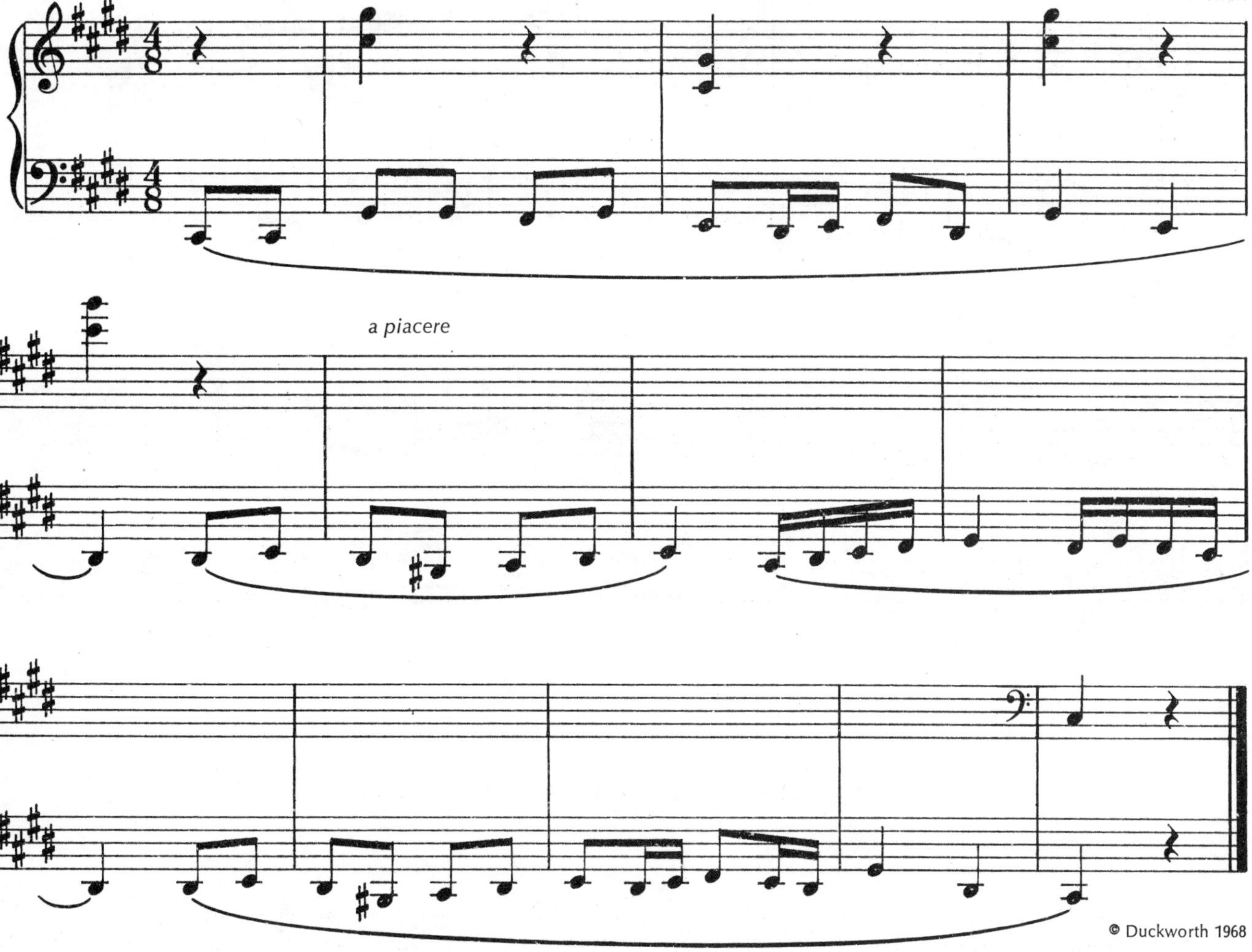

RHYTHMIC PATTERN REPETITION

15

Dutch

PARALLEL AT THE OCTAVE

16

Dutch

PARALLEL FIFTHS IN STACCATO

17

German

HORNPIPE

18

British

TRIADS—BROKEN AND SOLID

19

German

PARALLEL SIXTHS IN STACCATO

20

Lithuanian

ECCOSSAISE

21

F. Schubert

MENUET (Duet)

22

From Sonatina II for four hands

SECONDO

W. A. Mozart

MENUET (Duet)

22

From Sonatina II for four hands

PRIMO

W. A. Mozart

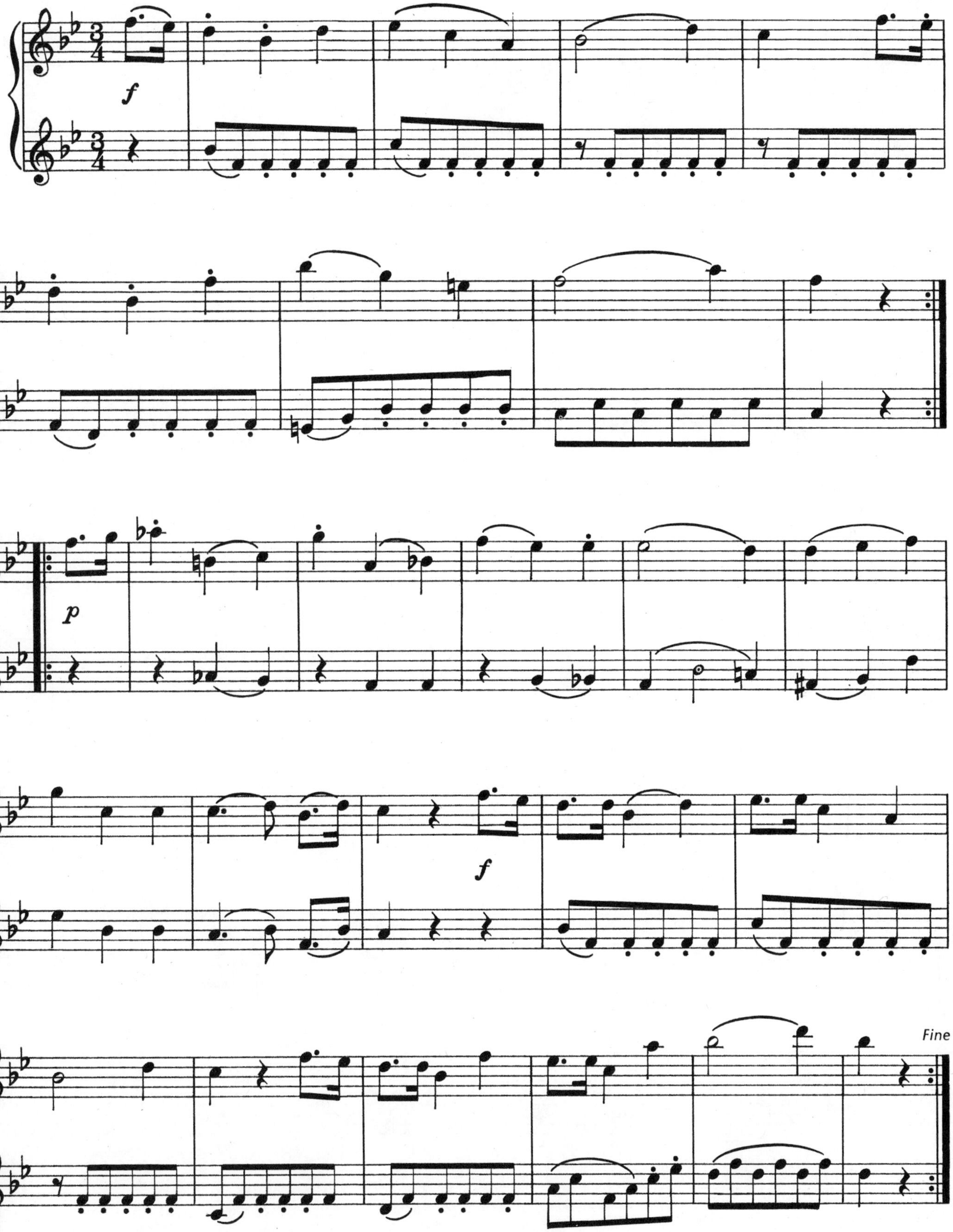

Trio
p
(D. C.) al Fine

Trio
p
(D. C.) al Fine

CROSSES-LIMITED RANGE

The following compositions continue to have a range of a sixth or seventh with the phrases themselves exceeding a range of a fifth. The student needs additional means through crossings so as to accommodate the pitches he is required to play WITHIN phrases.

READING

These major and modal compositions are written so as to provide reading experiences in all keys while emphasizing the need for crossing over the thumb or passing the thumb under to accommodate pitches beyond a pentachord. Step patterns WITHIN phrases facilitate crossings. It is advisable to play the melody alone before reading the complete composition.

FINGERING

The ideal place on the keyboard to cross-over or pass the thumb under the hand is when the pitches require movement from a black to a white or a white to a black key. The cross-over occurs most naturally when going from a white to black key, and the pass-under occurs when going from a black to a white key. When a step pattern is located in which a crossing is appropriate to accommodate the pitches required, the fingers used for crossing should be written in the score. For example:

INVERSIONS OF TRIADS

French

Brackets [ ] are indicated in the score of the first few compositions to show where crossings are required.

Change of hand position between phrases and stretches within phrases are still required in the performance of this material.

TRANSPOSING

Extending the ability to think within any key center by transposing these piano pieces continues. It is important to select key centers now which approximate as much as possible the same keyboard topography as the original key center—relationship of black to white keys—so as to maintain with relative ease the same fingering on transposition. (See Harmonizing.)

IMPROVISING

Patterns in the compositions are to be completed as before. The student continues to improvise to verse using these patterns as well as traditional settings for accompaniments. (See Harmonizing.)

HARMONIZING

Harmonizing the major and minor melodies that are set in a contemporary or contrapuntal manner continues. Transposing these same traditional settings as well as those set to improvised melodies to the verse in Resource Materials remains important for student progress.

MAJOR—MINOR

1

British

INVERSIONS OF TRIADS

2

French

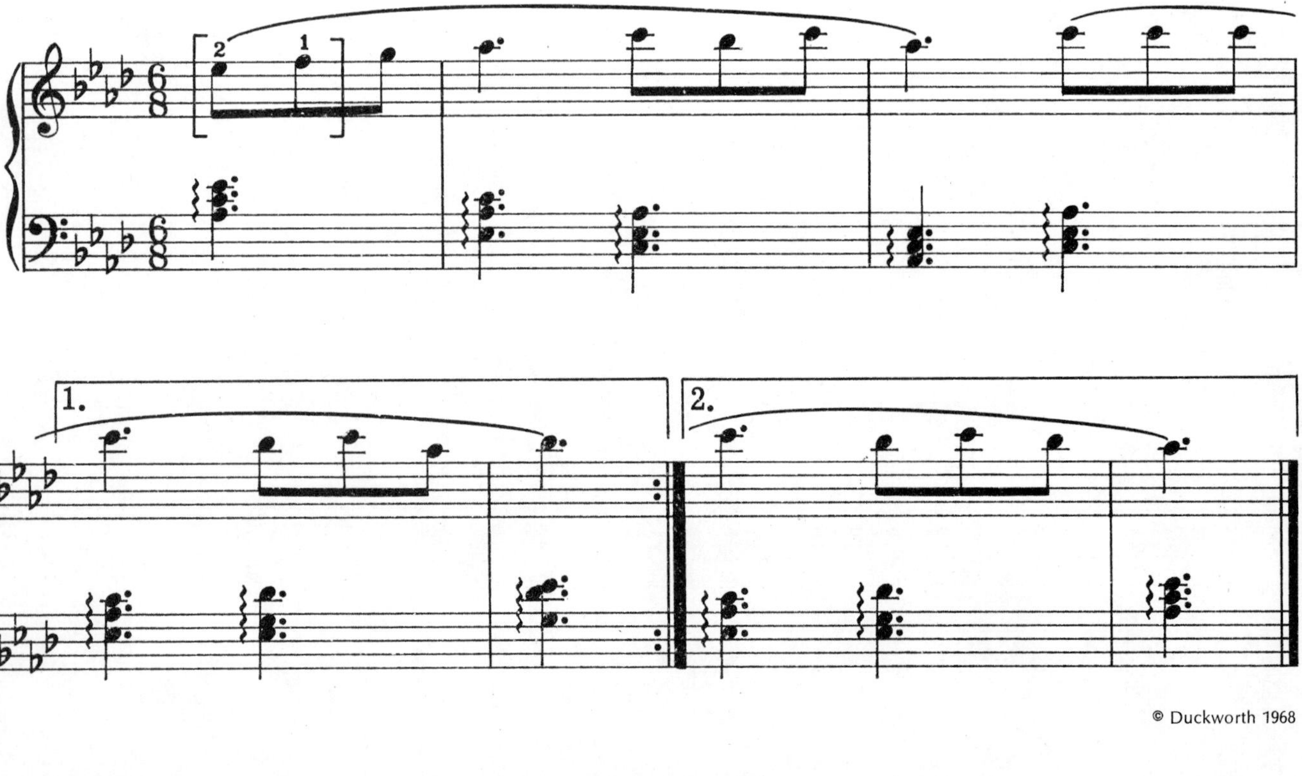

FOURTHS AND FIFTHS

3

Serbian

SUPERTONIC

4

German

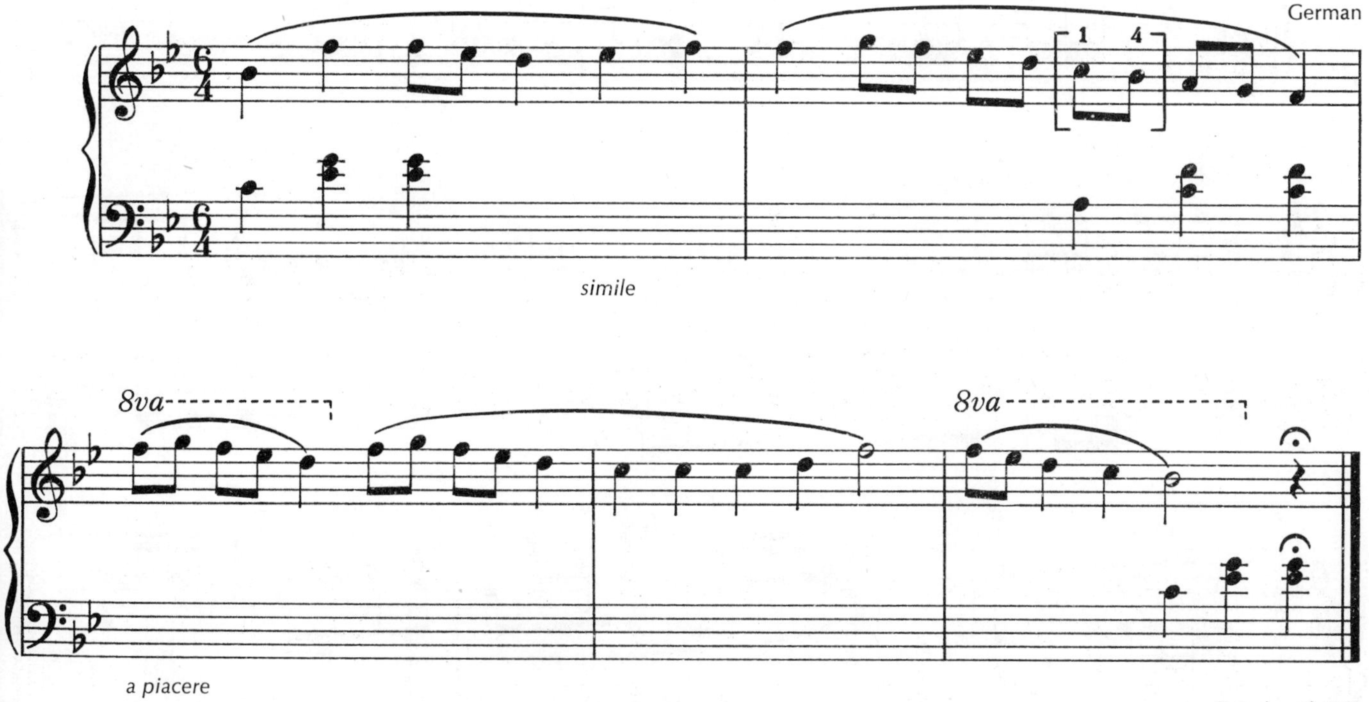

CHORDS IN FOURTHS

5

Croatian

REPEATED PITCHES

6

Czechoslovakian

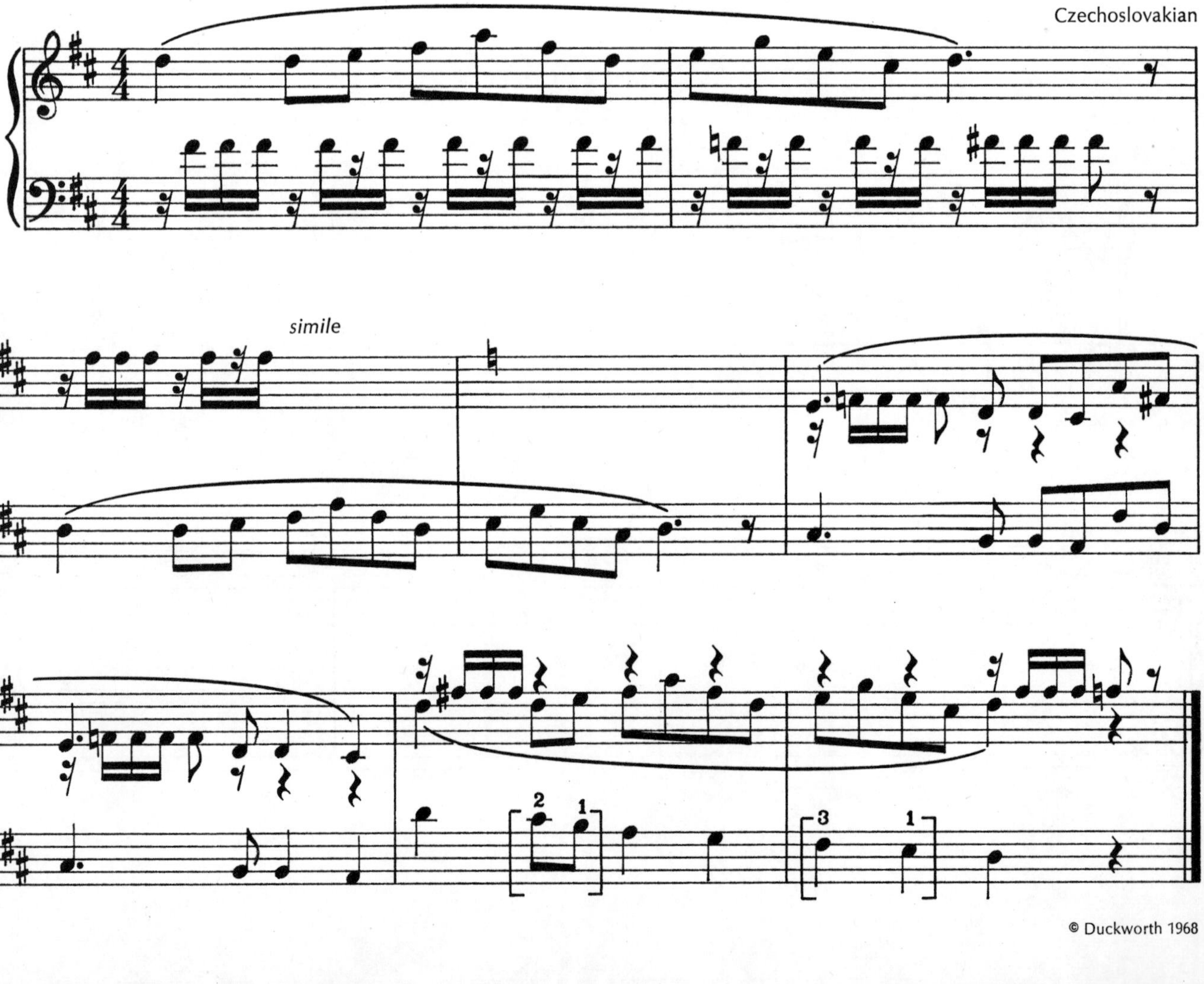

FIRST INVERSION TRIADS

7

Russian

CHORD SEQUENCE IN SECOND INVERSION

8

Dutch

CONTRARY MOTION

9

British

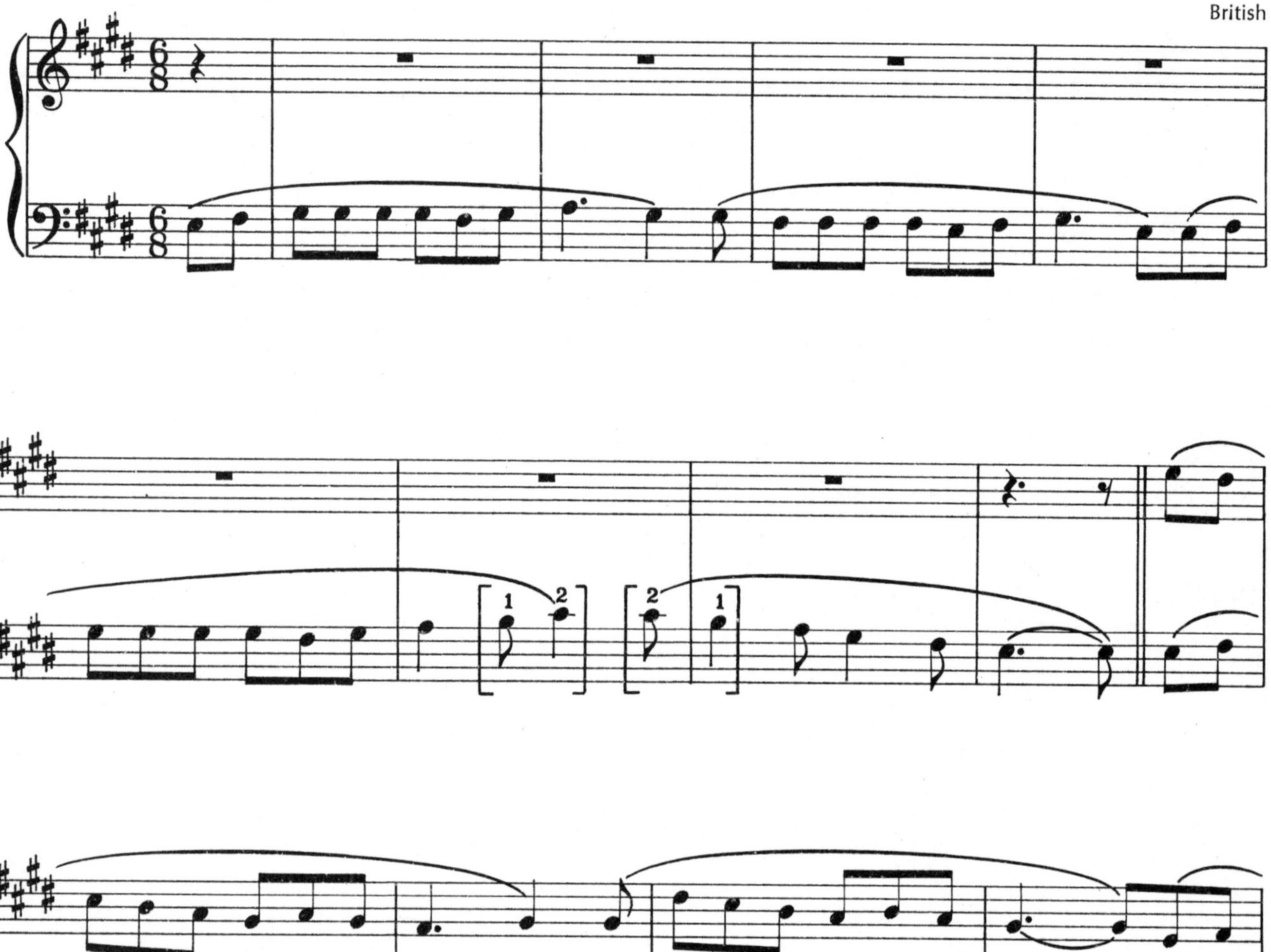

PARALLEL MOTION

10

A

B

IMITATION

11

Polish

MUSIC BOX

12

French

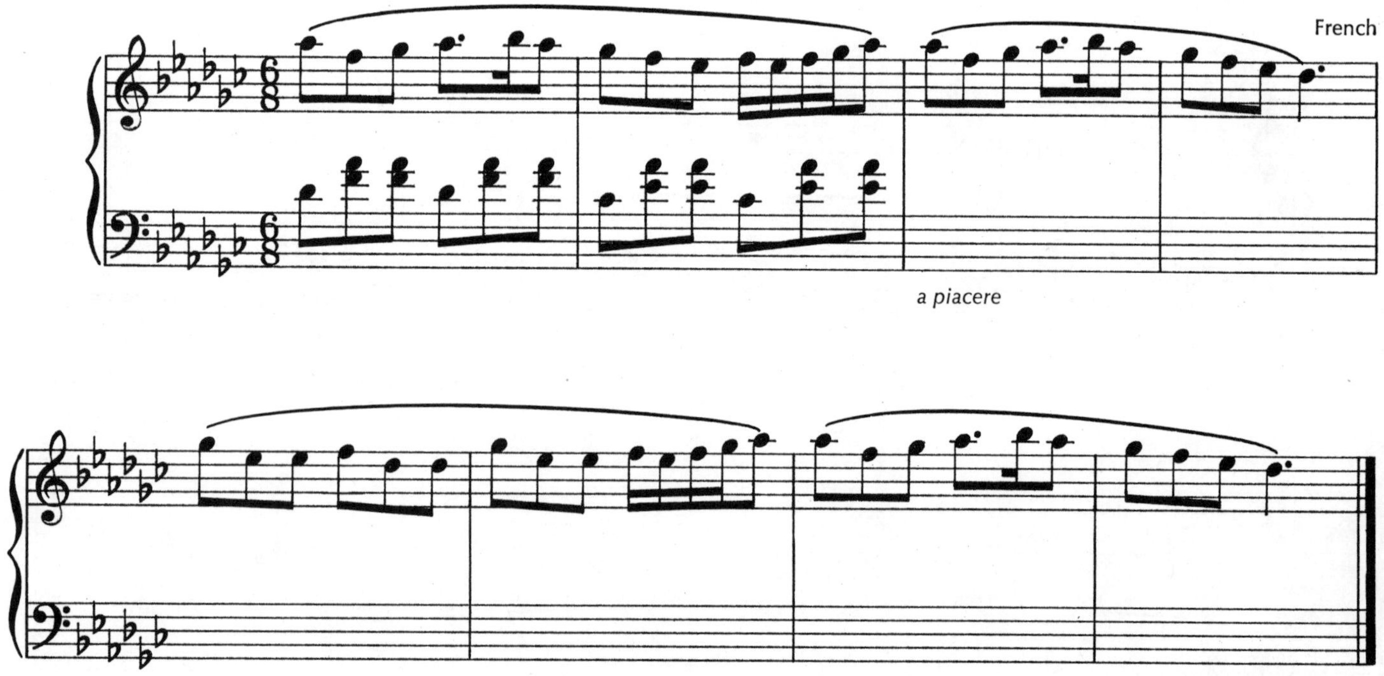

PERFECT FIFTHS

13

French

TRIADS WITH SECONDS

14

Swedish

ALBERTI BASS

15

Polish

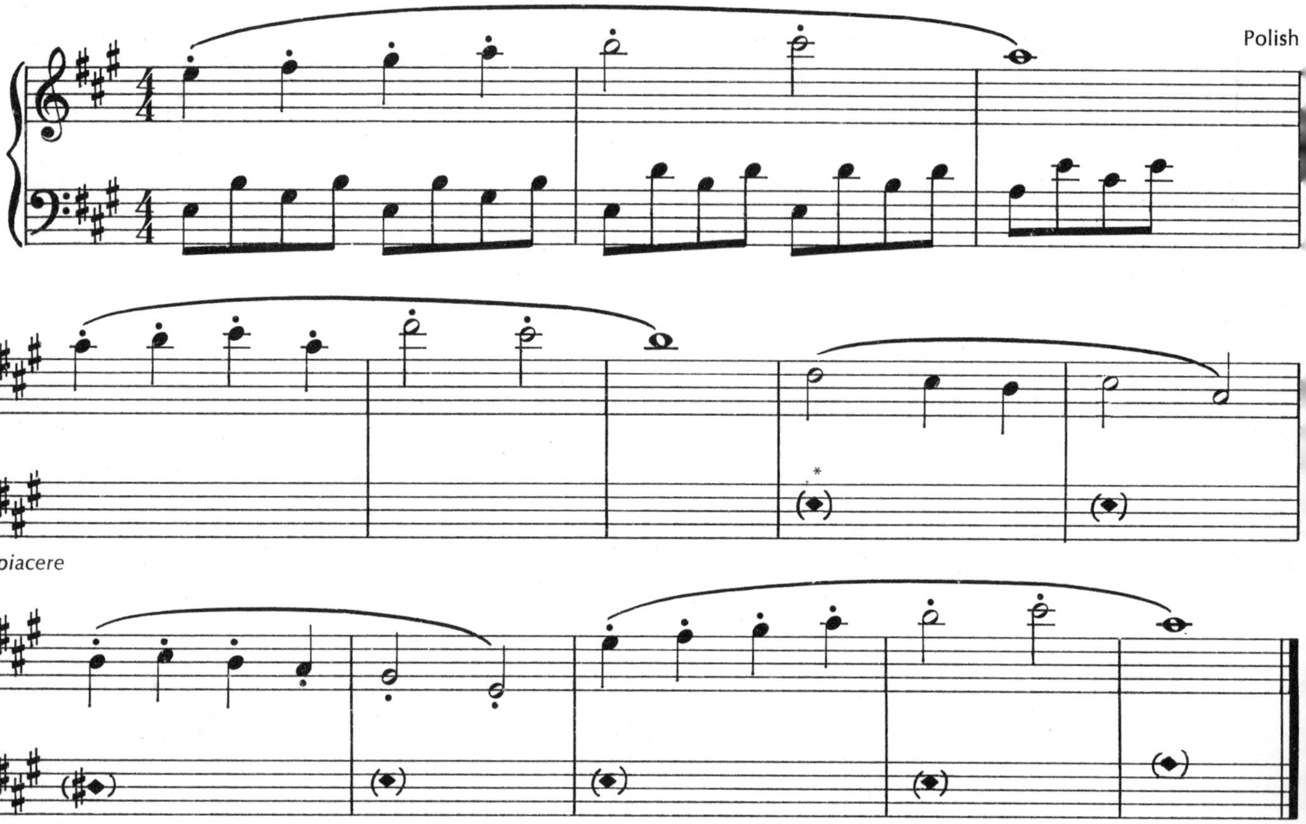

*These notes in parentheses are only suggestions for a bass line.

SCALE PATTERNS

16

Luxembourgian

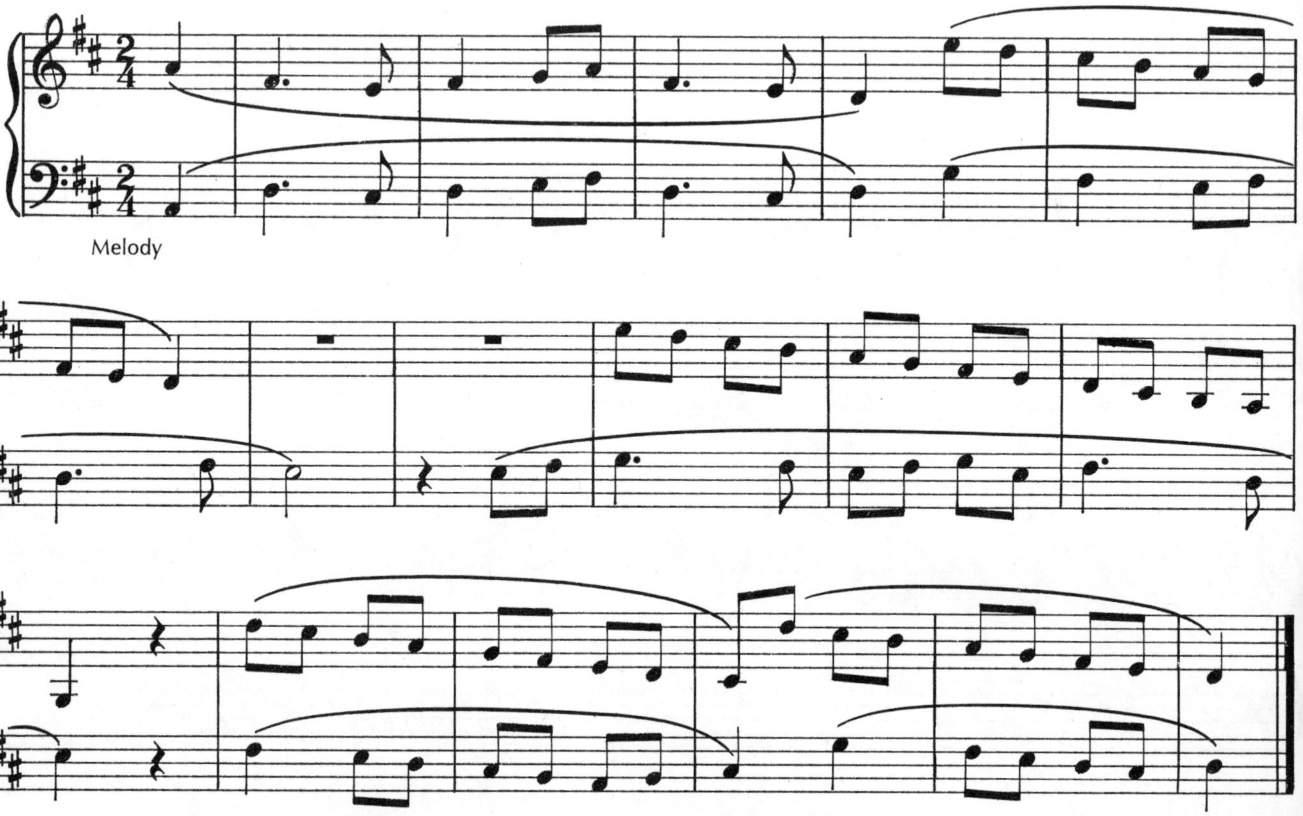

1

German

PHRYGIAN

2

Greek

REPEATED PATTERN

3

A

Basque

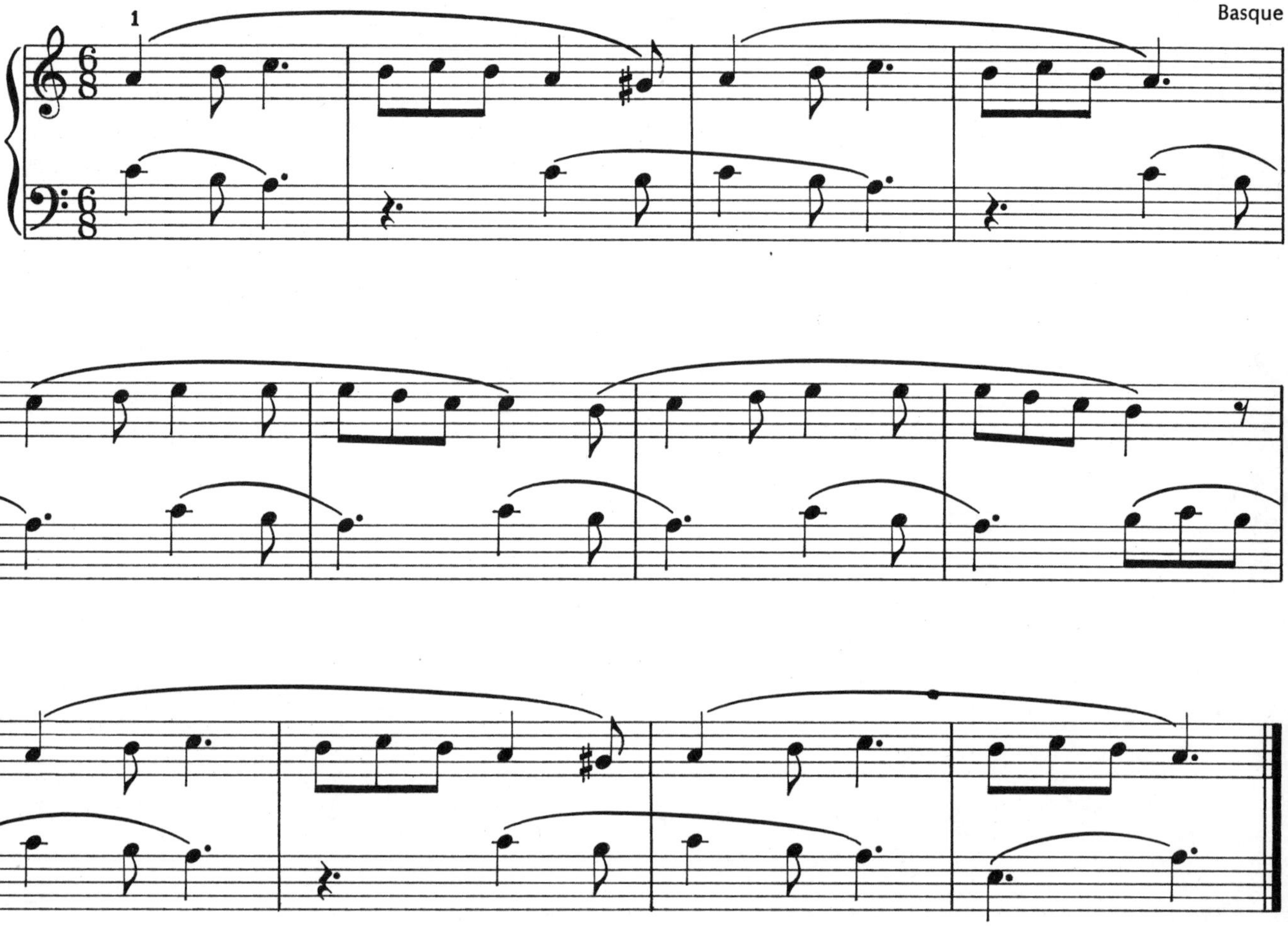

B

British

SUPERTONIC AND MEDIANT

4

Russian

MINOR SECONDS

5

British

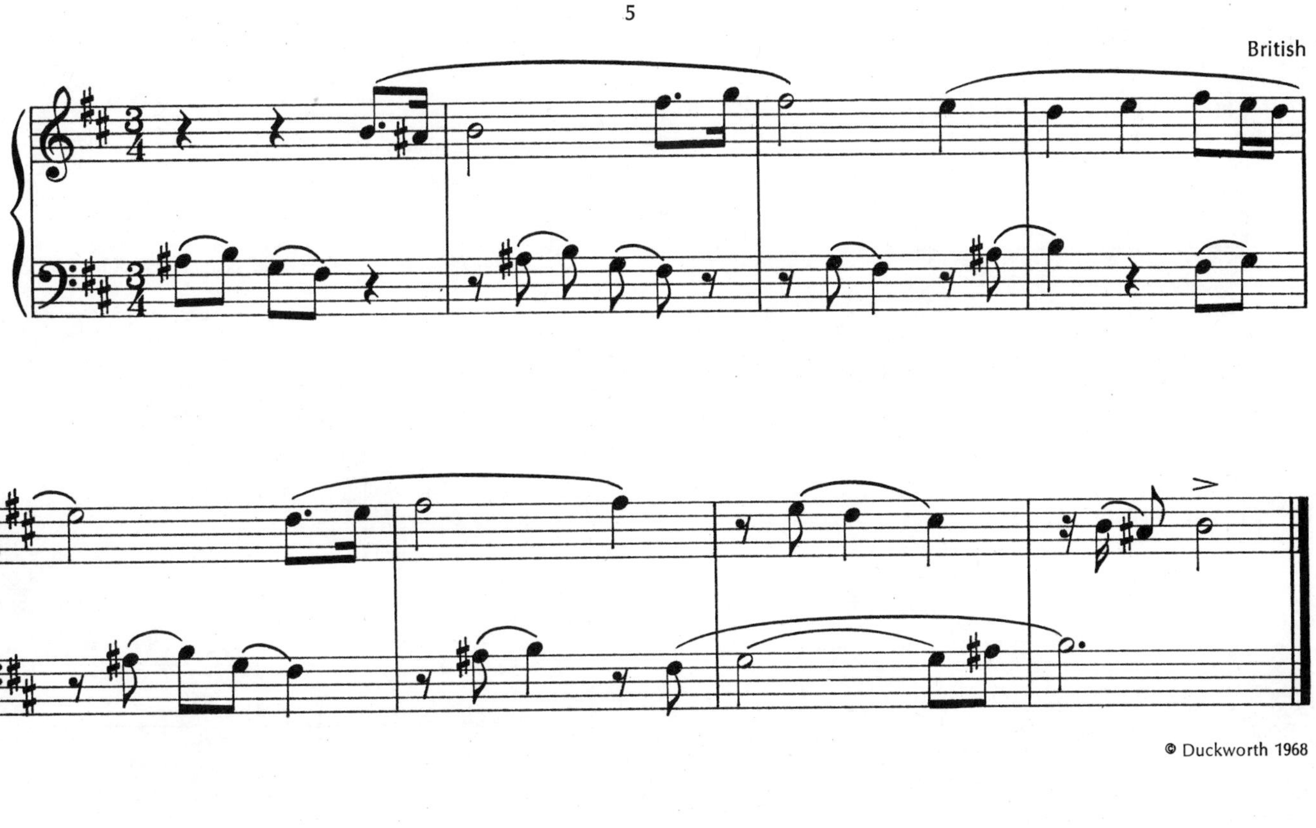

BROKEN TRIADS

6

British

OSTINATO

7

Finnish

REPEATED PATTERN

8a

German

REPEATED PATTERNS

8b

Russian

a piacere

SONATINE (Duet)

10

SECONDO

D. G. Türk

SONATINE (Duet)

10

PRIMO

D. G. Türk

REIGEN MIT ZWEI ZWISCHENSPIELEN (Duet)

11

SECONDO

D. G. Türk

REIGEN MIT ZWEI ZWISCHENSPIELEN (Duet)

11

PRIMO

Moderato e con dolcezza

D. G. Türk

Trio I

Trio II

ECCOSSAISE

9

J. Haydn

section 4.

REPERTOIRE-LIMITED RANGE

MINUET

1

J. S. Bach

Fine

Trio

MINUET

2

G. P. Telemann

MENUET

3

G. F. Handel

MINUET

4

L. Mozart

TRUMPET PIECE

5

Allegro ma non troppo

L. Mozart

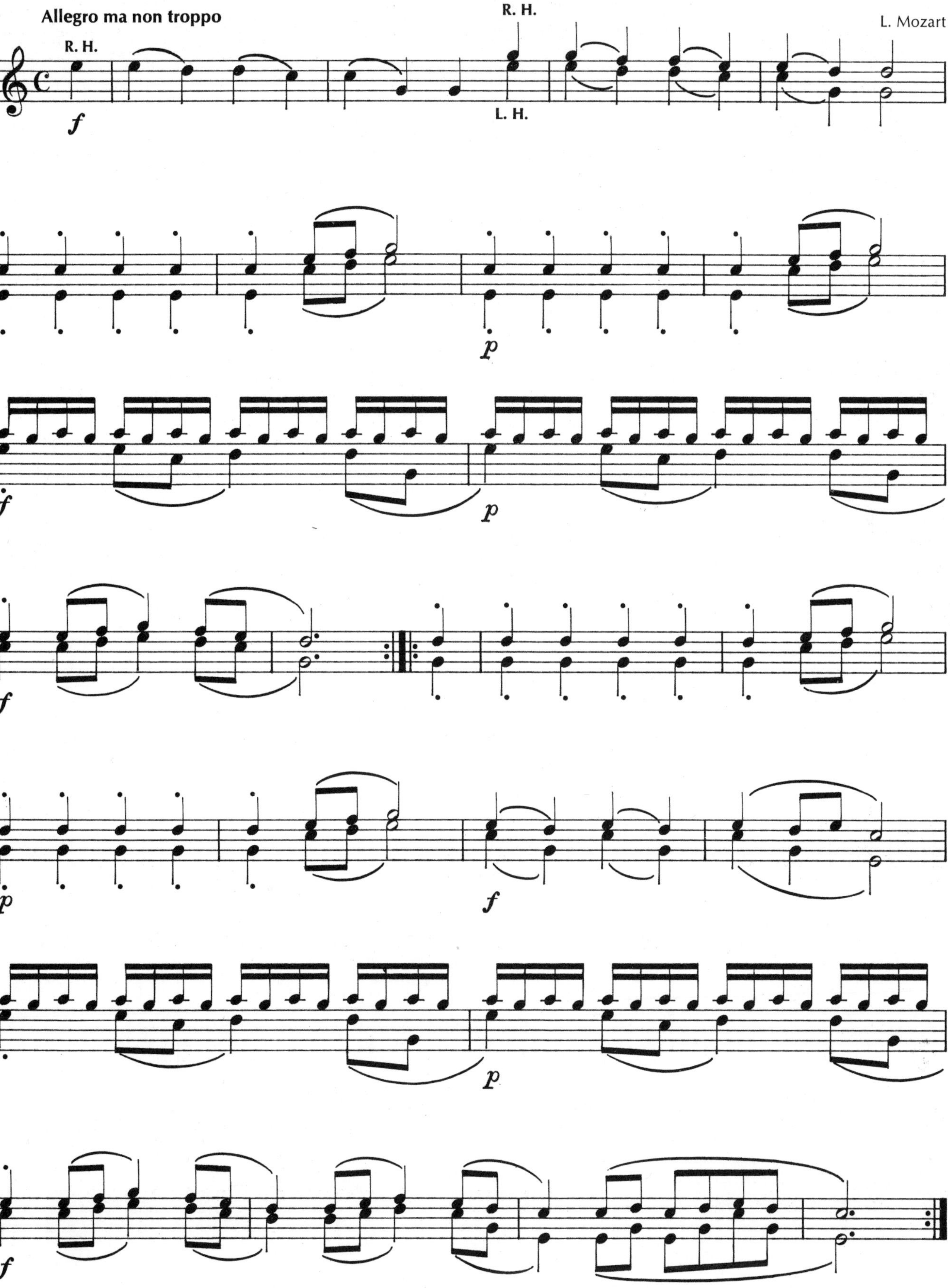

LANDLER

6

J. C. F. Bach

THE HUNT

7

Moderato D. G. Türk

ECCOSSAISE

8

Andantino F. Schubert

POLONAISE (Duet)

9

OP. 149 #14

SECONDO

A. Diabelli

POLONAISE (Duet)

9

OP. 149 #14

PRIMO

Allegretto

A. Diabelli

Trio
p
f
p
ff
sf
D. C. al Fine

Trio
p
f
p
ff
D. C. al Fine

ANDANTE (Duet)

10

OP. 149 #27

SECONDO

A. Diabelli

ANDANTE (Duet)

10

OP. 149 #27

PRIMO

A. Diabelli

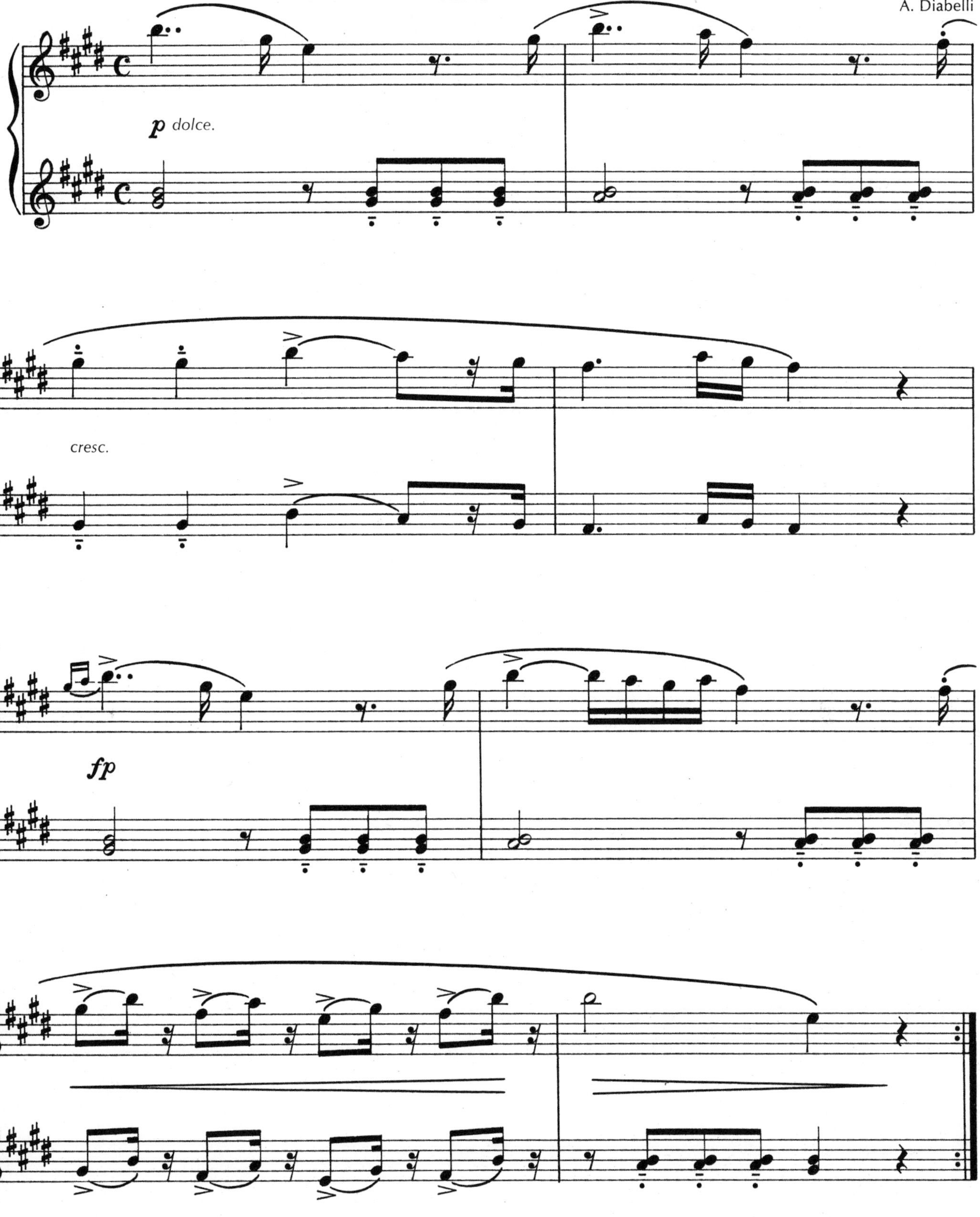

UNIT THREE

section 1.

CROSSES-UNLIMITED RANGE
Scale Playing

In this section the melodic range is unlimited. It extends the performer's understanding of his use of crossings in step patterns with phrases of wider range, thus enabling him to begin his scale playing.

READING and FINGERING

The piano pieces are written for duet performance. Although all are written with a key signature of two flats, each is written in a different mode. By reading through this material the performer realizes that the fingering for any scale depends more upon the topography of the keyboard (pattern of black and white keys) rather than the key center of the scale. Stated simply, crossing over the thumb occurs when approaching the first black key of a group and passing the thumb under occurs when leaving the last black key of a group. For example:

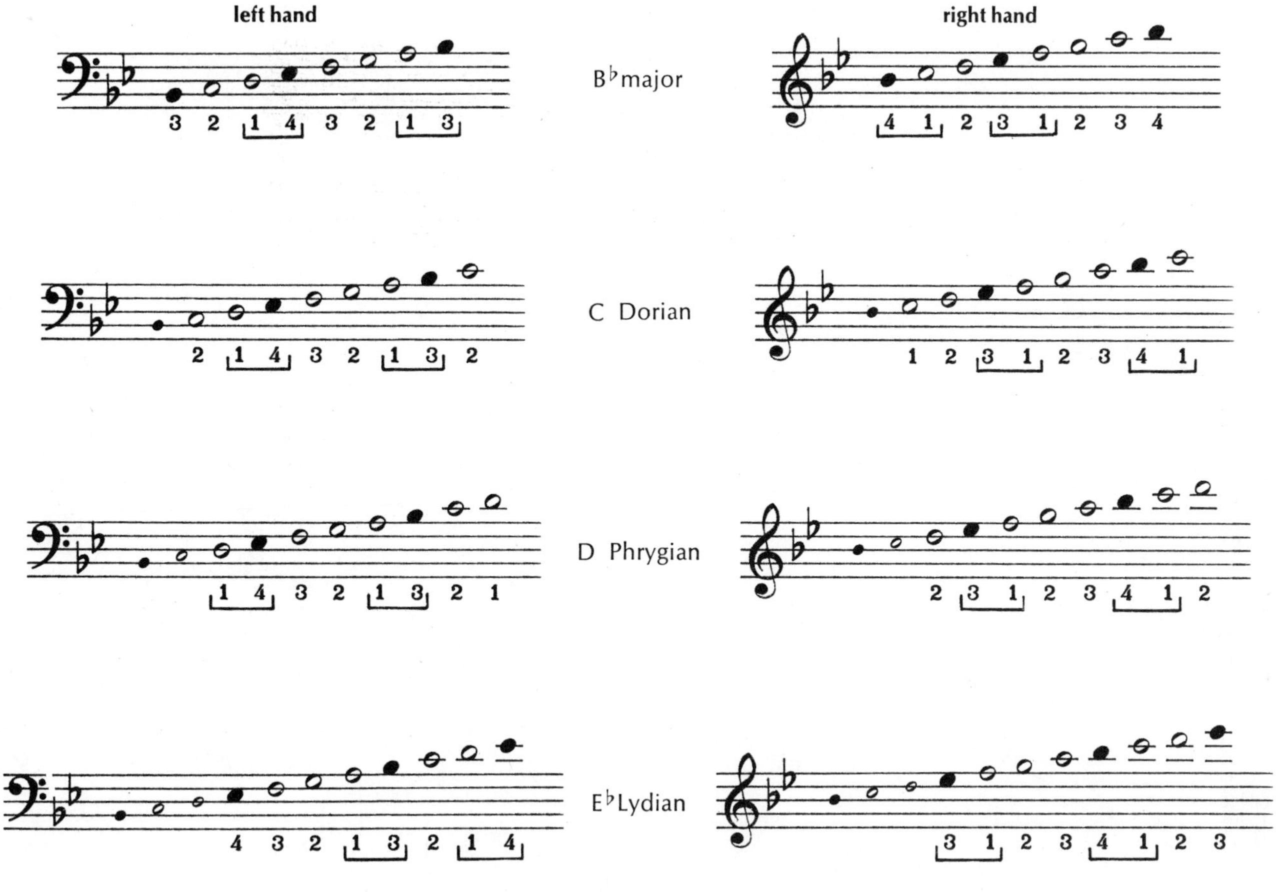

F Mixo-Lydian

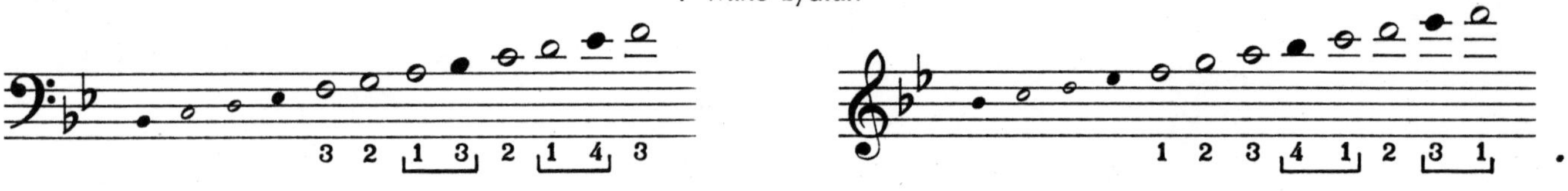

G Aeolian

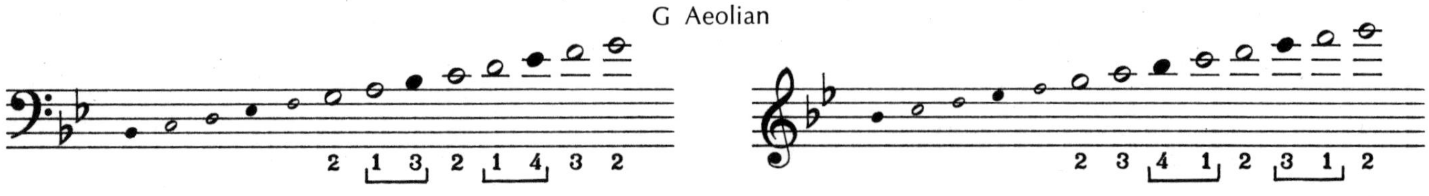

Brackets [ ] are indicated in the score to show where scale fingerings can be used.

TRANSPOSING

These piano pieces should be transposed to every key center. The fingering will have to be changed according to the keyboard topography of the new key center—the relationship of black keys to white. Organizing the scales in a given key signature should follow the transposition of each composition. Consult Resource Materials for the organization of major scales.

MAJOR SCALE

1

French

DORIAN SCALE

2

Polish

PHRYGIAN SCALE (Duet)

3

Dutch

LYDIAN SCALE (Duet)

4

British

MIXOLYDIAN SCALE (Duet)

Swedish

AEOLIAN SCALE (Duet)

6

American

ALLEGRO (Duet)

3

SECONDO

D. G. Türk

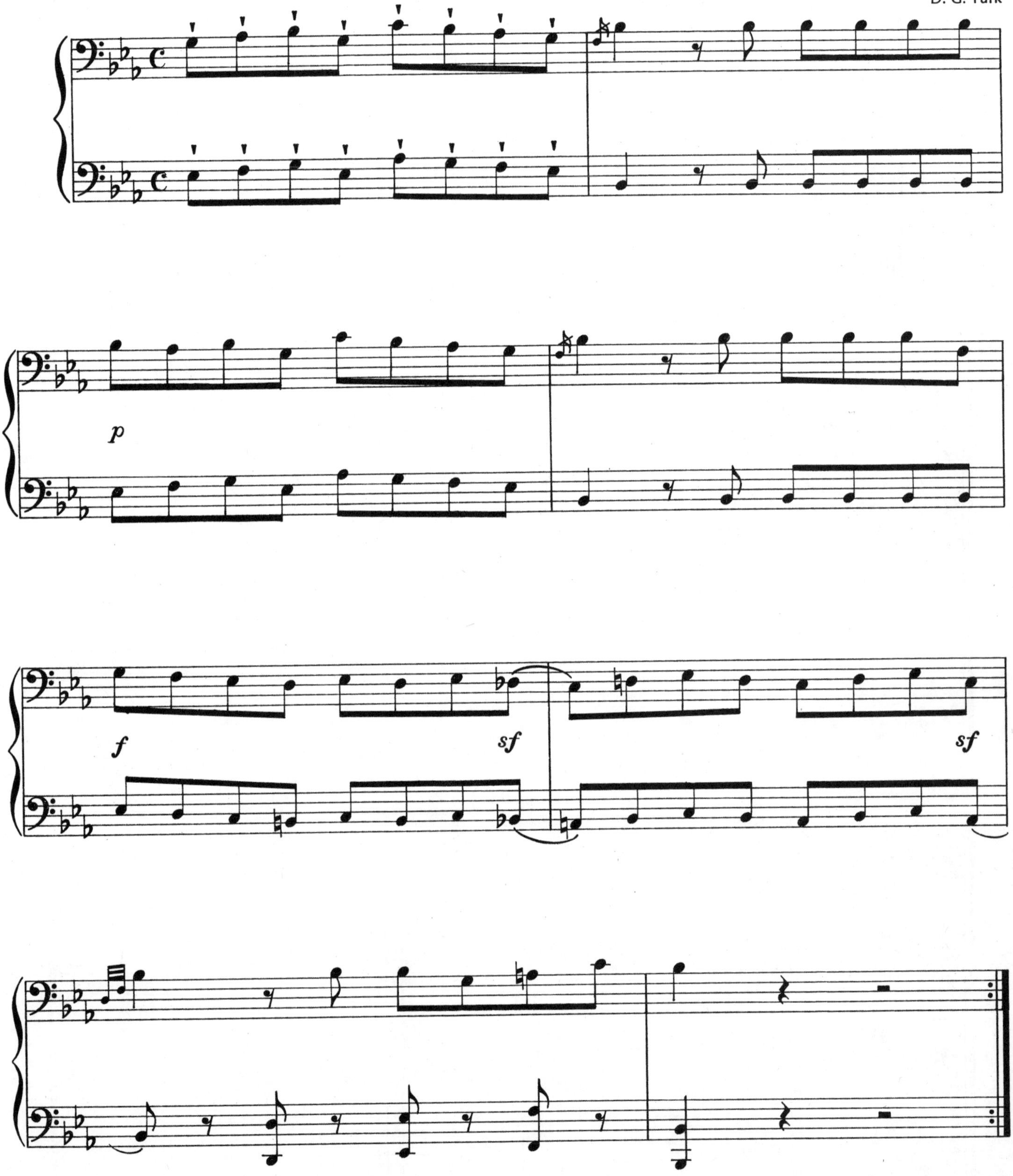

ALLEGRO (Duet)

3

PRIMO

D. G. Türk

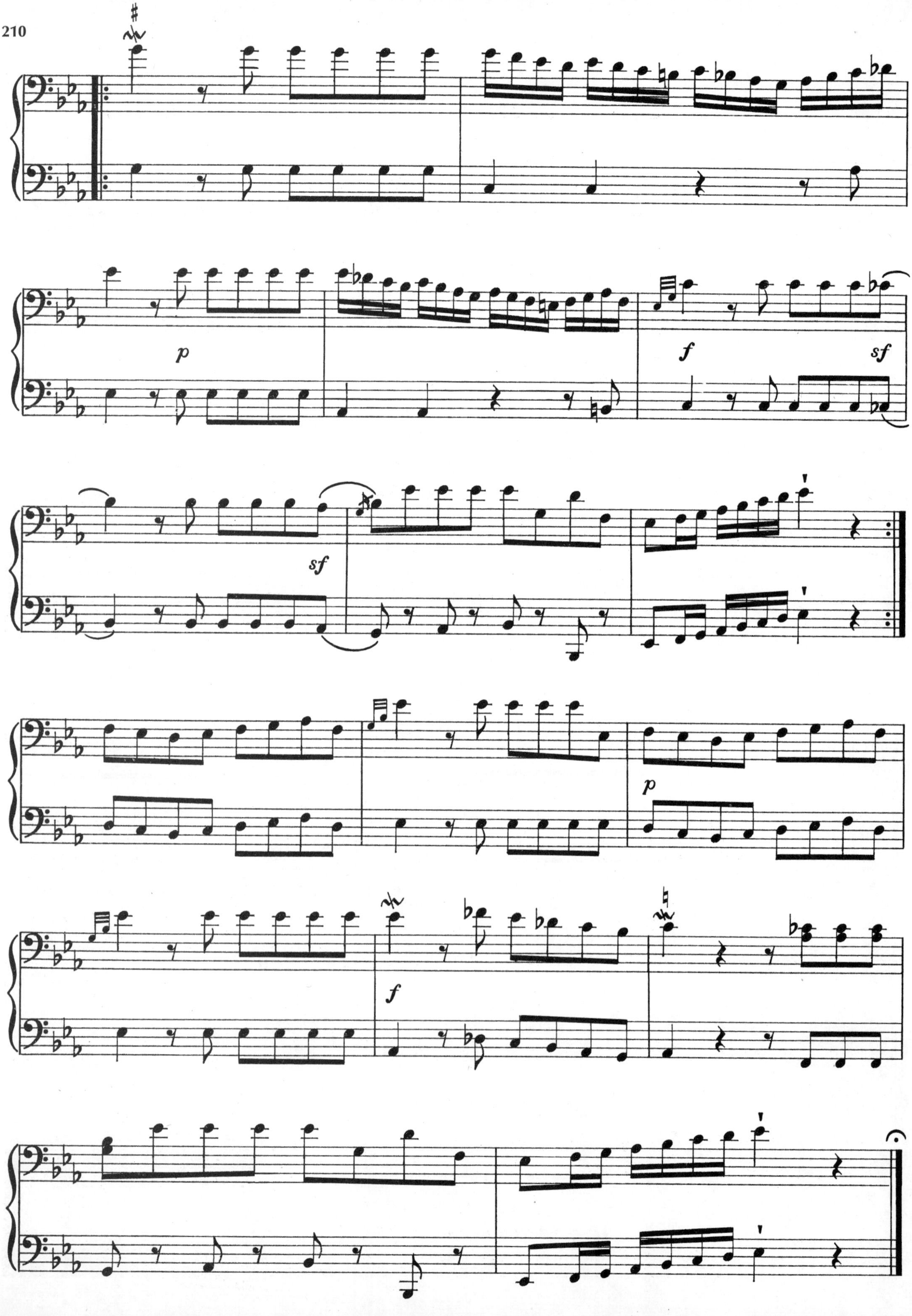
p
f
sf
sf
p
f

p
f
sf
sf
p
f

COURANTE

8

G. F. Handel

1.
2.

section 2.

CROSSES-UNLIMITED RANGE
Arpeggio Playing

In this section the melodic range is unlimited. It extends the performer's understanding of his use of crossings in skip patterns within a phrase, thus enabling him to begin his arpeggio playing.

READING and FINGERING

The topography of the keyboard remains important in skip patterns for determining the place for crossings. The concept stated for crossings in step patterns remains the same in skip patterns. Crosses and passes must occur as much as possible when leaving the last black key of a group or when approaching the first black key of a group. Brackets [ ] are indicated in the major and modal material to show where some of the crosses may occur.

TRANSPOSING

These pieces should be transposed to key centers which have approximately the same topography as the original key. Organizing triad arpeggios in three positions should result from this activity. In Resource Materials a pattern for playing all triad arpeggios in three positions is suggested. (See Harmonizing.)

IMPROVISING

Complete patterns in the reading material continues, along with improvising to verse and using these same patterns for accompaniments. (See Harmonizing.)

HARMONIZING

Harmonizing and transposing the major and minor pieces that are set in a contemporary and contrapuntal manner continue. Using these same settings for improvising to the verse in Resource Materials also continues.

CONTRARY MOTION

1

Danish

SEQUENCE IN ROOT POSITION

2A

Lithuanian

B

Swedish

SEQUENCE IN FIRST INVERSION

3

Polish

MELODY AND HARMONY COMBINED

4

German

SARABANDE (Duet)

5

Spanish

ECCOSSAISE

L. van Beethoven

CHOPIN

7

FROM CARNAVAL, OP. 9

PRELUDE

8

D. Scarlatti

section 3.

CONTRACTIONS-UNLIMITED RANGE

This section of the text emphasizes disjunct melodic lines. Until this time the performer has been primarily concerned with material that moves for some time in one direction—up or down. Since this material often changes direction with one pitch new problems result.

READING and FINGERING

Frequent changes of direction in melodic material often provide new reading-fingering problems. To accommodate these melodic lines the hand may need to be contracted. Whether the pattern is skip or step, the hand contracts—becomes smaller—by skipping more fingers than keys. A bracket [ ] in the score indicates where contractions may take place. (There will be some situations in adjunct melodic movement where contractions will also be necessary.)

TRANSPOSING

This skill remains very important.

IMPROVISING

Improvising should be pursued utilizing the new settings encountered in this material.

HARMONIZING

The harmonic structure of the major and minor material is again left to the performer to construct.

PATTERN REPEATED AND INVERTED

1

German

BROKEN TRIADS

2

British

IMITATION

3

British

ARPEGGIOS

4

A.

British

ARPEGGIOS

5

B.

German

OSTINATO

6

Hungarian

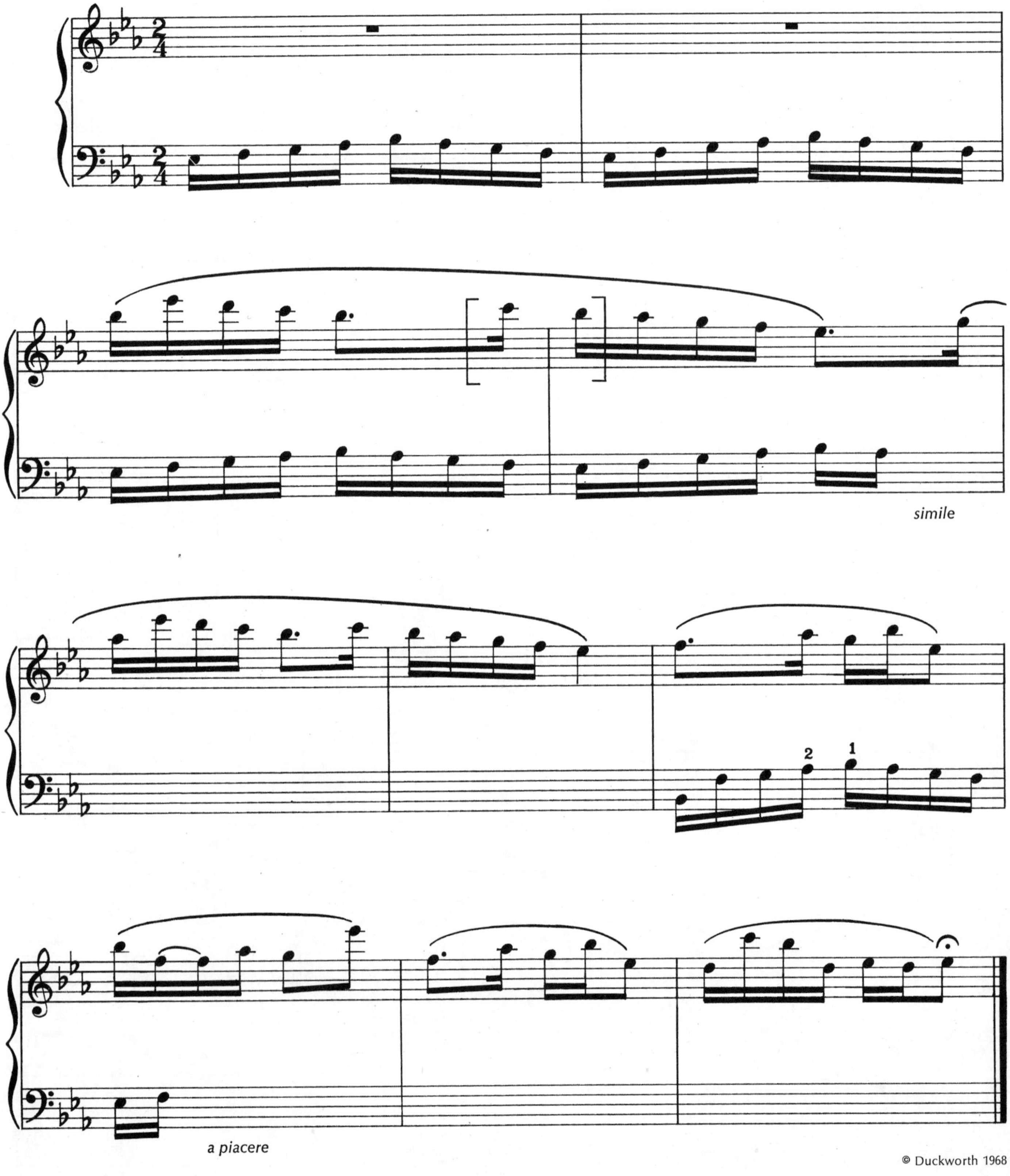

PRELUDE

7

J. S. Bach

LANDLER
8

L. van Beethoven

section 4.

REPEATED NOTES-
UNLIMITED RANGE

This section introduces the possibility of playing repeated notes by changing fingers. The author is concerned here with utilizing the repeated notes in a melody in such a way as to "get more fingers" for completing a phrase. His concern is not to change fingers to facilitate the articulation of repeated notes.

READING and FINGERING

Within a phrase repeated notes often occur upon which the performer can change fingers in order to obtain suffcient fingers to complete a given phrase. A bracket [ ] in the score indicates where the performer may accomplish this kind of fingering.

TRANSPOSING

This skill remains very important.

IMPROVISING

Improvising should be pursued utilizing the new settings encountered in this material.

HARMONIZING

The harmonic structure of the major and minor material should be harmonized by the performer in the styles he wishes.

BAGPIES IN DORIAN

1

French

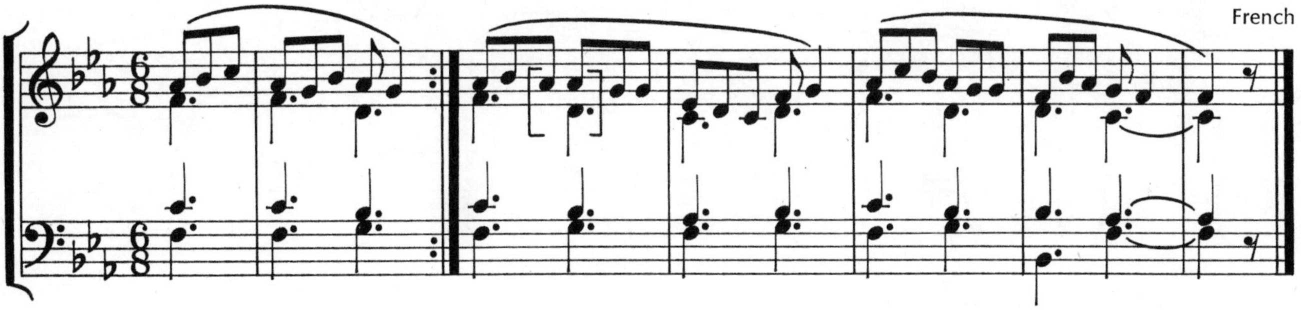

REPEATED PATTERNS

2

Slovakian

ECHO

3

German

PARALLEL MOTION AND IMITATION

4

Greek

TRIADS OUTLINED

5

German

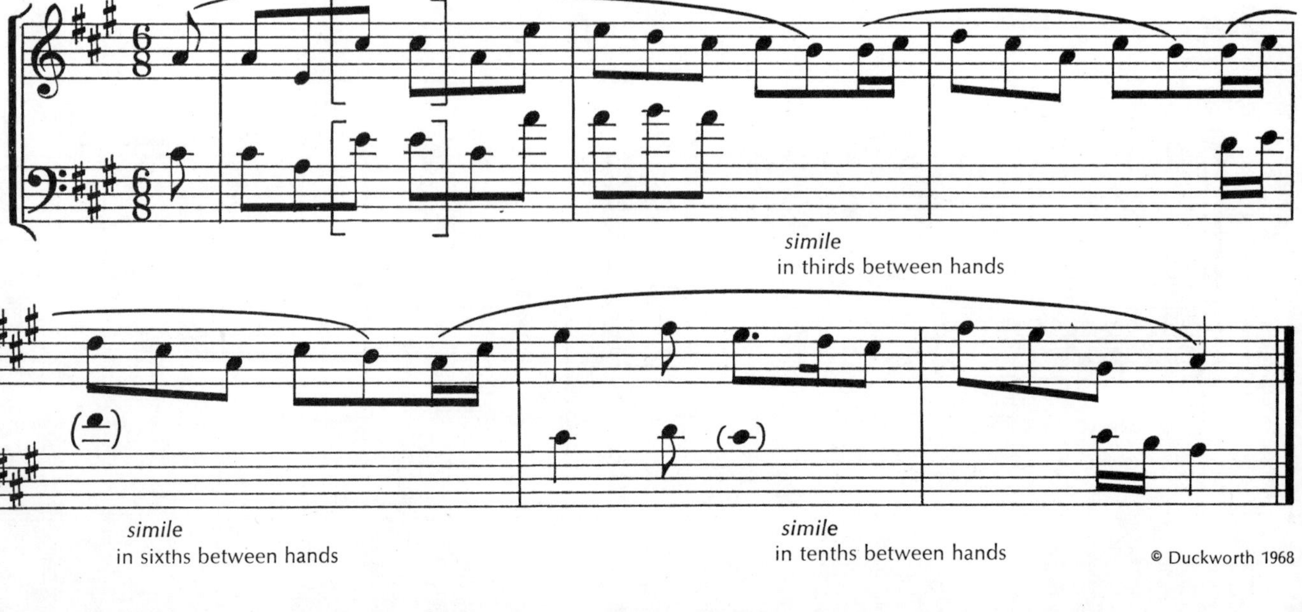

IMITATION

6

Russian

SARABANDE

7

G. Handel

WALTZ

OP. 9B #3

F. Schubert

8

WALTZ

C. M. von Weber

9

section 5.

REPERTOIRE-UNLIMITED RANGE

RONDEAU

1

J. P. Rameau

D. S.
2.
D. S.

LITTLE PRELUDE

2

J. S. Bach

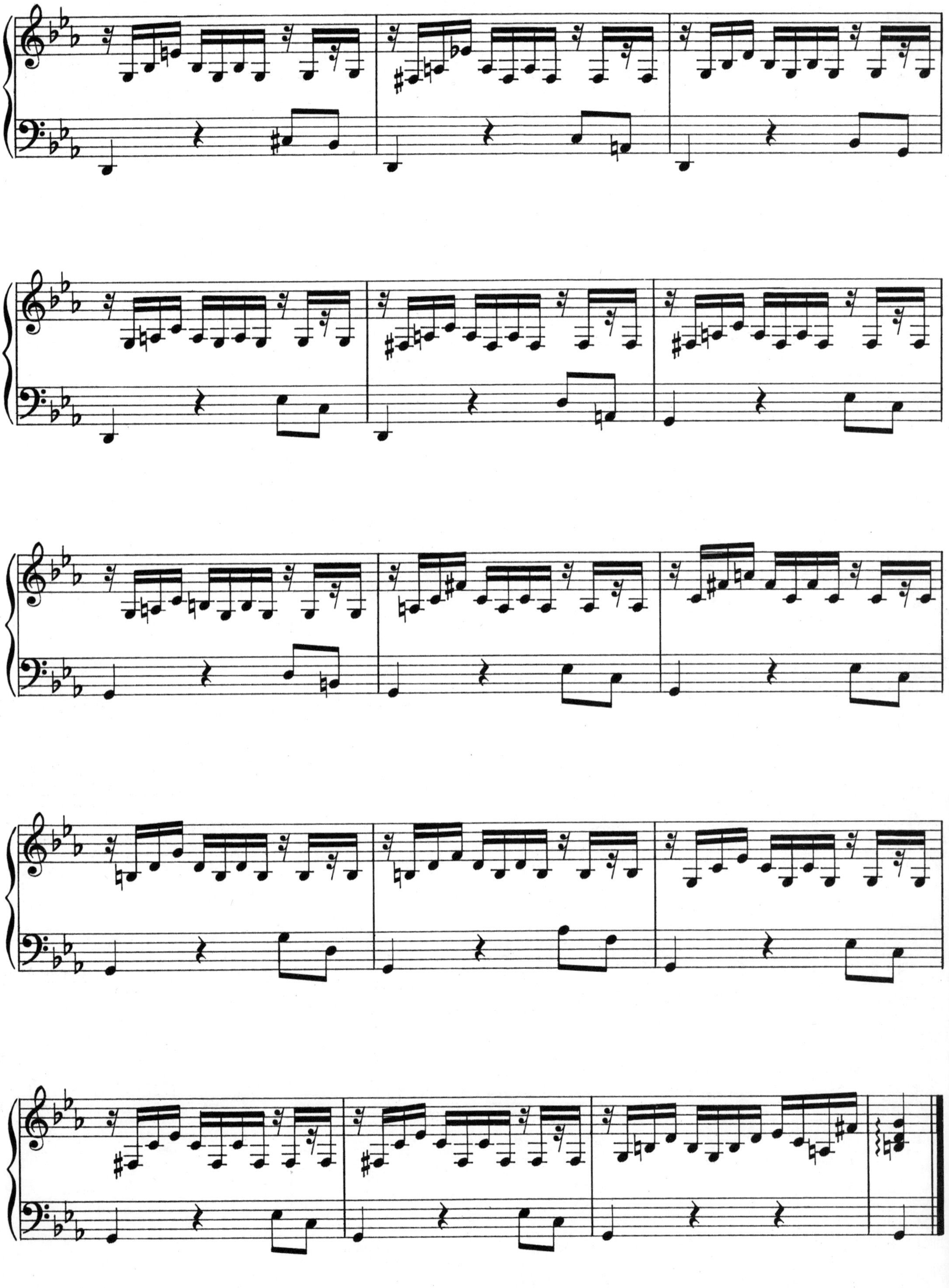

LA CHAROLAISE

3

F. Couperin

ALLEMANDE

4

L. van Beethoven

p
p
Coda
f
legato
p
f
p

ENTREE

5

L. Mozart

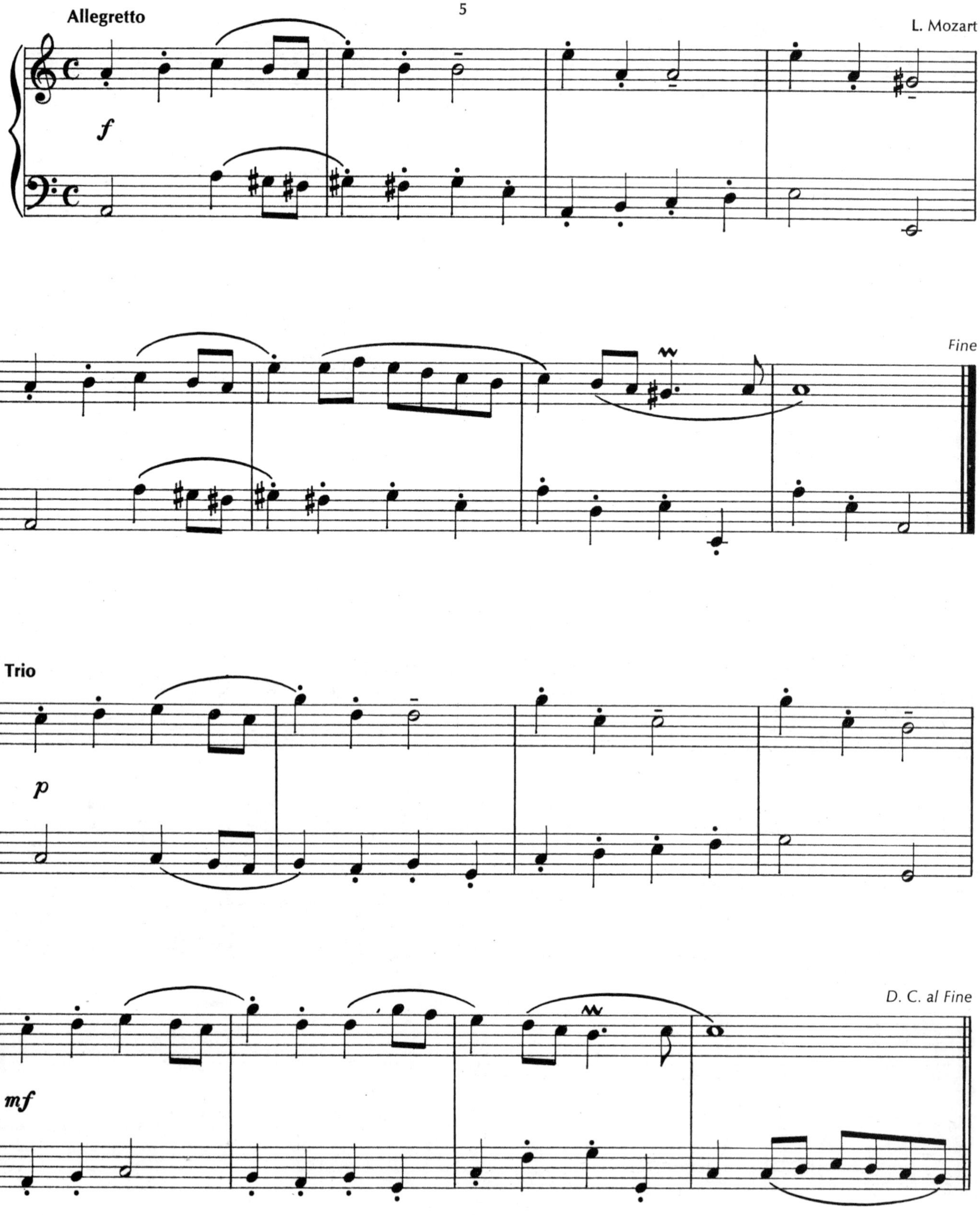

TURKISH MARCH

L. van Beethoven

WALTZ

Op. 33

7

F. Schubert

ETUDE

excerpt from Op. 25, #9

F. Chopin

PRELUDE

excerpt from Op. 28, #15

F. Chopin

ALLEGRETTO

10

F. Schubert

cresc.
f
ff
fz
fz
1
p
rit.
pp
p
a tempo
f
ff
p
rit
pp

WALTZ (Duet)

Op. 39, #15

11

SECONDO

J. Brahms

WALTZ (Duet)

Op. 39, #15

11

PRIMO

J. Brahms

ALLEMANDE

C. M. von Weber

RESOURCE MATERIALS

VERSE FOR IMPROVISING

In improvising songs, the performer must first determine where the accented syllables occur in the words of the poem. Recite some poetry rhythmically, exaggerating or emphasizing the stressed syllables. This emphasis on accents is called scanning. The accents are illustrated in the following example:

U - U - U - U -
Good people all, of every sort,
U - U - U - (U-)
Give ear unto my song;
U - U - U - U -
And if you find it wondrous short
U - U - U - (U-)
It can not hold you long.

Oliver Goldsmith

Scanning the words will indicate the poetic meter, which may be expressed by several different time signatures and note values. Note that two lines of the poem are generally required to complete a thought that would correspond to a phrase in music, commonly four measures in length. Note also that two four-measure phrases are required here to express the complete thought.

Scanning for accents: (U= weak, - = strong)

GOOD PEOPLE—Oliver Goldsmith

U - U - U - U
Good people all of every sort.

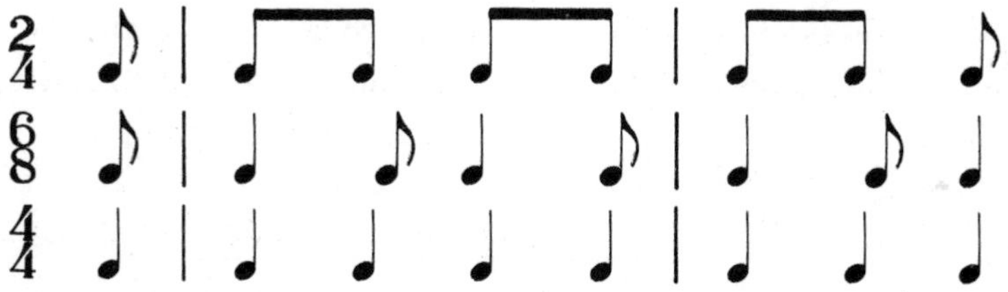

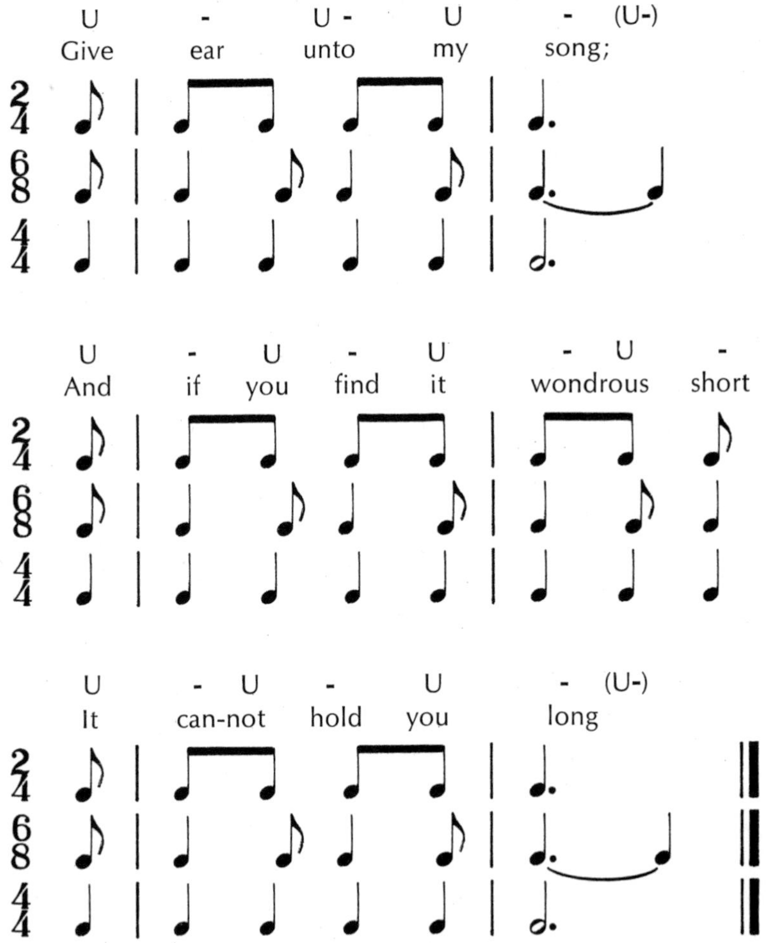

Experiment with melodies in the bass as well as in the upper register. Improvise in all keys, all modes. Apply understandings regarding range and fingering concepts to improvisations.

Probably the simplest melody is one made up entirely of chord skips, but some scale progressions and repeated tones are usually necessary for variety and balance. Experiment with various kinds of melodic progressions until this balance is achieved. The ear is the final arbiter.

After melodic improvisation is achieved with some ease, isolate the settings encountered in the text by selecting appropriate ones to complete the improvised compositions.

INCHAPE ROCK Robert Southey

No stir in the air, no stir in the sea,
The ship was still as she could be;
Her sails from heaven received no
motion;
Her keel was steady in the ocean.

JOHN GILPIN William Cowper

John Gilpin was a citizen
Of credit and renown
A train-band Captain eke was he
Of famous London town.

COLOR Larry E. Lawrence

A cloud outlined in silver,
Against the purple hill,
Reflecting blue-green shadows
Upon the valley still.

BLOW, BUGLE, BLOW
Alfred, Lord Tennyson

The splendor falls on castle walls
And snowy summits old in story:
The long light shakes across the
lakes
And the wild cataract leaps in
glory.

AUTUMN Emily Dickinson

The morns are meeker than they
were,
The nuts are getting brown;
The berry's cheek is plumper
The rose is out of town.

Vary the time signatures, choosing any which will make a normal four-measure phrase. Experiment by ending the last line of the poem with an evaded cadence and complete it by representing all or part of the line.

THE SEA GYPSY Richard Hovey

I am fevered with the sunset,
I am fretful with the bay,
For the wander-thirst is on me
And my soul is in Cathay.

THE DAY IS DONE
Henry W. Longfellow

The day is done, and the darkness
Falls from the wings of night,
As a feather is wafted downward
From an eagle in his flight.

ODE Arthur O'Shaughnessy

We are the music-makers
And we are the dreamers of
dreams,
Wandering by lone sea-breaders,
And sitting by desolate streams.

WHO HAS SEEN THE WIND
Christina Rossetti

Who has seen the wind?
Neither you nor I:
But when the trees bow down
their heads,
The wind is passing by.

THE REVEILLE—Brete Harte

Hark, I hear the tramp of
thousands,
And of armed men the hum:
Lo, a nation's hosts have gathered
Pound the quick alarming
drum.

NIGHT William Blake

The sun descending in the west,
The evening star does shine;
The birds are silent in their nest,
And I must seek for mine.

ROMANY Helena F. Schleich

The gypsy souls of you and me
Follow the roads together,
Over the hills and far away
In fair and stormy weather.

Experiment with any new time signatures such as $\frac{3}{8}$ $\frac{5}{8}$ $\frac{7}{8}$ within a phrase. Mix these time signatures with the more common ones.

HOW SHOULD I YOUR TRUE LOVE KNOW
from Shakespeare's Hamlet

How I should I your true love
know
From another one?
By his cockle hat and staff
And his sandal shoon.
He is dead and gone, lady,
He is dead and gone;
At his head a grass-green turf,
At his heels a stone.

THE VOICE OF THE SEA
T. B. Aldrich

In the hush of the autumn night
I hear the voice of the sea,
In the hush of the autumn night
It seem to say to me—
Mine are the winds above
Mine are the caves below,
Mine are the dead of yesterday
And the dead of long ago.

RIDDLES nursery rhyme

As I was going to St. Ives,
I met a man with seven wives,
Every wife had seven sacks,
Every sack had seven cats,
Every cat had seven kits,
Kits, cats, sacks, and wives,
How many were going to St. Ives?

Experiment with form. The form would depend on the number of stanzas in the poem: Two stanzas suggesting the A-B, and three stanzas the A-B-A- form.

TINK-A-TINK
William Makepeace Thackeray

Tink-a-tink, tink-a-tink,
By the light of the star,
On the blue river's brink,
I heard a guitar.

I heard a guitar,
On the blue water clear
And knew by its music
That Selim was near.

Tink-a-tink, tink-a-tink,
How the soft music swells,
And I hear the soft clink
Of the minaret bells.

THE THROSTLE
Alfred, Lord Tennyson

"Summer is coming, summer is
coming,
I know it, I know it, I know It,
Light again, leaf again, life again,
love again,
Yes, my wild little Poet.

"Love again, song again, nest
again, young again,
Never a prophet so crazy.
And hardly a daisy as yet, little
friend,
See, there is hardly a daisy.

WINDY NIGHTS
Robert Louis Stevenson

Whenever the moon and stars are
set,
Whenever the wind is high
All night long in the dark and wet,
A man goes riding by.
Late in the night when the fires
are out
Why does he gallop and gallop
about?

Whenever the trees are crying
aloud,
And the ships are tossed at sea,
By, on the highway, low and loud,
By at the gallop goes he.
By at the gallop he goes, and then
By he comes back at the gallop
again.

BLOW, BUGLE, BLOW
Alfred, Lord Tennyson

The splendor falls on castle walls
And snowy summits old in
story:
The long light shakes across the
lakes,
And the wild cataract leaps in
glory.
Blow, bugle, blow, set the wild
echoes flying,
Blow, bugle; answer, echoes,
dying, dying, dying.

Experiment with phrase lengths that are shorter or longer than four measures.

MARCH **William Cullen Bryant**

The stormy March is come at last,
With wind, and cloud, and
changing skies
I hear the rushing of the blast
That through the snowy valley
flies.

Then sing aloud the gushing rills
In joy that they again are free,
And brightly leaping down the
hills
Renew their journey to the sea.

THE FAIRY FOLK
William Allingham

Upon the airy mountain
Down the rushy glen,
We daren't go a-hunting
For fear of little men:
Wee fold, good folk,
Trooping all together
Green jacket, red cap,
And white owl's feather.

THE MERMAID
Alfred, Lord Tennyson

Who would be
A mermaid fair
Singing alone
Combing her hair
Under the sea
In a golden curl
With a comb of pearl,
On a throne.

Who would be
A mermaid bold,
Sitting alone,
Singing alone
Under the sea,
With a crown of gold,
On a throne?

KEYBOARD SEQUENCES

PRIMARY TRIADS *(Play also in minor)*

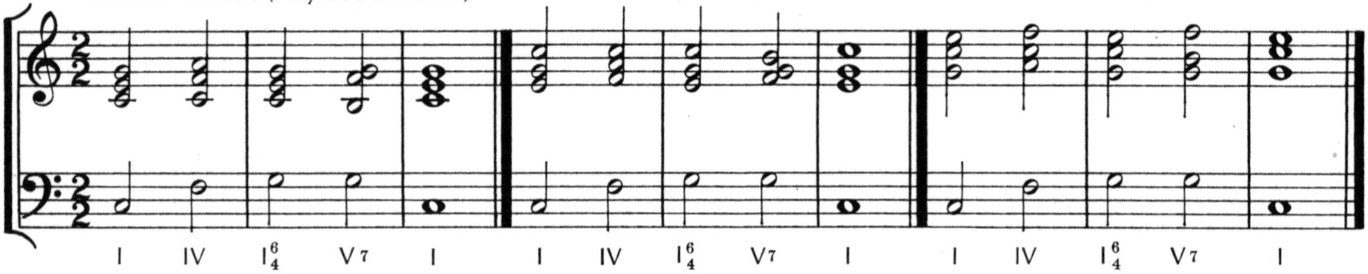

SECONDARY DOMINANTS *(See X chords. These indicate the dominant 7th or the following chord) (Play also in minor)*

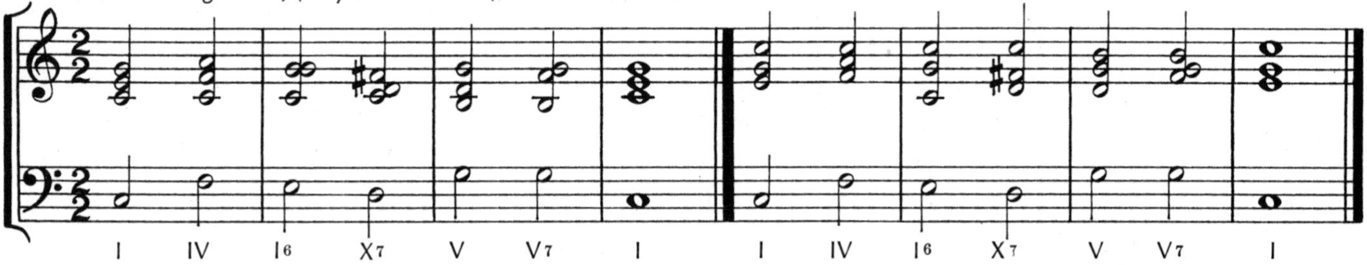

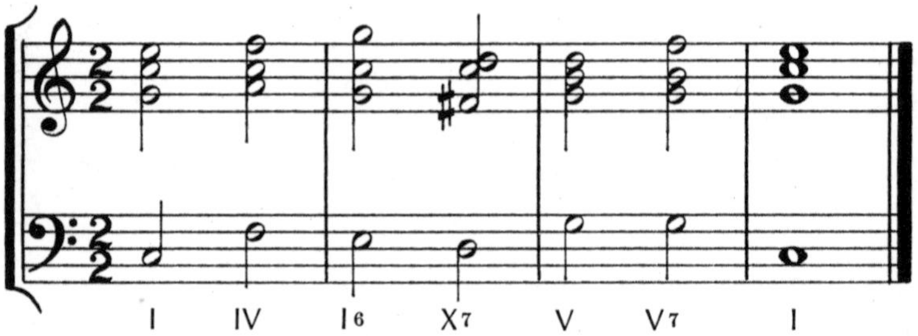

SECONDARY TRIADS *(Play also in minor)*

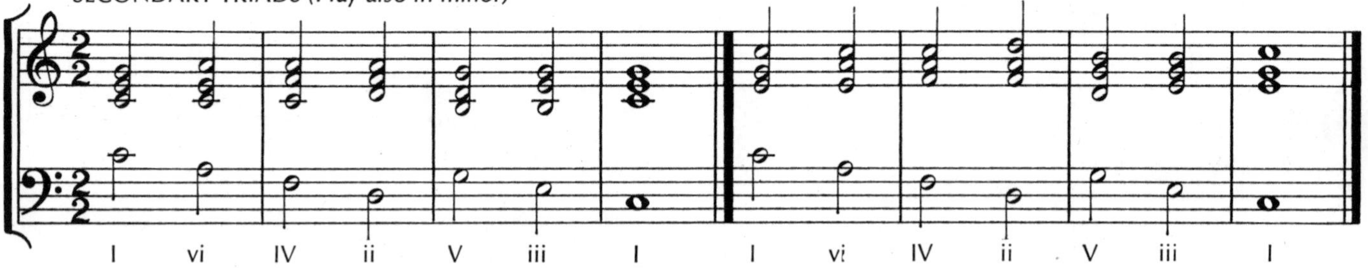

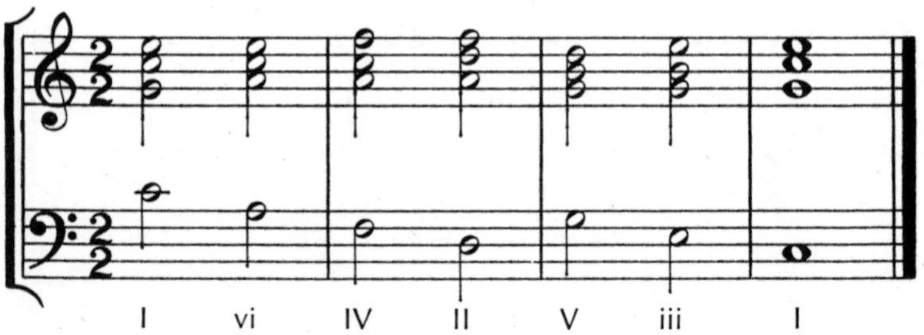

SCALE HARMONIZATION *Major*

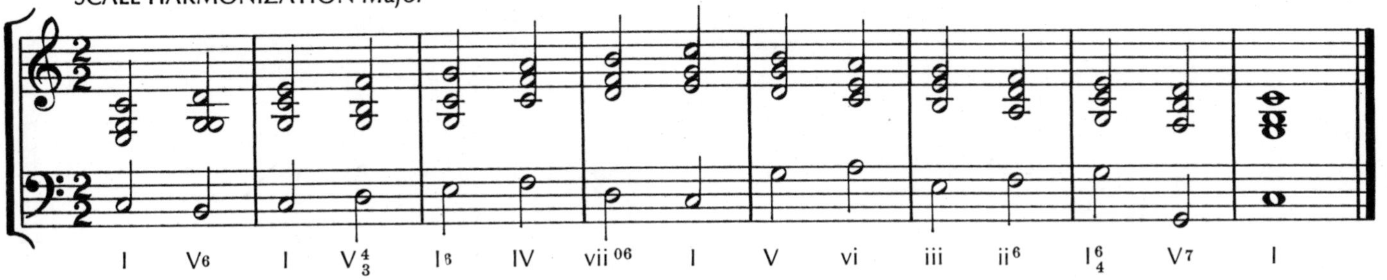

SCALE HARMONIZATION *Minor (melodic)*

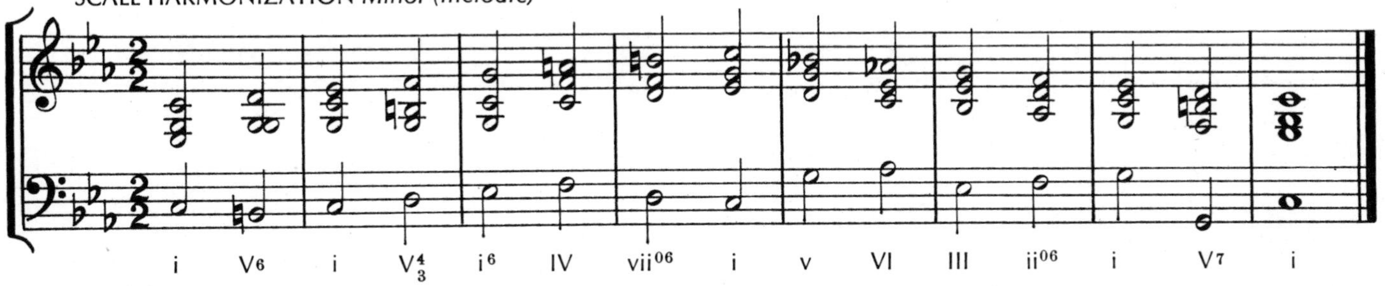

SEVENTHS IN THE KEY

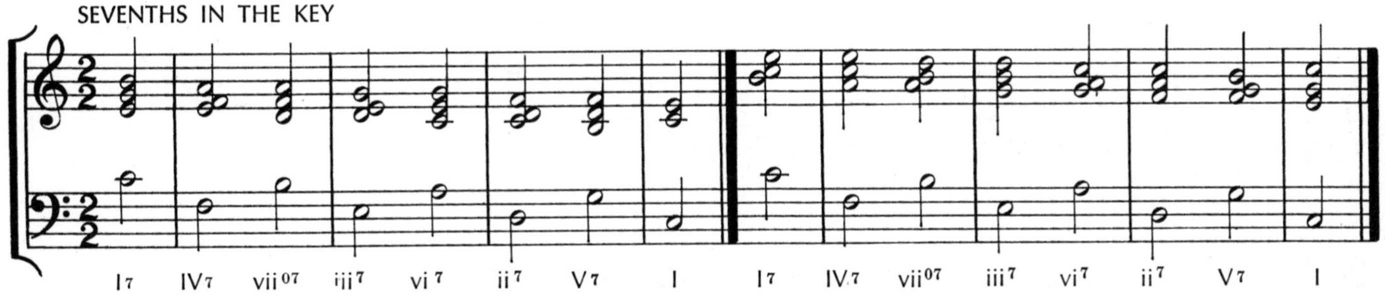

CIRCLE OF SEVENTHS (DOMINANTS) *Use Anticipations, Suspensions, Appoggiaturas, Echappes, Upper & Lower Neighbors as melodic material between chords.*

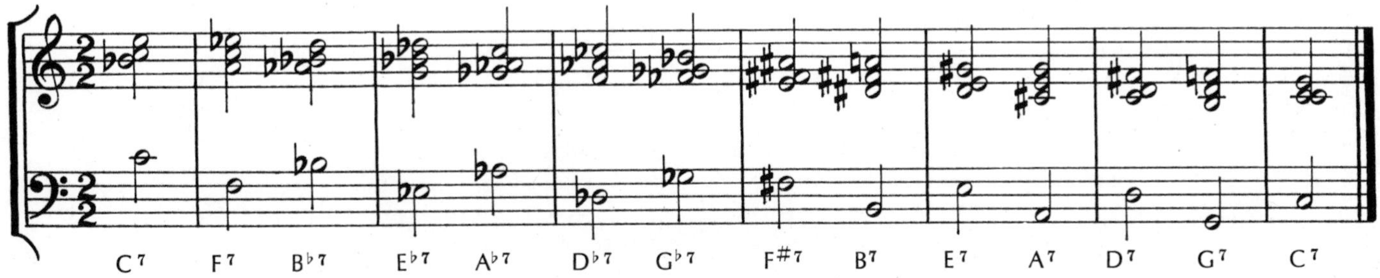

MAJOR SCALES

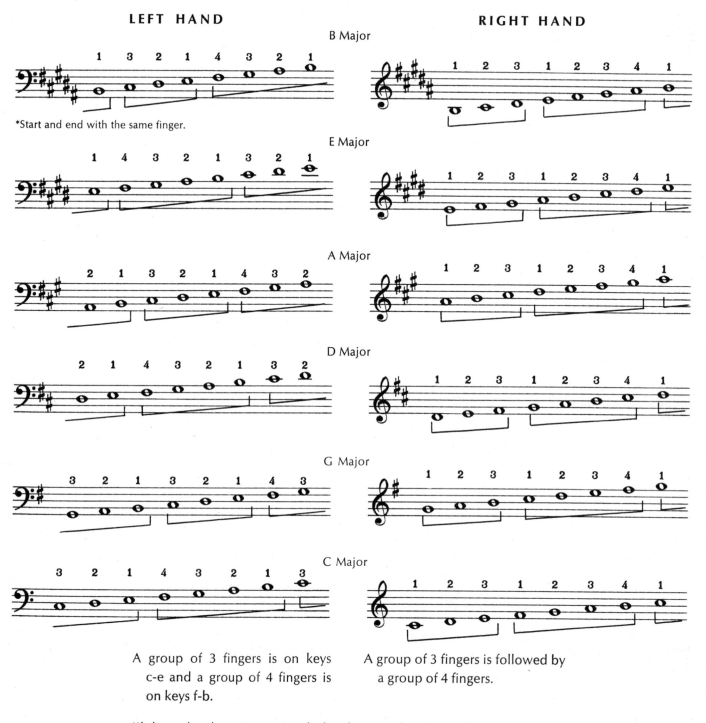

LEFT HAND | **RIGHT HAND**

B Major

*Start and end with the same finger.

E Major

A Major

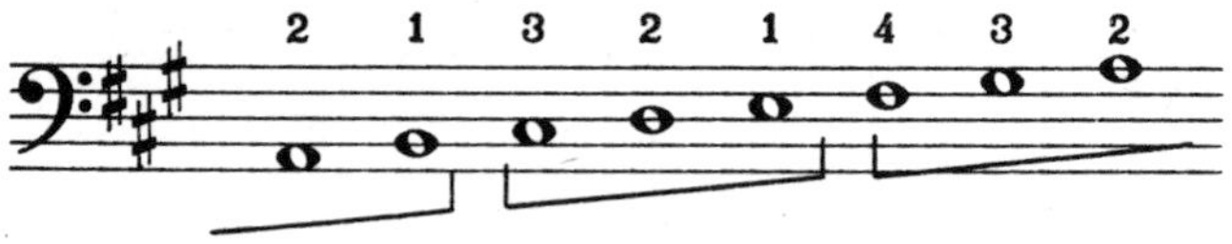

D Major

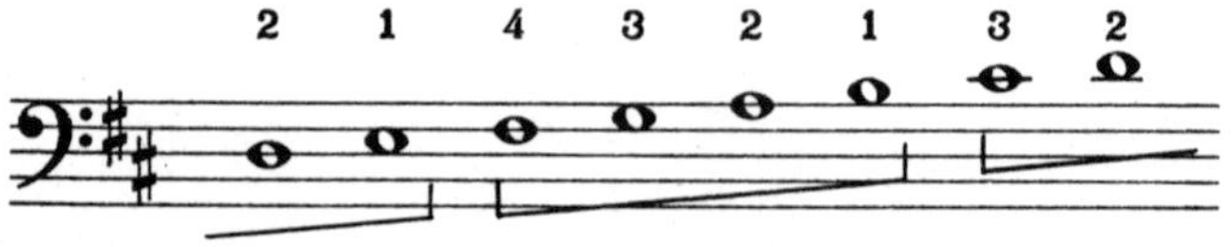

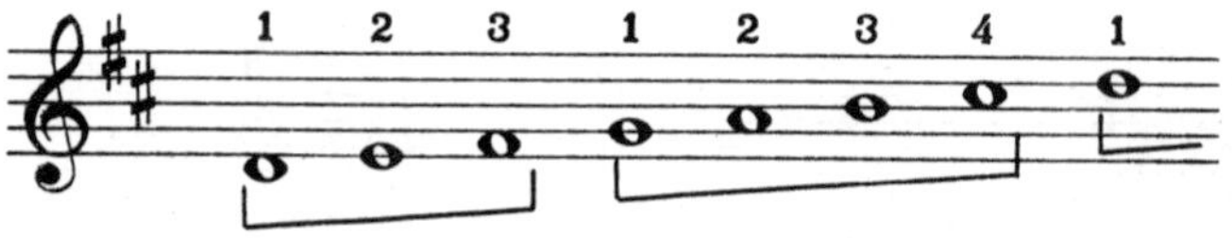

G Major

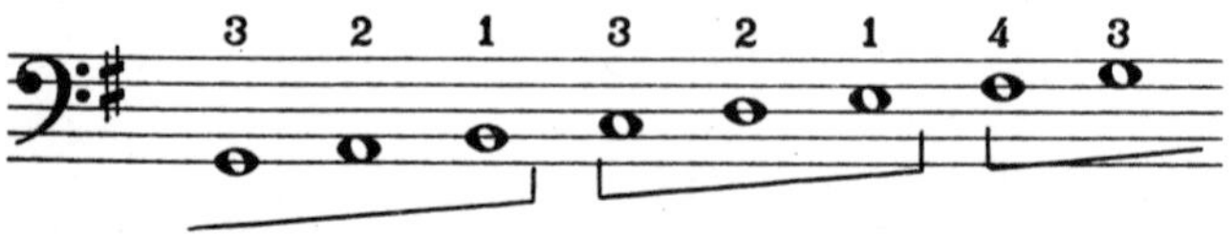

C Major

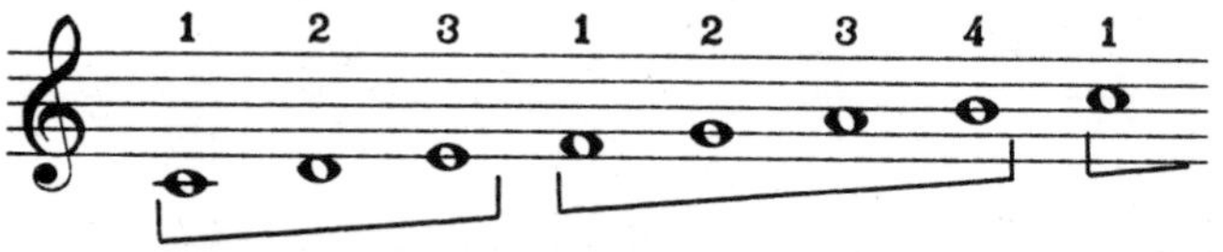

A group of 3 fingers is on keys c-e and a group of 4 fingers is on keys f-b.

A group of 3 fingers is followed by a group of 4 fingers.

*If the student learns to associate keyboard topography—black and white keys—with the notes on the staff and learns to draw implications for fingering accordingly, any technical problems he has can be related directly to how he perceives the score. J. C. Bach's rules on fingering scales facilitate this kind of thinking.

LEFT HAND—Place the thumb in front of the first black key ascending. This principle of J. C. Bach's changes the traditional 19th century fingering for the scales of C, G, D, and A. The key of C, of course, can be played with many different fingerings.

RIGHT HAND—Place the thumb after the last black key ascending. This principle of J. C. Bach's does not change any of the 19th century fingerings.

***LEFT HAND** ***RIGHT HAND**

Gb Major

Db Major

Ab Major

Eb Major

Bb Major

F Major

A group of 3 fingers is followed by a group of 4 fingers.

A group of 3 fingers is on keys c-e and a group of 4 fingers is on keys f-b.

*LEFT HAND—Place the thumb in front of the first black key ascending. J. C. Bach's principle only changes the scale fingering of F.

*RIGHT HAND—Place the thumb after the last black key ascending. This principle of J. C. Bach does not change any fingerings.

ARPEGGIOS

On C

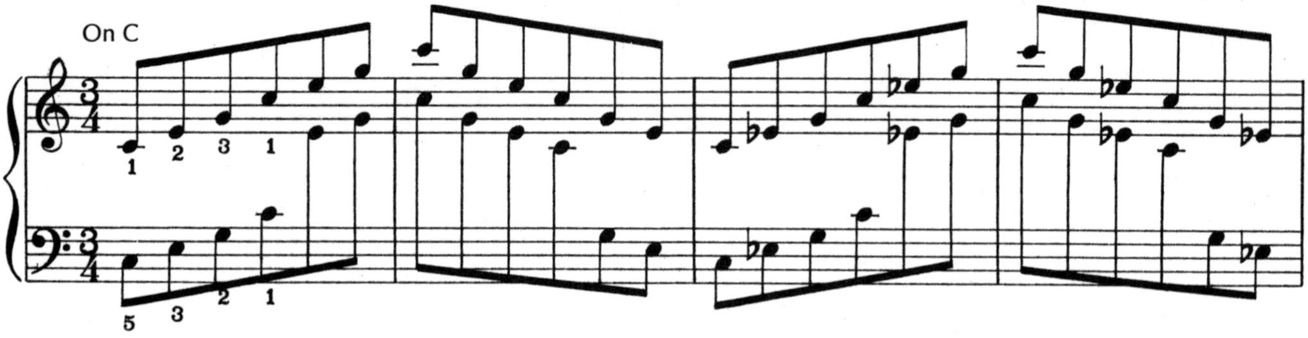

C major, root position — C minor, root position

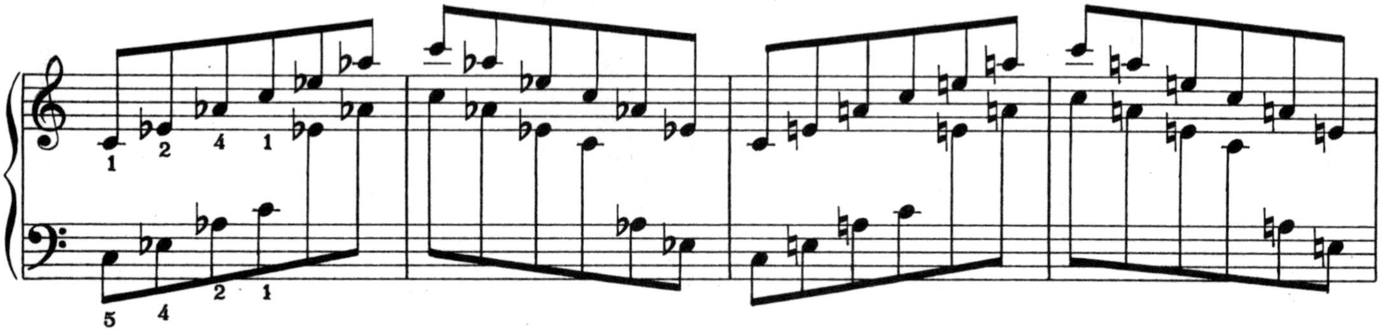

A♭ major, first inversion — A minor, first inversion

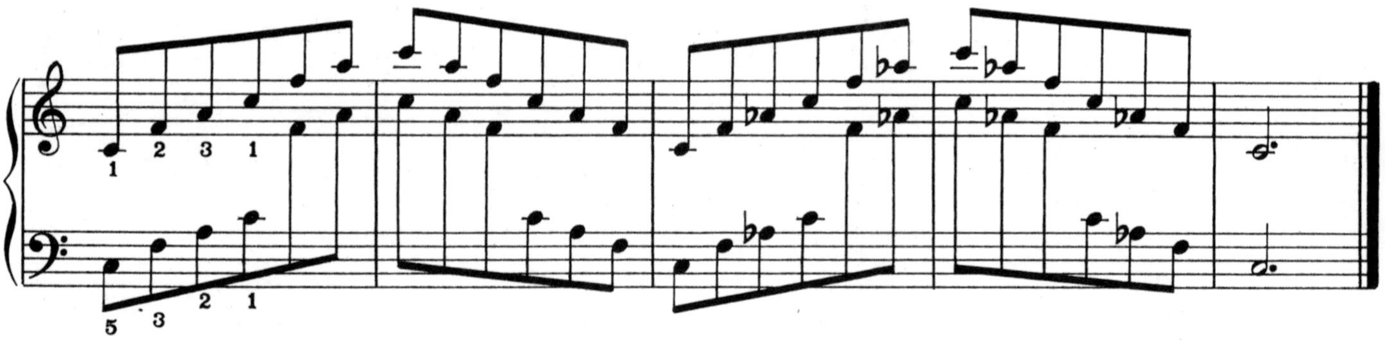

F major, second inversion — F minor, second inversion

On D
- D major, root position
- D minor, root position
- B♭ major, first inversion
- ♭ minor, first inversion
- G major, second inversion
- g minor, second inversion

On E
- E major, root position
- E minor, root position
- C major, first inversion
- C♯ minor, first inversion
- A major, second inversion
- A minor, second inversion

On F
- F major, root position
- F minor, root position
- D♭ major, first inversion
- D minor, first inversion
- B♭ major, second inversion
- B♭ minor, second inversion

On G
- G major, root position
- G minor, root position
- E♭ major, first inversion
- E minor, first inversion
- C major, second inversion
- C minor, second inversion

On A

- A major, root position
- A minor, root position
- F major, first inversion
- F# minor, first inversion
- D major, second inversion
- D minor, second inversion

On B

- B major, root position
- B minor, root position
- G major, first inversion
- G# minor, first inversion
- E major, second inversion
- E minor, second inversion

G♭ Major

root position

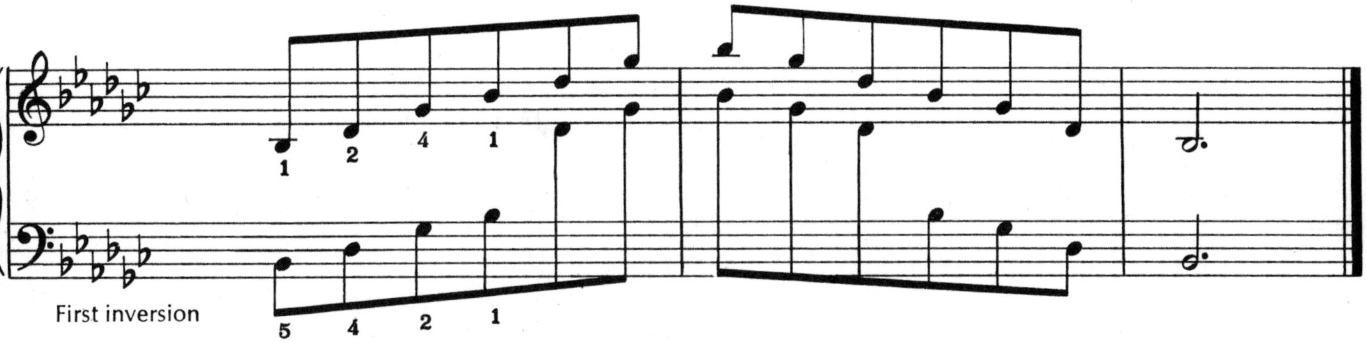

First inversion

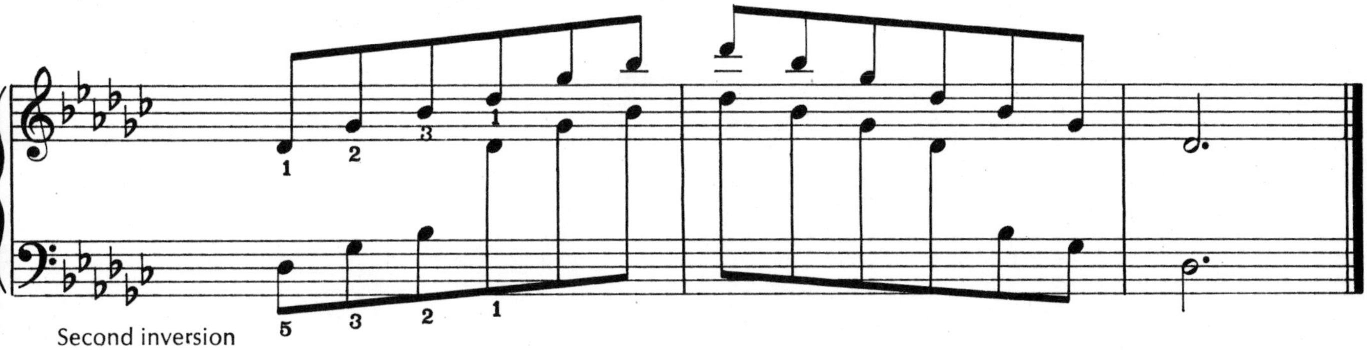

Second inversion